ANNUAL REVIEW OF PSYCHOLOGY

ANNUAL REVIEW OF PSYCHOLOGY

VOLUME 51, 2000

SUSAN T. FISKE, *Editor*
University of Massachusetts at Amherst

DANIEL L. SCHACTER, *Associate Editor*
Harvard University

CAROLYN ZAHN-WAXLER, *Associate Editor*
National Institute of Mental Health

www.AnnualReviews.org   science@annurev.org   650-493-4400

ANNUAL REVIEWS
4139 El Camino Way • P.O. Box 10139 • Palo Alto, California 94303-0139

ANNUAL REVIEWS
Palo Alto, California, USA

International Standard Serial Number: 0066-4308
International Standard Book Number: 0-8243-0251-6
Library of Congress Catalog Card Number: 50-13143

Annual Review and publication titles are registered trademarks of Annual Reviews.

♾ The paper used in this publication meets the minimum requirements of American National Standards for Information Sciences—Permanence of Paper for Printed Library Materials, ANSI Z39.48-1992.

Annual Reviews and the Editors of its publications assume no responsibility for the statements expressed by the contributors to this *Annual Review*.

Typeset by Impressions Book and Journal Services, Inc., Madison, WI
Printed and Bound in the United States of America

Preface

Fall in New England makes transitions salient, and the incoming editorial team salutes the outgoing editorial team, who served admirably for five years: Janet Spence, as Editor, with John Darley and Donald Foss as Associate Editors. That team and their 1997 editorial committee invited the authors appearing in the current table of contents, though the resulting articles were edited by the new team. The *Annual Review of Psychology* has thrived under their care, its articles ranked number 2 of 53 journals in citation impact, with a cited half-life of about 8 years. Knowing this, the current editorial team arrives both humbled and determined. We aim to maintain the brilliant annual display that draws readers from all over the world.

The *Annual Review of Psychology* resembles conventional review journals, in its goal to represent current knowledge in the field, in all its varieties. The *Annual Review of Psychology* differs, however, in its goal to provide timely perspectives by planful request, rather than by spontaneous submissions. Instead of waiting for submitted snapshots, and holding a contest, the AR commissions landscapes from different perspectives and different styles. Not every area is recorded every year, but over time, we hope to cover the territory. Choices of chapters are guided by a Master Plan of topics in psychology (just revised at the end of the previous team's watch, for which the current team is thankful). Topics come up in rotation, and the editorial committee assembles every spring to issue invitations. The joy of this job is that 90% of the invited authors accept, and 90% of those then deliver.

The *Annual Review of Psychology* holds a unique position for another reason. Its intended audience includes not only one's immediate colleagues expert in the same specialized subarea, but also other psychology colleagues catching up, graduate students coming in, adjacent scientists stopping by, undergraduates exploring around, and teachers keeping up. As such, we aim for articles that people want to read, accessible at several levels, with a lively point-of-view, as well as a scholarly respect for the range of evidence.

In acknowledging this transition and carrying on a tradition, we are grateful to Janet Spence for her instrumental and expressive skills in conveying *Annual Review of Psychology* traditions, standards, and trends; to John Darley for his wise help, unfailing interventions, and policy perspectives, as well as his altruism in easing the editorial committee's transition for two extra years; and to Donald Foss, for his deep comprehension and enlightened discourse over his term. Thanks to the Editorial Committee for their thoughtful legwork resulting in inspired and judicious choices. We also appreciate the organized, intelligent, unflappable skills of Lisa Dean, our sterling Production Editor, who makes our jobs possible.

SUSAN T. FISKE, Amherst
DANIEL L. SCHACTER, Cambridge
CAROLYN ZAHN-WAXLER, Washington

CONTENTS

PARENTING AND ITS EFFECTS ON CHILDREN: ON READING AND
MISREADING BEHAVIOR GENETICS, *Eleanor E. Maccoby*   1

THE PAIN OF BEING SICK: IMPLICATIONS OF IMMUNE-TO-BRAIN
COMMUNICATION FOR UNDERSTANDING PAIN, *L. R. Watkins and
S. F. Maier*   29

THOUGHT SUPPRESSION, *Richard M. Wenzlaff and Daniel M. Wegner*   59

SOCIAL COGNITION: THINKING CATEGORICALLY ABOUT OTHERS,
C. Neil Macrae and Galen V. Bodenhausen   93

ARE THERE KINDS OF CONCEPTS?, *Douglas L. Medin,
Elizabeth B. Lynch, and Karen O. Solomon*   121

NEW PERSPECTIVES AND EVIDENCE ON POLITICAL COMMUNICATION
AND CAMPAIGN EFFECTS, *Shanto Iyengar and Adam F. Simon*   149

GOAL THEORY, MOTIVATION, AND SCHOOL ACHIEVEMENT: AN
INTEGRATIVE REVIEW, *Martin V. Covington*   171

APPLICATIONS OF STRUCTURAL EQUATION MODELING IN
PSYCHOLOGICAL RESEARCH, *Robert C. MacCallum and
James T. Austin*   201

THE ENVIRONMENTAL PSYCHOLOGY OF CAPSULE HABITATS,
Peter Suedfeld and G. Daniel Steel   227

FOOD INTAKE AND THE REGULATION OF BODY WEIGHT,
*Stephen C. Woods, Michael W. Schwartz, Denis G. Baskin,
and Randy J. Seeley*   255

NEGOTIATION, *Max H. Bazerman, Jared R. Curhan, Don A. Moore,
and Kathleen L. Valley*   279

PARENTAL AND CHILD COGNITIONS IN THE CONTEXT OF THE
FAMILY, *Daphne Blunt Bugental and Charlotte Johnston*   315

EVALUATION METHODS FOR SOCIAL INTERVENTION, *Mark W. Lipsey
and David S. Cordray*   345

ADULT PSYCHOPATHOLOGY: ISSUES AND CONTROVERSIES,
T. A. Widiger and L. M. Sankis   377

SCIENTIFIC AND SOCIAL SIGNIFICANCE OF ASSESSING INDIVIDUAL
DIFFERENCES: "SINKING SHAFTS AT A FEW CRITICAL POINTS",
David Lubinski   405

THE EFFECTS OF FAMILY AND COMMUNITY VIOLENCE ON CHILDREN, *Gayla Margolin and Elana B. Gordis* 445

TOWARD A PSYCHOLOGY OF MEMORY ACCURACY, *Asher Koriat, Morris Goldsmith, and Ainat Pansky* 481

ATTITUDE CHANGE: PERSUASION AND SOCIAL INFLUENCE, *Wendy Wood* 539

CULTURAL PSYCHOPATHOLOGY: UNCOVERING THE SOCIAL WORLD OF MENTAL ILLNESS, *Steven Regeser López and Peter J. Guarnaccia* 571

MEMORY SYSTEMS IN THE BRAIN, *Edmund T. Rolls* 599

PERSONNEL SELECTION: LOOKING TOWARD THE FUTURE– REMEMBERING THE PAST, *Leaetta M. Hough and Frederick L. Oswald* 631

EMOTION, REGULATION, AND MORAL DEVELOPMENT, *Nancy Eisenberg* 665

NEURAL BASIS OF HEARING IN REAL-WORLD SITUATIONS, *Albert S. Feng and Rama Ratnam* 699

INDEXES

Author Index 727

Subject Index 769

Cumulative Index of Contributing Authors, Volumes 41–51 803

Cumulative Index of Chapter Titles, Volumes 41–51 807

Related Articles

From the *Annual Review of Anthropology,* Volume 28, 1999:

Life History Traits in Humans: Theory and Empirical Studies, Kim Hill and
Hillard Kaplan
The Chemical Ecology of Human Ingestive Behaviors, Timothy Johns
Evolutionary Psychology, Doug M. Jones
*Whither Primatology? The Place of Primates in Contemporary
Anthropology,* P.S. Rodman
The Human Adaptation for Culture, Michael Tomasello
Moving Bodies, Acting Selves, B. Farnell
Sociolinguistics and Linguistic Anthropology of US Latinos, Norma
Mendoza-Denton
Discourse and Racism: European Perspectives, R. Wodak and M. Reisigl
*MIRRORS AND WINDOWS: Sociocultural Studies of Human-Animal
Relationships,* Molly H. Mullin
War: Back to the Future, Anna Simons

From the *Annual Review of Neuroscience,* Volume 22, 1999:

Cellular and Molecular Determinants of Sympathetic Neuron Development,
Nicole J. Francis and Story C. Landis
Central Nervous System Neuronal Migration, Mary E. Hatten
Development of the Vertebrate Neuromuscular Junction, Joshua R. Sanes
and Jeff W. Lichtman
Growth Cone Guidance: First Steps Towards a Deeper Understanding,
Bernhard K. Mueller
Retinal Waves and Visual System Development, Rachel O. L. Wong
*The Specification of Dorsal Cell Fates in the Vertebrate Central Nervous
System,* Kevin J. Lee and Thomas M. Jessell
Monoamine Oxidase: From Genes to Behavior, J. C. Shih, K. Chen, and M.
J. Ridd
Birdsong and Human Speech: Common Themes and Mechanisms, Allison J.
Doupe and Patricia K. Kuhl
*Making Brain Connections: Neuroanatomy and the Work of TPS Powell,
1923–1996,* Edward G. Jones
The Cell Biology of the Blood-Brain Barrier, L. L. Rubin and J. M. Staddon
Neurotrophins and Synaptic Plasticity, A. Kimberley McAllister, Lawrence
C. Katz, and Donald C. Lo
Stress and Hippocampal Plasticity, Bruce S. McEwen

Molecular Biology of Odorant Receptors in Vertebrates, Peter Mombaerts
Autoimmunity and Neurological Disease: Antibody Modulation of Synaptic Transmission, K. D. Whitney and J. O. McNamara
Monitoring Secretory Membrane with FM1-43 Fluorescence, Amanda J. Cochilla, Joseph K. Angleson, and William J. Betz
Presynaptic Ionotropic Receptors and the Control of Transmitter Release, Amy B. MacDermott, Lorna W. Role, and Steven A. Siegelbaum
Computational Neuroimaging of Human Visual Cortex, Brian A. Wandell
Neural Selection and Control of Visually Guided Eye Movements, Jeffrey D. Schall and Kirk G. Thompson
Space and Attention in Parietal Cortex, Carol L. Colby and Michael E. Goldberg

From the *Annual Review of Public Health,* Volume 20, 1999:

Teen Pregnancy Prevention: Do Any Programs Work?, Josefina J. Card
The Social Environment and Health: A Discussion of the Epidemiologic Literature, I. Yen and S. L. Syme
Patient Outcomes Research Teams: Contribution to Outcomes and Effectiveness Research, Deborah Freund, Judith Lave, Carolyn Clancy, Gillian Hawker, Victor Hasselblad, Robert Keller, Ellen Schneiter, and James Wright

From the *Annual Review of Sociology,* Volume 25, 1999:

Game Theory in Sociology: A Reintroduction, Elisa Jayne Bienenstock
Gender and Sexual Harassment, Sandy Welsh
Sexuality in the Workplace: Organizational Control, Sexual Harassment, and the Pursuit of Pleasure, Christine L. Williams, Patti A. Giuffre, and Kirsten Dellinger
The Estimation of Causal Effects from Observational Data, Christopher Winship and Stephen L. Morgan
The Gender System and Interaction, Cecelia L. Ridgeway and Lynn Smith-Lovin
Bringing Emotions into Social Exchange Theory, Edward J. Lawler and Shane R. Thye
A Retrospective on the Civil Rights Movement: Political and Intellectual Landmarks, Aldon D. Morris
Women's Movements in the Third World: Identity, Mobilization, and Autonomy, R. Ray and A. C. Korteweg
Cultural Criminology, Jeff Ferrell
Organizational Innovation and Organizational Change, J. T. Hage
Perspectives on Technology and Work Organization, Jeffrey K. Liker, Carol J. Haddad, and Jennifer Karlin

Politics and Institutionalism: Explaining Durability and Change, Elisabeth S. Clemens and James M. Cook

The Dark Side of Organizations; Mistake, Misconduct, and Disaster, Diane Vaughan

Declining Violent Crime Rates in the 1990s: Predicting Crime Booms and Busts, Gary LaFree

Feminization and Juvenilization of Poverty: Trends, Relative Risks, Causes and Consequences, Suzanne M. Bianchi

Inequality in Earnings at the Close of the Twentieth Century, Martina Morris and Bruce Western

Social Networks and Status Attainment, Nan Lin

The Determinants and Consequences of Workplace Sex and Race Composition, Barbara F. Reskin, Debra B. McBrier, and Julie A. Kmec

Socioeconomic Position and Health: The Independent Contribution of Community Socioeconomic Context, Stephanie A. Robert

Eleanor E. Maccoby

Annu. Rev. Psychol. 2000. 51:1–27

PARENTING AND ITS EFFECTS ON CHILDREN:
On Reading and Misreading Behavior Genetics

Eleanor E. Maccoby

Department of Psychology, Stanford University, Building 420, Jordan Hall, Stanford, California 94305-2130; e-mail: maccoby@psych.stanford.edu

■ **Abstract** There is clear evidence that parents can and do influence children. There is equally clear evidence that children's genetic makeup affects their own behavioral characteristics, and also influences the way they are treated by their parents. Twin and adoption studies provide a sound basis for estimating the strength of genetic effects, although heritability estimates for a given trait vary widely across samples, and no one estimate can be considered definitive. This chapter argues that knowing only the strength of genetic factors, however, is not a sufficient basis for estimating environmental ones and indeed, that attempts to do so can systematically underestimate parenting effects. Children's genetic predispositions and their parents' childrearing regimes are seen to be closely interwoven, and the ways in which they function jointly to affect children's development are explored.

CONTENTS

Introduction 1
How Strong is the Connection Between Parent and Child Behaviors 5
The Challenge from Behavior Genetics 9
    The Focus on Variation 9
    The Claim for Substantial Genetic Effects 11
    Estimating the Size of Environmental Effects 12
    Shared and Unshared Environmental Effects 13
Interpreting Parent-Child Covariance 17
The Interaction of Genetic and Environmental Factors.................................19
    G × E Interactions in Animal Studies 19
    G × E Interactions in Adoption Studies...20
    Studies of Interactions with Temperament...21
Overview 22

INTRODUCTION

What are the forces that affect when and how children will change as they grow older? Can development be seen as a progressive process whereby children move toward a specifiable outcome or end state that we can call maturity? What conditions determine differences among children in their rates of development or their ultimate outcomes? These questions have been at the heart of much of the work in developmental psychology since the inception of the field. In pursuing the answers, the broad forces of nature and nurture, and the interplay between them, have been of central concern. It has long been clear that there are powerful maturational time-tables governing developmental change: e.g. the progression in infancy from sitting to crawling to standing to walking, or in the acquisition of language, the transition from rudimentary one-word utterances through intermediate phrases to the production of full, well-formed sentences. However, it has been equally obvious that children are learning many things through their daily experiences in interacting with the physical and social world, and that what is learned is not encoded in the genes. Some of the experiences children have are random—not planned or organized by any outside agency—but some occur according to what might be called a socialization time table. It is here that parenting has its place.

All societies prescribe certain characteristics that their members are expected to possess and certain things people must not do, if they are to function adequately as members of their society. Some of these prescriptions and proscriptions are nearly universal across cultures, such as the requirement for parents, or specified parent surrogates, to provide nurturance and protection for children. Other standards and values vary greatly from one cultural setting to another. In all societies, training of children occurs, and social controls are in place to ensure that children are socialized—that is, brought up in such a way that each new generation acquires the prescribed patterns of beliefs and behaviors. Of course, cultures do change, either slowly or rapidly, so that the cross-generational transmission is by no means absolute. A new generation may need to adapt to conditions that the parent generation did not face. And transmission of values, even when they continue to be appropriate for succeeding generations, is not always successful. Some children in every cohort may be seen to be inadequately socialized by the criteria that the society applies.

Not all socialization occurs in childhood. People are socialized into the customs and standards of an occupational culture when they take up an entry-level job. Socialization and resocialization occur when adults enter into new life roles (e.g. marriage, parenthood). In considering the role of parents, however, we are mainly concerned with childhood socialization. Some of the socialization that occurs throughout childhood is in a sense anticipatory, in that it functions to prepare children for adaptation to a fairly wide range of life roles and the various contexts children will encounter as they grow older. But childhood socialization also concerns the training of children in modes of behavior that are acceptable for the stage of childhood they currently occupy. Societies set different standards for people at different stages of their life cycle, and there are requirements that loom especially large in childhood. These include requirements for children to comply with adult demands, to avoid irritating adults or disrupting their activities, to accept age-appropriate responsibility, and to function as a pleasant, cooperative family member.

In modern societies, there are least three major contexts in which childhood socialization takes place: families, peer groups, and out-of-home contexts such as school classrooms or day-care centers in which the daily experiences of children are structured and overseen by adults. The enormous body of literature on childhood socialization has strongly emphasized the role of parents. This emphasis has a long and deep tradition. The idea that "as the twig is bent, so grows the tree" can be traced at least as far back as Greek and Biblical times—(probably earlier), and in most societies parents are the ones assigned primary responsibility for "bending" the children in desirable directions, by supervising, teaching, and disciplining them as they grow up. Early childhood in particular has long been thought to be a period in the life cycle when humans are especially plastic—a time when children are especially open to social influences on characteristics they will carry with them long after they have left their family of origin. Things thought to be especially vulnerable to influence in the first 5–7 years of children's lives include the language they speak, their food preferences, their religious beliefs, and certain enduring personality traits.

In the twentieth century, assumptions about the importance of within-family childhood socialization have been part of the fabric of mainstream psychological theories. From roughly the 1920s through the 1960s, behaviorist learning theories held sway, emphasizing the "blank slate" status of infants and the power of adults to teach young children, for good or ill, what they must learn. Parents, of course, were seen as the most available teachers, and the ones responsible for carrying out the training of their children. The physiological drive states (hunger, fatigue) with which children are innately endowed were not ignored in the learning theories of the time, so there was some blending of nature and nurture, but the major emphasis was on the control of learning processes exercised by environmental inputs. Psychoanalytic theories of this period emphasized the importance of early in-family experience in determining subsequent inner conflicts, defense mechanisms, and internalization of values. In more recent decades, as the cognitive revolution took hold and learning theory (as it related to socialization) was reformulated as cognitive social learning theory, the active role of children as participants in their own socialization was increasingly stressed. Currently, there is increasing emphasis on the role of parents' and children's mutual perceptions and understandings about each other's dispositions and intentions as determiners of their influence upon one another. But none of these theoretical shifts has greatly affected the underlying assumption that parents have a powerful impact on the characteristics children develop and the directions their lives take. The child development research literature has continued to include a wide range of studies on such things as (a) familial risk factors (i.e. aspects of family functioning that are related to the subsequent development of externalizing or internalizing disorders in children); (b) social conditions that affect such parenting practices as how well parents are able to monitor their children, or how warm and responsive they are; and (c) parenting behaviors as mediators of the connection between societal risk factors (e.g. poverty or dangerous neighborhoods) and children's adjustment.

In recent decades, there has been a countervailing ground swell of research and theorizing about nature—the genetic endowment of parents and children—as exerting a powerful influence on the characteristics that children develop. Of course, for many decades, elementary psychology textbooks have carried tables comparing identical and fraternal twins with respect to their degree of similarity on IQ or other traits. Studies of adopted children were also widely reported many years ago, and inferences were routinely drawn from both twin and adoption studies concerning the importance of genetic factors in development. Still, for many years, thinking remained largely compartmentalized, and readers continued to believe in both the importance of genetic factors and the importance of socialization factors as though they were in no way incompatible. In recent years, however, there has been more sophisticated work in behavior genetics, and there are insistent voices claiming that the findings from this work are indeed incompatible with many widely-held views about the power of within-family socialization.

These messages from behavior genetics have been picked up and synthesized with other misgivings about the weaknesses of socialization research into a more broad-based attack on traditional assumptions concerning parenting and its effects. Rowe's book, *The Limits of Family Influence* (1994), stated the case strongly, and Harris's more popular book *The Nurture Assumption* (1998) attracted a flurry of media attention to the issues. These authors have drawn together the findings from some well-known studies of parenting effects and findings from behavior genetics to make the following claims:

1. The connections that studies have found between the way parents deal with their children and how the children turn out are actually quite weak and have proved difficult to replicate. When parent "effects" are found, they tend to be effects on the way children behave at home and the relationships they develop with their parents. There is little carry-over from at-home experiences to the way children function in out-of-home contexts

2. When studies do establish connections between parenting and children's attributes, these are correlational findings. An example is Baumrind's early finding—now widely replicated—that the children of parents who are both responsive and firm tend to be more competent and cooperative than children of parents who are either authoritarian or permissive (Baumrind & Black 1967). Such findings have traditionally been interpreted as showing that authoritative parenting has beneficial effects on children, ignoring the possibility that the causal connection may run the other way—i.e. that competent, cooperative children may make it easier for their parents to be firm and responsive. In fact, the critics argue, parent behavior is substantially driven by the behavior of children, and much if not most of the parent/child correlation can be accounted for by the child's genetic predispositions.

3. Parental influence has been emphasized at the expense of sources of influence that in fact have great—or perhaps greater—importance in shaping children's development. Two kinds of influence which critics argue have been underemphasized are genetic predispositions and the influence of peers.

In the popular media, these critiques have been condensed into the oversimplified message "Parents don't matter" or "matter very little"—news bites that, on their face, have little relation to reality as it is experienced daily in family life. Often, reports in the popular media do not reflect what the cited authors actually said. For example, late in her book, Harris (1998) says she believes parents can foster the development of specific talents (e.g. by providing music lessons) and can influence such things as children's leisure time activities, their food preferences, their religious beliefs and practices, and the acquisition of knowledge and skills and preferences that will contribute to their ultimate choice of a profession. Yet, the burden of her book is to down-play such influences and stress the respects in which parents are not influential. Rowe says: " . . . parents in most working to professional-class families may have little influence on what traits their children may eventually develop as adults." (1994:7). His use of the word "may" does not greatly soften the import of his message. He goes on to say that he doubts whether any undesirable trait displayed by a child can be significantly modified by anything a parent does. Scarr (1992) expresses a similarly skeptical view about the possible effects of interventions. Such views, of course, when picked up and simplified in the popular press, can have serious implications for public policies concerning whether to invest in remedial or supportive programs for children and families.

These critiques constitute serious efforts to present a point of view that is clearly different from the traditional emphasis on the importance of parenting. They cite large bodies of data and have attracted the support of highly reputable psychologists. They deserve to be taken seriously. Nonetheless, I believe that they are out of date with respect to both the genetic studies and the parenting-effects studies they cite, and that they seriously misinterpret the pertinent body of research.

I turn first to the question of how strong the connections are between what parents do with their children and how the children turn out. I then turn to issues of genetic factors, in particular the ways in which these factors may determine or limit how we can interpret parenting effects.

HOW STRONG IS THE CONNECTION BETWEEN PARENT AND CHILD BEHAVIORS?

As noted above, critics charge that interpreters of traditional socialization studies have exaggerated the importance of parenting in children's lives—that in fact, the effect sizes reported in many widely-cited studies are really quite small. Indeed, reviews of research done before the mid-1980s did show weak correlations between parenting processes and children's characteristics (e.g. Maccoby & Martin 1983). Since then, many studies have come up with more robust findings, no doubt reflecting improvements in the ways in which parent and child characteristics are assessed. Leading researchers no longer rely on a single measure, such as a parent or child interview or a parent or child self-report scale, as a measure of parent or child attributes. Instead information is obtained from multiple sources—from parents, children, teachers, school records, sometimes from children's peers and police records as well—and importantly, from direct observation of parent-child interactions and of children in out-of-home settings. When several measures such as these are aggregated, associations between parent attributes and children's behavior can be quite substantial. Parenting variables have typically accounted for 20% to 50% of the variance in child outcomes (Conger & Elder 1994, Reiss et al 1995). Exceptionally robust connections are reported in the recent large-scale study of adolescents in never-divorced and step-families, Hetherington and colleagues (Hetherington et al 1999). Using composite scores for both parenting styles and children's attributes, report a concurrent coefficient of 0.76 between mothers' "authoritative parenting" and adolescents' "social responsibility" (the coefficient for fathers is 0.49). Parental negativity has very strong connections for both parents with adolescents' depression and internalizing behavior.[1] Patterson and colleagues have also found substantial correlations between parental characteristics (e.g. disciplinary practices and monitoring) and children's antisocial behavior (Patterson & Forgatch 1995). They are able to show connections between parental behaviors and the children's negative, coercive behavior both at home and in out-of-home contexts.

Concurrent correlations are usually considerably larger than predictive ones. Longitudinal studies present the opportunity to examine the connections, if any, between child-rearing styles at one point in time and subsequent attributes of the child. The strength of the connections that have been found depends on many things, such as what "packages" or clusters of parent and child variables are considered, the way they are measured, the length of time between predictive and outcome measures, and whether background variables are statistically controlled. A few examples will illustrate the range of findings. Kochanska 1997b:94 has been able to show that aspects of early parenting account for a significant but moderate (Beta coefficient 0.29, F 9.96) portion of the variance in young children's self-regulation and internalization assessed a year later. Pettit and colleagues (1997:908) found some—but fewer and weaker—predictive relationships between parenting as assessed at the beginning of the kindergarten year and children's adjustment and academic performance seven years later, in the sixth grade. Strong predictive power of family interaction processes over much longer spans of time have been found in longitudinal studies of antisocial behavior (see Loeber & Dishion 1983). In current socialization studies, simple first-order correlations between parenting characteristics and child outcomes are seldom relied on. Indeed, sometimes they are not even reported. Instead, multivariate analyses are used to investigate such questions as whether a given aspect of parenting has different effects on different kinds of children or in families living in different circumstances; or whether different aspects of parenting have independent, addi-

---

[1]The coefficient connecting mothers' negative/conflictual behavior with children's externalizing behavior was 0.82; for fathers this coefficient was 0.79. These coefficients are path coefficients in structural models in which two aspects of parenting (authoritative parenting parental negativity/conflict) are considered simultaneously along with measures of sibling relationships. Scores derived from videotapes of parent-child interactions were a contributing element (though a minor one) in the composite scores of both parenting characteristics and child outcomes.

tive effects, whether they are interchangeable, or whether they interact so that the effects of one depend on the level of another.

In longitudinal work, the initial level of a child's characteristic at time 1 is sometimes statistically controlled to determine whether a time-1 parent attribute is associated with subsequent *change* change in the child's behavior. As an example, Patterson & Bank (1989) studied families when their sons were in grade school, and again when the boys were adolescents. They found that changes in parenting during these years were strongly related to the chances of a boy's being arrested for delinquent activities in adolescence, even after the boy's anti-social tendencies at grade-school age were controlled. We see, then, that a variety of questions are being asked in current and recent research—questions to which simple parent/child correlations, either concurrent or time-lagged, will not provide answers.

A word should be said, too, about how large a correlation between some aspect of parenting and a child outcome is required for the relationship to be considered important or meaningful. Along with the rest of the psychological discipline, developmental psychologists are currently turning away from reporting the outcomes of studies primarily (or only) in terms of significance levels (*p* values) that indicate degree of departure from the null hypothesis. Instead, results are beginning to be reported in terms of effect sizes. For purposes of policy decisions in the medical arena, correlations as small as 0.03 between the use of a medication and reduction of disease have been considered strong enough to justify FDA approval of the drug (Rosenthal 1999). The importance of a medical intervention can be estimated in terms of such outcomes as the number of heart attacks averted or the number of people for whom a debilitating, chronic disease can be arrested or reversed. In the past, correlations in the 0.20s or 0.30s between aspects of family functioning and children's outcomes have often been dismissed as inconsequential. But when translated into the number of children who are at risk, for example, for failing in school or becoming delinquent or seriously depressed, predictive coefficients of this magnitude can be seen as by no means trivial. From the standpoint of social policy, the issue becomes one of how much importance a society attaches to social/behavioral outcomes, as compared with medical ones. This is obviously a matter of values, not statistics.

Studies continue to vary considerably with respect to the size of first-order correlations between parent and child characteristics. Clearly, a given parent behavior may have different effects on different children, depending on such things as age, sex, temperament, and distinctive prior experiences. If such differential effects exist, aggregating data across a whole sample of children will wash out parent/child effects—effects that might be quite robust within sub-groups of children. (See section on interactions, below.) It is not possible to arrive at any general rule as to when dividing by subgroups will increase or decrease a parent-child correlation. That will depend on the researcher's theoretical and empirical skill in identifying what the pertinent groupings might be. The use of more sophisticated statistical methods has contributed significantly to the ability of present-day researchers to identify parenting effects within the matrix of other factors with which they often co-vary.

Not only have methods of assessment been improved, but current socialization research includes a broader array of parenting attributes and focuses on a set of parenting processes that were not so clearly delineated in times past. One aspect of parental skill that has emerged in several recent studies as related to children's well-being is household organization; another concerns the ability of some parents to develop a reciprocal form of interaction with their children (e.g. shared positive affect, mutual responsivity). Studies of the predictive power of parent-child reciprocation in early childhood have yielded quite robust parenting effects (See Kochanska & Thompson 1997 for a review of this work). These examples illustrate the ways in which the field of family-impact studies has been growing in conceptual as well as methodological strength. Nevertheless we must be reconciled to the fact that there are important aspects of parenting that will never be revealed in studies that, by necessity, try to encapsulate parental characteristics into measurable clusters or traits. There are the memorable little socialization moments when the members of a parent/child dyad are, for some reason, especially attuned to one another—when the child, perhaps by virtue of having encountered a new and salient issue, is ready to both explain and listen. At such a moment, the parent may do or say something that makes a deep impression and can have a lasting influence. Conversely, a broken promise or a revealed deception may break the prevailing relationship of trust between the two, changing the nature of the influence that is possible between them. Such moments are unique to a dyad and may not be captured in socialization studies, even though our awareness of them is highlighted in biographies, autobiographies, and fiction.

I do not want to claim too much for the strength of parental influence in children's lives. Critics are right in pointing out that we have overemphasized these influences at the expense of other kinds of environmental influences. To what extent early childhood is a time of especially great plasticity, during which environmental inputs will be more likely to have a lasting influence than inputs later in life is an open question. Probably the answer will vary, depending on what domain of children's development we are talking about. (See for example, Neville's finding [Neville 1995] that the openness to influence by early experience differs between the semantic and syntactic language systems). Because parents are usually the ones who spend the most time with young children over extended periods of time, these questions of changing plasticity do matter in our efforts to understand the parental realm of influence. Still, parents are never the only source of influence on children, and as children grow older, they are more and more subject to the influence of peers, of schools and teachers, and of television. Also, there are the random events—a serious illness or accident, an unexpected success, a residential move, an environmental catastrophe—that can alter the trajectory of a child's life in ways that have little to do with parenting.

Of course, when we do see robust correlations between parent and child attributes, the question of the direction of effects arises at once. In making their argument that we may be seeing child-to-parent effects rather than the reverse, critics have relied heavily on the findings of behavior genetics[2], especially on studies of twins and adopted children. They have also relied on these findings to urge that nonparental aspects of a child's environment have greater weight than parental inputs in determining how a child will develop.

THE CHALLENGE FROM BEHAVIOR GENETICS

Some of the major findings of behavior genetics are powerful and require students of socialization to rethink some of their assumptions. Many of these findings are well known, and I do not summarize them in any detail here, but focus on the main lines of argument that bear on the issue of parenting effects.

The Focus on Variation

Behavior geneticists seek to understand the sources of variation in some human trait or characteristic. Their approach is to be distinguished from that of evolutionary psychologists, who seek to understand the genetic underpinnings of characteristics that are relatively uniform across a species.

There are important effects of both genes and environment that are overlooked in studies that focus on the variation of a characteristic within a given population. A human characteristic such as being born with two eyes is entirely genetic, yet its heritability would be computed as zero in a twin or adoption study since it is a characteristic that does not vary within the population studied. Similarly, there may be an environmental factor that affects the mean level of a characteristic—raising or lowering all scores to a similar degree—without greatly disturbing the rank-order of individuals on the characteristic. Thus, adoption studies have found that the correlation of adopted children's IQs with those of their biological parents can remain substantial, while at the same time the average IQ of the adopted children is higher than that of their natural parents, as though children receive an IQ bonus from being adopted into relatively stable, middle-class homes, while nevertheless continuing to differ from each other according to their genetic endowment. In a study of French children adopted at about the age of 5, it was found that the amount of increase in their IQs (assessed again in adolescence) was considerably greater for children adopted into affluent, well-educated families than for those adopted into underprivileged homes (Duyme et al 1999).

Secular trends illustrate the same point. The "Flynn effect" (Flynn 1987, 1999)—the substantial, monotonic rise in mean IQ scores over many decades in

---

[2]The term "behavior genetics" is a commonly used term for twin studies, adoption studies, and epidemiological studies of family resemblance. Currently, since molecular geneticists also study certain "behavioral" phenotypes in their relation to genes, the term quantitative genetics is sometimes used to distinguish studies that rely on statistical genetic analyses of family resemblance rather than on molecular gene identifiers. However the term "behavior genetics" is used here because it is more familiar to readers.

Western industrialized countries—is well known. There has been a substantial rise in the rates of smoking among American women in the last several decades, and the rates of drinking alcohol dropped during prohibition. These changes, of course, have occurred during periods of time that are much too short to reflect any genetic changes and they have occurred despite the fact that heritability estimates for IQ, drinking, and smoking have remained quite stable over the same time periods during which the average levels were changing. A similar phenomenon is seen in some migration studies, in which second-generation immigrants are on average quite different from their foreign-born grandparents, even on highly heritable traits such as height (Angoff 1988) or obesity (Price at all 1993, Ravussin et al 1994). The implication of these phenomena for parenting effects is this: There may have been secular changes in parenting—triggered perhaps by such things as changes in family structure or overall economic level—that have had widespread effects on children without affecting heritability estimates for the outcome characteristics being affected.

These powerful environmental effects are missed in the estimates of E (environment) derived from behavior genetics studies of twins and adopted children. Another way of putting this point is to note that high heritability of a trait does not imply that it is not also subject to the influence of environmental factors, or that it cannot be changed by alterations in environmental conditions. It is for this reason that, when comparing group means (by race, sex, or socioeconomic status) it is not legitimate to interpret any group differences in terms of estimates of genetic or environmental effects derived from quantitative behavior genetic studies.

Experimental Interventions with Parents   If large-scale environmental events can change mean levels of a characteristic without greatly changing the rank-order of individuals, it follows that experimental interventions might do the same. It is difficult to change actual parenting practices through parent-training programs, and then to document that program-induced changes in parenting change the mean levels of children's characteristics. Such programs must be longitudinal, of course, and must have an untreated control group for comparison. Studies that intervene with the parents but do not simultaneously treat the children, and that have random assignment of families to treatment or control groups, are understandably rare, but several have clearly shown that when treatment is able to change parental behavior toward children in specified ways, the behavior of children changes correspondingly (e.g. Patterson & Forgatch 1995, Van den Boom 1994, Forehand et al 1980). Dishion et al (1992) were able to show that it was indeed the reduction of parent-to-child coercive behavior, brought about by a parent-training intervention with a randomly assigned experimental group, that produced declining levels of antisocial behavior in a group of aggressive children. An intervention program that changes the mean of a group of parents (and consequently, of their children's behavior as well) may or may not change the initial rank order of the children. Researchers commonly find that some parents are influenced more than others by an intervention, and some children are affected more than others by improvements in parental disciplinary or monitoring practices. These differential effects might either increase or decrease the range of outcome scores in the treatment group, depending on whether it was the initially better-functioning or poorly-functioning families who were most affected by the intervention. However, expanding or shrinking the range of outcome scores does not necessarily change the initial rank-order. The point here is that changes in a mean can be independent of any changes in rank order. Thus, changes in a mean can clearly demonstrate an environmental effect, quite apart from any correlational information (based on rank orders of individuals) that might be used to compute genetic or environmental effects in a genetic analysis. The environmental effects revealed by the mean change would go undetected in a correlational analysis.

The Claim for Substantial Genetic Effects

In traditional behavior genetic research, data from studies of twins and adopted children are used to compute heritability estimates (h^2), which are interpreted as estimates of the proportion of variance accounted for by genetic factors. Many such studies have yielded substantial heritability estimates. Identical twins have been found to be more similar to each other than are same-sex fraternal twins with respect to a wide range of characteristics, including susceptibility to certain diseases, intelligence, temperament, and a number of personality characteristics. The inference is that this must be due to their greater genetic similarity, because the important aspects of their environments—parenting received, neighborhood, presence of a same-age, same-sex sibling—are presumably equally similar for the two kinds of twin pairs. Adopted children have been found to be more similar to their biological parents than to their adoptive parents with respect to a selected set of characteristics for which researchers have been able to obtain measures from both biological and adoptive parents.

In a general sense, the behavior geneticists have made their case. Children's genetic endowments do clearly affect how individuals will develop—in comparison to other children—to a much greater extent than was thought to be the case during the years of the ascendancy of reinforcement learning theories and psychodynamic theories (the middle decades of the twentieth century.)

How substantial is this genetic contribution? Critics have argued that estimates derived from twin studies systematically overestimate the genetic contribution to a trait because identical twins in fact have more similar environments than do same-sex fraternal twins. Identical twins (compared with fraternals) are treated more similarly by their parents, spend more time together (and hence constitute a greater proportion of each other's social environment), and more often share the same friends (Dunn & Plomin 1986, Plomin et al 1988, Reiss et al 1999, Rowe 1983). Probably, the greater similarity in the environments of identical twins is not sufficiently strong to negate the findings on genetic effects, but it does weaken them. Very likely, it helps to account for the fact that heritability estimates are usually larger in twin studies than in adoption studies.

Of course, the genetic contribution might be expected to be greater for some human attributes than others. It appears to be more substantial for measures of intelfjlectual abilities than for social or personality attributes. However, it is difficult to establish a reliable, generalizable estimate for any given trait. For one thing, estimates vary depending on the source of information for measuring a trait. When children's characteristics are assessed through parents' ratings, heritability estimates are often considerably higher than when assessments are derived from behavioral observations of the children, from children's self-reports, or from teacher ratings. It appears that parents see their children as more different from one another than other sources of information find them to be (a contrast effect). In a recent review of studies of the heritability of aggressive behavior, Cadoret and colleagues (Cadoret et al 1997) report a very wide range of heritability coefficients, (from near zero to over 0.70), with the higher figures coming from studies using parent report measures, and the lower ones from observational studies. Miles & Carey (1997), in a meta-analysis of 24 twin and adoption studies, report substantially greater values for h^2 based on parent reports than for those based on adolescent self-reports.

Especially important is the fact that the size of a heritability coefficient depends greatly on the range of both genetic and environmental factors in the population being studied (G. Patterson, under review). Estimates of the heritability of a given trait can change considerably when a new estimate is based on a culturally different population, or especially when a new estimate includes families from a wider range of subcultures and socioeconomic levels.

All this means that while the fact of a genetic contribution to human variability is not in doubt, the size of this contribution is indeterminate for any given trait. More specifically, the size of a heritability estimate cannot be generalized from the specific population—in its specific environment—assessed with the specific set of measures used in a given study.

Estimating the Size of Environmental Effects

In twin and adoption studies, estimates of the power of environmental factors are derived by adopting the additive assumption, i.e. by assuming that that the sources of variation in a trait can be separated into independent genetic (G) and environmental (E) components that together (along with error variance) add to 100% of the variance to be accounted for. On the basis of this assumption, the heritability coefficient can be subtracted from 100% to yield an estimate of the environmental contribution to variance. Estimating E in this way can be done without utilizing any direct measures of environmental factors. Obviously, if the estimates of h^2 are indeterminate, so are the estimates of E derived by subtracting h^2 from 100%.

The validity of the additive assumption has been widely challenged (Feldman & Lewontin 1975, Gottlieb 1995, Block 1995, Rose 1995, Turkheimer 1998) A number of these critiques have appeared in connection with the controversy over Hernstein & Murray's book *The Bell Curve* (1994), but they are equally pertinent to the current debate over parenting effects. If one adopts the additive assumption, it follows that when h^2 is large, the effects of all environmental factors—including parenting—must be correspondingly small. A major counter-argument has been that in fact, everything that human beings are or do must be a joint function of both their genes and their life experiences. The pathway between genes and phenotypes is a long one, with G and E being interwoven all along the way (see Elman et al 1996). The effects of genes depend on environmental triggers or enabling conditions, and the effects of different environments depend on the genetic characteristics of the individuals encountering an environment. When genes and environment act jointly, this can emerge empirically in behavior genetics studies in the form of either G × E correlations or G × E interactions. In estimating environmental effects, much depends on how these joint processes are handled (or not handled). Both kinds of coaction are considered below, but the main point here is that neither G × E covariances nor interactions fit into an additive model

Shared and Unshared Environmental Effects

In twin and adoption studies, once an overall estimate of E has been derived by subtracting h^2 from 100%, E can be further subdivided into two environmental components: Es (shared environment) and Eus (unshared environment). Once again, this can be done without utilizing direct measures of either. If fraternal twins are quite similar—more similar than would be expected from their shared genetics alone—or if adopted children are more similar to the parents or siblings in their adopted families than they are to adults or children in other households, this would imply an effect of their rearing environment, including of course the parents' child-rearing methods. Es is estimated from sibling similarities, and any variance still unexplained after the effects of G and Es have been accounted for are attributed to unshared environment or error of measurement.

An especially surprising finding emerging from the body of behavior genetics work has been that the effects of nonshared environment appear to be much greater than those of shared environment (see Plomin & Daniels 1987 and Plomin et al 1994). Recent estimates of nonshared environmental effects are much reduced when measurement error is taken into account (Rutter et al 1999). And a number of studies of social behavior or pathology have found substantial shared-environment effects. Nevertheless, shared environmental effects consistently emerge as small, and indeed are often reported as being close to zero (Plomin & Bergeman 1991). Adopted children do not appear to resemble their adoptive siblings or parents any more closely than they resemble children growing up in different households. Also, in many respects fraternal twins—or ordinary siblings, for that matter—do not greatly resemble each other or their parents.

Critics have urged that it is not valid to estimate environmental effects, either shared or unshared, without measuring them (Goodman 1991, Hoffman 1991, Rose 1995, Stoolmiller 1999, Patterson 1975). Recent work has involved designs in which both genetic and environmental factors have been directly assessed. For example, a group of leading behavior geneticists and leading students of parent-child interaction collaborated in a study comparing children of different degrees of genetic relatedness (twins, full siblings, half siblings, step siblings), in which parental child-rearing inputs were assessed through observations of parent-child interactions, as well as through parent and child reports (Reiss 1997, Reiss et al 1999, Hetherington et al 1999).

Relying on the additive assumption, these investigators have partitioned the variance in child adjustment outcomes into the three components: G, Es, and Eus, reporting substantial contributions from genetics. Effects of shared environment are variable, making clear contributions to some outcomes but not others; in general, though, they are considerably smaller than the substantial contributions from unshared environment. Unfortunately the design of this study confounds genetic similarities and family structures: the group in which siblings are most genetically unlike (stepsiblings) is also the group in which the two siblings receive the most discordant parenting (Hetherington et al 1999). It should be noted, too, that the range of environmental variation is restricted in this study. Thus, many of the reported findings of this important study are difficult to interpret.

The inference of behavior geneticists' claims concerning shared and unshared environments might be that children are not greatly affected by the characteristics of the household in which they are growing up. The weak shared-environment effects have been interpreted to mean that such factors as the parents' income or education, parental pathology, the level of harmony or conflict between the parents, or the neighborhood where the family lives must have little impact on how well the child will do in school, how socially competent the children will be, and so forth (Plomin et al 1994, Scarr & Grajek 1982).

These findings on weak shared-environment effects are startling, considering how consistently studies of parenting effects have found substantial relationships between these family characteristics and child outcomes. As an example, McLoyd (1998) made a strong case for the mediating role of parenting in the deleterious effects of poverty. In McLoyd's analysis, it emerges that the great stresses on impoverished parents—stresses stemming from the day-to-day struggle to find the resources to pay for food and rent, and the stresses of trying to cope with living in crowded housing and deteriorated, dangerous neighborhoods—bring about a weakening of parenting skills and a disorganization of family life. It is the deterioration of parenting, McLoyd found, that in its turn is responsible for many of the adjustment difficulties of children growing up in impoverished families. (See also Conger et al 1994 and Pettit et al 1997 for findings supporting this conclusion.)

It is difficult to reconcile findings such as these with the claim that the aspects of family environments that are shared by siblings do not affect their development. An obvious possibility is that while the family environment does have an effect on each child, its effects are different for different children. There probably was an unspoken assumption, in traditional socialization work, that the effects of shared environments would be to make siblings similar to one another. What the behavior geneticists are telling us is that any influences of familial circumstances—such as parental illness or health, economic prosperity or adversity, good or poor parenting—often function to make siblings different rather than similar. It is possible that a dysfunctional family environment may have effects on both members of a sibling pair, but that the effects are not such as to make siblings more alike, but indeed might function to make them more different. We know from Elder's work on effects of the Great Depression (Elder 1974) that when a father loses his job, the effects on the child will depend on the age and sex of the child at the time that this stressful event occurs. Even for same-sex twins, we can imagine that if they were adolescents at the time, one might react to a father's job loss by going out to get an after-school job to help support the family while the other might distance himself from the family and spend more time "hanging out" with friends. Both children would be affected by the change in the family environment, but differently.

Any familial or parental factors that serve to make siblings different rather than similar to one another are assigned, in behavior genetics, to the unshared rather than the shared environmental component when computing environmental effects. Behavior geneticists have never said that estimates of unshared environments did not include parent effects, but they argue that if parenting does have effects it must take one of two forms: parents must be treating different children in their families differently (or providing different environments for them), or different children in the same family who are exposed to similar parenting must react to the same parental inputs differently.

A considerable body of recent work has focussed on the question, What is it that makes siblings different from one another? (see Hetherington et al 1994). In these studies evidence is presented that siblings tend to join different peer groups and that siblings have considerably different experiences within the context of the sibling relationship itself. The question of how differently they are treated by their parents remains open. Studies done during a single time period often show that two siblings are treated differently by their parents (see summary by Brody & Stoneman 1994) However, in a longitudinal study Dunn found that parents were fairly consistent in how they treated children at a specific age. That is, a second child, when reaching the age of four, is treated in a similar way to the way his/her older sibling was treated at that age, even though the older sibling may now be receiving different treatment. Thus, over the span of the "growing up" years, different children in the same family received comparable treatment. This fact, of course, would be missed in any study that did not look for it longitudinally; the extent of differential treatment is likely to be overestimated in cross-sectional studies (except in the case of twins). Whether or not children actually are treated differently over the whole span of childhood, there is reason to believe that children's perceptions of how differently they are treated may be of considerable importance in children's development, so concurrent differences are important in their own right (Dunn & McGuire 1994).

In general, the exploration of siblings' unshared environments has been a productive and instructive enterprise. We now know that the environments of children growing up in the same family can indeed be different. But this does not solve the problem of how to interpret aspects of the environment that are truly shared, such as a parental illness, family income, parents' education, or the neighborhood where the family lives—factors that have an impact even when they function to make siblings different rather than alike. As noted above, behavior geneticists tend to conclude that, since it is clear that these aspects of environment are truly shared, they must not be having an effect because Es effects are negligible. As Plomin and colleagues say, "So often, we have assumed that the key influences on children's development are shared: their parents' personality and childhood experiences, the quality of their parents' marriage relationship, children's educational background, the neighborhood in which they grow up, and their parents' attitude to school or to discipline. Yet to the extent that these influences are shared, they cannot account for the differences we observe in children's outcomes" (Plomin et al 1994:23).

On the contrary, it seems plausible that these shared factors may indeed have powerful effects that do not show up in computations of shared environmental effects because of the requirement that only an environmental factor that makes siblings more similar can be called "shared." A behavior geneticists might say about the effect of a shared environmental factor that makes siblings different, "Oh, but we are calling those unshared effects." But to call an environmental input unshared even though it is experienced by all children in a family (e.g. a father's job-loss, a mother's depression, a move to a better neighborhood) is an unfortunate distortion of the simple meaning of the word "shared." We could see this as only a trivial matter of terminology choice, but it can lead to serious misunderstandings of behavior geneticists' findings. By definition, they have ruled out the possibility that a truly shared aspect of the environment could have a significant effect on at least one child, when the effects on different children are not the same.

When we deal with a shared environmental factor that impacts different children in the family differently, it could be argued—and behavior geneticists do so argue—that the effect stems from the fact that some children are more genetically vulnerable to an environmental event than others. In the usual computations of heritability, such an effect would then be assigned to the G component of the equation, rather than to the environmental one. Surely, it is equally plausible that both G and E are important here. Risk factors, such as poverty, a father's unemployment, or a mother's depression, are indeed environmental conditions that are shared by all the children in a family. In large population studies they will rightly emerge as having a negative impact on children, even though some children are more vulnerable to them than others. In the extreme case, we could imagine that in every two-child family, one of the children would show the deleterious effects of poverty and the other would not (perhaps because of genetic differences between them). Across many families, there would be a very powerful effect of poverty and it would be rightly identified as a strong risk factor, even though the shared environment effect would be computed at zero. The obvious danger here is that low estimates for Es can be interpreted as meaning that family environmental conditions that children share do not have an impact on their development, whereas in fact the opposite can be true, and often is.

The findings from behavior genetics on shared and unshared environments have profound implications for the way we think about child-rearing practices and their effects. For one thing, they focus attention on sibling differences. This is something that traditional research on child-rearing—almost always involving only one child per family—did not deal with. It should be noted that there is nothing about the findings of these traditional studies that is invalidated by their having studied only one child. The connections identified between the parental inputs to this child and the child's characteristics can be reliable, replicable ones, even though if we had studied a different parent-child pair in the same family we might have gotten a different constellation of parenting and outcomes. The picture emerging from aggregating data across a set of one-child cases is valid as well, though the findings are surely attenuated by the within-family sibling variation. Still, we get a less differentiated picture than the one that emerges from the study of siblings. Family systems theorists have alerted us to "niche-picking" by different children in a family—the effort of children to find distinctive roles. Evolutionary theorists have argued that there is natural competition among siblings for parental attention and other resources provided by parents. In short, there is reason to believe that there are forces motivating children to differentiate themselves from their siblings, and these may counterbalance, or transform, the effects of parental inputs that might otherwise function to make them the same. Of course, some of the differentiation between siblings can come directly from differential treatment by the parents, or it can stem from differential reactions by different children to the same parental inputs.

INTERPRETING PARENT-CHILD COVARIANCE

As noted above, quantitative geneticists have raised serious questions concerning the direction of effects when parental behaviors and child characteristics are found to be correlated. They point out that parent-child correlations could stem from genetic predispositions shared by parents and children that are directly transmitted from one generation to the next. In addition, evocative covariance occurs when children with different genetic predispositions elicit correspondingly different reactions from their parents. Thus, when a child is predisposed to be resistive or distractible and does not pay attention to the parent, the parent reacts by becoming more authoritarian, whereas a cooperative child will evoke a different reaction. (See Ge et al 1996, which shows clearly how the parenting by adoptive parents is affected by the predispositions of their adopted children.) Active covariance occurs when children select from a range of potential environmental influences only certain features with which to engage—certain TV programs, certain friends, certain sports—presumably on the basis of their own predispositions. Although children do not have the freedom to choose their parents, they do have some power to select which aspects of parental inputs they will attend to. Children with different genetic predispositions no doubt react differently to the same parental input, depending either on what they attend to, how they interpret their parents' actions, or what behavioral predisposition of their own has been triggered. In twin and adoption studies, all these forms of covariance between parent and child are thought to imply that genetics—either the child's own or the genes shared with parents—are driving the parental behaviors. For these reasons, it has seemed reasonable, in behavior genetic analyses, to assign parent-child covariances to the genetic component in the $G + E = 100\%$ equation.

I would argue that to assign parent-child covariance to G systematically underestimates the strength of parenting effects. It does so by ignoring the feed-back loop whereby parents, in reacting to a given child's distinctive input, reciprocate with counter influences of their own.

The fact that parents respond differently to children with different predispositions is not in doubt, and it has been one of the contributions of behavior genetics to bring this fact into the foreground of our thinking. Socialization researchers, too, have for some time been centrally aware of this issue and in the past several decades have by no means ignored the problem of direction of effects. A great deal of effort has been devoted to examining the processes whereby parents and children influence one another. The predominant modern viewpoint among students of socialization is an interactionist one, in which it is assumed that in any ongoing relationship, each member of an interacting pair is a significant feature of the other's environment to which each must adapt. In addition, it has become clear that the developmental level of a child is a powerful determiner of what kind of socialization inputs a parent will provide and what kind of receptiveness, resistance, or negotiation the child will bring to a parent-child encounter. We cannot expect to find generalizations about the nature and effects of specific parent/child interactions that will span all the ages and stages of a child's development.

From an interactionist perspective, the idea that in a long-standing relationship such as the one between a parent and child, the child would be influencing the parent but the parent would not be influencing the child is absurd. While it is entirely reasonable to assign the child's part in parent-child covariance (i.e. evocative effects) to the genetic component, it is not reasonable to assign the reciprocal parent contribution to the child's genetics. The parent's response is surely a function not only of the child's initiative but also of the parent's genetics, learned modes of behavior, perceptions of the child's needs and characteristics, and socialization objectives. And, just as surely, the parent's response to the child's initiatives is a central element in the child's environment. Thus, to assign the whole of parent-child covariance to G is surely to overestimate G and underestimate E.

A recent study from the Rutter-Plomin research group in London (O'Connor et al 1998) beautifully identifies the contributions of correlated G and E factors to developmental outcomes. Using longitudinal data from the Colorado Adoption Study, these researchers identified two groups of adoptees: one at genetic risk for anti-social behavior (i.e. a history of anti-social behavior in the biological mother) and the other not at risk. At several points during the adoptees' childhood, both the children's characteristics and the adoptive parents' child-rearing methods were assessed. Findings were that children carrying a genetic risk for antisocial behavior were more likely to receive negative socialization inputs from their adoptive parents—an evocative effect. But parental negative behavior made an independent contribution to children's externalizing, over and above the children's genetic predispositions.

This study illustrates what an interactionist perspective would lead us to expect: Parent-child covariance reflects the reciprocal effects of both parent and child inputs to a relationship. The issue here is not to compare G and E effects to see which is stronger. Instead, it is to explore how they intersect or how one mediates the effect of the other. Such issues remain largely unexplored. The relative strength of each contribution is difficult to assess and is almost entirely unknown in the large body of research literature on within-family socialization. The study by O'Connor et al illustrates the futility of efforts to compartmentalize the variance in children's characteristics into separate G and E components without getting independent measures of each. What this study shows is that G and E operate jointly to produce an outcome.

THE INTERACTION OF GENETIC AND ENVIRONMENTAL FACTORS

Interactions are found when a given environment has different effects on an organism, depending on the organism's genetic traits. Interactions are also seen when organisms with a given set of genetic traits react in one way under one set of environmental conditions, but another way under different environmental conditions. Plant biologists are able to point to dramatic examples, such as when there are two genetic strains of a grain, and strain 1 grows taller than strain 2 at high altitudes and shorter than strain 2 at low altitudes.

G × E Interactions in Animal Studies

A careful review of animal studies that looked for G × E interactions (Plomin 1986) reported that though interactions were sometimes found, they were not consistent within or across studies and accounted for only a small portion of variance. Since that review, some progress has been made in the difficult enterprise of mapping the complex processes that intervene between genotype and phenotype, and recently there has been some success in uncovering interactions with respect to these better-defined processes. In several mammalian species, it is now known that there are genetic factors underlying variation in "reactivity," that is, in the tendency to become emotionally aroused and fearful. Different levels of reactivity in rats are associated with both neuroendocrine and behavioral functioning (Caldji et al 1998, Liu et al 1997). Reactive animals appear jittery and hesitate to explore novel environments. In Rhesus monkeys, a gene has been isolated one of whose alleles is associated with the emergence of a reactive temperament (Suomi 1999). It has been found that young animals carrying the "reactive" allele are particularly vulnerable to variations in early rearing experience. If they are subjected to maternal deprivation during their first six months (reared with peers but no adult females) their neuroendocrine functioning is affected and they display a variety of pathological symptoms into adulthood, including incompetence in social interactions, low status in peer groups, and incompetence in mothering their own offspring (Suomi 1997). By contrast, young animals who do not carry the genetic risk factor are much less affected by maternal deprivation. In current work, genetically reactive newborn monkeys are being cross-fostered to non-reactive mothers, and preliminary observations indicate that calm mothering does indeed buffer them from the development of strongly reactive behavior. Cross-fostering work with rodents is also showing the positive effects of rearing genetically at-risk infants by a nurturant mother (Anisman et al 1998).We see here that the effects of a genetic predisposition are strongly seen under one set of environmental (rearing) conditions but not another.

G × E Interactions in Adoption Studies

Of course it is not possible to carry out systematic experiments of this sort with humans, but quantitative genetic studies can be used to test for G × E interactions. However, in such studies it is no longer possible to bypass measures of the environment and estimate E effects only as a residual after G effects have been estimated and subtracted out. Instead, there must be direct measures of both G and E. In most twin studies, the environments of twin pairs are too homogeneous to permit good estimates of G × E interactions, and there are difficulties in interpreting the differences between identical and fraternal twins in interaction terms. As Plomin said, "
. . . it is difficult if not impossible to use the twin design to estimate the overall contribution of genotype-environment interaction to phenotypic variance" (Plomin 1986:96).[3] Since that time, there have been some innovations in utilizing twin studies to study interactions. One method is to use one twin's characteristic as an index to the co-twin's genetic risk; when the two are not highly concordant for the trait, their respective environments can then be examined for clues as to the origins of their non-genetic differences. Another method is simply to compare the heritability estimates found in two different environments.

In studies of adopted children, adoptive families vary with respect to the kind of environments they provide (though the range of environmental variation is usually consistently narrower than in unselected populations), and interactions can be effectively studied. In a large-scale study of adopted children in Finland (Tienari et al 1994), children with a schizophrenic biological parent were contrasted with adopted children who did not carry this genetic risk factor. It was found that the at-risk children were more likely to develop a range of psychiatric problems, but only if they were adopted into dysfunctional adoptive families. A study of adopted children whose biological parents did or did not have a history of criminality (Bohman 1996) yielded similar results: Among adoptees who carried a risk factor from their biological parents, those who had been adopted into dysfunctional homes were over three times more likely to become petty criminals than those whose adoptive parents had provided a stable, supportive environment.

These findings from adoption studies are consistent with studies of cross-generational transmission of psychiatric disorders (Ge et al 1996, Downey & Walker 1992). These studies point to a mediating role of parenting: Children whose parents suffer from a psychiatric disorder are usually no more likely than children with normal parents to develop psychiatric disorders, unless the children are exposed directly

---

[3]In studies of twins reared apart more variation in environments is of course usually present but the Ns for such studies are small and environmental information fragmentary.

to harsh parenting and/or an otherwise dysfunctional family environment by the parents who are rearing them.

Taken together, these studies indicate that genetic risks may or may not become manifest, depending on the quality of the parenting children receive. In other words, whatever genetic risks a child carries can require an environmental trigger to emerge into phenotypic expression. Well-functioning parents can buffer children against the emergence of negative genetic potentials.

Studies of Interactions with Temperament

It is possible to approximate the study of G × E interactions even when no direct information on children's genetics is available. Since several dimensions of temperament are known to have a significant genetic component,[4] researchers have identified children with different temperaments, and studied how they differ in the way they interact with their parents and in the impact parental inputs have on them. Children's temperamental characteristics appear to set the stage for the kind of bi-directional processes that will emerge between them and their parents (Collins et al 1999). Evidence has been emerging that a given parental practice can have different effects on children with different temperaments. Kochanska (1995, 1997a) studied the development of conscience in young children. She reported that for shy, temperamentally fearful children, parental power-assertion does not appear to promote conscience development—gentler techniques are called for. But with bold assertive children, effective parenting involves firmness, along with maternal responsiveness and the formation of a close emotional bond with the child. In a similar way, it has been found that for children who are initially difficult, impulsive, and/or resistive, parental firmness and restrictiveness are more important ingredients in preventing the subsequent development of externalizing behavior than is the case for children with easier temperaments (Bates et al 1998). Other studies finding interactions between children's temperament and parenting effects are those by Belsky et al (1997) and Deater-Deckard & Dodge (1997).

In Plomin's (1986) review of the studies on G × E interactions in children that were available at that time, significant interactions were found to be quite rare. It is possible at this time to be more positive—though guardedly so—concerning the prevalence and power of these interactions. They may be more prevalent with respect to personality dimensions and psychopathology than they are with respect to cognitive dimensions, but they obviously cannot be detected by using the traditional additive approach to partitioning variance between G and E. Indeed, the presence of interactions constitutes strong evidence against the validity of this approach. In molecular genetics, it is axiomatic that interactions are the rule, not the exception and that efforts to partition variance into the two traditional components are counterproductive.

---

[4]Temperament is currently defined as " . . . constitutionally based individual differences in reactivity and self-regulation . . . " (Rothbart & Ahadi 1994:54).

OVERVIEW

Behavior genetics studies have made substantial contributions to our understanding of the factors that underlie the variation among children in their intellectual and personality characteristics. Studies of twins and adopted children have shown beyond reasonable doubt that a wide range of children's attributes are influenced substantially by the genes they inherit from their biological parents. These studies first began to appear in the 1930s, and work done since that time has continued to confirm the power of genetic factors. The precise magnitude of the genetic contribution to a given trait, however, has proved to be difficult to establish: Heritability estimates vary widely, and indeed there is no reason to expect that there exists any one valid number for any given trait. Instead, heritability inevitably depends on the range of variation within a given sample being studied, and on the socio-cultural milieu in which the studied population lives. No single estimate can ever be taken as definitive.

I have argued that when genetic factors are strong, this does not mean that environmental ones, including parenting, must be weak. The relation between the two is not a zero-sum game, and the additive assumption is untenable. There are environmental factors that can affect a group or population without greatly rearranging the rank order of individuals within that group. In such a case, estimates of heritability can remain high while at the same time powerful environmental forces are at work. For this reason, it is not legitimate to extrapolate G or E estimates derived from a behavior genetic analysis to differences between groups (e.g. between races, social classes, or genders) that differ in their environmental milieu.

Experimental interventions have been designed to change children's behavior by means of changing the child-rearing practices of their parents. These intervention programs have amply demonstrated that parenting does have direct effects on how children behave, both inside and outside the home. When families are randomly assigned to an intervention group, the children show a reduction in problem behaviors by comparison with an untreated control group, and these effects are clearly independent of any genetic contribution to the outcome behavior being studied. Equally important is the presence of interactions between genes and environment, such that an environmental trigger is needed to evoke a genetic predisposition. Included here would be instances in which competent, supportive parenting protects a child from developing a dysfunction for which he or she is genetically predisposed. Such interactions have been largely ignored in traditional behavior genetic studies. What I argue here is that while the contribution of genetic factors to children's characteristics has been solidly documented in behavior genetics work, the contribution of environmental factors as derived from these studies has not.

A crucially important contribution of behavior genetics has been to draw our attention to the unlikeness of siblings. While we may have been marginally aware of sibling disparities, the traditional studies of childhood socialization included only one child per family, and there was an implicit assumption that parents treated their various children much alike and that the effects of what they did would be similar for all their children. We must now seriously reexamine these assumptions. We now know that the correlations between siblings with respect to many of their characteristics are very low—indeed, sometimes lower than their genetic relatedness would predict. Is the unlikeness of siblings due to their being· treated differently by their parents? To some extent, yes, though findings are not consistent across studies. What the behavior geneticists have shown is that the genetic predispositions of different children often drive the responses of parents, determining to some degree the kind of parenting a child will receive. Understandably then, behavior geneticists have assigned correlations between parent and child behaviors to the child's genetics, but I argue that this is a mistake, in that it ignores the return feed-back loop whereby a parent, whose behavior has been triggered by the child, responds with actions which in their turn influence the child. To ignore this reciprocal influence is to seriously underestimate parenting effects.

The unlikeness of siblings continues to be something we do not fully understand. It has been interpreted to mean that aspects of environment which siblings share— amount of inter-parental conflict, good or poor neighborhoods, poverty or affluence, level of parental education or the "cultural" level of the home environment, household organization or disorganization, the amount of good humor characterizing the family atmosphere—all these things must have very little influence on children's development. This interpretation flies in the face of the large body of research on risk factors, which repeatedly finds strong relationships between these aspects of family functioning and children's outcomes. I argue that the risk-factor findings are indeed valid, but that they need not have the same effects on all children in a family nor function to make siblings more alike. It begins to seem likely that there are strong factors pushing siblings toward differentiation from one another, including perhaps competition for parental attention or other resources, "niche picking," counteridentification, and differential perceptions of the sibling relationship on the part of the participants in it. Such factors could function as counter forces, working against parental inputs that might otherwise make siblings more alike. But this is speculation. Much remains to be learned about this complex matter.

Many factors other than parents' actions influence how children grow and develop. As children grow beyond the preschool years, they are exposed more and more to other adult socialization agents (teachers, coaches) and, of course, to individual friends and larger peer groups. Within the matrix of factors that affect children's development, it is clear that parenting effects are real, though they often combine with genetic effects in influencing an outcome. Along with many other students of these phenomena, I urge that we give up the effort to partition the causal factors influencing children's development into two separate "nature" and "nurture" components, and that we abstain from asking ourselves which is more important. The two are inextricably interwoven all along the pathway from birth to maturity. So be it. Let us not underestimate either, but concentrate on the ways in which they function jointly.

ACKNOWLEDGMENTS

During the time I have been working on this chapter, I have also been participating with four colleagues in writing a closely related paper. These colleagues are W Andrew Collins, E Mavis Hetherington, Lawrence Steinberg, and Marc Bornstein. I gratefully acknowledge their help in searching out references and the clarifying value of our discussions. Others who have been helpful in providing materials for this chapter are Michael Rutter, Andrew Heath, Gerald Patterson, Stephen Suomi, Rich Weinberg, Megan Gunnar, John Flavell, Grazyna Kochanska, Robert Cairns, and Tom Dishion.

Visit the Annual Reviews home page at www.AnnualReviews.org.

LITERATURE CITED

Angoff WH. 1988. The nature-nurture debate, aptitudes and group differences. *Am. Psychol.* 43:713–20

Anisman H, Zaharia MD, Meaney MJ, Merali Z. 1998. Do early-life events permanently alter behavioral and hormonal responses to stressors. *Int. J.Dev. Neurosci.* 16:149–64

Bates J, Pettit G, Dodge K, Ridge B. 1998. Interaction of temperamental resistance to control and restrictive parenting in the development of externalizing behavior. *Dev. Psychol.* 34:982–95

Baumrind D, Black AE. 1967. Socialization practices associated with dimensions of competence in preschool boys and girls. *Child Dev.* 38:291–327

Belsky J, Hsieh K, Crnic K. 1997. Mothering, fathering and infant negativity as predictors of boys' externalizing problems and inhibition. *Dev. Psychopathol.* 10:301–19

Block N. 1995. How heretability misleads about race. *Cognition* 56:99–128

Bohman M. 1996. Predispositions to criminality: Swedish adoption studies in retrospect. In *Genetics of Criminal and Anti-Social Behavior, Ciba Found. Symp. 194,* ed. GR Bock, JA Goode, pp. 99–114. Chickester/New York: Wiley. 283 pp.

Brody G, Stoneman Z. 1994. Sibling relationships and their association with parental differential treatment. See Hetherington et al 1994, pp. 129–42

Cadoret RJ, Leve LD, Devor E. 1997. Genetics of aggressive and violent behavior. *Psychol. Clin. N. Am.* 20:301–22

Caldji C, Tannenbaum B, Sharma S, Francis D, Plotsky PM, Meaney MJ. 1998. Maternal care during infancy regulates the development of neural systems mediating the expression of fearfulness in the rat. *Proc. Nat. Acad. Sci.* 95:5335–40

Collins WA, Maccoby EE, Steinberg L, Hetherington EM, Bornstein M. 1999. Contemporary research on parenting: the case for nature *and* nurture. *Am. Psychol.* In press

Conger RD, Elder GH. 1994. *Families in Troubled Times: Adapting to Change in Rural America.* Hawthorne, NY: Aldine

Conger RD, Ge X, Elder GH, Lorenz FO, Simons R. 1994. Economic stress, coercive family process, and developmental problems of adolescents. *Child Dev.* 65:541–61

Deater-Deckard K, Dodge K. 1997. Spare the rod, spoil the authors: emerging themes in research on parenting. *Psychol. Inq.* 8:230–35

Dishion TJ, Patterson GR, Kavanagh K. 1992. An experimental test of the coercion model: linking theory, measurement, and intervention. In *The Interaction of Theory and Practice: Experimental Studies of Interventions,* ed. J McCord, R Trembly, pp. 253–82. New York: Guilford. 29 pp.

Downey G, Walker E. 1992. Distinguishing family-level and child-level influences on the development of depression and aggression. *Dev. Psychopathol.* 4:81–96

Dunn J, McGuire S. 1994. Young children's nonshared experiences: a summary of studies in Cambridge and Colorado. See Hetherington et al 1994, pp. 111–28

Dunn J, Plomin R. 1986. Determinants of maternal behavior toward three-year-old siblings. *Br. J. Dev. Psychol.* 57:348–56

Duyme M, Dumaret AC, Stanislaw T. 1999. How can we boost IQs of "dull" children?: a late adoption study. *Proc. Nat. Acad. Sci.* In press

Elder GH. 1974. *Children of the Great Depression.* Chicago: Univ. Chicago Press. 400 pp.

Elman JL, Bates EA, Johnson MH, Karmiloff-Smith A, Parisi D, Plunkett K. 1996. *Rethinking Innateness: A Connectionist Perspective on Development.* Cambridge, MA: MIT Press

Feldman MW, Lewontin RC. 1975. The heritability hangup. *Science* 190:1163–68

Flynn JR. 1999. Searching for justice: the discovery of IQ gains over time. *Am. Psychol.* 54:5–20

Flynn JR. 1987. Massive IQ gains in 14 nations: what IQ tests really measure. *Psychol. Bull.* 101:171–91

Forehand R, Wells KC, Griest DL. 1980. An examination of the social validity of a parent training program. *Behav. Ther.* 11:488–502

Ge X, Conger R, Cadoret R, Neiderhiser J, Yates W, et al. 1996. The developmental interface between nature and nurture: a mutual influence model of child antisocial behavior and parent behavior. *Dev. Psychol.* 32:574–89

Goodman R. 1991. Growing together and growing apart: the non-genetic forces on children in the same family. In *The New Genetics of Mental Illness,* ed. R McGuffin, R Murray, pp. 212–24. Oxford: Oxford Univ. Press

Gottlieb G. 1995. Some conceptual deficiencies in "developmental" behavior genetics. *Hum. Dev.* 38:131–41

Harris JR. 1998. *The Nurture Assumption: Why Children Turn Out the Way They Do.* New York: Free Press. 462 pp.

Hernnstein RJ, Murray C. 1994. *The Bell Curve: Intelligence and Class Structure in American Life.* New York: Free Press

Hetherington EM, Reiss D, Plomin R, eds. 1994. *Separate Social Worlds of Siblings.* Hillsdale, NJ: Erlbaum. 232 pp.

Hetherington EM, Henderson SH, Reiss D. 1999. *Adolescent Siblings in Stepfamilies: Family Functioning and Adolescent Adjustment.* Monog. Soc. Res. Child Dev. In press

Hoffman LW. 1991. The influence of the family environment on personality: accounting for sibling differences. *Psychol. Bull.* 110:187–203

Kochanska G. 1995. Children's temperament, mothers' discipline, and security of attachment: multiple pathways to emerging internalization. *Child Dev.* 66:597–615

Kochanska G. 1997a. Multiple pathways to conscience for children with different temperaments: from toddlerhood to age five. *Dev. Psychol.* 33:228–40

Kochanska G. 1997b. Mutually responsive orientation between mothers and their young children: implications for early socialization. *Child Dev.* 68:908–23

Kochanska G, Thompson RA. 1997. The emergence and development of conscience in toddlerhood and early childhood. In *Parenting and Children's Internalization of Values,* ed. JE Grusec, L Kuczunski pp. 53–77. New York: Wiley

Liu D, Diorio J, Tannenbaum B, Cladji C, Francis D, et al. 1997. Maternal care, hippocampal glucocorticoid receptors and hypothalamic-pituitary-adrenal responses to stress. *Science* 277:1659–62

Loeber R, Dishion TJ. 1983. Early predictors of male delinquency: a review. *Psychol. Bull.* 94:68–99

Maccoby EE, Martin JA. 1983. Socialization in the context of the family: parent-child interaction. In *Handbook of Child Psychology,* Vol. 4, ed. PH Messen, EM Herrington, 4:1–102. New York: Wiley. 4th ed. pp.1–102

McLoyd VC. 1998. Socioeconomic disadvantage and child development. *Am. Psychol.* 53:185–204

Miles D, Carey G. 1997. Genetic and environmental architecture of human aggression. *J. Pers. Soc. Psychol.* 72:207–17

Neville HJ. 1996. Developmental specificity in neurocognitive development in humans. In *The Cognitive Neurosciences,* ed. M Gazzaniga, pp. 219–31 Cambridge, MA: MIT Press

O'Connor TG, Deater-Deckard K, Fulker D, Rutter M, Plomin R. 1998. Genotype-environment correlations in late childhood and early adolescence: antisocial behavioral problems and coercive parenting. *Dev. Psychol.* 34:970–81

Patterson GR. 1975. Multiple evaluations of a parent-training program. In *Applications of Behavior Modification,* ed. T Thompson, W Dockens, pp. 299–322. New York: Academic

Patterson GR, Bank LI. 1989. Some amplifying mechanisms for pathologic processes in families. In *Systems and Development: The Minnesota Symposium on Child Psychology,* ed. MR Gunnar, E. Thelen pp. 167–209. Hillsdale, NJ

Patterson GR, Forgatch M. 1995. Predicting future clinical adjustment from treatment outcome and process variables. *Psychol. Assess.* 7:275–85

Pettit GS, Bates JE, Dodge KA. 1997. Supportive parenting, ecological context, and children's adjustment: a seven-year longitudinal study. *Child Dev.* 68:908–23

Plomin R. 1986. *Development, Genetics, and Psychology.* Hillsdale, NJ: Erlbaum. 372 pp.

Plomin R, Bergman CS. 1991. The nature of nurture: genetic influences on "environmental" measures. *Behav. Brain Sci.* 14:1–15

Plomin R, Chipuer HM, Neiderhiser JM. 1994. Behavioral genetic evidence for the importance of nonshared environment. See Hetherington et al 1994, pp. 1–31

Plomin R, Daniels D. 1987. Why are children in the same family so different from each other? *Behav. Brain Sci.* 10:1–16

Plomin R, DeFries J, Fulker D. 1988. *Nature and Nurture During Infancy and Early Childhood.* Pacific Grove, CA: Brooks-Cole

Price RA, Charles MA, Pettit DJ, Knowler WC. 1993. Obesity in Pima Indians: large increases in post- World War II birth cohorts. *Am. J. Phys. Anthropol.* 92:473–79

Ravussin E, Bennett PH, Valencia ME, Schulz LO, Esparaz J. 1994. Effects of a traditional lifestyle on obesity in Pima Indians. *Diabetes Care* 17:1067–74

Reiss D. 1997. Mechanisms linking genetic and social influences in adolescent development: beginning a collaborative search. *Curr. Dir. Psychol. Sci.* 6:100–6

Reiss D, Hetherington EM, Plomin R, Howe GW, Simmens SJ, et al. 1995. Genetic questions for environmental studies: differential parenting and psychopathology in adolescence. *Arch. Gen. Psychol.* 52:925–36

Reiss D, Neiderhiser J, Hetherington EM, Plomin R. 1999 *The Relationship Code: Deciphering Genetic and Social Patterns in Adolescent Development.* Cambridge, MA: Harvard Univ. Press. In press

Rose R. 1995. Genes and human behavior. *Annu. Rev. Psychol.* 46:625–54

Rosenthal R. 1999. *Discussion on effect sizes at symposium on, "Does Child Care Quality matter?"* Presented at Biennial Meet. Soc. Res. Child Dev., April, Albuquerque, NM

Rothbart M, Ahadi S. 1994. Temperament and the development of personality. *J. Abnorm. Psychol.* 103:55–66

Rowe D. 1994. *The Limits of Family Influence: Genes, Experience, and Behavior.* New York: Guilford

Rowe D. 1983. A biometrical analysis of perceptions of family environment: a study of twin and singleton sibling kinship. *Child Dev.* 54:416–23

Rutter M, Silberg J, O'Connor T, Simonoff E. 1999. Genetics and child psychiatry: I. Advances in quantitative and molecular genetics. *Child Psychol. Psychol.* 40:3–18.

Scarr S. 1992. Developmental theories for the 1990's: development and individual differences. *Child Dev.* 63:1–19

Scarr S, Grajek S. 1982. Similarities and differences among siblings. In *Sibling Relationships: Their Nature and Significance Across the Lifespan,* ed. ME Lamb, B Sutton-Smith, pp. 357–82. Hillsdale, NJ: Erlbaum

Stoolmiller M. 1999. Implications of the restricted range of family environments for estimates of heritability and nonshared environment in behavior genetic adoption studies. *Psychol. Bull.* In press

Suomi SJ. 1999. A biobehavioral perspective on developmental psychopathology: excessive aggression and serotonergic dysfunction in monkeys. In *Handbook of Developmental Psychopathology,* ed. AJ Samaroff, M Lewis, S Miller. New York: Plenum. In press

Suomi SJ. 1997. Long-term effects of different early rearing experiences on social, emotional and physiological development in non-human primates. In *Neurodevelopmental Models of Adult Psychopathology,* ed. MS Kesheven, RM Murra, pp. 104–16. Cambridge: Cambridge Univ. Press

Tienari P, Wynne LC, Moring J, Lahti I, Naarala M, et al. 1994. The Finnish adoptive family study of schizophrenia: implications for family research. *Br. J. Psychiatry* 23(Suppl. 164):20–26

Turkheimer E. 1998. Heritability and biological explanation. *Psychol. Rev.* 105:1–10

Van den Boom DC. 1994. The influence of temperament and mothering on attachment and exploration: an experimental manipulation of sensitive responsiveness among lower-class mothers with irritable infants. *Child Dev.* 65:1457–77

Annu. Rev. Psychol. 2000. 51:29–57

THE PAIN OF BEING SICK: Implications of Immune-to-Brain Communication for Understanding Pain

L. R. Watkins and S. F. Maier

Department of Psychology, University of Colorado at Boulder, Boulder, Colorado 80309–0345; e-mail: lwatkins@psych.colorado.edu, smaier@psych.colorado.edu

Key Words   review, interleukin-1, tumor necrosis factor, nerve growth factor, hyperalgesia, allodynia

■ **Abstract**   This review focuses on the powerful pain facilitatory effects produced by the immune system. Immune cells, activated in response to infection, inflammation, or trauma, release proteins called proinflammatory cytokines. These proinflammatory cytokines signal the central nervous system, thereby creating exaggerated pain as well as an entire constellation of physiological, behavioral, and hormonal changes. These changes are collectively referred to as the sickness response. Release of proinflammatory cytokines by immune cells in the body leads, in turn, to release of proinflammatory cytokines by glia within the brain and spinal cord. Evidence is reviewed supporting the idea that proinflammatory cytokines exert powerful pain facilitatory effects following their release in the body, in the brain, and in the spinal cord. Such exaggerated pain states naturally occur in situations involving infection, inflammation, or trauma of the skin, of peripheral nerves, and of the central nervous system itself. Implications for human pain conditions are discussed.

CONTENTS

Introduction 30
A Brief Overview of Pain Modulation 30
   Analgesia and Antianalgesia 32
   Hyperalgesia and Allodynia 33
Immune-to-Brain Communication: Organizing the Sickness Response...............35
Pain as a Natural Part of the Sickness Response.......................................39
Role of the Immune System in Pain 41
   Skin Infection and Inflammation 41
   Nerve Infection and Inflammation 43
   Central Nervous System Infection and Inflammation 45
Implications for Human Pain Conditions 47
Conclusions 49

0084–6570/00/0201–0029$12.00

INTRODUCTION

Interactions between the central nervous system and the body have generally been regarded as involving regulation of peripheral processes by the brain. However, a variety of recent research suggests that the interaction between brain and body is far more dynamic than previously recognized, with peripheral systems and products exerting potent effects on neural processes and thereby behavior. This bidirectionality of communication has become clear with regard to interactions between the brain and the immune system. Initial interest in brain-immune relationships focused on how neural processes could regulate immune function, but it is now clear that immune products signal the central nervous system and regulate its activity (for review see Maier & Watkins 1998). Immune-to-brain communication plays an unrecognized role in many psychological phenomena. The purpose of this review is to describe what is known about its role in pain.

A BRIEF OVERVIEW OF PAIN MODULATION

The sensation of pain is a dynamic, rather than passive, process. Research spanning well over a century has shown that highly organized neural circuits existing in the brain and spinal cord regulate pain. Some of these circuits suppress pain; others magnify it. Thus, a person's perception of pain may have little to do with the actual intensity of the pain.

A central organizational theme revealed by the study of pain inhibitory (analgesia) and pain facilitatory (hyperalgesia) circuits is that, by and large, the central nervous system regulates pain perception by regulating the pain message while it is still in the spinal cord (Kelly 1986). Thus, regulation occurs before pain reaches a person's consciousness (Figure 1). The analgesia and hyperalgesia circuits do this by modulating pain signals as they first arrive in the spinal cord from the body. In the absence of modulation, nociceptive (pain responsive) peripheral nerves become activated by intense stimuli (e.g. heat, crush, pinprick, acid), and this activation causes these nerves to relay electrical signals to neurons in the spinal cord dorsal horns. Here, the incoming sensory nerve fibers synapse, so neurotransmitters released in response to the incoming electrical signals carry the pain message forward to the second neuron in line. These spinal cord dorsal horn neurons become activated in turn, causing electrical signals encoding the pain message to be sent up to the brain, toward consciousness (Figure 1). From this description, it becomes clear that at the level of the spinal cord dorsal horns, there are two ways for pain to be modulated. One is to modulate how much neurotransmitter is released by the incoming nociceptive sensory nerves. The second is to modulate how excitable the spinal cord dorsal horn neurons are in response to the pain signals they receive. Analgesia and hyperalgesia circuits can regulate both (Figure 1), thereby allowing for dramatic suppression or enhancement

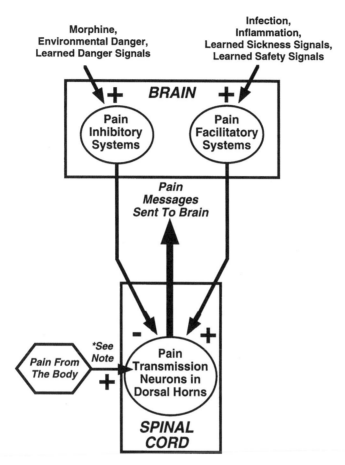

Figure 1 Dynamic modulation of pain. The brain contains distinct circuits that either inhibit pain (pain inhibitory systems) or facilitate pain (pain facilitatory systems). Pain inhibitory systems are activated by opiate drugs such as morphine, by environmental dangers, and by learned danger signals. Pain facilitatory systems, in contrast, are activated by infection, inflammation, learned sickness signals, and learned safety signals. Once activated, pain inhibitory systems suppress pain by inhibiting neurons in the spinal cord dorsal horns that relay pain information from the body to the brain (pain transmission neurons in dorsal horn). Pain facilitatory systems, on the other hand, exaggerate pain by making these spinal pain transmission neurons hyperexcitable to incoming sensory information. +, Excitatory connection; −, inhibitory connection. Note: There is also dynamic modulation of the release of neurotransmitter from pain fibers arriving in the spinal cord from the body. Although not illustrated in the figure, pain inhibitory systems can inhibit release of neurotransmitter from these sensory fibers, and pain facilitatory systems can exaggerate the release of neurotransmitter from these sensory fibers.

of the pain message being relayed to the brain (Sandkuhler 1996, Watkins & Maier 1997, Yaksh 1997, Zimmermann & Herdegen 1996).

Analgesia and Antianalgesia

Neural circuits that function to suppress pain are thought to have evolved to enhance survival of the organism during fight/flight. That is, suppressing the pain of wounds facilitates the ability of animals, including humans, to defend themselves during attack and to successfully escape from further harm. In keeping with such a notion, analgesia is produced by a variety of stressful environmental stimuli (e.g. environmental "dangers" such as electric shock, cold water, swims, conspecific aggression, the sight of a cat by a rat, military combat) (Kelly 1986). In addition, analgesia can be classically conditioned, whereby initially innocuous stimuli (e.g. lights or sounds) paired with an environmental danger (e.g. shock) become capable of eliciting analgesia by themselves (Watkins & Mayer 1986). Thus, learned danger signals, in addition to unlearned danger signals, can produce analgesia (Figure 1). Studies of the neural pathways and neurochemistries mediating these so-called stress-induced analgesias reveal that there are multiple pain suppression systems (Kelly 1986, Watkins & Mayer 1986). What these circuits have in common is that, in the end, they send axons from sites in the brain down to the spinal cord, where pain signals are inhibited (Figure 1). These circuits can also be activated directly, by systemic administration of drugs, such as morphine, or by implantation of either fine wires or tubes into discrete sites along these pathways that allow their activation by electrical stimulation or drug microinjection, respectively (Richardson 1995, Sandkuhler 1996, Yaksh 1997). Animal studies of analgesia produced by such direct activation of these pathways led to the development of many analgesic drugs and to the use of brain stimulators and epidural drug injections for control of pain in humans.

Although for many years only suppression of pain was thought to occur, this is not the case. Pain facilitation occurs as well (Figure 1). Two types of pain facilitation are now recognized: antianalgesia and hyperalgesia (Maier et al 1992).

Antianalgesia, as the name implies, refers to removal of pain inhibition. Antianalgesia was predicted long before it was experimentally demonstrated (Maier et al 1992). As noted above, it has long been known that danger signals activate analgesia systems. However, what brought these analgesic states to an end was a mystery. Recent studies have demonstrated that analgesia produced by signals indicating danger can be actively terminated by signals indicating safety (Wiertelak et al 1992b). These so-called antianalgesia circuits are activated by learned safety signals that predict that danger will not occur. Antianalgesia is created by a brain-to-spinal cord circuit that is anatomically distinct from those creating analgesia (Watkins et al 1998). Where analgesia and antianalgesia circuits come together is in the spinal cord. Antianalgesia actively opposes the ability of analgesia circuits to suppress pain transmission at the level of the spinal cord dorsal horns (Watkins et al 1997b, Wiertelak et al 1992a). The power of antianalgesia goes beyond simply abolishing stress-induced analgesia. It can also abolish the analgesic effects of a variety of drugs, including morphine (Watkins et al 1997b, Wiertelak et al 1992a). Learned safety signals abolish analgesia through the release of specific peptide transmitters within the spinal cord (Wiertelak et al 1992a, 1994). A family of such peptides has now been characterized, with cholecystokinin receiving by far the most study (Baber et al 1989, Cesselin 1995). Direct administration of cholecystokinin into the cerebrospinal fluid surrounding the spinal cord [intrathecal (i.t.) administration] effectively blocks analgesias produced by morphine, by environmental danger signals, and by learned danger signals (Baber et al 1989, Faris et al 1983). Animal studies led to the proposal that antianalgesic peptides may play a key role in the development and expression of morphine tolerance (Cesselin 1995, Kellstein & Mayer 1991, Payza et al 1993, Watkins et al 1984). Furthermore, animal studies have provided strong evidence that antianalgesic peptides such as cholecystokinin (*a*) may naturally suppress a variety of pain control procedures (e.g. morphine, acupuncture, placebo effects) (Benedetti & Amanzio 1997, Tang et al 1997, Watkins et al 1984) and (*b*) may be overexpressed in chronic pain states known to be resistant to such analgesic drugs as morphine (Nichols et al 1995, Xu et al 1994). Thus, the existence of antianalgesia systems has great implications for both normal and pathological pain states.

Hyperalgesia and Allodynia

In contrast to antianalgesia, hyperalgesia actually exaggerates pain transmission rather than simply oppose analgesia (Maier et al 1992). The existence of neurocircuitry that creates hyperalgesia has great implications for human pain and suffering, which is the focus of the remainder of this review. Like analgesia and antianalgesia, the actual modulation of pain occurs within the spinal cord dorsal horns. Also like analgesia and antianalgesia, hyperalgesia can be created by brain-to-spinal cord circuits (Kaplan & Fields 1991, Watkins & Maier 1997). Hyperalgesia is often assumed to also be created by direct peripheral nerve-to-spinal cord circuits. Events in the body that trigger exaggerated pain states include localized trauma, infection, and inflammation. It seems logical to assume that such events would cause exaggerated pain via their activation of peripheral nerves in the region, causing direct signaling to the spinal cord. Until recently, the possibility that the brain might be involved in creating such exaggerated pain states was not considered. It is therefore notable that in the few cases where the potential involvement of a brain-to-spinal cord circuit has been assessed, such a pathway again proved key for creating exaggerated pain states (Bian et al 1998, Pertovaara 1998, Ren & Dubner 1996, Wiertelak et al 1997).

The general term hyperalgesia is most accurately subdivided into two forms: hyperalgesia and allodynia (Willis 1992). Hyperalgesia, as used here, refers to a lowering of pain threshold such that stimuli that were not originally painful now are. Hyperalgesia is typically assessed in the laboratory using radiant heat stimuli. In the studies cited in this review, thermal hyperalgesia is almost always the form assessed. Hyperalgesia involves a "plastic" change in the spinal cord dorsal horn response (Liu & Sandkuhler 1998, Sandkuhler & Liu 1998), similar if not identical to the long-term potentiation (LTP) that some believe underlies learning and memory in the hippocampus (Doyere et al 1993). For both, LTP reflects a use-dependent increase in synaptic strength between presynaptic terminals of incoming nerve fibers and neuronal cell bodies within the region. Thus, such neuronal plasticity results in exaggerated electrical activity for a period of time, in response to synaptic input. This LTP-like process in spinal cord dorsal horn neurons can occur either after activation of a brain-to-spinal cord circuit or after "pain" neurons in this region receive a barrage of activity from peripheral nerves carrying pain messages. In either case, the signals arriving at the spinal cord dorsal horns release neurotransmitters, such as substance P and glutamate, that create a depolarization of spinal cord dorsal horn pain neurons that is sufficiently large and prolonged that N-methyl-d-aspartate ion channels become activated. When this key step occurs, the resulting influx of calcium ions sets into motion a whole cascade of intracellular events culminating in the formation of nitric oxide and prostaglandins (Willis 1992). Both nitric oxide and prostaglandins diffuse from the neuronal cell body where they are formed, causing dramatic increases in the excitability of the neuron that made them, of nearby neurons, and of presynaptic terminals of the peripheral sensory "pain" neurons that synapse in the region (Vasko 1995, Willis 1992). The end result is a dramatic change in spinal cord dorsal horn function. Sensory "pain" fibers arriving in the dorsal horn from the body release exaggerated quantities of transmitter. In response, spinal cord dorsal horn neurons overreact to the "pain" signals they receive from the body (Willis 1992).

Allodynia, on the other hand, is a less easily defined concept. Basically, allodynia (at least as assessed by laboratory animal behavior) may or may not be "pain" in the way that one normally thinks of pain. It refers to increased distress/reactivity to a stimulus that is normally innocuous (e.g. nonthreatening and nonstressful, in addition to nonpainful) (Willis 1992). The light touch of a wisp of cotton or the feeling of loose clothing against the body are examples of such innocuous stimuli. When allodynia occurs to such mechanical (touch/pressure) stimuli, the organism responds vigorously and often emotionally. Human pain patients complain of being greatly distressed by clothing, by bedsheets, or by a soft breeze across their skin (Gilmer 1995, Rowbotham & Fields 1996, Swanson et al 1998). Allodynic rats begin motorically reacting and often vocalizing to light-touch stimuli that evoke nothing but curious investigation from control animals (Slart et al 1997). How innocuous stimuli that do not release any of the "pain" neurotransmitters in the spinal cord dorsal horn become capable of causing distress and possibly pain in allodynic animals is a mystery. Many pain transmission neurons in the spinal cord dorsal horns are well known to receive sensory information from both sensory "pain" fibers and "light-touch" fibers arriving from the body. Under normal conditions, these dorsal horn neurons readily distinguish between pain and light-touch information, responding vigorously to pain and barely responding at all to light touch. Currently, the general view is that some (currently mysterious) process causes spinal cord dorsal horn pain transmission neurons to become so hyperexcitable that they respond to light touch as if it were pain. That is, light touch evokes a vigorous response by the pain transmission neurons comparable to that normally elicited only by pain.

Classically, hyperalgesia and allodynia have been assumed to be due entirely to alterations in neural function. For example, nerve crush or other trauma was thought to cause physical and functional changes in the membrane of the damaged nerve (Willis 1992). The abnormal nerve would then send barrages of electrical activity to spinal cord dorsal horn neurons, setting LTP-like processes within these neurons into motion. Thus, this view focused on direct damage to the nerve itself and the resulting neuronally mediated LTP-like cascades.

What is exciting is that this view is changing. The change is being brought about by the recognition that neurons do not simply act alone: They can be remarkably regulated by the immune system. The argument to be made is that substances released by immune cells can dynamically and dramatically modulate pain. Hyperalgesia and allodynia are the result of such immune-neuron interactions and occur following the release of immune cell-derived substances in the body, the brain, and/or the spinal cord. In the sections that follow, four interrelated aspects of immune modulation of pain are examined. First, hyperalgesia as a natural consequence of sickness is examined. To do this, the concept of immune-to-brain communication is introduced and the sickness response described. It is then argued that hyperalgesia is simply one component of a brain-mediated constellation of responses to immune challenge. The second topic examines hyperalgesia and allodynia that result from infection and inflammation of the skin. It is argued that what has previously been thought of as purely neurally created exaggerated pain states actually arise via the release of immune-derived substances. The third topic focuses on nerve trauma and inflammation, and it is argued that hyperalgesia and allodynia resulting from even this classic pain model needs to be reevaluated in terms of mediation by immune cells. The fourth topic examines the pain modulatory role of immune-like cells of the central nervous system: astrocytes and microglia. The case is presented that creation of hyperalgesia and allodynia in the spinal cord dorsal horns actually results from dynamic interactions between neurons and these glia. It is argued that spinal cord microglia and astrocytes actually play an important role in allodynia and hyperalgesia observed following infection, inflammation, or injury in the body. Furthermore, the case is made that spinal cord glia activated by infection of the central nervous system are sufficient to create exaggerated pain states. The concluding section explores the implications of these new roles of the immune system and spinal cord glia for developing new strategies for pain control in humans.

IMMUNE-TO-BRAIN COMMUNICATION: ORGANIZING THE SICKNESS RESPONSE

Defense of the organism against infection by pathogens (e.g. bacteria, viruses, parasites) is an evolutionarily old, survival-oriented response (Hart 1988, Maier & Watkins 1998). Organisms as primitive as sponges have specialized cells called immunocytes that recognize "nonself," causing foreign invaders to be attacked, engulfed, and destroyed (Smith & Hildemann 1986). Immunocytes are a type of phagocyte (literally eating cell), similar in function to phagocytes in our own bodies (including macrophages, meaning big eaters). As more complex species evolved, their immune systems evolved as well, adding a wide variety of specialized cell types dedicated to performing various functions required for host defense (Kuby 1992).

Evolution of the vertebrate brain provides for the ability to orchestrate broad changes in behavior and physiology to further enhance host survival during immune challenge. This brain-mediated set of changes is called the sickness response (Hart 1988). The sickness response consists of a constellation of physiological changes (fever, increased sleep, alterations in blood chemistry), behavioral changes (decreased locomotion, decreased sexual behavior, decreased exploration, decreased aggression, decreased food and water intake), and hormonal changes (release of classic stress hormones from the sympathetic nervous system and hypothalamo-pituitary-adrenal axis). Sickness occurs rapidly, beginning within minutes to a few hours after immune challenge in organisms as diverse as reptiles, fish, birds, and mammals (Hart 1988, Kluger 1978, Maier & Watkins 1998).

It has been argued that the immune system signals the brain about infection because the brain-mediated sickness response enhances host survival (Hart 1988, Maier & Watkins 1998). The key feature of the sickness response appears to be fever. Fever raises the core body temperature to the point where viruses and bacteria do not readily multiply, bacteria lose their ability to form protective outer coats, the host's white blood cells multiply rapidly, phagocytes are optimized for destruction of pathogens, and liver metabolism shifts to alter blood chemistry to deprive pathogens of nutrients and chemicals they need while maximizing the needs of the host (Kluger 1978, 1991). Although all these changes clearly enhance host survival, fever comes with a cost. Fever is extremely energy intensive, requiring a 10–15% increase in energy expenditure for every degree of fever (Kluger 1978, 1991). One can view many aspects of the sickness response as aimed at providing energy for fever, by saving energy used by nonessential behaviors (increased sleep, decreased exploration, decreased aggression, and so forth), and by releasing energy from bodily stores (one of the effects of classic stress hormones). Even decreased food and water intake can be viewed as "up front" energy saving if one takes into account the energy cost associated with running down prey and foraging, as well as the energy costs associated with digestion (Hart 1988, Maier & Watkins 1998).

Exactly how the immune system signals the brain is a matter of ongoing debate (Watkins et al 1995c). What is clear is that immune-to-brain communication occurs early in the immune response to infection and injury. During an immune challenge, macrophages and other immune cells rapidly create and release proteins called proinflammatory cytokines. These proteins are proinflammatory because they orchestrate the early immune response to infection and injury by communicating with white blood cells, attracting them to the site of infection/injury, and causing them to become activated to respond (Kuby 1992). The proinflammatory cytokine family includes tumor necrosis factor (TNF), interleukin (IL)-1, and IL-6. These proinflammatory cytokines frequently are sequentially formed in a cascade, where typically TNF is made first, causing the induction of IL-1, which in turn causes the induction of IL-6 (Kuby 1992). These proinflammatory cytokines (especially IL-1 and TNF) are thought to be key mediators of immune-to-brain communication (Maier & Watkins 1998, Watkins et al 1995c). They are both necessary and sufficient for eliciting sickness responses. That is, sickness responses can be blocked by administering antagonists that disrupt proinflammatory cytokine actions, and sickness responses can be elicited by administering proinflammatory cytokines in the absence of viral or bacterial challenge (Maier & Watkins 1998, Watkins et al 1995c).

What is far less clear is the signaling pathway between release of proinflammatory cytokines and brain activation. One popular idea is that proinflammatory cytokines build up at the site of infection/injury, spill over into the blood stream, and are carried by the blood to the brain. Because proinflammatory cytokines are large proteins that cannot passively cross the blood-brain barrier, they have been variously argued to (*a*) enter the brain at the few sites where the blood-brain barrier is weak or absent (e.g. circumventricular structures), (*b*) be actively transported across the blood-brain barrier, or (*c*) bind to receptors expressed in blood vessels of the brain, inducing the creation of other chemicals (such as prostaglandins) that can easily pass across the blood-brain barrier (Watkins et al 1995c). Although each of these views has its proponents, detractors point out that sickness responses can still be observed when infection is so localized that no proinflammatory cytokines can be detected in blood (Kluger 1991). Indeed, very localized infection/injury may most realistically model actual host defense against the initial stages of immune challenge. In this latter situation, immune-to-brain communication appears to be mediated by activation of specialized sensory nerves that carry immune information to the brain (Maier et al 1998).

To date, most research on this topic has focused on sensory nerves in the vagus as a neural pathway for immune-to-brain communication (Figure 2) (Maier et al 1998). Sensory nerves in the vagus are excited both by proinflammatory cytokines and by bacterial challenge, as evidenced by their increased expression of neuronal activation markers (e.g. cFos, an immediate-early gene product) (Gaykema et al 1998, Goehler et al 1998). Furthermore, a wide variety of sickness responses are blocked by cutting the vagus nerve, including fever, decreased food-motivated behavior, increased sleep, decreased activity, decreased social interaction, changes in brain activity, and release of stress hormones (Maier et al 1998). Substances released by activated immune cells may either directly (Ek et al 1998) or indirectly (Goehler et al 1997) activate sensory fibers in the vagus. For example, IL-1 can bind either to receptors expressed on sensory neurons of the vagus (Ek et al 1998) or to specialized sensory end-organs called paraganglia (Goehler et al 1997). These sensory end-organs synapse onto sensory vagal fibers, allowing communication to occur (Figure 2). Paraganglia are tiny chemoreceptive structures that have been called "the taste buds of the blood." Their location along lymph capillaries and blood capillaries perfectly positions them to "sample" these fluids for substances released by immune cells (Goehler et al 1997). In addition, the connective tissues surrounding the paraganglia contain dense accumulations of immune cells (macrophages, dendritic cells, mast

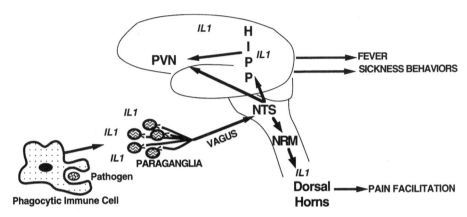

Figure 2 Immune-to-brain communication. On encountering pathogens (bacteria, viruses, etc), phagocytic immune cells become activated. Activated phagocytes both engulf the pathogens and release proinflammatory cytokines including interleukin-1 (IL-1). IL-1 binds to and activates sensory paraganglia, which send sensory information to sensory nerve fibers in the vagus. Vagal sensory information is relayed to the nucleus tractus solitarius (NTS) of the medulla, which then relays this information to brain areas that create sickness responses, including the hippocampus (HIPP) and paraventricular nucleus of the hypothalamus (PVN). For hyperalgesia, the pathway includes the NTS, the nucleus raphe magnus (NRM), and the dorsal horns of the spinal cord. Activation of these brain circuits leads to the release of IL-1 from glia, leading to the production of sickness responses.

cells) (Goehler et al 1999). These immune cells respond to localized immune challenge by rapidly producing and releasing proinflammatory cytokines and other substances (Goehler et al 1999). Taken together, this immune-to-vagus-to-brain pathway appears to form a rapid response system for triggering brain-mediated sickness responses (Figure 2).

Given that sensory vagal fibers synapse predominantly in the nucleus tractus solitarius (see Figure 2) (Ritter et al 1992), it would not be surprising if this medullary structure played a key role in the generation of brain-mediated sickness responses. Indeed, the nucleus tractus solitarius sends axons to numerous brain areas that create the various aspects of sickness (Figure 2) (Maier & Watkins 1998, Ritter et al 1992). Studies of how the brain creates sickness, after it is signaled to do so by the immune system, revealed an intriguing finding. That is, that proinflammatory cytokines again play a pivotal role. Within the brain, glia (which are immune-like cells of the central nervous system) respond to immune-to-brain signaling by synthesizing IL-1 de novo (Laye et al 1995). The brain expresses receptors for IL-1, and blocking IL-1 actions in the brain blocks sickness responses (Maier & Watkins 1998, Rothwell & Luheshi 1994).

To summarize, infection/injury in the body leads to the activation of immune cells. In the early stages of this immune response, a variety of substances, including proinflammatory cytokines (TNF, IL-1, IL-6), are released at the infection/injury site. For abdominal immune activation at least, this may trigger the activation of sensory paraganglia that communicate to sensory nerves in the vagus. The vagus may also be activated by direct receptor binding of immune products. The sensory vagal fibers, in turn, trigger brain-mediated sickness responses via activation of brain circuitry originating within the nucleus tractus solitarius. In addition, systemic signals for sickness may travel via the blood to the brain, providing an additional blood-borne pathway for immune-to-brain communication. In either case, glia become activated and these immune-like cells make and release IL-1, a key mediator within the central nervous system for creating sickness responses.

PAIN AS A NATURAL PART OF THE SICKNESS RESPONSE

We have recently suggested that exaggerated pain responses (hyperalgesia) be added to the list of classic sickness responses reviewed above (Watkins et al 1995d). Hyper-algesia would be advantageous to the survival of the organism, by directing recu-perative behaviors (like licking and favoring) to the site of injury or infection. Furthermore, by encouraging the organism to curl up and remain immobile, exag-gerated pain would also serve to save energy. Thus, from several regards, hyperalgesia seems a logical candidate for a sickness response.

Such an argument leads to three predictions: (*a*) that experimental manipulations that elicit classic sickness responses should also elicit hyperalgesia, (*b*) that the neu-rocircuitry mediating classic sickness responses and hyperalgesia should at least par-tially overlap, and (*c*) that like classic sickness responses, hyperalgesia should be dependent on IL-1 released in the central nervous system, in addition to proinflam-matory cytokines released at the site of infection. As is reviewed below, each of these predictions is true.

Hyperalgesia, like other sickness responses, is elicited by immune activation in the periphery. Intraperitoneal (i.p.) (intraabdominal) administration of either bacterial cell walls (endotoxin) or live bacteria elicits thermal hyperalgesia in rats (Mason 1993, Watkins et al 1995a,d). The fact that i.p. IL-1 and i.p. TNF can each produce hyperalgesia and allodynia supports the idea that proinflammatory cytokines are suf-ficient to elicit these responses (Ferreira et al 1988, Maier et al 1993, Oka et al 1996a, Watkins et al 1995b,d). Furthermore, proinflammatory cytokines are necessary for this so-called sickness-induced hyperalgesia because pharmacologically blocking the action of IL-1 or TNF prevents sickness-induced hyperalgesia induced by either bacterial cell walls or the proinflammatory cytokines themselves (Maier et al 1993, Watkins et al 1995d). A classic cytokine cascade is involved (Kuby 1992) because TNF actually creates hyperalgesia by inducing the release of IL-1 (Watkins et al 1995b).

Regarding similarity of neurocircuitry, what is known to date is that the initial portions of the circuit are shared by hyperalgesia and the other sickness responses. That is, cutting the vagus nerve disrupts sickness-induced hyperalgesias elicited by i.p. administration of bacterial cell walls, IL-1, or TNF (Watkins & Maier 1999a). Sickness-induced hyperalgesia is also disrupted by lesions of the nucleus tractus solitarius (Wiertelak et al 1997), the major termination site of sensory vagal nerves (Ritter et al 1992). From this point, the neurocircuitry for each sickness response likely diverges as axons from the nucleus tractus solitarius project to the multiple brain regions mediating various sickness outcomes. From lesion studies it is known that sickness-induced hyperalgesia involves, at least, the nucleus tractus solitarius and the nucleus raphe magnus (see Figure 2), with the latter structure sending its axons down to the spinal cord dorsal horns where exaggerated pain responses are created (Watkins & Maier 1999a).

Like other sickness responses, sickness-induced hyperalgesia involves proinflammatory cytokines within the central nervous system (Oka & Hori 1999). By i.p. administration, IL-1 appears to produce thermal hyperalgesia via de novo production and release of IL-1 within the brain, because this hyperalgesia is blocked by intracerebroventricular (i.c.v.) (into the cerebrospinal fluid–filled ventricles of the brain) administration of alpha-melanocyte–stimulating hormone (α-MSH), an endogenous peptide that functions as an IL-1 antagonist (Oka et al 1996a). By i.c.v. administration, TNF (Oka et al 1996b), IL-1 (Oka et al 1993, Watkins et al 1994, Yabuuchi et al 1996), and IL-6 (Oka et al 1995b) are each sufficient to produce thermal hyperalgesia, and α-MSH blocks hyperalgesia produced by i.c.v. IL-1 (Oka et al 1993). A classic cytokine cascade (Kuby 1992) again appears to be involved because i.c.v. TNF creates hyperalgesia by inducing the release of brain IL-1 (Oka et al 1996b). IL-1 exerts its effects on pain by selectively exaggerating neuronal electrical responses to intense stimuli applied to the skin (Oka et al 1994a). One site of IL-1 action is the hypothalamic preoptic area because microinjection of IL-1 into this site is sufficient to produce thermal hyperalgesia (Oka et al 1995a). All three proinflammatory cytokines (TNF, IL-1, IL-6) produce hyperalgesia via the release of prostaglandins (Oka et al 1993, 1995b, 1996b; Yabuuchi et al 1996), substances repeatedly implicated in exaggerated pain states (Willis 1992) and known to produce hyperalgesia following i.c.v. administration (Oka et al 1994b). Indeed, in keeping with the idea that IL-1 acts via prostaglandin release, prostaglandin likewise selectively exaggerates neuronal electrical activity in response to intense stimuli applied to the skin (Oka et al 1997).

Although brain IL-1 can increase pain responses, spinal cord IL-1 is also key. By i.p. administration, injection of bacterial cell walls not only induces hyperalgesia (Maier et al 1993) and increases brain IL-1 (Nguyen et al 1998; KT Nguyen, T Deak, MK Hansen, M Fleshner, LE Goehler et al, submitted for publication), it also rapidly increases IL-1 in the spinal cord dorsal horns (Watkins & Maier 1999a; KT Nguyen, T Deak, MK Hansen, M Fleshner, LE Goehler et al, submitted for publication). This is important because the spinal cord dorsal horns contain the neurons that receive and modulate pain information arriving from the body (Willis 1992). The IL-1 produced in the spinal cord dorsal horns by peripheral immune activation is used to create hyperalgesia. This is so because preventing spinal cord IL-1 effects, by microinjecting a selective IL-1 receptor antagonist into the cerebrospinal fluid surrounding the spinal cord, blocks thermal hyperalgesia produced by inflammation of a paw (Watkins et al 1997a). It has recently been reported that application of IL-1 directly onto the spinal cord, using electrophysiological techniques, causes exaggerated responses of spinal cord dorsal horn neurons only to incoming pain signals (Reeve et al 1998). Although the lack of IL-6 antagonists has prevented the potential role of IL-6 in sickness hyperalgesia from being tested, it should be noted that i.t. IL-6 produces hyperalgesia and allodynia in rats (DeLeo et al 1996).

Regarding the source of IL-1, spinal cord IL-1 is thought to be made and released by glia (astrocytes and microglia). As noted above, the neural circuit that leads to sickness-induced hyperalgesia involves a nucleus tractus solitarius–to–nucleus raphe magnus–to–spinal cord pathway. Spinal cord glia express receptors for, and are activated by, neurotransmitters released by the nucleus raphe magnus, including substance P and glutamate (Watkins & Maier 1999a). Activated astrocytes and microglia begin releasing glial products, including IL-1. IL-1 then likely acts on the cells in the region to stimulate further release of more IL-1 and, in addition, to stimulate the release of a variety of neuroactive substances, including nitric oxide, excitatory amino acids, and nerve growth factor (NGF). All these glially derived substances are known to be key mediators of sickness-induced hyperalgesia at the level of the spinal cord (Watkins & Maier 1999a, Watkins et al 1997a). Indeed, using light microscopy, spinal cord astrocytes and microglia are visibly activated in response to infection/inflammation in body. Immunohistochemical analyses of astrocyte- and microglial-specific activation markers reveal that both of these glial populations are activated by peripheral infection and inflammation (Fu et al 1998, Sweitzer et al 1999, Watkins et al 1995a). The importance of astrocytes and microglia in creating sickness-induced hyperalgesia is emphasized by the finding that hyperalgesia induced by infection and inflammation in the body is blocked by spinal administration of drugs that selectively disrupt glial function (Meller et al 1994; Watkins et al 1995a, 1997a).

ROLE OF THE IMMUNE SYSTEM IN PAIN

Skin Infection and Inflammation

Subcutaneous (s.c.) injection of a variety of immune stimuli causes thermal hyperalgesia and mechanical allodynia. Such stimuli include chemical irritants such as dilute formalin (Watkins et al 1997a), killed bacteria (Poole et al 1999, Poole & Woolf 1999), yeast cell walls (Meller et al 1994), and the algae protein, carrageenan (Poole et al 1999). These all recruit a variety of immune cells to the site of injection. Once there, these immune cells produce and release proinflammatory cytokines and NGF (Johnson & Krenger 1992, Kuby 1992).

A role for proinflammatory cytokines in creating such hyperalgesias is supported by the fact that s.c. injection of either IL-1 (Ferreira et al 1988, Follenfant et al 1989), TNF (Cunha et al 1992), or IL-6 (Cunha et al 1992) induces hyperalgesia and allodynia, with the following order of potency: IL-1 $>$ TNF $>>>$ IL-6 (Poole et al 1999). Such injections directly excite peripheral nociceptive fibers (e.g. nerves that become excited by intense stimuli that would be perceived as pain by humans) (Sorkin et al 1997, Xiao et al 1996). By s.c. administration, proinflammatory cytokines also sensitize these nociceptive fibers to overrespond to subsequent stimuli (Sorkin et al 1997, Xiao et al 1996). Poole and colleagues have extensively characterized the response cascades initiated by a variety of s.c. immune activators (Poole et al 1999, Poole & Woolf 1999). From their work, it is clear that all the proinflammatory cytokines act via release of IL-1. That is, hyperalgesias caused by all of the proinflammatory cytokines are reduced or abolished by blocking IL-1 actions with anti–IL-1 antibodies, IL-1 receptor antagonist, or the IL-1 functional antagonist α-MSH (Follenfant et al 1989; Poole et al 1992, 1999). In addition, at least TNF simultaneously exaggerates pain also via a second pathway, namely sympathetic activation (Poole et al 1999).

IL-1 actions have been variously argued to (a) reflect direct IL-1 binding and activation of sensory nerves, (b) be dependent on the release of prostaglandins that sensitize pain fibers (Ferreira 1972), (c) work via pathways that are independent of prostaglandins, or (d) be dependent on the release of NGF (Poole et al 1999, Poole & Woolf 1999). All four mechanisms actually do appear to mediate IL-1 actions to varying degrees, depending on the exact circumstances under study (Poole et al 1999, Poole & Woolf 1999).

NGF clearly plays a role in exaggerated pain states. By s.c. administration, NGF produces both hyperalgesia and allodynia (Woolf et al 1994), s.c. injection of killed bacteria causes the release of NGF, and hyperalgesia and allodynia produced by either NGF or killed bacteria are blocked by drugs that disrupt NGF action (McMahon et al 1995, Woolf et al 1994). During inflammation, NGF levels increase in immune cells at the site of infection, in inflammatory fluids (for example in the fluid space of inflamed joints), and in inflamed skin (Poole & Woolf 1999, Woolf et al 1994). NGF exerts both direct and indirect effects on peripheral nerves. Direct actions are exerted by NGF binding to receptors on nociceptive ("pain" responsive) fibers, thereby altering excitability of these nerves. Indirect actions of NGF arise from its cytokine-like actions, which cause immune cells that accumulate at the site of infection/injury to release their cellular contents. Many of these substances can, in turn, excite nociceptive fibers (Poole & Woolf 1999).

Several lines of evidence indicate that IL-1 acts, at least in part, via NGF release. In tissue culture, IL-1 causes NGF release from immune cells (Lindholm et al 1987, 1988). By s.c. administration, IL-1 also releases NGF (Safieh-Garabedian et al 1995), and blocking NGF actions blocks hyperalgesia induced by s.c. IL-1 (Safieh-Garabedian et al 1995). As reviewed above, because all proinflammatory cytokines release IL-1, this implies that NGF is likely a common pathway to pain. Furthermore, administering an IL-1 receptor antagonist blocks the ability of s.c.-killed bacteria either to produce hyperalgesia (Poole et al 1999) or to increase NGF (Poole & Woolf 1999). Because TNF exerts at least part of its hyperalgesic actions by inducing the release of IL-1 (Poole et al 1999), it is not surprising that TNF likewise releases NGF and, in fact, acts synergistically with IL-1 to do so (Hattori et al 1993, Woolf et al 1997).

Lastly, blocking NGF actions attenuates TNF-induced hyperalgesia (Woolf et al 1997), again in keeping with TNF actions being mediated partially by IL-1.

Like hyperalgesia following i.p. injections (Watkins & Maier 1999b), hyperalgesia induced via peripheral nerve activation by s.c. immune activators ultimately results in exaggerated responses of pain transmission neurons in the spinal cord dorsal horns. In fact, parallel to the activation of spinal cord glia observed after i.p. injections (Watkins et al 1995a, Watkins & Maier 1999b), s.c. injections of immune stimuli also activate glia in this key pain modulatory area. Both s.c. chemical irritants (formalin) (Fu et al 1998, Sweitzer et al 1999, Watkins et al 1995a) and s.c. yeast cell walls (Sweitzer et al 1999) activate microglia and astrocytes in the spinal cord dorsal horns. In addition, both s.c. formalin and s.c. yeast cell walls increase IL-1 production by spinal cord glia (Sweitzer et al 1999). The importance of this glial IL-1 is illustrated by the fact that blocking spinal cord IL-1 actions abolishes s.c. formalin-induced hyperalgesia (Watkins et al 1997a). That spinal cord glia are key to such changes in pain responsivity is supported by the finding that drugs that disrupt glial function block hyperalgesias elicited by both s.c. formalin (Watkins et al 1997a) and s.c. yeast cell walls (Meller et al 1994).

Nerve Infection and Inflammation

Both nerve trauma and nerve infection/inflammation create exaggerated pain states characterized by hyperalgesia and allodynia. Abnormal pain responses resulting from nerve trauma are referred to clinically as neuropathic pains, and they include such human pain conditions as deafferentation pain following loss of a body part or nerve crush, pain associated with diabetes, cancer pain, and pain that develops after viral infection of peripheral nerves (e.g. postherpetic neuralgia that results from shingles) (DeLeo & Colburn 1999, Willis 1992). When nerve infection/inflammation, rather than physical trauma, is the diagnosed cause, these same exaggerated pain responses are referred to clinically as neuritis. The potential of immune involvement in both neuropathic and neuritic pain states has now been recognized in such diverse species as the mollusk *Aplysia* and laboratory rats.

Like sponges (Smith & Hildemann 1986), the principle cell in mollusks that attacks, engulfs, and destroys foreign invaders is a phagocyte called an immunocyte. These immunocytes travel via the hemolymph (molluscan blood) and tissues to reach sites of injury and infection. They appear to be the source of IL-1– and TNF-like factors in hemolymph (Clatworthy 1999, Clatworthy et al 1994, Hughes et al 1992). IL-6–like factors have also been identified in mollusks (Clatworthy 1999), so these invertebrates appear to have the same proinflammatory cytokines as mammals. Certainly evidence to date is that molluscan proinflammatory cytokines cause the same biological responses as do their mammalian counterparts (Clatworthy 1999).

Responses to nerve injury in the mollusk *Aplysia* have been intensively studied. From single cell recordings, it is clear that sensory nerve injury induces dramatic increases in both excitability and synaptic transmission of nociceptive neurons (Clatworthy & Walters 1994, Walters et al 1991). The changes appear to reflect both direct effects at the site of trauma as well as indirect effects induced by axonal transport of signal molecules from the site of trauma back up to the cell body, causing excitability changes there as well (Gunstream et al 1995). Proinflammatory cytokines released from immunocytes attracted to the site of axonal injury appear to be the cause of all these changes (Clatworthy 1999). IL-1 and TNF increase excitability of neurons in mollusks such as *Aplysia* by altering ion channel function (Clatworthy 1999). Indeed, nerve damage is not even necessary for molluscan proinflammatory cytokine-induced excitability changes to occur. Simply attracting immunocytes close to the sensory nerves by "baiting" the area with killed bacteria leads to marked increases in neuronal excitability and synaptic transmission (Clatworthy & Grose 1997). Even in cell culture, *Aplysia* sensory neurons become hyperexcitable when incubated in solutions that previously contained immunocytes or when incubated in the presence of immunocytes stimulated by killed bacteria (Clatworthy & Grose 1997). Such data again implicate immunocyte-derived substances as the cause of the excitability changes.

Parallel to the situation just described in *Aplysia,* nerve trauma in rats is associated with attraction of macrophages and other phagocytic immune cells to the area and release of proinflammatory cytokines (DeLeo & Colburn 1999, Rotshenker et al 1992, Sommer & Schafers 1998) and NGF (Herzberg et al 1997) by these immune cells. In addition, Schwann cells that enwrap the damaged nerves become activated, causing these immune-derived cells to release proinflammatory cytokines and NGF as well (Myers et al 1999, Wagner & Myers 1996b). There is even evidence that sensory neurons begin creating NGF (Herzberg et al 1997) and proinflammatory cytokines (DeLeo & Colburn 1999, Richardson et al 1998) following trauma to their peripheral nerve fibers. The timecourse of hyperalgesia correlates well with the time-course of phagocyte invasion into the area of damage (Sommer et al 1993). Indeed, if phagocyte invasion of the area is experimentally delayed, neuropathic pain is like-wise delayed (Myers et al 1999, Sommer & Schafers 1998). Immune-derived sub-stances are implicated in the development of hyperalgesia and allodynia following nerve damage because the exaggerated pain responses can be reduced by blocking TNF (Illich et al 1997; Sommer et al 1997, 1998b; Wagner et al 1998), IL-1 (Sommer et al 1998a,c), or NGF (Herzberg et al 1997) at the site of nerve trauma.

It is intriguing that the very same types of responses can be observed in the absence of physical trauma to nerves, simply by attracting and activating immune cells in the region. Schwann cells, for example, begin producing proinflammatory cytokines in response to local injections of killed bacteria, TNF, IL-6, or IL-1 (Bolin et al 1995). Simply injecting TNF onto the sensory nerve both elicits hyperalgesia and allodynia (Wagner & Myers 1996a) and directly activates peripheral nerves that normally respond only to painful stimuli in the skin (Sorkin et al 1997). As noted above for *Aplysia* (Clatworthy 1999), it has been proposed that hyperexcitability induced by TNF results directly from alterations of ion channels in the sensory neuron (Baldwin et al 1996, Kagan et al 1992). Placing killed bacteria (Clatworthy et al 1995, Eliav et al 1996), viral coat proteins (Herzberg et al 1998), algae protein (Eliav et al 1996), or a foreign body such as chromic gut surgical sutures (Maves et al 1993) near sensory nerves also induces both hyperalgesia and allodynia. Taken together, these findings are striking in that they clearly demonstrate that proinflammatory cytokines can rapidly induce aberrant responses in peripheral nociceptive nerves, independent either of damage to the nerve or of any action at receptors expressed by peripheral nerve terminals (Sorkin et al 1997).

As was the case following either i.p. or s.c. injections of immune activators, there is growing evidence that neuritis and neuropathic pain models induce glial activation within the spinal cord dorsal horns. Damage of peripheral sensory nerves inducing neuropathic pain also leads to activation of both microglia and astrocytes within the spinal cord dorsal horns (Coyle 1998, DeLeo & Colburn 1999, Garrison et al 1991), correlated with increased spinal cord expression of the proinflammatory cytokines IL-1 (Coyle 1998, Sweitzer et al 1999), TNF (DeLeo & Colburn 1999), and IL-6 (DeLeo & Colburn 1999, DeLeo et al 1996). The importance of spinal cord IL-1 and IL-6 for exaggerated pain responses by the spinal cord was noted previously. Indeed, simply placing immune activators near sensory nerves, in the absence of trauma, causes intense activation of both astrocytes and microglia in the spinal cord dorsal horns, correlated with the expression of exaggerated pain responses (Herzberg et al 1998). Furthermore, we recently demonstrated a key role for spinal cord IL-1 in mediating neuritis-induced exaggerated pain states. We found that i.t. IL-1 receptor antagonists block exaggerated pain induced by immune activators (yeast cell walls) placed near healthy sciatic nerves (Hammack et al 1999).

Central Nervous System Infection and Inflammation

As noted above, infection and inflammation in the abdomen, in the skin, and around peripheral nerves all result in activation of astrocytes and microglia in the spinal cord. For s.c., periaxonal, and i.p. inflammation/infection, such glial activation actually mediates the exaggerated pain state (Hammack et al 1999; Meller et al 1994; Watkins et al 1995a, 1997a). This raises the issue of whether glial activation would be sufficient to create exaggerated pain states in the absence of infection, inflammation, or injury in the body.

This possibility presents itself because astrocytes and microglia are immunocompetent cells, which means these two types of glia act like immune cells within the central nervous system. They express specific receptors that recognize and bind bacteria and viruses (Becher et al 1996, Ma et al 1994, Peterson et al 1995, Sharpless et al 1992), and these glia become activated as a result. On activation, these cells begin releasing a variety of substances (nitric oxide, prostaglandins, IL-1, NGF, excitatory amino acids) that induce a positive feedback circuit (Watkins & Maier 1999b; ED Milligan K Mehmert, JL Hinde, D Martin, SF Maier, et al, submitted for publication). That is, substances released by activated microglia stimulate nearby astrocytes to release substances that further excite microglia, and so forth. Furthermore, as noted previously, all these substances excite neurons and are key mediators within the spinal cord dorsal horns of exaggerated pain states (Willis 1992).

This leads to the hypothesis that exaggerated pain would be expected to occur on infection of the spinal cord. A number of bacteria and viruses are neurotropic; that is, they "home" to the central nervous system and invade it. An example of one such virus is HIV-1, the virus that causes AIDS in humans. Various strains of HIV-1 infect the brain and spinal cord early in the course of the disease and continue throughout disease progression (Diederich et al 1988). Within the central nervous system, a specific portion of the outer surface of HIV-1 binds to activation receptors expressed on microglia and astrocytes. The portion of HIV-1 that activates these glia is a glycoprotein called gp120 (Tyor et al 1992).

Rats do not get AIDS because HIV-1 simply cannot multiply inside infected rat cells. However, glial activation is a process distinct from glial infection. gp120 does indeed bind to and activate rat microglia and astrocytes (Codazzi et al 1996, Opp et al 1996). This glial activation occurs in a manner identical to that in humans, and the same neuroexcitatory substances are released from rat glia as a result. Thus, this similarity between rat and human cellular responses allows laboratory rats to be used to examine whether viruses such as HIV-1 might cause exaggerated pain states through activation of spinal cord glia.

We have recently undertaken such studies. Although still in its infancy, this work has already been revealing. When gp120 is administered i.t. into the cerebrospinal fluid space surrounding the lumbosacral cord (that is, to the spinal levels receiving sensation from the lower body), remarkable thermal hyperalgesia results (Watkins & Maier 1999b; ED Milligan, K Mehmert, JL Hinde, D Martin, SF Maier, et al, submitted for publication). Altered responsivity extends beyond thermal stimuli. By i.t. administration, gp120 induces allodynia as well (Milligan et al 1998, 1999; Watkins & Maier 1999b). Thus, gp120, like peripheral immune activation by infection and injury, alters responsivity in ways paralleling clinically relevant aspects of pain.

Spinal cord glia do appear to be key mediators of these effects of i.t. gp120. By i.t. administration, drugs that disrupt glial function abolish both gp120-induced hyperalgesia and allodynia, and anatomical evidence of glial activation can be readily observed using immunohistochemistry for glial activation markers (Milligan et al 1998, Watkins & Maier 1999b; ED Milligan, K Mehmert, JL Hinde, D Martin, SF Maier, et al, submitted for publication). Investigation into the mediators released from spinal cord glia in response to gp120 is just beginning. In cell culture, at least, gp120 is able to induce the release of a variety of substances previously implicated in exaggerated pain states, for example nitric oxide (Koka et al 1995), prostaglandins (Ushijima et al 1995), IL-1 (Koka et al 1995), excitatory amino acids (Vesce et al 1997), and IL-6 (Yeung et al 1995). To date, we have only examined gp120-induced changes in IL-1. Our preliminary studies (Watkins & Maier 1999b; ED Milligan, K Mehmert, JL Hinde, D Martin, SF Maier, et al, submitted for publication) indicate that gp120 rapidly increases IL-1 gene activation, as evidenced by increases in mRNA content in spinal cord dorsal horns. We also know that IL-1 protein rapidly increases as well, specifically in the lumbosacral spinal cord region where gp120 was injected. That this IL-1 protein is actually released, and thus biologically relevant, is supported by the fact that IL-1 protein released from lumbosacral spinal cord rapidly and dramatically accumulates in the cerebrospinal fluid surrounding only this spinal cord level (Milligan et al 1998, 1999; Watkins & Maier 1999b). Spinal cord glia appear to be the source of this IL-1, given that drugs that disrupt glial function block gp120-induced increases in IL-1 protein both in spinal cord and in the surrounding cerebrospinal fluid (Milligan et al 1999). Lastly, and of key importance, gp120-induced thermal hyperalgesia and mechanical allodynia are both blocked by i.t. administration of a specific IL-1 receptor antagonist (Milligan et al 1999). These data provide strong support that IL-1 is a critical mediator of HIV-1 gp120-induced exaggerated pain states (Milligan et al 1998, Watkins & Maier 1999b).

IMPLICATIONS FOR HUMAN PAIN CONDITIONS

The finding in animal models that proinflammatory cytokines in the body, in the brain, and in the spinal cord create exaggerated pain states has major implications for human pain. Indeed, it has been stated that up-regulation of proinflammatory cytokines may well be the single most important and treatable factor linked to the development of chronic pain (Poole & Woolf 1999). As in the animal models reviewed above, implications for human pain states arise from the fact that proinflammatory cytokines can markedly influence pain at these levels: the peripheral nerve terminals, along the nerve bundles, within the brain, and within the spinal cord itself.

The role of spinal cord glia in creating exaggerated pain in humans is entirely unexplored. However, from the work reviewed above, this is clearly an issue that warrants serious consideration. In AIDS, as the example, upwards of 80% of patients suffer from chronic pain, and of these, a shockingly high percentage suffer from vague and diffuse pains of unknown origin (Breitbart et al 1996, Hewitt et al 1997). Clearly, AIDS patients suffer from pain from a variety of readily identifiable causes, including nerve damage, opportunistic cancers, and opportunistic infections, resulting both from the drugs used in therapy and from the disease process itself (Breitbart et al 1996, Hewitt et al 1997). Our work suggests that HIV-1 activation of spinal cord glia may also contribute to the pain and suffering. That is, HIV-1–induced glial activation in spinal cord would be expected to both create pain for which there is no definable etiology in the body and exaggerate pain resulting from identifiable peripheral causes.

Beyond the numerous bacteria and viruses known to "home" to the central nervous system, other triggers for spinal cord glial activation exist. For example, from the animal studies reviewed above, infection and damage of peripheral nerves leads both to exaggerated pain states and to astrocyte and microglial activation in the spinal cord (Coyle 1998, DeLeo & Colburn 1999). Although no studies of animal models of arthritis have yet examined spinal cord glial activation, the prolonged sensory pain fiber activity known to be induced by such conditions would cause prolonged release of pain transmitters into the spinal cord dorsal horns. As noted previously, this pattern of effects predicts glial activation at spinal levels. In none of these cases has the effect of drugs that disrupt glial function or specific glial mediators yet been tested. Furthermore, spinal cord trauma recruits immune cells from the general circulation into the region (Carlson et al 1998, Popovich et al 1997), activates both astrocytes (Hadley & Goshgarian 1997) and microglia (Popovich et al 1997), and causes exaggerated pain states in both laboratory animals and humans (Christensen & Hulsebosch 1997, Wang et al 1997, Xu et al 1993). The potential role of glia and proinflammatory cytokines in these pain states has yet to be explored.

Proinflammatory cytokines also directly activate peripheral nerves that carry the sensation of pain. TNF and IL-1 have each been repeatedly implicated in directly activating the sensory nerve bundles as they course toward the spinal cord. Indeed, TNF has been linked to demyelination and degeneration of axons (Redford et al 1995, Said & Hontebeyrie-Joskowicz 1992), leading to the suggestion that peripheral demyelinating neuropathies and multiple sclerosis may be linked to TNF release (Myers et al 1999). Such findings in laboratory animals again suggest examination of human conditions involving infection, inflammation, and damage involving or contacting peripheral sensory nerves. Some of these sites of proinflammatory cytokine production may be less than obvious. For example, herniated disks, which are sites both directly apposed to sensory nerves and associated with exaggerated pain states, are also sites of greatly elevated proinflammatory cytokines (Kang et al 1997, Rand et al 1997). Whether these cytokines contribute to pain and suffering of the patient remains to be investigated.

Lastly, proinflammatory cytokines act at peripheral nerve terminals to exaggerate pain. Their release at sites of skin infection and damage has obvious implications for human pain. Sensory nerves are in intimate contact with immune cells that reside in the skin (Misery 1998); they are also affected by immune cells attracted to sites of infection and trauma. Sites of proinflammatory cytokine production where tissue damage is less obvious are more subtle. One example is rheumatoid arthritis. Remarkable accumulations of activated immune cells occur in joint linings and fluid within the joint space of arthritic sites (Martin 1999). From animal models it is known that IL-1 injected into joints causes arthritis and worsens preexisting arthritic states. Furthermore, injection of IL-1 into the joints of laboratory animals increases sensory nerve activity, which is supportive of pain transmission (Fukuota et al 1994, Kelly et al 1996). Because of the immediacy of the effects observed, it appears that IL-1 again is acting directly on the nerve itself to increase sensory signaling (Kawatani & Birder 1992). Human arthritis patients show elevated IL-1 levels both in the general blood circulation and in the affected joint. In addition, their immune cells are primed to overrespond to new challenges with exaggerated IL-1 release (Martin 1999). The key involvement of IL-1 in arthritic pain is supported by recent placebo-controlled double-blind clinical trials over a 6-month period in patients with rheumatoid arthritis. Patients given an IL-1 receptor antagonist to disrupt IL-1 actions showed significant reductions in tender joint scores and both physician and patient assessment of their condition, compared with patients given the placebo (Nuki et al 1997). TNF appears to be involved in human arthritis as well. TNF levels are greatly increased in the general circulation as well as in the joints and joint fluids of patients with rheumatoid arthritis (Martin 1999). These elevations of TNF are correlated with joint pain, and TNF antagonists decrease symptoms in rheumatoid arthritis. Similar to the findings for IL-1, carefully controlled human clinical trials have provided evidence that TNF inhibitors produce significant improvement in patient quality of life indices and significantly reduce pain (Moreland et al 1997). Indeed, based on preclinical and clinical data, Martin has suggested that proinflammatory cytokines may be important targets for novel analgesic drugs for conditions such as phantom limb pain, reflex sympathetic dystrophy, traumatic nerve injuries, herpes zoster virus associated with both shingles and postherpetic neuralgia, trigeminal neuralgia, and diabetic neuropathy, all of which are currently poorly managed by available drugs and therapies.

CONCLUSIONS

Regardless of the precise details and the ultimate mechanisms that prove to be involved, it can be concluded that immune cells and products of immune cells signal the central nervous system and modulate pain. Indeed, activation of glia within the spinal cord dorsal horns and consequent release of IL-1 at this site may prove to be a final common pathway for many exaggerated pain states. Furthermore, a consideration of this immune regulation of pain may help to make functional sense out of what would not seem to be adaptive, namely hyperalgesia and allodynia. Thus, pain processes may participate in the larger scheme of host defense and be better understood in this context. The next few years will likely witness more attempts to understand immune-pain interactions, and we believe an unraveling of the mechanisms involved may well produce real advances in the ability to treat pain.

ACKNOWLEDGMENTS

This work was supported by NIH grants MH01558, MH50479, MH45045, MH55283, and NS38020.

Visit the Annual Reviews home page at www.AnnualReviews.org.

LITERATURE CITED

Baber NS, Dourish CT, Hill DR. 1989. The role of CCK caerulein, and CCK antagonists in nociception. *Pain* 39:307–28

Baldwin RL, Stolowitz ML, Hood L, Wisnieski BJ. 1996. Structural changes of tumor necrosis factor alpha associated with membrane insertion and channel formation. *Proc. Natl. Acad. Sci. USA* 93:1021–26

Becher B, Fedorowicz V, Antel JP. 1996. Regulation of CD14 expression on human adult central nervous system-derived microglia. *J. Neurosci. Res.* 45:375–81

Benedetti F, Amanzio M. 1997. The neurobiology of placebo analgesia: from endogenous opioids to cholecystokinin. *Prog. Neurobiol.* 52:109–25

Bian D, Ossipov MH, Zhong C, Malan TP Jr, Porreca F. 1998. Tactile allodynia, but not thermal hyperalgesia, of the hindlimbs is blocked by spinal transection in rats with nerve injury. *Neurosci. Lett.* 241: 79–82

Bolin LM, Verity AN, Silver JE, Shooter EM, Abrams JS. 1995. Interleukin-6 production by Schwann cells and induction in sciatic nerve injury. *J. Neurochem.* 65:850–58

Breitbart W, McDonald M, Rosenfeld B, Passik S, Hewitt D, et al. 1996. Pain in ambulatory AIDS patients: pain characteristics and medical correlates. *Pain* 68:315–21

Carlson SL, Parrish ME, Springer JE, Doty K, Dossett L. 1998. Acute inflammatory response in spinal cord following impact injury. *Exp. Neurol.* 151:77–88

Cesselin F. 1995. Opioid and anti-opioid peptides. *Fundam. Clin. Pharmacol.* 9:409–33

Christensen MD, Hulsebosch CE. 1997. Chronic central pain after spinal cord injury. *J. Neurotrauma* 14:517–37

Clatworthy AL. 1999. Evolutionary perspectives of cytokines in pain. See Watkins & Maier 1999c, pp. 21–38

Clatworthy AL, Grose EF. 1997. Immune cells release factors that modlate the excitability of nociceptive sensory neurons in Aplysia. *Soc. Neurosci. Abstr.* 23:166

Clatworthy AL, Hughes TK, Budelmann BU, Castro GA, Walters ET. 1994. Cytokines may act as signals for the injury-induced hyperexcitability in nociceptive sensory neurons in Aplysia. *Soc. Neurosci. Abstr.* 23:166

Clatworthy AL, Illich PA, Castro GA, Walters ET. 1995. Role of periaxonal inflammation in the development of thermal hyperalgesia and guarding behavior in a rat model of neuropathic pain. *Neurosci. Lett.* 184:5–8

Clatworthy AL, Walters ET. 1994. Comparative analysis of hyperexcitability and synaptic facilitation induced by nerve injury in cerebral and pleural mechanosensory neurons in Aplysia. *J. Exp. Biol.* 190:217–38

Codazzi F, Racchetti G, Grohovaz F, Meldolesi J. 1996. Transduction signals induced in the rat brain cortex astrocytes by the HIV gp120 glycoprotein. *FEBS Lett.* 384:135–37

Coyle DE. 1998. Partial peripheral nerve injury leads to activation of astroglia and microglia which parallels the development of allodynic behavior. *Glia* 23:75–83

Cunha Q, Poole S, Lorenzetti BB, Ferreira SH. 1992. The pivotal role of tumour necrosis factor alpha in the development of inflammatory hyperalgesia. *Br. J. Pharmacol.* 107:660–64

DeLeo JA, Colburn RW. 1999. Proinflammatory cytokines and glial cells: their role in neuropathic pain. See Watkins & Maier 1999c, pp. 159–82

DeLeo JA, Colburn RW, Nichols M, Malhotta A. 1996. Interleukin-6-mediated hyperalgesia/allodynia and increased spinal IL-6 expression in a rat mononeuropathy model. *J. Interferon Cytokine Res.* 16:695–700

Diederich N, Acermann R, Jurgens R, Ortseifen M, Thun F, et al. 1988. Early involvement of the nervous system by human immune deficiency virus (HIV). A study of 79 patients. *Eur. Neurol.* 28:93–103

Doyere V, Burette F, Redinidel-Negro CR, Laroche S. 1993. Long-term potentiation of hippocampal afferents and efferents to prefrontal cortex: implications for associative learning. *Neuropsychologia* 31:1031–53

Ek M, Kurosawa M, Lundeberg T, Ericsson A. 1998. Activation of vagal afferents after intravenous injection of interleukin-1beta: role of endogenous prostaglandins. *J. Neurosci.* 18:9471–79

Eliav E, Ruda MA, Bennett GJ. 1996. An experimental neuritis of the rat sciatic nerve produces ipsilateral hindpaw allodynia and hyperalgesia. *Proc. Soc. Neurosci.* 22:865

Faris PL, Komisaruk B, Watkins LR, Mayer DJ. 1983. Evidence for the neuropeptide cholecystokinin as an antagonist of opiate analgesia. *Science* 219:310–12

Ferreira SH. 1972. Aspirin-like drugs and analgesia. *Nat. New Biol.* 240:200–3

Ferreira SH, Lorenzetti BB, Bristow AF, Poole S. 1988. Interleukin-1β as a potent hyperalgesic agent antagonized by a tripeptide analogue. *Nature* 334:698–700

Follenfant RL, Nakamura-Craing M, Henderson B, Higgs GA. 1989. Inhibition by neuropeptides of interleukin-1-beta-induced, prostaglandin-independent hyperalgesia. *Br. J. Pharmacol.* 98:41–43

Fu K, Light AR, Maixner W. 1998. Long-lasting inflammation and hyperalgesia evoked by subcutaneous formalin injection: associated with spinal microglial activation. *Proc. Soc. Neurosci.* 24:152.2

Fukuota H, Kawatani M, Hisamitsu T, Takeshige C. 1994. Cutaneous hyperalgesia induced by peripheral injection of interleukin-1 beta in the rat. *Brain Res.* 657:133–40

Garrison CJ, Dougherty PM, Kajander KC, Carlton SM. 1991. Staining of glial fibrillary acidic protein (GFAP) in lumbar spinal cord increases following a sciatic nerve constriction injury. *Brain Res.* 565:1–7

Gaykema RPA, Goehler LE, Tilders FJH, Bol JGJM, McGorry M, et al. 1998. Bacterial endotoxin induces Fos immunoreactivity in primary afferent neurons of the vagus nerve. *NeuroImmunoModulation* 5:234–40

Gilmer WS. 1995. Neurologic conditions affecting the lower extremities in HIV infection. *J. Am. Podiatr. Med. Assoc.* 85:352–61

Goehler LE, Gaykema RPA, Hammack SE, Maier SF, Watkins LR. 1998. Interleukin-1 induces c-Fos immunoreactivity in primary afferent neurons of the vagus nerve. *Brain Res.* 804:306–10

Goehler LE, Gaykema RPA, Nguyen KT, Lee JE, Tilders FJH, et al. 1999. Interleukin-1beta in immune cells of the abdominal vagus nerve: a link between the immune and nervous systems? *J. Neurosci.* 19:2799–2806

Goehler LE, Relton JK, Dripps D, Kiechle R, Tartaglia N, et al. 1997. Vagal paraganglia bind biotinylated interleukin-1 receptor antagonist (IL-1ra) in the rat: a possible mechanism for immune-to-brain communication. *Brain Res. Bull.* 43:357–64

Gunstream JD, Castro GA, Walters ET. 1995. Retrograde transport of plasticity signals in Aplysia sensory neurons following axonal injury. *J. Neurosci.* 15:439–48

Hadley SD, Goshgarian HG. 1997. Altered immunoreactivity for glial fibrillary acidic protein in astrocytes within 1 h after cervical spinal cord injury. *Exp. Neurol.* 146:380–87

Hammack S, Milligan E, Nguyen K, Hansen M, Martin D, et al. 1999. Sciatic nerve neuritis-induced allodynia and hyperalgesia is blocked by intrathecal application of IL-1 receptor antagonist. *Proc. Soc. Neurosci.* 25: In press

Hart BL. 1988. Biological basis of the behavior of sick animals. *Neurosci. Biobehav. Rev.* 12:123–37

Hattori A, Tanaka E, Murase K, Ishida N, Chatani Y, et al. 1993. Tumor necrosis factor stimulates the synthesis and secretion of biologically active nerve growth factor in non-neuronal cells. *J. Biol. Chem.* 268:2577–82

Herzberg U, Eliav E, Dorsey JM, Gracely RH, Kopin IJ. 1997. NGF involvement in pain induced by chronic constriction injury of the rat sciatic nerve. *NeuroReport* 8:1613–18

Herzberg U, Frydel BR, Sagen J. 1998. Epineural exposure to HIV viral envelope protein gp120 induces painful peripheral mononeuropathy and spinal gliosis. *Proc. Soc. Neurosci.* 24:547.4

Hewitt D, McDonald M, Pertenoy R, Rosenfeld B, Passik S, et al. 1997. Pain syndromes and etiologies in ambulatory AIDS patients. *Pain* 70:117–23

Hughes TK, Smith EM, Leung MK, Stefano GB. 1992. Immunoreactive cytokines in Mytilus edulis nervous and immune interactions. *Acta Biol. Hung.* 43:269–73

Illich PA, Martin D, Castro GA, Clatworthy AL. 1997. TNF binding protein attenuates thermal hyperalgesia but not guarding behavior following loose ligation of rat sciatic nerve. *Soc. Neurosci. Abstr.* 23:166

Johnson D, Krenger W. 1992. Interactions of mast cells with the nervous system—recent advances. *Neurochem. Res.* 17:939–51

Kagan BL, Baldwin R, Munoz D, Wisnieski BJ. 1992. Formation of ion-permeable channels by tumor necrosis factor-alpha. *Science* 255:1427–30

Kang JD, Stefanovic-Racic M, McIntyre LA, Georgescu HI, Evans CH. 1997. Toward a biochemical understanding of human intervertebral disc degeneration and herniation.

Contributions of nitric oxide, interleukins, prostaglandin E2, and matrix metalloproteinases. *Spine* 22:1065–73

Kaplan H, Fields HL. 1991. Hyperalgesia during acute opioid abstinence: evidence for a nociceptive facilitating function of the rostral ventromedial medulla. *J. Neurosci.* 11:1433–39

Kawatani M, Birder L. 1992. Interleukin-1 facilitates Ca2 + release in acutely dissociated dorsal root ganglion (DRG) cells of rat. *Proc. Soc. Neurosci.* 18:691

Kellstein DE, Mayer DJ. 1991. Spinal co-administration of cholecystokinin antagonists with morphine prevents the development of opioid tolerance. *Pain* 47:221–29

Kelly DC, Asghar AUR, McQueen DS, Perkins MN. 1996. Effects of bradykinin and desArg9-bradykinin on afferent neural discharge in interleukin-1beta-treated knee joints. *Br. J. Pharmacol.* 117:90P

Kelly DD, ed. 1986. *Annals of the New York Academy of Sciences: Stress Induced Analgesia,* Vol. 467. New York: NY Acad. Sci.

Kluger MJ. 1978. The evolution and adaptive value of fever. *Am. Sci.* 66:38–43

Kluger MJ. 1991. Fever: role of pyrogens and cryogens. *Physiol. Rev.* 71:93–127

Koka P, He K, Ja Z, Kitchen S, Peacock W, et al. 1995. Human immunodeficiency virus 1 envelope proteins induce interleukin 1, tumor necrosis factor alpha, and nitric oxide in glial cultures derived from fetal, neonatal and adult human brain. *J. Exp. Med.* 182:941–51

Kuby J. 1992. *Immunology.* New York: Freeman

Laye S, Bluthe R-M, Kent S, Combe C, Medina C, et al. 1995. Subdiaphragmatic vagotomy blocks the induction of interleukin-1b mRNA in the brain of mice in response to peripherally administered peripheral lipopolysaccharide. *Am. J. Physiol.* 268:R1327–31

Lindholm D, Heumann R, Hengerer B, Thoenen H. 1988. Interleukin-1 increases stability and transcription of mRNA encoding nerve growth factor in cultured rat fibroblasts. *J. Biol. Chem.* 263:16348–51

Lindholm D, Heumann R, Meyer M, Thoenen H. 1987. Interleukin-1 regulates synthesis of nerve growth factor in non-neuronal cells of rat sciatic nerve. *Nature* 330:658–59

Liu XG, Sandkuhler J. 1998. Activation of spinal N-methyl-D-aspartate or neurokinin receptors induces long-term potentiation of spinal C-fibre-evoked potentials. *Neuroscience* 86:1209–16

Ma M, Geiger JD, Nath A. 1994. Characterization of a novel binding site for the human immunodeficiency virus type 1 envelope protein gp120 on human fetal astrocytes. *J. Virol.* 68:6824–28

Maier SF, Goehler LE, Fleshner M, Watkins LR. 1998. The role of the vagus nerve in cytokine-to-brain communication. *Ann. NY Acad. Sci.* 840:289–300

Maier SF, Watkins LR. 1998. Cytokines for psychologists: implications of bi-directional immune-to-brain communication for understanding behavior, mood, and cognition. *Psychol. Rev.* 105:83–107

Maier SF, Wiertelak EP, Martin D, Watkins LR. 1993. Interleukin-1 mediates behavioral hyperalgesia produced by lithium chloride and endotoxin. *Brain Res.* 623:321–24

Maier SF, Wiertelak EP, Watkins LR. 1992. Endogenous pain facilitatory systems: anti-analgesia and hyperalgesia. *Am. Pain Soc. J.* 1:191–98

Martin D. 1999. Interleukin-1 and tumor necrosis factor: rheumatoid arthritis and pain. See Watkins & Maier 1999c, pp. 205–20

Mason P. 1993. Lipopolysaccharide induces fever and decreases tail flick latency in awake rats. *Neurosci. Lett.* 154:134–36

Maves TJ, Pechman PS, Gebhart GF, Meller ST. 1993. Possible chemical contribution from chromic gut sutures produces disorders of pain sensation like those seen in man. *Pain* 54:57–69

McMahon SB, Bennett DLH, Priestley JV, Shelton DL. 1995. The biological effects of endogenous NGF in adult sensory neurones revealed by a trkA IgG fusion molecule. *Nat. Med.* 1:774–80

Meller ST, Dyskstra C, Grzybycki D, Murphy S, Gebhart GF. 1994. The possible role of glia in nociceptive processing and hyperalgesia in the spinal cord of the rat. *Neuropharmacology* 33:1471–78

Milligan E, Nguyen K, Hansen M, Martin D, Maier SF, et al. 1999. HIV-1 gp120-enhanced pain responsivity is mediated by activated spinal cord glia. *Proc. Soc. Neurosci.* 25: In press

Milligan ED, Nguyen KT, Hansen M, Maier SF, Watkins LR. 1998. Allodynia and increased dorsal spinal cord interleukin-1beta induced by intrathecal (IT) gp120, an HIV-1 envelope glycoprotein. *Proc. Soc. Neurosci.* 24:155.1

Misery L. 1998. Langerhans cells in the neuro-immuno-cutaneous system. *J. Neuroimmunol.* 89:83–87

Moreland LW, Baumgartner SW, Schiff MH, Tindall EA, Fleischmann RM, et al. 1997. Treatment of rheumatoid arthritis with a recombinant human tumor necrosis factor receptor (p75)-Fc fusion protein. *N. Engl. J. Med.* 337:141–47

Myers RR, Wagner R, Sorkin LS. 1999. Hyperalgesic actions of cytokines on peripheral nerves. See Watkins & Maier 1999c, pp. 133–58

Nguyen KT, Deak T, Owens SM, Kohno T, Fleshner M, et al. 1998. Exposure to acute stress induces brain interleukin-1beta protein in the rat. *J. Neurosci.* 18:2239–46

Nichols ML, Bian D, Ossipov MH, Lai J, Porreca F. 1995. Regulation of morphine antiallodynic efficacy by cholecystokinin in a model of neuropathic pain in rats. *J. Pharmacol. Exp. Ther.* 275:1339–45

Nuki G, Rozman B, Pavelka K, Emery P, Lockabaugh J, et al. 1997. Interleukin-1 receptor antagonist continues to demonstrate clinical improvement in rheumatoid arthritis. *Arthritis Rheum.* 40:S224

Oka T, Aou S, Hori T. 1993. Intracerebroventricular injection of interleukin-1β induces hyperalgesia in rats. *Brain Res.* 624:61–68

Oka T, Aou S, Hori T. 1994a. Intracerebroventricular injection of interleukin-1β enhances nociceptive neuronal responses of the trigeminal nucleus caudalis in rats. *Brain Res.* 656:236–44

Oka T, Aou S, Hori T. 1994b. Intracerebroventricular injection of prostaglandin E2 induces thermal hyperalgesia in rats: the possible involvement of EP3 receptors. *Brain Res.* 663:287–92

Oka T, Hori T. 1999. Brain cytokines and pain. See Watkins & Maier 1999c, pp. 183–204

Oka T, Hori T, Hosoi M, Oka K, Abe M, et al. 1997. Biphasic modulation in the trigerminal nociceptive neuronal responses by the intracerebroventricular prostaglandin E2 may be mediated through different EP receptor subtypes in rats. *Brain Res.* 771:278–84

Oka T, Oka K, Hosoi M, Aou S, Hori T. 1995a. The opposing effects of interleukin-1β microinjected into the preoptic hypothalamus and the ventromedial hypothalamus on nociceptive behavior in rats. *Brain Res.* 700:271–78

Oka T, Oka K, Hosoi M, Hori T. 1995b. Intracerebroventricular injection of interleukin-6 induces thermal hyperalgesia in rats. *Brain Res.* 692:123–28

Oka T, Oka K, Hosoi M, Hori T. 1996a. Inhibition of peripheral interleukin-1β-induced hyperalgesia by the intracerebroventricular administration of diclofenac and α-melanocyte-stimulating hormone. *Brain Res.* 736:237–42

Oka T, Wakugawa Y, Hosoi M, Oka K, Hori T. 1996b. Intracerebroventricular injection of tumor necrosis factor-α induces thermal hyperalgesia in rats. *NeuroImmunoModulation* 3:135–40

Opp M, Rady P, Hughes T, Cadet P, Tyring S, et al. 1996. Human immunodeficiency virus envelope glycoprotein 120 alters sleep and induces cytokine mRNA expression in rats. *Am. J. Physiol.* 270:R963–70

Payza K, Akar CA, Yang HYT. 1993. Neuropeptide FF receptors: structure-activity relationship and effect of morphine. *J. Pharmacol. Exp. Ther.* 267:88–94

Pertovaara A. 1998. A neuronal correlate of secondary hyperalgesia in the rat spinal dorsal horn is submodality selective and facilitated by supraspinal influence. *Exp. Neurol.* 149:193–202

Peterson PK, Gekker G, Hu S, Sheng WS, Anderson WR, et al. 1995. CD14 receptor-mediated uptake of nonopsonized *Mycobacterium tuberculosis* by human microglia. *Infect. Immun.* 63:1598–602

Poole S, Bristow AF, Lorenzetti BB, Das REG, Smith TW, et al. 1992. Peripheral analgesic activities of peptides related to alpha-MSH and interleukin-1 beta 193–195. *Br. J. Pharmacol.* 106:489–92

Poole S, Cunha FDQ, Ferreira SH. 1999. Hyperalgesia from subcutaneous cytokines. See Watkins & Maier 1999c, pp. 59–88

Poole S, Woolf CJ. 1999. Cytokine-nerve growth factor interactions in inflammatory hyperalgesia. See Watkins & Maier 1999c, pp. 89–132

Popovich PG, Wei P, Stokes BT. 1997. Cellular inflammatory response after spinal cord injury in Sprague-Dawley and Lewis rats. *J. Comp. Neurol.* 377:443–64

Rand N, Reichert F, Florman Y, Rotshenker S. 1997. Murine nucleus pulposus-derived cells secrete interleukins-1-beta, -6, and -10 and granulocyte-macrophage colony-stimulating factor in cell culture. *Spine* 22:2598–602

Redford EJ, Hall SM, Smith KJ. 1995. Vascular changes and demyelination induced by the intraneural injection of tumour necrosis factor. *Brain* 118:869–78

Reeve AJ, Fox A, Walker MJK, Urban L. 1998. Electrophysiological study on the spinal effects of interleukin-1β on the responses of dorsal horn neurones. *Proc. Soc. Neurosci.* 24:155.3

Ren K, Dubner R. 1996. Enhanced descending modulation of nociception in rats with persistent hindpaw inflammation. *J. Neurophysiol.* 76:3025–37

Richardson DE. 1995. Deep brain stimulation for the relief of chronic pain. *Neurosurg. Clin. N. Am.* 6:135–44

Richardson PM, Murphy PG, Ramer MS, Borthwick L, Bisby MA. 1998. Endogenous interleukin 6 contributes to peripheral neuropathic pain. *Proc. Soc. Neurosci.* 24:548.7

Ritter S, Ritter RC, Barnes CD. 1992. *Neuroanatomy and Physiology of Abdominal Vagal Afferents.* Ann Arbor, MI: CRC

Rothwell NJ, Luheshi G. 1994. Pharmacology of interleukin-1 actions in the brain. *Adv. Pharmacol.* 25:1–20

Rotshenker S, Aamar S, Barak V. 1992. Interleukin-1 activity in lesioned peripheral nerve. *J. Neuroimmunol.* 39:75–80

Rowbotham MC, Fields HL. 1996. The relationship of pain, allodynia and thermal sensation in post-herpetic neuralgia. *Brain* 119:347–54

Safieh-Garabedian B, Poole S, Allchorne A, Winter J, Woolf CJ. 1995. Contribution of interleukin-1b to the inflammation-induced increase in nerve growth factor levels and inflammatory hyperalgesia. *Br. J. Pharmacol.* 115:1265–75

Said G, Hontebeyrie-Joskowicz M. 1992. Nerve lesions induced by macrophage activation. *Res. Immunol.* 143:589–99

Sandkuhler J. 1996. The organization and function of endogenous antinociceptive systems. *Prog. Neurobiol.* 50:49–81

Sandkuhler J, Liu X. 1998. Induction of long-term potentiation at spinal synapses by noxious stimulation or nerve injury. *Eur. J. Neurosci.* 10:2476–80

Sharpless NE, O'Brien WA, Verdin E, Kukta CV, Chen IS, et al. 1992. Human immunodeficiency virus type 1 tropism for brain microglial cells is determined by a region of the env glycoprotein that also controls macrophage tropism. *J. Virol.* 66:2588–93

Slart R, Yu AL, Yaksh TL, Sorkin LS. 1997. An animal model of pain produced by systemic administration of an immunotherapeutic anti-ganglioside antibody. *Pain* 69:119–25

Smith LC, Hildemann WH. 1986. Allogeneic cell interactions during graft rejection in *Callyspongia diffusa* (Porifera, Demospongia); a study with monoclonal antibodies. *Proc. R. Soc. London Ser. B* 226:465–77

Sommer C, Galbraith JA, Heckman HM, Myers RR. 1993. Pathology of experimental compression neuropathy producing hyperesthesia. *J. Neuropath. Exp. Neurol.* 52:223–33

Sommer C, Lindenlaub L, Petrausch S, George A. 1998a. Neutralizing antibodies to interleukin-1-receptor attenuate hyperalgesia in experimental painful mononeuropathy. *Proc. Soc. Neurosci.* 24:495.4

Sommer C, Marziniak M, Myers RR. 1998b. The effect of thalidomide treatment on vascular pathology and hyperalgesia caused by chronic constriction injury of rat nerve. *Pain* 74:83–91

Sommer C, Schafers M. 1998. Painful mononeuropathy in C57BL/Wld mice with delayed Wallerian degeneration: differential effects of cytokine production and nerve regeneration on thermal and mechanical hypersensitivity. *Brain Res.* 784:154–62

Sommer C, Schmidt C, George A. 1998c. Hyperalgesia in experimental neuropathy is dependent on the TNF receptor 1. *Exp. Neurol.* 151:138–42

Sommer C, Schmidt C, George A, Toyka KV. 1997. A metalloprotease-inhibitor reduces pain associated behavior in mice with experimental neuropathy. *Neurosci. Lett.* 237:45–48

Sorkin LS, Xiao WH, Wagner R, Myers RR. 1997. Tumor necrosis factor-alpha induces ectopic activity in nociceptive primary afferent fibers. *Neuroscience* 81:255–62

Swanson B, Zeller JM, Paice JA. 1998. HIV-associated distal symmetrical polyneuropathy: clinical features and nursing management. *J. Assoc. Nurses AIDS Care* 9:77–80

Sweitzer SM, Colburn RW, Rutkowski M, DeLeo JA. 1999. Acute peripheral inflammation induces moderate glial activation and spinal IL-1β expression that correlates with pain behavior in the rat. *Brain Res.* In press

Tang NM, Dong HW, Wang XM, Tsui ZC, Han JS. 1997. Cholecystokinin antisense RNA increases the analgesic effect induced by electroacupuncture or low dose morphine: conversion of low responder rats into high responders. *Pain* 71:71–80

Tyor WR, Glass JD, Griffin J, Becker PS, McArthur JC, et al. 1992. Cytokine expression in the brain during the acquired immunodeficiency syndrome. *Ann. Neurol.* 31:349–60

Ushijima H, Nishio O, Klocking R, Perovic S, Muller WEG. 1995. Exposure to gp120 of HIV-1 induces an increased release of arachidonic acid in rat primary neuronal cell culture followed by NMDA receptor-mediated neurotoxicity. *Eur. J. Neurosci.* 7:1353–59

Vasko MR. 1995. Prostaglandin-induced neuropeptide release from spinal cord. *Prog. Brain Res.* 104:367–80

Vesce S, Bezzi P, Rossi D, Meldolesi J, Volterra A. 1997. HIV-1 gp120 glycoprotein affects the astrocyte control of extracellular glutamate by both inhibiting the uptake and stimulating the release of the amino acid. *FEBS Lett.* 411:107–9

Wagner R, Janjigian M, Myers RR. 1998. Anti-inflammatory interleukin-10 therapy in CCI neuropathy decreases thermal hyperalgesia, macrophage recruitment, and endoneurial TNF-alpha expression. *Pain* 74:35–42

Wagner R, Myers RR. 1996a. Endoneurial injection of TNF-alpha produces neuropathic pain behaviors. *NeuroReport* 7:2897–901

Wagner R, Myers RR. 1996b. Schwann cells produce tumor necrosis factor alpha: expression in injured and non-injured nerves. *Neuroscience* 73:625–29

Walters ET, Alizadeh H, Castro GA. 1991. Similar neuronal alterations induced by axonal injury and learning in Aplysia. *Science* 253:797–99

Wang CX, Olschowka JA, Wrathall JR. 1997. Increase of interleukin-1b mRNA and protein in the spinal cord following experimental traumatic injury of the rat. *Brain Res.* 759:190–97

Watkins LR, Deak T, Silbert L, Martinez J, Goehler L, et al. 1995a. Evidence for involvement of spinal cord glia in diverse models of hyperalgesia. *Proc. Soc. Neurosci.* 21:897

Watkins LR, Goehler LE, Relton J, Brewer MT, Maier SF. 1995b. Mechanisms of tumor necrosis factor-α (TNF-α) hyperalgesia. *Brain Res.* 692:244–50

Watkins LR, Kinscheck IB, Mayer DJ. 1984. Potentiation of opiate analgesia and apparent reversal of morphine tolerance by cholecystokinin antagonists. *Science* 224:395–96

Watkins LR, Maier SF. 1997. The case of the missing brain: arguments for a role of brain-to-spinal cord pathways in pain facilitation. *Behav. Brain Sci.* 20:469–70

Watkins LR, Maier SF. 1999a. Illness-induced hyperalgesia: mediators, mechanisms and implications. See Watkins & Maier 1999c, pp. 39–58

Watkins LR, Maier SF. 1999b. Implications of immune-to-brain communication for sickness and pain. *Proc. Natl. Acad. Sci. USA.* In press

Watkins LR, Maier SF, eds. 1999c. *Cytokines and Pain.* Basel: Birkhauser

Watkins LR, Maier SF, Goehler LE. 1995c. Cytokine-to-brain communication: a review and analysis of alternative mechanisms. *Life Sci.* 57:1011–26

Watkins LR, Maier SF, Goehler LE. 1995d. Immune activation: the role of pro-inflammatory cytokines in inflammation, illness responses and pathological pain states. *Pain* 63:289–302

Watkins LR, Martin D, Ulrich P, Tracey KJ, Maier SF. 1997a. Evidence for the involvement of spinal cord glia in subcutaneous formalin induced hyperalgesia in the rat. *Pain* 71:225–35

Watkins LR, Mayer DJ. 1986. Multiple endogenous opiate and non-opiate analgesia systems: evidence for their existence and clinical implications. *Ann. NY Acad. Sci. 1st Int. Conf. Stress-Induced Analgesia,* ed. DD Kelly, 467:273–99. New York: NY Acad. Sci. Press

Watkins LR, McGorry M, Schwartz B, Sisk D, Wiertelak EP, et al. 1997b. Reversal of spinal cord non-opiate analgesia by conditioned antianalgesia in the rat. *Pain* 71:237–47

Watkins LR, Wiertelak EP, Goehler LE, Smith KP, Martin D, et al. 1994. Characterization of cytokine-induced hyperalgesia. *Brain Res.* 654:15–26

Watkins LR, Wiertelak EP, McGorry M, Martinez J, Schwartz B, et al. 1998. Neurocircuitry of conditioned inhibition of analgesia: effects of amygdala, dorsal raphe, ventral medullary, and spinal cord lesions on antianalgesia. *Behav. Neurosci.* 112:360–78

Wiertelak EP, Maier SF, Watkins LR. 1992a. Cholecystokinin antianalgesia: safety cues abolish morphine analgesia. *Science* 256:830–33

Wiertelak EP, Roemer B, Maier SF, Watkins LR. 1997. Comparison of the effects of nucleus tractus solitarius and ventral medulla lesions on illness-induced and subcutaneous formalin-induced hyperalgesias. *Brain Res.* 748:143–50

Wiertelak EP, Watkins LR, Maier SF. 1992b. Conditioned inhibition of analgesia. *Anim. Learn. Behav.* 20:339–49

Wiertelak EP, Yang H-YT, Mooney-Heiberger K, Maier SF, Watkins LR. 1994. The nature of conditioned anti-analgesia: spinal cord opiate and antiopiate neurochemistry. *Brain Res.* 634:214–26

Willis WD, ed. 1992. *Hyperalgesia and Allodynia.* New York: Raven

Woolf CJ, Allchorne A, Safieh-Garabedian B, Poole S. 1997. Cytokines, nerve growth factor and inflammatory hyperalgesia: the contribution of tumour necrosis factor α. *Br. J. Pharmacol.* 121:417–24

Woolf CJ, Safieh-Garabedian B, Ma Q-P, Crilly P, Winter J. 1994. Nerve growth factor contributes to the generation of inflammatory sensory hypersensitivity. *Neuroscience* 62:327–31

Xiao WH, Wagner R, Myers RR, Sorkin LS. 1996. TNFa in the peripheral receptive field or on the sciatic nerve trunk evokes activity in primary afferent fibres. *Proc. Soc. Neurosci.* 22:1811

Xu XJ, Hao JX, Seiger A, Hughes J, Hokfelt T, et al. 1994. Chronic pain-related behaviors in spinally injured rats: evidence for functional alterations of the endogenous cholecystokinin and opioid systems. *Pain* 56:271–77

Xu XJ, Hao JX, Seiger A, Wiesenfeld-Hallin Z. 1993. Systemic excitatory amino acid receptor antagonists of the alpha-amino-3-hydroxy-5-methyl-4-isoxazolepropionic acid (AMPA) receptor and of the N-methyl-D-aspartate (NMDA) receptor relieve mechanical hypersensitivity after transient spinal cord ischemia in rats. *J. Pharmacol. Exp. Ther.* 267:140–44

Yabuuchi K, Nishiyori A, Minami M, Satoh M. 1996. Biphasic effects of intracerebroventricular interleukin-1β on mechanical-nociception in the rat. *Eur. J. Pharmacol.* 300: 59–65

Yaksh TL. 1997. Pharmacology and mechanisms of opioid analgesic activity. *Acta Anaesthesiol. Scand.* 41:94–111

Yeung M, Pulliam L, Lau A. 1995. The HIV envelope protein gp120 is toxic to human brain-cell cultures through the induction of interleukin-6 and tumor necrosis factor-alpha. *AIDS* 9:137–43

Zimmermann M, Herdegen T. 1996. Plasticity of the nervous system at the systematic, cellular and molecular levels: a mechanism of chronic pain and hyperalgesia. *Prog. Brain Res.* 110:233–59

Annu. Rev. Psychol. 2000. 51:59–91

THOUGHT SUPPRESSION

Richard M. Wenzlaff and Daniel M. Wegner

Division of Behavioral and Cultural Sciences, The University of Texas at San Antonio, San Antonio, Texas 78249–0652; e-mail: rwenzlaff@utsa.edu
Department of Psychology, Gilmer Hall, University of Virginia, Charlottesville, Virginia 22903; e-mail: dwegner@virginia.edu

Key Words   mental control, intrusive thought, rebound effect, ironic processes

■ **Abstract**   Although thought suppression is a popular form of mental control, research has indicated that it can be counterproductive, helping assure the very state of mind one had hoped to avoid. This chapter reviews the research on suppression, which spans a wide range of domains, including emotions, memory, interpersonal processes, psychophysiological reactions, and psychopathology. The chapter considers the relevant methodological and theoretical issues and suggests directions for future research.

> Again and again I have said to myself, on lying down at night, after a day embittered by some vexatious matter, 'I will *not* think of it any more!. . . It can do no good whatever to go through it again. I *will* think of something else!'
> And in another ten minutes I have found myself, once more, in the very thick of the miserable business, and torturing myself, to no purpose, with all the old troubles.
> Lewis Carroll (1893)
> *Curiosa Mathematica*

CONTENTS

Introduction 60
The Phenomena 61
   Emptying the Head 61
   Postsuppression Rebound...62
   Enhanced Accessibility During Suppression 64
Theoretical Accounts..66
   Distracter Associations 66
   Goal Interruption..67
   Ironic Process Theory...67
   The Role of Metacognition 68
Key Variables..69
   Target Characteristics...69
   Instructed vs Spontaneous Suppression 71

0084–6570/00/0201–0059$12.00   **59**

Individual Differences..72
Assessment of Thinking 73
Personal Consequences 75
  Emotional Reactions 75
  Substance Cravings 75
  Pain and Psychophysiological Reactions 76
  Memory 77
Interpersonal Consequences 78
  Impression Formation...78
  Stereotyping and Prejudice..79
Psychopathology..80
  Trauma 80
  Obsessive-Compulsive Disorder..81
  Depression...82
  Treatment Implications...83
Conclusions 83

INTRODUCTION

There is a certain predictability to unwanted thoughts, a grim precision in the way our mental clockwork returns such thoughts to mind each time we try to suppress them. As a result, it is tempting to attribute special significance or power to suppressed thoughts, to see them as expressions of sinister workings of mind—and in fact, it was exactly this approach that led Freud (e.g. 1953) to focus his attention on the nature of thoughts that are expelled from consciousness. As it turns out, however, it may not be especially useful to ascribe significance to unwanted thoughts themselves.

Contemporary research suggests that it is the process of thought suppression, not the product, that should be examined for its significance and power. This realization has emerged from studies in which people are instructed to spend time trying not to think about some particular thought, however neutral or mundane, with the consequences of their activity being measured. Early research hinted that such instructions might make such a thought tend to return (e.g. Antrobus et al 1964, Langfeld 1910). This finding was most pronounced in the "white bear" studies of Wegner et al (1987), and the introduction of this standardized laboratory paradigm has yielded substantial evidence that the paradoxical nature of the process of thought suppression is responsible for the returning of unwanted thoughts to mind.

Evidence on thought suppression is accumulating broadly at a rapid pace. Although there are reviews of aspects of this literature (Beevers et al 1999; Bodenhausen & Macrae 1996; Monteith et al 1998a; Purdon & Clark 1999; Wegner 1989, 1992; Wegner et al 1994a; Wegner & Wenzlaff 1996), the topic deserves an integrated and current review. We endeavor to provide this by focusing on research on the process of thought suppression that has accrued since the white bear studies. We begin by describing the phenomenon—when suppression is apt to backfire—and the methodological considerations relevant to the detection of this paradoxical effect. Next, we consider the main theoretical accounts for this outcome and examine the key variables that may mediate the effects of thought suppression. We then review the impact of suppression on intrapersonal states (e.g. emotional, cognitive) and interpersonal processes (e.g. attraction, prejudice), and finally we consider the relationship of thought suppression to psychopathology.

THE PHENOMENA

Researchers have identified three classes of suppression-related effects: (*a*) enhanced occurrence of target thoughts following a period of suppression; (*b*) an immediate, suppression-induced surge in target thoughts; and (*c*) an intensification of intrusions during suppression, triggered by cognitive demands. In this section, we examine the evidence for these different suppression-related phenomena. First, however, we briefly discuss the importance of baseline considerations in assessing suppression-related effects.

Emptying the Head

What exactly does it mean not to think of something? If thought suppression were a perfect process, it would ideally leave a person with no vestige of the unwanted thought at all. The initial "white bear" experiments of Wegner et al (1987) compared thought suppression to this ideal and found it wanting. It was assumed in these studies that college students in Texas would almost never think of a white bear spontaneously, and therefore that any evidence of such a thought during suppression was an indication that suppression had failed. And indeed, many such indications were observed. Participants' signals that the thought was occurring during a 5-minute suppression session—in the form of verbal reports or bell-rings to indicate the thought's return—on average exceeded one per minute.

This frequency of thinking seems excessive if people can indeed suppress a thought completely, but perhaps this is too much to ask. After all, the instruction to suppress is a sort of reminder of the unwanted thought. Perhaps this instruction cues people to think of the target more than they would have normally. To control for such cuing, investigators have examined several comparisons, each implying a different baseline level of spontaneous thinking.

One baseline approach is the "free monitoring" method, in which participants are asked to report whatever comes to mind. This approach is appealing because it does not produce artificially high rates of target thoughts and avoids potential ceiling and exhaustion effects. It does not, however, control for cuing effects that can result when the suppression group is specifically instructed to inhibit a particular thought. Moreover, the monitoring condition can risk floor effects when natural baseline levels for a particular thought are very low. To avoid the problem of a zero baseline and to minimize differential cuing, this free-monitoring method typically requires that the experimental procedure expose participants to the thought target (e.g. in a film or a reading) prior to the thought reporting period.

Another possible comparison involves a "cued monitoring" or "mention" control. In this case, instructions mention the target thought, either alone or in the context of other thoughts, optionally with some instruction indicating that these are things the participant may or may not consider during the thought report period. In some cases, the participant is also asked to monitor the occurrence of the cued thought. This approach helps equate cuing for the suppression and control groups while minimizing ceiling and floor effects. Although this approach has several advantages, the "mention" instructions may promote excessive attention to the target and could distort responses by making participants suspicious about its role in the study. Indeed, the attempt to monitor a thought may be a component of the mental process of suppression, in which case monitoring serves as a seriously flawed baseline.

The third potential comparison is the "expression" method, in which control participants are instructed to think about the item that the suppression group is trying to inhibit. Not surprisingly, this control method produces high rates of target thoughts in the control condition, and so makes instructed suppression look very successful. Trying not to think of something produces far fewer thoughts than does trying to think of it on purpose—but this effect seems attributable to the effectiveness of expression, not the effectiveness of suppression. Expression is thus used more as an informative comparison condition than as a control. And expression conditions have come to be important in suppression research because of the discovery that prior suppression can enhance the degree of subsequent expression—the post-suppression rebound effect (Wegner et al 1987).

Postsuppression Rebound

In the first experimental demonstration of a suppression-related increase in target thoughts, Wegner et al (1987) compared the thought reports of two groups during a period when each had been instructed to think aloud about a white bear. One group focused on the target from the outset, whereas the other first spent a period of time suppressing white-bear thoughts. Compared with the group that thought about a white bear at the outset, the initial suppression group reported a higher rate of target thoughts during a subsequent expression period. This paradoxical finding prompted follow-up studies that assessed the reliability of this postsuppression rebound effect and addressed some of the methodological issues involved in the original study.

One of the methodological issues concerned comparing the expression thought reports of the suppression group that had already engaged in a think-aloud session with the expression-only group that had no prior exposure to the thought-report protocol. Investigators (e.g. Clark et al 1991) point out that this design precludes distinguishing the potential effects of practice from those of suppression. Moreover, critics contend that the expression-control method lacks ecological validity (Merckelbach et al 1991) and might artificially obscure any immediate suppression-induced surge in target thoughts (Clark et al 1991).

In response to the practice issue, researchers have enlisted a modified design where participants engage in a common subsequent expression period after initial expression or suppression, thus eliminating differential effects of practice. In addition, investigators have addressed the issue of the contrived nature of the expression condition by replacing it with thought-monitoring instructions. A variety of studies using one or more of these methodological modifications have replicated the original postsuppression rebound effect (Clark et al 1991, 1993, Harnden et al 1997, Harvey & Bryant 1998b, Johnston et al 1997a, Kelly & Kahn 1994, Lavy & van den Hout 1994, McNally & Ricciardi 1996, Wegner et al 1991, Wegner & Gold 1995, Wenzlaff et al 1991).

The addition of a second reporting period for the monitoring group raises a new issue concerning differential "exhaustion" of the target thought. Some studies indicate that target thoughts among expression or monitor control groups decrease over time (Roemer & Borkovec 1994, Wegner et al 1991, Wenzlaff et al 1988). Thus, the higher rates of target thoughts for participants who had previously suppressed may be fueled by a decrease in target thoughts among the control group. The viability of this alternative explanation, however, is weakened by findings from a study by Clark et al (1993). The investigators found evidence for the postsuppression rebound even after statistically controlling for the percentage of target thoughts and time spent on the target during the first reporting period. They concluded that the observed rebound was a consequence of thought suppression, and not a methodological artifact.

The viability of an exhaustion interpretation of the rebound effect is further diminished by the results of studies employing a unique comparison group (Wenzlaff & Bates 1999). Participants unscrambled a series of sentences by rearranging five of six available words (e.g. "very looks future the dismal bright") to form either a positive or negative statement (e.g. "the future looks very dismal" or "the future looks very bright"). A monitor control group formed whatever statements came to mind and the suppression group was instructed to suppress either positive or negative thoughts. The unique addition to these groups was a concentration control, which was instructed to focus on either positive or negative thoughts. During a subsequent time period participants unscrambled a second set of sentences, with all groups receiving instructions to form whatever statement came to mind first. The result was that a rebound effect occurred for the suppression group only, even though both the suppression and the concentration groups produced equal levels of positive and negative statements during the first phase. Thus, an exhaustion account for the rebound effect in this instance is untenable.

Although the preponderance of published studies provides evidence for a postsuppression rebound, some investigations have found only partial support (Kelly & Kahn 1994; Rutledge et al 1993, 1996; Smari et al 1994), and others have failed to find the effect at all (Merckelbach et al 1991; Muris et al 1992, 1993; Roemer & Borkovec 1994). The results of studies that have not fully replicated the rebound effect suggest either that individual differences mediated the effect

(Rutledge et al 1993, 1996; Smari et al 1994) or that the type of thought made a difference (Kelly & Kahn 1994). In some remaining studies that did not find a rebound, methodological limitations preclude adequate control comparisons (e.g. Muris et al 1993).

Enhanced Accessibility During Suppression

The evidence indicates that when thought suppression is relinquished, it leads to more thoughts about the target than would have occurred if suppression had never been undertaken. This finding suggests that thought suppression increases the accessibility of the target (Higgins 1989) and raises the possibility that it may produce a surge in target thoughts during attempted suppression. Research investigating this has assessed the immediate effectiveness of thought suppression under normal circumstances and in the special case where a cognitive demand is imposed to undermine mental-control abilities.

Immediate Enhancement Without Load   In the absence of added cognitive demands, most research has failed to find that suppression produces an immediate enhancement of target thoughts. However, these same studies uniformly find some significant incidence of target-related thoughts among suppressing participants— even though it is typically less than in the nonsuppressing group. It is unclear whether the relatively low but notable occurrence of target thoughts during suppression indicates a suppression-related enhancement or whether it simply signals occasional failures of mental control.

The identification of an immediate suppression-induced surge in target thoughts is complicated by a potential interpretive dilemma that occurs when there is no difference in the number of target thoughts reported under suppression or control instructions. In this situation it is unclear whether suppression failed or participants simply did not follow instructions. Under these circumstances, the possibility of a manipulation failure would seem more likely if there were an accompanying absence of postsuppression effects (e.g. Merckelbach et al 1991).

It is less plausible, however, to dismiss as a manipulation failure results that show a higher frequency of target thoughts during suppression than during control monitoring. For example, Salkovskis & Campbell (1994) found a higher rate of personally intrusive thoughts for participants who tried to suppress the thoughts than for those who simply monitored them. In a study by Lavy & van den Hout (1990), participants reported a higher rate of thoughts about a neutral target (vehicles) during suppression than during control monitoring. In a subsequent experiment, Lavy & van den Hout (1994) used a modified version of the Stroop test to detect suppression-related changes in thought accessibility. The investigators found that, compared to a control group, the suppression group showed more selective attentional bias toward target words.

It is not clear why—in the absence of added cognitive demands—a few studies have found an immediate enhancement effect of suppression, whereas most have not. Conscious biases not to report intrusions might be operating, as most measurements in these experiments depend on self-report (Wegner & Smart 1997). As we see next, the imposition of cognitive demands increases the frequency with which immediate enhancement effects are found.

Immediate Enhancement With Load The evidence we have considered suggests that the paradoxical effects of suppression are most apt to occur when mental control is voluntarily relinquished (i.e. postsuppression rebound). If terminating suppression enhances the accessibility of the target thought, then disrupting the process of mental control during suppression may produce paradoxical effects as well. Operating on the assumption of a limited-capacity information-processing model (Bargh 1994, Gilbert 1989), researchers have reasoned that if suppression is an effortful process (Muraven et al 1998, Wegner 1992), it can be undermined by concurrent cognitive demands.

A variety of studies have found that the imposition of cognitive demands (e.g. time pressures, concurrent memory tasks) during suppression has the effect of not merely diminishing control but also of making the target material more accessible and influential than it would have been without suppression. For example, Wegner & Erber (1992) instructed participants to think or not to think about a target word (e.g. "house") and then assessed their tendency to respond with the target word to related prompts (e.g. "home") and unrelated cues (e.g. "adult"). With the imposition of time pressure, participants who were engaged in suppression responded to the prompts with the target word more often than did either suppressing participants not under time constraints or nonsuppressing participants.

In a second experiment, Wegner & Erber (1992) measured the accessibility of target words using a Stroop-type color-naming interference task, in which the participants' latency to name the color in which the word was printed was taken as a measure of the accessibility of the word. Participants attempting to suppress a target word showed greater accessibility of the word than did participants trying to think of the target word, but only when they were given a mental load—in the form of a nine-digit number to rehearse during the Stroop task. This paradoxical phenomenon was termed the hyperaccessibility of suppressed thought.

Macrae et al (1997) found that instructions to suppress stereotypical material produced enhanced recall of the information when attentional capacity was depleted. During instructed thought suppression, participants in another study (Wenzlaff & Bates 1999) were especially likely to unscramble sentences to form suppression-relevant themes when they were given a cognitive load. Wegner et al (1993) found that participants who tried to suppress thoughts of personal successes or failures experienced increased accessibility of those thoughts in the Stroop task. This effect was only observed on Stroop trials for which participants were given a mental load (a six-digit number). More evidence of a load-induced surge of suppression-related material has been found in other studies using different types of cognitive demands and different types of outcome measures (e.g.

Ansfield et al 1996, Arndt et al 1997, Lane & Wegner 1995, Newman et al 1996, Wegner et al 1998, Wenzlaff & Bates 1998).

Our review indicates that an enhancement of suppression-related thoughts ensues when thought suppression is either voluntarily relinquished or disabled by cognitive demands. Next, we consider theoretical accounts that could help explain these paradoxical effects.

THEORETICAL ACCOUNTS

Several theoretical perspectives are relevant to understanding the paradoxical effects of thought suppression. Although some of these explanations cannot account for the full range of suppression-related effects, they do shed light on potentially important aspects of the mental-control process.

Distracter Associations

In the first study to demonstrate a postsuppression rebound effect, Wegner et al (1987) noted that suppressing participants used many different distracters to divert attention from the prohibited thought. The wide assortment of items mentioned in thought reports during suppression suggested that the distraction target was constantly shifting. This observation led the investigators to hypothesize that such unfocused self-distraction during suppression may be responsible for the rebound effect. The picture that emerged from an analysis of the thought protocols was that participants were relying on cues in the immediate environment for distraction. Most of these highly accessible distractions (e.g. the wall, the chair, the person's attire, etc), however, did not compel sustained attention and allowed awareness to drift back to the suppression target.

The result of this unfocused cycle of self-distraction is that it creates associations between the unwanted thought and all the various distracters. When suppression is ultimately relinquished, the items previously used as distracters become reminders of the suppression target, thereby producing the rebound effect. This explanation is supported by studies showing that the rebound effect is attenuated by either the use of a single distracter during suppression (Wegner et al 1987) or changes in the environmental context (Muris et al 1993, Wegner et al 1991; but see Macrae et al 1994) or mood context (Wenzlaff et al 1991).

Although distracter association can account for the rebound effect, it has difficulty accommodating the finding that cognitive demands produce especially high levels of intrusions during suppression. Distracter association would predict that the introduction of a cognitive load during suppression could interfere with the process of distraction and allow unwanted thoughts to drift into awareness. The research indicates, however, that load-induced intrusions during suppression do not simply rise to the level of the nonsuppressing group: They exceed it. Distracter-association does not offer a mechanism to explain this paradoxical effect, which suggests that we must look elsewhere for a more comprehensive account.

Goal Interruption

Martin et al (1993; see also Martin & Tesser 1989) propose that the postsuppression rebound of target thoughts stems from the motivation to fulfill a blocked goal. This idea relies on the Zeigarnik effect—the motivated perseverance of goal-related thoughts (Lewin 1951). Zeigarnik (1938) found participants were most apt to recall an experimental task if they had not completed it because of an interruption. Similar results have been obtained by other investigators (Millar et al 1988, Wicklund & Gollwitzer 1982; but see Martin et al 1993) and taken as evidence that thoughts related to an incomplete task remain active in the person's cognitive system. From this perspective, if a person is unsuccessful in accomplishing the goal of suppressing a thought, it should make the target thought especially compelling.

Martin et al (1993) argued that the postsuppression rebound may be fueled by an unfulfilled desire to complete the goal of thought suppression. The goal is typically unfulfilled because intermittent intrusions are likely to occur during suppression (the theory does not explain these sporadic target thoughts). When the individual later relinquishes active suppression efforts, the lingering memory of those occasional failures fosters a preoccupation with suppression-relevant thoughts. In support of this notion, Martin et al (1993) describe an unpublished study in which they instructed participants to suppress or monitor white-bear thoughts prior to a timed word-recognition task. Before the word task, the experimenter gave half the suppression participants success feedback in an attempt to foster a sense of closure. The results indicated that the success feedback eliminated the rebound effect, thereby providing support for the goal-interruption interpretation.

Although Martin et al (1993) believe this formulation can help shed light on some of the paradoxical effects of suppression, they also acknowledge its limitations. For example, a goal-completion motive cannot explain the context-dependent effects involving suppression rebound (Wegner et al 1991, Wenzlaff et al 1991). It also has difficulty explaining both the attenuating effects of focused self-distraction and the intrusion-promoting effects of cognitive load, described earlier. Most crucial, the theory is unable to account for the return of intrusive thoughts during suppression (Erber & Wegner 1996). Despite these limitations, the goal-interruption perspective does highlight the potential importance of motivational considerations, foreshadowing issues having to do with natural suppression targets (discussed below).

Ironic Process Theory

The theory of ironic processes (Wegner 1992, 1994, 1997; Wegner & Wenzlaff 1996) states that thought suppression involves two mechanisms: an intentional operating process that seeks thoughts that will promote the preferred state (i.e.

anything other than the unwanted thought), and an ironic monitoring process that remains in the background of consciousness and searches for mental contents that signal the failure to achieve the desired state (i.e. the unwanted thought). The operating process is effortful and conscious, whereas the monitoring system is usually unconscious and less demanding of mental effort. The monitoring process is ironic in the sense that it opposes the overall goal of suppression by remaining vigilant for occurrences of the unwanted item. Despite its ironic nature, this vigilance is necessary for successful mental control because it alerts the operating process of the need to renew distraction when conscious awareness of the unwanted thought becomes imminent.

The ironic sensitivity supplied by the monitoring process normally exerts only a minor influence over conscious awareness, subtly alerting the operating system of deviations from its intended mental course. However, when the operating process is voluntarily terminated by the individual or disrupted by cognitive demands, the monitoring process continues its vigilance for unwanted thoughts. Once initiated, then, the monitoring process can linger after effortful distraction has abated, thereby enhancing the mind's sensitivity to unwanted material. This can explain both the occurrence of postsuppression rebound and the ironic effects of cognitive demands during thought suppression.

The ironic process theory thus accounts for several features of thought suppression. The theory, however, is not specific regarding if and when the monitoring process ceases its search for occurrences of the target thought. This issue is relevant to questions concerning the cumulative impact of repeated suppression attempts and the role of practice in the mental-control process (Kelly & Kahn 1994, Monteith et al 1998a). Moreover, the theory involves a cognitive model that does not make clear predictions concerning the mediating influences of motivational states (Shoham & Rohrbaugh 1997), and the theory may be overly general (Navon 1994). Nevertheless, ironic process theory is currently the most complete account for suppression-related phenomena.

The Role of Metacognition

Beliefs, expectations, and judgments about our own mental processes and products may contribute in important ways to the effectiveness of thought suppression. These metacognitions (Flavell 1979) arise during cognitive development, as people accrue an understanding of the contents and processes of mind. The sense that some thoughts or mental states are controllable whereas others are not, for example, unfolds with development, and the idea that it might be difficult to suppress a thought is only achieved with development as well (Flavell et al 1998).

The most important metacognition underlying thought suppression, of course, is the belief that suppression could succeed. Feelings of success or failure in controlling one's thoughts are likely to influence the person's propensity to undertake suppression, and fear of not having such control may also motivate people to undertake suppression. Metacognitions of this kind have been implicated in a variety of disorders that are defined in large part by the dysfunctional nature and high frequency of intrusive cognitions. For example, theories of obsession such as those proposed by Rachman (1997, 1998) and Salkovskis (1998) argue that intrusive thoughts become obsessions by virtue of distorted cognitive processes that magnify the significance, danger, and personal responsibility associated with unwanted thoughts (see Purdon & Clark 1999). Similar distortions in metacognitive processes have been observed in depressed individuals (Beck 1967) and chronic worriers (Wells 1994) and in those with phobias (Thorpe & Salkovskis 1995).

Although metacognitions may not produce the ironic effects associated with thought suppression, they probably help perpetuate attempts at mental control. For example, people can become excessively self-critical and alarmed by their unsuccessful thought-suppression attempts if they have unrealistically high expectations concerning their mental-control abilities or if they tend to magnify the significance of unwanted thoughts (Kelly & Kahn 1994). The resulting distress could rob them of adequate cognitive resources, thereby further undermining their mental-control efforts, setting into motion a downward spiral of mental-control failures. Eventually, this state of affairs would erode the sense of personal control and contribute to anxiety, despondency, and hopelessness. Clinical theorists implicitly suggest this scenario (Rachman 1998, Salkovskis 1998), but they have not yet explicitly integrated the thought-suppression research into their theoretical models (Beevers et al 1999, Clark & Purdon 1993).

KEY VARIABLES

Researchers have identified several variables that can influence the effects of thought suppression, including the valence and relevance of the target, variations in how suppression is experimentally induced, thought assessment techniques, and individual differences. Here we describe these variables and the evidence of their relationship to thought suppression.

Target Characteristics

Emotional Valence   Most studies that have varied the emotional valence of the suppression target have found that when other variables are equal, emotional material is more difficult to suppress than is neutral information. For example, Petrie et al (1998) found that participants had more difficulty suppressing thoughts related to personal emotional issues than about everyday events. Davies & Clark (1998) found that a distressing film produced a postsuppression rebound, whereas a film about polar bears did not. In another study, mock jurors who were instructed to disregard murder evidence were more likely to experience recurrence of those thoughts when the evidence was presented in a graphic and upsetting manner rather than in a sterile and legalistic one (Edwards & Bryan 1997). Similarly,

Roemer & Borkovec (1994) found that participants who had suppressed a depressing topic later expressed more target-relevant thoughts than did individuals who had suppressed anxious or neutral thoughts. In contrast, although Harvey & Bryant (1998b) found a postsuppression rebound among participants who had initially suppressed thoughts about a violent, humorous, or neutral film, it was not mediated by the valence of the film.

Although the research indicates that emotional aspects of the target may undermine suppression, it is unclear precisely what those elements are. Possibilities include the personal threat posed by the material (Higgins 1997), the concreteness and vividness of its mental imagery (East & Watts 1994, Erdelyi 1993, Stoeber 1998), its distinctiveness (England & Dickerson 1988, Levinson 1994), or its congruence to the person's mood state (Bower 1981, Wenzlaff et al 1988). The latter notion was tested in a study by Howell & Conway (1992), which found that the induction of a positive or negative mood made it more difficult to suppress, respectively, positive or negative material. In another study (Wenzlaff & Bates 1998), depressed participants had particular difficulty inhibiting the depressive content of ambiguous sentences. Other research indicates that depressed or anxious individuals have special difficulty inhibiting mood-related items in the Stroop task (Gotlib & McCann 1984, Mathews & MacLeod 1985, Mogg et al 1989, Segal et al 1988).

Natural Suppression Targets   For purposes of experimental control, suppression researchers typically supply participants with the material to be suppressed. A number of investigators have pointed out that this approach potentially limits generalizability, leaving it unclear whether naturally occurring intrusive thoughts are subject to the same vagaries of mental control as are experimental stimuli. A few studies have addressed this issue by using participant-supplied intrusive thoughts as the target of suppression. Although overall the findings are mixed, some studies suggest that naturally occurring intrusive thoughts are less susceptible to suppression-enhancement effects in the laboratory than are experimentally supplied targets. However, whatever suppression advantage exists for naturally occurring intrusive thoughts in the laboratory seems to erode when mental control is exerted in natural settings for more prolonged periods of time.

Evidence that natural suppression targets are more amenable to suppression in the laboratory was provided in a study by Kelly & Kahn (1994), which found a postsuppression rebound for white-bear thoughts but not for naturally occurring intrusive thoughts. The possibility that naturally occurring intrusive thoughts are more amenable to mental control than are neutral thoughts was also suggested by the results of a study by Wegner & Gold (1995). The investigators asked participants to suppress thoughts of either a previous romantic partner who was still the object of their desires (hot flame) or a former intimate whom they no longer desired (cold flame). The thought reports revealed a rebound effect for the cold flame but not the hot flame, which presumably was a more natural target of suppression. Other published studies have also failed to find a postsuppression rebound for naturally occurring intrusive thoughts, although neither employed a neutral comparison condition (Rutledge 1998, Smari et al 1995). The situation is complicated by the fact that other laboratory studies have found suppression-related enhancement of naturally occurring intrusive thoughts (McNally & Ricciardi 1996, Salkovskis & Campbell 1994).

One explanation for the studies that fail to find a postsuppression rebound for naturally intrusive targets involves the effects of practice (Kelly & Kahn 1994, Monteith et al 1998a). Because these thoughts occur frequently in everyday life, the person might develop techniques that are relatively effective for suppressing them—at least in a laboratory setting (e.g. an effective set of distracters). It is also possible that repeated efforts to suppress a personally relevant thought make the process of distraction more automatic and efficient (Wegner 1994). Thus, when these thoughts are selected for suppression in an experimental setting, people are better equipped to suppress them than they are to suppress the infrequently encountered thoughts that experimenters are apt to supply (e.g. white bear).

This practice notion, however, begs the fact that the natural suppression targets are, by definition, intrusive in the real world. Thus, whatever laboratory-setting benefits may accrue through real-world experience with these thoughts are likely to be short-lived and not extend to the natural environment. This idea is supported by the results of Trinder & Salkovskis (1994), in which participants identified a negative intrusive thought and recorded its occurrence over a period of four days. One group was instructed to record intrusions, another was told to try to think about the thoughts whenever they occurred, and a third group was advised to suppress the thoughts. The results over the four days indicated that the suppression group experienced more intrusive thoughts and found them more uncomfortable than did participants in the other two groups.

Another reason that natural targets may not lead to paradoxical effects in the lab as often as experimental targets do involves motivational differences. Participants may expend more effort and persist longer in suppressing natural targets. Consequently, for the short time they spend in the lab, participants may never completely relinquish suppression as instructed, thereby precluding a postsuppression rebound (Wegner & Gold 1995). This notion is supported by the finding that boosting incentives to suppress thoughts can lead to increased persistence and extend short-term success on the mental-control task (Letarte et al 1997).

Instructed vs Spontaneous Suppression

Most suppression experiments manipulate mental control by instructing participants to suppress, express, or monitor certain thoughts. Although this approach has the advantage of controlling extraneous variables, it raises questions concerning the relevance of the findings to the real world, where thought suppression is typically a self-initiated enterprise. Asking participants to suppress or monitor naturally occurring intrusive thoughts does not eliminate the problem because it still involves the artificial constraints associated with instructed mental control.

A few studies, however, have addressed this issue by creating circumstances that are likely to produce spontaneous suppression in the laboratory, thereby eliminating the need for suppression instructions and allowing a more naturalistic assessment of the mental-control process.

Arndt et al (1997) implicitly fostered suppression by exposing participants to a mortality salience treatment that primed death-related thoughts. The mortality priming appeared to activate suppression, as evidenced by a decrease in accessibility of death-related thoughts with low cognitive load and an increase with high cognitive load. This is precisely the pattern of results obtained with similar research using instructed suppression.

Wenzlaff & Bates (1998) found that individuals with a recent history of depression reported routinely suppressing depressive thoughts since their recovery. Presumably they were trying to preserve their emotional well-being by warding off the lingering negative thoughts associated with their recent depressive episode. This suppression was reflected in their performance on a laboratory task that involved unscrambling sentences that could form either positive or negative statements. Without a cognitive load they formed a high percentage of positive statements. However, the introduction of a cognitive load caused an increase in the number of negative statements they formed. In fact, the load manipulation led the previously depressed participants to form negative statements at a rate that resembled their actively depressed counterparts.

Macrae et al (1998) indirectly manipulated thought suppression by inducing participants to experience heightened self-focus. The investigators reasoned that because high self-focus increases the salience of internalized standards (Duval & Wicklund 1972), it should lead individuals to suppress prejudicial stereotypes. In support of their hypotheses they found that elevated self-focus reduced stereotype tendencies initially but produced a subsequent rebound effect when self-focus diminished. Wyer et al (1998) also obtained a suppression-related rebound of stereotypic judgments by varying the salience of relevant social standards to trigger spontaneous suppression.

Smart & Wegner (1999) observed spontaneous suppression among women with eating disorders who were asked to play the role in an interview of someone without such a disorder. These women, as compared to those who did not have an eating disorder, showed greater self-reports of suppression and intrusion of eating-related thoughts, higher accessibility of body-related thoughts, and a tendency to perceive the interviewer as likely to have an eating disorder as well.

The conclusion from these studies is that spontaneous suppression leads to the same type of paradoxical effects as does instructed suppression. This correspondence provides some assurance that the experimental benefits of instructed thought suppression do not come at the expense of ecological relevance.

Individual Differences

People vary in their natural tendency to suppress unwanted thoughts. Wegner & Zanakos (1994) developed the White Bear Suppression Inventory as a self-report measure of the tendency to suppress thoughts. The measure shows good internal and temporal reliability and correlates sensibly with other individual-difference variables, such as obsession, depression, dissociation, and anxiety (Muris & Merckelbach 1997, Muris et al 1996, van den Hout et al 1996, Wegner & Zanakos 1994). Although correlational ambiguities preclude conclusions about causality, these studies show that individuals who report a relatively strong desire for suppression are especially apt to suffer from recurrent intrusive thoughts. There are some indications that this tendency to rely on thought suppression may have its origins in childhood, where certain parental practices are apt to promote avoidant coping (Cooper et al 1998, Eisenberg et al 1998, Fraley & Shaver 1997, Wenzlaff & Eisenberg 1998). In a related vein, recent work suggests that the ability to inhibit unwanted thoughts diminishes in old age (Jacoby 1999, von Hippel et al 1999).

Kelly & Nauta (1997) identified another individual difference relevant to the outcome of thought suppression. The investigators found that thought-suppression instructions made individuals high in reactance feel especially out of control and disturbed by their intrusive thoughts. The investigators suggest that being motivated to restore one's freedom may paradoxically leave one feeling more out of control following attempted suppression.

A suppression-relevant individual difference of another sort has emerged from recent research involving hypnosis. Bowers & Woody (1996) instructed high- and low-hypnotizable participants to suppress thoughts in a normal state and in a hypnotic state. The results showed that both high- and low-hypnotizable participants experienced significant suppression-related intrusions when they were in a normal, waking state. When hypnotized, however, the number of intrusions reported by highly hypnotizable participants dropped to almost zero, whereas the level of intrusive thoughts of low-hypnotizable participants remained high. Investigators found a similar pattern of results with a cognitive load manipulation (King & Council 1998) and with pain tolerance as the dependent variable (Eastwood et al 1998). This research indicates that highly suggestible individuals may be able to suppress mental states with impunity when induced to do so under hypnosis. The reasons for this enhanced suppression ability are unclear and could include factors such as susceptibility to experimenter-demand effects, reporting biases, or unusual mental-control strategies.

Assessment of Thinking

The most obvious variables of interest in thought-suppression research involve cognitive processes and their products. Because investigators lack the means to observe mentation directly, they have employed a variety of self-report techniques, including verbalizing one's stream of consciousness (Clark et al 1991, Wegner et al 1987), writing down thoughts as they occur (Wenzlaff et al 1988), ringing a bell (Wegner et al 1987), clicking a hand counter (Salkovskis & Reynolds 1994), and making tally marks (Kelly & Kahn 1994). Although the correspondence among these various measures has not been systematically assessed, each has been shown to be sensitive to suppression-related effects in one or more instances.

Despite the fact that these self-report measures have proven useful, there is the obvious issue about the veracity of people's self-reported mental activity. First, the deliberate process of reporting thoughts may itself heighten self-consciousness or otherwise alter the person's frame of mind, thereby producing an unnatural state of mentation (see Whetstone & Cross 1998). In addition, the verity of the thought reports may be undermined by a person's conscious or unconscious defenses. Self-report biases of this sort are especially likely to occur when the thought involves emotionally disturbing or personally unfavorable material (Wegner & Smart 1997). This situation mitigates the odds of detecting suppression-related effects, especially with the added demand characteristics arising from instructions to suppress the target. Finally, it can be difficult to identify target occurrences when the target thought is not discretely defined (e.g. stereotypes, emotions), making it difficult for the participant or experimenter to assess the relevance of various potentially related thoughts.

The issues surrounding cognitive measures highlight the value of using objective behavioral indices that reflect target-relevant thinking. Indeed, a growing number of investigators have detected suppression-related paradoxical effects using behavioral correlates of cognition, including physiological states (Wegner et al 1990), physical avoidance (Macrae et al 1994), motor behavior (Wegner et al 1998), pain tolerance (Cioffi & Holloway 1993), and sleep (Ansfield et al 1996). These behavioral measures of mental state reveal the same susceptibility to the paradoxical effects of suppression as is reflected in the more common method of self-report.

Another approach to overcoming the deficiencies of self-report cognitive measures is the use of measures of automatic cognitive processes (see Bargh & Chartrand 1999, Wegner & Bargh 1998). Measures can be made, for example, of processes of which participants are unaware, of processes that occur before the participant is able to establish conscious control over a response, or of processes that occur when cognitive resources are diverted from attempts at conscious control. The several measures of this kind used in suppression research—such as Stroop interference (Wegner & Erber 1992), sentence unscrambling (Wenzlaff & Bates 1998), word completion (Arndt et al 1997, Smart & Wegner 1999), and recall priority (Lane & Wegner 1995)—suggest that suppression has effects on cognitive processes even when those processes are beyond conscious control. Indeed, it appears that suppression has paradoxical effects on uncontrollable or unconscious cognitive processes, but has more predictable and intended effects on conscious reports. Suppression may succeed in clearing consciousness of a thought, even while measures of cognitive processes beneath consciousness indicate that suppression prompts remarkable levels of activation. Wegner & Smart (1997) describe this influence of suppression as the production of "deep cognitive activation"—an increase in cognitive accessibility that is not accompanied by an increase in conscious experience of the thought.

PERSONAL CONSEQUENCES

Emotional Reactions

To the extent that thoughts influence emotions, one would expect that the paradoxical effects of suppression would promote the mood state associated with the target. This is precisely what Wegner et al (1993) found when they imposed a cognitive load on participants who were trying to control their moods. Unlike participants without load, those under load reported moods that were significantly in opposition to the ones they had tried to achieve.

Wenzlaff et al (1991) tested the idea that thought suppression creates a bond between the suppressed item and one's mood state, such that the reactivation of one leads to the reinstatement of the other. In the first experiment, participants who were induced by music to experience positive or negative moods reported their thoughts while trying to think or not think about a white bear. When all participants were subsequently asked to think about a white bear, those who were in similar moods during thought suppression and a later expression period displayed a particularly strong rebound of the suppressed thought. In the second experiment, the investigators assessed participants' moods following the expression of a previously suppressed or expressed thought. Mood reports showed that participants who had initially tried to suppress their thoughts experienced a reinstatement of the mood that existed during the initial period of suppression.

Ironic emotional effects of suppression have also been found with physiological indices of emotional arousal. For example, Wegner et al (1990) found that trying not to think about sex, like thinking about sex, increased electrodermal responding in comparison to thinking about or not thinking about less exciting topics (e.g. dancing). Wegner et al (1997) found that participants who were instructed to relax under cognitive load experienced more relaxation-incompatible physiological arousal than did a group who was given a load with no relaxation instructions. More evidence that suppression has emotional consequences comes from studies showing that elevated blood pressure is especially prevalent among individuals who chronically suppress anger (Cottington et al 1986, Dimsdale et al 1986, Thomas 1997).

Substance Cravings

People who should be highly motivated to control their dangerous substance cravings (e.g. drinking, eating, smoking, etc) are often the very ones for whom inhibition seems to backfire (Polivy 1998, Wenzlaff & Wegner 1998). Despite the obvious relevance of mental-control issues to addiction, few studies have examined the impact of suppression on substance-related thoughts. In one study, Salkovskis & Reynolds (1994) found that efforts by abstaining smokers to suppress cigarette-related thoughts produce especially high levels of intrusions. However, a longitudinal study found no relationship between thought suppression and smoking relapse (Haaga 1989, Haaga & Allison 1994).

In a study on dieting, Harnden et al (1997) instructed participants to suppress thoughts about weighing themselves. When suppression was later relinquished, nondieters experienced a rebound of target-related thoughts. Although dieters consistently reported more target-related thoughts than did nondieters, they did not exhibit a rebound effect. Herman & Polivy (1993) discuss the unique aspects of food-related thoughts that can potentially mediate the effectiveness of mental control. The authors highlight the need for more research on the role of thought suppression in eating-related problems—a recommendation that we echo and suggest applies equally to other types of cravings.

Pain and Psychophysiological Reactions

When one is experiencing physical pain, it seems clear that thinking about it intensifies the discomfort. The alternative, of course, is to suppress thoughts about the pain in an effort to reduce or eliminate the suffering. Although thought suppression is a common method for dealing with pain, few studies have tested its effectiveness (cf Cioffi 1993). With what we know about thought suppression, we would expect that attempts to suppress the experience of pain could backfire. Indeed, Cioffi & Holloway (1993) found that participants who were attempting to suppress pain of a cold pressor experienced more lingering discomfort than did participants who were involved in monitoring or distraction. Moreover, the suppression group later rated an innocuous vibration as more unpleasant than did the other groups, which suggests a postsuppression rebound related to the earlier pain. Sullivan et al (1997) also found that participants who were asked to suppress thoughts about an upcoming pain procedure experienced more thought intrusions during the suppression period and experienced more pain during the ice-water immersion than did a control group.

Although attempts to suppress thoughts about pain intensify subjective discomfort, does thought suppression have more direct physiological effects? As noted earlier, autonomic arousal does appear to be a common physiological reaction to the suppression of emotional thoughts (Cottington et al 1986; Dimsdale et al 1986; Gross 1998; Thomas 1997; Wegner et al 1990, 1997). For example, Gross & Levenson (1993) found that, compared to nonsuppressing participants, those instructed to suppress their emotions while watching a distressing film showed greater constriction of peripheral vasculature and greater electrodermal activity. Individuals who suppress thoughts on a chronic basis show a pattern of physiological responses that are consistent with anxiety (Lorig et al 1995).

Because persistent autonomic reactivity is associated with early disease processes (Jemmott & Locke 1984), one could expect that chronic suppression of emotional material would lead to health-related problems (Pennebaker 1997a).

Indeed, inhibition-related health problems have been associated with individuals who hide their gay status (Cole et al 1996), conceal traumatic experiences in their past (Pennebaker 1993, 1997a,b), suppress anger (Thomas 1997), or are considered inhibited or shy by others (e.g. Kagan et al 1988). Petrie et al (1998) found that thought suppression may compromise immunological functioning. Instructions to suppress either emotional or neutral thoughts produced effects on circulatory immune variables, causing a decrease in circulating T lymphocytes as well as marginal decreases in T suppressor cells and total lymphocyte numbers. In sum, the research suggests that thought suppression can affect physiological states in ways that are likely to have negative repercussions for physical well-being.

Memory

If thought suppression enhances the accessibility of the target, one might expect that the enhanced attention would foster better memory for the information as well. The finding that people often continue to remember items they have been asked to forget is consistent with this possibility (see Bjork 1989, Golding & Long 1998, Wegner et al 1994a, Whetstone & Cross 1998). More direct evidence for the notion that suppression can enhance memory for target material comes from studies by Macrae and his colleagues (1996, 1997). The studies found that the suppression of stereotype-congruent memories is especially demanding of cognitive resources, and when suppression is relinquished or interrupted, memory for the target information is enhanced. In related research, Sherman et al (1997) instructed participants to suppress their use of stereotypes while forming impressions of an Asian woman who revealed stereotypical and nonstereotypical behaviors. This suppression group later displayed better recognition memory for the stereotypical behaviors than did nonsuppressors.

Wegner et al (1996) found that although instructions to suppress thoughts about a recently viewed film did not affect later retrieval of the contents of the film relative to controls, it did disrupt the organization of the material. The suppression instructions undermined retrieval of information about the sequence in which items of content were encountered. Participants who had suppressed the film were also more likely than others to report their memories of the film as having the character of snapshots rather than of moving film. The idea that suppression can disrupt the sequence of events in memory is consistent with findings by Kuyken & Brewin (1995) that depressed patients who reported high levels of suppression of childhood physical or sexual abuse reported memories that were temporally vague or distorted. Suppression-induced disruption of sequence memory, however, may depend on as-yet-unidentified variables. For example, although Rassin et al (1997) found a suppression-induced enhancement of target thoughts, the suppression group did not differ from controls in recall of the sequence of stimulus material.

INTERPERSONAL CONSEQUENCES

Impression Formation

Research on the impact of thought suppression on impression formation has revealed several paradoxical effects. Newman et al (1997) examined how suppressing awareness of unwanted aspects of the self affects judgments of others. They reasoned that as a result of suppression, unwanted personal characteristics would become chronically accessible and would influence the interpretation of others' behavior. The idea of suppression-induced projection was supported in studies showing that people who avoid thinking about having threatening personality traits and deny possessing them are especially apt to impute those traits to others. When participants were either naturally predisposed to suppress personally unfavorable traits or were instructed to do so, they subsequently projected them onto someone else.

Newman et al (1996) hypothesized that priming a concept through thought suppression should have effects on trait inferences that are similar to those resulting from more direct forms of priming. Research on trait priming shows that when people are not distracted, they usually try to eliminate bias by avoiding the use of the primed trait to interpret social information (Lombardi et al 1987, Martin et al 1990, Newman & Uleman 1990). This contrast effect, however, can be eliminated when cognitive demands arise or when motivation to make accurate judgments is low, leading to the biased assimilation of social information, in accord with the primed trait (Martin et al 1990, Thompson et al 1994). Using thought suppression as a priming procedure, Newman et al (1996) found that when impressions were formed with no cognitive load, suppression led to contrast, whereas with a cognitive load it produced assimilation. The investigators concluded that suppression can also adversely affect interpersonal judgments.

A different type of assimilation and contrast process can involve the rejection of undesirable social models. The ironic effects of thought suppression do not bode well for someone who is actively trying not to be like someone else (e.g. an abusive parent, a racist associate, etc). Hodges & Wegner (1997) report the results of a study in which participants tried to assume or reject the perspective of another person. Participants read a story where two boys play in a house that is described in considerable detail. The key experimental conditions involved instructions for the readers either to think like a burglar or to try not to think like a burglar. Without a cognitive load, the "think like a burglar" group recalled more burglar-relevant information about the story than did the suppression group. However, the imposition of a cognitive load caused the suppression group to recall more burglar-related information than did a suppression group without load.

Research has also suggested that thought suppression—in the form of keeping socially relevant information secret—can increase interpersonal attraction (Lane & Wegner 1994). Wegner et al (1994b) found that past relationships that remained a secret were more likely to occupy a person's attention than previous public relationships. They also found that mixed-sex couples who were induced to play footsie under a table were more strongly attracted to their experimental partner if they tried to keep the activity a secret from others. Lane & Wegner (1995) found that secrets were associated with enhanced cognitive accessibility that was positively correlated with relevant suppression efforts. The findings suggest that secrecy promotes suppression of secretive thoughts, which can produce a preoccupation with the material even after disclosure. Smart & Wegner (1999) observed similarly that individuals with eating disorders who were assigned to role-play having no disorder for an interview then showed higher levels of suppression, intrusion, and accessibility of disorder-related thoughts.

Stereotyping and Prejudice

Several studies have found support for the paradoxic prediction that the suppression of stereotypes should lead to more use of the stereotype concept. In a series of experiments, Macrae et al (1994) found that, compared to a nonsuppression group, participants who had suppressed stereotypes about skinheads subsequently displayed increased accessibility of stereotype-relevant thoughts, formed more biased judgments, and were more apt to avoid skinheads. In another series, Macrae et al (1998) obtained similar findings when they indirectly manipulated the suppression of stereotypes by increasing or decreasing self-focus. Wyer et al (1999) also used an implicit suppression manipulation and found a postsuppression rebound of stereotypic judgments.

Monteith et al (1998b) found that the stereotype rebound associated with suppression may be mediated by the level of prejudice of the suppressor. Participants with low-prejudice attitudes toward gays were not prone to the rebound effect when it was assessed using an overt measure of stereotype use. Bodenhausen & Macrae (1996) and Monteith et al (1998a) provide a more detailed consideration of the potential mediating variables in the suppression of stereotypes.

In the studies that have found suppression-enhanced stereotyping, the enhancement occurred after suppression was relinquished. During suppression itself, stereotyping was actually reduced. Although controlled cognitive processes may correct for the automatic activation of stereotypes that would otherwise prejudice judgments (Devine 1989, Fiske 1989), such compensation is apt to require cognitive resources (Wegner 1994). Thus, relying on thought suppression to control the influence of stereotypes is likely to produce ironic effects when cognitive resources are in short supply. Wyer et al (1999) provided support for this prediction by showing that a cognitive load caused participants who were trying to suppress a stereotype to form more stereotypical judgments than were formed by their counterparts with no load or with no suppression instruction.

Finally, as noted above, paradoxical effects of stereotype suppression have also been observed with regard to memorial processes. For example, when suppression is relinquished or interrupted, memory for the previously suppressed stereotype is enhanced (Macrae et al 1996, 1997; Sherman et al 1997).

PSYCHOPATHOLOGY

One way to view the relation of thought suppression to disordered thought or emotion is simply to suggest that when people have unwanted symptoms, they may try not to think about them. This interpretation is reasonable for many of the studies that have found correlations between self-reported thought suppression and various clinical disorders. In other cases, however, evidence suggests that thought suppression might be implicated in the etiology or maintenance of disorders. Experimental findings showing that instructed suppression promotes the development of symptoms, in particular, suggests a causal rather than a reactive role for thought suppression. It may be, too, that in some cases feedback systems develop in which suppression and symptoms fuel each other cyclically. In this section, we examine clinical disorders—trauma, obsessive-compulsive disorder, and depression—that are associated with disturbing, intrusive thoughts and frequent suppression attempts, and for which there exists at least some experimental evidence that thought suppression may play a role in the production or maintenance of the disorder (see also Beevers et al 1999, Purdon 1999).

Trauma

Exposure to a traumatic event can produce posttraumatic stress disorder (PTSD), which is characterized by recurrent, intrusive thoughts and repeated efforts to suppress the intrusions and avoid situations that might cue more thoughts of the trauma. Although trauma-relevant suppression has sometimes been associated with unconscious repression, the more common scenario involves the conscious, intentional suppression of traumatic thoughts (Christianson & Engelberg 1997, Gold & Wegner 1995, Koutstaal & Schacter 1997).

Shipherd & Beck (1999) assessed baseline rape-related thoughts in an open-ended thought-report period using a sample of women who had recently been raped, approximately half of whom were experiencing PTSD. Following the baseline reporting, participants tried to suppress rape-related thoughts and then subsequently engaged in another open-ended thought-report period. Analysis of the thought protocols and participants' ratings of mental control indicated that although both groups reported equally low levels of rape-related thoughts during the suppression period, the PTSD group reported more difficulty controlling their thoughts. During the postsuppression period, the PTSD group's level of rape-related thoughts returned to the relatively high levels associated with the baseline period. In contrast, the non-PTSD groups' level of rape-related thoughts during the postsuppression period remained at low levels.

Harvey & Bryant (1998a) compared the thought reports of survivors of motor vehicle accidents with and without acute stress disorder to a normal control group using the suppression paradigm of baseline monitoring followed by suppression/monitoring and then monitoring. The results suggested a rebound effect for the acute stress disorder suppression group by showing that it had the highest occurrence of accident-related thoughts in the final reporting period.

A study of the victims of the Perth flood revealed that thought suppression was one of the best predictors of symptom severity, even after statistically controlling for the emotional intensity of the specific circumstances (Morgan et al 1995). The possibility that thought suppression contributes to the persistence of PTSD was also suggested by a prospective longitudinal study of patients injured in motor vehicle accidents (Ehlers et al 1998). The investigators found that the tendency to suppress accident-related thoughts at three months was an important predictor of PTSD symptoms one year later. Aaron et al (1999) have also found that early reports of thought suppression following physical trauma in children and adolescents are predictive of subsequent rumination and impaired coping.

Individual differences in thought suppression show substantial correlations with self-report measures of anxiety (Muris et al 1996, Wegner & Zanakos 1994), which suggests a broad connection between these dispositions. The desire not to be anxious might underlie attempts to suppress anxiety-related thoughts, and the intrusive return of such thoughts could fuel renewed anxiety (Wegner et al 1997, Wegner et al 1990). Muris et al (1997) observed, for example, that spider-phobic individuals tried harder to suppress spider-related thoughts during an instructed suppression period than did nonphobic participants. The tendency to avoid thinking about traumatic or anxiety-producing topics may prompt the return of those topics to mind, and so activate a cycle that could perpetuate anxiety disorders.

Obsessive-Compulsive Disorder

Among the cardinal symptoms of obsessive-compulsive disorder (OCD) are recurrent unwanted thoughts accompanied by repeated attempts to ignore or avoid them. Despite the obvious relevance of thought suppression to this disorder, there is a dearth of research testing the effects of thought suppression with obsessive-compulsive patients. In one of the only published clinical studies, Janeck & Calamari (1999) asked OCD patients and nonclinical control participants to suppress personally intrusive thoughts in the context of a suppression paradigm. The findings indicated that although the OCD group devoted more effort to thought suppression than did normal controls, they had more intrusive thoughts both during suppression and during the monitoring periods. The OCD participants also were more distressed by their intrusive thoughts and found the thoughts less acceptable and controllable than did control participants. These results are consistent with findings reported by Purdon & Clark (1994) of a positive relationship between perceived uncontrollability and thought intrusions. In the Janeck & Calamari study (1999), however, there were no suppression enhancement effects.

Smari et al (1994) used a normal sample to examine the relationship between scores on a measure of obsessionality and the effects of suppressing thoughts about a depressing story. Participants recorded their thoughts about the story during periods of instructed suppression and monitoring. Although participants' suppression-effort ratings indicated that they were responsive to the experimental instructions, those high in OCD tendencies reported equally high levels of target thoughts for both suppression and monitor instructions. In contrast, participants low in OCD reported fewer target thoughts under suppression instructions. In a subsequent study, Smari et al (1995) found that obsessionality scores were correlated with intrusions during the suppression of a personally disturbing thought. Rutledge (1998) obtained a similar correlation but only for women; the males in her sample showed a tendency in the opposite direction. Wegner & Zanakos (1994) found that among individuals with high levels of self-reported OCD symptoms, the White Bear Suppression Inventory measure of thought suppression provided a further increment in prediction of an interview-based assessment of obsessive thinking; the thought-suppression measure was not similarly predictive of the interview assessment of compulsive behavior.

Although it is risky to draw conclusions from so few studies, one commonality of the studies is that OCD symptoms are associated with a general failure of suppression (but see Rutledge 1998). The possibility that individuals with OCD have a generalized deficit in the ability to suppress thoughts has been the topic of some debate (Clayton et al 1999, de Silva 1992, Enright & Beech 1997, Salkovskis et al 1995). Future research examining the reliability and extent of thought-suppression deficits among individuals with OCD may help resolve this issue.

Depression

Depression involves a disturbance not only of mood but also of cognition. Depressed individuals are plagued by excessive self-criticism, pessimism, and a generally negative frame of mind (Beck 1967). One of the most popular psychological treatments for the disorder seeks to discourage negative cognitions in favor of more functional, positive thoughts (Sacco & Beck 1995). On their own, however, depressed individuals have considerable difficulty inhibiting their negative thoughts, despite the fact that they often expend considerable time and effort trying to do just that (Wenzlaff 1993, Wenzlaff & Bates 1998).

One of the mental-control problems depressed individuals encounter is that the distracters they find most accessible are tainted by the same negativity that characterizes the thoughts they are trying to suppress. By virtue of their close emotional association with the suppression target, these negative distracters can ultimately lead awareness back to the unwanted thought. This state of affairs explains the results of a study by Wenzlaff et al (1988), which found that compared to their nondepressed counterparts, depressed participants chose more negative distracters that eventually led to a breakdown in their ability to suppress negative material. A similar pattern of findings was obtained by Conway et al (1991), who found that dysphoric participants had more difficulty initially suppressing negative thoughts than positive ones. Howell & Conway (1992) replicated those results and also showed the converse effect by finding that nondysphoric individuals had more difficulty suppressing positive thoughts.

The idea that mood-related distracters create an association between the suppression target and the relevant mood was tested in a pair of studies by Wenzlaff et al (1991). The investigators found that reinstating the original mood (using a mood manipulation) that existed during suppression facilitated the return of the suppressed thought. Conversely, participants who were induced to think about a previously suppressed topic experienced a reinstatement of the mood they experienced during the original period of suppression.

One implication of this research is that thought suppression may prolong or worsen depression by strengthening mood-relevant associations. Some preliminary evidence supports this idea. Wenzlaff & Bates (1998) assessed depression over a 4- to 6-week period and found that higher levels of self-reported suppression of depressive thoughts were associated with a worsening of depressive symptoms. The study also found that participants who were not currently depressed but were at risk because of a previous episode were especially likely to employ suppression and were most apt to reveal depressive thinking under cognitive load. Taken together, the results suggest that by exacerbating negative cognitions, thought suppression may represent a cognitive risk factor for depression.

Treatment Implications

Investigators have only recently begun to consider the treatment implications of the thought-suppression research (Beevers et al 1999, Johnston et al 1997b, Purdon & Clark 1999, Shoham & Rohrbaugh 1997, Wegner 1997; Wenzlaff & Bates, 1998). One obvious recommendation for individuals plagued by unwanted thoughts is to abandon thought suppression in favor of alternative, more effective methods of mental control. Investigators have suggested a variety of options, including concentrating on desirable goals, learning how to use more effective distracters, and accepting and expressing unwanted thoughts. Decisions about the best alternatives to thought suppression should be informed by research examining the relative merits and potential risks of the various options. Much of this work remains to be done.

CONCLUSIONS

Virtually nonexistent fewer than 15 years ago, the study of thought suppression has grown into a significant area of scientific inquiry with a growing database that spans several psychological domains. What has compelled the interest of the scientific and clinical communities is that suppression is not simply an ineffective tactic of mental control; it is counterproductive, helping assure the very state of mind one had hoped to avoid. The problem of thought suppression is aggravated by its intuitive appeal and apparent simplicity, which help mask its false promises.

Despite the fact that the accumulated research is impressive in scope and consistency, our knowledge of the intricacies and idiosyncracies of thought suppression is far from complete. Questions remain concerning the potential mediating effects of certain target characteristics, the role of motivational and personality factors, and the clinical and practical implications, including the relative merits of alternative strategies.

Visit the Annual Reviews home page at www.AnnualReviews.org.

LITERATURE CITED

Aaron JD, Zaglul H, Emery RE. 1999. Post-traumatic stress following acute physical injury. *J. Pediatr. Psychol.* In press

Ansfield ME, Wegner DM, Bowser R. 1996. Ironic effects of sleep urgency. *Behav. Res. Ther.* 34:523–31

Antrobus JS, Antrobus JS, Singer JL. 1964. Eye movements accompanying daydreaming, visual imagery, and thought suppression. *J. Abnorm. Soc. Psychol.* 69:244–52

Arndt J, Greenberg J, Solomon S, Pyszczynski T, Simon L. 1997. Suppression, accessibility of death-related thoughts, and cultural worldview defense: exploring the psychodynamics of terror management. *J. Pers. Soc. Psychol.* 73:5–18

Bargh JA. 1994. The four horsemen of automaticity: awareness, intention, efficiency, and control in social cognition. In *Handbook of Social Cognition,* ed. RS Wyer Jr, TK Srull, 1:1–40. Hillsdale, NJ: Erlbaum

Bargh JA, Chartrand T. 1999. Studying the mind in the middle: a practical guide to priming and automaticity research. In *Research Methods in Social Psychology,* ed. H Reis, C Judd. New York: Cambridge Univ. Press. In press

Beck AT. 1967. *Depression: Clinical, Experimental, and Theoretical Aspects.* New York: Harper & Row

Beevers CG, Wenzlaff RM, Hayes AM, Scott WD. 1999. Depression and the ironic effects of thought suppression. *Clin. Psychol. Sci. Pract.* 6:133–48

Bjork RA. 1989. Retrieval inhibition as an adaptive mechanism in human memory. In *Varieties of Memory and Consciousness: Essays in Honor of Endel Tulving,* ed. HL Roediger, FIM Craik, pp. 309–30. Hillsdale, NJ: Erlbaum

Bodenhausen GV, Macrae CN. 1996. The self-regulation of intergroup perception: mechanisms and consequences of stereotype suppression. In *Stereotypes and Stereotyping,* ed. CN Macrae, C Stangor, M Hewstone, pp. 227–53. New York: Guilford

Bower GH. 1981. Mood and memory. *Am. Psychol.* 36:129–48

Bowers KS, Woody EZ. 1996. Hypnotic amnesia and the paradox of intentional forgetting. *J. Abnorm. Psychol.* 105:381–90

Christianson SA, Engelberg E. 1997. Remembering and forgetting traumatic experiences: a matter of survival. In *Recovered Memories and False Memories. Debates in Psychology,* ed. MA Conway, pp. 230–50. Oxford, UK: Oxford Univ. Press

Cioffi D. 1993. Sensate body, directive mind: physical sensations and mental control. See Wegner & Pennebaker 1993, pp. 410–42

Cioffi D, Holloway J. 1993. Delayed costs of suppressed pain. *J. Pers. Soc. Psychol.* 64:274–82

Clark DA, Purdon C. 1993. New perspectives for a cognitive theory of obsessions. *Aust. Psychol.* 28:161–67

Clark DM, Ball S, Pape D. 1991. An experimental investigation of thought suppression. *Behav. Res. Ther.* 29:253–57

Clark DM, Winton E, Thynn L. 1993. A further experimental investigation of thought suppression. *Behav. Res. Ther.* 31:207–10

Clayton IC, Richards JC, Edwards CJ. 1999. Selective attention in obsessive-compulsive disorder. *J. Abnorm. Psychol.* 108:171–75

Cole SW, Kemeny MW, Taylor SE, Visscher BR. 1996. Elevated health risk among gay men who conceal their homosexual identity. *Health Psychol.* 15:243–51

Conway M, Howell A, Giannopoulos C. 1991. Dysphoria and thought suppression. *Cogn. Ther. Res.* 15:153–66

Cooper ML, Shaver PR, Collins NL. 1998. Attachment styles, emotion regulation, and adjustment in adolescence. *J. Pers. Soc. Psychol.* 74:1380–97

Cottington EM, Matthews KA, Talbott E, Kuller LH. 1986. Occupational stress, suppressed anger, and hypertension. *Psychosom. Med.* 48:249–60

Davies MI, Clark DM. 1998. Thought suppression produces rebound effect with analogue post-traumatic intrusions. *Behav. Res. Ther.* 36:571–82

de Silva P. 1992. Obsessive-compulsive disorder. In *Adult Psychological Problems: An Introduction. Contemp. Psychol. Ser. 5,* ed. LA Champion, MJ Power, pp. 113–29. London: Falmer Press/Taylor & Francis

Devine P. 1989. Stereotypes and prejudice: their automatic and controlled components. *J. Pers. Soc. Psychol.* 56:5–18

Dimsdale JE, Pierce C, Schoenfeld D, Brown A. 1986. Suppressed anger and blood pressure: the effects of race, sex, social class, obesity, and age. *Psychosom. Med.* 48:430–36

Duval S, Wicklund RA. 1972. *A Theory of Objective Self-Awareness.* New York: Academic

East MP, Watts FN. 1994. Worry and the suppression of imagery. *Behav. Res. Ther.* 32:851–55

Eastwood JD, Gaskovski P, Bowers KS. 1998. The folly of effort: ironic effects in the mental control of pain. *Int. J. Clin. Exp. Hypn.* 46:77–91

Edwards K, Bryan TS. 1997. Judgmental biases produced by instructions to disregard: the (paradoxical) case of emotional information. *Pers. Soc. Psychol. Bull.* 23:849–64

Ehlers A, Mayou RA, Bryant B. 1998. Psychological predictors of chronic posttraumatic stress disorder after motor vehicle accidents. *J. Abnorm. Psychol.* 107:508–19

Eisenberg N, Cumberland A, Spinrad TL. 1998. Parental socialization of emotion. *Psychol. Inq.* 9:241–73

England SL, Dickerson M. 1988. Intrusive thoughts: unpleasantness not the major cause of uncontrollability. *Behav. Res. Ther.* 26:279–82

Enright S, Beech A. 1997. Schizotypy and obsessive-compulsive disorder. In *Schizotypy: Implications for Illness and Health,* ed. G Claridge, pp. 202–33. Oxford, UK: Oxford Univ. Press

Erber R, Wegner DM. 1996. Ruminations on the rebound. In *Ruminative Thoughts. Advances in Social Cognition,* ed. RS Wyer Jr, 9:73–79. Mahwah, NJ: Erlbaum

Erdelyi MH. 1993. Repression: the mechanism and the defense. See Wegner & Pennebaker 1993, pp. 126–48

Fiske ST. 1989. Examining the role of intent, toward understanding its role in stereotyping and prejudice. See Uleman & Bargh 1989, pp. 253–83

Flavell JH. 1979. Metacognition and metacognitive monitoring. A new area of cognitive-developmental inquiry. *Am. Psychol.* 34:906–11

Flavell JH, Green FL, Flavell ER. 1998. The mind has a mind of its own: developing knowledge about mental uncontrollability. *Cogn. Dev.* 13:127–38

Fraley RC, Shaver PR. 1997. Adult attachment and the suppression of unwanted thoughts. *J. Pers. Soc. Psychol.* 73:1080–91

Freud S. 1953 (1900). *The Interpretation of Dreams.* London: Holgarth

Gilbert DT. 1989. Thinking lightly about others: automatic components of the social inference process. See Uleman & Bargh 1989, pp. 189–211

Gold DB, Wegner DM. 1995. Origins of ruminative thought: trauma, incompleteness, nondisclosure, and suppression. *J. Appl.*

Soc. Psychol. 25:1245–61

Golding JM, Long DL. 1998. There's more to intentional forgetting than directed forgetting: an integrative review. In *Intentional Forgetting: Interdisciplinary Approaches,* ed. JM Golding, CM MacLeod, pp. 59–102. Mahwah, NJ: Erlbaum

Gotlib IH, McCann CD. 1984. Construct accessibility and depression: An examination of cognitive and affective factors. *J. Pers. Soc. Psychol.* 47:427–39

Gross JJ. 1998. The emerging field of emotion regulation: an integrative review. *Rev. Gen. Psychol.* 2:271–99

Gross JJ, Levenson RW. 1993. Emotional suppression: physiology, self-report, and expressive behavior. *J. Pers. Soc. Psychol.* 64:970–86

Haaga DAF. 1989. Articulated thoughts and endorsement procedures for cognitive assessment in the prediction of smoking relapse. *Psychol. Assess. J. Consult. Clin. Psychol.* 1:112–17

Haaga DAF, Allison ML. 1994. Thought suppression and smoking relapse: a secondary analysis of Haaga 1989. *Br. J. Clin. Psychol.* 33:327–31

Harnden JL, McNally RJ, Jimerson DC. 1997. Effects of suppressing thoughts about body weight: a comparison of dieters and nondieters. *Int. J. Eating Disord.* 22:285–90

Harvey AG, Bryant RA. 1998a. The effect of attempted thought suppression in acute stress disorder. *Behav. Res. Ther.* 36:583–90

Harvey AG, Bryant RA. 1998b. The role of valence in attempted thought suppression. *Behav. Res. Ther.* 36:757–63

Herman CP, Polivy J. 1993. Mental control of eating: excitatory and inhibitory food thoughts. See Wegner & Pennebaker 1993, pp. 491–505

Higgins ET. 1989. Knowledge accessibility and activation: subjectivity and suffering from unconscious sources. See Uleman & Bargh 1989, pp. 75–123

Higgins ET. 1997. Beyond pleasure and pain. *Am. Psychol.* 52:1280–1300

Hodges SD, Wegner DM. 1997. Automatic and controlled empathy. In *Empathic Accuracy,* ed. W Ickes, pp. 311–39. New York: Guilford

Howell A, Conway M. 1992. Mood and the suppression of positive and negative self-referent thoughts. *Cogn. Ther. Res.* 16:535–55

Jacoby LL. 1999. Ironic effects of repetition measuring age-related differences in memory. *J. Exp. Psychol.: Learn. Mem. Cogn.* In press

Janeck AS, Calamari JE. 1999. Thought suppression in obsessive-compulsive disorder. *Cogn. Ther. Res.* In press

Jemmott JB, Locke SE. 1984. Psychosocial factors, immunologic mediation, and human susceptibility to infectious diseases: How much do we know? *Psychol. Bull.* 95:78–108

Johnston L, Hudson SM, Ward T. 1997a. The suppression of sexual thoughts by child molesters: a preliminary investigation. *Sex. Abuse J. Res. Treat.* 9:303–19

Johnston L, Ward T, Hudson SM. 1997b. Deviant sexual thoughts: mental control and the treatment of sexual offenders. *J. Sex Res.* 34:121–30

Kagan J, Reznick JS, Snidman N. 1988. Biological bases of childhood shyness. *Science* 240:161–71

Kelly AE, Kahn JH. 1994. Effects of suppression of personal intrusive thoughts. *J. Pers. Soc. Psychol.* 66:998–1006

Kelly AE, Nauta MM. 1997. Reactance and thought suppression. *Pers. Soc. Psychol. Bull.* 23:1123–32

King BJ, Council JR. 1998. Intentionality during hypnosis: an ironic process analysis. *Int. J. Clin. Exp. Hypn.* 46:294–313

Koutstaal W, Schacter DL. 1997. Intentional forgetting and voluntary thought suppression: two potential methods for coping with childhood trauma. *Am. Psychiatr. Press Rev. Psychiatr.* 16:II-79–121. Washington, DC: Am. Psychiatr.

Kuyken W, Brewin CR. 1995. Autobiographical memory functioning in depression and reports of early abuse. *J. Abnorm. Psychol.* 104:585–91

Lane JD, Wegner DM. 1994. Secret relationships: the back alley to love. In *Theoretical Frameworks for Personal Relationships,* ed. R Erber, R Gilmour, pp. 67–85. Hillsdale, NJ: Erlbaum

Lane JD, Wegner DM. 1995. The cognitive consequences of secrecy. *J. Pers. Soc. Psychol.* 69:237–53

Langfeld HS. 1910. Suppression with negative instruction. *Psychol. Bull.* 7:200–8

Lavy EH, van den Hout MA. 1990. Thought suppression induces intrusions. *Behav. Psychother.* 18:251–58

Lavy EH, van den Hout MA. 1994. Cognitive avoidance and attentional bias: causal relationships. *Cogn. Ther. Res.* 18:179–91

Letarte H, Ladouceur R, Freeston M, Rheaume J. 1997. Incentive to suppress a neutral thought. *Behav. Cogn. Psychother.* 25:219–29

Levinson RW. 1994. Emotional control: variations and consequences. In *The Nature of Emotion,* ed. P Eckman, RJ Davidson, pp. 273–79. New York: Oxford Univ. Press

Lewin K. 1951. *Field Theory in Social Science: Selected Theoretical Papers.* New York: Harper & Row

Lombardi WJ, Higgins ET, Bargh JA. 1987. The role of consciousness in priming effects on categorization: assimilation versus contrast as a function of awareness of the priming task. *Pers. Soc. Psychol. Bull.* 13:411–29

Lorig TS, Singer JL, Bonanno GA, Davis P. 1995. Repressor personality styles and EEG patterns associated with affective memory and thought suppression. *Imagin. Cogn. Pers.* 14:203–10

Macrae CN, Bodenhausen GV, Milne AB. 1998. Saying no to unwanted thoughts: self-focus and the regulation of mental life. *J. Pers. Soc. Psychol.* 74:578–89

Macrae CN, Bodenhausen GV, Milne AB, Ford RL. 1997. On regulation of recollection: the intentional forgetting of stereotypical memories. *J. Pers. Soc. Psychol.* 72:709–19

Macrae CN, Bodenhausen GV, Milne AB, Jetten J. 1994. Out of mind but back in sight: stereotypes on the rebound. *J. Pers. Soc. Psychol.* 67:808–17

Macrae CN, Bodenhausen GV, Milne AB, Wheeler V. 1996. On resisting the temptation for simplification: counterintentional effects of stereotype suppression on social memory. *Soc. Cogn.* 14:1–20

Martin LL, Seta JJ, Crelia R. 1990. Assimilation and contrast as a function of people's willingness and ability to expend effort in forming an impression. *J. Pers. Soc. Psychol.* 59:27–37

Martin LL, Tesser A. 1989. Toward a motivational and structural theory of ruminative thought. See Uleman & Bargh 1989, pp. 306–26

Martin LL, Tesser A, McIntosh WD. 1993. Wanting but not having: the effects of unattained goals on thoughts and feelings. See Wegner & Pennebaker 1993, pp. 552–72

Mathews AM, MacLeod C. 1985. Selective processing of threat cues in anxiety states. *Behav. Res. Ther.* 23:563–69

McNally RJ, Ricciardi JN. 1996. Suppression of negative & neutral thoughts. *Behav. Cogn. Psychother.* 24:17–25

Merckelbach H, Muris P, van den Hout M, de Jong P. 1991. Rebound effects of thought suppression: instruction-dependent? *Behav. Psychother.* 19:225–38

Millar KU, Tesser A, Millar M. 1988. The effects of a threatening life event on behavior sequences and intrusive thought: a self-disruption explanation. *Cogn. Ther. Res.* 12:441–57

Mogg K, Mathews A, Weinman J. 1989. Selective processing of threat cues in anxiety states. A replication. *Behav. Res. Ther.* 27:317–23

Monteith MJ, Sherman JW, Devine PG. 1998a. Suppression as a stereotype control strategy. *Pers. Soc. Psychol. Rev.* 2:63–82

Monteith MJ, Spicer CV, Tooman GD. 1998b. Consequences of stereotype suppression:

stereotypes on AND not on the rebound. *J. Exp. Soc. Psychol.* 34:355–77

Morgan IA, Matthews G, Winton M. 1995. Coping and personality as predictors of posttraumatic intrusions, numbing, avoidance, and general distress: a study of victims of the Perth flood. *Behav. Cogn. Psychother.* 23:251–64

Muraven M, Tice DM, Baumeister RF. 1998. Self-control as limited resource: regulatory depletion patterns. *J. Pers. Soc. Psychol.* 74:774–89

Muris P, Merckelbach H. 1997. Suppression and dissociation. *Pers. Individ. Differ.* 23:523–25

Muris P, Merckelbach H, de Jong PF. 1993. Verbalization and environmental cueing in thought suppression. *Behav. Res. Ther.* 31:609–12

Muris P, Merckelbach H, Horselenberg R. 1996. Individual differences in thought suppression. The White Bear Suppression Inventory: factor structure, reliability, validity and correlates. *Behav. Res. Ther.* 34:501–13

Muris P, Merckelbach H, Horselenberg R, Susenaar M, Leeuw I. 1997. Thought suppression in spider phobia. *Behav. Res. Ther.* 35:769–74

Muris P, Merckelbach H, van den Hout M, de Jong P. 1992. Suppression of emotional and neutral material. *Behav. Res. Ther.* 30:639–42

Navon D. 1994. From pink elephants to psychosomatic disorders: paradoxical effects in cognition. *Psycholoquy* [On-line serial], 5(36) Available: http://journals.ecs.soton.ac.uk/resource/psycoloquy?5.36

Newman LS, Duff KJ, Baumeister RF. 1997. A new look at defensive projection: thought suppression, accessibility, and biased person perception. *J. Pers. Soc. Psychol.* 72:980–1001

Newman LS, Duff KJ, Hedberg DA, Blitstein J. 1996. Rebound effects in impression formation: assimilation and contrast effects following thought suppression. *J. Exp. Soc. Psychol.* 32:460–83

Newman LS, Uleman JS. 1990. Assimilation and contrast effects in spontaneous trait inference. *Pers. Soc. Psychol. Bull.* 16:224–40

Pennebaker JW. 1993. Social mechanisms of constraint. See Wegner & Pennebaker 1993, pp. 200–19

Pennebaker JW. 1997a. *Opening Up: The Healing Power of Expressing Emotions.* New York: Guilford

Pennebaker JW. 1997b. Writing about emotional experiences as a therapeutic process. *Psychol. Sci.* 8:162–66

Petrie KJ, Booth RJ, Pennebaker JW. 1998. The immunology effects of thought suppression. *J. Pers. Soc. Psychol.* 75:1264–72

Polivy J. 1998. The effects of behavioral inhibition: integrating internal cues, cognition, behavior, and affect. *Psychol. Inq.* 9:181–204

Purdon C. 1999. Thought suppression and psychopathology. *Behav. Res. Ther.* In press

Purdon C, Clark DA. 1994. Perceived control and appraisal of obsessional intrusive thoughts: a replication and extension. *Behav. Cogn. Psychother.* 22:269–85

Purdon C, Clark DA. 1999. Meta-cognition and obsessions. *Clin. Psychol. Psychother.* In press

Rachman S. 1997. A cognitive theory of obsessions. *Behav. Res. Ther.* 35:793–802

Rachman S. 1998. A cognitive theory of obsessions: elaborations. *Behav. Res. Ther.* 36:385–401

Rassin E, Merckelbach H, Muris P. 1997. Effects of thought suppression on episodic memory. *Behav. Res. Ther.* 35:1035–38

Roemer L, Borkovec TD. 1994. Effects of suppressing thoughts about emotional material. *J. Abnorm. Psychol.* 103:467–74

Rutledge PC. 1998. Obsessionality and the attempted suppression of unpleasant personal intrusive thoughts. *Behav. Res. Ther.* 36:403–16

Rutledge PC, Hancock RA, Rutledge JH III. 1996. Predictors of thought rebound. *Behav. Res. Ther.* 34:555–62

Rutledge PC, Hollenberg D, Hancock RA. 1993. Individual differences in the Wegner rebound effect: evidence for a moderator variable in thought rebound following thought suppression. *Psychol. Rep.* 72:867–80

Sacco WP, Beck AT. 1995. Cognitive theory and therapy. In *Handbook of Depression,* ed. EE Beckham, WR Leber, pp. 329–51. New York: Guilford

Salkovskis PM. 1998. Psychological approaches to the understanding of obsessional problems. In *Obsessive-Compulsive Disorder: Theory, Research, and Treatment,* ed. RP Swinson, MM Antony, pp. 33–50. New York: Guilford

Salkovskis PM, Campbell P. 1994. Thought suppression induces intrusion in naturally occurring negative intrusive thoughts. *Behav. Res. Ther.* 32:1–8

Salkovskis PM, Reynolds M. 1994. Thought suppression and smoking cessation. *Behav. Res. Ther.* 32:193–201

Salkovskis PM, Richards HC, Forrester E. 1995. The relationship between obsessional problems and intrusive thoughts. *Behav. Cogn. Psychother.* 23:281–99

Segal ZV, Hood JE, Shaw BF, Higgins ET. 1988. A structural analysis of the self-schema construct in major depression. *Cogn. Ther. Res.* 12:471–85

Sherman JW, Stroessner SJ, Loftus ST, Deguzman G. 1997. Stereotype suppression and recognition memory for stereotypical and nonstereotypical information. *Soc. Cogn.* 15:205–15

Shipherd JC, Beck JG. 1999. The effects of suppressing trauma-related thoughts on women with rape-related posttraumatic stress disorder. *Behav. Res. Ther.* 37:99–112

Shoham V, Rohrbaugh M. 1997. Interrupting ironic processes. *Psychol. Sci.* 8:151–53

Smari J, Birgisdottir AB, Brynjolfsdottir B. 1995. Obsessive-compulsive symptoms and suppression of personally relevant unwanted thoughts. *Pers. Individ. Differ.* 18:621–25

Smari J, Sigurjonsdottir H, Saemundsdottir I. 1994. Thought suppression and obsession-compulsion. *Psychol. Rep.* 75:227–35

Smart L, Wegner DM. 1999. Covering up what can't be seen: concealable stigma and mental control. *J. Pers. Soc. Psychol.* In press

Stoeber J. 1998. Worry, problem elaboration and suppression of imagery: the role of concreteness. *Behav. Res. Ther.* 36:751–56

Sullivan MJL, Rouse D, Bishop S, Johnston S. 1997. Thought suppression, catastrophizing, and pain. *Cogn. Ther. Res.* 21:555–68

Thomas SP. 1997. Women's anger: relationship of suppression to blood pressure. *Nurs. Res.* 46:324–30

Thompson EP, Roman RJ, Moskowitz GB, Chaiken S, Bargh JA. 1994. Accuracy motivation attenuates covert priming: the systematic reprocessing of social information. *J. Pers. Soc. Psychol.* 66:474–89

Thorpe SJ, Salkovskis PM. 1995. Phobia beliefs: Do cognitive factors play a role in specific phobias? *Behav. Res. Ther.* 33:805–16

Trinder H, Salkovskis PM. 1994. Personally relevant intrusions outside the laboratory: long-term suppression increases intrusion. *Behav. Res. Ther.* 32:833–42

Uleman JS, Bargh JA, eds. 1989. *Unintended Thought.* New York: Guilford

van den Hout M, Merckelbach H, Pool K. 1996. Dissociation, reality monitoring, trauma, and thought suppression. *Behav. Cogn. Psychother.* 24:97–108

von Hippel W, Silver LA, Lynch ME. 1999. Stereotyping against your will: the role of inhibitory ability in stereotyping and prejudice among the elderly. *Pers. Soc. Psychol. Bull.* In press

Wegner DM. 1989. *White Bears and Other Unwanted Thoughts.* New York: Viking/Penguin

Wegner DM. 1992. You can't always think what you want: problems in the suppression of unwanted thoughts. *Adv. Exp. Soc. Psychol.* 25:195–225

Wegner DM. 1994. Ironic processes of mental control. *Psychol. Rev.* 101:34–52

Wegner DM. 1997. When the antidote is the poison: ironic mental control processes. *Psychol. Sci.* 8:148–50

Wegner DM, Ansfield M, Pilloff D. 1998. The putt and the pendulum: ironic effects of the mental control of action. *Psychol. Sci.* 9:196–99

Wegner DM, Bargh JA. 1998. Control and automaticity in social life. In *Handbook of Social Psychology,* ed. D Gilbert, ST Fiske, G Lindzey, 1:446–96. New York:McGraw Hill. 4th ed.

Wegner DM, Bjork RA, Eich E. 1994a. Thought suppression. In *Learning, Remembering, Believing: Enhancing Human Performance,* ed. D Druckman, RA Bjork, pp. 277–93. Washington, DC: Natl. Acad.

Wegner DM, Broome A, Blumberg SJ. 1997. Ironic effects of trying to relax under stress. *Behav. Res. Ther.* 35:11–21

Wegner DM, Erber R. 1992. The hyperaccessibility of suppressed thoughts. *J. Pers. Soc. Psychol.* 63:903–12

Wegner DM, Erber R, Zanakos S. 1993. Ironic processes in the mental control of mood and mood-related thought. *J. Pers. Soc. Psychol.* 65:1093–104

Wegner DM, Gold DB. 1995. Fanning old flames: emotional and cognitive effects of suppressing thoughts of a past relationship. *J. Pers. Soc. Psychol.* 68:782–92

Wegner DM, Lane JD, Dimitri S. 1994b. The allure of secret relationships. *J. Pers. Soc. Psychol.* 66:287–300

Wegner DM, Pennebaker JW, eds. 1993. *Handbook of Mental Control.* Englewood Cliffs, NJ: Prentice Hall

Wegner DM, Quillian F, Houston CE. 1996. Memories out of order: thought suppression and the disturbance of sequence memory. *J. Pers. Soc. Psychol.* 71:680–91

Wegner DM, Schneider DJ, Carter SR, White TL. 1987. Paradoxical effects of thought suppression. *J. Pers. Soc. Psychol.* 53:5–13

Wegner DM, Schneider DJ, Knutson B, McMahon SR. 1991. Polluting the stream of consciousness: the effect of thought suppression on the mind's environment. *Cogn. Ther. Res.* 15:141–52

Wegner DM, Shortt JW, Blake AW, Page MS. 1990. The suppression of exciting thoughts. *J. Pers. Soc. Psychol.* 58:409–18

Wegner DM, Smart L. 1997. Deep cognitive activation: a new approach to the unconscious. *J. Consult. Clin. Psychol.* 65:984–95

Wegner DM, Wenzlaff RM. 1996. Mental control. In *Social Psychology: Handbook of Basic Principles,* eds. ET Higgins, AW Kruglanski, pp. 466–92. New York: Guilford

Wegner DM, Zanakos S. 1994. Chronic thought suppression. *J. Pers.* 62:615–40

Wells A. 1994. Attention and the control of worry. In *Worrying: Perspectives on Theory, Assessment and Treatment. Wiley Ser. Clin. Psychol.,* ed. GCL Davey, F Tallis, pp. 91–114. Chichester, UK: Wiley

Wenzlaff RM. 1993. The mental control of depression: psychological obstacles to emotional well-being. See Wegner & Pennebaker 1993, pp. 239–57

Wenzlaff RM, Bates DE. 1998. Unmasking a cognitive vulnerability to depression: how lapses in mental control reveal depressive thinking. *J. Pers. Soc. Psychol.* 75:1559–71

Wenzlaff RM, Bates DE. 1999. The relative efficacy of concentration and suppression strategies of mental control. *Pers. Soc. Psychol. Bull.* In press

Wenzlaff RM, Eisenberg AR. 1998. Parental restrictiveness of negative emotions: sowing the seeds of thought suppression. *Psychol. Inq.* 9:310–312

Wenzlaff RM, Wegner DM. 1998. The role of mental processes in the failure of inhibition. *Psychol. Inq.* 9:231–33

Wenzlaff RM, Wegner DM, Klein SB. 1991. The role of thought suppression in the bonding of thought and mood. *J. Pers. Soc. Psychol.* 60:500–8

Wenzlaff RM, Wegner DM, Roper DW. 1988. Depression and mental control: the resurgence of unwanted negative thoughts. *J. Pers. Soc. Psychol.* 55:882–92

Whetstone T, Cross MD. 1998. Control of conscious contents in directed forgetting and thought suppression. *Psyche* 4(16) (http://psyche.cs.monash.edu.au/v4/psyche-4-16-whetstone.html)

Wicklund RA, Gollwitzer PM. 1982. *Symbolic Self-Completion.* Hillsdale, NJ: Erlbaum

Wyer NA, Sherman JW, Stroessner SJ. 1998. The spontaneous suppression of racial stereotypes. *Soc. Cogn.* 16:340–62

Wyer NA, Sherman JW, Stroessner SJ. 1999. The roles of motivation and ability in controlling the consequences of stereotype suppression. *Pers. Soc. Psychol. Bull.* In press

Zeigarnik B. 1938 (1927). On finished and unfinished tasks. In *A Source Book of Gestalt Psychology,* ed. WD Ellis, pp. 300–14. New York: Harcourt, Brace & World (Reprinted and condensed from *Psychol. Forsch.* 9:1–85)

Annu. Rev. Psychol. 2000. 51:93–120

SOCIAL COGNITION: Thinking Categorically about Others

C. Neil Macrae and Galen V. Bodenhausen

Department of Experimental Psychology, University of Bristol, Bristol, BS8 1TN; United Kingdom; e-mail: c.n.macrae@bristol.ac.uk
Department of Psychology, Northwestern University, Evanston, Illinois 60204–3060; e-mail: galen@nwu.edu

Key Words automaticity, inhibition, memory, stereotypes, person perception

■ **Abstract** In attempting to make sense of other people, perceivers regularly construct and use categorical representations to simplify and streamline the person perception process. Noting the importance of categorical thinking in everyday life, our emphasis in this chapter is on the cognitive dynamics of categorical social perception. In reviewing current research on this topic, three specific issues are addressed: (*a*) When are social categories activated by perceivers, (*b*) what are the typical consequences of category activation, and (*c*) can perceivers control the influence and expression of categorical thinking? Throughout the chapter, we consider how integrative models of cognitive functioning may inform our understanding of categorical social perception.

CONTENTS

Introduction 93
Category Activation.. 96
   Automatic Category Activation 96
   Determinants of Category Activation 98
Category Application 103
   Forms of Category Application.. 103
   Conditions of Category Application 105
   Category Application in the Behavioral Domain.......................... 107
Category Inhibition.. 109
   The Mechanics of Mind Control 109
   Ironic Consequences of Stereotype Suppression......................... 110
   Spontaneous Stereotype Suppression 112
Conclusions... 113

INTRODUCTION

In order to successfully propel their owners through complex and demanding social environments, minds must be equipped with two complementary cognitive skills. On the one hand, they must sensitize perceivers to the invariant features of their immediate stimulus worlds. To behave in a purposive manner, perceivers must possess stable internal representations (i.e. mental models) of the environments in which they operate (Johnson-Laird 1983, Johnston & Hawley 1994, McClelland et al 1995). Knowing what to expect—and exactly where, when, and from whom to expect it—is information that renders the world a meaningful, orderly, and predictable place. On the other hand, however, to guide behavior in a truly flexible manner, minds must also be responsive to the presence of unexpected (i.e. novel, surprising) stimulus inputs (Baars 1997, McClelland et al 1995, Metcalfe 1993, Norman & Shallice 1986). An adaptive mind, after all, is one that enables its owner to override automated action plans and produce novel behavioral outputs as and when these responses are required. That minds routinely achieve this level of cognitive flexibility is one of the acknowledged triumphs of mental life. As Johnston & Hawley have argued, "[o]pposing biases toward both what is expected and what is least expected are among the most adaptive and revealing features of the mind" (1994:56). But how, exactly, is this flexibility attained and what implications does it have for a range of issues in person perception?

According to recent developments in the cognitive neurosciences, flexible processing is believed to be attained through the operation of two complementary mental modules: the neocortical and the hippocampal learning/memory systems (see McClelland et al 1995). The neocortical system (i.e. slow-learning system) comprises people's generic beliefs about the world (i.e. semantic memory), beliefs that accumulate gradually through repeated exposure to particular stimulus events. Given the need for stability in people's perceptions of the world, the contents of the neocortical system (e.g. beliefs, expectancies, norms) are highly resistant to modification or change. The hippocampal system (i.e. fast-learning system), in contrast, serves a different function in mental life in that it enables perceivers to form temporary representations of novel or surprising stimulus events, representations that commonly gain access to consciousness (i.e. episodic memory). Generally speaking, these episodic traces exert little impact on the status of generic knowledge, unless of course they are activated on a regular basis. Then, through a process of consolidation, they are passed to the neocortical system where they have the power to update or modify a perceiver's knowledge base (McClelland et al 1995).

There are good reasons why the mind requires the operation of two independent processing systems. As schematic knowledge (i.e. neocortical system) provides the cognitive backdrop against which the stimulus world is construed, it would be problematic if these mental contents were susceptible to modification following a single surprising experience. Under such conditions, purposive action would be a desirable though unattainable behavioral goal. At the same time, however, perceivers must also be able to respond rapidly and adaptively to novelty and surprise; indeed survival may depend on this ability (Norman & Shallice 1986, Shallice 1988). It is through the possession of two complementary learning systems that mental functioning is accorded the stability and plasticity it requires if perceivers are to chart a smooth passage through life's potentially turbulent waters (Johnston & Hawley 1994;

McClelland et al 1995; Schacter & Tulving 1994; Smith 1990, 1998; Smith & DeCoster 1999).

Of course, the ability to deal with both expected and unexpected stimulus information is a fundamental requirement of the person perception process (Macrae et al 1999, Sherman et al 1998, Smith & DeCoster 1999, von Hippel et al 1993). While anticipating consistency in the behavior of others, perceivers must also be responsive to the presence of unexpected information, as this material frequently demands the execution of nonstereotyped behavioral responses (see Macrae et al 1999, Norman & Shallice 1986, Shallice 1988). But how does the mind realize these diverse information-processing objectives? The answer lies in the application of schematic knowledge structures (i.e. neocortical system) when perceivers think about, and interact with, others. As Gilbert & Hixon observed "[t]he ability to understand new and unique individuals in terms of old and general beliefs is certainly among the handiest tools in the social perceiver's kit" (1991:509).

Given basic cognitive limitations and a challenging stimulus world, perceivers need some way to simplify and structure the person perception process. This they achieve through the activation and implementation of categorical thinking (Allport 1954, Bodenhausen & Macrae 1998, Brewer 1988, Bruner 1957, Fiske & Neuberg 1990). Rather than considering individuals in terms of their unique constellations of attributes and proclivities, perceivers prefer instead to construe them on the basis of the social categories (e.g. race, gender, age) to which they belong, categories for which a wealth of related material is believed to reside in long-term memory. Of course, it is also through the activation of categorical thinking that perceivers are sensitized to the presence of unexpected information. After all, one can only be surprised by a person's behavior if one has prior expectations about how that individual should behave. Thus, in one way or another, categorical thinking provides the flexibility (i.e. stability/plasticity) that the person perception process demands (Macrae et al 1999, Sherman et al 1998).

Once implemented, categorical thinking can shape person perception in at least two important ways. First, perceivers may use the activated knowledge structure to guide the processing (e.g. encoding, representation) of any target-related information that is encountered (Bodenhausen 1988). As a result, categorical thinking can exert a profound influence on the nature of a perceiver's recollections of others (Hamilton & Sherman 1994, Srull & Wyer 1989). Second, perceivers may use the contents of the activated knowledge structure (e.g. trait and behavioral expectancies) to derive evaluations and impressions of a target, a process that commonly gives rise to stereotype-based judgmental outcomes (Brewer 1988, Fiske & Neuberg 1990). Acknowledging the importance of these efforts, this chapter emphasizes the cognitive dynamics of categorical social perception; in particular, how expectations drive people's evaluations and recollections of others (see also Bodenhausen & Macrae 1998, von Hippel et al 1995). In reviewing current research on this topic, three specific issues are addressed: (*a*) When are social categories activated by perceivers, (*b*) what are the typical consequences of category activation, and (*c*) can perceivers control the influence and expression of categorical thinking? Throughout the chapter, we describe how integrative models of cognitive functioning (Johnston & Hawley 1994, McClelland et al 1995, Norman & Shallice 1986) may inform our understanding of the issues addressed herein.

CATEGORY ACTIVATION

In attempting to make sense of other people, we regularly construct and use categorical representations to simplify and streamline the person perception process. A debate that has dominated recent theorizing about the nature and function of these representations concerns the conditions under which they may or may not be activated when we interact with others (see Devine 1989, Bargh 1999, Fiske 1989, Gilbert & Hixon 1991, Lepore & Brown 1997). Early writings on this issue were quite unequivocal—category activation was believed to be an inescapable mental event. As Allport memorably noted, "the human mind must think with the aid of categories . . . We cannot possibly avoid this process. Orderly living depends upon it . . . Every event has certain marks that serve as a cue to bring the category of prejudgment into action . . . A person with dark brown skin will activate whatever concept of Negro is dominant in our mind" (1954:21). Such was the force of Allport's message that few researchers thought it necessary to contest the assumption that category activation is an unavoidable facet of the person perception process. Indeed, this belief served as the hub of conventional wisdom in person perception for almost 40 years. But is it entirely true? Is category activation really an unconditionally automatic mental process? Our attention now turns to a consideration of this important theoretical issue.

Automatic Category Activation

The term category is commonly used to describe the totality of information that perceivers have in mind about particular classes of individuals (e.g. Germans, plumbers, pastry chefs), and this knowledge can take many forms (e.g. visual, declarative, procedural) (see Andersen & Glassman 1996; Smith 1990, 1998). Once these categorical representations are triggered, of course, so too are their associated cognitive contents. Hence, content accessibility is commonly utilized as an index of category activation (e.g. Dovidio et al 1986, Perdue & Gurtman 1990). This methodological approach derives from related research in cognitive psychology, primarily work on semantic priming (see Neely 1991). If the associates of a particular concept (e.g. nurse) display enhanced accessibility following the prior presentation of a priming stimulus (e.g. hospital), it is assumed that a mental representation of the priming stimulus has been activated in memory (Anderson & Bower 1972, Collins & Loftus 1975). Similar reasoning is applied in person perception, with category activation also evidenced through the heightened accessibility of material following the presentation of a priming stimulus (Devine 1989, Dovidio et al 1986, Lepore & Brown 1997). Just as "hospital" primes "nurse," "drugs," and "illness," so too "librarian" activates "shy," "studious," and "responsible."

By endorsing the view that semantic priming is an inevitable consequence of mere stimulus exposure, social psychologists logically concluded that category activation must also be an unconditionally automatic mental process. As a result, a spate of experiments emerged in which researchers measured the accessibility of categorical contents (i.e. personality traits) following the presentation of a priming stimulus, usually (although not always) a verbal label (e.g. Italian). In one of the earliest studies of this kind, Dovidio et al (1986) presented participants with a priming category label (i.e. black or white), followed by a series of personality characteristics (e.g. musical). The target items were either stereotypic or nonstereotypic with respect to the priming stimulus, and a participant's task was to report, as quickly as possible, whether the item could ever be true (i.e. descriptive) of the primed category. As expected, participants responded more quickly when stereotypic rather than nonstereotypic items were preceded by the priming label, which suggests that the categorical representation was automatically activated during the task (Allport 1954). Notwithstanding this empirical demonstration, however, it is premature to infer the unconditional automaticity of category activation on the basis of these findings. To perform the experimental task, the participants in the Dovidio et al (1986) study were explicitly required to assess the descriptive applicability of the prime-target relationship (i.e. could X ever be true of Y?). By drawing attention to the priming stimulus in this manner, it is not possible to argue that category activation is an unconditionally automatic event, requiring only the registration of the priming stimulus for its occurrence (see Bargh 1994, 1997).

Noting this difficulty with the Dovidio et al (1986) procedure, subsequent investigations of category activation have employed a range of semantic priming techniques (e.g. lexical decision tasks) that attempt to obscure the relationship between the prime and target stimuli. This is typically achieved in one of two ways: Either the priming stimuli are presented below a perceiver's threshold for conscious detection (Devine 1989; Dovidio et al 1997; Lepore & Brown 1997; Macrae et al 1994b, 1995; Wittenbrink et al 1997) or the task instructions are framed in such a way that they conceal any associative relationship between the items (Banaji & Hardin 1996; Fazio & Dunton 1997; Fazio et al 1995; Gilbert & Hixon 1991; Kawakami et al 1998; Locke et al 1994; Macrae et al 1997b, 1998b; Spencer et al 1998). The logic underlying these studies is straightforward. If perceivers are unable to avoid category activation when the triggering stimulus lies outside consciousness or is seemingly irrelevant to the task at hand (Bargh 1990, 1994; Greenwald & Banaji 1995), then this would support the notion that category activation is an unconditionally automatic mental process (Allport 1954, Devine 1989). As it turns out, the available empirical evidence appears to corroborate this viewpoint (Bargh 1999). Presenting perceivers with a priming category label apparently makes them unable to prevent the activation of the corresponding representation (and its associated contents) in memory (Devine 1989, Perdue & Gurtman 1990). But does this really signal that category activation is an unconditionally automatic mental process, at least in the way that Allport (1954) suggested?

On the basis of the evidence presented thus far, there are two grounds for questioning the unconditional automaticity of category activation. First, under empirical scrutiny, most mental operations fail to satisfy the multiple criteria needed to qualify a process as exclusively automatic in character (Bargh 1990, 1994; Logan & Cowan 1984; Wegner & Bargh 1998). Indeed, even prototypic examples of automatic mental processes, such as Stroop and semantic priming effects, fail in this respect (e.g. Logan 1989, Smith et al 1983). It turns out that most automatic operations are controllable to some degree, an observation that daily experience confirms on a regular basis (Logan 1989). Category activation should be no exception to this rule. Second, given Allport's (1954) assertion that category activation follows the registration of a triggering stimulus—specifically, another person—why is it that researchers have typically used verbal labels to investigate this process? If one could assume a symbolic equivalence between words and persons, then clearly this would not be a problematic experimental strategy. In person perception, however, this assumption of symbolic equivalence may be unwarranted (Gilbert & Hixon 1991, Macrae et al 1997b, Zárate & Smith 1990).

Consider, for example, the following scenario. On encountering a dentist, in no sense is one psychologically compelled to categorize the individual as such. Instead, the person could just as easily be construed as female, elderly, Asian, or indeed any other applicable categorization (Bodenhausen & Macrae 1998, Macrae et al 1995, Pendry & Macrae 1996). This is obviously not the case with category labels, however. Once the label has been detected, mental life may demand that its associates are activated (Neely 1991). As Gilbert & Hixon suggested, " . . . to do otherwise would be to fail to understand what one has read" (1991:516). Simply stated, whereas perceivers must make a categorization when they encounter another person, no equivalent processing is required for verbal labels, as the categorization and the stimulus are one and the same thing. It remains unclear, therefore, the extent to which the presentation of verbal labels can inform our understanding of the earliest stages of the person perception process, stages where perceivers must extract a stable construal of multiply categorizable persons (Bodenhausen & Macrae 1998, Brewer 1988, Fiske & Neuberg 1990).

Given these difficulties, recent years have witnessed something of a sea change in research investigating the automaticity of category activation (Bargh 1999). Following trends in cognitive psychology (Logan 1989), current work is motivated by a revised empirical question. Rather than assuming that category activation is an unconditionally automatic mental operation, recent research has explored the possibility that the process may actually be conditionally automatic, occurring only under certain triggering conditions (Bargh 1994, Wegner & Bargh 1998). But if so, what are these triggering conditions?

Determinants of Category Activation

According to recent thinking on the topic, mere exposure to a stereotyped target may be insufficient to trigger category activation. Instead, activation may only occur under certain precipitating conditions. The impetus for this work came from an influential article by Gilbert & Hixon (1991). Backed by a revised conception of automaticity (Bargh 1994), Gilbert & Hixon proposed that category activation may be conditional on the availability of attentional resources. Exposing their participants to a videotaped presentation of an Asian card turner, Gilbert & Hixon argued that the attentional demands of the task environment may determine whether or not an applicable category (i.e. Asian) is activated. Drawing a distinction between the activation and application of categorical thinking, Gilbert & Hixon argued that whereas deficits in cognitive capacity increase the likelihood that perceivers will apply previously activated categories in their dealings with others, these same deficits also reduce the probability that perceivers will be able to activate the relevant category in the first place. Their data suggested that although mentally preoccupied participants knew the category membership of the target, they were too busy to activate associated stereotypic content. Spears & Haslam (1997) went even further, suggesting that cognitive load disrupts the very process of category identification. However, this claim was effectively refuted by Klauer & Wegener (1998), who used a rigorous formal modeling approach to decompose the components of performance in a memory task in which participants had to recall which of several speakers had made various comments in a group discussion. Although the imposition of a cognitive load did impair memory performance for certain components of the model, it had no impact on gender category discrimination (i.e. ability to recall correctly the gender of the speaker). Thus, in contrast to Spears & Haslam's (1997) claims, mental load did not interfere with the process of identifying the category membership of social targets.

A number of studies have sought to identify other factors that may moderate the activation of categorical knowledge structures (Blair & Banaji 1996, Lepore & Brown 1997, Locke et al 1994, Macrae et al 1997b, Wittenbrink et al 1997). On the basis of the evidence that has been collected to date, two factors appear to play a prominent role in the regulation of category activation: perceivers' temporary processing goals (Blair & Banaji 1996, Macrae et al 1997b, Spencer et al 1998) and their general attitudes (i.e. prejudice level) toward the members of the category in question (e.g. Lepore & Brown 1997, Wittenbrink et al 1997). In a recent study, for example, Macrae et al (1997b) demonstrated that category activation does not occur under conditions in which the social meaning of a target is irrelevant to a perceiver's current information-processing concerns. In a similar vein, Blair & Banaji (1996) purported to show that the operation of a counterstereotypic processing expectancy can thwart category activation, at least under certain conditions (but see Bargh 1999).

The effects of temporary processing objectives do not stop here, however. Not only can goal states eliminate category activation, they can also promote categorical thinking. Extending Gilbert & Hixon's (1991) findings, Spencer et al (1998) have shown that even resource-depleted perceivers are capable of activating categorical knowledge structures, if such activation can enhance their feelings of self-worth. Category activation thus appears to be goal dependent (Bargh 1994), with its occurrence conditional upon the complex interplay of both cognitive and motivational forces.

In addition to temporary processing objectives, a perceiver's chronic beliefs about others also appear to moderate the activation of categorical thinking (Lepore & Brown 1997, Locke et al 1994, Wittenbrink et al 1997). It is interesting, however, that this observation is at odds with conventional thinking on the dynamics of the categorization process. Based on Devine's (1989) seminal article, it has been widely accepted that both prejudiced and egalitarian individuals activate categories (and their associated stereotypes) to the same degree when they encounter members of stigmatized social groups. Through common socialization experiences, all individuals are assumed to have the same cultural stereotypes stored in memory, stereotypes that are accessed as soon as a group member (or symbolic equivalent) is encountered (Allport 1954, Devine 1989, Dovidio et al 1986). The cognitive difference between humanitarians and bigots is that whereas the former group overrides the automatic effects of category activation by replacing stereotypic thoughts with their own nonprejudiced personal beliefs (i.e. controlled inhibition), the latter group does not engage in such an activity. Thus, differences between the groups emerge only at the level of controlled cognitive processing. Where automatic operations are concerned (i.e. category activation), bigots and humanitarians are believed to be psychologically indistinguishable (see Devine 1989).

But is this strictly true? Some recent research casts doubt on the veracity of this assumption. Unlike their prejudiced counterparts, egalitarians display no evidence whatsoever of stereotype activation when presented with priming categorical stimuli (Lepore & Brown 1997, Locke et al 1994, Wittenbrink et al 1997). In other words, bigots and humanitarians appear to be distinguishable at the level of automatic cognitive operations (cf Devine 1989). The implication of this finding is obvious: Bigots and humanitarians must differ with respect to material they hold in memory about the members of stigmatized social groups, with humanitarians holding substantially less prejudiced beliefs about these groups (Hilton & von Hippel 1996, Wittenbrink et al 1998). Taken together, these findings suggest that category activation is sometimes amenable to control, at least in the sense of being responsive to a perceiver's cognitive limitations, temporary processing objectives, and chronic beliefs about certain social groups.

Notwithstanding the emergence of the view that category activation is a conditionally automatic mental process, doubts have been cast about the solidity of the empirical foundation upon which this claim is based. Variables that seem to qualify stereotype activation in one study have been found to be uninfluential in other studies. For example, whereas some studies suggest that category activation is contingent upon prejudice levels, some researchers (Dunning & Sherman 1997) have found that implicit gender activation (in the form of tacit inferences) is independent of a participant's level of sexism. Recently, Bargh (1999) provided a provocative review of the literature on the conditional automaticity of category activation. Echoing Allport's (1954) belief that social categories are spontaneously activated when a perceiver encounters a group member, Bargh has critiqued the emerging literature that takes precisely the opposite view—that category activation is avoidable under certain circumstances (e.g. Blair & Banaji 1996, Gilbert & Hixon 1991, Macrae et al 1997b).

Noting some methodological and interpretive problems with this research, Bargh has argued that "the field of social cognition has become overly optimistic about the 'cognitive monster' of automatic stereotype activation. . . . contrary to what research is actually showing, the conclusions drawn from the data have overestimated the degree to which automatically activated stereotypes can be controlled through good intentions and effortful thought" (Bargh 1999:362). Given the acknowledged perils of stereotypical thinking, Bargh's message is decidedly pessimistic in flavor. But, in the context of category activation, is it entirely correct? Have researchers really over-estimated the extent to which category activation is controllable (Fiske 1989), or are there indeed conditions under which perceivers reliably fail to activate social categories and their associated stereotypes?

One notable weakness of the existing research in this domain is that is has tended to rely on verbal stimulus materials (i.e. category labels) to investigate the cognitive dynamics of the category activation process. Indeed, virtually all the empirical evidence that suggests that category activation is an unconditionally automatic process has been collected in studies of this kind (Devine 1989, Dovidio et al 1986, Perdue & Gurtman 1990). While providing experimental expedience, the use of verbal stimulus materials is problematic, as it necessarily obscures the true information-processing puzzle that confronts perceivers when they encounter other people. The issue is one of stimulus complexity. Whereas people are obviously multiply classifiable entities for which a given categorization must be drawn by perceivers, the same cannot be said of verbal labels. Thus, when presented with words and people, the mind is faced with distinct cognitive puzzles, puzzles that may require different information-processing solutions (Gilbert & Hixon 1991, Macrae et al 1997b, Pendry & Macrae 1996). To assume, therefore, that the processing of verbal labels elucidates the manner in which perceivers categorize and construe others may be a dangerous assumption. Thus, whether category activation is a conditionally or an unconditionally automatic process remains open to question and further empirical scrutiny (Bargh 1999, Devine 1989, Macrae et al 1997b, Spencer et al 1998). To clarify matters, additional work will be required in which researchers investigate the construal processes that are implemented when perceivers encounter real people.

Of course, by presenting perceivers with real people, another puzzle arises: How does the mind deal with the problem of multiple category memberships? Suppose, for example, you meet a thin elderly man who is holding a stethoscope and who is introduced to you as Dr. Jones. Such a person clearly offers multiple opportunities for classification. Will he be categorized in terms of his sex, his age, his somatype, or perhaps even his occupation? One possibility is that the target may be categorized in all of these ways and that each of the applicable stereotypes will simultaneously be activated (Kunda & Thagard 1996). This task could be daunting, however, as a large number of the relevant associates may be semantically or affectively incompatible, prompting cognitive confusion and target ambiguity.

In an attempt to resolve this problem, recent research has suggested that category selection may be facilitated through the operation of low-level inhibitory processes

(Bodenhausen & Macrae 1998, Macrae et al 1995, Stroessner 1996; see also Smith et al 1996). When a perceiver encounters a multiply categorizable target, all applicable categories are believed to be activated in parallel, and a competition for mental dominance then ensues (see Gernsbacher & Faust 1991, Neumann & DeSchepper 1992, Tipper 1985). Category salience, chronic accessibility, and goal relevance are factors that confer an activational advantage to particular categories in such a competition (Bodenhausen & Macrae 1998).

But once a particular categorization achieves significant activation to win the competition, a critical question concerns the fate of the losing categories during the struggle for mental dominance. One viewpoint is that these competing categorizations are actively inhibited during the category selection process (Bodenhausen & Macrae 1998). That is, potentially distracting (hence disruptive) categorizations are removed from the cognitive landscape through a process of spreading inhibition (Neumann & DeSchepper 1992). A perceiver's motivational state also seems to play an important role in the active inhibition of social categories. In a provocative demonstration, Sinclair & Kunda (1999) showed that after participants received favorable performance feedback from a black doctor, associates of the category "blacks" became significantly less accessible in their minds (compared to negative-feedback and no-feedback conditions), whereas associates of the category "doctors" became significantly more accessible. Thus, when motivated to view a black doctor as competent (because he had praised them), participants inhibited the category "blacks" and activated the category "doctors." They did just the reverse when the black doctor provided negative feedback, and they were thus motivated to view him as incompetent. Under these conditions, they inhibited the category "doctors" and activated the category "blacks." Motivational factors thus appear to be as important in the inhibition of social categories as they are in their activation.

Although exciting, research on the role of inhibitory mechanisms in category activation is still in its infancy. Indeed, it has yet to be demonstrated just how important inhibitory processes may be in shaping critical aspects of the category selection process. If other areas of psychology are to serve as a useful guide, however, inhibitory mechanisms are likely to play a prominent role in person perception. In the same way that inhibitory processes contribute to our capacity to see complex patterns of motion, initiate complex actions, comprehend written text, and select relevant rather than irrelevant objects from a stimulus array (Gernsbacher & Faust 1991, Neumann & DeSchepper 1992, Norman & Shallice 1986, Tipper 1985), so too they are likely to facilitate our ability to categorize others when competing classifications are readily available. A categorization process that operated in any other way would surely not be flexible enough to deal with the myriad demands of everyday life. Thus, in trying to understand the dynamics of the categorization process, it may be necessary to consider how perceptual, cognitive, and motivational forces modulate the excitatory and inhibitory mechanisms that prompt the activation of categorical thinking.

CATEGORY APPLICATION

If categorical representations are to be of any value in the social perceiver's quest to navigate social life effectively, obtaining satisfactory outcomes with a minimum of pain and embarrassment, then they must not merely be activated, they must also be used. As Gilbert & Hixon (1991) took pains to point out, the two processes are separable, and the nature and determinants of each must be considered independently. In this section, we outline recent research addressing the forms, conditions, and domains of category application.

Forms of Category Application

The principal function of activated categorical representations is to provide the perceiver with expectancies that can guide the processing of subsequently encountered information (Olson et al 1996). As previously noted, there are two primary ways that expectancies can influence subsequent information processing. First, they can serve as frameworks for the assimilation and integration of expectancy-consistent information, leading the perceiver to emphasize stereotype-consistent information to a greater extent than he or she would have in the absence of category activation (e.g. Fiske 1998, Fyock & Stangor 1994, Macrae et al 1994b,c). At the same time, expectancies also sensitize the perceiver to unexpected data, leading to a greater emphasis on stereotype-inconsistent information following category activation (e.g. Hastie & Kumar 1979, Srull & Wyer 1989). If the available evidence fails to contradict stereotypic expectancies in a clear way, then category activation would be expected to produce an assimilative bias, leading to judgmental and memory effects that are substantially more stereotypic compared to a case in which the same information was presented without category activation (e.g. Bodenhausen 1988). However, if both stereotypic and counterstereotypic information is presented, which kind of information dominates? In the domain of memory, at least, it is clear that counterstereotypic information is most likely to dominate subsequent processing, particularly during impression formation (Stangor & McMillan 1992).

An ability to deal with the unexpected is obviously an essential requirement for successful social interaction. In dealing with surprising social stimuli, such as extraverted librarians and adventurous senior citizens, two mental abilities are of paramount importance. Recognizing the inconsistency confronting them in such instances, social perceivers need to make sense of the situation by resolving the discrepancy between prior expectations and current actualities (Hastie & Kumar 1979). In addition, they need to be able to remember that the encountered individual does not conform to available stereotypic expectations. In other words, they must individuate the target (Fiske & Neuberg 1990), organizing their memories around the individual's personal identity rather than in terms of his or her superordinate group memberships. But how exactly do perceivers do this? Recent research has speculated that these two crucial processes of person perception (i.e. inconsistency resolution and individuation) come under the purview of executive cognitive functioning (Macrae et al 1999).

According to current thinking, the term executive function can be used to characterize a raft of higher-order cognitive operations that are involved in the planning, execution, and regulation of behavior (Baddeley 1996, Goldman-Rakic 1998, Shallice & Burgess 1998). Where memory function is concerned, these operations coordinate the activities of working memory by determining which specialized systems should be activated at any given time and how the products of these systems should be integrated and combined (Baddeley & Della Sala 1998).

If inconsistency resolution and individuation are indeed executive cognitive operations, then they should be susceptible to impairment or disruption only under dual-task conditions that are known to promote executive dysfunction (see Baddeley 1996). When concurrent activities do not challenge executive operations in any way, attentional depletion should not obstruct the implementation (and products) of these processes: These are precisely the effects that Macrae et al (1999) reported in a recent article. Under conditions of executive impairment, perceivers' recollective preference for unexpected information was eliminated, they were no longer able to organize their memories of others in an individuated manner, and they were unable to identify the source of their recollections, particularly when these recollections were counter-stereotypic in implication (Johnson et al 1993). When attentional depletion did not obstruct executive functioning, however, none of these effects emerged. These findings are theoretically noteworthy because they confirm that it is not attentional depletion per se that obstructs inconsistency resolution and individuation (Dijksterhuis & van Knippenberg 1995, Pendry & Macrae 1994); rather, it is executive dysfunction that impairs a perceiver's ability to process unexpected material. These findings can be integrated with work in the cognitive neurosciences that considers how dysexecutive syndrome can impair aspects of cognitive functioning, such as the accuracy of source memory (Johnson et al 1993). In linking these literatures, it may be possible to begin to chart the neuropsychological origins of social information processing (see Klein et al 1996, Klein & Kihlstrom 1998), thereby providing an integrative theoretical account of the process and consequences of categorical thinking in person perception.

So far, we have seen that category application can influence memories in two different ways, depending on whether consistent or inconsistent information is encountered and emphasized in the processing of target information. In the realm of social judgment, research has also focused on a number of interesting determinants of whether category activation will result in judgmental outcomes that are biased in a manner that is consistent with or opposite to stereotypic expectancies. One important determinant is the nature of the judgment being made, in particular whether it relies on an objective response metric (such as judging height in meters or salary in dollars) versus a subjective scale (such as judging height on a scale ranging from 1 to 10, with appropriate anchors). Whereas objective judgments are assimilated to categorical expectancies, subjective judgments often are contrasted against these expectancies (Biernat et al 1998, Biernat & Kobrynowicz 1997, Kobrynowicz & Biernat 1997). This work shows that stereotype application can take an interesting form in the case of subjective judgments. Specifically, judgments of individuals may be calibrated against a category-specific standard, which shifts the meaning of the subjective response scale. When judging how tall Sally is on a rating scale, the subjective meaning of "tall" may be calibrated in terms of expectations that are specific to the category "women," providing an implicit qualification of the judgment (e.g. "pretty tall, for a woman"). However, when judging how tall Sally is in meters, no such category-specific calibration can occur, because a meter is a meter, regardless of whether it is a man or a woman whose height is being estimated.

Stapel & Koomen (1998) took a different approach to understanding when assimilation versus contrast is likely to result from category activation. Their research showed that assimilation effects are likely to occur when abstract categorical associates (i.e. stereotypic traits) are activated, but contrast effects are the likely result when a category is activated via the presentation of specific category members. They argued that abstract concepts are used as an assimilative framework, whereas specific exemplars typically serve as standards for comparison against which targets are contrasted. Thus, the manner of category activation appears to influence how the category is applied in subsequent judgments.

Conditions of Category Application

Having described some of the processes through which stereotype application occurs, we now consider the question of when these processes are most likely to be implemented. Based on Lippmann's (1922) functional analysis of categorical social perception (see also Allport 1954), an expansive literature has confirmed that category application is likely to occur when a perceiver lacks the motivation, time, or cognitive capacity to think deeply (and accurately) about others (Bodenhausen et al 1999, Brewer & Feinstein 1999, Fiske et al 1999). Among recent demonstrations of this general idea is additional evidence that judgment becomes more stereotypic under cognitive load (e.g. van Knippenberg et al 1999), as long as there is not a demonstrably poor fit between the categorical expectations and the available target information (e.g. Blessum et al 1998, Pratto & Bargh 1991).

Given that categorical stereotypes seem most likely to be used when mental capacity and motivation are low, it is perhaps not surprising that Gilbert & Hixon characterized stereotypes as "a sluggard's best friend" (1991:509). Although consistent with much available data, this viewpoint nevertheless obscures some basic cognitive benefits that a perceiver can accrue from the application of categorical thinking, especially during times of cognitive duress. Perhaps perceivers enlist the services of categorical thinking not because they are inherently lazy but because this mode of thought offers tangible cognitive benefits, such as rapid inference generation and the efficient deployment of limited processing resources (Macrae et al 1994b, Pendry & Macrae 1994, Sherman & Bessenoff 1999, Sherman & Frost 1999, Sherman et al 1998). But if categorical thinking really does promote efficient cognitive functioning, how is this efficiency achieved, and through which processing operations is it realized?

According to the "encoding flexibility model" of Sherman et al (1998), categorical thinking is efficient because it facilitates the encoding of both category-consistent and category-inconsistent information when processing resources are in short supply (cf Dijksterhuis & van Knippenberg 1995, Macrae et al 1994b, Stangor & Duan 1991). Following the activation of categorical knowledge structures, expected material can be processed in a conceptually fluent manner (von Hippel et al 1993, 1995), even when a perceiver's attentional capacity is low. Any spare processing resources can therefore be directed to unexpected material, material that is notoriously difficult to process (and comprehend) under conditions of attentional depletion (Dijksterhuis & van Knippenberg 1995, Stangor & Duan 1991). Thus, the benefits of categorical thinking in demanding environments are twofold. First, expected material is processed in a conceptually fluent (i.e. relatively effortless) manner. Second, residual attentional resources are redirected to any unexpected information that is present, thereby enabling perceivers to process (and remember) this potentially important material (Sherman et al 1998).

Of notable theoretical significance is the explication by Sherman et al (1998) of their findings in terms of Johnston & Hawley's (1994) "mismatch" theory. According to this account of mental functioning, the mind does not waste valuable attentional resources on familiar (i.e. expectancy redundant) items that can be encoded easily and efficiently through conceptually driven processing. Instead, once expected information has been matched to an existing knowledge structure or template in memory, attention is redirected to the encoding of unexpected or novel stimuli, as these items are potentially highly informative to perceivers (see also McClelland et al 1995). Given the multifaceted ways that categorical representations can promote efficient and effective information processing, especially when processing resources are constrained, Sherman (1999) proposed a "Swiss Army knife" metaphor to capture this flexibility. Just as anticipated in the seminal writings of Lippmann (1922), a theoretical focus on cognitive economy continues to yield important insights into the nature of category activation and use.

In addition to the plethora of studies examining the role of cognitive load on category application, other approaches have been taken in attempting to understand the conditions under which activated categorical knowledge is likely to influence social information processing. A variety of motivational states seem to be important. It is fairly well established that accuracy motivation undermines the use of stereotypes in judgment (Fiske 1998). In contrast, category application is significantly enhanced by other motivational states, such as when application can serve an ego-protective function by providing a basis for downward social comparisons (Fein & Spencer 1997). A different perspective on the moderation of category application is embodied in the "social judgeability" approach (Yzerbyt et al 1997a, 1998), which emphasizes the idea that metacognitive concerns often dictate whether perceivers will be willing to render category-based judgments of social targets. Specifically, unless perceivers subjectively believe that there is a legitimate informational basis for a stereotypic judgment (whether or not such a basis actually exists), they are unlikely to report category-based assessments. Finally, in a different vein, Levy et al (1998) demonstrated that whether or not people are likely to apply stereotypes in their judgments of others depends to a considerable extent on whether they hold an "entity" theory of human nature. Such a theory emphasizes the notion that the traits possessed by individuals and groups are fixed and enduring. Individuals who endorsed such a view of human nature were substantially more likely to render stereotypic judgments of category members. Research of this sort indicates that a full appreciation of the conditions promoting the application of categorical beliefs must go beyond the traditionally emphasized moderator variables—processing capacity and motivation for effortful analysis—to include a variety of additional motivational and informational conditions.

Category Application in the Behavioral Domain

Our consideration of category application has so far focused on the domains of memory and judgment. Recently, some particularly adventurous social psychologists have ventured beyond these highly cognitive response domains and have begun to examine motoric behavioral responses following category activation. The importance and interest value of this research resides in its ability to illuminate a fundamental misconception concerning the origins of human action. Specifically, although perceivers routinely attribute the origins of their own actions to the operation of strategic (i.e. conscious, goal directed) mental processes, such attributions may be based on little more than an introspective illusion (Bargh 1990, 1997; Bargh & Gollwitzer 1994; Dennett 1991; Wegner & Bargh 1998). Although it may typically seem as if we are consciously directing our own behavior, the reality of the situation is that frequently we are not. Instead, many of our complex social actions have their origin in the impenetrable and silent workings of the unconscious mind. As Bargh noted, "many of the processes believed to be the product of conscious intention . . . could in fact be nonconsciously produced; to wit, even the activation and operation of intentions (goals) themselves could occur without an act of will" (1997:231). The observation that complex social behavior can be driven by preconscious cognitive processes is not, of course, a novel one; this idea has taken central stage in many influential treatments of human action (Bargh 1990, James 1890, Norman & Shallice 1986). The noteworthy contribution of recent research on the topic, however, has been to demonstrate the impact that these implicit forces can have on a range of everyday behaviors (see Bargh 1997). Residing in long-term memory are cognitive structures (e.g. scripts, exemplars) that are believed to specify a host of schema-related behavioral tendencies (Bargh 1990, Bargh & Gollwitzer 1994). Critically, all that it takes for one's behavior to be shaped by these action tendencies is the activation (i.e. priming) of the relevant cognitive representation, and consciousness need play no part in either the instigation or the maintenance of this process (Dennett 1991). Once triggered, action tendencies can guide social behavior in an entirely autonomous manner (Bargh 1997).

Of relevance in the current context, category activation is but one such route through which automatic action can be elicited. Not only are semantic contents (e.g.

personality characteristics) and affective evaluations represented in categorical knowledge structures, so too are a range of associated behavioral tendencies. Once activated, these implicit action tendencies have the power to guide and shape a perceiver's behavioral products (Bargh 1997, Bargh & Gollwitzer 1994). For example, following the covert activation of the stereotype of the elderly, perceivers have been shown to reduce their walking speed to a dawdle (Bargh et al 1996, Dijksterhuis et al 1998). In a similar vein, surreptitiously activating the stereotype of African-Americans has prompted perceivers to emit decidedly hostile nonverbal behaviors (Bargh et al 1996). The logic underlying these effects is straightforward. The essence of behavioral priming is that perceivers adopt the mental and motoric characteristics of primed cognitive representations, and consciousness need play no part in this process—perception can lead directly to action (Bargh 1997, Bargh et al 1996, Chartrand & Bargh 1996, Chen & Bargh 1997, Dijksterhuis & van Knippenberg 1998, Macrae et al 1998b). Even the cognitive abilities of a perceiver appear susceptible to the effects of this kind. Dijksterhuis & van Knippenberg (1998), for example, demonstrated that following the activation of the stereotype of university professors, participants displayed enhanced performance on a test of their general knowledge (see also Dijksterhuis et al 1998). But what exactly are the limits of these automatic effects? Can priming experiences prompt the occurrence of any behavioral outcome, such as an outburst of violence?

Understandably perhaps, demonstrations of automatic priming are a cause for concern when one considers the possible behavioral implications of such a process. This is essentially because these consciously unprovoked effects may promote the occurrence of undesirable or antisocial behavioral outcomes. For example, if the stereotype of robbers were activated, would this prompt a perceiver to go out and buy a shotgun and raid the nearest bank? As it turns out, there is little reason to suspect that behavioral priming manipulations (e.g. category activation) should propel people to commit calamitous personal actions, although this message is arguably obscured in the available literature on this topic. This is not, of course, because these effects play only a trivial role in the causation of action; clearly they are important determinants of human behavior (Bargh 1997). Rather, it is because in a complex mental system, the influence of activated categorical action schemas is constantly tempered by a variety of other mental events, triggered by a combination of exogenous (e.g. environmental cues) and endogenous (e.g. perceiver goals) forces (Macrae & Johnston 1998). At any point in time, it is probable that numerous behavioral schemas will simultaneously compete for the control of behavior, with some action tendencies triggered by internal processes (e.g. goals, rumination) and others by features of the immediate task environment (see Norman & Shallice 1986). Whether or not a specific action occurs will therefore be determined by the relative strengths of the activated schemas, with schemas routinely provoking antagonistic behavioral responses. According to this account, then, behavioral control is a competition between activated schemas, with various environmental cues and inner psychological states either facilitating or inhibiting the elicitation of certain action patterns (Shallice 1988). How much, when, and for whom activated categories shape behavior, however, are questions that require empirical clarification and theoretical elaboration. Although automatic forces undeniably shape a person's behavioral products (Bargh 1997), the extent (e.g. time course, malleability) and implications (e.g. are people morally responsible for their automatic behavioral outputs?) of these effects have yet to be fully understood (but see Fiske 1989).

CATEGORY INHIBITION

Having considered the activation and application of categorical thinking, our attention now turns to the equally important issue of category inhibition. As Dovidio & Gaertner (1986) observed, concerns about egalitarianism and fairness toward minority groups have been on the rise in recent decades. Public opinion polls now reveal nearly universal endorsement of the general principles of equal opportunity and equal treatment under the law (Schuman et al 1997). Increased awareness of the dangers of categorical thinking has had several important consequences. In particular, perceivers now attempt to prevent the expression of discriminatory thinking, either because legal sanctions may follow (Fiske et al 1991) or because stereotyping violates their personal standards of fairness and equality (Devine et al 1991). In other words, whether the motivation arises from personal or societal sources, there may be many conditions under which social perceivers desire to avoid the influence of activated stereotypes on their evaluations of others. But just how readily can a perceiver regulate the expression of categorical thinking? Is mind control an attainable cognitive goal?

The Mechanics of Mind Control

Although mental control is a topic with a venerable past (Freud 1957), recent years have witnessed a resurgence of interest in the question of how perceivers achieve mastery over their thoughts and recollections (Bodenhausen & Macrae 1998, Carver & Scheier 1990, Jacoby et al 1999, Wegner 1994, Wegner & Pennebaker 1993, Wilson & Brekke 1994). Of course, for perceivers to avoid or make adjustments for the possible influence of unwanted mental contents, such as stereotypic thoughts (Monteith et al 1998a), they must first be aware that such influences are a possibility in the first place (Strack & Hannover 1996). If they do not entertain even the possibility that such effects can occur, perceivers will take no steps to avoid or mitigate the resulting biases (Bodenhausen et al 1998, Greenwald & Banaji 1995, Stapel et al 1998). However, when people become cognizant of the potential for stereotypic bias in their reactions toward others, a variety of regulatory procedures can be used. One possible strategy, for instance, is simply to make direct adjustments to social judgments in the direction opposite to that of the presumed bias (e.g. Wegener & Petty 1997, Wilson & Brekke 1994). More ambitious, however, is a second possible regulatory strategy whereby perceivers may actively attempt to prevent stereotypic thoughts and recollections from ever entering into their deliberations (Bodenhausen

& Macrae 1998, Macrae et al 1997a, Monteith et al 1998a). These direct attempts at thought stopping implicate the mechanisms of mental control identified by Wegner and his colleagues in their impressive and influential program of research (see Wegner 1994).

Stopping unwanted thoughts turns out to be a common human goal (Wegner & Pennebaker 1993); consequently, a sizable literature has addressed the process and consequences of mind control. After examining processes of mental control in a variety of domains, Wegner (1994) developed a general theoretical model of thought suppression. The model postulates that when people desire to avoid a certain type of thought (e.g. categorical thinking), this goal is realized by the joint operation of two cognitive processes. The first is a monitoring process that scans the mental environment looking for signs of the unwanted thought. If detected, a second operating process is initiated that directs consciousness away from the unwanted thought by focusing attention on a suitable distracter. Crucially, whereas the monitoring process is assumed to operate in a relatively automatic manner, the operating process is postulated to be effortful and to require adequate cognitive resources for its successful execution. Thus, detecting the presence of stereotypic ideas is a task that can be accomplished with ease, independently of any other demands that are imposed on a perceiver's processing resources. Replacing these thoughts with suitable distracters, however, is an altogether more demanding affair that can happen only when sufficient attentional resources are available (Wegner 1994).

To detect unwanted thoughts, one must keep in mind what it is one is trying to avoid. Thus, the monitoring process must involve at some level the mental activation of the to-be-avoided material. Otherwise, there would be no criterion on which to conduct the search of consciousness. One of the ironic things about mental control that is apparent from this theoretical perspective is that trying to avoid a particular thought may result in its hyperaccessibility (Wegner & Erber 1992). That is, the very act of trying not to think in categorical terms may actually increase the extent of category activation. Of course, as long as perceivers have adequate resources and consistent motivation, the operating process may be able to keep the focus of attention away from the stereotypic material (Wegner 1994). But if a perceiver is cognitively busy, distracted, under time pressure, or indeed if the motivation for suppression has been relaxed for any reason, the hyperaccessibility created by suppression efforts may not be checked by the operating process. Inhibitory efficiency can also be undermined by such diverse factors as depressive affect (Linville 1996) and the cognitive changes associated with aging (von Hippel et al 1999, Zacks et al 1996). If the inhibitory system is compromised, whatever the reason, then the intention to avoid biased judgments and reactions may actually backfire, producing even more of the unwanted reaction than would otherwise have been the case. We now turn to a consideration of the recent literature examining such counterintentional outcomes.

Ironic Consequences of Stereotype Suppression

Several studies have documented the ironic consequences of stereotype suppression, as manifest in a perceiver's reactions (e.g. evaluations, recollections, behavior) toward stereotyped targets (e.g. Macrae et al 1994a, 1996, 1997a, 1998a; Sherman et al 1997;

Wyer et al 1998). For example, when evaluating a target (i.e. a skinhead), a prior period of suppression can prompt an increase in stereotyping, once the initial inhibitory intention has been relaxed (Macrae et al 1994a, Wyer et al 1998). As is the case with other mental contents (Wegner 1994, Wegner & Erber 1992), it would appear that an explicit instruction to suppress stereotypes can actually serve to enhance the accessibility of this material in memory (Macrae et al 1994a), thereby setting the stage for postsuppression rebound effects. With stereotypic concepts highly accessible and no operating process in place to direct attention elsewhere (Wegner 1994), construals of social targets are driven by stereotype-based preconceptions, often to a degree that is greater than if a perceiver had never sought to suppress the stereotype in the first place (Macrae et al 1994a, Wyer et al 1998). Ironic effects of this kind also extend to a perceiver's recollections of stereotyped targets. Following the cessation of a well-intentioned period of suppression, perceivers display a recollective preference (both in recall and recognition) for the very material (i.e. stereotype-consistent items) they were formerly trying to dismiss (Macrae et al 1996, 1997a; Sherman et al 1997). Finally, rebound effects have also been shown to shape a perceiver's overt behavior toward the members of stereotyped groups, with suppression promoting an increase in discriminatory action (Macrae et al 1994a). Thus, although the road to stereotype avoidance may be paved with good intentions, without consistent motivation and processing capacity these laudable goals may be unsatisfied, indeed even reversed (Bodenhausen & Macrae 1998, Fiske 1989, Wegner 1994, Wegner & Bargh 1998).

Notwithstanding the aforementioned demonstrations of stereotype rebound, doubts remain over the generality of these ironic effects (see Monteith et al 1998a). For example, does the suppression of any stereotype promote rebound and a subsequent increase in stereotyping? One limitation of early research on this topic was that it employed stereotypes that perceivers are not highly motivated to avoid (e.g. skinheads) (see Macrae et al 1994a). Thus, the question remains whether rebound effects would emerge for groups where there are strong personal or societal prohibitions against stereotyping (e.g. African-Americans, women, homosexuals). As it turns out, the evidence on this issue is equivocal. In a recent article, Monteith et al (1998b) revealed that participants with low-prejudice attitudes toward gays were not susceptible to rebound effects (on either overt or covert measures of stereotyping) following a period of suppression. In contrast, suppression did prompt the hyperaccessibility of stereotypes among participants who were prejudiced toward gays.

Further evidence that suppression can increase stereotyping for even socially sensitive groups can be garnered from recent work by Sherman et al (1997) and Wyer et al (1998). In each of these studies, racial stereotyping was exacerbated following a period of suppression. However, a study by Wyer et al (1999) does suggest that people may be more consistent in their efforts to avoid stereotyping highly sensitive social groups. Because consistency of suppression motivation is an important factor in the avoidance of ironic suppression effects, this work does suggest that rebound effects arising from the suspension of suppression motivation may indeed be less likely when a highly sensitive social category is involved. Clearly, further research is required to establish the extent and boundary conditions of stereotype-based rebound effects. In this respect, several factors are likely to play a critical role in determining the efficacy of the suppression process. For example, whether perceivers are internally or externally motivated to avoid prejudice (Dunton & Fazio 1997, Plant & Devine 1998) and the extent to which they are practiced at suppression (Kelly & Kahn 1994, Wegner 1994) are likely to shape the process and consequences of mental self-regulation.

Spontaneous Stereotype Suppression

Ambiguity also surrounds the conditions under which self-regulatory processes are initiated by perceivers. Despite growing interest in the topic of stereotype suppression, surprisingly little is known about how and when inhibitory processes are spontaneously implemented. A characteristic feature of much of the available research on this topic is that the intention to suppress a particular thought or impulse is provided to participants by the experimenter in the form of an explicit admonishment not to think about a particular person in a stereotype-based manner (e.g. Macrae et al 1994a, 1996; Monteith et al 1998a; Sherman et al 1997). Although such a strategy offers obvious methodological advantages, it does sidestep a number of important theoretical questions, most notably the spontaneity issue. It is one thing to suppress stereotypes in response to an explicit experimental instruction, but it may be an entirely different matter to do so spontaneously. So when, exactly, does a perceiver attempt to regulate the expression of stereotypical thinking? Insight into the determinants of uninstructed self-censorship can be gleaned from the work of Devine et al (1991) and Monteith (1993). Monteith (1993), for example, has shown that attempts at self-regulation are implemented when a perceiver experiences a discrepancy between his or her internalized standards and actual behavior. When people are committed to egalitarian, nonprejudiced standards and their behavior apparently violates these standards, they feel guilty, experience compunction, become self-focused, and direct their efforts at reducing this discrepancy. That is, having reacted in an ostensibly prejudiced manner, a perceiver implements self-regulatory procedures in an attempt to avoid a potential repetition of the action.

But is the commission of a prejudiced action, or indeed the belief that such an action has occurred, a necessary precursor of stereotype inhibition? Recent research would tend to suggest not (Macrae et al 1998a, Wyer et al 1998). Instead, heightened self-focus (i.e. self-directed attention) would appear to be sufficient to trigger the spontaneous suppression of unwanted stereotypic thoughts (Bodnehausen & Macrae 1998, Macrae et al 1998a). A common experimental finding is that when the self becomes the focus of attention, perceivers are especially likely to behave in accordance with internalized standards and norms (Carver & Scheier 1990). Under these conditions, behavioral self-regulation is governed by the process of feedback control (Miller et al 1960). In feedback control, an existing condition of the system (e.g. "What am I doing?") is compared against some standard or reference value in memory (e.g. "What should I be doing?"). If a discrepancy between these two states is detected, an operating process is implemented in an attempt to get the system back on track (Carver & Scheier 1990, Miller et al 1960, Wegner 1994). Of relevance in the current context, stereotype suppression is also believed to operate in such a manner. Triggered by situational cues, stereotype suppression does not demand a conscious inhibitory intention on the part of a perceiver (Macrae et al 1998a).

But what are the cues that reliably trigger stereotype suppression? According to Wyer et al (1998), any cue that makes salient social norms (personal or societal) against stereotyping is likely to promote the spontaneous suppression of stereotypical thinking. Thus, task context, the presence of others, and current information-processing goals are factors that are likely to moderate stereotype suppression. How, when, and for whom personal beliefs and situational cues interact to shape stereotype suppression are issues that require empirical clarification. Additionally, most research and theory on category inhibition has focused on cognitive mechanisms to the neglect of the possible role of affective forces. However, a recent model of willpower proposed by Metcalfe & Mischel (1999) suggests that self-regulation typically involves not only "cool" cognitive processes, such as the self-regulatory mechanisms embodied in Wegner's (1994) theory of mental control, but also "hot," emotional, and stimulus-driven factors. Application of their hot/cool-system analysis of self-regulation to the problem of category inhibition promises to be a fruitful avenue for future research.

CONCLUSIONS

Research on the nature of social cognition has proceeded at such an explosive pace that the idea of providing a comprehensive review of recent developments (within the severe constraints placed on this article) was daunting indeed. Whereas other recent reviews have done an excellent job of describing advances that have occurred in our understanding of the affective and social-pragmatic aspects of person perception and social cognition (e.g. Schwarz 1998), we focused our attention specifically on the cognitive dynamics of categorical social perception. Even within this circumscribed domain, it is not possible to consider fully all of the important and interesting developments of the past few years. For example, we have not touched on the highly promising application of the notion of subjective essentialism (Medin 1989) to the domain of social categories. This work suggests that certain social categories (such as gender and race) are seen as representing fundamental divides of the natural world, based on what are perceived to be deep and stable (presumably biological) foundations (e.g. Gelman et al 1994, Hirschfeld 1996, Rothbart & Taylor 1992, Yzerbyt et al 1997b). Categories may not all be alike in their potential for activation and application, nor in the manner in which they are applied, and much more research needs to address this intriguing issue. We have also not explored the related and burgeoning literature dealing with entitativity, which asserts both that there may often be important differences in the processing of information about groups versus individuals and that groups may vary in their "groupiness," with important consequences for social perception, memory, and judgment (e.g. Campbell 1958, Hamilton & Sherman 1996,

McConnell et al 1997, Yzerbyt et al 1998b). Lamentably, many other valuable topics have been neglected as well. It is surely a healthy sign that there is simply too much good work on social cognition taking place to distill it all into a single brief review. In the research we reviewed, progress has come in two important forms. First, theoretical coherence is beginning to emerge in a number of areas, especially when theoretical ideas and general principles that have proven to be fruitful in many domains of psychology and neuroscience are brought to bear on related phenomena of social cognition. At the same time, however, accounting for unique aspects of social life poses new challenges for many such existing theoretical frameworks and exposes explanatory gaps that invoke uniquely social concerns and principles. We look forward, with considerable excitement and anticipation, to the development of a truly social neuroscience that attempts to build explanations for social behavior that bridge multiple levels of explanation. Furthering our understanding of the neurobiological, personal, social, and cultural bases of category activation and use in social perception will undoubtedly be a key part of this endeavor, as social psychology enters the new millennium.

Visit the Annual Reviews home page at www.AnnualReviews.org.

LITERATURE CITED

Allport GW. 1954. *The Nature of Prejudice.* Reading, MA: Addison-Wesley

Andersen SM, Glassman NS. 1996. Responding to significant others when they are not there. Effects on interpersonal inference, motivation, and affect. In *Handbook of Motivation and Cognition,* ed. RM Sorrentino, ET Higgins, 3:262–321. New York: Guilford

Anderson JR, Bower GH. 1972. *Human Associative Memory.* Washington, DC: Winston

Baars BJ. 1997. *In the Theater of Consciousness.* New York: Oxford Univ. Press

Baddeley A. 1996. Exploring the central executive. *Q.J. Exp. Psychol.* 49A:5–28

Baddeley A, Della Sala S. 1998. Working memory and executive control. See Roberts et al 1998, pp. 9–21

Banaji MR, Hardin CD. 1996. Automatic stereotyping. *Psychol. Sci.* 7:136–41

Bargh JA. 1990. Automotives: preconscious determinants of thought and behavior. See Higgins & Sorrentino 1990, 2:93–130

Bargh JA. 1994. The four horsemen of automaticity: awareness, intention, efficiency, and control in social cognition. In *Handbook of Social Cognition.* Vol. 1: *Basic Processes,* ed. RS Wyer Jr, TK Srull, pp. 1–40. Hillsdale, NJ: Erlbaum. 2nd ed.

Bargh JA. 1997. The automaticity of everyday life. In *The Automaticity of Everyday Life: Advances in Social Cognition,* ed. RS Wyer Jr, 10:1–61. Mahwah, NJ: Erlbaum

Bargh JA. 1999. The cognitive monster: the case against the controllability of automatic stereotype effects. See Chaiken & Trope 1999, pp. 361–82

Bargh JA, Chen M, Burrows L. 1996. Automaticity of social behavior: direct effects of trait construct and stereotype activation on action. *J. Pers. Soc. Psychol.* 71:230–44

Bargh JA, Gollwitzer PM. 1994. Environmental control of goal-directed action: automatic and strategic contingencies between situations and behavior. In *Integrative Views of Motivation, Cognition, and Emotion,* ed. WD Spaulding, pp. 71–124. Lincoln: Univ. Nebraska

Biernat M, Crandall CS, Young LV, Kobrynowicz D, Halpin SM. 1998. All that you can be:

stereotyping of self and others in a military context. *J. Pers. Soc. Psychol.* 75:301–17

Biernat M, Kobrynowicz D. 1997. Gender- and race-based standards of competence: lower minimum standards but higher ability standards for devalued groups. *J. Pers. Soc. Psychol.* 72:544–57

Blair IV, Banaji MR. 1996. Automatic and controlled processes in stereotype priming. *J. Pers. Soc. Psychol.* 70:1142–63

Blessum KA, Lord CG, Sia T. 1998. Cognitive load and positive mood reduce typicality effects in attitude-behavior consistency. *Pers. Soc. Psychol. Bull.* 24:496–504

Bodenhausen GV. 1988. Stereotypic biases in social decision making and memory: testing process models of stereotype use. *J. Pers. Soc. Psychol.* 55:726–37

Bodenhausen GV, Macrae CN. 1998. Stereotype activation and inhibition. In *Stereotype Activation and Inhibition: Advances in Social Cognition,* ed. RS Wyer Jr, 11:1–52. Hillsdale, NJ: Erlbaum

Bodenhausen GV, Macrae CN, Garst J. 1998. Stereotypes in thought and deed: social-cognitive origins of intergroup discrimination. In *Intergroup Cognition and Intergroup Behavior,* ed. C Sedikides, J Schopler, CA Insko, pp. 311–36. Mahwah, NJ: Erlbaum

Bodenhausen GV, Macrae CN, Sherman JW. 1999. On the dialectics of discrimination: dual processes in social stereotyping. See Chaiken & Trope 1999, pp. 271–90

Brewer MB. 1988. A dual process model of impression formation. In *A Dual-Process Model of Impression Formation: Advances in Social Cognition,* ed. RS Wyer Jr, TK Srull, 1:1–36. Hillsdale, NJ: Erlbaum

Brewer MB, Feinstein A. 1999. Dual processes in the representation of persons and social categories. See Chaiken & Trope 1999, pp. 255–70

Bruner J. 1957. On perceptual readiness. *Psychol. Rev.* 64:123–52

Campbell DT. 1958. Common fate, similarity, and other indices of the status of aggregates of persons as social entities. *Behav. Sci.* 3:14–25

Carver CS, Scheier MF. 1990. Principles of self-regulation. See Higgins & Sorrentino 1990, 2:3–52

Chaiken S, Trope Y, eds. 1999. *Dual Process Theories in Social Psychology.* New York: Guilford

Chartrand TL, Bargh JA. 1996. Automatic activation of impression formation and memorization goals: nonconscious goal priming reproduces effects of explicit task instructions. *J. Pers. Soc. Psychol.* 71:464–78

Chen M, Bargh JA. 1997. Nonconscious behavioral confirmation processes: the self-fulfilling nature of automatically activated stereotypes. *J. Exp. Soc. Psychol.* 33:541–60

Collins AM, Loftus EF. 1975. A spreading activation theory of semantic processing. *Psychol. Rev.* 82:407–28

Dennett DC. 1991. *Consciousness Explained.* Boston: Little Brown

Devine PG. 1989. Stereotypes and prejudice: their automatic and controlled components. *J. Pers. Soc. Psychol.* 56:5–18

Devine PG, Monteith MJ, Zuwerink JR, Elliot AJ. 1991. Prejudice with and without compunction. *J. Pers. Soc. Psychol.* 60:817–30

Dijksterhuis A, Spears R, Postmes T, Stapel DA, Koomen W, et al. 1998. Seeing one thing and doing another: contrast effects in automatic behavior. *J. Pers. Soc. Psychol.* 75:862–71

Dijksterhuis A, van Knippenberg A. 1995. Memory for stereotype-consistent and stereotype-inconsistent information as a function of processing pace. *Eur. J. Exp. Soc. Psychol.* 25:689–93

Dijksterhuis A, van Knippenberg A. 1998. The relation between perception and behavior or how to win a game of Trivial Pursuit. *J. Pers. Soc. Psychol.* 74:865–77

Dovidio JF, Evans N, Tyler RB. 1986. Racial stereotypes: the contents of their cognitive representations. *J. Exp. Soc. Psychol.* 22:22–37

Dovidio JF, Gaertner SL. 1986. Prejudice, discrimination, and racism: historical trends and contemporary approaches. In *Prejudice, Discrimination, and Rracism,* ed. JF Dovidio, SL Gaertner, pp. 1–34. Orlando, FL: Academic

Dovidio JF, Kawakami K, Johnson C, Johnson B, Howard A. 1997. On the nature of prejudice: automatic and controlled components. *J. Exp. Soc. Psychol.* 33:510–40

Dunning D, Sherman DA. 1997. Stereotypes and tacit inference. *J. Pers. Soc. Psychol.* 73:459–71

Dunton BC, Fazio RH. 1997. An individual difference measure of motivation to control prejudiced reactions. *Pers. Soc. Psychol. Bull.* 23:316–26

Fazio RH, Dunton BC. 1997. Categorization by race: the impact of automatic and controlled components of racial prejudice. *J. Exp. Soc. Psychol.* 33:451–70

Fazio RH, Jackson JR, Dunton BC, Williams CJ. 1995. Variability in automatic activation as an unobtrusive measure of racial attitudes: a bona fide pipeline? *J. Pers. Soc. Psychol.* 69:1013–27

Fein S, Spencer SJ. 1997. Prejudice as self-image maintenance: affirming the self through derogating others. *J. Pers. Soc. Psychol.* 73:31–44

Fiske ST. 1989. Examining the role of intent: toward understanding its role in stereotyping and prejudice. See Uleman & Bargh 1989, pp. 253–83

Fiske ST. 1998. Stereotyping, prejudice, and discrimination. See Gilbert et al 1998, 2:357–411

Fiske ST, Bersoff DN, Borgida E, Deaux K. 1991. Social science on trial: use of sex stereotyping research in Price Waterhouse v. Hopkins. *Am. Psychol.* 46:1049–60

Fiske ST, Lin M, Neuberg SL. 1999. The continuum model: ten years later. See Chaiken & Trope 1999, pp. 231–54

Fiske ST, Neuberg SL. 1990. A continuum model of impression formation from category-based to individuating processes: influences of information and motivation on attention and interpretation. *Adv. Exp. Soc. Psychol.* 23:1–74

Freud S. 1957 (1915). The unconscious. In *The Standard Edition of the Complete Psychological Works of Sigmund Freud,* ed. J Strachey, 14:104–15. London: Hogarth

Fyock J, Stangor C. 1994. The role of memory biases in stereotype maintenance. *Br. J. Soc. Psychol.* 33:331–43

Gelman SA, Coley JD, Gottfried GM. 1994. Essentialist beliefs in children: the acquisition of concepts and theories. In *Mapping the Mind,* ed. LA Hirschfeld, SA Gelman, pp. 341–65. New York: Cambridge Univ. Press

Gernsbacher MA, Faust ME. 1991. The mechanism of suppression: a component of general comprehension skill. *J. Exp. Psychol.: Learn. Mem. Cogn.* 17:245–62

Gilbert DT, Fiske ST, Lindzey G, eds. 1998. *Handbook of Social Psychology.* Boston: McGraw-Hill. 4th ed.

Gilbert DT, Hixon JG. 1991. The trouble of thinking: activation and application of stereotypic beliefs. *J. Pers. Soc. Psychol.* 60:509–17

Goldman-Rakic PS. 1998. The prefrontal landscape: implications of functional architecture for understanding human mentation and the central executive. See Roberts et al 1998, pp. 87–102

Greenwald AG, Banaji MR. 1995. Implicit social cognition: attitudes, self esteem, and stereotypes. *Psychol. Rev.* 102:4–27

Hamilton DL, Sherman JW. 1994. Stereotypes. In *Handbook of Social Cognition,* ed. RS Wyer Jr, TK Srull, 2:1–68. Hillsdale, NJ: Erlbaum. 2nd ed.

Hamilton DL, Sherman SJ. 1996. Perceiving individuals and groups. *Psychol. Rev.* 103:336–55

Hastie R, Kumar P. 1979. Person memory: personality traits as organizing principles in memory for behaviors. *J. Pers. Soc. Psychol.* 37:25–38

Higgins ET, Sorrentino RM, eds. 1990. *Handbook of Motivation and Cognition.* New York: Guilford

Hilton JL, von Hippel W. 1996. Stereotypes. *Annu. Rev. Psychol.* 47:237–71

Hirschfeld LA. 1996. *Race in the Making: Cognition, Culture, and the Child's Construction of Human Kinds.* Cambridge, MA: MIT Press

Jacoby LL, Kelley CM, McElree BD. 1999. The role of cognitive control: early selection versus late correction. See Chaiken & Trope 1999, pp. 383–400

James W. 1890. *Principles of Psychology.* New York: Holt

Johnson MK, Hashtroudi S, Lindsay DS. 1993. Source monitoring. *Psychol. Rev.* 114:3–28

Johnson-Laird PN. 1983. *Mental Models.* Cambridge, UK: Cambridge Univ. Press

Johnston WA, Hawley KJ. 1994. Perceptual inhibition of expected inputs: the key that opens closed minds. *Psychom. Bull. Rev.* 1:56–72

Kawakami K, Dion KL, Dovidio JF. 1998. Racial prejudice and stereotype activation. *Pers. Soc. Psychol. Bull.* 24:407–16

Kelly AE, Kahn JH. 1994. Effects of suppression on personal intrusive thoughts. *J. Pers. Soc. Psychol.* 66:998–1006

Klauer KC, Wegener I. 1998. Unraveling social categorization in the "who said what?" paradigm. *J. Pers. Soc. Psychol.* 75:1155–78

Klein SB, Kihlstrom JF. 1998. On bridging the gap between social-personality psychology and neuropsychology. *Pers. Soc. Psychol. Rev.* 2:228–42

Klein SB, Loftus J, Kihlstrom JF. 1996. Self-knowledge of an amnesic patient: toward a neuropsychology of personality and social psychology. *J. Exp. Psychol.: Gen.* 125:250–60

Kobrynowicz D, Biernat M. 1997. Decoding subjective evaluations: how stereotypes provide shifting standards. *J. Exp. Soc. Psychol.* 33:579–601

Kunda Z, Thagard P. 1996. Forming impressions from stereotypes, traits, and behaviors: a parallel constraint satisfaction theory. *Psychol. Rev.* 103:284–308

Lepore L, Brown R. 1997. Category and stereotype activation: Is prejudice inevitable? *J. Pers. Soc. Psychol.* 72:275–87

Levy SR, Stroessner SJ, Dweck CS. 1998. Stereotype formation and endorsement: the role of implicit theories. *J. Pers. Soc. Psychol.* 74:1421–37

Linville P. 1996. Attention inhibition: Does it underlie ruminative thought? In *Ruminative Thoughts: Advances in Social Cognition,* ed. RS Wyer Jr, 9:121–34. Mahwah, NJ: Erlbaum

Lippmann W. 1922. *Public Opinion.* New York: Harcourt Brace Jovanovich

Locke V, MacLeod C, Walker I. 1994. Automatic and controlled activation of stereotypes: individual differences associated with prejudice. *Br. J. Soc. Psychol.* 33:29–46

Logan GD. 1989. Automaticity and cognitive control. See Uleman & Bargh 1989, pp. 52–74

Logan GD, Cowan WB. 1984. On the ability to inhibit thought and action: a theory of an act of control. *Psychol. Rev.* 91:295–327

Macrae CN, Bodenhausen GV, Milne AB. 1995. The dissection of selection in person perception: inhibitory processes in social stereotyping. *J. Pers. Soc. Psychol.* 69:397–407

Macrae CN, Bodenhausen GV, Milne AB. 1998a. Saying no to unwanted thoughts: self-focus and the regulation of mental life. *J. Pers. Soc. Psychol.* 74:578–89

Macrae CN, Bodenhausen GV, Milne AB, Castelli L, Schloerscheidt AM, Greco S. 1998b. On activating exemplars. *J. Exp. Soc. Psychol.* 34:330–54

Macrae CN, Bodenhausen GV, Milne AB, Ford RL. 1997a. On the regulation of recollection: the intentional forgetting of stereotypical memories. *J. Pers. Soc. Psychol.* 72:709–19

Macrae CN, Bodenhausen GV, Milne AB, Jetten J. 1994a. Out of mind but back in sight: stereotypes on the rebound. *J. Pers. Soc. Psychol.* 67:808–17

Macrae CN, Bodenhausen GV, Milne AB, Thorn TMJ, Castelli L. 1997b. On the activation of social stereotypes: the moderating role of processing objectives. *J. Exp. Soc. Psychol.* 33:471–89

Macrae CN, Bodenhausen GV, Milne AB, Wheeler V. 1996. On resisting the temptation for simplification: counterintentional effects of stereotype suppression. *Soc. Cogn.* 14:1–20

Macrae CN, Bodenhausen GV, Schloerscheidt AM, Milne AB. 1999. Tales of the unexpected: executive function and person perception. *J. Pers. Soc. Psychol.* 76:200–13

Macrae CN, Johnston L. 1998. Help, I need somebody: automatic action and inaction. *Soc. Cogn.* 16:400–17

Macrae CN, Milne AB, Bodenhausen GV. 1994b. Stereotypes as energy-saving devices: a peek inside the cognitive toolbox. *J. Pers. Soc. Psychol.* 66:37–47

Macrae CN, Stangor C, Milne AB. 1994c. Activating social stereotypes: a functional analysis. *J. Exp. Soc. Psychol.* 30:370–89

McClelland JL, McNaughton BL, O'Reilly RC. 1995. Why there are complementary learning systems in the hippocampus and neocortex: insights from the success and failures of connectionist models of learning and memory. *Psychol. Rev.* 102:419–57

McConnell AR, Sherman SJ, Hamilton DL. 1997. Target entatitivity: implications for information processing about individual and group targets. *J. Pers. Soc. Psychol.* 72:750–62

Medin DL. 1989. Concepts and conceptual structure. *Am. Psychol.* 44:1469–81

Metcalfe J. 1993. Novelty monitoring, metacognition and control in a composite holographic associative recall model: implications for Korsakoff amnesia. *Psychol. Rev.* 100:3–22

Metcalfe J, Mischel W. 1999. A hot/cool-system analysis of delay of gratification: dynamics of willpower. *Psychol. Rev.* 106:3–19

Miller GA, Galanter E, Pribram KH. 1960. *Plans and the Structure of Behavior.* New York: Holt, Rinehart Winston

Monteith MJ. 1993. Self-regulation of prejudiced responses: implications for progress in prejudice-reduction efforts. *J. Pers. Soc. Psychol.* 65:469–85

Monteith MJ, Sherman JW, Devine PG. 1998a. Suppression as a stereotype control strategy. *Pers. Soc. Psychol. Rev.* 2:63–82

Monteith MJ, Spicer CV, Tooman GD. 1998b. Consequences of stereotype suppression: stereotypes on and not on the rebound. *J. Exp. Soc. Psychol.* 34:355–77

Neely JH. 1991. Semantic priming effects in visual word recognition: a selective review of current findings and theories. In *Basic Processes in Reading: Visual Word Recognition,* ed. D Besner, G Humphreys, pp. 264–336. Hillsdale, NJ: Erlbaum

Neumann E, DeSchepper B. 1992. An inhibition-based fan effect: evidence for an active suppression mechanism in selective attention. *Can. J. Psychol.* 46:1–40

Norman DA, Shallice T. 1986. Attention to action: willed and automatic control of behavior. In *Consciousness and Self-Regulation: Advances in Research and Theory,* ed. RJ Davidson, GE Schwartz, D Shapiro, 4:1–18. New York: Plenum

Olson JM, Roese NJ, Zanna MP. 1996. Expectancies. In *Social Psychology: Handbook of Basic Principles,* ed. ET Higgins, AW Kruglanski, pp. 211–38. New York: Guilford

Pendry LF, Macrae CN. 1994. Stereotypes and mental life: the case of the motivated but thwarted tactician. *J. Exp. Soc. Psychol.* 30:303–25

Pendry LF, Macrae CN. 1996. What the disinterested perceiver overlooks: goal-directed social categorization. *Pers. Soc. Psychol. Bull.* 3:250–57

Perdue CW, Gurtman MB. 1990. Evidence for the automaticity of ageism. *J. Exp. Soc. Psychol.* 26:199–216

Plant EA, Devine PG. 1998. Internal and external motivation to respond without prejudice. *J. Pers. Soc. Psychol.* 75:811–32

Pratto F, Bargh JA. 1991. Stereotyping based upon apparently individuating information. Trait and global components of sex stereotypes under attention overload. *J. Exp. Soc. Psychol.* 27:26–47

Roberts AC, Robbins TW, Weiskrantz L, eds. 1998. *The Prefrontal Cortex: Executive and Cognitive Functions.* Oxford, UK: Oxford Univ. Press

Rothbart M, Taylor M. 1992. Category labels and social reality: Do we view social categories as natural kinds? In *Language, Interaction and Social Cognition,* ed. G Semin, K Fiedler, pp. 11–36. London: Sage

Schacter DL, Tulving E. 1994. *Memory Systems 1994.* Cambridge, MA: MIT Press

Schuman H, Steeh C, Bobo L, Krysan M. 1997. *Racial Attitudes in America: Trends and Interpretations.* Cambridge, MA: Harvard Univ. Press. Rev. ed.

Schwarz N. 1998. Warmer and more social: recent developments in cognitive social psychology. *Annu. Rev. Sociol.* 24:239–64

Shallice T. 1988. *From Neuropsychology to Mental Structure.* New York: Cambridge Univ. Press

Shallice T, Burgess P. 1998. The domain of supervisory processes and the temporal organization of behavior. See Roberts et al 1998, pp. 22–35

Sherman JW. 1999. The dynamic relationship between stereotype efficiency and mental representation. In *The Future of Social Cognition,* ed. G Moskowitz. New York: Guilford. In press

Sherman JW, Bessenoff GR. 1999. Stereotypes as source-monitoring cues: on the interaction between episodic and semantic memory. *Psychol. Sci.* 10:106–10

Sherman JW, Frost LA. 1999. On the encoding of stereotype-relevant information under cognitive load. *Pers. Soc. Psychol. Bull.* In press

Sherman JW, Lee AY, Bessenoff GR, Frost LA. 1998. Stereotype efficiency reconsidered: encoding flexibility under cognitive load. *J. Pers. Soc. Psychol.* 75:589–606

Sherman JW, Stroessner SJ, Loftus ST, DeGuzman G. 1997. Stereotype suppression and recognition memory for stereotypical and non-stereotypical information. *Soc. Cogn.* 15:205–15

Sinclair L, Kunda Z. 1999. Reactions to a black professional: motivated inhibition and activation of conflicting stereotypes. *J. Pers. Soc. Psychol.* In press

Smith ER. 1990. Content and process specificity in the effects of prior experiences. In *Content and Process Specificity in the Effects of Prior Experiences: Advances in Social Cognition,* ed. TK Srull, RS Wyer Jr, 3:1–59. Hillsdale, NJ: Erlbaum

Smith ER. 1998. Mental representation and memory. See Gilbert et al 1998, 1:391–445

Smith ER, DeCoster J. 1999. Associative and rule-based processing: a connectionist interpretation of dual-process models. See Chaiken & Trope 1999, pp. 323–36

Smith ER, Fazio RH, Cejka MA. 1996. Accessible attitudes influence categorization of multiply categorizable objects. *J. Pers. Soc. Psychol.* 71:888–98

Smith MC, Theodor L, Franklin PE. 1983. The relationship between contextual facilitation and depth of processing. *J. Exp. Psychol.: Learn. Mem. Cogn.* 9:697–712

Spears R, Haslam SA. 1997. Stereotyping and the burden of cognitive load. See Spears et al 1997, pp. 171–207

Spears R, Oakes PJ, Ellemers N, Haslam SA, eds. 1997. *The Social Psychology of Stereotyping and Group Life.* Cambridge, MA: Blackwell

Spencer SJ, Fein S, Wolfe CT, Fong C, Dunn M. 1998. Automatic activation of stereotypes: the role of self-image threat. *Pers. Soc. Psychol. Bull.* 24:1139–52

Srull TK, Wyer RS Jr. 1989. Person memory and judgment. *Psychol. Rev.* 96:58–83

Stangor C, Duan C. 1991. Effects of multiple task demands upon memory for information about social groups. *J. Exp. Soc. Psychol.* 27:357–78

Stangor C, McMillan D. 1992. Memory for expectancy-congruent and expectancy-incongruent information: a review of the social and social developmental literatures. *Psychol. Bull.* 111:42–61

Stapel D, Koomen W. 1998. When stereotype activation results in (counter)stereotypic judgments: priming stereotype-relevant traits and exemplars. *J. Exp. Soc. Psychol.* 34:136–63

Stapel D, Martin LL, Schwarz N. 1998. The smell of bias: What instigates correction processes in social judgments? *Pers. Soc. Psychol. Bull.* 24:797–806

Strack F, Hannover B. 1996. Awareness of influence as a precondition for implementing correctional goals. In *The Psychology of Action,* ed. PM Gollwitzer, JA Bargh, pp. 579–96. New York: Guilford

Stroessner SJ. 1996. Social categorization by race or sex: effects of perceived non-normalcy on response times. *Soc. Cogn.* 14:247–76

Tipper SP. 1985. The negative priming effect: inhibitory effects of ignored primes. *Q.J. Exp. Psychol.* 37A:571–90

Uleman JS, Bargh JA, eds. 1989. *Unintended Thought.* New York: Guilford

van Knippenberg A, Dijksterhuis A, Vermeulen D. 1999. Judgment and memory of a criminal act: the effects of stereotypes and cognitive load. *Eur. J. Soc. Psychol.* 29:191–202

von Hippel W, Jonides J, Hilton JL, Narayan S. 1993. Inhibitory effect of schematic processing on perceptual encoding. *J. Pers. Soc. Psychol.* 64:921–35

von Hippel W, Sekaquaptewa D, Vargas P. 1995. On the role of encoding processes in stereotype maintenance. *Adv. Exp. Soc. Psychol.* 27:177–254

von Hippel W, Silver LA, Lynch ME. 1999. Stereotyping against your will: the role of inhibitory ability in stereotyping and prejudice among the elderly. *Pers. Soc. Psychol. Bull.* In press

Wegener DT, Petty RE. 1997. The flexible correction model: the role of naive theories of bias in bias correction. *Adv. Exp. Soc. Psychol.* 29:141–208

Wegner DM. 1994. Ironic processes of mental control. *Psychol. Rev.* 101:34–52

Wegner DM, Bargh JA. 1998. Control and automaticity in social life. See Gilbert et al 1998, 1:446–96

Wegner DM, Erber R. 1992. The hyperaccessibility of suppressed thoughts. *J. Pers. Soc. Psychol.* 63:903–12

Wegner DM, Pennebaker JW. 1993. *Handbook of Mental Control.* Englewood Cliffs, NJ: Prentice Hall

Wilson TD, Brekke N. 1994. Mental contamination and mental correction: unwanted influences on judgments and evaluations. *Psychol. Bull.* 116:117–42

Wittenbrink B, Hilton JL, Gist PL. 1998. In search of similarity: stereotypes as naïve theories in social categorization. *Soc. Cogn.* 16:31–55

Wittenbrink B, Judd CM, Park B. 1997. Evidence for racial prejudice at the implicit level and its relationship with questionnaire measures. *J. Pers. Soc. Psychol.* 72:262–74

Wyer NA, Sherman JW, Stroessner SJ. 1998. The spontaneous suppression of racial stereotypes. *Soc. Cogn.* 16:340–52

Wyer NA, Sherman JW, Stroessner SJ. 1999. The roles of motivation and ability in controlling the consequences of stereotype suppression. *Pers. Soc. Psychol. Bull.* In press

Yzerbyt VY, Leyens J-P, Corneille O. 1998a. The role of naïve theories of judgment in impression formation. *Soc. Cogn.* 16:56–77

Yzerbyt VY, Leyens J-P, Schadron G. 1997a. Social judgeability and the dilution of stereotypes: the impact of the nature and sequence of information. *Pers. Soc. Psychol. Bull.* 23:1312–22

Yzerbyt VY, Rocher S, Schadron G. 1997b. Stereotypes as explanations: a subjective essentialist view of group perception. See Spears et al 1997, pp. 20–50

Yzerbyt VY, Rogier A, Fiske ST. 1998b. Group entatitivity and social attribution: on translating situational constraints into stereotypes. *Pers. Soc. Psychol. Bull.* 24:1089–103

Zacks RT, Radvansky G, Hasher L. 1996. Studies of directed forgetting in older adults. *J. Exp. Psychol.: Learn. Mem. Cogn.* 22:143–56

Zárate MA, Smith ER. 1990. Person categorization and stereotyping. *Soc. Cogn.* 8:161–85.

Annu. Rev. Psychol. 2000. 51:121–147

ARE THERE KINDS OF CONCEPTS?

Douglas L. Medin, Elizabeth B. Lynch, and Karen O. Solomon

Department of Psychology, Northwestern University, Evanston, Illinois 60208; e-mail: medin@nwu.edu, elynch@nwu.edu, k-solomon@nwu.edu

Key Words categorization, cognitive processes, mental representation, domain specificity

■ **Abstract** Past research on concepts has focused almost exclusively on noun-object concepts. This paper discusses recent research demonstrating that useful distinctions may be made among kinds of concepts, including both object and nonobject concepts. We discuss three types of criteria, based on structure, process, and content, that may be used to distinguish among kinds of concepts. The paper then reviews a number of possible candidates for kinds based on the discussed criteria.

CONTENTS

Introduction 122
Criteria for Kinds of Concepts 123
  Structural Differences 123
  Processing Differences 124
  Content-Laden Principles 124
Candidates for Kinds of Concepts Based on Structure 125
  Nouns Versus Verbs 125
  Count Nouns Versus Mass Nouns 125
  Isolated and Interrelated Concepts 126
  Objects Versus Mental Events 126
  Artifacts Versus Natural Kinds 127
  Abstract Concepts 128
  Basic Level Versus Subordinate and Superordinate Concepts 128
  Hierarchies Versus Paradigms 131
  Category Structure and the Brain 132
  Summary 132
Candidates for Kinds of Concepts Based on Processing 132
  Common Taxonomic Versus Goal-Derived Categories 132
  Social Information Processing and Individuation 133
  Stereotypes, Subtypes, and Subgroups 134
  Category Processing and the Brain 135
  Other Distinctions 135
  Summary 136

0084–6570/00/0201–0121$12.00

Candidates for Kinds of Concepts Based on Content: Domain Specificity 136
    Summary 138
Conclusions 138

INTRODUCTION

Many years ago, the cryptic but pointed comment of a collegue on a book by one of the present authors (Smith & Medin 1981) said, "This is an excellent overview but you two seem to think that concept is spelled, n o u n." The commentator may have been generous at that, because natural object concepts were the focus (with attempts made to justify the reasons). In this paper, we do not distinguish questions about kinds of categories from questions about kinds of concepts. Although the distinction between concepts and categories is important (see Solomon et al 1999), where there are distinct kinds of categories, the associated concepts will also be distinct. Although the reviewer's barbed comment is still relevant today, since that time there has been a continuous and substantial volume of research on categories and concepts. This has served to greatly broaden the topic's empirical and theoretical base, so that today there is a lot more to say about different kinds of concepts than there was in 1981. Accordingly, this review is organized around the question of whether there are distinct kinds of concepts.

On the surface it seems transparently true that there are kinds of concepts— notions like democracy seem different from things like party or from concepts such as "black-capped chickadee." But a little reflection suggests that the notion of kinds of concepts must be evaluated relative to the theoretical work a kind or domain is going to be asked to do. For example, if one is interested in concept learning, the relevant issue might be whether different kinds of concepts are acquired in the same way. Note that this shifts but does not remove the explanatory burden: For the question to be meaningful, criteria are needed for deciding whether concepts are "acquired in the same way." In brief, questions about kinds of concepts should be answered by theories rather than intuitions. In this paper, we attempt to bring together candidates for kinds of concepts that have emerged across the different theoretical perspectives of current research on concepts.

One motivation for the interest in kinds is that a number of scientists, especially researchers in the area of cognitive development, have argued that cognition is organized in terms of distinct domains, each characterized by (usually) innate constraints or skeletal developmental principles (e.g. Hirschfeld & Gelman 1994a). That is, cognition is said to be domain specific. Some researchers object to the claims about innateness as well as the claims about domain specificity (e.g. Jones & Smith 1993). To evaluate this debate, one needs criteria for domains (or kinds).

A less-contentious reason to worry about kinds concerns trade-offs between different levels of explanation and specificity or preciseness of generalizations. To use an analogy with biological kinds, there are interesting properties that all living things share, but there are further interesting generalizations that may hold only for mammals or only for primates or only for human beings. Treating all concepts as being of the same type may be useful for some purposes but we may be missing important principles that apply robustly only for subsets of concepts.

Another reason to care about kinds of concepts is that even universal aspects of concepts may be more salient and easier to study in some concepts than in others. Neurologists study the squid axon not because squids are the only things that have axons but because the squid axon is large. Finally, the most obvious reason to worry about kinds is that exploring different kinds allows us to test the generality of our theories and models.

The rest of this review is organized as follows. First, a variety of criteria for establishing distinct kinds of concepts is presented. Then some candidates for kinds are discussed and the corresponding literature is evaluated with respect to our criteria. Finally, a descriptive summary and prescriptive advice are presented.

In evaluating the literature from a specific perspective, we take advantage of a number of other recent review papers and edited volumes (e.g. Nakamura et al 1993, Van Mechelen et al 1993, Lamberts & Shanks 1997, Ward et al 1997a, Medin & Heit 1999). Komatsu (1992) analyzes research on the role of intuitive theories and other forms of knowledge versus the role of similarity in categorization (for related analyses, see also Goldstone 1994a; Hahn & Chater 1997; Hampton 1997, 1998; Heit 1997; Malt 1995; Murphy 1993; Sloman & Rips 1998). Solomon et al (1999) focus on the role and implications of multiple conceptual functions for concept theories. A review by Medin & Coley (1998) traces relationships between laboratory studies using artificially created categories and research using natural (lexical) concepts (see also Estes 1994).

CRITERIA FOR KINDS OF CONCEPTS

We consider three types of interrelated criteria for distinguishing concept types: (*a*) structural differences, (*b*) processing differences, and (*c*) content-laden principles.

Structural Differences

A great deal of research on the psychology of concepts has been directed at their componential structure, especially as it relates to categorization. Virtually everyone believes that concepts should be analyzed in terms of constituent attributes or features. For example, the concept of stallion may be understood in terms of features such as animate, four-legged, male, adult, and so on. Thus, criteria for kinds of concepts based on structural differences would be based primarily on differences in the kinds of features in a concept and the relations among these features. The 1970s were characterized by a shift from the position that categories are organized in terms of defining (singly necessary and jointly sufficient) features (the so-called classical view) to the view that category membership is more graded and structured in terms of features that are only typical or characteristic of categories—the so-called probabilistic or prototype view (for seminal papers, see Rosch & Mervis 1975, Smith et al 1974; for an early general review, see Smith & Medin 1981).

As noted earlier, much of the discussion and research on conceptual structure has employed object concepts (e.g. chair, bird, tool, etc). The possibility remains that other categories conform to a classical view structure or exhibit entirely novel structure.

Processing Differences

One might also distinguish among kinds of concepts based on the types of processing that are done to develop and maintain them. For example, categories formed through data-driven, bottom-up processes may be different from categories formed through top-down categorical processes. It is an obvious but important point that claims about either structure or processing cannot be evaluated in isolation, that structure-process pairs must be considered (e.g. Anderson 1978). For example, a hypothesis-testing mechanism for learning classical view categories would likely fail to acquire probabilistic categories. Researchers interested in processing principles have generally assumed that differences in structure are associated with processing differences. Of course, process may drive structure. For example, categories created in the service of goals may be fundamentally different from natural object categories. An alternative idea is that there may be multiple processes that operate on the same structure.

It is fair to say that theories about conceptual structure and processing are based primarily on research with object categories, though the conclusions from this work are thought to apply to a wide range of concepts. Are object categories analogous to the squid axon mentioned above? That is, are object concepts just easy-to-study representatives of all concepts? One may also wonder whether object concepts are themselves uniform in kind. Below we discuss recent research that suggests that there are principles of conceptual structure and processing that cannot be generalized across all concepts. We then turn to the question of whether important variations exist among object categories.

Content-Laden Principles

In contrast to the view that there are general, abstract principles of conceptual structure and processing, advocates of domain specificity focus on principles that apply uniquely to concepts with specific contents. For example, in this view, kinds of concepts may be divided into domains of concepts, such as naïve biology, naïve psychology, and naïve physics. Given that the contents of concepts in different domains are almost surely going to be different, it is tempting to conclude that these advocates have created kinds (or domains) simply by defining them into existence. As we shall see, the domain specificity view does have empirical content. First, however, we consider candidates for kinds based on structure and those based on processing.

CANDIDATES FOR KINDS OF CONCEPTS BASED ON STRUCTURE

Nouns Versus Verbs

It appears that the distinction between nouns and verbs is universal (Sapir 1944). Gentner and colleagues (Gentner 1981, 1982; Gentner & France 1988; Gentner & Boroditsky 1999) have marshaled theoretical and empirical arguments for the view that nouns and verbs map onto ontologically distinct aspects of the environment (see also MacNamara 1972). Although the contrast is not without exception, the general idea is that nouns refer to clusters of correlated properties that create chunks of perceptual experience. Languages honor these perceptual discontinuities, as evidenced by good cross-cultural consistency in the presence of lexical entries corresponding to these chunks. In contrast, predicative concepts in general and verbs in particular focus on relations among these entities involving such things as causal relations, activity, or change of state. Given that relations presuppose arguments or objects, it would seem that nouns are conceptually simpler than verbs and, Gentner (1981) argues, more constrained by perceptual experience. If so, one might expect that (*a*) (concrete) nouns should be learned before verbs (see Bloom et al 1993, Choi & Gopnik 1995, Au et al 1994, Tardif et al 1999, Tomasello 1992, Waxman 1998, Waxman & Markow 1995, Woodward & Markman 1997; for review, see Gentner & Boroditsky 1999), (*b*) there should be more cross-linguistic variability in verbs than in nouns (see Bowerman 1996; Levinson 1994, 1999; Waxman et al 1997), and (*c*) linguistic (syntactic) structure should play a greater role in verb learning than in noun learning (see Naigles 1990, Choi & Bowerman 1991, Pinker 1994). Although there is not universal agreement on any of these claims, the weight of evidence appears to agree with each of them.

The distinction between nouns and verbs no doubt needs to be somewhat nuanced. For example, motion is associated with both nouns and verbs (e.g. Kersten & Billman 1995), but there is a bias for nouns to be associated with motion intrinsic to an object and for verbs to be associated with motions involving relations between objects (Kersten 1998a,b).

Count Nouns Versus Mass Nouns

Another lexical distinction that reveals differences in conceptual structure is the mass/count distinction. For example, although you can say "a dog" (count noun), you cannot say "a rice" or "a sand." Wisniewski et al (1996) note that the mass/count distinction applies to superordinate categories as well: Some superordinate concepts are mass nouns (e.g. "some" furniture), and others are count nouns (e.g.

"an" animal). In a series of studies, Wisniewski et al demonstrate that the linguistic distinction between mass and count superordinates reflects conceptual differences as well. They found that members of mass superordinates tend to co-occur and people tend to interact with many members of a mass superordinate at one time, but they tend to only interact with single members of count-noun superordinates. Furthermore, they found that properties that characterize individuals are a more salient aspect of count superordinates. Wisniewski et al conclude that mass superordinates refer to unindividuated groups of objects, rather than to single objects, and that, unlike count superordinates, mass superordinates are not true taxonomic categories. Markman (1985) also noted conceptual differences between mass and count superordinates. Specifically, she found that across languages, terms for categories at more abstract levels of a hierarchy are more likely to be mass nouns than are terms for categories at low levels of a hierarchy. She also found that children learned concepts with the same extension faster when they were referred to by a mass noun than by a count noun (Markman et al 1980).

Isolated and Interrelated Concepts

The structural difference between noun and verb concepts in terms of clusters of features versus relational properties may also usefully distinguish among kinds of nouns. Some noun concepts are intrinsically defined, whereas others appear to be more relational in character (Barr & Caplan 1987, Caplan & Barr 1991). For example, the concept of grandmother seems to centrally involve the relational notion of being a female parent of a parent. Barr & Caplan (1987) found that relational concepts show more graded membership and smaller differences between gradients of typicality and membership judgments than do intrinsically defined concepts. Given that the literature has tended to focus on intrinsic concepts, perhaps other phenomena associated with categorization and other uses of concepts may not generalize to relational concepts. There is not sufficient evidence to hazard a guess with respect to this possibility.

Goldstone (1996) has marshaled evidence for the distinction between isolated and interrelated concepts where a concept is interrelated to the extent that it is influenced by other concepts. He further showed that current models of categorization (e.g. exemplar models) can account for some but not all of the phenomena associated with interrelated concepts. However, he offers a recurrent network model that successfully describes varying amounts of intercategory influence. The fact that a unitary computational model accounts for both isolated and interrelated concepts undermines the view that these are distinct kinds of categories.

Objects Versus Mental Events

Although some researchers have focused on parallels between object and event concepts (e.g. Rifkin 1985; for social events, see Morris & Murphy 1990), Rips and his associates have demonstrated important differences between objects and mental events (e.g. Rips & Conrad 1989, Rips & Estin 1998). For example, part-whole relations seem to behave differently for objects and mental events. The steering wheel of a car is not a kind of vehicle but a part of planning, such as evaluating competing plans is a type of thinking (Rips & Estin 1998). Evidence from other experiments suggests that parts of mental events (and, to an intermediate degree, scripts) are less bounded (discriminable) and more homogeneous than parts of objects (Rips & Estin 1998). Finally, if the categories that describe mental events are less bounded, then they may be more difficult to learn than object categories (see Keil 1983).

Artifacts Versus Natural Kinds

Numerous studies have shown that different kinds of features are important to natural kind verses artifact categories (Barton & Komatsu 1989, Gelman 1988, Keil 1989, Rips 1989). These studies indicate that functional features are more important for artifacts, and features referring to internal structure are more important for natural kinds. For example, Barton & Komatsu (1989) presented participants with natural kind and artifact categories that had changes either in molecular structure (e.g. a goat with altered chromosomes or a tire not made of rubber) or in function (e.g. a female goat not giving milk or a tire that cannot roll). Changes in molecular structure were more likely to affect natural kind categories than artifact categories (e.g. a goat with altered chromosomes is less likely to be a goat), whereas changes in function were more likely to affect artifact categories (e.g. a tire that cannot roll is less likely to be a tire). Later research does suggest some ambiguity with regard to the criterial features of artifact categories. Malt & Johnson (1992) found that artifact category membership decisions were more influenced by physical than by functional features. (For another view on the nature of artifact categories see Bloom 1996, 1998; Malt & Johnson 1998.) Overall, these studies suggest that natural kind and artifact categories may differ on the basis of the kinds of features that are criterial for membership in the category.

Research by Ahn (1998) may explain why different kinds of features are criterial for natural kind and artifact categories. Ahn claims that the centrality of a feature to a category depends on the causal status of that feature relative to the other features in the category (see also Ahn 1999, Sloman & Ahn 1999, Sloman et al 1998). Specifically, if a feature is thought to give rise to other features in the category, removing that causal feature affects category identity more than the removal of a noncausal feature does. Ahn showed that the causal status hypothesis accounted for the results of Barton & Komatsu (1989) and Malt & Johnson (1992). That is, the features in these studies that had been judged as criterial to their categories were also rated as the most causal. In artificial category studies, Ahn (1998) showed that regardless of whether the category was a natural kind or an artifact, when functional features caused compositional features, functional features were considered more essential to category membership, whereas when compositional features caused functional features, compositional features were considered more essential to category membership. This suggests that the differences between artifact and natural kind categories may result from the fact that different kinds of features are causal in natural kind and artifact categories (for further discussion, see Keil 1995). The original problem of determining whether artifacts and natural kinds constitute distinct kinds of categories thus becomes the problem of determining whether the causal status of the features of a category can be determined independently of its status as a natural kind or an artifact.

Abstract Concepts

Abstract concepts, such as truth and justice, seem different from object concepts, such as dogs and boats. Yet little work has addressed how we understand abstract concepts. One suggestion has been that abstract concepts are understood through conceptual metaphors (Gibbs 1997, Lakoff & Johnson 1980). During this process, representations of concrete concepts are mapped onto the abstract concepts to facilitate understanding. For example, justice might be understood through a conceptual representation of a scale, and anger might be understood through a conceptual representation of boiling water. If abstract concepts are understood via a metaphorical representation of an object concept, we might not expect to find structural differences between these two types of concepts. Clearly more work needs to be done on how abstract categories are formed and understood.

Basic Level Versus Subordinate and Superordinate Concepts

The observation by Markman (1985) that mass categories are likely to be superordinate categories suggests that differences in taxonomic level may correspond to differences in conceptual structure. Although most objects can be described or named at a number of different levels of abstractness (e.g. rocking chair, chair, furniture item, human artifact), the "best name" for objects (Brown 1958) is at one particular level. In a classic paper, Rosch et al (1976) argued that bundles of correlated properties associated with objects form natural discontinuities or chunks that create a privileged level of categorization. They showed that the basic level is the most inclusive level, at which many common features or properties are listed, the most abstract level at which category members have a similar shape (for a more detailed analysis of comparability and levels, see Markman & Wisniewski 1997), and the level above which much information was lost. Furthermore, the basic level is preferred in adult naming, first learned by children, and the level at which categorization is fastest. In short, these and other measures all converged on a single level as privileged. The findings by Rosch el al (1976) presented a powerful picture of a single taxonomic level as privileged across a wide range of conceptual measures. The authors suggested that the basic level is the level that provides the most cognitively accessible information about the correlational structure of the environment. Are basic-level categories different in kind from categories at other levels? Surprisingly, a number of lines of research suggest that this may not be the case.

First of all, recent evidence suggests that, at least on some tasks, the basic level may change as a function of expertise (e.g. Tanaka & Taylor 1991; Palmer et al 1989; Johnson & Mervis 1997, 1998). For example, experts may prefer to name at subordinate levels, and they verify category labels equally fast at subordinate and basic levels. Although Rosch et al (1976) had contemplated this possibility, this evidence compromises their explanation of the basic level by suggesting that the cognitive accessibility of feature correlations is expertise dependent, rather than universal and absolute. An interesting possibility is that learning may modify the constituent features or attributes of a concept. A number of recent findings and models provide support for this possibility (e.g. Gauthier & Tarr 1997, Goldstone 1994b, Livingston et al 1998, Norman et al 1992, Schyns & Rodet 1997, Schyns 1998; for an overview and commentary, see Schyns et al 1998; for an edited volume, see Goldstone et al 1997). In short, the salience of feature clusters may not be absolute and invariant but rather variable as a function of learning.

Another complication is that although ethnobiologists (Berlin 1992) and psychologists both find evidence for a privileged taxonomic level, they disagree about where in the taxonomy this level is located. Berlin (1992) pinpoints privilege at the level that would typically correspond to genus (e.g. blue jay, bass, beech), whereas Rosch et al (1976) found the privileged level to be a more abstract level, corresponding more nearly with class (e.g. bird, fish, tree). One explanation is that this represents an expertise effect. The people in traditional societies studied by ethnobiologists may be biological experts relative to undergraduates in a technologically oriented society—the population of choice for psychologists. Another possibility is that ethnobiologists and psychologists use different measures of basicness and that these measures do not converge (see also Barsalou 1991).

Coley et al (1997; see also Atran et al 1997, Medin et al 1997) did direct cross-cultural comparisons of these two types of populations using a single measure, inductive confidence. They assumed that if the basic level is the most abstract level at which category members share many properties, then inductive confidence (reasoning from one member having some novel property to all members having that property) should drop abruptly for reference categories above the basic level. Surprisingly, both the Itzaj of Guatemala (members of a traditional society) and US undergraduates consistently showed the same level as privileged, and this level corresponded to genus, consistent with expectations derived from anthropology. This finding raises the possibility that different levels within an object hierarchy are useful for different kinds of tasks (different types of processing). At least for novices, there is a disparity between the level privileged for induction and that favored in naming and speeded category verification tests (though experts may show a convergence across these three tasks). Despite the admirable thoroughness of the original studies of Rosch et al (1976), evidence is increasingly challenging their claim that a single taxonomic level is privileged across the divergent processing demands of particular tasks.

Although Rosch et al have claimed that informativeness determines the basic level, Barsalou (1991) has suggested that perceptual factors may be more central. Barsalou argues that entities are categorized first by shape, because the visual system extracts the low-spatial-frequency information that is used to recognize shape faster than it extracts the high-spatial-frequency information that is necessary to recognize more detailed information (e.g. texture). For example, shape has fairly low variance across birds, making shape a strongly predictive feature for the category bird. This argument is strengthened by the fact that entities that do not share the same shape as their fellow basic-level category members (defined by informativeness) are usually not categorized initially at the basic level but instead are categorized initially at the subordinate level (Jolicoeur et al 1984). For example, a chicken is first categorized as a chicken rather than a bird, presumably because it has an atypical shape for a bird. Barsalou (1991) suggests that there may be a perceptual basic level, based primarily on shape and used largely during perception, and a more informational basic level, carrying more conceptual information and used for secondary categorizations during reasoning and communication. This idea may help explain the discrepancy between the privileged level discovered by Rosch et al 1976) on perceptual tasks and that discovered by Coley et al (1997) on the induction task.

Murphy & Wisniewski (1989) present further evidence that different taxonomic levels serve different functions. Specifically, superordinates may be used to conceptualize scenes or other types of schemas where interconceptual relations are important, whereas basic-level concepts may be used to conceptualize entities in isolation. (For a recent review of research on hierarchical category structure, see Murphy & Lassaline 1997.)

Another claim by Rosch et al (1976) that is under examination is the idea that the basic level is the level at which categories are first learned by children. Specifically, recent studies have raised the possibility that superordinate categories may be learned as early as, or earlier than, basic-level categories. For example, Mandler et al (1991) found that children 18 months old were able to distinguish between members of the superordinate categories of animals and vehicles, but they were not able to distinguish between members within each of these categories (such as dogs and rabbits, and cars and boats). Mandler et al argued from this finding that children acquire certain kinds of superordinate categories, which they call global categories, prior to basic-level categories.

Other evidence suggests that the categories that a child first acquires are not determined by their position within a taxonomic hierarchy but rather depend on the particular objects to which the child has been previously exposed. For example, infants 3–4 months old trained on domestic cats in a habituation paradigm dishabituate to members of contrasting basic-level categories (e.g. dogs, birds, tigers) but not to novel domestic cats. This suggests that during training, the infants formed a representation of the basic-level category "domestic cats" (Eimas & Quinn 1994, Eimas et al 1994). However, infants also appear to be facile at learning categories at superordinate levels. When infants 3–4 months old are trained on different members of the superordinate category "mammal" (e.g. dogs, cats, tigers, zebras), they dishabituate to nonmammal category members (birds, fish) but not to novel mammals (e.g. deer, beavers) (Behl-Chadha 1996). Apparently, the infants were able to form a representation of the superordinate category "mammal."

These studies suggest that children can form both basic-level and global concepts depending on the stimuli presented (see also Quinn & Johnson 1997.) Although these findings appear to be robust, there may be less unanimity with respect to their interpretation. A critical question concerns the criteria for the claim that a child has learned a concept. For example, is sensitivity to perceptual discontinuities that correspond to concepts equivalent to having a concept? (For one point of view on this issue, see Mandler 1997, Mandler & McDonough 1998.)

Overall, recent research tends to weaken the claim for a qualitative distinction between the different levels of a taxonomic hierarchy. The blurring of the distinction between levels undermines the notion that basic-level concepts are special kinds of concepts that reflect the structure of the world, independent of knowledge, expectations, goals, and experience.

Hierarchies Versus Paradigms

The previous discussion of levels is premised on categories being hierarchically organized. But social categories based on factors such as race, age, gender, and occupation (e.g. female teenager, Asian mail carrier) represent more of a cross-classification or paradigm than a taxonomy. Is there a notion of privilege for social categories, as there is for hierarchical categories? It appears that a key factor in social information processing is accessibility of categories (e.g. Smith & Zarate 1992, ER Smith et al 1996) and that some social categories may be accessed automatically (e.g. Bargh 1994, Devine 1989, Banaji et al 1993, Greenwald & Banaji 1995, Zarate & Smith 1990). Some intriguing evidence even suggests that the activation of one social category leads to the inhibition of competing social categories (Macrae et al 1995). Although the structural difference between paradigms and taxonomies is important, it is too early to tell if processing principles also differ between social categories and taxonomic categories, mainly because direct comparisons have not been done.

Ross & Murphy (1999) studied categories associated with foods and their consumption, a context that is interesting because it allows one to study relations between taxonomic categories (e.g. breads, meats, fruits) and script categories that cut across taxonomic categories (e.g. snack foods, dinner foods, junk foods). They report evidence that script categories are less accessible than are common taxonomic categories. Both types of categories were used in inductive reasoning, but their use varied with the type of inference involved. This work points to the fact that even hierarchically organized object categories may admit to other organizations.

Category Structure and the Brain

Studies of patients with selective cognitive impairments have often provided important clues to normal functioning. One intriguing observation concerns category-specific deficits, where patients may lose their ability to recognize and name category members in a particular domain of concepts. Perhaps the most studied domain difference has been living versus nonliving kinds. For example, Nelson (1946) reported a patient who was unable to recognize a telephone, a hat, or a car but could identify people and other living things (the opposite pattern is also observed and is more common).

These deficits raise the possibility that living and nonliving things are represented in anatomically and functionally distinct systems (Sartori & Job 1988). An alternative view (e.g. Warrington & Shallice 1984) is that these patterns of deficits can be accounted for by the fact that different kinds of information are needed to categorize different kinds of objects. For example, sensory information may be relatively more important for recognizing living kinds, and functional information more important for recognizing artifacts (for computational implementations of these ideas, see Farah & McClelland 1991, Devlin et al 1998). Although the weight of evidence appears to favor the kinds-of-information view (see Damasio et al 1996, Forde 1999, Forde & Humphreys 1999), the issue continues to be debated (for a strong defense of the domain-specificity view, see Caramazza & Shelton 1998).

Summary

Researchers are beginning to systematically explore a variety of structural principles according to which conceptual representations vary. There is fairly good support for the idea that nouns and verbs are different kinds of concepts, or at least that the distinction serves to organize an interesting body of research on linguistic and conceptual development. The lexical distinction between nouns and verbs appears to be mirrored in conceptual structure. Another factor that emerges across a number of candidates for kinds of concepts is the difference between those that are composed of clusters of features and those composed of relations. In the next section, we focus on processing-related differences, but given that processing affects structure, this can be seen as an addition to our list of structural distinctions.

CANDIDATES FOR KINDS OF CONCEPTS BASED ON PROCESSING

Common Taxonomic Versus Goal-Derived Categories

Barsalou (1983, 1985) pointed out that many categories are created in the service of goals and that these goal-derived categories may differ in important ways from object categories. Examples of goal-derived categories include "things to take out of your house in case of a fire" or "foods to eat when on a diet." Goal-derived categories may activate context-dependent properties of category members. For example, the fact that a basketball is round is a stable property that should be accessed independent of context, but the fact that basketballs float may only be accessed in contexts where a goal relies on its buoyancy. Barsalou's research also shows that members of goal-derived categories are not especially similar to one another and, thus, that they violate the correlational structure of the environment that basic-level categories are said to exploit. In addition, Barsalou has determined that the basis for typicality effects differs for goal-derived versus common taxonomic categories. Typicality or goodness of example is generally assumed to be based on similarity relationships—a good example of a category (e.g. robin for the category "bird") is similar to other category members and not similar to nonmembers, whereas an atypical example (e.g. penguin as a bird) shares few properties with category members and may be similar to nonmembers. Barsalou (1985) found that typicality for goal-derived categories was based on proximity to ideals rather than on central tendency. For instance, the best example of diet foods is not one that has the average number of categories for a diet food but one that meets the ideal of zero categories. In short, it appears that goals can create categories and that these categories are organized in terms of ideals.

Is this distinction between taxonomic and goal-derived categories fundamental? It is difficult to say. Barsalou notes that the repeated use of goal-derived categories (e.g. things to take on a camping trip for an experienced camper) may lead to them being well established in memory. Perhaps more surprising are recent observations that suggest that ideals play more of a role in organizing common taxonomic categories than previously had been suspected. Atran (1998) reports that for the Itzaj Maya of Guatemala, the best example of the category "bird" is the wild turkey, a distinctive bird that is culturally significant and prized for both its beauty and its meat. Lynch et al (1999) found that tree experts based judgments of tree typicality on the positive ideal of height and on the absence of undesirable characteristics or negative ideals—central tendency played at most a minor role. It may be that typicality is organized in terms of central tendency only for relative novices. Actually, Barsalou's original investigation (1985) found that although common taxonomic categories were most strongly based on central tendency, proximity to ideals made a reliable and independent contribution to goodness of example judgements. In short, common taxonomic and goal-derived categories may be more similar than is suggested by first appearance.

Social Information Processing and Individuation

One could make a case for the view that processing associated with social categories is different from the processing of object categories. For example, there is the intriguing observation by Wattenmaker (1995) that linear separability (separating categories by a weighted additive function of features) is important for social categories but not for object categories. More generally, people appear to be flexible in social information processing. Fiske et al (1987) proposed a continuum model whereby people may form impressions either by top-down, category-based processes or by bottom-up, data-driven processes. (For a parallel constraint satisfaction model of impression formation in which stereotypical and individuating information are processed simultaneously, see Kunda & Thagard 1996.) Factors such as the typicality of examples and the goals of the learner influence the relative prominence of these two processes. This general framework has held up well and serves to organize a great deal of research on social information processing (for a review, see Fiske et al 1999). It is not clear, however, whether there are corresponding processes that operate for nonsocial categories because this question has been relatively neglected. The only relevant study we know of (Barsalou et al 1998) did identify at least some conditions under which individuation of examples took place. The dearth of comparisons derives in part from the relative neglect of different kinds of processing associated with object categories.

Stereotypes, Subtypes, and Subgroups

Although people clearly rely on stereotypes based on categories such as race, gender, and age, increasing evidence suggests that people may be more likely to use more specific social categories in their daily interactions. For example, people appear to have and use several different subcategories for the elderly, such as grandmother-type and elder statesman (Brewer et al 1981).

Do these subcategories share properties with subordinate object categories? Some kinds of subcategories may operate similarly to subordinate object categories, but others may operate differently. Fiske (1998) argues that social subcategories can be divided into two different kinds based on the goals of a perceiver. When a perceiver is trying to understand why a few individuals differ from her stereotype of a group, she might form a subtype to explain their aberrant behavior (Hewstone et al 1994, Johnston et al 1994). For example, a person may form a subtype for black lawyers to explain why several black individuals she knows speak differently and live in a different part of town than her stereotype of blacks. Notably, forming a subtype allows one to maintain his or her current stereotypes.

Fiske (1998) points out that the amount of experience one has with a group also plays a role in whether a subtype is formed. When people have little experience with a group, they tend to perceive less variability among individuals, requiring subtypes to explain any aberrant behavior. With more knowledge about a group, however, people tend to perceive more variability among individuals, which in turn may lead them to form category subgroups. Subgroups consist of category members who are more similar to one another than category members of another subgroup. The key distinction between subgroups and subtypes is that subtypes are made up of a group of people who disconfirm the stereotype in some way, whereas subgroups are usually made up of people who are consistent with the stereotype but in a different way from another subgroup. For example, as Fiske (1998) notes, housewives and secretaries might both be consistent with the stereotype of female, but in different ways.

The most common examples of subordinate object categories (e.g. rocking chair, kitchen chair; song birds, birds of prey) seem to be more analogous to subgroups than subtypes, although there may be some examples of subtype-like object categories as well (e.g. birds that do not fly). A question that needs to be addressed is why subtypes appear more common for social categories than for object categories. (For an analysis of motivational processes aimed at preserving stereotypes, see Kunda 1990.)

Category Processing and the Brain

Process dissociations have often been used as markers of distinct systems, and recently this logic has been applied to categorization. Specifically, Knowlton & Squire (1993; see also Squire & Knowlton 1995) have reported dissociations between categorization and recognition in amnesic and normal individuals, which they interpreted as indicating that multiple memory systems underlie these two tasks. These findings pose challenges for categorization models that assume that categorization and recognition are mediated by a common system. This challenge has not gone unanswered. Nosofsky & Zaki (1998) showed that an exemplar model of categorization can account for the Knowlton & Squire (1993) dissociations, and a strong methodological critique has been made of the Squire & Knowlton (1995) study (Palmeri & Flanery 1999). No doubt the debate will continue.

Ashby et al (1998) offered a neuropsychological theory that assumes that category learning involves both an explicit verbal system and an implicit decision-bound learning system (see also Erickson & Kruschke 1998; for multi-strategy category learning models, see Nosofsky et al 1994). The Ashby et al model is promising in that it integrates neuropsychological and computational modeling, but it is premature to evaluate either its success or the illumination it might provide on kinds of categories.

Other Distinctions

We are necessarily limited in the scope and depth of our coverage; other reviewers would no doubt highlight other differences. One intriguing idea that should at least be mentioned is the proposition that categories are grounded by emotional responses and that stimuli that trigger the same emotion category are seen as similar and are categorized together (Niedenthal et al 1999). Another idea is that different kinds of categories may be represented in memory through different kinds of representational formats. For example, although object categories may be organized in memory in a spatial format, events may be organized in more of a temporal format (Barsalou 1999).

Summary

Our reading of the evidence is that the case for kinds of concepts based on processing is somewhat weaker than the case for kinds based on structure. In addition, the work on goal-derived categories serves to reinforce structural distinctions. It could also be said that we have imposed something of an artificial bound between structure and processing—the strongest case for distinct kinds will require computational models that make concrete assumptions about both structure and processing. We turn now to the third candidate for kinds of concepts, those based on content.

CANDIDATES FOR KINDS OF CONCEPTS BASED ON CONTENT: DOMAIN SPECIFICITY

A general trend in the cognitive sciences has been a shift from viewing human beings as general-purpose computational systems to seeing them as adaptive and adapted organisms whose computational mechanisms are specialized and contextualized to our particular environment (Tooby & Cosmides 1992). In this view, learning may be guided by certain skeletal principles, constraints, and (possibly innate) assumptions about the world (e.g. see Keil 1981, Kellman & Spelke 1983, Spelke 1990, Gelman 1990). In an important book, Carey (1985) developed a view of knowledge acquisition as built on framework theories that entail ontological commitments in the service of a causal understanding of real-world phenomena. Two domains can be distinguished from one another if they represent ontologically distinct entities and sets of phenomena. A criterion used to determine whether two concepts refer to ontologically distinct entities is that these concepts are embedded within different causal explanatory frameworks (Solomon et al 1996, Inagaki & Hatano 1993). These ontological commitments serve to organize knowledge into domains such as naïve physics (or mechanics), naïve psychology, or naïve biology (see Wellman & Gelman 1992; Spelke et al 1995; Keil 1992, 1994; Au 1994; Carey 1995; Hatano & Inagaki 1994; Johnson & Solomon 1997; Gopnik & Wellman 1994).

Researchers advocating domain specificity have suggested that concepts from different domains are qualitatively different. Although it is difficult to give a precise definition of domain (for a review, see Hirschfeld & Gelman 1994a), the notion of domain specificity has served to organize a great deal of research, especially in the area of conceptual development. For example, studies of infant perception and causal understanding suggest that many of the same principles underlie both adults' and children's concepts of objects (e.g. Baillargeon 1994, 1998; Spelke et al 1992). For example, common motion appears to be a key determinant of 4-month-old infants' notion of an object. The Gestalt principle of good continuation, however, plays no detectable role in the concepts of object for infants at that age.

One of the most contested domain distinctions, and one that has generated much research, is that between psychology and biology (e.g. Carey 1991; Johnson & Carey 1998; Coley 1995; Hatano & Inagaki 1994, 1996, 1999; Inagaki 1997; Inagaki & Hatano 1993, 1996; Kalish 1996, 1997; Gelman & Wellman 1991; Rosengren et al 1991; Gelman & Gottfried 1996; Springer 1992, 1995; Springer & Keil 1989,1991; Simons & Keil 1995; Keil 1995; Keil et al 1999; Au & Romo 1996, 1999). Carey (1985) argues that biological concepts like animal are initially understood in terms of folk psychology. Others (Keil 1989, Springer & Ruckel 1992) argue that young children do have biologically specific theories, albeit more impoverished than those of adults. Ultimately, the question breaks down to whether one accepts the criterion used to define "ontologically distinct entities." For example, Springer & Keil (1989) show that preschoolers think biological properties are more likely to be passed from parent to child than are social or psychological properties. They argue that this implies that the children have a biology-like inheritance theory. Solomon et al (1996) claim that preschoolers do not have a biological concept of inheritance because they do not have an adult-like understanding of the biological causal mechanism involved. But is there really a single adult understanding of biology? To address this question, one would need to examine adult understandings from a variety of samples both within and across cultures (Keil et al 1999).

What criteria should be used to define a particular domain? Domain-specificity theorists claim that domain-defining framework theories are qualitatively different from other theories in that "they allow and inspire the development of more specific theories but do so by defining the domain of inquiry in the first place" (Wellman & Gelman 1992:342). Do domains yield distinct kinds of concepts? Of necessity, our concepts refer to different kinds of things in the world. A fear is that domain-specificity theorists simply define kinds into existence by stating a priori that certain kinds of content (e.g. physics, biology, psychology) are important. In response, we point to the fact that claims about constraints or contents are always subject to skepticism and counter-attack in the form of both research and theory (e.g. for infant perception, see Cohen 1998, Cohen & Amsel 1999, Needham 1998, Needham & Baillargeon 1997, Xu & Carey 1996, Wilcox & Baillargeon 1998; for the role of conceptual knowledge in naming and linguistic development, see Jones & Smith 1993; Soja et al 1991, 1992; LB Smith et al 1996; Landau et al 1998; Landau 1996; Diesendruck et al 1999; Gelman & Eberling 1998). In short, claims about domains are anything but taken for granted.

It is one thing to stake out a domain and quite another to work out the details of how the associated competencies develop, how they are manifest in adults, and how cross-domain interactions emerge. Addressing these questions sets a research agenda that promises to increase our understanding of concept formation and use. For example, Gelman and her associates have been studying the linguistic cues in parental speech that are correlated with distinct ontological kinds (Gelman et al 1999, Gelman & Tardif 1998). In addition, adult folkbiological models and associated reasoning strategies may differ substantially both within and across cultures (Lopez et al 1997, Coley et al 1999) in a way that sharpens discussions of universal principles of biological understanding (see Atran 1998).

To briefly mention cross-domain interactions, one key idea and candidate for a universal principle in folkbiology has been psychological essentialism, the theory that people act as if biological kinds have a (hidden) essence that provides conceptual stability over changes in more superficial properties (e.g. Atran 1990, Hall 1998, Medin & Ortony 1989; see also Margolis 1998). But people also appear to essentialize social as well as biological categories (Rothbart & Taylor 1992, Miller & Prentice 1999, Hirschfeld 1996), which raises a number of further interesting questions. Does this essentialism bias arise independently in these two domains, does it start in one and transfer to the other, or is it possibly a bias that initially is highly general and only later on is restricted to biological and social kinds (see Atran 1995; Gelman et al 1994; Hirschfeld 1995; Gelman & Hirschfeld 1999; Kalish 1995; Gottfried et al 1999; Gelman 1999; Keil 1994; Braisby et al 1996; Malt 1994; Malt & Johnson 1992, 1998; Bloom 1998; Ghisilen 1999; Gelman & Diesendruck 1999; for a related discussion and debate, see Rips 1994)?

Summary

Although we remain agnostic or even skeptical about some of the claims arising from the domain-specificity framework, we believe that it is undeniable that this framework has been enormously helpful in organizing a large body of intriguing findings and observations, coupled with progress on the theoretical front.

CONCLUSIONS

One should not expect a definitive answer to the question of whether there are distinct kinds of concepts. As suggested earlier, this question has to be addressed relative to theories. What does seem clear, however, is that sensitivity to kinds of concepts is quite an effective research strategy. Far from creating insularity, questions about kinds are fostering richer theories of conceptual behavior.

Visit the Annual Reviews home page at www.AnnualReviews.org.

LITERATURE CITED

Ahn W. 1998. Why are different features central for natural kinds and artifacts?: the role of causal status in determining feature centrality. *Cognition* 69:135–78

Ahn W. 1999. Effect of causal structure on category construction. *Mem. Cogn.* In press

Anderson J. 1978. Arguments concerning representations for mental imagery. *Psychol. Rev.* 85:249–77

Ashby FG, Alfonso-Reese LA, Turken AU, Waldron EM. 1998. A neuropsychological theory of multiple systems in category learning. *Psychol. Rev.* 105:442–81

Atran S. 1990. *Cognitive Foundations of Natural History.* Cambridge, UK: Cambridge Univ. Press

Atran S. 1995. Causal constraints on categories and categorical constraints on biological reasoning across cultures. See Sperber et al 1995, pp. 205–33

Atran S. 1998. Folk biology and the anthropology of science: cognitive universals and cultural particulars. *Behav. Brain Sci.* 21:547–611

Atran S, Estin P, Coley JD, Medin DL. 1997. Generic species and basic levels: essence and appearance in folk biology. *J. Ethnobiol.* 17:22–45

Au TK. 1994. Developing an intuitive understanding of substance kinds. *Cogn. Psychol.* 27:71–111

Au TK, Dapretto M, Song Y. 1994. Input versus constraints: early word acquisition in Korean and English. *J. Mem. Lang.* 33:567–82

Au TK, Romo LF. 1996. Building a coherent conception of HIV transmission: a new approach to AIDS education. In *The Psychology of Learning and Motivation,* ed. D Medin, 35:193–241. San Diego: Academic

Au TK, Romo LF. 1999. Mechanical causality in children's "Folkbiology." See Medin & Atran 1999, pp. 355–401

Baillargeon R. 1994. How do infants learn about the physical world? *Curr. Dir. Psychol. Sci.* 3:133–40

Baillargeon R. 1998. Infants' understanding of the physical world. In *Advances in Psychological Science,* Vol. 2: *Biological and Cognitive Aspects,* ed. M Sabourin, F Craik, pp. 503–29. Hove, UK: Psychol. Press/Erlbaum

Banaji MR, Hardin C, Rothman AJ. 1993. Implicit stereotyping in person judgement. *J. Pers. Soc. Psychol.* 65:272–81

Bargh JA. 1994. The four horsemen of automaticity: awareness, intention, efficiency, and control in social cognition. In *Handbook of Social Cognition,* ed. RS Wyer, TK Srull, 1:1–40. Hillsdale, NJ: Erlbaum

Barr RA, Caplan LJ. 1987. Category representations and their implications for category structure. *Mem. Cogn.* 15:397–418

Barsalou LW. 1983. Ad hoc categories. *Mem. Cogn.* 11:211–27

Barsalou LW. 1985. Ideals, central tendency, and frequency of instantiation as determinants of graded structure of categories. *J. Exp. Psychol.: Learn. Mem. Cogn.* 11:629–54

Barsalou LW. 1991. Deriving categories to achieve goals. In *The Psychology of Learning and Motivation: Advances in Research and Theory,* ed. GH Bower, 27:1–64. San Diego: Academic

Barsalou LW. 1999. Perceptual symbol systems. *Behav. Brain Sci.* In press

Barsalou LW, Huttenlocher J, Lamberts K. 1998. Basing categorization on individuals and events. *Cogn. Psychol.* 36:203–72

Barton ME, Komatsu LK. 1989. Defining features of natural kinds and artifacts. *J. Psycholinguist. Res.* 18:433–47

Behl-Chadha G. 1996. Basic-level and superordinate-like categorical representations in early infancy. *Cognition* 60:105–41

Berlin B. 1992. *Ethnobiological Classification: Principles of Categorization of Plants and Animals in Traditional Societies.* Princeton, NJ: Princeton Univ. Press

Bloom L, Tinker E, Margulis C. 1993. The words children learn: evidence against a noun bias in early vocabularies. *Cogn. Dev.* 8:431–50

Bloom P. 1996. Intention, history, and artifact concepts. *Cognition* 60:1–29

Bloom P. 1998. Theories of artifact categorization. *Cognition* 66:87–93

Bowerman M. 1996. Learning how to structure space for language: a crosslinguistic perspective. In *Language and Space. Language, Speech, and Communication,* ed. P Bloom, MA Peterson, pp. 385–436. Cambridge, MA: MIT Press

Bowerman M, Levinson S, eds. 1999. *Language Acquisition and Conceptual Development.* Cambridge, UK: Cambridge Univ. Press. In press

Braisby N, Franks B, Hampton J. 1996. Essentialism, word use, and concepts. *Cognition* 59:247–74

Brewer MB, Dull V, Lui L. 1981. Perceptions of the elderly: stereotypes as prototypes. *J. Pers. Soc. Psychol.* 41:656–70

Brown R. 1958. *Words and Things.* New York: Free Press

Caplan LJ, Barr RA. 1991. The effects of feature necessity and extrinsicity on gradedness of category membership and class inclusion relations. *Br. J. Psychol.* 84:427–40

Caramazza A, Shelton JR. 1998. Domain-specific knowledge systems in the brain: the animate-inanimate distinction. *J. Cogn. Neurosci.* 10:1–34

Carey S. 1985. *Conceptual Change in Childhood.* Cambridge, MA: Bradford Books

Carey S. 1991. Knowledge acquisition: enrichment or conceptual change? In *The Epigenesis of Mind: Essays on Biology and Cognition,* ed. S Carey, R Gelman, pp. 257–91. Hillsdale, NJ: Erlbaum

Carey S. 1995. On the origins of causal understanding. In *Casual Understanding in Cognition and Culture,* ed. A Premack, pp. 268–308. New York: Oxford Univ. Press

Choi S, Bowerman M. 1991. Learning to express motion events in English and Korean: the influence of language-specific lexicalization patterns. *Cognition* 41:83–121

Choi S, Gopnik A. 1995. Early acquisition of verbs in Korean: a cross-linguistic study. *J. Child Lang.* 22:497–529

Cohen LB. 1998. An information processing approach to infant perception and cognition. In *Development of Sensory, Motor, and Cognitive Capacities in Early Infancy: From Sensation to Cognition,* ed. G Butterworth, F Simion, pp. 277–300. Sussex, UK: Taylor & Francis

Cohen LB, Amsel G. 1999. Precursors to infants' perception of the causality of a simple event. *Infant Behav. Dev.* In press

Coley JD. 1995. Emerging differentiation of folkbiology and folkpsychology: attributions of biological and psychological properties to living things. *Child Dev.* 66:1856–74

Coley JD, Medin DL, Atran S. 1997. Does rank have its privilege? Inductive inferences within folkbiological taxonomies. *Cognition* 64:73–112

Coley JD, Medin DL, Proffitt JB, Lynch E, Atran S. 1999. Inductive reasoning in folkbiological thought. See Medin & Atran 1999, pp. 205–32

Damasio H, Grabowski TJ, Tranel D, Hichwa RD, Damasio A. 1996. A neural basis for lexical retrieval. *Nature* 380:499–505

Devine PG. 1989. Stereotypes and prejudice: their automatic and controlled components. *J. Pers. Soc. Psychol.* 56:680–90

Devlin JT, Gonnerman LM, Andersen ES, Seidenberg MS. 1998. Category-specific semantic deficits in focal and widespread brain damage: a computational account. *J. Cogn. Neurosci.* 1:77–94

Diesendruck G, Gelman SA, Lebowitz K. 1999. Conceptual and linguistic biases in children's word learning. *Dev. Psychol.* In press

Eimas PD, Quinn PC. 1994. Studies on the formation of perceptual based basic-level categories in young infants. *Child Dev.* 65:903–17

Eimas PD, Quinn PC, Cowen P. 1994. Development of exclusivity in perceptually based categories of young infants. *J. Exp. Child Psychol.* 58:418–31

Erickson MA, Kruschke JK. 1998. Rules and exemplars in category learning. *J. Exp. Psychol.: Gen.* 127:107–40

Estes WK. 1994. *Classification and Cognition.* New York: Oxford Univ. Press

Farah MJ, McClelland JL. 1991. A computational model of semantic memory impairment: modality specificity and emergent category specificity. *J. Exp. Psychol.: Gen.* 120:339–57

Fiske ST. 1998. Stereotyping, prejudice, and discrimination. In *The Handbook of Social Psychology,* ed. DT Gilbert, ST Fiske, pp. 357–411. Boston, MA: McGraw-Hill

Fiske ST, Lin M, Neuberg SL. 1999. The continuum model: ten years later. In *Dual Process Theories in Social Psychology,* ed. S Chaiken, Y Trope, pp. 231–54. New York: Guilford

Fiske ST, Neuberg SL, Beattie AE, Milberg SJ. 1987. Category-based and attribute-based reactions to others: some informational conditions of stereotyping and individuating processes. *J. Exp. Soc. Psychol.* 23:399–427

Forde EME. 1999. Category specific recognition impairments. In *Case Studies in the Neuropsychology of Vision,* ed. GW Humphreys. Hove, UK: Psychology Press. In press

Forde EME, Humphreys GW. 1999. Category-specific recognition impairments: a review of important case studies and influential theories. *Aphasiology.* In press

Gauthier I, Tarr MJ. 1997. Orientation priming of novel shapes in the context of viewpoint-dependent recognition. *Perception* 26:51–73

Gelman R. 1990. Structural constraints on cognitive development: introduction. *Cogn. Sci.* 14:3–9

Gelman SA. 1988. The development of induction within natural kind and artifact categories. *Cogn. Psychol.* 20:65–95

Gelman SA. 1999. Developing a doctrine of natural kinds. *Psychol. Lang. Commun.* In press

Gelman SA, Coley JD, Gottfried GM. 1994. Essentialist beliefs in children: the acquisition of concepts and theories. See Hirschfeld & Gelman 1994b, pp. 341–67

Gelman SA, Coley JD, Rosengren K, Hartman E, Pappas T. 1999. Beyond labeling: the role of maternal input in the acquisition of richly-structured categories. *Monogr. Soc. Res. Child Dev.* In press

Gelman SA, Diesendruck G. 1999. What's in a concept? Context, variability, and psychological essentialism. In *Theoretical Perspectives in the Concept of Representation,* ed. IE Sigel. Hillsdale, NJ: Erlbaum. In press

Gelman SA, Ebeling KS. 1998. Shape and representational status in children's early naming. *Cognition* 66:35–47

Gelman SA, Gottfried G. 1996. Causal explanations of animate and inanimate motion. *Child Dev.* 67:1970–87

Gelman SA, Hirschfeld LA. 1999. How biological is essentialism? See Medin & Atran 1999, pp. 403–46

Gelman SA, Tardif TZ. 1998. Generic noun phrases in English and Mandarin: an examination of child-directed speech. *Cognition* 66:215–48

Gelman SA, Wellman HM. 1991. Insides and essences: early understandings of the non-obvious. *Cognition* 38:213–44

Gentner D. 1981. Some interesting differences between nouns and verbs. *Cogn. Brain Theory* 4:161–78

Gentner D. 1982. Why nouns are learned before verbs: linguistic relativity versus natural partitioning. In *Language Development.* Vol. 2: *Language, Thought and Culture,* ed. SA Kuczaj, pp. 301–34. Hillsdale, NJ: Erlbaum

Gentner D, Boroditsky L. 1999. Individuation, relativity and early word learning. See Bowerman & Levinson 1999

Gentner D, France IM. 1988. The verb mutability effect: studies of the combinatorial semantics of nouns and verbs. In *Lexical Ambiguity Resolution: Perspectives from Psycholinguistics, Neuropsychology, and Artificial Intelligence,* ed. SL Small, GW Cottrell, MK Tanenhaus, pp. 343–82. San Mateo, CA: Kaufmann

Ghiselen MT. 1999. Natural kinds and supra organismal individuals. See Medin & Atran 1999, pp. 447–60

Gibbs RW. 1997. How language reflects the embodied nature of creative cognition. See Ward et al 1997b, pp. 351–73

Goldstone RL. 1994a. The role of similarity in categorization: providing a groundwork. *Cognition* 52:125–57

Goldstone RL. 1994b. Influences of categorization on perceptual discrimination. *J. Exp. Psychol.: Gen.* 123:178–200

Goldstone RL. 1996. Isolated and interrelated concepts. *Mem. Cogn.* 24:608–28

Goldstone RL, Schyns PG, Medin DL, eds. 1997. *The Psychology of Learning and Motivation.* Vol. 36. San Diego, CA: Academic

Gopnik A, Wellman HM. 1994. The theory theory. See Hirschfeld & Gelman 1994b, pp. 257–93

Gottfried GM, Gelman SA, Schultz J. 1999. Children's understanding of the brain: from early essentialism to biological theory. *Cogn. Dev.* In press

Greenwald AG, Banaji MR. 1995. Implicit social cognition: attitudes, self-esteem, and stereotypes. *Psychol. Rev.* 102:4–27

Hahn U, Chater N. 1997. Concepts and similarity. See Lamberts & Shanks 1997, pp. 43–92

Hall DG. 1998. Continuity and the persistence of objects: when the whole is greater than the sum of the parts. *Cogn. Psychol.* 37:28–59

Hampton JA. 1997. Associative and similarity-based processes in categorization decisions. *Mem. Cogn.* 25:625–40

Hampton JA. 1998. Similarity-based categorization and fuzziness of natural categories. *Cognition* 65:137–65

Hatano G, Inagaki K. 1994. Young children's naive theory of biology. *Cognition* 50:171–88

Hatano G, Inagaki K. 1996. Cognitive and cultural factors in the acquisition of intuitive biology. In *The Handbook of Education and Human Development: New Models of Learning, Teaching and Schooling,* ed. DR Olson, N Torrance, pp. 683–708. Oxford, UK: Blackwell

Hatano G, Inagaki K. 1999. A developmental perspective on informal biology. See Medin & Atran 1999, pp. 321–54

Heit E. 1997. Knowledge and concept learning. See Lamberts & Shanks 1997, pp. 7–41

Hewstone M, Macrae CN, Griffiths R, Milne AB, Brown R. 1994. Cognitive models of stereotype change: measurement, development, and consequences of subtyping. *J. Exp. Soc. Psychol.* 30:505–26

Hirschfeld LA. 1995. Do children have a theory of race? *Cognition* 542:209–52

Hirschfeld LA. 1996. *Race in the Making: Cognition, Culture, and the Child's Construction of Human Kinds.* Cambridge, MA: MIT Press

Hirschfeld LA, Gelman SA. 1994a. Domain-specificity: an introduction. See Hirschfeld & Gelman 1994b, pp. 3–55

Hirschfeld LA, Gelman SA, eds. 1994b. *Mapping the Mind: Domain Specificity in Cognition and Culture.* Cambridge, UK: Cambridge Univ. Press

Inagaki, K. 1997. Emerging distinctions between naive biology and naive psychology. In *The Emergence of Core Domains of Thought: Children's Reasoning About Physical, Psychological, and Biological Phenomena. New Directions for Child Development,* ed. HM Wellman, K Inagaki, 75:27–44. San Francisco: Jossey-Bass

Inagaki K, Hatano G. 1993. Young children's understanding of the mind-body distinction. *Child Dev.* 64:1534–49

Inagaki K, Hatano G. 1996. Young children's recognition of commonalties between animals and plants. *Child Dev.* 67:2823–40

Johnson KE, Mervis CB. 1997. Effects of varying levels of expertise on the basic level of categorization. *J. Exp. Psychol.: Gen.* 126:248–77

Johnson KE, Mervis CB. 1998. Impact of intuitive theories on feature recruitment throughout the continuum of expertise. *Mem. Cogn.* 26:382–401

Johnson SC, Carey S. 1998. Knowledge enrichment and conceptual change in folkbiology: evidence from Williams syndrome. *Cogn. Psychol.* 37:156–200

Johnson SC, Solomon GEA. 1997. Why dogs have puppies and cats have kittens: the role of birth in young children's understanding of biological origins. *Child Dev.* 68:404–19

Johnston L, Hewstone M, Pendry L, Frankish C. 1994. Cognitive models of stereotype change: motivational and cognitive influences. *Eur. J. Soc. Psychol.* 24:581–92

Jolicoeur P, Gluck MA, Kosslyn SM. 1984. Pictures and names: making the connection. *Cogn. Psychol.* 16:243–75

Jones S, Smith L. 1993. The place of perception in children's concepts. *Cogn. Dev.* 8:113–39

Kalish CW. 1995. Essentialism and graded membership in animal and artifact categories. *Mem. Cogn.* 23:335–53

Kalish CW. 1996. Causes and symptoms in preschoolers' conceptions of illness. *Child Dev.* 67:1647–70

Kalish CW. 1997. Preschoolers' understanding of mental and bodily reactions to contamination: What you don't know can hurt you, but cannot sadden you. *Dev. Psychol.* 33:79–91

Keil FC. 1981. Children's thinking: What never develops? *Cognition* 10:159–66

Keil FC. 1983. On the emergence of semantic and conceptual distinctions. *J. Exp. Psychol.: Gen.* 112:357–85

Keil FC. 1989. *Concepts, Kinds, and Cognitive Development.* Cambridge, MA: MIT Press

Keil FC. 1992. The origins of an autonomous biology. In *Modularity and Constraints in Language and Cognition. The Minnesota Symp. Child Psychol.,* ed. MR Gunnar, M Maratsos, 25:103–37. Hillsdale, NJ: Erlbaum

Keil FC. 1994. The birth and nurturance of concepts by domains: the origins of concepts of living things. See Hirschfeld & Gelman 1994b, pp. 234–54

Keil FC. 1995. The growth of causal understandings of natural kinds. See Sperber et al 1995, pp. 234–67

Keil FC, Levin DT, Richman BA, Gutheil G. 1999. Mechanism and explanation in the development of biological thought: the case of disease. See Medin & Atran 1999, pp. 385–19

Kellman PJ, Spelke ES. 1983. Perception of partly occluded objects in infancy. *Cogn. Psychol.* 15:483–524

Kersten AW. 1998a. A division of labor between nouns and verbs in the representation of motion. *J. Exp. Psychol.: Gen.* 127:34–54

Kersten AW. 1998b. An examination of the distinction between nouns and verbs: associa-

tions with two different kinds of motion. *Mem. Cogn.* 26:1214–32

Kersten AW, Billman DO. 1995. The roles of motion and moving parts in noun and verb meanings. In *Proc. 17th Annu. Conf. Cogn. Sci. Soc.,* pp. 625–30. Hillsdale, NJ: Erlbaum

Knowlton BJ, Squire LR. 1993. The learning of categories: parallel brain systems for item memory and category knowledge. *Science* 262:1747–49

Komatsu LK. 1992. Recent views of conceptual structure. *Psychol. Bull.* 112:500–26

Kunda Z. 1990. The case for motivated reasoning. *Psychol. Bull.* 108:480–98

Kunda Z, Thagard P. 1996. Forming impressions from stereotypes, traits, and behaviors: a parallel-constraint-satisfaction theory. *Psychol. Rev.* 103:284–308

Lakoff G, Johnson M. 1980. The metaphorical structure of the human conceptual system. *Cogn. Sci.* 4:195–208

Lamberts K, Shanks DR, eds. 1997. *Knowledge, Concepts and Categories.* Cambridge, MA: MIT Press

Landau B. 1996. Multiple geometric representations of objects in languages and language learners. In *Language and Space. Language, Speech, and Communication,* ed. P Bloom, MA Peterson, pp. 317–63. Cambridge, MA: MIT Press

Landau B, Smith L, Jones S. 1998. Object shape, object function, and object name. *J. Mem. Lang.* 38:1–27

Levinson SC. 1994. Vision, shape, and linguistic description: Tzeltal body-part terminology and object description. *Linguistics* 33:791–855

Levinson SC. 1999. Covariation between spatial language and cognition and its implications for language learning. See Bowerman & Levinson 1999

Livingston KR, Andrews JK, Harnad S. 1998. Categorical perception effects induced by category learning. *J. Exp. Psychol.: Learn. Mem. Cogn.* 24:732–53

López A, Atran S, Coley JD, Medin DL. 1997. The tree of life: universal and cultural features of folkbiological taxonomies and inductions. *Cogn. Psychol.* 32:251–95

Lynch E, Coley JD, Medin DL. 1999. Tall is typical: central tendency, ideal dimensions and graded category structure among tree experts and novices. *Mem. Cogn.* In press

MacNamara J. 1972. Cognitive basis of language learning in infants. *Psychol. Rev.* 79:1–13

Macrae CN, Bodenhausen GV, Milne AB. 1995. The dissection of selection in person perception: inhibitory processes in social stereotyping. *J. Pers. Soc. Psychol.* 69:397–407

Malt BC. 1994. Water is not H_2O. *Cogn. Psychol.* 27:41–70

Malt BC. 1995. Category coherence in cross-cultural perspective. *Cogn. Psychol.* 29:85–148

Malt BC, Johnson EC. 1992. Do artifact concepts have cores? *J. Mem. Lang.* 31:195–217

Malt BC, Johnson EC. 1998. Artifact category membership and the intentional-historical theory. *Cognition* 66:79–85

Mandler JM. 1997. Development of categorization: perceptual and conceptual categories. In *Infant Development: Recent Advances,* ed. G Bremner, A Slater, G Butterworth, pp. 163–89. East Sussex, UK: Erlbaum/Psychol. Press

Mandler JM, Bauer PJ, McDonough L. 1991. Separating the sheep from the goats: differentiating global categories. *Cogn. Psychol.* 23:263–98

Mandler JM, McDonough L. 1998. Studies in inductive inference in infancy. *Cogn. Psychol.* 37:60–96

Margolis H. 1998. Tycho's illusion and human cognition. *Nature* 392:857

Markman AB, Wisniewski EJ. 1997. Similar and different: the differentiation of basic level categories. *J. Exp. Psychol.: Learn. Mem. Cogn.* 23:54–70

Markman EM. 1985. Why superordinate category terms can be mass nouns. *Cognition* 19:311–53

Markman EM, Horton MS, McLanahan AG. 1980. Classes and collections: principles of organization in the learning of hierarchical relations. *Cognition* 8:227–41

Medin DL, Atran S, eds. 1999. *Folkbiology.* Cambridge, MA: MIT Press

Medin DL, Coley JD. 1998. Concepts and categorization. In *Handbook of Perception and Cognition Perception and Cognition at Century's End: History, Philosophy, Theory,* ed. J Hochberg, JE Cutting, pp. 403–39. San Diego: Academic

Medin DL, Heit EJ. 1999. Categorization. In *Handbook of Cognition and Perception,* ed. D Rumelhart, B Martin, pp. 99–143. San Diego: Academic

Medin DL, Lynch EB, Coley JD, Atran S. 1997. Categorization and reasoning among tree experts: Do all roads lead to Rome? *Cogn. Psychol.* 32:49–96

Medin DL, Ortony A. 1989. Psychological essentialism. See Vosniadou & Ortony 1989, pp. 179–95

Miller DT, Prentice DA. 1999. Some consequences of a belief in group essence: the category divide hypothesis. In *Cultural Divides: Understanding and Resolving Group Conflict,* ed. DA Prentice, DT Miller. New York: Sage Found. In press

Morris MW, Murphy GL. 1990. Converging operations on a basic level in event taxonomies. *Mem. Cogn.* 18:407–18

Murphy GL. 1993. A rational of concepts. In *Categorization by Humans and Machines. The Psychology of Learning and Motivation: Advances in Research and Theory,* ed. GV Nakamura, DL Medin, 29:327–59. San Diego: Academic

Murphy GL, Lassaline ME. 1997. Hierarchical structure in concepts and the basic level of categorization. See Lamberts & Shanks 1997, pp. 93–131

Murphy GL, Wisniewski EJ. 1989. Categorizing objects in isolation and in scenes: what a superordinate is good for. *J. Exp. Psychol.: Learn. Mem. Cogn.* 15:572–86

Naigles L. 1990. Children use syntax to learn verb meaning. *J. Child Lang.* 17:357–74

Nakamura GV, Taraban R, Medin DL, eds. 1993. *The Psychology of Learning and Motivation: Categorization by Humans and*

Machines, Vol. 28. San Diego, CA: Academic

Needham A. 1998. Infants' use of featural information in the segregation of stationary objects. *Infant Behav. Dev.* 21:47–75

Needham A, Baillargeon R. 1997. Object segregation in 8-month-old infants. *Cognition* 62:121–49

Nelson JM. 1946. *Agnosia, Apraxia, Aphasia: Their Value in Cerebral Localization.* New York: Hoeben. 2nd ed.

Niedenthal PM, Halberstadt JB, Innes-Ker AH. 1999. Emotional response categorization. *Psychol. Rev.* In press

Norman GR, Brooks LR, Coblentz CL, Babcock CJ. 1992. The correlation of feature identification and category judgments in diagnostic radiology. *Mem. Cogn.* 20:344–55

Nosofsky RM, Palmeri TJ, McKinley SC. 1994. Rule-plus-exception model of classification learning. *Psychol. Rev.* 101:53–79

Nosofsky RM, Zaki S. 1998. Dissociations between categorization and recognition in amnesic and normal individuals: an exemplar-based interpretation. *Psychol. Sci.* 9:247–55

Palmer CF, Jones RK, Hennessy BL, Unze MG, Pick AD. 1989. How is a trumpet known? The "basic object level" concept and the perception of musical instruments. *Am. J. Psychol.* 102:17–37

Palmeri TJ, Flanery MA. 1999. Investigating the relationship between perceptual categorization and recognition memory through induced profound anmesia. *Proc. 21st Annu. Conf. Cogn. Sci. Soc.,* pp. 513–18. Hillsdale, NJ: Erlbaum

Pinker S. 1994. How could a child use verb syntax to learn verb semantics? *Lingua* 92:377–410

Quinn P, Johnson M. 1997. The emergence of a perceptual category representations in young infants: a connectionist analysis. *J. Exp. Child Psychol.* 66:236–63

Rifkin A. 1985. Evidence for a basic level in event taxonomies. *Mem. Cogn.* 13:538–56

Rips LJ. 1989. Similarity, typicality, and categorization. See Vosniadou & Ortony 1989, pp. 21–59

Rips LJ. 1994. *The Psychology of Proof: Deductive Reasoning in Human Thinking.* Cambridge, MA: MIT Press

Rips LJ, Conrad FG. 1989. Folk psychology of mental activities. *Psychol. Rev.* 96:187–207

Rips LJ, Estin PA. 1998. Components of objects and events. *J. Mem. Lang.* 39:309–30

Rosch E, Mervis CB. 1975. Family resemblances: studies in the internal structure of categories. *Cogn. Psychol.* 7:573–605

Rosch E, Mervis CB, Gray WD, Johnson DM, Boyes-Braem P. 1976. Basic objects in natural categories. *Cogn. Psychol.* 8:382–439

Rosengren K, Gelman SA, Kalish C, McCormick M. 1991. As time goes by: children's early understanding of biological growth. *Child Dev.* 62:1302–20

Ross B, Murphy GL. 1999. Food for thought: cross-classification and category organization in a complex real-world domain. *Cogn. Psychol.* In press

Rothbart M, Taylor M. 1992. Category labels and social reality: Do we view social categories as natural kinds? In *Language, Interaction and Social Cognition,* ed. GR Semin, K Fiedler, pp. 11–36. London: Sage

Sapir E. 1944. *Language.* New York: Harcourt Brace & World

Sartori G, Job R. 1988. The oyster with four legs: a neuropsychological study on the interaction of visual and semantic information. *Cogn. Neuropsychol.* 5:105–32

Schyns PG. 1998. Diagnostic recognition: task constraints, object information, and their interactions. *Cognition* 67:147–79

Schyns PG, Goldstone RL, Thilbaut J. 1998. The development of features in object concepts. *Behav. Brain Sci.* 21:1–54

Schyns PG, Rodet L. 1997. Categorization creates functional features. *J. Exp. Psychol.: Learn. Mem. Cogn.* 23:681–96

Simons DJ, Keil FC. 1995. An abstract to concrete shift in the development of biological thought: the insides story. *Cognition* 56:129–63

Sloman SA, Ahn W. 1999. Feature centrality: naming versus imagining. *Mem. Cogn.* In press

Sloman SA, Love BC, Ahn W. 1998. Feature centrality and conceptual coherence. *Cogn. Sci.* 22:189–228

Sloman SA, Rips LJ. 1998. Similarity as an explanatory construct. *Cognition* 65:87–101

Smith EE, Medin DL. 1981. *Categories and Concepts.* Cambridge, MA: Harvard Univ. Press

Smith EE, Shoben EJ, Rips LJ. 1974. Structure and process in semantic memory: a featural model for semantic decisions. *Psychol. Rev.* 81:214–41

Smith ER, Fazio RH, Cejka MA. 1996. Accessible attitudes influence categorization of multiply categorizable objects. *J. Pers. Soc. Psychol.* 71:888–98

Smith ER, Zarate MA. 1992. Exemplar-based model of social judgment. *Psychol. Rev.* 99:3–21

Smith LB, Jones SB, Landau B. 1996. Naming in young children: a dumb attentional mechanism? *Cognition* 60:143–71

Soja NN, Carey S, Spelke ES. 1991. Ontological categories guide young children's inductions of word meaning: object terms and substance terms. *Cognition* 38:179–211

Soja NN, Carey S, Spelke ES. 1992. Perception, ontology, and word meaning. *Cognition* 45:101–7

Solomon GEA, Johnson SC, Zaitchik D, Carey S. 1996. Like father, like son: young children's understanding of how and why offspring resemble their parents. *Child Dev.* 67:151–71

Solomon KO, Medin DL, Lynch E. 1999. Concepts do more than categorize. *Trends Cogn. Sci.* 3:99–104

Spelke ES. 1990. Principles of object perception. *Cogn. Sci.* 14:29–56

Spelke ES, Breinlinger K, Macomber J, Jacobson K. 1992. Origins of knowledge. *Psychol. Rev.* 99:605–32

Spelke ES, Phillips A, Woodward AL. 1995. Infants' knowledge of object motion and human action. See Sperber et al 1995, pp. 44–78

Sperber D, Premack D, Premack AJ, eds. 1995. *Casual Cognition: A Multidisciplinary Debate. Symposia of the Fyssen Foundation.* New York: Clarendon Press/Oxford Univ. Press

Springer K. 1992. Children's awareness of the biological implications of kinship. *Child Dev.* 63:950–59

Springer K. 1995. Acquiring a naive theory of kinship through inference. *Child Dev.* 66:547–58

Springer K, Keil FC. 1989. On the development of biologically specific beliefs: the case of inheritance. *Child Dev.* 60:637–48

Springer K, Keil FC. 1991. Early differentiation of causal mechanisms appropriate to biological and nonbiological kinds. *Child Dev.* 62:767–81

Springer K, Ruckel J. 1992. Early beliefs about the cause of illness: evidence against immanent justice. *Cogn. Dev.* 7:429–43

Squire LR, Knowlton BJ. 1995. Memory, hippocampus, and brain systems. In *The Cognitive Neurosciences,* ed. MS Gazzaniga, pp. 825–37. Cambridge, MA: MIT Press

Tanaka JM, Taylor M. 1991. Object categories and expertise: Is the basic level in the eye of the beholder? *Cogn. Psychol.* 23:457–82

Tardif TZ, Gelman SA, Xu F. 1999. Putting the 'noun bias' in context: a comparison of Mandarin and English. *Child Dev.* In press

Tomasello M. 1992. *First Verbs: A Case Study of Early Grammatical Development.* New York: Cambridge Univ. Press

Tooby J, Cosmides L. 1992. The psychological foundations of culture. In *The Adapted Mind,* ed. J Barkow, L Cosmides, J Tooby, pp. 19–136. Oxford, UK: Oxford Univ. Press

Van Mechelen I, Hampton J, Michalski RS, Theuns P, eds. 1993. *Categories and Concepts: Theoretical Views and Inductive Data Analysis.* London: Academic

Vosniadou S, Ortony A, eds. 1989. *Similarity and Analogical Reasoning.* New York: Cambridge Univ. Press

Ward TB, Smith SM, Vaid J. 1997a. Conceptual structures and processes in creative thought. See Ward et al 1997b, pp. 1–27

Ward TB, Smith SM, Vaid J, eds. 1997b. *Creative Thought: An Investigation of Conceptual Structures and Processes.* Washington, DC: Am. Psychol. Assoc.

Warrington EK, Shallice T. 1984. Category-specific semantic impairment. *Brain* 107:829–54

Wattenmaker WD. 1995. Knowledge structures and linear separability: integrating information in object and social categorization. *Cogn. Psychol.* 28:274–328

Waxman SR. 1998. Linking object categorization and naming: early expectations and the shaping role of language. In *The Psychology of Learning and Motivation,* ed. DL Medin, 38:249–91. San Diego: Academic

Waxman SR, Markow DB. 1995. Words as invitations to form categories: evidence from 12-month-old infants. *Cogn. Psychol.* 29:257–302

Waxman SR, Senghas A, Benveniste S. 1997. A cross-linguistic examination of the noun-category bias: its existence and specificity in French- and Spanish-speaking pre-school-aged children. *Cogn. Psychol.* 43:183–218

Wellman HM, Gelman SA. 1992. Cognitive development: foundational theories of core domains. *Annu. Rev. Psychol.* 62:1070–90

Wilcox T, Baillargeon R. 1998. Object individuation in infancy: the use of featural information in reasoning about occlusion events. *Cogn. Psychol.* 37:97–155

Wisniewski EJ, Imai M, Casey L. 1996. On the equivalence of superordinate concepts. *Cognition* 60:269–98

Woodward AL, Markman EM. 1997. Early word learning. In *Handbook of Child Psychology.* Vol. 2: *Cognition, Perception and Language,* ed. W Damon, D Kuhn, R Siegler, pp. 371–420. New York: Wiley

Xu F, Carey S. 1996. Infants' metaphysics: the case of numerical identity. *Cogn. Psychol.* 30:111–53

Zarate MA, Smith ER. 1990. Person categorization and stereotyping. *Soc. Cogn.* 8:161–85

Annu. Rev. Psychol. 2000. 51:149–169

New Perspectives and Evidence on Political Communication and Campaign Effects

Shanto Iyengar and Adam F. Simon

Departments of Communication and Political Science, Stanford University, Stanford, California 94305–2050; e-mail: siyengar@leland.stanford.edu
Department of Political Science, University of Washington, Box 353530 Seattle, Washington 98105–3530; e-mail: asimon@u.washington.edu

Key Words   politics, campaigns, elections, review

■ **Abstract**   We review recent empirical evidence that shows political campaigns are more potent than widely believed, focusing on the conceptual and methodological advances that have produced these findings. Conceptually, a broader definition of effects—that includes learning and agenda-control, as well as vote choice—characterizes contemporary research. This research also features two kinds of interactive models that are more complex than the traditional hypodermic (message-based) approach. The resonance model considers the relationship between message content and receivers' predispositions, while the strategic model highlights the interactions between competing messages. Finally, we attribute the emergence of stronger evidence in favor of campaign effects to the use of new methodologies including experimentation and content analysis, as well as the more sophisticated use of sample surveys.

CONTENTS

Introduction 150
Conceptual and Methodological Roadblocks 151
Bypassing the Roadblocks 154
   Multiple Effects 154
   Learning 154
   Agenda Control 156
New Theoretical Perspectives 158
   The Resonance Model 158
   The Strategic Model 161
Beyond Survey Methods 163
   Experimentation 163
   Content Analysis 164
Conclusion.. 165

0084–6570/00/0201–0149$12.00

INTRODUCTION

These are heady times for students of political communication. To an extent not previously seen, politicians' use—even manipulation—of the mass media to promote political objectives is now not only standard practice but in fact essential to survival. Recent months have seen political practitioners engage in high-stakes media games, including the apparently intentional leaking of secret grand jury proceedings to reporters, the national telecast of presidential deposition testimony, and the forced resignation of Speaker Newt Gingrich in the immediate aftermath of a failed advertising campaign. At the same time, the attention of political theorists, not to mention of other students of political processes, is turning toward the public arena. These scholars, especially those who style themselves "deliberative democrats," argue that the health of democratic societies depends on the quality of political communication.

Public relations and media advocacy have penetrated virtually all governmental arenas, even extending into the traditionally invisible judicial process. However, it is in the context of political campaigns that these strategies are most extensive and likely to have the greatest real-world impact. Electoral reforms and the influence of the broadcast media have gradually rendered grassroots organizations and party infrastructure less relevant, thereby transforming political campaigns from labor-intensive clashes between disciplined party organizations to capital-intensive, choreographed media spectacles. The ever-increasing level of investment made by the candidates is truly stunning—estimated at over one billion dollars for the 1998 cycle alone.

One question that defies analysis is why the participants in the political marketplace continue to invest at these levels when decades of academic research into the effects of media-based political campaigns purports to demonstrate that exposure to campaigns mainly reinforces voters' preexisting partisan loyalties. Political scientists still routinely attribute electoral outcomes to structural variables—most notably, the state of the national economy and the level of the incumbent president's popularity—giving short shrift to the specifics of day-to-day campaign events. These are generally viewed as having "minimal consequences" (see Abramowitz 1996, Gelman & King 1993, Campbell & Mann 1996). Aside from this straightforward empirical claim, there are deeper questions concerning the aggregate effect of this communication on our system of governance.

Our objective in this chapter is to demonstrate that the conventional academic wisdom is mistaken. Campaigns do matter and can be pivotal. In the current regime, the consequences of campaigns are far from minimal. Our view is that the conventional academic wisdom is compromised by conceptual, as well as methodological, inadequacies. Our approach is to identify the existing roadblocks—both conceptual and methodological—to a better understanding of the effects of campaigns, and then to describe cases where scholars have documented the significance of campaigns. We conclude by discussing how new theoretical and methodological vantage points can revive the study of modern, media-based campaigns while linking them to the central concerns of democratic theory.

CONCEPTUAL AND METHODOLOGICAL ROADBLOCKS

Perhaps the most fundamental obstacle to understanding the real-world role of political campaigns is a conceptual limitation on what effects are deemed relevant. Traditional research has looked mainly at persuasion (i.e. the effect of a campaign on voter preference). Within this definition, the law of minimal consequences has some validity because the evidence tends to suggest that exposure to campaigns merely activates voters' prevailing partisan sentiments (for a recent review of the evidence, see Iyengar & Petrocik 1998). Limiting the search to persuasion effects necessarily ignores a variety of other highly relevant campaign effects, the most significant of which may be turnout. Changes in the size and composition of the electorate can alter the distribution of candidate support. The single-minded quest for persuasion effects has also ignored the transmission of information, the setting of campaign agendas, and alteration of the criteria by which candidates are judged. Moreover, even if one were to accept persuasion as the benchmark for campaign effects, identifiable traces of persuasion are bound to be minimal because most campaigns feature offsetting messages. Observable effects should thus be limited to campaigns in which one candidate has a significant resource or skills advantage. This condition occurs rarely, if at all, in presidential campaigns, the races most often studied.

Turning to methodological issues, researchers have been (and still are) limited by their dependence on survey methods. The founding fathers of the field (including Lazarsfeld, Berelson, and their successors at the University of Michigan) capitalized on survey research. However, like all scientific techniques, survey methods have weaknesses, of which the logic of treating respondents' self-reported exposure to campaign communication as a reliable surrogate for actual exposure is particularly dubious. In this tradition, the standard test for campaign effects is the differences in voting behavior between respondents who self-report high or low levels of exposure to the campaign.

The assumption that self-reported exposure converges with actual exposure is problematic on several grounds. Most important, people have notoriously weak memories for past events, especially when the "event" in question concerns an encounter with a particular political campaign (e.g. see Bradburn et al 1987, Pierce & Lovrich 1982). In the experiments conducted by Ansolabehere & Iyengar (1998) concerning the effects of campaign advertising, for example, over 50% of the participants who were exposed to an advertisement were unable, some 30 minutes later, to recall having seen the advertisement. Respondents also make errors in the opposite direction, over-reporting exposure, possibly because these affirmative responses speak well of their civic virtue. In short, the considerable measurement error in self-reports necessarily attenuates estimates of the effects of political campaigns (see Bartels 1993, 1997).

Adding further confusion to the evaluation of campaigns, self-reported exposure to campaign messages is often endogenous to political attitudes, including candidate preference. That is, those who choose to tune in to the campaign differ systematically (in ways that matter to their vote choice) from those who do not. To take the case of campaign advertising, people who can recall an advertisement are likely to differ in innumerable ways from those who cannot. In addition to having better memories, the former are likely to be more interested in politics, more attached to the candidates, more informed about the issues, and more likely to vote. The presence of feedback between vote intention and recall of advertising seriously undermines claims about the impact of exposure to advertising on participation. The 1992 National Election Study survey shows that respondents who recalled a "negative" campaign advertisement were more likely to intend to vote (Wattenberg & Brians 1999) than those who did not, leading to the conclusion that negative campaigning stimulated turnout. But was it exposure to negative advertising that prompted turnout, or was the greater interest in campaigns among likely voters responsible for their higher level of recall? When recall of advertising in the same survey was treated as endogenous to vote intention and the effects reestimated using appropriate two-stage methods, the sign of the coefficient for recall was reversed: Those who recalled negative advertisements were less likely to intend to vote (see Ansolabehere et al 1999). Unfortunately, most survey-based analyses fail to disentangle the reciprocal effects of self-reported exposure to the campaign and partisan attitudes/behaviors.

Survey researchers have turned to longitudinal designs for monitoring the effects of campaigns. This obviates some of the problem with "one-shot" designs and is understandable in light of the fact that modern presidential campaigns are year-long affairs (if not longer). The Iowa caucuses occur in January, the primary season ends in June, the nominating conventions are held in August, and serious "campaigning" begins after Labor Day. In this environment, most voters are likely to arrive at their presidential candidate choice well before September 1 (see Iyengar & Petrocik 1998, Bartels 1997). Despite a handful of studies that track campaigns over their entire life span, most of the longitudinal evidence is derived from surveys administered after September 1. Not surprisingly, this evidence has hardly dented the conventional wisdom. Finkel's (1993) thorough analysis of the 1980 National Election Study panel survey typifies the literature: Precampaign attitudes and beliefs could account for almost 80% of the variance in vote choice. In addition, when attitudes did change during the campaign, they invariably did so in a manner consistent with voters' longstanding partisanship.

Aggregate-level longitudinal studies, by tracking changes in national sentiment, also provide estimates of campaign-based "interventions" in public opinion. Given the importance of contextual factors such as the state of the economy, these studies have the especially valuable ability to compare the effects of short-term campaign events on voter preference with the effects of the campaign context. Holbrook's (1994, 1995) studies of trends in candidate support during recent presidential campaigns finds that voters' initial attitudes are paramount. Although campaign events (such as conventions and debates) contribute modestly to net changes in the level of each candidate's support, the effects of the economy and the incumbent president's popularity dwarf these effects (Holbrook 1994, 1995).

Although aggregate time series and panels can generate estimates for the effects of specific events, like the cross-sectional survey, neither addresses the daily variation in campaign communication. In the case of panels, this would require that each respondent be matched to a particular set of media outlets for which the messages are coded for political content and slant—a virtual impossibility. In the case of the few time series studies that do incorporate measures of media content, because they necessarily aggregated to the national level, all voters in a given campaign are assumed to have received the identical message; the only variation in campaign communication occurs between elections. The problem with this aggregate approach, of course, is that it masks the considerable cross-sectional variation in the volume and tone of advertising. For example, Bill Clinton's advertisements were nowhere to be seen in California during the 1992 campaign simply because George Bush had conceded the state. Viewers in the "battleground" states, on the other hand, would have been exposed to much higher doses of advertising (see Shaw 1999, Goldstein 1999). This variation also lends itself to the study of campaign effects (discussed below). Even if one assumes that the candidates choose to campaign everywhere, they are hardly likely to deliver the same message to farmers in South Dakota as to high-technology workers in California. All this contemporaneous diversity in the content and tone of campaigning is ignored in aggregate time series methods (e.g. see Finkel & Geer 1998).

The survey design offering the greatest potential for the study of campaigns combines the panel and time series approaches. This is the repeated cross section in which interviews are carried out sufficiently frequently (on a daily basis) to yield reliable weekly or biweekly national samples that span the entire life of the campaign. This much more expensive design, dubbed the "rolling cross section," was implemented by the National Election Study group for the 1984 presidential campaign and featured a January-November time frame. More recently, a similar design was implemented to study the Canadian election of 1988 (Johnston et al 1992). Because respondents are interviewed more or less continuously from the earliest stages of the campaign, it is relatively easy to aggregate groups of respondents into precise temporal groupings corresponding to "pretest" and "posttest." Not surprisingly, the published reports based on these data sets (some of which are described in the next section) reveal several instances of campaigns that "work."

In summary, the study of campaigns has been impeded by a "drunkard's search" syndrome of sorts, in which researchers congregate at the persuasion "lamppost," and by methodological "correctness." By excluding effects other than persuasion and by remaining committed to the flawed logic of survey design, the state of campaign effects research is often mired in the uninteresting rut of minimal consequences.

BYPASSING THE ROADBLOCKS

Multiple Effects

The diminishing marginal returns from research into the persuasive effects of presidential and other campaigns has naturally encouraged scholars to explore other facets of voter behavior, none of which requires the abandonment of long-held partisan loyalties but which undermine the case for minimal consequences. Based on this research, we can add voter "learning"—the acquisition of information about the candidates and issues—and "agenda control"—the use of campaign rhetoric to set the public's political agenda—to the catalogue of robust campaign effects.

Learning

Because voters tend to be risk averse and are loathe to support unknown candidates (see Alvarez & Franklin 1994, Bartels 1986, Westlye 1991), information is a precious campaign commodity. Typically, to be known is to be liked, and campaigns generate large quantities of "knowns" on subjects as diverse as family background, military service, and the details of policy proposals. As campaigns have evolved into media affairs, however, the information-function of campaigns has fallen into disrepute. The candidates' media presentations, especially their reliance on the 30-second televised advertisement, appear superficial, and it is suspected that those superficial campaigns breed superficial voters.

The fears that campaigns are nonsubstantive are based on several observed regularities. The news media tend to treat the campaign first and foremost as a horse race. The candidates are entries, the consultants the jockeys, and the electorate the bettors (for evidence of the predominance of horse-race coverage, see Robinson & Sheehan 1980, Lichter 1988, Task Force on Campaign Reform 1998). Given this framework, daily events are accorded coverage in proportion to their bearing on the "odds." The Dukakis campaign's detailed position paper on education policy received no coverage in 1988, but the Massachusetts governor's brief answer (during a televised debate) to a question about the hypothetical rape of his wife attracted headlines and endless commentary about the candidate's diminishing chances to win.

In addition to the media's preoccupation with the political game, market-based journalism must keep voters interested (see Kalb 1998). What better enticement than sex, sleaze, and scandal? In recent months, Americans have become all too familiar with the details of President Clinton's relationship with Monica Lewinsky, as well as the moral quotient of some of his Republican antagonists (such as

Congressman Henry Hyde). In what might be called Gary Hart's Law, news about character drives out news about public policy (see Sabato 1991).

The final piece of evidence cited by critics of modern campaigns is that even when the candidates and the press do turn their attention to the issues or questions of performance and ideology, the rhetoric takes the form of truncated soundbites rather than well-developed and detailed arguments (Hallin 1994). Moreover, because of the strategic imperatives facing the candidates, these sound bites are generally ambiguous and one-sided (Simon 1997).

Given the rampant cynicism about the information value of media campaigns, it comes as a considerable surprise that campaign exposure—in the form of either paid advertising or news coverage—boosts citizens' political information. The evidence comes in several forms. In a series of experiments carried out by Ansolabehere & Iyengar (1995b, 1996), participants (ordinary citizens of southern California) exposed to a single 30-second advertisement were more able (by a significant margin) than those not exposed to the advertisement to identify the sponsoring candidate's position on the "target" issue. Exposure to issue-oriented advertising also increased the likelihood that participants would cite the candidates' positions on issues as a basis for supporting the sponsoring candidate. Brians & Wattenberg (1996) and Patterson & McClure (1976) obtained similar results using national and regional surveys, respectively. Both these studies found that exposure to campaign advertising (measured in terms of recall of campaign ads) contributed more to issue information than did exposure to newspaper or television coverage of the campaign. However, the question of which source looms larger in voter learning is still a matter of controversy.

There is evidence, contrary to the studies cited above, that news coverage has a greater informational value than do advertisements (Chaffee et al 1994, Zhao & Chaffee 1996). It is, however, difficult to compare results because Chaffee et al employed statewide and local surveys utilizing different designs and indicators. One possible explanation is that presidential advertisements [found to be informative by Ansolabehere & Iyengar (1995b, 1996), Brians & Wattenberg (1996), and Patterson & McClure (1976)] are more likely to feature issue appeals, whereas advertising in statewide or congressional races is more evenly divided between "issue" and "image" appeals (see West 1994, Kern 1989).

The conclusion that campaigns provide voters with substantive information is buttressed by survey designs that rely on alternative indicators of information. The most common framework examines the uncertainty in respondents' knowledge concerning candidates' positions. Franklin's (1991) study of US Senate campaigns in 1988 found that voters exposed to a senatorial campaign were more precise in their perceptions of their incumbent senator's position on a liberal-conservative scale. Alvarez (1997) confirmed this result for a broad array of knowledge and attitudes in analyses of contemporary presidential elections. Using more direct measures of voter knowledge, Bartels (1988) also found significant information gains during the presidential primaries of 1984. In a later study, he found that after accounting for measurement error, respondents in a panel survey absorbed substantial amounts of information in the 1980 presidential campaign (Bartels 1993). Several scholars have demonstrated that voters exposed to a "hard fought" race, which makes larger volumes of information available, are more engaged and cast better-informed votes (Kahn & Kenney 1997). Generally, as expected, respondents most attuned to the campaign tend to learn faster and end up knowing more.

Although the conclusion that voters gain substantive information from campaigns may seem counterintuitive given what we know about the behavior of reporters, it should come as no surprise that information about the candidates' personal traits and electoral chances is there for the taking. Popkin's work (1992, 1996) has shown that voters, like good psychologists, make inferences about the candidates' personalities based on what they see and read. The sight of President Ford attempting to eat an unshucked tamale sent Hispanic voters a clear signal about Ford's sensitivity to their concerns; the Republicans' unrelenting focus on impeachment in 1998 was understood by voters as a sign that Democrats were more concerned about education and social security. Popkin's work is especially revealing because it shows that voters' information about the candidates is highly sensitive to the ebb and flow of news. During the 1992 presidential campaign, Bill Clinton was saddled with the "Slick Willie" image in the aftermath of news coverage of his marital difficulties and avoidance of military service. Following his triumphant acceptance speech at the convention and the Clinton campaign's masterful use of "alternative" media outlets, voters began to learn about Clinton's economic plan and his track record on welfare reform and other issues. As information about Clinton's policy expertise came to the forefront, impressions of Clinton's character began to be couched more in terms of "the man from Hope" than "draft-dodger" (Popkin 1996). Finally, there is evidence that the barrage of horse-race stories raises the public's consciousness of the candidates' prospects (Mutz 1997). Experimental studies demonstrate that favorable poll results can lead to increased voter support (Brady 1984, Ansolabehere & Iyengar 1995a). Thus, especially during the initial rounds of primaries, communication can set campaign "bandwagons" in motion (for evidence from the 1984 primaries, see Bartels 1988).

In sum, campaigns are information-rich events. Contrary to the prevailing wisdom, the information they yield is multifaceted, encompassing the candidates' chances of winning, their personal traits and mannerisms, and most important, their policy and ideological bearings. Media campaigns may appear superficial, but they do educate citizens.

Agenda Control

If there is one issue on which political scientists and communications specialists agree, it is that ordinary citizens remain at arm's length from the world of public affairs. As casual observers of the political scene, individuals do not monitor the entire political universe; instead, they attend selectively to a few issues that appear important at the moment. Of course, the appearance of importance is very much a matter of what editors and journalists choose to cover or ignore. The more prominent some issue in the news media is, the higher the level of importance people accord that issue (see Iyengar & Kinder 1987, Baumgartner & Jones 1993, Rogers et al 1996, McCombs & Estrada 1996). Because candidates are the principal sources of news during campaigns, they are in an advantageous position to simultaneously influence the media and public agendas (see Semetko et al 1991, Dalton et al 1995)

The core implication of agenda setting for the study of campaign effects is that issues deemed significant by the electorate become the principal yardsticks for evaluating the candidates. This pattern (which is consistent with what the social psychologist calls priming) of weighting issues in accordance with their perceived salience has been documented in a series of experimental and nonexperimental studies (for a recent review of priming research, see Krosnick & Miller 1996). Iyengar & Kinder (1987), for instance, found that the news media's sudden preoccupation with the Iranian hostage issue in the closing days of the 1980 presidential campaign caused voters to think about the candidates' ability to control terrorism when choosing between Carter and Reagan. Naturally, this phenomenon proved disadvantageous to President Carter.

Given the number of considerations that the average voter employs, and the consequences of priming (which are tantamount to indirect persuasion in that altering the criteria can alter the choice), candidates are motivated to introduce and pursue issues on which they enjoy a comparative advantage. The candidate closer to the median voter on an issue like tax reform would want to address that topic, as opposed to discussing issues where he or she might be some distance away. Accordingly, a great deal of campaign rhetoric and strategy (discussed in the next section) is designed to capitalize on this "disequilibrium of tastes" (Riker 1980, Iyengar 1993). The rapid turn of events in the aftermath of the Gulf War bears this out. During the conflict, George Bush's popularity soared, but the end of the war prompted a shift in news coverage toward the economy. This cost President Bush dearly in the 1992 election because voters preferred Clinton by a wide margin on the economic dimension. Had the media continued to focus on security issues, we suspect that given Bush's edge on matters of national defense, the tables may have been turned (see Iyengar & Simon 1993, Krosnick & Brannon 1993).

The most compelling evidence of priming effects in the course of campaigns comes from the Canadian election study of 1988. The authors (Johnston et al 1992) show how the free trade agreement between Canada and the United States, as a result of the candidates' and parties' rhetorical posturing, came to the forefront of the public issue agenda. The candidates' efforts to position themselves on this issue had clear consequences; as the campaign progressed, voters' preferences on the issue increasingly came to influence their vote choice. Particularly striking in this case is the fact that a rival issue of equal, if not greater, relevance to Canadian politics—the Meech Lake Accords concerning Anglo-French relations—remained dormant. As the authors of this paradigmatic study conclude, "[r]hetoric, then, does play an important role in campaigns, but not just by persuading people. Rhetoric also plays a role—possibly its biggest role—by directing voters towards a specific agenda and considerations surrounding that agenda" (Johnston et al 1992:249).

As the examples of learning and agenda control suggest, campaigns can influence voters in more than one way. Confronted with partisan messages, most voters are loathe to roll over and declare their conversion; instead, they resist and rebut messages at odds with their prior preference. The acquisition of information and agenda control are more subtle forms of influence, often occurring "automatically" without the voters' awareness. Their net impact on the bottom line, however, can be just as electorally significant.

NEW THEORETICAL PERSPECTIVES

The earliest and still predominant way of thinking about the effects of campaigns has been to assume that candidates persuade voters simply by "injecting" them with appropriately designed messages. Assuming that the message is perfected (by carefully crafting the content and form of presentation), adequate exposure is all that candidates need; the more people they reach, the more likely they are to win. In this view, the all-absorbing task of the campaign consultant is to predict which variety of messages will be most advantageous and to design the campaign accordingly. In effect, campaigns are as good as the amount of resources and talents behind them.

The hypodermic model presumes that an effective campaign will be effective regardless of the office at stake, the political leanings of the electorate, the nature of the opposing candidate, or the circumstances of the moment. In contrast, more-promising theorizing about campaigns has emphasized the importance of the "environmental surrounding" and strategic logic of campaigns.

The Resonance Model

Although accepting the premise that voters can be persuaded, the distinctive premise of the "resonance" model is that campaign messages—whatever form they take—work their influence in concert with voters' prevailing predispositions and sentiments. In contrast to the hypodermic model, which assumes that effects are due entirely to particular characteristics of each campaign, the resonance model anticipates that effects are contingent on the degree of fit between campaign messages and prevailing attitudes. New information intermingles with the old, and depending on the chemistry, voters' choices will or will not be affected.

The most strongly charged ingredient of the electorate's prior predispositions is, of course, party identification. Acquired during early childhood, this psychological anchor is known to withstand the vicissitudes of events and the passage of time (Jennings & Niemi 1981, Niemi & Jennings 1991). Although much has been made of recent increases in the percentage of Americans who reject partisan labels, a good many of these "independents" are, in fact, closet partisans (Keith et al 1992). Party identification remains the salient feature of the American electoral landscape.

The importance of partisanship suggests an obvious prediction about the impact of campaigns. In hard-fought races, such as presidential contests, where virtually everyone is likely to encounter snippets of the campaign and where the contestants attain approximately the same decibel level, the principal impact of the campaign will be to push partisans into their respective corners. This prediction has been substantiated in nearly every systematic study of presidential elections since the 1940s: Campaigns reinforce voters' partisanship.

From the perspective of the resonance framework, the reinforcing effects of campaigns can be attributed to the interaction between the content of campaign messages (their slant) and voters' prior preferences. As part of one's attitudinal endowment, party identification is unlikely to be relinquished because of a particularly attractive advertisement or nasty news report. Messages that are counterattitudinal will be actively resisted, whereas those that are consonant are accepted (for the classic discussion of acceptance factors in the persuasion process, see McGuire 1968; for the McGuire model extended to political campaigns, see Zaller 1992, 1996). It is this interaction between message content and prior attitudes that governs the reinforcement or "polarization" effect. Because it may be expected that the most intense partisans are least in need of reinforcement, it is often the less-intense Democrats and Republicans who will move the most during campaigns. In the experimental studies of Ansolabehere & Iyengar (1995a), partisan reinforcement was significantly higher among partisans with lower levels of political interest. Similarly, Iyengar & Petrocik (1998) found that as campaigns progress, weak partisans and younger voters become especially likely to adopt candidate preferences in accord with their partisanship.

The relevance of voters' partisanship extends well beyond the mere fact that Democrats will be more responsive to the Democratic candidate and vice-versa. Not only do most voters acquire a partisan identity, they also acquire beliefs about the groups served by the political parties and, by inference, the issues or problems on which they will deliver (see Petrocik 1996). For example, the public generally considers Democrats more able than Republicans to deal with the problem of education. Conversely, Republicans are seen as better than Democrats on taxation. These stereotypes about the differential policy responsiveness of the parties influence campaign strategy (the nature and effects of this influence are articulated in the next section). Campaigns that take advantage of (or resonate with) voters' expectations are considered most likely to be effective; a Democrat should be better off using appeals that emphasize his or her intent to strengthen public education, whereas a Republican should promote his or her support for lower taxes.

Ansolabehere & Iyengar (1995a) have tested this hypothesis experimentally by examining differences in the persuasiveness of Democratic and Republican campaign advertisements on the issues of crime and unemployment. The identical message was attributed to either the Democratic or the Republican candidate for US Senate in California in 1992. Gains from advertising on unemployment tended to be greater for the Democrats than the Republicans, with the opposite pattern holding for crime, leading the researchers to suggest that candidates have differing degrees of credibility on issues they address. In a later study, Iyengar & Valentino (1998) asked experimental participants to rate campaign ads aired by presidential candidates Dole and Clinton during the 1996 presidential campaign. They found that Republicans were more likely to rate Dole's ads as informative (and less likely to rate them as misleading) when the ads addressed "Republican" issues (drug abuse, crime, and illegal immigration). Conversely, Democrats were more impressed by Clinton's ads when they dwelled on "Democratic" issues (social security, welfare reform, health care).

The logic of what Petrocik (1996) calls "issue ownership" extends easily to attributes of the candidates other than their party affiliation. Gender is an especially visible attribute, and the popular culture provides several cues about the traits of males and females, cues that are amply reinforced by the media's depiction of women candidates (Kahn 1994). Given the availability of gender stereotypes, it might be anticipated that issues would have differential effects across candidates. "Masculine" issues such as defense or crime will be especially persuasive as campaign material when the candidate is a male war hero, whereas child care and matters of educational policy will resonate well with voters' beliefs about a female candidate who happens to be a mother. Ansolabehere & Iyengar (1995a), Iyengar et al (1996), and Iyengar & Valentino (1999) designed experimental tests of the predictions of the resonance model as it applies to the issue appeals of male and female candidates. This research compared the success of US senatorial candidates Barbara Boxer and Dianne Feinstein with presidential candidate Bill Clinton when they broadcast an advertisement that dealt with sexual harassment. Advertising on gender-related issues yielded significant gains for Boxer and Feinstein but virtually no advantage for Clinton.

Given the presence of built-in differences between candidates in their ability to gain from specific issue appeals, these results suggest strongly that candidates should emphasize issues on which they enjoy comparatively favorable stereotypes. As we describe in the next section, this is an important ingredient of campaign strategy.

In sum, the insight offered by the resonance approach is that campaigns do not occur in vacuums but instead blend in with voters' partisan motives and attitudes. As such, the effects of interest are inherently interactive—either involving interactions between the content or source of campaign messages and voters' partisanship or involving higher-order interactions that also capture individual differences in exposure to campaign messages.

The Strategic Model

Another theoretical entry into political communication specifies campaign effects as interactions but focuses instead on the competition between message strategies. This perspective recognizes the ability of the strategic interactions between the competing candidates and between candidates and the press to create different campaign contexts. These new approaches are not exclusive but the emphasis differs; the resonance framework centers on the candidates' actions vis-a-vis the electorate, with little regard for the actions of their opponents. The strategic model, on the other hand, sees the effects of any particular message as conditioned by the effects of other "elite" actors; thus, in contrast to the hypodermic view, candidates and the media are interdependent rather than autonomous actors.

The recognition that campaigns are interdependent is especially important in the political world. Unlike commercial advertisers, candidates for public office feel freer to air advertisements that feature their opponents. Campaigns have increasingly turned to "attack advertising," in which candidates or their surrogates directly attack or seek to discredit their opponents (see Jamieson 1992, Ansolabehere & Iyengar 1995b, 1996). Although the impact of attack messages is thought to depend on certain qualities of the sponsoring candidates (such as their popularity), practitioners generally acknowledge that it is the response of the attacked candidate that is more important. Generally, the attacked candidate is thought to suffer if he or she fails to rebut or otherwise discredit the attack. According to Roger Ailes' "First Law" of political advertising, "[o]nce you get punched, you punch back" (Ansolabehere et al 1993).

The question of advertising tone (i.e. attack versus self-promotion) is only one element of the strategic equation. For example, presidential campaigns mask further interactions between campaign messages. The level of exposure to one candidate's campaign is bound to fluctuate with the comparative volume of that campaign as well as with individual differences in political engagement and involvement (see above). Some campaigns will be louder than others, and some people are more likely than others to tune in. The combination of these effects can produce profound shifts in certain circumstances. These systematic differences in exposure produce, in Zaller's (1996) terminology, "reception gaps" whereby some voters are likely to encounter a message from one candidate but not the other. These voters tend to be drawn disproportionately from the middle level of the political involvement strata; as a result, the relationship between involvement and support for the louder candidate is curvilinear (for several tests of this model involving House elections where incumbents are presumptively the louder candidates, see Zaller 1992).

Game theory provides an elementary yet powerful tool for studying campaign strategy. The theory of games provides insights into the joint behavior of instrumentally rational actors, which can lead to an enriched and often counterintuitive understanding of campaigns. Candidates for elective office would seem to meet the definition of rational actors. They have clearly defined interests (gaining election), and they invest considerable time, money, and effort in order to maximize their own "utility," namely their probability of winning. Moreover, they are less than certain about the motives and actions of their competitor(s); as such, campaigns can be modeled as simple games of incomplete information (Austen-Smith 1992, Banks 1990). For example, Simon (1997) developed a game-theoretic model that, consistent with issue ownership, predicts the absence of dialogue. If, in any campaign, there is a range of themes on which communication can occur and candidates choose to discuss only the themes that will maximize their vote share, then candidates will never address the same topic. Moreover, experimental techniques can be used to estimate game-theoretic payoffs, which yields a potent combination for research.

A study of the 1994 California gubernatorial race bears out this model and result. In this campaign, incumbent governor Pete Wilson exploited challenger Kathleen Brown's attempt to dialogue. Using the model as a guide, the options available to each candidate whenever he or she made a strategic decision concerning communication can be experimentally reconstructed. This reconstruction explains the candidates' behavior as well as Wilson's eventual victory. Four scenarios (experimental conditions) are required to fully capture this logic with respect to the issue of crime, of which three were counterfactual and one was actually observed. For example, under one scenario, neither candidate advertised. In this, the control condition, the estimate of the game-theoretic payoff indicated Brown would have won by 12%, roughly the skew in the partisanship of Californians. Three other conditions estimate the joint payoffs of the candidates' strategic choices. When participants were exposed to only a Wilson ad on crime, he won by 13% whereas when he showed a crime ad and she responded by talking about the economy, the contest ended in a statistical dead heat. In the final condition, both candidates discussed crime, and Wilson won by 12%, roughly the actual outcome of the election. These results have been corroborated with extant survey data (Simon 1997).

In structuring an advertising campaign, a candidate must anticipate not only his or her opponent's probable strategy but also the evolving behavior of the news media. In the aftermath of the 1988 presidential campaign, reporters have shown a penchant for examining campaign advertisements. In 1992, all major news outlets regularly offered "ad watch" reports that scrutinized particular campaign advertisements for accuracy and fairness. The intent behind this new genre of campaign journalism is, of course, to deter candidates from using false, distorted, or exaggerated claims. However, this form of news coverage also has the potential to provide the candidates with considerable free exposure by recirculating the campaign message to a larger audience. Some studies of ad watch reports have concluded that they actually have the effect of strengthening the impact of the scrutinized advertisement; others have shown that ad watch reporting works as intended (for a review of the evidence, see Task Force on Campaign Reform 1998).

The emergence of ad watch journalism provides candidates with incentives to design advertisements that are especially likely to attract news coverage. By making their advertisements newsworthy, candidates obtain additional (and free) exposure on subjects of their choosing. In 1996, the Republican National Committee produced an advertisement criticizing President Clinton for attempting to use his status as Commander-in-Chief of the US military to evade prosecution on sexual harassment charges. This controversial attack attracted front-page and primetime coverage for several days, but not once did it air as an advertisement.

In sum, interactions define campaign effects. At one level there is the interaction between candidates and a voter, at another there is the interaction between candidates, and finally there is the interaction between the candidates and the press. The deeper one looks, the more voting behavior seems a complex function of the volume/intensity of the contestants' appeals, voters' partisan preferences, and voters' level of exposure to the campaign. From the perspective of the candidate, accordingly, the goal is to design advertisements that simultaneously fit the voters' expectations, counter the opponent's strategy, and also succeed in attracting extensive news coverage. The clear implication of the resonance and strategic models are that efforts to study campaigns as "main effects" (for example, by simply regressing media exposure indicators against attitude change) are doomed to fail.

BEYOND SURVEY METHODS

Experimentation

As outlined above, the field's commitment to survey research has impeded researchers' ability to detect the traces of campaigns in public opinion. The scientific benefits of experimental design are well known, and there is no need to reiterate the standard argument here (for a recent discussion, see Ansolabehere & Iyengar 1995b). A 30-second advertisement is a concatenated sequence of images and text. What was it that moved viewers in the infamous "revolving door" advertisement of 1988? Was it, as is widely alleged, Mr. Horton's race? Or was it the violent and brutal nature of his behavior, the fact that he was a convict, the race of his victim, or what? Modern, digital-based techniques of audiovisual editing make it possible to zero in on the explanation, whether text based or in the form of audio or visual cues. In the case of the Horton advertisement, for instance, we might construct identical facial composites of Mr. Horton but vary his skin color so as to estimate the effects of race. Alternatively, we might present the convict's face with and without a beard. In short, it is possible to dissect a message into core visual components and input these components into experimental manipulations.

Nevertheless, experimentation has its limits. Most experiments are administered on "captive" populations—college students who must participate in order to gain course credit. Hovland's (1959) warning that college sophomores are not comparable to "real people" is especially apt for the field of political communication, given the well-known gap in political participation between the young and the old. Experiments also feature a somewhat sterile, laboratory-like environment that bears little resemblance to what William James (cited in Lippmann 1922:54) called the "blooming, buzzing confusion" of election campaigns. It is true that experiments can be made more realistic (by resorting to experimental procedures and settings that closely reflect the typical citizen's media experiences and by administering the experiments during ongoing campaigns). However, no matter how realistic their designs, experimenters must strive to replicate their results using alternative sources of evidence. Content analysis merged with surveys provides one such opportunity.

Content Analysis

Traditionally, content analysis has been used as a descriptive tool to identify characteristics of messages. This descriptive function often enables researchers to identify the relevant experimental manipulations. In the past, this process was sufficiently labor intensive to deter most researchers. Attempts to increase the rate of return by using computers to interpret and categorize language have yet to bear fruit. Nonetheless, technological developments have introduced dramatic economies of scale. These developments will accelerate the ability to simultaneously identify the distribution of campaign messages and incorporate these messages into experimental manipulations.

Until recently, researchers attempting to analyze the content of news coverage had to either subscribe to a representative set of newspapers from across the country or rely on one or two prestige outlets. Either method required vast amounts of labor, storage, and organization. The process was tedious, expensive, and subject to considerable human error. Today, most newspapers can be accessed through electronic databases offering full-text retrieval of articles that can be digitally searched and transferred to digital storage in a matter of minutes. Online services, such as Nexis and Westlaw, include major newspapers as far back as 1980. By using all the electronic archives available, contemporary research has access to virtually every newspaper published in the United States. What would take months to collect and compile can be accomplished in a week in a format already suitable for analysis. For instance, for research on candidate strategy in US Senate campaigns between 1988 and 1992, we compiled over 14,000 newspaper articles bearing on 50 races. The raw data set was constructed within a period of 6 weeks (for details, see Simon & Iyengar 1996).

Using this approach, experimental findings can be replicated with relative ease. One of the more consistent results from experimental studies is that exposure to negative (rather than positive) advertising reduces voter turnout (see Ansolabehere & Iyengar 1995a, Houston & Roskos-Ewoldsen 1998, Houston et al 1999). This result has been replicated by analyzing the content of newspaper coverage of all 34 US Senate campaigns in 1992. Based on the news reports of the candidates' advertising, the races were classified as either positive or negative in tone. The content-based measure of advertising tone was then used to predict voter turnout in the various senate elections (see Ansolabehere et al 1999).

CONCLUSION

As suggested in this review, research has begun to take a toll on the long-dominant minimalist view of campaigns. A major stimulus to this progression has been the increasing volume of traffic between political science, communications, and allied disciplines. The work of the eminent social psychologists Carl Hovland and William McGuire has served as an invaluable beacon for the current generation of campaign researchers. Calls by Hovland (1959) for methodological pluralism led gradually to the current flourishing of experimental and quasi-experimental work, which, as shown, provides the most unequivocal evidence of campaign effects. McGuire's (1968) theorizing about the exposure-acceptance matrix has been no less fertile, contributing to the current interest in interactive specifications of campaign effects.

We may anticipate further growth in campaign research from exchanges on other cross-disciplinary fronts, particularly the synthesizing of empirical work on campaign effects with rational-choice, game-theoretic models of communication. These models provide a well-developed set of analytic and mathematical tools from which to derive testable propositions. Game theory, with its emphasis on strategic interactions and the dependency of outcomes on individual choices, would seem especially appropriate to the study of campaign strategy and decision making.

Movements elsewhere in political science warrant further optimism. Many scholars have claimed that public deliberation is a vital and beneficial feature of democracy (Mansbridge 1980, Cohen 1989, Benhabib 1994, Gutmann & Thompson 1996). Their logic builds from John Stuart Mill's (1975) notion of a marketplace of ideas; put simply, free speech makes for better collective political decisions. Fishkin (1997) presents perhaps the clearest statement, arguing that the legitimacy of democratic government depends on the quality of public deliberation. Thus, theorists routinely call for a revitalized public sphere featuring vigorous debate. Empirical research into political communication stands ready to aid in answering this call through increased understanding of deliberative processes.

In sum, the study of campaign effects stands poised to make significant theoretical and methodological advances. As ongoing interdisciplinary efforts mature, we may expect an outpouring of evidence that campaigns contribute to the selection of political leaders and the formulation of public policy.

Visit the Annual Reviews home page at www.AnnualReviews.org.

LITERATURE CITED

Abramowitz AI. 1996. Bill and Al's excellent adventure: forecasting the 1996 presidential elections. *Am. Polit. Q.* 24:434–43

Alvarez RM. 1997. *Information and Elections.* Ann Arbor: Univ. Mich. Press

Alvarez RM, Franklin CH. 1994. Uncertainty and political perceptions. *J. Polit.* 56:671–88

Ansolabehere S, Behr R, Iyengar S. 1993. *The Media Game: American Politics in the Television Age.* New York: Macmillan

Ansolabehere S, Iyengar S. 1995a. Of horseshoes and horse races: experimental studies of the impact of poll results on electoral behavior. *Polit. Commun.* 5:413–29

Ansolabehere S, Iyengar S. 1995b. Going Negative: how Political Advertisements Shrink and Polarize the Electorate. New York: Free Press

Ansolabehere S, Iyengar S. 1996. The craft of political advertising: a progress report. See Mutz et al 1996, pp. 1–24

Ansolabehere S, Iyengar S. 1998. Messages forgotten: misreporting in surveys and the bias toward minimal effects. Dept. Polit. Sci., unpublished paper

Ansolabehere S, Iyengar S, Simon A. 1999. Replicating experiments using aggregate and survey data: the case of negative advertising and turnout. Unpublished manuscript.

Austen-Smith D. 1992. Strategic models of talk in political decision making. *Int. Polit. Sci. Rev.* 3:45–58

Banks J. 1990. A model of electoral competition with incomplete information. *J. Econ. Theory* 50:309–25

Bartels LM. 1986. Issue voting under uncertainty. *Am. J. Polit. Sci.* 30:709–28

Bartels LM. 1988. *Presidential Primaries and the Dynamics of Public Choice.* Princeton, NJ: Princeton Univ. Press

Bartels LM. 1993. Messages received: the political impact of media exposure. *Am. Polit. Sci. Rev.* 87:267–85

Bartels LM. 1997. Three virtues of panel data for the analysis of campaign effects. Unpublished manuscript

Baumgartner FR, Jones BD. 1993. *Agendas and Instability in American Politics.* Chicago: Univ. Chicago Press

Benhabib S. 1994. Deliberative rationality and models of democratic legitimacy. *Constellations* 1:26–52

Bradburn NM, Rips LJ, Shevell SK. 1987. Answering autobiographical questions: the impact of memory and inference in surveys. *Science* 236:157–61

Brady HE. 1984. *Chances, utilities, and voting in presidential primaries.* Presented at Annu. Meet. Public Choice Soc., San Francisco

Brians CL, Wattenberg MP. 1996. Campaign issue knowledge and salience: comparing reception from TV commercials, TV news, and newspapers. *Am. J. Polit. Sci.* 40:305–24

Campbell JE, Mann TE. 1996. Forecasting the presidential election: What can we learn from them models? *Brook. Rev.* 14:26–32

Chaffee SH, Zhao X, Leshner G. 1994. Political knowledge and the campaign media of 1992. *Commun. Res.* 21:305–24

Cohen J. 1989. Deliberation and democratic legitimacy. In *The Good Polity: Normative Analysis of the State,* ed. A Hamlin, P Pettit, pp. 17–34. Oxford, UK: Blackwell

Dalton RJ, Beck PA, Huckfeldt R, Koetzle W. 1995. *Agenda-setting in the 1992 campaign: the flow of campaign information.* Presented at Annu. Meet. Midwest Polit. Sci. Assoc, Chicago

Finkel SE. 1993. Reexamining the 'minimal effects' model in recent presidential campaigns. *J. Polit.* 55:1–21

Finkel SE, Geer JG. 1998. A spot check: casting doubt on the demobilizing effect of attack advertising. *Am. J. Polit. Sci.* 42:573–96

Fishkin J. 1997. *The Voice of the People.* New Haven, CT: Yale Univ. Press

Franklin CH. 1991. Eschewing obfuscation? Campaigns and the perception of U.S. senate incumbents. *Am. Polit. Sci. Rev.* 85:1193–214

Gelman A, King G. 1993. Why are American presidential election campaign polls so variable when votes are so predictable? *Br. J. Polit. Sci.* 23:409–54

Goldstein K. 1999. Measuring the effects of spot advertising on vote choice in the 1996 presidential election. Unpublished manuscript

Gutmann A, Thompson D. 1996. *Democracy and Disagreement.* Cambridge, MA: Belknap

Hallin D. 1994. *We Keep America on Top of the World: Television Journalism and the Public Sphere.* London: Routledge

Holbrook TM. 1994. Campaigns, national conditions, and U.S. presidential elections. *Am. J. Polit. Sci.* 38:973–98

Holbrook TM. 1995. *Do Campaigns Matter?* Thousand Oaks, CA: Sage

Houston DA, Doan K, Roskos-Ewoldsen DR. 1999. Negative political advertising and choice conflict. *J. Exp. Psychol: Appl.* 5:3–16

Houston DA, Roskos-Ewoldsen DR. 1998. Cancellation and focus model of choice and preference for political candidates. *Basic Appl. Soc. Psychol.* 20:305–12

Hovland C. 1959. Reconciling conflicting results derived from experimental and survey studies of attitude change. *Am. Psychol.* 14:8–17

Iyengar S. 1993. Agenda-setting and beyond: television news and the strength of political issues. In *Agenda Formation,* ed. W Riker, pp. 1–27. Ann Arbor: Univ. Mich. Press

Iyengar S, Kinder DR. 1987. *News That Matters: Television and American Opinion.* Chicago: Univ. Chicago Press

Iyengar S, Petrocik JR. 1998. *Basic rule voting: the impact of campaigns on party and approval based voting.* Presented at Conf. Polit. Advert. Elect. Camp., American Univ., Washington, DC

Iyengar S, Reeves R, eds. 1996. *Do the Media Govern?* Thousand Oaks, CA: Sage

Iyengar S, Simon AF. 1993. News coverage of the Gulf War and public opinion: a study of agenda-setting, priming, and framing. *Commun. Res.* 20:365–83

Iyengar S, Valentino N. 1999. Who says what: source credibility as a mediator of campaign advertising. In *Elements of Reason,* ed. A Lupia, M McCubbins, S Popkin. In press. New York: Cambridge Univ. Press

Iyengar S, Valentino N, Simon AF, Ansolabehere S. 1996. To be or not to be: campaigning as a woman. In *Women, Media and Politics,* ed. P Norris, pp. 77–98. Cambridge, MA: Harvard Univ. Press.

Jamieson KH. 1992. *Dirty Politics.* New York: Oxford Univ. Press

Jennings MK, Niemi RG. 1981. *Generations and Politics: A Panel Study of Young Adults and Their Parents.* Princeton, NJ: Princeton Univ. Press

Johnston R, Blais A, Brady HE, Cret J. 1992. *Letting the People Decide: Dynamics of a Canadian Election.* Stanford, CA: Stanford Univ. Press

Kahn KF. 1994. Does gender make a difference? An experimental examination of sex stereotypes and press patterns in statewide campaigns. *Am. J. Polit. Sci.* 38:162–95

Kahn KF, Kenney PJ. 1997. A model of candidate evaluations in senate elections: the impact of campaign intensity. *J. Polit.* 59:1173–206

Kalb M. 1998. *The Rise of the New News: A Case Study of Two Root Causes of the Modern Scandal Coverage.* Washington, DC: John F. Kennedy Sch. Gov.

Keith BE, Magleby DB, Nelson CJ, Orr E, Westlye MC, Wolfinger RE. 1992. *The Myth of the Independent Voter.* Berkeley, CA: Univ. Calif. Press

Kern M. 1989. *Thirty-Second Politics: Political Advertising in the 1980s.* New York: Praeger

Krosnick JA, Brannon LA. 1993. The impact of the Gulf War on the ingredients of presidential evaluations: multidimensional effects of political involvement. *Am. Polit. Sci. Rev.* 87:963–78

Krosnick JA, Miller JM. 1996. The anatomy of news media priming. See Iyengar & Reeves 1996, pp. 258–75

Lichter SR. 1988. *The Video Campaign: Network Coverage of the 1988 Presidential Primaries.* Washington, DC: Am. Enterprise Inst.

Lippmann W. 1922. *Public Opinion.* New York: Free Press

Mansbridge J. 1980. *Beyond Adversary Democracy.* New York: Basic Books

McCombs MC, Estrada G. 1996. The news media and the pictures in our heads. See Iyengar & Reeves 1996, pp. 237–47

McGuire WJ. 1968. Personality and susceptibility to social influence. In *Handbook of Personality Theory and Research,* ed. EF Borgatta, WW Lambert, pp. 1130–87. Chicago: Rand McNally

Mill JS. 1975. *On Liberty.* New York: Norton

Mutz D, Sniderman P, Brody R, eds. 1996. *Political Persuasion and Attitude Change.* Ann Arbor: Univ. Mich. Press

Mutz DC. 1997. Mechanisms of momentum: Does thinking make it so? *J. Polit.* 59:104–24

Niemi RG, Jennings MK. 1991. Issues and inheritance in the formation of party identification. *Am. J. Polit. Sci.* 35:970–89

Patterson TE, McClure RD. 1976. *The Unseeing Eye: The Myth of Television Power in National Elections.* New York: Putnam

Petrocik JR. 1996. Issue ownership in presidential elections with a 1980 case study. *Am. J. Polit. Sci.* 40:825–50

Pierce JC, Lovrich NP. 1982. Survey measurement of political participation. *Soc. Sci. Q.* 63:164–71

Popkin SL. 1992. *The Reasoning Voter.* Chicago: Univ. Chicago Press

Popkin SL. 1996. Voter learning in the 1992 presidential election. See Iyengar & Reeves 1996, pp. 171–80

Riker WH. 1980. Implications from the disequilibrium of majority rule for the study of institutions. *Am. Polit. Sci. Rev.* 74:432–46

Robinson M, Sheehan M. 1980. *Over the Wire and on TV.* New York: Sage Found.

Rogers EM, Hart WB, Dearing JW. 1996. A paradigmatic history of agenda-setting research. See Iyengar & Reeves 1996, pp. 225–36

Sabato L. 1991. *Feeding Frenzy: How Attack Journalism Has Transformed American Politics.* New York: Free Press

Semetko H, Blumler JG, Gurevitch M, Weaver DH. 1991. *The Formation of Campaign Agendas: A Comparative Analysis of Party and Media Roles in Recent U.S. and British Election Campaigns.* Hillsdale, NJ: Erlbaum

Shaw DR. 1999. The impact of TV ads and candidate appearances on statewide presidential votes. *Am. Polit. Sci. Rev.* 93: In press

Simon AF. 1997. *The winning message? Campaign discourse, candidate behavior and democracy.* PhD thesis. Univ. Calif., Los Angeles. 230 pp.

Simon AF, Iyengar S. 1996. Toward theory-based research in political communication. *PS: Polit. Sci. Polit.* 29:29–32

Task Force on Campaign Reform. 1998. *Campaign Reform: Insights and Evidence.* Princeton, NJ: Woodrow Wilson Sch. Public Int. Affairs

Wattenberg MP, Brians CL. 1999. Negative campaign advertising: mobilizer or demobilizer. *Am. Polit. Sci. Rev.* In press

West DM. 1994. Political advertising and news coverage in the 1992 California U.S. senate campaigns. *J. Polit.* 56:1053–75

Westlye MLC. 1991. *Senate Elections and Campaign Intensity.* Baltimore, MD: Johns Hopkins Univer. Press

Zaller J. 1992. *The Nature and Origins of Mass Opinion.* New York: Cambridge Univ. Press

Zaller J. 1996. The myth of massive media impact revived: new support for a discredited idea. See Mutz et al 1996, pp. 17–78

Zhao X, Chaffee SH. 1996. Campaign ads versus television news as information sources. *Public Opin. Q.* 59:41–65

Annu. Rev. Psychol. 2000. 51:171–200

GOAL THEORY, MOTIVATION, AND SCHOOL ACHIEVEMENT: An Integrative Review

Martin V. Covington

Department of Psychology, University of California at Berkeley, Berkeley, California 94720

Key Words   self-worth, school reform, self-processes, self-protective mechanisms

■ **Abstract**   The purpose of this review is to document the directions and recent progress in our understanding of the motivational dynamics of school achievement. Based on the accumulating research it is concluded that the quality of student learning as well as the will to continue learning depends closely on an interaction between the kinds of social and academic goals students bring to the classroom, the motivating properties of these goals and prevailing classroom reward structures. Implications for school reform that follow uniquely from a motivational and goal-theory perspective are also explored.

CONTENTS

Introduction 171
   Motives as Drives 173
   Motives as Goals 173
Achievement Goal Theory 174
   Academic Goals 174
   Prosocial Goals 178
Self-Processes 180
   Self-Worth Theory 181
   Self-Protective Mechanisms 181
   Developmental Dynamics 183
Classroom Incentive Structures 184
   Ability Games 185
   Equity Games 189
Conclusions: Future Directions for Research 191

INTRODUCTION

The concept of motivation stands at the center of the educational enterprise. Terrel Bell, former Secretary of Education, put the point emphatically: "There are three things to remember about education. The first is motivation. The second one is motivation. The third one is motivation" (Maehr & Meyer 1997:372).

This review examines the directions and recent progress in our understanding of the motivational dynamics of school achievement. As we will see, it is the interaction between (*a*) the kinds of social and academic goals that students bring to the classroom, (*b*) the motivating properties of these goals, and (*c*) the prevailing classroom reward structures that jointly influence the amount and quality of student learning, as well as the will to continue learning.

Taken in its entirety, the substantial body of research reviewed here provides a relatively complete picture of the motivational dynamics of school achievement. For this reason, this review is more an unfolding narrative than a comprehensive cataloguing of numerous individual studies—a narrative broad in scope, with many intertwining themes, that ultimately provides for an overall cohesiveness. The fact that such a story can now be told is a tribute to the tireless, cumulative efforts of hundreds of investigators, many of whom are cited here. This is by no means to suggest, however, that the story is complete. Much has yet to be learned. But we understand enough to recognize gaps in our knowledge and what research steps need be taken next.

Basically, our inquiries are placed in a historical perspective around the distinction between motive-as-drives and motives-as-goals (Kelly 1955). The first section reviews research inspired by goal theory and in particular the evidence for the proposition that, depending on their purposes, achievement goals differentially influence school achievement and the will to learn via cognitive, self-regulation mechanisms.

The second section examines the motivational properties of these achievement goals from a drive-theory perspective. This allows us to account for otherwise puzzling behaviors not easily explained by strictly cognitive, goal-directed interpretations. For example, if the highest goal of many students is to achieve the best grades possible, then why do some of them sabotage their chances for success by procrastinating in their studies, or by setting unrealistically high goals that doom them to failure?

The third section examines how achievement goals are influenced by classroom incentive systems, either to the benefit or to the detriment of achievement. More specifically, two incentive systems that have commanded the attention of researchers over the past several decades are considered. The first system assumes that students are optimally motivated by there being fewer rewards than there are players in the learning game, i.e. turning students into competitors for recognition and further advancement. This model derives much of its justification from the view of motives-as-drives, which typically considers motivation an enabling factor, i.e. the means to superior performance. This scarcity of rewards disrupts learning by encouraging negative achievement goals, such as avoiding failure, rather than positive goals, such as striving for success. Special attention is given to the particularly devastating impact of reward scarcity on disenfranchised students and students of color, as well as on teachers themselves.

The second broad incentive system that has recently attracted considerable interest, largely as an alternative to the competitive model, assumes that motivation is optimal when there exists an abundance of payoffs for learning, and payoffs of many kinds, not just tangible, extrinsic rewards like grades or gold stars but also intrinsic sources of satisfaction, as well as a variety of ways in which to earn these rewards, ways suited to individual learning styles. This model reflects an emphasis on motives-as-goals that draw, not drive, individuals toward action, and generally for ennobling reasons: for the sake of curiosity, exploration, and self-improvement. We consider the evidence for how reward systems inspired by goal theory can encourage both prosocial and positive academic goals.

Finally, I end with some implications for school reform that follow uniquely from a motivational and goal-theory perspective and identify some future directions for research.

Motives as Drives

Over the past half century, two broadly different conceptions of achievement motivation have emerged. First came the perspective that views motivation as a drive, i.e. an internal state, need, or condition that impels individuals toward action. In this tradition needs were thought to reside largely within the individual, such that they were spoken of as being trait-like. These drive notions evolved from earlier theories of motivation that emphasized the satisfaction of such basic tissue needs as hunger and thirst (e.g. Woodworth 1918). However, because of the limitations of applying a strictly physiological approach to understanding human behavior, researchers eventually broadened their focus to postulate learned drives or such psychological motives as the needs for social approval, power, and achievement.

The most sophisticated view of achievement motivation as a learned drive was developed in the 1950s and early 1960s by Atkinson (1957, 1964) and McClelland (1961). This theory held that achievement is the result of an emotional conflict between striving for success and avoiding failure. These two motivational dispositions were characterized largely in emotional terms. For example, hope for success and the anticipation of pride at winning or prevailing over others was said to encourage success-oriented individuals to strive for excellence. On the other hand, a capacity for experiencing shame was thought to drive failure-oriented persons to avoid situations where they believed themselves likely to fail. It was the balance—or more aptly the imbalance—between these two factors that was believed to determine the direction, intensity, and quality of achievement behavior. For example, failure-avoiding individuals were thought likely to avoid all but the simplest tasks, unless extrinsic incentives such as money or the threat of punishment were introduced to overcome their resistance. In effect, it was this difference in emotional reactions (pride vs shame) that was thought to answer the question of why some individuals approach learning with enthusiasm and others only with reluctance, and why some choose easy tasks for which success is assured and others tackle problems for which the likelihood of success is exquisitely balanced against the chances of failure.

Motives as Goals

Over the years, this approach/avoidance distinction has undergone significant modifications, especially with the rise of the alternative view of motives-as-goals that entice individuals toward action (e.g. Elliott & Dweck 1988). Researchers in this tradition assume that all actions are given meaning, direction, and purpose by the goals that individuals seek out, and that the quality and intensity of behavior will change as these goals change. Obviously, this drive/goal distinction is somewhat arbitrary, i.e. the same achievement behavior can often be construed as either satisfying a need or the result of pursuing a goal. In this sense, neither view discounts the validity of the other; rather they are complementary and each is additive to our understanding. For instance, goal theory leaves largely unaddressed the question of why individuals choose one goal over another, an issue that remains a central focus of need-achievement theory. On the other hand, goal theory offers a practical surrogate for a concept—motivation—whose nature is not yet fully understood and for which many differing perspectives have been put forward over the years (for a historical review, see Maehr & Meyer 1997). By rewarding some goals and not others, teachers can change the reasons students learn, which is to say change their motives. Thus, by this analysis, we need not await final, all-encompassing definitions or ultimate clarification before taking eminently practical steps to solve more immediate, pressing problems that are basically motivational in nature.

ACHIEVEMENT GOAL THEORY

Academic Goals

The most recent embodiment of the motives-as-goals tradition is achievement goal theory (e.g. Ames 1992, Dweck 1986, Urdan 1997, Urdan & Maehr 1995). The basic contention of achievement goal theory is that depending on their subjective purposes, achievement goals differentially influence school achievement via variations in the quality of cognitive self-regulation processes. Cognitive self-regulation refers to students being actively engaged in their own learning, including analyzing the demands of school assignments, planning for and mobilizing their resources to meet these demands, and monitoring their progress toward completion of assignments (Pintrich 1999, Zimmerman 1990, Zimmerman et al 1994). In effect, then, one's achievement goals are thought to influence the quality, timing, and appropriateness of cognitive strategies that, in turn, control the quality of one's accomplishments.

Two general kinds of goals that closely follow the original approach/avoidance designation of need theory have been made a particular focus of study: learning goals and performance goals, respectively. Although researchers have favored different designations for learning goals, such as task-goals (Anderman & Midgley 1997, Kaplan & Midgley 1997, Midgley et al 1998, Nicholls 1984) or mastery goals (Ames 1992, Roberts 1992), there is general agreement that irrespective of these variations, learning goals refer to increasing one's competency, understanding, and appreciation for what is being learned. Likewise, there is general agreement that performance goals, whether referred to as ego-goals (Nicholls 1989, Thorkildsen & Nicholls 1998) or self-enhancing goals (Skaalvik 1997), involve outperforming others as a means to aggrandize one's ability status at the expense of peers.

The specific hypothesis put forward by achievement goal theorists is twofold: first, that learning goals favor deep-level, strategic-processing of information, which in turn leads to increased school achievement; and second, that performance goals trigger superficial, rote-level processing that exerts a stultifying influence on achievement. These twin hypotheses have stimulated a considerable body of research in recent years, the bulk of which examines one link at a time in the proposed trichotomous sequence, with a few studies testing the entire sequence simultaneously (e.g. goals → cognitions → achievement).

Goals → Cognitions   First, consider briefly the evidence for the first link of this proposed causal sequence, namely that achievement goals influence the quality of self-regulated learning exhibited by students.

Regarding learning goals, both correlational and laboratory studies indicate that students who espouse a learning-goal orientation report engaging in more self-regulated learning than do those students who endorse these same learning goals but to a lesser degree (Ames 1992, Dweck & Leggett 1988, Pintrich & De Groot 1990, Pintrich & Schrauben 1992). These differences in self-regulation include a greater effort among learning-oriented students (*a*) to monitor their understanding of what is being learned—in short, recognizing when they know something sufficient to the demands of the task and when they do not (Meece & Holt 1993, Middleton & Midgley 1997), (*b*) to employ organizing strategies such as paraphrasing and summarizing (Archer 1994), and (*c*) to make positive, adaptive attributions for one's occasional failures to understand. In this latter connection, learning-oriented students tend to believe that effort is the key to success and that failure, despite trying hard, does not necessarily imply incompetence but simply not having employed the right learning strategies (Nicholls 1984, Pintrich & Schunk 1996). The benefits of adopting a learning orientation also extend to affective reactions. For example, learning goals are positively associated with pride and satisfaction in success and negatively associated with anxiety in the event of failure (Ames 1992, Jagacinski & Nicholls 1984, 1987).

The evidence concerning the presumed relationship between adopting performance goals and the quality of self-regulated learning is more complex and less consistent than that just summarized for learning goals (for commentary, see Harackiewicz et al 1998). Although researchers have generally reported that performance goals are positively associated with superficial, rote rehearsal strategies and are unrelated or negatively associated with deep-level processing (e.g. Karabenick & Collins-Eaglin 1997, Pintrich et al 1993), it is also true that no clear pattern has emerged from those studies exploring the association between performance goals and either task persistence (e.g. Bouffard et al 1995, Pintrich et al 1993) or the degree of effort extended (e.g. MacIver et al 1991, Wentzel 1996). This failure to confirm the expectation that effort level and persistence are negatively associated with performance goals likely occurs because, initially, researchers did not distinguish, as some subsequently have (e.g. Elliot & Harackiewicz 1996), between performance/approach goals and performance/avoidance goals. When performance goals are properly parsed into their respective approach and avoidance components, the evidence suggests that those performance-oriented students who approach success invest considerable effort in highly sophisticated study strategies, which is not surprising given their goal of outperforming others (Wolters et al 1996). By contrast, performance-oriented subjects whose goal is to avoid failure reflect a pattern of reduced effort and task persistence (Bouffard et al 1995). By not trying, this latter group is thought to create face-saving excuses for having done poorly (Pintrich 1999).

Thus, from a self-protective point of view, performance-oriented students, whether approach or avoidant, are driven by fears of incompetency, with the former group striving to avoid failure by succeeding and the latter group setting up failures when necessary, but in ways that deflect the implication that they are incompetent.

Cognitions → Achievement   Does the quality of different cognitive processing strategies translate into different achievement outcomes, thus confirming the final link in the trichotomous goal theory framework? The available evidence also supports this contention. A number of studies conducted in the years prior to the advent of goal theory had already established a convincing case for deep-level processing as the optimal condition for achievement in a variety of subject-matter areas, including English composition and science (for a review, see Covington 1992). Moreover, recent anecdotal observations provide indirect corroboration for these linkages. For example, Borkowski & Thorpe (1994) report that underachieving students are impulsive and inaccurate in their self judgements regarding prior knowledge of a topic to be learned and in judging their own capacities, given specific task demands. Conversely, academically successful minority high school students demonstrate a greater degree of self-regulation and willingness to persist on task than their less-successful peers (CR Wibrowski 1992).

Cultural variations in the cognitive, self-regulation element of this trichotomous sequence have also been reported. For instance, Purdie & Hattie (1996) found that compared with Anglo high school students, native Japanese favor memorizing and rote rehearsal strategies when studying and, incidentally, rely on feelings of obligation to others as the primary motivating imperative (see also Rosenthal & Feldman 1991). By contrast, Anglo students are more likely to favor self-testing as a means to assess their level of understanding, as well as to create plans and goals for both motivating and organizing their studies. As to the cognition/achievement linkage itself, the highest achievers in both the Anglo and Japanese groups tended to employ all the above-mentioned strategies—in effect, studying in more-complex ways—compared with the study practices of the low achievers in both groups.

Goals → Cognitions → Achievement   Several multiple-regression studies have confirmed the entirety of this trichotomous framework. Elliot et al (1999) report that the presence of performance/avoidance goals was associated with superficial processing and disorganizing tendencies (i.e. inefficient use of study time), factors that in turn were linked to decreases in subsequent academic performance. It is interesting to note that adopting a performance/approach goal also was associated with superficial processing, but in this case inefficiency was offset by a tendency for extra rehearsal so that the net effect was a gain in performance. By contrast, adopting learning goals was positively associated with deep-level processing, persistence, and high effort, a combination that also led to increases in achievement. Parenthetically, achievement gains were equal for both learning-oriented and performance/approach students (also see Elliot & Harackiewicz 1996), which suggests that achievement per se, even superior performances, may be less important to the larger objectives of schooling than the means by which superior status is achieved. More specifically, successful achievement driven by fear can make learning an ordeal, no matter how well one does academically.

Several other investigations corroborate the Elliot et al (1999) study by confirming a direct association between student goals on the one hand and academic outcomes on the other (e.g. Meece & Holt 1993, Pokay & Blumenfeld 1990). Perhaps most noteworthy for establishing causal, not merely correlational, relationships is a study reported by Schunk (1996) in which young children who were directed to work under a learning-goal set demonstrated greater task involvement and greater subsequent achievement than children who worked under a performance-goal set. In an additional series of studies, Roney et al (1995) manipulated approach and avoidance orientations with college students by inviting some to focus on the specific number of anagram problems they would try to solve (approach) and others to estimate the number they would be unable to solve (avoidance). Subjects operating under an approach set performed better and were more persistent in working on unsolvable anagrams. Similar differences have been produced by other investigators using a variety of approach/ avoidance primers, including solving problems while imagining either positive or negative selves (Ruvolo & Markus 1992) or operating under a self-initiated vs an obligatory achievement set (Roney & Sorrentino 1995).

Little is known about the ethnic and cultural correlates of the trichotomous goal-theory framework. To date, most research has focused on ethnic variations in achievement attributions. Basically, Asian youngsters, in particular Chinese Americans (Hess et al 1987, Whang & Hancock 1994) and native Japanese (Hamilton et al 1989), tend to attribute their successes to trying hard and their failures to lack of effort whereas Anglo American students tend to divide their attributional explanations more evenly between good luck, ability, and effort (for a review, see Holloway 1988). Similar patterns favoring effort attributions for achievement have also been found among native-born Mexicans (Snyder 1994).

Although attributional mechanisms are clearly implicated in the pursuit of achievement goals, they are not the same as goals. One of the few investigations concerned with the compound relationship between academic goals, ethnicity and school achievement involved comparisons among Anglo, Aboriginal (Australian), and Native American (Navaho) high school students (McInerney et al 1997). The findings generally corroborated the previously cited work in that learning goals were positively associated with school grades, whereas performance goals were essentially uncorrelated with grades. Most important was the fact that this pattern was common to all three ethnic groups. It would appear that diverse ethnic groups may be more similar than different, perhaps not only in their preferred goals but also in the causal impact of these goals on academic achievement.

In summary, the accumulated evidence overwhelmingly favors the goal-theory hypothesis that different reasons for achieving, nominally approach and avoidance, influence the quality of achievement striving via self-regulation mechanisms. Although much remains to be learned about these relationships, especially regarding potential ethnic and gender variations, this trichotomous framework nonetheless provides the basis for a rapprochement with motivational issues (see below). Moreover, this framework openly invites a consideration of additional goals, which typically have not been considered part of traditional academic achievement. It is to this point that we now turn.

Prosocial Goals

The bulk of research inspired by achievement goal theory has focused on academic outcomes. A separate line of inquiry with different origins and emphases, but that will almost certainly contribute to a deeper understanding of academic achievement, focuses on the interpersonal world of students and on the expression of social goals, including peer acceptance and respectability. From the time that McClelland (1955) and others (e.g. Veroff 1969) first identified the need for approval as an important social motivator in the drive-theory tradition, investigators have recognized a broad range of social concerns and behaviors as important aspects of school-related motivation, including the willingness to cooperate, to comply with rules, and to help others.

Recently, investigators have located the need to achieve a sense of belonging, integrity, and the respect of others in the larger context of goal theory (e.g. Farmer et al 1991). Such prosocial goals as gaining acceptance share much in common with academic goals (Schneider et al 1996). Like academic goals, the pursuit of social goals can help organize, direct, and empower individuals to achieve more fully. For example, the desire of individuals to achieve for the sake of the group is a well-known phenomenon, and it forms the basis for much of the success of cooperative learning (Hertiz-Lazarowitz et al 1992). Moreover, like many academic goals, especially those associated with intrinsic curiosity and creative expression, prosocial goals are also valued in their own right, apart from any justification that they may contribute to academic success. This valuation is part of the larger commitment of American schools to encourage moral character and social responsibility among upcoming generations.

Currently, our understanding of how the pursuit of social goals fits into the larger dynamics of classroom achievement is not nearly as advanced as our understanding of the role of academic goals in this regard. Nonetheless, the prosocial literature appears sufficiently developed to support several generalizations proposed by Wentzel (1996) and others (e.g. Wentzel & Wigfield 1998).

First, it is clear that the pursuit of such social goals as making friends and being responsible to others is given high priority by children of virtually all ages (Allen

1986, Ford 1992), often even higher than the pursuit of academic goals (Wentzel 1991a, 1992).

Second, the pursuit of these prosocial goals is closely related to students being liked and respected by their peers (Wentzel 1994). Conversely, students who are identified by their peers as being less well-liked report trying to achieve these same prosocial goals less often. Teachers, too, are judged in much the same manner. According to Wentzel (1996), teachers who are well liked by students are rated as willing to treat children's ideas with respect, to give of their time and resources unstintingly, and to provide positive encouragement and feedback.

Third, prosocial behavior including being cooperative, compliant, and willing to share is positively associated with academic success (Wentzel 1989, 1991b, 1993). The reasons for this relationship are not entirely clear, except to say that, motivationally speaking, both prosocial goals and academic achievement are intimately linked. One possible moderator involves level of academic effort. For example, tutoring others is not only a valued expression of prosocial cooperation, but the benefits to the tutor of consolidating his/her own understanding of the subject matter in the process also bode well for subsequent achievement. Wentzel (1996) found indirect support for the prosocial/effort portion of this potential linkage with achievement in a study of seventh-grade English classes. The amount of time students spent on their homework (effort) depended on the degree to which they endorsed socially responsible goals, such as helping peers understand their assignments. Longitudinal analyses of the same data also indicated that increases in effort levels from the sixth-grade to eight-grade depended not only on the degree to which students pursued social goals within that time period, but also on the pursuit of learning goals as well.

This latter finding serves to illustrate a fourth and final point: Not only do prosocial goals likely influence achievement in their own right, but as was just implied by the Wentzel study, they also likely act jointly with academic goals to influence achievement. At the moment, the precise nature of such a complex causal network of goals is not well understood, and interest in this possibility has far outrun the available evidence (see Wentzel 1993, Wentzel & Wigfield 1998). Whatever the dynamics eventually prove to be, however, varying combinations of goals will likely exert negative as well as positive influences on academic achievement. For instance, whether the willingness to share becomes a positive factor in the achievement equation will almost certainly depend on which academic goals predominate. As only one example, Wentzel (1996) reports that the tendency of students to pursue social goals, like sharing, is positively related to learning goals but not to performance goals. This finding likely reflects the fact that by their very nature, learning goals—exploring, experimenting, and discovering—depend heavily on the acquiescence, if not the active cooperation, of others whereas the main objective of performance goals— doing better than others—is patently contrary to positive social values, involving as they do sabotage, deception, and a reluctance to cooperate (Covington 1992).

Other academic/social goal combinations will likely act in positive, compensatory ways, such as when, for example, an otherwise boring subject matter is mastered merely for the social value of doing so. And finally, there is the possibility of a direct conflict between social and academic goals that present painful dilemmas for young-sters and, in the process, bode ill for the successful pursuit of any academic goals to which they might aspire. A classic example involves the special dilemma for many minority students who must accept dominant Anglo achievement values (e.g. com-petition, autonomy, independence) sufficiently to do well in school but not enough to incur the wrath of their minority peers and family as betrayers of their cultural heritage (Arroyo & Zigler 1995, Fordham & Ogbu 1986; but see Bergin & Cooks 1995, Collins-Eaglin & Karabenick 1993).

Not only will the impact on achievement likely depend on the composition of various multiple-goal alliances, but teachers will also certainly emerge as key mod-erators of these dynamics (Perry & Weinstein 1998). A few recent findings attest to this point. For instance, the willingness of students to form a consensus around the goals of doing well and helping peers academically depends on their perceptions that teachers care about them both as persons and students (Feldlaufer et al 1988, Good-enow 1993, Harter 1996, Wentzel 1995); conversely, when students perceive teachers as having failed to provide support, they feel no obligation to behave in socially responsible ways, nor do they particularly enjoy school (Dray et al 1999). Of special interest is the fact that perceptions of teacher support are positively associated with instructional techniques that feature mastery and learning goals and frequent displays of feedback (Wentzel 1995). Clearly, then, the quality of the student/teacher relation-ship depends not only on the personal actions of teachers, but also on the instructional climate in which these actions occur (see below).

SELF-PROCESSES

Research inspired by goal theory has substantially advanced our understanding of classroom achievement dynamics. In essence, it is now clear that the quality of self-regulation forms an essential link between academic goals on the one hand and the quality of achievement behavior on the other. And the stage is set for further reve-lations with the inclusion of prosocial goals in the on-going study of multiple-goal influences on achievement. Yet despite these advances, we are left wondering about the larger motivating function of these goals. Although achievement goals organize behavior via self-regulation mechanisms, thereby addressing the sustaining function of motives, what about the arousal and selection functions of motives? Why, for example, do individuals choose to pursue some goals and not others, and pursue the chosen goals with different degrees of energy? And what of the adaptive function of motives? If the highest goal of most students is to get the best grades possible, as appears to be the case (Covington & Wiedenhaupt 1997), then why do some of them sabotage their chances by procrastinating in their studies or setting unrealistically high goals that doom them to failure?

These questions imply that achievement goals may serve more fundamental adap-tive, even survival, functions than has previously been acknowledged by goal theo-rists. However, perspectives are changing rapidly. Within the past decade there has been a growing recognition that neither motivational nor cognitive models by themselves can fully describe all aspects of academic achievement (see especially Garcia & Pintrich 1994, Graham & Golan 1991). Several approaches to establishing a theoretical rapport between a cognitive agenda and motivational concerns have been advanced. Some investigators have suggested infusing achievement goals with self-motivating processes (Kluger & De Nisi 1996, Maehr 1998, Roeser et al 1996), including internalized self-talk to help monitor and sustain long-term task engagement (R Butler, MV Covington & S Wiedenhaupt, unpublished data). Other researchers propose conceptualizing goal orientations as highly personal in nature, i.e. based on stable, trait-like dispositions rather than being treated as more situated reactions that are subject to prevailing environmental demands (Emmons 1986, Pintrich 1999). The treatment of achievement goals as enduring, adaptive drives has remained a central emphasis in the need-achievement tradition. The most recent expression of this focus was the advent of the self-worth theory.

Self-Worth Theory

The self-worth theory (Covington 1992, 1998; Covington & Beery 1976) assumes that the achievement goals adopted by students, whether learning oriented or performance oriented, reflect a Promethean, life-spanning struggle to establish and maintain a sense of worth and belonging in a society that values competency and doing well. In effect, in our society individuals are widely considered to be only as worthy as their ability to achieve. For these reasons, the kinds of grades students achieve are the unmistakable measure by which many, if not most, youngsters judge their worth as students.

Yet although a grade focus dominates, it is the way students define success that is the all-important factor by which self-esteem mechanisms operate to affect achievement. For example, those students previously described as success-oriented (Atkinson 1957; Covington 1992) define success in terms of becoming the best they can be, irrespective of the accomplishments of others. They also value pushing the envelope of their current skills and understanding through diligence and hard work. Success-oriented students value ability as much as do others, but as a tool or resource to achieve personally meaningful goals. By contrast, other students value ability as a matter of status, which means defining competency in terms of doing better than others academically, and in the process they are often forced to avoid failure, or at least avoid the implications of failure, i.e. that they are incompetent, because the rules of competition dictate that only a few can succeed. The failure-avoiding tactics involved here have many guises, but whatever their form or character, they are all linked to the fear of failure, which is to say they are part of the defensive repertoire of those individuals who tie their sense of worth to grades and as a result are dominated by performance goals (Fried-Buchalter 1992, Thompson et al 1998).

Self-Protective Mechanisms

The past decade has witnessed a renewal of interest in the nature and consequences of these defensive strategies, which have been divided into three conceptually related categories (Thompson 1993, 1994): (*a*) self-worth protection, (*b*) self-handicapping strategies, and (*c*) defensive pessimism.

Self-worth protection describes a general strategy of withholding effort when risking failure so that the perceived causes of failure, should failure occur, remain ambiguous owing to the possibility that not trying is the culprit rather than incompetency (Mayerson & Rhodewalt 1988, Rhodewalt et al 1991, Thompson et al 1995). From this defensive perspective, not trying becomes a virtue for failure-threatened students, even though inaction is typically reprimanded by teachers (Weiner & Kukla 1970). Thus effort becomes a double-edged sword: valued by students because teachers reward it, yet also feared by students for its potential threat to their sense of worth when anticipating failure (Covington 1998).

Self-handicapping behavior involves the creation of some impediment to one's performance—either imagined or real—so that the individual has a ready excuse for potential failure. This strategy encompasses a wealth of specific tactics, including procrastination (McCown & Johnson 1991) and establishing unrealistically high achievement goals (Covington 1992). By studying only at the last moment, one's failures can hardly be blamed on inability, and if procrastinators should do well, they will appear highly able, because they have succeeded with so little effort. Likewise, individuals may handicap themselves by striving for unattainable goals, but such a failure would not reflect significantly on their ability, since under the circumstances no one else could be expected to succeed either. At other times, students may attempt to maintain a sense of worth by merely stating a worthy goal, e.g. announcing that they will do better on the next test—even if that is unlikely. Here individuals attempt to compensate for failure with an alternative source of gratification. In this case, however, the person has substituted fantasies for actual accomplishments. From the vantage point of self-protective dynamics, such irrational goal setting becomes a reasonable, even logical and self-justified, response to situations in which one is required to perform, but in which the likelihood of success is low and failure abrasive.

A third distinctive strategy involves defensive pessimism, in which individuals maintain unrealistically low expectations for ever succeeding or discount the importance of an assignment, all in an effort to minimize feelings of anxiety that might otherwise overwhelm their studies if they took an assignment seriously (Cantor & Harlow 1994, Cantor & Norem 1989, Norem & Illingworth 1993; AJ Martin 1998).

The accumulated evidence suggests that although strategies such as claiming a handicap for one's failure may afford short-term protection from feelings of diminished self-esteem (Isleib et al 1988, Rhodewalt et al 1991), substantial long-term costs are also likely to be extracted, especially when avoidance strategies become habitual and are incorporated into the individuals characteristic mode of achievement for extended periods of time. Ultimately, these costs translate into diminished achievement (Rhodewalt 1990; AJ Martin 1998). This diminution takes many forms, including achieving inconsistently, i.e. sometimes performing well and at other times poorly, depending on how likely failure is perceived to be the outcome (Thompson 1993). Diminished achievement in turn is likely to be accompanied by heightened anxiety. For example, procrastinators with high neuroticism scores and elements of perfectionism find that studying actually increases their anxiety rather than reducing it (McCown & Johnson 1991). Emotional exhaustion and eventually burnout are also frequently cited consequences of the excessive use of these failure-avoiding strategies, as well as reduced interest in achieving (Higgins & Berglas 1990, Thompson 1994, Topping & Kimmel 1985).

Defensive posturing is more likely to occur among males than females, and these gender differences emerge in the earliest years of schooling. For example, Craske (1988) reported that primary grade boys are more likely than girls to withdraw from difficult tasks or not to try following failure. Miller (1986) has also found similar patterns among middle-school boys. Furthermore, Urdan et al (1998) report excessive handicapping among boys in the upper-elementary grades, behaviors that are associated with a diminished grade-point average.

Developmental Dynamics

Research inspired by the drive-theory tradition has demonstrated a clear relationship between child-rearing practices and the characteristic ways that individuals resolve the inherent conflict implied in the approach/avoidance distinction. In brief, early pioneering studies established that the parents of success-oriented youngsters encourage them to exercise independence and explore options on their own (Winterbottom 1953) in the context of warm nurturing and guidance, a combination that accelerates the development of the skills necessary for handling the responsibility implied in making one's own choices and trying out new ideas (Rosen & D'Andrade 1959, Hermans et al 1972). These parents were also found to reward the praiseworthy accomplishments of their children, yet ignore disappointing performances. This overall pattern is essentially reversed when it comes to the parents of failure-oriented youngsters (RC Teevan & R Fischer, unpublished data). Here the disappointing performances of children were perceived as violations of adult expectations and punished accordingly, usually severely, whereas success was met with faint praise and even indifference.

More recent research has confirmed these earlier findings (Eskilson et al 1986, Ginsburg & Bronstein 1993, Jacobs et al 1998, Strage 1999). For example, success-oriented college students recall their parents employing praise more often in success, and punishment less often in failure compared with the recollections of failure-avoiding students who report the opposite pattern (K Tomiki 1997).

Several variations in these basic child-rearing patterns have also been documented recently, all of which are associated with uncertain self-estimates of personal worth among children, chronic achievement anxiety, and an increased likelihood of self-handicapping behavior (Kernis et al 1992, Kimble et al 1990). These debilitating patterns include giving children inconsistent, noncontingent feedback, such as when parents sometimes punish what they perceive as their child's successes and at other times disregard or even reward poor performances (Kohlmann et al 1988). Similar parental reactions have been implicated in the development of learned helplessness, a phenomenon in which learners give up trying because they come to believe, often rightly, that they have no control over their own destiny (Mineka & Henderson 1985). Another debilitating parental reaction involves consistently providing false feedback, e.g. telling children that they have performed poorly when they have done reasonably well or pronouncing the child's performance adequate when it is clearly not. Other disastrous patterns involve aggressive, often overbearing demands for excellence but with little or no guidance for how to achieve it (Chapin & Vito 1988). In this case, children hopelessly outclass themselves by maintaining unrealistically high self-standards with no way to attain them.

Recent investigations have also extended the study of these dynamics to include ethnic factors. For example, Asian students appear more subject than Anglo students to demanding family values that imply the threat of personal rejection should they fail academically (Hess et al 1987; K Tomiki 1997), and as a result they are often driven to succeed more out of a fear of failure than for intrinsic reasons (Eaton & Dembo 1997).

Given the apparent consistency of such child-rearing practices at different points in time as well as their early onset, one gains the impression that the tendencies to approach success and to avoid failure found among adults likely reflect fundamental personality structures laid down at the deepest levels. Yet if the quality of child rearing contributes to later achievement styles in such straight forward, discernable ways, as suggested here, then cannot negative dispositions be changed or at least offset and positive ones reinforced by rewarding positive achievement goals? To address this question we need to consider the kinds of incentive systems used in schools to motivate students to achieve.

CLASSROOM INCENTIVE STRUCTURES

Every classroom reflects rules that determine the basis on which students will be evaluated and how rewards such as grades, praise, or gold stars are distributed (Doyle 1983). This arrangement has been compared to a game, albeit a serious one, in which students attempt to earn as many points (rewards) as possible (Alschuler 1973). A wide array of rewards are available, including positive reinforcers, which range from the internalized satisfaction of having done one's best (which abets learning goals) to public recognition for doing better than others (reinforcing of performance goals) or at least being praised for complying with the rules of the game, which supports such prosocial behaviors as submission to teacher authority and a willingness to try hard. Negative reinforcers also abound for noncompliance with a work ethic, ranging from the threat of poor grades to teacher warnings and the enforced isolation of rule breakers.

In effect, then, not only are the causal linkages between achievement goals and subsequent academic performance mediated by cognitive mechanisms, but achievement goals are themselves controlled in turn by prevailing classroom incentive systems. Two incentive systems have been the subject of intensive research in recent years.

Ability Games

Many classrooms employ rules that turn schooling into what has been described as a failure-oriented (competitive) ability game (Ames 1990, Covington & Teel 1996), i.e. rules that encourage performance goals whose purpose is variously to enhance one's reputation for ability by outperforming others, to avoid failure, or at least to avoid the implications of failure, that one is incompetent. These negative achievement goals are provoked largely by a scarcity of rewards (e.g. good grades) because these top marks are distributed unequally, with the greatest number going to those students who perform the best or learn the quickest. This arrangement amounts to a zero-sum scoring system. When one student (player) wins (or makes points), other students must loose (points). In such a competitive game, the main obstacles to overcome are other students, not the challenge of mastering subject-matter material. Thus, good grades become valued not necessarily because they indicate that one has learned a stipulated amount or learned it well, but because they imply that one is able, whereas poor grades imply a lack of ability that triggers feelings of worthlessness.

Failure-oriented students are placed at the greatest risk in an ability game because they have tied their sense of worth to grades. As a consequence, unlike success-oriented students, there are few if any alternative, personally meaningful incentives available to failure-oriented students other than striving for high grades, which are in scarce supply. Thus, sadly enough, for these students trying one's best provides little satisfaction if performance failure is the anticipated outcome. Indeed, as documented previously (Covington 1998), having studied hard but failing anyway, far from providing any comfort, actually creates the ultimate threat: the implication that one is incompetent. Consequently, failure-oriented students must satisfy themselves with the thin consolation provided by the relief of not failing, or at least of not failing in ways that imply low ability.

The Dynamics of Achievement Failure Competitive ability games gain a measure of credibility from a popular misinterpretation of drive theory, which assumes that students will comply with prevailing academic demands if teachers can only provide the right rewards or threaten sufficient punishments, and that the fewer the rewards offered, the harder students will attempt to attain them. The evidence does not support these propositions. Several studies have explored the various consequences of falling short of one's grade goals in competitive circumstances and how these dynamics play themselves out over time in actual classrooms, ranging from the elementary level (Schwarzer & Cherkes-Julkowski 1982, Schwarzer et al 1983) to middle school (Hagtvet 1984) and college settings (Covington & Omelich 1981). As a group these studies, one of which tracked German high school students over a 2-year period (Schwarzer et al 1984), typically employed either path analytic interpretations of multiple regression or structural equation modeling, techniques that strengthen a causal interpretation of the events observed.

These studies reveal a common thread. Basically, the degree of shame (an ability-linked emotion) that follows a first classroom failure experience depends largely on the individual's initial self-concept of ability—the lower the student's self-estimate, the more he or she experiences shame and feelings of hopelessness. Then as one failure follows another over time, these feelings intensify for the individual, driven by several interlocking processes. First, nonability explanations for failure become increasingly implausible, and as a result, self-estimates of ability steadily deteriorate. Second, failures are increasingly attributed to a lack of ability. These dynamics are intensified by competitive pressures. In short, then, as failures mount, failure-prone students believe themselves to be more and more deficient in the very factor—ability—that emerges in their minds as the most important ingredient to competitive success. These dynamics are typically accompanied by increasing levels of anxiety or, for some subsamples of students, the reverse: lower levels of anxiety accompanied by an increasing sense of hopelessness (Schwarzer et al 1984). This latter pattern appears akin to a state of resignation and growing indifference to events.

Other complementary, multivariate studies have also examined these same dynamics but within the foreshortened time frame of a single study/test cycle (Covington & Omelich 1979, 1988). Students whose achievement goals are defensive in nature, i.e. failure avoiding, initially assess their chances of succeeding on an upcoming test as marginal and report being riddled with anxiety (Carver & Scheier 1988). These fears, especially concerns about being unmasked as incompetent (Laux & Glanzmann 1987), cascade forward through time to interfere with both test preparation and eventual performance. As to the quality of test preparation, multivariate findings not only corroborate those previously cited correlational studies that merely demonstrate an association between achievement goals and the quality of study, they also place them in a larger dynamic context. More specifically, students preoccupied with defensive performance/avoidance goals are foreclosed from deep-level processing, largely because of the distracting effects of anxiety triggered by fears of incompetency (Covington & Omelich 1988). As a consequence, what is learned by these students is learned sparingly, if not superficially, and often on a rote basis, so that later recall in the face of continuing test anxiety is marginal at best, thereby completing the causal, trichotomous network associated with achievement goal theory.

Incidently, these findings suggest that poor performance is often less the result of anxiety interfering with the retention of what is learned than of the fact that anxious students typically learn less to begin with (Culler & Holahan 1980, Tobias 1986, Topman & Jansen 1984). By this reasoning, achievement anxiety may best be thought of as a noncausal, emotional byproduct that accompanies the realization that the individual is inadequately prepared and will do poorly.

Returning to the microdynamics of the study/test cycle, feelings of incompetency also drive a host of self-protective actions—which, according to the findings of several multiple-regression studies, disrupt the quality of test preparation even further (Covington & Omelich 1988). For instance, failure-avoiding students indulge in blame projection (e.g. "If I had a better teacher, I might do better") and in wishful thinking (e.g. "I wish that the test would somehow go away"). Not only do these multivariate analyses corroborate the operation of self-handicapping tendencies among failure-avoiding students, they also place such self-sabotage at the very heart of the achievement process when students risk their sense of worth in a competitive learning game.

The general fear-of-failure dynamics described here have been differentiated for a subgroup of students who closely resemble the performance/approach type of Elliot & Harackiewicz (1996). These individuals, referred to as overstrivers by other investigators (Covington 1998, Depreeuw 1990), do in fact approach success, but for defensive reasons: to avoid failure. Overstrivers experience great emotional tension throughout the achievement cycle, equal to that of performance/avoidance students. But for overstrivers, the direction of the impact of tension on the quality of test preparation is reversed. Instead of impairing their studies, as it does for failure avoiders, the presence of emotional tension actually mobilizes the enormous capacity of overstrivers for study, which typically takes the form of slavish overpreparation. However, although anxiety arouses the considerable resources of overstrivers, the tension that persists during test-taking itself appears to cause a massive failure to recall what was originally learned (Covington & Omelich 1987). There is no evidence of a skill deficit here, and certainly no lack of involvement. Rather, overstrivers appear to suffer from a retrieval deficit in which anxiety acts to inhibit the recall of even well-learned material.

Implications The importance of multivariate studies that trace the joint impact of cognitive, motivational, and emotional factors on achievement over time cannot be overestimated, for several reasons. First, these studies make clear that school achievement is most properly viewed as a clustering of interrelated causal factors—cognitions (goals), self-protective mechanisms, and feelings whose relationships to one another and ultimately to school performance itself change as students progress from one achievement event to another (Pekrun 1992, Ratner & Stettner 1991). Moreover, these dynamics are highly situated and subject to prevailing work demands and incentive systems.

In short, researchers now possess conceptual blueprints within which they can locate and trace an enormous array of complex, interacting factors that form the essence of achievement behavior. This means that researchers are now able to document with unprecedented precision just how classroom achievement processes unfold and, of equal importance, just how these dynamics change as a function of individual learner differences. And these latter revelations hold enormous practical importance. A case in point is the discovery that the nature of the relationship between anxiety and performance—whether a skill deficit or a retrieval deficit—appears to depend on the prevailing achievement goals of the individual learner. Clearly, then, from the standpoint of helping anxious students, no single intervention is likely to be equally effective for all. Different types of students suffer different deficits and require different kinds of treatment, a fact neatly demonstrated by the research of Naveh-Benjamin (1985). This researcher administered relaxation therapy to a group of highly anxious students with good study strategies, akin to overstrivers. Another group of anxious students who possessed poor study habits were instructed in how to improve their study skills. These same treatments were administered to two other identical groups, but in the reverse order to provide a control comparison. The benefits of therapy were minimal for these latter two groups because the interventions did not compensate them for their particular weaknesses, whereas when a proper match between deficit and remediation was achieved, school test performance improved for both kinds of anxious students.

Second, these multivariate analyses also provide important insights into the structural causes of the record of poor school achievement among many minority youngsters from the urban ghettos and barrios of America. These youngsters are put at a considerable disadvantage by the ability-game mentality, for two reasons. For one thing, for many of these minority youngsters the primary achievement goals to which they aspire—caring for others, maintaining kinship roles for the sake of survival, and assuming adult work roles—lie outside the more traditional mainstream realm of academic achievement, and as a result, they are not particularly honored or encouraged. For another thing, given the middle-class emphasis on competitive values, on independence, and on the scramble for improved social status, minority students are also deprived of their preferred means of achieving their goals, which is largely through cooperation, sharing, and close social cohesion (Losey 1995). Numerous case studies make clear that minority students are capable of extraordinary achievements despite these institutional obstacles, but only if the benefits of schooling are perceived by them to fit their unique needs (Reyes & Jason 1993). For example, Suarez-Orozco (1989) documented the various reasons that many Hispanic refugees from war-torn Central America won top honors in American schools and often went on to professional careers. Their goals were neither self-indulgence nor personal financial gain. These youngsters were driven to rescue family members who had been left behind in their war-devastated homelands, and who had sacrificed much so that these youngsters could immigrate to America.

This conflict of cultural values (goals) is intensified for minority youngsters in the transition from the elementary years to middle school, when evaluation becomes more formal and competitive as the function of schools focuses more and more on the selection and sorting out of talent (for a review, see Wigfield et al 1987). As a consequence, minority youngsters must increasingly play by competitive rules if they are to play at all, rules that for them are often frightening and confusing.

Third, the multivariate study of school dynamics via achievement goal theory also serves notice that teachers are at risk as much as are students. The broad outlines of a demoralizing downward cycle of student achievement and deteriorating teacher/ student relationships have emerged in recent years (Wentzel 1996). When excessive emphasis is placed on performance goals and success is narrowly defined as outperforming others, teachers pressure students. They use controlling autocratic teaching techniques, which means relying on extrinsic rewards, allowing students little choice for how they go about learning, and threatening to withdraw emotional support as a means of control (Maehr & Stallings 1972). It is ironic that these are the very instructional practices, noted earlier, that lead students to reject positive social goals, including sharing and cooperation, and in the process to become passive-resistant, if not outright defiant, of teacher authority. These disruptive behaviors are frequently cited by teachers as one of the main reasons for leaving the profession.

Fourth, and perhaps most important, achievement goal theory and the multivariate evidence inspired by it provide a sound scientific basis for reshaping American educational practices.

Equity Games

Motives-as-goal adherents have championed radically different perspectives on classroom incentive structures, which in addition to enjoying considerable empirical support make common cause with the pedagogical views of many influential educational philosophers, beginning with Dewey (1916). Goal theorists believe that the basic impediment to classroom learning is the scarcity of rewards, which forces most youngsters to struggle to avoid failure rather than to approach success. The solution, they suggest, involves substituting new rules of engagement that recognize students' efforts for self-improvement, for task diligence, and for making progress as well as for correcting their own learning errors—yardsticks of accomplishment that are open to all, irrespective of ability, status, or past experience. Obviously, not everyone is equally bright, nor can all children compete on an equal footing intellectually. But at least, these goal theory proponents argue, schools can provide all students with a common heritage in the reasons they learn. In effect, goal theorists seek to establish a condition of motivational equity (Covington 1998, Nicholls 1989).

Central to creating motivational equity is the need for teachers to set the absolute standards of excellence they require of all their students and to make explicit the relationship between goal attainment and payoffs. One equity approach that has been studied extensively in recent years involves a mastery paradigm in which students must demonstrate a minimum level of skill or task proficiency before receiving a payoff, which may simply be the chance to proceed to the next level of challenge (for a review, see Covington 1992). For those students who do not achieve the minimums initially, there are options for remediation through the help of teachers, fellow students, or both (Slavin 1983, Slavin et al 1984). Elements of task choice, individual goal setting, and autonomy of student action have also been introduced into the basic paradigm. In perhaps the most sophisticated case, students are permitted to work for any grade they choose by amassing credits, e.g. so many points for an A, a B, etc, with the caveat that the higher the grade to which students aspire, the better they must perform or the more they must accomplish (Covington 1998, Covington & Omelich 1984).

Researchers have investigated the advantages of equity paradigms across grade levels. In general, the findings favor the motivational and learning benefits of such paradigms compared with those of incentive structures that embody competitive ability games. Several complementary, interlocking research strands can be identified.

First, a number of studies have assessed the motivational impact of individual components of the equity paradigm, taken singly and in isolation from each other but under rigorous laboratory conditions. Consider, for example, the alleged benefits of individual goal setting as studied by Ames and her colleagues (see Ames & Ames 1984). Elementary school children who were directed to establish their own learning goals perceived failure experiences as temporary, compared with otherwise comparable subjects who adopted a competitive goal. This latter group was more likely to interpret failure as a matter of personal incompetency. Moreover, when students succeeded under competitive goal conditions, they were more likely to perceive themselves as smarter than their companions (adversaries), and to engage in more self-praise at the expense of their failing competitors, whom they saw as less deserving. As for the losing competitors, failure created self-loathing, especially among those students who were high in self-perceived ability. This suggests that under competitive goals, individuals are likely to continue striving only for as long as they remain successful. No one wants to continue if the result is shame and self-recrimination.

In complementary research, experimentally induced learning goals as contrasted to ability-focused performance goals were found to generate less task anxiety and an increased willingness to risk failure in the pursuit of challenging tasks (Meece 1991), greater metacognitive self-regulation and thoughtfulness in approaching problems (Schunk 1996), a greater sense of personal control over events (Covington & Omelich 1984), and greater interest in the subject matter being covered (Bergin 1995).

Second, the findings of these fixed-design studies have generally been replicated under actual classroom conditions in a number of correlational-based investigations. For instance, Garcia & Pintrich (1994) demonstrated that the degree to which college students exhibited learning as opposed to performance goals in a given class was closely associated with the extent to which they judged the class to be encouraging of individual goal setting and allowing for student choice of assignments. Similar relationships have also been found among middle-school youngsters (Pintrich et al 1994). Likewise, in a study of some 20 elementary classrooms, Ames & Archer (1987) reported that variations in the effective use of learning strategies, the perceived value of effort, and positive feelings toward learning were all related to the extent to which children perceived their job to be the mastering of subject-matter material, not competing with others. Other similar studies using a variety of methodologies, including qualitative analysis of classroom observations, have uncovered similar positive patterns (Meece 1991; Meece et al 1988, 1989).

Third, a series of applied field studies have successfully incorporated elements of the equity paradigm in various combinations as a regular part of the curriculum among such diverse groups as college undergraduates (Covington & Omelich 1984) and at-risk minority students in middle school (Covington & Teel 1996, Teel et al 1994). In the latter instance, researchers controlled the quality and quantity of student work by applying a simple rule: The better the grade students wanted, the more credit they had to earn, irrespective of how well others were doing. Substantial amounts of grade credit were given based on how much students improved and for redoing assignments after having received corrective feedback. Also, grading criteria honored a variety of ways to demonstrate what was learned, including the use of drawings, poetry, and skits. These procedures appeared particularly effective for at-risk youngsters who, because of a long history of academic failure, had come to despair of their academic promise. In an additional example, Ames (1990) and Ames & Maehr (1989) modified the rules of the learning game in 100 elementary school classrooms favoring noncompetitive successes and the sharing of authority among teacher and students. Results indicate that this restructuring changed the learning climate for the better.

In order to institutionalize the kinds of restructuring cited here, the climate of an entire school must change. This involves negotiating a shared instructional vision among teachers, staff, and administration (Maehr & Midgley 1991). The pioneering efforts of Weinstein and her colleagues to carry out such school-wide change alerts us to the problems and promise of pursuing sustainable educational reform (Weinstein 1998, Butterworth & Weinstein 1996, Weinstein et al 1995) .

CONCLUSIONS: FUTURE DIRECTIONS FOR RESEARCH

Several directions for future research have been implied in the course of this review, perhaps the most important being the need to understand more fully the nature and costs of the continuing mismatch of cultural values that confronts many minority students, both with respect to the goals of schooling and the means by which these goals are achieved. In this regard, the pathway to responsible educational change would seem to lie in widening the legitimate reasons for learning as well as the permissible means for achieving excellence, including cooperation and sharing. The work of Suarez-Orozco (1989) cited earlier regarding Central American immigrants emphasizes the fact that the values of the dominant white middle class (autonomy, independence, and competition) are not the only pathways to personal excellence. Rather, an almost endless variety of as-yet largely unexplored avenues from other cultures can be equally effective and motivating (Valdéz 1998). These alternative reasons for learning (goals) and the means to encourage them deserve our immediate attention (see Maehr 1998).

A second proposal echoes the first. Although we are relatively well informed about the role of academic goals in motivating achievement, our understanding of how social goals enter into the process lags behind. It is interesting to note that it was drive-theory proponents who first offered a theoretical model—the dynamics of action model (Atkinson 1981, McClelland 1980)—that captured the common-sense proposition that many motives, not just one, operate in any achievement setting, and that the individual's behavior may be best understood in terms of the moment-to-moment changes in the relative strength of these motives. The perspective afforded by this action model is useful because it portrays achievement behavior in its full richness and complexity. Moreover, it stands as a challenge to the current limits of our theory building and taxes our ingenuity to develop ways to measure instability as well as stability in achievement behavior. We would do well to revisit these earlier offerings.

A third proposal concerns the fact that our understanding of achievement dynamics as amassed over the past half century is limited largely to students striving in the context of clear goals against explicit standards, usually relative in nature, that define success and failure (Brophy 1999). By comparison, we are far less knowledgeable about achievement dynamics as they relate to exploratory learning, to the appreciation and valuing of what one is learning, and to the role motivation plays in the pursuit of one's unique, individual interests. In this exploratory world, learners cannot say with any certainty what will become of what they learn, or even how much of their studies they have completed, but only that they have undertaken a task that can never be finished. It is in this sense that one's learning goals can be intangible—but motivating nonetheless—and what counts as success and failure comes to be defined idiosyncratically, not by consensus or by comparison with the accomplishments of others.

It is time that we redress this imbalance and give more attention to the valuing aspects of motivation. This is especially imperative because many observers have lamented the prospects of ever encouraging such intrinsic values as subject-matter appreciation in a context in which many students are grade driven and a common motivational strategy involves the threat of poor grades. Fortunately, there is a limited but growing body of evidence that suggests that striving for good grades and caring for learning are not necessarily incompatible goals, and that in some situations they may actually be mutually reinforcing (Covington 1999).

Finally, a note about educational reform. The accumulated research inspired by achievement goal theory and its motivational correlates has indicted the practice of limiting rewards as a short-sighted, destructive strategy for motivating students. But to indict only the most blatant mechanisms of competition, such as grading on the curve, is to miss the larger point. Competition is more than a dubious way to arouse children to learn. Competitive practices are only the obvious manifestations of more subtle but powerfully entrenched obstacles to educational change. The larger culprit is an ethos, or world view, held by many policy makers and ordinary citizens alike regarding the essential nature of the process of schooling. This world view is best expressed metaphorically when schools are likened to factories (see Marshall 1990): First comes children cast in the role of workers whose job it is to learn, followed by teachers in the role of supervisors whose task it is to guarantee quality control, capped off by school boards (akin to management) who wield ultimate authority over the entire process. Metaphors such as this establish the customs, espouse ideals, and above all determine the rules by which people relate to each other—in this case, rules that can set person against person and discourage cooperation. Many beliefs and practices detrimental to positive educational change form the vanguard of this metaphor, not the least of which are the hardened institutional lines of authority that run top down from school boards to teachers, a practice that disenfranchises teachers and undercuts their ongoing struggle for professional status (Maehr & Midgley 1991). Another fallout of the factory model is the misplaced yet surprisingly pervasive view of children as passive recipients of knowledge—vessels to be filled, or blank slates to be etched—not at all reflective of the active, willful, ingenious human beings that psychological research has shown children to be.

Before true educational reform can occur, this outdated factory metaphor of schooling must be replaced with new metaphors that more fully respond to the demands and opportunities of the twenty-first century. We need not look far for tantalizing possibilities, including an odds-on favorite: schooling as future-building, and personal goals as mediators of the future. In this connection, one is reminded of Harry Lauder's remark that "the future is not a gift, it is an achievement." If the future is an achievement, as Lauder argued, then teachers are futurists, along with politicians, filmmakers, and journalists: those individuals who make people's futures more real to them.

Psychologists can aid in creating new, more constructive public visions regarding the role and mission of schools in a variety of ways, not the least of which would involve redoubling research into children's perceptions of the future and their place in it. They can also continue developing promising lines of thought involving the concept of motivation, not as a matter of drives—with the underlying assumption that children must be forced to learn—but as a matter of goals, personal visions that beguile and draw, indeed entice, youngsters toward a future of their own creation.

Visit the Annual Reviews home page at www.AnnualReviews.org.

LITERATURE CITED

Allen JD. 1986. Classroom management: students' perspectives, goals, and strategies. *Am. Educ. Res. J.* 23:437–59

Alschuler AS. 1973. *Developing Achievement Motivation in Adolescents.* Englewood Cliffs, NJ: Educ. Technol.

Ames C. 1990. *Achievement goals and classroom structure: Developing a learning orientation.* Presented at Annu. Meet. Am. Educ. Res. Assoc., Boston

Ames C. 1992. Classrooms: goals, structures, and student motivation. *J. Educ. Psychol.* 84:261–71

Ames C, Ames R. 1984. Systems of student and teacher motivation: Toward a qualitative definition. *J. Educ. Psychol.* 76:535–56

Ames C, Archer J. 1987. *Achievement goals in the classroom: Student learning strategies and motivation processes.* Presented at Annu. Meet. Am. Educ. Res. Assoc., Washington, DC

Ames C, Maehr M. 1989. *Home and school cooperation in social and motivational development. (Contract No. DE-H023T80023).* Research funded by the Office of Special Education and Rehabilitative Services. Technical Report

Anderman EM, Midgley C. 1997. Changes in achievement goal orientations, perceived academic competence, and grades across the transition to middle-level schools. *Contemp. Educ. Psychol.* 22:269–98

Archer J. 1994. Achievement goals as a measure of motivation in university students. *Contemp. Educ. Psychol.* 19:430–46

Arroyo CG, Zigler E. 1995. Racial identity, academic, and the psychological well-being of economically disadvantaged adolescents. *J. Pers. Soc. Psychol.* 69:903–14

Atkinson JW. 1957. Motivational determinants of risk-taking behavior. *Psychol. Rev.* 64:359–72

Atkinson JW. 1964. *An Introduction to Motivation.* Princeton, NJ: Van Nostrand

Atkinson JW. 1981. Studying personality in the context of an advanced motivational psychology. *Am. Psychol.* 36:117–28

Bergin DA. 1995. Effects of a mastery versus

competitive motivation situation on learning. *J. Exp. Educ.* 63:303–14

Bergin DA, Cooks HC. 1995. *"Acting white": Views of high school students in a scholarship incentive program.* Presented at Annu. Meet. Am. Educ. Res. Assoc., San Francisco

Borkowski JG, Thorpe PK. 1994. Self-regulation and motivation: a life-span perspective on underachievement. See Schunk & Zimmerman 1994, pp. 45–74

Bouffard T, Boisvert J, Vezeau C, Larouche C. 1995. The impact of goal orientation on self-regulation and performance among college students. *Br. J. Educ. Psychol.* 65:317–29

Brophy J. 1999. Toward a model of the value aspects of motivation in education: developing appreciation for particular learning domains and activities. *Educ. Psychol.* Special Issue: *The Value Aspects of Motivation in Education,* ed. PR Pintrich, 34 (No. 2): Spring 1999 J Brophy, Guest ed.

Butterworth B, Weinstein RS. 1996. Enhancing motivational opportunity in elementary schooling: a case study of the ecology of principal leadership. *Elem. Sch. J.* 97:57–80

Cantor N, Harlow RE. 1994. Personality, strategic behavior, and daily-life problem solving. *Curr. Dir. Psychol. Sci.* 3:169–72

Cantor N, Norem JK. 1989. Defensive pessimism and stress and coping. *Soc. Cogn.* 7:92–112

Carver CS, Scheier MF. 1988. A control-process perspective on anxiety. *Anxiety Res.* 1:17–22

Chapin SL, Vito R. 1988. *Patterns of family interaction style, self-system processes and engagement with schoolwork: an investigation of adolescents rated as at-risk, or not-at-risk for academic failure.* Presented at Annu. Meet. Am. Educ. Res. Assoc., New Orleans

Collins-Eaglin J, Karabenick SA. 1993. *Devaluing of academic success by African-American students: on "acting white" and "selling out."* Presented at Annu. Meet. Am. Educ. Res. Assoc., Atlanta

Covington MV. 1992. *Making the Grade: A Self-Worth Perspective on Motivation and School Reform.* New York: Cambridge Univ. Press

Covington MV. 1998. *The Will to Learn.* New York: Cambridge Univ. Press

Covington MV. 1999. Caring about learning: the nature and nurturing of subject-matter appreciation. *Educ. Res.* 34:127–36

Covington MV, Beery RG. 1976. *Self-Worth and School Learning.* New York: Holt, Rinehart & Winston

Covington MV, Omelich CL. 1979. Are causal attributions causal? A path analysis of the cognitive model of achievement motivation. *J. Pers. Soc. Psychol.* 37:1487–504

Covington MV, Omelich CL. 1981. As failures mount: affective and cognitive consequences of ability demotion in the classroom. *J. Educ. Psychol.* 73:799–808

Covington MV, Omelich CL. 1984. Task-oriented versus competitive learning structures: motivational and performance consequences. *J. Educ. Psychol.* 76:1038–50

Covington MV, Omelich CL. 1987. "I knew it cold before the exam": a test of the anxiety-blockage hypothesis. *J. Educ. Psychol.* 79:393–400

Covington MV, Omelich CL. 1988. Achievement dynamics: the interaction of motives, cognition and emotions over time. *Anxiety J.* 1:165–83

Covington MV, Teel KM. 1996. *Overcoming Student Failure: Changing Motives and Incentives for Learning.* Washington, DC: Am. Psychol. Assoc.

Covington MV, Wiedenhaupt S. 1997. Turning work into play: the nature and nurturing of intrinsic task engagement. In *Effective Teaching in Higher Education: Research and Practice,* ed. R Perry, JC Smart, pp. 101–14. New York: Agathon

Craske ML. 1988. Learned helplessness, self-worth protection and attribution retraining for primary school children. *Br. J. Educ. Psychol.* 58:152–64

Culler RE, Holahan CJ. 1980. Test anxiety and academic performance: the effects of study-related behaviors. *J. Educ. Psychol.* 72:16–20

Depreeuw E. 1990. *Fear of Failure: A Complex Clinical Phenomenon.* Belgium: Univ. Leuven

Dewey J. 1916. *Democracy and Education.* New York: Macmillan

Doyle W. 1983. Academic work. *Rev. Educ. Res.* 53:159–99

Dray L, Beltranena R, Covington MV. 1999. *Nurturing intrinsic motivation in schools: a developmental analysis.* Presented at Annu. Meet. Am. Educ. Res. Assoc., Montreal

Dweck CS. 1986. Motivational processes affecting learning. *Am. Psychol.* 41:1040–48

Dweck CS, Leggett EL. 1988. A social-cognitive approach to motivation and personality. *Psychol. Rev.* 95:256–73

Eaton MJ, Dembo MH. 1997. Differences in the motivational beliefs of Asian American and non-Asian students. *J. Educ. Psychol.* 89:433–40

Elliot AJ, Harackiewicz JM. 1996. Approach and avoidance achievement goals and intrinsic motivation: a mediational analysis. *J. Pers. Soc. Psychol.* 70:968–80

Elliot AJ, McGregor HA, Gable SL. 1999. Achievement goals, study strategies, and exam performance: a mediational analysis. *J. Educ. Psychol.,* 91:In press

Elliott ES, Dweck CS. 1988. Goals: an approach to motivation and achievement. *J. Pers. Soc. Psychol.* 53:5–12

Emmons R. 1986. Personal strivings: an approach to personality and subjective well-being. *J. Pers. Soc. Psychol.* 51:1058–68

Eskilson A, Wiley MG, Muehlbauer G, Dodder L. 1986. Parental pressure, self-esteem and adolescent reported deviance: bending the twig too far. *Adolescence* 21(83):501–14

Farmer HS, Vispoel W, Maehr ML. 1991. Achievement contexts: effect on achievement values and causal attributions. *J. Educ. Res.* 85:26–38

Feldlaufer H, Midgley C, Eccles J. 1988. Student, teacher, and observer perceptions of the classroom before and after the transition to junior high school. *J. Early Adolesc.* 8:133–56

Ford ME. 1992. *Motivating Humans: Goals, Emotions, and Personal Agency Beliefs.* Newbury Park, CA: Sage

Fordham S, Ogbu JU. 1986. Black students' school success: coping with the burden of "acting white." *Urban Rev.* 18:176–206

Fried-Buchalter S. 1992. Fear of success, fear of failure, and the impostor phenomenon: a factor-analytic approach to convergent and discriminate validity. *J. Pers. Assess.* 58:368–79

Garcia T, Pintrich PR. 1994. Regulating motivation and cognition in the classroom: the role of self-schema and self-regulatory strategies. See Schunk & Zimmerman 1994, pp. 371–402

Ginsburg GS, Bronstein P. 1993. Family factors related to children's intrinsic/extrinsic motivational orientation and academic performance. *Child Dev.* 64:1461–74

Goodenow C. 1993. Classroom belonging among early adolescents: relationships to motivation and achievement. *J. Early Adolesc.* 13:21–43

Graham S, Golan S. 1991. Motivational influences on cognitive: task involvement, ego involvement, and depth of information processing. *J. Educ. Psychol.* 83:187–96

Hagtvet KA. 1984. Fear of failure, worry and emotionality: their suggestive causal relationships to mathematical performance and state anxiety. *Adv. Test Anxiety Res.* 3:211–24

Hamilton VL, Blumenfeld PC, Akoh H, Miura K. 1989. Japanese and American Children's reasons for the things they do in school. *Am. Educ. Res. J.* 26:545–71

Harackiewicz JM, Barron KE, Elliot AJ. 1998. Rethinking achievement goals: When are they adaptive for college students and why? *Educ. Psychol.* 33:1–21

Harter S. 1996. Teacher and classmate influences on scholastic motivation, self-esteem, and level of voice in adolescents. In *Social Motivation: Understanding Children's School Adjustment,* ed. J Juvonen, K Wentzel, pp. 11–42. New York: Cambridge Univ. Press

Hermans HJM, ter Laak JF, Maes CJM. 1972. Achievement motivation and fear of failure in family and school. *Dev. Psychol.* 6:520–28

Hertiz-Lazarowitz R, Kirdus VB, Miller N. 1992. Implications of current research on cooperative interaction for classroom application. In *Interaction in Cooperative Groups: The*

Theoretical Anatomy of Group Learning, ed. R Hertz-Lazarowtiz, N Miller, pp. 253–80. New York: Cambridge Univ. Press

Hess RD, Chih-Mei C, McDevitt TM. 1987. Cultural variations in family beliefs about children's performance in mathematics: comparisons among People's Republic of China, Chinese-American, and Caucasian-American families. *J. Educ. Psychol.* 79:179–88

Higgins RL, Berglas S. 1990. The maintenance and treatment of self-handicapping. See Higgins et al 1990, pp. 187–238

Higgins RL, Snyder CR, Berglas S, eds. 1990. *Self-Handicapping: The Paradox That Isn't.* New York: Plenum

Holloway SD. 1988. Concepts of ability and effort in Japan and the United States. *Rev. Educ. Res.* 58:327–45

Isleib RA, Vuchinich RE, Tucker JA. 1988. Performance attributions and changes in self-esteem following self-handicapping with alcohol consumption. *J. Soc. Clin. Psychol.* 6:88–103

Jacobs JE, Hyatt S, Tanner J. 1998. *Lessons learned at home: relations between parents' child-rearing practice and children's achievement perceptions.* Presented at Annu. Meet. Am. Educ. Res. Assoc., San Diego

Jagacinski CM, Nicholls JG. 1984. Conceptions of ability and related affects in task involvement and ego involvement. *J. Educ. Psychol.* 76:909–19

Jagacinski CM, Nicholls JG. 1987. Competence and affect in task involvement and ego involvement: the impact of social comparison information. *J. Educ. Psychol.* 79:107–14

Kaplan A, Midgley C. 1997. The effect of achievement goals: Does level of perceived academic competence make a difference? *Contemp. Educ. Psychol.* 22:415–35

Karabenick SA, Collins-Eaglin J. 1997. Relation of perceived instructional goals and incentives to college students' use of learning strategies. *J. Exp. Educ.* 65:331–41

Kelly GA. 1955. *Psychology of Personal Constructs.* Vol. 1: *A Theory of Personality.* New York: Norton

Kernis MH, Grannemann BD, Barclay LC. 1992. Stability of self-esteem: assessment, correlates, and excuse making. *J. Pers.* 60:621–44

Kimble CE, Funk SC, DaPolito KL. 1990. The effects of self-esteem uncertainty on behavioral self-handicapping. *J. Soc. Behav. Pers.* 5:137–49

Kluger AN, De Nisi A. 1996. The effects of feedback interventions on performance: a historical review, a meta-analysis, and a preliminary feedback intervention theory. *Psychol. Bull.* 119:254–85

Kohlmann CW, Schumacher A, Streit R. 1988. Trait anxiety and parental child-rearing behavior: support as a moderator variable? *Anxiety Res.* 1:53–64

Laux L, Glanzmann P. 1987. A self-presentational view of test anxiety. *Adv. Test Anxiety Res.* 5:31–37

Losey KM. 1995. Mexican American students and classroom interaction: an overview and critique. *Rev. Educ. Res.* 65:283–318

MacIver D, Stipek D, Daniels D. 1991. Explaining within-semester changes in student effort in junior high school and senior high school courses. *J. Educ. Psychol.* 83:201–11

Maehr ML. 1998. *Confronting culture with culture: creating optimum learning environments for students of diverse socio-cultural backgrounds.* Presented at Annu. Meet. Am. Educ. Res. Assoc., San Diego

Maehr ML, Meyer HA. 1997. Understanding motivation and schooling: Where we've been, where we are, and where we need to go. *Educ. Psychol. Rev.* 9:371–409

Maehr ML, Midgley C. 1991. Enhancing student motivation: a school-wide approach. *Educ. Psychol.* 26:399–427

Maehr ML, Stallings WM. 1972. Freedom from external evaluation. *Child Dev.* 43:177–85

Marshall H. 1990. Beyond the workplace metaphor: toward conceptualizing the classroom as a learning setting. *Theory Pract.* 29:94–101

Martin AJ. 1998. *Self-handicapping and defensive pessimism: predictors and consequences from a self-worth motivation perspective.* PhD diss., Univ. Western Sydney

Mayerson NH, Rhodewalt F. 1988. The role of self-protective attributions in the experience of pain. *J. Soc. Clin. Psychol.* 6:203–18

McClelland DC. 1955. Some social consequences of achievement motivation. In *Nebraska Symposium on Motivation*, ed. MR Jones, pp. 41–65. Lincoln: Univ. Nebr. Press

McClelland DC. 1961. *The Achieving Society.* Princeton, NJ: Van Nostrand

McClelland DC. 1980. Motive dispositions: the merits of operant and respondent measures. *Rev. Pers. Soc. Psychol.* 1:10–41

McCown W, Johnson J. 1991. Personality and chronic procrastination by university students during an academic examination period. *Pers. Individ. Differ.* 12:413–15

McInerney DM, Roche LA, McInerney V, Marsh HW. 1997. Cultural perspectives on school motivation: the relevance and application of goal theory. *Am. Educ. Res. J.* 34:207–36

Meece JL. 1991. The classroom context and students' motivational goals. *Advances in Motivation and Achievement,* ed. M. Maehr, P. Pintrich, 7:261–86. Greenwich, CT: JAI

Meece JL, Blumenfeld PC, Hoyle RH. 1988. Students' goal orientations and cognitive engagement in classroom activities. *J. Educ. Psychol.* 80:514–23

Meece JL, Blumenfeld PC, Puro P. 1989. A motivational analysis of elementary science learning environments. In *Looking Into Windows: Qualitative Research in Science Education,* ed. M Matyas, K Tobin, B Fraser, pp. 13–23. Washington, DC: Am. Assoc. Adv. Sci.

Meece JL, Holt K. 1993. A pattern analysis of students' achievement goals. *J. Educ. Psychol.* 85:582–90

Middleton MJ, Midgley C. 1997. Avoiding the demonstration of lack of ability: an under-explored aspect of goal theory. *J. Educ. Psychol.* 89:710–18

Midgley C, Kaplan A, Middleton M, Maehr ML. 1998. The development and validation of scales assessing students' achievement goal orientations. *Contemp. Educ. Psychol.* 23:113–31

Miller AT. 1986. A development study of the cognitive basis of performance impairment after failure. *J. Pers. Soc. Psychol.* 40:529–38

Mineka S, Henderson RW. 1985. Controllability and predictability in acquired motivation. *Annu. Rev. Psychol.* 36:495–529

Naveh-Benjamin M. 1985. *A comparison of training programs intended for different types of test-anxious students.* Presented at Symp. Inf. Process. Motiv., Am. Psychol. Assoc., Los Angeles

Nicholls JG. 1984. Achievement motivation: conceptions of ability, subjective experience, task choice, and performance. *Psychol. Rev.* 91:328–46

Nicholls JG. 1989. *The Competitive Ethos and Democratic Education.* Cambridge: Harvard Univ. Press

Norem JK, Illingworth KS. 1993. Strategy-dependent effects of reflecting on self and tasks: some implications of optimism and defensive pessimism. *J. Pers. Soc. Psychol.* 65:822–35

Pekrun R. 1992. The impact of emotions on learning and achievement: towards a theory of cognitive/motivational mediators. *Appl. Psychol. Int. Rev.* 41(4):359–76

Perry KE, Weinstein RS. 1998. The social context of early schooling and children's school adjustment. *Educ. Psychol.* 33(4):177–94

Pintrich PR. 1999. The role of goal orientation in self-regulated learning. In *Handbook of Self-Regulation: Theory, Research and Applications,* ed. M Boekaerts, PR Pintrich, M Zeidner, San Diego: Academic

Pintrich PR, De Groot EV. 1990. Motivational and self-regulated learning components of classroom academic performance. *J. Educ. Psychol.* 82:33–40

Pintrich PR, Roeser RW, De Groot EV. 1994. Classroom and individual differences in early adolescents' motivation and self-regulated learning. *J. Early Adolesc.* 14:139–61

Pintrich PR, Schrauben B. 1992. Students' motivational beliefs and their cognitive engagement in classroom tasks. See Schunk & Meece 1992, pp. 149–83

Pintrich PR, Schunk DH. 1996. *Motivation in*

Education: Theory, Research and Applications. Englewood Cliffs, NJ: Prentice Hall Merrill

Pintrich PR, Smith D, Garcia T, McKeachie WJ. 1993. Reliability and predictive validity of the Motivated Strategies for Learning Questionnaire (MSLQ). *Educ. Psychol. Meas.* 53:801–13

Pokay P, Blumenfeld PC. 1990. Predicting achievement early and late in the semester: the role of motivation and use of learning strategies. *J. Educ. Psychol.* 82:41–50

Purdie N, Hattie J. 1996. Cultural differences in the use of strategies for self-regulated learning. *Am. Educ. Res. J.* 33:845–71

Ratner H, Stettner L. 1991. Thinking and feeling: putting Humpty together again. *Merrill-Palmer Q.* 37:1–26

Reyes O, Jason LA. 1993. Pilot study examining factors associated with academic success for Hispanic high school students. *J. Youth Adolesc.* 22:57–71

Rhodewalt F. 1990. Self-handicappers: individual differences in the preference for anticipatory, self-protective acts. See Higgins et al 1990, pp. 69–106

Rhodewalt F, Morf CC, Hazlett S, Fairfield M. 1991. Self-handicapping: the role of discounting and augmentation in the preservation of self-esteem. *J. Pers. Soc. Psychol.* 61:122–31

Roberts GC. 1992. Motivation in sport and exercise: conceptual constraints and convergence. In *Motivation in Sports and Exercise*, ed. GC Roberts, pp. 3–29. Champaign, IL: Human Kinetics

Roeser RW, Midgley C, Urdan TC. 1996. Perceptions of the school psychological environment and early adolescents' psychological and behavioral functioning in school: the mediating role of goals and belonging. *J. Educ. Psychol.* 88:408–22

Roney C, Higgins ET, Shah J. 1995. Goals and framing: how outcome focus influences motivation and emotion. *Pers. Soc. Psychol. Bull.* 21:1151–60

Roney C, Sorrentino R. 1995. Reducing self-discrepancies or maintaining self-congruence? Uncertainty orientation, self-regulation, and performance. *J. Pers. Soc. Psychol.* 68:485–97

Rosen BC, D'Andrade R. 1959. The psychosocial origins of achievement motivation. *Sociometry* 22:185–218

Rosenthal DA, Feldman SS. 1991. The influence of perceived family and personal factors on self-reported school performance of Chinese and western high school students. *J. Res. Adolesc.* 1:135–54

Ruvolo A, Markus H. 1992. Possible selves and performance: the power of self-relevant imagery. *Soc. Cogn.* 10:95–124

Schneider RJ, Ackerman PL, Kanfer R. 1996. To "act wisely in human relations": exploring the dimensions of social competence. *Pers. Individ. Differ.* 21:469–81

Schunk DH. 1996. Goal and self-evaluative influences during children's cognitive skill learning. *Am. Educ. Res. J.* 33:359–82

Schunk DH, Meece J, eds. 1992. *Student Perceptions in the Classroom: Causes and Consequences.* Hillsdale, NJ: Erlbaum

Schunk DH, Zimmerman BJ, eds. 1994. *Self-Regulation of Learning and Performance: Issues and Educational Applications.* Hillsdale, NJ: Erlbaum

Schwarzer R, Cherkes-Julkowski M. 1982. Determinants of test anxiety and helplessness. *Adv. Test Anxiety Res.* 1:33–43

Schwarzer R, Jerusalem M, Schwarzer C. 1983. Self-related and situation-related cognition in test anxiety and helplessness: a longitudinal analysis with structural equations. *Adv. Test Anxiety Res.* 2:35–43

Schwarzer R, Jerusalem M, Stiksrud A. 1984. The developmental relationship between test anxiety and helplessness. *Adv. Test Anxiety Res.* 3:73–79

Skaalvik E. 1997. Self-enhancing and self-defeating ego orientations: relations with task and avoidance orientation, achievement, self-perceptions, and anxiety. *J. Educ. Psychol.* 89:71–81

Slavin RE. 1983. When does cooperative learning increase student achievement? *Psychol. Bull.* 94:429–45

Slavin RE, Madden NA, Leavey MB. 1984. Effects of team assisted individualization on the mathematics achievement of academically handicapped and non-handicapped students. *J. Educ. Psychol.* 76:813–19

Snyder ML. 1994. British and Mexican Students' attributes of academic success. *Psychol. Rep.* 75:815–18

Strage A. 1999. Family context variables and the development of self-regulation in college students. *Adolescence.* In press

Suarez-Orozco MM. 1989. *Central American Refugees and US High Schools: A Psychological Study of Motivation and Achievement.* Stanford, CA: Stanford Univ. Press

Teel KM, Covington MV, De Bruin-Parecki A. 1994. Promoting and sustaining a shift in motivation among low achieving African-American middle school students. *Int. J. Educ.* 8:138–51

Thompson T. 1993. Characteristics of self-worth protection in achievement behavior. *Br. J. Educ. Psychol.* 63:469–88

Thompson T. 1994. Self-worth protection: implications for the classroom. *Educ. Rev.* 46:259–74

Thompson T, Davis H, Davidson JA. 1998. Attributional and affective responses of impostors to academic success and failure feedback. *Pers. Individ. Differ.* 25:381–96

Thompson T, Davidson JA, Barber JG. 1995. Self-worth protection in achievement motivation: Performance effects and attitudinal behaviour. *J. Educ. Psychol.* 87:598–610

Thorkildsen TA & Nicholls JG. 1998. Fifth graders' achievement orientations and beliefs: Individual and classroom differences. *J. Educ. Psychol.,* 90:179–201.

Tobias S. 1986. Anxiety and cognitive processing of instruction. In *Self-Related Cognitions in Anxiety and Motivation,* ed. R Schwarzer, pp. 35–54. Hillsdale, NJ: Erlbaum

Tomiki K. 1997. *Influences of cultural values and perceived family environments on achievement motivation among college students.* Master's thesis. Univ. Calif. Berkeley

Topman RM, Jansen T. 1984. "I really can't do it, anyway": the treatment of test anxiety. *Adv. Test Anxiety Res.* 3:243–51

Topping ME, Kimmel EB. 1985. The impostor phenomenon: feeling phony. *Acad. Psychol. Bull.* 7:213–26

Urdan T. 1997. Achievement goal theory: past results, future directions. *Advances in Motivation and Achievement.* ed. PR Pintrich, ML Maehr, Vol. 10:99–142. Greenwich, CN: JAI

Urdan T, Midgley C, Anderman EM. 1998. The role of classroom goal structure in students' use of self-handicapping strategies. *Am. Educ. Res. J.* 35:101–22

Urdan TC, Maehr ML. 1995. Beyond a two-goal theory of motivation and achievement: A case for social goals. *Rev. Educ. Res.* 65(3):213–43

Valdéz G. 1998. The world outside and inside schools: language and immigrant children. *Educ. Res.* 27:4–18

Veroff J. 1969. Social comparison and the development of achievement motivation. In *Achievement-Related Motives in Children,* ed. CP Smith, pp. 46–101. New York: Sage

Weiner B, Kukla A. 1970. An attributional analysis of achievement motivation. *J. Pers. Soc. Psychol.* 15:1–20

Weinstein RS. 1998. Promoting positive expectations in schooling. In *How Students Learn: Reforming Schools Through Learner-Centered Education,* ed. NM Lambert, BL McCombs, pp. 81–111. Washington, DC: Am. Psychol. Assoc.

Weinstein RS, Madison SM, Kuklinski MR. 1995. Raising expectations in schooling: obstacles and opportunities for change. *Am. Educ. Res. J.* 32:121–59

Wentzel KR. 1989. Adolescent classroom goals, standards for performance, and academic achievement: an interactionist perspective. *J. Educ. Psychol.* 81:131–42

Wentzel KR. 1991a. Relations between social competence and academic achievement in early adolescence. *Child Dev.* 61:1066–78

Wentzel KR. 1991b. Social competence at school: the relation between social responsibility and academic achievement. *Rev. Educ. Res.* 61:1–24

Wentzel KR. 1992. Motivation and achievement in adolescence: a multiple goals perspective. See Schunk & Meece 1992, pp. 287–306

Wentzel KR. 1993. Motivation and achievement in early adolescence: the role of multiple classroom goals. *J. Early Adolesc.* 13: 4–20

Wentzel KR. 1994. Relations of social goal pursuit to social acceptance, classroom behavior, and perceived social support. *J. Educ. Psychol.* 86:173–82

Wentzel KR. 1995. *Teachers Who Care: Implications for Student Motivation and Classroom Behavior.* Washington, DC: Off. Educ. Res. Improve.

Wentzel KR. 1996. Social and academic motivation in middle school: concurrent and long-term relations to academic effort. *J. Early Adolesc.* 16:390–406

Wentzel KR, Wigfield A. 1998. Academic and social motivational influences on students' academic performance. *Educ. Psychol. Rev.* 10:155–75

Whang PA, Hancock GR. 1994. Motivation and mathematics achievement: comparisons between Asian-American and non-Asian students. *Contemp. Educ. Psychol.* 19:302–22

Wibrowski CR. 1992. *Self-regulated learning processes among inner city students.* PhD diss., Graduate School of the City Univ. New York

Wigfield A, Eccles JS, Pintrich PR. 1987. Development between the ages of 11 and 25. *The Handbook of Educational Psychology,* ed. DC Berliner, RC Calfee. New York: Prentice Hall International

Winterbottom MR. 1953. The relation of need for achievement of learning experiences in independence and mastery. In *Motives in Fantasy, Action, and Society,* ed. J Atkinson, pp. 453–78. Princeton, NJ: Van Nostrand

Wolters CA, Yu SL, Pintrich PR. 1996. The relation between goal orientation and students' motivational beliefs and self-regulated learning. *Learn. Individ. Differ.* 8:211–38

Woodworth RS. 1918. *Dynamic Psychology.* New York: Columbia Univ. Press

Zimmerman BJ. 1990. Self-regulated learning and academic achievement: an overview. *Educ. Psychol.* 25:3–17

Zimmerman BJ, Greenspan D, Weinstein CE. 1994. Self-regulating academic study time: a strategy approach. See Schunk & Zimmerman 1994, pp. 181–99

Annu. Rev. Psychol. 2000. 51:201–226

APPLICATIONS OF STRUCTURAL EQUATION MODELING IN PSYCHOLOGICAL RESEARCH

Robert C. MacCallum and James T. Austin

The Ohio State University, Department of Psychology, 142 Townshend Hall, Columbus, Ohio 43210–1222; e-mail: maccallum.1@osu.edu, austin.38@osu.edu

Key Words   structural equation models, covariance structures, LISREL

■ **Abstract**   This chapter presents a review of applications of structural equation modeling (SEM) published in psychological research journals in recent years. We focus first on the variety of research designs and substantive issues to which SEM can be applied productively. We then discuss a number of methodological problems and issues of concern that characterize some of this literature. Although it is clear that SEM is a powerful tool that is being used to great benefit in psychological research, it is also clear that the applied SEM literature is characterized by some chronic problems and that this literature can be considerably improved by greater attention to these issues.

CONTENTS

Introduction 202
Overview of SEM 202
Literature Review 203
    Previous Reviews of Applications 203
    Current Review... 204
Uses of SEM in Psychological Research 204
    Cross-Sectional Designs.. 205
    Longitudinal Designs 205
    Measurement Studies.. 208
Experimental Studies 210
    Twin Studies 211
    Other Areas of Application.. 211
Problematic Issues in Applications of SEM 211
    Generalizability of Findings 211
    Confirmation Bias 213
    The Issue of Time... 213
    Model Specification, Design, and Analysis Issues 215
    Reporting of Results... 219
Conclusion... 220

0084–6570/00/0201–0201$12.00   **201**

INTRODUCTION

The development of structural equation modeling (SEM) methods and software has proceeded rapidly since the 1970s. A historical review of the development of SEM was provided by Bentler (1986), and annotated bibliographies of the technical SEM literature have been provided by Austin & Wolfe (1991) and Austin & Calderón (1996). Methodological developments also have been reviewed (Bentler 1980, Bentler & Dudgeon 1996). Software development, with respect to both implementation of methodological advances as well as improvement of user interfaces, has made this sophisticated and powerful method readily accessible to substantive researchers, and these researchers have found SEM to be well-suited to addressing a variety of questions arising in psychological research. This combination of methodological advances, improved software, and applicability to problems of interest has resulted in wide usage of SEM in psychology and related disciplines (Tremblay & Gardner 1996), which has in turn yielded advances in substantive knowledge. At the same time, this ease of access and application of such a complex and sophisticated technique has given rise to a variety of problems and chronic misuses and oversights in practice.

In this review we assess positive and negative aspects of the applied SEM literature in psychology. We describe a range of issues and designs to which SEM has been applied productively. We also discuss a number of problematic issues in this literature, ranging from concerns regarding perspective, design, and strategy to chronic errors in conducting analyses and presenting and interpreting results. Our goal is to promote improved usage of SEM by increasing awareness of the range of research questions that can be addressed using this method and by helping users avoid some common pitfalls.

OVERVIEW OF SEM

To provide a basis for subsequent discussion, we present a brief overview of SEM along with some important special cases and extensions of the usual model. SEM is a technique used for specifying and estimating models of linear relationships among variables. Variables in a model may include both measured variables (MVs) and latent variables (LVs). LVs are hypothetical constructs that cannot be directly measured. In SEM each such construct is typically represented by multiple MVs that serve as indicators of the construct. A structural equation model, then, is a hypothesized pattern of directional and nondirectional linear relationships among a set of MVs and LVs. Directional relationships imply some sort of directional influence of one variable on another. Nondirectional relationships are correlational and imply no directed influence. In the most common form of SEM, the purpose of the model is to account for variation and covariation of the MVs.

Some special cases of SEM are of particular interest and are commonly used in practice. For example, path analysis provides for the testing of models of relationships among MVs; no LVs are included in the model. Path analysis models are used when MVs are of primary interest or when multiple indicators of LVs are not available. Factor analysis, another special case, provides for testing models of relationships between LVs, which are common factors, and MVs, which are indicators of common factors. The factor analysis model allows for correlational (nondirectional) relationships among LVs but does not include directional influences as in general SEM.

The usual form of SEM can be extended to great advantage in a variety of ways. We focus here on two such extensions that are well developed, easily accessible, and probably underutilized in practice. These extensions have been described in various SEM texts (e.g. Bollen 1989, Kline 1998, Loehlin 1998, Maruyama 1998) as well as in the LISREL software manual (Jöreskog & Sörbom 1996). The first such extension is multisample modeling, wherein a model is fit simultaneously to sample data from different populations. A key aspect of this approach involves the testing of invariance of critical parameters across groups. Similarities in the covariance structure of the MVs across groups may be attributable to parameters that are invariant across groups, and differences attributable to parameters that vary across groups. A second extension involves the modeling of MV means as well as variances and covariances. This is especially useful in multisample models where, for example, group differences in means on MVs could be accounted for as a function of group differences in means on LVs. Modeling of means is also used extensively in analysis of repeated measures data. In this context, a model may account for variances and covariances among repeated measures of a MV as well as for change in mean level of the MV over time. By using one or both of these extensions in various ways and contexts, investigators have developed an array of powerful and elegant models applicable to particular research designs. Many of these models are described below.

There exist other extensions and generalizations of SEM that undoubtedly will eventually become widely used but that are not as yet fully developed or accessible. One involves the incorporation of interactions and other nonlinear effects among LVs into models. Early developments in this area (e.g. Kenny & Judd 1984) have proved difficult to implement in practice, and there is a clear need for better methods. Schumacker & Marcoulides (1998) reviewed and illustrated recent efforts to extend SEM in this way. Another developing extension involves the application of SEM to multilevel data structures, where units at one level of observation are nested within units at another (e.g. students within schools), and variables may be measured at each level. Some structural equation models for such data structures have been discussed by Muthén (1994, 1997) and McDonald (1994).

LITERATURE REVIEW

Previous Reviews of Applications

Several within-domain reviews of published applications of SEM have appeared. All limit themselves to four to six journals over variable time periods (6–18 years). Breckler (1990) reviewed 72 applications published between 1977 and 1987 in major journals in personality and social psychology. He presented problematic issues, guidelines for reporting, and an analysis of a typical application. Two evaluative reviews of applications have appeared in marketing journals. Hulland et al (1996) identified 186 applications published between 1980 and 1994, whereas Baumgartner & Homburg (1996) located 149 applications published between 1977 and 1994. Hulland et al coded models on dimensions of theory, measurement, evaluation, and descriptive adequacy, then attempted to replicate published results for a subset of 112 models; successful replication was achieved in only 75% of these cases. Baumgartner & Homburg (1996) coded articles in terms of specification, data screening, and model evaluation. Two reviews of applications of SEM in organizational research have appeared. James & James (1989) coded 55 applications (1978–1987) separately for manifest variable (72%) and latent variable (28%) designs. They found that most a priori models were disconfirmed and that specification searches were routinely undertaken without checking for assumptions. Similarly, Medsker et al (1994) coded 28 applications in five major journals (1988–1993). They described a variety of usage trends by comparing their sample to that of James & James.

Current Review

We reviewed approximately 500 published applications of SEM appearing in 16 psychological research journals from 1993 to 1997. The journals, grouped by domain, were *Journal of Applied Psychology, Journal of Vocational Behavior, Organizational Behavior & Human Decision Processes,* and *Personnel Psychology* (Industrial-Organizational); *Journal of Abnormal Psychology, Journal of Consulting and Clinical Psychology, Journal of Counseling Psychology,* and *Psychological Assessment* (Counseling-Clinical); *Psychology and Aging, Child Development,* and *Developmental Psychology* (Developmental); *Journal of Personality, Journal of Personality and Social Psychology, Journal of Research in Personality,* and *Personality and Social Psychology Bulletin* (Social-Personality). We also included *Multivariate Behavioral Research* and *Structural Equation Modeling.*Our collection of studies included those using the full SEM framework as well as those using special cases of SEM, such as path analysis and confirmatory (not exploratory) factor analysis.

USES OF SEM IN PSYCHOLOGICAL RESEARCH

In this section we organize, describe, and cite examples of usage of SEM in substantive research in psychology. By necessity our categories are fuzzy and overlapping and by no means exhaustive. Furthermore, although we have endeavored to identify and cite sound exemplars of various uses of SEM, virtually any such application might be critiqued on specific aspects of design, specification, or analysis. From this perspective, we begin with some comments about research design. In general, psychological research investigating relationships among variables can be categorized as either observational (correlational) or experimental. SEM is by far more heavily used in observational studies. In fact, there seems to be a common misconception that its use is restricted to that category. To the contrary, SEM can be used in experimental studies to great advantage, as we discuss below.

Within the realm of observational studies, designs can be broken down roughly into two categories: cross-sectional and longitudinal. SEM is heavily used for both kinds of designs, with applications to cross-sectional designs being more common in social/personality and industrial/organizational psychology, and applications to longitudinal designs being more common in studies of development and aging. We consider applications to these two designs in turn.

Cross-Sectional Designs

As the name suggests, a cross-sectional design is a single-occasion snapshot of a system of variables and constructs. Its key feature is the concurrent measurement of variables. The use of SEM in cross-sectional designs is common, with applications to manifest variable, latent variable, or measurement studies. Multisample models and models with structured means are often used. For example, Rice et al (1997) used a cross-sectional design with multiple groups to compare African-American and Caucasian, as well as male and female, adolescents to investigate predictors of emotional well-being. Judge & Locke (1993) used reports from individuals and significant others to estimate the effects of dysfunctional thought processes on subjective well-being and job satisfaction.

A notable feature of many models used in cross-sectional studies is the specification of directional influences among variables. The perspective that directional influences require some finite amount of time to operate suggests that interpretation of such effects in cross-sectional designs may be problematic because concurrent measurement of variables precludes such effects from occurring (Gollob & Reichardt 1987, 1991). Nevertheless, numerous cross-sectional studies that we reviewed framed models as involving noninstantaneous processes or change over time. This potential conflict between design and model is discussed in more detail below.

Longitudinal Designs

There are two sorts of longitudinal designs to which SEM is often applied. Both involve measurements obtained from the same individuals on repeated occasions. In one type of longitudinal design, which we call a sequential design, different variables are measured at successive occasions and the model specifies effects of variables at a given occasion on other variables at later occasions. The researcher is interested in the pattern of influences operating over time among different variables. The sequence and timing of measurements are designed to allow for these hypothesized effects to operate. In another type of longitudinal design, a repeated measures design, the same variable or variables are measured at each occasion. Here the researcher is interested in relationships among the repeated measures of the same variables as well as the pattern of change over time. Occasions of measurement are chosen to represent the range of time and intervals during which change is of interest. Of course these two kinds of designs are not mutually exclusive; many studies incorporate elements of both.

In applications of SEM to sequential designs, directional influences in a model are hypothesized as operating over some time interval, and fitting the model to observed data yields estimates of such effects. The interpretation of such effects is bolstered by the use of a design that allows appropriate time for the effects to occur. Examples include a study by Holohan et al (1997) of effects of social support and social stressors on subsequent depressive symptoms, a study by Gest (1997) of relationships between behavioral inhibition and peer relations over time, and a study by Gold et al (1995) of stability and predictors of intellectual abilities measured 40 years apart. An important aspect of such designs and models is the desirability of including autoregressive influences. That is, if one hypothesizes that variable A at time 1 (A_1) influences B at time 2 (B_2), one should also measure B_1 and include in the model the influence of B_1 on B_2 as well as the correlation of A_1 with B_1. Failure to do so can result in a highly biased estimate of the effect of A_1 on B_2 (Gollob & Reichardt 1991). That is, one might conclude that there is a strong influence of A_1 on B_2 when in fact that apparent influence is in part spurious and due to the autoregressive influence of B_1 on B_2 and the correlation of B_1 with A_1.

Turning to repeated measures designs, the application of SEM to such designs represents an area of highly creative development of models and novel applications in recent years. There are two general frameworks for model specification in such designs. In both approaches it is possible and often desirable to include means in the model, so that the model accounts for changes in the mean of the MV over time, as well as for variances and covariances of repeated measures of the MV. One general approach involves the use of autoregressive models (Jöreskog 1979, McArdle & Aber 1990). Given measures of X at occasions 1, 2, . . . , t, . . . , T, such a model specifies a series of autoregressive effects wherein each X_t influences X_{t+1}. Such models are often called simplex models because they account for a simplex correlational structure, wherein the correlation between repeated measures decreases as the lag between the measures increases. The basic autoregressive model allows for many extensions and variations, many of which are described by Jöreskog (1979) and McArdle & Aber (1990). These include modeling of effects over various time lags, modeling of the structure of correlations among error terms, and evaluating whether parameters of interest are stable across occasions or intervals. One can also model autoregressive effects for LVs, where a given LV is represented by multiple indicators at each occasion. Examples of the use of autoregressive models in repeated measures designs include a study of drug abuse by Aiken et al (1994) and a study of anxiety in children by Lopez

& Little (1996). Both of these two-wave studies used multisample models with structured means. Examples of modeling data with more than two waves can be found in McArdle & Aber (1990) and Curran et al (1997b).

A second general class of models for repeated measures designs is latent curve models, often called growth curve models. Originating in early work by Tucker (1958) and Rao (1958), latent curve models represent a rich domain of methodological development in recent years (Collins & Horn 1991, Sayer & Collins 1999) and have been used in many elegant applications. A technical overview is provided by Meredith & Tisak (1990); less technical discussions are offered by Willett & Sayer (1994), Duncan et al (1994), and Duncan et al (1999). The objective of such models is to capture information about interindividual differences in intraindividual change (Nesselroade 1991). In their simplest forms, latent curve models can be viewed as a type of confirmatory factor analysis model, where the variances, covariances, and means of repeated measures of a MV are modeled. Factors, or latent curves, represent aspects of change over time, such as level, linear change, or acceleration. According to the model, each individual's vector of repeated measures on the MV is represented as a linear combination of these latent curves. Jones & Meredith (1996) presented an application of this model in a study of personality change across 30–40 years.

There is an array of important extensions of this model, many of which have been discussed and illustrated by McArdle & Aber (1990) and Duncan et al (1999). One can introduce additional variables representing predictors, correlates, or consequences of aspects of change. Such a model would involve an extension of the latent curve model into a full SEM model, specifying hypothesized associations between the latent curves and other LVs or MVs. Willett & Sayer (1994) described and illustrated this approach in a study using gender and exposure to deviant behavior to predict change in deviant behavior during adolescence. Raykov (1994) also used this method to study correlates of change in factors of fluid intelligence. Another extension involves investigating change on more than one MV simultaneously. In such multiple-outcome models, latent curves are specified for each MV, and one can then investigate relationships between latent curves representing different outcome variables. Such models have been discussed by MacCallum et al (1997), Tisak & Meredith (1990), and Willett & Sayer (1995). Curran et al (1997a,b) and Stoolmiller (1994) used this approach in empirical studies. Latent curve models can also be used in multisample designs, where repeated measures of a variable of interest are collected from samples of individuals from distinct populations. Such a design and model allow for the study of group differences in aspects of change. Muthén & Curran (1997) have proposed the use of such multisample latent curve models to analyze data from intervention studies. Given control and experimental groups, repeated measures of a dependent variable are obtained. The groups differ in that some treatment or intervention is applied in the experimental group after the baseline measure is observed. A latent curve model is specified to model change over time in the control group; the same latent curves are specified for the experimental group along with an additional latent curve to represent differential change after treatment. This approach had been used in an earlier application by Raykov (1995) to investigate the effect of a cognitive intervention on change in fluid intelligence during aging. Multisample latent curve models are also useful in sequential cohort designs in aging and developmental research. Such designs avoid the problems associated with obtaining repeated observations on a single sample for an extended period of time. Rather, multiple cohorts are followed for shorter periods of time, where cohorts differ with respect to age at the first occasion of measurement. Duncan et al (1996) described and illustrated the modeling of such data.

Measurement Studies

Confirmatory factor analysis (CFA) models, a special case of SEM, are widely used in measurement applications for a variety of purposes. Designs for construct validation and scale refinement, multitrait-multimethod validation, and measurement invariance can be evaluated through specification and testing of CFA models. We discuss each category in turn.

Construct Validation and Scale Refinement   Development of a measure of a construct requires validation of the hypothesized relationship between the construct and its indicators. The indicators are typically single items or composites consisting of multiple items. One or more models of this relationship are often evaluated using CFA. Methods for developing and validating multi-item assessment scales using factor analysis have been described by Floyd & Widaman (1995). Jackson et al (1993) used such methods to develop five scales for assessing job control, cognitive demand, and production responsibility. They tested a series of nested measurement models using two samples of shop employees, confirming a hypothesized five-factor model as well as invariance for four of the five factors across their samples. Novy et al (1994) used CFA to evaluate a theoretical model of ego development. Neuberg et al (1997) illustrated how CFA can be used to critique an existing scale, specifying and supporting a two-dimensional interpretation for a scale of need for closure that had been thought to be unidimensional. Similarly, some CFA analyses of personality inventories (e.g. Church & Burke 1994, Parker et al 1993) have yielded poor support for the popular five-factor theory of personality. McCrae et al (1996) criticized usage of CFA to validate such dimensional theories and recommended instead the use of exploratory factor analysis with target rotation. In our view, the phenomenon underlying such controversies involves the lack of correspondence between the highly structured nature of a confirmatory factor model and the somewhat looser criteria used to develop assessment instruments. Floyd & Widaman (1995) have discussed some aspects of this issue.

If construct validity is supported by confirmation of a hypothesized dimensional structure, other types of scale refinement or assessment may be considered. These include the development of short forms, as done by Donders (1997) with the WISC-III, or the assessment of construct validity in a different context, as done by Meyer et al (1993) in extending their measure of the construct of commitment from the context of organizations to the context of occupations. On the other hand, if CFA results do not support construct validity, it is possible to use results to revise the scale for future reevaluation. For example, items with a complex loading structure or high unique variance might be omitted, or additional items might be constructed to better represent a LV. Walker et al (1997) used this approach in refining a pain-response scale for children.

Multitrait-Multimethod Studies   Multitrait-multimethod (MTMM) studies represent a specific design for construct validation, in which multiple traits are measured by multiple methods (Campbell & Fiske 1959). Models for such matrices represent trait and method factors (LVs) as combining either additively (Widaman 1985) or multiplicatively (Cudeck 1988) to yield observed correlations among MVs. Reichardt & Coleman (1995), Kenny & Kashy (1992), and Widaman (1985) showed how evidence for convergent and discriminant validity can be obtained through the comparative evaluation of alternative additive models. Brannick & Spector (1990) demonstrated problems with fitting the additive formulation. They described common identification and specification problems and reanalyzed data from 18 published MTMM studies, finding estimation problems in 17 of 18. Applications of the additive model for MTMM designs typically encounter problems of empirical indeterminacy unless restrictions such as equality constraints are imposed on model parameters. An application by Coovert et al (1997) compared the additive and multiplicative models for performance rating data across seven military jobs and concluded that the multiplicative formulation performed better.

Measurement Invariance   When an investigator wishes to use a given measure or set of measures to make comparisons across populations or across time, the validity of those comparisons depends on the assumption that the same construct is being measured in different groups or at different occasions. This assumption of measurement invariance can be tested using CFA (Meredith 1993), usually including mean structures so as to allow for comparison of latent variable means across groups or occasions. The assessment of measurement invariance across groups involves the use of multisample CFA. Methods have been described and illustrated by Widaman & Reise (1997) and Reise et al (1993). Horn & McArdle (1992) and Tisak & Meredith (1990) described and illustrated methods for studying measurement invariance over time. In either context, one is interested in testing the invariance of parameters of the factor model, including factor means, across groups or time. Studies of measurement invariance are common in the literature. Little (1997) investigated invariance of factors of control expectancy across gender and four cultural groups. Kim et al (1996) studied invariance of world views and religious beliefs of older adults over time. Pentz & Chou (1994) described and illustrated the study of measurement invariance across both groups and time simultaneously in a study of adolescent drug abuse. Millsap (1997) extended research on invariance by examining the relationship between measurement invariance and predictive bias. Given a predictor and criterion set measured in multiple groups, he found that measurement invariance ordinarily implies predictive bias (group differences in regression coefficients), and that an absence of predictive bias ordinarily implies an absence of measurement invariance. Millsap showed how these conditions can be investigated using simple structural equation models.

Experimental Studies

We return now to the issue of observational versus experimental designs. Most of the applications described to this point involve observational studies. As mentioned earlier, there seems to be a common misconception that SEM is applicable only to observational studies and not to experimental studies. This misconception apparently stems from the fact that models for data gathered in experimental studies would incorporate categorical independent variables, and the inclusion of such variables appears to violate the assumption of multivariate normality underlying the commonly used maximum likelihood method of estimation. However, as clarified by Bollen (1989:126–28), the assumption of multivariate normality need not apply to exogenous measured variables. Rather, this assumption can be stated as referring to all other variables conditional on the levels of exogenous measured variables. Thus, given experimentally manipulated independent variables, one can use SEM to model the relationships of those variables, represented by coded variables such as dummy variables, to other variables, including covariates, mediators, and outcomes. Russell et al (1998) provided a discussion of procedures, issues, and advantages in the use of SEM in experimental studies, along with illustrations. The social cognition literature provides numerous examples of the use of SEM to study mediational effects in experimental designs. For example, Prussia & Kinicki (1996) used SEM to investigate mediators of effects of performance feedback and vicarious experience on group effectiveness, and Hoyle (1993) used SEM to study mediational effects of perceived attitudinal similarity on attraction toward a stranger. Another approach to using SEM in experimental studies is to treat different levels of experimental variables as representing different populations and to conduct multisample SEM, where the model of interest is fit simultaneously to samples representing different experimental conditions. Muthén & Curran (1997) used this approach to fit latent curve models to control and treatment groups. They illustrated this method using data from a study of the effectiveness of an intervention intended to reduce aggressive behavior in school children. In general, the application of SEM in experimental studies represents a significant but relatively untapped potential area of application. The conceptual boundary that is usually defined between observational and experimental research is probably far too rigid. SEM clearly cuts across that boundary.

Twin Studies

In recent years SEM has become a valuable tool in twin and family designs to model genetic and environmental influences on variables of interest (Loehlin 1989, Plomin & Rende 1991). In the most basic model, relevant data consist of measures on an observed variable collected from samples of siblings of different levels of relatedness (monozygotic twins, dizygotic twins, nontwin siblings, etc). Genetic and environmental influences are then investigated using a form of multisample confirmatory factor analysis, in which groups are defined according to relatedness, and factors represent shared or nonshared genetic and environmental influences. Results provide estimates of the impact of each source of variation and covariation. Methodological details have been provided by Loehlin (1998), Neale & Cardon (1992), McArdle & Prescott (1997), and McArdle et al (1998). There are many applications in the literature, often including other capabilities of SEM described above. Examples include a study of temperament (Saudino et al 1995), a study of memory performance including a multisample analysis of Swedish and American twin data (Finkel et al 1995), and a study of genetic and environmental components of latent curves representing aspects of change in alcohol consumption (Prescott & Kendler 1996).

Other Areas of Application

We reemphasize that our discussion of types of applications of SEM is by no means exhaustive, and that many applications involve aspects of several different categories described above. In addition, many applications and special cases address problems that fall outside the domain we have described. Such methods include, for instance, the use of SEM in meta-analysis (Rounds & Tracey 1993) and test-retest designs (McArdle & Woodcock 1997), the use of multisample models to study moderator effects (e.g. Eisenberg et al 1997, Harnish et al 1995), and the longitudinal study of reliability and validity (Tisak & Tisak 1996).

PROBLEMATIC ISSUES IN APPLICATIONS OF SEM

We now turn to methodological problems and issues of concern that emerged in our review of published applications. We consider several global concerns before turning to problems involving details of analysis, interpretation, and presentation of results.

Generalizability of Findings

In our view, much of the applied SEM literature is characterized by inadequate understanding or acknowledgment of the limitations of single studies. Even in a well-designed study where analyses are conducted properly, conclusions may be limited to the particular sample, variables, and time frame represented by the design. Such limitations are seldom acknowledged, let alone addressed as a topic of research. Rather, results are usually interpreted as if substantial generalizability exists.

More specifically, researchers using SEM must recognize that results are subject to sampling or selection effects with respect to at least three aspects of a study: individuals, measures, and occasions (Nesselroade 1991). Most researchers are familiar with the notion of sampling effects with respect to individuals. Such effects are taken into account via sampling procedures and the use of inferential statistics. Another mechanism for taking such effects into account in SEM is cross-validation (Browne & Cudeck 1989, Cudeck & Browne 1983). Researchers can use the expected cross-validation index (ECVI) (Browne & Cudeck 1989, 1993), which is computed from a single sample, as an index of how well a solution obtained in one sample is likely to fit an independent sample. This index is useful for comparison of alternative models, especially when sample size is not large, providing an indication of which model yields a solution with greatest generalizability.

Another aspect of selection effects at the level of observations involves the population of interest. A structural equation model is a hypothesis about the structure of relationships among MVs in a specific population. Researchers should explicitly define the population of interest, although this is often not done in practice, and should acknowledge that the generalizability of a model beyond that population may be uncertain. Of course, many studies do address this issue explicitly, especially those that involve multisample SEM, where the focus of the study is the evaluation of model fit and parameter estimates across samples from distinct populations (e.g. Aiken et al 1994, Lindenberger & Baltes 1997).

Selection effects are also inherent in the choice of measured variables used in a given study. In SEM this issue is especially prominent with regard to the choice of indicators to represent latent variables. In any given study, a particular latent variable is effectively defined as that which its indicators have in common. The nature of the construct can shift with the choice of indicators, which in turn can influence results and interpretation. Clearly, valid results and interpretation depend on having appropriate operationalizations of the latent variables under study. Little et al (1999) discussed and demonstrated selection effects involving indicators and offered guidelines for selection of good indicators.

An additional aspect of selection effects involves occasions of measurement. In any study where one investigates effects that operate over time, those effects may vary with the length of the time interval (Gollob & Reichardt 1987, 1991). From this perspective, there is no single true effect of one variable on another, unless the variables themselves do not change over any time period of interest. In addition to acknowledging this point explicitly, researchers could conduct studies of effects of interest over different time lags to more fully understand the nature of such effects.

In general, we urge researchers to be more aware of the limitations of single studies with respect to these issues. Such an awareness could manifest itself via explicit acknowledgments, qualified interpretations, and studies that investigate generalizability of findings with respect to these issues.

Confirmation Bias

Results of our review suggested that researchers using SEM are quite susceptible to a confirmation bias (Greenwald et al 1986), i.e. a prejudice in favor of the model being evaluated. We see two symptoms of this bias: (*a*) a moderately frequent, overly positive evaluation of model fit, to be discussed below; and (*b*) a routine reluctance to consider alternative explanations of data. Reichardt (1992) discussed the fallibility of judgments about models, noting that it is easy to accept an explanation that fits our data well, and that researchers are not then motivated to consider alternatives. This is especially problematic in SEM. Given a study where support is obtained for a specific model, other models that would fit the data equally well, or approximately so, routinely exist. It is important for researchers to consider this possibility and to employ strategies and methods that provide for examination of alternatives. One such approach is to specify and evaluate multiple a priori models. Although many studies use this strategy (about 50% in our review), most such studies investigate a series of nested models, where parameters of one model in the series are a subset of those in the next model. Although this approach helps to indicate which parameters are needed to account for observed data, it does not address the possible existence of qualitatively distinct models of approximately equal complexity that provide alternative meaningful explanations of data. Millsap & Meredith (1994) provide an illustration of the investigation of qualitatively distinct nonnested models in their study of models of salary discrimination.

An especially interesting phenomenon in the context of alternative models is the existence of equivalent models, which are alternative models that fit any data to the same degree. Such models can be distinguished only in terms of substantive meaning. Lee & Hershberger (1990) provided some simple rules for generating equivalent models from a given model. In a study of published applications of SEM, MacCallum et al (1993) showed that equivalent models occur routinely in practice, often in very large numbers. Investigators are apparently almost universally unaware of this phenomenon, or else they choose to ignore it. We urge researchers to generate and evaluate the substantive meaningfulness of equivalent models in empirical studies. Ruling out their existence or meaningfulness would strengthen the support of a favored model. More generally, any effort to examine alternative models can provide some protection against a confirmation bias and bolster support of a favored model.

The Issue of Time

Gollob & Reichardt (1987, 1991) suggested that directional effects in structural equation models can be considered as causal effects in a loose sense wherein a change in one variable somehow results in a change in another variable, and they described three properties of such effects: (*a*) these effects take some finite amount of time to operate; (*b*) a variable may be influenced by the same variable at an earlier point in time, i.e. autoregressive effects may exist; and (*c*) the magnitude of an effect may vary as a function of the time lag. Our review showed that directional effects are routinely studied using cross-sectional designs, which as pointed out by Gollob & Reichardt (1987, 1991) cannot incorporate any of the three properties just defined. Cross-sectional designs allow only for the evaluation of relationships among variables at one point in time and do not allow for auto-regressive effects or time lags. Thus, it may be problematic to infer causality or directional influence in cross-sectional studies. For such an inference to be valid, a researcher must take one of two positions. One option is to argue that the time lag during which the causal influence operates is essentially instantaneous, thereby justifying concurrent measurement of variables in a cross-sectional design. Such situations may not be unusual. For example, Pajares & Miller (1995), in a study of the effect of mathematics self-efficacy on performance on mathematics tests, argued explicitly that the effect of interest was essentially instantaneous, meaning that the variables should be measured as closely together as possible in time. If the time lag of interest is not of extremely short duration, then to justify the study of directional influences in cross-sectional designs the investigator must assume that the causal variables under study do not change over the time period of interest, i.e. between the time the causal effect occurs and the time the causal variable is measured. If this assumption is not valid or if effects of interest are not essentially instantaneous, estimates of directional effects obtained in a cross-sectional design may be highly biased (Gollob & Reichardt 1987, 1991). Given the prevalence in the literature of models incorporating directional effects estimated and tested using data from cross-sectional studies, such biased estimates of effects are probably a chronic problem in the literature.

We suggest that one or the other of these justifications should be stated explicitly for cross-sectional models that include directional influences. In the absence of such justification, a cross-sectional design may be inappropriate and a longitudinal design preferred to allow for representation of the properties described by Gollob & Reichardt (1987, 1991). Furthermore, as noted earlier, longitudinal designs and models should provide for assessment of autoregressive effects. Our review showed that such effects are routinely overlooked in practice, resulting in substantial potential bias in estimates of directional influences (for further discussion of this point and for an application, see Wagner et al 1994). Also, in designing longitudinal studies to evaluate causal effects, one must not forget Cliff's (1983) admonition that a temporal sequence in itself is not sufficient to imply causality. Even given a temporal sequence, an apparent causal influence may be due to an intervening variable or to some correlate of the putative cause, so it is important to make efforts to avoid omitting important variables of this kind. The critical general point is that many studies show inadequate consideration of the issue of time in design, and that greater consideration of this issue would result in improved information about directional influences among variables.

Model Specification, Design, and Analysis Issues

Latent Variable Versus Measured Variable Models   Approximately 25% of the studies we reviewed used path analysis models, with no LVs. Many researchers may be unaware of advantages of LV models over MV models. Theories in psychology typically postulate patterns of relationships among LVs. Single MVs generally do not provide adequate representation of such constructs because of imperfect (often modest) reliability and validity. Nevertheless, path analysis models treat single MVs as exact, error-free representations of the constructs of interest. This approach can result in estimates of effects that are highly biased due to the influence of error (Bollen 1989:151–76, Maruyama 1998:79–87). An alternative is to obtain multiple indicators of each LV. A given LV is then defined in effect as whatever its indicators have in common. Little et al (1999) have discussed issues and important phenomena relevant to the selection of indicators. A full LV model then specifies relationships of the indicators to the LVs as well as relationships of the LVs to each other. Such a model allows for estimation of the unique variance in each indicator, and estimates of relationships among LVs are not biased by the presence of error in the indicators.

However, let us consider those situations in which only a single indicator is available for each LV of interest. The relatively common use of path analysis in such settings is of concern because results are susceptible to the biasing effects of error just described. Fortunately, there is a simple method for resolving this problem in many cases. Given a LV represented by a single multiitem scale, one approach to obtaining multiple indicators might be to use each item as an indicator. However, this strategy is often ineffective because of the potentially large number of items, the lack of unidimensionality of the scale, or the relatively low reliability of single items. An alternative approach that is often viable is to construct parcels. A parcel is simply a sum of a subset of items from the scale. Multiple parcels can be defined by aggregating distinct subsets of items, and the parcels then serve as multiple indicators of the given LV. An investigator can thus gain the advantages inherent in full LV models and avoid some of the difficulties associated with MV path analysis models. Our review indicated that such an approach could have been taken in many published studies using path analysis. Methods for constructing parcels have been described by Kishton & Widaman (1994). Examples of the use of parcels can be found in Lent et al (1997) and Lopez & Little (1996).

Sample Size   Our review indicated a wide range of sample sizes used in SEM applications, with small-sample studies not being uncommon. About 18% of the studies we reviewed used samples of fewer than 100 individuals. Published applications rarely include explicit consideration of whether the available sample is sufficiently large, and few well-founded guidelines are available. Developments in recent years make it feasible to address this question from a power analysis perspective. MacCallum et al (1996) provided a method for determining the minimum sample size necessary to achieve a given level of power for tests of model fit. As noted by MacCallum et al, however, a minimum sample size determined by power analysis for tests of overall fit is not necessarily adequate for other purposes, such as obtaining sufficiently precise parameter estimates. In any case, lacking a power analysis or other justification, SEM analyses of small samples are almost certainly problematic. We are reluctant to recommend rules of thumb regarding sample size in SEM. Recent work (MacCallum et al 1999) on the question of sample size in factor analysis has shown rules of thumb to be generally invalid in that context, which is a special case of SEM, and that minimum sample size necessary to accurately recover population factor loadings is highly dependent on characteristics such as communality level of the MVs. We expect that similar phenomena operate in the more general context of SEM, and we anticipate further research and improved guidelines regarding the sample size question.

The issue of sample size is also relevant in the context of model evaluation. Hu & Bentler (1998) reviewed literature regarding effects of sample size on fit indexes. Although important effects exist, investigators should not necessarily favor measures of fit that are independent of sample size, especially when comparing alternative models. This issue has been examined carefully by Cudek & Henly (1991). Consider the case where sample size is relatively small and one wishes to compare alternative models of varying complexity, where more complex models have more parameters. As one estimates larger numbers of parameters, one loses some precision in those estimates, more so with smaller samples. A small sample may not be large enough to support the estimation of more complex models. Thus, the model that can be best supported may depend on sample size, with simpler models favored when sample size is smaller. In comparing models when sample size is small, it is advisable to use an index such as ECVI (Browne & Cudeck 1989, 1993), which is sensitive to the phenomenon just described.

Strategy   Jöreskog & Sörbom (1996) described three strategies in model specification and evaluation: (*a*) strictly confirmatory, wherein a single a priori model is studied; (*b*) model generation, wherein an initial model is fit to data and then modified as necessary until it fits adequately well; and (*c*) alternative models, wherein multiple a priori models are specified and evaluated. Our review showed approximately the following percentages of studies using each of these strategies: strictly confirmatory, 20%; model generation, 25%; alternative models, 55%. The relatively common usage of the first two strategies is unfortunate. The strictly confirmatory strategy is highly restrictive, requiring the investigator to evaluate a single model in isolation and leaving little recourse if that model does not work well. The model generation strategy is potentially misleading and easily abused. Studies have shown that such data-driven model modifications may lack validity (MacCallum 1986) and are highly susceptible to capitalization on chance (MacCallum et al 1992). Any use of a model generation strategy must be subject to conditions. First, it must be acknowledged that the resulting model is in part data driven; second, modifications must be substantively meaningful; and third, the modified model must be evaluated by fitting it to an independent sample. Although some applications using this strategy meet the first and second conditions, very few meet the third. Fortunately, there are some pleasant exceptions providing cross-validation of modified models (e.g. Belsky et al 1996, Marsiske et al 1997). The alternative models strategy provides an attractive alternative to the other strategies, avoiding the difficulties just described and providing comparative information about alternative explanations of the data, thus lending some protection against a confirmation bias.

Correlation Versus Covariance Matrices   In typical applications of SEM, users must decide whether to fit a model to a covariance matrix, S, or a correlation matrix, R. In some designs, such as multisample or repeated measures designs, it is necessary to use covariance matrices so as to retain information about variances of variables. Differences in variances of variables among groups or across time represent important information to be accounted for by a model. This recommendation is followed closely in practice. In most other designs the user may choose to analyze either S or R, but there are interpretational advantages to using R. If latent variables are standardized and the model is fit to R, then parameter estimates can be interpreted in terms of standardized variables. In practice, about 50% of the published applications we reviewed fit models to correlation matrices. Unfortunately, however, most users seem unaware that fitting a model to R versus S introduces a subtle but potentially serious problem (Cudeck 1989, Lawley & Maxwell 1971:100–3). Conventional estimation methods in SEM are based on statistical distribution theory that is appropriate for S but not for R. It is not correct to fit a model to R while treating R as if it were a covariance matrix. As discussed by Cudeck (1989), the consequences of treating R as a covariance matrix depend on properties of the model being fit. In all cases, standard errors of parameter estimates as well as confidence intervals and test statistics for parameter estimates will be incorrect. Correct standard errors will generally be smaller than the incorrect values, resulting in narrower confidence intervals and larger test statistics. In some cases, parameter estimates themselves may be incorrect, and in some cases values of fit indexes will also be incorrect. As noted by Cudeck, these facts have significant implications for published applications of SEM where popular programs are used to fit models to correlation matrices; such studies undoubtedly include some incorrect results.

At the time of this writing (August 1999) various computer programs for SEM deal with this issue in different ways. Currently, two programs automatically provide for correct estimation when analyzing a correlation matrix (RAMONA) Browne & Mels 1998; SEPATH, Steiger 1999). This same facility is expected to be implemented in the next release of EQS (PM Bentler, personal communication). Correct estimation of a correlation structure can be done in LISREL (Jöreskog & Sörbom 1996) and Mx (Neale 1997) but requires the user to introduce specific constraints on parameters. The AMOS program (Arbuckle & Wothke

1999) does not accept correlation matrices for analysis. Given this variation in treatment of this issue and the rapid pace of software development, along with the potential impact of incorrect analyses of correlation structures, we offer a test whereby users can determine whether a specific SEM program provides correct estimation of a model fit to a correlation matrix. Jöreskog & Sörbom (1996) present the widely used stability-of-alienation example (Wheaton et al 1977). Their model B (Figure 6.3, p. 218, excluding error covariances) can be fit to the correlation matrix obtained by rescaling the covariance matrix in their Table 6.5 (p. 216). A check of correctness of results can be made with reference to a single parameter. The correct maximum likelihood estimate of the factor loading of Alienation67 on Powerlessness67 is 0.999. The correct estimate of the standard error for this loading is 0.036. If the correlation matrix is treated incorrectly as a covariance matrix, the resulting incorrect estimate of the standard error is 0.047. If this latter value is obtained, the implication is that the software in question provides incorrect results for analysis of correlation matrices, as described above and as discussed in detail by Cudeck (1989). We urge users fitting models to correlation matrices to be certain that their SEM software treats such matrices correctly. Otherwise, it would be preferable to fit models to covariance matrices, ensuring correct results but sacrificing some ease of interpretation.

Interpretation of Results   Our review produced a variety of concerns about assessment of model fit and interpretation of parameter estimates. With respect to model fit, researchers do not seem adequately sensitive to the fundamental reality that there is no true model (Browne & Cudeck 1993, Cudeck & Henly 1991), that all models are wrong to some degree, even in the population, and that the best one can hope for is to identify a parsimonious, substantively meaningful model that fits observed data adequately well. At the same time, one must recognize that there may well be other models that fit the data to approximately the same degree. Given this perspective, it is clear that a finding of good fit does not imply that a model is correct or true, but only plausible. These facts must temper conclusions drawn about good-fitting models.

In addition, a finding of good fit does not imply that effects hypothesized in the model are strong. In fact, it is entirely possible for relationships among variables to be weak, or even zero, and for a hypothesized model to fit extremely well. The resulting parameter estimates would reflect weak relationships among variables and large residual variances for endogenous variables. Thus, it is critically important to pay attention to parameter estimates, even when fit is very good. We found this to be a common oversight in applications. For instance, in nearly 50% of the studies reviewed, researchers failed to report residual variances for endogenous variables. For example, a model might hypothesize an influence of LV *A* on LV *B*. The model would be found to fit well; the researcher would report the estimate of the effect of *A* on *B* but would not report the residual variance in *B*, which may well be substantial. Good fit does not imply at all that such residual variances are small. Such information is critical to a full understanding of the magnitude of effects and should always be reported and discussed.

We observed a wide variety of measures of fit being used, as well as a range of criteria for determining what constitutes good fit. There was little consistency in choice of fit indexes or criteria for their evaluation. We encountered numerous cases of clearly overly positive assessment of fit, with authors stating that fit was acceptable even though values of fit indexes fell well short of any proposed criteria for adequate fit. Researchers using SEM need better guidelines regarding selection and interpretation of fit measures. Some useful information has been provided in recent papers by Hu & Bentler (1998, 1999). In studies of the performance of various fit measures with respect to sensitivity to model misspecification, Hu & Bentler (1998) recommended the use of the standardized root mean square residual (SRMSR) in tandem with one of several other indexes that they see as more or less interchangeable. These include the non-normed fit index (NNFI; Bentler & Bonett 1980) and the root mean square error of approximation (RMSEA; Browne & Cudeck 1993, Steiger & Lind 1980), among others. Significantly, Hu & Bentler (1998) recommended against usage of some common indexes such as the goodness of fit index (GFI) and adjusted goodness of fit index (AGFI), measures that are widely used in the SEM literature. In addition to being insufficiently and inconsistently sensitive to model misspecification, these indexes have also been shown to be strongly influenced by sample size (Marsh et al 1988). Hu & Bentler (1998, 1999) also emphasized that commonly used criteria for interpretation of popular fit indexes have a clear tendency to result in acceptance of poorly specified models. They propose rules of thumb that are more conservative than popular criteria and are also more conservative than criteria recommended in the heavily cited early paper by Bentler & Bonett (1980). We would add one strong recommendation to those of Hu and Bentler. We especially encourage use of RMSEA for several reasons: (*a*) It appears to be adequately sensitive to model misspecification (Hu & Bentler 1998); (*b*) commonly used guidelines for interpretation seem to yield appropriate conclusions about model quality (Hu & Bentler 1998, 1999); and (*c*) most importantly, a confidence interval is available. This confidence interval provides important information about precision of the estimate of fit, which is not available for almost all other fit indexes. We urge the routine use of RMSEA and the reporting and discussion of the associated confidence interval. Finally, we also encourage use of methods for the assessment of model fit at the individual level (Neale 1997, Reise & Widaman 1999). These procedures provide a measure of the contribution of each individual to the overall lack of model fit, allowing for identification of individuals for whom a model fits well or poorly, as well as subsequent analysis of such information to assess possible predictors or correlates of person-fit.

Reporting of Results

In our review we encountered many difficulties associated with presentation of information about models, methods, analyses, and results. For example, in about

10% of the articles reviewed we were unable to determine precisely either the model or the indicators of LVs. In about 25% we could not determine if the model was fit to R or S. In about 50% reporting of parameter estimates was incomplete (omission of nonsignificant estimates, unique variances, and/or residual variances). Many of these issues can be resolved by attention to published guidelines for presenting results of SEM (Hoyle & Panter 1995, Raykov et al 1991). We urge investigators as well as journal editors to adhere to these guidelines and suggest that every application of SEM should provide at least the following information: a clear and complete specification of models and variables, including a clear listing of the indicators of each LV; a clear statement of the type of data analyzed, with presentation of the sample correlation or covariance matrix (or making such data available upon request); specification of the software and method of estimation; and complete results. We define complete results to mean multiple measures of fit as recommended above, with confidence intervals when available, along with all parameter estimates and associated confidence intervals or standard errors. Criteria for evaluating values of fit indexes should be clearly stated.

CONCLUSION

Our review confirmed that SEM is a highly versatile tool heavily used in the psychology research literature to investigate a variety of problems. Although there are high-quality applications that provide important insights or advances in particular substantive areas, there are also problematic aspects of this literature. These range from problems of perspective, design, and strategy to mechanical aspects of model specification, data analysis, interpretation, and presentation. The problems we have described can have a substantial impact on the quality of information produced in these applications as well as on the validity of interpretations and conclusions. Paying attention to the concerns raised in this review should enhance the quality of applications of SEM and in turn increase the quality of knowledge gained from its use.

ACKNOWLEDGMENTS

We wish to thank the following individuals for valuable comments and suggestions provided at various stages of this project: Michael Browne, Roger Millsap, Chip Reichardt, Keith Widaman, Joe Rodgers, Jack McArdle, John Nesselroade, Jim Steiger, and Ken Bollen. We also thank Scott Davies for his enormous assistance in conducting the literature review and Tom Sidick for assistance in checking the manuscript and references.

Visit the Annual Reviews home page at www.AnnualReviews.org.

LITERATURE CITED

Aiken L, Stein JA, Bentler PM. 1994. Structural equation analyses of clinical subpopulation differences and comparative treatment outcomes: characterizing the daily lives of drug addicts. *J. Consult. Clin. Psychol.* 62:488–99

Arbuckle JL, Wothke W. 1999. *Amos 4.0 User's Guide.* Chicago: SmallWaters

Austin JT, Calderón RF. 1996. Theoretical and technical contributions to structural equation modeling: an updated annotated bibliography. *Struct. Equ. Model.* 3: 105–75

Austin JT, Wolfle LM. 1991. Annotated bibliography of structural equation modeling: technical work. *Br. J. Math. Stat. Psychol.* 44:93–152

Baumgartner H, Homburg C. 1996. Applications of structural equation modeling in marketing and consumer research: a review. *Int. J. Res. Market.* 13:139–61

Belsky J, Hsieh K, Crnic K. 1996. Infant positive and negative emotionality: one dimension or two? *Dev. Psychol.* 32:289–98

Bentler PM. 1980. Multivariate analysis with latent variables: causal modelling. *Annu. Rev. Psychol.* 31:419–56

Bentler PM. 1986. Structural modelling and psychometrika: an historical perspective on growth and achievements. *Psychometrika* 51:35–51

Bentler PM, Bonett DG. 1980. Significance tests and goodness-of-fit in the analysis of covariance structures. *Psychol. Bull.* 88:588–606

Bentler PM, Dudgeon P. 1996. Covariance structure analysis: statistical practice, theory, and directions. *Annu. Rev. Psychol.* 47:563–92

Bollen KA. 1989. *Structural Equations with Latent Variables.* New York: Wiley

Brannick MT, Spector PE. 1990. Estimation problems of the block diagonal model of the multitrait-multimethod matrix. *Appl. Psychol. Meas.* 14:325–40

Breckler SJ. 1990. Applications of covariance structure modeling in psychology: cause for concern? *Psychol. Bull.* 107:260–73

Browne MW, Cudeck R. 1989. Single sample cross-validation indices for covariance structures. *Multivar. Behav. Res.* 24: 445–55

Browne MW, Cudeck R. 1993. Alternative ways of assessing model fit. In *Testing Structural Equation Models,* ed. KA Bollen, JS Long, pp. 136–61. Newbury Park, CA: Sage

Browne MW, Mels G. 1998. Path analysis: RAMONA. In *SYSTAT for Windows: Advanced Applications* (Ver 8), pp. 607–65. Evanston, IL: SYSTAT

Campbell DT, Fiske DW. 1959. Convergent and discriminant validation by the multitrait-multimethod matrix. *Psychol. Bull.* 56:81–105

Church AT, Burke PJ. 1994. Exploratory and confirmatory tests of the Big Five and Tellegen's three- and four-dimensional models. *J. Pers. Soc. Psychol.* 66:93–114

Cliff N. 1983. Some cautions concerning the application of causal modelling methods. *Multivar. Behav. Res.* 18:115–26

Collins LM, Horn JL, eds. 1991. *Best Methods for the Analysis of Change.* Washington, DC: Am. Psychol. Assoc.

Coovert MD, Craiger JP, Teachout MS. 1997. Effectiveness of the direct product versus confirmatory factor model for reflecting the structure of multimethod-multirater job performance data. *J. Appl. Psychol.* 82:271–80

Cudeck R. 1988. Multiplicative models and MTMM matrices. *Multivar. Behav. Res.* 13:131–47

Cudeck R. 1989. Analysis of correlation matrices using covariance structure models. *Psychol. Bull.* 105:317–27

Cudeck R, Browne MW. 1983. Cross-validation of covariance structures. *Multivar. Behav. Res.* 18:507–34

Cudeck R, Henly SJ. 1991. Model selection in covariance structures analysis and the "problem" of sample size: a clarification. *Psychol. Bull.* 109:512–19

Curran P, Harford T, Muthén BO. 1997a. The relation between heavy alcohol use and bar patronage: a latent growth model. *J. Stud. Alcohol* 57:410–18

Curran P, Stice E, Chassin L. 1997b. The relation between adolescent alcohol use and peer alcohol use: a longitudinal random coefficients model. *J. Consult. Clin. Psychol.* 65:130–40

Donders J. 1997. A short form of the WISC-III for clinical use. *Psychol. Assess.* 9:15–20

Duncan TE, Duncan SC, Hops H. 1996. Analysis of longitudinal data within accelerated longitudinal designs. *Psychol. Methods* 1:236–48

Duncan TE, Duncan SC, Stoolmiller M. 1994. Modeling developmental processes using latent growth structural equation methodology. *Appl. Psychol. Meas.* 18:343–54

Duncan TE, Duncan SC, Strycker LA, Li F, Alpert A. 1999. *An Introduction to Latent Variable Growth Curve Modeling.* Mahwah, NJ: Erlbaum

Eisenberg N, Guthrie IK, Fabes RA, Reiser M, Murphy BC, et al. 1997. The relations of regulation and emotionality to resilience and competent social function in elementary school children. *Child Dev.* 68:295–311

Finkel D, Pederson N, McGue M. 1995. Genetic influences on memory performance in adulthood: comparison of Minnesota and Swedish twin data. *Psychol. Aging* 10:437–46

Floyd FJ, Widaman KF. 1995. Factor analysis in the development and refinement of clinical assessment instruments. *Psychol. Assess.* 7:286–99

Gest SD. 1997. Behavioral inhibition: stability and associations with adaptation from childhood to early adulthood. *J. Pers. Soc. Psychol.* 72:467–75

Gold DP, Andres D, Etezadi J, Arbuckle T. 1995. Structural equation model of intellectual change and continuity and predictors of intelligence in older men. *Psychol. Aging* 10:294–303

Gollob HF, Reichardt CS. 1987. Taking account of time lags in causal models. *Child Dev.* 58:80–92

Gollob HF, Reichardt CS. 1991. Interpreting and estimating indirect effects assuming time lags really matter. In *Best Methods for the Analysis of Change,* ed. LM Collins, JL Horn, pp. 243–59. Washington, DC: Am. Psychol. Assoc.

Greenwald AG, Pratkanis AR, Leippe MR, Baumgardner MH. 1986. Under what conditions does theory obstruct research progress? *Psychol. Rev.* 93:216–29

Harnish JD, Dodge KA, Valente E. 1995. Mother-child interaction quality as a partial mediator of the roles of maternal depressive symptomatology and socioeconomic status in the development of child behavior problems. *Child Dev.* 66:739–53

Holohan CJ, Moos RH, Holohan CK, Brennan P. 1997. Social context, coping strategies, and depressive symptoms: an expanded model with cardiac patients. *J. Pers. Soc. Psychol.* 72:918–28

Horn JL, McArdle JJ. 1992. A practical guide to measurement invariance in research on aging. *Exp. Aging Res.* 18:117–44

Hoyle RH. 1993. Interpersonal attraction in the absence of explicit attitudinal information. *Soc. Cogn.* 11:309–20

Hoyle RH, Panter AT. 1995. Writing about structural equation modeling. In *Structural Equation Modeling: Concepts, Issues, and Applications,* ed. RH Hoyle, pp. 158–76. Thousand Oaks, CA: Sage

Hu L, Bentler PM. 1998. Fit indices in covariance structure modeling: sensitivity to underparameterized model misspecification. *Psychol. Methods* 3:424–53

Hu L, Bentler PM. 1999. Cutoff criteria for fit indexes in covariance structure analysis:

conventional criteria versus new alternatives. *Struct. Equ. Mod.* 6:1–55

Hulland J, Chow YH, Lam S. 1996. Use of causal models in marketing research: a review. *Int. J. Res. Mark.* 13:181–97

Jackson PR, Wall TD, Martin R, Davids K. 1993. New measures of job control, cognitive demand, and production responsibility. *J. Appl. Psychol.* 78:753–62

James LR, James LA. 1989. Causal modelling in organizational research. In *International Review of Industrial and Organizational Psychology 1989,* ed. C Cooper, I Robertson, pp. 371–404. Chichester, UK: Wiley

Jones C, Meredith W. 1996. Patterns of personality change across the life span. *Psychol. Aging* 11:57–65

Jöreskog KG. 1979. Statistical models and methods for analysis of longitudinal data. In *Advances in Factor Analysis and Structural Equation Models,* ed. KG Jöreskog, D Sörbom, pp. 129–69. Cambridge, MA: Abt

Jöreskog KG, Sörbom D. 1996. *LISREL 8 User's Reference Guide.* Chicago: Sci. Software Int.

Judge TA, Locke EA. 1993. Effect of dysfunctional thought processes on subjective well-being and job satisfaction. *J. Appl. Psychol.* 78:475–90

Kenny DA, Judd CM. 1984. Estimating the nonlinear and interactive effects of latent variables. *Psychol. Bull.* 96:201–10

Kenny DA, Kashy D. 1992. Analysis of the multitrait-multimethod matrix by confirmatory factor analysis. *Psychol. Bull.* 112:165–72

Kim J, Nesselroade JR, Featherman DL. 1996. The state component in self-reported worldviews and religious beliefs of older adults: the MacArthur successful aging studies. *Psychol. Aging* 11:396–407

Kishton JM, Widaman KF. 1994. Unidimensional versus domain representative parceling of questionnaire items: an empirical example. *Educ. Psychol. Meas.* 54:757–65

Kline RB. 1998. *Principles and Practice of Structural Equation Modeling.* New York: Guilford

Lawley DN, Maxwell AE. 1971. *Factor Analysis as a Statistical Method.* New York: Elsevier

Lee S, Hershberger S. 1990. A simple rule for generating equivalent models in covariance structure modeling. *Multivar. Behav. Res.* 25:313–34

Lent RW, Brown SD, Gore PA. 1997. Discriminant and predictive validity of academic self-concept, academic self-efficacy, and mathematics-specific self-efficacy. *J. Counsel. Psychol.* 44:307–15

Lindenberger U, Baltes PB. 1997. Intellectual functioning in old and very old age: cross-sectional results for the Berlin Aging Study. *Psychol Aging* 12:410–32

Little TD. 1997. Mean and covariance structures (MACS) analyses of cross-cultural data: practical and theoretical issues. *Multivar. Behav. Res.* 32:53–76

Little TD, Lindenberger U, Nesselroade JR. 1999. On selecting indicators for multivariate measurement and modeling with latent variables: when 'good' indicators are bad and 'bad' indicators are good. *Psychol. Methods* 4:192–211

Loehlin JC. 1989. Partitioning environmental and genetic contributions to behavioral development. *Am. Psychol.* 44:1285–92

Loehlin JC. 1998. *Latent Variable Models: An Introduction to Factor, Path, and Structural Analysis.* Hillsdale, NJ: Erlbaum. 3rd ed.

Lopez DF, Little TD. 1996. Children's action-control beliefs and emotional regulation in the social domain. *Dev. Psychol.* 32:299–312

MacCallum RC. 1986. Specification searches in covariance structure modelling. *Psychol. Bull.* 100:107–20

MacCallum RC, Browne MW, Sugawara HM. 1996. Power analysis and determination of sample size for covariance structure modeling. *Psychol. Methods* 1:130–49

MacCallum RC, Kim C, Malarkey WB, Kiecolt-Glaser JK. 1997. Studying multivariate change using multilevel models and latent curve models. *Multivar. Behav. Res.* 32:215–53

MacCallum RC, Roznowski M, Necowitz LB. 1992. Model modifications in covariance structure analysis: the problem of capitalization on chance. *Psychol. Bull.* 111:490–504

MacCallum RC, Wegener DT, Uchino BN, Fabrigar LR. 1993. The problem of equivalent models in applications of covariance structure analysis. *Psychol. Bull.* 114:185–99

MacCallum RC, Widaman KF, Zhang S, Hong S. 1999. Sample size in factor analysis. *Psychol. Methods* 4:84–99

Marsh HW, Balla JR, McDonald RP. 1988. Goodness-of-fit indexes in confirmatory factor analysis: the effect of sample size. *Psychol. Bull.* 103:391–410

Marsiske M, Klumb P, Baltes MM. 1997. Everyday activity patterns and sensory functioning in old age. *Psychol. Aging* 12:444–57

Maruyama G. 1998. *Basics of Structural Equation Modeling.* Thousand Oaks, CA: Sage

McArdle JJ, Aber MS. 1990. Patterns of change within latent variable structural equation modeling. In *New Statistical Methods in Developmental Research,* ed. A von Eye, pp. 151–224. New York: Academic

McArdle JJ, Prescott CA. 1997. Contemporary models of the biometric genetic analysis of intellectual abilities. In *Contemporary Intellectual Assessment: Theories, Tests, and Issues,* ed. DP Flanagan, JL Genshaft, PL Harrison, pp. 403–36. New York: Guilford

McArdle JJ, Prescott CA, Hamagami F, Horn JL. 1998. A contemporary method for developmental-genetic analyses of age changes in intellectual abilities. *Dev. Neuropsychol.* 14:69–114

McArdle JJ, Woodcock RW. 1997. Expanding test-retest designs to include developmental time-lag components. *Psychol. Methods* 2:403–35

McCrae RR, Zonderman AB, Costa PT, Bond MH, Paunonen SV. 1996. Evaluating replicability of factors in the revised NEO Personality Inventory: confirmatory factor analysis versus Procrustes rotation. *J. Pers. Soc. Psychol.* 70:552–66

McDonald RP. 1994. The bilevel reticular action model for path analysis with latent variables. *Sociol. Methods Res.* 22:399–413

Medsker GM, Williams LJ, Holohan P. 1994. A review of current practices for evaluating causal models in organizational behavior and human resources management research. *J. Manage.* 20:439–64

Meredith W. 1993. Measurement invariance, factor analysis, and factorial invariance. *Psychometrika* 58:525–43

Meredith W, Tisak J. 1990. Latent curve analysis. *Psychometrika* 55:107–22

Meyer JP, Allen NJ, Smith CA. 1993. Commitment to organizations and occupations: extension and test of a three-component conceptualization. *J. Appl. Psychol.* 78:475–90

Millsap RE. 1997. Invariance in measurement and prediction: their relationship in the single-factor case. *Psychol. Methods* 3:248–60

Millsap RE, Meredith W. 1994. Statistical evidence in salary discrimination studies: nonparametric inferential conditions. *Multivar. Behav. Res.* 29:339–64

Muthén BO. 1994. Multilevel covariance structure analysis. *Sociol. Methods Res.* 22:376–98

Muthén BO. 1997. Latent variable modeling of longitudinal and multilevel data. In *Sociological Methodology,* ed. A Raftery, 27:453–80. Oxford, UK: Basil Blackwell

Muthén BO, Curran PJ. 1997. General longitudinal modeling of individual differences in experimental designs: a latent variable framework for analysis and power estimation. *Psychol. Methods* 2:371–402

Neale MC. 1997. *Mx: Statistical Modeling.* Richmond, VA: Dept. Psychiatry, Med. Coll. Virginia

Neale MC, Cardon LR, eds. 1992. *Methodology for Genetic Studies of Twins and Families. NATO ASI Ser. D, Vol. 67.* Dordrecht, The Netherlands: Kluwer

Nesselroade JR. 1991. Interindividual differences in intraindividual change. In *Best Methods for the Analysis of Change,* ed. LM Collins, JL Horn, pp. 92–105. Washington, DC: Am. Psychol. Assoc.

Neuberg SL, Judice TN, West SG. 1997. What the need for closure scale measures and what it does not: toward differentiating among related epistemic motives. *J. Pers. Soc. Psychol.* 72:1396–1412

Novy DM, Frankiewicz RG, Francis DJ, Liberman D, Overall JE, Vincent KR. 1994. An investigation of the structural validity of Loevinger's model and measure of ego development. *J. Pers.* 62:86–118

Pajares F, Miller MD. 1995. Mathematics self-efficacy and mathematics performances: the need for specificity of assessment. *J. Couns. Psychol.* 42:190–98

Parker JDA, Bagby RM, Summerfeldt LJ. 1993. Confirmatory factor analysis of the Revised NEO Personality Inventory. *Pers. Individ. Differ.* 15:463–66

Pentz MA, Chou C. 1994. Measurement invariance in longitudinal clinical research assuming change from development and intervention. *J. Consult. Clin. Psychol.* 62:450–62

Plomin R, Rende R. 1991. Human behavioral genetics. *Annu. Rev. Psychol.* 42:161–90

Prescott CA, Kendler KS. 1996. Longitudinal stability and change in alcohol consumption among female twins: contributions of genetics. *Dev. Psychopathol.* 8:849–66

Prussia GE, Kinicki AJ. 1996. A motivational investigation of group effectiveness using social cognitive theory. *J. Appl. Psychol.* 81:187–98

Rao CR. 1958. Some statistical methods for comparison of growth curves. *Biometrics* 14:1–17

Raykov T. 1994. Studying correlates and predictors of longitudinal change using structural equation modeling. *Appl. Psychol. Meas.* 18:63–77

Raykov T. 1995. Multivariate structural modeling of plasticity in fluid intelligence of

aged adults. *Multivar. Behav. Res.* 30:255–87

Raykov T, Tomer A, Nesselroade JR. 1991. Reporting structural equation modeling results in *Psychology and Aging:* some proposed guidelines. *Psychol. Aging* 6:499–503

Reichardt CS. 1992. The fallibility of our judgments. *Eval. Pract.* 13:157–63

Reichardt CS, Coleman SC. 1995. The criteria for convergent and discriminant validity in a multitrait-multimethod matrix. *Multivar. Behav. Res.* 30:513–38

Reise SP, Widaman KF. 1999. Assessing the fit of measurement models at the individual level: a comparison of item response theory and covariance structure approaches. *Psychol. Methods* 4:3–21

Reise SP, Widaman KF, Pugh RH. 1993. Confirmatory factor analysis and item response theory: two approaches for exploring measurement invariance. *Psychol. Bull.* 114:552–66

Rice KG, Cunningham TJ, Young MB. 1997. Attachment to parents, social competence, and emotional well-being: a comparison of black and white late adolescents. *J. Couns. Psychol.* 44:89–101

Rounds J, Tracey TJ. 1993. Prediger's dimensional representation of Holland's RIASEC circumplex. *J. Appl. Psychol.* 78:875–90

Russell DW, Kahn JH, Spoth R, Altmaier EM. 1998. Analyzing data from experimental studies: a latent variable structural equation modeling approach. *J. Couns. Psychol.* 45:18–29

Saudino KF, McGuire S, Reiss D, Hetherington EM, Plomin R. 1995. Parent ratings of EAS temperaments in twins, full siblings, half siblings, and step siblings. *J. Pers. Soc. Psychol.* 68:723–33

Sayer A, Collins LM, eds. 1999. *New Methods for the Analysis of Change.* Washington, DC: Am. Psychol. Assoc.

Schumacker RE, Marcoulides GA, eds. 1998. *Interaction and Nonlinear Effects in Structural Equation Modeling.* Mahwah, NJ: Erlbaum

Steiger JH. 1999. Structural equation modeling (SEPATH). In *Statistica for Windows,* Vol. 3. Tulsa, OK: StatSoft

Steiger JH, Lind A. 1980. *Statistically based tests for the number of common factors.* Presented at the Annu. Meet. Psychometric Soc., Iowa City, IA

Stoolmiller M. 1994. Antisocial behavior, delinquent peer association, and unsupervised wandering for boys: growth and change from childhood to early adolescence. *Multivar. Behav. Res.* 29:263–88

Tisak J, Meredith W. 1990. Descriptive and associative developmental models. In *Statistical Methods in Longitudinal Research,* ed. A von Eye, 2:387–406. San Diego, CA: Academic

Tisak J, Tisak M. 1996. Longitudinal models of reliability and validity: a latent curve approach. *Appl. Psychol. Meas.* 20:275–88

Tremblay PF, Gardner RC. 1996. On the growth of structural equation modeling in psychological journals. *Struct. Equ. Model.* 3:93–104

Tucker LR. 1958. Determination of parameters of a functional relationship by factor analysis. *Psychometrika* 23:19–23

Wagner RK, Torgeson JK, Rashotte CA. 1994. Development of reading-related phonological processing abilities: new evidence of bidirectional causality from a latent variable longitudinal study. *Dev. Psychol.* 30:73–87

Walker LS, Smith CA, Garber J, Van Slyke DA. 1997. Development and validation of the Pain Response Inventory for children. *Psychol. Assess.* 9:392–405

Wheaton B, Muthén B, Alwin D, Summers G. 1977. Assessing reliability and stability in panel models. In *Sociological Methodology,* ed. DR Heise, pp. 84–136. San Francisco: Jossey-Bass

Widaman KF. 1985. Hierarchically nested covariance structure models for multitrait-multimethod data. *Appl. Psychol. Meas.* 9:1–26

Widaman KF, Reise S. 1997. Exploring the measurement invariance of psychological instruments: applications in the substance use domain. In *The Science of Prevention: Methodological Advances from Alcohol and Substance Abuse,* ed. KJ Bryant, M Windle, SG West, pp. 281–324. Washington, DC: Am. Psychol. Assoc.

Willett JB, Sayer AG. 1994. Using covariance structure analysis to detect correlates and predictors of individual change over time. *Psychol. Bull.* 116:363–81

Willett JB, Sayer AG. 1995. Cross-domain analyses of change over time: combining growth modeling and covariance structure analysis. In *Advanced Structural Equation Modeling: Issues and Techniques,* ed. GA Marcoulides, RE Schumacker, pp. 125–57. Mahwah, NJ: Erlbaum

Annu. Rev. Psychol. 2000. 51:227–253

THE ENVIRONMENTAL PSYCHOLOGY OF CAPSULE HABITATS

Peter Suedfeld and G. Daniel Steel

The University of British Columbia, Vancouver, British Columbia, Canada, and Lincoln University, Canterbury, New Zealand, e-mail: psuedfeld@cortex.psych.ubc.ca, steelg@kahu.lincoln.ac.hz

Key Words isolation, confinement, unusual environments, enclosed habitats

■ **Abstract** Capsule habitats make it possible for human beings to survive and function in environments that would otherwise be lethal, such as space, the ocean depths, and the polar regions. The number of people entering capsules in the course of their work or for purposes of recreation is constantly increasing. However, long-term living in such habitats imposes physical and psychological risks as well as offering opportunities and benefits. This paper reviews what is known about the environmental, social, and personality aspects of adaptation to capsules, including sources of stress, selection criteria, obstacles to and facilitators of adequate coping, changes in group interaction, the role of temporal factors, and post-mission consequences.

CONTENTS

Introduction 227
Definitions..228
Positive Capsule Psychology...229
Psychologically Relevant Aspects of the Capsule Environment 230
  Physical Stressors 231
  Psycho-Environmental Factors 233
  Social Factors..234
  Temporal Factors 237
  Postmission Reentry..239
Applications of Psychology 239
  Selection 239
  Environmental Design...243
  Countering Boredom..244
Other Interesting Issues...246

INTRODUCTION

To appreciate the nature of life in a capsule, people have to open, and perhaps to bend, their minds a bit. Our lives are full of variety, stimulation, change, and surprise. Most of the situations we encounter are pleasant and interesting, offering a chronic "surfeit of attractive stimuli" (Lipowski 1971). Capsule habitats are different. They protect their occupants from an outside environment that is harsh, dangerous, and potentially lethal. But the inside also imposes challenges and difficulties.

Today, technology is making it possible for human beings to live in places that in the past we could neither reach nor have survived in. And, for a multitude of reasons, more and more people are not only working in such places, they are playing there, too: Antarctic tourism is flourishing, and plans for space tourism are developing (Wichman 1996). Capsules, the people who populate them, and the organizations that support them offer unique opportunities for research and applications of psychology.

DEFINITIONS

Capsule environments are one type of isolated, confined environment (ICE). This classification overlaps with the category of extreme and unusual environments (EUEs) (Suedfeld 1987), also called exotic, abnormal, or stressful environments (e.g. Bachrach 1982, Harrison & Connors 1984). Of course, almost any environment is extreme and unusual for some individuals and groups and familiar and survivable for others: A life-long New Yorker suddenly alone in the frozen Arctic tundra would find the surroundings no less strange and dangerous, and probably would live no longer, than would the Inuk hunter plunked down in the middle of a Times Square intersection. Here, we use the term extreme to indicate physical parameters that are substantially outside the optimal range for human survival (even though some groups may exist in them) and the term unusual to denote conditions that deviate seriously from the accustomed milieux of most (but not necessarily all) human communities. Some environments qualify as EUEs only during temporary disruption, such as natural or industrial disasters or war. Many EUEs involve physical remoteness or lack of access from accustomed locales and a circumscribed spatial range. These are further classified as ICEs.

ICEs located in non-EUEs include prisons, prison camps, resource-extraction communities (e.g. mining and logging camps), the habitats of hermits and lone prospectors, transoceanic vessels, stimulus-restriction laboratories, spaceship and other simulators, and the control areas of missile silos. ICEs located in EUEs that do involve extreme and unusual physical conditions include deserts, unpopulated islands, mountain peaks, and capsules.

Typically, capsule environments are remote from other communities, are located in places where the physical parameters are inimical to human life, and are difficult to enter or leave. They are inhabited by artificially composed groups of people who are removed from their normal social networks and who carry out specific tasks and procedures. Excursions into the surrounding environment are relatively rare, usually uncomfortable, and frequently dangerous. The capsule therefore has to contain workspaces and living quarters, as well as facilities for recreation, health maintenance, medical treatment, sanitation, food preparation and consumption, and communication.

The life-support systems of the capsule may be relatively ordinary, as in polar stations, or the epitome of sophisticated technology, as in space stations and submarines. The capsule may be stationary or moving, either more or less in circles—for example, in orbit—or toward a specific goal. The natural surround may change with the seasons or with travel, or it may be uniform throughout the life of the capsule. However, "striking similarities seem to exist between the problems facing groups in the polar regions, space, underwater establishments, and expeditions. . . ." (Ursin et al 1991:778).

Opportunities for psychological research abound. Polar stations, space vehicles, and undersea habitats are the most common field locales for capsule research (Rivolier 1997a, Stuster 1996), but many studies are conducted in simulators, which are cheaper, easier, and safer to run. Appropriate methods span the full range: psychometric and projective tests, interviews, laboratory experiments, participant observations, field studies, simulations, and qualitative methods, including content analyses (Stuster 1996, Taylor et al 1986). The available literature includes a body of scientific data, much of it recent, as well as a sizable library of autobiographies, memoirs, diaries, letters, histories, stories in popular media, and government and corporate reports that go back a long time. Aside from research in simulators, capsule data tend to be based on small (and by definition non-random) samples. On the other hand, many of the findings reported in this review have been replicated in more than one group of sojourners and/or in more than one capsule environment, increasing the credibility of the conclusions.

POSITIVE CAPSULE PSYCHOLOGY

Most accounts of capsule living emphasize its strangeness, deprivations, dangers, and stresses. Emphasis is placed on episodes of mental disturbance, group conflict, and disagreements with the sponsoring organization or with the person in charge (these last often referred to as rebellions or mutinies); no mention is made of the frequency of similar events in humdrum, familiar environments (Douglas 1991). We, too, address the adverse consequences of capsule living, but we start by looking at the salutogenic (Antonovsky 1987), positive (Seligman 1998) aspects of the experience.

Despite book titles to the contrary (Cherry-Garrard 1970, Ransmayr 1991), the evidence is overwhelming that for many, perhaps most, capsule dwellers—at least, for those whose mission did not end in total disaster—the sojourn is a cherished and important part of their life, perceived as an impetus to growing, strengthening, and deepening, to be remembered with pride and enjoyment. Along with their accounts of hardship, cold, hunger, and possible doom, early explorers, stuck in the ice in crumbling ships or ramshackle shelters, made diary entries exalting the grandeur of the polar environment, the transcendental feelings, and the sense of appreciation for their colleagues (Mocellin & Suedfeld 1991). Autobiographical accounts of astronauts are crammed with a sense of adventure and accomplishment, enjoyment and fulfillment (Collins 1974, White 1987). Current-day polar crews report many more positive than negative experiences (Stuster et al 1999, Wood et al 1999a). Both to space and to the polar regions, the return rate is high, and the disappointment of those who are frustrated in their desire to go back is profound (Steel 1999a, Taylor 1969, Wolfe 1979). Twenty-six of 28 participants in a dangerous and uncomfortable undersea habitat study were willing to do it again (Radloff & Helmreich 1968).

The long-term aftereffects of such experiences are also strikingly positive. Both self-reports and scientific data show that people who have come through a demanding capsule mission are mentally and physically healthier, more successful, and more insightful than they had been or than were matched controls (e.g. Burr & Palinkas 1987, Palinkas 1986).

Harrison & Summit (1991) argue that "third force"—humanistic—psychology may be the best framework for interpreting these phenomena. People are "active organisms that seek challenges and engage in activities for their own sake" (Harrison & Summit 1991:186). Peak and flow experiences (Csikszentmihalyi 1996, Maslow 1968) occur in capsule environments; the whole enterprise of entering such a novel and engrossing situation calls to something deep inside many people (Anderson 1970). People who go into capsules usually like challenges, and most do quite well in meeting the ones they encounter there. Although many experience some stress, and may show negative signs, the vast majority of studies find little if any serious deterioration or psychiatric symptomatology (e.g. Peri et al 1991, 1999; Taylor 1987). Members of crews often come back with a less superficial set of values, more tolerance and affection toward other people, and higher self-confidence (Suedfeld 1998).

PSYCHOLOGICALLY RELEVANT ASPECTS OF THE CAPSULE ENVIRONMENT

One important fact, which has emerged during decades of research, is that in the study of capsule environments there are few main effect variables. Almost every outcome is due to an interaction among a host of physical and social environmental variables and personality factors. Thus, although we conceptually deconstruct the situation into particular sources of variance, we must remember that how people experience an environment is more important than the objective characteristics of the environment (Suedfeld 1991).

During early space flights, fears of psychological deterioration were not borne out, probably because of the short mission durations and the high stimulus levels

(Sharpe 1969). The situation may be different for certain kinds of long-duration capsule living. There was early recognition by NASA that long-term space flight could exacerbate problems arising from boredom, interpersonal difficulties, and alienation from the organization "back home" (Connors et al 1985), but only a few such episodes have been recorded.

On the other hand, the popular and professional polar literature has made much ado about "winter-over syndrome." A subset of winter-over crew members exhibit some combination of depression, irritability, cognitive impairment, sleep disturbance, and altered states of consciousness (Palinkas & Browner 1995, Rivolier et al 1995, Strange & Klein 1973). The last two of these have acquired popular nicknames: "Big eye" refers to the chronic polar insomnia and "long eye" to the "20-foot stare in the 10-foot room," a state in which thoughts drift from current reality into a vague absence that even the individual cannot always recollect afterward. Other symptoms reported during winter-over are withdrawal, apathy, psychosomatic problems, and neglect of personal hygiene among some crew members (e.g. Taylor 1987). Paradoxically, the greatest increase in symptoms can occur in the least hostile environment (Palinkas 1991, Palinkas & Houseal 1999), and it may be that some "symptoms" reflect an attempt to live up to the local version of the "old hand" image (Cravalho 1996). In any case, the changes are temporary and seldom interfere seriously with work and other activities.

Below, we look selectively at a few of the challenging aspects of capsule living. Sources of stress can be divided into four interacting categories: physical stressors; psycho-environmental factors, which arise from individual reactions to the restricted environment of the capsule; social factors, related to interpersonal relations (identified as the primary concern in the first quantitative content analysis of contemporary Antarctic diaries) (Stuster et al 1999); and temporal factors, having to do with the passage of time. Postmission stress, sometimes called re-entry shock, is another challenge but is, strictly speaking, outside the boundaries of capsule psychology.

Physical Stressors

Capsules tend to be located in dangerous places—that is why they are needed. Although in spacecraft and submarines the complicated life-support systems are sources of concern, the greatest Antarctic dangers have been identified as unforeseen deterioration in weather conditions and not having appropriate equipment (including a radio) or clothing when going off station or crossing sea ice (Burns & Sullivan 1999). However, such physical danger is rated at moderate levels, perhaps because most expeditioners consider themselves competent in dealing with it.

A capsule's life-support system is important for survival in polar regions and crucial in space and under water. It must provide for appropriate temperatures, breathable air at near-normal pressure, adequate food and water, and protection from environmental dangers. Occasional trips outside expose the person to the hazards of the surround, some aspects of which may in fact permeate the shelter as well (e.g. radiation and microgravity in space). Some capsules, such as submarines, may be engaged in combat operations, but even in nonmilitary contexts, in space, undersea, and polar missions, the risk of death exists and injuries occur at fairly high levels. Fires, equipment failures, accidents while using tools, and so on, could happen anywhere, but other hazards are unique to these environments.

The etiology of some adverse effects is uncertain: For example, there is increased reactivation and shedding of latent viruses (herpes and Epstein-Barr) among both Antarctic winter personnel and space crews, although no increase in actual occurrence of either disease has been demonstrated (Tingate et al 1997). The phenomenon may be related to stress, but may also be due to the lack of immunological challenges while the crew is encapsulated. In other cases, even the extent of the physical threat is unknown. One example is the long-term impact of microgravity on the human body (Space Studies Board 1998). Some of the serious medical consequences that have been identified may be counteracted by regimens of diet and exercise (Bluth & Helppie 1986, Money 1981, Ross 1975, SIMIS 1991), but some—e.g. massive loss of bone mineral density—so far have not been preventable and may not be completely reversible (van Loon et al 1993).

Many physical problems have complex effects. Unusual interior atmospheres in undersea habitats (helium-oxygen mixtures) result in high-pitched Donald Duck voices, loss of body heat, and greater chances of ear infections and sleep disturbances; high oxygen content in spacecraft atmospheres causes increased risks of fire and explosion, as well as difficulties in communication (Bachrach 1982, Darby & Darby 1971, Miller & Koblick 1984, Radloff & Helmreich 1968, Weybrew & Noddin 1979a).

Noise is another problem. Constant, monotonous noise and vibration from life-support machinery can interfere with sleep and concentration. Crew members also experience subtle, chronic tension as they listen "unconsciously" for mechanical failure indicated by any change in the sound (Bluth & Helppie 1986, Radloff & Helmreich 1968). The loud, persistent noises of polar and ocean storms are nerve-racking. Background noise is punctuated by thumps—the ship hitting an ice floe, a small and harmless fish or meteorite hitting the habitat, glaciers rumbling—that may trigger a startle response, interfering with ongoing activities. Of course, sound is also used positively, as in the relaxing effects of music, radio or television broadcasts, and taped nature sounds (Bluth & Helppie 1986).

In microgravity, spilled items—particles of food, drops of body fluids or drinks—float around until they are captured and put into a container. Sloppy eating, or allowing drops of urine to escape, may elicit adverse comments from one's colleagues. Long-duration space capsules can become disgustingly unsanitary (Collins 1974), the stench discommoding the ground crews who open the hatch after reentry.

Without gravity, the discrepancy between bodily cues ("local vertical") and visual cues is psychologically disorienting and may cause space motion sickness

(Stuster 1996). Vestibular orientation can be disrupted even under normal gravity. SEALAB II, nicknamed the Tiltin' Hilton, was found to tilt some 6° simultaneously in two directions, causing a disconcerting confusion between visual cues and local vertical (Radloff & Helmreich 1968).

Psycho-Environmental Factors

Psycho-environmental sources of stress arise because the individual is exposed to an unusually restricted environment.

Density One group of psycho-environmental factors violates accustomed norms of how human beings use physical space. Capsules tend to be small, for practical reasons (cost of construction and emplacement, payload mass and size, crew size). Notable exceptions are the larger Antarctic stations during the winter. The summer-to-winter population ratio can be as high as 10:1; in the winter, there are X satisfied people in the area where $10X$ summer occupants felt crowded.

There is disagreement about the acceptable amount of space per person, with estimates ranging from 84 to 700 ft^3 (Connors et al 1985, Stuster 1996), but most capsules provide insufficient levels of the interrelated factors of territoriality, privacy, and interpersonal distance. Preferred interpersonal distances are disrupted by lack of privacy (Christensen & Talbot 1986, Smith 1969), which also infringes on confidential telecommunications (e.g. with spouses, or space-faring patient and earth-bound physician).

Anecdotal evidence from many capsule sources attests to the need to have a place where people can be alone (Stuster 1996). Sleeping areas are a case in point. There is probably no territory more personal than one's own bed. The importance of this area to confined individuals is evident by the rapidity with which they claim a particular bed as their own (Altman & Haythorn 1967); it is routinely violated both in space vessels and submarines. In the latter, "hot-bunking" (each bunk being occupied by a different person during each workshift) has been an official policy—at least for low-ranking crew members.

The Capsule as ICE A second group of psycho-environmental stressors is related to the ICE aspect shared by most capsules. In an early review, Sells (1973) found that most researchers commonly identify three dimensions with a negative impact on the psychological well-being of mission personnel: social isolation, confinement, and sensory restriction (Altman 1973, Haythorn 1970, Kubis 1972, Sells 1973). All three overlap and interact, and little research has been done to disaggregate their effects.

Capsule isolation Capsule isolation can lead to neurotic reactions, general drowsiness, sleep disorders, psychological stress resulting from exhaustion, information exhaustibility, and post-isolation hypomanic syndrome (Bluth & Helppie 1986). Short-term isolation in high-altitude aircraft has been associated with the "break-off phenomenon," a feeling of disconnection from the earth, but this did not seem to happen in the early space flights (Space Science Board 1972).

Confinement   Confinement was at its worst in early space missions. Early US astronauts were compared to "Spam in a can"—lying essentially immobilized while the vessel blasted off, did its orbits, and landed (Wolfe 1979). Later versions provide much more room and demand much more activity. Most capsules now allow for at least occasional emergence into the surrounding environment, although such trips may be uncomfortable, dangerous, and focused on a specific task. Nevertheless, they break the monotony, provide a scope for physical exercise and perhaps adventure, and expose the person to the interesting and sometimes beautiful natural milieu. Even seeing the external environment is important and may in fact be the crew's major or only contact with it. Astronauts are entranced by the view out the windows (Haines 1991), and aquanauts in undersea habitats are fascinated by the ebb and flow of water and the marine life visible through portholes (Miller & Koblick 1984, Radloff & Helmreich 1968). One hypothesis worth testing is that the inclusion of live animals and plants in the capsule would reduce stress and especially boredom (as it did in the Biosphere 2 analogue environment; Walford et al 1996).

Confinement is frequently accompanied by limited physical exercise and subsequent deconditioning. Subjects experience "sleeplessness, depression, and general mood declines; compulsive behavior; psychosomatic problems" (Smith 1969:386) and hypodynamia, the result of insufficient motor activity (Bluth & Helppie 1986). This condition can bring about muscle atrophy and lowered cognitive and motor performance (Bennett et al 1985), and it is especially irksome for crew members used to highly active physical exercise.

Monotony   Monotony, the lack of sensory variation and novelty, is the third factor (Berry 1973). The capsule environment is invariant; often, the external surround is equally unchanging. Extreme monotony leads to increasing boredom, which in turn can motivate coping attempts (some of which may be dangerously risky). Another response is "long eye," possibly a mild fugue state.

Social Factors

Social Monotony   Kubis (1972) felt it likely that space crews would experience the social counterpart of the sensory monotony discussed above. Enforced togetherness plus social monotony are indeed major social stressors. Smith (1969) concluded that after 2 weeks or more of confinement, the foremost psychological irritants were inadequate leadership and the behavior of others. The former, of course, may be a subset of the latter. Disruptive effects on the group have been noted in Antarctica (Smith 1969), in submarines (Sandal et al 1999), and also in the Soviet space program (Bluth & Helppie 1986).

The arrival of visitors or replacements alleviates social monotony (Bluth & Helppie 1986) and may cause elevation of the arousal component of mood (Steel & Suedfeld 1992). The ability of new personnel to relieve boredom is a double-edged sword, however. Visitors and incoming crew members disrupt established routines, need special attention, and pose problems of integration into the existing group. Those who remain on station must be socialized to the group's norms. As well, tolerance for additional—i.e. not replacement—crew members will be in inverse proportion to the degree of crowding (Bluth & Helppie 1986).

Conflict   In even the best-conducted projects, conflict can occur among crew members, or between the leader and the followers. Admiral Byrd (1938) decided to winter in Antarctica alone rather than risk being cooped up with a companion whose very way of chewing his food might become infuriating. There have been physical assaults, as well as complaints about other people's trivial habits, among both early and recent polar dwellers—among the former, a murderous attack over a chess game (Palinkas 1990) and a 1996 assault with a hammer (New Zealand Herald 1996). In fact, a speculative article (Schwetje 1991) proposed that psychological irritability might be a legal defense for crimes committed in long-term spaceflight.

Conflict may also arise due to the mix of individual characteristics in the group (Altman & Haythorn 1967, Haythorn 1970, Kubis 1972, Smith 1969). Questions as to the assessment of interpersonal compatibility persist; some national space programs emphasize selecting a group rather than individuals (Santy 1994), and it has been suggested that cooperative group training is equally important (Kass et al 1995). With the advent of the International Space Station and financial cutbacks in support for Antarctic research, cross-cultural mixtures are on the increase. In general, these have not caused much trouble, although some foreign visitors in Russian and American space vehicles have felt marginalized (Kanas 1997).

Social Roles   In normal environments, most adults encounter a wide variety of people, with relationships recognized to exist within particular networks of affective ties, status hierarchies, and behavior settings. The people in all these groups have typical roles enacted in the particular setting, which mesh with the roles of other people in the group. By contrast, the individual arriving in the capsule is removed from his or her accustomed social circles and put into a strange situation with a group, usually a small group, of relative or absolute strangers. New people are assessing the individual, to some extent by new criteria; self-evaluation and self-esteem may lose their firm structure. Role expectations may become confused. Guidelines for one's own behavior and for predicting the behavior of others are eroded. New sources of stress arise (Harrison et al 1991, Rasmussen 1973, Taylor 1987, Weybrew & Noddin 1979a) as new role expectations, self-concepts, and micro-cultures develop in the station (Nelson 1973).

Incompatible roles (e.g. of military personnel versus civilian scientists) have led to conflict, generally centered on mission priorities (Radloff & Helmreich 1968), reactions to organizational hierarchy and discipline (Suedfeld 1995), and different values and goals (Gunderson 1966). Such tension may split the group by dividing it into cliques or by pitting one individual against the rest (Suedfeld 1987).

Communication   The capsule has a major effect on interpersonal exchanges. Altman & Haythorn (1965, 1967) showed that simulator confinement increases the intimacy and depth of self-disclosure. Crewmates who disclose very private matters about themselves may later come to regret this loss of informational privacy and to resent its recipients. Rumors, true or not, circulate rapidly and frequently and may lead to a variety of negative feelings (Cornelius 1991); it is difficult to keep anything secret (Law 1960). Among predominantly male crews, women may be especially vulnerable to gossip about their sexual availability (Rothblum et al 1998).

Isolation has a direct impact on both official and personal communications with the outside. Increased ease of communication, through satellite technology, the Internet, etc, has both good and bad aspects. In emergencies, experts back at the "home office," representing a wider span of knowledge and less distracted by danger and moment-to-moment demands, may be able to provide life-saving information and advice. On a more mundane level, keeping in touch with friends, family, and colleagues is generally a source of pleasure and relief to most isolates (Bluth & Helppie 1986, Smith 1969, Taylor 1987). Even talking to strangers can be fun: A Christmas day ham radio hookup between a Canadian high Arctic weather station and an American Antarctic station brought excitement into the lives of both groups (P Suedfeld, unpublished observation), as did an attempted radio conversation between French and American aquanauts that was complicated both by language difficulties and the Donald Duck effect of the artificial atmospheres (Radloff & Helmreich 1968).

On the other hand, the crew's relationship with the parent organization can be strained when mission controllers use communication technology to micromanage its activities. With teams probably self-selected to be high in self-confidence and control (Smith & Jones 1962), it is a bad idea to infringe on group autonomy and privacy (Deutsch 1971, Kanas 1990, Lebedev 1983, Radloff & Helmreich 1968, Sandal et al 1995, Walford et al 1996). Personal relationships may come under stress because of bad news, or no news, from home; the capsule dweller may experience depression, anger, and frustration when he or she is powerless to help out or participate when something is happening in the family (Earls 1969; NE Thagard, personal communication). And one US Antarctican had to be relieved of duty because of a "communication obsession" (Stuster 1996).

Sex   Most Antarctic programs and both the Russian and the American space programs now regularly include female crew members. In the Antarctic, results have been generally good, although some sexual competition and jealousy have arisen and some women find the attention uncomfortable (Rothblum et al 1998). In space, no adverse effects on group functioning have been reported (Bluth & Helppie 1986, Harrison & Connors 1984, Oliver 1991). Although NASA has found no sex-related performance differences in its short-term missions (Wood et al 1999b), the Russians have noted that "for some of the work on board that requires carefulness and accuracy, women are capable of acting more efficiently than men" (Gubarev 1983:38). Greeting a newly arrived female cosmonaut with a broom and dustpan and instructions to start cleaning up (as happened in the Soviet program) depicts a view somewhat different from the official one, however.

As to sexual deprivation and its amelioration—in space, on ships, and at the poles—this has been a sensitive topic with untold potential for bad publicity. It is clear that sexual activity does go on in capsules and, if masturbation is included, probably in most long-duration capsules. There has been much speculation about homosexual relations in all-male (or, nowadays, all-female) crews and about the varieties of heterosexual activity in mixed ones. Most reports "don't ask, don't tell" about the former and shy away from the latter; we follow their cautious example.

Temporal Factors

Altman (1973) has suggested that in ICE teams, "group processes should be studied in a dynamic sense, with an understanding of how they occur over time. . ." (p. 244). The same is true for individual processes. Various aspects of time have consequences for capsule crews.

Duration   One critical characteristic is the length of occupancy in the capsule. This factor interacts with all the physical and psychological variables mentioned previously (Baum et al 1981, Kubis 1972). Partly because some of the stressors are not dramatic and their impact is cumulative over time, the crew may not become aware of them until their effects are serious. For this reason, it is important—especially, though not only, for leaders—to monitor the symptoms of accumulating stress and to apply appropriate countermeasures (Suedfeld 1995).

Motivation and overall morale may show a decline during confinement (Harrison & Connors 1984, Smith 1969). As a mission unfolds, nuclear submariners become more aware of possible health problems (Weybrew & Molish 1979), and Antarctic expeditioners increasingly recognize shortcomings in their preparations and the dangers involved in polar travel, work, and recreation (Pekkarinen et al 1992, Rothblum et al 1995). Regardless of total duration (and of the specific kind of capsule), important changes in crew morale and performance consistently occur shortly past the halfway point (Bechtel & Berning 1991, Curley et al 1979, Harrison et al 1989, Kanas 1990, Kanas et al 1999, Sandal et al 1995, Steel 1999b, Stuster et al 1999).

Not all aspects of increasing mission duration are negative. Confidence and coping tend to increase as time passes in the capsule environment (Sandal et al 1996, Palinkas et al 1989), thus reducing apprehension with regard to the potentially hazardous tasks the crew member may need to undertake (Radloff & Helmreich 1968). Expressions of tension and similar negative moods among capsule dwellers seem to rise in the final stages of short-term capsule situations (Bergan et al 1993); but the opposite is true in long-term ones (Kanas et al 1996, Mocellin & Suedfeld 1991), which also show more positive affect generally (Stuster el al 1999).

The fact that studies in this area cover a mixture of short- and long-term capsule periods (e.g. Altman 1973, Smith 1969, Altman & Haythorn 1967) underscores the need for theories and research procedures that recognize the importance of duration, and several theorists have proposed such models (Harrison & Connors 1984). It is unlikely that we can validly generalize across data collected from Mercury missions lasting a few hours, Shuttle missions of a week or two, Mir space station missions of 6–12 months, and a possible 3-year voyage to Mars. A month or two in the polar summer is a different proposition from an 8-month winter-over, much less 2 or 3 years in a ship frozen into the ice, a common experience among early explorers (Connors et al 1985, Holland 1994).

Cycles   Circadian rhythms, particularly sleep-wake cycles, may be disrupted and social cues for time may become more critical (Sorokin et al 1996). These rhythms are intimately linked to both social and physical time cues; any disparity between these cues tends to put both physiological and psychological stress on the individual. As well, a paucity of time cues can lead to internal desynchronization, in which the body's systems or functions become "out of phase" with each other (Ross 1975).

Scheduling   Another temporal factor is the ratio of work to leisure time. Capsules can be paradoxical, providing long stretches of boring, unstructured time and—sometimes equally long—periods of frantic activity (Connors et al 1985). Both submariners (Beare et al 1981) and astronauts in space simulators (Steel & Suedfeld 1998) spend much of their leisure time actually working. In space, though, excessively high workloads have led to conflict between crews and controllers—as when the Skylab 4 crew forcefully insisted on reasonable time off and some control over what tasks they would perform when (Douglas 1991). The demands of medical and psychological research, being both time-consuming and intrusive (e.g. lengthy and repetitive questionnaires, frequent blood sampling), may be particularly resented, even by scientist-subjects (Rivolier et al 1989).

"Empty" time is even more stressful than overwork, because it provides no distraction from the unpleasant aspects of the capsule situation. Altered states of consciousness and slowing of cognitive and motor tempo [comparable to hibernation (Taylor 1989)] emerge to fill in the time, both sometimes being misinterpreted as symptoms of mental deterioration (AF Barabasz 1991, White et al 1983).

Fortunately, it is relatively easy to devise diversions to reduce the impact of suboptimal workload (Blair 1991, Johnson & Suedfeld 1996).

Postmission Reentry

Relatively little attention has been paid to psychological issues revolving around the voyager's return home. Medical treatment and physical rehabilitation are carefully applied, but emotional decompression and readjustment, reintegration into the family, getting used to routines of working, commuting, shopping, socializing, and so on, are to a great extent left up to the individual.

APPLICATIONS OF PSYCHOLOGY

Below, we look in some detail at only three of the most important applications of psychology in capsule programs. They cover three primary aspects of living in capsules: selection, the attempt to staff the capsule with people who can function well in it; design, approaches to making the capsule a livable environment; and countermeasures (systemic and individual) to ameliorate the adverse effects of prolonged pyscho-environmental and social stressors by reducing boredom and other negative emotions.

Selection

There is probably no more striking depiction of the rigors of capsule selection and training than the film *The Right Stuff* and the book on which it was based (Wolfe 1979). The sequences of astronaut candidates being poked, prodded, and punctured by physicians, and persecuted by psychologists, show not necessarily how it was but certainly how it felt. No wonder one response was that "the astronauts won't be happy until the last flight surgeon is strangled in the guts of the last aviation psychologist (or vice versa)" (unpublished data). They retaliated as best they could, from Conrad complaining that the blank white TAT card had been presented to him upside down (Wolfe 1979) to Collins's (1974:28) interpreting it as "nineteen polar bears fornicating in a snowbank." We should note Douglas's (1991) vehement argument that the hostility has been sensationalized and that in fact the astronaut corps respects the professionalism of physicians and psychologists.

In general, the selection process consists of two distinct steps: selecting out and selecting in.

Screening: Selecting Out   In the first stage, candidates are screened for inadequate preparation, overt psychopathology, and problematic life history. Interviews, biographical data, and tests (both objective and projective) are typically used. Candidates who are "flagged" at this point are removed from further consideration. Screening has been emphasized because selectors view the environment as psychologically dangerous and "pathogenic" (Antonovsky 1987): Isolation, with restricted access to an (often life-threatening) external environment, is thought to be so stressful that only those with the "right stuff" could stand up to the challenge (Santy 1994).

Some screening procedures have been overly demanding. To paraphrase the comment of Radloff & Helmreich (1968) about undersea habitats, those who were considered best suited to working under water could also walk on it. On the other hand, it could be argued that high standards ensure successful missions. Despite a few highly publicized episodes, studies examining the effects of encapsulated life have not shown psychological breakdowns. The interesting question is whether this was due to the rigorous, valid selection or to the exaggerated expectations of "experts" concerning the stressfulness of the capsule environment. As agencies have become more realistic about potential problems, some screening criteria have loosened to the point where candidates for space flight no longer have to be test pilots (or even pilots) and being a septuagenarian is not always a cause for disqualification.

Choosing: Selecting In   The goal of the second stage, selecting in, is to choose the best of the remaining candidates. Criteria regarding what constitutes desirability probably vary only slightly from environment to environment. They can be grouped under Gunderson's (1973) Antarctic triarchy of task ability, sociability, and emotional stability. These may be outweighed or supplemented by considerations of desirable public image (Wolfe 1979) and, according to some observers, organizational politics and personal biases (for details concerning the Mir-Shuttle astronauts, see Burrough 1998; for selection of Yuri Gagarin as the first man in space, see Rivolier 1997a). The fact that the first seven candidates selected for the Mercury program did not significantly differ from the 24 nonselected finalists either in test scores or in stress tolerance on a series of performance, projective, and psychometric measures (Santy 1994) indicates the role of nonobvious criteria. Still another limitation on selectivity is the limited size of a volunteer pool within a crucial occupation, such as principal investigators conducting research during the circumpolar winter and medical officers in polar stations.

All current space programs have some form of personality assessment (Santy 1994). This is also true of selection for submarine crews (Flin 1996) and polar winter crews (Rivolier 1997b). Biodata, interviews, situational tests, and standardized psychometric instruments all have their proponents (Stuster 1996). The Soviet (now Russian) space program uses a massive array of interviews and tests, with one stress test requiring a group of candidates to drive a small car cross-country. As this particular simulation indicates, the program selects crews, not just individuals; group compatibility is a major consideration in mission planning. Other European programs have a variety of emphases and use a variety of instruments. The National Space Development Agency of Japan uses personality questionnaires, projective tests, encounter groups, participant observations, and interviews in attempting to select for positive social interaction characteristics (Santy 1994).

These national differences reflect both cultural factors and the nature of each space program. The European and Japanese selectors could be most demanding; their astronauts have flown only occasionally, in American or Russian spacecraft. The Russian program has been geared to small groups of cosmonauts living together for many months in a cramped station. Americans are moving from relatively short-duration missions, through the recent Shuttle-Mir missions, on to the International Space Station and the voyage to Mars. This may force NASA to pay more attention to psychosocial factors, as urged by Norman E Thagard, the first American on Mir. In fact, plans are being made for NASA's new "expedition" astronauts—those in line for service on the space station and Martian or lunar bases—to receive greatly expanded psychological assessment and preparation (Behavioral Health and Performance Team, 1999).

Space mission durations and activities are likely to become more homogenized, as all national programs begin to focus on the International Space Station. As a result, the various programs can begin to select astronauts for the same set of conditions. An attempt to develop a standardized selection procedure is being pursued by the European Space Agency. Some of the scientists involved in that project are also working to develop a standard Antarctic selection battery, to be validated in a number of national programs (Grant et al 1998). Instruments chosen for the battery assess mood, depression, interpersonal confidence, optimism, anxiety-proneness, coping strategies, self-perceptions, and the Big Five personality dimensions.

Research needs to be done on what combination of personality measures, performance tests, simulations, and other techniques would optimize the select-in process. Which personality traits are important in capsule environments has been a debated topic and the focus of many studies (Gunderson 1973, Harrison & Connors 1984, Harrison et al 1989, Kubis 1972, Santy 1994, Suedfeld 1987, Torrance 1954). Although the personality factors relevant to particular habitats are not fully identified, we may tentatively group them along two dimensions. "Self-related" characteristics include emotional stability, feelings of competence, self-reliance and/or a high degree of autonomy, good motivation, goal orientation, and demographic characteristics (e.g. age, sex, cultural background). The "other-related" dimension includes social versatility, agreeableness or friendliness, and openness. A sense of humor, often mentioned by both capsule dwellers and those who study them (Cravalho 1996), is important; with the growing incidence of international crews, so are cultural sensitivity and tolerance (Burrough 1998). These traits have been tested, if at all, only in relatively gross ways.

Among established personality approaches, the "Big Five" model (Costa & McCrae 1992) has considerable face validity for capsule selection programs. Arctic and Antarctic workers score higher than the norm group on all factors except neuroticism (Steel et al 1997), which is related to Gunderson's "emotional stability" dimension and to essentially identical (but differently labeled) categories used as criteria in the American, European, and Japanese space programs (Santy 1994) and submarine crew selection (Weybrew & Noddin 1979b). A high score is clearly a select-out criterion. High scores on two of the other Big Five would clearly be favorable signs. One is conscientiousness, related to Gunderson's "task ability" (Gunderson 1973, Moes et al 1996, Rosnet et al 1999, Santy 1994, Steel & Suedfeld 1998); the other is agreeableness (Gunderson's "sociability"), although it does include modesty, a problem in low-privacy environments (Galarza & Holland 1998). The other two dimensions have mixed indicators. Openness to experience subsumes enjoyment of inner life (M Barabasz 1991) but also desire for novelty, activity, and excitement. Extraversion includes sincerity, sensitivity, and altruism, which are good. Its gregariousness component is not desirable: Somewhat reserved "sociable introverts"—who enjoy, but do not need, social interaction—seem optimally suited for capsule living (de Monchaux et al 1979, Moes et al 1996, Strange & Youngman 1971).Ursin et al (1992) specified ten personality characteristics of the ideal astronaut. These are more detailed than, but overlap significantly with, Gunderson's list (with the addition of "medium initiative and creativity" and "high patience"). Ability to tolerate frustration and some degree of failure would probably also be good traits (Abraini et al 1998).

The Personality Paradox   Two aspects of capsule selection pose an interesting paradox that cries out for research.

The first is that most volunteers for anything as challenging and unusual as space, undersea habitats, and polar work will score toward the upper end of any scale of thrill-seeking, novelty-seeking, competence/effectance motivation, and similar dimensions. Aside from other incentives (and there are many), they want adventure and challenges. Many discover only too soon that they have committed themselves to monotonous, routine, boring tasks in a monotonous, confining environment, cooped up with the same unvarying group, and they can not get out.

The second is that volunteers also tend to be high on the need for personal control and autonomy (Smith & Jones 1962, Stuster 1996). They find that capsule life is in fact controlled by environmental requirements and organizational regulations. In most capsules, the crew has very circumscribed spheres of free choice of activities, companions, or behavior settings.

Given that programs recruit from exactly the kinds of people most likely to be unhappy on site, what can we do to improve recruitment, orientation, training, or the capsule conditions to diminish the gap? The most promising strategy is a combination of two approaches. First, potential recruits should be familiarized with what the experience will really be like by thorough orientation and experience in analogue environments such as capsule simulators. Second, both the physical environment and procedural guidelines (work schedules, recreational opportunities, decision-making rules) should maximize variety, flexibility, and control by the crew rather than base staff.

Environmental Design

Generally, the size of human habitations is inversely proportional to the harshness of the outside environment (Strub 1996); capsules are usually small for their population. Limited fuel can lead to inadequate provision of light, heat, and hot water. In polar and especially in space capsules, transportation difficulties and payload capacity are obvious critical factors. The physical structure and internal layout tend to be designed to emphasize survivability in a harsh environment and economic and functional requirements.

But the capsule should also provide for psychosocial needs. It is, after all, a small total institution whose inhabitants are totally dependent on it for all the amenities of life. Here, designers have been less successful. Most capsules tend to be on the no-frills side: stark, monochromatic, inflexible, and hard, perhaps with some amelioration of these features in a limited portion of the station (Incoll 1990).

The detailed analysis by Carrére et al (1991) of space use in a small American Antarctic station suggests guidelines for the location of rooms used for different purposes (e.g. active or passive recreation; private or public socializing). She recommends the provision of locales for both group and individual pursuits, noisy and quiet times, formal and informal interaction, etc. Her findings also point to the importance of solitude—60% of people's waking time was spent alone—and of designing to safeguard privacy, particularly auditory privacy (which is more difficult to achieve than visual).

Space stations, with their much more rigid limitations on size and construction, pose a more serious problem—but one that has been recognized and that has brought forth recommendations for remedies (Stuster 1996). The preference for solitude and privacy should alert both researchers and practitioners to the inappropriateness of popular ideas that wanting to be alone is a symptom of unhappiness or maladjustment.

Control over one's own area has been a problem in space capsules. For one thing, in space capsules there is less of "one's own area." Most areas are shared, and even the provision of private sleeping facilities (such as a cocoon attached to a wall) is a recent idea. In addition, surfaces are more fully utilized for work—unlike in normal gravity, it is possible to attach apparatus to almost the entire "wall" space in all six directions, as all parts are equally accessible when the users are floating around inside the capsule. As already noted, this may also result in disorientation. To reduce this difficulty, designers can color-code walls, floors, and ceilings using a common system throughout the environment and can orient furniture, controls, and other physical features in an "earth-normal" position vis-á-vis each other (Bluth & Helppie 1986, Johnson 1975). For instance, table surfaces should be parallel to each other and facing the "ceiling," whereas all cupboard doors should swing open on an axis parallel or perpendicular to the "floor."

Stuster (1996), in a thorough review of the psychological aspects of space capsule design, has urged that stations be designed to allow for more personalization and variety. The performance of at least some crew members may be affected by wall color (Kwalleck & Lewis 1993), and a diversity of colors, shapes, and textures throughout the habitat would help to ward off boredom (Stuster 1996). No matter how efficient the capsule design is, the psychological needs of its occupants require that it also be varied, interesting, and attractive (Berry 1973).

Lighting types and levels can be critical to performance and safety in any habitat (Ross 1975, Miller & Koblick 1984). It has been recommended that capsule lighting be as similar to daylight as possible (Bluth & Helppie 1986). Additionally, the brightness contrast produced by the light (Ross 1975) and the safety of the illuminating agent itself need to be considered (Miller & Koblick 1984).

A somewhat different aspect of lighting involves wake-sleep cycles and circadian rhythms. Both are disrupted in the artificial environment of all capsules as well as in some of their natural environments: The usual 24-h cycle is absent alike from submarines, spacecraft, and the high polar regions. Sleep disturbances may be related to this distortion; fortunately, it is relatively easy to solve this problem by imposing a normal light-dark cycle within the capsule, at least in areas that are not operational around the clock.

Countering Boredom

Capsule dwellers have their own methods for combating the negative effects of crowding, isolation, confinement, and monotony. Many of these have been known for centuries and have been practiced by the officers and crews of isolated ships on long voyages. Some focus on aspects of the capsule environment or its surround (the reappearance of the sun after the polar winter always evokes a major celebration), whereas others are nostalgic recreations of the crew's far-away home (Johnson & Suedfeld 1996). They include conversation, letter writing and reading, games, books, hobbies, puzzles, studies, lectures, music, theatrical performances, and parties to celebrate events such as a birthday or established holiday— nowadays supplemented by videos, radio, TV, and calls home. Wise leaders and groups from nineteenth century exploring ships to the astronauts also engage everyone in regularly scheduled vigorous activity (Stuster 1996).

Both space voyagers and Antarctic winterers relish their own taped music and special foods. If allowed, they also bring special clothing to enrich the stimulus world, assert their personality, and recapture a sense of home. Carrére et al (1991) found "dressing up" for special occasions important enough to be enforced by group norms.

Food is a preeminent reliever of boredom and stress. The cook is typically one of the most important people on a polar station or submarine. The general quality of the food, special meals, and the role of mealtime for socializing and marking the passage of time are all of intense interest to the crew, and many polar winterers and submariners gain considerable weight (Peri 1988, Stuster 1996). In the early, hungry days, cooped-up Antarctic crews enjoyed the local game, such as seal and penguin meat, as well as novel ways of preparing the food they had brought along. One specialty was hoosh, made by boiling or frying a variety of meats, biscuit crumbs, and fats or, in a dessert version, everything sweet that was available: cocoa powder, raisins, bits of chocolate.

In space, there is little scope for creative food preparation; however, personal favorites and delicacies such as caviar have been provided by resupply rocket to the Mir station and are much appreciated. In one well-known episode, Mir's normal larder was supplemented by gourmet items brought by a visiting French "spationaute." After the departure of the guest, a Russian crewman said that although he had enjoyed the treats, "it was good to get back to plain black bread" (Stuster 1996:341).

Alcohol is closely related to food in relieving boredom. It has been a standby of encapsulated teams for centuries, going back to the wine, beer, or rum rations (and home brews) of far-voyaging sailing vessels (Johnson & Suedfeld 1996). Drunkenness was a serious problem on the sailing ships and still can cause difficulties at times; but most current-day capsule crews are sufficiently well trained to know that it can be dangerous. Alcohol does help to lower anxiety, defuse tension, and make things less monotonous; it is also an important adjunct to meals and celebrations. Drinking increases during the Antarctic winter (e.g. Rothblum et al 1998)—as does smoking (Bhargava et al 1999). Because on most capsules supplies are easily controlled by the home organization, the abuse problem is manageable (Stuster 1996).

Everyone in the Carrére et al study (1991) personalized his or her living quarters with decorations, paint, new furniture, and reminders of home. Some devised virtual "windows," others put up posters of tropical and other idyllic places where they had been or would like to go. Simulator research has shown the importance of such things as personal mementos and photographs (Altman 1973), and these were even more significant in the Antarctic.

The public areas of the station were also modified to reflect the personality of the group, with photographs, plaques, and paint, some of which are kept by crews in subsequent years to produce an environmental archive of the station. Modifying the environment to suit one's desires has been relatively free and easy in polar environments. It still is, within the new requirements of political correctness to avoid offending one's colleagues.

Less innocuous is a craving for excitement that can lead to life-threatening recklessness. Experienced polar personnel go outside without appropriate equipment or clothing, neglect to tell anyone where they were going, ignore warnings of deteriorating weather; a veteran cosmonaut begins an extravehicular activity without fastening his safety tether. These and similar acts, directed perhaps by the eagerness for diverse activity that can lead to a lack of attention, can be—and in polar milieux have been—fatal.

OTHER INTERESTING ISSUES

Capsule life involves myriad interesting psychological concerns. Applied studies should be done on personnel selection and training, capsule design, and the development of interventions and countermeasures against emotional problems or performance deterioration. As for basic research, capsules are a natural laboratory: The environment imposes various levels of interesting independent variables, many extraneous factors can be controlled, and there is a steady supply of potential participants. Table 1 is based on recent recommendations for psychological studies in space (Space Studies Board 1998), and analogous lists can be drawn up for other kinds of capsules. The word "countermeasures" refers to preventive

TABLE 1   Recommended research topics

Basic research	Countermeasure development
Environmental issues	
Microgravity effects on	Filling unstructured time
cognition, perception, physiology	Provide novelty and surprises
Responses to perceived risk	Train about privacy-related issues
Predictors of territoriality	Interior design to reduce monotony
Psychophysiological issues	
Characteristics of sleep	Develop spaceworthy instrumentation
Psychophysiological stress patterns	
Individual issues	
Measure stress	Improve screening and selection
Indicators of coping strategies	Assess stress countermeasures
Stress and performance	Assess psychoactive medications
Personality and performance	for use in space
Postflight changes	
Interpersonal issues	
Assess group compatibility	Interpersonally oriented selection
Training in group dynamics	Team-oriented training modules
Different group compositions	Alternate methods of monitoring interaction
Monitoring group dynamics in flight	Reducing capsule-ground conflict
Organizational issues	
Effects of flight duration, phases	Sharing knowledge, attitudes, etc
Requirements for effective management	

steps designed to avoid or minimize problems rather than to interventions applied after a problem occurs.

Some needed investigations relate to the effects of various environmental features on basic processes such as cognition, perception, memory, motor performance, psychophysiological reactions, and the like. Others are more complicated: What kind of crew composition is best for performance and for emotional adaptation? Are the same variables optimal for both? How should capsule crews be trained, and how can the transition from selection to training to operations be eased (Holland & Curtis 1998)? This shift has been problematic in the recent past (Burrough 1998; JE Blaha, personal communication).

What about leadership? Many capsule leaders are in an unusual situation: Far from the parent organization, and almost completely shorn of reward or punishment power, living just as the crew does without the mystique of remoteness and special privileges, how do they maintain control and discipline? How do capsule micro-cultures develop, and what makes them different from each other even in similar environments (or the same one as crews change)? What is the best way to help the crew's family to adjust to the voyager's departure and reappearance?

Some of the necessary research can be conducted in laboratories, archives, and simulators, but there may be an increasing presence of psychologists in remote capsule environments. As the data show, such participation can be surprisingly enjoyable and stimulating. Solzhenitsyn put it well:

> Zoyenka, how can you tell which part of the world you'd be happy in, and which you'd be unhappy in? Who can say he knows that about himself?

A Solzhenitsyn, *The Cancer Ward*

ACKNOWLEDGMENTS

We thank numerous colleagues who sent us reprints as well as copies of the technical reports, conference presentations, and other relatively inaccessible materials that contain much of the relevant knowledge about capsule living. We are also grateful to PJ Johnson, DJ Lugg, LA Palinkas, A Peri, J Stuster, and others who made helpful comments on previous drafts of the manuscript.

Visit the Annual Reviews home page at www.AnnualReviews.org.

LITERATURE CITED

Abraini JH, Ansseau M, Bisson T, de Mendoza JLJ, Therme P. 1998. Personality patterns of anxiety during occupational deep dives with longterm confinement in a hyperbaric chamber. *J. Clin. Psychol.* 54:825–30

Altman I. 1973. An ecological approach to the functioning of socially isolated groups. See Rasmussen 1973, pp. 241–69

Altman I, Haythorn WW. 1965. Interpersonal exchange in isolation. *Sociometry* 28:411–26

Altman I, Haythorn WW. 1967. The ecology of isolated groups. *Behav. Sci.* 32:169–82

Anderson JRL. 1970. *The Ulysses Factor: The Exploring Instinct in Man.* London: Hodder, Stoughton

Antonovsky A. 1987. *Unraveling the Mystery of Health: How People Manage Stress and Stay Well.* San Francisco: Jossey-Bass

Bachrach AJ. 1982. The human in extreme environments. In *Advances in Environmental Psychology.* Vol. 4: *Environment and Health,* ed. A Baum, JE Singer, pp. 211–36. Hillside, NJ: Erlbaum

Barabasz AF. 1991. Effects of isolation on states of consciousness. See Harrison et al 1991, pp. 201–8

Barabasz M. 1991. Imaginative involvement in Antarctica: applications to life in space. See Harrison et al 1991, pp. 209–15

Baum A, Singer JE, Baum CS. 1981. Stress and the environment. *J. Soc. Issues* 37:4–35

Beare AN, Bondi KR, Biersner RJ, Naitoh P. 1981. Work and rest on nuclear submarines. *Ergonomics* 24:593–610

Bechtel R, Berning A. 1991. The third-quarter phenomenon: Do people experience discomfort after stress has passed? See Harrison et al 1991, pp. 261–66

Behavioral Health and Performance Team. 1999. *Behavioral health and performance program plan: Definition and implementation guide.* Houston, TX: Medical Operations Branch, NASA Johnson Space Center

Bennett BL, Schlichting CL, Bondi KR. 1985. *Cardiorespiratory Fitness and Cognitive Performance Before and After Confinement in a Nuclear Submarine. Rep. No. 1030.* Groton, CT: Nav. Submarine Med. Res. Lab.

Bergan T, Sandal G, Warncke M, Ursin H, Vaernes RJ. 1993. Group functioning and communication. *Adv. Space Biol. Med.* 3:59–80

Berry CA. 1973. View of human problems to be addressed for long-duration space flights. *Aerospace Med.* 44:1136–46

Bhargava R, Mukerji S, Sachdeva U. 1999. Psychological impact of the Antarctica winter on Indian expeditioners. *Environ. Behav.* In press

Blair SM. 1991. The Antarctic experience. See Harrison et al 1991, pp. 57–64.

Bluth BJ, Helppie M. 1986. *Russian Space Stations as Analogs, NASA Grant NAGW-659.* Washington, DC: NASA. 2nd ed.

Burns R, Sullivan P. 1999. Perceptions of danger, risk taking and outcomes in a remote community. *Environ. Behav.* In press

Burr RG, Palinkas LA. 1987. Health risks among submarine personnel in the U.S. Navy, 1974–1979. *Undersea Biomed. Res.* 14:535–44

Burrough B. 1998. *Dragonfly: NASA and the Crisis Aboard Mir.* New York: Harper Collins

Byrd RE. 1938. *Alone.* New York: Ace

Carrére S, Evans GW, Stokols D. 1991. Winter-over stress: physiological and psychological adaptation to an Antarctic isolated and confined environment. See Harrison et al 1991, pp. 229–37

Cherry-Garrard A. 1970 (1922). *The Worst Journey in the World: Antarctic 1910–1913.* Harmondsworth, UK: Penguin

Christensen JM, Talbot JM. 1986. A review of the psychological aspects of space flight. *Aviat. Space Environ. Med.* 57:203–12

Collins M. 1974. *Carrying the Fire: An Astronaut's Journeys.* New York: Farrar, Straus, Giroux

Connors MM, Harrison AA, Akins FR. 1985. *Living Aloft: Human Requirements for Extended Space Flight.* Washington, DC: NASA

Cornelius PE. 1991. Life in Antarctica. See Harrison et al 1991, pp. 9–14

Costa PT, McCrae RR. 1992. *The NEO PI-R Professional Manual.* Odessa, FL: Psychol. Assess. Resour.

Cravalho MA. 1996. Toast on ice: the ethno-psychology of the winter-over experience in Antarctica. *Ethos* 24:628–56

Csikszentmihalyi M. 1996. *Creativity: Flow and the Psychology of Discovery and Invention.* New York: HarperCollins

Curley MD, Berghage TE, Raymond LW, Sode J, Leach C. 1979. Emotional stability during a chamber saturation dive to 49.5 atmospheres absolute. *J. Appl. Psychol.* 64:310–14

Darby R, Darby P. 1971. *Conquering the Deep-Sea Frontier.* New York: McKay

de Monchaux C, Davies A, Edholm OG. 1979. Psychological studies in the Antarctic. *Br. Antarct. Surv. Bull.* 46:93–97

Deutsch S. 1971. A man-systems integration study of the behavior of crews and habitability in small spaces. In *Scientists in the Sea,* ed. JW Miller, JG VanDerwalker, RA Waller, Chapt. VIII. Washington, DC: US Dept. Interior

Douglas WK. 1991. Psychological and sociological aspects of manned spaceflight. See Harrison et al 1991, pp. 81–87

Earls JH. 1969. Human adjustment to an exotic environment. *Arch. Gen. Psychiatry* 20:117–23

Flin R. 1996. *Sitting in the Hot Seat: Leaders and Teams for Critical Incident Management.* New York: Wiley

Galarza L, Holland AW. 1998. *Identifying and Measuring Psychological Predictors of Astronaut Adaptation to Long-Duration Space Missions.* Houston, TX: Johnson Space Center

Grant I, Palinkas LA, Suedfeld P, Eriksen HR, Ursin H. 1998. *SOAP: Selection of Antarctic Personnel.* Bergen, Norway: Univ. Bergen

Gubarev V. 1983. "I like this work." *USSR Rep. Space 20.* Arlington, VA: Joint Publ. Res. Serv.

Gunderson EKE. 1966. *Adaptation to Extreme Environments: Prediction of Performance. Unit Rep. 66–17.* San Diego: US Navy Med. Neuropsychiatr. Res. Unit

Gunderson EKE. 1973. Individual behavior in confined or isolated groups. See Rasmussen 1973, pp. 145–64

Haines RF. 1991. Windows: their importance and functions in confining environments. See Harrison et al 1991, pp. 349–58

Harrison AA, Clearwater YA, McKay CP. 1989. The human experience in Antarctica: applications to life in space. *Behav. Sci.* 34:253–71

Harrison AA, Clearwater YA, McKay CP, eds. 1991. *From Antarctica to Outer Space: Life in Isolation and Confinement.* New York: Springer-Verlag

Harrison AA, Connors MM. 1984. Groups in exotic environments. In *Advances in Experimental Social Psychology,* ed. L Berkowitz, 18:49–87. Orlando: Academic

Harrison AA, Summit J. 1991. How "Third Force" psychology might view humans in space. *Space Power* 10:185–203

Haythorn WW. 1970. Interpersonal stress in isolated groups. In *Social and Psychological Factors in Stress,* ed. JE McGrath, pp. 159–76. Chicago: Holt, Rinehart & Winston

Holland AW, Curtis K. 1998. Operational psychology countermeasures during the Lunar-Mars Life Support Test Project. *Life Support Biosphere Sci.* 5:445–52

Holland C, ed. 1994. *Farthest North: A History of North Polar Exploration in Eye-Witness Accounts.* New York: Carroll, Graf

Incoll P. 1990. *The Influence of Architectural Theory on the Design of Australian Antarctic Stations.* Melbourne: Aust. Constr. Serv.

Johnson CC. 1975. Skylab experiment M487: habitability/crew quarters. Adv. Astronaut. Sci: the Skylab results. In *Proc. 20th Annu. Meet. Am. Astronaut. Soc., Torrance, CA*

Johnson PJ, Suedfeld P. 1996. Coping with stress through creating microcosms of home and family among Arctic whalers and explorers. *Hist. Fam.* 1:41–62

Kanas N. 1990. Psychological, psychiatric, and interpersonal aspects of long-duration space missions. *J. Spacecr. Rockets* 27:457–63

Kanas N. 1997. Psychosocial value of space simulation for extended spaceflight. *Adv. Space Biol. Med.* 6:81–91

Kanas N, Salnitskiy V, Grund E, Gushin V, Kozerenko O, et al. 1999. Crewmember interactions during joint U.S./Russian Mir missions: purpose and panel overview. Presented at Aerospace Med. Assoc. Meet., Detroit

Kanas N, Weiss DS, Marmar CR. 1996. Crewmember interactions during a Mir space station simulation. *Aviat. Space Environ. Med.* 67:969–75

Kass J, Kass R, Samaltedinov I. 1995. Psychological considerations of man in space: problems and solutions. *Acta Astronaut.* 36:657–60

Kubis JF. 1972. Isolation, conflict, and group dynamics in long duration spaceflight. *Acta Astronaut.* 17:45–72

Kwallek N, Lewis CM. 1993. The impact of interior colors on the crew in the habitation space module. In *Proc. IDEEA Two Conf.*, p. 213. Montreal: Cent. North. Stud. Res., McGill Univ.

Law P. 1960. Personality problems in Antarctica. *Med. J. Aust.*, Feb. 20:273–81

Lebedev V. 1983. *Diary of a Cosmonaut.* College Station, TX: Phytoresour. Res.

Lipowski ZJ. 1971. Surfeit of attractive information inputs: a hallmark of our environment. *Behav. Sci.* 16:461–71

Maslow AH. 1968. *Toward a Psychology of Being.* Princeton, NJ: Van Nostrand

Miller JW, Koblick IG. 1984. *Living and Working in the Sea.* New York: Van Nostrand Reinhold

Mocellin JSP, Suedfeld P. 1991. Voices from the ice: diaries of polar explorers. *Environ. Behav.* 23:704–22

Moes GS, Lall R, Johnson B. 1996. Personality characteristics of successful submarine personnel. *Mil. Med.* 161:239–42

Money KE. 1981. Biological effects of space travel. *Can. Aeronaut. Space J.* 27:195–201

Nelson PD. 1973. Indirect observation of groups. See Rasmussen 1973, pp. 167–94

New Zealand *Herald.* 1996. FBI sent in to Antarctic base. *Herald,* Oct. 14, p. 83.

Oliver D. 1991. Psychological effects of isolation and confinement of a winter-over group at McMurdo Station, Antarctica. See Harrison et al 1991, pp. 217–28

Palinkas LA. 1986. Health and performance of Antarctic winter-over personnel: a follow-up study. *Aviat. Space Environ. Med.* 57:549–59

Palinkas LA. 1990. Psychosocial effects of adjustment in Antarctica: lessons for long-duration spaceflight. *J. Spacecr.* 27:471–77

Palinkas LA. 1991. Effects of physical and social environments on the health and well-being of Antarctic winter-over personnel. *Environ. Behav.* 23:782–99

Palinkas LA, Browner D. 1995. Effects of prolonged isolation in extreme environments on stress, coping, and depression. *J. Appl. Soc. Psychol.* 25:557–76

Palinkas LA, Gunderson EKE, Burr RG. 1989. *Psychophysiological Correlates of Human Adaptation in Antarctica. Rep. 89–5.* San Diego, CA: Nav. Health Res. Cent.

Palinkas LA, Houseal M. 1999. Stages of change in mood and behavior during a winter in Antarctica. *Environ. Behav.* In press

Pekkarinen A, Soini S, Hassi J, Laapio H. 1992. Accident and risk evaluation on Finnish Antarctic expeditions. *Polar Rec.* 28:145–48

Peri A. 1988. L'alimentazione in ambienti remoti—Il caso Antartide. *Cent. Stud. Ric. Ligabue,* June, pp. 9–17

Peri A, Ruffini M, Taylor AJW. 1991. Le reazioni della coppia durante le spedizioni nazionali in Antartide. *Ann. Med. Nav.* 96:65–75

Peri A, Scarlata C, Barbarito M. 1999. Preliminary studies on the psychological adjustment in the Italian Antarctic summer campaigns. *Environ. Behav.* In press

Radloff R, Helmreich R. 1968. *Group Under Stress: Psychological Research in SEALAB II.* New York: Appleton-Century-Crofts

Ransmayr C. 1991. *The Terrors of Ice and Darkness.* London: Weidenfeld & Nicolson

Rasmussen JE, ed. 1973. *Man in Isolation and Confinement.* Chicago: Aldine

Rivolier J. 1997a. *L'Homme dans l'Espace: Une Approche Psycho-Écologique des Vols Habitués.* Paris: Presses Univ. France

Rivolier J. 1997b. *Review of Present Methods of Selection and Preparation as Adopted by Certain Member Countries.* Cambridge, UK: Work. Group Hum. Biol. Med., Sci. Ctee Antarct. Res.

Rivolier J, Cazes G, Bachelard C. 1995. *Summary of the French Research in Medicine and Psychology in the French Antarctic and Austral Territories.* Brest: Institut Rech. Technol. Paris: Com. Fr. Res. Antarct.

Rivolier J, Goldsmith R, Lugg DJ, Taylor AJW, eds. 1989. *Man in the Antarctic.* London: Taylor, Francis

Rosnet E, Le Scanff C, Sagal M-C. 1999. How self image and personality influence performance in an isolated environment. *Environ. Behav.* In press

Ross HE. 1975. *Behavior and Perception in Strange Environments.* New York: Basic Books

Rothblum ED, Morris JF, Weinstock JS. 1995. Women in the Antarctic: risk-taking and social consequences. *World Psychol.* 1:83–112

Rothblum ED, Weinstock JS, Morris JF, eds. 1998. *Women in the Antarctic.* Binghamton, NY: Harrington Park

Sandal GM, Endresen IM, Vaernes RJ, Ursin H. 1999. Personality and coping strategies during submarine missions. *Mil. Psychol.* In press

Sandal GM, Vaernes R, Bergan T, Warncke M, Ursin H. 1996. Psychological reactions during polar expeditions and isolation in hyperbaric chambers. *Aviat. Space Environ. Med.* 67:227–34

Sandal GM, Vaernes R, Ursin H. 1995. Interpersonal relations during simulated space missions. *Aviat. Space Environ. Med.* 66:617–24

Santy PA. 1994. *Choosing the Right Stuff: The Psychological Selection of Astronauts and Cosmonauts.* London: Praeger

Schwetje FK. 1991. Justice in the Antarctic, space, and the military. See Harrison et al 1991, pp. 383–94

Seligman MEP. 1998. What is the 'good life'? *APA Monit.* 29(10):2

Sells SB. 1973. The taxonomy of man in enclosed space. See Rasmussen 1973, pp. 280–303

Sharpe MR. 1969. *Living in Space.* London: Aldus

SIMIS (Simulation Mission Study Group). 1991. *Report of the Activities and Conclusions of a Group of Experts on Simulation of Manned Space Flight. Publ. LTPO-SR-91–01.* Paris: Eur. Space Agency

Smith S. 1969. Studies of small groups in confinement. In *Sensory Deprivation: Fifteen Years of Research,* ed. JP Zubek, pp. 374–403. New York: Appleton-Century-Crofts

Smith WM, Jones MB. 1962. Astronauts, Antarctic scientists, and personal autonomy. *Aerospace Med.* 33:162–66

Sorokin AA, Maksimov AL, Letuchikh VI, Konovalov YV, Turdiev A. 1996. Human circadian rhythm synchronization with social timers: the role of motivation. *Hum. Physiol.* 22:682–88

Space Science Board. 1972. *Human Factors in Long-Duration Space Flight.* Washington, DC: Natl. Acad. Sci.

Space Studies Board. 1998. *A Strategy for Research in Space Biology and Medicine in the New Century.* Washington, DC: Natl. Acad. Sci.

Steel GD. 1999a. Polar bonds: environmental relationships in the polar regions. *Environ. Behav.* In press

Steel GD. 1999b. *The third-quarter phenomenon in Antarctica.* Presented at the Victoria Univ. Wellington Antarct. Semin., Wellington, NZ

Steel GD, Suedfeld P. 1992. Temporal patterns of affect in an isolated group. *Environ. Behav.* 23:749–65

Steel GD, Suedfeld P. 1998. Use of free time in a simulated space shuttle mission. See Sullivan et al 1998, pp. 121–26

Steel GD, Suedfeld P, Peri A, Palinkas LA. 1997. People in high latitudes: the "Big Five" personality characteristics of the circumpolar sojourner. *Environ. Behav.* 29:324–47

Strange RE, Klein WJ. 1973. Emotional and social adjustment of recent US winter-over parties in isolated Antarctic stations. In *Polar Human Biology,* ed. OG Edholm, EKE Gunderson, pp. 410–16. London: Heinemann

Strange RE, Youngman SA. 1971. Emotional aspects of wintering over. *Antarct. J. US* 6:255–57

Strub H. 1996. *Bare Poles: Building Designs for High Latitudes.* Ottawa, Can.: Carleton Univ. Press

Stuster J. 1996. *Bold Endeavors: Lessons from Space and Polar Exploration.* Annapolis, MD: Nav. Inst.

Stuster J, Bachelard C, Suedfeld P. 1999. *In the Wake of the Astrolabe: Review and Analysis of Diaries Maintained by the Leaders and Physicians of French Remote Duty Stations.* Santa Barbara, CA: ANACAPA Sci.

Suedfeld P. 1987. Extreme and unusual environments. In *Handbook of Environmental Psychology,* ed. D Stokols, I Altman, 1:863–86. New York: Wiley

Suedfeld P. 1991. Groups in isolation and confinement: environments and experiences. See Harrison et al 1991, pp. 135–46

Suedfeld P. 1995. *Leadership and group behavior in isolated, confined environments.* Presented to Astronaut Candidate class, Johnson Space Cent., Houston, TX

Suedfeld P. 1998. Homo invictus: the indomitable species. *Can. Psychol.* 38:164–73

Sullivan P, Casgrain C, Hirsch N, eds. 1998. *CAPSULS: A 7-Day Space Mission Simulation—Final Report and Scientific Results.* Saint-Hubert, PQ, Can.: Can. Space Agency

Taylor AJW. 1969. Professional isolates in New Zealand's Antarctic research programme. *Int. Rev. Appl. Psychol.* 18:135–38

Taylor AJW. 1987. *Antarctic Psychology.* Wellington, NZ: Dept. Sci. Ind. Res.

Taylor AJW. 1989. Polar winters: chronic deprivation or transient hibernation? *Polar Rec.* 25:239–46

Taylor AJW, Robinson RD, McCormick IA. 1986. Written personal narratives as research documents—the case for their restoration. *Int. Rev. Appl. Psychol.* 35:197–208

Tingate TR, Lugg DJ, Muller HK, Stowe RP, Pierson DL. 1997. Antarctic isolation: immune and viral studies. *Immunol. Cell Biol.* 75:275–83

Torrance EP. 1954. The behavior of small groups under the stress conditions of "survival." *Am. Sociol. Rev.* 19:751–55

Ursin H, Bergan T, Collet J, Endresen IM, Lugg DJ, et al. 1991. Psychobiological studies of individuals in small, isolated groups in the Antarctic and in space analogues. *Environ. Behav.* 23:766–81

Ursin H, Comet B, Soulez-Larivieres C. 1992. An attempt to determine the ideal psychological profiles for crews of long-term space missions. *Adv. Space Res.* 12:310–14

van Loon JJ, van den Bergh LC, Schelling R, Veldhuijzen JP, Huijser RH. 1993. *Development of a centrifuge for acceleration research in cell and development biology.* Presented at Int. Astronaut. Fed. Congr., Graz, Austria

Walford RL, Bechtel R, MacCallum T, Paglia DE, Weber LJ. 1996. "Biospheric medicine" as viewed from the two-year first closure of Biosphere 2. *Aviat. Space Environ. Med.* 67:609–17

Weybrew BB, Molish HB. 1979. Attitude changes during and after long submarine missions. *Undersea Biomed. Res.* 6:S175–89

Weybrew BB, Noddin EM. 1979a. Psychiatric aspects of adaptation to long submarine missions. *Aviat. Space Environ. Med.* 50:575–80

Weybrew BB, Noddin EM. 1979b. The mental health of nuclear submariners in the United States Navy. *Mil. Med.* 144:189–91

White F. 1987. *The Overview Effect.* Boston: Houghton Mifflin

White KG, Taylor AJW, McCormick IA. 1983. A note on chronometric analysis of cognitive ability: Antarctic effects. *NZ J. Psychol.* 12:36–40

Wichman H. 1996. Designing user-friendly civilian spacecraft. *Adv. Astronaut. Sci.* 91:583–99

Wolfe T. 1979. *The Right Stuff.* New York: Bantam

Wood J, Hysong SJ, Lugg DJ, Harm DL. 1999a. Is it really so bad? A comparison of positive and negative experiences in Antarctic winter stations. *Environ. Behav.* In press

Wood J, Hysong SJ, Lugg DJ, Harm DL. 1999b. *Gender differences in psychological adaptation to extreme environments?* Presented at Internatl. Workshop on Human Factors in Space, Tokyo

Annu. Rev. Psychol. 2000. 51:255–277

Food Intake and the Regulation of Body Weight

Stephen C. Woods[1], Michael W. Schwartz[2],
Denis G. Baskin[2], and Randy J. Seeley[1]

[1]*Department of Psychiatry, University of Cincinnati Medical Center, Cincinnati, Ohio 45267; e-mail: steve.woods@psychiatry.uc.edu*
[2]*Division of Metabolism, Endocrinology and Nutrition, Department of Medicine, University of Washington, and the Puget Sound Veterans Administration Health Care System, Seattle, Washington 98195*

Key Words satiety, energy homeostasis, neuropeptides, leptin, insulin, hypothalamus

■ **Abstract** This chapter reviews the recent literature on hormonal and neural signals critical to the regulation of individual meals and body fat. Rather than eating in response to acute energy deficits, animals eat when environmental conditions (social and learned factors, food availability, opportunity, etc.) are optimal. Hence, eating patterns are idiosyncratic. Energy homeostasis, the long-term matching of food intake to energy expenditure, is accomplished via controls over the size of meals. Individuals who have not eaten sufficient food to maintain their normal weight have lower levels of adiposity signals (leptin and insulin) in the blood and brain, and one consequence is that meal-generated signals (such as CCK) are less efficacious at reducing meal size. The converse is true if individuals are above their normal weight, when they tend to eat smaller meals. The final section reviews how these signals are received and integrated by the CNS, as well as the neural circuits and transmitters involved.

CONTENTS

Introduction 256
Energy Homeostasis 256
Patterns of Food Intake 257
Meal Initiation... 258
   Correlates of Meal Onset.. 259
   The Role of Learning 260
The Control of Meal Size 261
The Regulation of Adiposity 263
   Adiposity Signals 265
Central Control Mechanisms 266

0084–6570/00/0201–0255$12.00

INTRODUCTION

Tremendous advances are being made in our understanding of the physiology of food intake. There are many reasons for this, perhaps foremost being the revolution in molecular biology and its application to behavior. A different, albeit not totally independent, factor has been a change in the federal government's view of obesity and its treatment (see World Health Org. 1998). Obesity is now recognized as a chronic disorder with biologic causes that may require chronic medical therapy, much as is the case for hypertension or diabetes mellitus. Prior to this change of policy, antiobesity drugs approved by the Federal Drug Administration were expected to induce weight loss that was sustained even after drug treatment was discontinued. Consequently, there was little interest on the part of pharmaceutical companies in the development of new drugs for the treatment of obesity. Fortunately, common sense and the weight of medical evidence prevailed and led to a reassessment. A major consequence of this new policy is the potential for new opportunities for the pharmaceutical industry, which once again has turned its attention (and immense resources) toward the development of antiobesity drugs and their lucrative market.

A second major contributor to the accelerating pace of research on the controls of food intake was the discovery in 1994 of the adipose tissue hormone leptin (Zhang et al 1994) and the finding that it interacts with specific receptors in the brain to control food intake and energy homeostasis. The realization that specific gene products have a profound influence on food intake and body weight paved the way for biotechnology companies to enter the fray, and the stream of new gene products and drugs that are now under investigation is impressive. One consequence is that the center of gravity of research on food intake has spread from its roots in psychology and physiology toward biochemistry and molecular biology, and many investigators new to the field are making seminal observations. In this review we attempt to unravel some of the myriad new molecules important in the control of eating and integrate them into what is understood about the biology of energy homeostasis.

ENERGY HOMEOSTASIS

Food intake serves many purposes. It provides energy in the form of calories as well as all the macronutrients, with their essential building blocks for cellular structure and function, vitamins, and minerals, and a variable amount of water. We focus on the intake of calories and its regulation while recognizing that regulation of specific macro- and micronutrients also occurs, often in the form of specific appetites, and that these can interact with the intake of calories. Energy intake in the form of food, and energy expenditure in the form of cellular metabolism and exercise, are precisely coupled over long intervals in healthy adults, resulting in stable body fat stores. The processes that regulate these behaviors are collectively called energy homeostasis.

PATTERNS OF FOOD INTAKE

Humans enjoy diverse lifestyles, and this complexity is reflected in their eating customs and habits. Although the stereotyped "three meals a day" may typify many individuals, both the number and size of eating bouts, as well as the total amount of food consumed each day, tend to be variable (de Castro 1998). There is also considerable day-to-day variability within individuals as they integrate eating with other activities. Yet, assuming that adequate food is available in the environment, most individuals (at least as adults) maintain relatively stable amounts of stored fat (adiposity) over long intervals (Bray 1976, Schwartz & Seeley 1997b, Stallone & Stunkard 1991). This implies that energy intake and expenditure are matched to one another despite a considerable variety of eating patterns.

Energy is continuously expended by living organisms, the rate varying with activity, ambient temperature, and many other factors. By comparison, eating generally occurs in distinct bouts or meals, the size and number of which vary considerably both within and among individuals. Vertebrates are able to cope with this variability because they store excess caloric energy when ample food is available and draw on those reserves when times are leaner. This natural ebb and flow of energy is easily illustrated by seasonal fluctuations of energy balance in many species, with more food being available, consumed, and stored as energy in the summer and autumn and with fat reserves becoming depleted again in the winter. But analogous fluctuation occurs on a daily basis as well, with the organism living off recently ingested energy during and immediately after meals and storing the excess to support bodily activities until it eats again. The entry of calories into the blood from either the gut or energy stores, as well as the uptake and utilization of these calories by the various tissues, is controlled by the brain and the liver. Both organs detect energy available in the blood, and the two intercommunicate via direct neural connections. The liver additionally has the ability to convert energy from one molecular form to another (e.g. from carbohydrate to fat, or from amino acids to carbohydrate) as needed, and it is the primary site for delivery of glucose to the circulation when glucose is no longer being absorbed from the gastrointestinal tract. This is important because some tissues rely relatively exclusively on one or another molecular form of energy (the brain has a large obligatory glucose requirement and the liver must utilize fats), whereas others (e.g. skeletal muscle) utilize whatever is available (glucose or fats).

Concordant with its continuous need for adequate levels of energy derived from fat, the liver is able to detect local reductions of fat availability and/or usage. In response, the liver activates distinct neural pathways that enter the brainstem and pass anteriorly to the forebrain, where they interact with controllers of energy homeostasis (Grill et al 1995, Ritter & Dinh 1994). Analogously, sensors in the hindbrain (Calingasan & Ritter 1993, Ritter et al 1981, Ritter & Dinh 1994, Ritter et al 1998) detect reductions of glucose availability and/or usage and activate parallel but separate pathways to the forebrain (Ritter et al 1998, Singer & Ritter 1996). Hence, separate but interacting (see Friedman 1998, Friedman & Tordoff 1986, Horn et al 1999, Singer-Koegler et al 1996) pathways regarding the availability of fats and glucose influence food consumption and perhaps choice, as well as energy expenditure (Park et al 1995, 1996; Ritter et al 1995; Scheurink & Ritter 1993; van Dijk et al 1995). Davidson and colleagues have provided evidence that animals differentiate specific stimuli associated with fat or carbohydrate consumption (Altizer & Davidson 1999, Davidson et al 1997). Furthermore, they are able to make appropriate responses for these different nutrients when challenged by drugs that selectively compromise fat or carbohydrate utilization by the body.

MEAL INITIATION

The brain and liver are incredibly efficient at controlling the provision of what is needed, and as a result, adequate amounts of utilizable fuels (glucose and fats) are generally always available to tissues via the blood. Fluctuations in the circulating levels of these fuels generally occur only during and after meals as ingested energy passes from the gut into the circulation, and from there into tissues and energy storage organs. Decreases of plasma fuels below levels adequate to meet tissue requirements are rare in normal individuals although they can be experimentally induced. For example, if the amount of energy derived from glucose is decreased, either by drugs that deplete it from the blood [exogenous insulin (Grossman 1986, Lotter & Woods 1977, MacKay et al 1940)] or drugs that prevent its cellular oxidation [2-deoxy-D-glucose (Grossman 1986, Smith & Epstein 1969)], an emergency situation occurs as the brain detects its requisite fuel supply dwindling. One result is that animals seek and ingest food (Langhans 1996a). Likewise, if fat consumption is experimentally compromised (Langhans & Scharrer 1987b, Scharrer & Langhans 1986), the source of usable fuel by the liver is challenged, the liver sends critical neural messages to the brain, and again animals seek and ingest food (Langhans 1996a,b).

A key point is that under usual circumstances, the supply of energy in the blood does not decrease to anywhere near the threshold necessary to trigger eating. Rather, animals initiate meals even though ample energy is readily available. Eating is in fact a relatively inefficient way to get calories into the blood rapidly. Unless pure glucose is available (rare in natural settings), foods must be processed and digested in the stomach, passed to the intestine where they are further processed, and then absorbed into the blood. Despite this time lag between the ingestion of food and the appearance of nutrients in the bloodstream, the concept that eating is triggered as a means to replenish dwindling fuel supplies has persisted for many decades. Early in this century blood glucose was thought to be a critical determinant of meals (Carlson 1916), and this concept was formalized and popularized by Mayer with his glucostatic hypothesis (Mayer 1955, Mayer & Thomas 1967). In a nutshell, Mayer postulated that eating is initiated when glucose availability and utilization by specific cells in the hypothalamus are reduced. Analogously, meals were hypothesized to terminate when glucose levels and/or availability are restored to adequate levels. Besides the problem of the temporal sluggishness, such a process forces animals to attain dangerously low levels of glucose prior to the initiation of every meal. More important, it is not clear what the consequences would be if glucose availability dipped to the threshold for initiating meals at a time when it was inconvenient or impossible to eat. It is now generally recognized that this protective system is probably activated to the point of initiating a meal only in extreme metabolic emergencies (Epstein et al 1975, Grossman 1986, Langhans 1996a).

Correlates of Meal Onset

Nonetheless, when the level of glucose in the blood is continuously monitored by means of an indwelling intravenous catheter, Campfield & Smith (1986b, 1990b) observed that beginning a few minutes prior to when a "spontaneous" meal is initiated in freely feeding rats, blood glucose decreases. More recently, that group reported a similar phenomenon in humans (Campfield et al 1996). This is an important observation because, at least in rats, every observed spontaneous meal was preceded by the small (approximately 12%) but reliable decline of plasma glucose (Campfield et al 1985). The premeal decline of blood glucose reverses just prior to the actual initiation of eating, and if food is removed at that point (and no eating occurs), glucose returns to the baseline that was present before the decline began. Campfield & Smith interpreted the premeal glucose decline as providing a signal that is monitored by the brain (Campfield & Smith 1990a,b; Smith & Campfield 1993). When its parameters are "correct," a meal is initiated. If metabolic conditions preclude the decline meeting the "correct" parametric criteria, no meal is initiated. In their schema, Campfield & Smith believe that the brain is the initiator of the decline of plasma glucose. Consistent with this, there is a small increase of plasma insulin at the beginning of the premeal decline of glucose (Campfield & Smith 1986a, 1990a), and cutting the vagus nerve (via which the brain can regulate insulin secretion) disrupts the relationship between changes of glucose and the start of meals (Campfield & Smith 1990a). One particularly appealing aspect of the hypothesis that premeal declines of glucose trigger meals is that extreme life- or consciousness-threatening declines of glucose need not be present for normal meals to occur. It also suggests that small, physiological fluctuations of glucose provide important signals that the brain uses to help determine ingestive responses. There is also evidence that the liver responds to small fluctuations of fatty acids and their metabolites by sending signals to the brain via the vagus nerves (Langhans et al 1985, Langhans & Scharrer 1987a).

There are other events that occur prior to, and hence are predictive of, the onset of meals. Implanted thermistors allow body temperature to be monitored continuously in freely moving and feeding animals. Just prior to spontaneous meals, the body temperature of rats begins to increase (de Vries et al 1993). When the meal begins, temperature continues to increase and then declines as the meal is terminated. Likewise, metabolic rate has been found to decrease prior to the start of spontaneous meals, and to increase as eating begins (Even & Nicolaidis 1985, Nicolaidis & Even 1984). All these parameters (blood glucose, temperature, metabolic rate, and no doubt others as well) begin a slow change 10–15 min before meals begin, and all are therefore highly correlated with meal onset. With a slightly different time course, laboratory rats increase their activity (e.g. running in a wheel) prior to spontaneous meals (Aravich et al 1995, Rieg & Aravich 1994, Sclafani & Rendel 1978, Stevenson & Rixon 1957). All these observations support the hypothesis that animals eat because these changes are occurring, i.e. that the decrease of blood glucose or of metabolic rate, or the exercise-induced use of fuels, is causally related to meal onset. However, a compelling case can also be made that, based upon factors such as habit or opportunity, the brain determines when a meal is going to start, and that as part of the overall meal process it initiates metabolic changes to prepare the body to receive the food (Woods & Strubbe 1994). As an example, a premeal decline of blood glucose can limit the magnitude of the otherwise much larger postprandial increase of blood glucose. In this schema, animals do not initiate meals because one or another tissue's supply of available energy is about to be compromised, but rather an animal eats when it is accustomed to eating, or when its predators have left, or when it has a break between classes. We take the position that the timing of meals is idiosyncratic and dictated by an individual's lifestyle, convenience, and opportunity. This accounts for the extreme variability of meal patterns among individuals in a species, but it cannot account, by itself, for the remarkable ability of animals to maintain a constant level of adiposity.

The Role of Learning

An important question concerns the factors that actually cause an individual to initiate a meal, or to experience "hunger." That is, if, under normal conditions, decreases of blood glucose or fats (or their correlated utilization) do not cause an animal to eat, what does? Although there are no clear answers to this question, there are compelling data that environmental stimuli previously associated with the ingestion of calories can elicit eating (Sclafani 1997, Warwick 1996, Woods & Strubbe 1994). Time of day is a particularly salient cue (Woods & Strubbe 1994), and a large literature documents the observation that when animals are habitually fed at the same, arbitrarily-selected time each day, they learn to synthesize and secrete hormones and neurotransmitters that are important controllers of food intake [e.g. insulin (Woods et al 1996, 1977) and neuropeptide Y (Yoshihara et al 1996a,b)]. Animals readily learn associations based upon the caloric content of food they receive, and the later presence of these cues in turn contributes to how much food is consumed during meals (Sclafani 1997, Warwick & Schiffman 1992). There is even evidence that the ability of "satiety" factors such as cholecystokinin (see below) to reduce meal size is modifiable by learning (Goodison & Siegel 1995). Finally, the argument has been made that diurnal fluctuations of hormones and neurotransmitters that are important determinants of meals and meal size are in fact entrained to the time that animals normally eat the largest meals of the day (Woods & Strubbe 1994). It is therefore reasonable to conclude that based upon an individual's history, idiosyncratic stimuli in the environment contribute to the timing of meals, and that associations based upon the caloric (and nutrient) content of previously consumed foods contribute to how much is eaten (e.g. Altizer & Davidson 1999, Davidson et al 1997, Sclafani 1997, Warwick & Weingarten 1996).

THE CONTROL OF MEAL SIZE

Given that the timing and frequency of meals are driven more by lifestyle than by immediate need, and given that caloric intake is matched to caloric expenditure over long intervals, the regulation of energy homeostasis can be manifest via control of how many calories are consumed when eating actually occurs. In other words, energy homeostasis can be achieved if there is control over meal size. Consistent with this, there is compelling evidence that the amount of food consumed during individual meals is under the control of signals generated in response to the food being eaten (Smith 1998, Smith & Gibbs 1992). And there is further evidence that the sensitivity of the brain to these meal-generated signals is in turn determined in part by the size of the adipose mass. That is, when animals are administered compounds that indicate to the brain that body fat has increased (leptin or insulin, see below), they become far more sensitive to the meal-suppressing action of meal-generated signals such as cholecystokinin (CCK) (Barrachina et al 1997, Figlewicz et al 1995, Matson & Ritter 1999, Matson et al 1997, Riedy et al 1995). The point is that an individual who has recently eaten insufficient food to maintain its weight will be less sensitive to meal-ending signals and, given the opportunity, will consume larger meals on the average. Analogously, an individual who has enjoyed excess food and consequently gained some weight will, over time, become more sensitive to meal-terminating signals.

Gibbs et al (1973) were the first to demonstrate conclusively that certain meal-generated peptides are able to reduce meal size, and more recently Smith & Gibbs (1992) provided a theoretical framework to account for these observations. It is based upon the well-described process that occurs when ingested food interacts with receptors in the proximal intestine. General omnivores such as humans and rats consume a wide spectrum of foods. Consistent with this, their digestive systems can draw on an analogously wide spectrum of digestive enzymes and secretions to customize the digestive process with what has actually entered the gut. This is accomplished via sensors in the mouth and digestive tract that analyze what is consumed and that coordinate the precise blend of digestive juices to be added to the food and that control the speed with which the material moves through the system. Enteroendocrine sensory cells lining the gut secrete compounds that signal distant organs such as the liver and exocrine pancreas to release the appropriate secretions into the intestine. Smith & Gibbs (1992) postulated that some of these secreted compounds (mainly peptides) additionally stimulate sensory nerves and thereby provide a signal related to the number and type of calories being consumed to the brain. The brain consequently integrates this information with other controllers and thereby determines meal size.

The gut peptide CCK is the best-known example of these meal-generated and meal size–controlling signals. CCK is secreted by the intestines during normal meals, and there are specific receptors for it, among many other places, on sensory fibers of the vagus nerve near the point where food passes from the stomach into the intestine (Smith et al 1984). More precisely, these vagal nerve endings contain CCK-A receptors (Corp et al 1993, Mercer & Lawrence 1992). Hence, during a meal, locally secreted CCK can stimulate these nerves and thereby send a signal to the lower brainstem where they synapse with neurons controlling digestive reflexes and responses as well as with neurons passing anteriorly to the forebrain (see Moran & Schwartz 1994, Rinaman et al 1995). When selective CCK-A receptor antagonists are administered to animals prior to a meal (Hewson et al 1988, Moran et al 1993, Reidelberger & O'Rourke 1989), meal size is increased significantly. Such results imply that endogenous CCK normally acts to reduce meal size. Consistent with this, if exogenous CCK is administered prior to a meal, meal size is decreased significantly and dose dependently (Gibbs et al 1973; Kulkosky et al 1976; Smith & Gibbs 1992, 1998). The importance of the CCK-to-vagus-to-brainstem circuitry is revealed when the receptive fields of the sensory fibers (Moran et al 1988), the sensory fibers themselves (Smith et al 1981, Smith et al 1985), or their entry point into the brainstem (Edwards et al 1986) is compromised. In each instance, exogenous CCK no longer reduces meal size. Consistent with these observations, when these same sensory fibers have been acutely compromised, there is an increase of meal size, which suggests that they normally send signals to the brain that limit intake (Chavez et al 1997, Kelly et al 1999).

Several further points can be emphasized. One is that the reduction of meal size elicited by exogenous CCK occurs at doses that do not create malaise (for reviews, see Smith & Gibbs 1992, 1998). Another is that the sensations elicited by CCK comprise but one portion of meal-related signals that influence meal size. There are several other gut peptides that have similar actions, although the route(s) by which their signals are passed to the brain differs. These include members of the bombesin family of peptides (gastrin releasing peptide and neuromedin B in mammals) (Gibbs et al 1979, Smith & Gibbs 1998), glucagon (Geary 1998, Salter

1960), somatostatin (Lotter et al 1981), amylin (Morley & Flood 1991), enterostatin (Erlanson-Albertsson & York 1997, Okada et al 1991, Shargill et al 1991), and perhaps others.

There are also other kinds of signals that normally help limit meal size, including the amount of distension or stretch in the stomach. Endings on vagal sensory nerves in the muscle layers of the stomach are situated to function as tension or stretch receptors. These same nerves have other branches with different kinds of sensory endings (Berthoud & Powley 1992), which suggests that two or more kinds of sensory information can be integrated within single vagal neurons. Consistent with this anatomical observation, it was recently reported that vagal activity elicited by exogenous CCK combines synergistically with that caused by distension of either the stomach (Schwartz et al 1993) or the duodenum (Schwartz et al 1995). The important point is that signals conveying information about numerous key parameters related to food intake converge in the brainstem (Schwartz & Moran 1996, Wang et al 1998). These include, in addition to gastric stretch, information on the specific types and amounts of food being processed, the relative amounts of water and solutes, the possible presence of toxins in the food, and so on.

THE REGULATION OF ADIPOSITY

In most adult mammals, the level of adiposity tends to remain constant over long intervals (Bray 1976, Keesey & Hirvonen 1997, Schwartz & Seeley 1997b, Stallone & Stunkard 1991). This is in spite of the fact that daily energy intake and expenditure, as well as meal patterns, may vary considerably over the same intervals. This is usually explained in thermodynamic terms, i.e. the energy equation tends to be balanced over long intervals (Keesey & Hirvonen 1997). Energy that is expended through metabolism, heat production, and physical exercise is precisely matched by energy that is consumed, for even a small discrepancy between the two will lead to gradual weight gain or weight loss. The precision of the regulatory mechanism is revealed when the system is perturbed. If an individual voluntarily diets (or has its food supply forcibly reduced), it loses weight, and the loss is mainly body fat. However, when the diet ends, or the food supply is restored, the individual eats more food than normal and regains the lost weight. Likewise, if individuals voluntarily or experimentally eat sufficient extra food to gain weight, they readily become hypophagic and lose the excess weight when conditions permit. Many reviews have documented these points (Bray 1976, Keesey & Hirvonen 1997, Schwartz & Seeley 1997b, Stallone & Stunkard 1991, Woods et al 1974). Even more compelling is the observation that if adipose tissue is surgically removed, the suddenly below-normal-weight individual, if s/he has a nutritionally adequate diet, eats sufficient extra calories to regain the weight lost to the scalpel (Faust et al 1977, 1979). In all these examples, food intake is not the sole means of correcting displaced adiposity. Rather, there are parallel changes of metabolic rate that work in concert with changes of food intake as adiposity is restored (Keesey & Hirvonen 1997).

There are several important implications of these observations. The first is that the amount of fat in the body is under strict negative feedback control. When it is displaced (whether voluntarily or involuntarily) and free feeding with ample food is allowed, its preperturbation level is soon restored. The second is that regulatory control systems in the brain appear to sense the amount of fat that actually exists at any moment. The third is that when perturbations in adiposity occur, the brain has corrective responses at its command that, in this case, control both the amount of calories eaten and the rate that energy is expended.

The size of the adipose mass that individuals maintain and defend obviously varies considerably within a species. Evidence suggests that in humans, the amount of fat carried is a complex interaction of genes and environment (Bjorntorp 1997b, Bouchard 1995, Comuzzie & Allison 1998, Hill & Peters 1998, Perusse et al 1998, Ravussin & Gautier 1999, Ravussin & Tataranni 1997). It is clear that as environmental conditions change for any given individual, the amount of fat they maintain also changes. For example, persistent exercise (Brownell 1998, Doucet & Tremblay 1998, Rippe & Hess 1998, Saris 1998) or stress (Bjorntorp 1997a,b) can result in maintenance of altered levels of adiposity. The nutritional content of the diet is also a major factor, with higher proportions of calories consumed as fat being associated with maintaining a greater amount of adiposity (Bray & Popkin 1998, Hill & Peters 1998, Willett 1998). There is also evidence that nutritional factors present during critical periods of development are important (Jackson et al 1996; West et al 1982, 1987). An important principle, however, is that in any given environment, an individual will maintain and defend a specific amount of body fat, and whereas changing the environment may change the absolute level of fat maintained, it does not interfere with the ability to regulate.

The regulation of body weight can be likened to the regulation of other homeostatically controlled variables, such as body temperature. Being homeotherms, mammals are able to maintain relatively constant internal temperatures in the face of variable and often extreme ambient temperatures. This feat is easily accomplished by means of coupled afferent and efferent mechanisms. Thermal receptors in the skin, liver, brain, and presumably elsewhere continuously send messages to the central nervous system (CNS). The CNS in turn combines this information with other relevant information (activity level, needs of various tissues, cognitive information) and adjusts the gain of some subset of possible effector mechanisms (blood flow in superficial veins, breathing rate, perspiration, closing a window, etc). The result is that the temperature inside the body remains relatively constant over time, and it is accomplished via adjustments in both behavioral and autonomic responses (see Gordon 1993, Ramsay & Woods 1997).

Until recently, the mechanisms that transduce body fat into afferent signals to the brain were far-less-well understood. Many traditionally studied sensory systems have specialized receptors that convert mechanical, thermal, or electromagnetic energy into action potentials in afferent neurons traveling to the CNS. The sensing of body fat is unusual in that it follows a different pattern and is accomplished via detection of the levels of circulating compounds whose levels are highly correlated with the size of the fat mass. Hence, the sensory organ for body fat is comprised of a set of brain neurons that express receptors for adiposity-correlated compounds and that have synaptic connections with brain areas that control food intake and metabolism.

Adiposity Signals

At least two circulating compounds meet the criteria for being "adiposity" signals to the brain, the pancreatic hormone insulin and the adipose tissue hormone leptin. Leptin is secreted in direct proportion to the amount of fat stored in individual adipocytes (fat cells), such that leaner individuals secrete less and fatter individuals secrete more leptin (Considine et al 1996, Rosenbaum et al 1996). When an individual fasts (or diets) and loses weight, plasma leptin decreases (Ahren et al 1997, Boden et al 1996, Havel et al 1996, Keim et al 1998); analogously, an increase of energy balance and associated weight gain is associated with an increase in leptin secretion (Ahren et al 1997, Seeley et al 1996). The importance of leptin as an adiposity signal to the brain is revealed by animals that either do not synthesize it [*ob/ob* mice, which have a mutation in the leptin gene (Zhang et al 1994)] or that have genetic mutations that compromise functioning of the leptin receptor [*db/db* mice and fatty Zucker, *fa/fa* rats (Chua et al 1996)]. These animals are characterized by hyperphagia and extreme obesity, and administering small amounts of leptin into the brains of *ob/ob* mice reverses this syndrome (for reviews, see Schwartz & Seeley 1997a, Seeley & Schwartz 1997, Woods et al 1998).

Insulin is the major hormone that enables tissues to remove glucose from the blood. Hence, its secretion is directly responsive to the level of blood glucose, and its absence (as exists in insulin-deficiency diabetes mellitus) is characterized by elevated blood glucose. Insulin secretion is also directly correlated with adiposity (Bagdade et al 1967, Polonsky et al 1988), and this is true in the resting or basal state as well as in response to elevated blood glucose during and after meals (Bagdade et al 1967, Polonsky et al 1988). The importance of insulin as an adiposity signal to the brain is revealed by the observation that insulin-deficient animals are hyperphagic and that the administration of small amounts of insulin locally into the brain of such animals eliminates their hyperphagia (Sipols et al 1995). Furthermore, the administration of antibodies to insulin into the brain of normal animals increases their food intake (Strubbe & Mein 1977) and body weight (McGowan et al 1992). Insulin-deficient individuals are not obese (like leptin-deficient individuals) in spite of extreme hyperphagia because fat cells cannot store fat in its absence. Hence, the brain of the insulin-deficient individual continuously strives to increase body fat and the excess calories consumed accumulate in the blood and are often lost in the urine.

The important point is that at least two hormones, leptin and insulin, provide important afferent information to the brain. The secretion of each is highly correlated with adiposity, a transport system in brain capillary endothelial cells passes each from the plasma into the brain, specific receptors for each exist in areas of the brain that control energy homeostasis, and manipulation of the levels of either locally within the brain causes predictable changes in food intake and body weight. There are several reviews of this literature (Porte et al 1998, Schwartz et al 1992a, Schwartz & Seeley 1997b, Seeley & Schwartz 1997, Woods et al 1998).

CENTRAL CONTROL MECHANISMS

To modulate energy homeostasis effectively, the actions of leptin and insulin within the brain must be transduced into motor patterns that influence the consumption of food on the one hand and energy expenditure on the other. The anatomical and neurochemical nature of the circuits that are sensitive to leptin and insulin are currently the subject of intense study. Because of this, new information concerning the role of long-described but only recently understood neural pathways is being generated at an unprecedented pace. In particular, neuronal circuits downstream of the initial actions of insulin and leptin are recognized as being attractive targets for pharmaceutical intervention in the treatment of obesity. In this section we provide an overview of this rapidly developing area, emphasizing the actions of leptin within the brain.

Mounting evidence supports the hypothesis that neuronal pathways in the hypothalamus are the primary targets for leptin action in energy homeostasis. Receptors for leptin are found throughout the body, as well as in many areas of the brain. However, the so-called long-form or signaling form of the leptin receptor is expressed in particularly high levels in several cell groups of the medial hypothalamus, including the arcuate (ARC), ventromedial, and dorsomedial nuclei (Baskin et al 1999a,b; Schwartz et al 1996b). It is important that these leptin receptors are located on neurons whose neurotransmitters have been implicated as important mediators of energy homeostasis.

Neuropeptide Y (NPY) is a peptide neurotransmitter that is ubiquitously synthesized in many areas of the brain. However, within the ARC, one group of NPY neurons containing leptin receptors is under the control of local levels of leptin. These neurons in turn project to the paraventricular nuclei (PVN), where NPY is released. Reduced leptin signaling such as would occur when an individual is underweight activates these ARC neurons to synthesize and release more NPY into the PVN (Schwartz et al 1996a, Stephens et al 1995). Increased NPY in the PVN and adjacent regions in turn promotes increased food intake, body weight gain (Kalra et al 1988, Stanley et al 1986), and reduced energy expenditure (Billington et al 1991, 1994). Hence, an individual who is underweight secretes less leptin and consequently activates this NPY-to-PVN pathway, thereby contributing to adaptive behavioral and metabolic responses that promote the recovery of the lost weight (Schwartz & Seeley 1997b, Seeley & Schwartz 1997, Woods et al 1998). Analogously, insulin receptors are also expressed in ARC neurons (Baskin et al 1990, Schwartz et al 1992a), and administration of insulin into the adjacent third cerebral ventricle reduces the weight loss–induced elevation of ARC NPY (Schwartz et al 1991, 1992b).

This leptin-NPY control system works in both directions. Individuals who are rendered overweight secrete increased leptin (Frederich et al 1995). Increased leptin in turn attenuates the activation of the ARC NPY neurons, simulating the effect that would normally occur in response to elevated body fuel stores (Schwartz et al 1996a,b). Leptin inhibition of orexigenic neuronal pathways in the hypothalamus is therefore proposed as playing a major role in energy homeostasis.

The melanocortins are a family of peptides that include adrenocorticotropic hormone and α-melanocyte–stimulating hormone (α-MSH). Within the hypothalamus, some melanocortins, including α-MSH, have effects on energy homeostasis opposite to those of NPY [i.e. they cause anorexia and weight loss (Tsujii & Bray 1989)]. The precursor of α-MSH, proopiomelanocortin (POMC), is synthesized in a subset of ARC neurons situated just adjacent to those that make NPY (Baskin et al 1999a, Kiss et al 1984). Fasting and its associated weight loss reduce POMC expression in the ARC, and local administration of leptin reverses the reduction, stimulating melanocortin synthesis (Schwartz et al 1997, Thornton et al 1997). Thus, conditions associated with reduced leptin signaling cause increased NPY production and reduced melanocortin production (Schwartz et al 1997, Thornton et al 1997). Moreover, leptin administration to these animals increases hypothalamic POMC while inhibiting NPY gene expression, a combination that may play a major role in leptin's ability to reduce food intake and body weight. The observation that the long-form of the leptin receptor is expressed by both NPY- and POMC-containing neurons in the ARC suggests that they are direct targets of leptin signaling in the hypothalamus (Baskin et al 1999a, Cheung et al 1997).

Some of the POMC neurons of the ARC project to the PVN where α-MSH (and perhaps other melanocortins) stimulate melanocortin (MC) receptors [specifically, MC3 and MC4 receptors (Schioth et al 1996)]. A unique feature of this melanocortin signaling system is the presence of both endogenous agonists (α-MSH) as well as antagonists of MC3 and MC4 receptors. The first endogenous melanocortin agonist to be described was a protein called "agouti protein" that is normally expressed in skin and hair follicles, where it is an endogenous modulator of pigmentation (coat color). "Agouti" mice have a mutation that causes them to express agouti protein in the brain inappropriately. As might be expected, agouti mice have chronically antagonized melanocortin receptors in the brain and are obese (Cone et al 1996, Huszar et al 1997). Furthermore, and consistent with the importance of the leptin-modulated ARC-to-PVN pathway, agouti mice do not reduce their food intake and body weight when administered leptin (Halaas et al 1997). An important implication from these findings is that chronic antagonism at MC3/MC4 receptors produces obesity by reducing the actions of leptin to initiate a cascade of events that results in increased agonistic activity at MC3MC4 receptors via α-MSH. Consistent with this hypothesis, local administration of antagonists to MC3/MC4 receptors into the brain blocks the actions of exogenous leptin to reduce food intake (Seeley et al 1997).

Agouti-related protein (AgRP) is a more-recently identified antagonist of MC3/MC4 receptors. Unlike agouti protein, which is normally made only in the skin, AgRP is made in the ARC (Rossi et al 1998, Shutter et al 1997), and its local administration into the brain potently stimulates food intake and weight gain. It is interesting that AgRP is made in the same ARC neurons that make NPY and that they are sensitive to changes in energy balance and leptin signaling (Hahn et al 1998). Thus, conditions associated with weight loss (i.e. reduced leptin signaling to the brain) potently induce both AgRP and NPY expression in these ARC neurons while inhibiting the POMC/α-MSH neurons. As a result, when an individual loses weight, the reduced signal to the brain results in the activation of transmitters that increase food intake and reduce energy expenditure (such as NPY). That results in inhibition of transmitters that reduce food intake and increase energy expenditure (such as α-MSH), and the activation of transmitters that antagonize α-MSH (such as AgRP). As discussed below, this level of complexity and apparent redundancy appear to be characteristic of the central controls involved in energy homeostasis.

The neuronal pathways downstream of the leptin-sensitive ARC neurons that participate in energy homeostasis are beginning to be dissected. Both AgRP/NPY neurons and POMC neurons originating in the ARC project heavily to the PVN and the perifornical hypothalamic area, regions long recognized to be important in the control of food intake. Neurons in the PVN synthesize many neuropeptides important in energy homeostasis, including corticotropin-releasing hormone, oxytocin, and thyrotrophin-releasing hormone. Each of these (and others) is a potential downstream target that could be regulated by input from ARC neurons, and each has been found to reduce food intake (for reviews, see Elmquist et al 1998, 1999; Trayhurn et al 1999; Woods et al 1998).

Peptides in the lateral hypothalamic area have also been implicated as downstream mediators of the actions of ARC neurons. Melanin-concentrating hormone (MCH) is expressed in the perifornical and lateral hypothalamic areas in neurons that receive synaptic input from both AgRP/NPY- and α-MSH–containing neurons (Elias et al 1998, Tritos et al 1998). MCH is an endogenous stimulant of feeding behavior (Qu et al 1996), and mice with a genetic MCH deficiency have reduced food intake and body fat stores, which suggests that MCH is another critical determinant of normal energy homeostasis (Qu et al 1996, Shimada et al 1998). Since hypothalamic MCH neurons project to diverse forebrain and hindbrain areas involved in food intake regulation, they may provide a key link between hypothalamic neurocircuits that respond to leptin and those that are involved in the short-term control of feeding. Other orexigenic [e.g. the orexins/hypocretins (de Lecea et al 1998, Sakurai et al 1998)] and anorexic [e.g. cocaine-amphetamine-related transcript (Kristensen et al 1998, Vrang et al 1999)] peptides have also recently been discovered in the hypothalamus and have been linked to leptin's actions (e.g. Lambert et al 1998, Trayhurn et al 1999).

Taken together, all these observations support a model in which the adipose tissue hormone leptin exerts opposing regulatory effects on ARC neurons containing NPY/AgRP on the one hand and melanocortins on the other. These neurons in turn project to secondary hypothalamic neuronal systems that are presumably regulated by inputs from myriad other systems pertinent to energy homeostasis. Ultimately, signals are generated that influence feeding behavior, energy expenditure, and the metabolic state of the individual. A major focus for the future is to identify critical neural networks in the brain that carry out these downstream effects. The importance of this objective is highlighted by the growing evidence that resistance to leptin, occurring at a "postreceptor" site in the CNS, is present in most forms of rodent obesity, and it likely exists in at least some forms of human obesity as well (Pi-Sunyer et al 1999, Trayhurn et al 1999, Woods et al 1998). We anticipate that the successful long-term treatment of obesity will require an appreciation of the multiple mechanisms responsible for this leptin resistance and the development of strategies to overcome it.

ACKNOWLEDGMENTS

Preparation of this review was supported in part by NIH grants DK 17844, DK 54080, DK-12829, DK-52989, DK 54890, and NS-32273; by the Diabetes Endocrinology Research Center and Clinical Nutrition Research Unit at the University of Washington; and by the VA Merit Review program. We thank Stephen C Benoit and Mary M Hagan for their critical comments.

Visit the Annual Reviews home page at www.AnnualReviews.org.

LITERATURE CITED

Ahren B, Mansson S, Gingerich RL, Havel PJ. 1997. Regulation of plasma leptin in mice: influence of age, high-fat diet and fasting. *Am. J. Physiol.* 273:R113–20

Altizer AM, Davidson TL. 1999. The effects of NPY and 5-TG on responding to cues for fats and carbohydrates. *Physiol. Behav.* 65:685–90

Aravich PF, Stanley EZ, Doerries LE. 1995. Exercise in food-restricted rats produces 2DG feeding and metabolic abnormalities similar to anorexia nervosa. *Physiol. Behav.* 57:147–53

Bagdade JD, Bierman EL, Porte D Jr. 1967. The significance of basal insulin levels in the evaluation of the insulin response to glucose in diabetic and nondiabetic subjects. *J. Clin. Invest.* 46:1549–57

Barrachina MD, Martinez V, Wang L, Wei JY, Tache Y. 1997. Synergistic interaction between leptin and cholecystokinin to reduce short-term food intake in lean mice. *Proc. Natl. Acad. Sci. USA* 94:10455–60

Baskin DG, Breininger JF, Schwartz MW. 1999a. Leptin receptor mRNA identifies a subpopulation of neuropeptide Y neurons activated by fasting in rat hypothalamus. *Diabetes* 48:828–33

Baskin DG, Marks JL, Schwartz MW, Figlewicz DP, Woods SC, Porte D Jr. 1990. Insulin and insulin receptors in the brain in relation to food intake and body weight. In *Endocrine and Nutritional Control of Basic Biological Functions,* ed. H Lehnert, R Murison, H Weiner, D Hellhammer, J Beyer, pp. 202–22. Stuttgart, Ger.: Hogrefe & Huber

Baskin DG, Schwartz MW, Seeley RJ, Woods SC, Porte D Jr, et al. 1999b. Leptin receptor long form splice variant protein expression in neuron cell bodies of the brain and colocalization with neuropeptide Y mRNA in the arcuate nucleus. *J. Histochem. Cytochem.* 47:353–62

Berthoud HR, Powley TL. 1992. Vagal afferent innervation of the rat fundic stomach: morphological characterization of the gastric tension receptor. *J. Comp. Neurol.* 319:261–76

Billington CJ, Briggs JE, Grace M, Levine AS. 1991. Effects of intracerebroventricular injection of neuropeptide Y on energy metabolism. *Am. J. Physiol.* 260:R321–27

Billington CJ, Briggs JE, Harker S, Grace M, Levine AS. 1994. Neuropeptide Y in hypothalamic paraventricular nucleus: a center coordinating energy metabolism. *Am. J. Physiol.* 266:R1765–70

Bjorntorp P. 1997a. Body fat distribution, insulin reistance, and metabolic diseases. *Nutrition* 13:795–803

Bjorntorp P. 1997b. Obesity. *Lancet* 350:423–26

Boden G, Chen X, Mozzoli M, Ryan I. 1996. Effect of fasting on serum leptin in normal human subjects. *J. Clin. Endocrinol. Metab.* 81:3419–23

Bouchard C. 1995. The genetics of obesity: from genetic epidemiology to molecular markers. *Mol. Med. Today* 1:45–50

Bray GA. 1976. *The Obese Patient.* Philadelphia: Saunders

Bray GA, Popkin BM. 1998. Dietary fat does affect obesity. *Am. J. Clin. Nutr.* 68:1157–73

Brownell KD. 1998. Diet, exercise and behavioral intervention: the nonpharmacological approach. *Eur. J. Clin. Invest.* 28(Suppl. 2):19–21

Calingasan NY, Ritter S. 1993. Lateral parabrachial subnucleus lesions abolish feeding induced by mercaptoacetate but not by 2-deoxy-D-glucose. *Am. J. Physiol.* 265:R1168–78

Campfield LA, Brandon P, Smith FJ. 1985. On-line continuous measurement of blood glucose and meal pattern in free-feeding rats: the role of glucose in meal initiation. *Brain Res. Bull.* 14:605–16

Campfield LA, Smith FJ. 1986a. Blood glucose and meal initiation: a role for insulin? *Soc. Neurosci. Abstr.* 12:109

Campfield LA, Smith FJ. 1986b. Functional coupling between transient declines in blood glucose and feeding behavior: temporal relationships. *Brain Res. Bull.* 17:427–33

Campfield LA, Smith FJ. 1990a. Systemic factors in the control of food intake: evidence for patterns as signals. In *Handbook of Behavioral Neurobiology. Neurobiology of Food and Fluid Intake,* ed. EM Stricker, pp. 183–206. New York: Plenum

Campfield LA, Smith FJ. 1990b. Transient declines in blood glucose signal meal initiation. *Int. J. Obes.* 14(Suppl. 3):15–31

Campfield LA, Smith FJ, Rosenbaum M, Hirsch J. 1996. Human eating: evidence for a physiological basis using a modified paradigm. *Neurosci. Biobehav. Rev.* 20:133–37

Carlson AJ. 1916. *Control of Hunger in Health and Disease.* Chicago: Univ. Chicago Press

Chavez M, Kelly L, York DA, Berthoud HR. 1997. Chemical lesion of visceral afferents causes transient overconsumption of unfamilar high-fat diets in rats. *Am. J. Physiol.* 272:R1657–R63

Cheung CC, Clifton DK, Steiner RA. 1997. Proopiomelanocortin neurons are direct targets for leptin in the hypothalamus. *Endocrinology* 138:4489–92

Chua SC, Chung WK, Wu-Peng XS, Zhang Y, Liu S, et al. 1996. Phenotypes of mouse diabetes and rat fatty due to mutations in the OB (Leptin) receptor. *Science* 271:994–96

Comuzzie AG, Allison DB. 1998. The search for human obesity genes. *Science* 280:1374–77

Cone RD, Lu D, Koppula S, Vage DI, Klungland H, et al. 1996. The melanocortin receptors: agonists, antagonists, and the hormonal control of pigmentation. *Recent Prog. Horm. Res.* 51:287–320

Considine RV, Sinha MK, Heiman ML, Kriaucinas A, Stephens TW, et al. 1996. Serum immunoreactive-leptin concentrations in normal-weight and obese humans. *N. Engl. J. Med.* 334:292–95

Corp ES, McQuade J, Moran TH, Smith GP. 1993. Characterization of type A and type B CCK receptor binding sites in rat vagus nerve. *Brain Res.* 623:161–66

Davidson TL, Altizer AM, Benoit SC, Walls EK, Powley TL. 1997. Encoding and selective activation of "metabolic memories" in the rat. *Behav. Neurosci.* 111:1014–30

de Castro JM. 1998. Genes and environment have gender-independent influences on the eating and drinking of free-living humans. *Physiol. Behav.* 63:385–95

de Lecea L, Kilduff TS, Peyron C, Gao XB, Foye PE, et al. 1998. The hypocretins: hypothalamus-specific peptides with neuroexcitatory activity. *Proc. Natl. Acad. Sci. USA* 95:322–27

de Vries J, Strubbe JH, Wildering WC, Gorter JA, Prins AJA. 1993. Patterns of body temperature during feeding in rats under varying ambient temperatures. *Physiol. Behav.* 53:229–35

Doucet E, Tremblay A. 1998. Body weight loss and maintenance with physical activity and diet. *Coron. Artery Dis.* 9:495–501

Edwards GL, Ladenheim EE, Ritter RC. 1986. Dorsomedial hindbrain participation in cholecystokinin-induced satiety. *Am. J. Physiol.* 251:R971–77

Elias CF, Saper CB, Maratos-Flier E, Tritos NA, Lee C, et al. 1998. Chemically defined projections linking the mediobasal hypothalamus and the lateral hypothalamic area. *J. Comp. Neurol.* 402:442–59

Elmquist JK, Elias CF, Saper CB. 1999. From lesions to leptin: hypothalamic control of food intake and body weight. *Neuron* 22:221–32

Elmquist JK, Maratos-Flier E, Saper CB, Flier JS. 1998. Unraveling the central nervous system pathways underlying responses to leptin. *Nat. Neurosci.* 1:445–50

Epstein AN, Nicolaidis S, Miselis R. 1975. The glucoprivic control of food intake and the glucostatic theory of feeding behavior. In *Neural Integration of Physiological Mechanisms and Behavior,* ed. GJ Mogenson, FR Calaresci, pp. 148–68. Toronto: Univ. Toronto Press

Erlanson-Albertsson C, York D. 1997. Enterostatin—a peptide regulating fat intake. *Obes. Res.* 5:360–72

Even P, Nicolaidis S. 1985. Spontaneous and 2DG-induced metabolic changes and feeding: the ischymetric hypothesis. *Brain Res. Bull.* 15:429–35

Faust IM, Johnson PR, Hirsch J. 1977. Adipose tissue regeneration following lipectomy. *Science* 197:391–93

Faust IM, Johnson PR, Hirsch J. 1979. Adipose tissue regeneration in adult rats. *Proc. Soc. Exp. Biol. Med.* 161:111–14

Figlewicz DP, Sipols AJ, Seeley RJ, Chavez M, Woods SC, Porte D Jr. 1995. Intraventricular insulin enhances the meal-suppressive efficacy of intraventricular cholecystokinin octapeptide in the baboon. *Behav. Neurosci.* 109:567–69

Frederich RC, Hamann A, Anderson S, Lollmann B, Lowell BB, Flier JS. 1995. Leptin levels reflect body lipid content in mice: evidence for diet-induced resistance to leptin action. *Nat. Med.* 1:1311–14

Friedman MI. 1998. Fuel partitioning and food intake. *Am. J. Clin. Nutr.* 67(Suppl. 3):513–18S

Friedman MI, Tordoff MG. 1986. Fatty acid oxidation and glucose utilization interact to control food intake in rats. *Am. J. Physiol.* 251:R840–45

Geary N. 1998. Glucagon and the control of meal size. See Smith 1998, pp. 164–97

Gibbs J, Fauser DJ, Rowe EA, Rolls ET, Maddison SP. 1979. Bombesin suppresses feeding in rats. *Nature* 282:208–10

Gibbs J, Young RC, Smith GP. 1973. Cholecystokinin decreases food intake in rats. *J. Comp. Physiol. Psychol.* 84:488–95

Goodison T, Siegel S. 1995. Learning and tolerance to the intake suppressive effect of cholecystokinin in rats. *Behav. Neurosci.* 109:62–70

Gordon CJ. 1993. *Temperature Regulation in Laboratory Rodents.* New York: Cambridge Univ. Press

Grill HJ, Friedman MI, Norgren R, Scalera G, Seeley RJ. 1995. Parabrachial nucleus lesions impair feeding response elicited by 2,5-anhydro-D-mannitol. *Am. J. Physiol.* 268:R676–82

Grossman SP. 1986. The role of glucose, insulin and glucagon in the regulation of food intake and body weight. *Neurosci. Biobehav. Rev.* 10:295–315

Hahn TM, Breininger JF, Baskin DG, Schwartz MW. 1998. Coexpression of Agrp and NPY in fasting-activated hypothalamic neurons. *Nat. Neurosci.* 1:271–72

Halaas JL, Boozer C, Blair-West J, Fidahusein N, Denton DA, Friedman JM. 1997. Physiological response to long-term peripheral and central leptin infusion in lean and obese mice. *Proc. Natl. Acad. Sci. USA* 94:8878–83

Havel PJ, KasimKarakas S, Mueller W, Johnson PR, Gingerich RL, Stern JS. 1996. Relationship of plasma leptin to plasma insulin and adiposity in normal weight and overweight women: effects of dietary fat content and sustained weight loss. *J. Clin. Endocrinol. Metab.* 81:4406–13

Hewson G, Leighton GE, Hill RG, Hughes J. 1988. The cholecystokinin receptor antagonist L364,718 increases food intake in the rat by attenuation of endogenous cholecystokinin. *Br. J. Pharmacol.* 93:79–84

Hill JO, Peters JC. 1998. Environmental contributions to the obesity epidemic. *Science* 280:1371–74

Horn CC, Addis A, Friedman MI. 1999. Neural substrate for an integrated metabolic control of feeding behavior. *Am. J. Physiol.* 276:R113–19

Huszar D, Lynch CA, Fairchild-Huntress V, Dunmore JH, Fang Q, et al. 1997. Targeted disruption of the melanocortin-4 receptor results in obesity in mice. *Cell* 88:131–41

Jackson AA, Langley-Evans SC, McCarthy HD. 1996. Nutritional influences in early life upon obesity and body proportions. *CIBA Found. Symp.* 201:129–37

Kalra SP, Clark JT, Sahu A, Dube MG, Kalra PS. 1988. Control of feeding and sexual behaviors by neuropeptide Y: physiological implications. *Synapse* 2:254–57

Keesey RE, Hirvonen MD. 1997. Body weight set-points: determination and adjustment. *J. Nutr.* 127:1875–83

Keim NL, Stern JS, Havel PJ. 1998. Relation between circulating leptin concentrations and appetite during a prolonged, moderate energy deficit in women. *Am. J. Clin. Nutr.* 68:794–801

Kelly LA, Chavez M, Berthoud HR. 1999. Transient overconsumption of novel foods by deafferented rats: effects of novel diet composition. *Physiol. Behav.* 65:793–800

Kiss JZ, Cassell MD, Palkovits M. 1984. Analysis of the ACTH/beta-End/alpha-MSH-immunoreactive afferent input to the hypothalamic paraventricular nucleus of rat. *Brain Res.* 324:91–99

Kristensen P, Judge ME, Thim L, Ribel U, Christjansen KN, et al. 1998. Hypothalamic CART is a new anorectic peptide regulated by leptin. *Nature* 393:72–76

Kulkosky PJ, Breckenridge C, Krinsky R, Woods SC. 1976. Satiety elicited by the C-terminal octapeptide of cholecystokinin-pancreozymin in normal and VMH-lesioned rats. *Behav Biol.* 18:227–34

Lambert PD, Couceyro PR, McGirr KM, Vechia SE, Smith Y, Kuhar MJ. 1998. CART peptides in the central control of feeding and interactions with neuropeptide Y. *Synapse* 29:293–98

Langhans W. 1996a. Metabolic and glucostatic control of feeding. *Proc. Nutr. Soc.* 55:497–515

Langhans W. 1996b. Role of the liver in the metabolic control of eating: what we know–and what we do not know. *Neurosci. Biobehav. Rev.* 20:145–53

Langhans W, Egli G, Scharrer E. 1985. Selective hepatic vagotomy eliminates the hypophagic effect of different metabolites. *J. Auton. Nerv. Syst.* 13:255–62

Langhans W, Scharrer E. 1987a. Evidence for a vagally mediated satiety signal derived from hepatic acid oxidation. *J. Auton. Nerv. Syst.* 18:13–18

Langhans W, Scharrer E. 1987b. Role of fatty acid oxidation in control of meal pattern. *Behav. Neural Biol.* 47:7–16

Lotter EC, Krinsky R, McKay JM, Treneer CM, Porte D Jr, Woods SC. 1981. Somatostatin decreases food intake of rats and baboons. *J. Comp. Physiol. Psychol.* 95:278–87

Lotter EC, Woods SC. 1977. Injections of insulin and changes of body weight. *Physiol. Behav.* 18:293–97

MacKay EM, Calloway JW, Barnes RH. 1940. Hyperalimentation in normal animals produced by protamine insulin. *J. Nutr.* 20:59–66

Matson CA, Ritter RC. 1999. Long-term CCK-leptin synergy suggests a role for CCK in the regulation of body weight. *Am. J. Physiol.* 276:1038–45

Matson CA, Wiater MF, Kuijper JL, Weigle DS. 1997. Synergy between leptin and cholecystokinin (CCK) to control daily caloric intake. *Peptides* 18:1275–78

Mayer J. 1955. Regulation of energy intake and the body weight: the glucostatic and lipostatic hypothesis. *Ann. NY Acad. Sci.* 63:14–42

Mayer J, Thomas DW. 1967. Regulation of food intake and obesity. *Science* 156:328–37

McGowan MK, Andrews KM, Grossman SP. 1992. Chronic intrahyphothalamic infusions of insulin or insulin antibodies alter body weight and food intake in the rat. *Physiol. Behav.* 51:753–66

Mercer JG, Lawrence CB. 1992. Selectivity of cholecystokinin receptor antagonists, MK-329 and L-365,260 for axonally transported CCK binding sites in the rat vagus nerve. *Neurosci. Lett.* 137:229–31

Moran TH, Ameglio PJ, Peyton HJ, Schwartz GJ, McHugh PR. 1993. Blockade of type A, but not type B, CCK receptors postpones satiety in rhesus monkeys. *Am. J. Physiol.* 265:R620–24

Moran TH, Schwartz GJ. 1994. Neurobiology of cholecystokinin. *Crit. Rev. Neurobiol.* 9:1–28

Moran TH, Shnayder L, Hostetler AM, McHugh PR. 1988. Pylorectomy reduces the satiety action of cholecystokinin. *Am. J. Physiol.* 255:R1059–63

Morley JE, Flood JF. 1991. Amylin decreases food intake in mice. *Peptides* 12:865–69

Nicolaidis S, Even P. 1984. Mesure du métabolisme de fond en relation avec la prise alimentaire: hypothese iscymétrique. *C. R. Acad. Sci. Paris* 298:295–300

Okada S, York DA, Bray GA, Erlanson-Albertsson C. 1991. Enterostatin (Val-Pro-Asp-Pro-Arg), the activation peptide of procolipase, selectively reduces fat intake. *Physiol. Behav.* 49:1185–89

Park CR, Benthem L, Seeley RJ, Wilkinson CW, Friedman MI, Woods SC. 1996. A comparison of the effects of food deprivation and of 2–5 anhydrous-D-mannitol on metabolism and ingestion. *Am. J. Physiol.* 270:R1250–56

Park CR, Seeley RJ, Benthem L, Friedman MI, Woods SC. 1995. The effect of 2–5 anhydro-D mannitol on whole body metabolic parameters. *Am. J. Physiol.* 268:R299–302

Perusse L, Chagnon YC, Bouchard C. 1998. Etiology of massive obesity: role of genetic factors. *World J. Surg.* 22:907–12

Pi-Sunyer FX, Laferrere B, Aronne LJ, Bray GA. 1999. Therapeutic controversy: obesity—a modern-day epidemic. *J. Clin. Endocrinol. Metab.* 84:3–12

Polonsky BD, Given E, Carter V. 1988. Twenty-four-hour profiles and pulsatile patterns of insulin secretion in normal and obese subjects. *J. Clin. Invest.* 81:442–48

Porte D Jr, Seeley RJ, Woods SC, Baskin DG, Figlewicz DP, Schwartz MW. 1998. Obesity, diabetes and the central nervous system. *Diabetologia* 41:863–81

Qu DQ, Ludwig DS, Gammeltoft S, Piper M, Pelleymounter MA, et al. 1996. A role for melanin-concentrating hormone in the central regulation of feeding behaviour. *Nature* 380:243–47

Ramsay DS, Woods SC. 1997. Biological consequences of drug administration: implications for acute and chronic tolerance. *Psychol. Rev.* 104:170–93

Ravussin E, Gautier JF. 1999. Metabolic predictors of weight gain. *Int. J. Obes. Relat. Metab. Disord.* 23(Suppl. 1):37–41

Ravussin E, Tataranni PA. 1997. Dietary fat and human obesity. *J. Am. Diet. Assoc.* 97(Suppl. 7):S42–46

Reidelberger RD, O'Rourke MF. 1989. Potent cholecystokinin antagonist L-364,718 stimulates food intake in rats. *Am. J. Physiol.* 257:R1512–18

Riedy CA, Chavez M, Figlewicz DP, Woods SC. 1995. Central insulin enhances sensitivity to cholecystokinin. *Physiol. Behav.* 58:755–60

Rieg TS, Aravich PF. 1994. Systemic clonidine increases feeding and wheel running but does not affect rate of weight loss in rats subjected to activity-based anorexia. *Pharmacol. Biochem. Behav.* 47:215–18

Rinaman L, Hoffman GE, Dohanics J, Le WW, Stricker EM, Verbalis JG. 1995. Cholecystokinin activates catecholaminergic neurons in the caudal medulla that innervate the paraventricular nucleus of the hypothalamus in rats. *J. Comp. Neurol.* 360:246–56

Rippe JM, Hess S. 1998. The role of physical activity in the prevention and management of obesity. *J. Am. Diet. Assoc.* 10(Suppl. 2):S31–38

Ritter RC, Slusser PG, Stone S. 1981. Glucoreceptors controlling feeding and blood glucose: location in the hindbrain. *Science* 213:451–52

Ritter S, Dinh TT. 1994. 2-Mercaptoacetate and 2-deoxy-D-glucose induce Fos-like immunoreactivity in rat brain. *Brain Res.* 641:111–20

Ritter S, Llewellyn-Smith I, Dinh TT. 1998. Subgroups of hindbrain catecholamine neurons are selectively activated by 2-deoxy-D-glucose induced metabolic challenge. *Brain Res.* 805:41–54

Ritter S, Scheurink AJW, Singer LK. 1995. 2-Deoxy-D-glucose but not 2-mercaptoacetate increases Fos-like immunoreactivity in adrenal medulla and sympathetic preganglionic neurons. *Obes. Res.* 3(Suppl. 5):729–34S

Rosenbaum M, Nicolson M, Hirsch J, Heymsfield SB, Gallagher D, et al. 1996. Effects of gender, body composition, and menopause on plasma concentrations of leptin. *J. Clin. Endocrinol. Metab.* 81:3424–27

Rossi M, Kim MS, Morgan DGA, Small CJ, Edwards CMB, et al. 1998. A C-terminal fragment of Agouti-related protein increases feeding and antagonizes the effect of alpha-melanocyte stimulating hormone in vivo. *Endocrinology* 139:4428–31

Sakurai T, Amemiya A, Ishii M, Matsuzaki I, Chemelli RM, et al. 1998. Orexins and orexin receptors: a family of hypothalamic neuropeptides and G protein-coupled receptors that regulate feeding behavior. *Cell* 92:573–85

Salter JM. 1960. Metabolic effects of glucagon in the Wistar rat. *Am. J. Clin. Nutr.* 8:535–39

Saris WH. 1998. Fit, fat and fat free: the metabolic aspects of weight control. *Int. J. Obes. Relat. Metab. Disord.* 22(Suppl. 2):S15–21

Scharrer E, Langhans W. 1986. Control of food intake by fatty acid oxidation. *Am. J. Physiol.* 250:R1003–6

Scheurink AJW, Ritter S. 1993. Sympathoadrenal responses to glucoprivation and lipoprivation in rats. *Physiol. Behav.* 53:995–1000

Schioth HB, Muceniece R, Wikberg JE. 1996. Characterisation of the melanocortin 4 receptor by radioligand binding. *Pharmacol. Toxicol.* 79:161–65

Schwartz GJ, McHugh PR, Moran TH. 1993. Gastric loads and cholecystokinin synergistically stimulate rat gastric vagal afferents. *Am. J. Physiol.* 265:R872–76

Schwartz GJ, Moran TH. 1996. Subdiaphragmatic vagal afferent integration of meal-related gastrointestinal signals. *Neurosci. Biobehav. Rev.* 20:47–56

Schwartz GJ, Tougas G, Moran TH. 1995. Integration of vagal afferent responses to duodenal loads and exogenous CCK in rats. *Peptides* 16:707–11

Schwartz MW, Baskin DG, Bukowski TR, Kuijper JL, Foster D, et al. 1996a. Specificity of leptin action on elevated blood glucose levels and hypothalamic neuropeptide Y gene expression in *ob/ob* mice. *Diabetes* 45:531–35

Schwartz MW, Figlewicz DP, Baskin DG, Woods SC, Porte D Jr. 1992a. Insulin in the brain: a hormonal regulator of energy balance. *Endocr. Rev.* 13:387–414

Schwartz MW, Marks J, Sipols AJ, Baskin DG, Woods SC, et al. 1991. Central insulin administration reduces neuropeptide Y mRNA expression in the arcuate nucleus of food-deprived lean (Fa/Fa) but not obese (fa/fa) Zucker rats. *Endocrinology* 128:2645–47

Schwartz MW, Seeley RJ. 1997a. Neuroendocrine responses to starvation and weight loss. *N. Engl. J. Med.* 336:1802–11

Schwartz MW, Seeley RJ. 1997b. The new biology of body weight regulation. *J. Am. Diet. Assoc.* 97:54–58

Schwartz MW, Seeley RJ, Campfield LA, Burn P, Baskin DG. 1996b. Identification of hypothalmic targets of leptin action. *J. Clin. Invest.* 98:1101–6

Schwartz MW, Seeley RJ, Weigle DS, Burn P, Campfield LA, Baskin DG. 1997. Leptin increases hypothalamic proopiomelanocoritin (POMC) mRNA expression in the rostral arcuate nucleus. *Diabetes* 46:2119–23

Schwartz MW, Sipols AJ, Marks JL, Sanacora G, White JD, et al. 1992b. Inhibition of hypothalamic neuropeptide Y gene expression by insulin. *Endocrinology* 130:3608–16

Sclafani A. 1997. Learned controls of ingestive behavior. *Appetite* 29:153–58

Sclafani A, Rendel A. 1978. Food deprivation-induced activity in dietary obese, dietary lean, and normal-weight rats. *Behav. Biol.* 24:220–28

Seeley RJ, Matson CA, Chavez M, Woods SC, Schwartz MW. 1996. Behavioral, endocrine and hypothalamic responses to involuntary overfeeding. *Am. J. Physiol.* 271:R819–23

Seeley RJ, Schwartz MW. 1997. Regulation of energy balance: peripheral endocrine signals and hypothalamic neuropeptides. *Curr. Dir. Psychol. Sci.* 6:39–44

Seeley RJ, Yagaloff KA, Fisher SL, Burn P, Thiele TE, et al. 1997. Role of melanocortin receptors in leptin effects. *Nature* 390:349

Shargill NS, Tsujii S, Bray GA, Erlanson-Albertsson C. 1991. Enterostatin suppresses food intake following injection into the third ventricle of rats. *Brain Res.* 544:137–40

Shimada M, Tritos NA, Lowell BB, Flier JS, Maratos-Flier E. 1998. Mice lacking melanin-concentrating hormone are hypophagic and lean. *Nature* 396:670–74

Shutter JR, Graham M, Kinsey AC, Scully S, Luthy R, Stark KL. 1997. Hypothalamic expression of ART, a novel gene related to agouti, is up-regulated in obese and diabetic mutant mice. *Genes Dev.* 11:593–602

Singer LK, Ritter S. 1996. Intraventricular glucose blocks feeding induced by 2-deoxy-D-glucose but not mercaptoacetate. *Physiol. Behav.* 59:921–23

Singer-Koegler LK, Magluyan P, Ritter S. 1996. The effects of low-, medium-, and high-fat diets on 2-deoxy-D-glucose- and mercaptoacetate-induced feeding. *Physiol. Behav.* 60:321–23

Sipols AJ, Baskin DG, Schwartz MW. 1995. Effect of intracerebroventricular insulin infusion on diabetic hyperphagia and hypothalamic neuropeptide gene expression. *Diabetes* 44:147–51

Smith FJ, Campfield LA. 1993. Meal initiation occurs after experimental induction of transient declines in blood glucose. *Am. J. Physiol.* 265:R1423–29

Smith GP, ed. 1998. *Satiation: From Gut to Brain.* New York: Oxford Univ. Press

Smith GP, Epstein AN. 1969. Increased feeding in response to decreased glucose utilization in rat and monkey. *Am. J. Physiol.* 217:1083–87

Smith GP, Gibbs J. 1992. The development and proof of the cholecystokinin hypothesis of satiety. In *Multiple Cholecystokinin Receptors in the CNS,* ed. CT Dourish, SJ Cooper, SD Iversen, LL Iversen, pp. 166–82. Oxford, UK: Oxford Univ. Press

Smith GP, Gibbs J. 1998. The satiating effects of cholecystokinin and bombesin-like peptides. See Smith 1998, pp. 97–125

Smith GP, Jerome C, Cushin BJ, Eterno R, Simansky KJ. 1981. Abdominal vagotomy blocks the satiety effect of cholecystokinin in the rat. *Science* 213:1036–37

Smith GP, Jerome C, Norgren R. 1985. Afferent axons in abdominal vagus mediate satiety effect of cholecystokinin in rats. *Am. J. Physiol.* 249:R638–41

Smith GT, Moran TH, Coyle JT, Kuhar MJ, O'Donohue TL, McHugh PR. 1984. Anatomic localization of cholecystokinin receptors to the pyloric sphincter. *Am. J. Physiol.* 246:R127–30

Stallone DD, Stunkard AJ. 1991. The regulation of body weight: evidence and clinical implications. *Ann. Behav. Med.* 13:220–30

Stanley BG, Kyrkouli SE, Lampert S, Leibowitz SF. 1986. Neuropeptide Y chronically injected into the hypothalamus: a powerful neurochemical inducer of hyperphagia and obesity. *Peptides* 7:1189–92

Stephens TW, Basinski M, Bristow PK, Bue-Vallesky JM, Burgett SG, et al. 1995. The role of neuropeptide Y in the antiobesity action of the obese gene product. *Nature* 377:530–34

Stevenson JAF, Rixon RH. 1957. Environmental temperature and deprivation of food and water on the spontaneous activity of rats. *Yale J. Biol. Med.* 29:575–84

Strubbe JH, Mein CG. 1977. Increased feeding in response to bilateral injection of insulin antibodies in the VMH. *Physiol. Behav.* 19:309–13

Thornton JE, Cheung CC, Clifton DK, Steiner RA. 1997. Regulation of hypothalamic proopiomelanocortin mRNA by leptin in ob/ob mice. *Endocrinology* 138:5063–67

Trayhurn P, Hoggard N, Mercer JG, Rayner DV. 1999. Leptin: fundamental aspects. *Int. J. Obes. Relat. Metab. Disord.* 23(Suppl. 1):22–28

Tritos NA, Vicent D, Gillette J, Ludwig DS, Flier ES, Maratos-Flier E. 1998. Functional interactions between melanin-concentrating hormone, neuropeptide Y, and anorectic neuropeptides in the rat hypothalamus. *Diabetes* 47:1687–92

Tsujii S, Bray GA. 1989. Acetylation alters the feeding response to MSH and beta-endorphin. *Brain Res. Bull.* 23:165–69

van Dijk G, Scheurink AJW, Ritter S, Steffens AB. 1995. Glucose homeostasis and sympathoadrenal activity in mercaptoacetate-treated rats. *Physiol. Behav.* 57:759–64

Vrang N, Tang-Christensen M, Larsen PJ, Kristensen P. 1999. Recombinant CART peptide induces c-Fos expression in central areas involved in control of feeding behaviour. *Brain Res.* 818:499–509

Wang L, Martinez V, Barrachina MD, Tache Y. 1998. Fos expression in the brain induced by peripheral injection of CCK or leptin plus CCK in fasted lean mice. *Brain Res.* 791:157–66

Warwick ZS. 1996. Probing the causes of high-fat diet hyperphagia: a mechanistic and behavioral dissection. *Neurosci. Biobehav. Rev.* 16:585–96

Warwick ZS, Schiffman SS. 1992. Role of dietary fat in calorie intake and weight gain. *Neurosci. Biobehav. Rev.* 16:585–96

Warwick ZS, Weingarten HP. 1996. Flavor-postingestive consequence associations incorporate the behaviorally opposing effects of positive reinforcement and anticipated satiety: implications for interpreting two-bottle tests. *Physiol. Behav.* 60:711–15

West DB, Diaz J, Roddy S, Woods SC. 1987. Long-term effects of adiposity following preweaning nutritional manipulations in the gastrostomy-reared rat. *J. Nutr.* 117:1259–64

West DB, Diaz J, Woods SC. 1982. Infant gastrostomy and chronic formula infusion as a technique to overfeed and accelerate weight gain of neonatal rats. *J. Nutr.* 112:1339–43

Willett WC. 1998. Is dietary fat a major determinant of body fat? *Am. J. Clin. Nutr.* 67(Suppl.):S56–62

Woods SC, Chavez M, Park CR, Riedy C, Kaiyala K, et al. 1996. The evaluation of insulin as a metabolic signal controlling behavior via the brain. *Neurosci. Biobehav. Rev.* 20:139–44

Woods SC, Decke E, Vasselli JR. 1974. Metabolic hormones and regulation of body weight. *Psychol. Rev.* 81:26–43

Woods SC, Seeley RJ, Porte D Jr, Schwartz MW. 1998. Signals that regulate food intake and energy homeostasis. *Science* 280:1378–83

Woods SC, Strubbe JH. 1994. The psychobiology of meals. *Psychonom. Bull. Rev.* 1:141–55

Woods SC, Vasselli JR, Kaestner E, Szakmary GA, Milburn P, Vitiello MV. 1977. Conditioned insulin secretion and meal feeding in rats. *J. Comp. Physiol. Psychol.* 91:128–33

World Health Org. 1998. Obesity: Preventing and Managing the Global Epidemic. Geneva, Switzerland: WHO

Yoshihara T, Honma S, Honma K. 1996a. Effects of restricted daily feeding on neuropeptide Y release in the rat paraventricular nucleus. *Am. J. Physiol.* 270: E589–95

Yoshihara T, Honma S, Honma K. 1996b. Prefeeding release of paraventricular neuropeptide Y is mediated by ascending noradrenergic neurons in rats. *Am. J. Physiol.* 270:E596–600

Zhang YY, Proenca R, Maffei M, Barone M, Leopold L, Friedman JM. 1994. Positional cloning of the mouse obese gene and its human homologue. *Nature* 372:425–32

Annu. Rev. Psychol. 2000. 51:279–314

NEGOTIATION

Max H. Bazerman[1], Jared R. Curhan[2], Don A. Moore[3], and Kathleen L. Valley[4]

[1]*Kellogg Graduate School of Management, Northwestern University, Evanston, Illinois 60208; e-mail: mbazerman@hbs.edu*
[2]*Graduate School of Business Administration, Harvard University, Boston, Massachusetts 02163; e-mail: curhan@psych.stanford.edu,*
[3]*Department of Psychology, Stanford University, Stanford, California 94305; Kellogg Graduate School of Management, Northwestern University, Evanston, Illinois 60208; e-mail: dmoore@nwu.edu*
[4]*Graduate School of Business Administration, Harvard University, Boston, Massachusetts 02163; e-mail: kvalley@hbs.edu*

Key Words bargaining, mental models, ethics, culture, communications media, multiparty negotiation

■ **Abstract** The first part of this paper traces a short history of the psychological study of negotiation. Although negotiation was an active research topic within social psychology in the 1960s and 1970s, in the 1980s, the behavioral decision perspective dominated. The 1990s has witnessed a rebirth of social factors in the psychological study of negotiation, including social relationships, egocentrism, motivated illusions, and emotion. The second part of this paper reviews five emerging research areas, each of which provides useful insight into how negotiators subjectively understand the negotiation: (*a*) mental models in negotiation; (*b*) how concerns of ethics, fairness, and values define the rules of the game being played; (*c*) how the selection of a communication medium impacts the way the game is played; (*d*) how cross-cultural issues in perception and behavior affect the negotiation game; and (*e*) how negotiators organize and simplify their understandings of the negotiation game when more than two actors are involved.

CONTENTS

Introduction 280
A short History of the Psychological Study of Negotiation 280
   The Early Social Psychology of Negotiations 280
   The Behavioral Decision Perspective on Negotiations 282
   The Rebirth of the Social Psychology of Negotiations 283
A Psychological Definition of the Negotiation Game 286
   Mental Models in Negotiation 287
   Ethics and Sacredness in Negotiation 291
   Choosing a Medium of Communication 293

Cross-Cultural Issues in Negotiation 296
Negotiation with More than Two Players 300
Conclusion 302

INTRODUCTION

The past 25 years have seen dramatic shifts in the psychological study of negotiation. The study of negotiation was an active field within the domain of social psychology in the 1960s and 1970s, but the cognitive revolution in the late 1970s left little room for interpersonal processes, leaving the study of negotiation to decline. By the early 1980s, negotiations blossomed anew as perhaps the fastest growing area of teaching and research in schools of management. Much of this growth was based on psychological research, specifically a behavioral decision-making perspective. The 1980s and 1990s have witnessed an explosion of research on the negotiator as decision maker. But the late 1990s brought many calls to reintroduce the social aspects of the negotiation process—with an explicit criticism of the behavioral decision paradigm of negotiation as overly restrictive. In this paper, we review these developments and also explore an emergent body of work integrating cognitive and social aspects of negotiation. This new work examines the negotiation as it is perceived and constructed by the negotiators themselves.

We organize this paper around two sections. In the first section, we provide a selective history of the development of the psychological study of negotiation. This history briefly explores the demise of the early social psychology of negotiations, overviews the behavioral decision perspective of negotiation, and explores recent efforts to create a new social psychology of negotiations. In the second section, we explore emerging trends that broaden the study of negotiation and connect negotiations to a broader spectrum of psychological literatures. Specifically, this section focuses on research that, rather than assuming negotiators respond to an objectively specified game structure, explores how negotiators psychologically understand the negotiation game they are playing.

A SHORT HISTORY OF THE PSYCHOLOGICAL STUDY OF NEGOTIATION

The Early Social Psychology of Negotiations

Negotiation was the subject of hundreds of empirical papers by social psychologists in the 1960s and 1970s (Rubin & Brown 1975). During this time, the study of negotiations in social psychology primarily focused on two subdomains: individual differences of negotiators and situational characteristics. In the sections that follow, we discuss the general conclusions arising out of these areas of research. As the field of social psychology moved toward research on social cognition, negotiation, like many interpersonal topics, drifted from the forefront of social psychology.

Individual differences   Rubin & Brown (1975) documented the extensive literature on individual differences in negotiation, including both demographic characteristics and personality variables. Despite hundreds of investigations, these factors typically do not explain much variance in negotiator behavior (Thompson 1998), just as they fail to account for much variance in other behaviors (Ross & Nisbett 1991). When individual differences do influence negotiated outcomes, slight changes in situational features swamp these effects (Ross & Nisbett 1991, Thompson 1998). Although true believers in individual differences still exist (Barry & Friedman 1998), many authors have reached the conclusion that simple individual differences offer limited potential for predicting negotiation outcomes (Lewicki et al 1993, Pruitt & Carnevale 1993). Furthermore, individual differences are of limited use because they are not under the negotiator's control (Bazerman & Carroll 1987). Finally, ample evidence shows that even experts are poor at making clinical assessments about another person's personality in order to accurately formulate an opposing strategy (Morris et al 1999, 1995).

Structural variables   Social psychological research on negotiation in the 1960s and 1970s also explored a series of situational/structural variables. These are the variables that define the context of the negotiation. Examples of situational variables include the presence of constituencies (Druckman 1967), parties' incentives and payoffs (Axelrod & May 1968), power (Marwell et al 1969), deadlines (Pruitt & Drews 1969), the number of people on each side (Marwell & Schmitt 1972), and the presence of third parties (Pruitt & Johnson 1972). Although research on situational variables has contributed to our understanding of negotiation, the objective features of a negotiation are often beyond the control of an individual negotiator. Recent research has turned its attention to how negotiators perceive and construct the negotiation problem, which is more (although certainly not fully) under the control of the negotiator. Unfortunately, the older social psychological study of negotiation did not explore the creation or construal of the negotiation structure but tended to offer data on the impact of objective alternative structures. As a result, the effects were typically consistent with naïve intuition.

Overall, the dominant social psychological approaches suffered from critical shortcomings and were of limited use for enhancing the effectiveness of negotiation scholarship or practice. As we will argue, the problem was not inherent in the psychological perspective; the problem was with the specific analytic lens chosen, which relied on description without clear standards of rationality or optimality against which behavior could be evaluated.

The Behavioral Decision Perspective on Negotiations

The cognitive revolution in psychology strongly influenced research in negotiation. The research moved in the direction of behavioral decision research (BDR) in the 1980s and 1990s. Greater interaction between descriptive and prescriptive researchers facilitated research on this decision perspective (Bazerman & Neale 1992). Prescriptive research on negotiations prior to 1982 focused primarily on game theory, the mathematical analysis of fully rational negotiators. Raiffa's (1982) focus on providing the best advice to a focal negotiator was a key turning point in negotiation research. First, from a prescriptive perspective, Raiffa explicitly acknowledged the importance of developing accurate descriptions of opponents rather than assuming the opponent negotiator to be fully rational. Second, the notion of using negotiation analysis to give advice implicitly acknowledged that negotiators themselves do not intuitively follow purely rational strategies. Most important, from the perspective of psychology, Raiffa initiated the groundwork for dialog between prescriptive and descriptive researchers, creating a prescriptive need to descriptively understand how negotiators actually make decisions. Following Raiffa's structure, Bazerman and Neale (1992) outlined a psychological understanding of negotiation designed to use description to prescribe strategies that would help the focal negotiator increase the likelihood that the parties would grow a larger pie, while simultaneously giving the focal negotiator the needed understanding to maximize how much of the pie they obtained, subject to concerns for fairness and the ongoing relationship.

The 1980s and 1990s witnessed a large number of studies that address the questions Raiffa's work left unexamined (Bazerman 1998, Neale & Bazerman 1991, Thompson 1990, 1998). This line of work uses the field of BDR as a core for ideas about how negotiators actually make decisions. The field of BDR delineates the systematic ways in which decision makers deviate from optimality or rationality (Dawes 1998, Kahneman & Tverksy 1973, 1979). Individuals are presumed to attempt to act rationally but to be bounded in their ability to achieve rationality (Simon 1957). This field has allowed researchers to predict, a priori, how people will make decisions that are inconsistent, inefficient, and based on normatively irrelevant information. To document the biases that lead negotiators to deviate from optimally rational behavior is not to deny the amazing feats of which the human mind is capable (Pinker 1997). We navigate complex social worlds with amazing dexterity and solve enormously complex problems with breathtaking ease, but we are not perfect. Human cognition suffers from a variety of predictable mistakes, and it is precisely these mistakes that give us insight into the functioning of the mind (Kahneman & Tversky 1982).

The core argument of much of BDR is that people rely on simplifying strategies, or cognitive heuristics (Bazerman 1998). Although these heuristics are typically useful shortcuts, they also lead to predictable mistakes (Tversky & Kahneman 1974). It is the systematic and predictable nature of these biases, and what they reveal about the human mind, that makes them so intriguing to researchers.

Specifically, research on two-party negotiations suggests that negotiators tend to (*a*) be more concessionary to a positively framed specification of the negotiation than to a negatively framed specification (Bazerman et al 1985, Bottom & Studt 1993, De Dreu & McCusker 1997, Lim & Carnevale 1995, Olekalns 1997); (*b*) be inappropriately affected by anchors in negotiation (Kahneman 1992, Kristensen & Garling 1997, Northcraft & Neale 1987, Ritov 1996, Thompson 1995, Whyte & Sebenius 1997); (*c*) be inappropriately affected by readily available information (Neale 1984, Pinkley et al 1995); (*d*) be overconfident and overly optimistic about the likelihood of attaining outcomes that favor themselves (Bazerman et al 1999, Bazerman & Neale 1982, Kramer et al 1993, Lim 1997); (*e*) falsely assume that the negotiation pie is fixed and miss opportunities for mutually beneficial trade-offs between the parties (Bazerman et al 1985, Fukuno & Ohbuchi 1997, Thompson & DeHarpport 1994, Thompson & Hastie 1990); (*f*) falsely assume that their preferences on issues are incompatible with those of their opponent (Thompson & Hrebec 1996); (*g*) escalate conflict even when a rational analysis would dictate a change in strategy (Bazerman 1998, Bazerman & Neale 1983, Bizman & Hoffman 1993, Diekmann et al 1999, 1996, Keltner & Robinson 1993); (*h*) ignore the perspective of other parties (Bazerman & Carroll 1987, Carroll et al 1988, Samuelson & Bazerman 1985, Valley et al 1998); and (*i*) reactively devalue any concession made by the opponent (Curhan et al 1998, Ross & Stillinger 1991).

Behavioral decision theory perspective largely reframed psychological research on negotiation in the 1980s and early 1990s. This behavioral research departed from previous psychological research on negotiation, as it emphasized how actual decisions were different from what would be predicted by normative models. Clearly, a goal to provide useful information that could lead to the debiasing of negotiators guided this research. As we move forward, our goal is to outline a future for negotiation research that keeps this strength, yet allows for a broader understanding of the psychological task of negotiation.

The Rebirth of the Social Psychology of Negotiation

The behavioral decision perspective had a significant influence on the scholarship and practice of negotiation. However, many authors criticized this perspective for ignoring too many factors that were obviously important in negotiation (Greenhalgh & Chapman 1995). Recent research adds social psychological variables consistent with a BDR perspective. In this research, the social factors argued to be missing from earlier research on decision making have become specific topics of study. However, this new social psychology of negotiations accepts some of the features of the BDR perspective, including the backdrop of rationality (Murnighan 1994, Thompson 1998). This section highlights four sets of questions, building off of the review by Bazerman et al (2000).

Social relationships in negotiation   The importance of relationships in negotiation has been noted throughout the field's history (e.g. Follett 1940, Rubin &

Brown 1975, Walton & McKersie 1965). However, this topic has reemerged strongly in the 1990s (for reviews see Greenhalgh & Chapman 1998, Valley et al 1995). The study of relationships and negotiation can be trichotomized into three basic levels: the individual, the dyad, and the network.

The first level includes studies of how judgment and preferences of individual negotiators are influenced by social context (for review see Clark & Chrisman 1994). An example of this work is a study by Loewenstein et al (1989), which found that disputants' reported preferences for monetary payoffs were greatly influenced by payoffs to and relationships with their hypothetical counterparts.

The second level examines how social relationships within dyads can influence negotiation processes and outcomes (for review see Valley et al 1995). Bazerman et al (1998a) demonstrated that certain behaviors that appear irrational from the individual perspective may be rational from the perspective of the dyad. For example, given the opportunity to communicate freely, negotiators often appear irrational in their individual decision making yet reach dyadic outcomes that outperform game theoretic models (Valley et al 1998).

Finally, the third level is concerned with the influence of relationships on the broader network of actors (Baker 1984, 1990; Shah & Jehn 1993; Sondak & Bazerman 1989; Valley 1992). As an example of this third category, Tenbrunsel et al (1996) examined the implications of relationships on the selection of a negotiation partner. Essentially, they argued that people "satisfice" (March & Simon 1958) by matching with other people they already know rather than seeking out new partners (Tenbrunsel et al 1996), at the cost of finding better-fitting matches.

Egocentrism in negotiation   Negotiators' fairness judgments are not purely objective. Rather, parties tend to overweight the views that favor themselves—resulting in a motivational bias (Babcock & Loewenstein 1997, Diekmann et al 1997, Walster et al 1978) in addition to the cognitively based biases reviewed earlier. This motivational bias is called egocentrism. Thompson & Loewenstein (1992) found negotiators to be egocentric, and the more egocentric the parties were, the more difficulty they had coming to agreement. This pattern has been replicated both in studies that used financial incentives for performance and across negotiation contexts (Babcock et al 1995, Camerer & Loewenstein 1993, Loewenstein et al 1993). Furthermore, Thompson & Loewenstein (1992) found that the provision of more (neutral) information increases egocentrism. Those participants who received this additional neutral information tended to make more extreme estimates of a fair outcome. Participants also showed self-serving recall bias, remembering better those facts that favored themselves.

A large amount of research has gone into explaining this egocentric pattern of behavior. We are most persuaded by the view of Messick & Sentis (1983) that preferences are basic and immediate, but fairness judgments must be determined through reflection, a process that is vulnerable to bias. As ambiguity creates uncertainty around what a fair outcome would be, negotiators tend to interpret fairness in ways that favor themselves (Babcock & Olson 1992, Camerer & Loewenstein 1993, De Dreu 1996, Diekmann 1997, Diekmann et al 1997, Messick & Sentis 1979). Experimental manipulations that reduce potential ambiguity also reduce egocentrism. For example, when players occupy symmetric roles, egocentrism is weaker than when their roles are asymmetric (Wade-Benzoni et al 1996). Communication between the players that allows them to form a shared understanding of the situation also reduces egocentrism (Thompson & Loewenstein 1992, Wade-Benzoni et al 1996).

Motivated illusions in negotiation   Most people view themselves, the world, and the future in a considerably more positive light than reality can sustain (Taylor 1989, Taylor & Brown 1988). People tend to perceive themselves as being better than others on desirable attributes (Gabriel et al 1994, Messick et al 1985, Svenson 1981) and have unrealistically positive self-evaluations (Brown 1986). In the negotiations domain, Kramer et al (1993) found that in a negotiation class taken by candidates for masters in business administration, 68% of the students predicted that their bargaining outcomes would fall in the upper 25% percent of the class.

In part, negotiators' optimism may be traceable to overestimation of their ability to control uncontrollable events (Crocker 1982, Kramer 1994, Miller & Ross 1975). Negotiators in a prisoner's dilemma act as if their decision will control the simultaneous decision of the other party, even when that is logically impossible (Morris et al 1998, Shafir & Tversky 1992). This research argues that one reason parties cooperate in one-shot prisoner dilemma games is the illusion that their own cooperation will create cooperation in the other party. Other evidence points to the social costs of positive illusions. Unsuccessful negotiators tend to denigrate their more successful counterparts by attributing their success to uncooperative and unethical bargaining tactics (Kramer 1994). Positive illusions, especially when accompanied by egocentrism and vilification of opponents, are likely to increase the costs of conflict by inhibiting integrative gains and by delaying agreement (De Dreu et al 1995b).

Emotion and negotiation   Although the laboratory-based cognitive approach that dominated negotiation research in the 1980s and 1990s has ignored most emotion-relevant variables, some research has explored the important role of emotion in negotiation. This research finds that positive moods tend to increase negotiators' tendencies to select a cooperative strategy (Forgas 1998) and enhance their ability to find integrative gains (Carnevale & Isen 1986). Angry negotiators are less accurate in judging the interests of opponent negotiators and achieve lower joint gains (Allred et al 1997). Anger makes negotiators more self-centered in their preferences (Loewenstein et al 1989) and increases the likelihood that they will reject profitable offers in ultimatum games (Pillutla & Murnighan 1996).

In these experiments, fairly mild manipulations created moderately strong effects. Nevertheless, the nature of emotion manipulations that are ethically possible in the lab may be sufficiently "cold" (Janis 1982) that they are qualitatively different from the "hot" emotions that lead people to find the role of emotion in negotiation so compelling. The hotter emotions create strong internal conflicts in people, and tell us emotions are important in negotiation. These are more likely to create a divide between what people think they should do (cognitive) and what they want to do (emotional) (Bazerman et al 1998b), leading to self-destructive choices (O'Connor et al 1998). Nevertheless, some authors see a functional role for emotions (Keltner & Kring 1999), and some have pointed to the potential strategic use of emotion (Barry 1999, Thompson et al 1999).

In sum, the behavioral decision perspective has been enriched by renewed attention to social factors. More important, because this recent research relies on a backdrop of rational optimality for assessing decisions, it can be useful in offering advice to actual negotiators. It gives the negotiator useful hints about the likely behavior of opponents and suggests ways in which the individual's own decisions may be biased.

A PSYCHOLOGICAL DEFINITION OF THE NEGOTIATION GAME

We believe that the research just reviewed provides an excellent base for the future development of the psychological study of negotiation. The rationality backdrop to this research is key. This creates the opportunity for a useful dialogue with economic perspectives. It is also crucial in creating a psychological field that is capable of providing advice to negotiators. Yet, as the contemporary social psychological critiques suggest, the behavioral decision perspective became narrow in order to develop these strengths. Although the recent exploration of social factors has broadened the field, we see even further broadening by thinking about how to help negotiators become more rational in order to better obtain what they value in the negotiation process.

An important emerging feature of research on negotiation is the study of how players define and create the negotiation game—both psychologically and structurally. Interdependence theory explored the ways in which social actors transform the given matrix of outcomes into an effective matrix by their own personal interpretations, relationship-specific motives, and social norms (Kelley & Thibaut 1978, Rusbult & Van Lange 1996). More recently, Brandenburger & Nalebuff (1996) changed the focus of game theory by arguing that how competitors define the game may be more important than the moves they make within the game. In the present section, we explore this perspective through the lens of psychology, suggesting that how parties understand the game is a critical determinant of how they play the game. To give rational advice, we need to understand the actual preferences and mental models of negotiators, rather than simply inferring that they accept the utility structure that an experimentalist provides. Understanding how negotiators differentially define the game may be key to better understanding why parties do not reach agreements when we think they should.

At first appearance, this focus on the definition of the game would seem to be a throwback to the structural research of the 1960s and 1970s earlier criticized. However, the new focus is on how negotiators define and create the game, rather than on how structural features of the game predict negotiators' behavior. We argue that negotiators' mental models (Gentner & Stevens 1983) are central to understanding how the negotiation game is defined. We then examine how other critical factors determine the definition. Specifically, we explore how concerns of ethics, fairness, and values define the rules of the game; how the selection of a communication medium impacts the play of the game; how cross-cultural issues in perception and behavior affect the game; and how negotiators organize and simplify their understandings of the game when more than two actors are involved.

Mental Models in Negotiation

Much of the work on negotiation assumes that the structure of a negotiation is exogenous to the parties and that the cognition and affect of the parties is exogenous to the structure. But work on mental models of negotiation suggests that the parties' perceptions of the negotiation structure are critical and endogenous to the negotiation and that, similarly, the cognition and affect of the parties are critical and endogenous to the negotiation.

The concept of mental models is related to some other psychological constructs. Although we recognize the substantial overlap, both within the literature and within our definitions, we see the construct of mental models differing from frames, scripts, and schemata in its expansiveness and its reliance on both social and cognitive processes (Gentner & Stevens 1983; L Thompson, D Gentner & J Loewenstein, unpublished data). This paper defines a mental model as a cognitive representation of the expected negotiation, a representation that encompasses understanding of the self, negotiator relationships, attributions about the other, and perceptions and knowledge of the bargaining structure and process. Mental models can be studied as individually held cognitive concepts or as shared definitions that develop interactively. We use this distinction between individually and mutually shared models to organize the literature. Although the authors were not studying mental models per se in much of the research discussed below, we extrapolate from their findings to explore the role of mental models in negotiations.

Individually held mental models   In an integrative task, Thompson & Hastie (1990) directly measured individual negotiators' perceptions of the negotiation structure. They asked their respondents whether the structure of the situation allowed for integrative trade-offs and found that the majority assumed their interests were strictly opposed to those of the other party. This assumption was held across all the various issues, even those for which the two parties had identical, compatible interests (see Thompson & Hrebec 1996). Thompson & Hastie (1990) provided evidence that individuals who modified their initial perceptions, or mental model, did so immediately at the onset of the interaction; otherwise the fixed-pie assumption tended to persist throughout the negotiation. They showed that fixed-pie biases result in a largely predictable outcome that fails to capture gains from integration.

In a creative examination of how the individually held definition of the situation affects processes and outcomes of negotiations, Larrick & Blount (1997) addressed the question of why cooperation levels differ between ultimatum games and two-person social dilemmas that are identical in their objective structures. Larrick & Blount (1997) found that when the interaction is framed as a social dilemma, the second party accepts substantially lower payoffs than when the interaction is framed as an ultimatum game. Through a series of studies, they show that the critical difference is whether the second party is given the role of "claimer" or "acceptor or rejector." Apparently, when the subjects perceive themselves to be claimers, they do not perceive their roles as including the right to reject the first party's proposal. Rejection is not included as an appropriate behavior in the rules prescribed by their mental model.

Investigators (see Ross & Ward 1995) crossed individual reputations (cooperative/competitive) with the definition, or more precisely the name, of the game ("community game"/"Wall Street game"). All participants played the same seven-round prisoner's dilemma game. The effects of the construal manipulation were dramatic. The manipulation affected play throughout the seven rounds, with nearly twice as much cooperation in the community game as in the Wall Street game. In contrast, individual dispositions showed virtually no effect, despite the fact that three steps were taken to maximize their impact: (a) The dispositional predictions were based on evaluations by people who knew the subjects well; (b) only those judged to be extreme cooperators or competitors were used as subjects; and (c) all dyads were composed of subjects with the same extreme disposition. Simply changing the name of the game changed the mental models the parties brought to the situation, and with it their definitions of what was acceptable or appropriate behavior.

Loewenstein et al (1999) address the question of creating an appropriate mental model for a new situation, based on analogical reasoning. Past research has shown that when trying to understand a situation, people often attend to information that has surface, rather than structural, similarity to the situation in which they are engaged (Gentner & Markman 1997, Gentner et al 1993). Explicitly comparing examples, rather than experiencing examples sequentially, allows negotiators to adjust their models of the current negotiation to incorporate past learning (L Thompson, D Gentner & J Loewenstein, unpublished data). Loewenstein et al (1999) showed that this learning affects subsequent negotiation behavior. Parties taught to draw analogies between cases were almost three times more likely to apply useful frames from other negotiations than were parties exposed to the cases sequentially. Others (L Thompson, D Gentner & J Loewenstein, unpublished data) argue for the use of analogies in teaching people to apply more useful mental models across negotiations.

The research just discussed focuses on mental models of the situation. Mental models can also focus on the other parties in the negotiation. There is a long research tradition in attribution and interpersonal perception (Gilbert 1994). In addition, researchers have explored the role of these attributions in conflict resolution (e.g. Betancourt & Blair 1992; Bradbury & Fincham 1990; De Dreu et al 1994, 1995a; Forgas 1994; Friedland 1990; Johnson & Rule 1986; Kette 1986; Lord & Smith 1983). For example, researchers have explored the problem of naïve realism in mental models of social conflict and the resulting false polarization effect (Keltner & Robinson 1996, Robinson & Keltner 1996, Robinson et al 1995). In one study, participants who identified themselves as either pro-life or pro-choice responded to a variety of questions relevant to their attitudes about abortion, both for themselves and in the way that they believed the average pro-life or pro-choice person would respond. Participants overestimated the degree of ideological difference between themselves and their opponents and saw their ideological opponents as more extreme than they actually were (Robinson & Keltner 1997).

In addition to defining the situation and the other parties or resources in a negotiation, mental models can also be seen in the way people perceive themselves in the negotiation. Montgomery (1998) developed a formal model of strategic play in which players are constrained to follow the meta-rules consistent with their role in a given interaction. Thus, in games with exactly the same economic structure, "a business person" and "a friend" will act differently, in ways that reflect their different roles. A central tenet of role theory is that individuals do not hold immutable roles, rather their roles change with the situation. The "business person" and the "friend" could be the same person in different situations. These models can improve on standard game-theoretic models of bargaining in accounting for empirical findings. Describing what we would call the search for an appropriate mental model, Montgomery (1998) asserted that people in social situations are struggling with "a constantly recurring problem of pattern recognition."

Shared mental models   The research just discussed posits mental models as individually held. Within a given negotiation, one party could hold one model, whereas the other holds an orthogonal or even contradictory model. The research discussed in this section suggests that these asymmetries are unlikely to continue through the negotiation—that negotiators quickly create shared understandings of the situation, the parties, and the rules of acceptable behavior (Messick 1999).

Most of the research on shared mental models holds as a basic assumption that these models are dynamic. The phenomenon of one party's beliefs changing the reality for both parties is well documented in the literature on the self-fulfilling prophecy (e.g. Rosenthal 1974), expectancy confirmation (e.g. Darley & Fazio

1980), and behavioral confirmation (Snyder 1992). In short, this literature provides substantial evidence that interpersonal beliefs actively guide social interaction, creating a social world that fits the expectations of the actors. Actors engaged in social interaction behave as if their beliefs about the others are true, and their targets, in turn, tend to act in ways that verify these beliefs. The demonstrations of this effect "are sufficiently numerous that the existence of the phenomenon need not be questioned" (Jones 1986:43). In negotiations, too, the parties, through their belief systems, create the interaction and its outcomes. Negotiators can and do, as Brandenburger & Nalebuff (1996) advocate, "change the game."

Conflict research in communication and anthropology takes as a given that a negotiation script is shared and dynamic (Felstiner et al 1980, Mather & Yngvesson 1981, Merry & Silbey 1984, Putnam & Holmer 1992, Putnam & Poole 1987, Todd 1978). In communications research, the interaction itself, as it evolves in the negotiation, defines the meanings for the involved parties. In anthropological research, the dispute is a series of interpretive acts that define the parties' understanding of and acceptable behavior for the next stage of the dispute.

Pruitt & Carnevale (1993) proposed that negotiations entail collective scripts with "interlocking roles." A working relationship is one of the collective scripts where the interaction flows along a predictable, contingent path, with reciprocity as an important subroutine. When and how negotiators evoke the working relationship script depends on the strength of the relationship. As is true with individually held mental models, norms and rules are likely to accompany this script—specifically, the norms of responsiveness, reciprocity, and truth telling.

Negotiation research is only beginning to adopt the notion that mental models can be developed mutually in interaction. In one of the few studies directly addressing this issue, Pinkley & Northcraft (1994) measured three dimensions of disputant frames before and after a multi-issue negotiation: relationship versus task, cooperate versus win, and emotional versus intellectual (Pinkley 1990). They found that the parties' frames mutually influence each other, converging during the interaction. In turn, these frames affect individual and joint monetary outcomes, as well as satisfaction with the outcomes.

Exploring the same issue at a more cognitive level, De Dreu et al (1995a) found that a negotiator's behavior is influenced by the other party's gain-loss frame. The focal negotiator sends messages that communicate the held frame (e.g. profits and benefits versus expenses or costs). In return, the responding negotiator sends messages adopting this frame. This mutual influence holds primarily when the adopting party has a gain rather than a loss frame (De Dreu et al 1992). Thus, if one party in a negotiation holds a loss frame, the bulk of the communication during the negotiation process will reflect this frame, regardless of the other party's frame at the onset of the negotiation.

Valley and Keros (unpublished data) explicitly traced the process of the interaction with a two-party, distributive negotiation. The investigators found that a very short segment of initial interaction solidifies the mental models of the negotiators (Thompson & Hastie 1990), resulting in either a trusting or a competitive script that carries through the negotiation. When the parties do not come to a common model of the interaction, the negotiation is much more likely to result in impasse or widely disparate payoffs than when a single model is shared, regardless of whether the shared model defines the interaction as trusting or competitive.

Wegner et al (1991) proposed that shared mental models within close relationships need not rely on interaction but result from shared memory systems. Friends are likely to classify, describe, and evaluate information about others and themselves in similar ways (Deutsch & Mackesy 1985). Extending this work into negotiations, a growing body of work (Barsness & Tenbrunsel 1998, Halpern 1997; KL Valley & AT Keros, unpublished data) provides evidence of a shared model of appropriate bargaining behavior between friends. It was found (KL Valley & AT Keros, unpublished data) that many of the touted positive effects of friendship and rich communication media in bargaining are mediated through a shared script.

Taken as a whole, a growing body of research provides evidence that the process and outcome of negotiations cannot be fully understood without a clearer understanding of negotiators' mental models. To come to this clearer understanding, psychological researchers need to devise ways of investigating the presence and role of these models (Rouse & Morris 1986). We need to pay increased attention to how process and outcome are interrelated if we are to obtain more accurate descriptions of negotiations and more useful prescriptions.

Ethics and Sacredness in Negotiation

Ethical standards in negotiation are inextricably tied to the definition of the game. Understanding what sort of game is being played conveys information about rules, boundaries, and which strategies are permissible. There have been some attempts to evaluate the perceived permissibility of the most frequently used bargaining tactics (Lewicki & Stark 1996, Robinson et al 1997). These attempts are consistent with the desire to articulate a general formulation of ethical guidelines, against which any tactic or behavior can be evaluated (e.g. Applbaum 1996). Although ethics, interpreted superficially, impose clear limits on allowable negotiation strategies, much of the evidence on their use in actual negotiations highlights their ambiguity and flexibility.

According to Lewicki & Litterer, "lying and deceit are an integral part of effective negotiation" (1985:324). Certainly it is the case that deception is used in negotiation (Schweitzer 1997) and can be an effective strategy for increasing one's own outcomes (O'Connor & Carnevale 1997). The 1990s saw an active debate on the ethics of deception in negotiation. Some have argued that deception in negotiation is to be expected and is morally acceptable (Strudler 1995, Wokutch & Carson 1993). Others, however, have maintained that the world would be better off without deception and that it is always morally regrettable (Dees & Cramton 1991, 1995).

Interests, motivations, and incentives influence the interpretation of ethical standards. Kronzon & Darley (1999) show that individuals' perceptions of how ethics apply in a specific situation depend fundamentally on which rules favor themselves. They had participants in their experiment observe an ethically questionable act of deception in a videotaped negotiation. Partisans who allied with the victim perceived the act as more reprehensible than did either partisans allied with the perpetrator or neutral observers. Deception in negotiation increases as the incentives for performance increase (Tenbrunsel 1998). Furthermore, deception is more likely to occur when people have individualistic motivations than when they have cooperative motivations (O'Connor & Carnevale 1997). Despite the influence that situational factors exert on negotiators' perceptions both of the ethical permissibility of various strategies and on actual behavior, research suggests that people underestimate differences in construal and thus are overconfident in their predictions of both their own and others' behavior (Griffin et al 1990).

People are motivated to think of themselves as ethical, and rate themselves as more ethical than the average person (Tenbrunsel 1998). When people do engage in ethically questionable behavior, they often justify it as self-defense (see Shapiro 1991). Consistent with this notion, negotiators' expectations that their opponents will deceive them are influenced by their own tendency to deceive. Tenbrunsel (1998) varied the amount of money participants could win for negotiating successfully. Participants who could win $100 expected significantly more deception from their opponents and were significantly more likely to deceive than those who could only win $1. However, participants' expectations of their opponents' deception were not influenced by whether the opponent could win $1 or $100.

Players can harmonize their mental models and gain insight into the rules of the game they are playing by communicating with others. However, ethical disagreements may be more difficult to resolve if their goal is not accuracy but moral correctness based on some internal, subjective standard, especially when that internal standard is egocentrically biased (Kronzon & Darley 1999, Wade-Benzoni et al 1996). Tenbrunsel (1999) suggested that construal differences across parties may actually lead to greater expectations of unethical behavior than uniformly high incentives to behave unethically. Disagreements about ethics are likely to be an enduring fixture of real negotiations, on which parties may not be motivated to seek agreement. Yet the existence of multiple conflicting models of fairness need not make conflicts insoluble. Messick (1995) pointed out that different decision rules can be implemented simultaneously.

Sometimes, negotiation itself can be seen as immoral. When issues are tied to sacred values, compromise or trade becomes exceedingly difficult. For example, most people resist setting a price on human life or creating markets for human body parts. Not only will people resist trades or compromises on sacred issues, but even the consideration of such trades may be seen as reprehensible (Tetlock et al 1996). Tetlock et al (1996) explored how people respond to "taboo trade-offs" that pit sacred values against each other. Taboo trade-offs lie outside the permissible bounds of the game and tend to elicit responses of moral outrage, avoidance, or outright denial (Tetlock et al 1996). Fiske & Tetlock (1997) recently specified a model of misdirected matches of transaction frames. They argued that people code relationships as based on (*a*) community, (*b*) authority, (*c*) equality, or (*d*) market mechanisms. Perceptions of deviant, unethical, or taboo behavior are most likely to occur when parties hold differing models.

Although Tetlock et al (1996) explicitly avoided endorsing any particular way of responding to taboo trade-offs, Thompson & Gonzalez (1997) took a stronger stand. They pointed out that the daily decisions of life force us to make trades between values we hold dear, even if we do not routinely understand our choices in these terms. Thompson & Gonzalez (1997) suggested that in many negotiations where one side claims an issue is sacred, the issue is not, in fact, sacred but pseudosacred. Issues are pseudosacred when negotiators would consider trading that issue, given adequate compensation. In desperate times, people have sold their kidneys and even their children.

Tough bargaining strategies aside, insincere claims of sacredness may lock parties into suboptimal negotiation outcomes. Integrative negotiation depends fundamentally on parties' ability to trade issues against each other (Froman & Cohen 1970, Walton & McKersie 1965). Claims of sacredness that rule out certain trades or compromises restrict the game. An unwillingness to consider trades because of sacred values may constrain the set of permissible agreements in ways that reduce the value of negotiated outcomes for all parties by turning negotiations into win-lose battles in highly restricted domains (Thompson & Gonzalez 1997).

Concerns about ethics and sacredness pose as general rules of allowable and appropriate conduct in negotiation. Ethical guidelines define the rules and permissible negotiation strategies. Negotiators tend to make decisions of ethical appropriateness in an egocentric fashion and to favor those rules that favor themselves. However, negotiators can also hurt themselves by claiming certain issues to be sacred when in fact they are not, thereby placing constraints on the game and on their ability to find integrative trade-offs.

Choosing a Medium of Communication

One way in which negotiators can influence the mental model held by other parties is by their choice of communications media. As we enter the new millennium, we see an expanding universe of technologically mediated communication channels, such as telephone, fax, express mail, videophone, and electronic mail. Whereas in the 1960s when little was known about the influence of communication media on negotiation (Smith 1969), today researchers generally agree that medium of communication affects social conflict in a number of important ways (Carnevale & Probst 1997, Roth 1995, Valley et al 1998). The technology we use to negotiate affects our definition of the negotiation game and the behavior deemed appropriate for the interaction (KL Valley & AT Keros, unpublished data).

Therefore, from the perspective of an individual negotiator, the choice of communication medium can be critical to the process and outcome of a negotiation. In this section, we review research findings that bear on the question of whether or not a negotiator should seek face-to-face communication.

The case for face-to-face communication in bargaining   Most researchers studying the impact of communication media conceptualize the various forms of media along a continuum of "social presence" (Fulk et al 1990, Rutter & Robinson 1981). That is, face-to-face communication has the richest level of social presence, followed by audio/visual, audio, and finally written or computer-mediated communication. Accordingly, in a study by Drolet & Morris (1999), face-to-face communication enabled participants to develop greater rapport and cooperation than audio-only communication. Thus, unless a close relationship already exists or rapport can be generated by some alternative means (see Moore et al 1999), rapport is more likely to be developed and consequently more likely to improve negotiated outcomes in face-to-face interaction. This research suggests that in negotiations where rapport is more likely (e.g. face-to-face, between closely related parties, where cooperation is primed), we can expect to see a more shared, dynamic evolution of the mental model.

Truth telling is higher in face-to-face negotiations than in other media. In a two-person negotiation exercise involving asymmetric information, Valley et al (1998) found that participants negotiating face-to-face achieve higher joint benefit, due to higher levels of truth telling than those negotiating by telephone or in writing. In the game used by Valley et al (1998), the seller held the informational advantage. Buyers' trust was higher in verbal interaction than in written interaction, regardless of whether the verbal communication took place face-to-face or over the telephone, yet trustworthiness among the sellers was higher only in face-to-face interaction. In other words, deceit may be less common in the context of face-to-face interaction, increasing the likelihood of mutually beneficial agreements, whereas suspicion of deceit and actual deceit may be higher in the context of written interaction, increasing the likelihood of impasse. In telephone interaction, the players do not seem to share the same mental model: The buyer appears to be operating under a model assuming trustworthiness, whereas the seller is operating under a model allowing deception. The result is likely to be a bad deal for the trusting buyer.

A significant proportion of a message's meaning comes from facial and vocal cues rather than the actual words themselves (DePaulo & Friedman 1998). Therefore, it is no surprise that removal of such cues can reduce a message's clarity. Evidence for this assertion is found in the results of studies that utilize dilemma games (Sally 1995). Without the presence of clear communication, participants are less likely to coordinate their moves to achieve mutual cooperation. Accordingly, in a study by Wichman (1970), 87% of participants playing 78 trial prisoner's dilemma games cooperated when they could see and hear one another,

72% when they could only hear one another, 48% when they could only see one another, and 41% when they could neither hear nor see one another.

The case against face-to-face communication in bargaining   The aforementioned advantages of conducting negotiations face-to-face notwithstanding, under certain conditions, conducting negotiations via telephone or other audio-only channels might be preferable. In a study by Lewis & Fry (1977), individualistically oriented negotiators used fewer pressure tactics, were less likely to impasse, and obtained higher joint profit when they negotiated with a barrier that prevented them from seeing each other. Participants with a more cooperative problem solving orientation were not significantly affected by the presence of the barrier. Other studies have found similar tension-enhancing effects of face-to-face communication when negotiators possess high levels of accountability (Carnevale et al 1981) or when low-Machiavellian negotiators are matched with high-Machiavellian negotiators (Christie & Geis 1970, Fry 1985).

Carnevale et al concluded that, under certain conditions, ". . .the other party's gaze may be interpreted as an effort to dominate. . . . [B]argainers will make pressure statements only if they can accompany them with efforts to stare the other down" (1981:113). Lewis & Fry (1977) noted that the negative consequences that sometimes accompany face-to-face interaction are consistent with Zajonc's (1965) theory that the visible presence of others has arousal-inducing properties. Arousal leads to dominant behavioral responses, and dominant behavioral responses to conflict typically involve either attack or retreat (Selye 1976). Therefore, under conditions of high arousal, audio-only communication may facilitate more sophisticated, adaptive negotiating strategies.

Although written communication may share some of these mitigating effects on arousal, e-mail communication in particular—especially in the context of high arousal—could make things worse rather than better. When a communication medium like e-mail lacks social context cues, people tend to become more forthright in their communication, even to the point of weakening inhibitions on socially undesirable behavior, either because of reduced evaluation anxiety or because of reduced attention to social norms (Kiesler & Sproull 1992). Moreover, a feeling of anonymity that tends to accompany e-mail communications may exacerbate such disinhibition (Griffith & Northcraft 1994, Thompson 1998, Zimbardo 1969). Dubrovsky et al (1991) found that, among 24 four-person decision-making groups interacting via computer, there were 102 instances of rude or impulsive behavior, whereas another 24 groups that interacted face-to-face produced only 12 such remarks. Among computer aficionados, this uninhibited or antisocial behavior is referred to as flaming (Sproull & Kiesler 1991). Perhaps as a result of this uninhibited behavior, e-mail negotiations suffer from higher rates of breakdown (Croson 1999). Therefore, audio-only communication may be the best choice of media when it comes to negotiating under conditions of high arousal.

One potential benefit of e-mail interaction is its tendency to cut across social hierarchies. In three experiments comparing the effects of face-to-face and computer-mediated communication, Siegel et al (1986) found that the amount of participation is more equally distributed among group members interacting via computer than among group members interacting face-to-face. Whereas face-to-face discussions often involve status differentials that determine talk time (Bales et al 1951), computer-mediated discussions have fewer social status cues (Sproull & Kiesler 1991). Although some interpret this lack of social regulation in computer-mediated communication as disorganized (i.e. lacking in efficiency) (Williams 1977), many see it as egalitarian.

In summary, a negotiator often can influence the negotiation game and its outcome through his or her choice of a communication medium. Research indicates that this decision should depend in large part on the circumstances of the negotiation. Conducting negotiations face-to-face appears to be more likely to foster development of rapport, less likely to involve deceit, and less likely to involve misunderstanding. However, when rapport already exists and/or tension (i.e. arousal) is high, audio-only communication may reduce the likelihood of pressure tactics that might otherwise result in domination or hostility. Moreover, in other cases, where conflicts involve low levels of arousal and meeting by phone or in person is overly costly or prohibited, computer-mediated negotiations may allow for certain benefits, such as more evenly distributed participation. Because the choice of medium so clearly changes the negotiation game, prescriptive advice should take these contingencies into consideration.

Cross-Cultural Issues in Negotiation

In their review of research on negotiation and mediation, Carnevale & Pruitt (1992) predicted that cultural differences in negotiation would increase in importance as a result of growing interrelationships among nations. Indeed, over the past decade, we have seen an expansion of research on culture and negotiation (Weiss 1996). In this section, we review two types of literature. The first type includes research on cross-cultural differences in negotiation behavior as well as how these affect and are affected by the parties' conceptions of negotiation. The second type deals with negotiating across cultural boundaries and prescriptive techniques for doing so successfully. Put differently, we review both differences in the negotiation game between cultures and how negotiators might change their game (or even change their mental models) to facilitate negotiation across cultures.

The nature of the negotiation game within cultures   Over the past decade, dozens of studies have examined how the meaning and practice of negotiation varies across cultures (for reviews see Cohen 1997, Leung 1998, Markus & Lin 1998). Although a growing number of studies have examined organizational culture (e.g. Chatman et al 1998, Mannix et al 1995), for the purposes of this paper, we focus on national cultures.

Of the multiple dimensions of cultural variability recognized by cultural psychologists, the most relevant to the culture and negotiation literature have been collectivism-individualism, power distance, communication context, and conception of time (Brett et al 1998, Cohen 1997, Leung 1998). The first two dimensions emerged from a much-cited survey of international values conducted by Hofstede (1980, 1983). The last two dimensions emerged from the work of Hall (1976).

Although individualism-collectivism may in fact represent a number of cultural factors rather than a single trait (Triandis 1995), it is perhaps the most important (Triandis 1990) as well as the most frequently cited cultural dimension in studies of negotiation (Leung 1998). Members of individualist cultures are said to have loose ties among individuals and to value independence, uniqueness, and individual goals, whereas members of collectivist countries are said to have tight ties among individuals and to value interdependence, doing one's duty, and the goals of the collective (Hofstede 1983, Markus & Kitayama 1991, Triandis 1990).

Many researchers have explored how the individualism-collectivism dimension applies to conflict management. Generally speaking, the individualist negotiator (e.g. United States, Great Britain, The Netherlands) is more concerned with preserving individual rights and attributes, whereas the collectivist negotiator (e.g. Colombia, Pakistan, Taiwan) is more concerned with preserving relationships (Markus & Lin 1998). A number of cross-cultural studies of negotiation-related behavior and cognition have provided data consistent with the generalization that members of individualist cultures are more likely to handle conflicts directly through competition and problem solving, whereas members of collectivist cultures are more likely to handle conflict in indirect ways that attempt to preserve the relationship (Leung 1998, Starr & Yngvesson 1975). For example, Americans (individualists) were more likely than Japanese (collectivists) to hold egocentric notions of fairness and to defect in asymmetric social dilemmas (i.e. placing individual goals ahead of group goals) (KA Wade-Benzoni, T Okumura, JM Brett, DA Moore, AE Tenbrunsel et al, unpublished data). In a conflict scenario study (E Weldon, KA Jehn, L Doucet, X Chen & W Zhong-Ming, unpublished data), Chinese (collectivists) more frequently addressed the conflict with the express interest of maintaining relationships, whereas Americans simply wanted to address the incident itself. Members of collectivist cultures were more likely than members of individualist cultures to use deception, typically as a means of saving face, avoiding confrontation or preserving harmony (HC Triandis, P Carnevale, M Gelfand, C Robert, A Wasti, et al, unpublished data).

In comparison to the collectivism-individualism dimension, three other dimensions—power distance, communication context, and conception of time—have received only minimal attention in cross-cultural studies of negotiation. Power distance refers to the relative prevalence of social or professional hierarchies in a society (Hofstede 1980). High power distance societies reflect inequalities among individuals on the basis of these hierarchies, whereas low power distance societies reflect more egalitarian values. Communication context is the degree to which communicated messages inherit meaning from the settings in which they are transmitted (Hall 1976). The Low communication context cultures use explicit, direct language, whereas high communication context cultures use implicit, indirect language in which words and phrases derive their meanings from contextual clues. Finally, conception of time refers to the way in which people perceive and manage their time. A polychronic conception of time is the notion that time is plentiful and many tasks can be undertaken simultaneously, whereas a monochronic conception of time is the notion that time is scarce and only one task can be handled at a time (Hall 1983).

In a conflict scenario study, Tinsley (1998) found each of the three cultural dimensions described above to account partially for normative models of conflict resolution in Japan, Germany, and the United States. Moreover, in his review of the literature on culture and negotiation, Leung (1998) provided evidence for the following associations. First, members of high-power-distance cultures (e.g. the Philippines, Venezuela, India, France, Belgium) have fewer conflicts with their superiors and are more likely to have superiors intervene in settling their conflicts than do members of low-power-distance cultures (e.g. Denmark, Israel, Austria) (Bond et al 1985, Gudykunst & Ting-Toomey 1988; for review see James 1993). Second, members of low-context cultures (e.g. United States, Germany, Scandinavia, Switzerland) have been found to communicate more directly than members of high-context cultures (e.g. Japan, China, Korea, Vietnam) (Chua & Gudykunst 1987). More recent evidence suggests, however, that the more important differences may be in the goals of the communication and not the amount of direct communication (E Weldon, KA Jehn, L Doucet, X Chen & W Zhong-Ming, unpublished data). Third, negotiators who hold monochronic conceptions of time (e.g. North American, Western Europe) are more likely to process issues sequentially and to negotiate in a highly organized fashion, whereas negotiators with polychronic conceptions of time (e.g. Asia, Africa, South America, Middle East) are more likely to process issues simultaneously while ignoring conversational turn-taking (i.e. speaking simultaneously) and using frequent interruptions (Foster 1992).

Overall, attempts to correlate cultural value dimensions with cross-cultural differences in intracultural negotiations have produced only partial success (Tinsley & Brett 1997; E Weldon, KA Jehn, L Doucet, X Chen & W Zhong-Ming, unpublished data). Tinsley & Brett (1997) argued that value dimensions such as the four just discussed lack predictive power and therefore should not be used to predict negotiation behavior. Instead, they advocate domain-specific, normatively based predictors such as asking study participants to rate the appropriateness of a given conflict-handling behavior, explaining each party's underlying concerns, or seeking help from a boss (Tinsley & Brett 1997). However, Weldon & Jehn (1995) suggested that the problem of low predictive power could be mitigated through the use of inductive approaches to the generation of conflict scenarios and the measurement of conflict behaviors (E Weldon, KA Jehn, L Doucet, X Chen & W Zhong-Ming, unpublished data).

Difficulties predicting behavior based on cultural value dimensions recall the failure of individual-differences research to predict specific behaviors (Ross & Nisbett 1991, Thompson 1998). Perhaps a more fertile avenue for research lies in studying how cultural traits, in conjunction with individual definitions of the game, influence negotiation behavior (Neuberg 1988). Such a relationship is suggested by investigators (DA Briley, MW Morris & I Simonson, unpublished data), who demonstrated how individually held mental models moderate the effect of culture on choice behavior. When individuals were made introspective by having to provide reasons before making choices, their choices varied more on the basis of their culture than when no reasons were required. A similar interaction between culture and individually held mental models may also govern negotiation behavior.

Negotiation across cultures—changing the game   Cross-cultural differences are substantial, and negotiating across cultures (intercultural negotiations) differs dramatically from negotiating within the same culture (Adler & Graham 1989). Indeed, tales of "cross-cultural conflict—faux pas and 'blunders'—abound" (Weiss 1994:52). Tinsley et al (1999) described the process of intercultural negotiation as akin to a dance in which one person does a waltz and another a tango. Different cultures may not share some of the most basic assumptions; evidence suggests that there is cultural variation in the tendency to fall victim to the fixed-pie assumption (Starr & Yngvesson 1975) and the fundamental attribution error (Morris & Peng 1994).

According to Tinsley et al (1999), intercultural negotiations present a sort of "dilemma of differences." On the one hand, differences between cultural scripts present procedural conflict at the bargaining table; on the other hand, differences in preferences present opportunities for logrolling. For example, cultures that differ in their perceptions of risk (see Weber & Hsee 1999) can create value by sharing risks and benefits proportionally but asymmetrically (Bontempo et al 1997). However, the price of realizing such joint gains is high. In a study of intercultural negotiations by Brett & Okumura (1998), Japanese and American participants negotiated a hypothetical mixed-motive conflict with either a same-culture partner or an other-culture partner. As expected, intercultural dyads reached outcomes that were of lower joint value than intracultural dyads. Responses to a postnegotiation questionnaire revealed that intercultural dyads had less-accurate mutual understanding of each other's priorities (although Japanese negotiators understood more about American priorities than vice versa). Consistent with the power-distance dimension, Americans viewed their walk-away option as a source of power, whereas Japanese had preexisting notions of power based on role assignments (i.e. buyer versus seller). Finally, consistent with the collectivism-individualism dimension, Americans were more focused on self-interest than were Japanese—a factor that, when asymmetrical between negotiators, has been found to lead to premature closure of negotiations (Huber & Neale 1987). The authors speculate that a combination of these factors—insufficient information sharing, power struggle, and asymmetric focus on self-interest—led to lower levels of joint gains among intercultural negotiation dyads.

A growing literature has emerged to address the intercultural negotiation challenge through prescriptive advice to practitioners (e.g. Corne 1992, Morrison et al 1994, Shapiro & von Glinow 1999, Weiss 1994). This advice usually suggests modifying how one plays the game or, even better, modifying how one's opponent plays the game. The problem is that even if negotiators were to agree on a cultural norm by which to conduct their business, there is no evidence that an individual negotiator could transcend his or her own cultural background (Brett & Okumura 1998). Shapiro & von Glinow (1999) conceded that "stepping out" of one's culture would be difficult. A more plausible suggestion was offered by Weiss (1994), who instructed intercultural negotiators to jointly follow the culture with which both negotiators are most familiar. Clearly, more research is necessary to determine the feasibility and effectiveness of these strategies.

In sum, cross-cultural differences in the negotiation game can be conceptualized along four basic dimensions—collectivism-individualism, power distance, communication context, and conception of time (Brett et al 1998, Cohen 1997). Most empirical research has focused on the first of these dimensions—collectivism-individualism—and has documented both behavioral and cognitive manifestations related to negotiation. Although the research using cultural value dimensions alone has suffered from predictive shortcomings (Tinsley & Brett 1997), perhaps the use of mental models in conjunction with culture (e.g. DA Briley, MW Morris & I Simonson, unpublished data) will prove more fruitful. The prescriptive literature is growing, but the most common suggestion for negotiation across cultures involves deliberate changes to the negotiation game. Although in theory such changes seem reasonable, research has not, to our knowledge, confirmed its viability for the typical negotiator.

Negotiation With More Than Two Players

Increasing the number of players involved in a negotiation dramatically increases the complexity of the situation in at least five ways: informational, computational, procedural, social, and strategic (Kramer 1991). As new players are added to a conflict, the number of potential dyadic connections between players increases exponentially. Different parties are likely to bring a variety of interests to the table, and simply understanding these interests, let alone finding ways to integrate them, can become an exceedingly complex task. Multiparty negotiations are situations in which a full understanding of the situation, with the variety of potential strategies and outcomes, may simply be impossible. Making the problem tractable often necessitates simplification of the structure or organization of the interaction, and there may be many justifiable ways to accomplish this simplification. Different ways will have different consequences for the outcome of the negotiation.

Developing a manageable understanding of the situation is essentially the problem of how people structure and define the negotiation game when there are more than two players. Empirical research has highlighted some of the ways that they do this.

One procedural tool for managing conflict in the face of that complexity is to implement decision-making rules that control participants' opportunities to communicate or specify how the group will make a decision (e.g. dictatorship, majority rule, unanimity). However, many procedures designed to reduce conflict or organize the process of multiparty negotiation also serve to reduce the opportunities for negotiators to learn about each others' interests and to find integrative gains (Bazerman et al 1988). For example, an agenda that leads negotiators to resolve issues one at a time dramatically reduces their ability to improve the quality of the agreement using trade-offs across issues (Mannix et al 1989, Weingart et al 1993). On the other hand, a unanimity decision rule, which requires agreement from all parties, can be cumbersome to implement, but tends to increase the quality of agreements (Thompson et al 1988). Groups without any shared mental model for dealing with the negotiation are likely to seek some such coordination; simply telling a group about a guideline without requiring its use can nevertheless be a large influence on group norms and future group agreements (Mannix & Blount White 1992).

Another way to structure the information-processing complexity of multiparty negotiations is to limit communication to subsets of the group. Even when all parties' participation is necessary for an agreement, constraining communication to dyadic encounters results in lower levels of cooperation, less-equal outcomes, and a decrease in integrative trade-offs involving more than two parties (Palmer & Thompson 1995). When parties can be excluded from the final agreement, caucusing increases the likelihood of coalition agreements (Kim 1997, Mannix 1993a).

The possibility of shutting some parties out of an agreement is one distinguishing feature of multiparty disputes. Although some multiparty conflicts require the participation of all parties for an agreement, many can be resolved by a coalition. Analysis of coalition games has a long history (Gamson 1961, Luce & Raiffa 1957). Forming coalitions to reduce the number of parties to an agreement is one way to simplify a complex multiparty deal. Research finds that various factors that increase the complexity of multiparty negotiations, such as asymmetry between parties (Mannix 1993b) or uncertainty regarding outcomes (Mannix & Blount White 1992), also increase the occurrence of coalition agreements.

The embeddedness of negotiated outcomes in social relations can also be an important factor in the resolution of multiparty negotiations. Although structural analyses of coalition formation suggest that coalitions will often be unstable (Murnighan & Brass 1991), the social context of interpersonal relationships in which coalitions form may contribute to their stability (Polzer et al 1995). Negotiators tend to form coalitions with those who have been allies in the past, even if better partners exist, based on the congruence of interests (Polzer et al 1998). Furthermore, the spoils from coalition games tend to be allocated more equally (Mannix 1994) and include more parties (Mannix 1991) when the players care about future interactions with their negotiating partners.

Increases in the informational and computational complexity of the negotiation situation extend the length of time it takes to reach agreement (Polzer 1996) and may lead to information overload (Morely 1982), which increases the use of cognitive heuristics. Therefore, we might expect simplifying strategies or cognitive mistakes to be more common in complex multiparty negotiations. For example, we might expect multiparty negotiations to have more trouble achieving integrative gains than dyadic negotiations, and we might expect outcomes to gravitate toward social heuristics or focal points such as equal division (Debusschere & van Avermaet 1984, Messick 1993), rather than more complex allocation rationales. However, given that people interpret fairness in egocentric ways (Diekmann et al 1997), additional complexity is likely to increase dissention about what a fair outcome would be (Thompson & Loewenstein 1992). This dissention may increase the chances of delays, stalemates, and impasses.

There is more optimistic evidence from experiments that compare individual with team negotiation. These experiments, which have only two sides represented in a negotiation but which vary the number of people representing each side, suggest that teams have some distinct advantages. When teams negotiate against individuals, the teams tend to claim a larger portion of the bargaining surplus (Polzer 1996, Thompson et al 1996). At the same time, teams exchange more information (Thompson et al 1996), generate more high-quality ideas for solutions (Polzer 1996), and tend to enhance the integrative value of the resulting agreement (Polzer 1996, Thompson et al 1996). However, teams perceive themselves, and are perceived by their opponents, to be less cooperative and less trustworthy than are individual negotiators (Polzer 1996). In addition, team members tend to be less satisfied with both the negotiation process and the outcome than are individuals (Polzer 1996).

As the number of parties in a negotiation increases, the complexity of the dispute rises quickly. Negotiators may respond to this complexity by simplifying the negotiation game in several ways. They may rely on group norms. They may form coalitions that reduce the number of parties to an agreement. They may implement procedures that establish decision rules. Although there are reasons to assume that increased complexity would increase reliance on cognitive simplifications of the negotiation landscape, evidence suggests that negotiating teams are better than individuals at exchanging information that allows them to find wise agreements.

CONCLUSION

The psychological study of negotiation has witnessed an amazing set of shifts over the past 25 years, often in parallel with more global changes in the field of psychology and the broader society. We view these changes as useful and exciting.

We have seen the birth and death of the study of personality and structural variables that were common in the precognitive era of social psychology (Bazerman et al 2000). We have seen the development of a behavioral decision perspective in the 1980s and 1990s shift the attention of researchers to the decision processes of the actor, and we have witnessed the criticism that resulted from the narrowness of this perspective. We have seen the reemergence of the role of social psychology in the study of how social context affects negotiator decision making. And, finally, this paper has attempted to integrate recent research that calls for a better understanding of how negotiators define the negotiation game that they are playing.

We see the backdrop of rationality as critical to the impact of the psychological study of negotiation on related fields. We believe that the main reason the behavioral decision perspective dominated negotiation research in the 1980s and 1990s is that this perspective made it explicitly clear what was needed to improve negotiation behaviors—the debiasing of the mind of the negotiator. This perspective has now spilled over into the new social psychology of negotiations that we overviewed in this chapter. And we see this perspective as relevant to creating useful research about how the negotiator defines the game.

As laboratory researchers, we are sympathetic to the constraints of the laboratory methodology. However, it is also important to realize the resulting biases in the definition of the field. Most negotiation experiments are easiest to create when it is in the power of the researcher to specify the game. Unfortunately, this researcher specification may have inhibited the study of how negotiators psychologically define the game. Many of us have been annoyed by the "weird" things that our experimental participants do, particularly when they "ruin" the significance of our effects. However, one important source of error may be in not understanding how our participants redefine the game.

Finally, we offer our review as a call for better integration of the multiple subfields of psychology to understand negotiation. The psychological study of negotiation was once a subfield of social psychology (Rubin & Brown 1975), but this is no longer the case. We now have important contributions from social psychology (Bazerman et al 2000), cognitive psychology (Loewenstein et al 1999), behavioral decision research (Thompson 1998), and clinical psychology (Greenhalgh & Chapman 1997, Greenhalgh & Okun 1998). Moreover, early work suggests that physiological factors can increase our understanding of negotiations as well (TC Burnham, unpublished data; ME Schweitzer, unpublished data). We hope that these multiple lenses can create a more unified understanding so that psychology can help the world overcome barriers to effective negotiation behavior.

ACKNOWLEDGMENTS

This paper benefited from useful and insightful suggestions offered by Adam Brandenburger, Carsten De Dreu, David Messick, Keith Murnighan, Jeff Polzer, and Leigh Thompson. We received support for this research from the Dispute

Resolution Research Center at Northwestern University, the Dean's office of the Kellogg School at Northwestern, and Faculty Research Support from the Harvard Business School.

Visit the Annual Reviews home page at www.AnnualReviews.org.

LITERATURE CITED

Adler N, Graham JL. 1989. Cross-cultural interaction: the international comparison fallacy? *J. Int. Bus. Stud.* 20:515–37

Allred KG, Mallozzi JS, Matsui F, Raia CP. 1997. The influence of anger and compassion on negotiation performance. *Organ. Behav. Hum. Decis. Process.* 70:175–87

Applbaum AI. 1996. Rules of the game, permissible harms, and the principle of fair play. In *Wise Choices: Decisions, Games, and Negotiations,* ed. RJ Zeckhauser, RL Keeney, JK Sebenius, pp. 301–21. Boston: Harvard Bus. Sch. Press

Axelrod S, May JG. 1968. Effect of increased reward on the two-person non-zero-sum game. *Psychol. Rep.* 11:109–26

Babcock L, Loewenstein G. 1997. Explaining bargaining impasse: the role of self-serving biases. *J. Econ. Perspect.* 11:109–26

Babcock L, Loewenstein G, Issacharoff S, Camerer C. 1995. Biased judgments of fairness in bargaining. *Am. Econ. Rev.* 85:1337–43

Babcock L, Olson C. 1992. The causes of impasses in labor disputes. *Ind. Relat.* 31:348–60

Baker WE. 1984. The social structure of a national securities market. *Am. J. Sociol.* 89:775–811

Baker WE. 1990. Market networks and corporate behavior. *Am. J. Sociol.* 96:589–625

Bales R, Strodtbeck FL, Mills TM, Roseborough ME. 1951. Channels of communication in small groups. *Am. Sociol. Rev.* 16:461–68

Barry B. 1999. The tactical use of emotion in negotiation. See Lewicki et al 1999, 7:93–121

Barry B, Friedman RA. 1998. Bargainer characteristics in distributive and integrative negotiation. *J. Pers. Soc. Psychol.* 74:345–59

Barsness Z, Tenbrunsel AE. 1998. *Technologically-mediated communication and negotiation: Do relationships matter?* Presented at Annu. Meet. Int. Assoc. Conflict Manage., College Park, MD

Bazerman MH. 1998. *Judgment in Managerial Decision Making.* New York: Wiley. 4th ed.

Bazerman MH, Carroll JS. 1987. Negotiator cognition. *Res. Organ. Behav.* 9:247–88

Bazerman MH, Curhan JR, Moore DA. 2000. The death and rebirth of the social psychology of negotiation. In *Blackwell Handbook of Social Psychology,* ed. M Clark, G Fletcher. In press. Cambridge, MA: Blackwell

Bazerman MH, Gibbons R, Thompson L, Valley KL. 1998a. Can negotiators outperform game theory? In *Debating Rationally: Nonrational Aspects in Organizational Decision Making,* ed. JJ Halpern, RN Stern, pp. 79–98. Ithaca, NY: ILR

Bazerman MH, Magliozzi T, Neale MA. 1985. The acquisition of an integrative response in a competitive market. *Organ. Behav. Hum. Decis. Process.* 34:294–313

Bazerman MH, Mannix EA, Thompson LL. 1988. Groups as mixed-motive negotiations. In *Advances in Group Processes,* ed. EJ Lawler, B Markovsky. 5:195–216. Greenwich, CT: JAI

Bazerman MH, Moore DA, Gillespie JJ. 1999. The human mind as a barrier to wiser environmental agreements. *Am. Behav. Sci.* 42:1254–76

Bazerman MH, Neale MA. 1982. Improving negotiation effectiveness under final offer arbitration: the role of selection and training. *J. Appl. Psychol.* 67:543–48

Bazerman MH, Neale MA. 1983. Heuristics in negotiation: limitations to effective dispute resolution. In *Negotiating in Organizations,* ed. MH Bazerman, RJ Lewicki, pp. 51–67. Beverly Hills, CA: Sage

Bazerman MH, Neale MA. 1992. *Negotiating Rationally.* New York: Free Press

Bazerman MH, Tenbrunsel AE, Wade-Benzoni KA. 1998b. Negotiating with yourself and losing: understanding and managing competing internal preferences. *Acad. Manage. Rev.* 23:225–41

Betancourt H, Blair I. 1992. A cognition (attribution)-emotion model of violence in conflict situations. *Pers. Soc. Psychol. Bull.* 18:343–50

Bies RJ, Lewicki RJ, Sheppard BH, eds. 1991. *Research on Negotiation in Organizations,* Vol. 3. Greenwich, CT: JAI

Bizman A, Hoffman M. 1993. Expectations, emotions, and preferred responses regarding the Arab-Israeli conflict: an attributional analysis. *J. Confl. Resolut.* 37:139–59

Bond MH, Wan KC, Leung K, Giacalone R. 1985. How are responses to verbal insults related to cultural collectivism and power distance? *J. Cross-Cult. Psychol.* 16:111–27

Bontempo RN, Bottom WP, Weber EU. 1997. Cross-cultural differences in risk perception: a model-based approach. *Risk Anal.* 17:479–88

Bottom WP, Studt A. 1993. Framing effects and the distributive aspect of integrative bargaining. *Organ. Behav. Hum. Decis. Process.* 56:459–74

Bradbury TN, Fincham FD. 1990. Attributions in marriage: review and critique. *Psychol. Bull.* 107:3–33

Brandenburger AM, Nalebuff BJ. 1996. *Co-opetition.* New York: Doubleday

Brett JM, Adair W, Lempereur A, Okumura T, Shikhirev P, et al. 1998. Culture and joint gains in negotiation. *Negot. J.,* Jan., pp. 61–86

Brett JM, Okumura T. 1998. Inter- and intra-cultural negotiation: US and Japanese negotiators. *Acad. Manage. J.* 41:495–510

Brown JD. 1986. Evaluations of self and others: self-enhancement biases in social judgments. *Soc. Cogn.* 4:353–76

Camerer C, Loewenstein G. 1993. Information, fairness, and efficiency in bargaining. See Mellers & Baron 1993, pp. 155–81

Carnevale PJD, Isen AM. 1986. The influence of positive affect and visual access on the discovery of integrative solutions in bilateral negotiation. *Organ. Behav. Hum. Decis. Process.* 37:1–13

Carnevale PJD, Probst TM. 1997. Conflict on the internet. In *Culture of the Internet,* ed. S Kiesler. pp. 233–55. Mahwah, NJ: Erlbaum

Carnevale PJD, Pruitt DG. 1992. Negotiation and mediation. *Annu. Rev. Psychol.* 43:511–82

Carnevale PJD, Pruitt DG, Seilheimer SD. 1981. Looking and competing: accountability and visual access in integrative bargaining. *J. Pers. Soc. Psychol.* 40:111–20

Carroll JS, Bazerman MH, Maury R. 1988. Negotiator cognitions: a descriptive approach to negotiators' understanding of their opponents. *Organ. Behav. Hum. Decis. Process.* 41:352–70

Chatman JA, Polzer JT, Barsade SG, Neale MA. 1998. Being different yet feeling similar: the influence of demographic composition and organizational culture on work processes and outcomes. *Adm. Sci. Q.* 43:749–80

Christie R, Geis FL. 1970. *Studies in Machiavellianism.* New York: Academic

Chua E, Gudykunst W. 1987. Conflict resolution styles in low- and high-context cultures. *Commun. Res. Rep.* 4:32–37

Clark MS, Chrisman K. 1994. Resource allocation in intimate relationships: trying to make sense of a confusing literature. In *Entitlement and the Affectional Bond,* ed.

MJ Lerner, G Mikula, pp. 65–88. New York: Plenum

Cohen R. 1997. *Negotiation Across Cultures.* Washington, DC: US Inst. Peace

Corne PH. 1992. The complex art of negotiation between different cultures. *Disput. Resolut. J.* 47:46–50

Crocker J. 1982. Biased questions in judgment of covariation studies. *Pers. Soc. Psychol. Bull.* 8:214–20

Croson RTA. 1999. Look at me when you say that: An electronic negotiation simulation. *Simul. Gaming.* 30:23–27

Curhan JR, Neale MA, Ross L. 1998. *Dynamic valuation: preference change in the context of active face-to-face negotiations.* Presented at Annu. Stanford/Berkeley talks, Stanford, CA

Darley JM, Fazio RH. 1980. Expectancy-confirmation processes arising in the social interaction sequence. *Am. Psychol.* 35:867–81

Dawes RM. 1998. Behavioral decision making and judgment. In *Handbook of Social Psychology,* ed. DT Gilbert, ST Fiske, G Lindzey, pp. 497–548. New York: McGraw-Hill. 4th ed.

Debusschere M, van Avermaet E. 1984. Compromising between equity and equality: the effects of situational ambiguity and computational complexity. *Eur. J. Soc. Psychol.* 14:323–33

De Dreu CKW. 1996. Gain-loss frame in outcome-interdependence: Does it influence equality or equity considerations? *Eur. J. Soc. Psychol.* 26:315–24

De Dreu CKW, Carnevale PJD, Emans BJM, van de Vliert E. 1994. Gain-loss frames in negotiation: loss aversion, mismatching, and frame adoption. *Organ. Behav. Hum. Decis. Process.* 60:90–107

De Dreu CKW, Carnevale PJD, Emans BJM, van de Vliert E. 1995a. Outcomes frames in bilateral negotiation: resistance to concession making and frame adoption. In *European Review of Ssocial Psychology,* ed. W Stroebe, M Hewstone, pp. 97–125. New York: Wiley

De Dreu CKW, Emans BJM, van de Vliert E. 1992. The influence of own cognitive and other's communicated gain or loss frame on negotiator cognition and behavior. *Int. J. Confl. Manage.* 3:115–32

De Dreu CKW, McCusker C. 1997. Gain-loss frames and cooperation in two-person social dilemmas: a transformational analysis. *J. Pers. Soc. Psychol.* 72:1093–106

De Dreu CKW, Nauta A, van de Vliert E. 1995b. Self-serving evaluations of conflict behavior and escalation of the dispute. *J. Appl. Soc. Psychol.* 25:2049–66

Dees JG, Cramton PC. 1991. Shrewd bargaining on the moral frontier: toward a theory of morality in practice. *Bus. Ethics Q.* 1:135–67

Dees JG, Cramton PC. 1995. Deception and mutual trust: a reply to Strudler. *Bus. Ethics Q.* 5:823–32

DePaulo BM, Friedman HS. 1998. Nonverbal communication. In *The Handbook of Social Psychology,* ed. DT Gilbert, ST Fiske, G Lindzey, 2:3–40. Boston: McGraw Hill. 4th ed.

Deutsch FM, Mackesy ME. 1985. Friendship and the development of self-schemas: the effects of talking about others. *Pers. Soc. Psychol. Bull.* 11:399–408

Diekmann KA. 1997. 'Implicit justifications' and self-serving group allocations. *J. Organ. Behav.* 18:3–16

Diekmann KA, Samuels SM, Ross L, Bazerman MH. 1997. Self-interest and fairness in problems of resource allocation: allocators versus recipients. *J. Pers. Soc. Psychol.* 72:1061–74

Diekmann KA, Tenbrunsel AE, Bazerman MH. 1999. Escalation and negotiation: two central themes in the work of Jeffrey Z. Rubin. In *Negotiation Ethics: Essays in Memory of Jeffrey Z. Rubin,* ed. D Kolb. Cambridge, MA: PON Books

Diekmann KA, Tenbrunsel AE, Shah PP, Schroth HA, Bazerman MH. 1996. The descriptive and prescriptive use of previous purchase price in negotiations. *Organ. Behav. Hum. Decis. Process.* 66:179–91

Drolet AL, Morris MW. 1999. Rapport in conflict resolution: accounting for how nonverbal exchange fosters coordination on mutually beneficial settlements to mixed motive conflicts. *J. Exp. Soc. Psychol.* In press

Druckman D. 1967. Dogmatism, prenegotiation experience, and simulated group representation as determinants of dyadic behavior in a bargaining situation. *J. Pers. Soc. Psychol.* 6:279–90

Dubrovsky VJ, Kiesler S, Sethna BN. 1991. The equalization phenomenon: status effects in computer-mediated and face-to-face decision-making groups. *Hum. Comp. Interact.* 6:119–46

Felstiner WLF, Abel RL, Sarat A. 1980. The emergence and transformation of disputes: naming, blaming, claiming. *Law Soc. Rev.* 15:631–54

Fiske AP, Tetlock PE. 1997. Taboo trade-offs: reactions to transactions that transgress the spheres of justice. *Polit. Psychol.* 18:255–97

Follett M. 1940. Constructive conflict. In *Dynamic Administration,* ed. H Metcalf, L Urwick, pp. 30–49. New York: Harper & Row

Forgas JP. 1994. Sad and guilty? Affective influences on the explanation of conflict in close relationships. *J. Pers. Soc. Psychol.* 66:56–68

Forgas JP. 1998. On feeling good and getting your way: mood effects on negotiator cognition and bargaining strategies. *J. Pers. Soc. Psychol.* 74:565–77

Foster DA. 1992. *Bargaining Across Borders.* New York: McGraw-Hill

Friedland N. 1990. Attribution of control as a determinant of cooperation in exchange interactions. *J. Appl. Soc. Psychol.* 20:303–20

Froman LA, Cohen MD. 1970. Compromise and logroll: comparing the efficiency of two bargaining processes. *Behav. Sci.* 30:180–83

Fry WR. 1985. The effect of dyad machiavellianism and visual access on integrative bargaining outcomes. *Pers. Soc. Psychol. Bull.* 11:51–62

Fukuno M, Ohbuchi K. 1997. Cognitive biases in negotiation: the determinants of fixed-pie assumption and fairness bias. *Jpn. J. Soc. Psychol.* 13:43–52

Fulk J, Schmitz J, Steinfield CW. 1990. A social influence model of technology use. In *Organizations and Communication Technology,* ed. J Fulk, CW Steinfield, pp. 117–40. Newbury Park, CA: Sage

Gabriel MT, Critelli JW, Ee JS. 1994. Narcissistic illusions in self-evaluations of intelligence and attractiveness. *J. Pers.* 62:143–55

Gamson WA. 1961. A theory of coalition formation. *Am. Sociol. Rev.* 26:373–82

Gentner D, Markman AB. 1997. Structure mapping in analogy and similarity. *Am. Psychol.* 52:45–56

Gentner D, Rattermann MJ, Forbus KD. 1993. The roles of similarity in transfer: separating retrievability from inferential soundness. *Cogn. Psychol.* 25:524–75

Gentner D, Stevens AL, eds. 1983. *Mental Models.* Hillsdale, NJ: Erlbaum

Gilbert D. 1994. Attribution and interpersonal perception. In *Advanced Social Psychology,* ed. A Tesser, pp. 99–147. New York: McGraw-Hill

Greenhalgh L, Chapman DI. 1995. Joint decision making: the inseparability of relationships and negotiation. See Kramer & Messick 1995, pp. 166–85

Greenhalgh L, Chapman DI. 1997. Relationships between disputants: an analysis of their characteristics and impact. In *Frontiers in Dispute Resolution and Human Resources,* ed. SE Gleason, pp. 203–29. East Lansing: Mich. State Univ.

Greenhalgh L, Chapman DI. 1998. Negotiator relationships: construct measurement, and demonstration of their impact on the process and outcomes of business transactions. *Group Decis. Negot.* 7:465–89

Greenhalgh L, Okun RL. 1998. Negotiation and conflict resolution. In *Encyclopedia of*

Mental Health, ed. HS Friedman, 1:759–74. San Diego: Academic

Griffin DW, Dunning D, Ross L. 1990. The role of construal processes in overconfident predictions about the self and others. *J. Pers. Soc. Psychol.* 59:1128–39

Griffith TL, Northcraft GB. 1994. Distinguishing between the forest and the trees: media, features, and methodology in electronic communication research. *Organ. Sci.* 5:272–85

Gudykunst WB, Ting-Toomey S. 1988. Culture and affective communication. *Am. Behav. Sci.* 31:384–400

Hall ET. 1976. *Beyond Culture.* Garden City, NY: Anchor

Hall ET. 1983. *The Dance of Life: The Other Dimension of Time.* Garden City, NY: Anchor/Doubleday

Halpern JJ. 1997. Elements of a script for friendship in transactions. *J. Confl. Resolut.* 41:835–68

Hofstede G. 1980. *Culture's Consequences: International Differences in Work-Related Values.* Beverly Hills, CA: Sage

Hofstede G. 1983. Cultural relativity of organizational theories. *J. Int. Bus. Stud.* 14.2:75–90

Huber VL, Neale MA. 1987. Effects of self and competitor's goals on performance in an interdependent bargaining task. *J. Appl. Psychol.* 72:197–203

James K. 1993. The social context of organizational justice: cultural, intergroup, and structural effects on justice behaviors and perceptions. In *Justice in the Workplace,* ed. R Cropanzano, pp. 21–50. Hillsdale, NJ: Erlbaum

Janis IL. 1982. *Groupthink: Psychological Studies of Policy Decisions and Fiascoes.* Boston: Houghton Mifflin

Johnson TE, Rule BG. 1986. Mitigating circumstance information, censure, and aggression. *J. Pers. Soc. Psychol.* 50:537–42

Jones EE. 1986. Interpreting personal behavior: the effects of expectancies. *Science* 234:41–46

Kahneman D. 1992. Reference points, anchors, norms, and mixed feelings. *Organ. Behav. Hum. Decis. Process.* 51:269–312

Kahneman D, Tversky A. 1973. On the psychology of prediction. *Psychol. Rev.* 80:237–51

Kahneman D, Tversky A. 1979. Prospect theory: an analysis of decision under risk. *Econometrica* 47:263–91

Kahneman D, Tversky A. 1982. The simulation heuristic. In *Judgment Under Uncertainty: Heuristics and Biases,* ed. D Kahneman, P Slovic, A Tversky, pp. 201–8. New York: Cambridge Univ. Press

Kelley HH, Thibaut JW. 1978. *Interpersonal Relations: A Theory of Interdependence.* New York: Wiley

Keltner D, Kring AM. 1999. Emotion, social function, and psychopathology. *Rev. Gen. Psychol.* In press

Keltner D, Robinson RJ. 1993. Imagined ideological differences in conflict escalation and resolution. *Int. J. Confl. Manage.* 4:249–62

Keltner D, Robinson RJ. 1996. Extremism, power, and the imagined basis of social conflict. *Curr. Dir. Psychol. Sci.* 5:101–5

Kette G. 1986. Attributions restore consistency in bargaining with liked/disliked partners. *Eur. J. Soc. Psychol.* 16:257–77

Kiesler S, Sproull L. 1992. Group decision making and communication technology. *Organ. Behav. Hum. Decis. Process.* 52:96–123

Kim PH. 1997. Strategic timing in group negotiations: the implications of forced entry and forced exit for negotiators with unequal power. *Organ. Behav. Hum. Decis. Process.* 71:263–86

Kramer RM. 1991. The more the merrier? Social psychological aspects of multiparty negotiations in organizations. See Bies et al 1991, 3:307–32

Kramer RM. 1994. The sinister attribution error: paranoid cognition and collective distrust in organizations. *Motiv. Emot.* 18:199–230

Kramer RM, Messick DM, eds. 1995. *Negotiation as a Social Process.* Thousand Oaks, CA: Sage

Kramer RM, Newton E, Pommerenke PL. 1993. Self-enhancement biases and negotiator judgment: effects of self-esteem and mood. *Organ. Behav. Hum. Decis. Process.* 56:110–33

Kristensen H, Garling T. 1997. The effects of anchor points and reference points on negotiation process and outcome. *Organ. Behav. Hum. Decis. Process.* 72:256–79

Kronzon S, Darley J. 1999. Is this tactic ethical? Biased judgments of ethics in negotiation. *Basic Appl. Soc. Psychol.* In press

Larrick RP, Blount S. 1997. The claiming effect: why players are more generous in social dilemmas than in ultimatum games. *J. Pers. Soc. Psychol.* 72:810–25

Leung K. 1998. Negotiation and reward allocations across cultures. In *New Perspectives on International Industrial/Organizational Psychology,* ed. PC Early, M Erez. San Francisco: Jossey-Bass

Lewicki RJ, Sheppard B, Bies RJ, eds. 1999. *Research on Negotiation in Organizations,* Vol. 7. Greenwich, CT: JAI

Lewicki RJ, Litterer JA. 1985. *Negotiation.* Homewood, IL: Irwin

Lewicki RJ, Litterer JA, Saunders DM, Minton JW. 1993. *Negotiation: Readings, Exercises, and Cases.* Burr Ridge, IL: Irwin. 2nd ed.

Lewicki RJ, Stark N. 1996. What is ethically appropriate in negotiations: an empirical examination of bargaining tactics. *Soc. Justice Res.* 9:69–95

Lewis SA, Fry WR. 1977. Effects of visual access and orientation on the discovery of integrative bargaining alternatives. *Organ. Behav. Hum. Decis. Process.* 20:75–92

Lim RG. 1997. Overconfidence in negotiation revisited. *Int. J. Confl. Manage.* 8:52–79

Lim RG, Carnevale PJ. 1995. Influencing mediator behavior through bargainer framing. *Int. J. Confl. Manage.* 6:349–68

Loewenstein G, Issacharoff S, Camerer C. 1993. Self-serving assessments of fairness and pretrial bargaining. *J. Legal Stud.* 22:135–59

Loewenstein G, Thompson L, Bazerman MH. 1989. Social utility and decision making in interpersonal contexts. *J. Pers. Soc. Psychol.* 57:426–41

Loewenstein J, Thompson L, Gentner D. 1999. Analogical encoding facilitates knowledge transfer in negotiation. *Psychon. Bull. Rev.* In press

Lord RG, Smith JE. 1983. Theoretical, information processing, and situational factors affecting attribution theory models of organizational behavior. *Acad. Manage. Rev.* 8:50–60

Luce RD, Raiffa H. 1957. *Games and Decisions: Introduction and Critical Survey.* New York: Wiley

Mannix E, Neale MA, Northcraft GB. 1995. Equity, equality, or need? The effects of organizational culture on the allocation of benefits and burdens. *Organ. Behav. Hum. Decis. Process.* 63:276–86

Mannix EA. 1991. Resource dilemmas and discount rates in decision making groups. *J. Exp. Soc. Psychol.* 27:379–91

Mannix EA. 1993a. The influence of power, distribution norms and task meeting structure on resource allocation in small group negotiation. *Int. J. Confl. Manage.* 4:5–23

Mannix EA. 1993b. Organizations as resource dilemmas: the effects of power balance on coalition formation in small groups. *Organ. Behav. Hum. Decis. Process.* 55:1–22

Mannix EA. 1994. Will we meet again? Effects of power, distribution norms, and scope of future interaction in small group negotiation. *Int. J. Confl. Manage.* 5:343–68

Mannix EA, Blount White S. 1992. The impact of distributive uncertainty on coalition formation in organizations. *Organ. Behav. Hum. Decis. Process.* 51:198–219

Mannix EA, Thompson LL, Bazerman MH. 1989. Negotiation in small groups. *J. Appl. Psychol.* 74:508–17

March JG, Simon HA. 1958. *Organizations.* New York: Wiley

Markus HR, Kitayama S. 1991. Culture and the self: implications for cognitions, emotion, and motivation. *Psychol. Rev.* 98:224–53

Markus HR, Lin LR. 1998. Conflictways: cultural diversity in the meanings and practices of conflict. In *Cultural Divides,* ed. D Miller, D Prentice. New York: Sage

Marwell G, Ratcliff K, Schmitt DR. 1969. Minimizing differences in a maximizing difference game. *J. Pers. Soc. Psychol.* 12:158–63

Marwell G, Schmitt DR. 1972. Cooperation in a three-person prisoner's dilemma. *J. Pers. Soc. Psychol.* 21:376–83

Mather L, Yngvesson B. 1981. Language, audience and the transformation of disputes. *Law Soc. Rev.* 15:775–822

Mellers BA, Baron J, eds. 1993. *Psychological Perspectives on Justice: Theory and Applications.* New York: Cambridge Univ. Press

Merry SE, Silbey S. 1984. What do plaintiffs want? Reexamining the concept of dispute. *Justice Syst. J.* 9:151–77

Messick DM. 1993. Equality as a decision heuristic. See Mellers & Baron 1993, pp. 11–31

Messick DM. 1995. Equality, fairness, and social conflict. *Soc. Justice Res.* 8:153–73

Messick DM. 1999. Alternative logics for decision making in social settings. *J. Econ. Behav. Organ.* 39:11–28

Messick DM, Bloom S, Boldizar JP, Samuelson CD. 1985. Why we are fairer than others. *J. Exp. Soc. Psychol.* 21:480–500

Messick DM, Sentis KP. 1979. Fairness and preference. *J. Exp. Soc. Psychol.* 15:418–34

Messick DM, Sentis KP. 1983. Fairness, preference, and fairness biases. In *Equity Theory: Psychological and Sociological Perspectives,* ed. DM Messick, KS Cook, pp. 61–94. New York: Praeger

Miller DT, Ross M. 1975. Self-serving biases in the attribution of causality: fact or fiction? *Psychol. Bull.* 82:213–25

Montgomery JD. 1998. Toward a role-theoretic conception of embeddedness. *Am. J. Sociol.* 104:92–125

Moore DA, Kurtzberg TR, Thompson LL, Morris MW. 1999. The long and short routes to success in electronically-mediated negotiations: group affiliations and good vibrations. *Organ. Behav. Hum. Decis. Process.* 77:22–43

Morely IE. 1982. Preparation for negotiation: conflict, commitment, and choice. In *Group Decision Making,* ed. H Brandstatter, JH Davis, G Stocker-Kreichgaure. New York: Academic

Morris MW, Larrick RP, Su SK. 1999. Misperceiving negotiation counterparts: when situationally determined bargaining behaviors are attributed to personality traits. *J. Pers. Soc. Psychol.* 77(1):52–67

Morris MW, Leung K, Sethi S. 1995. *Person perception in the heat of conflict: perceptions of opponents' traits and conflict resolution choices in two cultures.* Presented at Annu. Meet. Acad. Manage., Vancouver, Can.

Morris MW, Peng K. 1994. Culture and cause: American and Chinese attributions for social and physical events. *J. Pers. Soc. Psychol.* 67:949–71

Morris MW, Sim DLH, Girotto V. 1998. Distinguishing sources of cooperation in the one-round prisoner's dilemma: evidence for cooperative decisions based on the illusion of control. *J. Exp. Soc. Psychol.* 34:494–512

Morrison T, Conaway WA, Borden GA. 1994. *Kiss, Bow, or Shake Hands: How to Do Business in Sixty Countries.* Holbrook, MA: Adams Media Corp.

Murnighan JK. 1994. Game theory and organizational behavior. In *Research in Organizational Behavior,* ed. BM Staw, LL Cummings, 16:83–123. Greenwich, CT: JAI

Murnighan JK, Brass DJ. 1991. Intraorganizational coalitions. See Bies et al 1991, 3:283–306

Neale MA. 1984. The effects of negotiation and arbitration cost salience on bargainer behavior: the role of the arbitrator and constituency on negotiator judgment. *Organ. Behav. Hum. Decis. Process.* 34:97–111

Neale MA, Bazerman MH. 1991. *Cognition and Rationality in Negotiation.* New York: Free Press

Neuberg SL. 1988. Behavioral implications of information presented outside of conscious awareness: the effect of subliminal presentation of trait information on behavior in the Prisoner's Dilemma Game. *Soc. Cogn.* 6:207–30

Northcraft GB, Neale MA. 1987. Expert, amateurs, and real estate: an anchoring-and-adjustment perspective on property pricing decisions. *Organ. Behav. Hum. Decis. Process.* 39:228–41

O'Connor KM, Carnevale PJ. 1997. A nasty but effective negotiation strategy: misrepresentation of a common-value issue. *Pers. Soc. Psychol. Bull.* 23:504–15

O'Connor KM, De Dreu CK, Schroth H, Barry B, Lituchy T, et al. 1998. *What we want to do versus what we think that we should do: an empirical investigation of intrapersonal conflict.* Presented at Annu. Meet. Acad. Manage., San Diego, CA

Olekalns M. 1997. Situational cues as moderators of the frame-outcome relationship. *Br. J. Soc. Psychol.* 36:191–209

Palmer LG, Thompson L. 1995. Negotiation in triads: communication constraints and tradeoff structure. *J. Exp. Psychol. Appl.* 1:83–94

Pillutla MM, Murnighan JK. 1996. Unfairness, anger, and spite: emotional rejections of ultimatum offers. *Organ. Behav. Hum. Decis. Process.* 68:208–24

Pinker S. 1997. *How the Mind Works.* New York: Harper Collins

Pinkley RL. 1990. Dimensions of conflict frame: disputant interpretations of conflict. *J. Appl. Psychol.* 75:117–26

Pinkley RL, Griffith TL, Northcraft GB. 1995. Fixed pie a la mode: information availability, information processing, and the negotiation of suboptimal agreements. *Organ. Behav. Hum. Decis. Process.* 62:101–12

Pinkley RL, Northcraft GB. 1994. Conflict frames of reference: implications for dispute processes and outcomes. *Acad. Manage. J.* 37:193–205

Polzer JT. 1996. Intergroup negotiations: the effects of negotiating teams. *J. Confl. Resolut.* 40:678–98

Polzer JT, Mannix EA, Neale MA. 1995. Multiparty negotiation in its social context. See Kramer & Messick 1995, pp. 123–42

Polzer JT, Mannix EA, Neale MA. 1998. Interest alignment and coalitions in multiparty negotiation. *Acad. Manage. J.* 41:42–54

Pruitt DG, Carnevale PJ. 1993. *Negotiation in Social Conflict.* Pacific Grove, CA: Brooks/Cole

Pruitt DG, Drews JL. 1969. The effect of time pressure, time elapsed, and the opponent's concession rate on behavior in negotiation. *J. Exp. Soc. Psychol.* 5:43–69

Pruitt DG, Johnson DF. 1972. Mediation as an aid to face saving in negotiation. *J. Pers. Soc. Psychol.* 14:239–46

Putnam L, Holmer M. 1992. Framing, reframing, and issue development. In *Communication and Negotiation,* ed. L Putnam, M Roloff, pp. 128–55. Newbury Park, CA: Sage

Putnam LL, Poole MS. 1987. Conflict and negotiation. In *Handbook of Organizational Communication,* ed. F Jablin, L Putnam, K Roberts, L Porter, pp. 549–99. Newbury Park, CA: Sage

Raiffa H. 1982. *The Art and Science of Negotiation.* Cambridge, MA: Belknap

Ritov I. 1996. Anchoring in simulated competitive market negotiation. *Organ. Behav. Hum. Decis. Process.* 67:16–25

Robinson RJ, Keltner D. 1996. Much ado about nothing? Revisionists and traditionalists choose an introductory English syllabus. *Psychol. Sci.* 7:18–24

Robinson RJ, Keltner D. 1997. Defending the status quo: power and bias in social conflict. *Pers. Soc. Psychol. Bull.* 23:1066–77

Robinson RJ, Keltner D, Ward A, Ross L. 1995. Actual versus assumed differences in construal: 'naïve realism' in intergroup perception and conflict. *J. Pers. Soc. Psychol.* 68:404–17

Robinson RJ, Lewicki RJ, Donohue EM. 1997. A five factor model of unethical bargaining tactics: the SINS scale. In *Aust. Ind. Organ. Psychol. Best Pap. Proc. Australian Industrial and Organizational Society:* Melbourne, Australia, pp. 131–37.

Rosenthal R. 1974. *On the Social Psychology of the Self-Fulfilling Prophecy: Further Evidence for Pygmalion Effects and Their Mediating Mechanisms.* New York: MSS Inf. Corp. Modular Publ.

Ross L, Nisbett RE. 1991. *The Person and the Situation: Perspectives of Social Psychology.* New York: McGraw-Hill

Ross L, Stillinger C. 1991. Barriers to conflict resolution. *Negot. J.* 7:389–404

Ross L, Ward A. 1995. Psychological barriers to dispute resolution. *Adv. Exp. Soc. Psychol.* 27:255–303

Roth AE. 1995. Bargaining experiments. In *The Handbook of Experimental Economics,* ed. JH Kagel, AE Roth, pp. 253–348. Princeton, NJ: Princeton Univ. Press

Rouse WB, Morris NM. 1986. On looking into the black box: prospects and limits in the search for mental models. *Psychol. Bull.* 100:349–63

Rubin JZ, Brown BR. 1975. *The Social Psychology of Bargaining and Negotiation.* New York: Academic

Rusbult CE, Van Lange PAM. 1996. Interdependence processes. In *Social Psychology: Handbook of Basic Principles,* ed. ET Higgins, AW Kruglanski, pp. 564–96. New York: Guilford

Rutter ER, Robinson B. 1981. An experimental analysis of teaching by telephone: theretical and practical implications for social psychology. In *Progress in Applied Social Psychology,* ed. GM Stephenson, JH Davis, pp. 345–74. New York: Wiley

Sally DF. 1995. Conversation and cooperation in social dilemmas: experimental evidence from 1958 to 1992. *Ration. Soc.* 7:58–92

Samuelson WF, Bazerman MH. 1985. Negotiation under the winner's curse. In *Research in Experimental Economics,* ed. V Smith, 3:105–38. Greenwich, CT: JAI

Schweitzer ME. 1997. Omission, friendship, and fraud: lies about material facts in negotiation. Presented at Annu. Meet. Acad. Manage., Boston, MA

Selye H. 1976. *The Stress of Life.* New York: McGraw-Hill. Rev. ed.

Shafir E, Tversky A. 1992. Thinking through uncertainty: nonconsequential reasoning and choice. *Cogn. Psychol.* 24:449–74

Shah PP, Jehn KA. 1993. Do friends perform better than acquaintances? The interaction of friendship, conflict, and task. *Group Decis. Negot.* 2:149–65

Shapiro DL. 1991. The effects of explanation on negative reactions to deceit. *Adm. Sci. Q.* 36:614–30

Shapiro DL, von Glinow MA. 1999. Negotiation in multicultural teams: new world, old theories? See Lewicki et al 1999

Siegel J, Dubrovsky V, Kiesler S, McGuire TW. 1986. Group processes in computer-mediated communication. *Organ. Behav. Hum. Decis. Process.* 37:157–87

Simon HA. 1957. *Models of Man.* New York: Wiley

Smith DH. 1969. Communication and negotiation outcome. *J. Commun.* 19:248–56

Snyder M. 1992. Motivational foundations of behavioral confirmation. *Adv. Exp. Soc. Psychol.* 25:67–114

Sondak H, Bazerman MH. 1989. Matching and negotiation processes in quasi-markets. *Organ. Behav. Hum. Decis. Process.* 44:261–80

Sproull L, Kiesler SB. 1991. *Connections: New Ways of Working in the Networked Organization.* Cambridge, MA: MIT Press

Starr J, Yngvesson B. 1975. Scarcity and disputing: zeroing-in on compromise decisions. *Am. Ethnol.* 2:553–66

Strudler A. 1995. On the ethics of deception in negotiation. *Bus. Ethics Q.* 5:805–22

Svenson O. 1981. Are we less risky and more skillful than our fellow drivers? *Acta Psychol.* 47:143–51

Taylor SE. 1989. *Positive Illusions.* New York: Basic Books

Taylor SE, Brown JD. 1988. Illusion and well-being: a social psychological perspective on mental health. *Psychol. Bull.* 103:193–210

Tenbrunsel AE. 1998. Misrepresentation and expectations of misrepresentation in an ethical dilemma: the role of incentives and temptation. *Acad. Manage. J.* 41:330–39

Tenbrunsel AE. 1999. Trust as an obstacle in the economics-environment debates. *Am. Behav. Sci.* 42(8):1350–67

Tenbrunsel AE, Wade-Benzoni KA, Moag J, Bazerman MH. 1996. *When is a friend not a friend? A look at relationships and partner selection in negotiations.* Presented at Wharton Organ. Behav. Conf., Philadelphia

Tetlock PE, Peterson RS, Lerner JS. 1996. Revising the value pluralism model: incorporating social content and context postulates. In *Values: 8th Annu. Ontario Symp. Pers. Soc. Psychol.,* ed. C Seligman, J Olson, M Zanna, pp. 25–51. Hillsdale, NJ: Erlbaum

Thompson L. 1990. Negotiation behavior and outcomes: empirical evidence and theoretical issues. *Psychol. Bull.* 108:515–32

Thompson L. 1995. The impact of minimum goals and aspirations on judgments of success in negotiations. *Group Decis. Negot.* 4:513–24

Thompson L. 1998. *The Mind and Heart of the Negotiator.* Upper Saddle River, NJ: Prentice Hall

Thompson L, DeHarpport T. 1994. Social judgment, feedback, and interpersonal learning in negotiation. *Organ. Behav. Hum. Decis. Process.* 58:327–45

Thompson L, Hastie R. 1990. Social perception in negotiation. *Organ. Behav. Hum. Decis. Process.* 47:98–123

Thompson L, Hrebec D. 1996. Lose-lose agreements in interdependent decision making. *Psychol. Bull.* 120:396–409

Thompson L, Loewenstein G. 1992. Egocentric interpretations of fairness and interpersonal conflict. *Organ. Behav. Hum. Decis. Process.* 51:176–97

Thompson L, Mannix EA, Bazerman MH. 1988. Group negotiation: effects of decision rule, agenda, and aspiration. *J. Pers. Soc. Psychol.* 54:86–95

Thompson L, Nadler J, Kim PH. 1999. Some like it hot: the case for the emotional negotiator. In *Shared Cognition in Organizaitons: The Management of Knowledge,* ed. L Thompson, D Messick, J Levine, pp. 139–61. Hillsdale, NJ: Erlbaum

Thompson L, Peterson E, Brodt SE. 1996. Team negotiation: an examination of integrative and distributive bargaining. *J. Pers. Soc. Psychol.* 70:66–78

Thompson LL, Gonzalez R. 1997. Environmental disputes: competition for scarce resources and clashing of values. In *Environment, Ethics, and Behavior,* ed. MH Bazerman, DM Messick, AE Tenbrunsel, KA Wade-Benzoni, pp. 75–104. San Francisco: New Lexington

Tinsley C. 1998. Models of conflict resolution in Japanese, German, and American cultures. *J. Appl. Psychol.* 83:316–23

Tinsley C, Brett JM. 1997. *Managing workplace conflict: a comparison of conflict frames and outcomes in the U.S. and Hong Kong.* Presented at Annu. Meet. Acad. Manage., Boston

Tinsley C, Curhan J, Kwak RS. 1999. Adopting a dual lens approach for overcoming the dilemma of difference in international business negotiations. *Int. Negot.* 4:1–18

Todd HF. 1978. Litigious marginals: character and disputing in a Bavarian village. In *The Disputing Process,* ed. L Nader, HF Todd, pp. 86–121. New York: Columbia Univ. Press

Triandis HC. 1990. Cross-cultural studies of individualsim and collectivism. *Nebr. Symp. Motiv. 1989,* 37:41–133

Triandis HC. 1995. *Individualism and Collectivism.* Boulder, CO: Westview

Tversky A, Kahneman D. 1974. Judgment under uncertainty: heuristics and biases. *Science* 185:1124–31

Valley KL. 1992. *Relationships and resources: a network exploration of allocation deci-*

sion. PhD thesis. Northwestern Univ., Evanston, Ill. 115 pp.

Valley KL, Moag J, Bazerman MH. 1998. A matter of trust: effects of communication on the efficiency and distribution of outcomes. *J. Econ. Behav. Organ.* 34:211–38

Valley KL, Neale MA, Mannix EA. 1995. Friends, lovers, colleagues, strangers: the effects of relationships on the process and outcome of dyadic negotiations. In *Research on Negotiation in Organizations,* ed. RJ Bies, RJ Lewicki, BH Sheppard, 5:65–93. Greenwich, CT: JAI

Wade-Benzoni KA, Tenbrunsel AE, Bazerman MH. 1996. Egocentric interpretations of fairness in asymmetric, environmental social dilemmas: explaining harvesting behavior and the role of communciation. *Organ. Behav. Hum. Decis. Process.* 67:111–26

Walster E, Walster GW, Berscheid E. 1978. *Equity: Theory and Research.* Boston: Allyn & Bacon

Walton RE, McKersie RB. 1965. *A Behavioral Theory of Labor Negotiations.* New York: McGraw-Hill

Weber EU, Hsee CK. 1999. Cross-cultural differences in risk perception, but cross-cultural similarities in attitudes towards perceived risk. *Manage. Sci.* In press

Wegner DM, Erber R, Raymond P. 1991. Transactive memory in close relationships. *J. Pers. Soc. Psychol.* 61:923–29

Weingart LR, Bennett RJ, Brett JM. 1993. The impact of consideration of issues and motivational orientation on group negotiation process and outcome. *J. Appl. Psychol.* 78:504–17

Weiss SE. 1994. Negotiating with "Romans"—Part 1. *Sloan Manage. Rev.* 35:51–61

Weiss SE. 1996. International negotiations: bricks, mortar, and prospects. In *Handbook for International Management Research,* ed. BJ Punnett, O Shenkar. Cambridge, MA: Blackwell

Weldon E, Jehn KA. 1995. Examining cross-cultural differences in conflict management behavior: a strategy for future research. *Int. J. Confl. Manage.* 6:387–403

Whyte G, Sebenius JK. 1997. The effect of multiple anchors on anchoring in individual and group judgment. *Organ. Behav. Hum. Decis. Process.* 69:75–85

Wichman H. 1970. Effects of isolation and communication on cooperation in a two-person game. *J. Pers. Soc. Psychol.* 16:114–20

Williams E. 1977. Experimental comparisons of face-to-face and mediated communication: a review. *Psychol. Bull.* 84:963–76

Wokutch RE, Carson TL. 1993. The ethics and profitability of bluffing in business. See Lewicki et al 1993, pp. 499–504

Zajonc RB. 1965. Social facilitation. *Science* 149:269–74

Zimbardo PG. 1969. The human choice: individuation, reason, and order versus deindividuation, impulse, and chaos. In *Nebraska Symposium on Motivation,* ed. WJ Arnold, D Levine, pp. 237–307. Lincoln, NE: Univ. Nebr. Press

Annu. Rev. Psychol. 2000. 51:315–344

PARENTAL AND CHILD COGNITIONS IN THE CONTEXT OF THE FAMILY

Daphne Blunt Bugental[1] and Charlotte Johnston[2]

[1]Department of Psychology, University of California, Santa Barbara, Santa Barbara, California 93106; e-mail: bugental@psych.ucsb.edu
[2]Department of Psychology, University of British Columbia, Vancouver, British Columbia, Canada V6T 1Z4, ; e-mail: cjohnston@cortex.psych.ubc.ca

Key Words   social cognition, parent-child relations, socialization, attributions, beliefs

■ **Abstract**   Parent and child family-related cognitions are reviewed with respect to (*a*) their origins, (*b*) their linkage to affect and behavior, (*c*) their transmission and perpetuation, (*d*) their alteration on the basis of first-hand experience, and (*e*) their collaborative negotiation and renegotiation. A distinction is offered between the functioning of implicit, relatively unaware, schematic cognitions and relatively aware, explicit, event-dependent cognitions. Consideration is also given to the differential content (or topics) of cognitions. As a positive outcome of recent research, many new insights have emerged with respect to the linkage of family members' cognitions and their individual and shared patterns of behavior. However, several limitations remain, including too little consideration of the shared influences of parents' and children's cognitions and the changes in these cognitions over time. As a growth area, there is emerging interest in the application of our knowledge of cognitions to the clinical context in programs designed to remediate and prevent family problems.

CONTENTS

Introduction 316
How Have Cognitions Been Conceptualized?..316
  What Are the Relevant Cognitive Levels?.......................................317
  What Are the Topical Concerns of Cognitions?................................317
Schematic Cognitions of Individual Family Members: What Are Their
  Origins and What Are Their Consequences?......................................319
  Schematic Cognitions as Linear Links Within the Family.....................319
  Schematic Cognitions as Moderators...325
Family-Relevant Events and Characteristics and their Links to Event-
  Dependent Cognitions 327
  *Children's Behavior and Characteristics, and their Links to Event-Dependent
  Cognitions* 328
  Event-Dependent Cognitions as Contextually Organized.......................329
Family Cognitions as Interdependent or Joint Constructions 331

0084–6570/00/0201–0315$12.00

Interdependent Influences 332
Mutual Influences 332
Common Fate 334
Conclusions and Directions for the Future 334
Subject Matter of Cognitive Constructs 334
Restricted Focus within the Family 335
Theoretical and Methodological Issues 336
Implications for Remediation 337

INTRODUCTION

The past 15 years have seen an emergent focus on the role of cognitions in family life (e.g. Bugental & Goodnow 1998, Holden & Edwards 1989, Miller 1995, Murphey 1992). From a contemporary perspective, the actions and emotions of family members cannot be fully understood without recognition of the cognitive processes to which they are linked. Arguably, the first official recognition of the centrality of cognitions within family interactions appeared in the edited volume by Sigel (1985). The current review covers work conducted on cognitions in families during the past 10 years, with a focus on findings since the volume on parental beliefs by Sigel et al (1992). In places, earlier literature is cited to provide a historical framework for current research in this field. In considering the topic of cognitions in families, it is also necessary to set boundaries on the content of the literature included for review. We selectively focus attention on parent and child cognitions about shared, commonly occurring social events that have significance for family life as opposed to (*a*) cognitions about very specific or rare events (e.g. severe mental illnesses), (*b*) cognitions that are primarily concerned with other domains (e.g. children's academic performance), and (*c*) parents' cognitions concerning their relationships with their adult partners.

We first outline how family-related cognitions have been conceptualized in terms of levels of analysis and topical concerns. Relevant empirical literature is then reviewed from the standpoint of different conceptual models. The paper concludes with a consideration of strengths and limitations of past work, along with recommended directions for future research.

HOW HAVE COGNITIONS BEEN CONCEPTUALIZED?

In this chapter, our concern is with the dynamic nature of cognitions: How they come to be, the ways they are linked to affective and behavioral processes, the ways they are perpetuated, the ways they may change or be fine-tuned as a result of first-hand experience, and the ways they are collaboratively negotiated and renegotiated within family life.

What Are the Relevant Cognitive Levels?

As a central organizing feature, cognitions may be conceptualized as operating at different levels–levels that form the basis for our organization of this chapter. For individual family members, cognitions may be thought of as involving either schematic or event-dependent processes. Schematic cognitions involve stable knowledge structures that operate automatically and with little awareness (implicit processes). Examples of such cognitions would include internal working models or attributional styles. Event-dependent cognitions involve data-driven processes that operate with higher levels of awareness and reflection (explicit processes): for example, attributional inferences or problem solving in response to specific family events. The dual processes suggested reflect a frequently offered division within the social cognition literature (e.g. Fiske & Taylor 1991). Research that has focused on schematic cognitions has generally taken the cognitions of parents and/or children as a starting point and has explored their origins and consequences. Research that has focused on event-dependent cognitions has more typically taken family-relevant experiences as its starting point and explored the association between such events and family members' cognitions. However, it is generally recognized that schematic cognitions and event-dependent cognitions are in continuous interaction, and the distinction between the two is not always clear.

Alternative to the focus on cognitions of individuals, cognitions may be conceptualized as joint constructions that are continuously negotiated and renegotiated within the family. This body of work takes as its starting point the collaborative cognitions that operate within dyads, groups, and cultures (e.g. Valsiner et al 1997).

What Are the Topical Concerns of Cognitions?

As a cross-cutting theme, cognitions about family relationships also differ in terms of their contents or "topics." They may be concerned with (*a*) the ways things are perceived to be in family life (descriptive cognitions), (*b*) the perceived reasons for family-related events (analytical cognitions), (*c*) the way things "should" be within the family (evaluative-prescriptive cognitions), or (*d*) the convergence or divergence between the way things are and the ways things "should" be (efficacy cognitions). The questions posed by these different types of cognitions do not compete with each other nor do they differ in legitimacy as topics of study. Instead, they may be understood as addressing different issues and serving different purposes within the family.

Descriptive Cognitions   Much of the early literature concerned with family-relevant cognitions focused on parental beliefs and expectations regarding the nature of children. These formulations centered on the conscious reflections of family members, that is, what family members "knew," thought about, and could talk about. Current work of this sort is more likely to refer to family members' perceptions of other family members' behavior (e.g. Krech & Johnston 1992, Richters 1992, Webster-Stratton 1990). As interests emerged in different levels of cognitive processing, attention expanded to include less event-dependent forms of descriptive family cognitions. Within developmental psychology, Bowlby's notion of working models (Bowlby 1980, Bretherton 1995) opened the door for concerns with cognitive representations that operate at a relatively unaware, automatic level. Within social psychology, it was proposed that close relationships as a whole come to be represented schematically as a function of early experience (e.g. Andersen & Glassman 1996, Baldwin 1992). Such scripted or schematic accounts are thought of as affectively tagged (Fiske & Pavelchak 1986) and acting as organizers of expectations and guides to behavior (e.g. Bargh et al 1996).

Analytical Cognitions   Within the social cognition and social cognitive learning theory literatures, questions have emerged as to the ways in which humans think about causality: What makes things happen? What and who are the sources of causality (e.g. Kelley 1967, Lazarus & Folkman 1984, Rotter 1966, Weiner 1986)? Such cognitions have often been conceptualized in terms of attributional processes. Early interest in individual attributional processes was soon co-opted in the service of family-oriented questions. As pointed out by Miller (1995), a concern with parents' search for explanations of their children's behavior involves an important spontaneous, self-aware activity of parents. As this literature evolved, attention also turned to "attributional style" as a schematic, memory-based, less-aware cognitive construct (e.g. Alloy et al 1984, Bugental et al 1997, Nix et al 1999); here, the interest is in explanatory processes that are "chronically accessible" and that "come to mind" automatically.

Evaluative-Prescriptive Cognitions   A third type of question addressed by family cognitions has focused on evaluative processes and motives within family life. Early interests in this area focused on parental attitudes and values, reflecting views regarding the desirability of particular kinds of child behaviors or parental practices. However, it became apparent that parental attitudes and values were poor predictors of parental practices (Holden & Edwards 1989), and empirical interest in these constructs declined. More recently, we have seen a rebirth of such concerns with the introduction of the notion of parental goals. As a construct, parental goals include the evaluative and prescriptive component of values but have the advantage of being conceptually more closely linked to actions (Dix 1992, Hastings & Grusec 1998). That is, goals may be thought of as providing the means by which emotions, motives, or values are translated into actions (e.g. Martin & Tesser 1996). Goals may either be conceptualized as stable structures that operate relatively automatically or as event-dependent structures that involve reflective appraisal.

Efficacy Cognitions   From a fourth perspective, family-related cognitions have been considered in terms of the correspondence between perceived reality (descriptive cognitions) and desired reality (evaluative-prescriptive cognitions). Family members may be thought of as understanding their relational experiences in terms of perceived self-efficacy (Bandura 1989, Coleman & Karraker 1997, Teti & Gelfand 1991). Alternatively, Higgins & his colleagues (1998) have focused on the convergence between "actual" selves and "ought" selves, and between "actual" selves and "ideal" selves in their formulation of socialization processes. In well-functioning families, for example, hoped-for outcomes and realities may be closely matched, but in families experiencing conflict, there may be striking disparities between what "is" and what "ought" to be or what would be "ideal."

SCHEMATIC COGNITIONS OF INDIVIDUAL FAMILY MEMBERS: WHAT ARE THEIR ORIGINS AND WHAT ARE THEIR CONSEQUENCES?

Family-relevant cognitive schemas represent knowledge structures that influence and are influenced by most aspects of family life. A variety of theoretical approaches have been reflected in the research addressing this level of cognitive processing. For example, social cognitive learning theory has directed attention to the experiences that shape family members' global perceptions of self-efficacy and their summary cognitions about relationships with others (e.g. Bandura 1989). Attachment theory has focused on the origins and perpetuation of working models of relationships (e.g. Bowlby 1980, van IJzendoorn 1995). Attributional theories have been concerned primarily with stylistic differences in perceived controllability, intentionality, locus, and stability of family-related events (for review, see Bugental et al 1998).

Regardless of theoretical approach, the focus of research in this area is on the origins, consequences, and perpetuation of stable, knowledge-based cognitive structures in family life. Particular attention is often directed to the role of cognitive structures in the emergence and maintenance of behavioral and emotional problems within the family. However, a distinction can be made between models in which schematic cognitions are viewed (*a*) as linked in a linear fashion to the responses of self and others or (*b*) as moderators or qualifiers of the interaction between self and others.

Schematic Cognitions as Linear Links within the Family

As a general issue that transcends theoretical approaches, investigators have studied continuity in schematic cognitions across generations. Particular concern has been directed to the mechanisms of transmission of family cognitions–whether direct tuition, parenting practices, or the provision of experiences that foster or maintain cognitions. Implicit within research on transmission is the idea that parents are primary shapers of their children's cognitions. Parents may not only influence children's cognitions directly, they may also influence children's cognitions indirectly through their management of children's environments (e.g. Parke & O'Neil 1996). Indeed, it has even been suggested that cross-generational influence processes are primarily mediated through children's groups (Harris 1995). When, for example, parents select neighborhoods, schools, churches/synagogues, or play/sports/interest groups for their children, they are also selecting environments that serve to socialize particular types of prescriptive cognitions.

The preponderance of research that follows this approach has taken parental cognition as its starting point and then considered the linkage of such cognitions to (a) the emotional responses and parenting practices shown by parents, and (b) the behaviors and emotional responses shown by children. Although there is variability across research programs, increasing attention has been given to the mediating processes by which parents' schematic cognitions produce their effects. Thus, Patterson (1997) has argued strongly that the influences of parent cognitions on child and family outcomes are mediated via the effects that these cognitions (and associated emotions) have on parenting behaviors. A smaller body of research has taken child cognitions as its starting point and assessed the linkage of such cognitions to children's emotional and behavioral interactions with other family members. At this point, only limited (but much needed) attention has been given to the joint effects of parental and child cognitions on their individual and interactional responses.

In the sections that follow we have organized our review on the basis of types of cognitions. Within each category, we consider the ways in which linkages between parents and children have been studied.

Descriptive Cognitions   In the past decade, the preponderance of work on individual differences in descriptive family-relevant cognitions comes from an attachment framework (culturally shared descriptive cognitions are described in a later section). Working models of attachment represent descriptive cognitive-motivational accounts of the relationship between parents and children. In particular, there has been an interest in the cross-generational transmission of working models. van IJzendoorn (1995), in reviewing the literature, concluded that there is a very high degree of continuity in attachment styles across generations. The best evidence for such continuity is provided by the strong relationships found between parents' attachment styles, as measured by their retrospective accounts on the Adult Attachment Interview (M Main & R Goldwyn, unpublished data), and the attachment styles of their own children. The average effect size for such correspondence was reported as 1.06. Such continuity goes beyond the simple distinction between secure versus insecure attachment, and it extends to specific attachment categories.

Consistent with a model of parenting behavior as influenced by parental cognitions, several investigators have found relationships between parents' working models and their behavior in interactions with their children (e.g. Cohn et al 1992, Crowell et al 1991, Grusec et al 1994, Grusec & Mammone 1995). In general, this research suggests that parents whose working models reveal an insecure attachment history are more likely to be unsupportive and negatively reactive to their own children, and to have children who reciprocate such reactions.

Although much theoretical attention has been given to children's earliest representations of their parents (their working models), relevant measures of these have necessarily focused on inferences drawn from children's behavioral and affective responses to parents (and separation from parents). More direct measures of children's cognitive representations are available only at somewhat older ages. For example, Cassidy et al (1996) found that children who were categorized as avoidantly attached (as infants) provided less-positive responses to questions posed to them concerning anticipated maternal support following a hypothetical negative event (presented to them at age 3.5–4 years) than did other children. In addition, Fury & colleagues (1997) found that early attachment history predicted key features of the ways in which children depicted their relationships in drawings at age 8 or 9.

As a specialized area of interest, particular attention has been given to the ways in which maltreated children represent their relationships with parents (Toth et al 1997). For example, maltreated preschoolers (in a story completion task), in comparison with nonmaltreated children, represent parents as stepping in less often to relieve children's distress. Abused children (sexual or physical abuse) differed from neglected children (and nonmaltreated children) in their representations of children. That is, abused children were more likely to interject themselves into stories as intervening to help a child (or to role reverse with parents) than were neglected children (Macfie et al 1999).

Analytical Cognitions   Considerable attention has been given to the long-term influences of parents' analytical cognitions about children's behavior and family-related events—with a particular interest in attributional style. As a general concern, there has been an interest in the cross-generational transmission of the perceived causes of interpersonal outcomes within parent-child relationships. Burks & Parke (1996) compared mothers' and children's causal attributions; in general, good agreement was obtained. Bugental & Martorell (1999) have also demonstrated cross-generational continuity in causal attributions about family-related events within the family—in particular between mothers and sons. Stronger correspondence between the attributional styles of mothers and children (rather than fathers and children) was also found by Seligman & colleagues (1984). The possibility emerges that cross-generational transmission processes in causal reasoning are more likely to involve mothers than fathers (for complex effects involving gender of parent and gender of child, see Fincham et al 1998).

Attributional style   Research has focused on the relationships between attributional biases of parents and children and negative family (and individual) outcomes. In particular, parents' attributional biases have been linked to the coerciveness, harshness, or authoritarian nature of their interactions with children. In general, those parents who abuse or are physically coercive with their children are more likely to attribute defiant intentions to children and to perceive themselves as lacking power (Bradley & Peters 1991, Bugental et al 1989, Silvester et al 1995, Smith & O'Leary 1995). Even when not physically coercive, parents with this attributional style are more likely than other parents to be highly controlling (e.g. Mills 1998).

There is also evidence that blame-oriented attributions precede and foster harsher parental tactics. For example, Slep & O'Leary (1998) observed that parents became harsher in their disciplinary style if they were experimentally induced to see children as misbehaving intentionally. Nix et al's (1999) longitudinal analysis of the long-term correlates of parents' hostile attributional style also provides suggestive leads. That is, parents' hostile biases (measured during an initial home visit) predicted child aggression (at home and school), as mediated by parents' harsh disciplinary practices (as reported by parents and their spouses). Reported child aggression (assessed separately for teachers/peers, and parents) was averaged across a four-year time period that began with ratings made at the start of the project. Despite some inferential limitations (e.g., uncertainties regarding direction of effects), these findings provide an impressive extension of Dodge's past work on children's attributional biases(e.g. Dodge 1993) to the potential effects of parents' attributional biases.

A smaller body of work has been concerned with children's attributions concerning family-related events, for example, children's inferences regarding the causes of marital conflict (e.g. Brody et al 1996, Fincham 1998, Grych & Fincham 1993). The focus has been on the ways in which children's attributions influence their affective and behavioral responses to parents. For example, Fincham et al (1998) found that at 10–12 years of age, children's "conflict-promoting attributions" (high causality and responsibility attributed to parents for negative interactions) predicted both their own and their parents' reports of parent-child conflict. When objective measures were taken of parent-child interactions, children's conflict-promoting attributions only served to predict their negative relationship with fathers. As suggested by the authors, children's closer relationships with mothers may have led them to be less likely to act on their negative attributions.

Relatively little attention has been given to the joint processes by which parent and child cognitions come to influence their shared and individual outcomes. As an excellent example of this approach, research conducted by MacKinnon-Lewis and her colleagues (1990, 1992, 1994) gave joint attention to the predictive power of maternal and child cognitions. Specifically, the research focused on the role of attributions as predictors of aggressive behavior. Testing an affective-cognitive model of mother-child aggression with assessments at two points in time, these investigators studied the contributions of child attributions and maternal attributions to the aggressiveness of their interaction and to the aggressiveness of children outside the home. As predicted, the most aggressive dyads were those in which both mothers and sons attributed hostile intentions to each other. The observed predictive relationships were strongest when marital conflict was low and education was high. In addition, the hostile attributional bias of mothers predicted sons' aggressive behavior in the school environment.

Locus of control   A continuing interest has been shown in the relationship between parents' locus of control, associated parenting tactics, and children's locus of control. For example, parents with an external locus of control (i.e., who perceive reinfocing events to be controlled by luck or powerful others) are more likely to show an authoritarian control style (e.g. Janssens 1994), a pattern that is most pronounced among parents who perceive their children as demonstrating behavior problems. Supporting these findings, Roberts et al (1992), using the Parent Locus of Control Scale, found a significant relationship between parents' external locus and the observed resistive behavior of oppositional-defiant children. Carton & Carton (1998) demonstrated that mothers of children with a generalized internal locus of control were more likely to exhibit nonverbal warmth (e.g. smiles, hugs, gaze) than were the mothers of children with an external locus of control. In addition, mothers of sons with an internal locus of control were found to be more supportive of their sons on a difficult puzzle-solving task, whereas mothers of sons with an external locus of control were relatively more likely to simply watch or else take over on the task (Carton et al 1996). However, these findings were not replicated with mothers and daughters, perhaps, as the authors suggest, because of different learning histories in mother-daughter versus mother-son pairs. Within such research, it is, of course, difficult to draw secure causal inferences.

Evaluative-Prescriptive Cognitions   Concerns with parents' evaluative-prescriptive cognitions have traditionally focused on individual differences in their values, goals, or concerns (see Dix 1992). As a new direction within this long-standing area of interest, Gottman and his colleagues have focused attention on parents' beliefs about their own and their children's emotions (e.g. Gottman et al 1996). Such cognitions of parents and children may assume particular importance as sources of influence on children's responses to family conflict. For example, Katz & Gottman (1997) demonstrated that parents' "meta-emotion philosophy" (positive, differentiated awareness of own emotions and those of children) may buffer children against the negative effects of marital distress or dissolution.

Research has also examined the cross-generational transmission of these family-relevant, evaluative-prescriptive cognitions (e.g. what is valued, the ways in which things "should" be done). Such transmission may involve a variety of mediating processes. As an obvious route, children's cognitions may be shaped by direct tuitional processes. That is, parents, teachers, or other societal representatives guide the ideas as well as the actions of the young. Parents (and siblings) communicate their ideas about family life by a variety of means. They may influence children's cognitions through their conversation (Dunn 1996), proverbs (Palacios 1996b), guided recollections of past events (Fivush 1994), or guided plans for future activity (Rogoff 1991). At older ages, children's evaluative-prescriptive cognitions are likely to be increasingly influenced by children's groups (Harris 1995). For example, values regarding style of speech and play are perpetuated within peer cultures (e.g. Corsaro & Eder 1990, Opie & Opie 1969, Zukow 1989).

Self-Efficacy Cognitions   Research concerned with self-efficacy cognitions in the family has focused on parents, much of it drawing on general social learning ideas of efficacy (Bandura 1989). Primary attention has been given to the relationship between parents' stable perceptions of their own efficacy in the parenting role and their parenting styles. Several studies have linked feelings of parenting self-efficacy to elements of both parenting behavior and child outcomes (e.g. Coleman & Karraker 1997, Johnston & Mash 1989). For example, Bondy & Mash (1997) demonstrated that parents who are low in parenting self-efficacy are more likely to use a coercive disciplinary style than are parents who are high in self-efficacy. A relationship between parenting self-efficacy and parenting behavior has also been found in early relationships between mothers and infants. In a sample that included clinically depressed mothers, low maternal self-efficacy predicted low observed maternal competence even after depression and infant temperament were statistically controlled (Teti & Gelfand 1991). Parental feelings of efficacy appear to have their origins in actual experiences as a parent (e.g. Mash & Johnston 1983), as well as childhood experiences and the cultural and social context (Grusec et al 1994).

Linkages Across Cognitions   Beyond the links between specific types of cognitions and family outcomes, several recent studies have explored the additive and interactive effects associated with multiple types of parental cognitions. For example, Mize, Pettit, & Brown (1995) conducted research that explored the interactive influences of parenting knowledge and causal beliefs. Knowledge of socialization strategies proved to be a significant predictor of the quality of parents' supervision of children's peer play only when parents believed that social skills were both modifiable and important. As another type of bridge across cognitive constructs, Grusec & Mammone (1995) demonstrated that mothers with an insecure attachment history (as measured by the Adult Attachment Interview) were found to hold more power-oriented conceptions of parent-child interactions. That is, insecurely attached women described themselves as having exceptionally high or exceptionally low power, relative to children. Such findings highlight the importance of considering the differential contributions of different types of cognitions to the parenting process.

As still a different type of linkage, some research has been concerned with the combined effects of schematic cognitions and event-dependent cognitions. For example, Milner & Foody (1994) reported that adults at risk for child abuse did not use mitigating situational information to change their attributions for child misbehavior, whereas low-risk adults did. This suggests that the ability to incorporate multiple sources of causal information and the willingness to consider nonchild causes may be important aspects of attributions that are related to the likelihood of abusive parenting behavior. It also suggests the possible stability and inflexibility of negative social cognitions (Malle & Horowitz 1995).

Schematic Cognitions as Moderators

In addition to views of schematic cognitions as linear links, such cognitions may also be understood as moderators within family relationships. From this perspective, cognitions are viewed as providing individual differences of an if-then or conditional nature (Mischel & Shoda 1995), and they act as guides to differential response patterns in different contexts. In particular, explanatory cognitions are likely to be called into play in family settings that pose a source of difficulty or uncertainty (Bugental et al 1999a, Dix et al 1990, Strassberg 1995).

In testing moderating relationships, there has been a particular interest in the role of control attributions as qualifiers of reactions to family-relevant events. However, research programs have differed in the extent to which they have focused on the individual's attributions regarding his or her own control, the control attributed to children, or the balance of control (or power) between parents and children.

Self-Perceived Control   Research conducted within a learned helplessness framework has typically focused on family members' perceptions of their own level of control. Thus, sources of family stress are expected to have negative affective sequelae to the extent that they are interpreted as uncontrollable by self. Donovan and her colleagues have studied the role of mothers' control perceptions as moderators of their reactions to infant cries. They asked mothers to assess their ability to terminate infant cries in a laboratory-simulated child-care task (Donovan & Leavitt 1989, Donovan et al 1990). That is, mothers' control perceptions were explored as moderators of their differing responses to an aversive family-relevant event. Women with an illusory sense of control (who reported a high ability to terminate infant cries) showed a pattern of learned helplessness in their subsequent reactions to infant cries. When confronted with cries that they could not terminate, they showed a pattern of defensive arousal. Whereas other mothers showed increasing attention to impending infant cries (as reflected in decreased heart rate), mothers with an illusory sense of control demonstrated heart rate acceleration, a response pattern that is consistent with aversive conditioning. In addition, mothers who showed an illusory sense of control also revealed depressed affect. In a second experimental paradigm (Donovan et al 1997), mothers who differed in perceptions of control (realistic versus illusory) were exposed to different types of infant cries. Infant cries were varied in fundamental frequency, variations that are consistent with the cries of difficult versus easy infants. Women with an illusory sense of control showed deficits in their ability to distinguish between the different types of infant cries.

Relatively little attention has been given to children's attributions as moderators within family relationships. As an exception, Kerig (1998) demonstrated that children's cognitions may also serve to moderate the effects of interparental conflict. However, the nature of these effects were found to differ as a function of child gender. Whereas boys with high perceived control over parental conflict (illusory beliefs) were less likely to show externalizing problems, girls who held the (illusory) belief that they could control parents' quarrels were more likely to demonstrate internalizing problems. As a second exception, Granger et al (1994) observed neuroendocrine changes in clinic-referred children in response to a stressful interaction with mothers—as moderated by children's control-relevant beliefs. Children's salivary cortisol levels were measured before and after engaging in a conflictual discussion. Those children who showed low levels of perceived control over social outcomes responded with high levels of cortisol reactivity. Research of this type suggests that control cognitions may be important moderators of children's, as well as parents', reactions in family interactions.

Control Attributed to Others   Other researchers have turned their attention to the presumed control (or blame) assigned to children as a moderator of parental reactions to "difficult" child behavior. For example, Power et al (1990) demonstrated that mothers who interpreted infants' difficult behavior at 6 weeks of age as due to resistance/disinterest were more likely than other mothers to see infants as unpredictable and willful 3 months later. Sacco & Murray (1997) provided evidence supporting a different type of moderator pattern reflecting attributions to children. Mothers who held negative trait conceptions of their children were found to be particularly likely to show relationship dissatisfaction if they interpreted these traits as dispositional (internal, stable, controllable, global) in nature.

Balance of Control or Power   Another line of work has focused on parents' perceived balance of control as a moderator of family-related interactions. Parents who attribute greater control or power to children than to self (over negative events) have been found to be exceptionally (and negatively) reactive to caregiving challenge (Bugental 1992). Whether assessed on the basis of attributions for hypothetical events (as measured by the Parent Attribution Test) (Bugental et al 1989) or their spoken attributions (as coded by the Leeds Attributional Coding System) (Stratton et al 1988), parents who attribute disproportional power or control to children have been found to be at elevated risk for a variety of negative parenting outcomes (Bugental et al 1989, Silvester et al 1995).

When confronted with potential challenge (in particular if that challenge is ambiguous), adults with a low perceived balance of power show a sequence of responses that act to foster and maintain coercive interactions. The response pattern of "powerless" parents (mothers or fathers) begins with exceptionally fast retrieval of negatively biased ideation (thoughts of children as more powerful than self) (Bugental et al 1997). They subsequently demonstrate response patterns that reflect conflicted efforts to defend against perceived threat. Although they show submissive nonverbal behavior (Bugental et al 1996), they also show responses that reflect an apparent motivation to regain control. For example, they show (*a*) increases in autonomic arousal (Bugental et al 1993), (*b*) increases in negative affect (Bugental et al 1993; E Katsurada & AI Sugawara unpublished data), (*c*) decreases in use of positive control tactics (Bugental et al 1993), (*d*) increases in verbal derogation of children (Bugental & Happaney 1999), and (*e*) increases in use of physical force when giving punishment (Bradley & Peters 1991; Bugental et al 1999a). Children, in turn, respond to the inconsistent communication style of low-power adults with attentional avoidance (Bugental et al 1999).

Mills (1998) provided an extended understanding of the responses of "powerless" parents to variations in eliciting conditions. She found that mothers with low perceived power (as measured by the Parent Attribution Test) responded to increasing levels of fearfulness among their very young children with increasing levels of control. She suggested that child fearfulness acts as a signal to parents that the child has a power disadvantage, a circumstance that triggers paradoxical increases in levels of parental control. This mirrors Bugental & Lewis' (1998) finding that "powerless" parents show increases in vocal assertion when given a power advantage in their interactions with difficult children.

As a second extension of this line of work, Lovejoy et al (1996) demonstrated that "powerless" mothers (as measured by the Parent Attribution Test) show deficits both in their ability to (*a*) respond differentially to child characteristics and (*b*) distinguish perceptually among types of disruptive behavior shown by children. The limitations in the ability of powerless parents to adaptively respond to differences in child behavior is consistent with suggestions that coercive parents may be overly reliant on schematic cognitions and fail to use event-dependent levels of processing to draw distinctions among child-rearing situations or contexts (Korzilius et al 1999).

FAMILY-RELEVANT EVENTS AND CHARACTERISTICS, AND THEIR LINKS TO EVENT-DEPENDENT COGNITIONS

Complementing research beginning with the cognitions of individual family members, a second body of research has focused on the characteristics of children, families, and contexts and asked the implications of these factors for parental cognitions (e.g. attributions, appraisals, goals). In doing so, attention turns to the origins and functioning of relatively aware, explicit, event-dependent cognitions. Here concerns have more typically focused on variations in cognitions across partners and contexts—rather than to stable differences in cognitions across individuals. From this perspective, researchers have explored the ways in which cognitions operate—on an on-line basis—as organizers of family interactions. The quality and complexity of parents' reasoning about child-rearing events influence the success with which associated challenges are met (Dekovic et al 1991, Forgatch & DeGarmo 1997, Hansen et al 1995).

Children's Behavior and Characteristics Linked to Parental Cognitions

Response to Ownness   Research that follows this perspective has primarily been concerned with the relationship between parental cognitions and their experiences with their own children. The "ownness" of the child, perhaps because of the biological bond between parent and child (Bowlby 1980), appears to exert an affectively positive bias on parental cognitions (e.g. Kendziora & O'Leary 1998). Grusec & colleagues (1994) suggest that parents' experiences with their own children may have a greater impact at the level of specific cognitions (e.g. sense of parenting efficacy in managing a particular child), rather than global parental beliefs (e.g. belief in the value of education).

Response to Problematic Behavior   As has been noted in previous reviews (e.g. Joiner & Wagner 1996, Miller 1995), the preponderance of research on this general topic has been concerned with the relationship between parental cognitions and negative or problematic child behaviors. For example, there has been a continuing interest in the relationship between social cognitions (of parents and children) and children's internalizing problems (e.g. shyness, depression), children's externalizing problems (e.g. aggression, oppositional-defiant behavior, attention deficit hyperactivity disorder), and generalized problems of adaptation to changing life events.

The majority of this work has focused on the associations between aggressive or externalizing problems in children and parents' analytical cognitions. Across numerous studies (e.g. Baden & Howe 1992, Bickett et al 1996, Geller & Johnston 1995), relationships have been demonstrated between level of child aggression and the likelihood of parents' seeing child misbehavior as caused by factors that are stable, global, and internal to the child. As one example of this work, Strassberg (1995) found that mothers of behavior problem children were more likely than other mothers to attribute defiant intent to children in videotaped scenes that depicted ambiguous cues regarding child behavior. In a later study, Strassberg (1997) extended these findings and noted that mothers of aggressive and nonaggressive boys showed consistent differences in attributional processes but showed no such differences in their descriptive judgments, which suggests the special significance of analytical or inferential cognitions.

Investigators (Johnston & Freeman 1997, Johnston & Patenaude 1994, Johnston et al 1998) have extended this line of research by examining parent attributions specifically within families of children with attention deficit hyperactivity disorder (ADHD). In this research, parent attributions are examined in association with aspects of child misbehavior that may vary in their etiologies. Across a variety of assessment methods, parents of children with ADHD adopt a disease-model pattern of attributions, both for behaviors symptomatic of ADHD (e.g. inattention) and for oppositional behaviors. That is, in comparison to parents of non-problem children, parents of ADHD children see both types of misbehavior as more internally caused and stable but less controllable by the child. They also hold a more pessimistic view of positive child behaviors, seeing these as less dispositional and less durable. Finally, these parents also take less personal responsibility for their children's behavior than do parents of non-problem children. The experience of parenting a child with ADHD appears to have altered the analyses these parents offer regarding the causes of child behavior, and to have generally lowered the degree to which they see either themselves or their children as able to impact the child's problems.

Event-Dependent Cognitions as Contextually Organized

Event-dependent parental cognitions may also be viewed as qualified by relevant contextual features. From this standpoint, the potential effects of child behavior on adult cognitions are moderated by contextual factors (e.g. the parents' immediate mood state, the capabilities of the child, the goals that govern a particular interaction, the presence of change or transition).

Parental States   Dix has been a major voice calling attention to parents' changing interpretations of children's behavior in response to individual parents' own changing emotional states (Dix 1991). That is, as parents' negative mood increases, so does their tendency to provide a negative interpretation of children's behavior (Dix et al 1990, Geller & Johnston 1995, Krech & Johnston 1992). According to Dix and his colleagues, when parents' mood is negative (or if they have a general readiness to assign blame), they are more likely to interpret children's negative actions as dispositional, intentional and blameworthy; and these biased interpretations, in turn, increase the probability that parents will react with more negative affect and that they will make use of more power-assertive disciplinary strategies (Dix 1993). Also supporting this view, Smith & O'Leary (1995) found that when mothers watched videotapes of child negative affect, mothers' child-blaming attributions and their own negative arousal served as predictors of harsher parenting responses. The authors suggest that dysfunctional parental attributions and emotional arousal work in concert to maintain inappropriate parenting behaviors.

Capabilities of Children   Research concerned with differences in parental cognitions for children of different ages does not reveal an entirely clear picture. Although Dix et al (1986) found that parents see older children's actions as more intentional and controllable than those of younger children, Zeedyk (1997) found, among mothers of first-born children, that mothers of younger infants perceived more intentionality in children compared with mothers of older infants. Others have found general patterns of stability in parental cognitions across child development, with some qualifications involving complex interactions between child age and gender (e.g. Cote & Azar 1997, Mills & Rubin 1992). For example, Mills & Rubin (1992) found (in a longitudinal investigation) that mothers became increasingly negative about aggression in girls but decreasingly negative about aggression in boys.

Goals or Domains   It has also been suggested that parents may respond differently to children based upon their currently activated goal state (Dix 1992, Hastings & Grusec 1998). Beginning with the seminal work of Kuczynski (1984), there has been increasing interest in the role of parental goals as contextually based. Indeed, Smetana (1994a) points out that parenting goals are most likely to be predictive when they are considered as situationally dependent, rather than as trait characteristics. Research conducted by Hastings & Grusec (1998) has addressed the issue of the influence of parental goals on parental practices, as mediated by on-line appraisals and affective processes. In their study of parent-child interactions, parents who were focused on their own goals showed more negative affect and more controlling, punitive control strategies than did parents who were focused on child-centered or relationship-centered goals. Support was also found for the role of attributions (the perception of children's misbehavior as intentional and dispositional) as mediators of the link between parental goals and parental practices.

From a different perspective, it has been suggested that cognitions may be organized in terms of social domains—domains that vary in their motivational and cognitive features (Fiske 1992). Integrating an evolutionary and a cross-cultural perspective, Fiske suggested that—across time and culture—social life is cognitively represented in distinctive ways. Bugental & Goodnow (1998) have suggested that a similar conceptualization can be applied to socialization domains. They proposed that socialization may be regulated and cognitively represented in distinctive ways when it is organized in the service of the following: the attachment domain (proximity-seeking and safety-maintenance of related young), the social exchange domain (reciprocity and negotiation between functional equals), the hierarchical domain (power-based negotiation between those with unequal resources or control), and the group domain (influence based upon shared social identity and common interests).

Change or Transition   On-line cognitive appraisal processes are more likely to occur in families during periods of change, disequilibrium, or transition than during more static periods. As a classic example, parental cognitive appraisal activity escalates in response to the birth (or the anticipated birth) of a first child (Levy-Shiff et al 1998). The outcome of such cognitive activity may, in turn, influence long-term family outcomes. Thus, those parents who prenatally viewed the experience of parenting as a "challenge" or controllable were found to be more likely to experience positive adjustment outcomes than were those who viewed it as a "threat" or less controllable. In addition, prenatal cognitive appraisals of parenting served as significant predictors of infant developmental outcomes at age 1 year.

During periods of transition, disequilibrium, or change, parents are also more likely to make use of extra-familial social networks as (a) an additional source of explanation about caregiving events and (b) a potential buffer against—or exacerbation of—stress. This interaction with social networks may result in modifications in parents' own cognitive activity and the nature of their interpretations of parenting. The unavailability of such networks may, in turn, foster self-generated attributional activity. Thus, Melson et al (1993) observed that mothers who described themselves as having few people who supported them in their parenting role were more likely to show high spontaneous attributional activity (i.e. they selected a relatively large number of potential causes of "difficulty" in facilitating their child's social development).

Work in clinical contexts also supports a role for cognitions during times of change. For example, parental cognitions regarding the causes of child behavior problems may influence their receptivity to interventions. Reimers et al (1995) found that when parents attributed their children's behavior problems to physical causes, they were less accepting of involvement in behavioral treatments. Cross-cultural research also suggests moderating pathways that influence family receptivity to remediation. Weisz and colleagues have conducted several studies considering the influence of cultural context on adults' perceptions of children's problems, and on the likelihood that these problems will be referred for mental health services (e.g. Weisz et al 1997, Weisz & Weiss 1991). Finally, cognitions themselves may be targeted for retraining activities during periods of change (e.g. prebirth, adolescence). For example, cognitive retraining has been included as a component within programs directed to preventing child maltreatment at key points in the life course of at-risk populations (Wekerle & Wolfe 1998; Bugental 1999).

FAMILY COGNITIONS AS INTERDEPENDENT OR JOINT CONSTRUCTIONS

In contrast with research focusing on the cognitions of individual family members, family cognitions may also be understood as created and altered by a dyadic or group process that occurs within the family. Kenny (1996), in proposing methods of analyzing such processes, suggested that dyadic (or other group) processes may be understood as involving (a) partner effects (reciprocal or interdependent influences), (b) mutual influences, or (c) the influences of shared fate. Each of these processes has been reflected in the theoretical as well as the empirical framing of research questions. As this approach to family cognitions as group processes and joint constructions involves a large literature that bridges disciplines, we only present representative research.

Interdependent Influences

A long tradition in studying processes within the family has made use of reciprocal effects or interdependence models. That is, the cognitions held by each individual in the family influence the cognitions held by all other family members, a partner effect. Such notions are consistent with Kelley's interdependence theory (Kelley 1979). Cook (1993) applied a social relations model (Kenny & La Voie 1984) to cognitive processes within the family. Specifically, he assessed the interdependence of family members' beliefs about their ability to influence each other. The three dimensions identified for study were effectance (i.e. feelings of own effective influence within the relationship), acquiescence (the belief that one is influenced by the other person), and fate (belief that the relationship is controlled by fate). In the terms used here, he was concerned with both analytical and efficacy cognitions. His analysis revealed that the cognitions of individual family members are dependent on the characteristics of their partners and the relationship. This approach is consistent with our previous discussion of individual cognitions within those research programs that give consideration to reciprocal influences between parents and children.

Mutual Influences

Cognitions in the family have also been thought of as developing as a function of mutual coconstruction, collaboration, negotiation, and conflict. Such activities may either reflect family processes or broader processes within the culture as a whole. A number of investigators have focused on the mutual constructions of cognitions (in particular social and moral knowledge) within the family. For example, Smetana (1997) has proposed that reciprocal interactions between parents and children (and among children) provide the collaborative basis for the creation of shared knowledge. Parents and children regularly agree that moral and conventional decisions appropriately fall within the authority of parents. They also agree that personal decisions fall within the jurisdiction of children themselves. Conflicts are likely to emerge in connection with boundary issues, however. For example, decisions that parents may interpret as involving prudential issues and thus falling within their jurisdiction (e.g. children's activities with friends) may be understood as involving personal decisions by the young (Smetana & Asquith 1994).

In addition to reflecting differences in the underlying cognitions of family members, conflict within the family may also indicate a uniformity in members' negative, conflict-promoting cognitions. For example, Grace et al (1993) found that parent-adolescent conflict was associated with the beliefs of both parents and adolescents that the negative actions of the other were intentional, blameworthy, and selfishly motivated. Such similarities in parent and adolescent analytic cognitions may well contribute to a vicious cycle of conflict, which confirms and strengthens the negative attributions.

Alternatively, some types and levels of conflict may reflect reasonable disagreements between parents and the young (Goodnow 1994). Goodnow has challenged the usual view of disagreements as a problem and substituted the notion of disagreements as normative. From this standpoint, interest then turns to an understanding of the means by which agreement is reached and the circumstances under which disagreements are a source of concern. In order to understand such processes, she has proposed that greater attention should be given to parents' goals and intentions and argues that only within such a framework is it possible to understand the significance of cross-generational agreement and disagreement. As a specific example, Goodnow (1996) has explored the ways in which negotiation of household tasks forms the basis for ideas of responsibility and the expected nature of relationships between family members. It is, of course, important to recognize the conditions under which parent-child conflict is adaptive (e.g.. the relatively mild disagreements that occur in well-functioning families) versus the conditions under which it may be more problematic (e.g. the types of disagreements that occur between depressed mothers and their children [Hay et al 1998]).

Researchers whose work is embedded within a cultural psychology tradition have been concerned with the local character of cognitions; that is, they focus on intracultural processes. For example, Palacios (1996a) has been concerned with the heterogeneity of parental ideas within a single country (Spain). From this perspective, cognitions are mutually (but differentially) constructed within different segments of the population. Palacios identified three different systems of ideas about parenting: traditional (focused on the fixed nature of human characteristics), modern (focused on the malleable nature of human characteristics), and paradoxical (an inconsistent mixture of traditional and modern beliefs that reflects families' combined exposure to traditional village beliefs and to views acquired in formal schooling or from medical/educational experts). These ideas (strongly linked to educational differences) were widely observed and were transmitted and maintained across generations.

Valsiner et al (1997) have been major advocates of a coconstructionist position in understanding cognitions in families. The notion of coconstruction references the mutual and complementary construction of personal and collective cultures. As stated by them, "cultural messages are actively communicated (by parents) and equally actively reassembled by their recipient children, who are joint constructors of the new cultural knowledge through their constructive internalization/ externalization processes. Each new generation proceeds beyond the preceding generation, as it transforms the cultural system" (Valsiner et al 1997:284). Goal orientations are understood as resulting from continuous co-construction processes, and as leading to reorganization of belief orientations. Such belief orientations may then serve as guides to parent and child actions. From this framework, relevant research questions include those that consider the dynamic and emergent nature of the continuous coconstructions of beliefs and their selective links to action, for example, the extent to which coherent co-constructions predict effective family functioning. Recent research concerned with the narrative co-constructions of parents and children about family life issues (e.g., Fiese et al 1999; Macfie et al 1999; Oppenheim et al 1997) exemplify this approach.

Common Fate

Cognitions in the family also reflect a variety of shared experiences. That is, cognitions may be similar because of the factors that have jointly influenced the cognitions of the collective, whether family or cultural group. In contrast to Palacios' (1996a) work on intracultural differences, research has also been conducted examining differences across cultures in parental cognitions, particularly with regard to caregiving tasks. For example, Bornstein & his colleagues (1998) conducted a cross-national study of the variations (and uniformities) in maternal cognitions within seven countries. Primiparous mothers were asked to assess their own competence, satisfaction, investment, and role balance within the parenting relationship; in addition, they were asked for their attributions regarding the causes of success and failure on different parenting tasks. Across cultures, the strongest uniformities were found in mothers' attributions regarding the causes of caregiving failure (typically attributed to own level of ability, task difficulty, and child behavior); in general, success was more likely to be attributed to child behavior and mood. Mothers also shared high feelings of satisfaction. Although differences appeared across cultures, the similarities were also striking. As pointed out by Stevenson-Hinde (1998), variations within countries are typically as large or larger than variations across countries.

CONCLUSIONS AND DIRECTIONS FOR THE FUTURE

Subject Matter of Cognitive Constructs

The content of cognitive constructs has been described as differing in terms of a selective focus on description, analysis, evaluation or prescription, and efficacy. Within this literature, interest in descriptive cognitions has continued over the past 10 years—but in altered format from earlier concerns with individual parental beliefs and attitudes. The focus is now more on the ways in which family members perceive each other, often conceptualized in terms of working models of relationships or relationship schemas. Possibly the greatest amount of interest during the past 10 years has been with analytic cognitions—in particular family-related attributions. Attention has regularly been given to the attributional dimensions initially proposed within the learned helplessness literature, for example globality, stability, locus. In addition, measures have often included the dimension of controllability—typically a central dimension of importance for theoretical conceptions, as well as a subjectively important dimension for naive attributers. Across approaches, "conflict-promoting attributions" (e.g. attributions of blame and intent to others) have regularly been found both to follow from family problems and to foster family problems. Consistent with the history of interest in analytical cognitions (e.g. Alloy et al 1984), there has been a strong continuing concern with the relationship between causal attributions and psychopathology in the family.

Although interest in general child-rearing values and styles has declined, an emergent area of interest is that of parental goals. Parenting goals, representing desired outcomes for parent and/or child, are conceptualized as being relatively specific to the context of particular children and socialization tasks. Goals thus serve as a vehicle through which parents translate global parenting values into specific parenting actions, and as a mechanism for organizing these actions. Distinctions have been proposed in the types of parenting goals, including parent versus child focus and short-term versus long-term outcomes. Differences on these dimensions have been reliably associated with differences in parenting behaviors. In addition to their promise as predictors of parenting behavior, research has also suggested that goals are related to other forms of parent cognitions and may interact or act in concert with these other cognitions (e.g. attributions, self-efficacy) in influencing family outcomes.

Another thriving body of work has focused on parents' cognitions regarding their efficacy in the parenting role. Much of this research draws on more general social learning ideas of efficacy. A positive sense of efficacy as a parent has been related to positive elements in both parenting behavior and child outcomes, and it appears to develop out of actual experiences as a parent, as well as childhood experiences and the cultural and social context.

Given the clear differences in the "subject matter" of different types of cognitions, it should not be surprising to learn that there is low convergence across cognitive constructs (e.g. Bondy & Mash 1997, Lovejoy et al 1997) and high variability in the predictive value of different cognitive constructs (e.g. Mize et al 1995, Strassberg 1997). Greater recognition of these differences might, however, promote integrative research that assesses the influences of multiple types of cognitions. As an example, the social information-processing model used by Milner (1993) to describe abusive families incorporates perceptions, interpretations and expectations, response integration and selection, and monitoring as separate, but related, stages of parental cognitive processing.

Restricted Focus within the Family

Systematic biases were identified in terms of the family members who have been the focus of studies on family cognitions. There has been an historical focus on parental cognitions that continues in current research. Although there has been extensive work on children's causal cognitions in other domains [their relationships to peers (e.g. Dodge 1993), their achievement in the academic domain (e.g. Skinner et al 1998), and their health or medical problems (Compas et al 1991), there has been little systematic attention directed to their cognitions regarding parents and family-related events. More research is needed that includes an assessment of developmental changes in children's perceptions of the causal influences of both parent and child.

As a second constraint, little systematic attention has been given to gender effects. Although evidence reviewed here occasionally reported differences in the magnitude of effects for mothers versus fathers, no consistent patterns emerged, and often studies examined only mothers, precluding a comparison of mother versus father cognitions.

As a general restriction, there has been a focus on the cognitions of family members regarding either their own individual outcomes or the individual outcomes of their children. It is time to move on to consider family members' cognitions concerning the joint contributions of self and others to their shared outcomes and relationships.

Theoretical and Methodological Issues

A general failure to consider the theoretical underpinnings of cognitive constructs has led to limitations in the inferences that can be drawn from empirical findings. For example, the increasing awareness and elucidation of implicit versus explicit cognitive processes in other fields has not been matched with equivalent refinements in developmental research (see Brainerd et al 1998). Despite the general move we have seen toward an interest in implicit social cognitions (e.g. Greenwald & Banaji 1995), the preponderance of work on family cognitions remains tied to a focus on explicit cognitions. That is, the majority of work in this field makes the assumption that such processes operate in a conscious mode. Cognitions are, in turn, regularly assessed with direct, self-report measures that presume accurate introspection (and immunity from self-presentation artifacts). Efforts are needed to find ways to measure family cognitions as implicit processes in order to understand better their subtle, unaware influences on affect and behavior (see Bugental et al 1998).

At the same time, it is also essential to consider the relationships that exist among the multiple types and levels of family cognitions. The on-line functioning of cognitions may best be thought of as reflecting an active, evolving interplay between event-dependent cognitions (e.g. perceived successes or failures) and schematic cognitions (e.g. expected success or failure). Indeed, it may be that the ability of these two levels of cognition to be mutually influential is one marker of adaptive parenting. For example, although a stable sense of efficacy or perceived control may carry the parent through transitory periods of parenting difficulty, sensitivity to and ability to change adaptively in response to shifting contexts serves to optimize family relationships.

A major methodological (as well as conceptual) issue concerns the assessment of directions of effects among cognitions, behaviors, and affects in the family, and the nature of the processes mediating these relationships. The most common mode of research has been to take a one-time snapshot picture of one or perhaps two of these elements of family functioning. Although such research has proven useful, its cross-sectional nature and selective focus on one or two aspects of functioning result in inferential uncertainty. Such problems are compounded when reliance is placed exclusively on self-report—creating problems of shared method variance. The conditional and complex nature of the relationships among family cognitions, emotions, and behaviors must be tested through longitudinal designs that permit inferences regarding long-term effects, or by experimental paradigms in which key factors within relationships are systematically varied. Although the number of studies that allow such inferences is increasing, there is a continuing need for such designs.

Finally, the role of variables that may influence the cognitions of both parents and children needs to be given greater consideration. Some consideration has been given to cultural factors in this regard (Weisz et al 1997). However, the possibility of shared genetic influences are rarely considered—despite emerging evidence for genetic influences on perceptions of parenting (e.g. Neiderhiser et al 1998), as well as shared effects on parenting practices and outcomes of parenting.

Implications for Remediation

Throughout this review and elsewhere, we have pointed out the importance of considering the role of cognitions in the design of programs directed to remediating and preventing family problems (Johnston 1996; Bugental 1999). An understanding of cognitive contributions to dysfunction represents one step within this process. At another level, the cognitions of family members have been shown to influence their receptivity to different types of programs. Finally, the problematic cognitions of family members (e.g. hostile attributional biases, blame-oriented cognitions, perceived powerlessness) are themselves the appropriate targets of remedial efforts and prevention programs.

Visit the Annual Reviews home page at www.AnnualReviews.org.

LITERATURE CITED

Alloy LB, Peterson C, Abramson LY, Seligman MEP. 1984. Attributional style and the generality of learned helplessness. *J. Pers. Soc. Psychol.* 46:681–87

Andersen SM, Glassman NS. 1996. Responding to significant others when they are not there: effects on interpersonal inference, motivation, and affect. In *Handbook of Motivation and Cognition.* Vol. 3. *The Interpersonal Context,* ed. RM Sorrentino, ET Higgins, pp. 262–321. New York: Guilford. 646 pp.

Baden AD, Howe GW. 1992. Mothers' attributions and expectancies regarding their conduct-disordered children. *J. Abnorm. Child Psychol.* 20:467–86

Baldwin MW. 1992. Relational schemas and the processing of social information. *Psychol. Bull.* 112:461–84

Bandura A. 1989. Regulation of cognitive processes through perceived self-efficacy. *Dev. Psychol.* 25:729–35

Bargh JA, Chen M, Burrows L. 1996. Automaticity of social behavior: direct effects of trait construction and stereotype activation on action. *J. Pers. Soc. Psychol.* 71:230–44

Bickett LR, Milich R, Brown RT. 1996. Attributional styles of aggressive boys and their mothers. *J. Abnorm. Child Psychol.* 24:457–72

Bondy EM, Mash EJ. 1997. *Parenting efficacy, perceived control over caregiving failure, and mothers' reactions to preschool children's misbehavior.* Presented at Bienn. Meet. Soc. Res. Child Dev., Washington, DC

Bornstein MH, Haynes OM, Azuma H, Galperin C, Maital S, et al. 1998. A cross-national study of self-evaluations and attributions in parenting: Argentina, Belgium, France, Israel, Italy, Japan, and the United States. *Dev. Psychol.* 34:662–76

Bowlby J. 1980. *Attachment and Loss.* Vol. 3. *Loss.* New York: Basic Books. 462 pp.

Bradley EJ, Peters RD. 1991. Physically abusive and nonabusive mothers' perceptions of parenting and child behavior. *Am. J. Orthopsychiatr.* 61:455–60

Brainerd CJ, Stein LM, Reyna VF. 1998. On the development of conscious and unconscious memory. *Dev. Psychol.* 34:342–57

Bretherton I. 1995. Attachment theory and developmental psychopathology. Emotion, cognition, and representation. In *Rochester Symp. Dev. Psychopathol.,* ed. D Cicchetti, SL Toth, 6:231–60. Rochester, NY: Univ. Rochester Press. 437 pp.

Brody GH, Arias I, Fincham FD. 1996. Linking marital and child attributions to family processes and parent-child relationships. *J. Fam. Psychol.* 10:408–21

Bugental DB. 1992. Affective and cognitive processes within threat-oriented family systems. See Sigel et al 1992, pp. 219–48

Bugental DB. 1999. *Power-oriented cognitions as predictors of family violence.* Presented at Meet. Soc. Exp. Soc. Psychol., St. Louis, MO

Bugental DB, Blue J, Cortez V, Fleck K, Kopeikin H, et al. 1993. Social cognitions as organizers of autonomic and affective responses to social challenge. *J. Pers. Soc. Psychol.* 64:94–103

Bugental DB, Blue J, Cruzcosa M. 1989. Perceived control over caregiving outcomes: implications for child abuse. *Dev. Psychol.* 25:532–39

Bugental DB, Brown M, Reiss C. 1996. Cognitive representations of power in caregiving relationships: biasing effects on interpersonal interaction and information processing. *J. Fam. Psychol.* 10:397–407

Bugental DB, Goodnow JJ. 1998. Socialization processes. In *Handbook of Child Psychology.* Vol. 3. *Social, Emotional, and Personality Development,* ed. W Damon, N Eisenberg, pp. 389–462. New York: Wiley. 1208 pp. 5th ed.

Bugental DB, Happaney KH. 1999. Parent-child interaction as a power contest. *J. Appl. Dev. Psychol.* In press

Bugental DB, Johnston C, New M, Silvester J. 1998. Measuring parental attributions: conceptual and methodological issues. *J. Fam. Psychol.* 12:459–80

Bugental DB, Lewis J. 1998. Interpersonal power repair in response to threats to control from dependent others. In *Personal Control in Action: Cognitive and Motivational Mechanisms,* ed. M Kofta, G Weary, G Sedek, pp. 341–62. New York: Plenum. 459 pp.

Bugental DB, Lewis JC, Lin E, Lyon J, Kopeikin H. 1999a. In charge but not in control: The management of teaching relationships by adults with low perceived power. *Dev Psychol.* In press

Bugental DB, Lyon JE, Krantz J, Cortez V. 1997. Who's the boss? Differential accessibility of dominance ideation in parent-child relationships. *J. Pers. Soc. Psychol.* 72:1297–309

Bugental DB, Lyon JE, Lin E, McGrath EG, Bimbela A. 1999b. Children "tune out" in response to the ambiguous communication style of powerless parents. *Child Dev.* 70:214–30

Bugental DB, Martorell G. 1999. Competition between friends: the joint influence of self, friends, and parents. *J. Fam. Psychol.* 13:1–14

Burks VS, Parke RD. 1996. Parent and child representations of social relationships: linkages between families and peers. *Merrill-Palmer Q.* 42:358–78

Carton JS, Carton EER. 1998. Nonverbal maternal warmth and children's locus of control of reinforcement. *J. Nonverbal Behav.* 22:77–86

Carton JS, Nowicki S Jr, Balser GM. 1996. An observational study of antecedents of locus of control of reinforcement. *Int. J. Behav. Dev.* 19:161–75

Cassidy J, Kirsh SJ, Scolton KL, Parke RD. 1996. Attachment and representations of peer relationships. *Dev. Psychol.* 32:892–904

Cohn DA, Cowan PA, Cowan CP, Pearson J. 1992. Mothers' and fathers' working models of childhood attachment relationships, parenting styles, and child behavior. *Dev. Psychopathol.* 4:417–31

Coleman PK, Karraker KH. 1997. Self-efficacy and parenting quality: findings and future applications. *Dev. Rev.* 18:47–85

Compas BE, Banez GA, Malcarne V, Worsham N. 1991. Perceived control and coping with stress: a developmental perspective. *J. Soc. Issues* 47:23–34

Cook WL. 1993. Interdependence and the interpersonal sense of control: an analysis of family relationships. *J. Pers. Soc. Psychol.* 64:587–601

Corsaro WA, Eder D. 1990. Children's peer cultures. *Annu. Rev. Sociol.* 16:197–220

Cote LR, Azar ST. 1997. Child age, parent and child gender, and domain differences in parents' attributions and responses to children's outcomes. *Sex Roles* 36:23–50

Crowell JA, O'Connor E, Wollmers G, Sprafkin J, Rao U. 1991. Mothers' conceptualizations of parent-child relationships: relation to mother-child interaction and child behavior problems. *Dev. Psychopathol.* 3:431–44

Dekovic M, Gerris JRM, Janssens JMAM. 1991. Parental cognitions, parental behavior, and the child's understanding of the parent-child relationship. *Merrill-Palmer Q.* 37:523–41

Dix T. 1991. The affective organization or parenting: adaptive and maladaptive processes. *Psychol. Bull.* 110:3–25

Dix T. 1992. Parenting on behalf of the child: empathic goals in the regulation of responsive parenting. See Sigel et al 1992, pp. 319–46

Dix T. 1993. Attributing dispositions to children: an interactional analysis of attributions in socialization. *Pers. Soc. Psychol. Bull.* 19:633–43

Dix T, Reinhold DP, Zambarano RJ. 1990. Mothers' judgments in moments of anger. *Merrill-Palmer Q.* 36:465–86

Dix T, Ruble DN, Grusec JE, Nixon S. 1986. Social cognition in parents: inferential and affective reactions to children of three age levels. *Child Dev.* 57:879–94

Dodge KA. 1993. Social-cognitive mechanisms in the development of conduct disorder and depression. *Annu. Rev. Psychol.* 44:559–84

Donovan WL, Leavitt LA. 1989. Maternal self-efficacy and infant attachment: integrating physiology, perceptions, and behavior. *Child Dev.* 60:460–72

Donovan WL, Leavitt LA, Walsh RO. 1990. Maternal self-efficacy: illusory control and its effect on susceptibility to learned helplessness. *Child Dev.* 61:1638–47

Donovan WL, Leavitt LA, Walsh RO. 1997. Cognitive set and coping strategy affect mothers' sensitivity to infant cries: a signal detection approach. *Child Dev.* 68:760–72

Dunn J. 1996. Family conversations and the development of social understanding. In *Children, Research, and Policy: Essays for*

Barbara Tizard, ed. B Bernstein, J Brannen, pp. 81–95. Washington, DC: Taylor & Francis. 275 pp.

Fiese BH, Sameroff AJ, Grotevant HD, Wamboldt FS, Dickstein S, Fravel DL. 1999. The stories that families tell. *Monogr. Soc. Res. Child Dev.* 64(2):1–180

Fincham FD. 1998. Child development and marital relations. *Child Dev.* 69:543–74

Fincham FD, Beach SRH, Arias I, Brody GH. 1998. Children's attributions in the family: the Children's Relationship Attribution Measure. *J. Fam. Psychol.* 12:481–93

Fiske AP. 1992. The four elementary forms of sociality: framework for a unified theory of social relations. *Psychol. Rev.* 99:689–723

Fiske ST, Pavelchak MA. 1986. Category-based versus piecemeal-based affective responses: developments in schema-triggered affect. In *Handbook of Motivation and Cognition: Foundations of Social Behavior,* ed. RM Sorrentino, ET Higgins, pp. 167–203. New York: Guilford Press. 610 pp.

Fiske ST, Taylor SE. 1991. *Social Cognition.* New York: McGraw-Hill. 717 pp.

Fivush R. 1994. Constructing narrative, emotion, and self in parent-child conversations about the past. In *The Remembering Self: Construction and Accuracy in the Self-Narrative, Emory Symp. Cogn. 6,* ed. U Neisser, R Fivush, pp. 136–57. New York: Cambridge Univ. Press. 301 pp.

Forgatch MS, DeGarmo DS. 1997. Adults' problem solving: contributor to parenting and child outcomes in divorced families. *Soc. Dev.* 6:237–53

Fury G, Carlson EA, Sroufe LA. 1997. Children's representations of attachment relationships in family drawings. *Child Dev.* 68:1165–64

Geller J, Johnston C. 1995. Depressed mood and child conduct problems: relationships to mothers' attributions for their own and their children's experiences. *Child Fam. Behav. Ther.* 17:19–34

Gerris JRM, ed. 1999. *Dynamics of Parenting: Nature and Sources of Parenting in Child-hood and Adolescence.* Hillsdale, NJ: Erlbaum. In press

Goodnow JJ. 1994. Acceptable disagreement across generations. See Smetana 1994b, pp. 51–64

Goodnow JJ. 1996. From household practices to parents' ideas about work and interpersonal relationships. See Harkness & Super 1996, pp. 313–44

Gottman JM, Katz LF, Hooven D. 1996. Parental meta-emotion philosophy and the emotional life of families: theoretical models and preliminary data. *J. Fam. Psychol.* 10:243–68

Grace NC, Kelley ML, McCain AP. 1993. Attribution processes in mother-adolescent conflict. *J. Abnorm. Child Psychol.* 21:199–211

Granger DA, Weisz JR, Kauneckis D. 1994. Neuroendocrine reactivity, internalizing behavior problems, and control-related cognitions in clinic-referred children and adolescents. *J. Abnorm. Psychol.* 103:267–76

Greenwald AG, Banaji MR. 1995. Implicit social cognition: attitudes, self-esteem, and stereotypes. *Psychol. Rev.* 102:4–27

Grusec JE, Hastings P, Mammone N. 1994. Parenting cognitions and relationship schemas. See Smetana 1994b, pp. 5–19

Grusec JE, Kuczynski L, eds. 1997. *Parenting and Children's Internalization of Values: A Handbook of Contemporary Theory.* New York: Wiley. 439 pp.

Grusec JE, Mammone N. 1995. Features and sources of parents' attributions about themselves and their children. In *Review of Personality and Social Psychology,* ed. N Eisenberg, 15:49–73. Thousand Oaks, CA: Sage. 288 pp.

Grych JH, Fincham FD. 1993. Children's appraisals of marital conflict: initial investigations of the cognitive-contextual framework. *Child Dev.* 64:215–30

Hansen DJ, Pallota GM, Christopher JS, Conaway RL, Lundquist LM. 1995. The parental problem-solving measure: further evaluation with maltreating and nonmaltreating parents. *J. Fam. Violence* 10:319–36

Harkness S, Super CM, eds. 1996. *Parents' Cultural Belief Systems: Their Origins, Expressions and Consequences.* New York: Guilford. 558 pp.

Harris JR. 1995. Where is the child's environment? A group socialization theory of development. *Psychol. Rev.* 102:458–89

Hastings PD, Grusec JE. 1998. Parenting goals as organizers of responses to parent-child disagreement. *Dev. Psychol.* 34:465–79

Hay DF, Vespo JE, Zahn-Waxler C. 1998. Young children's quarrels with their siblings and mothers: Links with maternal depression and bipolar illness. *Br. J. Dev. Psychol.* 16:519–38.

Higgins ET, Fazio RH, Rohan MJ, Zanna MP, et al. 1998. From expectancies to world views: regulatory focus in socialization and cognition. In *Attribution and Social Interaction: The Legacy of Edward E. Jones,* ed. JM Darley, J Cooper, pp. 243–309. Washington, DC: Am. Psychol. Assoc. 550 pp.

Holden GW, Edwards LA. 1989. Parental attitudes toward child rearing: instruments, issues, and implications. *Psychol. Bull.* 106:29–58

Janssens JMAM. 1994. Authoritarian child rearing, parental locus of control, and the child's behaviour style. *Int. J. Behav. Dev.* 17:485–501

Johnston C. 1996. Addressing parent cognitions in interventions with families of disruptive children. In *Advances in Cognitive-Behavioral Therapy,* ed. KS Dobson, KD Craig, pp. 193–209. Thousand Oaks, CA: Sage. 305 pp.

Johnston C, Freeman W. 1997. Attributions for child behavior in parents of children without behavior disorders and children with attention deficit-hyperactivity disorder. *J. Consult. Clin. Psychol.* 65:636–45

Johnston C, Mash EJ. 1989. A measure of parenting satisfaction and efficacy. *J. Clin. Child Psychol.* 18:167–75

Johnston C, Patenaude R. 1994. Parent attributions for inattentive-overactive and oppositional-defiant child behaviors. *Cogn. Ther. Res.* 18:261–75

Johnston C, Reynolds S, Freeman WS, Geller J. 1998. Assessing parent attributions for child behavior using open-ended questions. *J. Clin. Child Psychol.* 27:87–97

Joiner TE Jr, Wagner KD. 1996. Parental, child-centered attributions and outcome: a meta-analytic review with conceptual and methodological implications. *J. Abnorm. Child Psychol.* 24:37–52

Katz LF, Gottman JM. 1997. Buffering children from marital conflict and dissolution. *J. Clin. Child Psychol.* 26:157–71

Kelley HH. 1967. Attribution theory in social psychology. *Nebr. Symp. Motiv.* 15:192–240

Kelley HH. 1979. *Personal Relationships: Their Structures and Processes.* Hillsdale, NJ: Erlbaum. 183 pp.

Kendziora KT, O'Leary SG. 1998. Appraisals of child behavior by mothers of problem and nonproblem toddlers. *J. Abnorm. Child Psychol.* 26:247–56

Kenny DA. 1996. Models of non-independence in dyadic research. *J. Soc. Pers. Relat.* 13:279–94

Kenny DA, La Voie L. 1984. The social relations model. *Adv. Exp. Soc. Psychol.* 18:141–82

Kerig PK. 1998. Moderators and mediators of the effects of interparental conflict on children's adjustment. *J. Abnorm. Child Psychol.* 26:199–212

Korzilius H, Gerris J, Felling A. 1999. Explorations of mental scripts of perceptions, cognitions, and emotions, explaining parenting behaviors. See Gerris 1999. In press

Krech KH, Johnston C. 1992. The relationship of depressed mood and life stress to maternal perceptions of child behavior. *J. Clin. Child Psychol.* 21:115–22

Kuczynski L. 1984. Socialization goals and mother-child interaction: strategies for long-term and short-term compliance. *Dev. Psychol.* 20:1061–73

Lazarus R, Folkman S. 1984. *Stress, Appraisal, and Coping.* New York: Springer. 445 pp.

Levy-Shiff R, Dimitrovsky L, Shulman S, Har-Even D. 1998. Cognitive appraisals, coping strategies, and support resources as correlates of parenting and infant development. *Dev. Psychol.* 34:1417–27

Lovejoy MC, Polewko J, Harrison B. 1996. Adult perceptions of interpersonal control and reactions to disruptive child behaviors. *Soc. Cogn.* 14:227–45

Lovejoy MC, Verda MR, Hays CE. 1997. Convergent and discriminant validity of measures of parenting efficacy and control. *J. Clin. Child Psychol.* 26:366–76

Macfie J, Toth SL, Rogosch FA, Robinson J, Emde RN. 1999. Effect of maltreatment on preschoolers' narrative representations of response to relieve distress and of role reversal. *Dev. Psychol.* 15:460–65

MacKinnon CE, Lamb ME, Belsky J, Baum C. 1990. An affective-cognitive model of mother-child aggression. *Dev. Psychopathol.* 2:1–13

MacKinnon-Lewis C, Lamb ME, Arbuckle B, Baradaran LP, Volling BL. 1992. The relationship between biased maternal and filial attributions and the aggressiveness of their interactions. *Dev. Psychopathol.* 4:403–15

MacKinnon-Lewis C, Volling BL, Lamb ME, Dechman K, Rabiner D, Curtner ME. 1994. A cross-contextual analysis of boys' social competence: from family to school. *Dev. Psychol.* 30:325–33

Malle BF, Horowitz LM. 1995. The puzzle of negative self-views: an explanation using the schema concept. *J. Pers. Soc. Psychol.* 68:470–84

Martin LL, Tesser A, eds. 1996. *Striving and Feeling: Interactions Among Goals, Affect, and Self-regulation.* Mahwah, NJ: Erlbaum. 408 pp.

Mash EJ, Johnston C. 1983. Parental perceptions of child behavior problems, parenting self-esteem, and mothers' reported stress in younger and older hyperactive and normal children. *J. Consult. Clin. Psychol.* 51:86–99

Melson GF, Ladd GW, Hsu H-C. 1993. Maternal social support networks, maternal cognitions, and young children's social and cognitive development. *Child Dev.* 64:1401–17

Miller SA. 1995. Parents' attributions for their children's behavior. *Child Dev.* 66:1557–84

Mills RS. 1998. Paradoxical relations between perceived power and maternal control. *Merrill-Palmer Q.* 44:523–37

Mills RS, Rubin KH. 1992. A longitudinal study of maternal beliefs about children's social behaviors. *Merrill-Palmer Q.* 38:494–512

Milner JS. 1993. Social information processing and physical child abuse. *Clin. Psychol. Rev.* 13:275–94

Milner JS, Foody R. 1994. The impact of mitigating information on attributions for positive and negative child behavior by adults at low- and high-risk for child-abusive behavior. *J. Soc. Clin. Psychol.* 13:335–51

Mischel W, Shoda Y. 1995. A cognitive-affective system theory of personality: reconceptualizing situations, dispositions, dynamics, and invariance in personality structure. *Psychol. Rev.* 102:246–68

Mize J, Pettit GS, Brown EG. 1995. Mothers' supervision of their children's peer play: relations with beliefs, perceptions and knowledge. *Dev. Psychol.* 31:311–21

Murphey DA. 1992. Constructing the child: relations between parents' beliefs and child outcomes. *Dev. Rev.* 12:199–232

Neiderhiser JM, Pike A, Hetherington EM, Reiss D. 1998. Adolescent perceptions as mediators of parenting: genetic and environmental contributions. *Dev. Psychol.* 34:1459–69

Nix RL, Pinderhughes EE, Dodge KA, Bates JE, Pettit GS. 1999. Do parents' hostile attribution tendencies function as self-fulfilling prophecies? An empirical examination of a theoretical sequence of aggressive transactions. *Child Dev.* 70:896–909

Opie J, Opie P. 1969. *Children's Games in Street and Playground.* London: Oxford University Press. 371 pp.

Oppenheim D, Nir A, Warren S, Emde RN. 1997. Emotion regulation in mother-child narrative co-construction: Association with children's narratives and adaptation. *Dev. Psychol.* 33:284–94.

Palacios J. 1996a. Parents' and adolescents' ideas on children, origins and transmission of intracultural diversity. See Harkness & Super 1996, pp. 215–53

Palacios J. 1996b. Proverbs as images of children and childrearing. In *Images of Childhood*, ed. CP Hwang, ME Lamb, IE Sigel, pp. 75–98. Mahwah, NJ: Erlbaum. 212 pp.

Parke RD, O'Neil R. 1996. The influence of significant others on learning about relationships. In *Learning About Relationships*, ed. S Duck, pp. 29–59. Newbury Park, CA: Sage. 252 pp.

Patterson GR. 1997. Performance models for parenting: a social interactional perspective. See Grusec & Kuczynski 1997, pp. 193–226

Power TG, Gershenhorn S, Stafford D. 1990. Maternal perceptions of infant difficultness: the influence of maternal attitudes and attributions. *Infant Behav. Dev.* 13:427–37

Reimers TM, Wacker DP, Derby KM, Cooper LJ. 1995. Relation between parental attributions and the acceptability of behavioral treatments for their child's behavior problems. *Behav. Disord.* 20:171–78

Richters JE. 1992. Depressed mothers as informants about their children: a critical review of the evidence for distortion. *Psychol. Bull.* 112:485–99

Roberts MW, Joe VC, Rowe-Hallbert A. 1992. Oppositional child behavior and parental locus of control. *J. Clin. Child Psychol.* 21:170–77

Rogoff B. 1991. Social interaction as apprenticeship in thinking: guidance and participation in spatial planning. In *Perspectives on Socially Shared Cognitions*, ed. LB Resnick, JM Levine, SD Teasley, pp. 349–64. Washington, DC: Am. Psychol. Assoc. 429 pp.

Rotter JB. 1966. Generalized expectancies for internal versus external control of reinforcement. *Psychol. Monogr.* 80(1):1–28

Sacco WP, Murray DW. 1997. Mother-child relationship satisfaction: the role of attri-

butions and trait conceptions. *J. Soc. Clin. Psycholol.* 16:24–42

Seligman MEP, Peterson C, Kaslow NJ, Tanenbaum RL, Alloy LB, Abramson LY. 1984. Attribution style and depressive symptoms among children. *J. Abnorm. Psychol.* 93:235–38

Sigel IE, ed. 1985. *Parental Belief Systems: The Psychological Consequences for Children.* Hillsdale, NJ: Erlbaum. 390 pp.

Sigel IE, McGillicuddy-deLisi AV, Goodnow JJ, eds. 1992. *Parental Belief Systems: The Psychological Consequences for Children.* Hillsdale, NJ: Erlbaum. 478 pp. 2nd. ed.

Silvester J, Bentovim A, Stratton P, Hanks HGI. 1995. Using spoken attributions to classify abusive families. *Child Abus. Negl.* 19:1221–32

Skinner EA, Zimmer-Gembeck MJ, Connell JP. 1998. Individual differences and the development of perceived control. *Monogr. Soc. Res. Child Dev.* 63(2–3):1–220

Slep AMS, O'Leary SG. 1998. The effects of maternal attributions on parenting: an experimental analysis. *J. Fam. Psychol.* 12:234–43

Smetana JG. 1994a. Parenting styles and beliefs about parental authority. See Smetana 1994b, pp. 21–36

Smetana JG, ed. 1994b. *Beliefs about Parenting: Origins and Developmental Implications.* San Francisco: Jossey-Bass. 104 pp.

Smetana JG. 1997. Parenting and the development of social knowledge reconceptualized: a social domain analysis. See Grusec & Kuczynski 1997, pp. 162–92

Smetana JG, Asquith P. 1994. Adolescents' and parents' conceptions of parental authority and personal autonomy. *Child Dev.* 65:1147–62

Smith AM, O'Leary SG. 1995. Attributions and arousal as predictors of maternal discipline. *Cogn. Ther. Res.* 19:459–71

Stevenson-Hinde J. 1998. Parenting in different cultures: time to focus. *Dev. Psychol.* 34:698–700

Strassberg Z. 1995. Social information processing in compliance situations by mothers of behavior-problem boys. *Child Dev.* 66:376–89

Strassberg Z. 1997. Levels of analysis in cognitive bases of maternal disciplinary dysfunction. *J. Abnorm. Child Psychol.* 25:209–15

Stratton P, Munton AG, Hanks HGI, Heard DH, Davidson C. 1988. *Leeds Attributional Coding System (LACS) Manual.* Leeds, UK: Leeds Fam. Ther. Res. Cent.

Teti DM, Gelfand DM. 1991. Behavioral competence among mothers of infants in the first year: the mediational role of maternal self-efficacy. *Child Dev.* 62:918–29

Toth SL, Cicchetti D, Macfie J, Emde RN. 1997. Representations of self and other in the narratives of neglected, physically abused, and sexually abused preschoolers. *Dev. Psychopathol.* 9:781–96

Valsiner J, Branco AU, Dantas CM. 1997. Co-construction of human development: heterogeneity within parental belief orientations. See Grusec & Kuczynski 1997, pp. 283–304

van IJzendoorn MH. 1995. Adult attachment representations, parental responsiveness, and infant attachment: a meta-analysis on the predictive validity of the Adult Attachment Interview. *Psychol. Bull.* 117:387–403

Webster-Stratton C. 1990. Stress: a potential disruptor of parent perceptions and family interactions. *J. Clin. Child Psychol.* 19:302–12

Weiner B. 1986. *An Attributional Theory of Motivation and Emotion.* New York: Springer-Verlag. 304 pp.

Weisz JR, McCarty CA, Eastman KL, Chaiyasit W, Suwanlert S. 1997. Developmental psychopathology and culture: ten lessons for Thailand. In *Developmental Psychopathology: Perspectives on Adjustment, Risk, and Disorder,* ed. SS Luthar, JA Burack, D Cicchetti, JR Weisz, pp. 568–92. New York: Cambridge Univ. Press. 618 pp.

Weisz JR, Weiss B. 1991. Studying the "referability" of child clinical problems. *J. Consult. Clin. Psychol.* 59:266–73

Wekerle C, Wolfe DA. 1998. Windows for preventing child and partner abuse: early childhood and adolescence. In *Violence Against Children in the Family and the Community,* ed. P Trickett, DJ Schellenbach, pp. 339–69. Washington, DC: Am. Psychol. Assoc. 511 pp.

Zeedyk MS. 1997. Maternal interpretations of infant intentionality: changes over the course of infant development. *Br. J. Dev. Psychol.* 15:477–93

Zukow PG. 1989. Siblings as effective socializing agents: Evidence from Central Mexico. In *Sibling Interaction Across Cultures: Theoretical and Methodological Issues,* ed. PG Zukow, pp. 79–104. New York: Springer-Verlag

Annu. Rev. Psychol. 2000. 51:345–375

EVALUATION METHODS FOR SOCIAL INTERVENTION

Mark W. Lipsey and David S. Cordray

Department of Psychology and Human Development, Vanderbilt University, Nashville, Tennessee 37203; e-mail: mark.lipsey@vanderbilt.edu, david.s.cordray@vanderbilt.edu

Key Words   program evaluation, treatment effectiveness, outcomes, field experiments, quasi-experiments, analysis of change

■ **Abstract**   Experimental design is the method of choice for establishing whether social interventions have the intended effects on the populations they are presumed to benefit. Experience with field experiments, however, has revealed significant limitations relating chiefly to (*a*) practical problems implementing random assignment, (*b*) important uncontrolled sources of variability occurring after assignment, and (*c*) a low yield of information for explaining why certain effects were or were not found. In response, it is increasingly common for outcome evaluation to draw on some form of program theory and extend data collection to include descriptive information about program implementation, client characteristics, and patterns of change. These supplements often cannot be readily incorporated into standard experimental design, especially statistical analysis. An important advance in outcome evaluation is the recent development of statistical models that are able to represent individual-level change, correlates of change, and program effects in an integrated and informative manner.

CONTENTS

Introduction 346
Problems and Progress in Experimental Methods..................................... 347
  Random Assignment.. 347
  Selection Modeling 348
  Within Program Variation 349
  Outcome Variables 354
  Elaboration of the Experimental Paradigm.. 357
Explanation and the Many Roles of Theory 357
  Describing and Explaining Change... 360
Advances in Statistical Modeling 363
  Analysis of Relative Group Change... 364
  Individual Growth Modeling... 366
Conclusion... 368

0084–6570/00/0201–0345$12.00   **345**

INTRODUCTION

The field of program evaluation presents a diversity of images and claims about the nature and role of evaluation that confounds any attempt to construct a coherent account of its methods or confidently identify important new developments. We take the view that the overarching goal of the program evaluation enterprise is to contribute to the improvement of social conditions by providing scientifically credible information and balanced judgment to legitimate social agents about the effectiveness of interventions intended to produce social benefits. Because of its centrality in this perspective, this review focuses on outcome evaluation, that is, the assessment of the effects of interventions upon the populations they are intended to benefit. The coverage of this topic is concentrated on literature published within the last decade with particular attention to the period subsequent to the related reviews by Cook and Shadish (1994) on social experiments and Sechrest & Figueredo (1993) on program evaluation.

The classical and still standard methodological paradigm for outcome evaluation is experimental design and its various quasi-experimental approximations. The superiority of experimental methods for investigating the causal effects of deliberate intervention is widely acknowledged. It is also widely acknowledged that the experimental paradigm as it is conventionally applied in outcome evaluation has significant limitations. In particular, the practice of outcome evaluation is marked by increased recognition of important variables that the experiment cannot control.

Random assignment, for instance, is recognized as a useful means of equating groups prior to the delivery of an intervention (Boruch 1997), though practical and ethical constraints often necessitate comparison of nonrandomized groups. Whereas assignment to treatment and control conditions is a defining event in outcome evaluation, decades of experience have shown that after assignment important processes occur that can seriously influence the quality of the evaluation design, the interpretability of the results, and the utility of the study. Among these processes are (*a*) poor program implementation, (*b*) augmentation of the control group with nonprogram services, (*c*) poor retention of participants in program and control conditions, (*d*) receipt of incomplete or inconsistent program services by participants, and (*e*) attrition or incomplete follow-up measurement. In addition, a host of participant characteristics (e.g. problem severity, motivation, ability level) can interact with exposure and response to treatment in ways that further complicate the situation.

Although efforts to minimize compromises to ideal experimental design should be encouraged, program circumstances typically permit little control over many variables that potentially have substantial influence on the outcomes under investigation. When such variables cannot be controlled and are too important to ignore, the only alternative is to measure them and incorporate the results into the statistical analysis. This approach not only permits some degree of statistical control over problem variables, but also supplies more information about factors that may explain why effects were or were not found. Therefore, in outcome evaluation, data collection has been increasingly extended to include measurement of such variables as program implementation, participants' exposure to services, and those participant characteristics and responses that may mediate or moderate the effects of treatment. In order for such variables to be measured, of course, they must first be identified as relevant and be defined with sufficient specificity to be operationalized. These are conceptual tasks, and correspondingly, outcome evaluation is increasingly being guided by theories of program and individual change.

Given the nature and number of the sources of uncontrolled variability in outcome evaluation, it is hardly surprising that different patterns of change across individuals can and have emerged in evaluation studies (e.g. Collins 1996, Krause et al 1998). An important advance in outcome evaluation has been the recent development of statistical models for growth (or decay) that are able to represent individual-level change, correlates of change, and program effects in a sophisticated and informative manner.

PROBLEMS AND PROGRESS IN EXPERIMENTAL METHODS

Evaluators have identified many practical and conceptual limitations in the experimental and quasi-experimental designs that for decades have been the primary tools for investigating program effects (Campbell & Stanley 1966, Cook & Campbell 1979). Recognition of those limitations, in turn, has stimulated significant methodological innovation. Indeed, much of the history of methodological development in evaluation research can be viewed as refinements of, or reactions to, the perceived deficiencies of experimental design for certain evaluation purposes. The major areas of problems and progress, summarized below, touch on almost every aspect of experimental design in field settings.

Random Assignment

The practicality of random assignment has been a continuing issue in the study of intervention effects (Dennis 1990) despite a steady cumulation of know-how about implementing it in field settings (Boruch 1997). Although it is not hard to find examples of successful randomization (e.g. Gueron 1997, Braucht & Reichardt 1993), its applicability is not uniform. In some cases there are too few units to randomize, a notable problem for community-level programs (Murray et al 1996), or no units available to be assigned to control conditions, as with full-coverage programs. In other instances, randomization raises ethical or legal questions about withholding services from otherwise eligible persons. In response to these concerns, alternative allocation methods have been proposed, such as sequential assignment (Staines et al 1999). However, even in favorable situations, the procedural difficulty of assigning persons to service conditions solely on the basis of chance and maintaining their participation through final data collection may thwart well-intentioned efforts. As a result, outcome evaluations often use the weakest of the quasi-experimental designs, nonequivalent comparisons, either by intent or because of degradation of an initial randomization through treatment and measurement attrition (Chalk & King 1998, Norman et al 1995, Speer & Newman 1996).

Under these circumstances, it would be comforting to have some assurance that the results of nonequivalent comparison designs were close approximations to those of randomized designs so the inferential strength of the experiment was preserved. Empirical comparisons, unfortunately, give no such assurance. Using meta-analysis summaries, Lipsey & Wilson (1993) found that randomized and nonrandomized designs in the same intervention area often gave quite divergent results. Though the average discrepancy was near zero, they ranged from large positive differences to large negative ones. Similarly, meta-analyses in selected intervention areas have found different results from randomized and nonrandomized comparisons, although the discrepancies were considerably diminished when the studies were equated for such features as amount of treatment to the control group, pretest effect size, selection, and attrition (Heinsman & Shadish 1996, Shadish & Ragsdale 1996). It thus appears that nonrandomized designs often yield biased estimates, but given favorable circumstances or effective statistical control, they are also capable of producing results comparable to randomized designs (Aiken et al 1998, Reynolds & Temple 1995).

Selection Modeling

The frequent bias in nonequivalent comparison designs justifies efforts to improve them. Most of the work on this issue has been directed toward statistical models for selection bias, in particular on ways to statistically control initial differences between intervention and comparison groups to better approximate results from random assignment.

One-stage statistical models, the prototype of which is ANCOVA (Analysis of Covariance), have long been recognized as problematic for adjusting selection bias between groups (Campbell & Erlebacher 1970). However, some analysts have argued that structural equation modeling with latent variables, particularly mean and covariance structure models, are capable of providing good estimates of treatment effects (Bentler 1991). Aiken et al (1994), for example, used this approach to compare the effects of two drug abuse treatments on the daily activities of drug addicts, and Wu & Campbell (1996) applied it to a reanalysis of the Westinghouse Head Start evaluation.

Two-stage models, introduced by Heckman in the mid-1970s, separately estimate the function describing group membership and that describing group differences in treatment outcome, using the predictions of the former as an instrumental variable in the latter (Heckman 1979). Selection bias may be represented directly in terms of the characteristics differentiating the groups or propensity scores reflecting the probability of group assignment (Rosenbaum 1995), or indirectly with an instrumental variable that is independent of group membership (Newhouse & McClellan 1998). The difficulty of specifying an appropriate instrumental variable and the analytic complexity of these two-stage models has inhibited their use in outcome evaluation despite persuasive advocacy (e.g. Humphreys et al 1996). Nonetheless, recent applications have been made in such diverse intervention areas as resocialization for homeless substance abusers (Devine et al 1997), compensatory education for low-income African American children (Reynolds & Temple 1998), home care under HMO and fee-for-service payment plans (Holtzman et al 1998), and antidepressant drug therapy (Croghan et al 1997).

The major problem with the available statistical approaches to selection bias is the sensitivity of the results to violation of the model assumptions, especially the requirement that all relevant variables be specified (Hartman 1991, Winship & Mare 1992). Much work remains to be done on the question of which models are best for which circumstances (for a good start on this issue, see Stolzenberg & Relles 1997).

Within-Program Variation

Experimental and quasi-experimental designs represent the independent variable as a categorical dichotomy—treatment and control. Within the treatment category there is no differentiation of program components or recognition of any variability in the type or amount of treatment provided to individual recipients. Thus, experimental outcome studies treat the program as a molar whole that is characterized only in terms of whether it is assigned as present or absent for a particular recipient. Looking inside the "black-box" of programs, however, reveals various sources of variation, most of which are beyond the evaluator's control, that can have profound effects on the outcomes that are observed. Program services may, for instance, be inconsistently or incompletely delivered, recipients may access or interact with services differently, and the same service regimen may have different effects for different recipients.

Assessments of program effects often do not consider these sources of variation when analyzing outcome data and instead examine only the mean effects for the overall treatment-control contrast. Such analyses produce unbiased statistical estimates of mean program effects if conducted with adequate statistical power, but furnish little information about the variation around those means and its sources. If that variation stems from important program characteristics, however, ignoring it can result in misleading conclusions about what effects the program produced and why. One of the more noteworthy developments in outcome evaluation is recognition that many forms of within-program variation can be crucial to understanding program effects. Some of the more significant forms of such variation are described below.

Delayed, Incomplete, or Failed Program Implementation   One of the more trenchant lessons from decades of evaluation practice is that intervention programs are characteristically difficult to implement. It may take a new or revised program years to be up and running in the intended manner if, indeed, that is ever accomplished. Moreover, even mature programs may deliver services incompletely, inconsistently, or not at all to some significant portion of their target clientele.

For example, Stecher et al (1994) contrasted residential and nonresidential treatments for dually diagnosed homeless adults. Both interventions involved two phases, the first of which had eight goals (e.g. client engagement, retention, assessment, and treatment planning) and an intended duration of three months. Interviews with administrators and counselors revealed that fewer than 20% of the goals were accomplished for the nonresidential program during its first nine months of operation. By the fifteenth month the implementation reached 75%, where it peaked. Moreover, even though the residential treatment had been operational for four years prior to the study, it was not until the eighteenth month that it attained all eight program goals.

Similar organizational development was discovered by ethnographers studying 14 projects associated with the Comprehensive Child Development Program (CSR Inc. 1997, St. Pierre et al 1997). With the organizational life cycle described in terms of four stages (Shortell & Kaluzny 1988), it was found that projects spent an average of 13 months in the start-up stage, 12 months in the growth stage, 10 months in the stabilization stage, and 6 months as stabilized programs. In addition, there was wide variation around each of these means, and some projects never reached maturity. Even if programs reach a mature stage of implementation, of course, they may not be able to maintain it. Carroll et al (1998), for instance, found modest reductions over time in the intensity of interventions for substance abuse problems. Similarly, McGrew et al (1994) documented "program drift" over several generations of the assertive community treatment (ACT) program.

Most programs involve multiple components, activities, or phases such that implementation can be incomplete for all or some elements at any given time. If a program is not implemented, it cannot be expected to produce effects. If distinct phases or components of programs are not implemented, and they are directed toward specific outcomes, it would hardly be a surprise to find no effects for those particular outcomes. If a program is changing over time, either advancing or deteriorating, clients receiving services at one time will be exposed to a different version of the program than their counterparts who experience it at another time. The evaluator cannot safely assume that a program provided any services, the intended services, or the same services to the designated clients and, indeed, can expect to find considerable variability in the nature and amount of services available to the individuals in any group of clients.

Individual Engagement in Services   Even if the structural features of a program (e.g. facilities, personnel, management, routine activities) are put in place as planned, and a complete and uniform service package is made available to each target client, it does not follow that a program is well and consistently implemented. Except in cases of mandatory and enforced participation, the target clients must also choose to accept the services and maintain their engagement until the completion of those services (Mowbray et al 1993). It is not at all unusual for program implementation to be severely compromised by low client retention and rendered inconsistent by variability among the target clients in their level of participation.

In one illustrative study that highlighted these individual differences, Maude-Griffin et al (1998) assessed the relative effectiveness of cognitive-behavioral therapy versus a 12-step program for cocaine abusers. Although the treatment plan called for 36 group and 12 individual therapy sessions, participants attended an average of 14 group and five individual sessions; fewer than 15% attended at least three-fourths of both types of sessions. Importantly, the standard deviations were large relative to the means and represented the full range from individuals who attended no sessions to those who attended all sessions.

Not all programs show low rates of service completion or great variability in amount of participation (e.g. Smith et al 1998), but these are nonetheless pervasive problems in many program areas. Moreover, there is not only reason to believe that persons who complete service are systematically different from those who drop out, but that there are differences among noncompleters as well. Kazdin & Mazurick (1994), for instance, found distinctively different client and family profiles for early versus late dropouts from psychotherapy. Evaluators, therefore, will often find that different treatment doses have been received by different types of clients despite a successful effort by the program to make a complete and consistent treatment regimen available to each participant.

Extracurricular Services   In open systems like the ones in which social programs are implemented, services are generally available from sources other than the program being evaluated. Some program participants may obtain such services and some of those services may resemble those the program provides or affect, for better or worse, the outcomes the program is attempting to achieve. Occasionally, evaluators have made efforts to assess the receipt of these services (e.g. Carroll et al 1998, Smith et al 1998, St. Pierre et al 1997), usually to determine if they differ between the treatment and control groups. However, little is known about the relationship of various forms of supplementary services to the outcomes of specific types of programs. This is clearly a topic that requires more systematic attention, but also one that involves another potentially significant source of variation among program participants with regard to the nature of the services they experience.

Aptitude by Treatment Interactions   Some sources of variation in program implementation can be linked to the propensities of individuals to engage in treatment (or not), seek more or fewer services, or drop out prior to completion of the program. In addition, there is ample evidence in the literature to indicate that individuals with certain characteristics (e.g. high versus low severity of presenting problem) are differentially affected by certain interventions. These aptitude by treatment interactions (ATI) represent a source of variability in program outcomes that can occur even when every individual receives exactly the same treatment (Smith & Sechrest 1991). ATIs are often uncovered through post-hoc analyses to identify subgroups of clients that show larger and smaller intervention effects. Increasingly, however, attempts are made to specify them a priori (e.g. Longabaugh et al 1995, Maude-Griffin et al 1998).

Differentiation of Treatment and Control Conditions   The topics discussed above relate to sources of variation within a program and its clientele that may be important for understanding outcomes. In experimental and quasi-experimental studies, however, program effects are observed in the form of differences between the outcomes for the treatment group and those for the control group. If the program is poorly implemented, treatment participants may receive services little different from control participants and have similar outcomes. However, it is also the case that there will be little contrast if the control group receives services comparable to those of the treatment group, even if the latter are well served.

As proposed in Kazdin's (1986) discussion of treatment differentiation in psychotherapy, the service difference between groups represents the relative strength of the intervention. That is, conditions or groups with overlapping service models, leakage of services across purportedly different interventions, and other forms of compensation can reduce the intended contrast between conditions with corresponding reductions in the size of the relative treatment effects.

Given these circumstances, it is somewhat surprising that little attention has been directed at understanding the types and amounts of service available to those in control conditions, especially "usual care" controls and other such conditions that are presumed to receive service of some kind. To emphasize this issue, Cordray & Pion (1993) recommended that the nature, amount, and presumed influence of the services available to the control group be characterized as thoroughly as those for the treatment group. In this regard, it should be noted that all the sources of variation within programs and program clientele that are discussed above also potentially apply within control groups as well.

One of the most comprehensive assessments of treatment differentiation was presented by Carroll et al (1998) as part of project MATCH (Matching Alcoholism Treatments to Client Heterogeneity) . Three scales were developed, each depicting the key features of a different manual-based therapy (cognitive behavioral, motivation enhancement, and 12-step facilitation). These were then used to rate the sessions for the three types of therapy according to the degree to which on-type and off-type intervention features were present. Multiple-group profile analysis showed substantial statistical differentiation between the conditions, although the scale means nonetheless indicated that each therapy was delivered with some features of the other therapies.

Implementation Assessment   As indicated above, it is now widely recognized that a program may not actually be implemented as intended, with the result that what is called the treatment condition may be little different from what is called the control condition. Moreover, even when implemented to some meaningful degree on average, there may be enormous variation in the actual treatment delivered to, and received by, different participants. This recognition has resulted in the rise of program description as a component of outcome evaluation, especially description of the extent of program implementation, delivery of services, and treatment dosage received by the intended clientele.

The techniques for examining the nature and adequacy of program implementation serve not only the purposes of outcome evaluators attempting to establish that the intended services were delivered, but also those of formative evaluators investigating ways to improve programs, and managers and sponsors seeking feedback and accountability. As a result, a bewildering variety of overlapping methods and terminology has evolved. The field now recognizes, however indistinctly, the activities of process evaluation (Scheirer 1994), implementation assessment, program monitoring, and management information systems. The most recent addition to this repertoire is performance measurement, a phrase associated with the various government initiatives at the federal and state levels that require agencies to identify their goals and report on their performance in attaining those goals (Hatry 1997, Martin & Kettner 1996).

Implementation assessment as part of outcome evaluation generally requires a multi-level assessment of the organizational functions associated with effective service delivery. These functions can be influenced by external context (e.g. laws, political support, organizational interdependencies), the character of the host organization (e.g. management structures), the nature of the program unit (e.g. required activities, personnel), and the type of services and the clients to whom they are provided (e.g. mode of treatment, nature of client and provider roles). Despite continuing dialogue about the roles of qualitative and quantitative methods in evaluation (Reichardt & Rallis 1994), in practice, multi-method approaches are commonly used for the task of documenting program implementation (e.g. ethnography, surveys, ratings, observations, interviews).

Implementation assessment is typically undertaken to gauge whether a program has reached some, often poorly specified, end state (e.g. "implemented as planned") or to support a judgment that the program is sufficiently mature to warrant an outcome evaluation. Fuller explication of what activities and services constitute adequate program implementation is often aided by the creation, refinement, and use of program "logic models" (Brekke 1987; Brekke & Test 1992; Cordray & Pion 1993; Julian 1997; Rog & Huebner 1991; Yin 1994, 1997) and "program templates" (Scheirer 1996) that depict the program activities in relationship to each other and the expected outcomes for service recipients. These constructions are usually derived inductively from stakeholders' descriptions of the program-as-intended and information about reputedly successful model programs and best practices.

If systematic descriptions of the intended program have been developed to give guidance, formal measures of program implementation (e.g. treatment strength and fidelity) can be constructed and used as the basis for determining what services were actually delivered and received (e.g. Carroll et al 1998, CSR Inc. 1997, McGrew et al 1994, Orwin et al 1998, Yeaton 1994). The development of such measures requires the same concern about the psychometric properties of the scales as does outcome measurement. Zanis et al (1997) have pointed out that because of low to moderate intercorrelations among service measures and biases in data recording, valid measurement of the type and quantity of services provided to clients can be difficult.

Nonetheless, the systematic assessment of program implementation as a component of outcome evaluation appears to be on the rise. In their review of 359 outcome studies conducted between 1980 and 1988, Moncher & Prinz (1991) found that the use of some form of treatment fidelity assessment increased from 40% to 60% over the course of the decade. Contemporary estimates may be even higher. The majority of these assessments, however, are based on either summary judgments of the overall treatment delivery or studies of adherence to protocol with small samples of clients. As such, the results are mainly indicative of average program implementation levels and do not necessarily speak to the issue of variation in program exposure and participation among individual clients.

A notable characteristic of implementation assessment done in conjunction with outcome studies is that it is most often conducted as a separate and relatively freestanding activity that is not directly integrated into the outcome analysis. Thus, an evaluator will describe the nature and extent to which an intervention is implemented with one set of observations and evidence, then conduct an experimental or quasi-experimental outcome study yielding additional data that is analyzed separately. This is not surprising given that the customary data analysis schemes do not readily permit differentiation of the intervention within the categorically independent variable defined in the experimental design. Nonetheless, fuller integration of information about program process and outcome would likely yield richer insight into the whys and wherefores of program effects. This is a topic to which we will return later in this chapter.

Outcome Variables

The dependent variables in outcome evaluation are measures of the social conditions the program is expected to change. Describing and evaluating such changes, as well as ascribing them to program activity, have generally been problematic in outcome evaluation (Rossi 1997). The problems are fundamental:

knowing what changes to expect, how to measure them, and how to evaluate them.

What Effects to Measure In the world of program practice within which outcome evaluation is conducted, the changes that programs are supposed to bring about are often not well-specified. A major endeavor in evaluation planning, therefore, is the attempt to convert program goals to measurable outcomes. This is an area in which increased use of program theory has made especially useful contributions. By describing the logic that connects program activities to program outcomes, the exercise of specifying program theory identifies the outcomes that can be reasonably expected. Moreover, attention to interim outcomes and mediator variables serves to identify proximal outcomes expected to follow rather directly from program activities as well as the more distal outcomes that the program hopes ultimately to achieve but that may be too remote or diffuse to measure adequately.

Related approaches involve focused investigation of the structure and substance of the outcome domain the program expects to affect. Dumka et al (1998), for instance, described an intensive qualitative inquiry into the nature of parenting stress among three ethnic groups, the results of which were used to develop an appropriate quantitative measure for the effects of an intervention program. In a similar spirit, Cousins & MacDonald (1998) used concept mapping techniques to describe the key dimensions of successful product development projects and thus identify appropriate outcome constructs for management training programs.

Evaluation practice with regard to delineating the intended program outcomes has evolved largely on the presumption that such outcomes are specific to the particular program being evaluated and, therefore, the identification of outcomes must be individually tailored to each program. Owen (1998) has suggested that generic outcome hierarchies, derived from program theory, may contribute the appropriate framework for specifying outcomes for any of a class of programs with similar characteristics that address similar social problems.

How to Measure Outcomes A relative lack of off-the-shelf, validated measures appropriate for many of the social conditions that programs attempt to change continues to cause difficulties for outcome evaluation (e.g. Chalk & King 1998). Moreover, even established measures may be susceptible to distinctive sources of measurement error when used for purposes of assessing treatment effects, e.g. self-serving biases or comprehension problems among low-functioning clients (Lennox & Dennis 1994).

Among the most distinctive measurement issues associated with assessment of intervention outcomes is sensitivity to change. The characteristics that make a measure sensitive to individual differences on a construct of interest are not necessarily the ones that make them sensitive to change on that construct over time (Eddy et al 1998). Although there is general recognition in the field that outcome measures must be sensitive to change, there has been surprisingly little systematic analysis of the ways sensitive measures can be identified and how sensitivity can be enhanced. Notable exceptions are Stewart & Archbold (1992, 1993), who described seven factors that bear on the sensitivity of a potential outcome measure to change.

Evaluating Effects   Given the results of an experimental or quasi-experimental outcome assessment, some determination must be made regarding whether an effect was found and, if so, its magnitude and meaning. Current practice continues to be dominated by statistical significance as the criterion for claiming an effect, despite vigorous and rather convincing arguments that this is a poor and misleading standard (Cohen 1994, Lipsey 1999, Posavac 1998, Schmidt 1996). Various alternatives have been proposed around the theme of reducing the privileged status of the null hypothesis under conditions of low statistical power. These include reliance on confidence intervals rather than point significance testing (Reichardt & Gollob 1997), reporting of the counternull value, that is, the nonnull magnitude of the effect size supported by the same amount of evidence as the null value (Rosenthal & Rubin 1994), and identifying the minimal detectable effect (Bloom 1995).

When an intervention effect is detected by some defensible criterion, the issue of assessing its magnitude and meaning within the context of the program and its goals remains. In current practice this issue is generally neglected; outcome evaluation reports typically say little about effect magnitude other than reporting statistical significance. Various alternatives have been proposed, but none has yet been widely adopted. One approach is to report effect sizes using the statistics developed in meta-analysis for this purpose, e.g. the standardized mean difference effect size or odds ratio (Posavac 1998). Jacobson & Truax (1991) proposed a definition of clinical significance based on attainment of posttreatment outcome scores more similar to those for functional than nonfunctional populations that has received some application (e.g. Ogles et al 1995). Sechrest et al (1996) argued that the measures used to describe psychotherapy outcomes should be calibrated against real behavior and events in people's lives. Many of their suggestions would apply to outcome measures in other intervention areas as well. It is a limitation of the evaluation field that no general consensus has yet emerged about how to handle this fundamental issue.

If we take into account the numerous sources of variability within programs and clients that were discussed earlier, their influence would be expected to produce many different patterns of change across individuals. This variability makes the issue of evaluating effects even more complex. Clearly, a single effect size estimate would not be adequate for summarizing a differentiated set of changes in response to intervention. The statistical methods for assessing individual-level reliable change (either growth or decay) and no-change that have begun to appear in the evaluation literature yield multiple indicators of effects such as the percentage of participants who improved, deteriorated, or exhibited no change (e.g. Speer & Greenbaum 1995).

Elaboration of the Experimental Paradigm

Program outcome evaluation shares a history with agricultural experiments and medical clinical trials in its use of the experimental paradigm to assess the effects of practical intervention regimens. Experimental methods work best, however, when the researcher can (*a*) operationalize the categorical independent variable in a consistent, well-defined manner, such as dispensing known quantities of pills and placebos or types of fertilizers uniformly to all experimental units; (*b*) control the assignment of units to the conditions defined by the independent variable and keep them in those conditions until the outcome data are collected; and (*c*) know what outcomes are important, how to measure them, and how to judge their practical significance.

As the discussion above indicates, it is rare for these circumstances to apply to the evaluation of social programs. Random assignment is often impractical or unsuccessful; treatments are inconsistent; recipients vary in their level of participation, drop out before treatment is completed, and respond differently; and expected outcomes are difficult to define, measure, and appraise. Nonetheless, this situation offers little justification for abandoning the experimental paradigm for outcome evaluation. No viable alternative method has yet been put forward for providing an equally credible answer to the question, "Does the program work?" That is, does the program have beneficial effects on the social conditions it seeks to improve? This question is at the heart of outcome evaluation for the good reason that it is what program stakeholders and policymakers generally want to know when they weigh the merits of investing valuable social resources in an intervention program.

What has occurred in outcome evaluation is a steady elaboration of concepts and methods to extend and supplement experimental and quasi-experimental design in ways that better capture and elucidate the often complex relationships between program activities and social change. Many such developments are mentioned above. Two interrelated and especially far-reaching trends in outcome evaluation, however, deserve fuller discussion. These are the increased attention to "theory" and the application of new statistical models for the analysis of change.

EXPLANATION AND THE MANY ROLES OF THEORY

Despite the associated practical difficulties and limitations, the experimental method persists as the principal tool for outcome evaluation because it produces the most scientifically credible answers to questions about the effects of social programs on the intended beneficiaries. However, in its basic form it renders essentially a yes or no answer with regard to each outcome investigated. This might well be sufficient if programs were disposable commodities that could easily be organized, implemented, tested, and discarded or replaced if they proved ineffective, and retained otherwise. On the contrary, social programs are politically, financially, and socially difficult to create and maintain, and it is not realistic to regard them as trials in a trial-and-error problem-solving exercise. Typically, poorly performing programs are expected to improve, at least incrementally, rather than be put out of business entirely. This circumstance puts a premium on learning why an intervention is effective or ineffective so that lessons can be learned and improvements can be made. One thing that has become clear in the evaluation field is that program stakeholders and policymakers want an explanation for the results of an outcome evaluation, not just a statement about whether effects were found on selected outcome variables.

The basic, unadorned experiment or quasi-experiment yields little explanatory information about the effects found or not found. Explaining the results requires a thorough description of the way the program functions and discussion of the relationship between program activity and program effects. In short, the explanation of program effects, or the lack thereof, requires some theory about the way the intervention is presumed to bring about the intended effects, a theory that can serve as a framework for organizing and interpreting information from both descriptive and experimental components of an outcome evaluation.

The relevance of program theory to the evaluation enterprise has long been recognized (e.g. Weiss 1972), but within the last decade it has emerged as a major topic (Rog & Fournier 1997). Despite the high level of interest and discussion, there is no evident consensus on what constitutes program theory or how it should be used (Weiss 1997). Instead, various different images of theory abound, and they are cast in several distinct roles in evaluation practice.

Most common is the use of theory as a planning tool for an evaluation (Julian et al 1995). The program models or logic models derived during evaluability assessment are of this sort (Wholey 1994). Their purpose is to determine whether an agreed-upon conceptualization of the program exists, what it is, and whether it is sensible and feasible. Such logic models typically show the key program activities, the program personnel and clients involved, and the expected results. Once laid out, they often lead to program reconceptualization or refinement, as well as serving to identify questions that might be asked and variables that might be measured in an evaluation.

This form of program theory gives the evaluator a road map that directs attention to what stakeholders view as the critical program activities, the intended outcomes, and the presumed relationships between those activities and the intended outcomes. Its purposes in outcome evaluation are to identify the important variables and relationships that should be studied and to furnish a conceptual framework for organizing and interpreting the results.

A problematic aspect of program theory for these purposes is that it is typically derived entirely from the assumptions and expectations of program stakeholders. As such, its basis is generally clinical experience, informed hunches, and common sense about how certain services might bring about the desired changes in social conditions (Campbell·1986, Chen et al 1997). Its value for organizing the outcome study and interpreting the results, therefore, depends on the extent to which the views on which it is based represent valid insights about the organizational activities and social change processes that affect the target social conditions.

This circumstance adds another dimension to outcome evaluation, that of assessing the feasibility and plausibility of the program theory itself. Some developments in this direction are beginning to take shape. Rossi et al (1999) presented an extended discussion of the steps and tools needed to evaluate program theories and models. Another effort by Scheirer (1996) centered around the use of program templates as tools for evaluating program content. Although principally descriptive, Scheirer and other contributors to her edited collection urged that the program templates be developed on the basis of "best" or "effective practices." Huberman (1996:102) noted that "careful sifting through research, development, and evaluation literature for the best exemplars to implement locally" is crucial but labor intensive.

Another perspective views theory as something that should emerge from an evaluation rather than function as a starting point. For example, ethnographic or other qualitative methods can be used to develop "grounded theory" (Strauss & Corbin 1990) about how and how well a program works (e.g. Kalafat & Illback 1998). Alternatively, quantitative researchers may engage in exploratory analysis of interactions and relationships to discover informative patterns in the data collected for an evaluation (e.g. Rosenheck et al 1995).

Although either of these forms of program theory might be useful as a framework for explaining program effects, they do not characteristically focus on the web of relationships between program actions and intended outcomes in a conceptually sophisticated way. Often, for instance, these theories stipulate a set of sequenced or chained activities, one of which is presumed to lead to another, without paying any attention to the nature or plausibility of the links that are assumed. Weiss (1997) reported that she could find few evaluations that actually tested any of the causal links implied within the program's chain of activities. Instead, she observed that much of what was done in practice focused on program implementation, e.g. attendance, treatment receipt, and so forth.

The form of program theory that Weiss (1997) found least often is the one that is most pertinent to the challenge of explaining why particular program effects are or are not produced by program actions, namely theory which focuses specifically on the causal mechanisms through which program actions have effects. One variation on this theme is the argument that evaluation research should be theory-driven—that is, it should begin with an articulated theory about how program actions cause the expected effects and organize inquiry around investigation of that theory (Chen 1990, Sidani & Braden 1998). The theories involved may take various forms, e.g. intervening variable theories that examine mediators hypothesized as links between program activity and social outcomes (Donaldson et al 1994), dose-response theories that presume differential outcomes as a function of the nature or amount of treatment contact (Brekke et al 1997), and individual differences theories in which differential outcomes are expected primarily as a function of characteristics of the recipient (Longabaugh et al 1995, Maude-Griffin et al 1998).

Another variation on the idea of organizing evaluation around a theory of the casual mechanism embodied in the program has been voiced from the perspective of scientific realism (Henry et al 1998, Pawson & Tilley 1997). In this view, programs are assumed to bring about social change through one or more "generative mechanisms" operating in the program context. For instance, a program to encourage homeowners to mark their property with identifying numbers might reduce theft through such mechanisms as increasing the difficulty for thieves to dispose of stolen goods or enhancing the detection of offenses by making it easier to establish that someone possesses stolen property (Pawson & Tilley 1997). Outcome evaluation in this scheme is oriented toward determining why a program works (i.e. through what mechanism), for whom, and under what circumstances.

One of the concepts central to discussions of the forms of theory relating to the causal or generative mechanisms in programs is that of change. For these theories, the key issue is explaining how problematic social conditions are transformed by the interaction of the program with those conditions. This concept seems especially promising for further development of the explanatory aspects of outcome evaluation and warrants additional attention.

Describing and Explaining Change

Assessing intervention effects is inherently an investigation of change, in particular, the changes in social conditions brought about by the intervention, which itself represents a deliberate change in the social environment. From this perspective, one of the more interesting trends in outcome evaluation is increased attention to change as an important concept for understanding intervention and its effects. Two domains of change are relevant in this regard, corresponding to the common distinction between program action and the mechanisms through which that action produces social changes (Chen 1990, 1994; Lipsey 1997; Weiss 1997).

First, consideration must be given to the matter of organizational change. Programs represent sets of activities that must be enacted within an organizational context influenced by factors both within and outside the organization. Evaluators investigating whether and why a program has been adequately implemented, or who attempt to assist program managers improve program functioning, must inevitably theorize about organizational change and the factors that inhibit or facilitate it.

The second domain of application for change theories relates to the causal process through which desired changes in social conditions come about as a result of program action. Thus, some set of cause-and-effect links is presumed to connect the intervention to the effects it is intended to achieve. Evaluators investigating whether and why the expected effects occurred must inevitably theorize about social change and the mechanisms that bring it about.

Organizational Change   That program implementation represents a form of organizational change was recognized early in the history of program evaluation. Concepts such as formative evaluation (Scriven 1967, 1991), process analysis (Weiss 1972), evaluability assessment (Wholey 1994), and implementation failure (Suchman 1967) highlighted the fact that effective service delivery did not follow automatically from the program status quo. Over the past three decades, recognition of the theories of action underlying programs (Bickman 1987, 1990; Chen 1990, 1994; Weiss 1997), coupled with the development of ways to systematically describe program components and activities (e.g. logic models), has placed organizational issues at center stage in the analysis of program implementation and process.

In addition, the role of the evaluator in relation to program organization has expanded over the decades. In early conceptions of evaluation, evaluators were characterized as "methodological servants to the experimenting society" (Campbell 1971), a role largely confined to assessing the effectiveness of programs devised and organized by others. Since then, the evaluator's role has expanded so that it often includes preintervention issues, such as program design and planning, and program implementation and refinement. Thus, evaluation specialists have increasingly infiltrated the organizational development process.

Despite this shift in roles and the heightened interest in program theory, there has been little systematic development of organizational theory focused on the process of implementing social programs. This deficiency is especially striking in light of the availability of a large body of general theory for organizational change that should be adaptable to program implementation issues (Rogers & Hough 1995). Similarly, organizational variables are not generally used to aid the understanding of specific programs undergoing evaluation, though there are notable exceptions (e.g. CSR Inc. 1997, Delany et al 1994).

Aside from involving little organizational change theory, the increasingly systematic efforts in evaluation practice to understand if and how programs are organized for effective delivery of services are often conducted independently of the outcome analyses. Implementation assessment is thus generally a separate, first step in outcome evaluation, but the results of that assessment relating, for instance, to variability in delivery and receipt of services, are not integrated into the analysis of outcome data. Sometimes this is appropriate because the implementation process does not produce or permit any variability, resulting in no individual differences in engagement, retention, and so on (e.g. Smith et al 1998). In many instances, though, better explanation of the observed outcomes would be possible if program implementation data were linked to change on outcome variables for individuals with varying kinds of interaction with the program.

Development and application of forms of organizational change theory for program implementation and service delivery, therefore, hold considerable potential for helping to explain program outcomes. Such theory would also be useful for program planning and formative evaluation aimed at program improvement, even without outcome evaluation. Work along these lines is not very advanced, however, and currently provides limited tools for program description and analysis.

Social Change   The conception of the way in which the intended social improvements come about as a result of program actions that is implicit in a program's activities, or sometimes explicitly articulated, constitutes the program's theory of social change. Such theories depend on assumptions about the etiology of the problems the program attempts to address and the mechanisms by which change can be induced. These theories vary quite dramatically in their level of specificity and applicability across problem domains, though several general theoretical frameworks are routinely encountered as justification for social programming. For example, Smith et al (1998) postulated that problem drinking is the result of environmental contingencies; modifying drinking behavior is a matter of altering the contingencies. Their intervention, the Community Reinforcement Approach (CRA), was derived directly from their theory. Similarly, Latkin et al (1996) used social network theory to craft an intervention to prevent HIV among injection drug users. The guiding principle was that social influence processes have strong effects on risky behavior. Therefore, altering the social processes among members of groups (e.g. social comparison processes, fear of social sanctions, socialization of new members, information exchange) should reduce risky behaviors of all members of the network.

Other meta-theories of change include knowledge-attitude-behavior models (Weiss 1997), in which changes in behavior are presumed to be a function of changes in attitudes, which in turn depend on the acquisition of knowledge (e.g. regarding the harmful consequences of smoking). Similar notions of change underlie interventions stemming from cognitive-behavior theory, e.g. in health (McGraw et al 1996) and substance abuse (Longabaugh et al 1995, Maude-Griffin et al 1998).

The relevance of models of change to social programs is particularly well illustrated by the transtheoretical model championed by Prochaska and his colleagues (Prochaska et al 1992). Although still evolving, the transtheoretical model identifies stages associated with the individual's predisposition to change an adverse behavior (i.e. precontemplation through maintenance of change). This model has become a basis for prevention programs in such areas as smoking (Dijkstra et al 1998), skin cancer (Hedeker & Mermelstein 1998), and substance abuse (see Prochaska et al 1992).

For purposes of this discussion, the transtheoretical change model highlights several important principles about the assessment of change. First, whereas outcome evaluation usually examines the magnitude of the mean change for an intervention group relative to a control group, theories of individual change direct attention to differential patterns of change within groups. By focusing on individual differences in susceptibility to the intervention (stage of change each person is in), we can get closer to the goal of understanding how programs affect individuals, who is most affected, and under what circumstances.

Increasingly, interventions are rooted in theories of change that stipulate individual difference variables presumed to moderate the direction and rate of change. Using these theories, program evaluators have the opportunity to identify and measure these individual difference variables and analyze them in relationship to individual-level change on outcome variables. Combined with information about the nature and amount of participation of each individual in the program, the results of such analysis should yield answers to both the questions of whether the program produced the expected effects and why or why not.

Integrating Theory, Design, and Analysis   The fullest and most informative scheme for outcome evaluation would take into consideration (*a*) the variability to be expected in program implementation, service participation, response to treatment, and the like, along with the organizational theory relating to those factors; (*b*) the causal mechanisms presumed to link program action with social change and the moderator and mediator variables associated with that theory; (*c*) the observable outcomes expected to result from the program action at the level of change in the individuals exposed to the program; and (*d*) the net program effects attributable to program action on the basis of an experimental or quasi-experimental design. A careful integration of this information should indicate whether the program brought about change, for whom, why or why not, and in the process, yield useful descriptive information to guide program improvement and general understanding about that particular form of intervention. While individual evaluation studies can be found with one or more of these elements, none combines them all in an integrated fashion. This is due to (*a*) practical constraints—not every evaluation situation affords the resources and opportunity for such a probing inquiry; (*b*) conceptual deficiencies—theoretical development is primitive in many intervention areas, though studies of the sort described would do much to improve it; and (*c*) technical limitations—combining experimental and correlational data in an integrated analysis oriented toward individual and group change issues presents many challenges. On the latter point, however, important and relatively recent statistical developments have equipped evaluators with powerful new tools that can be readily adapted for these purposes.

ADVANCES IN STATISTICAL MODELING

From a statistical point of view, the "core" (or initial) analysis of data from an experiment should follow the unit of assignment (Boruch 1997); this is often referred to as the "intent-to-treat" model of analysis. Even with many transgressions (e.g. crossovers, dropouts) unbiased estimates of net treatment effects can be derived. As a starting point, Boruch's advice is sound. But, for outcome evaluation also to yield information that helps explain how and why effects were produced, statistical analyses that produce more differentiated results are required.

In addition, theories of change such as those discussed above, when sufficiently well developed, should guide the form and scope of the analysis.

Evaluators have adapted various statistical approaches that have been around for some time to these purposes. The more interesting development, though, is the proliferation of statistical models and approaches to the study of change that has been generated in the last decade by statistical theorists and methodologists (Collins & Horn 1991, Francis et al 1991, Meredith & Tisak 1990, Muthén & Curran 1997, Willett & Sayer 1994). These methods can be grouped into two different analytic strategies. The first focuses on estimating relative group differences. What distinguishes these methods from the intent-to-treat model is the deliberate attempt to incorporate factors associated with program implementation, program theory, or both into the analysis of those group differences. The second analytic strategy is relatively new and focuses specifically on change, generally referred to as "growth."

In reviewing practices within each of these analytic strategies, we attempt to distinguish between sequenced and integrated assessments of change. Specifically, some programs involve change processes at several levels of the service system (e.g. community, program, and individual) such that changes at one level are presumed to be prerequisite to change at other levels. These models require a sequential assessment of the steps in the change process (Chen et al 1997). On the other hand, when the change processes all pertain to the same level of analysis (e.g. individuals) and relevant measures are obtained on all change parameters, an integrated model can be used. The most fully integrated model would examine change in the target clientele as a function of variables relating to receipt of service, characteristics of the recipients, and individual-level change processes operating through some sequence of mediating variables. Currently, illustrations of fully integrated models are rare.

Analysis of Relative Group Change

In general, analysis of relative program effects tends to represent change with simple before-after comparisons or, perhaps, longer time series for group means on performance indicators. For example, Smith et al (1998) compared the mean level of drinking behavior over several measurement occasions for program and control clients. Multivariate analysis may be used to link process and before-after change data on outcome variables. Spoth et al (1998), for instance, applied structural equation modeling to examine the direct and indirect effects of family-focused preventive interventions on changes in parenting behavior.

Within many of these studies, examination of program change involves a sequential assessment in which the first step is to determine if the program implementation has reached some criterion level. That is, in the spirit of a "manipulation check," the first stage of the analysis focuses on ascertaining whether the intervention has been applied or delivered as intended at the program or organizational level. If that is established, the analysis then turns to the observed change among those receiving services. The linkage between program implementation, program theory, and outcomes is chiefly a logical one; if the program was implemented as intended and effects were observed, then the program theory is presumed supported.

In the Smith et al (1998) study, for example, the effects of a Community Reinforcement Approach (CRA) for alcohol-dependent, homeless adults were assessed. A manual-based assessment of adherence to CRA was undertaken, attendance at CRA meetings was recorded, and clients in both the treatment and control groups were questioned about receipt of non-CRA services. This procedure showed that both groups received relevant services, but among CRA clients the overall amount of service was greater, and more of the alcohol-related components of the CRA protocol were received. In the next phase of the analysis, examination of the outcomes revealed change in both groups on the major dependent variables (alcohol consumption, employment, and residential stability), with the relative effects favoring the CRA group only for the alcohol outcomes.

A more integrated analysis involving program implementation variables is achieved by including variables related to individual-level receipt of services and outcomes in the same analytic model. This approach is a variation on the dose-response analysis conducted in studies of pharmaceutical treatments. Program performance is represented in this scheme by indicators of how much service each individual received. The link to outcome is made by examining the relationship between "dose" and change on the dependent variables. This link is analyzed correlationally, of course, since dosage is not assigned randomly other than at the level of the global treatment versus control conditions. Babcock & Steiner (1999) presented a useful illustration in the area of domestic violence of what can be learned from this type of analysis, as well as a discussion of the limitations.

In another application, McGraw et al (1996) used multiple regression to show that in a health education program, program fidelity, modifications made during implementation, and teacher characteristics had direct relationships to changes in dietary knowledge, intentions, and self-efficacy among elementary school students. Similarly, Van Ryzin (1996) conducted a path analysis to examine the indirect effects of the type of management of public housing on housing satisfaction among residents. An interesting aspect of this analysis is that it involved a series of mediator and moderator variables derived from an implicit program theory.

As these examples illustrate, it is not uncommon for outcome studies to incorporate variables relating to program implementation or the degree to which recipients are exposed to the intervention and relate them in some manner to the observed change on outcome variables. The program theories implicit or explicit in these analyses, however, are generally no more than assumptions about certain criterion levels a program should reach on key performance indicators before it can be expected to have effects. Little attention has been given to modeling more complex changes in organization or service delivery over the program life cycle, much less integrating such analysis with outcome data.

Individual Growth Modeling

Although there are important differences among the various approaches, the common theme in growth modeling is a focus on change at the level of the individual unit as the base upon which to construct any other analyses of interest. Using multiwave data on an outcome variable (observed or latent), these models involve at least two levels of analysis. At the first level, the repeated measures within subjects are analyzed, allowing individual change trajectories to be examined directly in terms of their starting values and the rate and shape of change. The second level of analysis compares the individual growth curves to investigate systematic differences among them. A variety of individual growth models, stemming from such fields as biostatistics, education, and psychometrics, have been developed and refined during the last decade (Mellenbergh & van den Brink 1998, Muthén & Curran 1997, Speer & Greenbaum 1995, Willett & Sayer 1994).

It is clearly the more sophisticated multivariate models of change that are most promising for purposes of analyzing change in outcome studies in ways that integrate information about exposure to the intervention, mediator variables, differential responsiveness to intervention among service recipients, and the degree to which effects are maintained over time. These methods are advancing at an impressive rate. In HLM (Hierarchical Linear Modeling) (Bryk & Raudenbush 1992), individual differences in growth or decline are represented by coefficients derived under a random effects model. Osgood & Smith (1995) reported a useful demonstration of how different HLM-based models could test different patterns of treatment effects. For example, treatment effects may be represented in terms of a simple change-from-baseline model, or group effects on growth trajectories with pre-existing factors controlled might be used.

Longabaugh et al (1995) used hierarchical latent growth modeling to assess the interactive effects of individual difference variables, time, and treatment type in an analysis of substance abuse outcomes. Their results are complex but they illustrate the modeling technique, effectively presenting the results using a three-dimensional graphic. Here, treatment fidelity, differentiation, drift, and therapist and site differences were examined prior to the growth modeling (see Carroll et al 1998). Fidelity and treatment differentiation were judged to be sufficient, and these factors were not included in the second phase of the analysis.

Willett & Sayer (1994) translated growth models into covariance structure analysis. Within their framework, predictors and correlates of change can be assessed and extended to between-group effects that represent intervention conditions. Statistical advances for models that prescribe noncontinuous or staged change have also appeared. For example, Hedeker & Mermelstein (1998) developed a threshold-based model of change for k stages of change (with a test for treatment effects and time x treatment effects). They illustrated the model with data from a multi-school skin cancer prevention study.

Muthén & Curran (1997) expanded the random coefficient model beyond a single response variable by incorporating it into a latent variables framework. As a practical guide to growth modeling for intervention studies, their paper is exceptional. In addition to elaborating the random coefficients model, they described a five step analytic process for testing differences between experimental groups and presented methods for estimating statistical power. The recommended steps include developing and testing a separate change model for the control group and the intervention group, testing for differences between those models, analyzing the equivalence of the groups and the effects of initial status on differential growth, and conducting sensitivity analyses on the models. Reanalysis of data from Kellem et al (1994), using these techniques, revealed larger effects, reflecting greater control over extraneous error.

In general, these recent developments (and others reviewed by Muthén & Curran 1997) share much common ground. The main differences revolve around issues of design (e.g. number of measurement waves) and whether manifest or latent variables are used in the analysis. There are also differences among analytic frameworks in their focus on change exclusively or on change plus variables thought to exercise causal influence on the change. What seems clear from the available literature on growth models is that they are sufficiently flexible to be applied to the sorts of program change models that have been described in the evaluation literature.

The evaluation literature, nonetheless, does not yet offer examples of integrated change models that incorporate program, client, mediator, and outcome variables in patterns suggested by program theory. An interesting example of the potential for such integrated analysis, however, is Osgood & Smith's (1995) Boy's Town follow-up study. Among other analyses, they showed how variation in length of treatment affected estimates of change in feelings of isolation, but did not attempt to model the causal mechanisms responsible for that change.

To date, the most complete attempts to incorporate assessments of program implementation into analyses of change among service recipients have followed the two-step logic mentioned earlier, in which implementation is separately checked as a prerequisite to investigating intervention effects. A good example is reported by CSR Inc. (1997), an elaborate implementation analysis of multiple sites associated with the Comprehensive Child Development Program. Using a common model across sites, the researchers assessed implementation at the organizational and individual family levels. Then, with summary indices for key features of the implementation process in hand, St. Pierre et al (1997) conducted growth curve analyses to assess the developmental outcomes for children. Finding no overall effects, they assessed project variation in service levels, along with the prevalence of nontreatment services obtained in both treatment and control groups. This is one of the few studies available that puts together evidence from the process and outcome evaluation components to assess whether no-effect findings were due to method, implementation, or theory failure.

The advances in statistical modeling have supplied the technical armamentarium to tackle complex evaluation designs that contain controlled and uncontrolled sources of variation. Unlike the intent-to-treat model, which ignores the sources of uncontrolled variation in treatment receipt, nontreatment service seeking, and other individual difference variables, these advanced techniques are more flexible and comprehensive. Yet, despite their advantages, the simple fact is that departures from randomization always leave room for uncertainty. In discussing their results pertaining to treatment exposure, for instance, Osgood & Smith (1995) were clear that this source of variation represents postassignment selection bias. Babcock & Steiner (1999) made the same point in their analysis of the relationship between treatment exposure and subsequent instances of spousal abuse.

As experience accumulates with these more sophisticated methods, we suspect that the next major developments will be in the area of modeling these sources of postassignment selection bias. As described earlier in this chapter, a great deal of attention has been directed toward modeling selection bias in nonrandomized comparisons through the use of propensity scoring and other two-stage selection modeling. With proper measurement of post-assignment selection processes (e.g. propensity to engage in treatment or seek services) additional progress (and controversy) might be made toward exerting some statistical control over these inherently difficult features of experimental methods in application to program outcome evaluation.

CONCLUSION

The strength of experimental methods for outcome evaluation is the scientific credibility with which they answer questions about the effects of intervention on the social conditions they are intended to ameliorate. They answer these questions, however, chiefly in terms of whether there were mean effects on the outcome variables examined and, sometimes, what the magnitudes of those effects were. As valuable and policy-relevant as this information is, it leaves much of the story untold. Knowing what services were delivered and received, what difference that made to the individuals receiving them, whether individuals responded differently, and generally, why certain effects were or were not found is also valuable and relevant.

These additional concerns cannot be easily addressed by experimental methods within the practical and ethical constraints inherent in social programs. Qualitative methods can tell much of this story and, in that regard, are a worthwhile adjunct to even the most comprehensive and rigorous experimental design. Increasingly, however, evaluators are incorporating additional variables into experimental and quasi-experimental designs to acquire more particularistic data about factors that might explain the variability in outcome. For the most part, the scope of these efforts has been limited and the associated analyses have been adjuncts to the experimental design. The trend, nonetheless, is appropriately in the direction of more fully integrating those variables and issues into the analysis of the experimental comparisons, greatly aided by powerful new statistical techniques.

However informative, statistical modeling of the sources of variability within experimental groups is nonetheless essentially based on correlational relationships. As such, it is only as good as the variables included and the assumptions made about the nature of those variables and their relationships. A notable weakness of the evaluation field in this regard is the paucity of information that has cumulated from decades of outcome evaluation in various intervention domains about the factors involved in selection bias, differential delivery and receipt of treatment, participation in treatment, differential response to treatment, and the predictors of outcome. Without better empirical and conceptual grounding, progress in outcome evaluation methods will continue to lag despite the impressive advances in statistical techniques.

A question critical to the future of program evaluation is whether useful generalization is indeed possible regarding the factors involved in social intervention and the manner in which they interrelate to produce beneficial effects for the target individuals and populations (Adelman & Taylor 1994). The alternative view is that every intervention situation is so distinctive that little useful input can be derived from prior evaluation studies and related research. If each intervention situation is virtually unique, as much evaluation research seems to assume, then there is little hope for either the cumulation of knowledge to aid the development of explanatory models for specific intervention programs or for generalization about what types of interventions are most effective for what types of problems.

There is an important complementarity between the evaluation of individual programs and the strength and completeness of the knowledge base regarding social intervention. The development of explanatory models of program behavior derived through the cumulation and synthesis of empirical findings would allow evaluators to direct their attention to assessing whether programs operate in a fashion consistent with effective practice. This would reduce the necessity of conducting separate, methodologically difficult, outcome evaluations for each individual program whose effectiveness is in question. The effort of designing and implementing high quality social experiments rich in potentially explanatory variables could then be reserved for innovative intervention strategies that are not yet well understood.

Visit the Annual Reviews home page at www.AnnualReviews.org.

LITERATURE CITED

Adelman HS, Taylor L. 1994. *On Understanding Intervention in Psychology and Education.* Westport, CT: Praeger. 279 pp.

Aiken LS, Stein JA, Bentler PM. 1994. Structural equation analyses of clinical subpopulation differences and comparative treatment outcomes: characterizing the daily lives of drug addicts. *J. Consult. Clin. Psychol.* 62:488–99

Aiken LS, West SG, Schwalm DE, Carroll JL, Hsiung S. 1998. Comparison of a randomized and two quasi-experimental designs in a single outcome evaluation: efficacy of a university-level remedial writing program. *Eval. Rev.* 22:207–44

Babcock JC, Steiner R. 1999. The relationship between treatment, incarceration, and recidivism of battering: a program evaluation of Seattle's coordinated community response to domestic violence. *J. Fam. Psychol.* 13:45–59

Bentler PM. 1991. Modeling of intervention effects. In *Drug Abuse Prevention Intervention Research: Methodological Issues,* ed. CG Leukefeld, WJ Bukoski, pp. 159–82. NIDA Research Monograph 107. Rockville, MD: Natl. Inst. Drug Abuse. 263 pp.

Bickman L. 1987. Functions of program theory. In *Using Program Theory in Evaluation: New Directions for Program Evaluation,* ed. L Bickman, 33:5–18. San Francisco: Jossey-Bass. 116 pp.

Bickman L, ed. 1990. *Advances in Program Theory: New Directions for Program Evaluation,* Vol. 47. San Francisco: Jossey-Bass. 124 pp.

Bloom HS. 1995. Minimum detectable effects: a simple way to report the statistical power of experimental designs. *Eval. Rev.* 19:547–56

Boruch RF. 1997. *Randomized Experiments for Planning and Evaluation: A Practical Guide.* Thousand Oaks, CA: Sage. 265 pp.

Braucht GN, Reichardt CS. 1993. A computerized approach to trickle-process, random assignment. *Eval. Rev.* 17:79–90

Brekke JS. 1987. The model-guided method for monitoring implementation. *Eval. Rev.* 11:281–99

Brekke JS, Long JD, Nesbitt N, Sobel E. 1997. The impact of service characteristics on functional outcomes from community support programs for persons with schizophrenia: a growth curve analysis. *J. Consult. Clin. Psychol.* 65:464–75

Brekke JS, Test MA. 1992. A model for measuring implementation of community support programs: results from three sites. *Comm. Mental Health J.* 28:227–47

Bryk AS, Raudenbush SW. 1992. *Hierarchical Linear Models: Applications and Data Analysis Methods.* Newbury Park, CA: Sage. 265 pp.

Campbell DT. 1971. Methods for the experimenting society. Presented at Meet. East. Psychol. Assoc., New York, and Meet. Am. Psychol. Assoc., Washington, DC

Campbell DT. 1986. Relabeling internal and external validity for applied social scientists. In *Advances in Quasi-Experimental Design Analysis: New Directions for Program Evaluation,* 31:67–77. San Francisco: Jossey-Bass. 113 pp.

Campbell DT, Erlebacher AE. 1970. How regression artifacts in quasi-experimental evaluations can mistakenly make compensatory education look harmful. In *Compensatory Education: A National Debate,* ed. J Hellmuth, 3:185–210. New York: Brunner/Mazel

Campbell DT, Stanley JC. 1966. *Experimental and Quasi-Experimental Designs for Research.* Boston, MA: Houghton Mifflin. 84 pp.

Carroll KM, Connors GJ, Cooney NL, DiClemente CC, Donovan DM, et al. 1998. Internal validity of project MATCH treatments: discriminability and integrity. *J. Consult. Clin. Psychol.* 66:290–303

Chalk R, King P, eds. 1998. *Violence in Families: Assessing Prevention and Treatment Programs.* Washington, DC: Natl. Acad. 392 pp.

Chen H-T. 1990. *Theory-Driven Evaluations.* Thousand Oaks, CA: Sage. 325 pp.

Chen H-T. 1994. Current trends and future directions in program evaluation. *Eval. Practice* 15:229–38

Chen H-T, Wang JCS, Lin L-H. 1997. Evaluating the process and outcome of a garbage reduction program in Taiwan. *Eval. Rev.* 21:27–42

Cohen J. 1994. The earth is round (p<.05). *Am. Psychol.* 49:997–1003

Collins LM. 1996. Is reliability obsolete? A commentary on "Are simple gain scores obsolete?" *Appl. Psychol. Meas.* 20:289–92

Collins LM, Horn JL. 1991. *Best Methods for the Analysis of Change.* Washington, DC: Am. Psychol. Assoc.

Cook TD, Campbell DT. 1979. *Quasi-Experimentation: Design and Analysis for Field Settings.* Boston, MA: Houghton Mifflin

Cook TD, Shadish WR. 1994. Social experiments: some developments over the past fifteen years. *Annu. Rev. Psychol.* 45:545–80

Cordray DS, Pion GM. 1993. Psychosocial rehabilitation assessment: a broader perspective. In *Improving Assessment in Rehabilitation and Health,* ed. R Glueckauf, G Bond, L Sechrest, B McDonel, pp. 215–40. Newbury Park, CA: Sage. 334 pp.

Cousins JB, MacDonald CJ. 1998. Conceptualizing the successful product development project as a basis for evaluating management training in technology-based companies: a participatory concept mapping application. *Eval. Prog. Plan.* 2: 333–44

Croghan TW, Lair TJ, Engelhart L, Crown WE, Copley-Merriman C, et al. 1997. Effect of antidepressant therapy on health care utilization and costs in primary care. *Psychiatric Serv.* 48:1420–26

CSR Incorporated. 1997. *Process Evaluation of the Comprehensive Child Development Program.* Washington, DC: CSR Inc. 404 pp.

Delany PJ, Fletcher BW, Lennox RD. 1994. Analyzing shelter organizations and the services they offer: testing a structural model using a sample of shelter programs. *Eval. Prog. Plan.* 17:391–98

Dennis ML. 1990. Assessing the validity of randomized field experiments: an example from drug abuse treatment research. *Eval. Rev.* 14:347–73

Devine JA, Brody CJ, Wright JD. 1997. Evaluating an alcohol and drug treatment program for the homeless: an econometric approach. *Eval. Prog. Plan.* 20:205–15

Dijkstra A, De Vries H, Roijackers J, Van Breukelen G. 1998. Tailored interventions to communicate stage-matched information to smokers in different motivational stages. *J. Consult. Clin. Psychol.* 66:549–57

Donaldson SI, Graham JW, Hansen WB. 1994. Testing the generalizability of intervening mechanism theories: understanding the effects of adolescent drug use prevention interventions. *J. Behav. Med.* 17:195–216

Dumka LE, Gonzales NA, Wood JL, Formoso D. 1998. Using qualitative methods to develop contextually relevant measures and preventive interventions: an illustration. *Am. J. Comm. Psychol.* 26:605–37

Eddy JM, Dishion TJ, Stoolmiller M. 1998. The analysis of intervention change in children and families: methodological and conceptual issues embedded in intervention studies. *J. Abnorm. Child Psychol.* 26:45–61

Francis DJ, Fletcher JM, Stuebing KK, Davidson KC, Thompson NM. 1991. Analysis of change: modeling individual growth. *J. Consult. Clin. Psychol.* 59:27–37

Gueron J. 1997. Learning about welfare reform: lessons from state-based evaluations. See Rog & Fournier, 1997, pp. 79–94

Hartman R. 1991. A Monte Carlo analysis of alternative estimators in models involving selectivity. *J. Bus. Econ. Stat.* 9:41–49

Hatry HP. 1997. Where the rubber meets the road: performance measurement for state and local public agencies. In *Using Performance Measurement to Improve Public and Nonprofit Programs: New Directions for Evaluation,* ed. KE Newcomer: 75:31–44. San Francisco: Jossey-Bass. 102 pp.

Heckman JJ. 1979. Sample selection bias as a specification error. *Econometrica* 47:153–61

Hedeker D, Mermelstein RJ. 1998. A multilevel thresholds of change model for analysis of stages of change data. *Mulivar. Behav. Res.* 33:427–55

Heinsman DT, Shadish WR. 1996. Assignment methods in experimentation: When do non-randomized experiments approximate answers from randomized experiments? *Psychol. Methods* 1:154–69

Henry GT, Julnes G, Mark MM, eds. 1998. Realist Evaluation: An Emerging Theory in Support of Practice. *New Directions for Evaluation* Vol. 78. San Francisco: Jossey-Bass. 109 pp.

Holtzman J, Chen Q, Kane R. 1998. The effect of HMO status on the outcomes of home-care after hospitalization in a Medicare population. *J. Am. Geriatrics Soc.* 46:629–34

Huberman M. 1996. A critical perspective on the use of templates as evaluation tools. See Scheirer 1996, pp. 99–108

Humphreys K, Phibbs CS, Moos RH. 1996. Addressing self-selection effects in evaluations of mutual help groups and professional mental health services: an introduction to two-stage sample selection models. *Eval. Prog. Plan.* 19:301–8

Jacobson NS, Truax P. 1991. Clinical significance: a statistical approach to defining meaningful change in psychotherapy research. *J. Consult. Clin. Psychol.* 59:12–19

Julian DA. 1997. The utilization of the logic model as a system level planning and evaluation device. *Eval. Prog. Plan.* 20:251–57

Julian DA, Jones A, Deyo D. 1995. Open systems evaluation and the logic model: program planning and evaluation tools. *Eval. Prog. Plan.* 18:333–41

Kalafat J, Illback RJ. 1998. A qualitative evaluation of school-based family resource and youth service centers. *Am. J. Comm. Psychol.* 26:573–604

Kazdin AE. 1986. Comparative outcome studies of psychotherapy: methodological issues and strategies. *J. Consult. Clin. Psychol.* 54:95–105

Kazdin AE, Mazurick JL. 1994. Dropping out of child psychotherapy: distinguishing early and late dropouts over the course of

treatment. *J. Consult. Clin. Psychol.* 62:1069–74

Kellem SG, Rebok GW, Ialongo N, Mayer LS. 1994. The course and malleability of aggressive behavior from early grade into middle school: results of a developmental epidemiologically-based preventive trial. *J. Child Psychol. Psychiatry* 35:963–74

Krause MS, Howard KI, Lutz W. 1998. Exploring individual change. *J. Consult. Clin. Psychol.* 66:838–45

Latkin CA, Mandell W, Vlahov D, Oziemkowska M, Celentano DD. 1996. The long-term outcome of a personal network-oriented HIV prevention intervention for injection drug users: the SAFE study. *Am. J. Comm. Psychol.* 24:341–64

Lennox RD, Dennis ML. 1994. Measurement error issues in substance abuse services research: lessons from structural equation modeling and psychometric theory. *Eval. Prog. Plan.* 17:399–407

Lipsey MW. 1997. What can you build with thousands of bricks? Musings on the cumulation of knowledge in program evaluation. See Rog & Fournier, 1997, pp. 7–24

Lipsey MW. 1999. Statistical conclusion validity for intervention research: a significant (p<.05) problem. In *Validity and Social Experimentation: Donald Campbell's Legacy,* Vol. I. ed. L Bickman. Thousand Oaks, CA: Sage.

Lipsey MW, Wilson DB. 1993. The efficacy of psychological, educational, and behavioral treatment: confirmation from meta-analysis. *Am. Psychol.* 48:1181–1209

Longabaugh R, Wirtz PW, Beattie MC, Noel N, Stout R. 1995. Matching treatment focus to patient social investment and support: 18-month follow-up results *J. Consult. Clin. Psychol.* 63:296–307

Martin LL, Kettner PM. 1996. *Measuring the Performance of Human Service Programs.* Thousand Oaks, CA: Sage. 138 pp.

Maude-Griffin PM, Hohenstein JM, Humfleet GL, Reilly PM, Tusel DJ, et al. 1998. Superior efficacy of cognitive-behavioral therapy for urban crack cocaine abusers: main and matching effects. *J. Consult. Clin. Psychol.* 66:832–37

McGraw SA, Sellars DE, Stone EJ, Bebchuk J, Edmundson E, et al. 1996. Using process data to explain outcomes: an illustration from the child and adolescent trial for cardiovascular health (CATCH). *Eval. Rev.* 20:291–312

McGrew JH, Bond GR, Dietzen L, Salyers M. 1994. Measuring the fidelity of implementation of a mental health program model. *J. Consult. Clin. Psychol.* 62:670–78

Mellenbergh GJ, van den Brink WP. 1998. The measurement of individual change. *Psychol. Methods* 3:470–85

Meredith W, Tisak J. 1990. Latent curve analysis. *Psychometrika* 55:107–22

Moncher FJ, Prinz RJ. 1991. Treatment fidelity in outcome studies. *Clin. Psychol. Rev.* 11:247–66

Mowbray CT, Cohen E, Bybee D. 1993. The challenge of outcome evaluation in homeless services: engagement as an intermediate outcome measure. *Eval. Prog. Plan.* 16:337–46

Murray DM, Moskowitz JM, Dent CW. 1996. Design and analysis issues in community-based drug abuse prevention. *Am. Behav. Sci.* 39:853–67

Muthén BO, Curran PJ. 1997. General longitudinal modeling of individual differences in experimental designs: a latent variable framework for analysis and power estimation. *Psychol. Methods* 2:371–402

Newhouse JP, McClellan M. 1998. Econometrics in outcomes research: the use of instrumental variables. *Annu. Rev. Public Health* 19:17–34

Norman J, Vlahov D, Moses LE, eds. 1995. *Preventing HIV Transmission: The Role of Sterile Needles and Bleach.* Washington DC: Natl. Acad. 334 pp.

Ogles BM, Lambert MJ, Sawyer JD. 1995. Clinical significance of the National Institute of Mental Health Treatment of Depression Collaborative Research Program data. *J. Consult. Clin. Psychol.* 63:321–26

Orwin RG, Sonnefeld LJ, Cordray DS, Pion GM, Perl HI. 1998. Constructing quantitative implementation scales from categorical services data: examples from a multisite evaluation. *Eval. Rev.* 22:245–88

Osgood DW, Smith GL. 1995. Applying hierarchical linear modeling to extended longitudinal evaluations: the Boys Town follow-up study. *Eval. Rev.* 19:3–38

Owen JM. 1998. Towards an outcomes hierarchy for professional university programs. *Eval. Prog. Plan.* 21:315–21

Pawson R, Tilley N. 1997. *Realistic Evaluation.* Thousand Oaks, CA: Sage. 235 pp.

Posavac EJ. 1998. Toward more informative uses of statistics: alternatives for program evaluators. *Eval. Prog. Plan.* 21:243–54

Prochaska JO, DiClemente CC, Norcross JC. 1992. In search of how people change: applications to addictive behaviors. *Am. Psychol.* 47:1102–14

Reichardt CS, Gollob HF. 1997. When confidence intervals should be used instead of statistical tests, and vice versa. In *What If There Were No Significance Tests?*, ed. LL Harlow, SA Mulaik, JH Steiger, pp. 259–84. Hillsdale, NJ: Erlbaum. 446 pp.

Reichardt CS, Rallis SE, eds. 1994. *The Qualitative-Quantitative Debate: New Perspectives: New Direction for Program Evaluation.* Vol. 61. San Francisco: Jossey-Bass. 98 pp.

Reynolds AJ, Temple JA. 1995. Quasi-experimental estimates of the effects of a preschool intervention: psychometric and econometric comparisons. *Eval. Rev.* 19:347–73

Reynolds AJ, Temple JA. 1998. Extended early childhood intervention and school achievement: age thirteen findings from the Chicago Longitudinal Study. *Child Dev.* 69:231–46

Rog DJ, Fournier D, eds. 1997. Progress and Future Directions in *Evaluation: Perspectives on Theory, Practice, and Methods: New Directions for Evaluation* Vol. 76. San Francisco: Jossey-Bass. 111 pp.

Rog DJ, Huebner RB. 1991. Using research and theory in developing innovative programs for homeless families. In *Using Theory to Improve Program and Policy Evaluations,* ed. H-T Chen, PH Rossi, pp. 129–44. New York: Greenwood. 278 pp.

Rogers PJ, Hough G. 1995. Improving the effectiveness of evaluations: making the link to organizational theory. *Eval. Prog. Plan.* 18:321–32

Rosenbaum PR. 1995. *Observational Studies.* New York: Springer-Verlag. 230 pp.

Rosenheck R, Frisman L, Gallup P. 1995. Effectiveness and cost of specific treatment elements in a program for homeless mentally ill veterans. *Psychiatric Serv.* 46: 1131–38

Rosenthal R, Rubin DB. 1994. The counternull value of an effect size: a new statistic. *Psychol. Sci.* 5:329–34

Rossi PH. 1997. Program outcomes: conceptual and measurement issues. In *Outcome and Measurement in the Human Services: Cross-Cutting Issues and Methods,* ed. EJ Mullen, J Magnabosco. Washington, DC: Natl. Assoc. Social Workers

Rossi PH, Freeman HE, Lipsey MW. 1999. *Evaluation: A Systematic Approach.* Thousand Oaks, CA: Sage. 500 pp. 6th ed.

Scheirer MA. 1994. Designing and using process evaluation. In *Handbook of Practical Program Evaluation,* ed. JS Wholey, HP Hatry, KE Newcomer, pp. 40–68. San Francisco: Jossey-Bass. 622 pp.

Scheirer MA, ed. 1996. A template for assessing the organizational base for program implementation. In *A User's Guide to Program Templates: A New Tool for Evaluating Program Content: New Directions for Evaluation.* 72:61–80. San Francisco: Jossey-Bass. 111 pp.

Schmidt FL. 1996. Statistical significance testing and cumulative knowledge in psychology: implications for training of researchers. *Psychol. Methods* 1:115–29

Scriven M. 1967. The methodology of evaluation. In *Perspectives of Curriculum Evaluation,* ed. RW Tyler, RM Gagne, M

Scriven, pp. 39–83. AERA Monograph Series on Curriculum Evaluation. Chicago: Rand McNally

Scriven M. 1991. Beyond formative and summative evaluation. In *Evaluation and Education: At Quarter Century,* ed. MW McLaughlin, DC Phillips, pp. 18–64. Chicago: Univ. Chicago Press

Sechrest L, Figueredo AJ. 1993. Program evaluation. *Annu. Rev. Psychol.* 44: 645–74.

Sechrest L, McKnight P, McKnight K. 1996. Calibration of measures for psychotherapy outcome studies. *Am. Psychol.* 51:1065–71

Shadish WR, Ragsdale K. 1996. Random versus nonrandom assignment in controlled experiments: Do you get the same answer? *J. Consult. Clin. Psychol.* 64:1290–1305

Shortell S, Kaluzny A. 1988. *Health Care Management: A Text in Organization Theory and Behavior.* New York: Wiley. 524 pp. 2nd ed.

Sidani S, Braden CJ. 1998. *Evaluating Nursing Interventions: A Theory-Driven Approach.* Thousand Oaks, CA: Sage

Smith B, Sechrest L. 1991. Treatment of aptitude x treatment interactions. *J. Consult. Clin. Psychol.* 59:233–44

Smith JE, Meyers RJ, Delaney HD. 1998. The community reinforcement approach with homeless alcohol-dependent individuals. *J. Consult. Clin. Psychol.* 66:541–48

Speer DC, Greenbaum PE. 1995. Five methods for computing significant individual client change and improvement rates: support for an individual growth curve approach. *J. Consult. Clin. Psychol.* 63:1044–48

Speer DC, Newman FL. 1996. Mental health services outcome evaluation. *Clin. Psychol. Sci. Practice* 3:105–29

Spoth R, Redmond C, Shin C. 1998. Direct and indirect latent-variable parenting outcomes of two universal family-focused preventive interventions: extending a public health-oriented research base. *J. Consult. Clin. Psychol.* 66:385–99

St. Pierre RG, Layzer JI, Goodson BD, Berstein LS. 1997. *National Impact Evaluation of the Comprehensive Child Development*

Program: Final Report. Cambridge, MA: Abt

Staines GL, McKendrick K, Perlis T, Sacks S, De Leon G. 1999. Sequential assignment and treatment-as-usual: alternatives to standard experimental designs in field studies of treatment efficacy. *Eval. Rev.* 23:47–76

Stecher BM, Andrews CA, McDonald L, Morton S, McGlynn EA, et al. 1994. Implementation of residential and nonresidential treatment for dually diagnosed homeless. *Eval. Rev.* 18:689–717

Stewart BJ, Archbold PG. 1992. Nursing intervention studies require outcome measures that are sensitive to change: Part one. *Res. Nursing Health* 15:477–81

Stewart BJ, Archbold PG. 1993. Nursing intervention studies require outcome measures that are sensitive to change: Part two. *Res. Nursing Health* 16:77–81

Stolzenberg RM, Relles DA. 1997. Tools for intuition about sample selection bias and its correction. *Am. Sociol. Rev.* 62:494–507

Strauss A, Corbin J. 1990. *Basics of Qualitative Research: Grounded Theory Procedures and Techniques.* Thousand Oaks, CA: Sage. 270 pp.

Suchman EA. 1967. *Evaluation Research: Principles and Practice in Public Service and Social Action Programs.* New York: Russell Sage Found.186 pp.

Van Ryzin GG. 1996. The impact of resident management on residents' satisfaction with public housing: a process analysis of quasi-experimental data. *Eval. Rev.* 20:485–506

Weiss CH. 1972. *Evaluation Research: Methods of Assessing Program Effectiveness.*

Englewood Cliffs, NJ: Prentice-Hall. 160 pp.

Weiss CH. 1997. Theory-based evaluation: past, present and future. See Rog & Fournier 1997, pp. 41–56

Wholey JS. 1994. Assessing the feasibility and likely usefulness of evaluation. In *Handbook of Practical Program Evaluation,* ed. JS Wholey, HP Hatry, KE Newcomer, pp. 15–39. San Francisco: Jossey-Bass. 662 pp.

Willett JB, Sayer AG. 1994. Using covariance structure analysis to detect correlates and predictors of individual change over time. *Psychol. Bull.* 116:363–81

Winship C, Mare RD. 1992. Models for sample selection bias. *Annu. Rev. Sociol.* 18:327–50

Wu P, Campbell DT. 1996. Extending latent variable LISREL analyses of the 1969 Westinghouse Head Start evaluation to Blacks and full year Whites. *Eval. Prog. Plan.* 19:183–91

Yeaton WH. 1994. The development and assessment of valid measures of service delivery to enhance inference in outcome-based research: measuring attendance at self-help group meetings. *J. Consult. Clin. Psychol.* 62:686–94

Yin RK. 1994. Discovering the future of the case study method in evaluation research. *Eval. Pract.* 15:283–90

Yin RK. 1997. Case study evaluations: a decade of progress? See Rog & Fournier 1997, pp. 69–78

Zanis DA, McLellan AT, Belding MA, Moyer G. 1997. A comparison of three methods of measuring the type and quantity of services provided during substance abuse treatment. *Drug Alcohol Depend.* 49:25–32

Annu. Rev. Psychol. 2000. 51:377–404

ADULT PSYCHOPATHOLOGY: Issues and Controversies

T. A. Widiger and L. M. Sankis

*Department of Psychology, University of Kentucky, Lexington, Kentucky 40506–0044;
e-mail: widiger@pop.uky.edu*

Key Words mental disorder, pathology, diagnosis, dyscontrol, dysfunction

■ **Abstract** This review discusses issues and controversies with respect to the construct of a mental disorder, models of etiology and pathology, and domains of psychopathology. Fundamental to the science of psychopathology is a conceptualization of mental disorder, yet inadequate attention is being given to the differentiation of normal and abnormal psychological functioning in current research. The boundaries between mental and physical disorders are equally problematic. Neurophysiological models are receiving particular emphasis in large part because of the substantial progress being made in documenting and clarifying the important role of neurophysiological structures and mechanisms in etiology and pathology. However, this attention might be at the expense of the recognition of equally valid psychological models. Problematic diagnostic boundaries are also considered, including those within and between different classes of disorder. Dimensional models may offer a more precise and comprehensive classification of psychopathology.

CONTENTS

Introduction 378
Construct of Psychopathology 378
  Normal Versus Abnormal Functioning 378
  Cultural Relativity 380
  Harmful Dysfunction or Dyscontrolled Maladaptivity 382
Models of Etiology and Pathology 384
  Substance Dependence 385
  Posttraumatic Stress Disorder 386
  Discussion 387
Domains of Psychopathology 390
  Diagnostic Boundaries 391
  Dyscontrolled Anger, Hostility, and Aggression 393
  Life Span Psychopathology 394
  Dimensional Versus Categorical Classification 396
Conclusions 398

INTRODUCTION

The goal of any chapter in an *Annual Review of Psychology* is to interpret the progress, direction, and purpose of current research. Prior chapters on adult psychopathology published in the 1990s have emphasized diagnosis and classification (e.g. Nathan & Langenbucher 1999, Widiger & Trull 1991), comorbidity (e.g. Clark et al 1995, Mineka et al 1998), and research methodology (e.g. Kessler 1997, Sher & Trull 1996). These reviews remain current and highly informative, although many of the concerns raised within them are also addressed in this volume. However, emphasis is given in this instance to major issues and controversies that continue to complicate a scientific understanding of adult psychopathology, organized with respect to the construct of psychopathology, models of etiology and pathology, and domains of psychopathology.

CONSTRUCT OF PSYCHOPATHOLOGY

An ongoing concern that is fundamental to the science of psychopathology is the absence of an established definition of the construct of mental disorder. Proposals, and compelling critiques of same, continue to be developed (e.g. Bergner 1997, Dammann 1997, Lilienfeld & Marino 1995, Nathan & Langenbucher 1999, Wakefield 1999). Wakefield's (1992, 1997) series of papers has been especially helpful in finding instructive faults with various alternative proposals.

Normal Versus Abnormal Functioning

Explicit within the definition of a mental disorder provided in the American Psychiatric Association's (APA) Diagnostic and Statistical Manual of Mental Disorders (DSM-IV) (APA 1994) is that the condition "must currently be considered a manifestation of a behavioral, psychological, or biological dysfunction in the individual" (APA 1994:xxi–xxii). Wakefield (1997) provided examples of criteria sets from DSM-IV that he argued failed to make necessary distinctions between maladaptive problems in living and true psychopathology, resulting from the reliance in DSM-IV on indicators of distress or impairment rather than the purportedly fundamental internal dysfunctions. For example, the DSM-IV criteria set for major depressive disorder (APA 1994) excludes uncomplicated bereavement, presumably because depressive reactions to the loss of a loved one are normal (nonpathological). However, DSM-IV makes no exclusion for comparably uncomplicated reactions of sadness to other major stressors, such as a terminal illness, divorce, or loss of job. Wakefield suggests that whatever distinction is being made between a major depressive disorder and uncomplicated bereavement should be made for all other circumstances in which the symptoms of depression would represent a normal response.

An alternative hypothesis is that purportedly normal bereavement is much more complicated than previously thought (Prigerson et al 1999). For example, the normality of a depressive response to the loss of a loved one might not be a matter of its rationality, commonality, understandability, or even symptom severity. If the reaction is maladaptive and not within adequate control of the person, then perhaps it should be classified as a mental disorder. A future investigation that might be of considerable scientific value would be one of the normality (or pathology) of purportedly normal depressive reactions to various losses. Even ostensibly normal cases of bereavement might display indicators of an irrational cognitive schema or a neurochemical dysregulation.

The importance of a meaningful demarcation between normal and abnormal psychological functioning is particularly apparent for epidemiological research (Leighton & Murphy 1997, Regier et al 1998). Regier and colleagues (1998) lament the inconsistent and potentially excessive prevalence rates that have been obtained in National Institute of Mental Health epidemiology research programs. Prevalence estimates have at times been so high that Regier et al (1998) question whether existing diagnostic criteria sets are in fact identifying instances of "true psychopathologic disorder" (1998:114). One caution, however, is that the presumption that there is an overdiagnosis might not itself be valid. Regier and his colleagues are forthright in their acknowledgment that their concerns reflect in part their efforts to convince social policy makers of the need for mental health services. "In the current US climate of determining the medical necessity for care in managed health care plans, it is doubtful that 28% or 29% of the population would be judged to need mental health treatment in a year. Hence, additional impairment and other criteria should be developed" (Regier et al 1998:114). The failure of government and insurance agencies to adequately fund research and treatment of mental disorders is of substantial social and clinical importance, but perhaps these concerns should not affect the answer to scientific questions regarding the actual prevalence rate of psychopathology (Spitzer 1998).

Critics of the DSM have questioned the increasing number of diagnoses within each edition, suggesting that the expansion is more political than scientific (e.g. Follette & Houts 1996, Rogler 1997). However, it might have been more surprising to find that scientific research and increased knowledge have led to the recognition of fewer instances of psychopathology (Wakefield 1998). It is also unclear why the prevalence rate of mental disorders should be so much lower than the prevalence rate of physical disorders. Optimal psychological functioning, as in the case of optimal physical functioning, might represent an ideal that is achieved by no one. The rejection of a high prevalence rate of psychopathology may reflect the best of intentions, such as concerns regarding the stigmatization of mental disorder diagnoses (Kutchins & Kirk 1997) or the inadequate funding of their research and treatment (Regier et al 1998), but these social and political concerns might be hindering a recognition of a more realistic and accurate estimate of the true rate of psychopathology.

Klein (1999) suggests that abnormal pathology can be inferred from the responsivity of a person to pharmacologic treatment. "Currently, our positive experience with psychopharmacological agents, that have little effect upon normals, but have marked benefits on patients with chronic disorders, leads to the inference of something chronically but reversibly wrong" (Klein 1999). Responsivity to pharmacologic agents has at times been useful as a diagnostic indicator, but a reliance on this responsivity to guide judgments regarding the presence of an underlying pathology can at times be mistaken (Barkley 1998). The neurochemical mechanisms of actions of pharmacologic interventions are in many respects diverse and nonspecific (e.g. Gorman & Kent 1999, Stahl 1998) and are unlikely to be confined to a specific or even identifiable neurochemical pathology. Antidepressants and anxiolytics might be effective simply by impairing, inhibiting, or blocking normal rather than dysregulated, dyscontrolled, or otherwise pathologic neurochemical mechanisms of sadness and anxiousness. In any case, there does not appear to be much research on the psychological, affective, behavioral, or even neurochemical effects of these pharmacologic agents within ostensibly normal persons. The assumption that they have no effect appears to be inferred "by the fact that [these drugs] are not sold on the street as euphorants" (Klein 1999). Simply because a drug does not have sufficient value as a euphoric to be marketable as a drug of abuse does not mean that it does not affect normal neurochemical processes. Antidepressants and anxiolytics are not being sold as euphorants, but they are being sold frequently by physicians to help people decrease their experience of negative affectivity (Munoz et al 1994).

In a double-blind study Knutson and his colleagues (1998) administered paroxetine, a selective serotonin reuptake inhibitor (SSRI), for 4 weeks to 23 of 48 ostensibly normal volunteers. They reported that SSRI administration (relative to placebo) reduced negative affectivity and increased social facilitation. The magnitude of changes was even correlated with plasma levels of SSRI within the SSRI group. "This is the first empirical demonstration that chronic administration of a selective serotonin reuptake blockade can have significant personality and behavioral effects in normal humans in the absence of baseline depression or other psychopathology" (Knutson et al 1998:378).

Cultural Relativity

One controversy has been the validity of the construct of a mental disorder across different cultural perspectives (Lopez & Guarnaccia 2000, Sher & Trull 1996). There is perhaps both a strong and a weak cross-cultural critique of current scientific understanding of psychopathology. The weak critique is that social and cultural processes affect and potentially bias the "science of psychopathology and diagnosis: *a*) by determining the selection of persons and behaviors as suitable material for analysis; *b*) by emphasizing what aspects of this material will be handled as relevant from a [clinical] standpoint; *c*) by shaping the language of diagnosis, including that of descriptive psychopathology; *d*) by masking the symptoms of any putative "universal" disorder; *e*) by biasing the observer and would-be diagnostician; and *f*) by determining the goals and endpoints of treatment" (Fabrega 1994:262). These concerns are not weak in the sense that they are trivial or inconsequential, but they are relatively weak in the sense that they do not necessarily question the fundamental validity of the construct of a mental disorder or the science of psychopathology. The strong critique, in contrast, is that the construct is itself a culture-bound belief that reflects the local biases of western society, and that the science of psychopathology could be valid only in the sense that it is an accepted belief system of a particular culture (Lewis-Fernandez & Kleinman 1995).

A diagnosis of a mental disorder is inherently a value judgment that there should be necessary, adequate, or optimal psychological functioning (Sadler 1997, Wakefield 1992). However, this same value judgment also applies to the construct of a physical disorder. In a world of persons who placed no value on necessary, adequate, or optimal physical functioning, or in a world in which there were in fact virtually no impairments or threats to physical functioning, the construct of a physical disorder might have no meaning and perhaps no validity (except as an interesting thought experiment). Meaningful and valid scientific research on the etiology, pathology, and treatment of physical disorders nevertheless does appear to occur in the world, as it currently exists, despite this value judgment. On the other hand, different species will not share the same perspective on what constitutes healthy biological functioning, and different societies, cultures, and even persons within a particular culture may disagree as to what constitutes optimal or pathological biological and psychological functioning (Lopez & Guarnaccia 2000). Diener & Suh (1999) report significant variation across cultures (or nations) in the relative importance persons place on, for example, happiness, autonomy, or social ties for the obtainment of subjective well-being. A fundamental issue for research in psychopathology is how to understand the differences between cultures with respect to what constitutes dysfunction and pathology.

For example, the fact that diagnostic criteria sets are acceptable to or applied reliably across different cultures does not necessarily make the constructs themselves valid within these cultures (Lewis-Fernandez & Kleinman 1995). A clinically acceptable and reliable criteria set can be developed for an entirely illusory diagnostic construct. On the other hand, it is perhaps equally unclear why it would be necessary for the documentation of a disorder's construct validity to obtain cross-cultural (i.e. universal) application or acceptance.

Lewis-Fernandez & Kleinman (1995) argue that a cross-cultural perspective is necessary "to produce a comprehensive nosology that is both internationally and locally valid" (p. 435). The universality of a diagnostic system can have significant theoretical implications and social value (Kessler 1999), and it is important to recognize and appreciate alternative belief systems (Lopez & Guarnaccia 2000). However, it is also apparent that belief systems vary in their veridicality, and cultures that emphasize a scientific method to develop and advance their belief systems might experience more success (although not always) in increasing the extent of accurate knowledge. One cannot prove the validity of a scientific method, but the advances to knowledge in the fields of physics, chemistry, biology, astronomy, and geology in cultures that have emphasized the scientific method do appear to provide fairly compelling evidence for the success of the approach (Bergner 1997). In fact, to the extent that different cultural belief systems are equally valid, the cultural relativity arguments of Lewis-Fernandez & Kleinman (1995) might themselves have no validity beyond their own particular social-cultural perspective (Lillard 1998).

Kirmayer and his colleagues (1995) illustrate many of the complexities of cross-cultural research. For example, a woman's housebound behavior might be diagnosed as agoraphobic within Western cultures but perhaps considered normative (or even virtuous) within a Muslim culture; submissive behavior that is diagnosed as pathologic dependency within Western societies might be considered normative within the Japanese culture. However, the fact that a behavior pattern is valued, accepted, encouraged, or even statistically normative within a particular culture does not necessarily mean it is conducive to optimal psychological functioning. For example, "in societies where ritual plays an important role in religious life . . . such societies may predispose individuals to obsessive-compulsive symptoms and mask the disorder when present" (Kirmayer et al 1995:507). "The congruence between religious belief and practice and obsessive-compulsive symptoms also probably contributes to relatively low rates of insight into the irrationality of the symptoms" (Kirmayer et al 1995:508). "This possible tension between cultural styles and health consequences is in urgent need of further research" (Kirmayer et al 1995:517), and it is important for this research to go beyond simply identifying differences in practices and belief systems across different cultures, and to address instead the extent to which these differences are valid indicators of, or perhaps even contributions to, the development of psychopathology. Further discussion of these issues is provided by Lopez & Guarnaccia (2000).

Harmful Dysfunction or Dyscontrolled Maladaptivity

Wakefield has provided many compelling and informative critiques of proposed models of psychopathology, but his own proposal for a "harmful dysfunction" definition of mental disorder (Wakefield 1992) has now itself received compelling critiques (e.g. Bergner 1997, Kirmayer & Young 1999, Lilienfeld & Marino 1999). In Wakefield's (1992, 1999) model, disorder means harmful dysfunction, where dysfunction is a failure of an internal mechanism to perform a naturally selected function; harm is a value judgment that the failure is harmful to the individual. A fundamental limitation of the model, however, might be its girding within evolutionary theory (Bergner 1997). Evolutionary theory has enriched current understanding of the etiology and pathology of various mental disorders (Buss et al 1998), but it is itself a particular theoretical model of etiology and pathology. Harmful dysfunction might then be inadequate in providing a general definition of mental disorder that allows for or is compatible with alternative models (Kirmayer & Young 1999).

Wakefield's model might even be inconsistent with some sociobiological models of psychopathology. For example, cultural evolution may at times outstrip the pace of biological evolution, rendering some designed functions that were originally adaptive within the Pleistocene age maladaptive in many current environments (Lilienfeld & Marino 1999). "The existence in humans of a preparedness mechanism for developing a fear of snakes may be a relic not well designed to deal with urban living, which currently contains hostile forces far more dangerous to human survival (e.g. cars, electrical outlets) but for which humans lack evolved mechanisms of fear preparedness" (Buss et al 1998:538). Harmful dysfunction, however, would not diagnose a genetically based irrational fear of a stimulus that was the result of a mismatch between past evolutionary design and the current environment (Wakefield 1999).

Wakefield (1999), however, might be disengaging harmful dysfunction from evolutionary theory by indicating that the model never implied or required that the judgment of harm arising from a failure of an evolutionarily designed function reflected in some respect the failure to perform that function. The judgment of harm is independent of the judgment of fitness or survival. This disengagement of the judgment of harm from the underlying sociobiological model, however, might also be regrettable, as one of the intriguing aspects of the model was the suggestion that the harms experienced by an organism were related conceptually to failures of naturally selected mechanisms to perform in the manner for which they were designed (Lilienfeld & Marino 1999). The harm experienced by an organism that justifies a diagnosis of a mental disorder could now even be in opposition to the purpose for which a mechanism was designed to function.

Missing entirely from Wakefield's (1999) definition of mental disorder is any reference to dyscontrol. The component of harm is concerned with a documentation of impairment; the component of dysfunction is the presence of a pathology. Mental disorders, however, are perhaps dyscontrolled organismic impairments in psychological functioning (Kirmayer & Young 1999, Klein 1999, Widiger & Trull 1991). "Involuntary impairment remains the key inference" (Klein 1999). Dyscontrol is not fundamental to the construct of a physical disorder, but it might be fundamental to the construct of a mental disorder, as the latter concerns impairments to feelings, thoughts, or behaviors over which a normal (healthy) person is believed to have adequate control.

A more appropriate conceptualization of a mental disorder might be dyscontrolled maladaptivity rather than harmful dysfunction (Widiger & Trull 1991). Fundamental to a judgment of mental disorder is perhaps the ability to control one's thoughts, behaviors, or feelings adequately (Bergner 1997). To the extent that a person is willfully, intentionally, freely, voluntarily, or with adequate self-control engaging in harmful sexual acts, drug usage, gambling, or child abuse, the person would not be considered to have a mental disorder. To the extent that a person could adequately control, modulate, manage, regulate, or resolve his or her depressed mood, the person would not be considered to have a mood disorder. Current diagnostic criteria are indicators of impairment, but they are also indicators of dyscontrol (e.g. continued usage of a drug despite social, legal, financial, physical, or other significant negative consequences). Distress is a fallible but valid indication of the presence of a mental disorder in part because it suggests that the person lacks adequate ability to simply change or resolve the problematic symptoms themselves. People seek professional intervention in large part to obtain the insights, techniques, skills, or other tools (e.g. medications) that increase their ability to better control their mood, thoughts, or behavior. The assessment of the boundary between adequate versus inadequate self-

ment of the boundary between adequate versus inadequate self-control is highly problematic (Golding et al 1999, Webster & Jackson 1998) and often controversial (Alper 1998), but the extent of dyscontrol should perhaps be a primary focus of research, as it might be fundamental to the documentation of the presence of psychopathology.

MODELS OF ETIOLOGY AND PATHOLOGY

Mental disorders are not equivalent to physical disorders, but the boundary between them is at best problematic. A mental disorder is described in DSM-IV as "a clinically significant behavioral or psychological syndrome or pattern" (APA 1994:xxi). Mental disorders, by and large, involve impairments in psychological or behavioral functioning, whereas physical disorders (general medical conditions) involve disorders of physiological functioning. The distinction is primarily with respect to phenomenology. Disorders in psychological or behavioral functioning can be the result of a neurophysiological etiology and pathology, but the phenomenology of the disorder is more psychological than physical.

Nevertheless, there is not a clear boundary between psychological and physiological functioning. For example, pain disorder is diagnosed when psychological factors are judged to have an important role in the experience of or difficulty tolerating pain. There are two subtypes: pain disorder associated with psychological factors, and pain disorder associated with both psychological factors and a general medical condition (APA 1994). In the former case, "medical conditions play either no role or a minimal role in the onset or maintenance of the pain" (APA 1994:458). Apparently, it is possible for there to be no physical basis for pain, despite the apparent contributions of the central nervous system. Fishbain and his colleagues (1998) indicated in a meta-analysis of pain disorder studies that antidepressants decreased significantly the intensity of psychogenic pain, but they indicated as well that this may simply reflect analgesic effects of antidepressants.

A diagnosis closely related to pain disorder is psychological factors affecting a medical condition (PFAMC) (APA 1994). This diagnosis was classified as a mental disorder in DSM-III-R (APA 1987) but is now classified in DSM-IV as simply a condition that might be the focus of clinical attention (APA 1994). "Consequently, the diagnosis has ceased to exist as a mental disorder" (Hales 1998:1084). PFAMC was a diagnosis used by specialists in behavioral medicine to indicate the contribution of psychological factors to the etiology, exacerbation, or maintenance of a physical disorder, such as an ulcer or obesity. However, in most instances the disorder that was being treated was physical rather than psychological. Psychological factors might have contributed to its etiology, exacerbation, and ultimately its treatment, but there is perhaps no physical disorder for which psychological factors could not make an important contribution (Baum & Posluszny 1999). Most important, the phenomenology and pathology of these disorders will in most of these cases be essentially physiological. If there is a psychological pathology underlying a physical abnormality (as in cases of conversion, factitious, or somatization disorders), then that particular mental disorder should perhaps be diagnosed (e.g. type A personality traits diagnosed as a personality disorder) rather than PFAMC.

DSM-IV also eliminated the section of DSM-III-R devoted to organic mental disorders, as the inclusion of this section was largely a historical artifact of an illusory distinction between organic and functional mental disorders (Spitzer et al 1992). "The essential feature of all these [organic mental] disorders is a psychological or behavioral abnormality associated with transient or permanent dysfunction of the brain" (APA 1987:9). This statement would now apply to many instances of anxiety, mood, psychotic, and other mental disorders. In fact, virtually all mental disorders are being increasingly redefined as brain disorders. An excellent account of this historical trend is provided by Kandel (1998). "To function effectively in the future, the psychiatrists we are training today will need more than just a nodding familiarity with the biology of the brain. They will need the knowledge . . . fully comparable to that of a well-trained neurologist" (Kandel 1998:466). This proactive shift to a neurological perspective is demonstrated below with respect to the substance-related and posttraumatic stress disorders.

Substance Dependence

An increasing emphasis on neurophysiological models of etiology and pathology is illustrated in part by three recent editorials concerning substance dependence research. O'Brien (1997), Kosten (1998), and Leshner (1999) go beyond simply highlighting the contributions made by neurophysiological research to argue that substance abuse and dependence are fundamentally neurophysiological disorders.

Substance dependence was synonymous with a physiological dependence in DSM-III (APA 1980). The diagnosis was confined to the presence of symptoms of either a physiological tolerance or withdrawal. However, dependence was affiliated with a more psychological construct of behavioral dependence in DSM-III-R (Carroll et al 1994). "Dependence is seen as a complex process that reflects the central importance of substances in an individual's life, along with a feeling of compulsion to continue taking the substance and subsequent problems controlling use" (Schuckit et al 1999:41).

Kosten (1998), Leshner (1999), and O'Brien (1997), however, suggest that current research indicates that any excessively maladaptive motivation, interest, desire, or craving for a drug is fundamentally a neurophysiological pathology. Tsai et al (1998), for example, provided a neurochemical model for a subtle and protracted physiological withdrawal that might explain future behavioral relapses that occur irrespective of the traditional (DSM-III) signs of withdrawal. "This persistent effect may be due to a self-perpetuating cycle of enhanced glutamatergic neurotransmission and increased oxidative stress" (Tsai et al 1998:731). Volkow et al (1997) used imaging techniques to indicate the neurophysiological correlates of the psychologically reinforcing experiences associated with drug usage. Dopamine transporter blockade "greater than 47% is required for cocaine to be subjectively perceived as reinforcing . . . These results consolidate the role of [dopamine transporter] blockade as a crucial mechanism in the reinforcing properties of cocaine in humans" (Volkow et al 1997:829). Volkow et al (1999) also used imaging techniques to assess the effects of two sequential doses of methylphenidate on regional brain glucose metabolism in 20 detoxified cocaine abusers. The cocaine abusers, in contrast to the normal subjects, displayed methyphenidate-induced increases in the superior cingulate gyrus and in the right thalamus, and Volkow et al (1999) concluded that "the striato-orbitofrontal circuit is involved with the salience of reinforcing stimuli, and thus its activation may be one of the mechanisms associated with the loss of control and the compulsive drug administration observed in cocaine-addicted subjects" (p. 25). Childress et al (1999) also used imaging techniques to assess whether limbic-related regions might be differentially activated during cue-induced cocaine craving by comparing cocaine-dependent and cocaine-naive participants' reactions to cocaine-related and non–drug-related videos. During the cocaine video, the cocaine users experienced craving and displayed increases in limbic (amygdala and anterior cingulate) cerebral blood flow that did not occur in the cocaine-naive participants. Perhaps even more intriguing, the cocaine-dependent participants also displayed a decrease in basal ganglia cerebral blood flow. "The lack of hippocampal activation during craving suggests the subordination of explicit (factual) memory to an amygdala-driven emotional state. The developing brain signature of cue-induced craving is thus consistent with its clinical phenomenology: the drug user is gripped by a visceral emotional state, experiences a highly focused incentive to act, and is remarkably unencumbered by the memory of negative consequences of drug taking" (Childress et al 1999:15).

In sum, "a modern conceptualization of addiction is that it acts as a chronic disease produced by thousands of exposures to drugs. Each drug-taking episode activates specific brain structures, leaving a memory trace that persists long after the drug has disappeared from the body" (O'Brien 1997:1195). Kosten (1998) concludes that, indeed, "addiction is a brain disease" (p. 711). "That addiction is tied to changes in brain structure and function is what makes it, fundamentally, a brain disease" (Leshner 1997:46). "Initially, drug use is a voluntary behavior, but when that switch is thrown, the individual moves into the state of addiction, characterized by compulsive drug seeking and use" (Leshner 1997:46). Even when this dyscontrolled usage reflects in part a social-learning history, "alterations in gene expression induced by learning give rise to changes in patterns of neuronal connections . . . [that] are responsible for initiating and maintaining abnormalities of behavior that are induced by social contingencies" (Kandel 1998:460).

Posttraumatic Stress Disorder

An additional illustration of an increasing neurophysiological emphasis is provided by a disorder that has traditionally been understood from a more psychosocial perspective. The DSM-III-R diagnosis of posttraumatic stress disorder (PTSD) required that the stressor be an event that was outside the range of usual human experience and would be markedly distressing to most anyone (APA 1987). This requirement was consistent with the belief that the occurrence of the disorder was due in large part to the nature or severity of the stressor. However, "studies of the prevalence, course, and comorbidity of PTSD have raised issues regarding the role of the stressor as the true etiologic factor in the development of this disorder" (Yehuda & McFarlane 1995:1705).

"The emergence of PTSD following exposure to a trauma may represent the manifestation of an underlying diathesis rather than a normative adaptation to environmental challenge" (Yehuda & McFarlane 1995:1709). The experience of a trauma, such as a violent rape, is not a sufficient determinant of PTSD (Bowman 1999). Yehuda (1998) suggests that a qualitatively distinct set of biological alterations occur in persons who develop the symptoms of PTSD. Rather than displaying a purportedly normal response to stress of increased adrenocortical activity and ultimately pituitary hyporesponsivity, the hypothalamic-pituitary-adrenal system appears to become more sensitized in cases of PTSD, manifested by a decreased cortisol release and an increased (rather than decreased) negative feedback inhibition. "This disruption may lead to alterations in the processing of traumatic memories. Indeed, low cortisol enhances the memory-potentiating effects of catecholamines in the central nervous system" (Yehuda et al 1998a:858).

An alternative understanding for this neurophysiological model is that Yehuda and her colleagues are simply documenting the neurophysiological correlates of the psychological horror that is experienced by some persons who suffer severe trauma. The neuroendocrinological abnormalities have in all instances been obtained after the person was traumatized and could simply represent a consequence of having been traumatized rather than providing the original etiology for the traumatization. Yehuda et al (1998b), however, interviewed 22 Holocaust survivors and their adult offspring. Psychopathology in offspring has traditionally been explained as a result of experiencing vicariously the horror of the Holocaust through the reports and stories of the older generation. Yehuda and her colleagues, however, again noted that not all of the offspring or all of the survivors of the Holocaust became impaired psychologically. They found that the development of PTSD symptomatology of Holocaust offspring depended largely on whether the parent had developed a chronic PTSD. "The findings supplement studies exploring biological concomitants of PTSD by raising the possibility of a genetically linked risk factor for PTSD" (Yehuda et al 1998b:843).

Discussion

There is much that is neurophysiological in psychopathology. The progress that has been made in understanding biogenetic and neurophysiological etiologies and pathologies of mental disorders has been remarkable, and we have certainly only scratched the surface of what will eventually become known (Kandel 1998). "We currently possess the ability to manipulate the mouse genome nearly at will" (Hyman 1998:38), and such research will "provide important insights into the pathophysiology of mental disorders" (Hyman 1998:38). For example, Thiele et al (1998) produced neuropeptide Y (NPY)-deficient mice by gene targeting. Prior research had indicated that alcohol-preferring rats have lower levels of NPY in several brain regions. Thiele et al reported that their NPY-deficient mice demonstrated, as predicted, increased consumption of alcohol and, perhaps even more intriguing, were less sensitive to the sedative and hypnotic effects of ethanol. In marked contrast, transgenic mice that overexpressed a marked NPY gene in areas of the brain, in which it is usually found, demonstrated a lower preference for alcohol and were more sensitive to sedative and hypnotic effects. These findings of Thiele et al might provide the neurophysiological explanation for research that has indicated that humans with a genetic vulnerability to dyscontrolled alcohol use are less susceptible to its effects.

Childress et al (1999) described how their imaging research can be helpful in clarifying the frustrating search for medications to prevent cocaine relapse. "'Antiwithdrawal' agents intended to restore or enhance the dopaminergic tone of hypoactive limbic regions may actually generate an internal state experienced as craving and/or may enhance the response to external cocaine cues. Conversely, 'anticraving' agents that block limbic dopamine receptors may reduce cue-related craving, but their blunting of mood and motivation makes compliance problematic" (Childress et al 1999:16). Neurophysiological methods can also themselves inform more psychologically-oriented perspectives (Miller 1996). For example, identification through imaging techniques of the activation of different brain regions for seemingly comparable expressions of a desire to use drugs might lead to more accurate differentiations among different psychological components of drug craving.

Nevertheless, there may also be a tendency to overstate the importance of neurophysiology and to understate the scientific importance of social-psychological variables. We have perhaps left the decade of the brain (Judd 1998) to enter a decade of the brain disease (Andreasen 1997, Hyman 1998). In an excellent discussion of this issue, Miller (1996) provided a number of illustrations of potentially excessive reductions of psychological events to neurophysiological events, as if this translation somehow provided a more complete, fundamental, or scientific explanation. Comparable concerns can be raised with respect to the studies described above.

For example, functional and structural changes in neurophysiology can be as much the result of experiences as the causes of future behaviors (Kolb & Whishaw 1998). Identifying the neurochemical basis for a behavior does not necessarily suggest that neurophysiology causes the behavior to occur (Alper 1998, Berman & Coccaro 1998), and identifying the neural basis for learning does not suggest that the neurophysiological perception of learning is the etiology for the resulting behavior rather than the psychosocial events that were originally perceived. In addition, neuroimages of cognitive activity do not suggest that cognitions do not have their own significance and importance in understanding and explaining a disorder's etiology or pathology. Statements that are made to oneself (by other persons or by oneself) will have an effect on other thoughts, feelings, and behaviors (Bandura 1995). Even if the neurophysiology of the perception of these statements can be fully understood, or even if this neurophysiology can someday be altered so that these perceptions will not occur, this should not diminish the scientific and clinical importance of the etiological significance of the psychological meaning of the statements or behaviors. For example, the etiology of PTSD in persons who experienced the Holocaust (or other traumas) is probably not reducible entirely (or perhaps even primarily) to genetic abnormalities that make a person vulnerable to severe trauma, or even to structural or functional changes to the brain that result from these experiences (King et al 1999). "It is [perhaps] a gross oversimplification" (Kirmayer et al 1995:506). There probably does remain substantial psychological significance of being the victim of torture, rape, and genocide (e.g. Holtz 1998, Neria et al 1998) and perhaps even to being the victim of more subtle but still personally significant pathogenic environmental events.

It might then be a bit one-sided "to adopt the position that the mind is the expression of the activity of the brain" (Andreasen 1997:1586). Judd (1998) stated that the National Institute of Mental Health "has avowed that a central feature of psychiatric research in the twenty-first century will be a focus on the brain, pursued through molecular and cellular biology, along with molecular genetics, complemented by sophisticated cognitive and behavioral science" (p. 7). Hyman (1998) affirms strongly that it is not his intention "to do away with psychosocial research" (p. 37). There does indeed remain substantial funding for psychosocial, behavioral, and clinical research. Nevertheless, Hyman (1998) also clearly espouses the theoretical model that "for all our major disorders . . . the situation is one in which genes, acting at different times in brain development in different locations in the brain, interact with epigenetic and environmental influences to produce vulnerabilities to mental disorders" (p. 37). "Mental illnesses are real, diagnosable, treatable brain disorders" (Hyman 1998:38).

There are even suggestions that a neurophysiological understanding of psychopathology is somehow more scientific (e.g. Andreasen 1997, Leshner 1997). For example, Lilienfeld & Marino (1995), in their otherwise compelling critique of Wakefield's (1992) construct of harmful dysfunction, argued that the construct of a mental disorder had to be defined by or reduced to neurophysiological variables in order for it have any viable scientific meaning. "It is in principle impossible to explicitly define mental disorder, because disorder is a mental construction that lacks a clear point of demarcation in the real world and possesses no criterial attributes" (Lilienfeld & Marino 1995:417). "Controversies regarding the inclusion or exclusion of specific conditions in the DSM result not from a failure to adequately define mental disorder . . . but rather from a failure to recognize that the question of whether a given condition constitutes a mental disorder cannot be answered by means of scientific criteria" (Lilienfeld & Marino 1995:417). In a manner reminiscent of Szasz (Dammann 1997), they indicated that the construct would remain nonscientific until its "inner nature" was discovered (p. 417), by which they meant its neurophysiological basis.

Mental disorder is indeed a hypothetical construct, but this does not render it nonscientific or even less scientific than constructs that are purportedly more within nature. Physiological constructs can be relatively more precise in their assessment than psychological constructs, but a physical disorder is itself a hypothetical construct that will lack a fully operational definition (Wakefield 1999). "Functional impairment or disability, not the presence of a lesion, is the essential element in the medical concept of disease" (Bergner 1997:245). A biological functional impairment is as conceptual as a psychological functional impairment. Equally important, psychological constructs may not need to be reduced to biological or neurochemical mechanisms in order to become scientifically viable. The absence of an operational definition that reduces a behavior, cognition, or speech to a neurophysiological mechanism complicates research, often substantially, but it does not prevent the occurrence of highly informative scientific research or scientific progress. Behavior, speech, and thought do have a natural, real existence in nature in a manner that is fundamentally equal to that of neurophysiology. In fact, Lilienfeld and Marino (1999) themselves argued that "the question of why certain conditions tend to be viewed as disorders or nondisorders is amenable to scientific inquiry." They concluded that a cognition (i.e. belief) that there are mental disorders is sufficiently within nature to be studied scientifically but, perhaps paradoxically, they argued that the maladaptivity of such cognitions was not sufficiently within nature to be studied scientifically.

Optimal scientific progress might be obtained by a more integrative perspective (Gabbard & Goodwin 1996, Miller 1996, Rutter 1997b), although equally intriguing might be efforts to empirically contrast neurophysiological and psychological models of psychopathology, such as the neurophysiological model of PTSD proposed by Yehuda and her colleagues (1998a,b), with the cognitive model of PTSD proposed by Basoglu et al (1997). For example, Klein (1999) has hypothesized that panic disorder is the expression of a dysregulated neurophysiological suffocation alarm. Panic attacks occur when rising arterial carbon dioxide (CO_2) levels signal imminent asphyxiation. In contrast, cognitive models of panic disorder have proposed that panic attacks are the result of catastrophic misinterpretations of benign symptoms. Schmidt et al (1997) suggested that "if a relatively stable suffocation monitor exists, patients with panic disorder should minimally habituate to serial CO_2 exposures" (Schmidt et al 1997:630–631). In contrast, "if the panicogenic effects of CO_2 reside in the tendency to catastrophically misinterpret CO_2 induced sensations, correcting the tendency to misinterpret sensations should result in reduction, or even complete extinction, of fearful responding to the challenges" (Schmidt et al 1997:631). Schmidt et al compared the responsivity to CO_2 challenge in panic disorder patients who either received cognitive-behavioral therapy with respiratory training, cognitive-behavioral therapy without respiratory training, or no therapy. At posttreatment, only 20% of the treated patients panicked in response to a CO_2 challenge, in comparison to 64% of the untreated patients (44% of the treated patients reported no anxiety, in comparison to 0% of the untreated patients). "These findings are consistent with psychological conceptualizations of panic disorder that postulate that fearful responding is mediated by catastrophic misinterpretation of bodily perturbations . . . . [and] the pronounced decrease in CO_2-induced fearful responding for treated patients is not consistent with a fixed biological chain of events produced by a faulty CO_2 monitoring system" (Schmidt et al 1997:636).

DOMAINS OF PSYCHOPATHOLOGY

The domains of psychopathology studied by researchers are influenced heavily by DSM-IV (Pincus et al 1992). DSM-IV is a well-validated nomenclature that is guided largely and governed mostly by scientific research (Nathan & Langenbucher 1999,

Wakefield 1998, Widiger et al 1998). However, researchers appear to be gradually converting to alternative forms of classification as the inadequacies of the existing categorical distinctions become increasingly problematic and unwieldy (Widiger 1997).

Diagnostic Boundaries

Mental disorders are organized by DSM-IV into 16 major diagnostic classes, largely for the purpose of maximizing clinical utility, not necessarily because they refer to distinct domains of psychopathology. The three illustrations provided below of problematic boundaries between diagnostic classes are acute and posttraumatic stress as dissociative disorders, body dysmorphic disorder as an eating disorder, and early onset dysthymia as a personality disorder, but many other illustrations are equally plausible (e.g. conversion disorder as a dissociative disorder, hypochondriasis as an anxiety disorder, or generalized social phobia as a personality disorder) (Widiger 1997).

PTSD may have more in common with respect to etiology, pathology, and treatment with the dissociative disorders than it does with the anxiety disorders. Both PTSD and dissociative disorders typically involve difficulties integrating, accepting, or absorbing a severe and even horrifying trauma, expressed through symptoms of gross denial, amnesia, avoidance, intrusive recollections, anxiety, and/or hypervigilance (Janoff-Bulman 1992, Spiegel 1993). Difficulty forgetting (or letting go of) a horrifying experience may simply be the opposite side of the same coin of difficulty remembering (accepting or acknowledging) a horrifying experience. However, a diagnostic system that emphasizes distinct classes of disorders may hinder efforts to recognize and validate common pathologies across diagnostic classes. A new diagnosis identified as brief reactive dissociative disorder was proposed for DSM-IV (Spiegel 1993) but, given its obvious similarity to PTSD, it was placed instead among the anxiety disorders and identified as acute stress disorder (APA 1994). The dissociative symptomatology included within the diagnosis of acute stress disorder might now appear to be excessive, particularly if it is conceptualized as an anxiety disorder (Bryant & Harvey 1997), despite the possibility that dissociative symptomatology in both acute and posttraumatic stress disorders is important to understanding the pathology of the disorder and predicting its future course (Bremner & Brett 1997, Classen et al 1998, Harvey & Bryant 1998). The optimal solution might have been to classify acute stress as a disorder of anxiety and dissociation so that clinicians would appreciate the presence of both mechanisms in their understanding of its pathology and treatment, but an option of multiple coding is not currently available within the APA (1994) diagnostic nomenclature.

Body dysmorphic disorder was a new addition to the DSM-III-R (APA 1987). It was classified as a somatoform disorder because its primary complaints are somatic and persons with this disorder will typically seek treatment within a medical rather than a psychiatric setting. However, substantial attention is being given to a possibly common pathogenesis with the obsessive-compulsive anxiety disorders (Phillips et al 1998a). Persons with these disorders share substantial anxiousness, overvalued (e.g. unreasonable and sustained) and/or intrusive ideation, rumination, and ritualistic behaviors. An equally compelling argument can be made for a close relationship to anorexia and bulimia. Body dysmorphia does not typically involve a maladaptive dyscontrol in eating behavior, but it does involve a pathological preoccupation with an imagined defect in physical appearance that is perhaps also fundamental to both anorexia and bulimia (Jarry 1998, Rosen & Ramirez 1998). These eating disorders are diagnosed substantially more often in females, but a masculine variant of anorexia might be a preoccupation with muscle strength, tone, and definition, or what Pope and his colleagues (Pope et al 1997) describe as a muscle dysmorphia. Males who are preoccupied with building their muscles may share much in common with females who are preoccupied with thinness. This hypothetical masculine variant of anorexia is not currently conceptualized as a disorder, in part because a preoccupation with body building provides only a minimal risk to physical health. However, the health risk might now be increasing with the growing use of steroids (Schwerin et al 1996), along with the ongoing psychological, social, and occupational costs of a preoccupation with a muscular body image (Pope et al 1997).

An issue left unresolved by the authors of DSM-IV was the differentiation of axis I disorders (e.g. anxiety, mood, schizophrenic, impulse dyscontrol, and others) from axis II disorders (e.g. avoidant, depressive, schizotypal, borderline, and others) (Gunderson 1998). A relatively clear statement of the distinction between axis I and axis II disorders was provided in DSM-III-R, where it was indicated that "the disorders listed on axis II, developmental disorders and personality disorders, generally begin in childhood or adolescence and persist in a stable form (without periods of remission or exacerbation) into adult life. With only a few exceptions (e.g. the gender identity disorders and paraphilias), these features are not characteristic of the axis I disorders" (APA 1987:16).

However, the conceptual distinction between axis I and axis II was deleted in DSM-IV (APA 1994). It is no longer the case that personality disorders (and mental retardation) are the only conditions known to generally begin in childhood or adolescence and persist without periods of remission into adulthood. Mood and anxiety disorders are now conceptualized as conditions that might also be chronic, characteristic of everyday functioning, and evident since childhood. For example, prior to DSM-III, chronic feelings of pessimism, helplessness, and inadequacy that were evident since childhood were conceptualized as a personality disorder but this symptomatology was placed within the mood disorders section in DSM-III-R because of a closer phenomenological resemblance to depressive mood disorders than to other personality disorders (Keller & Russell 1996). DSM-IV early onset dysthymia includes low self-esteem, feelings of inadequacy, pessimism, hopelessness, and social withdrawal that are characteristic for most of the day for more days than not and "has an early and insidious onset (i.e. in childhood, adolescence, or early adult life) as well as a chronic course" (APA 1994:347). Distinguishing this mood disorder from depressive personality disorder has been a focus of very informative research (e.g. Klein & Shih 1998, Phillips et al 1998b), but no meaningful distinction may in fact be possible (Clark 1999).

There are proposals to abandon the axis I and II distinctions altogether (Livesley 1998). One option would be to fold all but a few of the personality disorders into respective sections of axis I where they would have the most phenomenologic resemblance. Each of the axis I disorders could include a subtyping for chronic and early onset variants (e.g. characterologic variants of maladaptive anxiousness, depressiveness, and impulse dyscontrol). Some of the components of personality disorder symptomatology would not be readily captured by a chronic variant of an axis I disorder, such as submissiveness, dependency, gullibility, callousness, exploitation, intimacy problems, narcissism, arrogance, and deceitfulness (Clark et al 1996, Livesley et al 1998, Trull et al 1998). However, most of this remaining symptomatology could be captured by a new section of the manual devoted to disorders of interpersonal relatedness. This would be consistent with those models of personality that emphasize interpersonal relatedness (Wiggins & Pincus 1992) and might even facilitate the representation of marital and family relationship disorders within the diagnostic nomenclature. The professional activity and responsibility of many clinicians is devoted to the diagnosis and treatment of abusive, violent, conflicted, or otherwise pathological marital, familial, and social relationships (Fincham & Beach 1999) that are currently inadequately recognized within the diagnostic nomenclature (Kaslow 1996).

Dyscontrolled Anger, Hostility, and Aggression

There are also compelling proposals for an increased representation of disorders of dyscontrolled or dysregulated anger, hostility, and aggression. Aggressive and violent behavior are of substantial social and clinical importance. "The enormity of the problem of juvenile aggression and violence [alone] is difficult to grasp" (Loeber & Hay 1997:372), perhaps matched only by its enormity within adulthood (Monahan & Steadman 1994). "Despite the common occurrence of inappropriate, impulsive-aggressive behavior in our society, the [DSM-IV] continues to be deficient in identifying individuals with problematic behaviors of this type" (Coccaro et al 1998:368). Anger, scorn, revulsion, disgust, hostility, rage, irritability, annoyance, outrage, and other comparable affective states and traits are a major component of the broader construct of negative affectivity, along with the equally important components of anxiousness and depressiveness (Watson & Clark 1984, Clark et al 1994). Nevertheless, there is only one diagnosis within DSM-IV that is concerned explicitly with this important component of negative affectivity (i.e. intermittent explosive disorder) (APA 1994), whereas entire sections of DSM-IV are devoted to different manifestations and forms of expressions of dyscontrolled anxiousness and depression (anger, rage, aggression, and other related traits are included within the diagnostic criteria of various personality disorders, but these traits are not the primary features of any one of them).

A substantial amount of informative research is devoted to the study of the prevalence, association, and risk of violent behavior among persons with a recognized mental disorder such as schizophrenia, antisocial personality, or substance dependence (Monahan & Steadman 1994). Steadman and colleagues (Steadman et al 1998), for example, suggested in their extensive patient and community study that the presence of substance abuse provided a particularly noteworthy risk for violent, aggressive behavior. The possible mechanisms are varied but may include the disinhibiting contributions of a comorbid substance-related disorder (Giancola & Zeichner 1997). Most important, however, Steadman and colleagues emphasized that "the character of violence is remarkably similar whether the violence is committed by discharged patients or by their neighbors" (Steadman et al 1998:400), suggesting perhaps that the psychopathology of anger, violence, and aggression, as well as their comorbidity with other forms of psychopathology, should itself be the focus of research (Group Adv. Psychiatry, Comm. Prev. Psychiatry 1999).

The clinical importance of anger, hostility, and related constructs is evident by their importance in other domains of research (Loeber & Hay 1997). For example, expressed emotion (EE) is a measure of the family environment, typically assessed by how relatives spontaneously talk about the patient, that has been demonstrated to be a reliable psychosocial predictor of relapse in schizophrenia (Butzlaff & Hooley 1998). Butzlaff & Hooley indicated in a systematic meta-analysis of the existing research that EE may also be of considerable importance "in the understanding and prevention of relapse [for] a broad range of psychopathological conditions" (p. 547), including mood and eating disorders. Equally important perhaps is that the construct and assessment of EE does not give equal weight to the expression of just any emotion (e.g. joy, happiness, anxiousness, or depression) but emphasizes in particular the "number of critical comments or . . . signs of hostility" (Butzlaff & Hooley 1998:547). Butzlaff & Hooley (1998) concluded that "the time has now come for creative and sophisticated research that will tell us why EE is associated with relapse in such a wide range of psychopathological conditions" (p. 551), and the expression and experience of hostility, criticism, or anger might be central to this research.

Much of the research on the contribution of personality traits to the development of coronary heart disease has been concerned historically with a constellation of personality traits identified as type A, consisting of competitiveness, hostility, impatience, time urgency, achievement striving, workaholism, and pressured, explosive speech. Comparable to EE research, it is apparent that the hostility within this constellation "has emerged as the most important personality variable in psychosocial research on the etiology of coronary heart disease" (Miller et al 1996:340). Miller and his colleagues (Miller et al 1996) documented in an extensive meta-analysis "that chronic anger and hostility is an independent risk factor for the development of coronary heart disease and premature mortality" (p. 344).

Life Span Psychopathology

One notable exception to the phenomenological organization of DSM-IV is the section for disorders usually first diagnosed in infancy, childhood, or adolescence. However, "the provision of a separate section for disorders that are usually first diagnosed in infancy, childhood, or adolescence is for convenience only and is not meant to suggest that there is any clear distinction between 'childhood' and 'adult' disorders" (APA 1994:37). The separate classification may simply reflect in part the tradition that researchers and practitioners tend to focus primarily or exclusively on the mental disorders of children, adolescents, or adults, with an inadequate collaboration across the life span.

The authors of DSM-IV expended substantial effort in attempting to bridge the artificial boundary between childhood and adulthood. Diagnostic criteria sets were revised and additional information was provided in the text to indicate how each disorder varies in its presentation across the life span (Davis et al 1998). Some DSM-III-R disorders of childhood and adulthood were even collapsed into a single diagnosis that emphasized a more developmental, life span perspective. For example, it was misleading and artifactual in DSM-III-R to suggest that there are distinct gender identity disorders of childhood and adulthood (Bradley et al 1997). It is more accurate to indicate that this particular disorder varies in its expression across childhood, adolescence, adulthood, and perhaps into aging. Another oddity of DSM-III-R was the absence of any mood disorders of childhood, while including many anxiety disorders (Shaffer et al 1998). DSM-III-R avoidant disorder of childhood was therefore folded in DSM-IV into the anxiety disorder of social phobia, and DSM-III-R overanxious disorder of childhood was folded into generalized anxiety disorder. However, it is apparent that the amount of life span information that is provided in DSM-IV is only the tip of the iceberg of what should in fact be known. Prospective longitudinal studies from childhood into adulthood (and into aging) are sorely needed to document empirically how particular disorders sustain, alter, or remit in their presentation across the life span.

For example, longitudinal studies of persons diagnosed with attention-deficit hyperactivity disorder (ADHD) in childhood and followed prospectively into adulthood have provided particularly informative and intriguing results, documenting for example that a variety of disorders in adulthood have roots within seemingly quite different disorders of childhood, that the diagnostic criteria developed for children or adolescents are grossly inadequate in adulthood, and that disorders of childhood will often have clinically and socially significant consequences in adulthood even if these persons are no longer seeking treatment and no longer meet the threshold for an officially recognized mental disorder (e.g. Hansen et al 1999, Mannuzza et al 1997). One of the more difficult and controversial issues that has emerged, in part from this research, is whether there should be a diagnosis of ADHD that has an onset in adulthood (Barkley 1998). Comparable research with many other disorders of childhood (e.g. oppositional defiant disorder, conduct disorder, communication disorders, and learning disorders) might be equally informative.

There are perhaps few disorders of adulthood that will not have some roots or antecedents in childhood, for it is unlikely that a mental disorder could develop in adulthood in the absence of any clinically significant premorbid antecedents (Lynam 1996). One of the more remarkable gaps in knowledge is the childhood antecedents for the personality disorders of adulthood. DSM-III included four childhood antecedents of personality disorders: identity disorder as an antecedent of borderline personality disorder, avoidant disorder of childhood as an antecedent of avoidant personality disorder, oppositional defiant disorder as an antecedent of passive-aggressive personality disorder, and conduct disorder as the antecedent for antisocial personality disorder (APA 1980); only one has remained. It is unclear why there should be so much support for a childhood antecedent of antisocial personality disorder but almost none for any of the others. Research concerning these antecedents is now in progress (Sher & Trull 1996), and this research might even be helpful in identifying the environmental factors and processes that contribute to the eventual stability of the personality traits within adulthood (e.g. Bernstein et al 1996; Guzder et al 1996; Lynam 1996, 1998; Trull et al 1997).

Dimensional Versus Categorical Classification

"DSM-IV is a categorical classification that divides mental disorders into types based on criteria sets with defining features" (APA 1994:xxii). However, increasing amounts of attention and interest are being given to alternative dimensional models of classification, from the personality disorders (e.g. Livesley et al 1998, O'Connor & Dyce 1998, Trull et al 1998) through the mood and anxiety disorders (e.g. Brown et al 1998, Burns & Eidelson 1998, Krueger et al 1998, Mineka et al 1998, Zinbarg & Barlow 1996) to the schizophrenic and affective psychotic disorders (e.g. Grube et al 1998, Lenzenweger & Dworkin 1996, Ratakonda et al 1998, Toomey et al 1998).

Livesley et al (1998), for example, demonstrated in a community and clinical twin sample that the phenotypic and genotypic structure of personality disorder symptomatology replicated across clinical and community samples. "Personality disorders are not qualitatively distinct from normal personality functioning, they are simply maladaptive, extreme variants of common personality traits" (Widiger 1998:865). Equally important, however, was the finding that the genetic structure was not consistent with existing diagnostic boundaries, and that "the genetic structure of personality appears to involve multiple specific predispositions and a few general factors" (Livesley et al 1998:945), consistent with a comparable cross-cultural twin study by Jang et al (1998). "The suggestion that multiple distinct genetic factors shape the phenotype means that discrete categories are unlikely to occur" (Livesley et al 1998:946).

"As the rare Mendelian disorders such as cystic fibrosis and Huntington's disease are solved, the entire genetics community is, with great excitement, turning its attention to complex disorders . . . [and] psychiatric illnesses are fully and unquestionably viewed as part of the next challenge in mainstream genetics" (Hyman 1998:38). There has been substantial interest, even within personality disorder research, to identify a specific gene (or other form of specific etiology) for each mental disorder, modeled after the success obtained with some physical disorders. However, the complex disorders of psychopathology are unlikely to have specific etiologies, or even specific genetic etiologies (McGue & Bouchard 1998, Nigg & Goldsmith 1998), and initial successes in identifying specific genes have typically failed to replicate (e.g.

Sullivan et al 1998). For example, up to 85% of the susceptibility to schizophrenia appears to be attributable to genetic contributions, but the extensive genome scan studies of schizophrenia currently "do not support the hypothesis that a single gene causes a large increase in the risk of schizophrenia" (Levinson et al 1998:741).

"Categorical disease models are being challenged . . . by the recent data indicating that individuals may carry a genetic risk factor to develop a disorder that can be measured premorbidly . . . and that may or may not ultimately be expressed as the full form of the disorder, depending on the occurrence of a variety of factors" (Andreasen 1997:1587). Genetic contributions to the etiology of a mental disorder may at times constitute no more than a vulnerability that in some instances might be necessary for its development but may also prove to be insufficient (Andreasen 1997, McGue & Bouchard 1998). "It is thus most probable that genetic susceptibility to schizophrenic psychoses is polygenetic, and that their effects are dependent on inter-action with physical and psychosocial environmental factors" (Portin & Alanen 1997:73). There are continued efforts to demarcate "a clear-cut, natural, qualitative subgroup" of persons within a spectrum of schizophrenic pathology (Lenzenweger 1999:186), but this might be a rare instance in which Meehl's (1995) expectations (of eventually discovering a dominant, specific etiology) were largely mistaken. The effects of any specific gene are likely to be much broader than currently understood, with each gene influencing a variety of symptoms and disorders. Rather than search for the gene that is purportedly the specific etiology for a particular mental disorder, it might be more accurate and fruitful to identify the constellation of behaviors that are expressions of a particular gene. It is perhaps also unrealistic to expect the symp-tomatology of a mental disorder (i.e. the maladaptive cognitions, affects, and behav-iors) to have a specific etiology. Not only would this etiology have to have provided a strong contribution to the development of the symptomatology, but the phenome-nology of the disorder would also have to have been largely resilient to the influence of other genetic and environmental influences. The symptomatology of mental dis-orders appears to be, in contrast, responsive to a variety of neurochemical, interper-sonal, cognitive, and other mediating variables. Mental disorders are perhaps most likely the result of polygenetic dispositions and multifactorial etiologies (Rutter 1997a).

Even the boundaries between classes of mental disorders (i.e. anxiety, mood, schizophrenic, and personality) are beginning to collapse under the weight of the evidence (Clark 1999, Mineka et al 1998, Nathan & Langenbucher 1999). Further clarity regarding the genetic (and other etiologic) contributions to the development of mental disorders is perhaps more likely to be obtained with an increased recog-nition of the dimensions of psychopathology that underlie and are shared among the purportedly distinct diagnostic categories of DSM-IV (Livesley et al 1998, Mineka et al 1998, Ratakonda et al 1998, Sherman et al 1997). Diagnostic categories will still be useful in identifying constellations of symptomatology that describe particu-larly noteworthy, common, or problematic syndromes, such as the lethal and deadly constellation of personality traits that result in the syndrome identified as psychopathy, but an adequate understanding of the etiology and pathology of the disorder might require an appreciation of its underlying multifactorial nature and the arbitrariness of the diagnostic boundaries (Widiger & Lynam 1998).

A useful illustration is perhaps provided by the disorder of mental retardation, a disorder for which much is known regarding its etiology, pathology, and classification. Mental retardation is currently defined in large part as a level of intelligence below an IQ score of approximately 70 (APA 1994). This point of demarcation is not unreasonable, random, or meaningless, but it is arbitrary (Widiger 1997). There are no distinct breaks in the phenotypic distribution of intelligence that provide an absolute distinction between normal and abnormal intelligence. There are persons with an IQ below 70 for whom a qualitatively distinct disorder is evident that can be traced to a specific biological event (e.g. trisomy 21), but the disorder in such cases is not mental retardation; it is a physical disorder (e.g. Down's syndrome) that has a substantial effect upon the psychological components of intelligence. Intelligence itself is distributed as a continuous variable, as any particular person's level of intelligence is the result of a complex array of multiple genetic, fetal, infant development, socioeconomic, and other influences (Neisser et al 1996). Comparable dimensional models of classification and demarcation might be feasible for the mood, anxiety, personality, psychotic, and other domains of psychopathology.

CONCLUSIONS

Psychopathology research continues to advance our scientific understanding of the conceptualization, diagnosis, etiology, and pathology of mental disorders. This overview of ongoing issues and controversies will, we hope, be helpful in stimulating further progress. Studies that might be of particular value were noted explicitly and implicitly throughout the review, including (but certainly not limited to) research concerning the demarcation of clinically significant (or pathological) from clinically insignificant (or nonpathological) impairments, the pathology of purportedly normal functioning, the impact of cultural values on the conceptualization and validation of psychopathology, the integration and contrast of neurophysiological and psychological models of etiology and pathology, the validation or refutation of diagnostic boundaries, and the further development of dimensional models of psychopathology across the entire diagnostic nomenclature.

ACKNOWLEDGMENTS

We express our appreciation to Donald Lynam, Richard Milich, and Carolyn Zahn-Waxler for their very helpful suggestions; Philipp Kraemer for his support; and Heshimu Evans, Wayne Turner, and Scott Padgett for the many helpful points they made.

LITERATURE CITED

Alper JS. 1998. Genes, free will, and criminal responsibility. *Soc. Sci. Med.* 46:1599–611

American Psychiatric Assoc. 1980. *Diagnostic and Statistical Manual of Mental Disorders.* Washington, DC: Am. Psychiatr. Assoc. 494 pp. 3rd ed.

American Psychiatric Assoc. 1987. *Diagnostic and Statistical Manual of Mental Disorders.* Washington, DC: Am. Psychiatr. Assoc. 567 pp. 3rd ed. Rev.

American Psychiatric Assoc. 1994. *Diagnostic and Statistical Manual of Mental Disorders.* Washington, DC: Am. Psychiatr. Assoc. 886 pp. 4th ed.

Andreasen NC. 1997. Linking mind and brain in the study of mental illnesses: a project for a scientific psychopathology. *Science* 275:1586–93

Bandura A. 1995. Comments on the crusade against the causal efficacy of human thought. *J. Behav. Ther. Exp. Psychiatry* 27:323–45

Barkley RA, ed. 1998. *Attention-Deficit Hyperactivity Disorder. A Handbook for Diagnosis and Treatment.* New York: Guilford. 628 pp.

Basoglu M, Mineka S, Paker M, Aker T, Livanou M, et al. 1997. Psychological preparedness for trauma as a protective factor in survivors of torture. *Psychol. Med.* 27:1421–33

Baum A, Posluszny DM. 1999. Health psychology: mapping biobehavioral contributions to health and illness. *Annu. Rev. Psychol.* 50:137–63

Bergner RM. 1997. What is psychopathology? And so what? *Clin. Psychol. Sci. Pract.* 4:235–48

Berman AU, Coccaro EF. 1998. Neurobiologic correlates of violence: relevance to criminal responsibility. *Behav. Sci. Law* 16:303–18

Bernstein DP, Cohen P, Skodol A, Bezirganian S, Brook JS. 1996. Childhood antecedents of adolescent personality disorders. *Am. J. Psychiatry* 150:907–13

Bowman ML. 1999. Individual differences in posttraumatic stress: problems with the DSM-IV model. *Can. J. Psychiatry* 44:21–33

Bradley SJ, Blanchard R, Coates S, Green R, Levine SB, et al. 1997. Gender identity disorder. In *DSM-IV Sourcebook,* ed. TA Widiger, AJ Frances, HA Pincus, R Ross, MB First, et al, 3:317–26. Washington, DC: Am. Psychiatr. Assoc. 1048 pp.

Bremner JD, Brett E. 1997. Trauma-related dissociative states and long-term psychopathology in posttraumatic stress disorder. *J. Trauma Stress* 10:37–50

Brown TA, Chorpita BF, Barlow BF. 1998. Structural relationships among dimensions of the DSM-IV anxiety and mood disorders and dimensions of negative affect, positive affect, and autonomic arousal. *J. Abnorm. Psychol.* 107:179–92

Bryant RA, Harvey AG. 1997. Acute stress disorders: a critical review of diagnostic issues. *Clin. Psychol. Rev.* 17:757–73

Burns DD, Eidelson RJ. 1998. Why are depression and anxiety correlated? A test of the tripartite model. *J. Consult. Clin. Psychol.* 66:461–73

Buss DM, Haselton MG, Shackelford TK, Bleske AL, Wakefield JC. 1998. Adaptations, exaptations, and spandrels. *Am. Psychol.* 53:533–48

Butzlaff RL, Hooley JM. 1998. Expressed emotion and psychiatric relapse. *Arch. Gen. Psychiatry* 55:547–52

Carroll KM, Rounsaville BJ, Bryant KJ. 1994. Should tolerance and withdrawal be required for substance dependence disorder? *Drug Alcohol Depend.* 36:15–20

Childress AR, Mozley PD, McElgin W, Fitzgerald J, Reivich M, et al. 1999. Limbic activation during cue-induced cocaine craving. *Am. J. Psychiatry* 156:11–18

Clark LA. 1999. Personality, disorder, and personality disorder: towards a more rational conceptualization. *J. Pers. Disorders.* 13:142–51

Clark LA, Livesley WJ, Schroeder ML, Irish SL. 1996. Convergence of two systems for assessing specific traits of personality disorder. *Psychol. Assess.* 8:294–303

Clark LA, Watson D, Mineka S. 1994. Temperament, personality, and the mood and anxiety disorders. *J. Abnorm. Psychol.* 103:103–16

Clark LA, Watson D, Reynolds S. 1995. Diagnosis and classification of psychopathology: challenges to the current system and future directions. *Annu. Rev. Psychol.* 46:121–53

Classen C, Koopman C, Hales R, Spiegel D. 1998. Acute stress disorder as a predictor of posttraumatic stress disorder. *Am. J. Psychiatry* 155:620–24

Coccaro EF, Kavoussi RJ, Berman ME, Lish JD. 1998. Intermittent explosive disorder-revised: development, reliability, and validity of research criteria. *Compr. Psychiatry* 39:368–76

Dammann EJ. 1997. "The myth of mental illness": continuing controversies and their implications for mental health professionals. *Clin. Psychol. Rev.* 17:733–56

Davis W, Widiger TA, Frances AJ, Pincus HA, Ross R, et al. 1998. Introduction to final volume. See Widiger et al 1998, pp. 1–20

Diener E, Suh EM. 1999. National differences in subjective well-being. In *Well-Being: The Foundations of Hedonic Psychology,* ed. D Kahneman, E Diener, N Schwarz, pp. 434–50. New York: Russell Sage Found. In press

Fabrega H. 1994. International systems of diagnosis in psychiatry. *J. Nerv. Ment. Dis.* 182:256–63

Fincham FD, Beach SRH. 1999. Conflict in marriage: implications for working with couples. *Annu. Rev. Psychol.* 50:47–77

Fishbain DA, Cutler RB, Rosomoff HL, Rosomoff RS. 1998. Do antidepressants have an analgesic effect in psychogenic pain and somatoform pain disorder? A meta-analysis. *Psychosom. Med.* 60:503–9

Follette WC, Houts AC. 1996. Models of scientific progress and the role of theory in taxonomy development: a case study of the DSM. *J. Consult. Clin. Psychol.* 64:1120–32

Gabbard GO, Goodwin FK. 1996. Integrating biological and psychosocial perspectives. In *Review of Psychiatry,* ed. LJ Dickstein, MB Riba, JM Oldham, 15:527–48. Washington, DC: Am. Psychiatric Press

Giancola PR, Zeichner A. 1997. The biphasic effects of alcohol on human physical aggression. *J. Abnorm. Psychol.* 106:598–607

Golding SL, Skeem JL, Roesch R, Zapf PA. 1999. The assessment of criminal responsibility: current controversies. In *The Handbook of Forensic Psychology,* ed. AK Hess, IB Weiner, pp. 379–408. New York: Wiley. 756 pp. 2nd ed.

Gorman JM, Kent JM. 1999. SSRIs and SNRIs: broad spectrum of efficacy beyond major depression. *J. Clin. Psychiatry* 60(Suppl. 4):33–38

Group Adv. Psychiatry, Comm. Prev. Psychiatry. 1999. Violent behavior in children and youth: preventive intervention from a psychiatric perspective. *J. Am. Acad. Child Adolesc. Psychiatry* 38:235–41

Grube BS, Bilder RM, Goldman RS. 1998. Meta-analysis of symptom factors in schizophrenia. *Schizophr. Res.* 25:113–20

Gunderson J. 1998. DSM-IV personality disorders: final overview. See Widiger et al 1998, pp. 1123–40

Guzder J, Paris J, Zelkowitz P, Marchessault K. 1996. Risk factors for borderline pathology in children. *J. Am. Acad. Child Adolesc. Psychiatry* 35:26–33

Hales RE. 1998. DSM-IV psychiatric system interface disorders (PSID) work group: final overview. See Widiger et al 1998, pp. 1077–86

Hansen C, Weiss D, Last CG. 1999. ADHD boys in young adulthood: psychosocial adjustments. *J. Am. Acad. Child Adolesc. Psychiatry* 38:165–71

Harvey AG, Bryant RA. 1998. The relationship between acute stress disorder and posttraumatic stress disorder: a prospective evaluation of motor vehicle accident survivors. *J. Consult. Clin. Psychol.* 66:507–12

Holtz TH. 1998. Refugee trauma versus torture trauma: a retrospective controlled cohort study of Tibetan refugees. *J. Nerv. Ment. Disord.* 186:24–34

Hyman SE. 1998. NIMH during the tenure of Director Steven E. Hyman, M.D. (1996–present): the now and future of NIMH. *Am. J. Psychiatry* 155(Suppl.):36–40

Jang KL, McCrae RR, Angleitner A, Riemann R, Livesley WJ. 1998. Heritability of facet-level traits in a cross-cultural twin sample: support for a hierarchical model of personality. *J. Pers. Soc. Psychol.* 74:1556–65

Janoff-Bulman R. 1992. *Shattered Assumptions.* New York: Free Press. 256 pp.

Jarry JL. 1998. The meaning of body image for women with eating disorders. *Can. J. Psychiatry* 43:367–74

Judd LL. 1998. Historical highlights of the National Institute of Mental Health from 1946 to the present. *Am. J. Psychiatry* 155 (Suppl.):3–8

Kandel ER. 1998. A new intellectual framework for psychiatry. *Am. J. Psychiatry* 155:457–69

Kaslow FW, ed. 1996. *Handbook of Relational Diagnosis and Dysfunctional Family Patterns.* New York: Wiley. 566 pp.

Keller MB, Russell CW. 1996. Dysthymia. In *DSM-IV Sourcebook,* ed. TA Widiger, AJ Frances, HA Pincus, R Ross, MB First, et al, 2:21–36. Washington, DC: Am. Psychiatr. Assoc.

Kessler RC. 1997. The effects of stressful life events on depression. *Annu. Rev. Psychol.* 48:191–214

Kessler RC. 1999. The World Health Organization International Consortium in Psychiatric Epidemiology: initial work and future directions—the NAPE lecture. *Acta Psychiat. Scand.* 99:2–9

King DS, King LA, Foy DW, Keane TM, Fairbank JA. 1999. Posttraumatic stress disorder in a national sample of female and male Vietnam veterans: risk factors, war-zone stressors, and resilience-recovery variables. *J. Abnorm. Psychol.* 108:164–70

Kirmayer LJ, Young A. 1999. Culture and context in the evolutionary concept of mental disorder. *J. Abnorm. Psychol.* In press

Kirmayer LJ, Young A, Hayton BC. 1995. The cultural context of anxiety disorders. *Psychiatr. Clin. North Am.* 18:503–21

Klein DF. 1999. Harmful dysfunction, disorder, disease, illness, and evolution. *J. Abnorm. Psychol.* In press

Klein DN, Shih JH. 1998. Depressive personality: associations with DSM-III-R mood and personality disorders and negative and positive affectivity, 30-month stability, and prediction of course of Axis I depressive disorders. *J. Abnorm. Psychol.* 197:319–27

Knutson B, Wolkowitz OM, Cole SW, Chan T, Moore EA, et al. 1998. Selective alteration of personality and social behavior by serotonergic intervention. *Am. J. Psychiatry* 155:373–79

Kolb B, Whishaw IQ. 1998. Brain plasticity and behavior. *Annu. Rev. Psychol.* 49:43–64

Kosten TR. 1998. Addiction as a brain disease. *Am. J. Psychiatry* 155:711–13

Krueger RF, Caspi A, Moffitt TE, Silva PA. 1998. The structure and stability of common mental disorders (DSM-III-R): a longitudinal-epidemiological study. *J. Abnorm. Psychol.* 107:216–27

Kutchins H, Kirk SA. 1997. *Making Us Crazy. DSM: The Psychiatric Bible and the Creation of Mental Disorders.* New York: Free Press. 305 pp.

Leighton AH, Murphy JM. 1997. Nature of pathology: the character of danger implicit in functional impairment. *Can. J. Psychiatry* 42:714–21

Lenzenweger MF. 1999. Deeper into the schizotypy taxon: on the robust nature of maximum covariance analysis. *J. Abnorm. Psychol.* 108:182–87

Lenzenweger MF, Dworkin RH. 1996. The dimensions of schizophrenia phenomenology. Note one or two, at least three, perhaps four. *Br. J. Psychiatry* 168:432–40

Leshner AI. 1997. Addiction is a brain disease and it matters. *Science* 278:45–47

Leshner AI. 1999. Science is revolutionizing our view of addiction—and what to do about it. *Am. J. Psychiatry* 156:1–3

Levinson DF, Mahtani MM, Nancarrow DJ, Brown DM, Kruglyak L, et al. 1998. Genome scan of schizophrenia. *Am. J. Psychiatry* 155:741–50

Lewis-Fernandez R, Kleinman A. 1995. Cultural psychiatry. Theoretical, clinical, and research issues. *Psychiatr Clin. North Am.* 18:433–46

Lilienfeld SO, Marino L. 1995. Mental disorder as a Roschian concept: a critique of Wakefield's "harmful dysfunction" analysis. *J. Abnormal. Psychol.* 104:411–20

Lilienfeld SO, Marino L. 1999. Essentialism revisited: evolutionary theory and the concept of mental disorder. *J. Abnorm. Psychol.* In press

Lillard A. 1998. Ethnopsychologies: cultural variations in theories of mind. *Psychol. Bull.* 123:3–32

Livesley WJ. 1998. Suggestions for a framework for an empirically based classification of personality disorder. *Can. J. Psychiatry* 43:137–47

Livesley WJ, Jang KL, Vernon PA. 1998. Phenotypic and genotypic structure of traits delineating personality disorder. *Arch. Gen. Psychiatry* 55:941–48

Loeber R, Hay D. 1997. Key issues in the development of aggression and violence from childhood to early adulthood. *Annu. Rev. Psychol.* 48:371–410

López SR, Guarnaccia JJ. 2000. Cultural psychopathology: uncovering the social world of mental illness. *Annu. Rev. Psychol.* 51:571–98

Lynam DR. 1996. The early identification of chronic offenders: Who is the fledgling psychopath? *Psychol. Bull.* 120:209–34

Lynam DR. 1998. Early identification of the fledgling psychopath: locating the psychopathic child in the current nomenclature. *J. Abnorm. Psychol.* 107:566–75

Mannuzza S, Klein RG, Bessler A, Malloy P, Hynes ME. 1997. Educational and occupational outcome of hyperactive boys grown up. *J. Am. Acad. Child Adolesc. Psychiatry* 36:1222–27

McGue M, Bouchard TJ. 1998. Genetic and environmental influences on human behavioral differences. *Annu. Rev. Neurosci.* 21:1–24

Meehl PE. 1995. Bootstraps taxometrics: solving the classification problem in psychopathology. *Am. Psychol.* 50:266–75

Miller GA. 1996. How we think about cognition, emotion, and biology in psychopathology. *Psychophysiology* 33:615–28

Miller TQ, Smith TW, Turner CW, Guijarro ML, Hallett AJ. 1996. A meta-analytic review of research on hostility and physical health. *Psychol. Bull.* 119:322–48

Mineka S, Watson D, Clark LA. 1998. Comorbidity of anxiety and unipolar mood disorders. *Annu. Rev. Psychol.* 49:377–412

Monahan J, Steadman HJ, eds. 1994. *Violence and Mental Disorder.* Chicago: Univ. Chicago Press. 324 pp.

Munoz RF, Hollon SD, McGrath E, Rehm LP, VandenBos GP. 1994. On the AHCPR depression in primary care guidelines. *Am. Psychol.* 49:42–61

Nathan PE, Langenbucher JW. 1999. Psychopathology: description and classification. *Annu. Rev. Psychol.* 50:79–107

Neisser U, Boodoo G, Bouchard TJ, Boykin AW, Brody N, et al. 1996. Intelligence: knowns and unknowns. *Am. Psychol.* 51:77–101

Neria Y, Solomon Z, Dekel R. 1998. An eighteen-year follow-up study of Israeli prisoners of war and combat veterans. *J. Nerv. Ment. Disord.* 186:174–82

Nigg JL, Goldsmith HH. 1998. Developmental psychopathology, personality, and temperament: reflections on recent behavioral genetics research. *Hum. Biol.* 70:387–412

O'Brien CP. 1997. Progress in the science of addiction. *Am. J. Psychiatry* 154:1195–97

O'Connor BP, Dyce JA. 1998. A test of models of personality disorder configuration. *J. Abnorm. Psychol.* 107:3–16

Phillips KA, Gunderson CG, Mallya G, McElroy SL, Carter W. 1998a. A comparison study of body dysmorphic disorder and obsessive-compulsive disorder. *J. Clin. Psychiary* 59:568–75

Phillips KA, Gunderson JG, Triebwasser J, Kimble CR, Faedda G, et al. 1998b. Reliability and validity of depressive personality disorder. *Am. J. Psychiatry* 155:1044–48

Pincus HA, Frances AJ, Davis WW, First MB, Widiger TA. 1992. DSM-IV and new diagnostic categories: holding the line on proliferation. *Am. J. Psychiatry* 149:112–17

Pope HG, Gruber AJ, Choi P, Olivardia R, Phillips KA. 1997. Muscle dysmorphia. An underrecognized form of body dysmorphic disorder. *Psychosomatics* 38:548–57

Portin P, Alanen YO. 1997. A critical review of genetic studies of schizophrenia. II. Molecular genetic studies. *Acta Psychiatr. Scand.* 95:73–80

Prigerson HG, Shear MK, Jacobs SC, Reynolds CF, Maciejewski PK, et al. 1999. Consensus criteria for traumatic grief: a preliminary empirical test. *Br. J. Psychiatry* 174:67–73

Ratakonda S, Gorman JM, Yale SA, Amador XF. 1998. Characterization of psychotic conditions. Use of the domains of psychopathology model. *Arch. Gen. Psychiatry* 55:75–81

Regier DA, Kaelber CT, Rae DS, Farmer ME, Knauper B, et al. 1998. Limitations of diagnostic criteria and assessment instruments for mental disorders. Implications for research and policy. *Arch. Gen. Psychiatry* 55:109–15

Rogler LH. 1997. Making sense of historical changes in the Diagnostic and Statistical Manual of Mental Disorders: five propositions. *J. Health Soc. Behav.* 38:9–20

Rosen JC, Ramirez E. 1998. A comparison of eating disorders and body dysmorphic disorder on body image and psychological adjustment. *J. Psychosom. Res.* 44:441–49

Rutter ML. 1997a. Implications of genetic research for child psychiatry. *Can. J. Psychiatry* 42:569–76

Rutter ML. 1997b. Nature-nurture integration. The example of antisocial behavior. *Am. Psychol.* 52:390–98

Sadler JZ. 1997. Recognizing values: a descriptive-causal method for medical/scientific discourse. *J. Med. Philos.* 22:541–65

Schmidt NB, Trakowski JH, Staab JP. 1997. Extinction of panicogenic effects of a 35% CO_2 challenge in patients with panic disorder. *J. Abnorm. Psychol.* 106:630–38

Schuckit MA, Daeppen J-B, Danko GP, Tripp ML, Smith TL, et al. 1999. Clinical implications for four drugs of the DSM-IV distinction between substance dependence with and without a physiological component. *Am. J. Psychiatry* 156:41–49

Schwerin MJ, Corcoran KJ, Fisher L, Patterson D, Askew W, et al. 1996. Social physique anxiety, body esteem, and social anxiety in bodybuilders and self-reported anabolic steroid users. *Addict. Behav.* 21:1–8

Shaffer D, Widiger TA, Pincus HA. 1998. DSM-IV child disorders. II. Final overview. See Widiger et al 1998, pp. 963–78

Sher KJ, Trull TJ. 1996. Methodological issues in psychopathology research. *Annu. Rev. Psychol.* 47:3710–400

Sherman DK, Iacono WG, McGue MK. 1997. Attention-deficit hyperactivity disorder dimensions: a twin study of inattention and impulsivity-hyperactivity. *J. Am. Acad. Child Adolesc. Psychiatry* 36:745–53

Spiegel D. 1993. Dissociation and trauma. In *Dissociative Disorders. A Clinical Review,* ed. D Spiegel, pp. 117–31. Washington, DC: Am. Psychiatric Press. 134 pp.

Spitzer RL. 1998. Diagnosis and need for treatment are not the same. *Arch. Gen. Psychiatry* 55:120

Spitzer RL, First MB, Williams JBW, Kendler K, Pincus HA, et al. 1992. Now is the time to retire the term "organic mental disorder." *Am. J. Psychiatry* 149:240–44

Stahl SM. 1998. Basic psychopharmacology of antidepressants. 1. Antidepressants have seven distinct mechanisms of action. *J. Clin. Psychiatry* 59(Suppl. 4):5–14

Steadman HJ, Mulvey EP, Monahan J, Robbins PC, Appelbaum PS, et al. 1998. Violence by people discharged from acute psychiatric inpatient facilities and by others in the same neighborhoods. *Arch. Gen. Psychiatry* 55:393–401

Sullivan PF, Fifield WJ, Kennedy MA, Mulder RT, Sellman JD, et al. 1998. No association between novelty seeking and the type 4 dopamine receptor gene (DRD4) in two New Zealand samples. *Am. J. Psychiatry* 155:98–101

Thiele TE, Marsh DJ, Ste. Marie L, Bernstein IL, Palmiter RD. 1998. Ethanol consumption and resistance are inversely related to neuropeptide Y levels. *Nature* 396:366–69

Toomey R, Faraone SV, Simpson JC, Tsuang MT. 1998. Negative, positive, and disorganized symptom dimensions in schizophrenia, major depression, and bipolar disorder. *J. Nerv. Ment. Disord.* 186:470–76

Trull TJ, Useda D, Conforti R, Doan B-J. 1997. Borderline personality disorder features in nonclinical young adults. 2. Two-year outcome. *J. Abnorm. Psychol.* 106:307–14

Trull TJ, Widiger TA, Useda D, Holcomb J, Doan B-J, et al. 1998. A structured interview for the assessment of the five-factor model of personality. *Psychol. Assess.* 10:229–40

Tsai GE, Ragan P, Chang R, Chen S, Linnoila MI, et al. 1998. Increased glutamatergic neurotransmission and oxidative stress after alcohol withdrawal. *Am. J. Psychiatry* 155:726–32

Volkow NR, Wang G-J, Fischman MW, Foltin RW, Fowler JS, et al. 1997. Relationship between subjective effects of cocaine and dopamine transporter occupancy. *Nature* 386:827–39

Volkow NR, Wang G-J, Fowler JS, Hitzemann R, Angrist B, et al. 1999. Association of methylphenidate-induced craving with changes in right striato-orbitofrontal metabolism in cocaine abusers: implications in addiction. *Am. J. Psychiatry* 156:19–26

Wakefield JC. 1992. The concept of mental disorder: on the boundary between biological facts and social values. *Am. Psychol.* 47:373–88

Wakefield JC. 1997. Diagnosing DSM-IV—Part I: DSM-IV and the concept of disorder. *Behav. Res. Ther.* 35:633–49

Wakefield JC. 1998. The DSM's theory-neutral nosology is scientifically progressive: response to Follette and Houts (1996). *J. Consult. Clin. Psychol.* 66:846–52

Wakefield JC. 1999. Evolutionary versus Roschian analyses of the concept of disorder. *J. Abnorm. Psychol.* In press

Watson D, Clark LA. 1984. Negative affectivity: the disposition to experience aversive emotional states. *Psychol. Bull.* 96:465–90

Webster CD, Jackson MA, eds. 1998. *Impulsivity: Theory, Assessment, and Treatment.* New York: Guilford. 462 pp.

Widiger TA. 1997. Mental disorders as discrete clinical conditions: dimensional versus categorical classification. In *Adult Psychopathology and Diagnosis,* ed. SM Turner, M Hersen, pp. 3–23. New York: Wiley. 626 pp. 3rd ed.

Widiger TA. 1998. Four out of five ain't bad. *Arch. Gen. Psychiatry* 55:865–66

Widiger TA, Frances AJ, Pincus HA, Ross R, First MB, et al, eds. 1998. *DSM-IV Sourcebook.* Washington, DC: Am. Psychiatr. Assoc. 4th Vol. 1176 pp.

Widiger TA, Lynam DR. 1998. Psychopathy from the perspective of the five-factor model of personality. In *Psychopathy: Antisocial, Criminal, and Violent Behaviors,* ed. T Millon, E Simonsen, M Birket-Smith, RD Davis, pp. 171–87. New York: Guilford. 476 pp.

Widiger TA, Trull TJ. 1991. Diagnosis and clinical assessment. *Annu. Rev. Psychol.* 42:109–33

Wiggins JS, Pincus AL. 1992. Personality: structure and assessment. *Annu. Rev. Psychol.* 43:473–504

Yehuda R. 1998. Psychoneuroendocrinology of post-traumatic stress disorder. *Psychiatric. Clin. North Am.* 21:359–39

Yehuda R, McFarlane AC. 1995. Conflict between current knowledge about posttraumatic stress disorder and its original conceptual basis. *Am. J. Psychiatry* 152:1705–13

Yehuda R, Resnick HS, Schmeidler J, Yang R-K, Pitman RK. 1998a. Predictors of cortisol and 3-methoxy-4-hydroxy-phenylglycol responses in the acute aftermath of rape. *Biol. Psychiatry* 43:855–59

Yehuda R, Schmeidler J, Giller EL, Siever LJ, Binder-Brynes K. 1998b. Relationship between posttraumatic stress disorder characteristics of Holocaust survivors and their adult offspring. *Am. J. Psychiatry* 155:841–43

Zinbarg RE, Barlow DH. 1996. Structure of anxiety and the anxiety disorders: a hierarchical model. *J. Abnorm. Psychol.* 105:181–93

Annu. Rev. Psychol. 2000. 51:405–444

Scientific and Social Significance of Assessing Individual Differences: "Sinking Shafts at a Few Critical Points"

David Lubinski

Department of Psychology and Human Development, Vanderbilt University, Nashville, Tennessee 37203; e-mail: david.lubinski@vanderbilt.edu

Key Words   differential psychology, general intelligence, total evidence rule, consilience

■ **Abstract**   This chapter reviews empirical findings on the importance of assessing individual differences in human behavior. Traditional dimensions of human abilities, personality, and vocational interests play critical roles in structuring a variety of important behaviors and outcomes (e.g. achieved socioeconomic status, educational choices, work performance, delinquency, health risk behaviors, and income). In the review of their importance, the construct of general intelligence is featured, but attributes that routinely add incremental validity to cognitive assessments are also discussed. Recent experimental and methodological advances for better understanding how these dimensions may contribute to other psychological frameworks are reviewed, as are ways for determining their scientific significance within domains where they are not routinely assessed. Finally, some noteworthy models are outlined that highlight the importance of assessing relatively distinct classes of individual-differences attributes simultaneously. For understanding fully complex human phenomena such as crime, eminence, and educational-vocational development, such a multifaceted approach is likely to be the most productive.

CONTENTS

Introduction 406
    Literature Reviewed 407
Dispositional Attributes: Abilities, Interests, and Personality 407
    Cognitive Abilities 407
    Interests 420
    Personality 422
Constellations 424
    Intellectual Development 424
    Vocational Adjustment 426
    Work Performance 427
    Creativity and Eminence 428
    Crime 430

0084–6570/00/0201–0405$12.00

Health Risk Behavior... 431
Life Span Development.. 431
Methodological Issues.. 432
  Causal Modeling.. 432
  Causality and Confounds... 432
  Total Evidence Rule 433
Consilience.. 433

INTRODUCTION

Throughout most of this century, a broad introduction to the psychology of individual differences or differential psychology was standard background for graduate training in applied psychology. Its importance was underscored by Scott: "Possibly the greatest single achievement of the American Psychological Association is the establishment of the psychology of individual differences" (1920:85). Differential psychology comprises the psychometric assessment of abilities, personality, and vocational interests, with special emphasis devoted to their real-world significance and their developmental antecedents. Topics of interest included educational, interpersonal, and vocational behaviors, especially those relevant to facilitating optimal adjustment to life and work and tailoring opportunities for positive growth. Anastasi (1937), Tyler (1965), and Willerman (1979) all wrote classic texts covering these topics, and provided the conceptual underpinnings for psychologists working in educational, clinical, industrial, and military settings.

Emerging out of these early conceptual foundations, accumulating empirical evidence has made it clear that differential psychology can contribute to better understanding of academic achievement (Benbow & Stanley 1996, Snow 1991), the particulars of intellectual development (Ackerman 1996), creativity (Eysenck 1995, Jensen 1996), crime and delinquency (Gordon 1997, Lykken 1995), educational and vocational choice (Dawis 1992, Snow et al 1996), health-risk behavior (Caspi et al 1997, Lubinski & Humphreys 1997), income and poverty (Hunt 1995, Murray 1998), occupational performance (Hunter & Schmidt 1996, Hough 1997), social stratification (Gottfredson 1997), clinical prediction (Dawes 1994, Grove & Meehl 1996), and life-span development (Harris 1995, Holahan & Sears 1995, Rowe 1994, Schaie 1996). As a matter of fact, causal models of these phenomena that do not incorporate individual differences variables are likely to be underdetermined. In addition, as differential psychologists devote particular attention to socially relevant phenomena, their findings are germane to the work of medical and social scientists studying people at risk for negative outcomes or showing promise for positive outcomes.

As developments in differential psychology unfolded, however, and specialization progressed, the study of individual differences became less likely to be viewed (and reviewed) as a cohesive body of knowledge. Willerman's (1979) comprehensive text was the last of its kind. Basic researchers (and textbook writers) have tended since to restrict their activities to specific classes of attributes: e.g. either human abilities, interests, personality, or their biological and environmental antecedents. Indeed, few research programs have examined these attributes simultaneously or systematically for their collective role in explaining and predicting human psychological phenomena. Yet, a much richer picture of humanity and psychological diversity is brought into focus when constellations of individual-differences variables are assembled for research and practice. By teaming relatively independent individual-differences variables to model human behavior, it becomes easy to illustrate how they operate in many important contexts (whether they are measured or not). A new millennium marks a good time to examine the study of individual differences more holistically.

Literature Reviewed

Following an examination of Cattell's (1890) classic, wherein the term "mental test" was first introduced, Galton (1890: 380) appended two pages of profoundly influential remarks underscoring the importance of assessing psychological phenomena of substantive significance: "One of the most important objects of measurement is hardly if at all alluded to here and should be emphasized. It is to obtain a general knowledge of . . . capacities . . . by sinking shafts, as it were, at a few critical points. In order to ascertain the best points for the purpose . . . We thus may learn which of the measures are the most instructive."

The reviewed literature reveals a number of "deep shafts" that would likely impress Galton himself. First, three classes of dispositional attributes will be reviewed: abilities, interests, and personality. To keep this review down to manageable dimensions, abilities will be restricted to cognitive abilities, interests will focus on educational and vocational interests, and omitted from consideration in personality dimensions are the familiar psychopathological traits (e.g. schizophrenia, manic depressive disorders, etc). Without this curtailment, a wide-angle view of differential psychology would be prohibitive. Some research combining ability, interest, and personality variables will be reviewed, followed by a discussion of methodological issues pertaining to mis-specified causal modeling. This chapter concludes by explicating some ideas behind the concept of "niche building" (i.e. how individuals seek out, build, and create environments that correspond to their personal attributes). This analysis may resolve conflicts between various groups, e.g. the tensions observed between Snow's (1967) "two cultures" (the humanists and the scientists) or, closer to home, psychologists who work with people (see clients) versus psychologists who do not. As the psychology of individual differences illuminates issues surrounding human diversity, it may furnish tools for facilitating cross-cultural empathy (Dawis 1992).

DISPOSITIONAL ATTRIBUTES: ABILITIES, INTERESTS, AND PERSONALITY

Cognitive Abilities

The last two decades have witnessed many ambitious examinations of cognitive ability measures and the constructs they assess. Discussion has focused on the construct of general intelligence (g). However, discourse has also extended into cognitive abilities beyond *g* and grappled with the full dimensionality and psychometric organization of the resulting array of intellective components. At broader levels of analysis, group differences (e.g. sex, race) have been explored, along with attendant questions about whether test bias might place certain groups at a disadvantage in the assessment process. A further topic of inquiry has been an observed tendency for scores on intelligence tests to rise cross-culturally over the century. Finally, biological correlates of *g* have been explored, leading ultimately to speculation on the evolutionary derivation of general cognitive ability. Findings from each of these areas of investigation are reviewed below.

General Intelligence ("g")   Large-scale studies have addressed the psychological nature of *g,* biological interconnections, and the validity of well-known tools purporting to index *g* for predicting socially valued criteria. During the past decade, treatments have intensified exponentially (Carroll 1993, Jensen 1998, Neisser et al 1996), across both familiar (core) as well as less familiar (peripheral) criterion domains. Research has sharpened validity generalizations forecasting educational outcomes (Benbow 1992, Benbow & Stanley 1996, Snow 1996), occupational training, and work performance (Hunter & Schmidt 1996, Schmidt & Hunter 1998). More is also now known about periphery phenomena surrounding *g*'s nomological network: aggression, delinquency, and crime (Caspi & Moffitt 1993, Gordon 1997, Wiegman et al 1992); health risks (Lubinski & Humphreys 1997, Macklin et al 1998); and income and poverty (Hunt 1995, Murray 1998).

For some benchmarks, general cognitive ability covaries 0.70–0.80 with academic achievement measures, 0.40–0.70 with military training assignments, 0.20–0.60 with work performance (higher values reflect higher job complexity families), 0.30–0.40 with income, and 0.20 with law abidingness (Brody 1992, 1996; Gordon 1997). Willis & Schaie (1986) have shed considerable light on the role of general intelligence for practical intelligence in later life, and O'Toole (1990) has done the same for motor vehicle accident proneness. A nice compilation of positive and negative correlates of *g* is Brand's (1987) Table 2, which documents a variety of modest correlations between general intelligence and altruism, sense of humor, practical knowledge, response to psychotherapy, social skills, supermarket shopping ability (positive correlates), and impulsivity, accident proneness, delinquency, smoking, racial prejudice, and obesity (negative correlates), among others. These outer-layer peripheral correlates are especially thought provoking because they reveal how individual differences in *g* "pull" with them cascades of primary (direct) and secondary (indirect) effects (Gottfredson 1997).

Contemporary psychologists at opposite poles of the applied educational-industrial spectrum, such as Snow (1989) and Campbell (1990), respectively, have showcased *g* in law-like empirical generalizations.

> Given new evidence and reconsideration of old evidence, [*g*] can indeed be interpreted as 'ability to learn' as long as it is clear that these terms refer to complex processes and skills and that a somewhat different mix of these constituents may be required in different learning tasks and settings. The old view

that mental tests and learning tasks measure distinctly different abilities should be discarded. (Snow 1989:22)

General mental ability is a substantively significant determinant of individual differences in job performance for any job that includes information-processing tasks. If the measure of performance reflects the information processing components of the job and any of several well-developed standardized measures used to assess general mental ability, then the relationship will be found unless the sample restricts the variances in performance or mental ability to near zero. The exact size of the relationship will be a function of the range of talent in the sample and the degree to which the job requires information processing and verbal cognitive skills. (Campbell 1990:56)

These views are widely accepted among psychometricians (Barrett & Depinet 1991, Carroll 1997, Gottfredson 1997). They will be welcomed by researchers who have searched in vain for genuine moderator variables and felt compelled therefore to accept, however reluctantly, Ghiselli's (1972:270) influential but dyspeptic appraisal: "It is possible that moderators are as fragile and elusive as that other will-o-the-wisp, the suppressor variable." The following empirical generalization is now one of the most robust in all of psychology: The positive correlation between work performance (Y) and general intelligence (X) is moderated by job complexity (Z). Substituting general academic learning for Y and accelerated abstract-curriculum for Z, another robust empirical generalization of a moderated relationship is revealed for curriculum and instruction (Benbow & Stanley 1996).

Yet, contentious debate has been common for research pertaining to g (Campbell 1996). Indeed, psychologists can be found on all sides of the complex set of issues engendered by assessing general intelligence (Snyderman & Rothman 1987). This is not new, however. Heated debate has followed this important construct since shortly after Spearman's (1904) initial article (cf. Chapman 1988). Nevertheless, recently, many scientists have been determined to understand g and the means of assessing it better. Even prior to 1994, the date marking publication of Herrnstein & Murray's (1994) controversial book, a number of highly visible publications appeared that attempted (among other things) to explicate the social significance of g. For by the 1980s it was becoming clear that g played a prominent role in learning and work (Ackerman 1988, Thorndike 1985). This development bore out Cronbach's (1970:197) earlier evaluation: "The general mental test stands today as the most important technical contribution psychology has made to the practical guidance of human affairs." Thorndike (1994:150) summarized years of research findings on cognitive abilities: "[T]he great preponderance of the prediction that is possible from any set of cognitive tests is attributable to the general ability that they share. What I have called 'empirical g' is not merely an interesting psychometric phenomenon, but lies at the heart of the prediction of real-life performances . . . ." Meehl (1990:124) remarked: "Almost all human performance (work competence) dispositions, if carefully studied, are saturated to some extent with the general intelligence factor g, which for psychodynamic and ideological reasons has been somewhat neglected in recent years but is due for a comeback."

By 1995, largely in response to exchanges stimulated by the *Bell Curve* (Herrnstein & Murray 1994) (both within scholarly outlets and the popular press), the APA formed a special task force (Neisser et al 1996). Contemporaneously with the work of this task force, several major psychological outlets published special issues (Ceci 1996, Sternberg 1997, Gottfredson 1997).

The final chapter to this story is far from complete. However, one thing is clear: The intensity of research on intellectual abilities continues unabated. Jensen (1998) has just unveiled his most recent book which, like Carroll's (1993), is destined to become a classic (Bouchard 1999, Neisser 1999). In Meehl's (1998) words: "Verbal definitions of the intelligence concept have never been adequate or commanded consensus. Carroll's [1993] and Jensen's [1998] books, *Human Cognitive Abilities* and *The g Factor* (which will be the definitive treatises on the subject for many years to come), essentially solve the problem." In both works, general intelligence has been conceptualized through a (perhaps, the) fundamental predicate of science—covariation. General intelligence is defined by the covariation cutting across various problem solving mediums (numerical, pictorial, verbal), assessment modalities (group, individual), and populations (cross culturally); it reflects the general factor—or communality—shared by these multiple operations.

To the extent that this general factor reaches out and connects with external phenomena—covariation—a basis is formed for evaluating its scientific significance. Jointly, these two systems of covariation (internal operations of assessment tools and external links to extra-assessment phenomena) form the nexus of the general intelligence construct. g is viewed as the central node of this nexus, with its meaning successively clarified as conceptual and empirical interrelationships develop through research and establish the causal directionality of the network's strands. Spearman (1927:89) referred to the essence of g as "mental energy," which manifested itself in individual differences in "the eduction of relations and correlates." This was a respectable pioneering beginning but, as indicated below, there are other ways to construe this attribute.

While Meehl (1998) is correct that verbal definitions of intelligence have never been "adequate or commanded consensus" because writers tend to focus on the unique features of their formulation rather than the communality that they share (cf. Sternberg & Detterman 1986), literary definitions do have their place. For example, they frequently point to critical core criteria and relevant peripheral criteria that constitute differential degrees of importance for establishing construct validity of measures purporting to assess the attribute in question. Such distinctions can bring the fruitfulness of a particular line of research into focus. Early psychophysical measures of intelligence were rejected, for example, because they failed to covary with educational outcomes, rate of learning academic material, and teacher ratings—criteria thought to be central to the meaning of intelligence; for measures not to display an appreciable relationship with these criteria would violate the essence of what intelligence was intended to embody. It was natural, therefore, that when Binet and Spearman produced tests predictive of these core criteria, investigators shifted their focus and began using the new tools in their empirical research (Thorndike & Lohman 1990).

Today, for example, there is a fair amount of agreement among measurement experts that measures of g assess individual differences pertaining to "abstract thinking or reasoning," "the capacity to acquire knowledge," and "problem-solving ability" (see Snyderman & Rothman's 1987 survey of 641 experts and Gottfredson 1997). Naturally, individual differences in these attributes influence aspects of life outside of academic and vocational arenas because abstract reasoning, problem-solving, and rate of learning touch so many facets of life, especially now in our information intense society. These quoted characteristics fit with correlates at both the core and the periphery of g's nexus. They are compatible with empirical facts. Investigators who conceptualize intelligence differently are probably talking about something other than psychometric g, and something less central to learning and work performance.

Dimensionality and Organization Over the past 20 years, an understanding of how cognitive abilities are organized (hierarchically) has emerged, through hierarchical factor analysis (Carroll 1993, Humphreys 1994), radex scaling (Snow & Lohman 1989), and structural equation modeling (Gustafsson & Undheim 1996). To psychological researchers working outside the field of cognitive abilities, variations across these methods mirror Allport's distinction between his and Henry Murray's view of personality: "narcissisms of subtle difference." Most impressive is Carroll's (1993) treatment of cognitive abilities, which confirmed what a number of investigators have maintained all along. Cognitive abilities are organized hierarchically and, when administered to a wide range of talent, approximately 50% of the common variance in heterogeneous collections of cognitive tests comprise a general factor. There is clearly a conspicuous red thread running through variegated conglomerations of cognitive tests (and the items that form them). It reflects the largest vein of construct-valid variance uncovered by differential psychology in terms of its external connections. Yet, to be sure, there is psychological significance beyond the general factor. Quantitative, spatial, and verbal reasoning abilities all possess psychological import beyond g. This is especially true for predicting educational and career tracks that people self-select (Achter et al 1999, Austin & Hanisch 1990, Humphreys et al 1993), but also for individual differences in criterion performance (Carroll 1993, Jensen 1998). However, as Carroll (1993:689) has noted, the scientific significance of various abilities comes in degrees: "[A]bilities are analogous to elements in the periodic table: Some, like fluid intelligence ["g"], are obviously as important as carbon or oxygen; others are more like rare earth elements . . . "

Although Carroll's (1993) nomenclature is presented below, other approaches would paint a similar picture. All of the aforementioned treatments are centered by a general factor at the apex of a hierarchy (stratum III) that is defined by the communality running through a secondary tier of more content specific abilities (stratum II): mathematical, spatial/mechanical, and verbal reasoning abilities. The stratum III general factor is a global marker of intellectual complexity or sophistication, whereas the stratum II abilities are content specific strengths and relative weaknesses. There are others, but the above abilities command the most scientific significance. Finally, under these dimensions are more circumscribed abilities closely associated with specific tests (stratum I), such as arithmetic reasoning, block design, vocabulary, etc. Carroll's (1993) three-stratum theory is, in many respects, not new. Embryonic outlines are seen in earlier psychometric work (Burt, Cattell, Guttman, Humphreys, and Vernon, among others). But the empirical bases for Carroll's (1993) conclusions are unparalleled; readers should consult this source for a systematic detailing of more molecular abilities.

In view of these developments, some have concluded that a fairly comprehensive picture of the structure and forecasting capabilities of cognitive abilities has been drawn. Consequently, little is likely to come of further examining phenotypic aspects of intellectual behavior. For example, Jensen (1998) has argued that basic research needs to uncover more fundamental (biological) vertical paths and develop more ultimate (evolutionary) explanations, for genuine advances to occur. There are, however, at least two issues worthy of additional examination. The first involves the scientific significance of lower-order dimensions of human abilities (those beyond g) and how best to appraise their scientific worth. The second has to do with population changes and differences.

Cognitive Abilities Beyond g   Specific abilities beyond g contribute to real-world forecasts. This becomes especially true at higher g levels [e.g. continuous gradations extending from bright, to gifted, to profoundly gifted populations (cf. Achter et al 1996, Benbow 1992)], where the major markers of g successively pull apart (dissociate). In complex educational (graduate school) and vocational (doctoral-level occupational) environments, range truncation on g is intense because an appreciable amount of g is necessary to operate with competence in these ever-changing, symbolically dense environments (Hunt 1995, 1996). Hence, the predictive power of other factors increases relative to general intelligence, but again, only for populations highly selected on g. This is akin to Tanner's (1965) intriguing discriminant function analysis. The physical (body build) profiles of Olympic athletes enabled Tanner to identify their domains of excellence (events they were competing in) with great accuracy. Yet, within a given event, the individual differences dimensions utilized to classify these gifted athletes were not impressive performance predictors. [That the *American Psychologist* (1998) recently devoted nine letters and 12 pages to pointing out how range truncation can attenuate correlations is commentary on the poor cumulative nature of some psychological research. Reading McNemar's (1964) article would have forestalled the need for this exchange.]

Probably the simplest model of human cognitive abilities (beyond g) is Eysenck's (1995) two-dimensional model: the general factor and a bipolar spatial-verbal factor. Vernon (1961) used verbal-educational-numerical (v:ed) and mechanical-practical-spatial (k:m) as major group factors subservient to g, while Cattell (1971) has proposed a fluid/crystallized distinction. Snow and his colleagues (Snow 1991, Snow &

Lohman 1989) have discussed verbal/linguistic, quantitative/numerical, and spatial/ mechanical abilities, in addition to the general factor defined by what is common to these symbolic, problem-solving systems. Over a variety of educational/vocational contexts, these three regions represent important sectors of concentration; they have also demonstrated incremental validity relative to g. However, traditional factor-analytic treatments have not proceeded with incremental validity in mind. That is, factor analytic models of cognitive abilities have (for the most part) focused on the internal structure of assessment tools. Models have been based on within-instrument covariance structure.

Many factor analysts seem to hold as their implicit (if not explicit) goal accounting for all the common variance in a correlation matrix. However, this goal fails to consider the psychologically significant dimensionality that might result. For example, Carroll (1994:196) writes: "I have pointed out (Carroll 1993) that the general factor on the average contributes only a little more than half the common factor variance of a given test; thus, lower order factors can have almost as much importance as the general factor." But it must be asked, Is this view plausible? Given the breadth and depth of the g nexus, is it conceivable that, even collectively, lower-order cognitive factors, all independent of g, could evince external relationships as important as g by itself? Mathematically, of course, it is conceivable; but is it psychologically conceivable based on what we know about various ability dimensions that are independent of g when in competition with the general factor for predicting important external criteria? Based on existing evidence, it does not seem likely.

Furthermore, Carroll (1994) seems to imply that all the dimensions resulting from common variance among cognitive abilities have the potential of being psychologically important. Again, although this is technically possible, it is unlikely; in fact, there is reason to suspect otherwise. This is especially true when all of the variables in a factor analysis are assessed by the same (monomethod) modality (Carroll's "a given test"). Understanding this idea is important, because it generalizes to issues involving the number of dimensions needed to model both personality and vocational interests discussed in subsequent sections. For example, in the context of a discussion on the number of dimensions needed to characterize personality, Block (1995a:189) noted: "[T]he amount of variance 'explained' internally by a factor need not testify to the external psychological importance of the factor."

Within a domain of individual-differences measures, only a portion of the common variance should be expected to have psychological import. This can be illustrated through basic concepts from Campbell & Fiske's (1959) multi-trait multi-method matrix. When examining construct validity through multiple sources, monomethod correlations are essentially always larger than their heteromethod counterparts. Indeed, this comparison is most germane to calibrating the magnitude of methods variance operating. It indicates that some portion of common variance running through cognitive ability tests is methods variance and, as such, is construct irrelevant. Dimensions emerging primarily from this aspect of common variance are best viewed as undesirable contaminants for the ultimate psychological solution (but not necessarily for a mathematical solution aiming to account for all of the common variance regardless of construct relevance). The basic idea, carried to its logical conclusion, challenges the assumed desirability of accounting for all of the common variance in a correlation matrix through factor-analytic techniques (when attempting to understand the psychological structure underlying a representative collection of individual differences measures). It suggests that only a fraction of the common variance is construct relevant.

A factor solution accounting for 85% of the common variance among 50 variables with a three-factor solution, and reinforced by a sharp "elbowed" scree between eigenvalues three and four would constitute, by many, a clear-cut, if not elegant, triadic solution. But what if factors two and three provided little incremental validity over factor one in the prediction of relevant (group membership or performance) criteria, and none that held up under cross-validation (Lubinski & Dawis 1992, Schmidt et al 1998)? Should we consider these dimensions psychologically important too? Or, might these factors constitute nuisance variables—namely, reliable variance akin to what Cook & Campbell (1979) have referred to as construct irrelevancies, or "systematic bias" (Humphreys 1990), "constant error" (Loevinger 1954), "systematic ambient noise" (Lykken 1991), "crud" (Meehl 1990), or, "methods variance" (Campbell & Fiske 1959)? There is no a priori reason to assume that all of the common variance in a correlation matrix is psychologically significant; but to determine whether it is (and to what extent) is an empirical question (cf. Thurstone 1940:217).

If the amount of common variance accounted for in a factor analysis need not translate into the importance of a factor, what does? A proposal stemming from earlier recommendations by Humphreys (1962) and McNemar (1964) has been reinstated (Lubinski & Dawis 1992). Humphreys and McNemar stress the importance of incremental validity. That is, when attempting to ascertain the number of dimensions necessary to characterize cognitive abilities (or any domain of individual differences), consider the amount of incremental validity gleaned over and beyond what is already available. Given that the general factor accounts for about 50% of the common variance among cognitive tests (coupled with the breadth and depth of its external linkages), parsimony suggests that investigators begin here. By adding variables to multiple regression equations (following the general factor), investigators can work their way down the hierarchy of cognitive abilities and, as long as lower-tier dimensions add incremental validity to what prior dimensions provided and these increments hold up on cross-validation (Lubinski & Dawis 1992), more molecular dimensions thus achieve the status of psychologically significant parameters of individuality. Messick (1992:379) has communicated the same idea in a slightly different way: "Because IQ is merely a way of scaling measures of general intelligence, the burden of proof in claiming to move beyond IQ is to demonstrate empirically that . . . test scores tap something more than or different from general intelligence by, for example, demonstrating differential correlates with other variables (which is the external aspect of construct validity)." Just as incremental validity is important when appraising innovative measures (Dawis 1992, Lykken 1991, Sanders et al 1995), the same holds for the dimensional products of factor analysis. Innovative measures and variables worthy of scientific attention provide information not already available; nonincremental sources of variance do not.

Group Differences   When Jenkins & Paterson (1961) compiled their classic book illustrating the historical development of psychological measurement and individual differences, and searched "for a topic to serve as a model problem [they] quickly settled on intelligence" (1961:v). Then, like now, intellectual assessment was the richest vein of differential psychology. Furthermore, not unlike today (Herrnstein & Murray 1994), their preface stressed how controversial this area is. Campbell (1996) provides an excellent contemporary overview (see also Coleman 1990–1991). Humphreys (1995), moreover, has maintained that it is because of the magnitude of group differences on ability measures, and the real world performances that these measures are able to forecast, that differential psychology has been a neglected area in psychology.

At the apex as well as at the lower tiers of cognitive abilities, attention toward group contrasts has arisen for several reasons. Before proceeding, however, the magnitude of overlap between various groupings of human populations should be emphasized. In standard deviation units, the range within any given population (race, sex) is many times the range between population means. One noteworthy achievement of differential psychology is that it has moved human psychological appraisals from crude nominal categories (group membership) to more refined ordinal and interval measurement (continuous dimensions of human variation), and experimental procedures for ratio measurement are underway (Deary 1996). As a result of these refinements, all human populations have revealed exceptional talent (comparable ranges). Ordinal and interval assessments of individual differences illuminate the diversity of talent within all demographic groupings, which nominal scaling systems are ill equipped to do.

Since the onset of psychometric inquiry, however, differences among various racial groupings (sometimes reaching one standard deviation or slightly more) have been both stubborn and consistent (Cronbach 1975; Jensen 1980, 1998). Furthermore, the magnitude of these differences has been relatively stable even during periods of converging educational opportunities (Gottfredson & Sharf 1988). Beyond this, it is important to understand that, like demonstrable differences, seemingly minor differences in ability level (mean) and dispersion (variability) warrant critical scrutiny. Collectively and individually, small group differences in level and dispersion frequently create huge upper tail ratios when stringent cutting scores are implemented (e.g. for select educational and training opportunities). Asian and Jewish populations, for example, typically manifest superior test scores, relative to the general population, and are overrepresented when stringent selection is applied to test scores. Feingold (1995) presents data on sex differences and considers implications for group differences more generally. For example, meta-analytic reviews focus on level or aggregating effect sizes (differences in standard deviation units), but groups may also differ in variability, which meta-analyses typically do not address. Feingold highlights the importance of examining both.

Sex Differences   Most investigators concur on the conclusion that the sexes manifest comparable means on general intelligence (Halpern 1992); yet, there is some evidence for slightly greater male variability (Eysenck 1995, Jensen 1998, Lubinski & Dawis 1992). With respect to level, Jensen (1998) has provided a particularly detailed presentation of this topic, including an innovative methodology for arriving at this conclusion. However, a number of investigators—including Jensen (1998), using his new method—have reached a different consensus about sex differences in strengths and relative weaknesses on specific abilities (Benbow 1988, Geary 1998, Halpern 1996, Hedges & Nowell 1995, Stanley et al 1992). Females appear to excel in certain verbal abilities, males in certain mathematical and spatial abilities. Hedges & Nowell (1995) published probably the most compelling contemporary analysis on this topic. They analyzed data from six large-scale studies collected between 1960 and 1992. Their analysis is important because, as they point out, many studies on sex differences are based on nonrandom samples, whereas their probability samples consisted of stratified random samples of U.S. populations. This study compiled data from Project Talent, National Longitudinal Study of the High School Class of 1972, National Longitudinal Study of Youth, High School and Beyond 1980, National Educational Longitudinal Study 1988, and National Assessment of Educational Progress. Means, variances, and upper tail ratios >90% and >95% were computed. Findings were consistent with other reports: Females tend to score higher on several verbal/linguistic measures, while males score higher in certain quantitative and spatial/mechanical abilities. Moreover, with respect to spatial/mechanical abilities, males display higher means and larger variances on nonverbal reasoning tests, which, again, generate huge upper tail ratios. Hedges & Nowell (1995) discuss implications of these findings for male/female proportions in math/science domains.

Race Differences   Clearly, the most contentious area of contemporary research on individual differences is found in Black/White contrasts (Gordon 1997). The most noteworthy group difference in this regard is the approximately one standard deviation difference on the general factor mean, with Whites scoring higher than Blacks. There are other group differences as well. For example, Hispanic populations tend to score intermediately between Blacks and Whites, whereas Asian and Jewish populations are score slightly higher than Whites (Gottfredson 1997). Nevertheless, Black/White contrasts have generated the best data (Humphreys 1988, 1991) and, by far, the most attention (Campbell 1996). Over the years, these differences have motivated intense study of test bias (especially underestimating the performance of underrepresented groups). Some benchmarks are found in an *American Psychologist* (1965) special issue and two APA task force reports (Cleary et al 1975, Neisser et al 1996). Jensen (1980) is still an excellent source on test bias. Given that these reports, compiled over four decades, reached the same conclusion found in two National Academy of Science reports (Wigdor & Garner 1982, Hartigan & Wigdor 1989), an empirical generalization can be ventured: Professionally developed general ability measures do not underpredict performance of underrepresented groups.

Flynn Effect   Observed scores on intelligence tests have been steadily rising cross-culturally over this century. These raw-score increases on measures of general intelligence have been labeled the "Flynn effect," after the investigator who documented their occurrence (Flynn 1999). Whether these increases reflect genuine gains in g is, however, unclear. Increases can occur due to increases on a measure's construct relevant or construct irrelevant (nonerror unique) variance, or both. The problem is complex and has generated considerable discussion (Neisser 1998). As yet, a final answer is not available. However, evidence that changes are due, at least in part, to construct irrelevant aspects of measuring tools is available.

Across various g indicators, the Flynn effect is positively correlated with the amount of nonerror uniqueness. For example, gains on the Raven matrices are greater than gains on verbal reasoning composites of heterogeneous verbal tests, which, in turn, are greater than gains on broadly sampled tests of g (aggregates of heterogeneous collections of numerical, spatial, and verbal problems). The Raven matrices consist of approximately 50% g variance, whereas heterogeneous collections of cognitive tests aggregated to form a measure of g approach 85% (Lubinski & Humphreys 1997). (Broad verbal reasoning tests are intermediate.) Complexities are added by considering that test scores have probably increased (especially at the lower end of general intelligence) due to advances in medical care, dietary factors, and educational opportunities (Jensen 1998). Yet, at high levels of g, the gifted appear to have suffered some setbacks as a consequence of being deprived of developmentally appropriate opportunities—a challenging curriculum at the appropriate time (Benbow & Stanley 1996). This topic deserves intense study for a number of reasons (Moffitt et al 1993, Schaie 1996), one of which is especially noteworthy. Sorting out the complexities involved in assessing dysgenic trends (Loehlin 1997, Lynn 1996, Williams & Ceci 1997) is predicated on understanding the causal determinants of raw score fluctuations on measures of g.

Whatever these raw score gains are ultimately attributed to, they do not, as some have indicated, appreciably detract from the construct validity of measures of g. Mean gains on construct valid measures do not speak to changes in internal or external covariance structure (Hunt 1995). Populations at contrasting levels of development, for example, typically manifest the same covariance structure with respect to the trait indicators under analysis (Rowe et al 1994, 1995).

Horizontal and Vertical Inquiry   The idea that constructs may be analyzed at different levels of analysis is well known. For example, Embretson (1983) has contributed an important distinction to the construct validation process. She suggests a parsing of the nomological network into two regions: construct representation versus nomothetic span. The latter denotes the network of empirical relationships observed with measures at the behavioral level, whereas the former is aimed at underlying processes or mechanisms responsible for generating these phenotypic manifestations. Jensen (1998) has likewise pointed to two lines of empirical research on g, one vertical and the other horizontal. Both lines dovetail with MacCorquodale & Meehl's (1948) distinction between hypothetical constructs (HC) and intervening variables

(IV). Although both concepts carry denotative and explicative meaning, hypothetical constructs stress explanation, whereas intervening variables are more restricted to description. Spearman's (1927) initial formulation of g as "mental energy," was a HC, whereas the parameters describing the functional relationships between conceptually equivalent measures of g and external criteria were IVs. When cross-disciplinary linkages are drawn, the HCs of one discipline can become the IVs of another, but that discussion is beyond the scope of this review (see Maxwell 1961). What is important for our purposes is that connecting threads have been established between g and several biological phenomena. Ultimately, the causal paths of these interrelationships will need to be traced.

Pooling studies of a variety of kinship correlates on IQ (e.g. MZ and DZ twins reared together and apart and a variety of adoption designs), the heritability of general intelligence in industrialized nations has been estimated to be between 60%–80% (Hetherington et al 1994, McGue & Bouchard 1998). Using magnetic resonance imaging (MRI) technology, brain size controlled for body weight covaries 0.30–0.40 with general intelligence (Bouchard 1999, Jensen 1998, Willerman et al 1991). Haier (1993) reports that glucose metabolism is related to problem-solving behavior, and that the gifted appear to engage in more efficient problem solving behavior that expends less energy. Also, highly intellectually gifted individuals evince enhanced right hemispheric functioning (Haier & Benbow 1995, O'Boyle et al 1995). The complexity of electroencephalograph (EEG) waves is positively correlated with g, as are amplitude and latency of the average evoked potential (AEP) (Lutzenberger et al 1992). Some investigators have determined the negative correlation between g and inspection times, assessed through chronometric procedures, to be a biological phenomenon (Deary 1996). Anderson (1993) suggested that dendritic arborization is correlated with g. Although Anderson typically examines histological data across groups of individuals with documented IQ differences, he also has conducted an intriguing case study involving Albert Einstein's brain (Anderson & Harvey 1996). In contrast to a control group of autopsied men, the frontal cortex of Einstein's brain possesses a significantly greater neuronal density (cf. Diamond et al 1985). Given this, the following was perhaps inevitable: A multidisciplinary team appears to have uncovered a DNA marker associated with g (Chorney et al 1998).

It is virtually guaranteed that more biological linkages will be made to g (Vernon 1993). Like those already uncovered, they are likely to be heterogeneous and to vary in strength of association with g. These biological phenomena are in no way mutually exclusive and can be complementary to one another. Some may transcend phylogenetic orders and thus enhance our comparative understanding of general learning phenomena (Anderson 1993, 1994a,b, 1995). One provocative conjecture is the myelination hypothesis (Miller 1994): Individual differences in cognitive efficiency are a function of individual differences in the amount of myelin (the fatty substance coating the neurons).

Proximal and Ultimate Examinations of g   Given the biological connections to g (Vernon 1993), some researchers have gone beyond these proximal associations to speculate on their ultimate evolutionary basis. Bouchard et al (1996) have revised experience producing drives (EPD) theory, which speaks to human intellectual development. EPD theory-revised is a modification of an earlier formulation by Hayes (1962), a comparative psychologist and pioneer in language and socialization capabilities of nonhuman primates. His idea was that, like all organisms, humans were designed to do something, and that they possess EPDs to facilitate ability and skill acquisition through inherited dispositions that motivate individuals toward particular kinds of experiences and developmental opportunities. Such evolutionary selective sensitivities can operate, moreover, in a wide range of functionally equivalent environments (which fits with the idea that humans evolved in a highly fluctuating environment).

Other investigators have sought a synthesis between evolutionary psychology and chronometric procedures for measuring inspection time (Deary 1996). Inspection time is a measure of speed of perceptual discrimination on "simple" elementary cognitive tasks (responses to stimulus configurations that typically take less than one second for average adults to perform with essentially zero errors). Theoretically, performance on elementary cognitive tasks indexes the time course of information processing in the nervous system. There are a variety of technical measurement issues surrounding this area of research, but it does appear that the temporal dynamics of performance on elementary cognitive tasks covaries negatively with g (faster processing is associated with higher g levels). Washburn & Rumbaugh (1997) used inspection time measures to successfully assess individual differences in cognitive sophistication among nonhuman primates.

This intriguing line of research might provide a vehicle for comparative psychological inquiry into the biological underpinnings of general cognitive sophistication, comparable with what the sign-language modality fostered for language learning in nonhuman primates. This is certainly not far-fetched. Investigators have long remarked on the range of individual differences within primate conspecifics. For example, Premack (1983:125) noted in his discussion of language versus nonlanguage-trained groups of chimpanzees, "Although chimpanzees vary in intelligence, we have unfortunately never had any control over this factor, having to accept all animals that are sent to us. We have, therefore, had both gifted and nongifted animals in each group. Sarah is a bright animal by any standard, but so is Jessie, one of the non-language trained animals. The groups are also comparable at the other end of the continuum, Peony's negative gifts being well matched by those of Luvy."

Individual differences in processing stimulus equivalency (verbal/symbolic) relationships have been postulated by some experimentalists to index general intelligence (Sidman 1986). If such individual differences are ultimately linked to individual differences in central nervous system microstructure within and between the primate order, and these in turn are linked to observations like Premack's "teacher ratings," all of the ingredients are assimilated for advancing primate comparative psychology. The language-communicative performances now routinely displayed by chimpanzees and, especially, pigmy chimpanzees are truly remarkable (Savage-Rumbaugh et al 1993, Savage-Rumbaugh & Lewin 1994, Wasserman 1993). They encompass sign-language reports of emotional states and conspecific tutoring (Lubinski & Thompson 1993). Savage-Rumbaugh et al (1993) have connected these nonhuman primate findings with those from child language-development research. Will primate comparative-examinations someday provide clues to human individuality? If individual differences in acquiring cognitive skills could be linked to more fundamental biological mechanisms (like the phenomena discussed above), we might have an especially powerful lens through which to view common phylogenetic processes involved in cognitive development. Research developments on this front will be interesting to follow. Perhaps they might even obviate Wilson's (1998:184) recently expressed concern: "[S]ocial scientists as a whole have paid little attention to the foundations of human nature, and they have had almost no interest in its deep origins."

Interests

Interests have played a large role in differential psychology since the 1920s. Longitudinal inquiry comprising both temporal stability analyses (reliability) and forecasts of occupational group-membership (validity) established these measures as among the most important in applied psychology (Harmon et al 1994, Savickas & Spokane 2000). Going beyond adult populations, assessments conducted at more developmentally inchoate stages revealed that interests begin to crystallize during adolescence. They can forecast antecedents to occupational choice (e.g. college major) and, as such, serve as important tools in educational contexts (Dawis 1992). An especially critical aspect of these longitudinal studies is their incremental validity (Austin & Hanisch 1990, Humphreys et al 1993): Interests contribute important information relative to abilities. Further, the validity generalization of the unique contribution of interests has been extended to special populations. For example, Achter et al 1999 recently reported that age 13 interest assessments, among intellectually gifted students, forecast educational choice (four-year degree) over a 10-year temporal gap and add incremental validity to ability assessments. These are scientifically significant tools, which (like cognitive abilities) are predictive of a broad spectrum of criteria ranging from (core) educational/vocational settings to (more peripheral) activities in everyday life (Dawis 1992, Hogan et al 1996).

Although early research on interests was atheoretical, using empirical keying (group contrast) methodology to literally form a scale for every occupation, over the past few decades the push for deriving a general model of interest dimensions has intensified. A hexagonal structure of interest dimensions emerged (Holland 1996), which is helpful for understanding how people approach and operate within learning and work environments. Holland's model is defined by six general interest themes known as RIASEC: *r*ealistic [working with things and gadgets], *i*nvestigative [scientific pursuits], *a*rtistic [aesthetic pursuits and opportunities for self-expression], *s*ocial [people contact and helping professions], *e*nterprising [corporate environments: buying, marketing, selling], and *c*onventional [office practices and well-structured tasks].

While RIASEC is not embraced by everyone (Gati 1991), it is the most popular model available and, like the hierarchical organization of human abilities and personality's five-factor model (discussed below), innovative frameworks will need to be measured against it. RIASEC has emerged repeatedly in large samples (Rounds & Tracey 1993, Tracey & Rounds 1993), and its generalizability has held up cross-culturally (Day & Rounds 1998). RIASEC is organized around Holland's (1996) calculus assumption, which states that adjacent themes are most highly correlated, and opposite themes least correlated. Prediger (1982) has argued that Holland's model can be reduced to two relatively independent dimensions: people versus things, and data versus ideas. The former runs from Holland's social (people) to realistic (things) themes, whereas the latter runs perpendicular to people versus things splitting enterprising and conventional (data) and artistic and investigative (ideas). Prediger's two-dimensional model fits, as he maintains, within RIASEC, but most investigators feel that the parsimony achieved through this two-dimensional collapse does not offset the richness that is lost. Nevertheless, Prediger's work is important.

While the sexes do not appear to differ appreciably on data versus ideas, they routinely differ by a full standard deviation on people versus things (females tend to gravitate toward the former, males toward the latter). For example, Lippa (personal communication) computed all the effect sizes (female minus male) in his interesting multi-study article on the people versus things dimension (Lippa 1998). For all three studies, effect sizes were ≥ 1.20 on people versus things. This is typical, reflecting perhaps the largest of all sex differences on major psychological dimensions.

To be sure, there are more specific interest dimensions beyond RIASEC that carry psychologically significant import [religiosity being a noteworthy example (Waller et al 1990; see also Harmon et al 1994, Savickas & Spokane 2000)]. Nevertheless, RIASEC constitutes a cogent outline of this important arena of psychological diversity. Interestingly, like the constituents found in the hierarchy of human cognitive abilities, antecedents to RIASEC may be traced over many decades. RIASEC exemplifies how, through careful research (including cross-cultural inquiry), the nature and organization of an important domain can be successfully clarified. Guilford (1954), for example, examined and discussed very similar structures: mechanical, scientific, aesthetic expression, social welfare, business, and clerical. Holland's (1996) model stands on the shoulders of much that has gone before it.

As in our earlier discussion of range truncation (Olympic athletes), the most important dimensions for steering individuals to specific opportunities and settings are often uniformly high. With respect to forecasting continuous work-related criteria, range truncation among incumbents may generate equivocal empirical findings. So, with respect to predicting job satisfaction,

> A number of explanations can be advanced to account for the mixed results found for interests. If . . . subjects of follow-up studies were the survivors of a selection process, one might infer that in this process, the dissatisfied would have tended to leave, whereas the satisfied—and satisfactory—would have tended to remain. The restriction of range that would result could contribute to

the lowering of the true correlations. Unfortunately, the means and standard deviations of variables frequently go unreported so that a straightforward check on this simple explanation is often thwarted (Dawis 1991:851–52).

Indeed, psychological research would be more informative if it routinely described samples with means and standard deviations on major dimensions of abilities, interests, and personality for purposes of ecological validity. Doing so would reveal that some perplexing findings stem from nonrepresentative sampling.

Personality

A consensus has emerged on the major personality dimensions, but it is more opaque than for cognitive abilities and interests. Although the dimensions reviewed here appear relatively independent of abilities and interests (Ackerman 1996, Ackerman & Heggstad 1997), it is something of a misnomer to reserve the term "personality" for them. One could argue that abilities and interests are salient aspects of personality. (Cattell [1971], for example, thought so.) Like garden-variety personality measures, abilities and interests are enduring features of one's psychological make-up (Bouchard 1997, Rowe 1994, Scarr 1996). A complete understanding of one's character or reputation (Hogan et al 1996) is incomprehensible without them. Thus, while thinking about personality, it is important to keep in mind the wisdom of the great counseling psychologist, Roe, whose words are as true today as they were when she published them:

> I have become more and more convinced that the role of occupation in the life of the individual has much broader psychological importance than has generally been appreciated. I believe that psychological theory could profit greatly from the kinds of satisfactions that can be found in work. This is as true for developmental theory as it is for motivational theory . . . If one wishes to understand the total psychology of any person, it is at least as important to understand . . . occupational behavior as it is to understand . . . sexual behavior. (They are not unrelated.) . . . The fact is, of course, that one can start with any facet of human behavior and work through it to the 'total personality' (1956:vi).

With this in mind, and acknowledging that some of the best contemporary evidence for the scientific significance of broad dimensions of personality is found in predicting vocational criteria (Hogan et al 1996, Hough 1997), an examination of recent advances in personality follows.

The Big Five   The intensity of work on the dimensionality of personality during the 1980s and 1990s is comparable to that of validity generalization in abilities during the 1970s and 1980s. This work has been productive. For the most part, examinations of personality have followed the "lexical" approach suggested by Galton (1884), namely, that important dimensions of human behavior will be encoded in natural language for economy of thought. Hence, the dictionary, when systematically examined, should prove an invaluable source for identifying personality characteristics (Allport & Odbert 1936). A working model of descriptors from the dictionary is available: the "big five" (McCrae & Costa 1997) [but see Block's (1995a) "contrarian view" and replies from Costa & McCrae (1995) and Goldberg & Saucier (1995), and Block's (1995b) rejoinder].

Labels for the big five have varied, but include Extraversion (surgency, positive emotionality), Neuroticism (anxiety, negative emotionality), Agreeableness (antagonism reversed), Conscientiousness (will to achieve), and Openness (culture, intellect). Like abilities and interests, these five generic factors have a long history in psychology. For years, they were simply referred to as "Norman's five," following Norman's (1963) seminal treatment. However, the same dimensions surfaced at least 50 years ago (Fiske 1949) and were subsequently supported by large-scale analysis of military samples (cf Tupes & Christal 1992, initially published in 1961). It should be noted that Eysenck (1995) felt that conscientiousness and agreeableness can be combined to form his psychoticism (reversed) dimension, thus supporting his preference for a three-dimensional model (the "big three"): extraversion, neuroticism, and psychoticism.

The Big Seven   Waller (1999) has traced decisions concerning the item pool that Allport & Odbert (1936), Cattell, and Norman considered relevant to "authentic traits." Subsequent investigators who consulted Allport and Odbert's categorical lists apparently excluded practically all evaluative terms from efforts to develop scales of the basic dimensionality of personality. Terms such as special, important, immoral, disloyal, and nasty were not routinely examined in attempts at mapping personality.

For several years now, Tellegen and Waller have studied evaluative terms by systematically sampling from the dictionary (Tellegen 1993, Tellegen & Waller 2000, Waller 1999). They have a questionnaire purporting to assess evaluative traits and the Big Five dimensions (Tellegen et al 1991). Their analysis appears to warrant seven dimensions: the big five and Positive and Negative Valence. Positive Valence depicts a dimension with positive loadings on "outstanding," "first-rate," "excellent," "remarkable," which form a continuum from ordinary-to-exceptional, or common-to-impressive. Negative Valence is captured by terms such as "cruel," "evil," "wicked," and "sickening," which portray a continuum from worthy-to-evil, or decent-to-awful. These two dimensions have held up cross-culturally (Almagor et al 1995, Benet & Waller 1995). Because these highly evaluative terms were prematurely jettisoned from empirical analyses until recently, there has not been an opportunity to demonstrate their importance.

Interpretation and Future Directions   Tellegen (1993) has suggested that major dimensions of personality have adaptability import. Individual differences reflect one's "preparedness" or "tuning" to affordances in the social landscape (see also Snow 1991). Tellegen's (1993) big seven studies motivated him to adopt somewhat different labels (with the following interpretations). "Positive and Negative Valence reflect primal readiness to encode power and evilness; Positive Emotionality and Negative Emotionality reflect built-in responsiveness to signals of emotion and emotional-temperamental dispositions; and Dependability, Agreeability, and Conventionality (vs. Unusualness) reflect protoscientific propensities to encode a person's predictability, controllability, and comprehensibility, respectively" (1993:126). Tellegen also has advanced the idea that we consider these "folk concepts" as distinguished from psychological concepts advanced to describe or explain psychological phenomena and processes. Recent advances have placed personological inquiry into the broader context of evolutionary theory (Hogan & Hogan 2000).

CONSTELLATIONS

Hogan et al (1996) have recently cautioned against examining personality dimensions individually because the manner in which each operates depends on the full constellation of personal characteristics. Two extroverts will operate quite differently, for example, if their standings on conscientiousness are diametrically opposed. The point is well-taken, but the evidence indicates that we should move beyond Hogan et al's (1996) recommendation (sound as it is) and intermingle cross-domain attributes. Like contrasting constellations of personality attributes, similar interest and ability patterns often produce markedly different phenotypes as a result of differences on dimensions from other classes. The paths traveled by two spatially gifted students are likely to be quite distinct if, for example, they occupy contrasting locations on "people versus things." Assuming that more comprehensive assessments will enhance psychological theory and practice, some approaches that go beyond domain-constrained treatments follow.

Intellectual Development

Ackerman (1996, Ackerman & Heggstad 1997) has proposed an intriguing model of adult intellectual development that orchestrates abilities as process, personality, and interest dimensions simultaneously to describe changes in cognitive content and processes throughout the life span. Content denotes the pedagogical aspects of learning (knowledge), whereas process is more restricted to power of intellect [or e.g. working memory capacity (Carpenter et al 1990, Kyllonen & Christal 1990), perhaps a modern conceptualization of Spearman's (1927) mental energy]. Ackerman's theory is called PPIK, for intelligence-as-process, -personality, -interests, and -knowledge. Interests and personality attributes channel the development of knowledge structures down different paths, for example, CP Snow's (1967) two intellectual cultures, while intelligence-as-process determines the complexity and density of the knowledge assimilated. Ackerman's approach is reminiscent of Cattell's (1971) early formulation of investment theory, where fluid abilities are invested in the development of crystallized abilities as a function of nonintellectual personal attributes. Intellectual bodies develop from a common multidimensional core (abilities, interests, and personality) that are seemingly quite generic cross-culturally (Carroll 1993, Day & Rounds 1998, McCrae & Costa 1997).

This model provides an insightful basis for uncovering why individuals with similar cognitive profiles can, and frequently do, vary widely in their knowledge base or "crystallized abilities." Ackerman (1996, Ackerman & Heggstad 1997) has compiled ability/interest, ability/personality, and interest/personality correlates to support PPIK. Analysis has distilled four across-attribute (ability/interest/personality) trait complexes. They are social, clerical/conventional, science/math, and intellectual/cultural. Intellectual/cultural, for example, reflects light correlations between verbal ability and aesthetic and investigative interests, whereas science/math reflects light correlations between math/spatial abilities and realistic, investigative and social (reversed) interests. The psychological import behind these trait complexes is similar to Snow's (1991) aptitude complexes (ability + interest constellations for classifying educational treatments), and Dawis & Lofquist's (1984) taxons (ability + preference constellations for conceptualizing transactions between individuals and work environments; see below).

PPIK might be especially relevant to contexts where knowledge is more important than intellectual processing abilities for predicting performance (Ericsson 1996). Examinations of expert performance (Rolfhus & Ackerman 1996), for example, have often revealed that the greatest difference between experts and nonexperts is in the richness and depth of the knowledge structures of the former. Ackerman also has developed a typical intellectual engagement (TIE) measure for assessing how much an individual is likely to invest in developing his or her intellectual abilities. However, this measure tends to covary more deeply with humanistic than scientific knowledge domains (Ackerman 1996). Therefore, multiple TIE measures might be required to capture the multiple motives involved in developing intellect. Perhaps distinct TIE should be developed for each PPIK trait complex. Given that the current TIE is primarily relevant to the humanities, a more descriptively apt label might be "TIE-verbal/humanistic" (for trait complex: intellectual/cultural). A TIE measure focusing more on nonverbal ideation might better forecast development in more technical domains: "TIE-science/math" (for trait complex: science/math).

What one knows (knowledge) and how sophisticated one is at manipulating what one knows (thinking) are ostensibly two different things. Yet, with respect to measurement operations, content and process (knowledge and thinking) always have been inextricably intertwined (Roznowski 1987). As Ackerman (1996:245) remarks: "[A]n individual can strive for breadth of knowledge or depth of knowledge, but there is a trade off between these two orientations. Only the most exceptional intellectual talent will allow for high levels of knowledge domain depth and breadth." Does "exceptional intellectual talent" primarily stem from one dimension or two? Perhaps breadth and depth combine to map *g* in a manner analogous to area; or perhaps speed should be added to assess this central dimension akin to measuring volume? It seems as though we always return to Spearman's *g* in one way or another—a dominant dimension whose scientific significance is central. These observations notwithstanding, PPIK clearly takes an important step forward in conceptualizing the nature of intellectual development.

Vocational Adjustment

Are you able to do it? Are you happy doing it? Throughout most of this century, in one form or another, vocational psychologists have been asking clients these two questions. Often data were collected to help clients whose reactions were initially uncertain or unclear. Dawis & Lofquist (1984, Lofquist & Dawis 1991) developed a system to conceptualize vocational adjustment and counseling, the theory of work adjustment (TWA). TWA is helpful for understanding why abilities and interests show incremental validity relative to each other in learning and work settings. Katzell (1994), reviewing volumes one through three of the *Handbook of Industrial and Organizational Psychology*, used TWA as an integrative framework to synthesize research literature in I/O psychology. TWA has been applied to designing learning environments throughout the life span (Lubinski & Benbow 2000), and the *Journal of Vocational Behavior* (1993) has a special issue on TWA.

TWA is predicated on two dimensions: satisfaction and satisfactoriness. Satisfaction is a function of the correspondence between a person's preferences (needs, interests, and values) and the rewards offered in a particular occupational setting or career path. Satisfactoriness is determined by the correspondence between one's abilities and the competency requirements needed for effective performance in a given occupation. Equal emphasis is placed on assessing the individual and the environment; both are assessed in commensurate terms; and, when a high degree of correspondence is achieved across both dimensions (i.e. the individual is feeling satisfied and is performing satisfactorily), a symbiotic relationship develops to sustain the joint person-environment interaction. When satisfaction is high but satisfactoriness is low, the environment is likely to terminate the relationship; when the inverse occurs, the person is more likely to break off the relationship.

TWA uses the term "taxon"—akin to Ackerman's "trait complexes" and Snow's "aptitude complexes"—to depict ability-preference constellations related to differential performance and enjoyment outcomes within the world of work. Supporting data are found in two books (Dawis & Lofquist 1984, Lofquist & Dawis 1991), as well as throughout the applied psychological literature examining how ability/ preference constellations fit into relatively well-defined ecological settings (e.g. educational tracks, military classification systems, occupations). As Katzell (1994:13) noted, "[a]lthough not derived specifically from the theory, there have been many practical applications of parts of it in industry, such as the prediction of turnover from job satisfaction and the matching of ability with job requirements to predict performance." Support for TWA's validity is seen in positive results for Schneider et al's (1995) attraction-selection-attrition (ASA) model and the gravitational hypothesis (Dunnette 1998, Wilk et al 1995, Wilk & Sackett 1996). The basic idea is that people select environments congenial to their personal attributes and style of life and migrate from those that are not good fits.

Work Performance

The opening sentence of Schmidt & Hunter's (1998:262) review of 85 years of research on selection methods in personnel psychology is consistent with the desire of applied psychologists to uncover longitudinally stable dimensions: "From the point of view of practical value, the most important property of a personnel assessment method is the predictive validity."

Work performance is an important area of applied psychology, not only in terms of a society's economic well-being in internationally competitive markets, but also in terms of the emotional and physical well-being of citizens within a society (Hunter & Schmidt 1996, Schmidt & Hunter 1998). For a poignant example, see Hunter & Schmidt's (1996) powerful and compelling illustration of factors associated with the time it takes to catch a rapist (measured in number of crimes committed). Huge individual differences are found between competent and excellent police officers, in the effectiveness of their work and how expeditiously justice is served. When consulting with legal officials, Hunter & Schmidt point out that lawyers frequently appreciate individual differences between competent and poor workers, but they have a rather poor appreciation of differences between competent and exceptional workers.

Laypersons are unaware of the two primary ways to assess individual differences in performance: dollar value of output and percent of mean output. At minimum, the standard deviation of the dollar value of output across individuals has been found to be 40% of the mean salary of the job. Hence, if the average salary for a job is $50,000, the standard deviation of employees' dollar-value output is $20,000. The difference, therefore, between above-average workers (e.g. one standard deviation above the mean) and below-average workers (e.g. one standard deviation below the mean) would be: $70,000 − $30,000 = $40,000. Work performance measured as a percentage of mean output would be estimated as follows: An employee's output would be divided by the output of workers at the 50th percentile and then multiplied by 100. The standard deviation of output as a percentage of average output is moderated by job level. Schmidt & Hunter's (1998) review found that percentage to be around 19% for unskilled and semi-skilled jobs, 32% for skilled jobs, and 48% for managerial and professional jobs. There is an old saying in applied psychology: For a difference to be a difference it must make a difference.

In view of these important differences, uncovering predictors to model work performance has attracted much attention. This was anticipated in Lerner's (1983) discussion of "human capital." Research has added to validity generalization studies of the past two decades by combining personality measures with abilities. Conscientiousness, for example, adds incremental validity with probably as much breadth (but not quite as much depth) as general ability measures to predictions for many occupations. The longstanding belief that personality measures do not contribute to individual differences in work performance is not true. Increments for personality measures typically range between 0.05 and 0.15, which may seem small when contrasted with what ability constructs offer, but their economic and social gains are huge. Moreover, the troubling group differences on abilities reviewed earlier are not found on these measures, so personality measurement has the potential to minimize adverse impact. There are, however, differences in opinion on how best to carve up personality for predicting work performance (Hough 1997). Nevertheless, there is widespread agreement that increments in predicted performance beyond ability are achievable through personality assessment. These increments are especially evident when studying peak performance.

Creativity and Eminence

A number of dimensions relevant to creativity have been identified. Interestingly, they are similar to Galton's (1869) necessary ingredients for eminence. Investigators operating within frameworks distinct from differential psychology have confirmed many of these (Gardner 1993). A deeper appreciation of this area is gleaned by combining the differential psychology of Eysenck (1995) with the work of Gardner (1993) and Simonton (1990, 1994). These treatments are not incompatible and, in many respects, the latter two attach idiographic flesh to the normative skeleton outlined by Eysenck (1995). They also enlarge classics such as Roe's (1953) *The Making of a Scientist* and Zuckerman's (1977) *Scientific Elite*.

Galton defined genius (the ultimate label for one's track record of creative accomplishments leading to eminence) in terms of reputation: "those qualities of intellect and disposition, which urge . . . acts that lead to reputation, I do not mean capacity without zeal nor zeal without capacity, nor even a combination of both of them without an adequate power of doing a great deal of very laborious work. But I mean a nature which, when left to itself, will, urged by an internal stimulus, climb the path that leads to eminence, and has the strength to reach the summit—one which, if hindered or thwarted, will fret and strive until the hindrance is overcome . . . " (1869:33).

For criterion measurement, Eysenck (1995) and Simonton (1990, 1994) have adopted Galton's view for calibrating eminence. In Simonton's (1990) investigations into the psychometric properties of reputation assessments (using informed judges), he has reported internal consistency reliability coefficients >0.85 for artistic distinction, philosophical eminence, and scientific fame.

The dispositional package that Galton outlined is in agreement with modern views, although Galton went too far in attributing eminence almost exclusively to personal attributes. Today, spectacular forms of creativity, like lesser forms, are seen as confluences of endogenous and exogenous determinants, rather than primarily the former. Cultural factors and the zeitgeist play critical roles.

What attributes predict eminence? The personal attributes of individuals at the top of their respective domains include the anticipated (ability + interest) constellations (aptitude complexes, trait complexes, and taxons) that distinguish individuals in their chosen domain or profession from the general population. However, more intense abilities are characteristic (and more is better) (Benbow 1992). For example, extraordinary engineers and physical scientists possess pronounced quantitative-spatial abilities and interests in investigative and realistic pursuits, whereas humanists possess higher verbal abilities, relative to nonverbal abilities, and preferences for artistic and social arenas. Yet, what appears to move the highly creative apart from their peers is their passion for work. They are exceptional in their industriousness and perseverance; they tend to be almost myopically fixated on work. This is something well-known among academic scientists who train academic scientists (cf Wilson 1998:56). (Edison's familiar 1% inspiration 99% perspiration also comes to mind.) The sheer amount of time devoted to their area of excellence is one of the most exceptional things about them. Zuckerman's (1977) account of the extraordinary efforts that Nobel Laureates displayed to reach the right teachers (who were almost always Laureates themselves) supports this.

On the other hand, some antecedents contributing to the enormous energy reserves of certain individuals are not necessarily positive. For example, Jamison (1993) has observed a higher incidence of manic-depressive disorders among creative writers and artists. Jensen (1996) has discussed other endogenous factors pertinent to cortical stimulation, for example, blood serum urate (a cortical stimulant) level (SUL). Interestingly, SUL covaries positively with achievement. Eysenck (1995) focuses on other neurochemical underpinnings posited to give rise to "zeal" (Galton 1869).

In part because of the intensity with which these individuals approach their work, the highly creative, as a group, are also known to be difficult in interpersonal relationships, socially harsh, and abrasive. Gardner (1993) has discussed the "casualties" surrounding these individuals as they steadfastly focus on their work to the exclusion of other aspects of life. He discusses the "mixed blessings" associated with being close to such individuals. This supports Eysenck's (1995) view that the highly creative are, on average, high on trait psychoticism (or conscientiousness + agreeableness in reverse). Following Eysenck, this, among other things, enables the highly creative to look at things quite differently (unconventionally).

What appears to draw individuals toward particular environments, people, and opportunities is, in part, the personal attributes that they possess; but once in these arenas, what actually happens is contingent on opportunity. It might be helpful to construe dispositional antecedents to exceptional forms of creativity as "emergent phenomena" (Lykken et al 1992), namely, the proper configuration of personal attributes [including the psychological endurance necessary for developing and maintaining exceptional performance (Ericsson 1996)]. When such constellations find supportive environments, then, and only then, does Galton's depiction hold. Jensen (1996) maintains that: genius = high ability $\times$ high productivity $\times$ high creativity.

Underpinning this equation, ability = information processing efficiency, productivity = endogenous cortical stimulation, and creativity = trait psychoticism (unconventional ideation). This suggests kinds of inquiry that must at least be entertained for understanding how products that change culture develop and, ultimately, how such achievements are best facilitated, as well as inadvertently suppressed.

Crime

When Cronbach & Meehl (1955) introduced construct validation, they exemplified the process by compiling a heterogeneous collection of findings all related to the psychopathic deviate (Pd) scale of the Minnesota Multiphasic Personality Inventory. How, they asked, could a scale developed to isolate criminals and delinquents from the general population also reveal elevated scores for: Broadway actors, high-school dropouts, deer hunters who accidentally shoot people, police officers, and nurses who were rated by their supervisors as not especially afraid of psychotic patients? (Note this was before wide use of psychoactive drugs, when patients routinely experienced frightening psychotic episodes.) Pd also covaries negatively with trustworthiness ratings. What underlying construct representation could possibly support this nomothetic span?

Two years later, Lykken (1957) published positive findings for what these groups have in common: Relatively speaking, they are fearless or in possession of a "low anxiety IQ." Using a Pavlovian paradigm, Lykken showed that, as a group, hardened criminals, when contrasted with random samples of inmates, were "retarded" when it came to developing conditioned responses to neutral stimuli paired with shock. This has been replicated and studied in several laboratories, albeit with somewhat different labels and measures: "socialization" (reversed), "danger seeking," or "sensation seeking" (Wilson & Herrnstein 1985, Lykken 1995).

As Lykken (1995) points out, however, being fearless does not prescribe a particular developmental path. This is the stock from which astronauts, poised law enforcement officials, firefighters on elite rescue teams, war heroes, and fighter pilots are grown. When coupled with other attributes and opportunities, being fearless can be an asset. However, it can also be a liability because it makes conventional socialization procedures difficult. For instance, when low fearfulness is combined with agreeableness + conscientiousness (reversed), a 75–90 IQ range, mesomorphic body build, and reared in an abusive crime-ridden environment, a high-risk liability emerges (Lykken 1995, Wilson & Herrnstein 1985). One of the handicaps faced by individuals within lower IQ ranges is a limited temporal horizon, a deficit in foreseeing temporally remote consequences of actions.

Fortunately, however, if Lykken (1995) is correct, a "type like" psychopath is relatively infrequent, relative to the proportion of individuals engaged in criminal behavior. He suggests that most criminal behavior stems from a larger group of individuals—sociopaths who, with proper parenting, could have been socialized away from a life of crime. He adds that, while the behavior genetic data are compelling (for the major individual-differences dimensions of his model), typical twin and adoption studies do not include families deeply enmeshed in illegal activities. The behavior genetic studies are restricted to environmental ranges not abnormally deviant from the population norm. Lykken (1997) argues, however, that interventions are most likely to be effective in these maladaptive environments (but see Rowe 1997).

Health Risk Behavior

"If public health officials understood the characteristic behaviors, thoughts, and feelings of those young persons who engage in health-risk behaviors, they could be in a better position to design health campaigns and educational programs that would appeal to their target audience" (Caspi et al 1997:1053). Repeatedly, longitudinal inquiry has uncovered the significance of individual differences in channeling the development of harmful maladies not only to the individual at risk (Gordon 1997, Lubinski & Humphreys 1997, Schaie 1996) but to others occupying their purview.

Like contemporary treatments of creative achievement and crime, contemporary discussions of health risk behaviors are related to "delay of gratification" phenomena, which can have multiple (ability + personological) antecedents. Outcomes emanating from both wise and unwise actions, and conscientious versus risky behavior, are often not precipitous. They frequently develop slowly over time to result in a life threatening condition, an ostensibly discrete arrest, or a seemingly effortless masterpiece. Short-lived behavioral episodes are often products of years of development. Just as the development of excellence is in part traceable to comprehending the temporally remote consequences of immediate practice, aspects of maladaptive behavior are due to a limited temporal horizon.

Life Span Development

Scarr (1992, 1996; Scarr & McCartney 1983) has drawn on three kinds of genotype-environment (GE) correlations distinguished by behavioral geneticists—active, passive, and reactive—to build a developmental theory of individuality. Her formulation builds on what differential psychologists have uncovered about the normative dimensionality of human variation (abilities, interests, and personality) to gain a purchase on the development of the idiographic particulars of each individual. Scarr's formulation fits well with treatments of how personal-attribute constellations (aptitude complexes, trait complexes, or taxons) serve to guide behavioral development down distinctive paths (Harris 1995).

Personal dispositions interact with the environment in three ways: (*a*) Passive GE correlations are in operation, for example, when the genetic antecedents for the development of verbal reasoning ability covary with the vocabulary size of rearing environments. Above average parents, for example, provide the genetic basis for complex verbal reasoning as well as a stimulating learning environment for its development. (*b*) Reactive GE correlations come about when children, because of their genetic differences, evoke different responses from their environment (e.g. when a painfully shy child attenuates the likelihood of spontaneous social/verbal engagement). (*c*)

Active GE correlations are produced when a person takes an active role in seeking out particular environments—for example, when children, at promise for achieving excellence in athletics or the performing arts seek out, through their own initiative, opportunities for athletic participation or musical instruction. This kind of GE interaction has been especially prominent in Scarr's recent writings, in which she has explicated how this mechanism operates in niche building.

Scarr maintains that people (especially as they mature) seek out or strive to create environments for themselves—environments that are congruent with their personal point of view and which, in large part, reflect their abilities, interests, and personality. Finding appropriate niches facilitates positive development, an idea that has been a longstanding supposition in differential psychology (Lubinski 1996). Scarr (1996) drew on this literature to offer recommendations for parenting. She suggests that children need and deserve supportive loving environments to ensure that they become happy individuals adjusted to the complexities associated with the demands of societal roles. However, she cautions parents against trying to shape children's enduring characteristics reflexively; instead, parents should tailor educational curricula and opportunities for positive development to the unique assets of each child's individuality.

METHODOLOGICAL ISSUES

Causal Modeling

In structural equation modeling, designs that omit key determinants of phenomena under analysis are called mis-specified (the term used to depict errors of omission) or neglected aspects. One compelling aspect of Herrnstein & Murray (1994) worth underscoring is their simultaneous examination of two putative causal sources (viz. general intelligence and SES). Many social scientists found the concurrent competition of these two factors unfamiliar, as the social science literature is replete with causal inference stemming from correlations between SES and important outcome measures (Bouchard et al 1996), but g is seldom assessed concomitantly in such designs.

Causality and Confounds

Removing (partialing out) SES from ability-performance correlations has been repeatedly criticized because general intelligence and SES share common antecedents (Bouchard 1997, Bouchard et al 1996). Meehl's (1970) ex post facto design is the general rubric for this methodological shortcoming. Yet, Murray (1998) has offered a clever methodology for untangling the causal influence of SES on ability-performance and ability-outcome functions. Using 15-year longitudinal data, Murray studied income differences between biologically related siblings (reared together) who differed in general intelligence. As ability differences between siblings increased, so did their income differences; moreover, these income differences mirrored those in the general population at similar ability ranges. This investigation corroborates a handful of studies using a similar control for family environment (Waller 1971).

Total Evidence Rule

The same year Burks (1928) published her landmark treatment on decomposing environmental and hereditary sources of variation, Ellis (1928) introduced psychologists to a more general refinement. "The logicians point out that a cause of much incorrect thinking is what is known as the fallacy of *the neglected aspect*. Early students of certain diseases considered them to be due to hot weather or excessive rain—neglecting the activities of the fly or the mosquito in spreading the bacteria. Neglecting aspects of problems often hide variable agencies that must be understood before the problem can be solved" (Ellis 1928:9). Subsequently, Carnap (1950) formalized this fallacy as the total evidence rule, which maintains that, when evaluating the plausibility of a particular hypothesis, it is imperative to take into account all of the relevant information (Bouchard 1997, Lubinski & Humphreys 1997). As commonsensical as this seems, it frequently is not done.

For example, investigators readily assume that the covariation between parent and child in abilities, interests, and personality is due to parent nurturing (cf Thompson's 1955 review of Hart & Risley 1994). Yet, biometric analyses reveal that covariation among broad individual differences approaches zero as adulthood is reached among biologically-unrelated siblings reared together. As unrelated individuals who were reared together grow older, they appear to "grow apart" (McCartney et al 1990), with respect to the attributes examined here. It appears that an inconspicuous cause, namely shared genetic make-up, is responsible for the phenotypic covariation between biologically related parents and children. Parents do, indeed, have an influence on their children with respect to the major dimensions reviewed herein; however, this influence is transmitted through a different reared-in mechanism than many presupposed. This is also supported by a variety of kinship correlates, such as finding that, on "environmental measures" (e.g. Home Observation for Measurement of the Environment (HOME): Plomin & Bergeman 1991), identical twins reared apart assess their reared-in home environments as similarly as fraternal twins reared together do (Scarr 1996). This is not to say that abusive environments are not detrimental to optimal development; recall Lykken's (1997) point about the kinds of families that are typically not found in biometrically informed psychological studies. What these studies do speak to, however, is that, overall, many families are functionally equivalent in terms of fostering the development of broad individual differences (Harris 1995, Hetherington et al 1994).

CONSILIENCE

In *Consilience: The Unification of Knowledge,* Wilson writes:

> Today, the greatest divide within humanity is not between races, or religions, or even, as widely believed between literate and illiterate. It is the chasm that

separates scientific from prescientific cultures . . . . Without the instruments and accumulated knowledge of the natural sciences—physics, chemistry, and biology—humans are trapped in a cognitive prison. They invent ingenious speculations and myths about the origin of the confining waters, of the sun and the sky and the stars above, and the meaning of their own existence. But they are wrong, always wrong, because the world is too remote from ordinary experience to be merely imagined." (1998:45)

By consilience, Wilson (1998) means the joining together of ideas across disciplines in order to paint a more comprehensive picture of the nature of the universe. He bemoans how over-specialization among the educated elite makes important conceptual syntheses unlikely, and suggests that professional misunderstandings often arise from ignorance of other disciplines, "not from a fundamental difference in mentality"(1998:126). He cites Snow's (1967) "two cultures" as a familiar example, while also noting that social scientists frequently neglect modern biological findings.

Dawis (1992) has remarked that psychometric tools for assessing the attributes reviewed here provide unparalleled windows on humanity—akin to the microscope in biology and the telescope in astronomy. Over psychology's short history much has been learned about human diversity, especially for understanding the niches people seek out, as well as those that people attempt to avoid, build, or change. This body of knowledge has interconnected beautifully with other disciplines, yet frequently, individual differences are neglected in research design and interpretation. Whereas biologists interested in protein molecules are unlikely to say: "But I am not interested in carbon atoms. I'll leave that for others," many psychologists appear content in examining human behavior while neglecting relevant scientific information.

Kimble (1994) has scolded psychologists in "Anti-Intellectualism Masquerading as Human Sensitivity," for their use of huge jargon-to-substance and feeling-to-thinking ratios on politically correct topics. "How you feel about a finding has no bearing on its truth" (Kimble 1994:257). In reviewing Sternberg & Grigorenko's (1997) *Intelligence: Heredity and Environment,* Hunt (1997) sees certain chapters as excellent overviews, but others as nonscientific "cultural perspectives." Is there a way to render this variance in psychological discourse more understandable?

If psychological practice is the application of scientific principles to individuals and groups, perhaps the psychology of individual differences, combined with the history of psychology, can illuminate such contrasting points of view. Here, I suggest that contrasting points of view held by certain groups of psychologists reflect the individual differences that they possess, the niches they selected for professional development, and the scientific standards (role models) found therein. With respect to selection for professional training, for example, psychology, relative to other disciplines, clearly draws on multiple attribute patterns (aptitude complexes, taxons, trait complexes). Psychologically speaking, APA is a heterogeneous lot, relative to other disciplines. Some psychologists work with people, others do not, and yet, this seems reasonable. Distinctive sets of skills and interests are needed for psychology's multifaceted roles. Boring's (1950) familiar distinction between clinical and experimental psychologists (viz the former "like people") comes to mind. But are some psychologists becoming too specialized? Is some practice and writing drifting away from a scientific base only to result in a *House of Cards* (Dawes 1994)?

Although marked group differences in "people interests" across psychological specialties are conspicuous and familiar, ability profiles often vary too, sometimes in level (in contrast to Wilson's view), but more often in pattern (something not considered by Wilson). Indeed, it appears that group differences within the main historical branches of psychology, across people and their intellectual products, become more understandable by considering individual-differences profiles. Further, it is suggested that people attracted to certain specialties tend to approach problems with different criteria for what constitutes a satisfying explanation. This has intensified to the point of becoming scientifically problematic. Consider the following.

The history of systems of psychology may be traced to England (differential), Germany (experimental), and France (clinical); the three systems differentially emphasize quantitative, spatial, and verbal reasoning, respectively. They can be seen as subtle divides across Snow's (1967) two cultures. Over time, specialization in these areas increased. Clinical psychologists slowly drifted more toward people contact and intellectual content restricted to verbal reasoning and literary skill, whereas differential psychologists and experimentalists drifted toward quantitative models and technical instrumentation. These all depict niche building (Scarr 1996), a powerful tool for conceptualizing "climate" and organizational change (Bouchard 1997, Dunnette 1998).

It is important to keep in mind, however, that psychological diversity is not necessarily problematic. Individual differences can be enriching. When individual differences are anchored by common ground, they routinely give rise to effective solutions through different strategies. Consider Thurstone's (1935) *Vectors of the Mind* and Burt's (1941) *Factors of the Mind*. Thurstone, a former engineer, chose to highlight concepts with line drawings (spatial configurations: "vectors"), whereas Burt, a brilliant algebraist, used copious formulas ("factors") but few diagrams. Factor analysis can be presented either algebraically or geometrically, so both approaches are complementary (and one may serve some students better than others). Either is fine. But when disciplines become more complex and critical tools are difficult to master, psychological diversity can be problematic. Sometimes migration is necessary. As Terman (1954:222) noted: "Thorndike confessed to me once that his lack of mechanical skill was partly responsible for turning him to mental tests and to the kinds of experiments on learning that required no apparatus." Whereas of BF Skinner, it was said that all he needed to build an apparatus was cardboard, string, and a piece of chewing gum. Clearly Freud and William James were primarily literary in their approach (Freud's literary skills earned him the Goethe Prize, and James was arguably a better writer than his brother Henry). All were excellent psychologists, yet most certainly they possessed different individual-differences profiles. Nevertheless, along with their uniqueness, they were all highly scientific (investigative) in orientation. Has this latter interest changed in some modern psychological specialties? Have certain segments of the psychological community become scientifically problematic?

These considerations may shed light on contentious debate beyond the biological bases of human behavior. If this analysis has verisimilitude, marked group (individual-differences) profiles should be observed among individuals with contrasting views on facilitated communication, recovered memory, qualitative (versus quantitative) methods, clinical (versus statistical) prediction, and numerous alternative formulations of human intelligence (emotional, multiple, etc.). Perhaps one group places a premium on characterizing unique nuances attendant with all psychological phenomena (measured against criteria of eloquence and verbal cohesiveness), while another emphasizes the communality cutting across scientifically significant dimensions of human behavior and their external linkages (graphed or measured quantitatively). If so, the seeds for communicating at cross-purposes are planted and germinate from deep differences in fundamental qualities—nurtured and supported by distinct niches.

Differential psychology not only fosters consilience, it offers understanding for some of the most critical social issues of our time. A coherent picture of the human condition is incomprehensible without individual differences concepts and methods. Finally, and perhaps most profoundly, differential psychology might point to ways to enhance the scientific integrity of psychology, and the social sciences more generally, by revealing (through multidimensional models) ways to develop, select, and train students for coming to terms with human behavior from a scientific point of view.

ACKNOWLEDGMENTS

I am grateful to several colleagues and friends for providing me with invaluable discussions and feedback on this chapter: Britt Anderson, Camilla P Benbow, Thomas J Bouchard Jr, John B Carroll, Rene V Dawis, Lewis Goldberg, Robert A Gordon, Linda S Gottfredson, Robert Hogan, Lloyd G Humphreys, Douglas N Jackson, Arthur R Jensen, David T Lykken, Paul E Meehl, Martha Morelock, Robert Plomin, James Rounds, Frank L Schmidt, Lynne Schoenauer, Daniel L Shea, Julian C Stanley, Auke Tellegen, Mary L Tenopyr, Niels G Waller, and Rose Mary Webb.

Visit the Annual Reviews home page at www.AnnualReviews.org.

LITERATURE CITED

Achter JA, Lubinski D, Benbow CP. 1996. Multipotentiality among intellectually gifted: "It was never there and already it's vanishing." *J. Couns. Psychol.* 43:65–76

Achter JA, Lubinski D, Benbow CP, Eftekhari-Sanjani H. 1999. Assessing vocational preferences among gifted adolescents adds incremental validity to abilities. *J. Educ. Psychol.* 91:777–86

Ackerman PL. 1988. A review of Linda S Gottfredson ed. The g factor in employment. Journal of Vocational Behavior. *Educ. Psychol. Meas.* 48:553–58. Special issue

Ackerman PL. 1996. A theory of adult intellectual development: process, personality, interests, and knowledge. *Intelligence* 22: 227–57

Ackerman PL, Heggestad ED. 1997. Intelligence, personality, and interests: evidence for overlapping traits. *Psychol. Bull.* 121:218–45

Allport GW, Odbert HS. 1936. Trait names: a psycho-lexical study. *Psychol. Monogr: Gen. Appl.* 47 (whole No. 211: 1–171)

Almagor M, Tellegen A, Waller NG. 1995. The big seven model: a cross-cultural replication. *J. Pers. Soc. Psychol.* 69:300–7

Amer. Psychol. 1965 Testing and public policy. 20:859–993

Am. Psychol. 1998. Comments. 53:566–77

Anastasi A. 1937. *Differential Psychology.* NY: Macmillan

Anderson B. 1993. Evidence from the rat for a general factor that underlies cognitive performance that relates to brain size: intelligence? *Neurosci. Lett.* 153:98–102

Anderson B. 1994a. Role of animal research in the investigation of human mental retardation. *Am. J. Ment. Retard.* 99:50–59

Anderson B. 1994b. The volume of the cerebellar molecular layer predicts attention to novelty in rats. *Brain Res.* 641:160–62

Anderson B. 1995. G explained. *Med. Hypotheses.* 45:602–4

Anderson B, Harvey T. 1996. Alterations in cortical thickness and neuronal density in the frontal cortex of Albert Einstein. *Neurosci. Lett.* 210:161–64

Austin JT, Hanisch KA. 1990. Occupational attainment as a function of abilities and interests. *J. Appl. Psychol.* 75:77–86

Barrett GV, Depinet RL. 1991. A reconsideration for competence rather than for intelligence. *Am. Psychol.* 46:1012–24

Benbow CP. 1988. Sex differences in mathematical reasoning ability among the intellectually talented. *Behav. Brain Sci.* 11:169–232

Benbow CP. 1992. Academic achievement in mathematics and science of students between ages 13 and 23: Are there differences among students in the top one percent of mathematical ability? *J. Educ. Psychol.* 84:51–61

Benbow CP, Lubinski D, eds. 1996. *Intellectual Talent.* Baltimore: Johns Hopkins Univ. Press. 428 pp.

Benbow CP, Stanley JC. 1996. Inequity in equity: how "equity" can lead to inequity for high-potential students. *Psychol. Public Policy. Law* 2:249–92

Benet V, Waller NG. 1995. The big seven factor model of personality description: evidence for its cross-cultural generality in a Spanish sample. *J. Pers. Soc. Psychol.* 69:701–18

Berliner DC, Calfee RC, eds. 1996. *Handbook of Educational Psychology.* New York: Macmillan. 1071 pp.

Block J. 1995a. A contrarian view of the five factor approach to personality description. *Psychol. Bull.* 117:187–215

Block J. 1995b. Going beyond the five factors given: rejoinder to Costa and McCrae (1995) and Goldberg and Saucier (1995). *Psychol. Bull.* 117:226–29

Bouchard TJ. 1997. Genetic influence on mental abilities, personality, vocational interests, and work attitudes. *Int. Rev. Indus. Organ. Psychol.* 12:373–95

Bouchard TJ. 1999. The definitive case for g. *Contemp. Psychol.* 44:133–35

Bouchard TJ, Lykken DT, Tellegen A, McGue M. 1996. Genes, drives, environment, and experience: EPD theory revisited. See Benbow & Lubinski 1996, pp. 5–43

Brand C. 1987. The importance of general intelligence. In *Arthur Jensen: Consensus and Controversy,* ed. S Magil, C Magil, pp. 251–65. NY: Falmer. 420 pp.

Brody N. 1992. *Intelligence.* San Diego: Academic. 395 pp.

Brody N. 1996. Intelligence and public policy. *Psychol. Public Policy Law* 3/4:473–85

Boring EG. 1950. *A History of Experimental Psychology.* NY: Appleton-Century-Crofts. 777 pp.

Burks BS. 1928. The relative influence of nature and nurture upon mental development. *27th Yearbook of the National Society for Education,* pp. 219–316. Bloomington, IN: Public School

Burt C. 1941. *The Factors of the Mind.* NY: Macmillan

Campbell DT, Fiske DW. 1959. Convergent and discriminant validation by the multitrait-multimethod matrix. *Psychol. Bull.* 93:81–105

Campbell JP. 1990. The role of theory in industrial and organizational psychology. In *Handbook of I/O Psychology,* ed. MD Dunnette, LM Hough, pp. 39–74. Palo Alto, CA: Consulting Psychologists. 755 pp.

Campbell JP. 1996. Group differences and personnel decisions: validity, fairness, and affirmative action. *J. Vocat. Behav.* 49:122–58

Carpenter PA, Just MA, Shell P. 1990. What one intelligence test measures: a theoretical account. *Psychol. Rev.* 97:404–31

Carnap R. 1950. *Logical Foundations of Probability.* Chicago: Univ. Chicago Press

Carroll JB. 1993. *Human Cognitive Abilities.* Cambridge: Cambridge Univ. Press. 819 pp.

Carroll JB. 1994. An alternative Thurstonian view of intelligence. *Psychol. Inq.* 5:195–97

Carroll JB. 1997. Psychometrics, intelligence, and public perception. *Intelligence* 24:25–52

Caspi A, Begg D, Dickson N, Harrington H, Langley J, et al. 1997. Personality differences predict health-risk behaviors in young adulthood. *J. Pers. Soc. Psychol.* 73:1052–63

Caspi A, Moffitt TE. 1993. When do individual differences matter? A paradoxical theory of personality coherence. *Psychol. Inq.* 4:247–321

Cattell JM. 1890. Mental tests and measurements. *Mind* 15:373–80

Cattell RB. 1971. *Abilities: Their Structure and Growth.* Boston: Houghton Mifflin

Ceci SJ. 1996. IQ in society. *Psychol. Public Policy Law* 3/4:403–645. Special issue

Chapman PD. 1988. *School as Sorters.* NY: New York Univ. Press

Chorney MJ, Chorney K, Seese N, Owen MJ, McGuffin P, et al. 1998. A quantitative trait locus (QTL) associated with cognitive ability in children. *Psychol. Sci.* 9:159–66

Cleary TA, Humphreys LG, Kendrick SA, Wesman A. 1975. Educational uses of tests with disadvantaged students. *Am. Psychol.* 30:15–41

Coleman JS. 1990–1991. The Sidney Hook Memorial Award Address: on the self-suppression of academic freedom. *Acad. Q.* 4:17–22

Cook TD, Campbell DT. 1979. *Quasi-Experimentation.* Chicago: Rand McNally. 405 pp.

Costa PT, McCrae RR. 1995. Solid ground in the wetlands of personality: a reply to Block. *Psychol. Bull.* 117:216–20

Cronbach LJ. 1970. *Essentials of Psychological Testing.* NY: Harper & Row. 752 pp. 3rd ed.

Cronbach LJ. 1975. Five decades of public controversy over mental testing. *Am. Psychol.* 30:1–14

Cronbach LJ, Meehl PE. 1955. Construct validity in psychological tests. *Psychol. Bull.* 52:281–302

Dawes RM. 1994. *House of Cards.* NY: Free. 338 pp.

Dawis RV. 1991. Vocational interests, values, and preferences. In *Handbook of I/O Psychology,* Vol. 2, ed. MD Dunnette, LM Hough, pp. 833–71. Palo Alto, CA: Consulting Psychologists. 957 pp.

Dawis RV. 1992. The individual differences tradition in counseling psychology. *J. Couns. Psychol.* 39:7–19

Dawis RV, Lofquist LH. 1984. *A Psychological Theory of Work Adjustment.* Minneapolis: Univ. Minn. Press. 245 pp.

Day SX, Rounds J. 1998. The universality of vocational interest structure among racial/ethnic minorities. *Am. Psychol.* 53:728–36

Deary IJ. 1996. Intelligence and inspection time. *Am. Psychol.* 51:599–608

Diamond MC, Scheibel AB, Murphy GM, Harvey T. 1985. The brain of a scientist: Albert Einstein. *Exp. Neurol.* 88:198–204

Dunnette MD. 1998. Emerging trends and vexing issues in I/O psychology. *Appl. Psychol: Int. Rev.* 47:129–53

Ellis RS. 1928. *The Psychology of Individual Differences.* NY: Appleton. 533 pp.

Embretson S. 1983. Construct validity: construct representation versus nomothetic span. *Psychol. Bull.* 93:179–97

Ericsson KA. 1996. *The Road to Excellence.* Mahwah, NJ: Erlbaum. 369 pp.

Eysenck HJ. 1995. *Genius.* Cambridge: Cambridge Univ. Press. 344 pp.

Feingold A. 1995. The additive effects of differences in central tendency and variability are important in comparisons between groups. *Am. Psychol.* 50:5–13

Fiske DW. 1949. Consistency of the factorial structures of personality ratings from different sources. *J. Abnorm. Soc. Psychol.* 44:329–44

Flynn JR. 1999. Searching for justice. *Am. Psychol.* 54:5–20

Galton F. 1869. *Hereditary Genius.* London: Macmillan. 379 pp.

Galton F. 1884. Measurement of character. *Fortn. Rev.* 36:179–85

Galton F. 1890. Remarks. *Mind* 15:380–81

Gardner H. 1993. *Creating Minds.* NY: Basic. 464 pp.

Gati L. 1991. The structure of vocational interests. *Psychol. Bull.* 109:209–24

Geary DC. 1998. *Male, Female: The Evolution of Human Sex Differences.* Washington, DC: Am. Psychol. Assoc. 397 pp.

Ghiselli EE. 1972. Comment on the use of moderator variables. *J. Appl. Psychol.* 56:270

Goldberg LR, Saucier G. 1995. So what do you propose we use instead? A reply to Block. *Psychol. Bull.* 117:221–25

Gordon RA. 1997. Everyday life as intelligence test. *Intelligence* 24:203–320

Gottfredson LS. 1997. Intelligence and social policy. *Intelligence* 24:L–320. Special issue

Gottfredson LS, Sharf JC. 1988. Fairness in employment testing. *J. Vocat. Behav.* 33:225–477. Special issue

Grove WM, Meehl PE. 1996. Comparative efficiency of informal (subjective, impressionistic) and formal (mechanical, algorithmic) prediction procedures: the clinical-statistical controversy. *Psychol. Public Policy Law* 2:293–323

Guilford JP, et al. 1954. A factor analytic study of human interests. *Psychol. Monogr.* 68(4, whole No. 375)

Gustafsson J, Undheim JO. 1996. Individual differences in cognitive functions. See Berliner & Calfee 1996, pp. 186–242

Haier RJ. 1993. Cerebral glucose metabolism and intelligence. See Vernon 1993, pp. 317–73

Haier RJ, Benbow CP. 1995. Sex differences in lateralization in temporal lobe glucose metabolism during mathematical reasoning. *Dev. Neurobiol.* 11:405–14

Halpern DF. 1992. *Sex Differences in Cognitive Abilities.* Hillsdale, NJ: Erlbaum. 308 pp.

Halpern DF. 1996. Public policy implications of sex differences in cognitive abilities. *Psychol. Public Policy Law* 3/4:561–74

Harmon LW, Hansen JC, Borgen FH, Hammer AL. 1994. *Applications and Technical Guide for the Strong Interest Inventory.* Palo Alto, CA: Consult. Psychol. 392 pp.

Harris J. 1995. Where is the child's environment?: a group socialization theory of development. *Psychol. Rev.* 102:458–89

Hart B, Risley TR. 1995. *Meaningful Differences.* Baltimore: Brookes. 268 pp.

Hartigan JA, Wigdor AK. 1989. *Fairness in Employment Testing.* Washington, DC: Natl. Acad. 354 pp.

Hayes KJ. 1962. Genes, drives, and intellect. *Psychol. Rep.* 10:299–342

Hedges LV, Nowell A. 1995. Sex differences in mental test scores, variability, and numbers of high scoring individuals. *Science* 269:41–45

Herrnstein RJ, Murray C. 1994. *The Bell Curve.* NY: Free. 845 pp.

Hetherington EM, Reiss D, Plomin R. 1994. *Separate Worlds of Siblings.* Hillsdale, NJ: Earlbaum. 232 pp.

Hogan J, Hogan R. 2000. Theoretical frameworks for assessment. In *Individual Assessment,* ed. PR Jeanneret, R Silzer. San Francisco: Jossey Bass. In press

Hogan R, Hogan J, Roberts BW. 1996. Personality measurement and employment decisions. *Am. Psychol.* 51:469–77

Holahan CK, Sears RR. 1995. *The Gifted Group in Later Maturity.* Stanford, CA: Stanford Univ. Press. 363 pp.

Holland JL. 1996. Exploring careers with a typology. *Am. Psychol.* 51:397–406

Hough LM. 1997. The millennium for personality psychology: new horizons or good old daze. *Appl. Psychol.: Int. Rev.* 47:233–61

Humphreys LG. 1962. The organization of human abilities. *Am. Psychol.* 17:475–83

Humphreys LG. 1988. Trends in levels of academic achievement of blacks and other minorities. *Intelligence* 12:231–60

Humphreys LG. 1990. View of a supportive empiricist. *Psychol. Inq.* 1:153–55

Humphreys LG. 1991. Limited vision in the social sciences. *Am. J. Psychol.* 104:333–53

Humphreys LG. 1994. Intelligence from the standpoint of a (pragmatic) behaviorist *Psychol. Inq.* 5:179–92

Humphreys LG. 1995. Foreword. In *Assessing Individual Differences in Human Behavior,* ed. D Lubinski, RV Dawis, p. v. Palo Alto, CA: Consulting Psychologists. 386 pp.

Humphreys LG, Lubinski D, Yao G. 1993. Utility of predicting group membership and the role of spatial visualization in becoming an engineer, physical scientist, or artist. *J. Appl. Psychol.* 78:250–61

Hunt E. 1995. *Will We Be Smart Enough?* NY: Russell Sage Found. 332 pp.

Hunt E. 1996. When should we shoot the messenger?: issues involving cognitive testing, public policy, and law. *Psychol. Public Policy Law* 3/4:486–505

Hunt E. 1997. Nature versus nurture: The feeling of vuja de. In *Intelligence: Heredity and Environment,* JR Sternberg and E Grigorenko ed. pp. 531–51. NY: Cambridge Univ. Press. 608 pp.

Hunter JE, Schmidt FL. 1996. Intelligence and job performance: economic and social implications. *Psychol. Public Policy Law* 3/4:447–72

Jamison KR. 1993. *Touched With Fire.* NY: Free. 370 pp.

Jenkins JJ, Paterson DG. 1961. *Studies in Individual Differences: The Search for Intelligence.* NY: Appleton-Century-Crofts. 774 pp.

Jensen AR. 1980. *Bias in Mental Testing.* NY: Free. 786 pp.

Jensen AR. 1996. Giftedness and genius. See Benbow & Lubinski 1996, pp. 393–411

Jensen AR. 1998. *The g Factor.* Westport, CT: Praeger. 648 pp.

J. Vocat. Behav., ed. HEA Tinsley. 1993. Special issue on the Theory of Work Adjustment. 43(1):1–132 (whole issue)

Katzell RA. 1994. Contemporary meta-trends in industrial and organizational psychology. In *Handbook of I/O Psychology,* vol. 4, ed. HC Triandis, MD Dunnette, LM Hough, pp. 1–89. Palo Alto, CA: Consulting Psychologists. 869 pp.

Kimble GA. 1994. A new formula for behaviorism. *Psychol. Rev.* 101:254–58

Kyllonen PC, Christal RE. 1990. Reasoning ability is (little more than) working memory capacity?! *Intelligence* 14:389–433

Lerner B. 1983. Test scores as measures of human capital and forecasting tools. In *Intelligence and National Achievement,* ed. RB Cattell, pp. 70–99. Washington DC: Cliveden

Lippa R. 1998. Gender-related individual differences and the structure of vocational interests. *J. Pers. Soc. Psychol.* 74:996–1009

Loehlin JC. 1997. Dysgenesis and IQ. *Am. Psychol.* 52:1236–39

Loevinger J. 1954. Effect of distortion on item selection. *Educ. Psychol. Meas.* 14:441–48

Lofquist LH, Dawis RV. 1991. *Essentials of Person Environment Correspondence Counseling.* Minneapolis: Univ. Minn. Press. 171 pp.

Lubinski D. 1996. Applied individual differences research and its quantitative methods. *Psychol. Public. Policy. Law* 2:187–203

Lubinski D, Benbow CP. 2000. States of excellence. *Am. Psychol.* 54: In press

Lubinski D, Dawis RV. 1992. Aptitudes, skills, and proficiencies. In *Handbook of I/O Psychology,* Vol. 3, ed. MD Dunnette, LM Hough, pp. 1–59. Palo Alto, CA: Consulting Psychologists. 1095 pp.

Lubinski D, Humphreys LG. 1997. Incorporating general intelligence into epidemiology and the social sciences. *Intelligence* 24:159–201

Lubinski D, Thompson T. 1993. Species and individual differences in communication based on private states. *Behav. Brain Sci.* 16:627–80

Lutzenberg W, Burbaumer N, Flor H, Rockstroh B, Elbert T. 1992. Dimensional analysis of the human EEG and intelligence. *Neurosci. Lett.* 143:10–14

Lykken DT. 1957. A study of anxiety in the sociopathic personality. *J. Abnorm. Soc. Psychol.* 55:6–10

Lykken DT. 1991. What's wrong with psychology anyway? In *Thinking Clearly About Psychology,* ed. D Chiccetti, W Grove, pp. 3–39. Minneapolis: Univ. Minn. Press. 277 pp.

Lykken DT. 1995. *The Antisocial Personalities.* Hillsdale, NJ: Erlbaum. 259 pp.

Lykken DT. 1997. The American crime factory. *Psychol. Inq.* 8:261–70

Lykken DT, McGue M, Tellegen A, Bouchard TJ. 1992. Emergenesis. *Am. Psychol.* 47:1565–77

Lynn R. 1996. *Dysgenics.* Westport, CT: Praeger. 237 pp.

MacCorquodale K, Meehl PE. 1948. On a distinction between hypothetical constructs and intervening variables. *Psychol. Rev.* 55:95–107

Macklin ML, Metzger LJ, Litz BT, McNally RJ, Lasko NB, et al. 1998. Lower precombat intelligence is a risk factor for posttraumatic stress disorder. *J. Consult. Clin. Psychol.* 66:323–26

Maxwell G. 1961. Meaning postulates in scientific theory. In *Current Issues in Philosophy of Science,* ed. H Feigl, G Maxwell, pp. 169–95. NY: Holt, Rinehart, & Winston. 484 pp.

McCartney K, Harris MJ, Bernieri F. 1990. Growing up and growing apart: a developmental meta-analysis of twin studies. *Psychol. Bull.* 107:226–37

McCrae RR, Costa PT. 1997. Personality structure as a human universal. *Am. Psychol.* 52:509–16

McGue M, Bouchard TJ. 1998. Genetic and environmental influences on human behavioral differences. *Annu. Rev. Neurosci.* 21:1–24

McNemar Q. 1964. Lost: our intelligence? Why? *Am. Psychol.* 19:871–82

Meehl PE. 1970. Nuisance variables and the ex post facto design. In *Minnesota Studies in the Philosophy of Science IV* ed. M Radner, S Winokur. Minneapolis: Univ. Minn. Press. 441 pp.

Meehl PE. 1990. Appraising and amending theories. *Psychol. Inq.* 1:108–41

Meehl PE. 1998. *The Power of Quantitative Thinking.* Washington, DC: American Psychological Society Cattell Award Address.

Messick S. 1992. Multiple intelligences or multilevel intelligence? *Psychol. Inq.* 3:365–84

Miller EM. 1994. Intelligence and brain myelination: a hypothesis. *Pers. Individ. Differ.* 17:803–32

Moffitt TE, Caspi A, Harkness AR, Silva PA. 1993. The natural history of change in intellectual performance. *J. Child. Psychol. Psychiatry* 34:455–506

Murray C. 1998. *Income, Inequality, and IQ.* Washington, DC: Am. Enterprise Inst. 47 pp.

Neisser U. 1998. *The Rising Curve.* Washington, DC: Am. Psychol. Assoc. 415 pp.

Neisser U. 1999. The great g mystery. *Contemp. Psychol.* 44:131–33

Neisser U, Boodoo G, Bouchard TJ, Boykin AW, Brody N, et al. 1996. Intelligence: knowns and unknowns. *Am. Psychol.* 51:77–101

Norman WT. 1963. Toward a taxonomy of personality attributes. *J. Abnorm. Soc. Psychol.* 66:574–83

O'Boyle MW, Benbow CP, Alexander JE. 1995. Sex differences, hemispheric laterality, and brain activity in the intellectually gifted. *Dev. Neurobiol.* 11:415–44

O'Toole BJ. 1990. Intelligence and behavior and motor vehicle accident mortality. *Accid. Anal. Prev.* 22:211–21

Plomin R, Bergeman CS. 1991. The nature of nuture: genetic influence on "environmental" measures. *Behav. Brain Sci.* 14:373–427

Prediger DJ. 1982. Dimensions underlying Holland's hexagon: missing link between interests and occupations? *J. Vocat. Behav.* 21:259–87

Premack D. 1983. The codes of man and beasts. *Behav. Brain Sci.* 6:125–67

Roe A. 1953. *The Making of a Scientist.* NY: Dodd, Mead. 244 pp.

Roe A. 1956. *The Psychology of Occupations.* NY: Wiley. 340 pp.

Rolfhus EL, Ackerman PL. 1996. Self-report knowledge: at the crossroads of ability, interests, & personality. *J. Educ. Psychol.* 88:174–88

Rounds JB, Tracey TJ. 1993. Prediger's dimensional representation of Holland's RIASEC circumplex. *J. Appl. Psychol.* 78:875–90

Rowe DC. 1994. *The Limits of Family Influence.* NY: Guilford. 232 pp.

Rowe DC. 1997. Are parents to blame? A look at the antisocial personalities. *Psychol. Inq.* 8:251–60

Rowe DC, Vazsonyi AT, Flannery DJ. 1994. No more than skin deep: ethnic and racial similarity in developmental process. *Psychol. Rev.* 101:396–413

Rowe DC, Vazsonyi AT, Flannery DJ. 1995. Ethnic and racial similarity in developmental process. *Psychol. Sci.* 6:33–38

Roznowski M. 1987. Use of tests manifesting sex differences as measures of intelligence. *J. Appl. Psychol.* 72:480–83

Sanders CE, Lubinski D, Benbow CP. 1995. Does the Defining Issues Test measure psychological phenomena distinct from verbal ability?: an examination of Lykken's query. *J. Pers. Soc. Psychol.* 69:498–504

Savage-Rumbaugh S, Lewin R. 1994. *Kanzi: The Ape at the Brink of the Human Mind.* NY: Wiley. 299 pp.

Savage-Rumbaugh S, Murphy J, Sevcik RA, Brakke KE, et al. 1993. Language comprehension in ape and child. *Monogr. Soc. Res. Child. Dev.* 58:1–256

Savickas ML, Spokane AR. 2000. *Vocational Interests.* Palo Alto, CA: Davies-Black. In press

Scarr S. 1992. Developmental theories for the 1990s: development and individual differences. *Child Dev.* 63:1–19

Scarr S. 1996. How people make their own environments: implications for parents and policy makers. *Psychol. Public Policy Law* 2:204–28

Scarr S, McCartney K. 1983. How people make their own environments: a theory of genotype → environment effects. *Child Dev.* 54:424–35

Schaie KW. 1996. *Intellectual Development in Adulthood.* NY: Cambridge Univ. Press. 396 pp.

Schmidt DB, Lubinski D, Benbow CP. 1998. Validity of assessing educational-vocational preference dimensions among intellectually talented 13-year olds. *J. Couns. Psychol.* 45:436–53

Schmidt FL, Hunter JE. 1998. The validity and utility of selection methods in personnel psychology: practical and theoretical implications of 85 years of research findings. *Psychol. Bull.* 124:262–74

Schneider BS, Goldstein AW, Smith DB. 1995. The ASA framework: an update. *Personnel Psychol.* 48:747–73

Scott WD. 1920. Changes in some of our conceptions and practices of personnel. *Psychol. Rev.* 27:81–94

Sidman M. 1986. Functional analysis of emergent verbal classes. In *Analysis and Integration of Behavioral Units,* ed. T Thompson, MD Zeiler, pp. 213–45. Hillsdale, NJ: Erlbaum. 367 pp.

Simonton DK. 1990. *Psychology, Science, and History.* New Haven, CT: Yale Univ. Press. 291 pp.

Simonton DK. 1994. *Greatness.* NY: Guilford. 502 pp.

Snow CP. 1967. *The Two Cultures and a Second Look.* London: Cambridge Univ. Press. 107 pp.

Snow RE. 1989. Aptitude-treatment interaction as a framework for research on individual differences in learning. In *Learning and Individual Differences,* ed. PL Ackerman, RJ Sternberg, RG Glasser, pp. 13–59. NY: Freedman. 107 pp.

Snow RE. 1991. The concept of aptitude. In *Improving Inquiry in the Social Sciences,* ed. RE Snow, DE Wiley, pp. 249–84. Hillsdale, NJ: Earlbaum. 343 pp.

Snow RE. 1996. Aptitude development and education. *Psychol. Public Policy Law* 3/ 4:536–60

Snow RE, Corno L, Jackson D III. 1996. Individual differences in affective and conative functions. See Berliner & Calfee 1996, pp. 243–310

Snow RE, Lohman DF. 1989. Implications of cognitive psychology for educational measurement. In *Educational Measurement,* ed. R Linn, pp. 263–331. NY: Collier. 610 pp.

Snyderman M, Rothman S. 1987. Survey of expert opinion on intelligence and aptitude testing. *Am. Psychol.* 42:137–44

Spearman C. 1904. "General intelligence," objectively determined and measured. *Am. J. Psychol.* 15:201–92

Spearman C. 1927. *The Abilities of Man.* NY: Macmillan. 415 pp.

Stanley JC, Benbow CP, Brody LE, Dauber S, Lupkowski A. 1992. Gender differences on eighty-six nationally standardized tests. In *Talent Development,* ed. N Colangelo, SG Assouline, DL Ambroson, pp. 42–65. NY: Trillium. 432 pp.

Sternberg RJ. 1997. Intelligence and life long learning. *Am. Psychol.* 51:77–101

Sternberg RJ, Detterman DK. 1986. *What is Intelligence?* Norwood, NJ: Ablex. 173 pp.

Sternberg RJ, Grigorenko EL. 1997. *Intelligence: Heredity and Environment.* NY: Cambridge Univ. Press. 608 pp.

Tanner JM. 1965. Physique and athletic performance: a study of Olympic athletes. In *Penguin Science Survey 1965 B,* ed. SA Barnett, A McLaren. Baltimore: Penguin

Tellegen A. 1993. Folk concepts and psychological concepts in personality and personality disorder. *Psychol. Inq.* 4:122–30

Tellegen A, Grove W, Waller NG. 1991. *Inventory of Personal Characteristics #7 (IPC7).*

Unpublished materials, Dept. Psychology, Univ. Minnesota, Minneapolis

Tellegen A, Waller NG. 2000. Exploring personality through test construction: development of the Multidimensional Personality Questionnaire. In *Personality Measures: Development and Evaluation,* ed. SR Briggs, JM Cheek. Greenwich, CT: JAI. In press

Terman L. 1954. The discovery and encouragement of exceptional talent. *Am. Psychol.* 9:221–30

Thompson T. 1995. Children have more need of models than critics: early language experience and brain development. *J. Early Interv.* 19:264–72

Thorndike R, Lohman DF. 1990. *A Century of Ability Testing.* Chicago: Riverside. 163 pp.

Thorndike RL. 1985. The central role of general ability in prediction. *Multivar. Behav. Res.* 20:241–54

Thorndike RL. 1994. g (Editorial). *Intelligence* 19:145–55

Thurstone LL. 1935. *Vectors of the Mind.* Chicago: Univ. Chicago Press. 266 pp.

Thurstone LL. 1940. Issues in factor analysis. *Psychol. Bull.* 37:189–235

Tracey TJ, Rounds J. 1993. Evaluating Holland's and Gati's vocational-interest models: a structural meta-analysis. *Psychol. Bull.* 113:229–46

Tupes EC, Christal RE. 1992. Recurrent personality factors based on trait ratings. *J. Pers.* 60:225–51. (Reprinted from USAF ASD Tech. Rep. No. 61–97, 1961, Lackland Air Force Base, TX: US Air Force.)

Tyler LE. 1965. *The Psychology of Human Differences.* NY: Appleton-Century-Crofts. 572 pp.

Vernon PA. 1993. *Biological Approaches to the Study of Human Intelligence.* Norwood, NJ: Ablex

Vernon PE. 1961. *The Structure of Human Abilities.* London: Methuen. 208 pp. 2nd ed.

Waller JH. 1971. Achievement and social mobility: relationships among IQ score, education, and occupation in two generations. *Soc. Biol.* 18:252–59

Waller NG. 1999. Evaluating the structure of personality. In *Personality and Psychopathology*, ed. CR Cloninger. pp. 155–97. Washington, DC: Am. Psychiatric Assoc. 524 pp.

Waller NG, Kojetin BA, Bouchard TJ, Lykken DT, Tellegen A. 1990. Genetic and environmental influences on religious interests, attitudes, and values. *Psychol. Sci.* 2:138–42

Washburn DA, Rumbaugh D. 1997. Faster is smarter so why are we slower? *Am. Psychol.* 52:1147–48

Wasserman EA. 1993. Comparative cognition. *Psychol. Bull.* 113:211–28

Wiegman O, Kuttschreuter M, Baarda B. 1992. A longitudinal study of the effects of television viewing on aggressive and prosocial behavior. *Br. J. Soc. Psychol.* 31:147–64

Wigdor AK, Garner WR. 1982. *Ability Testing.* Washington, DC: National Academy

Wilk SL, Desmarais LB, Sackett PR. 1995. Gravitation to jobs commensurate with ability: longitudinal and cross-sectional tests. *J. Appl. Psychol.* 80:79–85

Wilk SL, Sackett PR. 1996. Longitudinal analysis of ability-job complexity fit and job change. *Personnel Psychol.* 49:937–67

Willerman L. 1979. *The Psychology of Individual and Group Differences.* San Francisco: Freedman. 531 pp.

Willerman L, Rutledge JN, Bigler ED. 1991. *In vivo* brain size and intelligence. *Intelligence* 15:223–28

Williams WM, Ceci SJ. 1997. Are Americans becoming more or less alike?: trends in race, class, and ability differences in intelligence. *Am. Psychol.* 52:1226–35

Willis SL, Schaie KW. 1986. Practical intelligence in later adulthood. In *Practical Intelligence,* ed. RJ Sternberg, RK Wagner, pp. 236–68. Cambridge: Cambridge Univ. Press. 386 pp.

Wilson EO. 1998. *Consilience: The Unity of Knowledge.* NY: Knopf. 332 pp.

Wilson JQ, Herrnstein RJ. 1985. *Crime and Human Nature.* NY: Simon & Schuster. 639 pp.

Zuckerman H. 1977. *Scientific Elite.* NY: Free. 235 pp.

Annu. Rev. Psychol. 2000. 51:445–479

THE EFFECTS OF FAMILY AND COMMUNITY VIOLENCE ON CHILDREN

Gayla Margolin and Elana B. Gordis

*Department of Psychology, University of Southern California, Los Angeles, California
90089–1061; e-mail: margolin@rcf.usc.edu
Department of Psychology, University of California at Los Angeles, California 90095–
1563; e-mail: gordis@psych.ucla.edu*

Key Words   child abuse, community violence, children's exposure to marital violence, child maltreatment, developmental psychopathology

■ **Abstract**   This review examines theoretical and empirical literature on children's reactions to three types of violence—child maltreatment, community violence, and interparental violence. In addition to describing internalizing and externalizing problems associated with exposure to violence, this review identifies ways that violence can disrupt typical developmental trajectories through psychobiological effects, post-traumatic stress disorder (PTSD), cognitive consequences, and peer problems. Methodological challenges in this literature include high rates of co-occurrence among types of violence exposure, co-occurrence of violence with other serious life adversities, heterogeneity in the frequency, severity, age of onset, and chronicity of exposure, and difficulties in making causal inferences. A developmental psychopathology perspective focuses attention on how violence may have different effects at different ages and may compromise children's abilities to face normal developmental challenges. Emphasis is placed on the variability of children's reactions to violence, on outcomes that go beyond diagnosable disorders, and on variables that mediate and moderate children's reactions to violence.

CONTENTS

Introduction 446
Rates of Exposure 447
Children's Vulnerability as Related to Development 449
Methodological Issues.. 452
Consequences of Exposure to Violence 454
   Aggression and Other Externalizing Behavior Problems...................... 454
   Depression and Other Internalizing Problems 457
   Psychobiological Effects.. 459
   Post Traumatic Stress Disorder and Symptoms 461
   Cognitive Consequences.. 462
   Peer Relations.. 464

0084–6570/00/0201–0445$12.00

Caveat Regarding Adaptive Versus Maladaptive Outcomes............................466
Summary of Long-Range Outcomes of Exposure to Violence..........................466
Mediating and Moderating Variables 467
Conclusion..469

INTRODUCTION

Children's experience with violence, either as victims or as witnesses, has been described as a public health problem of epidemic proportions (Glodich 1998, Koop & Lundberg 1992, Pynoos 1993). Despite evidence from the 1997 National Crime Victimization Survey (U.S. Department of Justice 1998a) that violent crimes such as rape, assault, and robbery, have been decreasing over the past several years, recent data on violence directed toward children do not show similar declines (National Center for Child Abuse and Neglect 1996, Wang & Daro 1998). Many children experience or observe violence within the confines of their own homes or within their own neighborhoods. The problems posed by children's exposure to violence not only affect children's physical health and safety, but also their psychological adjustment, social relations, and academic achievement. The impact of violence exposure goes beyond emotional and behavioral disorders. It affects children's views of the world and of themselves, their ideas about the meaning and purpose of life, their expectations for future happiness, and their moral development (Garbarino et al 1991, Ney et al 1994). Moreover, the impact of violence goes beyond the period of exposure and the immediate aftermath, and sometimes occurs many years later, affecting individuals into adulthood.

The decision to review child physical and sexual abuse, community violence, and interparental violence stems from similarities across these different types of violence exposure. In addition to posing threats to the child's personal safety, these forms of violence all violate the child's immediate environment as a safe haven, and render parents potentially less available for physical and emotional caretaking (Margolin 1998). Finkelhor & Kendall-Tackett define victimization "as harms that occur to individuals because of other human actors behaving in ways that violate social norms" (1997:2), thereby setting exposure to violence apart from other stressors, such as chronic illness or natural disaster. Children's immediate reactions to these three forms of victimization are likely to be some combination of helplessness, fear, anger, and high arousal. Because these forms of victimization generally are recurring events, over time the child may experience persistent, high levels of arousal that disrupt his or her efforts in age appropriate academic and social pursuits. Data on children's experiences in war-torn countries, although not reviewed here, also lend support to commonalities in children's reactions to violence (Cicchetti et al 1997, Wright et al 1997). As this chapter illustrates, the theoretical and empirical literatures for each of the three reviewed types of violence exposure are relatively overlapping and complementary, although sometimes problem specific, in explicating to what extent and through what pathways violence exposure affects children.

RATES OF EXPOSURE

Vastly discrepant statistics estimating the rates of violence exposure are due to different definitions of exposure as well as different methods of data collection. Data on the incidence of child abuse, for example, can be obtained from legal and social service agencies responding to abuse or obtained directly from parents' reports through community surveys. The most recent National Incidence Study (NIC-3), conducted by the National Center of Child Abuse and Neglect (NCCAN) is based on official reports collected from child protective services, other investigatory agencies, and professionals in schools, hospitals, and other agencies. The 1996 results indicate that approximately 1,554,000 children (23.1 per 1000 children 18 years or younger) were found to be victims of maltreatment; 734,000 (11.1 per 1000) were found to be victims of physical or sexual abuse or emotional abuse; and 879,000 (13.1 per 1000) were victims of neglect (Sedlack & Broadhurst 1996). The annual report of 1997 data from the National Committee for the Prevention of Child Abuse provides similar data, indicating that 1,054,000 children (15 out of every 1000 children) were confirmed by child protective services as victims of child maltreatment (Wang & Daro 1998). As noted in the report by the NCCAN (1996), different reporting policies across states result in children with similar experiences being classified as victims in some states and as "in need of services" in other states.

In contrast to studies of children who come to the attention of legal and social service agencies, the two National Family Violence Surveys (Straus 1979, Straus & Gelles 1986) provide prevalence data based on national probability sampling through in-person or telephone interviews of adults in households including at least one child aged 3–17. These data indicate that the rate of severe physical child abuse within a one year period was 140 per 1000 children in 1975 and 107 per 1000 in 1985. More recently, Straus et al (1997) reported prevalence rates for physical abuse of 49 per 1000, and for corporal punishment, 615 per 1000. Straus et al (1997) point out that their physical abuse rate is 11 times greater than the 1994 report of the NCCAN and 5 times greater than the rate in the NIC-3. Even with these broader sampling procedures, there still is the possibility that violence directed toward children is underreported due to parents' reluctance to endorse behaviors that are socially and legally unacceptable.

The official report on child sexual abuse in the NIC-3 reveals that approximately 217,700 children (3.2 per 1000), or 29% of all victims of maltreatment, experienced sexual abuse (Sedlack & Broadhurst 1996), whereas the 50-state survey for 1997 indicates that over 84,000 new cases of child sexual abuse (8% of all confirmed child abuse victims) were accepted for service (Wang & Daro 1998). In light of the number of unreported cases of child sexual abuse, it also is common to obtain prevalence rates of child sexual abuse through retrospective population surveys. The Ontario Health Survey of persons age 15 years and older, for example, indicates that 11.1% of females and 3.9% of males reported that they had been victims of severe child sexual abuse (MacMillan et al 1997). Whereas population surveys generally include sexual abuse by any adult, Finkelhor et al (1990) report that between 6–16% of sexual abuse is committed by parental figures.

Because children exposed to interparental violence have no formal designation as crime victims, prevalence and incidence data are estimated from statistics on violence among intimate partners and from population data on the average number of children per household. Recent data on violence by intimates reveal that each year from 1992–1996, 8 per 1000 women experienced a violent victimization by an intimate partner, with slightly more than half of female victims of intimate violence living in households with children under the age of 12 (U.S. Department of Justice 1998b). Extrapolating from 1975 and 1985 national surveys, Straus (1992) estimated that more than 10 million children in the U.S. witness physical aggression between their parents each year, with prevalence rates throughout childhood being at least triple the rates of exposure within a given year. The database of Fantuzzo and colleagues (Fantuzzo et al 1997), collected from police officers and female victims of misdemeanor domestic violence in five U.S. cities, examines the extent to which children were directly involved in reported abuse episodes. They found, for example, that in 19.8% of households in which domestic violence occurred, an issue pertaining to children was identified as being an influence in the abuse episode; in 11–12% of cases, a child placed the call to police, and in 6–7% of cases, a child was physically abused during the domestic violence episode.

The statistics on community violence, generally collected through interview or survey methods, reflect the number of children who were personally victimized, or who directly observed family members, schoolmates, neighbors, and peers being the target of violence. Whereas child abuse and interparental aggression often are kept private, community violence is discussed widely, often resulting in rapidly spreading ripple effects. Thus, even children who do not directly witness community violence often hear repeated accounts of a specific incident, and may form their own mental imagery of the event. The data suggest that in inner city neighborhoods, one-third or more of pre-teenage and teenage children have been directly victimized, and almost all children have been exposed to community violence. Boney-McCoy & Finkelhor's (1995) telephone sample reveals that over one-third of 10–16-year-olds had been victims of assault. According to a four-city anonymous survey of 3735 high school students, male adolescents report particularly high levels of neighborhood victimization, with 3–22% being beaten or mugged in their own neighborhoods (Singer et al 1995). Farrell & Bruce (1997) similarly found higher rates of being beaten up for males (37%) than females (16%). Richters & Martinez (1993) found that according to parents' reports, 84% of children in grades 1 and 2 had witnessed community violence (e.g. shootings, stabbings, chases by gang, drug use), and 21% had been directly victimized. Parent reports for children in grades 5 and 6 were 90% for witnessing and 35% for victimization; these older children's self reports indicate that 97% had witnessed violence and 59% had been victimized. Using similar methods with 9–12-year-old children in a different city, Osofsky et al (1993) report that 93% had witnessed community violence, and over half had been victims of violence.

Often the violence observed is quite severe, as reflected in Bell & Jenkins' (1993) survey of elementary school children in Chicago, in which three out of four children had witnessed a robbery, stabbing, shooting and/or killing. Reporting on youth living in a public housing development, Fitzpatrick & Boldizar (1993) found that approximately 70% had seen someone get shot at and 43% had witnessed a murder. Even young children are exposed to serious violence. A survey at a pediatric clinic in Boston indicated that 10% of children under the age of six reported witnessing a shooting or stabbing (Groves et al 1993). Moreover, a considerable amount of violence occurs in schools. A 1996–1997 survey of public school principals produced the following national estimates of victimization on school grounds or at school sponsored events: approximately 4000 rapes or sexual batteries, 7000 robberies, 11,000 physical attacks or fights with a weapon, and 188,000 physical attacks or fights without weapons (U.S. Department of Education 1997). Because most of the data on community violence are obtained from urban samples, less is known about children from rural and suburban communities.

CHILDREN'S VULNERABILITY AS RELATED TO DEVELOPMENT

Children are potentially quite vulnerable to the effects of violence because violence exposure may alter the timing of typical developmental trajectories (Boney-McCoy & Finkelhor 1995). That is, violence initially may result in primary effects, such as anxiety, depression, or PTSD symptoms, which cause secondary reactions by disrupting children's progression through age-appropriate developmental tasks. For example, exposure to violence in young children can result in regressive symptoms, such as increased bedwetting, decreased verbalization, or separation anxiety (Osofsky 1995). These symptoms secondarily may affect children's socialization skills or ability to concentrate in school. Moreover, at a time when children may have difficulty with typical developmental tasks, exposure to violence can result in having to acknowledge and cope with adult issues. As Garbarino and colleagues note, "in Western culture, childhood is regarded as a period of special protection and rights" (1992:1). The home and the neighborhood, generally considered the primary safe havens for the child, lose those protective and comforting qualities in the aftermath of family or neighborhood violence (Margolin 1998).

A frequent recommendation is that a developmental perspective be incorporated into theories and research on children's exposure to violence and abuse (National Research Council 1993). This recommendation translates into examining (*a*) how the consequences of violence vary in intensity and form at different developmental stages; (*b*) whether certain periods of development are particularly vulnerable to disruption due to violence; (*c*) how outcomes of exposure to violence are multiply determined rather than the result of a single precipitating cause; and (*d*) whether and under what circumstances violence exposure at one age affects later development (Cicchetti & Rizley 1981, Finkelhor & Kendall-Tackett 1997). From a developmental psychopathology perspective, the effects of violence can only be understood in the context of the changing child, and his or her changing environment, including the evolving familial and societal expectations for the child (Pynoos 1993). That is, the child's experience of violence is not only determined by the nature of the violent events but by the child's own capacities to appraise and understand violence, to respond to and cope with danger, and to garner environmental resources that offer protection and support (Finkelhor & Kendall-Tackett 1997). These responses are inextricably linked to the child's general cognitive, emotional, and physical capacities (Marans & Adelman 1997).

The recommendation for a developmental perspective also means viewing childhood exposure to violence in the context of normal developmental processes and identifying the links between disrupted and normal development (Cicchetti 1993, Pynoos 1993). At different stages, children face different developmental challenges that can be disrupted by abuse and violence. An understanding of the sequelae of exposure to violence must be informed by an understanding of normal adaptation across developmental stages. Violence, for example, can shatter the essential assumptions fundamental to the developmental task of learning to trust others and form secure attachment relationships (Janoff-Bulman 1992), in turn leading to difficulties in subsequent relationships throughout life.

Exposure to violence affects children as early as infancy. Because of their physical vulnerability, very young children are at risk for physical injury and death when abused or neglected. Although it can be argued that very young children are partially protected from psychological distress because they do not fully comprehend violent episodes and the risk involved, Osofsky (1995) challenges the belief that very young children are too young to be affected by or react to violence. Although infants cannot articulate what they perceive or think about violence, distress has been inferred from observed changes in behavior including irritability, sleep disturbances, emotional distress, somatic complaints, fears of being alone, and regression in toileting behavior and language (Osofsky & Scheeringa 1997, Zeanah & Scheeringa 1997). Infants and young toddlers rely strongly on parent figures to protect them from danger, to make the world predictable and safe as they begin to venture forth, and to guide their responses in ambiguous or threatening situations—all functions that are potentially compromised in families with violence.

School-aged children face the developmental challenges of adapting to the school environment and establishing relations with peers. These tasks require the ability to regulate emotions, show empathy, and attend to increasingly complex cognitive material. According to Aber & Allen (1987), children who have safe, secure relationships and are ready to venture out and explore the world show greater readiness to learn and overall higher levels of cognitive competence. Alternatively, an overconcern with security issues (Cicchetti & Toth 1995), possibly coupled with hypervigilance to aggressive responses may lead children to process social information with a bias toward interpreting hostile intent (Dodge et al 1997). Together, these processes may result in children having a limited array of competent social responses and responding primarily in a negative fashion. Although school-age children are less dependent on parents for specific cues regarding how to respond to threatening situations, parents' emotional responsiveness and monitoring of their children's behavior are still important to children's development.

Contrary to common perceptions, the incidence of abuse and neglect of adolescents is at least as high as that of younger children (Am. Med. Assoc. Counc. Sci. Aff. 1993). The fact that adolescents often suffer less severe physical injury, coupled with generally negative societal attitudes toward adolescents may lead to perceptions that adolescents do not need as much outside protection as do younger children or that adolescents may be responsible for their own maltreatment. According to Rossman & Rosenberg (1998a), the emergence of abuse in adolescence often is a function of an authoritarian family system along with the family's inability to negotiate the transition to children's increasing need for independence. These authors further speculate that the impact is quite different for adolescents who have been part of an abusive system since childhood versus those who are first abused in adolescence. In addition to the wide ranging psychological consequences associated with both physical and sexual abuse, for example anxiety, depression, and suicidal behavior (Brown & Finkelhor 1986, Lewis 1992, Rossman & Rosenberg 1998a), abuse may exacerbate adolescents' risk-taking and escape behaviors, for example running away, drug use, and premature sexual behavior. These behaviors may, in turn, increase the likelihood of other types of psychological or health problems. Moreover, adolescents may begin to assume an active role in family violence. Physical abuse directed toward adolescents is associated with them being physically injurious toward parents and siblings (Kratcoski 1985, Rossman & Rosenberg 1998a). For adolescents exposed to marital violence, a common reaction, particularly for males, is to intervene physically in their parents battles, thereby risking injury to themselves (Jaffe et al 1990).

At each developmental stage, parents' abilities to attend to their child and to guide and support their child's negotiation of new developmental tasks is essential. When parents physically, emotionally, or sexually abuse their children, the parents' salience as a source of protection and support certainly is diminished. As a result, children may learn to rely on themselves, to approach caretakers only after having assessed the caretaker's mood, or to attempt to develop other sources of interpersonal support. Likewise, husband-to-wife abuse can make each caretaker less available to the child, with the father unpredictable and frightening and the mother distracted by basic issues of safety and survival for herself and her children (Margolin 1998). Moreover, there is recent evidence that the punitive, belligerent style of communication exhibited by abusive males toward their female partners may carry over into their communications with their children, particularly their sons (Margolin et al 1996). In the case of community violence, parents' caretaking may be negatively affected by their own feelings of helplessness, fear, and grief. Efforts to protect the child may be exhibited in authoritarian and restrictive parenting practices, as well as in certain precautions that may heighten the child's anxiety, e.g. putting a young child to bed in a bathtub to avoid gunshots (Garbarino 1993). Children exposed to violence, although in greater need of nurturance and protection than children without such stressors, may have less access to social supports from their caretakers.

METHODOLOGICAL ISSUES

Children's exposure to violence does not occur in pure forms (Dodge et al 1997, Margolin 1998, Rossman & Rosenberg 1998b). There are high rates of co-occurrence between exposure to marital violence and child physical abuse (Appel & Holden 1998, Jouriles & LeCompte 1991, Straus et al 1980, Wolfe et al 1985), and between exposure to community violence and intrafamilial violence (Bell & Jenkins 1993, Garbarino et al 1992, Lynch & Cicchetti 1998). Data are beginning to show that exposure to combinations of maltreatment experiences are generally associated with more serious outcomes (Egeland 1997, Lynch & Cicchetti 1998, Wolfe & McGee 1994). Although there is considerable interest in identifying different types of adaptational outcomes associated with different types of abuse, the overlap among abuse categories makes this a difficult question to examine (e.g. Manly et al 1994). Because samples generally are not large enough to consider all subtypes and combinations of subtypes, a hierarchy is often used to classify children, e.g. children who are physically and sexually abused are classified as sexually abused. In such hierarchies, neglect and psychological abuse often are subsumed under another type of abuse. According to McGee et al (1997), however, psychological maltreatment was more consistently related to maladjustment than other forms of maltreatment and actually potentiated the contribution of other maltreatment types to overall symptomatology. In general, strategies that classify children by maltreatment type make it difficult to disentangle unique effects of abuse from cumulative and possible interactive effects of multiple types of abuse.

Even within a particular type of abuse, there can be considerable heterogeneity. Studies on the effects of sexual abuse, for example, do not always differentiate abuse perpetrated by a family member versus a non–family member or stranger. Clearly there is the potential for widely discrepant family interaction patterns associated with these two types of sexual abuse. The experience of any one type of abuse can range vastly depending on the dangerousness and seriousness of the acts, the age of initial onset, the chronicity, and the frequency.

Children living with violence typically experience a number of other adversities such as poverty, poor nutrition, overcrowding, substance abuse, lack of adequate medical care, parents' unemployment, and parents' psychopathology (Garmezy & Masten 1994, Smith & Thornberry 1995, Vig 1996). Not only are these variables inadequately accounted for in studies but associated mechanisms such as overall family disorganization and instability, lack of cognitive stimulation, and maternal social isolation also are not adequately examined (Dodge et al 1997). Sameroff and colleagues (1987) illustrated how the accumulation of risk possibly compromises development. Their data show lower than average intelligence scores associated with three or four risk factors, but no such association for children with one or two risk factors.

There are important differences between studies based on community samples and those based on samples of children identified as maltreated by legal or social service agencies. An advantage of identified samples is that there is a significant level of exposure and the exposure is externally validated. A disadvantage, however, is that in addition to whatever treatment and protection the identified children receive after abuse has been reported, they also may be uprooted from their familiar surroundings and from family members. Adequate control groups, particularly for children in shelters or foster care, often are lacking (Moore et al 1989). Community samples generally offer a wider range of exposure experiences but may not include the most severe forms of exposure.

The vast majority of the research on outcomes associated with childhood exposure to violence uses cross-sectional designs, thereby making it difficult to disentangle how the nature and the effects of violence exposure vary at different developmental stages, as well as to examine immediate versus delayed effects of violence and the cumulative risk over time. Clearly, there are challenges to conducting longitudinal research, such as mobility of these families, attrition, and shifting maltreatment status (Cicchetti 1994). Yet, a handful of recent studies have demonstrated the importance of longitudinal designs in examining the effects of early abuse on later functioning. Rogosch et al (1995), for example, not only show the relationship between early maltreatment and later peer problems but also show how that association is mediated by early cognitive and affective deficits associated with the abuse. Using multiple data points and multiple measures, Egeland (1997) showed that early maltreatment was associated with later school failure, drug and alcohol problems, and psychopathology. Three recent longitudinal studies have examined how exposure to community violence influences children's later violent behavior with effects demonstrated for girls' later violent behavior (Farrell & Bruce 1997), and boys' aggression and depression (Gorman-Smith & Tolan 1998). In addition, Miller et al (1999) found that exposure to high levels of community violence or parent-child fighting posed a risk of increased negative behavior over a 15 month period.

Although studies with longitudinal designs identify temporal links between exposure to violence and behavioral outcomes in children, they still cannot be used as conclusive evidence of causation. Conclusions about causation in this field are limited by the inability to manipulate experimentally the presence and dosage of violence. Thus, investigations examining violence exposure cannot fully account for the roles of co-occurring risk factors and pre-existing characteristics that children bring to the situation. Accordingly, the interpretation of data on the effects of exposure to violence are limited to empirical associations and temporal dependencies rather than causes.

Despite the frequent mention of the importance of the broader environmental variables in violence exposure, little attention has been paid to culture. Culture influences norms, beliefs, and values surrounding the use of violence, expectations and reactions by caretakers to victimized children, and the way children understand and label their own experiences. Even definitions of acceptable versus abusive physical punishment may vary by culture. Culture also is important to understanding family structure and parenting. Sternberg (1993) illustrated that attending to culture helps to delineate varied pathways by which violence affects children. A few studies examined the impact of conflict and violence in ethnically diverse samples (Lindahl & Malik 1999, McCloskey et al 1995, O'Keefe 1994), but more work in this area is needed.

CONSEQUENCES OF EXPOSURE TO VIOLENCE

Much of the research conducted on the association between violence exposure and children's adjustment is more descriptive than theoretical. Despite considerable research documenting this association, less is known about the processes that account for such associations. The following summary of the literature on the consequences of exposure to violence highlights promising new directions that suggest mechanisms of effect. Given the number of available studies, the research presented is intended to be representative, but not comprehensive. Although the effects of exposure to violence are presented in separate domains of functioning, the domains are interrelated and contribute to one another. For example, if children who are exposed to violence are less flexible and resourceful in their reasoning, these cognitive processes may be associated with problems with peers and school work.

Aggression and Other Behavior Problems

Social learning explanations provide a logical theoretical link between the experience of physical abuse in early life and later development of aggressive behaviors. That is, the experience of physical abuse teaches aggressive behaviors and acceptance of aggression as a norm in close relations (Dodge et al 1997). The empirical data suggest that a variety of childhood victimization experiences are related to a variety of aggressive and violent behavior problems.

Researchers have documented elevated levels of aggression and externalizing problems among maltreated children, particularly among those who have been physically abused (Dodge et al 1990, Kolko 1992). Several studies link physical abuse with aggressive behavior during play with peers (Alessandri 1991, Hoffman-Plotkin & Twentyman 1984, Kaufman & Cicchetti 1989), with higher peer ratings of aggression, fighting, meanness, and antisocial behavior (Manly et al 1994, Salzinger et al 1993), and with higher parent and teacher ratings on aggression and externalizing scales (Haskett & Kistener 1991, Hoffman-Plotkin & Twentyman 1984, Trickett 1993). Physically abused children have been found to have more disciplinary problems at school than nonmaltreated neglected, or sexually abused children (Eckenrode et al 1993, Hoffman-Plotkin & Twentyman 1984). Physical abuse appears to have a more consistent link with aggression than does neglect or emotional abuse (Hoffman-Plotkin & Twentyman 1984, Kaufman & Cicchetti 1989). Physically abused adolescents have been found to be at increased risk for disruptive behavior disorders (Kaplan et al 1998, Pelcovitz et al 1994).

Increased aggression and externalizing behavior have been reported among sexually abused children, especially among nonclinic samples (Kendall-Tackett et al 1993), with evidence less consistent among clinic samples (Beitchman et al 1991, Kendall-Tackett et al 1993). Sexual abuse has been linked with aggression, delinquency, destructiveness, and externalizing behavior according to parents and teachers (Einbender & Friedrich 1989, Tong et al 1987, Trickett et al 1994) though not as consistently according to child self-report (Tong et al 1987). The link between sexual abuse and aggression may be less consistent than that between physical abuse and aggression. Eckenrode et al (1993) found that although children who were both sexually abused and neglected had more problems than nonmaltreated children, children who were sexually abused only did not differ from nonmaltreated children in discipline problems.

In addition to aggression against others, abuse has been related to self-destructive behaviors. For example, runaway behavior has been documented in both sexually abused (Rimsza et al 1988) and physically abused (Farber et al 1984) children. Although this behavior can be considered self-destructive, it can also be considered self-preservative, given that children tend to be running away from home situations in which they are at risk for harm (Farber et al 1984). Physically and sexually abused adolescents are also at increased risk for drug abuse (Kaplan et al 1998, Kendall-Tackett et al 1993, Pelcovitz et al 1994). Sexually abused children may be particularly self-destructive compared with physically abused children. Taussig & Litrownik (1997) found that sexually abused children exhibit relatively more self- than other-destructive behaviors, in contrast to physically abused children. Another form of risky behavior exhibited by sexually abused more than nonabused and neglected children is their tendency to touch and solicit attention from adults, including strangers (Tong et al 1987, White et al 1988).

Other behavior problems of sexually abused children include excessive and inappropriate sexual behavior (Friedrich 1993, Kendall-Tackett et al 1993). Sexualized and inappropriate sexual behaviors, such as the tendency to engage in more sex play and more masturbation in socially stressful situations than other children, have been documented mainly among sexually abused children (Ein-bender & Friedrich 1989, White et al 1988), though some evidence exists for increased sexualized behavior among physically abused children as well (Deblin-ger et al 1989).

The effect of abuse on externalizing problems varies as a function of the comparison group used, suggesting that other types of disadvantage also may lead to behavior problems. Wolfe & Mosk (1983) found that abused children were rated as more externalizing than children from normal comparison families but not than those from generally distressed families. Toth et al (1992) found no differences in aggression between groups of abused, neglected, and nonmaltreated children all from low SES families; however, there was more aggression in all groups than in a normal sample. Eckenrode et al (1993) found smaller differences between maltreated and nonmaltreated groups on behavioral measures when comparing the abused group to families receiving public assistance than when comparing them to families not receiving such assistance. In addition, Reyome (1993) found that teachers rated sexually abused and neglected children higher than a lower middle class comparison group on externalizing problems, but found no differences between the maltreated groups and children receiving public assistance.

The literature regarding the link between exposure to spousal violence and externalizing problems provides mixed evidence for this effect. Whereas some studies failed to find the link between marital violence and child aggression, conduct, and externalizing problems (Jouriles et al 1987, Wolfe et al 1986), several studies document the link between marital violence and increased aggression (Graham-Berman & Levendosky 1998, Holden & Ritchie 1991, Rosenberg 1986), externalizing behavior (Graham-Berman & Levendosky 1998, Jaffe et al 1986), and conduct problems (Jouriles et al 1989, Kempton et al 1989, McCloskey et al 1995). Research regarding the relative contributions of observing interparental violence versus being the target of parental abuse has yielded mixed results. Dawud-Noursi et al (1998) found increased aggression and behavior problems among child observers of domestic violence, victims of physical abuse, and those who were both abused and witnesses, but few differences between these groups. O'Keefe (1994) found that observing violence was associated with externalizing problems even after controlling for parent-child aggression, and for boys, was a better predictor of behavior problems than was parent-child aggression. Hughes et al (1989) found that children who were both exposed and abused were rated as the most externalizing, nonexposed and nonabused children as the least externalizing, and children who were exposed but not abused rated in between on externalizing behavior.

Several recent studies, including three longitudinal investigations, document the link between exposure to community violence and aggressive behavior. Miller et al (1999) found that exposure to community violence was associated with increases in parents' reports of antisocial behavior, controlling for earlier antisocial behavior among children age 6–10. Gorman-Smith & Tolan (1998) found that exposure to community violence was associated with increased aggression, controlling for earlier aggression, in a sample of inner-city African-American and Latino fifth- and seventh-grade boys. These investigators measured boys' aggression by combining mothers', teachers', and boys' self-reports. Farrell & Bruce (1997) examined the relation between exposure and violence among urban adolescents at three time points over an eight-month period. They found that at each assessment point, exposure was positively related to self-reported violent behavior. However, exposure was related to increased violence, controlling for earlier violence, only among girls. Schwab-Stone et al (1995) found that exposure to violence was associated with self-reported alcohol use and aggression and antisocial activities among urban 6th, 8th, and 10th graders. DuRant et al (1994) found that among urban black adolescents, exposure to violence and victimization were associated with self-reports of violence.

Depression and Other Internalizing Problems

As Kazdin et al (1985) argue, the harsh and uncontrollable punishment and parental rejection found in an abusive home environment may cause learned helplessness, ineffectiveness, anxiety, and depression in the child. Violence exposure can be interpreted by the child to mean not only that the world is unsafe but also that the child is unworthy of being kept safe (Lynch & Cicchetti 1998). Whether related to violence in the home (Vondra et al 1989) or in the community (Fitzpatrick 1993), these attitudes potentially contribute to negative self-perceptions and internalizing problems.

Reviewers of the literature have noted links between depression, anxiety, and physical and sexual abuse (Kolko 1992, Kendall-Tackett et al 1993). Elevations of depression and hopelessness in physically abused versus non-maltreated children have been found in psychiatric inpatient samples as well as nonclinic samples of children and adolescents (Allen & Tarnowski 1989; Kazdin et al 1985, 1997; Kinard 1980; Pelcovitz et al 1994; Toth et al 1992). Kaplan et al (1998) found that physical abuse increased risk for depressive symptoms above and beyond several parenting risk factors among adolescents. Sexual abuse has also been linked with depression and anxiety (Koverola et al 1993, Merry & Andrews 1994, Oates et al 1994, Trickett & Putnam 1993). Although several investigators have found significant relations between abuse and depression based on mothers' reports, results based on children's self-reports have been less consistent (Einbender & Friedrich 1989; Kinard 1995, 1998; Shapiro et al 1990). Merry & Andrews (1994) found elevated rates of depressive and anxiety disorders among sexually abused children a year after the abuse was disclosed. Even 18 months following the initial assessment, Oates et al (1994) found elevated depression scores in 35% of the abused children, as compared with 17% of the controls. Moreover, Calam et al (1998) found continued high rates of depression and anxiety among sexually abused children two years after initial assessment.

It is not clear whether physical and sexual abuse have differential effects. Dykman et al (1997) found increased internalizing symptoms in both groups relative to nonabused children, but no differences between sexually abused and physically abused children. However, Toth & Cicchetti (1996) found that maltreated children have a marginal tendency to report less depression than nonmaltreated children, and that sexually abused children reported significantly more depression than neglected, physically abused, and nonmaltreated children. Because both physically and sexually abused children were included in the sexually abused group, it is difficult to disentangle differential effects for type of abuse.

Related to depression is the impact of abuse on children's self-esteem and perceived self-competence. Several studies document a link between sexual and physical abuse and low self-esteem in both psychiatric and nonclinic samples (Allen & Tarnowski 1989, Kazdin et al 1985, Oates et al 1994, Toth et al 1992). Toth & Cicchetti (1996) found that maltreated children had lower self-perception scores in all assessed areas. Tong et al (1987) found that sexually abused children rated themselves lower than comparison children on self-concept regarding intellectual and school status, physical appearance and attributes, anxiety, popularity, happiness, and satisfaction. The authors report a particularly pronounced group difference among girls, who were more likely in this sample to have been abused by a relative or acquaintance. Some researchers have found developmental effects, such that younger maltreated children have exaggerated perceived self-competence, whereas older maltreated children have lower scores (Black et al 1994, Vondra et al 1989). Others have not found a link between sexual abuse and self-concept (Einbender & Friedrich 1989) or perceived school competence (Trickett et al 1994).

The connection between internalizing problems and exposure to interparental physical aggression has received some support in the literature as well (Davies & Cummings 1994, Margolin 1998). Sternberg et al (1993) found that children who had been physically abused, had observed spouse abuse, or both did not differ in depression levels, but that all had higher depression scores than did comparison children. Internalizing problems in general have also been documented among groups exposed to spousal physical aggression (Graham-Berman & Levendosky 1998, Holden & Ritchie 1991, Jaffe et al 1986, O'Keefe 1994). Some evidence suggests that the combination of witnessing spousal aggression and being abused puts children at particular risk for internalizing symptoms (Hughes et al 1989, O'Keefe 1996).

The existing research suggests that both witnessing and being a victim of community violence may put children at risk for increased anxiety and depressive symptoms (Kliewer et al 1998, Lynch & Cicchetti 1998), though the results are not completely consistent. Martinez & Richters (1993) found that among fifth and sixth grade students, being victimized by or witnessing violence involving family, friends, and acquaintances was associated with children's self-reported depression levels, whereas being victimized by or witnessing violence involving strangers was not related to depression. In their study of inner-city boys, Gorman-Smith & Tolan (1998) found that exposure to community violence was related to anxiety and depression. Schwab-Stone et al (1995) found that exposure to violence predicted depressed/anxious mood among 6th, 8th, and 10th graders, and Singer et al (1995) found that violence exposure and victimization were related to anxiety and depression among 14 to 19 year olds. However, these authors did not distinguish in their analyses between intra- and extra-familial violence or between observing violence and being victimized. Fitzpatrick (1993) found that violent victimization, but not witnessing violence, was positively related to depression among African-American youth. Farrell & Bruce (1997) found that exposure to community violence was unrelated to emotional distress in urban adolescents.

Other internalizing sequelae of abuse and exposure to violence include specific fears and somatic complaints. Sexual and physical abuse have been associated with fear, separation anxiety, somatic complaints, elimination disorders, and avoidance (Dykman et al 1997, Green 1993, Kendall-Tackett et al 1993, Merry & Andrews 1994, Trickett & Putnam 1998, White et al 1988). Interparental aggression and maternal abuse have been associated with phobias, fears, and separation anxiety (Kempton et al 1989, Margolin 1998). Some researchers report links between abuse and PTSD but not other forms of anxiety (Wolfe et al 1989).

Psychobiological Effects

The literature (Perry 1997, Perry et al 1995) offers several routes by which exposure to violence affects children's neurobiology. The first concerns the overall malleability of the brain during the early years of life, as well as the importance of critical periods for organization and development of specific brain areas (Perry 1997). The literature on central nervous system plasticity suggests that the human brain is dramatically affected by early experience (Weiss & Wagner 1998). Moreover, there are critical periods during which the central nervous system is particularly responsive to specific types of organizing and structuring experiences. Hence, the child who receives inadequate positive sensory stimulation may have compromised function in specific brain regions (Green 1983). Alternatively, children chronically exposed to adverse input may suffer abnormal neurological development due to the overstimulation of certain brain structures.

Effects of abuse and exposure to violence may affect children's arousal and ability to react appropriately to stress. Perry (1997) reported that children exposed to trauma have alterations in their overall arousal, increased muscle tone, increased startle response, sleep disturbance, and abnormalities in cardiovascular regulation. More specifically, chronic stress may result in increased catecholamine activity (De Bellis & Putnam 1994). Elevations in the dopaminergic system may be related to hypervigilance, which during acute stress may be functional, but may be problematic over the long term and potentially associated with posttraumatic stress symptoms (De Bellis & Putnam 1994). As evidence for the effect of abuse on catecholamine activity, Putnam & Trickett (1997) found elevated 24-hour urinary catecholamines in sexually abused girls as compared with nonabused girls. There was also evidence to suggest sympathetic nervous system suppression of immune functioning. De Bellis et al (1994b) found elevated urinary catechol-amine and catecholamine metabolite concentrations in sexually abused, compared with nonabused girls. Although the literature on physiological effects of witnessing interparental violence is less developed, there is a related physiological finding regarding overall marital quality. Parents' marital adjustment has been reported to be inversely related to urinary dopamine levels in children (Gottman & Katz 1989).

In addition, exposure to chronic stress appears to lead to a dysregulation of the hypothalamic-pituitary-adrenal (HPA) axis, a major stress-regulating system. This system is regulated by a negative feedback mechanism such that stress initially causes an increase in cortisol production, but then an inhibitory feedback mechanism results in decreased cortisol (Nelson & Carver 1998). Initially, autonomic arousal occurs, including increases in heart rate, blood pressure, and exaggerated startle. However, two different types of physiological dysregulation may occur with chronic or traumatic stress. An enhanced negative feedback mechanism in the HPA axis leads to lower basal cortisol levels and is linked with prolonged "fight or flight" responses, increased responsiveness to stress, and symptoms of PTSD. A reduced negative feedback mechanism is linked with a decrease in responsiveness to stress and may lead to depression (Golier & Yehuda 1998). Whereas earlier theories regarding effects of trauma on HPA axis dysregulation rely heavily on adult retrospective studies (Stein et al 1997b), a few researchers have begun to examine these biological variables among children and have found evidence for both types of HPA axis dysregulation (De Bellis et al 1994a; Hart et al 1995, 1996; Putnam & Trickett 1997).

Exposure to stress and trauma are also linked with abnormal hypothalamic-pituitary-growth hormone (HPGH) axis functioning (De Bellis & Putnam 1994). Stress-related abnormalities in the HPGH axis may result in delays and disturbances in growth and pubertal timing. As evidence for HPGH axis dysregulation, Jensen et al (1991) found that physically abused boys had reduced growth hormone (GH) response patterns, and sexually abused boys had elevated GH response patterns compared with nonabused controls.

Trauma also appears to affect the timing of pubertal onset and sexual behavior, although the direction of the effect is not yet clear. Theoretically, stress may affect the hypothalamic-pituitary-gondal (HPGn) axis by suppressing reproductive function through inhibiting gonatotropin-releasing hormone (GnRH), and ultimately delaying puberty and inhibiting sexual behavior (De Bellis & Putnam 1994). Alternatively, some researchers suggest that sexual abuse may be associated with early onset of puberty (Trickett & Putnam 1993). These authors note that hormonal changes associated with the stress, such as elevated androstenedione (D4-

AD) and dehydroepiandrosterone (DHEA), may contribute to elevated levels of sexual and aggressive behavior among sexually abused girls.

Post Traumatic Stress Disorder and Symptoms

Physiological consequences of abuse appear to be intimately linked with symptoms of posttraumatic stress disorder (PTSD). PTSD is a disorder in response to a recognizable, serious stressor that is characterized by specific behaviors falling into the categories of reexperiencing the event, avoidance and psychic numbing, and increased arousal. Describing children's responses to trauma, Terr (1991) presents four specific PTSD symptoms: repeatedly perceiving memories of the event through visualization, engaging in behavioral reenactments and repetitive play related to the event, fears related to the trauma event, and pessimistic attitudes reflecting a sense of hopelessness about the future and life in general. Putnam (1997) and Emery & Laumann-Billings (1998) suggest that examining PTSD symptoms rather than diagnoses is more appropriate for children because many children who experience posttraumatic symptoms do not technically earn the PTSD diagnosis.

PTSD and PTSD symptoms have been linked with sexual and physical abuse (Deblinger et al 1989, Green 1993, Sadeh et al 1993). Emery & Laumann-Billings (1998) report that researchers have documented PTSD in one-quarter to one-half of child victims of physical and sexual abuse. Effects for sexual abuse have been found more consistently. McLeer et al (1993) found that in a clinical sample, PTSD was significantly more prevalent among sexually abused compared with nonabused children. Deblinger et al (1989) compared physically and sexually abused psychiatric patients and found that although no differences emerged between groups regarding meeting diagnostic criteria, the sexually abused children exhibited more reexperiencing of symptoms. Sadeh et al (1993) found increased PTSD among sexually abused but not physically abused psychiatric inpatients. Pelcovitz et al (1994) found no difference in the rate of PTSD among physically abused compared to nonabused adolescents. Researchers have also found elevations on dimensional scales of PTSD symptoms, for example dissociative hyperactivity (Trickett et al 1994), intrusive, ruminative thoughts about the traumas, including difficulty falling or staying asleep, nightmares, and fears related to sex (Wolfe et al 1989) among sexually abused children. Greater severity, chronicity, and earlier age of abuse appear to increase the risk of PTSD (Glod & Teicher 1996, Kiser et al 1991, Wolfe et al 1989).

Increased hyperactivity and attention deficit have been reported in abused children with PTSD (Glod & Teicher 1996, Kiser et al 1991), possibly representing consequences of PTSD-associated hyperarousal and hypervigilance (Glod & Teicher 1996, Perry 1997). Glod & Teicher propose several possible explanations for the links between PTSD and hyperactivity, including the possibility that hyperactivity makes early abuse more likely, that early abuse has biological effects increasing the likelihood of both PTSD and hyperactivity, and that hyperactivity may be a biological risk factor for development of PTSD.

Exposure to interparental aggression and community violence have been associated with PTSD symptoms in elementary school children and adolescents (Boney-McCoy & Finkelhor 1995, Burton et al 1994, Fitzpatrick & Boldizar 1993, Horowitz et al 1995, Kilpatrick & Williams 1997, Martinez & Richters 1993, Osofsky et al 1993). Kilpatrick and Williams (1997) found increased prevalence of PTSD among child witnesses of domestic violence as compared with children who did not witness such violence. Terr's (1991) distinction between single event traumas and repeated exposure to trauma suggests that chronic exposure to violence would be more harmful than a single exposure. Nonetheless, PTSD symptoms have been found even one year following exposure to a one-time seriously threatening experience such as a sniper attack (Nader et al 1990). In the aftermath of a sniper attack on a school playground, Pynoos et al (1987) reported that 40% of the children were suffering from moderate or severe PTSD. Physical proximity to the attack was related to severity of the PTSD. Horowitz et al (1995) found that among urban adolescent girls PTSD was significantly correlated with hearing about or witnessing violent events and with being a victim.

Cognitive Consequences

Abuse and exposure to violence have been linked to delayed cognitive development and poor academic functioning. Whereas early theories implicated brain trauma directly resulting from head injury, head trauma does not account for the observed difficulties of abused children without head trauma (Carrey et al 1995). Recent research provides some evidence for links between abuse and trauma and brain and cognitive functioning. Research on animals, adult humans, and children suggests neurocognitive consequences of exposure to trauma involving hippocampal damage and left hemisphere abnormalities affecting memory functioning and verbal skills. Extrapolating from research with primates and adults, the stress of abuse and violence exposure may result in damage to the hippocampus. Glucocorticoids, which are secreted during stress, have been found to cause damage to the hippocampus among primates (Sapolsky et al 1990). Researchers have found adult survivors of child physical and sexual abuse to have smaller hippocampal volumes (Bremner et al 1997, Stein et al 1997a). Bremner et al (1995) also suggest that enhanced norepinephrine activity is likely to cause hippocampal damage. Because the hippocampus is involved in memory integration, damage may result in the dissociative, fragmented, incoherent nature of traumatic memories, as well as intrusive, anxiety-provoking, trauma-related thoughts (Bower & Sivers 1998, McNally 1998, Teicher et al 1997).

Teicher et al (1993, 1997) also present evidence of limbic system dysfunction and left hemispheric abnormalities. In a retrospective study, adults who had been abused reported more symptoms associated with limbic system dysfunction, including brief hallucinatory events, visual phenomena, and dissociative experiences, than those who had not, with the most pronounced effects for those abused before age 18. Teicher et al (1997) also compared physically and sexually abused child and adolescent psychiatric patients to nonabused patients and found an increased probability of left-sided frontotemporal abnormalities and higher prevalence of left compared to right hemisphere deficits on neuropsychological tests, which suggests compromised verbal performance. The authors also report evidence for reversed hemispheric asymmetry, abnormalities in the corpus collosum, and abnormal cortical development in abused children.

Theoretically, the cognitive problems and the behavioral disturbances associated with exposure to violence and abuse logically would threaten academic performance (Trickett et al 1994). Several studies document links between maltreatment, particularly neglect and physical abuse, with poor intellectual and cognitive performance. Abused and neglected school-age children have been found to score lower than nonabused comparison children on tests of verbal ability and comprehension (Allen & Tarnowski 1989, Eckenrode et al 1993, Kurtz et al 1993, Trickett 1993), math skills (Kurtz et al 1993, Eckenrode et al 1993), and overall achievement on standardized tests (Leiter & Johnsen 1994). However, not all studies have found links between maltreatment and standardized test scores (Alessandri 1991). In addition, the relation between physical abuse and grades has not been consistently supported (Eckenrode et al 1993, Kurtz et al 1993). Physical abuse has also been linked to missing more school (Leiter & Johnsen 1994), to parents' and teachers' ratings of lower academic performance and competence (Kurtz et al 1993), and to being more likely to repeat grades (Eckenrode et al 1993, Kurtz et al 1993). Exposure to community violence has also been linked with lower school achievement (Schwab-Stone et al 1995).

The effects of sexual abuse on children's academic performance are somewhat less clear. Trickett et al (1994) found that controlling for age and ethnicity, sexual abuse was associated with lower verbal ability, lower ratings of being a competent learner, lower classroom social competence, and higher school avoidance, but not with grades. Cognitive ability, perceived self-competence, and behavior problems associated with abuse, such as dissociative hyperactivity and bizarre destructiveness, predicted various domains of academic performance. This study emphasizes how the deficits that may be caused by abuse are not independent of each other but affect each other, and that problems in one domain can cause problems across other domains as well.

Other research regarding the effects of sexual abuse have produced mixed results. Einbender & Friedrich (1989) found that sexually abused girls had lower IQ scores, and lower school achievement and achievement test scores than did nonabused comparison children matched on age, race, family income, and family constellation. However, Reyome (1993) found no difference between sexually abused and nonabused children receiving public assistance on measures of intellectual ability. In additon, sexually abused children were no more likely to repeat a grade than comparison children, though they scored lower in classes and were more likely to be in special classes and tutoring than were the comparison children. Eckenrode et al (1993) compared effects of various types of maltreatment and found that the children who experienced sexual abuse but not other forms of maltreatment did not differ from nonmaltreated children on the reading and math portions of the Iowa Test of Basic Skills, on academic success, grades, or likelihood of repeating a grade.

Relevant to these varied findings is the evidence from several studies showing that neglect may cause the most problems regarding children's academic achievement. Eckenrode et al (1993) compared various subtypes of abuse and found that neglect was most consistently associated with the worst outcomes. Allen & Oliver (1982) found that neglect accounted for unique variance in auditory comprehension and verbal ability, whereas abuse and the abuse by neglect interaction did not account for unique variance. These findings make it difficult to interpret studies that either do not explicitly exclude neglected children from the abuse groups or combine neglected children into other abuse groupings. In addition to the issue of neglect, the results regarding abuse and effects on cognitive and academic performance appear to vary depending on the nature of the comparison group and control variables.

Researchers have also documented links between abuse and exposure to interparental aggression and deficits in social cognition. Abused children have been found to be less interpersonally sensitive and attentive to social cues, less competent at social perspective taking, less able to identify others' emotional expressions and to understand complex social roles, less able to generate competent, and more likely to generate aggressive solutions to interpersonal problems, and more likely to attribute biased hostile intent (Barahal et al 1981, Camras et al 1983, Dodge et al 1990, Rosenberg 1986, Trickett 1993). These kinds of social cognitive consequences may mediate between exposure to abuse and aggression (Dodge et al 1990, Rogosch et al 1995).

Peer Relations

A sizeable body of research supports the contention that children exposed to violence and abuse experience difficulties in their peer relationships. According to attachment theory, abused children have disorganized and insecure attachments to their primary caregivers, and become sensitized to anger. Moreover, as Howes & Espinosa (1985) note, abusive parents are likely to be socially isolated, so that children have poor role models for appropriate social interactions. Davies & Cummings (1994) theorize that children who are exposed to interparental violence also lack emotional security at home and become sensitized to hostility and conflict in relationships beyond the family. Although little research has directly addressed the issue, Osofsky (1995) argues that like maltreatment, community violence is likely to have a negative impact on children's formation of relationships, noting that the stress associated with community violence affects mothers' parenting ability and resources and children's capacity to form secure attachments. Because recent research suggests that having quality friendships can help buffer the effects of maltreatment on children's self-esteem (Bolger et al 1998), understanding the social difficulties of these children may be an important avenue through which to improve their developmental trajectories.

Physically abused children in particular tend to have peer difficulties. Physically abused preschool and school-age children have been found to be less prosocial and more aggressive and negative when interacting with peers (Alessandri 1991, Hoffman-Plotkin & Twentyman 1984, Haskett & Kistener 1991, Howes & Eldridge 1985, Kaufman & Cicchetti 1989). Main & George (1985) found that physically abused toddlers were more likely than control toddlers to respond with physical distress, fear, and anger to the distress of their peers. Parker & Herrera (1996) found school-age, physically abused children's interactions to be less intimate than those of nonabused children. Physically abused children tend to be rated by their peers as less popular and more rejected, aggressive, and disruptive (Bolger et al 1998, Dodge et al 1994, Salzinger et al 1993). Salzinger et al (1993) found that abused children tended to have fewer of their positive ratings of peer friends reciprocated, suggesting that they have difficulty distinguishing between potentially supportive and unsupportive peers. Abused children named fewer classmates as best friends in their social networks, and named a greater proportion of younger children in their networks than did the comparison children. Abused children also tend to be rated as more socially rejected by parents, teachers, and camp counselors (Hoffman-Plotkin & Twentyman 1984, Manly et al 1994, Okun et al 1994). Although some researchers have found that maltreatment accounted for variance in ratings of social competence over and above socioeconomic disadvantage (Okun et al 1994), others have found that abused children had similar ratings to those in a welfare agency (Wolfe & Mosk 1983).

Results on peer relations are less clear regarding sexual abuse. Sexually abused children have been found to have lower social competence scores according to parents, teachers, and youth self-report and higher teacher ratings of social withdrawal and unpopularity (Tong et al 1987). However, Manly et al (1994) found that camp counselors rated sexually abused children as more socially competent than physical abused, physically abused/neglected, and nonmaltreated children. In a longitudinal, large-sample study of abuse and peer interactions, Bolger et al (1998) found that sexual abuse was not associated with peer relationship problems.

Evidence also suggests that spousal abuse is related to peer problems. Graham-Berman & Levendosky (1998) found that preschool children who had been exposed to the physical and emotional abuse of their mothers exhibited more negative affect and aggressive behavior toward their peers than did nonexposed children. Dawud-Noursi et al (1998) report that children exposed to domestic violence and physical abuse were rated lower than comparison children by teachers on measures of peer functioning. Children from a battered-women's shelter sample, compared with community families, were found to have lower social competence ratings (Wolfe et al 1985).

Caveat Regarding Adaptive Versus Maladaptive Outcomes

It is important to consider the context in evaluating whether behavior is adaptive or maladaptive. Certain characteristics in children who initially are more resilient to violence (e.g. lack of empathy with a victim, imperviousness to impending danger) are not necessarily positive mental health attributes (Pynoos 1993). Similarly, what appears to be adaptative in one situation may be maladaptive in another. Hypervigilance serves an important self-protective function when confronted with repeated episodes of violence. However, in nonviolent situations, this overawareness of danger cues may be result in inappropriate behavior (Vig 1996), e.g. being overly aggressive with playmates or experiencing concentration difficulties due to being overreactive to a teacher's yelling. Moreover, one consequence for children who are resilient is that they may not elicit sufficient helping responses from others and ultimately may not receive the assistance they need.

Summary of Long-Range Outcomes of Exposure to Violence

Although the primary focus of this review is not on long-range effects, there is a growing literature reflecting both retrospective as well as prospective data of how childhood victimization experiences affect the adult risk for mental health disorders and victimizing others. For example, retrospective data indicate that prevalence risk ratios for female victims of child rape and molestation, compared to nonvictims, range from 1.5 for major depressive episodes to 6.7 for obsessive-compulsive disorders (Saunders et al 1992). Widom's (1998) prospective data reveal that children with a documented history of childhood abuse and neglect, compared to nonabused children from the same neighborhood and born at the same time, are at a two times greater risk for arrest for a violent crime, and are also at greater risk for earlier and more chronic involvement in criminal behavior. Additional prospective studies similarly document the relationship between child maltreatment as a risk factor for delinquency, even after controlling for other variables such as race/ethnicity and social class, albeit with varying strengths of effects (Smith & Thornberry 1995, Zingraff et al 1993). Jaffe et al (1990) suggest that 30% of boys exposed to interparental violence will become violent themselves. More generally, the reviews by Kaufman & Zigler (1987) and Oliver (1993) suggest that approximately one third of child victims grow up to be abusive or neglectful parents. Kaufman & Zigler (1987) cite a six-fold increase in adult abuse rates for those who had been abused. That is, approximately 30% of those persons who as children are physically abused, sexually abused, or severely neglected later maltreat their own children, compared to the 5% abuse rates in the general population. Thus, on the one hand, studies consistently point to an increased risk for serious behavioral outcomes associated with exposure to violence. Yet, on the other hand, the same studies indicate that the majority of those who are exposed to violence do not have diagnosable problems, are not in trouble with the law, and do not perpetuate abuse on others. Although exposure to violence clearly is associated with later risk for psychological problems and for being abusive to others, these negative outcomes certainly are not inevitable.

Although assessing severe outcomes is important to determining the overall impact and cost of violence exposure, it also may be important to examine whether the exposure to violence affects adult adjustment in other ways, for example, in satisfaction from close relationships, or in productivity and success at work. By focusing mainly on negative outcomes, we fail to learn how the majority of people cope with horrific early experiences and what role those experiences ultimately play in their lives. Data on more global perspectives of adult adjustment would inform our understanding of long range resilience, and not just vulnerability, to serious childhood stressors such as exposure to violence.

MEDIATING AND MODERATING VARIABLES

An important direction in the recent literature is the identification of variables that mediate and/or moderate the impact of violence on children. The types of mediating factors proposed generally fall into three categories: (*a*) child characteristics; (*b*) factors related to the frequency, severity, and chronicity of the violence; and (*c*) quality of family and social relations, and more generally the level of disruption and chaos in the children's lives (Hughes 1997).

Children's appraisals and coping strategies are frequently theorized to be key components in understanding vulnerability versus resilience to various types of violence exposure. Dodge et al (1990) report support for their theory that deficits in processing social information, including a failure to attend to relevant cues, a bias to attribute hostile intentions to others, and a lack of competent problem solving strategies, mediate the relationship between exposure to physical harm and later child aggression. With a focus on marital conflict more than marital violence, Grych & Fincham (1990) propose that the impact of marital tension is mediated by children's understanding and appraisals of conflict, such as perceptions of threat, beliefs in one's own ability to cope, and attributions regarding the cause of the conflict. Similarly, with respect to sexual abuse, Spaccarelli (1994) concludes that self-attributions of blame, perceptions of threat, and cognitive avoidant coping are associated with psychological symptoms.

According to the child coping literature, children engage in two predominant strategies when responding to stressors, either attempting to control the stressor through active intervention or attempting to control their own arousal and distress. As Rossman & Rosenberg (1992) suggest, children's beliefs that they can actively intervene in situations beyond their control, such as exposure to violence, heighten children's vulnerability to stress, whereas beliefs that they can self-soothe and modulate their emotions serve as buffers to stress. Hence, the children who intervene in interparental violence, that is taking responsibility for stopping interparental violence, show more negative outcomes than children who simply try to protect themselves from the violence (O'Brien et al 1995).

With a focus on emotional regulation, Davies & Cummings (1994, 1998) propose that a child's exposure to threatening situations results in emotional insecurity which may be reflected in the child's immediate reactions of negative emotional arousal as well as the child's long-range functioning. The importance of emotional regulation has also received support from physiological studies. Katz & Gottman (1995) report that children's emotional regulation, as indexed through vagal tone, a measure of parasympathetic nervous system activity, moderates the negative outcomes associated with marital hostility, though they did not investigate violence per se. For children with low vagal tone, exposure to marital hostility at age 5 was predictive of children's antisocial behavior at age 8, whereas no such relationship was found for the children with high vagal tone.

There are a variety of additional emotional and cognitive variables that may play a role in mediating and moderating reactions to violence. Children who tend to be shy or anxious may internalize their reactions to the violence, whereas children with an acting out style may be more likely to exhibit more externalizing behaviors following violence (Pynoos 1993). Overall cognitive ability was found by Frodi & Smetana (1984) to mediate social-cognitive deficits in young maltreated youngsters. Moreover, cognitive flexibility, an adaptable temperament, and the ability to tolerate change may help a child maneuver through the myriad adjustments following exposure to violence (Osofsky 1995). There are multiple pathways of effect for these cognitive characteristics. The same cognitive resources and skills that assist in coping with the immediate effects of violence are also likely to be related to school success and other achievements. These successes secondarily tend to bring praise and popularity, which are also protective against the stress of violence (Jenkins & Smith 1991).

Factors describing the nature of the violence, often considered the more objective dimensions of risk, have been identified as influencing the impact of exposure. With respect to community violence, for example, the literature points to the proximity of the violence, the chronicity of the exposure, the emotional closeness with the victim, and the degree of brutality (Bell & Jenkins 1993, Garbarino et al 1992, Martinez & Richters 1993, Pynoos 1993). Bolger et al (1998), examining six types of maltreatment, report that chronicity, frequency, and early onset increased the negative effects of particular maltreatment subtypes. With respect to sexual abuse, the literature indicates that duration of abuse, force accompanying the abuse, and biological father as perpetrator contribute to the seriousness of outcomes (Browne & Finkelhor 1986, Trickett et al 1997, Trickett & Putnam 1998). Moreover, interactions between these variables can be important. According to Manly et al (1994), the interaction between frequency and severity of maltreatment predicts a number of outcome variables rated by both adult and peer observers.

Characteristics of the child's social and family environment also influence the impact of violence. The literatures on sexual abuse, child abuse, and exposure to marital violence provide evidence that the availability of a supportive relationship, particularly from a parent or other important caretaker, is associated with fewer symptoms resulting from childhood victimization (e.g. Boney-McCoy & Finkelhor 1995, Margolin 1998, Trickett 1997). According to Kaufman & Zigler (1987), a supportive relationship with one parent also reduces the likelihood of a transmission of violence across generations. Katz & Gottman (1997) report that parental warmth, parental scaffolding and praise, and low derogation in parenting buffer young children exposed to high marital conflict from negative outcomes on academic achievement, emotional regulation, peer relations, and physical illness. Similarly, Neighbors et al (1993) found that a strong relationship with their mothers was associated with adolescents' resilience to high levels of interparental conflict. Margolin & John (1997) provide evidence that, although exposure to marital aggression has some direct effects on children's adjustment, to a large extent those effects are mediated through parenting. Kliewer et al (1998) elaborate on one of the important dimensions provided by a supportive relationship. Their data indicate that the opportunity to talk about violence exposure to supportive others is associated with less intrusive thinking and, consequently, fewer internalizing symptoms. Although positive parenting can buffer the effects of violence, considerable evidence exists that marital conflict and violence, child abuse, and sexual abuse are associated with compromised parenting, reflected in harsher forms of discipline and more negative emotional attachments (Davies & Cummings 1994, Erel & Burman 1995, Trickett 1997).

Supportive relations with persons other than the parents also are important. Jenkins & Smith (1991) found a trusting relationship with an adult outside the immediate family to be an important protective factor. Children's perceptions of their peer relationships and reported use of social supports have moderating effects on the association between parental conflict and children's adjustment (Rogers & Holmbeck 1997). More specifically, Bolger et al (1998) found that both friendship quality and reciprocated friendship moderated the association between maltreatment and low self-esteem.

CONCLUSION

This chapter highlights connections between different types of childhood exposure to violence. A frequent conclusion in this literature is that outcomes associated with exposure to violence range in nature and severity. As the developmental psychopathology literature suggests, each type of victimization can lead to diverse outcomes, and alternatively, diverse types of exposure to violence can lead to the same developmental outcome. The effects of exposure to violence may be less dependent on the type of exposure and more dependent on the processes and pathways by which exposure affects individual children. Moreover, because the type and severity of outcomes experienced by a child may change as that child develops and matures, assessments of outcome must be viewed as highly time specific.

Without undermining the importance of studying connections between childhood exposure to violence and diagnosable outcomes, it should be noted that there are many important outcomes other than those meeting diagnostic criteria. The cutting edge of the theoretical literature in this area is characterized by a focus on processes and mechanisms that, in addition to explaining diagnosable outcomes, are themselves important phenomena. These processes, such as persistent effort in the classroom, social competence, ability to regulate emotions, and physiological reactivity, are generally not represented in commonly used clinical assessment procedures. Much remains to be learned about how children's behavioral, cognitive, affective, and physiological processes are disrupted by exposure to violence and about how functioning in these different systems is interconnected. Continued attention to identifying the variability in children's reactions to violence and how the nature of response relates to developmental stage and environmental circumstances will assist in identifying important targets for intervention and prevention.

ACKNOWLEDGMENTS

We want to thank Ashley Borders, Aileen Echiverri, Deborah Nezarian, and Heather Santoro for their help with library work. Preparation of this chapter was supported by NIMH Grants R01 36595 and R01 MH 57347.

Visit the Annual Reviews home page at www.AnnualReviews.org.

LITERATURE CITED

Aber JL, Allen JP. 1987. The effects of maltreatment on young children's socio-emotional development: an attachment theory perspective. *Dev. Psychol.* 23:406–14

Alessandri SM. 1991. Play and social behavior in maltreated preschoolers. *Dev. Psyopathol.* 3:191–205

Allen DM, Tarnowski K. 1989. Depressive characteristics of physically abused children. *J. Abnorm. Child Psychol.* 17:1–11

Allen RE, Oliver JM. 1982. The effects of child maltreatment on language development. *Child Abuse Negl.* 6:299–305

Am. Med. Assoc. Counc. Sci. Aff. 1993. Adolescents as victims of family violence. *JAMA* 270:1850–56

Appel AE, Holden GW. 1998. The co-occurrence of spouse and physical child abuse: a review and appraisal. *J. Fam. Psychol.* 12:578–99

Barahal RM, Waterman JW, Martin HP. 1981. The social cognitive development of abused children. *J. Consult. Clin. Psychol.* 49:508–16

Beitchman JH, Zucker KJ, Hood JE, DaCosta GA, Akman D. 1991. A review of the short-term effects of child sexual abuse. *Child Abuse Negl.* 15:537–56

Bell CC, Jenkins EJ. 1993. Community violence and children on Chicago's southside. See Reiss et al 1993, pp. 46–54

Black M, Dubowitz H, Harrington D. 1994. Sexual abuse: developmental differences in children's behavior and self-perception. *Child Abuse Negl.* 18:85–95

Bolger KE, Patterson CJ, Kupersmidt JB. 1998. Peer relationships and self-esteem among children who have been maltreated. *Child Dev.* 69:1171–97

Boney-McCoy S, Finkelhor D. 1995. Psychosocial sequelae of violent victimization in a national youth sample. *J. Consult. Clin. Psychol.* 63:726–36

Bower GH, Sivers S. 1998. Cognitive impact of traumatic stress. *Dev. Psychopathol.* 10:625–53

Bremner JD, Krystal JH, Southwick SM, Charney DS. 1995. Functional neuroanatomical correlates of the effects of stress on memory. *J. Trauma. Stress* 8:527–53

Bremner JD, Randall ER, Staib L, Bronen RA, Mazure C, Capelli S, et al. 1997. Magnetic resonance imaging-based measurement of hippocampal volume in posttraumatic stress disorder related to childhood physical and sexual abuse—a preliminary report. *Biol. Psychiatry* 41:21–32

Browne A, Finkelhor D. 1986. Impact of child sexual abuse: a review of the research. *Psychol. Bull.* 99:66–77

Burton D, Foy D, Bwanausi C, Johnson J, Moore L. 1994. The relationship between traumatic exposure, family dysfunction, and post-traumatic stress symptoms in male juvenile offenders. *J. Trauma. Stress* 7:83–93

Calam R, Horne L, Glascow D, Cox A. 1998. Psychological disturbance and child sexual abuse: a follow-up study. *Child Abuse Negl.* 22:910–13

Camras LA, Grow JG, Ribordy SC. 1983. Recognition of emotional expression by abused children. *J. Clin. Child Psychol.* 12:325–28

Carrey NJ, Hendrick JB, Persinger MA, Bialik RJ. 1995. Physiological and cognitive correlates of child abuse. *J. Am. Acad. Child Adolesc. Psychiatry* 34:1067–75

Cicchetti D. 1993. Developmental psychopathology: reactions, reflections and projections. *Dev. Rev.* 13:471–502

Cicchetti D. 1994. Advances and challenges in the study of the sequelae of child maltreatment. *Dev. Psychopathol.* 6:1–3

Cicchetti D, Rizley R. 1981. Developmental perspectives on the etiology, intergenerational transmission and sequelae of child maltreatment. In *Developmental Perspectives on Child Maltreatment*, ed. R Rizley,

D Cicchetti, pp. 31–55. San Francisco: Jossey-Bass

Cicchetti D, Toth SL. 1995. A developmental perspective on child abuse and neglect. *J. Am. Acad. Child Adolesc. Psychiatry.* 34:541–65

Cicchetti D, Toth SL, eds. 1997. *Rochester Symposium on Developmental Psychopathology* Vol. 8. *Developmental Perspectives on Trauma: Theory, Research, and Intervention.* Rochester, NY: Univ. Rochester Press

Cicchetti D, Toth SL, Lynch M. 1997. Child maltreatment as an illustration of the effects of war on development. See Cichetti & Toth 1997, pp. 227–62

Davies PT, Cummings EM. 1994. Marital conflict and child adjustment: an emotional security hypothesis. *Psychol. Bull.* 116:387–411

Davies PT, Cummings EM. 1998. Exploring children's emotional security as a mediator of the link between marital relations and child adjustment. *Child Dev.* 69:124–39

Dawud-Noursi S, Lamb ME, Sternberg KJ. 1998. The relations among domestic violence, peer relationships, and academic performance. In *Families, Risk and Competence,* ed. C Feiring, M Lewis, pp. 207–26. Mahwah, NJ: Erlbaum

De Bellis MD, Chrousos GP, Dorn LD, Burke L, Helmers K, et al. 1994a. Hypothalamic-pituitary-adrenal axis dysregulation in sexually abused girls. *J. Clin. Endocrinol. Metab.* 78:249–55

De Bellis MD, Lefter L, Trickett PK, Putnam FW. 1994b. Urinary catecholamine excretion in sexually abused girls. *J. Am. Acad. Child Adolesc. Psychiatry* 33:320–27

De Bellis MD, Putnam FW. 1994. The psychobiology of childhood maltreatment. *Child Abuse* 3:663–78

Deblinger E, McLeer SV, Atkins MS, Ralphe D, Foa E. 1989. Posttraumatic stress in sexually abused, physically abused, and non-abused children. *Child Abuse Negl.* 13:403–8

Dodge KA, Bates JE, Pettit GS. 1990. Mechanisms in the cycle of violence. *Science* 250:1678–83

Dodge KA, Pettit GS, Bates JE. 1994. Socialization mediators of the relation between socioeconomic status and child conduct problems. *Child Dev.* 65:649–65

Dodge KA, Pettit GS, Bates JE. 1997. How the experience of early physical abuse leads children to become chronically aggressive. See Cicchetti & Toth 1997, pp. 263–88

DuRant RH, Cadenhead C, Pendergrast RA, Slavens G, Linder CW. 1994. Factors associated with the use of violence among urban black adolescents. *Am. J. Public Health* 84:612–17

Dykman RA, McPherson B, Ackerman PT, Newton JEO, Mooney DM, et al. 1997. Internalizing and externalizing characteristics of sexually and/or physically abused children. *Integ. Physiol. Behav. Sci.* 32:62–74

Eckenrode J, Laird M, Doris J. 1993. School performance and disciplinary problems among abused and neglected children. *Dev. Psychol.* 29:53–62

Egeland B. 1997. Mediators of the effects of child maltreatment on developmental adaptation in adolescence. See Cicchetti & Toth 1997, pp. 403–34

Einbender AJ, Friedrich WN. 1989. Psychological functioning and behavior of sexually abused girls. *J. Consult. Clin. Psychol.* 57:155–57

Emery R, Laumann-Billings L. 1998. An overview of the nature, causes, and consequences of abusive family relationships: toward differentiating maltreatment and violence. *Am. Psychol.* 53:121–35

Erel O, Burman B. 1995. The linkage between marital quality and the parent-child relationship: a meta-analysis. *Psychol. Bull.* 118:108–32

Fantuzzo J, Boruch R, Beriama A, Atkins M, Marcus S. 1997. Domestic violence and children: prevalence and risk in five major U.S. cities. *J. Am. Acad. Child Adolesc. Psychiatry* 36:116–22

Farber ED, Kinast C, McCoard WD, Falkner D. 1984. Violence in families of adolescent runaways. *Child Abuse Negl.* 8:295–99

Farrell AD, Bruce SE. 1997. Impact of exposure to community violence on violent behavior and emotional distress among urban adolescents. *J. Clin. Child Psychol.* 26:2–14

Finkelhor D, Hotaling G, Lewis IA, Smith C. 1990. Sexual abuse in a national survey of adult men and women: prevalence, characteristics, and risk factors. *Child Abuse Negl.* 14:19–28

Finkelhor D, Kendall-Tackett K. 1997. A developmental perspective on the childhood impact of crime, abuse, and violent victimization. See Cicchetti & Toth 1997, pp.1–32

Fitzpatrick KM. 1993. Exposure to violence and presence of depression among low-income, African-American youth. *J. Consult. Clin. Psychol.* 61:528–31

Fitzpatrick KM, Boldizar JP. 1993. The prevalence and consequences of exposure to violence among African-American youth. *J Am. Acad. Child Adolesc. Psychiatry* 32:424–30

Friedrich WN. 1993. Sexual victimization and sexual behavior in children: a review of recent literature. *Child Abuse Negl.* 17:59–66

Frodi A, Smetana J. 1984. Abused, neglected and nonmaltreated preschoolers' ability to discriminate emotions in others: The effects of IQ. *Child Abuse Negl.* 10:5–15

Garbarino J. 1993. Children's response to community violence: What do we know? *Infant Ment. Health J.* 14:103–15

Garbarino J, Dubrow N, Kostelny K, Pardo C. 1992. *Children In Danger.* San Francisco: Jossey-Bass

Garbarino J, Kostelny K, Dubrow N. 1991. What children can tell us about living in danger. *Am. Psychol.* 46:376–83

Garmezy N, Masten AS. 1994. Chronic adversities. In *Child and Adolescent Psychiatry,* ed. M Rutter, L Herzov, E Taylor, pp. 191–208. Oxford, UK: Blackwell Sci.

Glod CA, Teicher MH. 1996. Relationship between early abuse, posttraumatic stress disorder, and activity levels in prepubertal children. *J. Am. Acad. Child Adolesc. Psychiatry* 34:1384–93

Glodich A. 1998. Traumatic exposure to violence: a comprehensive review of the child and adolescent literature. *Smith Coll. Stud. Soc. Work* 68:321–45

Golier J, Yehuda R. 1998. Neuroendocrine activity and memory-related impairments in posttraumatic stress disorder. *Dev. Psychopathol.* 10:857–69

Gorman-Smith D, Tolan P. 1998. The role of exposure to community violence and developmental problems among inner-city youth. *Dev. Psychopathol.* 10:101–16

Gottman JM, Katz LF. 1989. The effects of marital discord on young children's peer interaction and health. *Dev. Psychol.* 25:373–81

Graham-Berman SA, Levendosky AA. 1998. The social functioning of preschool-age children whose mothers are emotionally and physically abused. *J. Emot. Abuse* 1:59–84

Green AH. 1983. Dimensions of psychological trauma in abused children. *J. Am. Acad. Child Adolesc. Psychiatry* 22:213–37

Green AH. 1993. Child sexual abuse: immediate and long-term effects and intervention. *J. Am. Acad. Child Adolesc. Psychiatry* 32:890–902

Groves BM, Zuckerman B, Marans S, Cohen D. 1993. Silent victims: children who witness violence. *JAMA* 269:262–64

Grych JH, Fincham FD. 1990. Marital conflict and children's adjustment: a cognitive-contextual framework. *Psychol. Bull.* 108:267–90

Hart J, Gunnar M, Cicchetti D. 1995. Salivary cortisol in maltreated children: evidence of relations between neuroendocrine activity and social competence. *Dev. Psychopathol.* 7:11–26

Hart J, Gunnar M, Cicchetti D. 1996. Altered neuroendocrine activity in maltreated children related to symptoms of depression. *Dev. Psychopathol.* 8:201–14

Haskett ME, Kistener JA. 1991. Social interaction and peer perceptions of young physically abused children. *Child Dev.* 62:979–90

Hoffman-Plotkin D, Twentyman CT. 1984. A multimodal assessment of behavioral and cognitive deficits in abused and neglected preschoolers. *Child Dev.* 55:794–802

Holden GW, Ritchie KL. 1991. Linking extreme marital discord, child rearing, and child behavior problems: evidence from battered women. *Child Dev.* 62:311–27

Horowitz K, Weine S, Jekel J. 1995. PTSD symptoms in urban adolescent girls: compounded community trauma. *J. Am. Acad. Child Adolesc. Psychiatry* 34:1353–61

Howes C, Eldridge R. 1985. Responses of abused, neglected, and non-maltreated children to the behavior of their peers. *J. Appl. Dev. Psychol.* 6:261–70

Howes C, Espinosa MP. 1985. The consequences of child abuse for the formation of relationships with peers. *Child Abuse Negl.* 9:397–404

Hughes HM. 1997. Research concerning children of battered women: clinical implications. In *Violence and Sexual Abuse at Home: Current Issues in Spousal Battering and Child Maltreatment*, ed. R Geffner, SB Sorenson, PK Lundberg-Love, pp. 225–44. New York: Haworth

Hughes HM, Parkinson D, Vargo M. 1989. Witnessing spouse abuse and experiencing physical abuse: a "double whammy"? *J. Fam. Violence* 4:197–209

Jaffe P, Wolfe DS, Wilson S. 1990. *Children of Battered Women*. Newbury Park, CA: Sage

Jaffe P, Wolfe DW, Wilson S, Zak L. 1986. Similarities in behavioral and social maladjustment among child victims and witnesses to family violence. *Am. J. Orthopsychiatry* 56:142–46

Janoff-Bulman R. 1992. *Shattered Assumptions: Toward a New Psychology of Trauma*. New York: Free Press

Jenkins JM, Smith MA. 1991. Marital disharmony and children's behavior problems: aspects of poor marriage that affect children adversely. *J. Child Psychol. Psychiatry* 32:793–810

Jensen JB, Pease BS, Bensel RT, Garfinkel BD. 1991. Growth hormone response patterns in sexually or physically abused boys. *J. Am. Acad. Child Adolesc. Psychiatry* 30:784–90

Jouriles EN, Barling J, O'Leary KD. 1987. Predicting child behavior problems in maritally violent families. *J. Abnorm. Child Psychol.* 15:165–73

Jouriles EN, LeCompte SH. 1991. Husbands' aggression toward wives and mothers' and fathers' aggression toward children: moderating effects of child gender. *J. Consult. Clin. Psychol.* 59:190–92

Jouriles EN, Murphy CM, O'Leary KD. 1989. Interpersonal aggression, marital discord, and child problems. *J. Consult. Clin. Psychol.* 57:453–55

Kaplan SJ, Pelcovitz D, Salzinger S, Mandel F, Weiner M. 1997. Adolescent physical abuse and suicide attempts. *J. Am. Acad. Child Adolesc. Psychiatry* 36:799–808

Kaplan SJ, Pelcovitz D, Salzinger S, Weiner M, Mandel FS, et al. 1998. Adolescent physical abuse: risk for adolescent psychiatric disorders. *Am. J. Psychiatry* 155:954–59

Katz LF, Gottman JM. 1995. Vagal tone protects children from marital conflict. *Dev. Psychopathol.* 7:83–92

Katz LF, Gottman JM. 1997. Buffering children from marital conflict and dissolution. *J. Clin. Child Psychol.* 26:157–71

Kaufman J, Cicchetti D. 1989. Effects of maltreatment on school-age children's socioemotional development: assessments in a day-camp setting. *Dev. Psychol.* 25:516–24

Kaufman J, Zigler E. 1987. Do abused children become abusive parents? *Am. J. Orthopsychiatry* 57:186–92

Kazdin AE, Moser J, Colbus D, Bell R. 1985. Depressive symptoms among physically abused and psychiatrically disturbed children. *J. Abnorm. Psychol.* 94:298–307

Kempton T, Thomas AM, Forehand R. 1989. Dimensions of interparental conflict and adolescent functioning. *J. Fam. Violence* 4:297–307

Kendall-Tackett KA, Williams LM, Finkelhor D. 1993. Impact of sexual abuse on children: a review and synthesis of recent empirical studies. *Psychol. Bull.* 115:164–80

Kilpatrick KL, Williams LM. 1997. Post-traumatic stress disorder in child witnesses to domestic violence. *Am. J. Orthopsychiatry* 67:639–44

Kinard EM. 1980. Emotional development in physically abused children. *Am. J. Orthopsychiatry* 50:686–96

Kinard EM. 1995. Mother and teacher assessments of behavior problems in abused children. *J. Am. Acad. Child Adolesc. Psychiatry* 34:1043–53

Kinard EM. 1998. Depressive symptoms in maltreated children from mother, teacher, and child perspectives. *Violence Vict.* 13:131–47

Kiser LJ, Heston J, Millsap PA, Pruitt DB. 1991. Physical and sexual abuse in childhood: relationship with post-traumatic stress disorder. *J. Am. Acad. Child Adolesc. Psychiatry* 30:776–83

Kliewer W, Leport SJ, Oskin D, Johnson PD. 1998. The role of social and cognitive processes in children's adjustment to community violence. *J. Consult. Clin. Psychol.* 66:199–209

Kolko D. 1992. Characteristics of child victims of physical violence: research findings and clinical implications. *J. Interpers. Violence* 7:244–76

Koop CE, Lundberg GD. 1992. Violence in America: a public health emergency: time to bite the bullet back. *JAMA* 267:3075–76

Koverola C, Pound J, Heger A, Lytle C. 1993. Relationship of child sexual abuse to depression. *Child Abuse Negl.* 17:393–400

Kratcoski PC. 1985. Youth violence directed toward significant others. *J. Adolesc.* 8:145–157

Kurtz PD, Gaudin JM, Wodarski JS, Howing PT. 1993. Maltreatment and the school-aged child: school performance consequences. *Child Abuse Negl.* 17:581–89

Leiter J, Johnsen MC. 1994. Child maltreatment and school performance. *Am. J. Educ.* 102:154–89

Lewis DO. 1992. From abuse to violence: psycho-physiological consequences of maltreatment. *J. Am. Acad. Child Adolesc. Psychiatry* 31:383–91

Lindahl KM, Malik NM. 1999. Marital conflict, family processes, and boys' externalizing behavior in Hispanic American and European American families. *J. Clin. Child Psychol.* 28:12–24

Lynch M, Cicchetti D. 1998. An ecological-transactional analysis of children and contexts: the longitudinal interplay among child maltreatment, community violence, and children's symptomatology. *Dev. Psychopathol.* 10:235–57

MacMillan HL, Fleming JE, Troome N, Boyle MH, Wong M, et al. 1997. Prevalence of child physical and sexual abuse in the community: results from the Ontario health supplement. *JAMA* 278:131–35

Main M, George C. 1985. Responses of abused and disadvantaged toddlers to distress in agemates: a study in the day care setting. *Dev. Psychol.* 21:407–12

Manly JT, Cicchetti D, Barnett D. 1994. The impact of subtype, frequency, chronicity, and severity of child maltreatment on social competence and behavior problems. *Dev. Psychopathol.* 6:121–43

Marans S, Adelman A. 1997. Experiencing violence in a developmental context. In *Children in a Violent Society,* ed. J Osofsky, pp. 202–22. New York: Guilford

Margolin G. 1998. Effects of domestic violence on children. In *Violence against Children in the Family and the Community,* ed. PK Trickett, CJ Schellenbach, pp. 57–102. Washington, DC: APA

Margolin G, John RS. 1997. Children's exposure to marital aggression: direct and mediated effects. In *Out of the Darkness: Contemporary Perspectives on Family Violence,* ed. GK Kantor, JL Jasinski, pp. 90–104. Thousand Oaks, CA: Sage

Margolin G, John RS, Ghosh CM, Gordis EB. 1996. Family interaction process: an essential tool for exploring abusive relations. In *Family Violence from a Communication Perspective,* ed. DD Cahn, SA Lloyd, pp. 37–58. Thousand Oaks, CA: Sage.

Martinez P, Richters JE. 1993. The NIMH Community Violence Project. II. Children's distress symptoms associated with violence exposure. See Reiss et al 1993, pp. 22–35

McCloskey LA, Figueredo AJ, Koss MP. 1995. The effects of systemic family violence on children's mental health. *Child Dev.* 66:1239–61

McGee RA, Wolfe DA, Wilson SK. 1997. Multiple maltreatment experiences and adolescent behavior problems: adolescents' perspectives. *Dev. Psychopathol.* 9:131–49

McLeer SV, Callaghan M, Henry D, Wallen J. 1993. Psychiatric disorders in sexually abused children. *J. Am. Acad. Child Adolesc. Psychiatry* 33:313–19

McNally RJ. 1998. Experimental approaches to cognitive abnormality in posttraumatic stress disorder. *Clin. Psychol. Rev.* 18:971–82

Merry SN, Andrews LK. 1994. Psychiatric status of sexually abused children 12 months after disclosure of abuse. *J. Am. Acad. Child Adolesc. Psychiatry* 33:939–44

Miller LS, Wasserman GA, Neugebauer R, Gorman-Smith D, Kamboukos D. 1999. Witnessed community violence and antisocial behavior in high-risk-urban boys. *J. Clin. Child Psychol.* 28:2–11

Moore TE, Pepler D, Mae R, Kates M. 1989. Effects of family violence on children: new directions for research and intervention. In *Intervening with Assaulted Women: Current Theory, Research, and Practice,* ed. B Pressman, G Cameron, M Rothery, pp. 75–91. Hillsdale, NJ: Erlbaum

Nader K, Pynoos R, Fairbanks L, Frederick C. 1990. Children's PTSD reactions one year after a sniper attack at their school. *Am. J. Psychiatry* 147:1526–30

National Center of Child Abuse and Neglect. 1996. *Child Maltreatment 1996: Reports from the States to the National Child Abuse and Neglect Data System.* Washington, DC: U.S. Gov. Printing Off.

National Research Council. 1993. *Understanding Child Abuse and Neglect.* Washington, DC: National Academy

Neighbors B, Forehand R, McVicar D. 1993. Resilient adolescents and interparental conflict. *Am. J. Orthopsychiatry* 63:462–71

Nelson CA, Carver LJ. 1998. The effects of stress and trauma on brain and memory: a view from developmental cognitive neuroscience. *Dev. Psychopathol.* 10:793–809

Ney P, Fung T, Wickett A. 1994. The worst combinations of child abuse and neglect. *Child Abuse Negl.* 18:705–14

Oates RK, O'Toole BI, Lynch DL, Stern A, Cooney G. 1994. Stability and change in outcomes for sexually abused children. *J. Am. Acad. Child Adolesc. Psychiatry* 33:945–53

O'Brien M, Margolin G, John RS. 1995. Relation among marital conflict, child coping, and child adjustment. *J. Clin. Child Psychol.* 24:346–61

O'Keefe M. 1994. Linking marital violence, mother-child/father-child aggression, and child behavior problems. *J. Fam. Violence* 9:63–78

O'Keefe M. 1996. The differential effects of family violence on adolescent adjustment. *Child Adolesc. Soc. Work* 13:51–68

Okun A, Parker JG, Levendosky AA. 1994. Distinct and interactive contributions of physical abuse, socioeconomic disadvantage, and negative life events to children's social, cognitive, and affective adjustment. *Dev. Psychopathol.* 6:77–98

Oliver JE. 1993. Intergenerational transmission of child abuse: rates, research, and clinical implications. *Am. J. Psychiatry* 150:1315–24

Osofsky JD. 1995. The effects of exposure to violence on young children. *Am. Psychol.* 50:782–88

Osofsky JD, Scheeringa MS. 1997. Community and domestic violence exposure: effects of development and psychopathology. See Cichetti & Toth 1997, pp. 155–80

Osofsky JD, Wewers S, Hann DM, Fick AC. 1993. Chronic community violence: What is happening to our children? See Reiss et al 1993, pp. 36–45

Parker JG, Herrera C. 1996. Interpersonal processes in friendship: a comparison of abused and nonabused children's experiences. *Dev. Psychol.* 32:1025–38

Pelcovitz D, Kaplan S, Goldenberg B, Mandel F, Lehane J, Guarrera J. 1994. Posttraumatic stress disorder in physically abused adolescents. *J. Am. Acad. Child Adolesc. Psychiatry* 33:305–12

Perry B. 1997. Incubated in terror: neurodevelopmental factors in the "Cycle of Violence." In *Children in a Violent Society,* ed. JD Osofsky, pp. 124–49. New York: Guilford

Perry B, Pollard R, Blakley T, Baker W, Vigilante D. 1995. Childhood trauma, the neurobiology of adaptation, and "use-dependent" development of the brain: how "states" become "traits." *Infant Ment. Health J.* 16:271–91

Putnam FW. 1997. *Dissociation in Children and Adolescents: A Developmental Perspective.* New York: Guilford

Putnam FW, Trickett PK. 1997. Psychobiological effects of sexual abuse: a longitudinal study. In *Annals of the New York Academy of Sciences,* Vol. 821, ed. R Yehuda, AC McFarlane, pp. 150–59. New York: New York Acad. Sci.

Pynoos RS. 1993. Traumatic stress and developmental psychopathology in children and adolescents. In *American Psychiatric Review of Psychiatry,* Vol. 12, ed. J Oldham, M Riba, A Tasman, pp. 205–38. Washington, DC: American Psychiatric Press

Pynoos RS, Frederick C, Nader K, Arroyo W, Steinberg A, et al. 1987. Life threat and posttraumatic stress in school-age children. *Arch. Gen. Psychiatry* 44:1057–63

Reiss D, Richters JE, Radke-Yarrow M, Scharff D, eds. 1993. *Children and Violence.* New York: Guilford

Reyome ND. 1993. A comparison of the school performance of sexually abused, neglected, and non-maltreated children. *Child Stud. J.* 23:17–38

Richters JE, Martinez P. 1993. The NIMH Community Violence Project. I. Children as victims of and witnesses to violence. See Reiss et al 1993, pp. 7–21

Rimsza ME, Berg RA, Locke CL. 1988. Sexual abuse: somatic and emotional reactions. *Child Abuse Negl.* 12:201–8

Rogers MJ, Holmbeck GN. 1997. Effects of interparental aggression on children's adjustment: the moderating role of cognitive appraisal and coping. *J. Fam. Psychol.* 11:125–30

Rogosch FA, Cicchetti D, Aber JL. 1995. The role of child maltreatment in early deviation in cognitive and affective processing abilities and later peer relationship problems. *Dev. Psychopathol.* 7:591–609

Rosenberg MS. 1986. Children of battered women: the effects of witnessing violence on their social problem-solving abilities. *Behav. Ther.* 4:85–89

Rossman BBR, Rosenberg MS. 1992. Family stress and functioning in children: the moderating effects of children's beliefs about their control over parental conflict. *J. Child Psychol. Psychiatry* 33:699–715

Rossman BBR, Rosenberg MS. 1998a. Maltreated adolescents: victims caught between childhood and adulthood. See Rossman & Rosenberg 1998b, pp. 107–29

Rossman BBR, Rosenberg MS. 1998b. *Multiple Victimization of Children: Conceptual, Developmental, Research, and Treatment Issues.* New York: Haworth

Sadeh A, Hayden RM, McGuire JPD, Civita R. 1993. Somatic, cognitive, and emotional characteristics of abused children in a psy-chiatric hospital. *Child Psychiatry Hum. Dev.* 24:191–200

Salzinger S, Feldman RS, Hammer M, Rosario M. 1993. The effects of physical abuse on children's social relationships. *Child Dev.* 64:169–87

Sameroff A, Seifer R, Barocas R, Zax M, Greenspan S. 1987. Intelligence quotient scores of 4-year-old children: social-environmental risk factors. *Pediatrics* 79:343–50

Sapolsky RM, Uno H, Rebert CS, Finch CE. 1990. Hippocampal damage associated with prolonged glucocorticoid exposure in primates. *J. Neurosci.* 10:2897–902

Saunders BE, Villeponteaux LA, Lipovsky JA, Kilpatrick DG, Veronen LJ. 1992. Child sexual assault as a risk factor for mental disorders among women: a community survey. *J. Interpers. Violence* 7:189–204

Schwab-Stone ME, Ayers TS, Kasprow W, Voyce C, Barone C, et al. 1995. No safe haven: a study of violence exposure in an urban community. *J. Am. Acad. Child Adolesc. Psychiatry* 10:1343–52

Sedlack AJ, Broadhurst DD. 1996. *Third National Incidence Study of Child Abuse and Neglect.* National Center of Child Abuse and Neglect: U.S. Dep. Health Human Serv.

Shapiro JP, Leifer M, Martone MW, Kassem L. 1990. Multimethod assessment of depression in sexually abused girls. *J. Pers. Asses.* 55:234–48

Singer MI, Anglin TM, Song LY, Lunghofer L. 1995. Adolescents' exposure to violence and associated symptoms of psychological trauma. *JAMA* 273:477–82

Smith C, Thornberry TP. 1995. The relationship between childhood maltreatment and adolescent involvement in delinquency. *Criminology* 33:451–81

Spaccarelli S. 1994. Stress, appraisal, and coping in child sexual abuse: a theoretical and empirical review. *Psychol. Bull.* 116:340–62

Stein MB, Koverola C, Hanna C, Torchia MG, McClarty B. 1997a. Hippocampal volume in women victimized by childhood sexual abuse. *Psychol. Med.* 27:951–59

Stein MB, Yehuda R, Koverola C, Hanna C. 1997b. Enhanced dexamethasone suppression of plasma cortisol in adult women traumatized by childhood sexual abuse. *Biol. Psychiatry* 42:680–86

Sternberg KJ. 1993. Child maltreatment: implication for policy from cross-cultural research. In *Child Abuse, Child Development, and Social Policy: Advance in Applied Developmental Psychology,* Vol. 8, ed. D Cicchetti, SL Toth, pp. 191–212. Norwood, NJ: Ablex

Sternberg KJ, Lamb ME, Greenbaum C, Cicchetti D, Dawud S, et al. 1993. Effects of domestic violence on children's behavior problems and depression. *Dev. Psychol.* 29:44–52

Straus MA. 1979. Measuring intrafamily conflict and violence: the Conflict Tactics (CT) Scales. *J. Marriage Fam.* 41:75–88

Straus MA. 1992. Children as witnesses to marital violence: a risk factor of lifelong problems among a nationally representative sample of American men and women. In *Children and Violence: Report of the Twenty-Third Ross Roundtable on Critical Approaches to Common Pediatric Problems.* ed. DF Schwarz, pp. 98–109. Columbus, OH: Ross Lab.

Straus MA, Gelles RJ. 1986. Societal change and change in family violence from 1975 to 1985 as revealed by two national surveys. *J. Marriage Fam.* 48:465–79

Straus MA, Gelles RJ, Steinmetz SK. 1980. *Behind Closed Doors: Violence in the American Family.* Garden City, NY: Anchor

Straus MA, Hamby SL, Finkelhor D, Moore DW, Runyan D. 1997. *Identification of Child Maltreatment with the Parent-Child Conflict Tactics Scales: Development and Psychometric Data from a National Sample of American Parents.* Durham, NH: Univ. New Hampshire, Family Res. Lab.

Taussig HN, Litrownik AJ. 1997. Self- and other-directed destructive behaviors: assessment and relationship to type of abuse. *Child Maltreatment* 2:172–82

Teicher MH, Glod CA, Surrey J, Swett C. 1993. Early childhood abuse and limbic system ratings in adult psychiatric outpatients. *J. Neuropsychiatry Clin. Neurosci.* 5:301–6

Teicher MH, Ito Y, Glod CA, Andersen SL, Dumont N, Ackerman E. 1997. Preliminary evidence for abnormal cortical development in physically and sexually abused children using EEG coherence and MRI. *Ann. NY Acad. Sci.* 821:160–75

Terr L. 1991. Childhood traumas: an outline and overview. *Am. J. Psychiatry* 48:10–20

Tong L, Oates K, McDowell M. 1987. Personality development following sexual abuse. *Child Abuse Negl.* 11:371–83

Toth SL, Cicchetti D. 1996. Patterns of relatedness, depressive symptomatology, and perceived competence in maltreated children. *J. Consult. Clin. Psychol.* 1:32–41

Toth SL, Manly JT, Cicchetti D. 1992. Child maltreatment and vulnerability to depression. *Dev. Psychopathol.* 4:97–112

Trickett PK. 1993. Maladaptive development of school-aged, physically abused children: relationship with the child rearing context. *J. Fam. Psychol.* 7:134–47

Trickett PK. 1997. Sexual and physical abuse and the development of social competence. In *Developmental Psychopathology: Perspectives on Adjustment, Risk, and Disorder,* ed. SS Luther, JA Burack, D Cicchetti, J Weisz, pp. 390–416. New York: Cambridge: Cambridge Univ. Press

Trickett PK, McBride-Chang C, Putnam FW. 1994. The classroom performance and behavior of sexually abused females. *Dev. Psychopathol.* 6:183–94

Trickett PK, Putnam FW. 1993. Impact of child sexual abuse on females: toward a developmental, psychobiological integration. *Psychol. Sci.* 4:81–87

Trickett PK, Putnam FW. 1998. Developmental consequences of child sexual abuse. In *Violence against Children in the Family and the Community,* ed. PK Trickett, CJ Schellenbach, pp. 39–56. Washington, DC: Am. Psychol. Assoc.

Trickett PK, Reiffman A, Horowitz LA, Putnam FW. 1997. Characteristics of sexual abuse trauma and the prediction of developmental outcomes. See Cicchetti & Toth 1997, pp. 289–314

U.S. Department of Education. 1997. *Principal/School Disciplinarian Survey on School Violence. Fast Response Survey System, 63.* Washington, DC: Natl. Cent. Educ. Stat. (http://nces.ed.gov/pubs98/violence/98030003.html)

U.S. Department of Justice. 1998a. *National Crime Victimization Survey. Criminal Victimization 1997: Changes 1996–97 with Trends 1993–97.* Washington, DC: Bur. Justice Stat.

U.S. Department of Justice. 1998b. *Violence by Intimates (NCJ-167237).* Washington, DC: Bur. Justice Stat.

Vig S. 1996. Young children's exposure to community violence. *J. Early Interv.* 20:319–28

Vondra J, Barnett D, Cicchetti D. 1989. Perceived and actual competence among maltreated and comparison school children. *Dev. Psychopathol.* 1:237–55

Wang CT, Daro D. 1998. *Current Trends in Child Abuse Reporting and Fatalities: The Results of the 1997 Annual Fifty State Survey.* Chicago, IL: Natl. Comm. Prev. Child Abuse

Weiss MJS, Wagner SH. 1998. What explains the negative consequences of adverse childhood experiences on adult health? Insights from cognitive and neuroscience research. *Am. J. Prev. Med.* 14:356–60

White S, Halpin B, Strom GA, Santilli G. 1988. Behavioral comparisons of young sexually abused, neglected, and nonreferred children. *J. Clin. Child Psychol.* 17:53–61

Widom CS. 1998. Child victims: searching for opportunities to break the cycle of violence. *Appl. Prev. Psychol.* 7:225–34

Wolfe DA, Jaffe P, Wilson SK, Zak L. 1985. Children of battered women: the relation of child behavior to family violence and maternal stress. *J. Consult. Clin. Psychol.* 53:657–65

Wolfe DA, McGee R. 1994. Dimensions of child maltreatment and their relationship to adolescent adjustment. *Dev. Psychopathol.* 6:165–81

Wolfe DA, Mosk MD. 1983. Behavioral comparisons of children from abusive and distressed families. *J. Consult. Clin. Psychol.* 51:02–708

Wolfe DA, Zak L, Wilson S, Jaffe P. 1986. Child witnesses to violence between parents: critical issues in behavioral and social adjustment. *J. Abnorm. Child Psychol.* 14:95–104

Wolfe VV, Gentile CG, Wolfe DA. 1989. The impact of sexual abuse on children: a PTSD formulation. *Behav. Ther.* 20:215–28

Wright MO, Masten AS, Northwood A, Hubbard JJ. 1997. Long-term effects of massive trauma: developmental and psychobiological perspectives. See Cichetti & Toth 1997, pp. 181–226

Zeanah CH, Scheeringa MS. 1997. The experience and effects of violence in infancy. In *Children in a Violent Society.* ed. JD Osofsky, pp. 97–123. New York: Guilford

Zingraff MT, Leiter J, Myers KA, Johnsen MC. 1993. Child maltreatment and youthful problem behavior. *Criminology* 31:173–202

Annu. Rev. Psychol. 2000. 51:481–537

Toward a Psychology of Memory Accuracy

Asher Koriat, Morris Goldsmith, and Ainat Pansky

Department of Psychology, University of Haifa, Haifa, Israel, 31905; e-mail:
akoriat@psy.haifa.ac.il, mgold@psy.haifa.ac.il, pansky@psy.haifa.ac.il

Key Words   memory correspondence, false memory, memory distortion, memory illusions, memory metaphors

■ **Abstract**   There has been unprecedented interest in recent years in questions pertaining to accuracy and distortion in memory. This interest, catalyzed in part by real-life problems, marks a significant departure from the quantity-oriented approach that has characterized much of traditional memory research. We outline a correspondence metaphor of memory underlying accuracy-oriented research, and show how the features of this metaphor are manifested across the disparate bodies of research reviewed here. These include work in the Gestalt tradition, spatial memory, memory for gist, schema theory, source monitoring, fluency misattributions, false recall and recognition, postevent misinformation, false memories, eyewitness research, and auto-biographical memory. In examining the dynamics of memory accuracy, we highlight the importance of metacognitive monitoring and control processes. We end by discussing some of the methodological, theoretical, and metatheoretical issues inherent in accuracy-oriented research, attempting to prepare the groundwork for a more coherent psychology of memory accuracy.

CONTENTS

Introduction 482
   Basic Characteristics of the Accuracy-Oriented Approach to Memory 483
   Expressions of the Correspondence Conception in Accuracy-Oriented
     Memory Research 485
Accuracy-Oriented Research: How and Why Memory Can Go Wrong 487
   The Gestalt Approach to Memory Changes Over Time 488
   Spatial Memory and Distortion 489
   Memory for Gist versus Detail 491
   Schema-Based Effects on Memory Accuracy 493
   Source Monitoring 496
   Illusions Stemming from Fluency Misattributions 498
   False Recall and Recognition 500
   Misleading Postevent Information 503
   Real-Life False Memories and Their Creation 505
   Eyewitness Memory 507
   Autobiographical Memory 510

Metacognitive Processes and Accuracy 513
  Monitoring the Correctness of One's Own Knowledge: Metamemory Illusions 514
  The Strategic Regulation of Memory Accuracy 515
Toward a Psychology of Memory Accuracy: Methodological,
  Theoretical, and Metatheoretical Issues... 516
  Correspondence-Oriented Research: Phenomena, Questions, and Theories 517
  Experimental Paradigms and Assessment Procedures 519
  Memory Accuracy and Error Within a Broader Functional Perspective 521

INTRODUCTION

Despite the enormous amount of research and theorizing on memory in the past century, there is still no consensual conceptual framework for thinking about memory. In our view, this state of affairs reflects the multifarious nature of memory itself, calling for a pluralism of approaches to the study of memory (Koriat & Goldsmith 1996b, 1997).

One approach that has dominated the experimental study of memory during the past century has followed Ebbinghaus (1895) in adopting a quantity-oriented conception. In this conception, memory is seen as a storehouse into which discrete items of information are initially deposited and then later retrieved (Marshall & Fryer 1978, Roediger 1980). Memory is then evaluated in terms of the number of items that can be recovered over some retention interval. This approach to memory underlies the traditional list-learning paradigm that continues to produce much of the data that appear in scientific journals.

More recently, however, a very different approach to memory has been gaining impetus, inspired by real-life memory phenomena. In this accuracy-oriented approach, which may be traced to the seminal work of Bartlett (1932) among others, memory is viewed as a representation or reconstruction of past experience. Hence, memory is evaluated in terms of its correspondence or fit with past events, rather than in terms of the mere number of input items that can be recovered.

The vast amount of recent work on memory accuracy and distortion has produced many new findings and also a search for theoretical frameworks that can accommodate them. Yet, only very recently has there been an emerging recognition that the new wave of accuracy-oriented research calls for the development of a metatheoretical foundation that can help in organizing the data and in motivating specifically accuracy-oriented memory theories (Koriat & Goldsmith 1996b, Payne & Blackwell 1998, Roediger 1996, Schacter et al 1998). In this chapter, we present a selective review and analysis of accuracy-oriented memory research. We first outline the basic characteristics of the accuracy-oriented approach in terms of a correspondence conception of memory. We then survey some of the main accuracy-oriented research areas, in the attempt to bring out the common features and issues inherent in the study of memory accuracy and error. We go on to emphasize the role that metacognitive processes have come to play in current treatments of memory accuracy. Finally, we discuss some of the theoretical, metatheoretical, and methodological issues that must be faced on the road to a psychology of memory accuracy.

Basic Characteristics of the Accuracy-Oriented Approach to Memory

In order to appreciate the unique features of the accuracy-oriented approach to memory, it is helpful to contrast it with the traditional, quantity-oriented approach. These two approaches appear to reflect two fundamentally different conceptions or metaphors of memory—the storehouse and correspondence metaphors, respectively (Koriat & Goldsmith 1996a,b).

The Quantity-Oriented Storehouse Conception The quantity-oriented approach to memory, inherent in the storehouse metaphor, is well illustrated by the standard list-learning paradigm, perhaps the hallmark of traditional memory research (Neisser 1991). This paradigm essentially simulates the course of events presumed to take place when memory items are initially deposited into and then subsequently retrieved from a memory store. The contents of the store are assumed to consist of discrete, elementary units (items), whose basic characteristic is countability: Measures of memory can be based simply on the number of recovered elements. Moreover, memory is assessed in an input-bound manner: One begins with the input and asks how much of it was recovered in the output. In scoring free-recall performance as percent correct, for instance, commission errors are essentially ignored (Roediger et al 1997). Forgetting, then is conceived as simple item loss. Moreover, the items are completely interchangeable as far as the total memory score is concerned: The content of the recollected and forgotten items is immaterial. What matters is not what is remembered, but rather, how much.

These aspects of the list-learning paradigm characterize an approach to memory in which memory is studied primarily in terms of its amount (Schacter 1989). This emphasis guides not only the way in which memory is assessed, but also the phenomena investigated, the questions asked, and the methods and theories developed to answer them. Until recently, the dominance of this approach was virtually unrivalled (Payne & Blackwell 1998, Roediger 1980).

The Accuracy-Oriented Correspondence Conception The accuracy-oriented approach, in contrast, can be illustrated by a memory paradigm common in eye-witness research, in which subjects first observe a staged event and are later asked to recount the event, or are questioned about specific details (e.g. Belli & Loftus 1996, Fisher et al 1994). This paradigm embodies a different way of thinking about memory, one in which the focus is on the correspondence between what the person reports and what actually occurred (see Winograd 1994, Payne & Blackwell 1998). Indeed, much of the recent work inspired by real-life memory phenomena discloses a keen preoccupation with the reliability, accuracy, or faithfulness of memory that has no parallel in the traditional, quantity-oriented approach. In order to capture the essential features of this alternative view, Koriat & Goldsmith (1996b) explicated a *correspondence metaphor* of memory in terms of the following interrelated attributes:

1. Aboutness: Memory is considered to be about past events (Conway 1991). Thus, memory reports are treated as descriptions, consisting of propositional statements that have truth value, rather than as mere collections of recovered items.
2. Focus on accuracy: Interest lies primarily in the extent to which the memory report is reliable, trustworthy, and accurate, i.e. the extent to which it accords with reality (or some other criterion) (see Kruglanski 1989).
3. Forgetting: Forgetting is conceived as a loss of correspondence between the memory report and the actual event, that is, as a deviation from veridicality. Thus, in addition to a concern with information loss, this view leads to a focus on the many different types of qualitative memory distortions (e.g. Bartlett 1932, Schacter 1995)—simplification, fabrication, confabulation, and the like.
4. Content: Unlike the quantity-oriented approach, in which interest focuses on how much is remembered, in the correspondence-oriented approach (and virtually all real-life memory situations), it matters a great deal what is remembered and misremembered (Conway 1991).
5. Output-boundedness: The assessment of memory correspondence is inherently output bound. Unlike the storehouse approach, which leads one to begin with the input and ask how much of it is represented in the output, in a correspondence view of memory it is more natural to focus on the output (e.g. an eyewitness report) and examine to what extent it accords with the input (e.g. a witnessed event). In general, accuracy can be measured only for what a person reports, not for what is omitted.
6. Memory as the perception of the past: The correspondence view of memory has much in common with the way we think about perception. In perception, interest lies in the correspondence between what we perceive and what is out there (i.e. veridicality), and in the various ways in which percepts may deviate from reality (e.g. illusions). Likewise, under the correspondence metaphor, memory may be conceived as the perception of the past, and the question then becomes, To what extent is this perception veridical or illusory (Roediger 1996)?

Collectively, these ingredients of the correspondence conception characterize an accuracy-oriented approach to memory. This way of treating memory has become increasingly salient in memory research and theorizing, particularly in work prompted by real-life memory phenomena (e.g. Intons-Peterson & Best

1998, Lynn & McConkey 1998, Ross et al 1994, Schacter 1995, Winograd & Neisser 1992).

Expressions of the Correspondence Conception in Accuracy-Oriented Memory Research

Even a cursory survey of the recent wave of accuracy-oriented memory research reveals fundamental differences from traditional quantity-oriented research. In this section, we point out some of these differences as a backdrop for considering the specific research areas that will be reviewed later.

First, the assumptions underlying the traditional use of the list-learning paradigm provide quantity-oriented research with memory measures of very broad applicability. The standard measures of percent recall and recognition, based on the assumption of item interchangeability, provide a common denominator that allows a broad spectrum of quantity-oriented research findings to be compared and integrated. In contrast, accuracy-oriented research has yielded a plethora of paradigm-specific dependent measures that allow less cross-talk between different areas at the level of memory assessment. This situation derives from features of the correspondence conception. Because the study of memory accuracy is concerned with the content of the information reported, it is less amenable to global memory measures. Moreover, the many qualitative ways in which memory of the past can deviate from veridicality call for memory measures that are tailored to individual dimensions of miscorrespondence. The focus of quantity-oriented research on only one dimension of miscorrespondence, omission, helped circumvent the many serious methodological and metatheoretical issues facing the study of memory correspondence (see Methodological, Theoretical, and Metatheoretical Issues).

Second, the focus on memory accuracy has led to a far more extensive analysis of the memory output than has been customary in traditional quantity-oriented research (e.g. Bartlett 1932; Brewer 1988a,b; Neisser 1981). The dramatic increase of interest in commission errors and false memories in recent years epitomizes the departure from the input-bound storehouse conception of forgetting as loss of studied items. That conception has particular difficulty accommodating the idea that memory can be supplemental, i.e. that some of the changes that occur between study and test involve "memory" for information that was not contained in the input. As noted by Roediger et al (1998), false recall and false recognition responses have generally been considered a mere methodological nuisance in the study of memory, rather than an object of interest in their own right.

Third, the treatment of memory reports as propositional descriptions that have truth value brings to the fore relational aspects of correspondence and miscorrespondence that cannot easily be accommodated within a conception of memory as a store of elementary units. The treatment of list-learning memory responses as propositional-relational statements played an insignificant role in traditional memory theorizing and was essentially optional. In contrast, propositional relations have figured prominently in the study of semantic memory (e.g. "a canary is a bird") and now they constitute a core of interest in the accuracy-oriented study of episodic and autobiographical memory as well. Such relational judgments as when or where an event took place (e.g. Winograd & Neisser 1992), whether the source of a memory is perception or imagination (e.g. Johnson 1997), and so forth, are now integral both to memory assessment procedures and to theorizing about underlying memory mechanisms. Indeed, deficits in binding together the various features of complex events have been proposed to underlie such varied memory errors as the effects of postevent misinformation and confabulations resulting from frontal lobe pathologies (see Schacter et al 1998).

Fourth, the affinity between memory and perception inherent in the correspondence metaphor is apparent in much research and theorizing about memory accuracy and distortion. Several researchers have stressed the similarity between memory illusions and perceptual illusions (Roediger 1996), proposing that "we should consider the study of sensing and perceiving as a model for studying remembering" (Roediger et al 1998:238). Such an affinity is perhaps most clear in the study of visual and spatial memory, in which principles governing perception have often been extended to apply to memory (e.g. Shepard 1978). However, it is also evident in other research areas, for example in the application of Gestalt principles to describe changes in memory for depicted events (Allport & Postman 1945), and in cognitive social-psychological research on person perception and person memory (e.g. Wyer & Srull 1989). The affinity between perception and memory is incorporated in the perception/reperception framework (Payne & Blackwell 1998), which applies similar concepts to the analysis of perception and memory, as well as in the study of "memory psychophysics" (Algom 1992). In addition, the attributional approach of Jacoby and his associates (e.g. Kelley & Jacoby 1998), affords an analysis of perceptual and memory illusions within the same conceptual framework.

Fifth, perhaps also part of the legacy of perception in the study of memory correspondence, is the increased interest in the phenomenal qualities of recollective experience. Experiential, subjective qualities attracted little interest in traditional quantity-oriented memory research. In contrast, many current studies of memory accuracy incorporate measures of various subjective characteristics similar to those used in imagery research, such as vividness and perceptual-contextual detail (Conway et al 1996, Johnson 1997, Lampinen et al 1998). Also included are measures of the state of awareness accompanying remembering (the know-remember distinction) (Tulving 1985; see also Gardiner & Java 1993, Gardiner et al 1998), as well as metacognitive feelings like the sense of familiarity, the feeling of knowing, the feeling of recall imminence, and subjective confidence (Benjamin & Bjork 1996, Koriat & Levy-Sadot 1999, Schwartz 1998). Such subjective measures have been examined in connection with reality and source monitoring (Suengas & Johnson 1988), autobiographical memories (Brewer 1992), false recall (Payne et al 1997, Roediger & McDermott 1995, Schacter et al 1996), postevent misinformation (Zaragoza & Mitchell 1996), flashbulb memories (Conway 1995), and eyewitness testimony (Fruzzetti et al 1992). No longer mere epiphenomena, experiential qualities have been treated as an integral component of the process of remembering (e.g. Johnson 1997, Norman & Schacter 1996) and in particular, as diagnostic clues used by both rememberers and observers in the attempt to distinguish genuine from false memories (e.g. Conway et al 1996, Koriat 1995, Ross 1997, Schwartz 1998). The assumption is that the quality of phenomenal experience may be critical in leading the rememberer to accept a memory as true.

Finally, the conception of memory as being about something has spawned a departure from the passive storehouse conception toward a more active view, in which remembering is an intentional, goal-directed "effort after meaning" (Bartlett 1932:20). This, of course, is the hallmark of Bartlett's reconstructive approach, in which "remembering is not the re-excitation of innumerable fixed, lifeless and fragmentary traces. It is an imaginative reconstruction or construction" (1932:213). Thus, a vast amount of accuracy-oriented research has been devoted to examining the consequences of the assumption that information is not simply deposited into a memory store, but is assimilated and integrated into cognitive structures (e.g. schemas) and later recreated from those structures. More recently, the active role of the rememberer has also been gaining prominence in the expanded notion of retrieval processes (e.g. Norman & Schacter 1996) and in work emphasizing the metacognitive processes of monitoring and control that mediate accurate memory performance (Goldsmith & Koriat 1999, Koriat & Goldsmith 1996c). Many authors have emphasized complex evaluative and decisional processes used to avoid memory errors or to escape illusions of familiarity (e.g. Burgess & Shallice 1996, Kelley & Jacoby 1996, Koriat 2000, Schacter et al 1998). The operation of these processes is particularly crucial in real-life situations (e.g. eyewitness testimony) in which a premium is placed on accurate reporting.

The preceding list represents a rough attempt to characterize some of the unique features of the correspondence-oriented study of memory. We now turn to an examination of how these features manifest themselves in specific research areas.

ACCURACY-ORIENTED RESEARCH: HOW AND WHY MEMORY CAN GO WRONG

The following survey brings together and examines somewhat disparate lines of accuracy-oriented memory research. Because one of our aims is to demonstrate the broad scope and diversity of accuracy-oriented research, it is simply not possible to be comprehensive. Instead, this survey is both selective and deliberately biased to highlight the issues, experimental paradigms, and phenomena that are distinctive of the study of memory correspondence. The sections have been organized to preserve as much as possible the coherence of different bodies of research. Following this survey, we go on to an analysis of some of the common issues and challenges facing these various lines of research.

The Gestalt Approach to Memory Changes Over Time

Although Bartlett (1932) is generally credited as being the founder of the qualitative, accuracy-oriented approach to memory, many facets of this approach were already apparent in the study of memory by Gestalt psychologists (see Koffka 1935, Riley 1962). Rejecting the Ebbinghaus-type focus on the number of remembered nonsense syllables, they revived the emphasis on qualitative aspects of memory that had been pioneered as early as the late nineteenth century by several students of memory for visual form (see Estes 1997, Woodworth 1938, for reviews). These latter researchers found, for example, that observers' reproductions from memory were characterized not only by loss of detail, but also by substitution of new detail, and object assimilation—a tendency of reproductions to shift toward the typical form of familiar objects.

Gestalt psychologists, extending the Gestalt principles from perception to memory (see Koffka 1935, Riley 1962), explained these distortions as resulting from autochthonous cortical forces that transform perceptual traces into more regular, symmetrical, and simple memory forms (*Prägnanz*). Wulf (1922), who had subjects draw geometrical figures from memory, identified two opposite types of changes: "sharpening," which involves the exaggeration of selected characteristics of the original figure, and "leveling," which entails a weakening of one or more features. These changes were assumed to be progressive, such that later reproductions tend to exaggerate the deviations of the previous ones. Based on these results, Wulf postulated three causal factors underlying both leveling and sharpening: "normalizing," which refers to changes toward a well-known or conventional figure, "pointing," which refers to changes that emphasize a feature of the stimulus, and "autonomous changes," which reflect systematic self-governed modifications of the memory trace toward simpler and more regular patterns ("good form"). It is the postulation of autonomous, intrinsic changes operating on the memory trace that is unique to Wulf's Gestalt perspective. According to this perspective, the memory engram "cannot be regarded as an immutable impression which can only become blurred with time, similar to a drawing carved on a brick. Rather this engram undergoes changes by virtue of gestalt laws" (Wulf 1922:370).

Goldmeier's stress model (1982) specifies the conditions under which distortions in the direction of "good figure" will occur, conceptualizing *Prägnanz* in terms of the notion of "singularity." Singular features (e.g. a full circle) contain no stress and should remain stable and accurate over time. By contrast, nonsingular features, such as ambiguous or poorly integrated material, produce unstable and imprecise traces that gradually lose information. It is the nearly singular features (e.g. an almost closed circle), those having the strongest stress, that elicit the tendency to shift toward singularity and therefore should exhibit progressive distortions over time. The nearly singular traces originally have the structure of schema-plus-correction, and the gradual distortion in memory eliminates the correction but retains the schema. This change toward increased self-consistency is adaptive, because it achieves maximal compactness within the trace system while suffering only a minimal loss of information.

Rhodes' (1996) more recent work on distortions in face recognition can also be seen as an example of the operation of sharpening. Using a computer-implemented caricature generator to manipulate the distinctiveness of facial features, line drawings of faces were distorted by either exaggerating the metric differences between each target face and a norm (i.e. sharpening), thus creating a caricature of the original face, or, conversely, by reducing these differences (i.e. leveling), creating anticaricatures. Several studies (see Rhodes 1996 for a review) indicated that when subjects learned to associate a name with a face, naming the caricature version of the face was faster than naming its anticaricature version, suggesting that sharpening is less disruptive to recognition than leveling (Rhodes et al 1987, 1997). Furthermore, the recognition of the caricature versions was as good or even better than that of the original face (Benson & Perrett 1994, Rhodes et al 1987). Rhodes concluded, "In some cases caricatures are even *superportraits,* with the paradoxical quality of being more like the face than the face itself." (Rhodes 1996:1). She proposed that the effectiveness of caricatures in recognition may derive from the fact that the representations stored in long term memory are "schematized so as to emphasize the distinctive properties of what is being represented." (Rhodes et al 1987:474).

The Gestalt idea of distortion toward "better form" has also been very influential in social cognition, primarily in cognitive consistency theory and cognitive balance theory, following from the work of Fritz Heider (1958; see Gilbert et al 1998). This research too illustrates the continuity between memory and perception, and in fact in this type of research, the distinction between memory (i.e. person memory) and perception (i.e. person perception) is generally blurred.

Spatial Memory and Distortion

The study of spatial memory also brings to the fore various features of the correspondence metaphor. First, it discloses an explicit interest in the nature and basis of the correspondence between memory representations and their spatial referents. Second, it invites the application of assessment procedures that depart greatly from those that follow from the storehouse metaphor. Third, it highlights some inherent similarities between the study of memory and of perception, allowing both to be analyzed in terms of the same theoretical constructs.

Early studies were primarily concerned with demonstrating an isomorphic mapping between spatial layouts and their memory representations. Kosslyn et al (1978), for example, found that the time it took to scan between two points on a mental image of a memorized map increased with the actual distance between the

points. A similar isomorphism was demonstrated in studies comparing performance in the presence and in the absence of spatial maps (e.g. Kerst & Howard
1978, Thorndyke 1981). These studies laid the groundwork for exploring various
aspects of miscorrespondence.

Memory psychophysics (see Algom 1992) embodies the view of memory as
the perception of the past, bringing perceptual issues and techniques to bear on
the study of memory. For example, Kerst & Howard (1978) found that perceptual
and memorial estimates of distance were related to the actual distances by similar
power functions, but the exponent of the memorial function was equal to the
square of the exponent of the perceptual function. They proposed a "re-perceptual
hypothesis": The same psychophysical transformation that operates on the sensory input to produce a perceptual representation is reapplied to the perceptual
representation to produce the memorial estimates (but see Radvansky et al 1995
for alternative accounts). Thus, memorial judgments are performed via "internal
psychophysics" (Moyer 1973), causing a magnification of perceptual distortions.

Thorndyke (1981) found that for perceptual as well as memorial tasks, estimated distances increased as a linear function of the number of intervening points
(i.e. "clutter") along the route. Thus, although distance estimations made from
memory were not entirely faithful to the actual distances in the external environment, they were faithful to the information that perception delivered to memory.
In fact, Thorndyke, as well as others, implied that such memory distortions as the
clutter effect actually stemmed from misperception: perceptual biases or illusions.

However, accumulating evidence of systematic distortions in spatial memory
has motivated alternative accounts, attributing spatial distortion to error-prone
reconstructive heuristics. For example, Byrne (1979) found an overestimation of
distance for routes containing bends as opposed to linear routes, and for routes
within the town center as opposed to peripheral routes, as well as a tendency to
normalize the angles between urban roads to 90°. Byrne proposed that spatial
representations do not preserve the exact metrics of the spatial environment (e.g.
veridical distances or angles); rather, subjects base their estimates on heuristics
(e.g. "the more locations that are remembered along a route, the longer the route
must be") that are generally adequate, but are sometimes prone to bias or
inaccuracy.

Additional types of errors in distance estimation also challenge the assumption
that internal representations preserve metric spatial information. For example, the
finding that landmarks produce asymmetric distance estimates—nonlandmarks
judged as closer to landmarks than vice versa (e.g. McNamara & Diwadkar
1997)—clearly violates the symmetry of Euclidean distances. This bias too has
been explained in terms of the reconstructive view, which suggests that spatial
properties "are not retrieved from long-term memory and reported in pure form,
but rather, are interpreted and scaled by the context in which the retrieval takes
place." (McNamara & Diwadkar 1997:188). This approach can also account for
the "perspective effect": Subjects who imagined themselves in New York judged
the distance between New York and Pittsburgh to be longer than those who imag-

ined themselves in San Francisco, whereas the opposite was found for judgments of the distance between San Francisco and Salt Lake City (Holyoak & Mah 1982). Distance estimates have also been found to be under- or overestimated depending on whether the judged locations are in the same or different spatial regions or units (e.g. McNamara 1986). The latter phenomenon is reminiscent of Stevens & Coupe's (1978) finding of an inferential process underlying memory for direction relations, in which subjects' reproductions were distorted in the direction of the superordinate relationships (e.g. Reno remembered as east of San Diego because Nevada is generally east of California).

Tversky (1981) reported distortions of alignment and rotation (e.g. toward canonical axes) that she interpreted as reflecting simplifying heuristics (compared to leveling, normalizing, or assimilation to a schema) that facilitate both the encoding and reconstruction of complex spatial information. More generally, she also demonstrated that various spatial distortions were analogous to biases and errors in other cognitive domains, suggesting that they are a "result of general cognitive processes and not restricted to spatial thinking" (Tversky 1998:267).

In virtually none of these studies, then, is spatial memory treated as the mere retrieval of stored items of spatial information, nor is it evaluated in terms of the mere amount of information that can be recovered. Instead, these studies illustrate a concern with the qualitative aspects of accuracy and distortion, and attempt to explain these phenomena in terms of perceptual biases and reconstructive processes.

Memory for Gist versus Detail

The idea that people can often remember the gist of an event without being able to remember its details is difficult to accommodate within the traditional quantity-oriented approach to memory. Work on this topic raises two issues that are unique to the correspondence metaphor. First, the correspondence between an event and its subsequent memory can be assessed at different levels of generality. For example, in his analysis of John Dean's memory for conversations with the president, Neisser (1981) identified three levels at which correspondence could be achieved: (*a*) accurately reproducing the details of a conversation, (*b*) distorting the details but retaining the gist or overall meaning, or (*c*) distorting both details and gist, but remaining faithful to the overall theme or "narrative truth" of the events. This can severely complicate the assessment of memory correspondence (see later discussion). Second, the choice of level of achieved correspondence is generally under the strategic control of the rememberer. For example, Goldsmith et al (1998; see also Goldsmith & Koriat 1999), showed that subjects strategically adjust the grain-size of their report (e.g. reporting "he was in his 20's" rather than "he was 23 years old"), often trading precision for accuracy. Similarly, Neisser observed that in answering open-ended questions, subjects tend to choose "a level of generality at which they [are] not mistaken" (1988:553). While such control can complicate memory assessment, it is in fact an important topic of study in its own right (see Metacognitive Processes and Accuracy).

Most research on the topic of gist has focused on the relative memorability of gist versus verbatim information. Many studies have shown that the general representation or semantic content of studied material (gist) is better retained over time than memory for surface details or verbatim wording of that material (see Brainerd & Reyna 1993). Kintsch et al (1990), for example, found differential decay rates for three different levels of information, with surface information (i.e. verbatim memory) becoming inaccessible within four days, memory for the semantic content (i.e. gist) declining at a slower rate, and judgments based on situational memory (i.e. inferences from a relevant knowledge schema) remaining highly stable over time.

Schema-based interpretations of such findings generally hold that as a result of abstraction and integration processes, verbatim traces of the original information are either lost or become integrated with schematic-gist information (Alba & Hasher 1983; but see Brewer & Nakamura 1984). Subsequent memory performance is then based on reconstructive processing of gist. By contrast, Brainerd & Reyna's fuzzy-trace theory (Brainerd & Reyna 1992, Reyna & Brainerd 1995) contends that during encoding, verbatim and gist traces are formed in parallel, creating a hierarchy of independent representations at varying levels of precision. In accessing these representations, because of the superior memorability and accessibility of gist, especially over time, rememberers tend to choose the highest possible level that complies with task demands. In support of the verbatim-gist independence, Reyna & Kiernan (1994) showed that subjects sometimes falsely recognize gist representations despite having accurate verbatim memories. Using tests of stochastic dependence, they found that correct recognition of verbatim information and misrecognition of gist were independent.

Fuzzy-trace theory has also gained impetus as a theoretical framework that could explain a variety of memory errors, such as false recognition and recall in list learning and postevent misinformation effects (see below), verbal overshadowing (Schooler 1998), and some complex age-related differences [see e.g. the special issue of *Journal of Experimental Child Psychology* edited by Liben (November 1998)].

Other distinctions have been explored that seem to parallel the verbatim-gist distinction. For example, Posner & Keele (1970) found that memory for the unpresented prototype of classified dot patterns was more stable over time than memory for the individual studied patterns from which it was abstracted. Also, Dorfman & Mandler (1994) examined memory for categorical information in terms of the tendency of false recognition to be made from the same category as the studied target words (e.g. falsely recognizing "canary" when "sparrow" was actually presented). Retention of categorical information was found to exhibit a milder rate of forgetting than the retention of the studied target itself (see also Koutstaal & Schacter 1997). Coll & Coll (1994), using a three-level hierarchy, found that commission errors shift from those that preserve fine/specific attributes to those that preserve more coarse/general attributes as retention interval increases. Recently, however, A Pansky & A Koriat (in preparation) found bidirectional shifts in the memory for items presented at either subordinate (e.g. sports car) or superordinate (e.g. vehicle) levels of a hierarchy toward the intermediate basic level (e.g. car). These symmetrical shifts (including the surprising trend toward instantiation) were especially pronounced following a one-week retention interval.

A different realization of the fine-coarse distinction is in terms of remembering the particular item versus remembering attribute information. For example, subjects have been found to correctly identify the emotional-evaluative tone of a word even when verbatim recall of the word failed (Schacter & Worling 1985). A Koriat, E Edry & G de Marcas (submitted for publication) recently found that subjects have equal access to the evaluative, potency, and activity attributes of unrecalled words, both when this access is measured by explicit attribute identification, and when it is inferred from the nature of the commission errors made. Access to partial information was found to decline less steeply with retention interval than the recall of the full word.

The distinction between access to item information and access to attribute information tends to support current views of memory in which the memory representation of an event is seen to consist of a pattern of features that are bound together to different degrees (e.g. Johnson 1997, Schacter et al 1998). Such views permit greater variability in the completeness of memory retrieval than that provided by the verbatim versus gist distinction.

Schema-Based Effects on Memory Accuracy

Schema theory represents perhaps the most general framework for correspondence-oriented memory research. It has been used by both cognitive and social psychologists to explain a wide array of phenomena concerning accuracy and distortion in both perception and memory.

Drawing on the seminal work of Bartlett (1932), schema theory holds that what people remember is the result of an interaction between the input information and pre-existing "schemas," i.e. generic knowledge structures or expectancies that are developed through experience. Schemas have been shown to affect the correspondence between the input and remembered material in a variety of ways at different stages in the memory process. Thus, the research described here (see reviews by Alba & Hasher 1983, Brewer & Nakamura 1984) demonstrates the correspondence-oriented focus on qualitative rather than only quantitative memory changes, and the type of constructive and reconstructive mechanisms assumed to underlie them.

In their well known review, Alba & Hasher (1983) identified the effects of four basic types of schema processes that occur during encoding: selection, abstraction, interpretation, and integration, as well as a fifth process that may occur during remembering, reconstruction. Most of these effects concern ways in which memory can go wrong.

Selection   Strictly speaking, selection effects concern the amount of remembered information rather than its accuracy: Information that can be assimilated into an active schema is more likely to be remembered than schema-irrelevant information. For example, in the absence of a relevant activated schema or background knowledge during encoding, information is encoded less efficiently and is less likely to be recalled (e.g. Bransford & Johnson 1972). Also, information that is more central to an activated schema will be recalled better than information that is less central (e.g. Johnson 1970). However, inconsistent (rather than irrelevant) information is often remembered better than schema-consistent information (e.g. Davidson 1994). Different accounts have been proposed for this seeming anomaly (see e.g. Erdfelder & Bredenkamp 1998, Stangor & McMillan 1992). Note that although schema-based selection would seem to affect memory quantity performance rather than accuracy per se, unlike the traditional view of omission errors under the storehouse view, schema-based omissions are inherently biased in the direction of greater compatibility with the operative schemas.

Abstraction   Abstraction effects are similar to selection effects in that specific details of the input event or material are lost as they are encoded into the various "slots" of the generic schematic representation (e.g. Mandler 1979). For example, the finding that people tend to remember the semantic content or gist of textual messages rather than their verbatim format has been taken to imply the operation of schema-based abstraction processes, although other types of explanations have also been proposed (see Memory for Gist versus Detail). Abstraction effects, like selection effects, involve a reduction in the amount of encoded and subsequently remembered information. However, they can also play a critical role in memory error and distortion: When asked to remember details that are not available in the schematic representation, people may try to reconstruct the missing details using schema-based inference processes at the time of remembering (Bartlett 1932, Neisser 1967). These reconstructions replace the original input information with generic information from the schema, yielding commission errors or schema-consistent distortions.

Interpretation   Unlike selection and abstraction, interpretation effects involve actual changes and additions to the input information during encoding: Activated schematic knowledge is used to make inferences and suppositions that go beyond the actual input event, which then become incorporated as part of the event's memory representation. For example, subjects may falsely remember the presence of a hammer after reading a passage about a person pounding a nail (Johnson et al 1973) or they may falsely remember information that is consistent with their general knowledge about a famous person (Dooling & Cristiaansen 1977). Similar inferences have been observed for nonlinguistic information: For example,

Intraub et al (1998) report a "boundary extension" illusion, in which observers remember seeing a greater expanse of the scene than was actually shown. Interestingly, subjects are unable to avoid the illusion even when explicitly instructed to do so (Intraub & Bodamer 1993). Both linguistic and nonlinguistic interpretation effects have been found to increase with retention interval, apparently due to progressive loss of memory for detail (see Brewer & Nakamura 1984).

Integration   Integration effects result from the combining of various pieces of information into a unified schematic whole, either during (e.g. Bransford & Franks 1971) or subsequent to (e.g. Loftus et al 1978) the initial encoding. Integration subsequent to initial encoding has attracted a great deal of attention in the context of post-event misinformation effects (see below). It has also been implicated in explaining "hindsight bias" or the "knew-it-all-along" effect (Fischhoff 1977, Hawkins & Hastie 1990), in which the exposure to new information regarding an event's outcome distorts one's memory for one's initial estimation of its likelihood. Integration effects in general, and misinformation effects in particular, have generated a heated debate concerning the underlying mechanisms (see Ayers & Reder 1998). One basic issue is whether these effects derive from actual changes to the memory representation, or from inferential processes operating at the time of remembering (see Stahlberg & Mass 1998 for an extension of this issue to the hindsight bias).

Reconstruction   The schema effects considered so far are assumed to derive from constructive processes operating during the encoding of information. In contrast, reconstructive processes operating at the time of remembering use "whatever details were selected for representation and are still accessible together with general knowledge to essentially fabricate what might have happened" (Alba & Hasher 1983:204). In their review, Alba & Hasher noted that "the consensus is that reconstruction is quite rare, and occurs only under special circumstances" (1983:204). Since that time, the consensus seems to have changed.

Ross and colleagues (see Ross 1989) have shown in several elegant studies how people's personal memories are biased by their implicit theories of stability and change. For example, people's belief that their attitudes are stable over time tends to bias recall of their earlier attitudes in the direction of greater consistency with their current attitudes (e.g. McFarland & Ross 1987, Ross et al 1981; and see, e.g. Bahrick et al 1996). Furthermore, people's expectancy that an attribute should change over time can also bias recall: Students led to believe in the effectiveness of a study skills course remembered their initial self-evaluated study skills as being lower, and their subsequent test grades as being higher, than did students in a control condition (Conway & Ross 1984; see Hirt 1990 for similar results in a laboratory study).

Many theorists allow the coexistence of both reconstructive and reproductive (i.e. direct retrieval) memory processing (e.g. Bahrick 1984, Brewer 1986, Hall 1990), and some, in fact view the choice between them as being under the control of the rememberer (e.g. Reder 1987, Ross 1989, Winograd 1994). Hirt et al (1995) found that whereas subjects who encoded the information under comprehension or impression-formation instructions exhibited a substantial expectancy-driven bias in recall, those encoding the information under verbatim recall instructions did not. Furthermore, the degree of this difference increased with retention interval, supporting the view that reconstructive inference is particularly likely when the memory representation is weak (Brewer & Nakamura 1984; see Hirt et al 1998 for other moderators of reconstructive processing).

Accuracy motivation may also moderate constructive and reconstructive processing. Ross, for instance, suggests that "people can choose to engage in relatively effortless, theory-guided recall or a more effortful and extensive memory search" (1989:355), and this choice will depend, among other things, on how motivated people are to accurately reproduce the details (see also Winograd 1994). In line with this idea, a wide range of results in social cognition lead to a view of the perceiver/rememberer as "a motivational tactician, choosing among a number of possible strategies, depending on current goals" (Fiske 1993:172).

Source Monitoring

We now turn to several bodies of research that have gained prominence in recent years, beginning with work on source monitoring. Memory for the source of information attracted little attention in traditional quantity-oriented research (but see Winograd 1968). In that context, "experimental work has largely taken the item or event as the unit of analysis rather than attempting to assess the relative availability for complex events of various phenomenal qualities" (Johnson et al 1996:137). In contrast, the source monitoring framework, developed by Johnson and her associates (see Johnson et al 1993), stresses the processes involved in determining the origin of memories, such as how, when, and where a certain memory was acquired. They argued that virtually all memory distortions (other than omissions) involve source monitoring failures—taking mental experiences to be something they are not (Johnson et al 1996). Indeed, there has been a growing appreciation of the central role that source monitoring plays in memory accuracy, and ideas from the source monitoring framework have been incorporated in explaining various memory distortions, such as false recalls and recognition in list learning, postevent misinformation effects, source amnesia, and confabulations.

Memory For Source   According to the source monitoring framework (Johnson 1997), in discriminating the origin of information, subjects take advantage of the fact that mental experiences from different sources (e.g. perception versus imagination) differ on average in their phenomenal qualities (e.g. visual clarity and contextual details). These diagnostic qualities can support a rapid, heuristically-based source monitoring, but sometimes more strategic, deliberative processes may be needed. Both types of processes require setting criteria for making a judgment, and procedures for comparing activated information to the criteria.

Several results suggest that source memory may be independent of item (or occurrence) memory (e.g. Lindsay 1990). Glisky et al (1995), who tested elderly adults, demonstrated a double dissociation between item memory (found to be sensitive to medial temporal lobe functioning) and source memory (found to be sensitive to frontal lobe functioning). Koriat et al (1991) found that self-performed actions yielded better occurrence memory (old-new recognition) but inferior context memory (in which room had the task been performed) than other-performed actions, suggesting that memories for self-performed actions are less contextualized than memories for other-performed actions, and may be more susceptible to source confusions. Johnson et al (1996) found that having subjects focus on how they felt when hearing a person make certain statements yielded better old-new recognition but lower source-accuracy scores than having them focus on how the speaker felt.

The source monitoring framework emphasizes the importance of binding—the integration of the various features of an event into a coherent whole (see also Schacter et al 1998). Deficient binding may result in source confusions, as when words said by one speaker are attributed to a different speaker (Ferguson et al 1992). It may also lead to memory conjunction errors (e.g. Reinitz et al 1996), as when the components of different stimuli (e.g. "instruct" and "consult") are recombined and result in false recognition ("insult").

Factors Contributing to Source Confusions According to Johnson (1992, 1997), source confusions may arise because the activated information during retrieval is incomplete or ambiguous, and/or because the processes responsible for attributing information to sources are imperfect. For example, divided attention or emotional self focus during encoding have been found to impair source monitoring (Craik & Byrd 1982, Johnson et al 1996), presumably because they disrupt binding. High perceptual similarity between two sources, as well as similarity in the encoding processes engaged may also result in source confusions (Dodson & Johnson 1996, Ferguson et al 1992). Although thinking about a perceived event after it has happened helps maintain its visual details, thinking about imagined events also increases their vividness, and may therefore result in impaired reality monitoring for these events (Suengas & Johnson 1988). Goff & Roediger (1998) found that the more times subjects imagined an unperformed action, the more likely they were to recollect having performed it.

During testing, conditions that interfere with reviving an episode (e.g. discrepancy between study and test contexts) or with decision and inference processes (e.g. time pressure, divided attention) also tend to impair source monitoring. This is also true for conditions that encourage lax criteria (Dodson & Johnson 1993).

Reducing or Escaping Source Confusions   The fact that people know at one time that a certain piece of information was imagined, dreamt, or fictional does not prevent them from later attributing it to reality (Durso & Johnson 1980, Finke et al 1988, Johnson et al 1984). In general, however, manipulations that facilitate or encourage the encoding of distinctive, item-specific features help reduce source confusion (e.g. Johnson et al 1995). During testing, source monitoring can be improved by having subjects make source discriminations, which presumably encourage more stringent decision criteria (Dodson & Johnson 1993; see also Jacoby et al 1989c). Multhaup (1995) found this manipulation to be particularly effective with the elderly.

Age Differences   Several studies indicate that young children are particularly deficient in distinguishing between memories of real and imagined events (see Ceci 1995). Elderly adults too have particular difficulty in remembering contextual information. Spencer & Raz's (1995) meta-analysis indicates a stronger age decline in memory for context than in memory for content. This pattern results in a greater rate of "decontextualized" memories in old age, which can lead to deficient source monitoring.

Illusions Stemming from Fluency Misattributions

Closely related to the source-monitoring framework is the attributional view of Jacoby, Kelley, and their associates (see Jacoby et al 1989b, Kelley & Jacoby 1998), which has been used to examine a variety of memory illusions and misattributions. Their work demonstrates the intimate link between perceiving and remembering, and particularly between perceptual illusions and memory illusions, thus bringing to the fore some of the unique aspects of the correspondence metaphor of memory.

Illusions of Memory   According to the attributional view of memory, the subjective experience of familiarity does not derive directly from the retrieval of a memory trace, but results from the unconscious attribution of fluent processing to the past (Jacoby & Dallas 1981, Johnston et al 1985). Fluent processing of a stimulus is enhanced by its previous presentation, and when fluency is attributed to the past, it gives rise to a veridical recognition. However, fluent processing can also be produced by other factors. In that case, an illusion of familiarity may ensue if fluency is misattributed to the past. Whittlesea (1993) manipulated fluency by priming the target words before they appeared in the recognition test. Primed words were more likely to be falsely recognized than nonprimed words. Fluency can also be enhanced by perceptual manipulations: Showing a brief preview of a test word immediately prior to presenting the word in full view for a recognition memory test increased the likelihood that new (as well as old) words would be judged "old" (Jacoby & Whitehouse 1989). Similarly, when the visual clarity of words at test was varied, new words were more likely to be judged as old when they were visually clear (Whittlesea et al 1990).

Whittlesea & Williams (1998) refined Jacoby's view of familiarity, arguing that it is not fluency per se but rather fluent processing occurring under unexpected circumstances that gives rise to feelings of familiarity. Although unstudied pseudohomophones (e.g. PHRAWG) were processed less fluently than unstudied words, they yielded more false recognitions (when read aloud by the subject), presumably because the unexpected fluency produced by their meaning was attributed to past experience.

Fluency emanating from the characteristics of the task can also be misattributed to stable characteristics of one's memory. Winkielman et al (1998) found that subjects asked to recall 12 childhood events gave poorer judgments of their memory than subjects asked to recall 4 childhood events. Although the former subjects recalled three times more events than the latter, retrieval fluency was the critical factor affecting metamemory judgments.

Misattributions of Memory   Memory misattributions are essentially the converse of the memory illusions just described. These occur when fluency emanating from the prior presentation of the stimulus is incorrectly attributed to a current characteristic of the stimulus, resulting in perceptual illusions. For example, when previously heard and new sentences were presented at test under white noise, the noise was judged to be lower for old than for new sentences (Jacoby et al 1988). Also, when subjects judged the duration of presented words, previously read or generated words were judged as occurring for longer durations than new words (Masson & Caldwell 1998).

Memory can also be misattributed to nonphysical qualities of the stimulus: Anagrams were judged to be easier for others to solve when their solution words had been presented earlier than when they had not (Kelley & Jacoby 1996; see also Kelley 1999). Also, in the "mere exposure effect," previous exposure to a stimulus leads to more positive attitudes regarding that stimulus (e.g. Bornstein & D'Agostino 1994). Similarly, in the "illusory truth effect" (see Begg et al 1996), sentences are more likely to be judged as true when they have been presented previously than when they are new. In the "false fame effect" (Jacoby et al 1989a), nonfamous names tend to be judged more often as famous when they have been presented earlier than when they are new.

Escaping Illusions and Misattributions of Memory   Illusions of memory can be avoided when subjects become aware of the manipulations of the physical characteristics of the stimulus. For example, visual clarity does not affect judgments of oldness when subjects know that clarity is being manipulated (Whittlesea et al 1990). Also, when subjects are fully aware of the preview of the test word (Jacoby & Whitehouse 1989), the tendency to judge that word as old is eliminated. Similarly, when subjects in the Winkielman et al (1998) study mentioned earlier were informed that most people find it difficult to recall 12 childhood events, their memory judgments did not differ from those of subjects who were asked to recall 4 events (but see Lindsay & Kelley 1996).

Misattributions of memory, i.e. falsely attributing fluency to a current characteristic of the stimulus, are more difficult to escape. For example, warning people about the influence of a prior presentation of a sentence on the experienced intensity of a background noise did not eliminate the effects of misattribution (Jacoby et al 1992; see also Whittelsea et al 1990). However, such misattributions can be avoided by recollecting the actual source of familiarity: The false fame effect is eliminated when people initially read the list of nonfamous people under full rather than under divided attention, presumably because they can recollect the prior presentation of those names when making fame judgments (Jacoby et al 1989c). Hence, several factors that disrupt recollection (but do not affect the influence of familiarity), such as divided attention, a short deadline for retrieval, or old age, may increase the likelihood of misattributions of memory (Kelley & Jacoby 1998).

False Recall and Recognition

In the past several years there has been a dramatic increase in the study of false memories, spurred in part by real-life controversies. False memory reports can be induced in a variety of ways for a wide range of materials (see Lampinen et al 1998). In this section we focus on laboratory studies examining commission errors in list learning.

An unprecedented wave of studies on spontaneously occurring false recalls was sparked recently by the influential work of Roediger & McDermott (1995). In a paradigm adapted from Deese (1959), a study list is presented, composed of words associated to a critical, nonpresented word. This critical word tends to falsely intrude in a subsequent recall test. The new Deese-Roediger-McDermott (DRM) paradigm has yielded a wealth of findings in studying false recognition and false recall. Variants of this paradigm have also emerged, including the use of words or pictures belonging to the same semantic category (e.g. Brainerd & Reyna 1998b, Koutstaal & Schacter 1997) and the use of visual stimuli representing stereotypical scenes from which typical exemplars have been removed (Miller & Gazzaniga 1998).

What is interesting about the DRM paradigm is that it affords the study of many aspects of memory accuracy and error within a simple, list-learning paradigm. The critical difference from the traditional use of this paradigm lies first, in the focus on the content of the information that is remembered and second, in the focus on commission errors, which have traditionally been treated as a mere nuisance (Roediger 1996). The progress in this area has been primarily empirical, and we summarize the main findings here.

Rate of False Memory Response   An interesting finding concerns the high rate of false memories obtained with this paradigm. In immediate testing, rate of false recalls is either comparable to or slightly lower than that of recalling studied words from the middle of the list (assumed to reflect retrieval from long-term memory; Roediger & McDermott 1995, Schacter et al 1996), whereas in a delayed test, it is actually higher than that of studied items (McDermott 1996).

McDermott & Roediger (1998) included the critical word in half of the presented lists but not in the other half, and for each list, subjects judged whether the critical word had occurred or had not occurred in the list. Although judgments were generally accurate, the false alarm rate for the critical nonpresented words was still substantial (0.38).

Factors Affecting False Memory   The rate of false memories varies with a number of factors. Robinson & Roediger (1997) found the occurrence of false recalls and recognitions to increase with the number of associated words presented in the list. In fact, as the number of studied associates increased, the probability of recalling a study item decreased, whereas that of recalling the nonpresented item increased. The inclusion of unrelated items, however, depressed veridical recall, but left false recall unaffected. Tussing & Greene (1999) observed that repetition of list words increased recognition of these words but did not increase false recognition of semantically related lures.

With regard to study and test conditions, rate of false recognition was not affected by either level of processing or repetition, but was found to be lower when learning was incidental (Tussing & Greene 1997). Divided attention either during study or during test was also found to attenuate false recognition (Payne et al 1996b). These results contrast with those obtained in studies indicating stronger illusions of memory under divided attention (e.g. Jacoby et al 1989c).

An intriguing observation is that there are dramatic and reliable differences between different lists in the extent to which they induce false recall and recognition. These differences are correlated only slightly with differences in correct recall and recognition (see Roediger et al 1998).

Persistence Over Time   False memories in the DRM paradigm are remarkably persistent: In comparing the results for an immediate test with those for a test given two days later, the proportion of accurate recall declined over time, whereas false recall actually tended to increase (McDermott 1996). A similar pattern was obtained for false recognition (Brainerd & Reyna 1998a, Payne et al 1996a). Toglia et al (1999) observed that the recall of the nonpresented words remained high over a three-week period, whereas that of studied words revealed the typical decrement.

Multiple study and test opportunities caused the level of false recall to decline over trials, but it remained high even after five study-test trials, suggesting that subjects did not completely edit out the erroneous responses (McDermott 1996). On the other hand, when multiple tests followed a single presentation, the proportion of false recalls increased over repeated tests, but there was no increase in the proportion of veridical recalls (Payne et al 1996a). Once again, false memories appear to be more robust than true memories.

How Can False Memories Be Avoided?   Gallo et al (1997) found that warning subjects about the false recognition effect attenuated, but did not eliminate, false recognitions (see also McDermott & Roediger 1998). An interesting finding by Seamon et al (1998) is also relevant: False recognition of the critical word was obtained even under conditions in which subjects were unable to discriminate studied from unrelated nonstudied words, suggesting that false recognition can stem from nonconscious activation of semantic concepts during list presentation.

There is evidence suggesting that distinctive processing of individual items can help reduce false memories. Thus, false recognition rates can be reduced by presenting each word together with a picture representing it (Israel & Schacter 1997, Schacter et al 1999), by visual rather than auditory presentation (Smith & Hunt 1998), by having subjects rate the pleasantness of the words during study (Smith & Hunt 1998), or by instructing them to remember the order of presentation (Read 1996).

Qualitative Characteristics of True and False Memories   Do true and false memories differ phenomenologically? When know/remember judgments (Tulving 1985) were solicited, true and false recognitions were equally likely to give rise to remember responses (Payne et al 1996a, Roediger & McDermott 1995, Schacter et al 1996). Also, subjects have been found to be relatively confident in their false recalls, claiming to have detailed and vivid memories of these items (e.g. Payne et al 1996a). From the perspective of the subject, such false memories are as real as their memories for studied words.

In experiments that probed the qualitative characteristics of true and false memories, Norman & Schacter (1997) found that both types of memories were predominantly associated with access to semantic/associative information (see also Mather et al 1997). However, true memories were associated with greater access to perceptual/contextual information than were false memories.

Individual Differences   Older adults sometimes exhibit as much or more false recognition of related lures, despite showing lower levels of true recognition (Norman & Schacter 1997; see also Koutstaal & Schacter 1997, Schacter et al 1999, Intons-Peterson et al 1999). This may stem from the tendency of older adults for generic, indistinct encoding (Rabinowitz et al 1982), or from their tendency to rely on gist-based processing during memory testing (Tun et al 1998). Henkel et al (1998) proposed that both aging and damage to medial temporal and frontal brain regions are associated with impairment in binding features into complex memories, and in accessing contextual features of memories.

Theoretical Accounts   Several accounts of the DRM phenomena have been considered (see Roediger et al 1998). Unfortunately, however, there is still no consensus even about the proper conceptual framework within which false recognition and recall phenomena can be analyzed. Perhaps the most prominent candidate is fuzzy-trace theory, which assumes that false recall or recognition of the critical lures relies on a gist representation (see Brainerd & Reyna 1998a, Payne et al 1996a). It would seem, though, that elements from different frameworks may be needed because some of these (e.g. implicit associative response activation; see Nelson et al 1998) can explain the activation of false memories, whereas others (e.g. source monitoring or memory attributions) are needed to explain their confusion with studied items as well as their phenomenological characteristics.

Misleading Postevent Information

The seminal work of Loftus and her associates (Loftus 1979a) on the contaminating effects of misleading postevent information (MPI) was instrumental in stirring up interest in memory accuracy and distortion in general, and in reconstructive aspects of memory in particular. This work coalesced with the move toward the investigation of real-life memory phenomena (Neisser 1978), and with the increased interest in societal and legal issues concerning false memory (see Ayers & Reder 1998, Belli & Loftus 1996). Whereas some of the early studies were primarily designed to document the memory impairment that ensues from misinformation, later investigations were more concerned with the underlying mechanisms, and led to important theoretical distinctions.

In the prototypical MPI paradigm, participants are exposed to an event, are later misinformed about some detail, and are finally given a forced recognition test requiring a choice between the original and suggested detail. This manipulation has been shown to result in an apparently impaired memory for the original detail, testifying for the malleability of memory (Loftus 1979a). Variations of this procedure have been used that differ either in the format of the memory test or in the order in which the target information and suggested information are presented (see Ayers & Reder 1998, Wright & Loftus 1998).

Conditions that Affect the Magnitude of the Misinformation Effect The MPI effect is stronger (*a*) with peripheral than with central details (Cassel & Bjorklund 1995, Heath & Erickson 1998), (*b*) when retention interval is longer (Belli et al 1992, Higham 1998; but see Windschitl 1996), (*c*) when the misleading information is presented in the context of a question (possibly encouraging imagination of the original event) than when presented in the context of a statement (Zaragoza & Lane 1994), and (*d*) particularly when the question is presented in a presupposition format ("what was the color of the . . . "; Fiedler et al 1996) rather than in an open format.

Zaragoza & Mitchell (1996) found that repeated exposure to postevent suggestions augmented the MPI effect, particularly when contextual variability between the repeated exposures was increased. Presumably, the variability impaired subjects' ability to discriminate the precise source of the suggestion (Mitchell & Zaragoza 1996). Zaragoza & Lane (1994) found a stronger MPI effect when subjects were encouraged to engage in active mental reconstruction of the original series of events before testing. Ayers & Reder (1998) suggest that the conditions most conducive to the misinformation effects are those in which processing the misleading information requires retrieval of the originally presented information, thus encouraging integration of the original and interpolated misinformation.

Quality of Memories   Loftus et al (1989) found that falsely recognized suggested items were as quickly accessed and as confidently held as items that were actually presented. Studies by Zaragoza and her colleagues (e.g. Zaragoza & Mitchell 1996) also indicate that false reports of the misleading detail are often endorsed with strong confidence. Weingardt et al (1994) found that subjects were willing to bet nearly as much money on the authenticity of postevent items as they were on event items. Complementing these findings, memory for the suggested information is often accompanied by "remember" rather than "know" responses (Roediger et al 1996, Wright & Stroud 1998).

Escaping Misinformation Effects   The effects of misinformation are difficult to escape. Subjects continue to report misinformation despite warnings that some or even all of the details suggested to them were wrong or misleading (Belli et al 1994, Lindsay 1990). Furthermore, they exhibit MPI effects even when they are able to correctly identify the misleading items as originating from the postevent narrative in a separate source-monitoring test (Dodson & Johnson 1993, Lindsay & Johnson 1989). Fiedler et al (1996) observed that even propositions that are initially rejected as false can intrude into memory. Ackil & Zaragoza (1998) further found that after one week, subjects reported false memories for details that they were coerced to fabricate immediately after viewing the original videotape. Apparently, these results are not due simply to subjects being forced to provide a response. Higham (1998), using a source-monitoring test, found that subjects misattributed misleading information to the original event even when given the option of reporting that they could not remember the source.

Nevertheless, the size of the MPI effect can sometimes be reduced by encouraging subjects to make fine-grained source discriminations rather than yes/no recognition responses, the latter apparently inducing familiarity-based responding (e.g. Dodson & Johnson 1993; see Source Monitoring).

Age Differences   Children have been found to be particularly prone to misleading information (for reviews, see Bruck & Ceci 1999, Ceci & Bruck 1993). They also seem to be particularly sensitive to characteristics of the misinformer, such as age and credibility (Ceci et al 1987, Lampinen & Smith 1995). In addition, Cohen & Faulkner (1989) found that elderly participants were more often misled by misleading information and were also more confident in their erroneous responses than were younger participants.

Theoretical Accounts of the Misinformation Effect Despite the wealth of research on the misinformation effect, there is still debate concerning its explanation. Several accounts have been proposed (see Ayers & Reder 1998), attributing the misinformation effects to trace alteration (Loftus 1975, 1979b), task demands/strategic effects (McCloskey & Zaragoza 1985), blocked memory access (Bekerian & Bowers 1983), source confusion (Lindsay & Johnson 1989), activation-based effects (Ayers & Reder 1998), and reliance on gist (Brainerd & Reyna 1998a). The attempt to discriminate between these accounts has led to important insights that go beyond the specific phenomena of the MPI paradigm.

Real-Life False Memories and Their Creation

False Memory in Real-Life Situations Clearly, the issue of memory accuracy stands at the heart of the recent debate over the authenticity of recovered memories, particularly memories of childhood sexual abuse (see e.g. Brown et al 1998, Conway 1997, Loftus 1993). Clinical psychologists typically attribute recovered memories to a specialized mechanism of repression that maintains memories of traumatic events outside consciousness, and assume that repressed memories can be recovered even after many years, usually in the course of therapy (see e.g. Courtois 1997, Loftus 1993). Many cognitive psychologists, however, doubt these assertions (Lindsay 1998, Loftus et al 1994), pointing instead to evidence suggesting that false memories may arise from normal reconstructive memory processes.

A survey of the issue of recovered memory is beyond the scope of this review. What is clear, though, is that the social and legal implications of this issue have been a significant driving force behind the recent interest in memory accuracy. Furthermore, this issue has helped crystallize two specific questions that have won experimental attention. The first concerns the processes that are likely to give rise to false memories. For example, many discussions share the belief that "ironically, the techniques that are effective in aiding recall are the very ones that can distort memory" (Pennebaker & Memon 1996:383). The second is whether some diagnostic cues exist that can help evaluators differentiate true memories from false memories (Loftus 1997, Schooler et al 1997). We shall briefly mention some pertinent findings.

Memory Implantation Although several anecdotal reports as well as more systematic investigations of false memories occurring in real-life situations have appeared in the scientific literature (e.g. Crombag et al 1996), studies that attempted to experimentally implant memories for events that did not happen are of greater theoretical significance. In one study (Loftus & Pickrell 1995), young adults were asked to try to remember childhood events that had been reported by a relative. Among these were three events that had actually occurred and one that had not (e.g. being lost in a shopping mall). About 25% of the subjects recalled the false event in two follow-up interviews. Using a similar procedure, Hyman et al (1995) succeeded in implanting some rather unusual childhood memories in college students. While none of the subjects recalled the false event in the first interview, in the second and third interviews 18% and 25% of the subjects, respectively, said that the event had occurred.

A more extreme demonstration is provided by Spanos and his colleagues (see Spanos 1996:107). Subjects were implanted with a false memory that allegedly occurred one day after their birth (a colored mobile hanging over their crib). They were then administered procedures that they were told would enable them to remember events as far back as birth. A majority of the subjects were susceptible to these memory-planting procedures, reporting infant memories of the target event. Almost half of them insisted that these were real memories, not fantasies.

Pezdek et al (1997) found that false memories are more likely to be implanted if relevant script knowledge exists in memory, and if the memories are plausible. As with the MPI paradigm, children appear to be particularly suggestible (see Bruck & Ceci 1999). For example, Ceci et al (1994a) conducted repeated interviews with 3–6-year-old children about events that had happened and those that had not. Across interviews, about 30%–40% of the children claimed to remember the false events, and provided considerable detail about them.

These studies show that false memories can be implanted. Two procedures that are particularly conducive to the creation of false memories are imagination instructions and repeated testing. Whereas the former procedure is common in psychotherapy as a means of encouraging the recovery of repressed memories, the latter is common in police investigations.

Imagination Inflation   Garry et al (1996) demonstrated what they called imagination inflation: Asking subjects to imagine childhood events in detail increased their ratings that the event actually occurred during childhood. One explanation is that imagination enhances familiarity, which is then misattributed to past experience (see also Goff & Roediger 1998). Hyman et al (1995) showed that repeatedly thinking about whether a nonoccurring childhood event had happened increased the likelihood that subjects believed that it actually happened. Subsequent studies (Hyman & Billings 1998, Hyman & Pentland 1996) indicated that instructions to imagine an event, whether true or false, increased the likelihood of its later remembrance. These results suggest that the creation of false childhood memories involves both memory reconstruction and errors in source monitoring.

Repeated Testing   Findings with the DRM paradigm indicate that repeated testing can enhance both true and false memories (Roediger et al 1998). Indeed, both true and false memories have been found to be similarly affected by various experimental manipulations (Toglia et al 1999). Shaw (1996) also observed that postevent questioning increased subjects' confidence in both incorrect and correct responses.

Testing manipulations, however, may also destroy the balance between true and false memories when such testing is applied selectively to the memory of false events. Ackil & Zaragoza (1998) observed that false memories could be created simply by forcing subjects to answer questions about events that clearly never happened. Using the MPI paradigm, Roediger et al (1996) found that the magnitude of the misinformation effect was much greater if the subjects had received a prior test on the misinformation items than if they had not. Prior testing also increased the likelihood that the misinformation items would be classified as remembered rather than as known. Finally, in an eyewitness memory situation, Schooler et al (1988) found that forcing subjects to provide a false response on a first recognition test (e.g. by having them choose between two false lures), impaired performance on a later memory test.

The finding that repeated questioning—particularly when forced—can foster false memories has important implications for police investigations. A similarly important finding is that of Kassin & Kiechel (1996) that corroboration of an event by another person can instill false memories: Innocent subjects who initially denied the charge of damaging a computer, tended to admit that charge, express guilt, and provide confabulatory details when a confederate said that she had seen them perform the action.

Distinguishing True and False Memories   Can the authenticity of memory for a past event be diagnosed by external observers? Loftus & Pickrell (1995) found that subjects used more words when describing true memories and expressed more confidence in these memories than in false memories. They also rated the true memories as being somewhat more clear, although the clarity of false memories tended to rise from first to second interview. However, Ceci et al (1994a,b) showed videotapes of children's memory interviews to both clinical and research psychologists, who could not discriminate accounts of real and fictional events. Loftus notes, "without corroboration, there is little that can be done to help even the most experienced evaluator to differentiate true memories from ones that were suggestively implanted" (Loftus 1997:55; see also Schooler et al 1997).

In sum, as research on the experimental implantation of false memory continues, we are reminded that "achieving a better scientific understanding of memory distortion is not merely a matter of theoretical concern, but has significant implications for the day-to-day lives of many members of our society" Schacter (1995:20).

Eyewitness Memory

Much of the work surveyed in the preceding sections on false or implanted memories and misinformation effects is either inspired by or directly tied to issues concerning the accuracy of eyewitness testimony. As was pointed out, the impact of that work extends far beyond the arena of eyewitness testimony, into mainstream experimental research and theorizing. Beyond these bodies of research, however, several other topics of investigation have been motivated primarily by practical concerns relating to issues of eyewitness accuracy. We will briefly mention four of these: questioning procedures, lineup identification, children's testimony, and the confidence-accuracy relationship.

Questioning Procedures   It has long been known that the form in which a question is put to a witness can have a strong effect on the quality of the answer (e.g. Binet 1905). Building on these early insights and the more recent work on the potential contaminating effects of postevent misinformation, a basic distinction has been drawn between open-ended, free narrative forms of questioning, and more specific, directed, and recognition formats. Open-ended questioning consistently yields more accurate but less complete reports than the more directed forms (see e.g. Hilgard & Loftus 1979; but see Koriat & Goldsmith 1994, 1996b for a somewhat different interpretation of this difference). Particularly harmful to memory accuracy are leading questions, which, either by form or by content, suggest the desired answer to the witness (see Bruck & Ceci 1999). Thus, the general recommendation is that witnesses should first be allowed to tell their story in their own words before being subjected to more directed questioning, and that even then, greater faith should be placed in the accuracy of the former type of testimony (e.g. Fisher & Geiselman 1992).

The lessons of both eyewitness and traditional memory research have been incorporated into the "cognitive interview" (CI), developed by Fisher and Geiselman (Fisher 1999, Fisher & Geiselman 1992). The CI procedure includes a variety of memory enhancing mnemonics (e.g. context reinstatement, multiple perspectives) and communication techniques designed to increase the amount of accurate information obtained from witnesses. In a recent meta-analysis of over 50 experiments (Kohnken et al 1999), the CI consistently elicited more correct information than a standard police or other control interview (mean effect size of $d = 0.87$), with a much smaller increase in incorrect information ($d = 0.28$). Thus, more information can be obtained while maintaining equivalent output-bound accuracy rates (~85%), but the accuracy rates themselves cannot be improved (Fisher 1995; see also Memon & Stevenage 1996 and responses by Fisher 1996, Goldsmith & Koriat 1996 regarding the proper measure of memory accuracy in this context).

Lineup Studies   Another central topic in eyewitness research is person identification from police lineups and photospreads (for reviews, see Wells 1993, Wells et al 1998). Here the issue of accuracy is paramount, as false eyewitness identifications appear to be the primary cause of the conviction of innocent people. In a sobering examination of 40 cases of persons convicted of serious crimes (all of whom had served time in prison, several on death row, until recent DNA analyses proved their innocence), Wells et al (1998) observed that fully 36 (90%) involved false eyewitness identifications. One basic reason for such errors may lie in witnesses' use of a relativistic judgment process, in which they tend to identify the person from the lineup who most resembles their representation of the suspect (Wells 1993, Wells et al 1998). Thus, rates of false identification increase dramatically when only one member of the (culprit-absent) lineup fits the general description of the culprit (e.g. Wells et al 1993), but decrease when witnesses are explicitly warned that the culprit might not be present in the lineup (e.g. Steblay 1997), and when the members of the lineup are presented sequentially rather than simultaneously (e.g. Sporer 1993). In fact, it appears that many witnesses who correctly identify the culprit in a culprit-present lineup, would simply identify another suspect when the culprit's photo is removed (Wells 1993). These and other findings have important implications for actual police procedures (see Wells et al 1998).

Both interrogation and lineup procedures involve system variables (Wells 1978) over which the judicial system and law enforcement agencies have some amount of control. In addition, estimator variables have to do with characteristics of the event, the suspect, or the witness, which could potentially be used to gauge the reliability of testimony or identifications in particular cases (see e.g. Deffenbacher 1991). Of these, the two most researched areas involve developmental differences in memory accuracy (children versus adults) and the diagnosticity of witnesses' confidence for the accuracy of their testimony.

Children's Testimony   The increased importance of child testimony in the courtroom, combined with common doubts regarding its reliability, have spurred a large amount of experimental work dealing with various aspects of children's memory and its accuracy relative to that of adults. Without making any attempt to capture the wealth of issues and findings, we note that unlike the fairly consistent findings that children tend to remember less information than adults (Schneider & Bjorklund 1998), it appears that no general statement can be made about the relative accuracy of children's and adults' memory reports (see e.g. Poole & White 1993). Instead, the focus has been on identifying various potential moderator variables. One of these is type of questioning: As noted earlier, children tend to be more suggestible than adults and hence more susceptible to leading questions and other forms of postevent misinformation (see Goodman & Schaaf 1997), though the findings suggest that this is true primarily for children of preschool age (see Bruck & Ceci 1999 for a recent review). Children may be particularly sensitive to other aspects of the questioning as well, implying the need for special interviewing techniques (see e.g. Walker & Hunt 1998).

Confidence-Accuracy Relation   Another key issue in eyewitness research concerns the confidence-accuracy (CA) relation. On the one hand, it has been found that the single most important factor affecting jurors' beliefs about the credibility of eyewitnesses is the confidence they express in their identification choices (e.g. Lindsay 1994, Penrod & Cutler 1995). On the other hand, numerous studies and meta-analyses have indicated that the CA relation for witness identifications is either nonexistent or quite weak, though the findings vary (see Wells 1993). Proposed moderator variables include the optimality of encoding, storage, and retrieval conditions (Deffenbacher 1980), methodology, realism, and experience in self-evaluation (Wells 1993, Wells & Murray 1984), choosers (witnesses making a positive identification) versus non-choosers (Sporer et al 1995, Read et al 1998), response options (e.g. the option to respond "don't know"), retention interval, and variability in encoding conditions (Lindsay et al 1998, Read et al 1998). Thus, under some conditions, the CA correlations can be fairly high (overall $r = 0.41$ for choosers in the meta-analysis by Sporer et al 1995 and as high as $r = 0.72$ in Read et al 1998). Moderate to high CA correlations are also common in studies of memory for witnessed details, particularly using within-subject rather than between-subject designs (e.g. Perfect et al 1993; but see Smith et al 1989) and recall rather than recognition testing (e.g. Robinson & Johnson 1996, Stephenson et al 1986; see also Koriat & Goldsmith 1996c).

More objective and perhaps more reliable markers of accurate testimony have also been sought. Some of the studied candidates are response time (Robinson et al 1997), response consistency (Fisher & Cutler 1995), output order (Schwartz et al 1998), and the processes leading to an identification (Dunning & Stern 1994).

Autobiographical Memory

Autobiographical memory concerns memory for one's past life events and experiences. Although Tulving (1983) suggested that the terms 'autobiographical memory' and 'episodic memory' be treated as equivalent, students of autobiographical memory generally disagree (e.g. Brewer 1986, 1996; Conway 1990, 1996). One of the reasons for this disagreement is that "the term 'episodic memory' has come to refer to a particular way of studying memory" (Conway 1990:4), that is, the quantity-based, list-learning paradigm in which discrete and unconnected stimuli that have little personal significance for the subject are used. Autobiographical memory, in contrast, is "specific, personal, long-lasting, and (usually) of significance to the self-system. Phenomenally it forms one's personal life history" (Nelson 1993:8). Thus, meaning, self-reference, temporal-spatial context, and the various phenomenological correlates of "recollective experience" (Brewer 1996) are of fundamental interest in autobiographical memory research.

Diary Studies   The issue of accuracy has been a driving force in the study of autobiographical memory, but a major hurdle is how to determine the veridicality of the memory reports. One technique is the diary method, in which subjects (sometimes the researchers themselves) keep a diary of daily events and are later tested for their memory of these events. Barclay & Wellman (1986), for example, had subjects keep diaries during a 4-month period, followed by old-new recognition tests up to 2½ years later. Although hit rates were quite high (decreasing from an average of 95% after a 3-month interval to 79% after 31 months), false recognition of altered records averaged about 40% after 3 months, and reached rates of over 50% by the end of one year. False recognition of completely fabricated items was relatively stable over time, averaging 22% over the retention intervals. The high false-recognition rates were shown to depend on the semantic similarity between the foil and original entries (Barclay 1986). Subsequent findings (see Barclay 1993) indicated that people tend to falsely identify foils that are congruent with their general self perceptions, and that mood congruency between foil and actual events leads to higher rates of false recognitions. These and similar results were taken to support a strong reconstructive view of autobiographical memory, in which "acquired autobiographical self-knowledge drives the reconstruction of plausible, but often inaccurate, elaborations of previous experiences. Memories for most everyday life events are therefore transformed, distorted, or forgotten" (Barclay 1986:89). This view has also been put forward forcefully by Neisser (1981, 1984).

Brewer (1986, 1996), in contrast, has proposed a "partially" reconstructive view, in which "recent personal memories retain a relatively large amount of specific information . . . but that with time, or under strong schema-based processes, the original experience can be reconstructed to produce a new nonveridical personal memory" (1986:44; see also Bahrick 1998, Thompson et al 1996). A qualitative analysis of the recall errors for recorded events in his "beeper" study led Brewer (1988a,b) to argue against Barclay's strong reconstructive view: Although over 50% of the provided recall responses (excluding omissions) were in error, 90% of these were more likely to be retrieval errors than reconstruction errors. In fact, only 1.5% of the wrong responses were "true errors" containing information that was in conflict with the original recorded information.

Phenomenological Data   Work on autobiographical memory also illustrates a heightened concern with the phenomenal correlates of accurate and inaccurate remembering (see Brewer 1992). For example, Brewer (1988a,b) found that the strength of imagery differed markedly for seven different types of correct and erroneous recall responses. Interestingly, memory binding errors in which subjects mistakenly combined aspects of events that occurred at slightly different times yielded levels of visual imagery comparable to those of correct recall responses, indicating that from the rememberer's point of view, these items are much like correct recalls. In contrast, recall statements classified as "correct inferences" tended to be associated with moderate to weak imagery, suggesting that these responses are based on generic self-schema representations (but see Holmes et al 1998 for evidence of strong visual imagery associated with schema-based processing). In another diary study, Conway et al (1996) also reported phenomenological differentiation for true and false recognitions of recorded events and thoughts.

Flashbulb Memories   Studies of "flashbulb memories" (e.g. Conway 1995, Winograd & Neisser 1992) have also focused on memory accuracy and its phenomenological correlates. People report unusually vivid and detailed memories of the circumstances in which they heard about an extraordinary event. The idea that such flashbulb memories, with their live quality, are unique, representing a biological "now print" mechanism (Brown & Kulik 1977) has generated an intense debate (e.g. McCloskey et al 1988). A major point of contention is their presumed accuracy (Neisser 1982). Thus, for example, on the morning after the *Challenger* shuttle explosion, Neisser & Harsch (1992), had subjects record how they first heard the news of it. When the subjects were tested over 2 and a half years later, most described their memories as visually vivid; yet none was entirely correct, and fully half of them were substantially wrong in their memory reports. Moreover, neither vividness nor confidence ratings, which were both quite high, correlated significantly with accuracy. Using a similar methodology, McCloskey et al (1988) found somewhat higher, but still imperfect, accuracy for memories of hearing about the *Challenger* explosion.

Despite the growing number of flashbulb memory studies, the issue of whether flashbulb memories are inherently more accurate than other types of autobiographical memories is still under debate. Some researchers have maintained that there is good reason to distinguish flashbulb memories from other types of autobiographical memory, as long as several preconditions, such as personal importance, consequentiality, emotion, and surprise are met (Brown & Kulik 1977, Conway 1995, Pillemer 1990). Others have pointed out that ordinary memories can also be accurate and long lasting if they are highly distinctive, personally significant (McCloskey et al 1988, Weaver 1993), or repeatedly rehearsed (Neisser 1982).

Memory for Temporal Context   It is taken as self-evident that autobiographical memories are bound together by extensive contextual information—who, what, where, and when (e.g. Conway 1996, Thompson et al 1996). Temporal information, however, appears to have a special status and to be represented and processed differently than other aspects of past events. According to the emerging consensus (see e.g. Friedman 1993, Larsen et al 1996), people do not store and retrieve temporal information directly. Rather, they reconstruct the temporal location of past events on the basis of fragments of information remembered about the content of the event (temporal cues) and general knowledge about time patterns (temporal schemata).

The data regarding the accuracy of people's memory for temporal information are intriguing. Although temporal memory is unbiased, in that the average dating error is close to zero (Larsen et al 1996, Rubin & Baddeley 1989), the absolute magnitude of dating errors increases as a linear function of elapsed time, by a constant error (0.10–0.22 days) per elapsed day (see Rubin & Baddeley 1989), similar to what has been found for simple perceptual properties (Larsen et al 1996; cf. memory psychophysics).

Error patterns, however, reveal the reconstructive nature of temporal memory. "Scale effects" occur when temporal accuracy is higher at a more finely grained scale (e.g. the hour of day) than at a more coarsely grained scale (e.g. the week it took place) (e.g. Bruce & van Pelt 1989, Friedman 1987, White 1982), suggesting the use of independent temporal schemata at each level. Independent schemata are also implicated in the "day-of-the-week effect," in which people are often able to localize an event with respect to the day of the week (using a temporal "week schema"), although they are wrong about the absolute date. Hence, dating errors that are multiples of seven days are heavily overrepresented (Thompson et al 1996). "Telescoping effects" involve date estimates that are moved forward from the actual dates toward the present, so that time seems to be compressed (e.g. Bradburn et al 1987, Loftus & Marburger 1983). Such effects occur when the interval from which the events are drawn is known by the rememberer to have distinct boundaries at the end (e.g. last semester), allowing the selective screening of errors beyond the interval (Huttenlocher et al 1990, Rubin & Baddeley 1989).

In sum, many features of correspondence-oriented memory research find clear expression in the study of autobiographical memory: concern with issues of veridicality and error, the propositional, relational, and (self-) referential nature of memory, the active role of the rememberer in constructing the memory report, and the output-bound, qualitative approach to memory assessment.

METACOGNITIVE PROCESSES AND ACCURACY

Discussions of memory errors have brought to the fore a variety of metacognitive operations that mediate memory accuracy. Complementing the reconstructive view, these discussions imply an active rememberer who engages in a variety of inferential and decisional processes that are characteristic of problem solving and decision making (see Burgess & Shallice 1996, Goldsmith & Koriat 1999, Koriat 2000, Koriat & Goldsmith 1998b, Nelson & Narens 1994). Hence, the accuracy of one's memory report is seen to depend heavily on the effectiveness of these processes.

Decisional processes underlying remembering have of course received attention in more traditional approaches to memory, notably in the context of signal-detection theory. Rather than focusing on a single hypothetical dimension of "trace strength," however, current discussions emphasize the multidimensional qualities of phenomenal experience on which the rememberer must operate, such as the know-remember distinction, vividness and clarity, amount of contextual details, and the like. The rememberer is conceived as facing the challenge of interpreting an ambiguous mental record, applying heuristics that are of limited validity, and engaging in a variety of fallible inferential processes (see Johnson 1997). Inferential processes are assumed to operate not only in making decisions on the basis of phenomenal experience, but also in affecting subjective experience itself (Kelley & Jacoby 1998).

Metacognitive processes are implicated at various stages of learning and remembering (Barnes et al 1999, Koriat & Levy-Sadot 1999). However, those operating during remembering are particularly crucial in determining memory accuracy and error. The functions of these processes include specifying the origin of mental experience (Johnson 1997), avoiding the influence of contaminating factors by attributing them to their proper source (Förster & Strack 1998, Whittlesea & Williams 1998), formulating a focused, well circumscribed description of the sought for past event (Koriat 1999, Schacter et al 1998), monitoring the correctness of information that comes to mind (Kelley & Lindsay 1993, Koriat 1993), choosing the proper remembering strategy for the task at hand (Nhouyvanisvong & Reder 1998), regulating the reporting of information according to the incentive for accuracy (Koriat & Goldsmith 1996c), and so forth. Some of these processes were mentioned in the earlier review of accuracy-oriented research. Indeed, Norman & Schacter (1996) have argued that monitoring and retrieval processes are so intertwined that they should not even be distinguished.

In this section we focus somewhat narrowly on monitoring the correctness of information that comes to mind, and the ensuing decision regarding how and whether to report the information. Evidence collected thus far indicates that people can generally monitor the correctness of their memories and that this ability is critical for the strategic regulation of memory accuracy.

Monitoring the Correctness of One's Own Knowledge: Metamemory Illusions

While metamemory judgments have been shown to be moderately accurate in predicting memory performance (Schwartz 1994), recent work on the bases of metacognitive judgments has disclosed several conditions that produce a dissociation between memory and metamemory (Bjork 1999). These appear to stem from the fact that metacognitive judgments rely on error-prone heuristics (Benjamin & Bjork 1996, Koriat & Levy-Sadot 1999). Benjamin et al (1998), for instance, had subjects answer general-information questions and make judgments of learning (JOL) about the likelihood of recalling the answer at a later time. Whereas the probability of eventual recall increased with the time spent retrieving the answer, JOLs in fact decreased with retrieval latency. Benjamin et al proposed that JOLs are generally based on retrieval fluency, which may sometimes be misleading.

Similarly, feeling of knowing judgments (FOK) about the likelihood of recalling or recognizing a solicited piece of information in the future have been assumed to be based on the overall familiarity of the memory question (Schwartz & Metcalfe 1992) or on the extent to which it brings some fragmentary clues to mind (Koriat 1993). Because subjects often fail to specify the source of familiarity or accessibility, irrelevant influences may result in illusions of knowing (Koriat

1998). Thus, for example, advance priming of a recall cue was found to enhance FOK without correspondingly affecting actual recall (Nhouyvanisvong & Reder 1998). In one experimental condition, Koriat (1995) in fact obtained a negative correlation between FOK judgments and actual recognition performance: When subjects failed to provide an answer to a question, they reported inordinately high FOK for specially chosen questions that generally tend to bring a great deal of incorrect information to mind. Similar illusions have been found with confidence judgments that subjects give after reporting an answer: Chandler (1994), for instance, found that when studied pictures were made similar to nontarget foil pictures, they were less likely to be recognized, but the responses were made with stronger confidence than when the target pictures bore no similarity to the non-target pictures.

These metamemory illusions, however, are the exception rather than the rule. By and large, people are successful in monitoring the correctness of their memory. With respect to confidence judgments, the within-subject correlations are often moderate to high (e.g. Koriat & Goldsmith 1996c). These correlations contrast with the generally low confidence-accuracy relation observed using between-subjects designs in eyewitness research (see above).

The Strategic Regulation of Memory Accuracy

People's ability to monitor their own memories is not just of intrinsic interest; it is also a critical component of the strategic regulation of memory accuracy. Koriat & Goldsmith (1994, 1996c; see also Barnes et al 1999) showed that monitoring and control processes operating during memory reporting can have a substantial effect on the accuracy of the reported information. This work derived from the observation that people generally have much more control over the information they report than is typically allowed in laboratory experiments: They can choose which aspects of the event to relate and which to ignore, what perspective to adopt, how much detail to provide, and so forth.

Koriat & Goldsmith focused on one particular type of control, "report option," that is, the option to volunteer or withhold specific items of information (i.e. to respond "don't know"). Their results indicate that people utilize the option of free report to enhance the accuracy of the information that they report, by screening out incorrect candidate answers. Moreover, given stronger incentives for accuracy, people enhance their accuracy performance even further. The basic dynamic, however, is a quantity-accuracy trade-off: Accuracy can be enhanced by withholding answers, but because the screening process is not perfect, this generally comes at a cost in quantity performance.

According to Koriat & Goldsmith's (1996c) model, under conditions of free reporting, people utilize a monitoring process to assess the probability that each piece of information that comes to mind is correct, and a control process that volunteers information only if its assessed probability passes a preset threshold. The setting of the threshold is sensitive to competing demands for quantity and accuracy. Thus, memory performance depends not only on overall retention (memory), but also on two additional metacognitive factors: the setting of the control threshold (response criterion) and monitoring effectiveness, that is, the validity of the assessed probabilities for distinguishing correct and incorrect information. Although the implications of the first factor are well known from signal detection theory, Koriat & Goldsmith's model brings out the critical role of monitoring effectiveness: When monitoring effectiveness is poor, the selective screening of answers does not enhance accuracy much or at all (Koriat & Goldsmith 1996c: Experiment 2). As monitoring effectiveness improves, however, greater increases in memory accuracy can be achieved, and at a lower cost in memory quantity performance. Thus, according to the model, only when monitoring effectiveness is perfect can eyewitnesses tell "the whole truth" and also "nothing but the truth" as they are often sworn to do in courtroom situations. Based on their theoretical framework, Koriat & Goldsmith (1996b,c) proposed a general assessment procedure (QAP, Quantity Accuracy Profile) that isolates the unique contributions of retention, monitoring, and control to free-report accuracy and quantity performance.

The theoretical framework developed for report option has recently been extended to encompass a further means of subject control, control over "grain size," that is, the level of generality or detail of the information that is reported (Goldsmith & Koriat 1999, Goldsmith et al 1998). Here too, results indicate that people utilize monitoring and control processes to strategically regulate the grain size of the information they report, attempting to achieve a balance between competing demands for accuracy versus informativeness (see also Yaniv & Foster 1997).

In sum, metacognitive processes have gained increasing prominence in correspondence-oriented research, both as a means by which people validate the accuracy of their own memories, and as mediators of memory accuracy performance itself. As such processes become more and more integrated into memory research and theorizing, they may help increase our understanding of memory phenomena in such varied domains as aging (Hasher et al 1999), brain damage (Schacter et al 1998), children's memory (Bruck & Ceci 1999, Koriat et al 1999, Schneider & Bjorklund 1998), scholastic testing (Koriat & Goldsmith 1998b), survey research (Schwarz 1999), and more.

TOWARD A PSYCHOLOGY OF MEMORY ACCURACY: METHODOLOGICAL, THEORETICAL, AND METATHEORETICAL ISSUES

This chapter brought together a broad array of correspondence-oriented memory research. The work reviewed exhibits a great deal of heterogeneity in the kind of phenomena investigated, in the questions asked, and in the experimental paradigms employed. Nevertheless, it has in common a concern with the faithfulness of memory. This concern is the essential core of the correspondence metaphor outlined in the introduction. Throughout the review we attempted to show how the various ingredients of this metaphor are reflected in accuracy-oriented memory research and theorizing.

In an earlier analysis, Koriat & Goldsmith (1996b) showed how the correspondence metaphor can help bind together the "what" (phenomena, questions, theories), "how" (experimental paradigms, assessment procedures), and "where" (naturalistic versus laboratory research contexts) of accuracy-oriented memory research. In concluding this chapter, we first focus on the "what" and "how" aspects, ending with a discussion of the place of memory accuracy and error within a broader functional perspective.

Correspondence-Oriented Research: Phenomena, Questions, and Theories

Clearly, the phenomena of interest under the correspondence metaphor differ from those that have occupied traditional memory research. The storehouse metaphor, with its associated quantity-oriented approach, has directed researchers' thinking toward such aspects of memory as storage capacity, the internal architecture of the store, the transfer of units from one department to another, competition between units, and of course, information loss. This metaphor, with its associated list-learning paradigm, has also dictated the type of phenomena investigated, for instance, the effects of list length, retention interval, item spacing, serial order, and so forth.

In contrast, the correspondence-oriented research reviewed here has concentrated on phenomena that pertain to the congruence between what one remembers and the actual input, focusing on the content of what is recalled or recognized, rather than on the mere amount of remembered information. Thus, in addition to omissions, correspondence-oriented research stresses a wealth of other ways in which what is remembered can depart from what actually occurred. These can roughly be classified into five categories: (*a*) falsely recalling or recognizing items or events that never happened (e.g. false recognition and recall, false memory, confabulation, schema- or script-based importation); (*b*) wrongly recombining features or elements that belong to different objects or events (e.g. illusory conjunctions, fluency misattributions, source confusions, misinformation effects); (*c*) distorting remembered information (e.g. leveling, sharpening, increased symmetry or consistency, clutter and perspective effects, telescoping, retrospective bias); (*d*) remembering information at a different level of generality or abstraction than the actual input (e.g. remembering gist versus detail, substituting the actual input with a different exemplar from its category or from a different hierarchical level); and (*e*) metamemory errors (e.g. over- or underconfidence, illusions of knowing or not knowing).

The common preoccupation with issues of accuracy and error cuts across the various research domains reviewed here and is also reflected in the kind of questions that are asked: How faithful is memory and what are the factors that affect its faithfulness? What is the origin of memory errors and what are their underlying mechanisms? To what extent are the same processes responsible for both accuracy and error? To what extent are memory errors escapable or preventable? What are the distinctive phenomenological correlates of true and false memories? What cues can be used to diagnose the authenticity of memories? Are there systematic individual and group differences in memory accuracy and error? And, more generally, what does the occurrence of memory errors and distortions tell us about the functioning of memory in general? Of course, not all of these questions find expression in any one domain. However, it is encouraging to see that the increasing similarity of questions across different domains and paradigms has helped promote cross-talk between them.

Nevertheless, a major challenge for the psychology of memory accuracy lies in the integration of the various threads of memory accuracy research within a general conceptual framework. At present, there is a great deal of diversity in the status of theoretical development across the various domains. Whereas in some domains (e.g. eyewitness research, DRM), theory development has lagged behind data collection, possibly because of the practical importance of the empirical findings as such, in other domains (e.g. MPI, schema theory, spatial memory) research is more theory driven. In addition, many of the theoretical accounts are local and ad hoc, closely tied to the specific phenomena investigated, and the specific paradigms used.

Recently, however, there is increasing awareness of the need for more general conceptual frameworks that can handle several threads of accuracy-oriented research together. This has led to attempts to extend some of the existing frameworks to account for new phenomena. Thus, beyond the schema-reconstructive framework, which is perhaps the most general of the accuracy-oriented frameworks, Brainerd & Reyna's (1998a) fuzzy-trace theory, Johnson's (1997) source monitoring framework, and Jacoby and Kelley's (Jacoby et al 1989b) attributional approach are increasingly applied to explain phenomena for which they were not originally developed. These extensions appear to be paving the way for the emergence of more integrative, correspondence-oriented theories. Importantly, there seems to be a growing consensus about some of the theoretical notions that could serve as basic building blocks for the development of such theories: assimilation and interpretation during encoding, reconstructive inferences and heuristics, top-down processes in recollection, binding, distinctiveness, source monitoring, attribution and misattribution, the phenomenal quality of recollective experience, metacognitive judgments, control processes, and response criteria. These theoretical notions clearly differ from those included in the traditional quantity-oriented memory theories.

One recently proposed integrative framework that incorporates many of these notions is Schacter et al's (1998) constructive memory framework (CMF), which emphasizes feature binding, pattern separation, pattern completion, retrieval focusing, and criterion setting as mediators of accurate or inaccurate memory. Representations of events are conceptualized as patterns of features, and retrieval involves a process of pattern completion through spreading activation. When a match is produced, a decision must be made whether the information delivered to awareness constitutes an episodic memory of the sought for target. Memory errors can result from deficient binding of the features comprising a specific episode, insufficient source information, or from setting a lax criterion in source monitoring. Errors can also result from inadequate separation of the episodic feature pattern from other similar patterns, or from unfocused retrieval, when people fail to construct a sufficiently focused retrieval cue, thus activating extraneous information.

An important feature of the CMF is that it is neuropsychologically informed. In fact, neuropsychological investigation is currently providing a fertile meeting ground for researchers working within different accuracy-oriented paradigms. The data derived from such investigations have been found valuable in organizing the various patterns of memory error and distortion, and may ultimately help researchers home in on a set of core theoretical constructs for accuracy-oriented memory theorizing (see e.g. Moscovitch 1995, Norman & Schacter 1996).

Experimental Paradigms and Assessment Procedures

In discussing the implications of the correspondence metaphor, we noted earlier that one obstacle to the development of a psychology of memory accuracy stems from the difficulty of devising experimental paradigms and assessment procedures that can be applied across a broad spectrum of accuracy-oriented research. This difficulty derives from the fact that the correspondence metaphor admits many ways in which memory for the past can deviate from veridicality. Hence, experimental paradigms and memory measures tend to be tailored to individual facets of correspondence and miscorrespondence.

In the context of the storehouse metaphor, the availability of such all-purpose measures as percent recall and percent recognition provided quantity-oriented research with standard operational definitions that could be used to study the characteristics of "memory": to derive forgetting curves and to examine the general effects of such variables as study time, divided attention, level of processing, and so forth. Can we envisage the development of parallel all-purpose measures of memory correspondence that would allow a similar study of factors affecting the overall faithfulness of memory?

In their analysis, Koriat & Goldsmith (1996b) specified two types of assessment procedures that can, with certain limitations, yield global measures of memory correspondence. The first, the wholistic type of correspondence measure, can be illustrated within the domain of visual-spatial memory. Waterman & Gordon (1984) measured the correspondence between a studied and a remembered map by assessing the fit between each memory reproduction and the actual map: They first applied transformations to neutralize differences in rotation, translation, and scale, and then computed an overall "distortion index" in terms of the squared distances between corresponding points on the output map and the criterion map. Also, Siegel (1981) used multidimensional scaling techniques to compare remembered distances between landmarks on a campus route against the actual distances.

Such overall goodness of fit measures, however, are much more difficult to apply to verbal reconstructions of real-life events. Such events can submit to a multitude of different descriptions, each of which may be accurate in some sense (Neisser 1981). Thus, in order to specify the relevant dimensions of correspondence or miscorrespondence, how they are to be measured and integrated and at what level of grain, an assessment model is needed that incorporates functional assumptions regarding both the reasons for remembering and the particular circumstances of the memory report. Furthermore, Neisser (1996) points out that even when such a measure is developed, it may be global but not all-purpose: A "weighted accuracy score" developed for use in a flashbulb memory study concerning the *Challenger* explosion (Neisser & Harsch 1992) had to be adapted for use in a different study concerning an earthquake disaster (Neisser et al 1991).

One option that circumvents some of these problems is to rely on subjective global accuracy ratings. In a clever variation on this idea, Wells & Turtle (1988) assessed the faithfulness of memory for faces in terms of the proportion of correct target recognitions that could be achieved by independent judges on the basis of the subjects' memory reports alone.

The second type of global correspondence measure is more similar to the traditional item-based measures. In the context of item-based assessment, overall measures of memory quantity and accuracy can be derived in terms of the input-bound and output-bound proportion correct, respectively: The input-bound quantity measure (e.g. percent recall), traditionally used to tap the amount of studied information that can be recovered, reflects the likelihood that each input item is correctly recalled or recognized. The output-bound accuracy measure (e.g. percent of recalled items that are correct), in contrast, reflects the likelihood that each reported item is in fact correct. Hence, it uniquely evaluates the dependability of memory—the extent to which remembered information can be trusted to be correct. Essentially, whereas the input-bound measure holds the person responsible for what he or she fails to report, the output-bound measure holds the person accountable only for what he or she does report.

The conceptual distinction between these two measures is sometimes missed. To illustrate, consider the issue of the dependability of children's eyewitness testimony. The finding that children remember less information than adults (Schneider & Bjorklund 1998) is relevant if we are concerned that a child witness may not be able to provide as much information from memory as an adult. However, if our concern lies in whether or not we can trust what the child does report to be true, then the proper measure is output-bound accuracy; the quantity measure is in fact irrelevant. Focusing on the output-bound accuracy measure can allow researchers to answer questions such as, Is the testimony provided by children, or by elderly adults, less dependable? What are the underlying mechanisms (e.g. monitoring and control) that account for such differences? How might dependability be improved? Does the dependability measure change over time in the same way as the quantity measure? An interesting finding in this regard is that whereas quantity performance typically decreases as a decelerating function of retention interval, output-bound accuracy may in fact remain constant (Ebbesen & Rienick 1998). Clearly, in order to get a more complete picture of memory performance, it is necessary to consider both accuracy and quantity in tandem (see e.g. Koriat & Goldsmith 1996b,c; QAP procedure, mentioned earlier; and see the discussion regarding the evaluation of the cognitive interview technique, also mentioned earlier). Unfortunately, not many studies have done this.

In sum, it is possible to derive correspondence measures that reflect the overall faithfulness of a memory report. However, this derivation requires the researcher either to ignore the specific content of the remembered information (output-bound accuracy) or to derive and justify a complex assessment model. Hence, most experimental work on memory accuracy has used dependent measures that are tailored to the task at hand and to the targeted facet of correspondence. Such measures are sometimes narrowly content-specific: for example, the likelihood of recalling a particular critical word in the DRM paradigm, or the likelihood of reporting having seen a "yield" sign in a misinformation paradigm.

Beyond the issues just discussed, however, there is still another issue concerning the proper criterion for measuring memory correspondence. Should memory reports be validated against reality or against perception, i.e. the initially encoded representation of reality? Newby & Ross's argument is representative: "Perhaps researchers should evaluate memory against an individual's initial representation of the event, rather than against the supposed objective stimulus. After all, we cannot ask more of memory than that recollections reflect the person's original reality; otherwise, we confuse differences in memory with differences in perception" (1996:205). This issue is complex (see Koriat & Goldsmith 1996d, 1998a), and we do not propose to resolve it here. Many theories of course, most notably schema theory, hold that changes that occur during the initial encoding are part and parcel of memory itself. On the other hand, efforts should continue to be made to isolate errors and distortions that are due to the initial perception and encoding from those that occur at later stages (see e.g. Alba & Hasher 1983; and see Spatial Memory and Distortion).

Memory Accuracy and Error Within a Broader Functional Perspective

The work on memory accuracy reviewed in this chapter could leave a pessimistic impression about the general faithfulness of human memory. As Schacter recently noted with regard to some of the deficiencies of memory, these "could easily lead one to question the wisdom of Mother Nature in building such a seemingly flawed system" (1999:196). But is the memory system really as flawed as it seems? First, as Schacter (1999) points out, although some of the memory deficiencies may appear to reflect flaws in the system design, they are in fact by-products of otherwise adaptive features of memory. Thus, for example, remembering the gist rather than the details of stories and events, or inferring information not actually present in the input, is often what is required. Indeed questions about the functional utility of memory cannot be settled in the abstract because the same processes that contribute to adaptive functioning in one case may be detrimental in another.

Second, while memory may in fact be more fallible and malleable than is assumed by the layman, it seems to us that the interest in memory illusions and false memories, spurred perhaps by real life problems, has led researchers to selectively focus on the dark side of memory, resulting in a somewhat biased picture.

In fact, a great deal of the work on memory errors defies the principle of representative design advocated by Brunswik (1955; see also Gibson 1979, Gigerenzer et al 1991). Consider, for example, false recalls in the DRM paradigm. The results indicate that the rate of false recall is roughly equal to that of accurate recall. If this finding were representative of memory performance in general, that is, if information retrieved were as likely to be correct as wrong, then memory would be totally useless. However, this high rate of false memories for particular items was obtained under deliberately contrived conditions. Under more representative conditions, a recalled item is much more likely to be correct than false (Koriat 1993). Thus, the output-bound accuracy of free recall has been found to be remarkably high across many experiments, typically ranging from 0.85 to 0.95. That is, over 85% of the items typically recalled are correct (Fisher 1995; Koriat 1993; Koriat & Goldsmith 1994, 1996c). Fisher reached the conclusion that "when uninfluenced by external pressure, most of the recollections that we bring to conscious awareness are accurate" (1995:741).

Interestingly, this conclusion holds true even for the contrived circumstances of the DRM paradigm when the entire recall output is considered. In McDermott's (1996) Experiment 1, for example, in which lists of 15 words were used, rates of correct and false recall were 0.58 and 0.44, respectively, for an immediate test, and 0.50 and 0.46, respectively, for a delayed test. Fortunately, McDermott also reported data on extralist intrusions, which averaged 0.22 and 0.32 words, respectively, for each list (McDermott 1996:216). On the basis of these data, we calculated the output-bound accuracy for each test: It amounted to 0.93 for the immediate test and 0.91 for the delayed test! Thus, recall responses in the DRM paradigm are remarkably dependable overall.

Nevertheless, unrepresentative as they may be, memory errors deserve experimental attention for two reasons: First, even if they are relatively rare, the devastating consequences of some memory errors demand a better understanding of when, how, and why they occur. Second, errors are particularly useful in providing insight about the normal processes underlying memory. This has also been the main motivation behind the study of illusions in perception (Gregory 1980).

Finally, however, memory clearly does not operate in a vacuum, and hence memory accuracy and error may need to be analyzed in the context of the personal and social goals of the rememberer. In fact, several authors have argued that memory should be evaluated in terms of its utility (e.g. Neisser 1996, Winograd 1994). This pragmatic view of memory, which has gained prominence in social psychology (Fiske 1993, Swann 1984), entails the idea that "accuracy is not absolute, it depends on one's purpose" (Fiske 1993:156). Thus, Neisser's (1996) proposal that remembering should be seen as a form of purposive doing, resonates well with Fiske's (1992) assertion that "thinking is for doing" in social cognition. In general, the issue of accuracy has been examined within a much wider range of perspectives in social psychology than in cognitive memory research (e.g. Kruglanski 1989). This has proven valuable both in evaluating the accuracy of social judgments, and in studying their underlying processes. Perhaps the time has come for memory researchers to devote more attention to the place of accuracy and error within a broader functional framework (Neisser 1997, Schacter 1999, Winograd 1994).

ACKNOWLEDGMENTS

The preparation of this chapter was supported by a research grant from ZEIT Foundation Ebelin and Gerd Bucerius. We wish to thank Ravit Levy-Sadot for her valuable comments.

Visit the Annual Reviews home page at www.AnnualReviews.org.

LITERATURE CITED

Ackil JK, Zaragoza MS. 1998. Memorial consequences of forced confabulation: age differences in susceptibility to false memories. *Dev. Psychol.* 34:1358–72

Alba JW, Hasher L. 1983. Is memory schematic? *Psychol. Bull.* 93:203–31

Algom D. 1992. Memory psychophysics: an examination of its perceptual and cognitive prospects. In *Psychophysical Approaches to Cognition,* ed. D Algom, pp. 444–513. Amsterdam: Elsevier/North-Holland

Allport GW, Postman LJ. 1945. The basic psychology of rumor. *Trans. NY Acad. Sci.* 8:61–81

Ayers MS, Reder LM. 1998. A theoretical review of the misinformation effect: predictions from an activation-based memory model. *Psychonom. Bull. Rev.* 5:1–21

Bahrick HP. 1984. Replicative, constructive, and reconstructive aspects of memory: implications for human and animal research. *Physiol. Psychol.* 12:53–58

Bahrick HP. 1998. Loss and distortion of autobiographical memory content. In *Autobiographical Memory: Theoretical and Applied Perspectives,* ed. CP Thompson, DJ Herrmann, pp. 69–78. Mahwah, NJ: Erlbaum

Bahrick HP, Hall LK, Berger SA. 1996. Accuracy and distortion in memory for high school grades. *Psychol. Sci.* 7:265–71

Barclay CR. 1986. Schematization of autobiographical memory. See Rubin 1986, pp. 82–99

Barclay CR. 1993. Remembering ourselves. In *Memory in Everyday Life,* ed. GM Davies,

RH Logie, pp. 285–309. Amsterdam: Elsevier/North-Holland

Barclay CR, Wellman HM. 1986. Accuracies and inaccuracies in autobiographical memories. *J. Mem. Lang.* 25:93–103

Barnes AE, Nelson TO, Dunlosky J, Mazzoni G, Narens L. 1999. An intergrative system of metamemory components involved in retrieval. See Gopher & Koriat 1999, pp. 287–313

Bartlett FC. 1932. *Remembering: A Study in Experimental and Social Psychology.* New York: Cambridge Univ. Press

Begg IM, Robertson RK, Gruppuso V, Anas A, Needham DR. 1996. The illusory-knowledge effect. *J. Mem. Lang.* 35:410–33

Bekerian DA, Bowers JM. 1983. Eyewitness testimony: Were we misled? *J. Exp. Psychol.: Learn. Mem. Cogn.* 9:139–45

Belli RF, Lindsay DS, Gales MS, McCarthy TT. 1994. Memory impairment and source misattribution in postevent misinformation experiments with short retention intervals. *Mem. Cogn.* 22:40–54

Belli RF, Loftus EF. 1996. The pliability of autobiographical memory: misinformation and the false memory problem. See Rubin 1996, pp. 157–79

Belli RF, Windschitl PD, McCarthy TT, Winfrey SE. 1992. Detecting memory impairment with a modified test procedure: manipulating retention interval with centrally presented event items. *J. Exp. Psychol.: Learn. Mem. Cogn.* 18:356–67

Benjamin AS, Bjork RA. 1996. Retrieval fluency as a metacognitive index. In *Implicit Memory and Metacognition*, ed. LM Reder, pp. 309–38. Hillsdale, NJ: Erlbaum

Benjamin AS, Bjork RA, Schwartz BL. 1998. The mismeasure of memory: when retrieval fluency is misleading as a metmnemonic index. *J. Exp. Psychol.: Gen.* 127:55–68

Benson PJ, Perrett DI. 1994. Visual processing of facial distinctiveness. *Perception* 23:75–93

Binet A. 1905. La science du temoignage [The science of testimony]. *Ann. Psychol.* 11:128–36

Bjork RA. 1999. Assessing our own competence: heuristics and illusions. See Gopher & Koriat 1999, pp. 435–59

Bornstein RF, D'Agostino PR. 1994. The attribution and discounting of perceptual fluency: preliminary tests of a perceptual fluency/attributional model of the mere exposure effect. *J. Exp. Psychol.: Appl.* 12:103–28

Bradburn NM, Rips LJ, Shevell SK. 1987. Answering autobiographical questions: the impact of memory and inference on surveys. *Science* 236:157–61

Brainerd CJ, Reyna VF. 1992. Explaining "memory free" reasoning. *Psychol. Sci.* 3:332–39

Brainerd CJ, Reyna VF. 1993. Memory independence and memory interference in cognitive development. *Psychol. Rev.* 100:42–67

Brainerd CJ, Reyna VF. 1998a. Fuzzy-trace theory and children's false memories. *J. Exp. Child Psychol.* 71:81–129

Brainerd CJ, Reyna VF. 1998b. When things that were never experienced are easier to "remember" than things that were. *Psychol. Sci.* 9:484–89

Bransford JD, Franks JJ. 1971. The abstraction of linguistic ideas. *Cogn. Psychol.* 2:331–50

Bransford JD, Johnson MK. 1972. Contextual prerequisites for understanding: some investigations of comprehension and recall. *J. Verbal Learn. Verbal Behav.* 11:717–26

Brewer WF. 1986. What is autobiographical memory? See Rubin 1986, pp. 25–49

Brewer WF. 1988a. Memory for randomly sampled autobiographical events. In *Remembering Reconsidered: Ecological and Traditional Approaches to the Study of Memory*, ed. U Neisser, E Winograd, pp. 21–90. New York: Cambridge Univ. Press

Brewer WF. 1988b. Qualitative analysis of the recalls of randomly sampled autobiographical events. See Gruneberg et al 1988, 1:263–68

Brewer WF. 1992. Phenomenal experience in laboratory and autobiographical memory tasks. In *Theoretical Perspectives on Autobiographical Memory,* ed. MA Conway, DC Rubin, H Spinnler, WA Wagenaar, pp. 31–51. Dordrecht, The Netherlands: Kluwer

Brewer WF. 1996. What is recollective memory? See Rubin 1996, pp. 19–66

Brewer WF, Nakamura GV. 1984. The nature and functions of schemas. In *Handbook of Social Cognition,* ed. RS Wyer Jr, TK Srull, 1:119–60. Hillsdale, NJ: Erlbaum

Brown D, Scheflin AW, Hammond DC. 1998. *Memory, Trauma Treatment, and the Law.* New York: Norton

Brown R, Kulik J. 1977. Flashbulb memories. *Cognition* 5:73–99

Bruce D, van Pelt M. 1989. Memories of a bicycle tour. *Appl. Cogn. Psychol.* 3:137–56

Bruck M, Ceci SJ. 1999. The suggestibility of children's memory. *Annu. Rev. Psychol.* 50:419–39

Brunswik E. 1955. Representative design and probabilistic theory in a functional psychology. *Psychol. Rev.* 62:193–217

Burgess PW, Shallice T. 1996. Confabulation and the control of recollection. *Memory* 4:359–411

Byrne RW. 1979. Memory for urban geography. *Q. J. Exp. Psychol.* 31:147–54

Cassel WS, Bjorklund DF. 1995. Developmental patterns of eyewitness memory and suggestibility: an ecologically based short-term longitudinal study. *Law Hum. Behav.* 19:507–32

Ceci SJ. 1995. False beliefs: some developmental and clinical considerations. See Schacter 1995, pp. 91–125

Ceci SJ, Bruck M. 1993. Suggestibility of the child witness: a historical review and synthesis. *Psychol. Bull.* 113:403–39

Ceci SJ, Crotteau-Huffman ML, Smith E, Loftus EF. 1994a. Repeatedly thinking about a non-event: source misattributions among

preschoolers. *Consciousness Cogn.* 3:388–407

Ceci SJ, Loftus EF, Leichtman MD, Bruck M. 1994b. The possible role of source misattributions in the creation of false beliefs among preschoolers. *Int. J. Clin. Exp. Psychol.* 42:304–20

Ceci SJ, Ross DF, Toglia MP. 1987. Suggestibility of children's memory: psycholegal implications. *J. Exp. Psychol.: Gen.* 116:38–49

Chandler CC. 1994. Studying related pictures can reduce accuracy, but increase confidence, in a modified recognition test. *Mem. Cogn.* 22:273–80

Cohen G, Faulkner D. 1989. Age differences in source forgetting: effects on reality monitoring and on eyewitness testimony. *Psychol. Aging* 4:10–17

Coll R, Coll JH. 1994. Memory trace development along a coarse-to-fine dimension: a study supporting a progressively finer attributes theory. *Curr. Psychol.: Dev. Learn. Pers. Soc.* 13:60–76

Conway M, Ross M. 1984. Getting what you want by revising what you had. *J. Pers. Soc. Psychol.* 47:738–48

Conway MA. 1990. *Autobiographical Memory: An Introduction.* Milton Keynes, UK: Open Univ. Press

Conway MA. 1991. In defense of everyday memory. *Am. Psychol.* 46:19–26

Conway MA. 1995. *Flashbulb memories. Essays in Cognitive Psychology.* Hove, UK: Erlbaum

Conway MA. 1996. Autobiographical memory. In *Memory,* ed. EL Bjork, RA Bjork, pp. 165–94. San Diego, CA: Academic

Conway MA, ed. 1997. *Recovered Memories and False Memories.* Oxford, UK: Oxford Univ. Press

Conway MA, Collins AF, Gathercole SE, Anderson SJ. 1996. Recollections of true and false autobiographical memories. *J. Exp. Psychol.: Gen.* 125:69–95

Conway MA, Gathercole SE, Cornoldi C, eds. 1998. *Theories of Memory II.* Hove, Sussex: Psychological Press

Courtois CA. 1997. Delayed memories of child sexual abuse: critique of the controversy and clinical guidelines. See Conway 1997, pp. 206–29

Craik FI, Byrd M. 1982. Aging and cognitive deficits: the role of attentional resources. In *Aging and Cognitive Processes,* ed. FIM Craik, S Trehub, pp. 191–211. New York: Plenum

Crombag HFM, Wagenaar WA, van Koppen PJ. 1996. Crashing memories and the problem of "source monitoring." *Appl. Cogn. Psychol.* 10:95–104

Davidson D. 1994. Recognition and recall of irrelevant and interruptive atypical actions in script-based stories. *J. Mem. Lang.* 33:757–75

Deese J. 1959. On the prediction of occurrence of particular verbal intrusions in immediate recall. *J. Exp. Psychol.* 58:17–22

Deffenbacher KA. 1980. Eyewitness accuracy and confidence: can we infer anything about their relationship? *Law Hum. Behav.* 4:243–60

Deffenbacher KA. 1991. A maturing of research on the behaviour of eyewitnesses. *App. Cogn. Psychol.* 5:377–402

Dodson CS, Johnson MK. 1993. Rate of false source attributions depends on how questions are asked. *Am. J. Psychol.* 106:541–57

Dodson CS, Johnson MK. 1996. Some problems with the process-dissociation approach to memory. *J. Exp. Psychol.: Gen.* 125:181–94

Dooling DJ, Christiaansen RE. 1977. Episodic and semantic aspects of memory for prose. *J. Exp. Psychol.: Hum. Learn. Mem.* 3:428–36

Dorfman J, Mandler G. 1994. Implicit and explicit forgetting: When is gist remembered? *Q. J. Exp. Psychol.* 47a:651–72

Dunning D, Stern LB. 1994. Distinguishing accurate from inaccurate eyewitness identifications via inquiries about decision processes. *J. Pers. Soc. Psychol.* 67:818–35

Durso FT, Johnson MK. 1980. The effects of orienting tasks on recognition, recall, and modality confusion of pictures and words. *J. Verbal Learn. Verbal Behav.* 19:416–29

Ebbesen EB, Rienick CB. 1998. Retention interval and eyewitness memory for events and personal identifying attributes. *J. Appl. Psychol.* 83:745–62

Ebbinghaus H. 1895/1964. *Memory: A Contribution to Experimental Psychology.* New York: Dover

Erdfelder E, Bredenkamp J. 1998. Recognition of script-typical versus script-atypical information: effects of cognitive elaboration. *Mem. Cogn.* 26:922–38

Estes WK. 1997. Processes of memory loss, recovery, and distortion. *Psychol. Rev.* 104:148–69

Ferguson SA, Hashtroudi S, Johnson MK. 1992. Age differences in using source-relevant cues. *Psychol. Aging* 7:443–52

Fiedler K, Walther E, Armbruster T, Fay D, Naumann U. 1996. Do you really know what you have seen? Intrusion errors and presuppositions effects on constructive memory. *J. Exp. Soc. Psychol.* 32:484–511

Finke RA, Johnson MK, Shyi GC. 1988. Memory confusions for real and imagined completions of symmetrical visual patterns. *Mem. Cogn.* 16:133–37

Fischhoff B. 1977. Perceived informativeness of facts. *J. Exp. Psychol.: Hum. Percept. Perform.* 3:349–58

Fisher RP. 1995. Interviewing victims and witnesses of crime. *Psychol. Public Policy Law* 1:732–64

Fisher RP. 1996. Misconceptions in design and analysis of research with the cognitive interview. *Psycholoquy* 7(35) ftp:// ftp.princeton.edu/pub/harnad/Psycoloquy/ 1996.volume.7/psyc.96.7.35.witness-memory.12.fisher

Fisher RP. 1999. Probing knowledge structures. See Gopher & Koriat 1999, pp. 537–56

Fisher RP, Cutler BL. 1995. The relation between consistency and accuracy of eyewitness testimony. In *Psychology, Law, and Criminal Justice: International Developments in Research and Practice,* ed. G

Davies, S Lloyd-Bostock, pp. 21–28. Berlin: De Gruyter

Fisher RP, Geiselman RE. 1992. *Memory-Enhancing Techniques for Investigative Interviewing: The Cognitive Interview.* Springfield, IL: Thomas

Fisher RP, McCauley MR, Geiselman RE. 1994. Improving eyewitness testimony with the cognitive interview. See Ross et al 1994, pp. 245–69

Fiske ST. 1992. Thinking is for doing: portraits of social cognition from Daguerreotype to laserphoto. *J. Pers. Soc. Psychol.* 63:877–89

Fiske ST. 1993. Social cognition and social perception. *Annu. Rev. Psychol.* 44:155–94

Förster J, Strack F. 1998. Subjective theories about encoding may influence recognition: judgmental regulation in human memory. *Soc. Cogn.* 16:78–92

Friedman WJ. 1987. A follow-up to "Scale effects in memory for the time of events": the earthquake study. *Mem. Cogn.* 15:518–20

Friedman WJ. 1993. Memory for the time of past events. *Psychol. Bull.* 113:44–66

Fruzzetti AE, Toland K, Teller SA, Loftus EF. 1992. Memory and eyewitness testimony. In *Aspects of Memory,* ed. MM Gruneberg, PE Morris, 1:18–50. London: Routledge

Gallo DA, Roberts MJ, Seamon JG. 1997. Remembering words not presented in lists: can we avoid creating false memories? *Psychonom. Bull. Rev.* 4:271–76

Gardiner JM, Java RI. 1993. Recognising and remembering. In *Theories of Memory,* ed. AF Collins, SE Gathercole, pp. 163–88. Hove, UK: Erlbaum

Gardiner JM, Ramponi C, Richardson-Klavehn A. 1998. Experiences of remembering, knowing, and guessing. *Consciousness Cogn.* 7:1–26

Garry M, Manning CG, Loftus EF, Sherman SJ. 1996. Imagination inflation: imagining a childhood event inflates confidence that it occurred. *Psychonom. Bull. Rev.* 3:208–14

Gibson JJ. 1979. *The Ecological Approach to Visual Perception.* Boston: Houghton Mifflin

Gigerenzer G, Hoffrage U, Kleinboelting H. 1991. Probabilistic mental models: a Brunswikian theory of confidence. *Psychol. Rev.* 98:506–28

Gilbert DT, Fiske ST, Lindzey G, eds. 1998. *The Handbook of Social Psychology,* Vol. 1. Boston: McGraw-Hill

Glisky EL, Polster MR, Routhieaux BC. 1995. Double dissociation between item and source memory. *Neuropsychology* 9:229–35

Goff LM, Roediger HL III. 1998. Imagination inflation for action events: repeated imaginings lead to illusory recollections. *Mem. Cogn.* 26:20–33

Goldmeier E. 1982. *The Memory Trace: Its Formation and Its Fate.* Hillsdale, NJ: Erlbaum

Goldsmith M, Koriat A. 1996. The assessment and control of memory accuracy: commentary on Memon & Stevenage on witness-memory. *Psycholoquy* 7(23) ftp://ftp.princeton.edu/pub/harnad/Psycoloquy/1996.volume.7/psyc.96.7.23.witness-memory.9.goldsmith

Goldsmith M, Koriat A. 1999. The strategic regulation of memory reporting: mechanisms and performance consequences. See Gopher & Koriat 1999, pp. 373–400

Goldsmith M, Koriat A, Weinberg-Eliezer A, Pansky A. 1998. *The Strategic Regulation of the "Grain Size" of Memory Reports.* Presented at Congr. Eur. Soc. Cogn. Psychol., 10th, Jerusalem, Israel

Goodman GS, Schaaf JM. 1997. Over a decade of research on children's eyewitness testimony: What have we learned? Where do we go from here? *Appl. Cogn. Psychol.* 11:S5–20

Gopher D, Koriat A, eds. 1999. *Attention and Performance XVII. Cognitive Regulation of Performance: Interaction of Theory and Application.* Cambridge, MA: MIT Press

Gregory RL. 1980. Perceptions as hypotheses. *Philos. Trans. R. Soc. London* 290:181–97

Gruneberg MM, Morris PE, Sykes RN, eds. 1988. *Practical Aspects of Memory: Current Research and Issues*. Chichester, UK: Wiley

Hall JF. 1990. Reconstructive and reproductive models of memory. *Bull. Psychonom. Soc.* 28:191–94

Hasher L, Zacks RT, May CP. 1999. Inhibitory control, circadian arousal, and age. See Gopher & Koriat 1999, pp. 651–75

Hawkins SA, Hastie R. 1990. Hindsight: biased judgments of past events after the outcomes are known. *Psychol. Bull.* 107:311–27

Heath WP, Erickson JR. 1998. Memory for central and peripheral actions and props after varied post-event presentation. *Leg. Crimin. Psychol.* 3:321–46

Heider F. 1958. *The Psychology of Interpersonal Relations*. Hillsdale, NJ: Erlbaum

Henkel LA, Johnson MK, De Leonardis DM. 1998. Aging and source monitoring: cognitive processes and neuropsychological correlates. *J. Exp. Psychol.: Gen.* 127:251–68

Higham PA. 1998. Believing details known to have been suggested. *Br. J. Psychol.* 89:265–83

Hilgard ER, Loftus EF. 1979. Effective interrogation of the eyewitness. *Int. J. Clin. Exp. Psychol.* 27:342–57

Hirt ER. 1990. Do I see only what I expect? Evidence for an expectancy-guided retrieval model. *J. Pers. Soc. Psychol.* 58:937–51

Hirt ER, McDonald HE, Erickson GA. 1995. How do I remember thee—the role of encoding set and delay in reconstructive memory processes. *J. Exp. Soc. Psychol.* 31:379–409

Hirt ER, McDonald HE, Markman KD. 1998. Expectancy effects in reconstructive memory: when the past is just what we expected. See Lynn & McConkey 1998, pp. 62–89

Holmes JB, Waters HS, Rajaram S. 1998. The phenomenology of false memories: episodic content and confidence. *J. Exp. Psychol.: Learn. Mem. Cogn.* 24:1026–40

Holyoak KJ, Mah WA. 1982. Cognitive reference points in judgments of symbolic magnitude. *Cogn. Psychol.* 14:328–52

Huttenlocher J, Hedges LV, Bradburn NM. 1990. Reports of elapsed time: bounding and rounding processes in estimation. *J. Exp. Psychol.: Learn. Mem. Cogn.* 16:196–213

Hyman IE, Billings FJ. 1998. Individual differences and the creation of false childhood memories. *Memory* 6:1–20

Hyman IE, Husband TH, Billings FJ. 1995. False memories of childhood experiences. *Appl. Cogn. Psychol.* 9:181–97

Hyman IE Jr, Pentland J. 1996. The role of mental imagery in the creation of false childhood memories. *J. Mem. Lang.* 35:101–17

Intons-Peterson MJ, Best DL. 1998. *Memory Distortions and Their Prevention*. Mahwah, NJ: Erlbaum

Intons-Peterson MJ, Rocchi P, West T, McLellan K, Hackney A. 1999. Age, testing at preferred or nonpreferred times (testing optimality), and false memory. *J. Exp. Psychol.: Learn. Mem. Cogn.* 25:23–40

Intraub H, Bodamer JL. 1993. Boundary extension: fundamental aspect of pictorial representation or encoding artifact? *J. Exp. Psychol.: Learn. Mem. Cogn.* 19:1387–97

Intraub H, Gottesman CV, Bills AJ. 1998. Effects of perceiving and imagining scenes on memory for pictures. *J. Exp. Psychol.: Learn. Mem. Cogn.* 24:186–201

Israel L, Schacter DL. 1997. Pictorial encoding reduces false recognition of semantic associates. *Psychonom. Bull. Rev.* 4:577–81

Jacoby LL, Allan LG, Collins JC, Larwill LK. 1988. Memory influences subjective experience: noise judgments. *J. Exp. Psychol.: Learn. Mem. Cogn.* 14:240–47

Jacoby LL, Dallas M. 1981. On the relationship between autobiographical memory and perceptual learning. *J. Exp. Psychol.: Gen.* 110:306–40

Jacoby LL, Kelley C, Brown J, Jasechko J. 1989a. Becoming famous overnight: limits on the ability to avoid unconscious influences of the past. *J. Pers. Soc. Psychol.* 56:326–38

Jacoby LL, Kelley CM, Dywan J. 1989b. Memory attributions. In *Varieties of Memory and Consciousness: Essays in Honour of Endel Tulving,* ed. HL Roediger III, FIM Craik, pp. 391–422. Hillsdale, NJ: Erlbaum

Jacoby LL, Lindsay DS, Toth JP. 1992. Unconscious influences revealed: attention, awareness, and control. *Am. Psychol.* 47:802–9

Jacoby LL, Whitehouse K. 1989. An illusion of memory: false recognition influenced by unconscious perception. *J. Exp. Psychol.: Gen.* 118:126–35

Jacoby LL, Woloshyn V, Kelley C. 1989c. Becoming famous without being recognized: unconscious influences of memory produced by dividing attention. *J. Exp. Psychol.: Gen.* 118:115–25

Johnson MK. 1992. MEM: mechanisms of recollection. *J. Cogn. Neurosci.* 4:268–80

Johnson MK. 1997. Identifying the origin of mental experience. In *The Mythomanias: The Nature of Deception and Self Deception,* ed. MS Myslobodsky, pp. 133–80. Mahwah, NJ: Erlbaum

Johnson MK, Bransford JD, Solomon SK. 1973. Memory for tacit implications of sentences. *J. Exp. Psychol.* 98:203–5

Johnson MK, De Leonardis DM, Hashtroudi S, Ferguson SA. 1995. Aging and single versus multiple cues in source monitoring. *Psychol. Aging* 10:507–17

Johnson MK, Hashtroudi S, Lindsay DS. 1993. Source monitoring. *Psychol. Bull.* 114:3–28

Johnson MK, Kahan TL, Raye CL. 1984. Dreams and reality monitoring. *J. Exp. Psychol.: Gen.* 113:329–44

Johnson MK, Nolde SF, De Leonardis DM. 1996. Emotional focus and source monitoring. *J. Mem. Lang.* 35:135–56

Johnson RE. 1970. Recall of prose as a function of the structural importance of the linguistic units. *J. Verbal Learn. Verbal Behav.* 9:12–20

Johnston WA, Dark VJ, Jacoby LL. 1985. Perceptual fluency and recognition judgments.

J. Exp. Psychol.: Learn. Mem. Cogn. 11:3–11

Kassin SM, Kiechel KL. 1996. The social psychology of false confessions: compliance, internalization, and confabulation. *Psychol. Sci.* 7:125–28

Kelley CM. 1999. Subjective experience as a basis for "objective" judgments: effects of past experience on judgments of difficulty. See Gopher & Koriat 1999, pp. 515–36

Kelley CM, Jacoby LL. 1996. Adult egocentrism: subjective experience versus analytic bases for judgment. *J. Mem. Lang.* 35:157–75

Kelley CM, Jacoby LL. 1998. Subjective reports and process dissociation: fluency, knowing, and feeling. *Acta Psychol.* 98:127–40

Kelley CM, Lindsay DS. 1993. Remembering mistaken for knowing: ease of retrieval as a basis for confidence in answers to general knowledge questions. *J. Mem. Lang.* 32:1–24

Kerst SM, Howard JH. 1978. Memory psychophysics for visual area and length. *Mem. Cogn.* 6:327–35

Kintsch W, Welsch D, Schmalhofer F, Zimny S. 1990. Sentence memory: a theoretical analysis. *J. Mem. Lang.* 29:133–59

Koffka K. 1935. *Principles of Gestalt Psychology.* New York: Harcourt Brace

Kohnken G, Milne R, Memon A, Bull R. 1999. The cognitive interview: a meta-analysis. *Psychol. Crime Law* 5:3–27

Koriat A. 1993. How do we know that we know? The accessibility model of the feeling of knowing. *Psychol. Rev.* 100:609–39

Koriat A. 1995. Dissociating knowing and the feeling of knowing: further evidence for the accessibility model. *J. Exp. Psychol.: Gen.* 124:311–33

Koriat A. 1998. Metamemory: the feeling of knowing and its vagaries. In *Advances in Psychological Science,* ed. M Sabourin, F Craik, 2:461–79. Hove, UK: Psychology Press

Koriat A. 2000. Control processes in remembering. In *The Oxford Handbook of Mem-*

ory, ed. E Tulving, FIM Craik. Oxford, UK: Oxford Univ. Press. In press

Koriat A, Ben Zur H, Druch A. 1991. The contextualization of input and output events in memory. *Psychol. Res./Psychol. Forsch.* 53:260–70

Koriat A, Goldsmith M. 1994. Memory in naturalistic and laboratory contexts: distinguishing the accuracy-oriented and quantity-oriented approaches to memory assessment. *J. Exp. Psychol.: Gen.* 123:297–315

Koriat A, Goldsmith M. 1996a. Memory as something that can be counted vs. memory as something that can be counted on. In *Basic and Applied Memory Research: Practical Applications,* ed. DJ Herrmann, C McEvoy, C Hertzog, P Hertel, MK Johnson, 2:3–18. Hillsdale, NJ: Erlbaum

Koriat A, Goldsmith M. 1996b. Memory metaphors and the real-life/laboratory controversy: correspondence versus storehouse conceptions of memory. *Behav. Brain Sci.* 19:167–228

Koriat A, Goldsmith M. 1996c. Monitoring and control processes in the strategic regulation of memory accuracy. *Psychol. Rev.* 103:490–517

Koriat A, Goldsmith M. 1996d. The correspondence metaphor of memory: right, wrong, or useful. *Behav. Brain Sci.* 19:211–22

Koriat A, Goldsmith M. 1997. The myriad functions and metaphors of memory. *Behav. Brain Sci.* 20:27–28

Koriat A, Goldsmith M. 1998a. Methodological and substantive implications of a metatheoretical distinction: more on correspondence versus storehouse metaphors of memory. *Behav. Brain Sci.* 21:165–67

Koriat A, Goldsmith M. 1998b. The role of metacognitive processes in the regulation of memory performance. In *Metacognition and Cognitive Neuropsychology: Monitoring and Control Processes,* ed. G Mazzoni, TO Nelson, pp. 97–118. Mahwah, NJ: Erlbaum

Koriat A, Goldsmith M, Schneider W. 1999. *Metamemory processes mediate the credibility of children's reports.* Presented at Meet. Soc. Appl. Res. Mem. Cogn., Boulder, CO

Koriat A, Levy-Sadot R. 1999. Processes underlying metacognitive judgments: information-based and experience-based monitoring of one's own knowledge. In *Dual-Process Theories in Social Psychology,* ed. S Chaiken, Y Trope. New York: Guilford

Kosslyn SM, Ball TM, Reiser BJ. 1978. Visual images preserve metric spatial information: evidence from studies of image scanning. *J. Exp. Psychol.: Hum. Percept. Perform.* 4:47–60

Koutstaal W, Schacter DL. 1997. Gist-based false recognition of pictures in older and younger adults. *J. Mem. Lang.* 37:555–83

Kruglanski AW. 1989. The psychology of being "right": the problem of accuracy in social perception and cognition. *Psychol. Bull.* 106:395–409

Lampinen JM, Neuschatz JS, Payne DG. 1998. Memory illusions and consciousness: examining the phenomenology of true and false memories. *Curr. Psychol.* 16:181–224

Lampinen JM, Smith VL. 1995. The incredible (and sometimes incredulous) child witness: child eyewitnesses' sensitivity to source credibility cues. *J. Appl. Psychol.* 80:621–27

Larsen SF, Thompson CP, Hansen T. 1996. Time in autobiographical memory. See Rubin 1996, pp. 129–56

Liben LS, ed. 1998. Special issue. *J. Exp. Child Psychol.* 71(2):79–209

Lindsay DS. 1990. Misleading suggestions can impair eyewitnesses' ability to remember event details. *J. Exp. Psychol.: Learn. Mem. Cogn.* 16:1077–83

Lindsay DS. 1998. Depolarizing views on recovered memory experiences. See Lynn & McConkey 1998, pp. 481–94

Lindsay DS, Johnson MK. 1989. The eyewitness suggestibility effect and memory for source. *Mem. Cogn.* 17:349–58

Lindsay DS, Kelley CM. 1996. Creating illusions of familiarity in a cued recall remember/know paradigm. *J. Mem. Lang.* 35:197–211

Lindsay DS, Read JD, Sharma K. 1998. Accuracy and confidence in person identification: the relationship is strong when witnessing conditions vary widely. *Psychol. Sci.* 9:215–18

Lindsay RCL. 1994. Expectations of eyewitness performance: Jurors' verdicts do not follow from their beliefs. See Ross et al 1994, pp. 362–84

Loftus EF. 1975. Leading questions and the eyewitness report. *Cogn. Psychol.* 7:560–72

Loftus EF. 1979a. *Eyewitness Testimony.* Cambridge, MA: Harvard Univ. Press

Loftus EF. 1979b. Reactions to blatantly contradictory information. *Mem. Cogn.* 7:368–74

Loftus EF. 1993. The reality of repressed memories. *Am. Psychol.* 48:518–37

Loftus EF. 1997. Creating false memories. *Sci. Am.* 277:50–55

Loftus EF, Donders K, Hoffman HG, Schooler JW. 1989. Creating new memories that are quickly accessed and confidently held. *Mem. Cogn.* 17:607–16

Loftus EF, Garry M, Feldman J. 1994. Forgetting sexual trauma: What does it mean when 38% forget? *J. Consult. Clin. Psychol.* 62:1177–81

Loftus EF, Marburger W. 1983. Since the eruption of Mt. St. Helens, has anyone beaten you up? Improving the accuracy of retrospective reports with landmark events. *Mem. Cogn.* 11:114–20

Loftus EF, Miller DG, Burns HJ. 1978. Semantic integration of verbal information into a visual memory. *J. Exp. Psychol.: Hum. Learn. Mem.* 4:19–31

Loftus EF, Pickrell JE. 1995. The formation of false memories. *Psychiatr. Ann.* 25:720–25

Lynn SJ, McConkey KM, eds. 1998. *Truth in Memory.* New York: Guilford

Mandler JM. 1979. Categorical and schematic organization in memory. In *Memory Organization and Structure,* ed. RC Puff, pp. 259–99. New York: Academic

Marshall JC, Fryer DM. 1978. Speak memory! An introduction to some historic studies of remembering and forgetting. In *Aspects of Memory,* ed. MM Gruneberg, P Morris. London: Methuen

Masson MEJ, Caldwell JI. 1998. Conceptually driven encoding episodes create perceptual misattributions. *Acta Psychol.* 98:183–210

Mather M, Henkel LA, Johnson MK. 1997. Evaluating characteristics of false memories: remember/know judgments and memory characteristics questionnaire compared. *Mem. Cogn.* 25:826–37

McCloskey M, Wible CG, Cohen NJ. 1988. Is there a special flashbulb-memory mechanism? *J. Exp. Psychol.: Gen.* 117:171–81

McCloskey M, Zaragoza M. 1985. Misleading postevent information and memory for events: arguments and evidence against memory impairment hypotheses. *J. Exp. Psychol.: Gen.* 114:1–16

McDermott KB. 1996. The persistence of false memories in list recall. *J. Mem. Lang.* 35:212–30

McDermott KB, Roediger HL. 1998. Attempting to avoid illusory memories: Robust false recognition of associates persists under conditions of explicit warnings and immediate testing. *J. Mem. Lang.* 39:508–20

McFarland C, Ross M. 1987. The relation between current impressions and memories of self and dating partners. *Pers. Soc. Psychol. Bull.* 13:228–38

McNamara TP. 1986. Mental representations of spatial relations. *Cogn. Psychol.* 18:87–121

McNamara TP, Diwadkar VA. 1997. Symmetry and asymmetry of human spatial memory. *Cogn. Psychol.* 34:160–90

Memon A, Stevenage VS. 1996. Interviewing witnesses: what works and what doesn't? *Psycholoquy* 7(6) ftp://ftp.princeton.edu/pub/harnad/Psycoloquy/1996.volume.7/psyc.96.7.06.witness-memory.1.memon

Miller MB, Gazzaniga MS. 1998. Creating false memories for visual scenes. *Neuropsychologia* 36:513–20

Mitchell KJ, Zaragoza MS. 1996. Repeated exposure to suggestion and fales memory: the role of contextual variablity. *J. Mem. Lang.* 35:246–60

Moscovitch M. 1995. Confabulation. See Schacter 1995, pp. 226–51

Moyer RS. 1973. Comparing objects in memory: evidence suggesting an internal psychophysics. *Percep. Psychophys.* 13:180–84

Multhaup KS. 1995. Aging, source, and decision criteria: when false fame errors do and do not occur. *Psychol. Aging* 10:492–97

Neisser U. 1967. *Cognitive Psychology.* New York: Appleton-Century-Crofts

Neisser U. 1978. Memory: What are the important questions? In *Practical Aspects of Memory,* ed. MM Gruneberg, PE Morris. New York: Academic

Neisser U. 1981. John Dean's memory: a case study. *Cognition* 9:1–22

Neisser U. 1982. Snapshots or benchmarks. In *Memory Observed: Remembering in Natural Contexts,* ed. U Neisser, pp. 43–48. San Francisco: Freeman

Neisser U. 1984. Interpreting Harry Bahrick's discovery: What confers immunity against forgetting? *J. Exp. Psychol.: Gen.* 113:32–35

Neisser U. 1988. Time present and time past. See Gruneberg et al 1988, 2:545–60

Neisser U. 1991. A case of misplaced nostalgia. *Am. Psychol.* 46:34–36

Neisser U. 1996. Remembering as doing. *Behav. Brain Sci.* 19:203–4

Neisser U. 1997. The ecological study of memory. *Philos. Trans. R. Soc. London Ser. B* 352:1697–701

Neisser U, Harsch N. 1992. Phantom flashbulbs: false recollections of hearing the news about Challenger. In *Affect and Accuracy in Recall: Studies of "Flashbulb Memories,"* ed. E Winograd, U Neisser, pp. 9–31. Cambridge, UK: Cambridge Univ. Press

Neisser U, Winograd E, Weldon MS. 1991. *Remembering the earthquake: "What I experienced" vs. "How I heard the news."* Presented at Ann. Meet. Psychonom. Soc., 32nd, San Francisco, CA

Nelson DL, McKinney VM, Gee NR, Janczura GA. 1998. Interpreting the influence of implicitly activated memories on recall and recognition. *Psychol. Rev.* 105:299–324

Nelson K. 1993. The psychological and social origins of autobiographical memory. *Psychol. Sci.* 4:7–14

Nelson TO, Narens L. 1994. Why investigate metacognition? In *Metacognition: Knowing about Knowing,* ed. J Metcalfe, AP Shimamura, pp. 1–25. Cambridge, MA: MIT Press

Newby IR, Ross M. 1996. Beyond the correspondence metaphor: when accuracy cannot be assessed. *Behav. Brain Sci.* 19:205–6

Nhouyvanisvong A, Reder LM. 1998. Rapid feeling-of-knowing: a strategy selection mechanism. In *Metacognition: Cognitive and Social Dimensions,* ed. VY Yzerbyt, G Lories, B Dardenne, pp. 35–52. London: Sage

Norman KA, Schacter DL. 1996. Implicit memory, explicit memory, and false recollection: a cognitive neuroscience perspective. In *Implicit Memory and Metacognition,* ed. LM Reder, pp. 229–57. Mahwah, NJ: Erlbaum

Norman KA, Schacter DL. 1997. False recognition in younger and older adults: exploring the characteristics of illusory memories. *Mem. Cogn.* 25:838–48

Payne DG, Blackwell JM. 1998. Truth in memory: Caveat emptor. See Lynn & McConkey 1998, pp. 32–61

Payne DG, Elie CJ, Blackwell JM, Neuschatz JS. 1996a. Memory illusions: recalling, recognizing, and recollecting events that never occurred. *J. Mem. Lang.* 35:261–85

Payne DG, Lampinen JM, Cordero ML. 1996b. *Remembrances of things not passed: fur-*

ther evidence concerning false memories. Presented at Ann. Meet. Psychonom. Soc., Chicago

Payne DG, Neuschatz JS, Lampinen JM, Lynn SJ. 1997. Compelling memory illusions: the qualitative characteristics of false memories. *Curr. Dir. Psychol. Sci.* 6:56–60

Pennebaker JW, Memon A. 1996. Recovered memories in context: thoughts and elaborations on Bowers and Farvolden (1996). *Psychol. Bull.* 119:381–85

Penrod S, Cutler B. 1995. Witness confidence and witness accuracy: assessing their forensic relation. *Psychol. Public Policy Law* 1:817–45

Perfect TJ, Watson EL, Wagstaff GF. 1993. Accuracy of confidence ratings associated with general knowledge and eyewitness memory. *J. Appl. Psychol.* 78:144–47

Pezdek K, Finger K, Hodge D. 1997. Planting false childhood memories: the role of event plausibility. *Psychol. Sci.* 8:437–41

Pillemer DB. 1990. Clarifying flashbulb memory concept: comment on McCloskey, Wible, and Cohen (1988). *J. Exp. Psychol.: Gen.* 119:92–96

Poole DA, White LT. 1993. Two years later: effect of question repetition and retention interval on the eyewitness testimony of children and adults. *Dev. Psychol.* 29:844–53

Posner MI, Keele SW. 1970. Retention of abstract ideas. *J. Exp. Psychol.* 83:304–8

Rabinowitz JC, Craik FI, Ackerman BP. 1982. A processing resource account of age differences in recall. *Can. J. Psychol.* 36:325–44

Radvansky GA, Carlson-Radvansky LA, Irwin DE. 1995. Uncertainty in estimating distances from memory. *Mem. Cogn.* 23:596–606

Read JD. 1996. From a passing thought to a false memory in 2 minutes: confusing real and illusory events. *Psychonom. Bull. Rev* 3:105–11

Read JD, Lindsay DS, Nicholls T. 1998. The relation between confidence and accuracy in eyewitness identification studies: Is the conclusion changing? In *Eyewitness Memory: Theoretical and Applied Perspectives,* ed. CP Thompson, DJ Herrmann, pp. 107–30. Mahwah, NJ: Erlbaum

Reder LM. 1987. Strategy selection in question answering. *Cogn. Psychol.* 19:90–138

Reinitz MT, Verfaellie M, Milberg WP. 1996. Memory conjunction errors in normal and amnesic subjects. *J. Mem. Lang.* 35:286–99

Reyna VF, Brainerd CJ. 1995. Fuzzy-trace theory: an interim synthesis. *Learn. Indiv. Differ.* 7:1–75

Reyna VF, Kiernan B. 1994. Development of gist versus verbatim memory in sentence recognition: effects of lexical familiarity, semantic content, encoding instructions, and retention interval. *Dev. Psychol.* 30:178–91

Rhodes G. 1996. *Superportraits: Caricatures and Recognition.* Hove, Sussex: Psychology Press

Rhodes G, Brennan S, Carey S. 1987. Identification and ratings of caricatures: implications for mental representations of faces. *Cogn. Psychol.* 19:473–97

Rhodes G, Byatt G, Tremewan T, Kennedy A. 1997. Facial distinctiveness and the power of caricatures. *Perception* 26:207–23

Riley DA. 1962. Memory for form. In *Psychology in the Making: Histories of Selected Research Problems,* ed. L Postman, pp. 402–65. New York: Knopf

Robinson KJ, Roediger HL. 1997. Associative processes in false recall and false recognition. *Psychol. Sci.* 8:231–37

Robinson MD, Johnson JT. 1996. Recall memory, recognition memory, and the eyewitness confidence-accuracy correlation. *J. Appl. Psychol.* 81:587–94

Robinson MD, Johnson JT, Herndon F. 1997. Reaction time and assessments of cognitive effort as predictors of eyewitness memory accuracy and confidence. *J. Appl. Psychol.* 82:416–25

Roediger HL. 1980. Memory metaphors in cognitive psychology. *Mem. Cogn.* 8:231–46

Roediger HL III. 1996. Memory illusions. *J. Mem. Lang.* 35:76–100

Roediger HL, Jacoby JD, McDermott KB. 1996. Misinformation effects in recall: creating false memories through repeated retrieval. *J. Mem. Lang.* 35:300–18

Roediger HL, McDermott KB. 1995. Creating false memories: remembering words not presented in lists. *J. Exp. Psychol.: Learn. Mem. Cogn.* 21:803–14

Roediger HL, McDermott KB, Goff LM. 1997. Recovery of true and false memories: paradoxical effects of repeated testing. See Conway 1997, pp. 118–49

Roediger HL, McDermott KB, Robinson KJ. 1998. The role of associative processes in creating false memories. See Conway et al 1998, pp. 187–245

Ross DF, Read JD, Toglia MP, eds. 1994. *Adult Eyewitness Testimony: Current Trends and Developments.* New York: Cambridge Univ. Press

Ross M. 1989. Relation of implicit theories to the construction of personal histories. *Psychol. Rev.* 96:341–57

Ross M. 1997. Validating memories. In *Memory for Everyday and Emotional Events,* ed. NL Stein, B Ornstein, B Tversky, C Brainerd. Hillsdale, NJ: Erlbaum

Ross M, McFarland C, Fletcher GJ. 1981. The effect of attitude on the recall of personal histories. *J. Pers. Soc. Psychol.* 40:627–34

Rubin DC, ed. 1986. *Autobiographical Memory.* New York: Cambridge Univ. Press

Rubin DC, ed. 1996. *Remembering Our Past: Studies in Autobiographical Memory.* New York: Cambridge Univ. Press

Rubin DC, Baddeley AD. 1989. Telescoping is not time compression: a model of the dating of autobiographical events. *Mem. Cogn.* 17:653–61

Schacter DL. 1989. Memory. In *Foundations of Cognitive Science,* ed. MI Posner, pp. 683–725. Cambridge, MA: MIT Press

Schacter DL, ed. 1995. *Memory Distortion: How Minds, Brains, and Societies Reconstruct the Past.* Cambridge, MA: Harvard Univ. Press

Schacter DL. 1999. The seven sins of memory. *Am. Psychol.* 54:182–203

Schacter DL, Israel L, Racine C. 1999. Suppressing false recognition in younger and older adults: the distinctiveness heuristic. *J. Mem. Lang.* 40:1–24

Schacter DL, Norman KA, Koutstaal W. 1998. The cognitive neuroscience of constructive memory. *Annu. Rev. Psychol.* 49:289–318

Schacter DL, Verfaellie M, Pradere D. 1996. The neuropsychology of memory illusions: false recall and recognition in amnesic patients. *J. Mem. Lang.* 35:319–34

Schacter DL, Worling JR. 1985. Attribute information and the feeling-of-knowing. *Can. J. Psychol.* 39:467–75

Schneider W, Bjorklund DF. 1998. Memory. In *Handbook of Child Psychology: Cognition, Perception and Language,* Vol. 2, ed. W Damon, D Kuhn, RS Siegler. New York: Wiley

Schooler JW. 1998. The distinctions of false and fuzzy memories. *J. Exp. Child Psychol.* 71:130–43

Schooler JW, Bendiksen M, Ambadar Z. 1997. Taking the middle line: Can we accommodate both fabricated and recovered memories of sexual abuse? See Conway 1997, pp. 251–92

Schooler JW, Foster RA, Loftus EF. 1988. Some deleterious consequences of the act of recollection. *Mem. Cogn.* 16:243–51

Schwartz BL. 1994. Sources of information in metamemory: judgments of learning and feelings of knowing. *Psychonom. Bull. Rev* 1:357–75

Schwartz BL. 1998. Illusory tip-of-the-tongue states. *Memory* 6:623–42

Schwartz BL, Fisher RP, Hebert KS. 1998. The relation of output order and commission errors in free recall and eyewitness accounts. *Memory* 6:257–75

Schwartz BL, Metcalfe J. 1992. Cue familiarity but not target retrievability enhances feeling-of-knowing judgments. *J. Exp. Psychol.: Learn. Mem. Cogn.* 18:1074–83

Schwarz N. 1999. Self-reports: how the questions shape the answers. *Am. Psychol.* 54:93–105

Seamon JG, Luo CR, Gallo DA. 1998. Creating false memories of words with or without recognition of list items: evidence for nonconscious processes. *Psychol. Sci.* 9:20–26

Shaw JS III. 1996. Increases in eyewitness confidence resulting from postevent questioning. *J. Exp. Psychol.: Appl.* 2:126–46

Shepard RN. 1978. The mental image. *Am. Psychol.* 33:125–37

Siegel AW. 1981. The externalization of cognitive maps by children and adults: in search of ways to ask better questions. In *Spatial Representation and Behavior Across the Life Span,* ed. LS Liben, AH Patterson, N Newcombe. New York: Academic

Smith ER, Hunt RR. 1998. Presentation modality affects false memory. *Psychonom. Bull. Rev.* 5:710–15

Smith VL, Kassin SM, Ellsworth PC. 1989. Eyewitness accuracy and confidence: within- versus between-subjects correlations. *J. Appl. Psychol.* 74:356–59

Spanos NP. 1996. *Multiple Identities and False Memories.* Washington, DC: Am. Psychol. Assoc.

Spencer WD, Raz N. 1995. Differential effects of aging on memory for content and context: a meta-analysis. *Psychol. Aging* 10:527–39

Sporer SL. 1993. Eyewitness identification accuracy, confidence, and decision times in simultaneous and sequential lineups. *J. Appl. Psychol.* 78:22–33

Sporer SL, Penrod S, Read D, Cutler B. 1995. Choosing, confidence, and accuracy: a meta-analysis of the confidence-accuracy relation in eyewitness identification studies. *Psychol. Bull.* 118:315–27

Stahlberg D, Mass A. 1998. Hindsight bias: impaired memory or biased reconstruction? *Eur. J. Soc. Psychol.* 8:105–32

Stangor C, McMillan D. 1992. Memory for expectancy-congruent and expectancy-incongruent information: a review of the social and social developmental literatures. *Psychol. Bull.* 111:42–61

Steblay NM. 1997. Social influence in eyewitness recall: a meta-analytic review of lineup instruction effects. *Law Hum. Behav.* 21:283–97

Stephenson GM, Clark NK, Wade GS. 1986. Meetings make evidence? An experimental study of collaborative and individual recall of a simulated police interrogation. *J. Pers. Soc. Psychol.* 50:1113–22

Stevens A, Coupe P. 1978. Distortions in judged spatial relations. *Cogn. Psychol.* 10:422–37

Suengas AG, Johnson MK. 1988. Qualitative effects of rehearsal on memories for perceived and imagined complex events. *J. Exp. Psychol.: Gen.* 117:377–89

Swann WB. 1984. Quest for accuracy in person perception: a matter of pragmatics. *Psychol. Rev.* 91:457–77

Thompson CP, Skowronski JJ, Larsen SF, Betz A. 1996. *Autobiographical Memory: Remembering What and Remembering When.* Mahwah, NJ: Erlbaum

Thorndyke PW. 1981. Distance estimation from cognitive maps. *Cogn. Psychol.* 13:526–50

Toglia MP, Neuschatz JS, Goodwin KA. 1999. Recall accuracy and illusory memories: when more is less. *Memory* 7:233–56

Tulving E. 1983. *Elements of Episodic Memory.* Oxford, UK: Clarendon

Tulving E. 1985. Memory and consciousness. *Can. Psychol.* 26:1–12

Tun PA, Wingfield A, Rosen MJ, Blanchard L. 1998. Response latencies for false memories: gist-based processes in normal aging. *Psychol. Aging* 13:230–41

Tussing AA, Greene RL. 1997. False recognition of associates: How robust is the effect? *Psychonom. Bull. Rev.* 4:572–76

Tussing AA, Greene RL. 1999. Differential effects of repetition on true and false recognition. *J. Mem. Lang.* 40:520–33

Tversky B. 1981. Distortions in memory for maps. *Cogn. Psychol.* 13:407–33

Tversky B. 1998. Three dimensions of spatial cognition. See Conway et al 1998, pp. 259–75

Walker NE, Hunt JS. 1998. Interviewing child victim-witnesses: how you ask is what you get. In *Eyewitness Memory: Theoretical and Applied Perspectives,* ed. CP Thompson, DJ Herrmann, pp. 55–87. Mahwah, NJ: Erlbaum

Waterman S, Gordon D. 1984. A quantitative-comparative approach to analysis of distortion in mental maps. *Profess. Geog.* 36:326–37

Weaver CA. 1993. Do you need a "flash" to form a flashbulb memory? *J. Exp. Psychol.: Gen.* 122:39–46

Weingardt KR, Toland HK, Loftus EF. 1994. Reports of suggested memories: Do people truly believe them? See Ross et al 1994, pp. 3–26

Wells GL. 1978. Applied eyewitness-testimony research: system variables and estimator variables. *J. Pers. Soc. Psychol.* 36:1546–57

Wells GL. 1993. What do we know about eyewitness identification? *Am. Psychol.* 48:553–71

Wells GL, Murray DM. 1984. Eyewitness confidence. In *Eyewitness Testimony: Psychological Perpectives,* ed. GL Wells, EF Loftus, pp. 155–70. New York: Cambridge Univ. Press

Wells GL, Rydell SM, Seelau EP. 1993. The selection of distractors for eyewitness lineups. *J. Appl. Psychol.* 78:835–44

Wells GL, Small M, Penrod S, Malpass RS, Fulero SM, Brimacombe CAE. 1998. Eyewitness identification procedures: recommendations for lineups and photospreads. *Law Hum. Behav.* 22:603–47

Wells GL, Turtle JW. 1988. What is the best way to encode faces? See Gruneberg et al 1988, 1:163–68

White RT. 1982. Memory for personal events. *Hum. Learn.* 1:171–83

Whittlesea BWA. 1993. Illusions of familiarity. *J. Exp. Psychol.: Learn. Mem. Cogn.* 19:1235–53

Whittlesea BWA, Jacoby LL, Girard K. 1990. Illusions of immediate memory: evidence of an attributional basis for feelings of familiarity and perceptual quality. *J. Mem. Lang.* 29:716–32

Whittlesea BWA, Williams LD. 1998. Why do strangers feel familiar, but friends don't? A discrepancy-attribution account of feelings of familiarity. *Acta Psychol.* 98:141–65

Windschitl PD. 1996. Memory for faces: evidence of retrieval-based impairment. *J. Exp. Psychol.: Learn. Mem. Cogn.* 22:1101–22

Winkielman P, Schwarz N, Belli RF. 1998. The role of ease of retrieval and attribution in memory judgments: judging your memory as worse despite recalling more events. *Psychol. Sci.* 9:124–26

Winograd E. 1968. List differentiation, recall, and category similarity. *J. Exp. Psychol.* 78:510–15

Winograd E. 1994. The authenticity and utility of memories. In *The Remembering Self: Construction and Accuracy in the Self Narrative,* ed. U Neisser, R Fivush, pp. 243–51. New York: Cambridge Univ. Press

Winograd E, Neisser U, eds. 1992. *Affect and Accuracy in Recall: Studies of "Flashbulb" Memories.* New York: Cambridge Univ. Press

Woodworth RS. 1938. *Experimental Psychology.* New York: Holt

Wright DB, Loftus EF. 1998. How misinformation alters memories. *J. Exp. Child Psychol.* 71:155–64

Wright DB, Stroud JN. 1998. Memory quality and misinformation for peripheral and central objects. *Leg. Crim. Psychol.* 3:273–86

Wulf F. 1922. Beitrage zur Psychologie der Gestalt: VI. Uber die Veranderung von Vorstellungen (Gedachtniss und Gestalt). *Psychol. Forsch.* 1:333–75

Wyer RS Jr, Srull TK. 1989. *Memory and Cognition in its Social Context.* Hillsdale, NJ: Erlbaum

Yaniv I, Foster DP. 1997. Precision and accuracy of judgmental estimation. *J. Behav. Decis. Mak.* 10:21–32

Zaragoza MS, Lane SM. 1994. Source misattributions and the suggestibility of eyewitness memory. *J. Exp. Psychol.: Learn. Mem. Cogn.* 20:934–45

Zaragoza MS, Mitchell KJ. 1996. Repeated exposure to suggestion and the creation of false memories. *Psychol. Sci.* 7:294–300

Annu. Rev. Psychol. 2000. 51:539–570

ATTITUDE CHANGE: Persuasion and Social Influence

Wendy Wood

*Department of Psychology, Texas A&M University, College Station, Texas 77843;
e-mail: wlw@psyc.tamu.edu*

Key Words influence, motives, fear appeals, social identity

■ **Abstract** This chapter reviews empirical and theoretical developments in research on social influence and message-based persuasion. The review emphasizes research published during the period from 1996–1998. Across these literatures, three central motives have been identified that generate attitude change and resistance. These involve concerns with the self, with others and the rewards/punishments they can provide, and with a valid understanding of reality. The motives have implications for information processing and for attitude change in public and private contexts. Motives in persuasion also have been investigated in research on attitude functions and cognitive dissonance theory. In addition, the chapter reviews the relatively unique aspects of each literature: In persuasion, it considers the cognitive and affective mechanisms underlying attitude change, especially dual-mode processing models, recipients' affective reactions, and biased processing. In social influence, the chapter considers how attitudes are embedded in social relations, including social identity theory and majority/minority group influence.

CONTENTS

Introduction 540
Motives for Agreeing with Others 540
   Public Versus Private Influence 542
Motives in Persuasion Research 544
   Functional Theories 544
   Cognitive Dissonance Theory 546
Multiple Attitudes 548
   Sources of Multiple Attitudes 548
   Influence and Multiple Attitudes 549
Dual-Mode Processing Models of Persuasion 551
   Cognitive Response Mediation of Attitude Change 552
   Dual-Mode Processing Models and Social Influence 553
   Motivated Processing and Bias Correction 554
Affect and Influence 555
   Effects of Mood 555
   Fear Appeals 556
Group and Self-Identity 557

0084–6570/00/0201–0539$12.00

Social Consensus and Validity of Information 558
Multiple Motives Instigated by Groups 559
Opinion Minority and Majority Groups 560
Conclusion 561

INTRODUCTION

This chapter reviews the research on attitude change from what traditionally have been two separate areas of inquiry, the study of message-based persuasion and the study of social influence. In the persuasion paradigm, influence appeals typically include detailed argumentation that is presented to individual recipients in a context with only minimal social interaction. Social influence appeals, in contrast, usually consist solely of information about the source's position, but these are delivered in more complex social settings that may include interaction among participants. Because of the marked continuities in the theoretical analyses and in the empirical findings that have emerged across these research areas in the past few years, this review draws from both literatures. It emphasizes in particular research published during 1996 to 1998, since the prior review of Petty et al (1997).

Giving social influence research a significant role in the current review requires that limited attention be given to some other research areas that have been featured prominently in the past. Work on attitude structure and on attitude-behavior relations has continued to flourish, and Eagly & Chaiken (1998) provide an excellent review elsewhere. Also noteworthy, despite some overlap with the current review, are Petty & Wegener (1998a), Cialdini & Trost (1998), and Chaiken et al (1996b). Another research area beyond the scope of this chapter is the extensive work on intergroup attitudes and stereotypes (Brewer & Brown 1998, Fiske 1998).

MOTIVES FOR AGREEING WITH OTHERS

A hallmark of social influence research is the delineation of the multiple motives that spur agreement or disagreement with others. For over 40 years, the central organizing perspective in this area has been a dual-motive scheme that differentiates between informational influence, which involves accepting information obtained from others as evidence about reality, and normative influence, which involves conformity with the positive expectations of "another," who could be "another person, a group, or one's self" (Deutsch & Gerard 1955:629).

Yet contemporary theories of motives for attitude change and resistance appear to be converging instead on a tripartite distinction (e.g. Chaiken et al 1996a, Cialdini & Trost 1998, Johnson & Eagly 1989, Wood 1999; for an early presentation of this kind of framework, see Kelman 1958). Although these typologies each possess unique features, a common thread is the recognition that attitude change can be motivated by normative concerns for (*a*) ensuring the coherence and favorable evaluation of the self, and (*b*) ensuring satisfactory relations with others given the rewards/punishments they can provide, along with an informational concern for (*c*) understanding the entity or issue featured in influence appeals. Thus, for example, Cialdini & Trost (1998) identify the behavioral goals of social influence recipients as managing the self-concept, building and maintaining relationships, and acting effectively. Similarly, Chaiken et al (1996a) distinguished between people's ego-defensive motives to achieve a valued, coherent self-identity, impression-related motives to convey a particular impression to others, and validity-seeking motives to accurately assess external reality.

Social influence researchers traditionally assumed that informational and normative motives are each associated with unique mechanisms that generate attitude change and with unique forms of change. The desire for an informed, correct position supposedly orients message recipients to process the content of the appeal and results in enduring private change in judgments. The desire to meet normative expectations supposedly yields less informational analysis and public, context-dependent, transitory judgment change. This view has been challenged by dual-mode processing models of persuasion (Eagly & Chaiken 1993, Petty & Wegener 1998a), especially by the demonstration that informational, accuracy-seeking motives can lead either to extensive processing and enduring attitude change or to more superficial processing and temporary change. In the dual-mode framework, motives for change are not preferentially related to change mechanisms or outcomes.

Two recent studies support the persuasion analysis by providing evidence that normative and informational motives affect influence through a common set of information-processing mechanisms (Chen et al 1996, Lundgren & Prislin 1998). Lundgren & Prislin (1998) found that, when participants were motivated to be accurate, they selected arguments to read on both sides (i.e. pro and con) of the target issue, generated thoughts that were relatively balanced in evaluation of both sides, and indicated relatively neutral attitudes. In contrast, when participants were motivated to convey a favorable impression to an interaction partner, they selected arguments to read that were congruent with the view ostensibly held by the partner and generated thoughts and attitudes that were congenial with their partner's position. Finally, when participants were motivated to defend their own position, they selected arguments to read that supported their view, generated thoughts supportive of their position, and indicated relatively polarized attitudes. Furthermore, analyses to test mediation revealed that the favorability of participants' thoughts (at least partially) mediated the effects of motives on attitude change. Thus, it appears that the attitude effects emerged in part because accuracy motives generated a relatively open-minded processing orientation, impression motives generated an agreeable orientation, and defense motives generated a protective orientation that maintained existing judgments.

These two studies also challenge the assumption that recipients' motives are associated with unique forms of attitude change. Regardless of the initial motive directing attitude judgments, the attitudes participants expressed to their ostensible discussion partners persisted when participants later indicated their judgments privately (Chen et al 1996, Lundgren & Prislin 1998). Especially impressive is the persistence of attitudes designed to convey a favorable impression. Contrary to classic theories of social influence, attitudes directed by impression-related normative motives were no more "elastic" than were attitudes directed by accuracy-seeking, informational motives. Instead, it seems that impression and defense motives, much like the accuracy motives studied extensively in message-based persuasion research, can yield careful, systematic processing of relevant information that results in stable judgments. This finding augments the results of earlier research in which impression motives were linked to superficial processing and temporary judgment shifts (e.g. Cialdini et al 1976). The factors that determine whether motives instigate extensive or more superficial processing are discussed below.

Public Versus Private Influence

In social influence paradigms, researchers often have diagnosed the motive for attitude change from the continuity of recipients' judgments across public and private settings. In public settings, recipients believe that the source of the appeal or members of their experimental group have surveillance over their responses, whereas in private settings, recipients believe that these others are unaware of their judgments. Supposedly, attitudes that maintain across public and private measures are internalized responses that result from the thoughtful processing associated with accuracy motives, whereas attitudes that are expressed in public but not private reflect normative pressures such as acceptance from the source or group.

Recent empirical findings suggest instead that lack of continuity between public and private judgments is not reliably diagnostic of recipients' motives. As described above, enduring attitude change is not the unique province of informational motives; it also can emerge from social motives such as the desire to accommodate others (Chen et al 1996, Lundgren & Prislin 1998). Evidence of judgment stability across public and private settings has emerged also in influence in the Asch-type judgment paradigm. In this research, participants are exposed to others' obviously incorrect judgments of line length and participants' agreement with others typically is interpreted as public, superficial acquiescence to social pressure. Yet the meta-analytic synthesis by Bond & Smith (1996) of 97 studies using the Asch-type social influence paradigm revealed no greater agreement in public than in private contexts of attitude expression. It seems, then, that social motives for agreement affected attitudes in public as well as private settings.

The lack of systematic differences between public and private expressions of judgment can be attributed to a number of factors. One is that recipients' motives for agreement can have relatively extended effects that generalize to new contexts in which the original motives are no longer salient or relevant (e.g. Hardin &

Higgins 1996, Higgins 1981, Ruscher & Duval 1998). Extended effects can occur when the initial motivated judgment is retrieved in new settings or when the information on which the judgment was based is retrieved, given that the motivated processing yielded a biased representation of the original information. Thus, because motives affect the judgments and the judgment-relevant information available in memory, initial motivations for processing may have effects that transcend context, and positions stated in public contexts may be maintained in private. Kassin & Kiechel (1996) provide a compelling example of the extended consequences of motivated processing. They simulated procedures sometimes used in the interrogation of crime suspects by (falsely) accusing research participants of an act of negligence while they were typing data into a computer. When participants were subjectively uncertain about their innocence (because they were typing at a fast speed), they accepted a witness's report of their actions and (incorrectly) confessed to the allegation. For the majority of participants, the confession was not mere compliance. Over half reported in a subsequent discussion that they had performed the negligent act, and over a third actually confabulated details in support of the false allegation.

Furthermore, the distinction between public and private settings suggests an overly simplified view of social impact, one that equates social presence with surveillance. Allport's (1985) famous definition of social psychology provided a considerably more differentiated view of social impact, in which the effects of others emerge whether their presence is "actual, imagined, or implied." Because important features of social impact may hold across public and private contexts, attitudes that are affected by these features may also hold across settings. For example, the manipulation by Baldwin & Holmes (1987) of social impact involved simply instructing female participants to think about two of their older relatives. The women were later given sexually explicit material to read in a supposedly unrelated context, and they reported not liking it much. Presumably, others' conservative moral standards were activated in the initial manipulation and continued to exert impact on subsequent experiences.

Theoretical perspectives need to progress beyond the simple distinction between public and private attitude expression and consider whether the features of social pressure that are relevant to attitude change are stable across settings. For example, in a meta-analytic synthesis of the minority-influence literature (Wood et al 1994), the influence of opinion-minority, low-consensus sources proved comparable in public and private settings. Thus, it seemed that attitude change was not controlled by surveillance and the fear that aligning with a deviant minority source in public would lead to social embarrassment and rejection by others. Agreement did vary, however, with another feature of the influence context; how directly attitudes were measured. "Direct" measures assess attitudes on the issue in the appeal, and recipients are aware that their (public or private) judgment can align them with the source's position. "Indirect" measures might, for example, assess attitudes on issues tangentially related to the appeal, and recipients are less aware that their judgments can align them with the influence source. Minority impact was smaller on direct than on indirect measures. Wood et al (1994) concluded that recipients' resistance on direct measures is due to their own personal knowledge that their judgments could align them with a deviant minority source. It seems, then, that minority influence was inhibited by recipients' concern for the favorability and integrity of their self-concept and their place in their reference group, and that these motives held in both public and private contexts (see below).

The current analysis of attitude expressions in public and private contexts also calls into question the common assumption that when public and private judgments differ in accuracy, privately expressed ones are generally more trustworthy because public expressions may be biased to achieve social motives. Although some features of public contexts (e.g. politeness norms) may compromise the accuracy of attitude expressions, other features appear to enhance thoughtful analyses and sometimes to increase accuracy. Cowan & Hodge (1996) demonstrated that to the extent public contexts enhance perceived accountability for judgments, people give especially thoughtful, reasoned responses in public. Similarly, Lambert et al (1996) argued that the expectation of public discussion focuses people on their own attitudes and encourages them to bolster their beliefs; thus, attitudes were found to play a greater role in guiding thought and action in public than in private settings.

Finally, given that in social-influence paradigms respondents often give their judgments first publicly and then again privately, continuity across judgment contexts can emerge from the effects of initial judgments on subsequent ones. Research on the impact of behavior on attitudes has demonstrated that people's interpretations of their public statements and other attitude-relevant behaviors can instigate shifts in privately held attitudes to correspond to public acts (see Chaiken et al 1996b). This research also has demonstrated that public-attitude statements that are of questionable veracity (e.g. when a public statement is given with low choice or high reward) do not affect the attitudes expressed in private settings (see below). However, Maio & Olson (1998) provide intriguing evidence that even under low-choice conditions, the act of providing an attitude judgment can enhance the accessibility of one's own attitude in memory; accessible attitudes then may affect subsequent attitude-relevant judgments in seemingly unrelated contexts.

MOTIVES IN PERSUASION RESEARCH

Functional Theories

The motives underlying attitude change in message-based persuasion paradigms have been investigated primarily in research on attitude functions (see Eagly & Chaiken 1998). In addition to the basic adaptive function of enabling people to evaluate and appraise stimuli in their environment, attitudes also are thought to serve more specific functions. Functions identified in early work include securing utilitarian outcomes, ego defense, value expression, and social adjustment (Katz 1960, Smith et al 1956). These functions are reflected in the tripartite motive scheme suggested above: Accuracy motives correspond generally to a utilitarian concern with maximizing rewards and minimizing punishments, self-concept motives correspond to concerns for defending the ego against potential threats and for expressing one's values, and social relation motives correspond to concerns for social adjustment and for obtaining social rewards and avoiding social punishments.

In one account of the role of attitude functions in influence, persuasive attempts are likely to be effective to the extent that the function of, or reason for holding, the position outlined in the appeal matches the function underlying recipients' attitudes (Lavine & Snyder 1996, Murray et al 1996: Study 2). For example, Lavine & Snyder (1996) reported that for people who are generally sensitive to the social consequences of their behavior (i.e. high self-monitors), appeals that emphasized the social adjustive functions of voting (e.g. enhancing one's attractiveness to others) elicited more favorable evaluations and greater attitude change than appeals that emphasized its value-expressive functions (e.g. a way to express values). For people who rely on inner dispositions (i.e. low self-monitors), appeals with value-expressive arguments yielded more favorable evaluations and were more persuasive. Furthermore, certain issues may be associated with certain attitude functions for most people. Although not specifically couched within a functional framework, the analysis by Rothman & Salovey (1997) of health-related messages suggested that influence is greatest when the orientation of an appeal matches the orientation intrinsic to the health issue itself. Recommendations to perform illness-detecting behaviors (e.g. breast self-exams) potentially incur risk and thus loss-framed appeals are likely to be effective, whereas recommendations for preventative behaviors (e.g. exercise) potentially incur positive outcomes and thus gain-framed appeals are likely to be effective.

In another account, matching between attitude function and message orientation does not always enhance persuasion but instead enhances careful thought about an appeal. Petty & Wegener (1998b) demonstrated that matched messages increased scrutiny of message content but enhanced persuasion only when the message contained strong, cogent arguments and not when it contained weak arguments. Yet because functionally matched messages potentially address important aspects of recipients' self-concepts, this careful processing will not always be objective and unbiased. Such appeals may instigate a thoughtful but defensive orientation, as recipients try to maintain valued aspects of the self. For example, Tykocinski et al (1994) reasoned that messages framed to match people's current experiences and concerns can elicit distress by identifying seemingly relevant goals that have not been adopted. Thus, such messages are especially likely to yield counterarguing and resistance. Similarly, Marsh et al (1997) reported that persuasive messages that address an important attitude function (i.e. for college students, the value-relevant issue of sororities/fraternities on college campuses) are processed carefully yet defensively and as a result are minimally influential.

Cognitive Dissonance Theory

This classic motivational theory of how attitudes change to maintain cognitive consistency continues to spark interest. The original notion of Festinger (1957) that dissonance arises from psychological inconsistency between linked cognitions has been modified extensively in subsequent research. In Cooper & Fazio's (1984) "new look" approach, dissonance arises not from simple inconsistency but rather from freely chosen behavior that brings about some foreseeable negative consequence.

A central question for dissonance researchers has been the motivational bases for dissonance and the cause of the aversive state of dissonance arousal. In Aronson's (1992) self-concept analysis, dissonance arises from inconsistent cognitions that threaten the consistency, stability, predictability, competence, or moral goodness of the self-concept. In Steele's (1988) self-affirmation theory, dissonance arises from the violation of general self-integrity. From these self-related perspectives, negative consequences are powerful inducers of dissonance because it is inconsistent with most people's self-views to act in a way that results in foreseeable aversive consequences. An alternate perspective on dissonance arousal, which has yet to be integrated into mainstream theorizing, is the argument by Joule & Beauvois (1998) that dissonance reduction is oriented toward rationalizing behavior rather than attaining psychological consistency.

In an interesting integration that recognizes that both self-concept threat and aversive consequences can instigate dissonance, Stone & Cooper (see Petty & Wegener 1998a) proposed that dissonance arises when people fail to behave in a manner consistent with some valued self-standard. The specific motivation behind dissonance supposedly depends on the type of self-standard involved. Dissonance can emerge from behavior that is inconsistent with personal self-standards and does not reflect the way people want to be (ideal self) or think they should be (ought self), or dissonance can emerge from behavior that generates aversive consequences and does not reflect how others want them to be (normative self-standards).

Several studies support the conclusion that dissonance motivation can emerge in contexts devoid of negative consequences. Participants in a study by Harmon-Jones et al (1996) freely engaged in the nonconsequential behavior of privately taking a counterattitudinal position, yet they experienced increased arousal and attitude shifts toward their expressed position. Similarly, Prislin & Pool (1996) found little evidence that dissonance arises only when behavior has identifiably negative consequences and instead concluded that dissonance emerges when behavior and its consequences challenge existing ideas about the self.

The hypocritical advocacy paradigm was developed to study dissonance motivation in the absence of negative consequences. In this research, participants advocate a proattitudinal position, are made aware of their past failures to act in accordance with this position, and (in order to reduce dissonance) then engage in acts congruent with the position (e.g. Fried 1998, Stone et al 1997). Although the lack of immediate negative consequences to this proattitudinal advocacy might appear to indicate that such consequences are not critical for producing dissonance, proponents of the negative consequences view can rightly note that highlighting past failures to uphold one's stated beliefs identifies aversive consequences of past acts. However, Fried & Aronson (1995) argued for the importance of the self in instigating dissonance by noting that dissonance in this paradigm does not emerge when people are only reminded of past transgressions (i.e. negative consequences) and do not engage in proattitudinal advocacy and experience the self-related implications of this behavior.

The second major issue addressed in dissonance research is the multiple routes or modes through which dissonance can be reduced. Although self-affirming behavior that reestablishes personal integrity has been shown to reduce dissonance (Steele 1988), self-affirmations are not always the mode of choice. When multiple routes are available, people apparently prefer to reduce dissonance directly by changing attitudes and behaviors (i.e. modifying the inconsistent cognitions) rather than to alleviate it indirectly through self-affirmations (Stone et al 1997). Even people with high self-esteem, who should possess the resources to reduce dissonance by focusing on positive aspects of the self-concept, have been found instead to modify cognitions (Gibbons et al 1997). Other research has identified boundary conditions for the usefulness of self-affirmations. According to Blanton et al (1997), affirmations do not reduce dissonance if they remind people of the violated self-standard (e.g. reassurance of one's compassion when one has acted in a noncompassionate way), presumably because such affirmations make it more difficult to justify the dissonance-inducing act and lead one to dwell on the dissonant behavior.

Other research on modes of dissonance reduction has revealed individual differences in the route of choice. People who are high in attributional complexity and characteristically search for abstract, complex explanations appear to reduce the dissonance caused by counterattitudinal advocacy by considering possible external justifications for the attitude-discrepant act rather than by changing attitudes (Stadler & Baron 1998). In addition, suggesting that research has only begun to tap the variety of modes available, Burris et al (1997) documented the dissonance-reducing effects of transcendence (reconciling inconsistent beliefs under a broader principle) and reaffirmation of the attacked belief. A recognition of the full range of routes available for dissonance reduction can help to account for some of the seeming inconsistencies in the dissonance literature. For example, when Fried (1998) modified the hypocrisy paradigm to make public participants' past failures to live up to their attitudes, participants did not perform attitude-congruent compensating behaviors to reduce dissonance. Instead, they decreased the dissonance caused by public transgressions by changing their attitudes to be congruent with the behavioral transgression.

A new perspective worth watching is the development of formal mathematical models of dissonance-related processes. Parallel constraint satisfaction systems represent dissonance as a dynamic, holistic process and provide a means to evaluate consistency and other aspects of the relation between beliefs (Read et al 1997). In one application of this approach, researchers specify a network of attitudes and other cognitions, simulate changes in the network (according to pre-specified rules of how the attitudes/cognitions are related to each other) until it reaches a state of overall consistency, and compare the results of the simulation to data from research participants. Shultz & Lepper (1996) were able to use this technique to successfully account for judgment change in several classic dissonance paradigms.

MULTIPLE ATTITUDES

Sources of Multiple Attitudes

A central assumption of much attitude theorizing is that people's evaluations of a given object are stable across time, context, and form of assessment. Empirical evidence of this coherence has emerged with increasing clarity in recent years, in part due to improved understanding of the determinants of coherence in attitudinal responses [e.g. strong attitudes (Petty & Krosnick 1995)] and in part to improved methods to document coherence [e.g. compatibility in measurement (Ajzen 1996)]. However, empirical evidence that people can hold multiple attitudes toward a given object is emerging as well, and this profile of dissociation has been explained in a number of ways.

The evidence for multiple attitudes has sometimes been dismissed as reflecting epiphenomena (e.g. context effects, "nonattitudes" or weakly held attitudes). Yet multiple attitudes also can stem from more enduring effects. For example, attitudes that vary with context can represent temporary constructions (e.g. differential use of rating scales, anchoring, and adjustment effects) or more internalized tendencies to respond that are stably linked to certain contextual features (McConnell et al 1997). In addition, multiple evaluations of an attitude object can emerge from attitude structure. They can reflect the superficial responses associated with attitudes that have minimal cognitive and affective bases or the more stable reactions associated with attitudes that have inconsistent components, as when attitudes are structurally inconsistent (e.g. Chaiken et al 1995, Prislin et al 1998), held with ambivalence (Priester & Petty 1996, Thompson et al 1995), or associated with varied affective responses [e.g. immediate versus anticipated future affect (Richard et al 1996a,b, Van der Pligt et al 1998)].

In recent years, multiple attitudes have begun to generate interest in their own right, as increased theoretical understanding provides a basis for predicting both the coherence and the dissociation that occurs in attitude judgments (e.g. Mackie & Smith 1998, Wilson & Hodges 1992). This is a still-developing research area that encompasses a somewhat diverse set of effects, including context-dependent attitudes, multiply categorizable attitude objects, explicit versus implicit attitudes, subjective construals, and issue framing. The common theme linking these various research areas is that people's responses to a particular attitude object can reflect diverse evaluations, cognitive representations and interpretations, and affective reactions.

One source of dissociations is the variety of motivations that can underlie attitudes. Dissociation is implied in the claim of social influence theorists that people are motivated to adopt attitudes of relevant reference groups to the extent that the group identity is salient and desirable (Kelman 1958, Turner 1991). That is, people may possess multiple cognitive representations of attitudes on an issue that is important to more than one of the groups with which they identify. Preliminary support for this idea was provided in findings by Wood & Matz (unpublished data) that college students' attitudes toward welfare programs were more favorable when their social identities as religious people were salient (relative to a base-line attitude measure obtained with no salient group identity), whereas students' attitudes were less favorable when their identities as political conservatives were salient. Furthermore, these attitude shifts emerged most strongly among participants who considered religious or conservative social groups to be self-defining.

Dissociations also can arise from cognitive processes. To the extent that an attitude object (e.g. yogurt) is relevant to a diverse set of issues and values, people can select from multiple categories (e.g. dairy products, health foods) when construing the object. A number of factors determine the category selected, including the accessibility of category attitudes (ER Smith et al 1996). Furthermore, a single attitude object may generate multiple representations in memory when attitude-relevant information is stored separately from overall evaluations of the object (Hastie & Park 1986). Indeed, McConnell et al (1997) demonstrated that different attitudes can be generated in different contexts for a single attitude object when perceivers do not attempt, on-line, to form an integrated attitude. Multiple cognitive representations of an issue also can emerge from information processing in social influence settings. After being exposed to the judgments of others in an influence appeal, recipients may later retrieve this information without recognizing its source and, under some circumstances, unwittingly adopt it as their own response (Betz et al 1996).

Dissociations also can arise as by-products of the variety of processes through which attitude-relevant judgments are generated. Explicit, conscious judgments differ in a number of ways from judgments that are implicitly held, including the kinds of information considered (Ajzen 1996, Greenwald & Banaji 1995). For example, Wittenbrink et al (1997) suggest that explicit and implicit measures of racial prejudice are only moderately correlated because people are more likely to base explicit judgments on an egalitarian ideology; thus explicit attitudes toward racial minorities are more favorable than implicit ones.

Influence and Multiple Attitudes

Influence strategies have capitalized on the multiple cognitive representations, affective reactions, and evaluations that people can hold concerning a given object. Asch (1940) argued early on that the primary process in influence is not change in attitudes toward an object but rather change in the definition and meaning of the object. When meaning changes, attitudes change accordingly. The link between meaning and evaluation is suggested in the finding by Bosveld et al (1997) that people are more favorable toward "affirmative action" when others claim that it refers to equal opportunity rather than, for example, reverse discrimination. Even subtle aspects of the way an issue is framed or represented in an appeal, such as the apparent location and time at which a proposal will take place, can affect recipients' attitudes (Liberman & Chaiken 1996). This latter finding raises troubling questions for persuasion research that has varied personal relevance through the supposed time or location of a message proposal (e.g. instituting senior comprehensive exams at one's own university or another university). Typically, it has been assumed that recipients are responding to comparable attitude objects regardless of whether the time and location of the message proposal renders it personally relevant.

Issue framing is an influence strategy that capitalizes on multiple attitudes. In this approach, the importance and relevance of certain consequences or attributes of an issue are emphasized over other potential consequences (Ball-Rokeach & Loges 1996, Nelson & Kinder 1996, Nelson et al 1997, Price & Tewksbury 1997). For example, Eagly & Kulesa (1997) illustrate how persuasive appeals from both sides of environmental debates have framed desired positions as achieving values favored by recipients (e.g. a healthy economy based on tourism or based on logging and industry) and framed the nondesired position as achieving values most recipients reject.

Readers may wonder how appeals that use framing differ from ones that use the belief change strategies typical of message-based persuasion paradigms. Standard persuasion appeals typically address intraattitudinal relations and describe the specific attributes possessed by an attitude object. In contrast, as implied in the label, framing appeals typically address interattitudinal relations and place an issue or object in the context of other attitude issues, values, and goals. Furthermore, framing appears to highlight the relevance or importance of existing knowledge structures and values. Nelson et al (1997) reported that framing effects are typically stronger for participants familiar with an issue (i.e. possessing the relevant knowledge structures) than for those unfamiliar with it. Despite these unique features of framing, established models of attitude change seem appropriate for understanding its effects. For example, expectancy-value formulations can account for framing effects through variations in the salience and likelihood of relevant goals and values, as well as through variations in the evaluation given to them (Ajzen 1996).

The mechanisms underlying framing effects probably depend, as in standard persuasion paradigms, on the extent to which recipients are motivated and able to process message content and other relevant information (see discussion of the dual-mode information processing models in next section). For example, the impetus to adopt a new interpretation or frame for an issue can arise from motivational goals such as rejecting a strongly disliked group identity. In a demonstration of this process, college students informed that their attitudes corresponded to those of a hated group, the Ku Klux Klan, shifted their own interpretations of the issue away from a seemingly racist construal; they then were able to shift their attitudes away from those of the Klan (Wood et al 1996, Pool et al 1998).

DUAL-MODE PROCESSING MODELS OF PERSUASION

Persuasion research has continued in the highly successful tradition of the dual-mode processing theories, the heuristic/systematic model (Chaiken et al 1996a) and the elaboration likelihood model (Petty & Wegener 1998a). The central tenet of these theories is that the determinants and processes of attitude change depend on people's motivation and ability to process issue-relevant information. When people are not highly motivated (e.g. the issue is not personally involving) or they have low ability (e.g. they are distracted), attitude judgments are based on easily available attributes of a source, message, or situation that are evaluated via efficient processing strategies. For example, they might use the heuristic rule, consensus implies correctness, and thus agree with a majority position. When people are both motivated and able to process information carefully, then attitudes are based on a more thoughtful, systematic assessment of relevant information. According to the elaboration likelihood model, such high-elaboration processes include learning message content, generation of cognitive responses, and dissonance-induced reasoning (Petty & Wegener 1998a). For evaluations of the similarities and differences between the heuristic/systematic model and the elaboration likelihood model, see Chaiken et al (1996a), Eagly & Chaiken (1993), and Petty & Wegener (1998a).

Research has continued apace identifying the factors that enhance systematic, thoughtful processing. According to the heuristic/systematic model, people are motivated to engage in systematic thought in order to achieve a sufficient "desired level of confidence" in their judgments. Factors that have been found to increase systematic processing (presumably by decreasing actual confidence or increasing desired confidence) include the following: framing of persuasive messages in an unexpected manner (Smith & Petty 1996); self-relevance of messages, either because recipients self-reference or are made self-aware (Turco 1996); and use in messages of token phrases that ambiguously signal broader values, such as, for Democrats, "family values" rhetoric (Garst & Bodenhausen 1996). Systematic processing also has been found when recipients hold strong, accessible attitudes on the message topic (Fabrigar et al 1998), hold ambivalent attitudes (Maio et al 1996), or enjoy effortful cognitive activity (i.e. are high in need for cognition; for review, see Cacioppo et al 1996). In addition, recipients engage in systematic processing in circumstances in which careful thought is likely to generate judgment confidence, such as when recipients believe in their own efficacy and ability to evaluate (Bohner et al 1998b) and when the message is presented in accessible, not overly complex language (Hafer et al 1996).

Systematic processing also may be implicated in resistance to influence. Pfau's (1997) insightful review of resistance research focused in particular on inoculation procedures, in which recipients receive information that strengthens their attitudes before exposure to persuasive attack. He argues that inoculation effects emerge when anticipated threats (e.g. warning of a potential attack to one's attitudes) motivate thoughtful processing to support one's own position or to counter opposing ones. Furthermore, resistance to attitude change appears to increase at midlife (Visser & Krosnick 1998). Middle-aged people appear to have especially strong attitudes that enable them to counterargue opposing positions.

Heuristic processing is used when a low-effort strategy yields attitudes with a sufficient level of confidence (Chaiken et al 1996a). A variety of heuristic cues have been identified in recent research. For example, familiar sayings can provide cues to agreement (Howard 1997), and the subjective experience of thinking about an issue can be a cue, so that, for example, people adopt positions when they can easily generate supportive arguments and reject positions when they cannot (Rothman & Schwarz 1998). In addition, relevant to understanding the heuristic cues used in everyday contexts are Dickerson's (1997) observations of politicians bolstering their favored positions with references to unbiased, expert sources and sources with an apparent allegiance to the opposition.

Cognitive Response Mediation of Attitude Change

Research has continued to address the mechanics underlying systematic, high-elaboration processing. One question is whether the valence of recipients' cognitive responses mediates persuasion or whether valence represents either an alternate measure of attitude change or an after-the-fact justification of change. To test causal precedence, Romero et al (1996) and Killeya & Johnson (1998) directly manipulated thoughts and examined the effects on attitudes. Consistent with the perspective in which thoughts mediate change, acceptance of the position in the appeal corresponded to the extent and valence of the generated thoughts. Furthermore, correlational analyses in these studies, as well as in several studies that assessed recipients' spontaneously generated thoughts (e.g. Friedrich et al 1996, Hafer et al 1996), proved consistent with the mediational role of thoughts.

Conclusions concerning causal order are complicated, however, by the few studies that reordered the typical causal sequence tested in correlational designs and found that attitudes can successfully mediate the effects of independent variables on thoughts (Friedrich et al 1996, Maio & Olson 1998). Yet the evidence of mutual mediation through attitudes as well as thoughts does not necessarily represent a challenge to the cognitive response model. Mutual mediation could reflect the simultaneous use of dual processing modes. People may engage simultaneously in effortful processing, in which an appeal instigates thoughts that then affect attitudes, along with less effortful processing, in which attitudes are directly affected by an appeal through, for example, heuristic analyses (Chaiken et al

1996a). When appeals have a direct effect on attitudes, then thoughts may reflect an after-the-fact justification for attitude judgments.

Another question is whether cognitive responses provide a sufficient model of mediation. Munro & Ditto (1997) and Zuwerink & Devine (1996) report that attitude change on prejudice-related issues is linked to message recipients' subjective experience of affect in addition to the favorability of their thoughts. Although it is possible that the insufficiency of thoughts as a mediator stems from measurement limitations (e.g. poor reliability or validity of coding of thought protocols), it also is possible that for prejudice and other attitudes with a strong affective basis, changes in affective reactions impact attitudes independently of cognitive responses.

Dual-Mode Processing Models and Social Influence

Dual-mode models also can provide a framework for understanding attitude change in social influence settings. For example, careful scrutiny of other group members' answers to a judgment task appears to depend on participants' motivation to perform well and their ability to conduct their own evaluations of the task. Baron et al (1996) reported that highly motivated participants relied on their own evaluations except when judgment stimuli were presented too briefly to identify the correct answer; then they appeared to adopt the heuristic strategy of relying on others' judgments. In contrast, participants who were only moderately motivated used the heuristic-like strategy of relying on others' estimates regardless of whether they could determine the correct answer themselves. The heuristic cues important in social influence settings include not only others' judgments, but also aspects of social interaction and others' self-presentation. For example, group members who are more confident in their judgments have been found to be more influential in discussions, regardless of their actual task accuracy (Zarnoth & Sniezek 1997).

The group discussion research by Kelly et al (1997) also can be interpreted from a dual-mode perspective. When members were motivated and able to achieve accurate solutions (i.e. the task had a seemingly correct solution, time was sufficient), group discussions entailed considerable reasoning and argumentation. Furthermore, systematic reasoning was apparently successful in yielding valid solutions; more systematic thought during discussion was associated with greater solution accuracy. Also interpretable from this perspective is the finding by Shestowsky et al (1998) that in dyadic discussions, participants who were motivated to engage in cognitive activities (i.e. were high in need for cognition) had the greatest impact on group decisions. Although no direct evidence was obtained that motivated participants engaged in careful analysis during the discussion or that this is what made them influential, participants' self-ratings suggested that those who valued thinking activities presented many arguments, presented valid arguments, and tried hard to be persuasive.

Motivated Processing and Bias Correction

Research has continued to document how recipients' motives (i.e. to defend self, maintain desired relations with others, have accurate judgements) instigate and direct systematic processing and yield more favorable evaluations of goal-promoting than hindering information (Munro & Ditto 1997, Zuwerink & Devine 1996). Motives also can yield selective use of heuristic cues, such as relying on social consensus when it provides adequate support for one's desired position (Giner-Sorolla & Chaiken 1997).

A variety of factors appear to motivate biased processing, including recipients' broader values (Eagly & Kulesa 1997, Maio & Olson 1998, Seligman et al 1996) and self-interests (Giner-Sorolla & Chaiken 1997), and attitude issues that are highly important and involving (Zuwerink & Devine 1996). However, the role of ability in biased processing remains unclear. Although some have speculated that bias emerges when people rely on their (presumably predominantly attitude-supportive) personal beliefs and knowledge to evaluate an issue, Biek et al (1996) found knowledge alone to be insufficient; thoughtful biased processing emerged only when knowledgeable people were also highly motivated (e.g. by strong affect) to hold a particular position.

Asymmetries also have been noted in motivated processing. People sometimes respond more intensely to threatening information that disconfirms their desired view than to congenial information that confirms it (see also Cacioppo et al 1997). Ditto et al (1998) speculate that because threatening stimuli are likely to require an immediate behavioral response, it is adaptive for people to conduct an objective, critical analysis of preference-inconsistent information while responding more passively to congenial information (see also Edwards & Smith 1996). It seems likely, however, that people use a variety of processing strategies to meet defensive goals. For example, a strategy of defensive inattention to challenging information can explain the finding by Slater & Rouner (1996) that people more carefully process congenial than threatening health-related information (see below).

An interesting question that has emerged in the past few years is whether people are aware of and can counteract biases and shortcuts in their information processing strategies. Wegener & Petty (1997) suggest that people engage in bias correction processes to the extent that they believe factors unrelated to the true qualities of the attitude issue have influenced their judgments and to the extent that they are motivated and able to counteract the bias. Although an implicit assumption seems to be that validity-seeking motives instigate bias correction, other motives also are plausible (e.g. the self-related motive of being an objective, impartial judge, the other-related motive of conveying this impression to others).

In a test of bias correction, Petty et al (1998) simulated a context in which it would be illegitimate to rely on heuristic rules. Participants were instructed to avoid letting their biases about a seemingly likable or unlikable source influence their judgments of the source's proposal. The result was an apparent over-correction in which the dislikable source was more persuasive than the likable one. Furthermore, because the correction instructions appeared to affect processing independently of participants' motivation to scrutinize the message, Petty et al (1998) concluded that careful message scrutiny does not spontaneously include attempts to counteract potential biases.

Bias correction also emerges in jury trials when the evidence presented is subsequently ruled inadmissible by the court. In experimental trial simulations, whether such evidence is discounted appears to depend in part on the reason for it being inadmissible. Evidence excluded because it was unreliable or because it was presented for some personal motive had little effect on judgments, whereas evidence excluded for procedural reasons continued to exert impact (Fein et al 1997, Kassin & Sommers 1997). In addition, consistent with Wegener & Petty's (1997) model, people attempting to compensate for inadmissible evidence have been found to both over- and undercorrect, depending on whether they believe the evidence was likely to have a strong or a weak impact on their judgments (Schul & Goren 1997).

AFFECT AND INFLUENCE

Effects of Mood

Several models have been developed to explain the effects of mood on information processing and attitude change. According to Wegener & Petty (1996), mood effects vary with elaboration likelihood. Direct effects of mood on agreement emerge through low-elaboration processes, including association of a persuasive appeal with positive or negative feelings (e.g. classical conditioning) and use of heuristic rules based on those feelings (e.g. "I feel bad so I must dislike it"). When people are more extensively processing, how an attitude object makes them feel can serve as a persuasive argument. It also can bias the information considered, such as when people attend more to messages that match their mood or when they recall such information more accurately (Rusting 1998). When amount of elaboration is at some middle level, people respond strategically to "manage" moods. Happy people selectively process in order to maintain their positive mood (e.g. attending to information that makes them feel good), whereas sad people are less selective because there is greater potential for any activity to be mood enhancing.

Alternatively, in the feelings-as-information account, moods signal appropriate processing strategies (Bless et al 1996, Schwarz 1997, Schwarz & Clore 1996). Similar to the discussion in the prior section concerning asymmetrical effects of motives on processing, positive moods suggest a benign environment appropriate for heuristic strategies, whereas negative moods indicate a potential problem that may require systematic evaluation. Yet all negative emotions do not appear to have the same processing implications. Ottati et al (1997) found that anger (marginally) reduced systematic processing relative to neutral moods, perhaps because anger implies agonistic contexts requiring quick response.

Controversy has emerged concerning whether negative affect enhances processing through mood management, as suggested by the elaboration model of Wegener & Petty (1996), or through signaling a problematic situation, as suggested by the feelings-as-information account of Schwarz & Clore (1996). At present, the available empirical data can be interpreted as supporting either perspectives. In addition, research findings have been taken to support a third, affect-infusion model (Forgas 1995), in which affect infuses thoughts and behaviors primarily when people engage in systematic, substantive processing. Although Forgas (1998) concluded that empirical tests support affect infusion, the finding that moods bias and direct systematic processing of influence appeals also is consistent with the other two models considered here.

Fear Appeals

The effects of fear-inducing appeals have been of particular interest in the health domain. Several theories have outlined the proximal beliefs through which fear-inducing appeals affect influence. According to protection motivation theory (Rogers 1983), appeals that are threatening and that offer an effective means of coping with the threat instigate danger control processes, which include accepting the recommended coping strategy and changing the maladaptive behavior (Prentice-Dunn et al 1997, Sturges & Rogers 1996). Rogers & Prentice-Dunn (1997) concluded that about half of the studies to date that have performed appropriate tests have supported the theory's prediction of maximum acceptance when perceived threat and coping are both high.

The extended parallel process model (Witte 1992, 1998) has linked influence to fear-control as well as danger-control responses. When threat is greater than coping, fear reactions can instigate message rejection through defensive responses (McMahan et al 1998, Witte et al 1998). Consistent with this view, Aspinwall & Brunhart (1996) reported that people who are not very optimistic about their own health coping strategies are less likely to attend to threatening health information than those who are more optimistic. Because fear-control responses inhibit the adoption of self-protective acts suggested in the appeal, they can account for the sometimes obtained "boomerang" shifts in attitudes away from messages when people do not believe they can cope effectively (Rogers & Prentice-Dunn 1997).

Research also has continued to investigate the effects of fear on message processing and to integrate the study of fear appeals into the broader models of mood and influence covered above. Fear, like other affective responses, appears to impact extent of processing. At low-to-moderate levels, fear functions like personal involvement and increases processing (Rogers & Prentice-Dunn 1997). Increased processing (at least of strong messages) may explain the often-obtained finding that fear facilitates influence and acceptance of new coping strategies (e.g.

Dillard et al 1996, Millar & Millar 1996). But fear also can bias processing in a way that justifies existing coping (or noncoping) behaviors (Biek et al 1996). At high levels, fear appears to reduce systematic processing (e.g. Jepson & Chaiken 1990). In general, the nonlinear effects of fear on processing are compatible with the idea that fear is multidimensional and involves both arousal and negative affect. Measurement scales that have been designed to tap the activation component have found that greater reported fear (i.e. arousal) enhances influence, whereas scales that have been designed to tap the negative tension component have found that greater fear (i.e. negative affect) inhibits influence or has minimal effect (Celuch et al 1998, LaTour & Rotfeld 1997).

GROUP AND SELF-IDENTITY

Social identity theory (Tajfel 1981, 1982) has sparked considerable interest in group influence as well as in other aspects of group behavior (see Brewer & Brown 1998). In the social identity view, when people categorize themselves as an ingroup member, the ingroup serves as a reference for social comparison, and people adopt the prototypic ingroup attitudes and beliefs as their own. Building on this analysis, Turner (1982, 1991) proposed that groups exert influence through a specific process, which he called referent informational influence. In this view, agreement from others categorized as similar to self enhances one's subjective certainty and suggests that the shared attitudes reflect external reality and the objective truth of the issue. Disagreement from similar others yields subjective uncertainty and motivates people to address the discrepancy through, for example, mutual social influence or attributional reasoning to explain the disagreement.

Empirical data from a variety of research paradigms are congruent with the social identity approach. Content analyses by Reicher & Hopkins (1996a,b) of political and social speeches illustrate the central role of ingroup and outgroup definitions in everyday persuasion. For example, their analysis of an antiabortion speech delivered to medical doctors revealed that it defined doctors and anti-abortion activists as a common ingroup in their concern for others' welfare, defined antiabortion activity as consonant with the medical identity, and defined abortion-rights proponents as a derogated outgroup. Other work has supported the social identity claim that influence stems from prototypic group attitudes. In the small group discussions examined by Kameda et al (1997), final decisions were influenced most strongly by "cognitively central" group members, whose initial beliefs about the discussion topic overlapped the most with other members. The influence advantage of prototypic members was independent of whether their initial judgment preferences placed them in the group majority or minority. Kameda et al (1997) argued that the shared beliefs and knowledge provided social validation for other members' views and a basis on which others could recognize prototypic members' expertise.

The self-categorization analysis differs from standard persuasion models in locating the determinants of attitude change in people's construction of group identity rather than in their understanding of attitude issues. One kind of evidence presented in support of this analysis is that influence varies with group membership (e.g. Haslam et al 1995). Other evidence is that the influence of a group does not depend on recipients learning the content of the influence appeal (McGarty et al 1994; see also Haslam et al 1996). Although some research has suggested that ingroup influence is accompanied by acceptance and learning of the message (e.g. Mackie et al 1992), Haslam et al (1996) argue that such learning occurs after adoption of the ingroup position, as people try to understand the group view in order to be an effective group member.

The self-categorization theory claim that group identity can have a direct effect on influence is compatible with a heuristic-like reasoning process in which people are persuaded because of the seeming validity of ingroup positions (e.g. my kind of people believe X). Yet evidence also exists for other kinds of processing. Empirical research has identified a number of conditions under which group identity motivates recipients to conduct a systematic, careful evaluation and interpretation of the appeal, and attitude change or resistance depends on this evaluation. Systematic processing has been found when the identity of the source group is relevant to recipients' own self-definitions (Wood et al 1996), when the issue is relevant to recipients' membership group (Crano & Chen 1998, Mackie et al 1990), when the message position is representative of ingroup consensus and thus is informative about the true group norms (van Knippenberg & Wilke 1992), and when the influence appeal evaluates an ingroup member and thus has implications for recipients' self-evaluations (Budesheim et al 1996). Systematic processing also emerges when recipients are unable to process heuristically, such as when the group position is provided after the message (Mackie et al 1992), and when the context enables careful analysis, such as when people have sufficient time to process a message from a salient, potentially important ingroup (Hogg 1996). Thus, the empirical data suggest that group influence does not operate through a single process. People's motives to align with or differentiate from social groups can yield heuristic analyses and other forms of relatively superficial information processing, or they can yield careful, systematic processing of relevant information.

Social Consensus and Validity of Information

Social identity and self-categorization theories offer a new perspective on the question of what makes information influential (see also Moscovici 1976). In message-based persuasion paradigms, strong, cogent arguments typically have been defined as ones that link the attitude issue to highly valued outcomes and that generate favorable reactions from recipients, whereas weak arguments are ones that link the issue to less-valued outcomes and that generate more negative reactions (Eagly & Chaiken 1993). Recent work within this tradition, for example, has examined how inserting weak arguments into an otherwise strong message can impair persuasion (Friedrich et al 1996, Friedrich & Smith 1998).

Social identity perspectives instead have focused on the social determinants of information validity. This view was developed in opposition to Festinger's (1954) claim that people prefer objective reality testing and use social reality testing (e.g. comparison with others' views) primarily when objective standards are not available. In self-categorization theory, reality testing is a single process in which people use the normative standards of relevant reference groups to achieve a valid, consensually shared understanding of reality congruent with their social identity (Turner 1991). In a strong statement of the implications of this position, Turner & Oakes argued that consensual judgments "are rationally more likely to reflect a deeper truth about the world, not because agreement always indicates accuracy, but because they have emerged from, and survived processes of discussion, argument, and collective testing" (1997:369).

Empirical data, however, suggest that the relation between social consensus and the apparent accuracy of information is contingent on a variety of factors. Subjective validity emerges from consensus that is established through the convergence of independent rather than dependent views and through validation by an individual's own, private cognitive processing (Levine 1996, Mackie & Skelly 1994). Furthermore, social consensus appears to be more impactful for some kinds of issues than for others, presumably because ingroup consensus implies subjective validity more strongly for some issues than for others. For example, majority consensus has an especially strong impact on judgments of personal preference, and less impact on judgments of objective stimuli, presumably because consensus indicates preferences likely to be shared with similar others (Crano & Hannula-Bral 1994, Wood et al 1994).

Multiple Motives Instigated by Groups

In social identity and self-categorization theories, the motive for influence derives largely from the desire to establish and maintain a positive evaluation of the self. In support, Pool et al (1998) demonstrated that people maintain a favorable self-view by shifting their attitudes to align with positively valued groups and to deviate from negatively valued ones. Attitude change motivated by social identity also can be driven by other self-related concerns, such as striving to be true to oneself and to achieve a coherent, certain self-view (Abrams & Hogg 1988).

The tripartite analysis of motives presented in this chapter suggests additional reasons why people adopt or reject group positions (see also Wood 1999). One involves the positive and negative outcomes provided by others. For example, going along with others in order to get along with them (i.e. receive social rewards and avoid punishments) is likely to be important in close relationships and other ingroup settings in which social harmony is valued. Another potential motive for adopting or rejecting group positions is in order to achieve an accurate, valid understanding of reality. This possibility challenges perspectives that have associated group influence with bias. For example, in an analysis of democratic participation, Pratkanis & Turner (1996) proposed that active, deliberative discussion and analysis of political issues occurs when citizens view issues as personally relevant, whereas uncritical acceptance of political solutions and propaganda provided by a ruling elite occurs when citizens wish to assume a certain social identity (e.g. party allegiance). However, to the extent that some social and group identities (e.g. informed voter, responsible citizen) motivate people to adopt valid, accurate positions, then group-related motives are not necessarily associated with biased processing.

OPINION MINORITY AND MAJORITY GROUPS

The seeming paradox that "few can influence many" has continued to spark interest in minority influence. This work typically defines minorities as sources advocating infrequent, low consensus positions.

Recent research has progressed beyond the original notion that minority sources are influential because they elicit informational conflict and challenge recipients' understanding of issues (Moscovici 1985). Instead, the most consistent finding appears to be that the social identity of minorities inhibits influence. Minorities are most influential when their impact is assessed on "indirect" judgment measures—ones on which recipients are relatively unaware that their judgments could align them with the deviant minority source (Wood et al 1994). Yet even on indirect measures, evidence of minority impact often fails to emerge (Martin 1998). Minorities seem to face two impediments to exerting influence. They are, by definition, not important reference groups. Thus source group identity is unlikely to motivate people to attend to and evaluate an appeal (De Vries et al 1996). Furthermore, even when people process the appeal, the source's low consensus, deviant position is likely to yield a negatively biased processing orientation. As a result, recipients resist influence (Mugny 1980, Erb et al 1998) or demonstrate "boomerang" shifts away from the minority view (Pool et al 1998, Wood et al 1996).

In a series of elegant experiments, Crano and his colleagues (Alvaro & Crano 1996, 1997; Crano & Alvaro 1998; Crano & Chen 1998) demonstrated that these impediments to minority influence can be surmounted by ingroup minority sources (see also David & Turner 1996). It appears that the distinctiveness of ingroup minority positions encourages careful message processing, yet with the lenient, open-minded orientation typically accorded to ingroup members. The deviance of the minority view attenuates acceptance on direct attitude measures but the imbalance in attitude structure that results from message processing yields attitude change toward the minority view on measures indirectly related to the appeal.

Several lines of research have documented the kinds of thought recipients generate to minority appeals. Especially in problem-solving contexts in which novel solutions are valued (Nemeth 1986), minorities encourage recipients to think about issues in a divergent manner and to consider novel ideas and solution strategies (Butera et al 1996, Erb et al 1998, Gruenfeld et al 1998, Nemeth & Rogers 1996, Peterson & Nemeth 1996). Attributional reasoning is also likely to mediate influence, given that minority positions are often unexpected and require explanation. Research findings generally support the analysis by Eagly et al (1981) that influence is impaired when the advocated position can be attributed to a potentially biasing attribute of the source or situation, such as the source's personal self-interest (Moskowitz 1996). In like manner, influence is enhanced when the advocated position can be attributed to external reality or the truth about the issue (Bohner et al 1996, 1998a). Also suggesting attributional reasoning is the finding that minorities are influential when they express their views in contexts, such as face-to-face interaction, in which deviancy can incur costs (McLeod et al 1997). Advocacy then suggests a source who is sufficiently committed and certain to risk social rejection.

A useful goal for future research will be to identify the specific aspect(s) of minority identity that motivate agreement or resistance. Following the three-motive scheme of this chapter, it may be that the minority source has relevance for recipients' personal identities and represents, for example, a deviant other from whom they wish to differentiate or a valued innovator they wish to emulate (Wood et al 1996). Another motive concerns recipients' relations with others, such as the desire to be lenient with ingroup minority sources (Crano & Chen 1998). Finally, recipients could achieve an accurate understanding of an issue by agreeing with minorities whose positions appear to reflect external reality (Bohner et al 1996).

CONCLUSION

This chapter has drawn from the literatures on message-based persuasion and social influence to identify common themes in attitude change research. In these traditionally separate areas of investigation, theoretical and empirical work has begun to delineate the motives underlying recipients' responses to influence appeals and the variety of cognitive and affective processes involved in attitude change and resistance.

The *Annual Review* chapter on attitudes traditionally has focused on message-based persuasion research that examines attitudes at the individual level. From this standpoint, the current inclusion of social influence findings highlights the sometimes neglected point that attitudes are social phenomena, that they emerge from and are embedded in social interaction. Yet, enthusiasm for aggregating knowledge across these two areas of investigation should not overwhelm the equally important point that each area is associated with unique predictors and processes. Models of influence via complexly argued persuasive messages will need to address unique factors that are not as important in the study of simple messages, including recipients' ability to engage in extensive cognitive processing and their knowledge about the message topic. In like manner, models of influence in groups and other complex social contexts address unique factors such as the likelihood of information exchange and the interaction structure in the social setting.

A challenge for future investigation will be to continue to develop models of social and cognitive processes that are sufficiently inclusive to capture attitude change in the variety of social and informational settings in which it occurs. An important aspect of this challenge is to place persuasion and social influence within a framework that recognizes cross-cultural and ethnic effects. It is appropriate to end the chapter with a noteworthy example of such an approach, the meta-analytic synthesis by Bond & Smith (1996) of social influence experiments from 17 countries. The usefulness of integrating cultural-level phenomena into attitude theories is evident in the greater levels of conformity in experiments conducted in nations characterized by collective than by individualistic values.

ACKNOWLEDGMENTS

Preparation of this chapter was supported by National Science Foundation grant #SBR 95–14537. The author thanks William D Crano, Alice H Eagly, David Matz, Richard E Petty, and Radmila Prislin for their helpful comments on an earlier draft of the chapter.

Visit the Annual Reviews home page at www.AnnualReviews.org.

LITERATURE CITED

Abrams D, Hogg MA. 1988. Comments on the motivational status of self-esteem in social identity and intergroup discrimination. *Eur. J. Soc. Psychol.* 18:317–34

Ajzen I. 1996. The directive influence of attitudes on behavior. See Gollwitzer & Bargh 1996, pp. 385–403

Allport GW. 1985. The historical background of social psychology. See Lindzey & Aronson 1985, 1:1–46

Alvaro EM, Crano WD. 1996. Cognitive responses to minority- or majority-based communications: factors that underlie minority influence. *Br. J. Soc. Psychol.* 35:105–21

Alvaro EM, Crano WD. 1997. Indirect minority influence: evidence for leniency in source evaluation and counterargumentation. *J. Pers. Soc. Psychol.* 72:949–64

Aronson E. 1992. The return of the repressed: Dissonance theory makes a comeback. *Psychol. Inq.* 3:303–11

Asch SE. 1940. Studies in the principles of judgments and attitudes. II. Determination of judgments by group and by ego standards. *J. Soc. Psychol.* 12:433–65

Aspinwall LG, Brunhart SM. 1996. Distinguishing optimism from denial: optimistic beliefs predict attention to health threats. *Pers. Soc. Psychol. Bull.* 22:993–1003

Baldwin MW, Holmes JG. 1987. Salient private audiences and awareness of the self. *J. Pers. Soc. Psychol.* 52:1087–98

Ball-Rokeach SJ, Loges WE. 1996. Making choices: media roles in the construction of value-choices. See Seligman et al 1996, pp. 277–98

Baron RS, Vandello JA, Brunsman B. 1996. The forgotten variable in conformity research: impact of task importance on social influence. *J. Pers. Soc. Psychol.* 71:915–27

Betz AL, Skowronski J, Ostrom TO. 1996. Shared realities: social influence and stimulus memory. *Soc. Cogn.* 14:113–40

Biek M, Wood W, Chaiken S. 1996. Working knowledge, cognitive processing, and attitudes: on the determinants of bias. *Pers. Soc. Psychol. Bull.* 22:547–56

Blanton H, Cooper J, Skurnik I, Aronson J. 1997. When bad things happen to good feedback: exacerbating the need for self-justification with self-affirmations. *Pers. Soc. Psychol. Bull.* 23:684–92

Bless H, Clore GO, Schwarz N, Golisano V, Rabe C, Wolk M. 1996. Mood and the use of scripts: Does a happy mood really lead to mindlessness? *J. Pers. Soc. Psychol.* 71:665–79

Bohner G, Erb HP, Reinhard MA, Frank E. 1996. Distinctiveness across topics in minority and majority influence: an attributional analysis and preliminary data. *Br. J. Soc. Psychol.* 35:27–46

Bohner G, Frank E, Erb HP. 1998a. Heuristic processing of distinctiveness information in minority and majority influence. *Eur. J. Soc. Psychol.* 28:855–60

Bohner G, Rank S, Reinhard MA, Einwiller S, Erb HP. 1998b. Motivational determinants of systematic processing: Expectancy moderates effects of desired confidence on processing effort. *Eur. J. Soc. Psychol.* 28:185–206

Bond R, Smith PB. 1996. Culture and conformity: a meta-analysis of studies using Asch's (1952, 1956) line judgment task. *Psychol. Bull.* 119:111–37

Bosveld W, Koomen W, Vogelaar R. 1997. Construing a social issue: effects on attitudes and the false consensus effect. *Br. J. Soc. Psychol.* 36:263–72

Brewer MB, Brown RJ. 1998. Intergroup relations. See Gilbert et al 1998, 2:554–94

Budesheim TL, Houston DA, DePaola SJ. 1996. Persuasiveness of in-group and out-group political messages: the case of negative political campaigning. *J. Pers. Soc. Psychol.* 70:523–34

Burris CT, Harmon-Jones E, Tarpley WR. 1997. "By faith alone": religious agitation and cognitive dissonance. *Basic Appl. Soc. Psychol.* 19:17–31

Butera F, Mugny G, Legrenzi P, Perez JA. 1996. Majority and minority influence, task representation and inductive reasoning. *Br. J. Soc. Psychol.* 35:123–36

Cacioppo JT, Gardner WL, Berntson GG. 1997. Beyond bipolar conceptualizations and measures: the case of attitudes and evaluative space. *Pers. Soc. Psychol. Rev.* 1:3–25

Cacioppo JT, Petty RE, Feinstein J, Jarvis B. 1996. Dispositional differences in cognitive motivation: the life and times of individuals varying in need for cognition. *Psychol. Bull.* 119:197–253

Celuch K, Lust J, Showers L. 1998. A test of a model of consumers' responses to product manual safety information. *J. Appl. Soc. Psychol.* 28:377–94

Chaiken S, Giner-Sorolla R, Chen S. 1996a. Beyond accuracy: defense and impression motives in heuristic and systematic information processing. See Gollwitzer & Bargh 1996, pp. 553–78

Chaiken S, Pomerantz EM, Giner-Sorolla R. 1995. Structural consistency and attitude strength. See Petty & Krosnick 1995, pp. 387–412

Chaiken S, Wood W, Eagly AH. 1996b. Principles of persuasion. See Higgins & Kruglanski 1996, pp. 702–42

Chen S, Schechter D, Chaiken S. 1996. Getting at the truth or getting along: accuracy- versus impression-motivated heuristic and systematic processing. *J. Pers. Soc. Psychol.* 71:262–75

Cialdini RB, Levy A, Herman CP, Kozlowski LT, Petty RE. 1976. Elastic shifts of opinion: determinants of direction and durability. *J. Pers. Soc. Psychol.* 34:663–72

Cialdini RB, Trost MR. 1998. Social influence: social norms, conformity, and compliance. See Gilbert et al 1998, 2:151–92

Cooper J, Fazio RH. 1984. A new look at dissonance theory. *Adv. Exp. Soc. Psychol.* 17:229–66

Cowan G, Hodge C. 1996. Judgments of hate speech: the effects of target group, publicness, and behavioral responses of the target. *J. Appl. Soc. Psychol.* 26:355–74

Crano WD, Alvaro EM. 1998. The context/comparison model of social influence: mechanisms, structure, and linkages that underlie indirect attitude change. *Eur. Rev. Soc. Psychol.* 8:175–202

Crano WD, Chen X. 1998. The leniency contract and persistence of majority and minority influence. *J. Pers. Soc. Psychol.* 74:1437–50

Crano WD, Hannula-Bral KA. 1994. Context/categorization model of social influence: minority and majority influence in the formation of a novel response norm. *J. Exp. Soc. Psychol.* 30:247–76

David B, Turner JC. 1996. Studies in self-categorization and minority conversion: Is being a member of the out-group an advantage? *Br. J. Soc. Psychol.* 35:179–99

Deutsch M, Gerard HB. 1955. A study of normative and informational social influences upon individual judgment. *J. Abnorm. Soc. Psychol.* 51:629–36

De Vries NK, De Dreu CKW, Gordijn EH, Schuurman M. 1996. Majority and minority influence: a dual role interpretation. *Eur. Rev. Soc. Psychol.* 7:145–72

Dickerson P. 1997. 'It's not just me who's saying this . . . .' The deployment of cited others in televised political discourse. *Br. J. Soc. Psychol.* 36:33–48

Dillard JP, Plotnick CA, Godbold LC, Freimuth VS, Edgar T. 1996. The multiple affective outcomes of AIDS PSAs: Fear appeals do more than scare people. *Commun. Res.* 23:44–72

Ditto PH, Scepansky JA, Munro GD, Apanovitch AM, Lockhart LK. 1998. Motivated sensitivity to preference-inconsistent information. *J. Pers. Soc. Psychol.* 75:53–69

Eagly AH, Chaiken S. 1993. *The Psychology of Attitudes.* Orlando, FL: Harcourt Brace Jovanovich

Eagly AH, Chaiken S. 1998. Attitude structure and function. See Gilbert et al 1998, 1:269–322

Eagly AH, Chaiken S, Wood W. 1981. An attribution analysis of persuasion. In *New Directions in Attribution Research,* ed. JH Harvey, WJ Ickes, RF Kidd, 3:37–62. Mahwah, NJ: Erlbaum

Eagly AH, Kulesa P. 1997. Attitudes, attitude structure, and resistance to change: implications for persuasion on environmental issues. In *Environment, Ethics, and Behavior: The Psychology of Environmental Valuation and Degradation,* ed. MH Bazerman, DM Messick, AE Tenbrunsel, KA Wade-Benzoni, pp. 122–53. San Francisco: New Lexington

Edwards K, Smith EE. 1996. A disconfirmation bias in the evaluation of arguments. *J. Pers. Soc. Psychol.* 71:5–24

Erb H, Bohner G, Schmalzle K, Rank S. 1998. Beyond conflict and discrepancy: cognitive bias in minority and majority influence. *Pers. Soc. Psychol. Bull.* 24:620–33

Fabrigar LR, Priester JR, Petty RE, Wegener DT. 1998. The impact of attitude accessibility on elaboration of persuasive messages. *Pers. Soc. Psychol. Bull.* 24:339–52

Fein S, McCloskey AL, Tomlinson TM. 1997. Can the jury disregard that information? The use of suspicion to reduce the prejudicial effects of pretrial publicity and inadmissible testimony. *Pers. Soc. Psychol. Bull.* 23:1215–26

Festinger L. 1954. A theory of social comparison processes. *Hum. Relat.* 7:117–40

Festinger L. 1957. *A Theory of Cognitive Dissonance.* Evanston, IL: Row Peterson

Fiske ST. 1998. Stereotyping, prejudice, and discrimination. See Gilbert et al 1998, 2:357–414

Forgas JP. 1995. Mood and judgment: the affect infusion model (AIM). *Psychol. Bull.* 117:39–66

Forgas JP. 1998. Asking nicely? The effects of mood on responding to more or less polite requests. *Pers. Soc. Psychol. Bull.* 24:173–85

Fried CB. 1998. Hypocrisy and identification with transgressions: a case of undetected dissonance. *Basic Appl. Soc. Psychol.* 20:145–54

Fried CB, Aronson E. 1995. Hypocrisy, misattribution, and dissonance reduction. *Pers. Soc. Psychol. Bull.* 21:925–33

Friedrich J, Fetherstonhaugh D, Casey S, Gallagher D. 1996. Argument integration and attitude change: suppression effects in the integration of one-sided arguments that vary in persuasiveness. *Pers. Soc. Psychol. Bull.* 22:179–91

Friedrich J, Smith P. 1998. Suppressive influence of weak arguments in mixed-quality messages: an exploration of mechanisms via argument rating, pretesting, and order effects. *Basic Appl. Soc. Psychol.* 20:293–304

Garst J, Bodenhausen GV. 1996. "Family values" and political persuasion: impact of kin-related rhetoric on reactions to political campaigns. *J. Appl. Soc. Psychol.* 26:1119–37

Gibbons FX, Eggleston TJ, Benthin AC. 1997. Cognitive reactions to smoking relapse: the reciprocal relation between dissonance and self-esteem. *J. Pers. Soc. Psychol.* 72:184–95

Gilbert DT, Fiske ST, Lindzey G, eds. 1998. *The Handbook of Social Psychology,* Vols. 1, 2. Boston: McGraw-Hill. 4th ed.

Giner-Sorolla R, Chaiken S. 1997. Selective use of heuristic and systematic processing under defense motivation. *Pers. Soc. Psychol. Bull.* 23:84–97

Gollwitzer PM, Bargh JA, eds. 1996. *The Psychology of Action: Linking Cognition and Motivation to Behavior.* New York: Guilford

Greenwald AG, Banaji MR. 1995. Implicit social cognition: attitudes, self-esteem, and stereotypes. *Psychol. Rev.* 102:4–27

Gruenfeld DH, Thomas-Hunt MC, Kim PH. 1998. Cognitive flexibility, communication strategy, and integrative complexity in groups: public versus private reactions to majority and minority status. *J. Exp. Soc. Psychol.* 34:202–26

Hafer CL, Reynolds K, Obertynski MA. 1996. Message comprehensibility and persuasion: effects of complex language in counterattitudinal appeals to laypeople. *Soc. Cogn.* 14:317–37

Hardin CD, Higgins ET. 1996. Shared reality: How social verification makes the subjective objective. In *Handbook of Motivation and Cognition,* ed. RM Sorrentino, ET Higgins, 3:28–84. New York: Guilford

Harmon-Jones E, Brehm JW, Greenberg J, Simon L, Nelson DE. 1996. Evidence that the production of aversive consequences is not necessary to create cognitive dissonance. *J. Pers. Soc. Psychol.* 70:5–16

Haslam SA, McGarty C, Turner JC. 1996. Salient group memberships and persuasion: the role of social identity in the validation of beliefs. In *What's Social About Social Cognition? Research on Socially Shared Cognition in Small Groups,* ed. JL Nye, AM Brower, pp. 29–56. Thousand Oaks, CA: Sage

Haslam SA, Oakes PJ, McGarty C, Turner JC, Onorato RS. 1995. Contextual changes in the prototypicality of extreme and moderate outgroup members. *Eur. J. Soc. Psychol.* 25:509–30

Hastie R, Park B. 1986. The relationship between memory and judgment depends on whether the judgment task is memory-based or on-line. *Psychol. Rev.* 93:258–68

Higgins ET. 1981. "The communication game": implications for social cognition and persuasion. In *Social Cognition: The Ontario Symposium,* ed. ET Higgins, CP

Herman, MP Zanna, 1:343–92. Mahwah, NJ: Erlbaum

Higgins ET, Kruglanski AW, eds. 1996. *Social Psychology: Handbook of Basic Principles.* New York: Guilford

Hogg MA. 1996. Intragroup processes, group structure and social identity. In *Social Groups and Identities: Developing the Legacy of Henri Tajfel,* ed. WP Robinson, pp. 65–93. Oxford, UK: Butterworth-Heinemann

Howard DJ. 1997. Familiar phrases as peripheral persuasion cues. *J. Exp. Soc. Psychol.* 33:231–43

Jepson C, Chaiken S. 1990. Chronic issue-specific fear inhibits systematic processing of persuasive communications. *J. Soc. Behav. Pers.* 5:61–84

Johnson BT, Eagly AH. 1989. Effects of involvement on persuasion: a meta-analysis. *Psychol. Bull.* 106:290–314

Joule R, Beauvois J. 1998. Cognitive dissonance theory: a radical view. *Eur. Rev. Soc. Psychol.* 8:1–32

Kameda T, Ohtsubo Y, Takezawa M. 1997. Centrality in sociocognitive networks and social influence: an illustration in a group decision-making context. *J. Pers. Soc. Psychol.* 73:296–309

Kassin SM, Kiechel KL. 1996. The social psychology of false confessions: compliance, internalization, and confabulation. *Psychol. Sci.* 7:125–28

Kassin SM, Sommers SR. 1997. Inadmissible testimony, instructions to disregard, and the jury: substantive versus procedural considerations. *Pers. Soc. Psychol. Bull.* 23:1046–54

Katz D. 1960. The functional approach to the study of attitudes. *Public Opin. Q.* 24:163–204

Kelly JR, Jackson JW, Hutson-Comeaux SL. 1997. The effects of time pressure and task differences on influence modes and accuracy in decision-making groups. *Pers. Soc. Psychol. Bull.* 23:10–22

Kelman HC. 1958. Compliance, identification, and internalization: three processes of attitude change. *J. Conflict Resolut.* 2:51–60

Killeya LA, Johnson BT. 1998. Experimental induction of biased systematic processing: the directed thought technique. *Pers. Soc. Psychol. Bull.* 24:17–33

Lambert AJ, Cronen S, Chasteen AL, Lickel B. 1996. Private vs public expressions of racial prejudice. *J. Exp. Soc. Psychol.* 32:437–59

LaTour MS, Rotfeld HJ. 1997. There are threats and (maybe) fear-caused arousal: theory and confusions of appeals to fear and fear arousal itself. *J. Advert.* 26:45–59

Lavine H, Snyder M. 1996. Cognitive processing and the functional matching effect in persuasion: the mediating role of subjective perceptions of message quality. *J. Exp. Soc. Psychol.* 32:580–604

Levine J. 1996. *Solomon Asch's legacy for group research.* Presented at Annu. Meet. Soc. Pers. Soc. Psychol., Sturbridge, MA

Liberman A, Chaiken S. 1996. The direct effect of personal relevance on attitudes. *Pers. Soc. Psychol. Bull.* 22:269–79

Lindzey G, Aronson E, eds. 1985. *Handbook of Social Psychology,* Vols. 1, 2. New York: Random House

Lundgren SR, Prislin R. 1998. Motivated cognitive processing and attitude change. *Pers. Soc. Psychol. Bull.* 24:715–26

Mackie DM, Gastardo-Conaco MC, Skelly JJ. 1992. Knowledge of the advocated position and the processing of in-group and out-group persuasive messages. *Pers. Soc. Psychol. Bull.* 18:145–51

Mackie DM, Skelly JJ. 1994. The social cognition analysis of social influence: contributions to the understanding of persuasion and conformity. In *Social Cognition: Impact on Social Psychology,* ed. P Devine, D Hamilton, T Ostrom, pp. 259–89. New York: Academic

Mackie DM, Smith ER. 1998. Intergroup relations: insights from a theoretically integrative approach. *Psychol. Rev.* 105:499–529

Mackie DM, Worth LT, Asuncion AG. 1990. Processing of persuasive ingroup messages. *J. Pers. Soc. Psychol.* 58:812–22

Maio GR, Bell DW, Esses VM. 1996. Ambivalence in persuasion: the processing of messages about immigrant groups. *J. Exp. Soc. Psychol.* 32:513–36

Maio GR, Olson JM. 1998. Attitude dissimulation and persuasion. *J. Exp. Soc. Psychol.* 34:182–201

Marsh KL, Hart-O'Rourke DM, Julka DL. 1997. The persuasive effects of verbal and nonverbal information in a context of value relevance. *Pers. Soc. Psychol. Bull.* 23:563–79

Martin R. 1998. Majority and minority influence using the afterimage paradigm: a series of attempted replications. *J. Exp. Soc. Psychol.* 34:1–26

McConnell AR, Leibold JM, Sherman SJ. 1997. Within-target illusory correlations and the formation of context-dependent attitudes. *J. Pers. Soc. Psychol.* 73:675–86

McGarty C, Haslam SA, Hutchinson KJ, Turner JC. 1994. The effects of salient group memberships on persuasion. *Small Group Res.* 25:267–93

McLeod PL, Baron RS, Marti MW, Yoon K. 1997. The eyes have it: minority influence in face-to-face and computer-mediated group discussion. *J. Appl. Psychol.* 82:706–18

McMahan S, Witte K, Meyer J. 1998. The perception of risk messages regarding electromagnetic fields: extending the extended parallel process model to an unknown risk. *Health Commun.* 10:247–59

Millar MG, Millar KU. 1996. Effects of message anxiety on disease detection and health promotion behaviors. *Basic Appl. Soc. Psychol.* 18:61–74

Moscovici S. 1976. *Social Influence and Social Change.* London: Academic

Moscovici S. 1985. Social influence and conformity. See Lindzey & Aronson 1985, 2:347–412

Moskowitz GB. 1996. The mediational effects of attributions and information processing in minority social influence. *Br. J. Soc. Psychol.* 35:47–66

Mugny G. 1980. *The Power of Minorities.* London: Academic

Munro GD, Ditto PH. 1997. Biased assimilation, attitude polarization, and affect in reactions to stereotype-relevant scientific information. *Pers. Soc. Psychol. Bull.* 23:636–53

Murray SL, Haddock G, Zanna MP. 1996. On creating value-expressive attitudes: an experimental approach. See Seligman et al 1996, pp. 107–33

Nelson TE, Kinder DR. 1996. Issue frames and group-centrism in American public opinion. *J. Polit.* 58:1055–78

Nelson TE, Oxley ZM, Clawson RA. 1997. Toward a psychology of framing effects. *Polit. Behav.* 19:221–46

Nemeth CJ. 1986. Differential contributions of majority and minority influence. *Psychol. Rev.* 93:23–32

Nemeth CJ, Rogers J. 1996. Dissent and the search for information. *Br. J. Soc. Psychol.* 35:67–76

Ottati V, Terkildsen N, Hubbard C. 1997. Happy faces elicit heuristic processing in a televised impression formation task: a cognitive tuning account. *Pers. Soc. Psychol. Bull.* 23:1144–56

Peterson RS, Nemeth C. 1996. Focus versus flexibility: Majority and minority influence can both improve performance. *Pers. Soc. Psychol. Bull.* 22:14–23

Petty RE, Krosnick JA. 1995. *Attitude Strength: Antecedents and Consequences.* Mahwah, NJ: Erlbaum

Petty RE, Wegener DT. 1998a. Attitude change: multiple roles for persuasion variables. See Gilbert et al 1998, 1:323–90

Petty RE, Wegener DT. 1998b. Matching versus mismatching attitude functions: implications for scrutiny of persuasive messages. *Pers. Soc. Psychol. Bull.* 24:227–40

Petty RE, Wegener DT, Fabrigar LR. 1997. Attitudes and attitude change. *Annu. Rev. Psychol.* 48:609–47

Petty RE, Wegener DT, White PH. 1998. Flexible correction processes in social judgment: implications for persuasion. *Soc. Cogn.* 16:93–113

Pfau M. 1997. The inoculation model of resistance to influence. *Prog. Commun. Sci.* 13:133–71

Pool GJ, Wood W, Leck K. 1998. The self-esteem motive in social influence: agreement with valued majorities and disagreement with derogated minorities. *J. Pers. Soc. Psychol.* 75:967–75

Pratkanis AR, Turner ME. 1996. Persuasion and democracy: strategies for increasing deliberative participation and enacting social change. *J. Soc. Issues.* 52:187–205

Prentice-Dunn S, Jones JL, Floyd DL. 1997. Persuasive appeals and the reduction of skin cancer risk: the roles of appearance concern, perceived benefits of a tan, and efficacy information. *J. Appl. Soc. Psychol.* 27:1041–47

Price V, Tewksbury D. 1997. News values and public opinion: a theoretical account of media priming and framing. *Prog. Commun. Sci.* 13:173–212

Priester JR, Petty RE. 1996. The gradual threshold model of ambivalence: relating the positive and negative bases of attitudes to subjective ambivalence. *J. Pers. Soc. Psychol.* 71:431–49

Prislin R, Pool GJ. 1996. Behavior, consequences, and the self: Is all well that ends well? *Pers. Soc. Psychol. Bull.* 22:933–48

Prislin R, Wood W, Pool GJ. 1998. Structural consistency and the deduction of novel from existing attitudes. *J. Exp. Soc. Psychol.* 34:66–89

Read SJ, Vanman EJ, Miller LC. 1997. Connectionism, parallel constraint satisfaction processes, and gestalt principles: (re)introducing cognitive dynamics to social psychology. *Pers. Soc. Psychol. Rev.* 1:26–53

Reicher S, Hopkins N. 1996a. Seeking influence through categorizing self-categories: an analysis of anti-abortionist rhetoric. *Br. J. Soc. Psychol.* 35:297–311

Reicher S, Hopkins N. 1996b. Self-category constructions in political rhetoric; an analysis of Thatcher's and Kinnock's speeches concerning the British miners' strike (1984–5). *Eur. J. Soc. Psychol.* 26:353–71

Richard R, Van der Pligt J, De Vries NK. 1996a. Anticipated affect and behavioral choice. *Basic Appl. Soc. Psychol.* 18:111–29

Richard R, Van der Pligt J, De Vries NK. 1996b. Anticipated regret and time perspective: changing sexual risk-taking behavior. *J. Behav. Dec. Mak.* 9:185–99

Rogers RW. 1983. Cognitive and physiological processes in fear appeals and attitude change: a revised theory of protection motivation. In *Social Psychophysiology: A Sourcebook,* ed. JT Cacioppo, RE Petty, pp. 153–77. New York: Guilford

Rogers RW, Prentice-Dunn S. 1997. Protection motivation theory. In *Handbook of Health Behavior Research,* ed. D Gochman, 1:113–32. New York: Plenum

Romero AA, Agnew CR, Insko CA. 1996. The cognitive mediation hypothesis revisited: an empirical response to methodological and theoretical criticism. *Pers. Soc. Psychol. Bull.* 22:651–65

Rothman AJ, Salovey P. 1997. Shaping perceptions to motivate healthy behavior: the role of message framing. *Psychol. Bull.* 121:3–19

Rothman AJ, Schwarz N. 1998. Constructing perceptions of vulnerability: personal relevance and the use of experiential information in health judgments. *Pers. Soc. Psychol. Bull.* 24:1053–64

Ruscher JB, Duval LL. 1998. Multiple communicators with unique target information transmit less stereotypical impressions. *J. Pers. Soc. Psychol.* 74:329–44

Rusting CL. 1998. Personality, mood, and the cognitive processing of emotional information: three conceptual frameworks. *Psychol. Bull.* 124:165–96

Schul Y, Goren H. 1997. When strong evidence has less impact than weak evidence: bias, adjustment, and instructions to ignore. *Soc. Cogn.* 15:133–55

Schwarz N. 1997. Moods and attitude judgments: a comment on Fishbein and Middlestadt. *J. Consum. Psychol.* 6:93–98

Schwarz N, Clore GL. 1996. Feelings and phenomenal experiences. See Higgins & Kruglanski 1996, pp. 433–65

Seligman C, Olson JM, Zanna MP, eds. 1996. *The Psychology of Values: The Ontario Symposium,* Vol. 8. Mahwah, NJ: Erlbaum

Shestowsky D, Wegener DT, Fabrigar LR. 1998. Need for cognition and interpersonal influence: individual differences in impact on dyadic decision. *J. Pers. Soc. Psychol.* 74:1317–28

Shultz TR, Lepper MR. 1996. Cognitive dissonance reduction as constraint satisfaction. *Psychol. Rev.* 103:219–40

Slater MD, Rouner D. 1996. Value-affirmative and value-protective processing of alcohol education messages that include statistical evidence or anecdotes. *Commun. Res.* 23:210–35

Smith ER, Fazio RH, Cejka MA. 1996. Accessible attitudes influence categorization of multiply categorizable objects. *J. Pers. Soc. Psychol.* 71:888–98

Smith MB, Bruner JS, White RW. 1956. *Opinions and Personality.* New York: Wiley

Smith SM, Petty RE. 1996. Message framing and persuasion: a message processing analysis. *Pers. Soc. Psychol. Bull.* 22:257–68

Stadler DR, Baron RS. 1998. Attributional complexity as a moderator of dissonance-produced attitude change. *J. Pers. Soc. Psychol.* 75:449–55

Steele CM. 1988. The psychology of self-affirmation. *Adv. Exp. Soc. Psychol.* 21:261–302

Stone J, Wiegand AW, Cooper J, Aronson E. 1997. When exemplification fails: hypocrisy and the motive for self-integrity. *J. Pers. Soc. Psychol.* 72:54–65

Sturges JW, Rogers RW. 1996. Preventive health psychology from a developmental perspective: an extension of protection motivation theory. *Health Psychol.* 15:158–66

Tajfel H. 1981. *Human Groups and Social Categories: Studies in Social Psychology.* Cambridge, UK: Cambridge Univ. Press

Tajfel H. 1982. Social psychology of intergroup relations. *Annu. Rev. Psychol.* 33:1–39

Thompson MM, Zanna MP, Griffin DW. 1995. Let's not be indifferent about (attitudinal) ambivalence. See Petty & Krosnick 1995, pp. 361–86

Turco RM. 1996. Self-referencing, quality of argument, and persuasion. *Curr. Psychol. Dev. Learn. Pers. Soc.* 15:258–76

Turner JC. 1982. Towards a cognitive redefinition of the social group. In *Social Identity and Intergroup Relations,* ed. H Tajfel, pp. 15–40. Cambridge, UK: Cambridge Univ. Press

Turner JC. 1991. *Social Influence.* Pacific Grove, CA: Brooks/Cole

Turner JC, Oakes PJ. 1997. The socially structured mind. In *The Message of Social Psychology: Perspectives on Mind in Society,* ed. C McGarty, SA Haslam, pp. 355–73. Cambridge, MA: Blackwell

Tykocinski O, Higgins ET, Chaiken S. 1994. Message framing, self-discrepancies, and yielding to persuasive messages: the motivational significance of psychological situations. *Pers. Soc. Psychol. Bull.* 20:107–15

Van der Pligt J, Zeelenberg M, Van Dijk WW, De Vries NK, Richard R. 1998. Affect, attitudes, and decisions: Let's be more specific. *Eur. Rev. Soc. Psychol.* 8:33–66

van Knippenberg D, Wilke H. 1992. Prototypicality of arguments and conformity to ingroup norms. *Eur. J. Soc. Psychol.* 22:141–55

Visser PS, Krosnick JA. 1998. Development of attitude strength over the life cycle: surge and decline. *J. Pers. Soc. Psychol.* 75:1389–410

Wegener DT, Petty RE. 1996. Effects of mood on persuasion processes: enhancing, reducing, and biasing scrutiny of attitude-relevant information. In *Striving and*

Feeling: Interactions Between Goals, Affect, and Self-Regulation, ed. LL Martin, A Tesser, pp. 329–62. Mahwah, NJ: Erlbaum

Wegener DT, Petty RE. 1997. The flexible correction model: the role of naive theories in bias correction. *Adv. Exp. Soc. Psychol.* 29:141–208

Wilson TD, Hodges SD. 1992. Attitudes as temporary constructions. In *The Construction of Social Judgment,* ed. LL Martin, A Tesser, pp. 37–65. Mahwah, NJ: Erlbaum

Witte K. 1992. Putting the fear back into fear appeals: the extended parallel process model. *Commun. Monogr.* 59:329–49

Witte K. 1998. Fear as motivator, fear as inhibitor: using the extended parallel process model to explain fear appeal successes and failures. In *Handbook of Communication and Emotion: Research, Theory, Applications, and Contexts,* ed. PA Andersen, LK Guerro, et al, pp. 423–50. San Diego: Academic

Witte K, Berkowitz JM, Cameron KA, McKeon JK. 1998. Preventing the spread of genital warts: using fear appeals to promote self-protective behaviors. *Health Educ. Behav.* 25:571–85

Wittenbrink B, Judd CM, Park B. 1997. Evidence for racial prejudice at the implicit level and its relationship with questionnaire measures. *J. Pers. Soc. Psychol.* 72:262–74

Wood W. 1999. Motives and modes of processing in the social influence of groups. In *Dual-Process Theories in Social Psychology,* ed. S Chaiken, Y Trope, pp. 547–70. New York: Guilford

Wood W, Lundgren S, Ouellette J, Busceme S, Blackstone T. 1994. Minority influence: a meta-analytic review of social influence processes. *Psychol. Bull.* 115:323–45

Wood W, Matz. 1999. *Attitudes vary with salient group identity.* Unpublished data, Texas A & M Univ.

Wood W, Pool GJ, Leck K, Purvis D. 1996. Self-definition, defensive processing, and influence: the normative impact of majority and minority groups. *J. Pers. Soc. Psychol.* 71:1181–93

Zarnoth P, Sniezek JA. 1997. The social influence of confidence in group decision making. *J. Exp. Soc. Psychol.* 33:345–66

Zuwerink JR, Devine PG. 1996. Attitude importance and resistance to persuasion: It's not just the thought that counts. *J. Pers. Soc. Psychol.* 70:931–44

Annu. Rev. Psychol. 2000. 51:571–598

CULTURAL PSYCHOPATHOLOGY: Uncovering the Social World of Mental Illness

Steven Regeser López and Peter J. J. Guarnaccia

*Department of Psychology, Box 951563, University of California, Los Angeles, California
90095–1563, e-mail: lopez@psych.ucla.edu*
*Institute for Health, Health Care Policy and Aging Research, Rutgers, The State University
of New Jersey, 30 College Avenue, New Brunswick, New Jersey 08901–1293; e-mail:
gortch@rci.rutgers.edu*

Key Words   culture, mental disorders, anxiety, schizophrenia, childhood disorders

■ **Abstract**   We review cultural psychopathology research since Kleinman's (1988) important review with the goals of updating past reviews, evaluating current conceptualizations and methods, and identifying emerging substantive trends. Conceptual advances are noted, particularly developments in the definition of culture and the examination of both culture-specific and cultural-general processes. The contributions of the Culture and Diagnosis Task Force for DSM-IV and the World Mental Health Report are reviewed and contrasted. Selected research on anxiety, schizophrenia, and childhood disorders is examined, with particular attention given to the study of *ataque de nervios,* social factors affecting the course of schizophrenia, and cross-national differences in internalizing and externalizing problems in children. Within the last ten years, cultural psychopathology research has become a significant force. Its focus on the social world holds promise to make significant inroads in reducing suffering and improving people's everyday lives.

CONTENTS

Introduction 571
Key Developments 573
   Conceptual Contributions 573
   Major Advances: Diagnostic and Statistical Manual-IV *and the World*
   Mental Health Report 576
   Disorder-Related Research 579
   Emerging Trends 587
Conclusion 589

INTRODUCTION

In 1977 Kleinman heralded the beginning of a "new cross-cultural psychiatry," an interdisciplinary research approach integrating anthropological methods and conceptualizations with traditional psychiatric and psychological approaches.

Researchers were encouraged to respect indigenous illness categories and to recognize the limitations of traditional illness categories, such as depression and schizophrenia. Also, the new cross-cultural psychiatry distinguished between disease, a "malfunctioning or maladaptation of biological or psychological processes" and illness, "the personal, interpersonal, and cultural reaction to disease" (Kleinman 1977:9). (See Shweder 1991 for a critique of this distinction). The perspective that Kleinman and others (Fabrega 1975, Kleinman et al 1978) articulated in the 1970s reflected an important direction for the study of culture and psychopathology—to understand the social world within mental illness. Parallel research efforts in cross-cultural psychology also identified ways in which culture shapes distress and disorder (for reviews see Marsella 1980, Draguns 1980).

Many advances were made during the first decade of the new cross-cultural psychiatry. One was the establishment of the interdisciplinary journal, *Culture, Medicine, and Psychiatry*. This newly founded journal, in conjunction with the reviews and commentaries of *Transcultural Psychiatry,* continues to provide an important forum for cultural research. Also, during this ten-year span, large-scale epidemiologic studies were carried out. The second multinational World Health Organization (WHO) study of schizophrenia was launched, and preliminary findings were reported (Sartorius et al 1986). The Epidemiological Catchment Area (ECA) studies were conducted as well (Regier et al 1984). Although some may question how culturally informed these landmark studies were (Edgerton & Cohen 1994, Fabrega 1990, Guarnaccia et al 1990), most reviews of culture, ethnicity, and mental disorders today refer to the findings from the WHO and ECA studies to address how social, ethnic, and cultural factors might be related to the distribution of psychopathology. Also during this time, the National Institute of Mental Health funded research centers with the sole purpose of conducting research on and for specific ethnic minority groups (African Americans, American Indians, Latinos, and Asian Americans). Some of the research from these centers contributed to the growing cultural psychopathology database (e.g. Cervantes et al 1991, King 1978, Manson et al 1985, Neighbors et al 1989, Rogler et al 1989).

Dialogues across disciplines were also initiated during this time. For example, Kleinman & Good's (1985) classic volume, *Culture and Depression,* brought together the research of not only anthropologists, but also psychologists and psychiatrists. Another significant indicator of the field's development continues to be its success in attracting new investigators, as suggested by Kleinman and colleagues' long-standing cultural anthropology and mental health training grant (for a summary, see Kleinman 1988). In sum, these first ten years can be characterized as an exciting and fertile time for the study of the new cross-cultural psychiatry. Important critiques were made, the empirical database was developing, attention to US ethnic groups grew, interdisciplinary dialogues were being established, and new investigators were being attracted to the field.

Despite the many advances, the field's main messages were not reaching larger audiences. Investigators were communicating primarily among themselves in specialty journals and books. Those findings that did manage to be published in mainstream journals were scattered among a broad array of journals. Thus, the developments of the new cross-cultural psychiatry went largely unnoticed by mainstream investigators. On a rare occasion, one would find a special issue on cultural research in a mainstream journal (e.g. *Journal of Consulting and Clinical Psychology* 1987; Clark 1987). In an effort to bring the field's messages to a broader audience (general psychiatry and other mental health fields), Kleinman (1988) provided a comprehensive review of culture, psychopathology, and related research. Drawing on empirical data and theory, Kleinman eloquently argued that culture matters for the study and treatment of mental disorders. This volume serves as a significant marker in the development of the new cross-cultural psychiatry.

We have chosen Kleinman's 1988 review as the starting point for our review. In our opinion, it is the most comprehensive review of the field to date. However, many advances have taken place since its publication. Accordingly, one of our goals for this review is to identify significant developments in the most recent study of cultural psychopathology, that is, between the years 1988 through 1998. A second goal is to evaluate the conceptualizations and methods that have guided the most recent investigations. We have largely selected systematic lines of inquiry that we consider exemplary and that can serve as models for future investigations. The third goal of this review is to identify emerging substantive trends in the study of culture and psychopathology. We discuss some of the newer, less developed areas of research that show considerable promise. In pursuing each of these goals, we hope to share our enthusiasm for this exciting and dynamic field of inquiry.

KEY DEVELOPMENTS

Conceptual Contributions

Definition of Culture   Central to the study of cultural psychopathology is the definition of culture. Much past and even current research relies on an outdated definition of culture. In fact, Betancourt & López (1993) wrote a critical review of psychological research concerning culture in which culture was defined as the values, beliefs, and practices that pertain to a given ethnocultural group. The strength of this definition is that it begins to "unpack" culture. Instead of arguing that a given expression of distress resides within a given ethnocultural group, for example, researchers argue that the expression of distress is related to a specific value or belief orientation. This is a significant advancement. It helps researchers begin to operationalize what about culture matters in the specific context. Further, it recognizes the heterogeneity within specific ethnocultural groups. Knowing that someone belongs to a specific ethnic group provides guidelines to potential cultural issues in psychopathology, but it does not imply that that person adheres to all the cultural values and practices of the group (see also Clark 1987, Helms 1997).

Despite the contributions of the values, beliefs, and practices definition of culture, it has important limitations (Guarnaccia & Rodriguez 1996, Lewis-Fernandez & Kleinman 1995). A major weakness is that this definition depicts culture as residing largely within individuals. The emphasis on values and beliefs points out the psychological nature of culture. Moreover, situating practices (customs and rituals) with values and beliefs gives the impression that the practices in the social world are a function of values and beliefs. For example, people are thought to rely on their family in times of crisis because they are high in familism or family-orientation. Investigators rarely examine what about the social world facilitates or fosters reliance on family members. Perhaps harsh environmental conditions contribute to families coming together to overcome adversity. When applying the values and beliefs definition of culture, the social world is subjugated to the psychological world of the individual. Contrary to this perspective, we argue that it is action in the social and physical world that produces culture as much as people's ideas about the world; the social world interacts on an equal footing with the psychological world in producing human behavior.

A second limitation of this frequently used definition of culture is that it depicts culture as a static phenomenon. We believe that culture is as much a process as an entity (Greenfield 1997). Attempts to freeze culture into a set of generalized value orientations or behaviors will continually misrepresent what culture is. Culture is a dynamic and creative process, some aspects of which are shared by large groups of individuals resulting from particular life circumstances and histories. Given the changing nature of our social world and given the efforts of individuals to adapt to such changes, culture can best be viewed as an ongoing process, a system or set of systems in flux.

A related limitation of the values-based definition of culture is that it depicts people as recipients of culture from a generalized "society" with little recognition of the individual's role in negotiating their cultural worlds. More recent approaches to culture in anthropology, while not discarding the importance of a person's cultural inheritance of ideas, values, and ways of relating, have focused equally on the emergence of culture from the life experiences of individuals and small groups. People can change, add to, or reject cultural elements through social processes such as migration and acculturation. A viable definition of culture acknowledges the agency of individuals in establishing their social worlds.

In sum, current views of culture attend much more to people's social world than past views of culture that emphasized the individual. Of particular interest are people's daily routines and how such activities are tied to families, neighborhoods, villages, and social networks. By examining people's daily routines one can identify what matters most (Gallimore et al 1993) or is most at stake for people (Ware & Kleinman 1992). Furthermore, this perspective captures the dynamic nature of culture because it is a product of group values, norms, and experiences, as well as of individual innovations and life histories. The use of this broader definition of culture should help guide investigators away from flat, unidimensional notions of culture, to discover the richness of a cultural analysis for the study of psychopatholgy. An important component of this perspective is the examination of intracultural diversity. In particular, social class, poverty, and gender continue to affect different levels of mental health both within and across cultural groups.

Goal of Cultural Research   There are divergent views regarding the purpose of cultural research. Some writers imply that cultural research should be carried out to test the generality of given theoretical notions. For example, in a thoughtful analysis of cultural research, Clark noted: "Conceptual progress in psychology requires a unified base for investigating psychological phenomena, with culture-relevant variables included as part of the matrix" (1987:465). From Clark's point of view, cross-cultural work can serve to enhance the generality of given conceptual models by adding, when necessary, cultural variables to an existing theoretical model to explain between-group and within-group variance. Although Clark acknowledges the possibility that a construct developed in one country may not have a counterpart in another country, at no time does she discuss the value of deriving models of distinct clinical entities found in only one country or ethnocultural group. This suggests that for Clark the main purpose of studying culture is to enhance the validity of existing psychological models by attending to cross-cultural variations.

In contrast, both Fabrega (1990) and Rogler (1989) criticize researchers for not attending to the cultural specificity of mental illness and mental health. Fabrega examines researchers' use of mainstream instruments and conceptualizations in studying mental disorders among Latinos and challenges such researchers to be bold in their critiques of "establishment psychiatry." Rogler recommends a framework for mainstream psychiatric researchers that attends more fully to culture. For both Fabrega and Rogler the risk of overlooking cultural variations is much greater in current psychopathology research than overlooking cultural similarities. Thus, Fabrega and Rogler urge researchers to consider cultural specificity and recommend practical steps to integrate a cultural perspective in the study of psychopathology.

An important conceptual advancement is the recognition of both positions, that is, studying culture to identify general processes and culture-specific processes. By focusing only on generalities, we overlook the importance of culture-specific phenomena. Thus, Clark's line of research may be less likely to recognize how culture shapes the expression of affect in significant ways. On the other hand, by emphasizing culture-specific phenomena we overlook the possibility of generalities. By developing culture-specific measures of mental illness, as suggested by both Fabrega and Rogler, we may underestimate the commonality of mental disorders across cultures. We agree with Clark, Fabrega, and Rogler that past researchers have neglected the importance of culture. However, the purpose of cultural research is to advance our understanding of general processes and culture-specific processes and the manner in which they interact in specific contexts. Our aim is to identify culture's mark amidst the ubiquity of human suffering. (See Draguns 1990 for an elegant discussion of this conceptual tension in the study of culture.)

Major Advances: *Diagnostic and Statistical Manual-IV* and the World Mental Health Report

We now turn to selected recent developments in the study of culture and psychopathology. We begin with a discussion of two of the most important projects that were carried out during the last decade, the incorporation of cultural factors in *Diagnostic and Statistical Manual (DSM)-IV* (American Psychiatric Association 1994), and the publication of the *World Mental Health Report* (Desjarlais et al 1996).

Through the efforts of Parron and colleagues, the National Institute of Mental Health funded the establishment of a task force to develop cultural materials for incorporation into all sections of the *DSM-IV*. Led by the members of the steering committee (Horacio Fabrega, Byron Good, Arthur Kleinman, Keh-Ming Lin, Spero Manson, Juan Mezzich, and Delores Parron) the task force gathered together available research and recommended how best to integrate a cultural perspective. Three main contributions were published in *DSM-IV*: (*a*) the inclusion of how cultural factors can influence the expression, assessment, and prevalence of specific disorders; (*b*) an outline of a cultural formulation of clinical diagnosis to complement the multiaxial assessment; and (*c*) a glossary of relevant cultural-bound syndromes from around the world. A more complete documentation of the task force's findings is available in the *DSM-IV Sourcebook* (Mezzich et al 1997) and in other publications [e.g. a special issue of *Psychiatric Clinics of North America* (Alarcon 1995), a special issue of *Transcultural Psychiatry* (Kirmayer 1998), and a compilation of relevant papers (Mezzich et al 1996)]. Without a doubt, the attention given to culture in *DSM-IV* is a major achievement in the history of classifications of mental disorders. Never before had classification schemas or related diagnostic interviews addressed the role of culture in psychopathology to this degree (López & Núñez 1987, Rogler 1996).

Although the attention to culture in *DSM-IV* is a significant advancement, it also has its limitations. Some observers have noted that significant portions of what was recommended by the Culture and Diagnosis Task Force were left out by the final arbiters of *DSM-IV* (see Kirmayer 1998, Mezzich et al 1999). Those aspects of culture that were included are only a partial reflection of the significant and dynamic role culture plays in psychopathology. The very limited discussion of specific symptoms which can be both culturally normative experiences and signs of distress, and the placement of the cultural-bound syndromes in the appendix tend to exoticize the role of culture. Cultural researchers object to the view that culture only pertains to patients from specific "cultural minority" groups, which present with specific symptoms or syndromes. Instead, cultural researchers view culture as infusing the presentation of all disorders among all people. Along these lines, the Culture and Diagnosis Task Force recommended that *DSM-IV* disorders such as anorexia nervosa and chronic fatigue syndrome be included in the "Glossary of Culture Bound Syndromes" because they represent North American disorders strongly shaped by culture. It was thought that doing so would counteract the impression that cultural syndromes are only relevant to members of ethnic minorities. The *DSM-IV* developers rejected this proposal, claiming that these disorders are not cultural in nature, as they were already in the body of *DSM-IV.* Furthermore, culturally informed researchers are concerned that the cultural formulation that was included is a "bare-bones" version of what was originally proposed. It is presented as a short list of questions with little introduction, and the illustrative case examples were deleted. The use of the pared down formulation may lead diagnosticians to a false sense of understanding culture's role in the diagnostic picture of patients. However, although the attention to culture in *DSM-IV* does fall short in depicting the important role culture plays in the suffering of individuals with mental disorders, it is a significant advancement over past efforts.

A second major development within the last decade was the publication of the *World Mental Health Report* (Desjarlais et al 1996). Desjarlais and colleagues compiled research from across the world to identify the range of mental health and behavioral problems (e.g. mental disorders, violence, suicide), particularly among low-income countries in Africa, Latin America, Asia, and the Pacific. The authors derived several conclusions. Perhaps the most significant was that mental illness and related problems exact a significant toll on the health and well-being of people worldwide, and produce a greater burden based on a "disability-adjusted life years" index than that from tuberculosis, cancer, or heart disease. Depressive disorders alone were found to produce the fifth greatest burden for women and seventh greatest burden for men across all physical and mental illnesses.

A second important observation was that mental illness and behavioral problems are intricately tied to the social world. For example, the authors identified the social roots of the poor mental health of women. Among the many factors included are hunger—(undernourishment afflicts more than 60% of women in developing countries), work—(women are poorly paid for labor intensive jobs, oftentimes in dangerous work settings), and domestic violence—(surveys in some low-income communities worldwide report up to 50% and 60% of women having been beaten). Another example of the social world-mental health problem linkage concerns the complex social and economic factors that contribute to people developing substance abuse disorders. One such factor is the social disruption that occurs when adolescents and young men migrate from rural communities to urban cities in search of economic sustenance. The cultural shock, the lack of social supports, and the inability to find steady employment are among the many risk factors that predict substance abuse. The research on substance abuse and women's mental health illustrates that psychopathology is as much pathology of the social world as pathology of the mind or body.

Based on their findings, Desjarlais and associates (1996) make specific recommendations to advance both mental health policy and research to help reduce the significant burden of mental illness across the world. Their consideration of the social world leads easily to recommending specific interventions to address not only the clinical problem but also the social conditions in which they reside. In addressing the poor mental health of women, for example, they call for coordinated efforts to empower women economically as well as to reduce violence against women in all its forms. In addition, women's mental health is identified as one of the top five research priorities worldwide. Research is called for to examine the social factors that influence women's health in specific cultural contexts and to identify effective community-based interventions in improving women's health status.

Despite its many contributions, as an example of culture and psychopathology research, the *World Mental Health Report* has limitations. Because of its broad scope, there is little attention paid to methodological issues, which may be important in understanding some of the findings. For example, in the reviewed studies of domestic violence, it is not clear how "being beaten" was defined and measured across studies. Furthermore, the authors move into important social, economic, and political domains. However, as researchers of cultural psychopathology, and even as practitioners, these broader domains can extend well beyond our areas of expertise. Certainly, they are important and need to be addressed, but it is unclear what role mental health researchers or practitioners can play in carrying out some of the vitally important goals, such as increasing the economic independence and productivity of women.

Despite their limitations, *DSM-IV* and the *World Mental Health Report* make major contributions to the study of culture and psychopathology. Furthermore, they illustrate the range of conceptualizations of culture and the importance of the social domain. In *DSM-IV,* culture tends to be depicted as exotic through its influence on symptom expression, the noted culture-bound syndromes, and reference to persons from "culturally different" groups. There is little attention given to culture in a broader, multifaceted social context to which individuals react. The emphasis is given to culture-general notions with slight cultural variability. The *World Mental Health Report,* on the other hand, recognizes the dynamic, social processes linked to culture. Hunger, work, and education, for example, are integrally related to how people adapt or fail to adapt. Clinical phenomena are recognized, but so are behavioral problems not traditionally considered in psychiatric classification systems, such as domestic and sexual violence. Throughout, the authors recognize cultural variability, but their stance is not extreme cultural relativism, as they recognize the moral and health implications for controversial practices, such as female circumcision. Despite the considerable differences in the treatment of culture by the *DSM-IV* and the *World Mental Health Report,* both documents indicate that culture as a subject matter is no longer solely within the purview of cultural psychologists, psychiatrists, and anthropologists. It is now the subject matter of all users of *DSM-IV* and policy makers and mental health researchers worldwide.

Disorder-Related Research

We now turn to the examination of selected psychopathology research. We chose the study of anxiety, schizophrenia, and childhood psychopathology because within each of these areas there is a series of systematic studies that examines the cultural basis of these disorders. The review of the published research in these areas is not meant to be exhaustive. Rather, key studies were selected so that both conceptual and methodological issues could be discussed in some depth.

Anxiety   There have been a number of recent reviews concerning the study of culture and anxiety disorders (Al-Issa & Oudji 1998, Guarnaccia 1997, Kirmayer et al 1995, Marsella et al 1996), including Neal & Turner's (1991) thoughtful review of the study of anxiety disorders among African Americans. Each of these directly or indirectly builds on Good & Kleinman's (1985) earlier review. Rather than update recent reviews, we chose to focus our attention on one line of research, the study of *ataques de nervios*. This is an important line of research because it focuses on a culture-specific phenomenon for which the triangulation of ethnography, epidemiology, and clinical research has made important contributions. Thus, we will be able to examine some ways ethnography informs mainstream psychopathology research.

Ataque de nervios is an idiom of distress particularly prominent among Latinos from the Caribbean, but also recognized among other Latino groups. Its literal translation is "attack of nerves." Symptoms commonly associated with *ataque de nervios* include trembling, attacks of crying, screaming uncontrollably, and becoming verbally or physically aggressive. Other symptoms that are prominent in some *ataques* but not others are seizure-like or fainting episodes, dissociative experiences, and suicidal gestures. A general feature experienced by most sufferers of *ataques de nervios* is feeling out of control. Most episodes occur as a direct result of a stressful life event related to family or significant others (e.g. death or divorce). After the *ataque,* people oftentimes experience amnesia of what occurred, but then quickly return to their usual level of functioning.

Guarnaccia initiated a program of research by first carrying out ethnographic research in clinical settings (De La Cancela et al 1986, Guarnaccia et al 1989a). Drawing from the rich description of clinical cases and an understanding of the social history of Puerto Ricans living in the United States, these investigators pointed out an association between social disruptions (family and immediate social networks) and the experience of *ataques.* To build on the ethnographic base, Guarnaccia and colleagues turned to epidemiological research to examine the prevalence of *ataques de nervios* in Puerto Rico. After preliminary epidemiological research in which a somatic symptom scale index was used as a proxy measure of *ataques* (Guarnaccia et al 1989b), a subsequent study was carried out in which respondents were directly queried as to whether they had suffered an *ataque de nervios* and what the experience was like (Guarnaccia et al 1993). The prevalence rate was found to be high, from 16%–23% of large community samples (Ns = 912 and 1513), and *ataques de nervios* were found to be associated with a wide range of mental disorders, particularly anxiety and mood disorders. The social context continued to be important in understanding *ataques de nervios*. *Ataques* were found to be more prevalent among women, persons older than 45, and those from lower socioeconomic backgrounds and disrupted marriages. In the most recent study thus far, Guarnaccia and colleagues (1996) returned to the ethnographic mode to explicate the experience of *ataques* from those persons who had reported suffering an *ataque de nervios* in the epidemiological study. Through in-depth interviewing, the full range of symptoms and the specific social contexts were identified. This "experience-near" research approach enabled Guarnaccia and associates to examine carefully how the social world can become part of the physical self as reflected in *ataques de nervios*.

Recent clinical research has further explicated the relationship between *ataques de nervios* and clinical diagnoses. Liebowitz and colleagues (1994) carried out clinical diagnostic interviews of 156 Latino patients from an urban psychiatric clinic that specializes in the treatment of anxiety. They examined the relationship between patients having an *ataque de nervios* and meeting criteria for panic disorder, other anxiety disorders, or an affective disorder. Their fine-grained analysis suggests that the expression of *ataque de nervios* is influenced by the coexisting mental disorder. With a panic disorder persons with an *ataque de nervios* present largely panic-like symptoms; however, with an affective disorder *ataque de nervios* are characterized by emotional lability, especially anger (Salmán et al 1998). Thus, in addition to the social factors previously noted, these findings suggest that the clinical context may also play a role in understanding *ataques de nervios*.

The study of *ataques de nervios* is exemplary for many reasons. What is most striking is the systematic, ongoing dialogue between ethnographic, epidemiological, and now clinical research methods to advance our understanding of *ataques de nervios* and how the social world interacts with psychological and physical processes in the individual. With these multiple approaches, one observes the shifting of the researchers' lenses (Kleinman & Kleinman 1991). In the early ethnographic work, Guarnaccia and colleagues drew from a small number of clinical cases and interpreted their findings with broad strokes focusing on the "microcontexts of power" and migration into strange and hostile environments. In the epidemiological research, the investigators used large, representative samples to identify people with *ataques* and the social correlates of that experience. In this research, the social context is reduced to the respondents' gender, age, educational level, and marital status, which provides some basis for interpretation but certainly lacks the richness of ethnographic material. The clinical studies provide an in-depth profile of patients' symptomatology and the symptom patterns of those with and without an *ataque,* but they provide less sense of the social world of the sufferer. Each approach has its strengths and limitations. What matters, though, is not the strengths or limitations of a given study but the weaving of multiple studies with multiple approaches to understand the given phenomenon in depth.

In addition to the ongoing dialogue between research approaches, the research is also exemplary by placing *ataque de nervios* and related mental disorders in their social context. In almost all studies, *ataque de nervios* is presented not as a cultural syndrome or clinical entity that resides within individuals, but as a common illness that reflects the lived experience largely of women with little power and disrupted social relations. In adopting multiple approaches, the emphasis given to the social domain is likely to shift. Nevertheless, over several studies, Guarnaccia and his colleagues have maintained considerable attention to the social context. In so doing, they have demonstrated how to include the social in epidemiological (e.g. Guarnaccia et al 1993) and clinical (Salmán et al 1998), as well as ethnographic studies.

This research is not without its limitations. In particular, criteria for meeting *ataques de nervios* are simply whether a person responds affirmatively to the question, "Have you ever experienced an *ataque de nervios?"* This is a broad definition that is particularly useful in the initial stages of research to identify *ataques de nervios* and the varied experiences of many people with this syndrome. The downside to this open, single-item criterion becomes evident when investigators begin to examine its relationship with clinical disorders based on multiple criteria. Thus, in terms of probabilities alone, *ataques* are likely to be more prevalent than most disorders, as was the case in the Puerto Rico Disaster study. Our point is that using one criterion for *ataques* may introduce a methodological artifact in examining the interrelationship of *ataques* with mental disorders. Work is ongoing to develop a measure of *ataques* using multiple criteria that could be utilized in future studies.

Despite the question of criteria, the study of *ataques de nervios* reflects a model of the investigation of culture and psychopathology, particularly research that begins with a culture-specific form of distress. The important questions being raised suggest that the study of *ataques de nervios* will continue to make significant contributions to the study of culture and psychopathology in years to come and can serve as a model for researchers working across cultures.

Schizophrenia   Fabrega (1989) provided a thoughtful overview of how past anthropologically informed research contributed to the study of psychosis and how future studies can advance our understanding of the interrelations of culture and schizophrenia. An integral point of his review is that the cultural conception of the self is likely to influence the manner in which the disorder is expressed and understood by others, particularly among those with schizophrenia that has not developed into a chronic, deteriorated state. According to Fabrega, schizophrenia is likely to affect individuals and communities differently whether they conceive of personhood as being autonomous and separate from others or as connected and bound to others (Shweder & Bourne 1984, Triandis 1989, Markus & Kitayama 1991). The research that most directly addresses this notion is that which examines the role of social factors in the course of schizophrenia. Two prominent lines of inquiry include the World Health Organization (WHO) cross-national study of schizophrenia and a series of studies examining the relationship of families' emotional climate and to the course of illness.

The WHO's International Pilot Study on Schizophrenia (IPSS) and the follow-up Determinants of Outcomes of Severe Mental Disorder (DOSMD) study represent the largest multinational study of schizophrenia to date (IPSS: 9 countries, 1202 patients; DOSMD: 10 countries, 1379 patients; Jablensky et al 1992, World Health Organization 1979). Many contributions have been made by these investigations, including evidence of the comparability of schizophrenia's core symptoms across several countries (for a critique see Kleinman 1988). The finding that has received the most attention by cultural researchers (e.g. Weisman 1997) is that schizophrenia in developing countries has a more favorable course than in developed countries. Some investigators have referred to this as "arguably the single most important finding of cultural differences in cross-cultural research on mental illness." (Lin & Kleinman 1988:563). Others have been critical of the studies' methods and interpretations (see Cohen 1992, Edgerton & Cohen 1994, Hopper 1991). For example, Edgerton & Cohen point out that the distinction between "developed" and "developing" countries is unclear. Moreover, they argue that the cultural explanation for the differences in course is poorly substantiated. They then go on to discuss how such research could be more culturally informed through the direct measure of specific cultural factors in conjunction with observations of people's daily lives (see also Hopper 1991). What is clear is that the WHO findings have provided the basis for an important discussion of method and theory in the context of schizophrenia and the social world.

Another line of research addressing culture's role in the course of schizophrenia focuses on families' emotional climate. Based on the early research of Brown and associates (e.g. Brown et al 1972), it is clear that patients who return to households marked by criticism, hostility, and emotional involvement [high expressed emotion (EE)] are more likely to relapse than those who return to households that are not so characterized (Bebbington & Kuipers 1994, Kavanaugh 1992, Leff & Vaughn 1985). This line of investigation is important to the study of culture because it points out the importance of the social world and, more specifically, because cross-national and cross-ethnic studies have uncovered interesting differences in the level and nature of expressed emotion (Jenkins & Karno 1992).

The most systematic cultural analysis of families' role in schizophrenia has been carried out by Jenkins and her colleagues. In using both clinical research methods based on the prototypic contemporary study of expressed emotion (Vaughn & Leff 1976) and ethnographic methods based on in-depth interviews, Jenkins and associates extended this line of study to Mexican American families in Los Angeles. In the first major report, Karno et al (1987) replicated the general finding that patients who return to high EE families are more likely to relapse than patients who return to low EE families. Jenkins (1988a) then carried out an in-depth examination of Mexican American families' conceptualization of schizophrenia, specifically *nervios,* and how this differed from a comparable sample of Anglo American families who viewed schizophrenia largely as a mental illness (see also Guarnaccia et al 1992 and Salgado de Snyder et al in press). It should be noted that *nervios* among Mexican Americans and *ataque de nervios* among Puerto Ricans are similar in that the concept of *nervios* (nerves) reflects both a mental and physical state. The two concepts differ as well; for example, *ataque de nervios* is usually thought to have a suddon onset whereas *nervios* is more of a condition that befalls individuals who are thought to be weak or vulnerable. Based on both quantitative (coded responses to open-ended questions) and qualitative data, Jenkins (1988b) suggested that Mexican Americans' preference for *nervios* is tied to the family members' efforts to decrease the stigma associated with the illness and also to promote family support and cohesiveness. In subsequent papers, Jenkins (1991, 1993) critiqued the cultural basis of the EE construct in general and its components, criticism and emotional overinvolvement, in particular. A most important theoretical contribution to the study of the course of schizophrenia is that Jenkins situates families' EE, not in the family members' attitudes, beliefs, or even feelings, which is usually the case, but in the patient-family social interaction. Overall, Jenkins' work has brought much needed attention to how serious mental illness is embedded in specific social and cultural contexts.

Building on Jenkins work, López and colleagues have further critiqued the notion of EE with its focus on negative family functioning (López et al 1999). They point out that at an early juncture in the study of families and relapse, investigators (i.e. Brown et al 1972) opted to focus on aspects of family conflict that predict relapse rather than the prosocial aspects of family functioning that prevent relapse. In a reanalysis and extension of the Mexican American sample (Karno et al 1987) and a comparable Anglo American sample (Vaughn et al 1984), López et al (1998) found that a lack of family warmth predicted relapse for Mexican Americans, whereas criticism predicted relapse for Anglo Americans. In other words, Mexican American patients who returned to families marked by low warmth were much more likely to relapse than those who returned to families characterized by high warmth. For Anglo Americans, warmth was unrelated to relapse. These findings are consistent with the hypothesis that culture plays a role in the manner in which families respond to relatives with schizophrenia, which in turn relates to the course of illness. Studies carried out in Italy (Bertrando et al 1992) and Yugoslavia (Ivanović et al 1994) have also found that warmth serves as a protective factor in the course of the illness. A limitation of the López et al study is that ethnicity serves as a proxy for culture; further research requires a direct assessment of cultural processes. Nevertheless, the importance of this study is that the exploration of possible cultural variability led to the beginning of a line of inquiry that examines what families do to prevent relapse. Such research has the potential to add a much needed balance to family research by focusing on both positive and negative aspects of what families do that relates to relapse. The study of caregiving (e.g. Guarnaccia 1998, Lefley 1998) and families' day-to-day interactions with ill family members will likely shed further light on the importance of families' prosocial functioning.

Childhood Disorders   The study of child psychopathology is a rich field of inquiry for those interested in culture. As noted by Weisz and associates (1997), child psychopathology requires that attention be given to the behavior of children as well as the views of adults—parents, teachers, and mental health practitioners—for it is the adults who usually decide whether a problem exists. The fact that others determine whether children's behavior is problematic indicates the importance of the social world in defining mental illness and disorders of children and adolescents.

The most systematic line of culture and childhood psychopathology research has been carried out by Weisz and his colleagues (for a review see Weisz et al 1997). In the very first study that was conducted in Thailand and the United States, Weisz and associates (1987b) found that Thai children and adolescents who were referred to mental health clinics reported more internalizing problems (e.g. those related to anxiety and depression) than US children and adolescents. In contrast, US children and adolescents reported more externalizing problems (i.e. acting-out types of problems such as aggressive behavior) than Thai children and adolescents. In follow-up community studies, where the mental health referral process was not a factor in the identification of problem behaviors, the cross-national differences for internalizing problems were confirmed, but not for externalizing problems (Weisz et al 1987a, 1993b). US and Thai children and adolescents identified in their respective communities did not differ in terms of acting-out problems. Weisz and colleagues (1997) argue that the findings with regard to internalizing problems are consistent with the idea that culture shapes the manner in which children and adolescents express psychological distress. Coming from a largely Buddhist religious and cultural background that values self-control and emotional restraint, Thai children may be more likely than US children to express psychological distress in a manner that does not violate cultural norms.

Aside from these intriguing findings, two other factors stand out in Weisz and colleagues' research: the systematic nature of the research and the care with which the research has been conducted. Weisz et al (1987a) began this line of investigation in mental health clinics, then went to a community survey to rule out the possibility of referral factors. Based on these findings, Weisz & Weiss (1991) derived a referability index for specific problem behaviors (e.g. vandalism and poor school work) that indexes the likelihood that a given problem will be referred for treatment, taking into account the problem's prevalence in a given community. In this study, they demonstrated how gender and nationality influence whether a problem is brought to the attention of mental health professionals. Subsequently,

Weisz and colleagues examined teachers' reports of actual children (Weisz et al 1989) and both parents' and teachers' ratings of hypothetical cases (Weisz et al 1991). Each of Weisz and colleagues' studies systematically builds on their previous work in advancing an understanding of how adults with differing social roles define children's problem behaviors.

The care that Weisz and colleagues take with their research is best illustrated in their most recent study of teachers' ratings of problem behaviors (Weisz et al 1995), in which they found Thai teachers to rate more internalizing and externalizing problem behaviors than US teachers do. Given that this finding runs counter to the previous clinical and community studies, which only found differences for internalizing problems, they devised an innovative observational methodology to assess whether it was something about the children or the teachers that contributed to this contradictory finding. Weisz and associates (1995) employed independent observers of children's school behavior, as well as teachers to rate the same children who were observed in Thailand and in the United States. One of the independent raters was a bilingual Thai psychologist who had received graduate training in the United States. His being part of both teams of independent observers was critical to assessing the reliability of the Thai and US observers. The relationship between his ratings and those of the other US and Thai raters were equally high, suggesting that the ratings were reliable across both national sites. Interestingly, the observers rated Thai children as having less than half as many problem and off-task behaviors than US children, yet Thai teachers rated the observed students as having many more problem behaviors than US teachers rated their students. These data suggest that Thai teachers have a much lower threshold than US teachers for identifying problem behaviors in their students. Integrating a careful observational methodology in conjunction with rating scales enabled Weisz and colleagues to uncover this intriguing set of findings.

The possibility that culture shapes the type and degree of problem behaviors of children and adolescents is receiving increasing attention by developmental researchers. Weisz and associates extended their Thai-US research to Jamaica and Kenya (Lambert et al 1989, Weisz et al 1993a). Other investigators have compared rates of internalizing and externalizing problems in other parts of the world, including Australia (Achenbach et al 1990b), Denmark (Arnett & Balle-Jensen 1993), Holland (Achenbach et al 1987), and Puerto Rico (Achenbach et al 1990a). Still other researchers have specifically examined internalizing-type problem behaviors (Greenberger & Chen 1996) or externalizing-type problem behaviors (Chen et al 1998, Feldman et al 1991, Weine et al 1995) in cross-national or cross-ethnic samples. An important trend in this research is that the original epidemiologic type research which compares groups cross-nationally and suggests possible cultural explanations is now being complemented by recent studies of psychosocial processes associated with children and adolescents' adjustment or psychopathology. For example, Chen et al (1998) examined risk factors (parent-adolescent conflict and perceived peer approval of misconduct) and protective factors (parental warmth and parental monitoring) associated with acting-out problems across four groups of adolescents: European Americans, Chinese Americans, Taipei Chinese, and Beijing Chinese.

The strength of the more recent studies is that they examine processes that may underlie potential cross-national differences and similarities, including social (family and peers) and psychological (values) processes. Thus, an important step has been taken to understand why differences and similarities may occur in behavior problems cross-nationally. Although the conceptual models used to frame such research are rich, include social processes, and have a strong empirical tradition in psychological research, they are minimally informed by cultural-specific processes of the non-US groups under study; investigators apply models developed largely in the United States. Ethnographic research would be particularly valuable at this stage to identify what about the social and cultural world might play a role in the expression of distress and disorder among children. Such research could then lead to directly testing culturally related variables within a conceptual framework, as evidenced in the work of some developmental researchers (e.g. Fuligni 1998, Harwood 1992), and as advocated by others (Greenfield 1997, Schneider 1998). The growing interest of researchers in studying internalizing and externalizing problem behaviors cross-nationally and cross-ethnically attests to the utility of this approach for enhancing our understanding of culture and childhood psychopathology.

Another framework that has considerable promise for the study of culture and developmental psychopathology is the ecocultural model of accommodation developed by Weisner, Gallimore, and colleagues in the context of developmental disabilities (Weisner 1984, Gallimore et al 1993). The daily activities and routines that children participate in are central to this theory. Culture is reflected in these activities (they mirror what matters most to families) and in the psychological processes that result from children's participation in such activities, for example, the children's cultural goals, expectations, and knowledge. In contrast to much of the previously reviewed child psychopathology research, which is largely comparative in nature and attempts to identify "cultural" differences, this research is largely process oriented. Investigators are interested in identifying how children's developmental disabilities can disrupt the daily routines and activities of families and, most importantly, how families adapt (Gallimore et al 1996). By examining how families adjust daily routines to address their needs and those of their disabled children, one can learn about the transactional process between culture and disability—how the social world influences disability and how disability influences the social world. Moreover, such research has important implications for interventions. Symptom reduction or skill training is a laudable treatment goal. However, successful interventions require assisting families to establish sustainable and meaningful daily routines for all members (Bernheimer & Keogh 1995). Thus, according to these researchers, the identification of successful interventions requires an assessment of the families' social world.

Emerging Trends

Immigration   A number of recent findings highlight the importance of immigration in understanding mental health and mental illness. The Los Angeles Epidemiologic Catchment Area study reported that Mexican-born Mexican Americans had significantly lower prevalence rates across a wide range of disorders than US-born Mexican Americans (Burnam et al 1987). This finding was replicated in a recent epidemiologic study comparing the prevalence rates of rural and urban Mexican-origin adults in Fresno and nearby communities (Vega et al 1998). [See also a similar pattern of findings regarding academic achievement among Mexican and Mexican-American students (Suarez-Orozco & Suarez-Orozco 1995)]. An important contribution of the Fresno study is that evidence was provided from a Mexico City sample indicating that Mexico City residents had rates comparable to the Mexican immigrant sample, thus countering the "hardy" immigrant hypothesis. Thus, the available evidence suggests that the mental health status of Mexican-origin adults and children declines over generations. In Great Britain also, the role of migration has received considerable attention in studies that found Afro-Caribbean immigrants to have higher treated prevalence rates of schizophrenia than other ethnic groups (e.g. Harrison et al 1988; see Sashidharan 1993 for a review). The social and psychological mechanisms that are responsible for the differing prevalence rates for the immigrant groups at this time are unclear. An examination of the acculturation literature might prove useful in understanding the factors related to these intriguing findings (Berry 1997, Berry & Sam 1997, LaFromboise et al 1993). Furthermore, the prevalence studies of Great Britain are based on treated cases, thus reflecting important methodological limitations (See Dohrenwend & Dohrenwend 1974). Nevertheless, both sets of studies indicate that the investigation of immigration is a ripe area to examine how the social world and psychopathology interrelate (see also Rogler 1994). A particularly wide open area of study is the examination of immigration and mental health and illness among children and adolescents (see Guarnaccia & López 1998). Not only will immigration research be able to address important conceptual and methodological issues in the study of culture, but it will also have important policy implications for the delivery of mental health services to underserved communities (e.g. Salgado de Snyder et al 1998).

US Ethnic Minority Groups   We are encouraged by the growing interest in the study of psychopathology of US ethnic minority groups. With regard to African Americans, there has been an increase in the study of anxiety disorders since Neal & Turner's (1991) call for research. The most recent studies include clinical studies (e.g. Friedman et al 1994), epidemiologic studies (Horwath et al 1993), a combined ethnographic and epidemiological study (Heurtin-Roberts et al 1997), and a study of childhood fears (Neal et al 1993). Although these studies are largely descriptive in nature, there is some attention to the differential social world of African American and white patients. For example, Friedman and associates

(1994) found that, relative to white patients with panic disorder and agoraphobia, African American patients reported a greater likelihood of having been separated as children from their parents and of having experienced their parents' divorce.

In terms of American Indians, a systematic series of studies have examined the mental health problems of children (Beiser et al 1998, Dion et al 1998, Sack et al 1993). Other researchers have examined disorder and distress among American Indian adolescents (e.g. Duclos et al 1998, Keane et al 1996, O'Nell & Mitchell 1996). In addition, after providing a comprehensive and useful critique of American Indian and Alaska Native mental health literature, O'Nell (1989) carried out an in-depth examination of the social world and its relation to depression, suicide, and drinking among Flathead Indians (O'Nell 1993, 1996). Manson and his colleagues (1990) have examined, among other areas, how American Indians report psychological distress, particularly on the Center for Epidemiologic Studies Depression scale. In addition, a special issue was published of *Culture, Medicine, and Psychiatry* (Maser & Dinges 1992/93), addressing the comorbidity of depression, anxiety, and substance abuse among American Indians and Alaska Natives. Overall, we are impressed by recent systematic efforts of psychopathology researchers of American Indians to assess the interrelations of distress and disorder to the social world. This emphasis is continuing, as reflected in Manson and colleagues' current study of epidemiology of mental disorders and services among American Indians.

With regard to Asian American research, Sue and his associates (1991) have had a long-standing interest in treatment issues. Most recently, Sue and colleagues have broadened their interests to include psychopathology (Sue et al 1995). Of particular importance is the recently conducted epidemiologic survey of depressive disorders among Chinese Americans residing in the Los Angeles area (Takeuchi et al 1998). Researchers have been able to examine prevalence rates of traditional depressive and related disorders as well as *neurasthenia* (Zheng et al 1997), a concept that was retired in the classification of mental disorders in the United States, but is still in use in China and other parts of Asia. *Neurasthenia* usually refers to weakness or fatigue, often accompanied by a variety of psychological (e.g. poor concentration) and physical (e.g. diffuse aches and pains) symptoms. Cheung & Lin's (1997) cultural formulation of a Chinese-Vietnamese patient with neurasthenia further considers the utility of this category for Asian Americans by examining, among other factors, the social (migratory experience) and cultural factors (the patient's explanatory model of the illness) that contribute to the expression of this disorder.

Although we have given considerable attention to research concerning Latinos, this research almost exclusively concerned adults. It is worth noting that Vega and colleagues (1995) have conducted an important study regarding Latino adolescents in Miami. This research points out that the relationship between specific acculturative stressors (e.g. language conflicts, perceived discrimination) and problem behaviors varies by immigration status. In addition, in their prevalence study of adolescents in the Houston metropolitan area, Roberts and colleagues

(1997) found that of nine ethnic groups, Mexican Americans reported the highest rates of major depression. Both studies are characterized by rigor in sampling schools, multiethnic samples, and large sample sizes (Roberts et al, N = 5423; Vega et al, N = 2360).

Other Promising Areas   The study of psychopharmacology and ethnicity has received increasing attention (see Lin et al 1995, Rudorfer 1996). This raises a series of issues including the interrelation of culture and biology, which Browner and colleagues (1988) addressed by challenging cultural investigators to ground their interpretative orientation in the study of biologically based phenomena. We agree with their call to bring together both social and biological lenses to study phenomena of mutual interest. However, we agree with Good (1988) that when bringing divergent perspectives together it is important that no one perspective be given priority. Floersch et al (1997) made a compelling argument that in the study of genetics among the Amish, the genetic perspective greatly overshadowed the study of cultural processes, although the latter was not completely ignored (Egeland et al 1983). Future genetic and cultural researchers can build on past efforts to demonstrate how genes and environment interact in psychopathology (Reiss et al 1991).

Despite the dearth of empirical articles, we believe that the study of culture and personality disorders will prove to be a rich area of study. Important review articles concerning culture, personality, and personality disorders support this point of view (e.g. Alarcon et al 1998, Cooke 1996, Lewis-Fernandez & Kleinman 1994, Nuckolls 1992, Paris 1997). One line of research that shows particular promise is the application of item response theory (IRT) to the study of psychopathy in Scotland, Canada, and the United States (Cooke & Michie 1999). IRT models specify the relation between item responses or ratings (the observable characteristics e.g. psychopathy) and the latent trait or construct (the unobservable characteristics) thought to underlie the responses or ratings. What is particularly advantageous for cultural research is that the meaning of the item responses is not tied to the distribution of the latent trait. Thus, IRT models are most capable of detecting whether measures are valid cross-culturally, regardless of whether there are significant cross-national or cross-ethnic differences in sample characteristics.

CONCLUSION

Cultural psychopathology research is "on the map." Articles are being published in culture-focused as well as mainstream journals (e.g. *American Journal of Psychiatry, Journal of Abnormal Psychology, Child Development, Developmental Psychology, Journal of Nervous and Mental Disease*). Substantive areas of psychopathology research are being shaped by cultural research. Efforts to integrate idioms of distress with mainstream constructs, for example, are well under way (*ataques de nervios* and anxiety and affective disorders, *nervios* and families' conceptualization of serious mental illness). In 1988, it was important for Kleinman to get the message out that culture matters. The message has been received; cultural research is providing an innovative and fresh perspective to our understanding of several important aspects of psychopathology.

For cultural researchers to build on the empirical and conceptual foundation that has been established, it is important for us to continue to be critical of how culture is conceptualized and how such conceptualizations guide our research. It is clear from this review that culture can no longer be treated solely as an independent variable or as a factor to be controlled for. Rather, culture infuses the full social context of mental health research. Culture is important in all aspects of psychopathology research—from the design and translation of instruments, to the conceptual models that guide the research, to the interpersonal interaction between researcher and research participants, to the definition and interpretation of symptom and syndromes, to the structure of the social world that surrounds a person's mental health problems. Cultural psychopathology research requires a framework that incorporates culture in multifaceted ways. Accordingly, it is important that cultural research not obscure the importance of other social forces such as class, poverty, and marginality that work in conjunction with culture to shape people's everyday lives. The examination of both social and cultural processes is one way to help guard against superficial cultural analyses that ignore or minimize the powerful political economic inequalities that coexist with culture.

A corollary of the need for a broad framework for research is the need for approaches that integrate qualitative and quantitative methods. Cultural psychopathology research can serve as an important site for integrating ethnographic, observational, clinical, and epidemiological research approaches. Mental health problems cannot be fully understood through one lens. Ethnographic research provides insights into the meaning of mental health problems and how they are experienced in their sociocultural context. Observational research captures people's functioning in their daily lives. Clinical research can provide detailed phenomenologies of psychopathological processes and can contribute to developing treatments to alleviate suffering at the individual as well as social levels. Epidemiological research can broaden perspectives to more generalized processes and populations. It is the integration of these perspectives, both methodologies and in the composition of research teams, that will make the cultural agenda succeed.

The ultimate goal of cultural psychopathology research is to alleviate suffering and improve people's lives. This requires attention to the multiple levels of individual, family, community, and the broader social system. Our enhanced notion of culture leads to analysis of the expression and sources of psychopathology at all of these levels. Our commitment to making a difference in peoples' everyday lives argues for the development of treatment and prevention interventions at these multiple levels as well. The increasing cultural diversity of the United States and the massive movements of people around the globe provide both an opportunity and imperative for cultural psychopathology research.

ACKNOWLEDGMENTS

The authors would like to thank Arthur Kleinman and John Weisz for their helpful comments on a previous draft. Also, the preparation of this paper was supported by two grants to the first author, an NIH Fogarty International Center, Minority International Research Training Grant (TW00061) and NIMH grant K08MH0499. The research on *ataques de nervios* was funded by NIMH grant R29 MH45789, which was awarded to the second author.

Visit the Annual Reviews home page at www.AnnualReviews.org.

LITERATURE CITED

Achenbach TM, Bird HR, Canino G, Phares V, Gould MS, Rubio-Stipec M. 1990a. Epidemiological comparisons of Puerto Rican and U.S. mainland children: parent, teacher and self-reports. *J. Am. Acad. Child Adolesc. Psychiatry* 29:84–93

Achenbach TM, Hensley VR, Phares V, Grayson D. 1990b. Problems and competencies reported by parents of Australian and American children. *J. Child Psychol. Psychiatry* 31:265–86

Achenbach TM, Verhulst FC, Baron GD, Akkerhuis GW. 1987. Epidemiological comparisons of Dutch and American children. I. Behavioral/emotional problems and competencies reported by parents for ages 4 to 16. *J. Am. Acad. Child Adolesc. Psychiatry* 26:326–32

Alarcon RD. 1995. Culture and psychiatric diagnosis: impact on DSM-IV and ICD-10. *Psychiatr. Clin. North Am.* 18:449–65

Alarcon RD, Foulks EF, Vakkur M. 1998. *Personality Disorders and Culture: Clinical and Conceptual Interactions.* New York: Wiley. 310 pp.

Al-Issa I, Oudji S. 1998. Culture and anxiety disorders. In *Cultural Clinical Psychology: Theory, Research, and Practice,* ed. SS Kazarian, DR Evans, pp. 127–51. Oxford: Oxford Univ. Press. 410 pp.

Arnett J, Balle-Jensen L. 1993. Cultural bases of risk behavior: Danish adolescents. *Child Dev.* 64:1842–55

American Psychiatric Association. 1994. *Diagnostic and Statistical Manual: IV.* Washington, DC: Am. Psychiatr. Assoc. 886 pp.

Bebbington P, Kuipers L. 1994. The predictive utility of expressed emotion in schizophrenia: an aggregate analysis. *Psychol. Med.* 24:707–18

Beiser M, Sack W, Manson S, Redshirt R, Dion R. 1998. Mental health and the academic performance of First Nations and majority-culture children. *Am. J. Orthopsychiatry* 68:455–67

Bernheimer LP, Keogh BK. 1995. Weaving interventions into the fabric of everyday life: an approach to family assessment. *Top. Early Child. Spec. Educ.* 15:415–33

Berry JW. 1997. Immigration, acculturation and adaptation. *Appl. Psychol. Intern. Rev.* 46:5–68

Berry JW, Sam D. 1997. Acculturation and adaptation. In *Handbook of Cross-Cultural Psychology: Social Behavior and Applications,* ed. JW Berry, MH Segall, C Kagitcibasi, 3:291–326. Needham Heights, MA: Allyn & Bacon

Bertrando P, Beltz J, Bressi C, Clerici M, Farma T, et al. 1992. Expressed emotion and schizophrenia in Italy: a study of an urban population. *Br. J. Psychiatry* 161:223–29

Betancourt H, López SR. 1993. The study of culture, race and ethnicity in American psychology. *Am. Psychol.* 48:629–37

Brown GW, Birley JLT, Wing JK. 1972. Influence of family life on the course of schizophrenic disorders: a replication. *Br. J. Psychiatry* 21:241–58

Browner CH, Ortiz de Montellano BR, Rubel AJ. 1988. A methodology for cross-cultural ethnomedical research. *Curr. Anthropol.* 29:681–702

Burnam A, Hough RL, Karno M, Escobar JI, Telles C. 1987. Acculturation and lifetime prevalence of psychiatric disorders among Mexican Americans in Los Angeles. *J. Health Soc. Behav.* 28:89–102

Cervantes RC, Padilla AM, Salgado de Snyder VN. 1991. The Hispanic Stress Inventory: a culturally relevant approach to psychological assessment. *Psychol. Assess.* 3:438–447

Chen C, Greenberger E, Lester J, Dong Q, Guo M. 1998. A cross-cultural study of family and peer correlates of adolescent misconduct. *Dev. Psychol.* 34:770–81

Cheung F, Lin KM. 1997. Neurasthenia, depression and somatoform disorder in a Chinese-Vietnamese woman migrant. *Cult. Med. Psychiatry* 21:247–58

Clark LA. 1987. Mutual relevance of mainstream and cross-cultural psychology. *J. Consult. Clin. Psychol.* 55:41–70

Cohen A. 1992. Prognosis for schizophrenia in the Third World: a reevaluation of cross-cultural research. *Cult. Med. Psychiatry* 16:53–75

Cooke DJ. 1996. Psychopathic personality in different cultures: What do we know? What do we need to find out? *J. Pers. Disord.* 10:23–40

Cooke DJ, Michie C. 1999. Psychopathy across cultures: North America and Scotland compared. *J. Abnorm. Psychol.* 108:58–68

De La Cancela V, Guarnaccia P, Carrillo E. 1986. Psychosocial distress among Latinos. *Humanit. Soc.* 10:431–47

Desjarlais R, Eisenberg L, Good B, Kleinman A. 1996. *World Mental Health: Problems and Priorities in Low-Income Countries.* Oxford: Oxford Univ. Press. 382 pp.

Dion R, Gotowiec A, Beiser M. 1998. Depression and conduct disorder in Native and non-Native children. *J. Am. Acad. Child Adolesc. Psychiatry* 37:736–42

Dohrenwend BP, Dohrenwend BS. 1974. Social and cultural influences on psychopathology. *Annu. Rev. Psychol.* 25:417–52

Draguns JG. 1980. Disorders of clinical severity. See Triandis & Draguns 1980, pp. 99–174

Draguns JG. 1990. Culture and psychopathology: toward specifying the nature of the relationship. In *Nebraska Symposium on Motivation 1989: Cross-Cultural Perspectives,* ed. J Berman, pp. 235–77. Lincoln: Univ. Neb.

Duclos CW, Beals J, Novins DK, Martin C, Jewett CS, Manson SM. 1998. Prevalence of common psychiatric disorders among American Indian adolescent detainees. *J. Am. Acad. Child Adolesc. Psychiatry* 37:866–73

Edgerton R, Cohen A. 1994. Culture and schizophrenia: the DOSMD challenge. *Br. J. Psychiatry* 164:222–31

Egeland, JA, Hostetter AM, Eshleman S. 1983. Amish Study: III. The impact of cultural factors on diagnosis of bipolar illness. *J. Am. Psychiatry* 140:67–71

Fabrega H. 1975. The need for an ethnomedical science. *Science* 189:969–75

Fabrega H. 1989. On the significance of an anthropological approach to schizophrenia. *Psychiatry* 52:45–65

Fabrega H. 1990. Hispanic mental health research: a case for cultural psychiatry. *Hisp. J. Behav. Sci.* 12:339–65

Feldman S, Rosenthal DA, Mont-Reynaud R, Leung K, Lau S. 1991. Ain't misbehavin': adolescent values and family environments as correlates of misconduct in Australia, Hong Kong, and the United States. *J. Res. Adolesc.* 1:109–34

Floersch J, Longhofer J, Latta K. 1997. Writing Amish culture into genes: biological reductionism in a study of manic depression. *Cult. Med. Psychiatry* 21:137–59

Friedman S, Paradis CM, Hatch M. 1994. Characteristics of African-American and White patients with panic disorder and agoraphobia. *Hosp. Commun. Psychiatry* 45:798–803

Fuligni A. 1998. Authority, autonomy, and parent-adolescent conflict and cohesion: a study of adolescents from Mexican, Chinese, Filipino, and European backgrounds. *Dev. Psychol.* 34:782–92

Gallimore R, Coots J, Weisner T, Garnier H, Guthrie D. 1996. Family responses to children with early developmental delays II: accommodation intensity and activity in early and middle childhood. *Am. J. Ment. Retard.* 101:215–32

Gallimore R, Goldenberg CN, Weisner TS. 1993. The social construction and subjective reality of activity settings: implications for community psychology. *Am. J. Commun. Psychol.* 21:537–59

Good B. 1988. Comments. *Curr. Anthropol.* 29:693–94

Good BJ, Kleinman AM. 1985. Culture and anxiety: cross-cultural evidence for the patterning of anxiety disorders. In *Anxiety and the Anxiety Disorders,* ed. AH Tuma, JD Maser, pp. 297–323. Hillsdale, NJ: Erlbaum. 1020 pp.

Greenberger E, Chen C. 1996. Perceived family relationships and depressed mood in early and late adolescence: a comparison of European and Asian Americans. *Dev. Psychol.* 32:707–16

Greenfield PM. 1997. Culture as process: empirical methods for cultural psychology. In *Handbook of Cross-Cultural Psychology: Theory and Method,* ed. JW Berry, YH Poortinga, J Pandey, 1:301–46. Needham Heights, MA: Allyn & Bacon. 406 pp.

Guarnaccia PJ. 1997. A cross-cultural perspective on anxiety disorders. In *Cultural Issues in the Treatment of Anxiety,* ed. S Friedman, pp. 3–20. New York: Guilford. 261 pp.

Guarnaccia PJ. 1998. Multicultural experiences of family caregiving: a study of African American, European American and

Hispanic American families. See Lefley 1998, pp. 45–61

Guarnaccia PJ, Canino G, Rubio-Stipec M, Bravo M. 1993. The prevalence of *ataques de nervios* in the Puerto Rico study: the role of culture in psychiatric epidemiology. *J. Nerv. Ment. Dis.* 181:157–65

Guarnaccia PJ, De La Cancela V, Carrillo E. 1989a. The multiple meanings of ataques de nervios in the Latino community. *Med. Anthropol.* 11:47–62

Guarnaccia PJ, Kleinman A, Good BJ. 1990. A critical review of epidemiological studies of Puerto Rican mental health. *Am. J. Psychiatry* 147:449–56

Guarnaccia PJ, López S. 1998. The mental health and adjustment of immigrant and refugee children. *Child Adolesc. Clin. North Am.* 7:537–53

Guarnaccia PJ, Parra P, Deschamps A, Milstein G, Argiles N. 1992. Si Dios quiere: Hispanic families' experiences of caring for a seriously mentally ill family member. *Cult. Med. Psychiatry* 16:187–215

Guarnaccia PJ, Rivera M, Franco F, Neighbors C. 1996. The experiences of ataques de nervios: towards an anthropology of emotions in Puerto Rico. *Cult. Med. Psychiatry* 20:343–67

Guarnaccia PJ, Rodriguez O. 1996. Concepts of culture and their role in the development of culturally competent mental health services. *Hisp. J. Behav. Sci.* 18:419–43

Guarnaccia PJ, Rubio-Stipec M, Canino G. 1989b. Ataques de nervios in the Puerto Rican Diagnostic Interview Schedule: the impact of cultural categories on psychiatric epidemiology. *Cult. Med. Psychiatry* 13:275–95

Harrison G, Owens D, Holton A, Neilson D, Boot D. 1988. A prospective study of severe mental disorder in Afro-Caribbean patients. *Psychol. Med.* 18:643–57

Harwood RL. 1992. The influence of culturally derived values on Anglo and Puerto Rican mothers' perceptions of attachment behavior. *Child Dev.* 63:822–39

Helms JE. 1997. The triple quandary of race, culture, and social class in standardized cognitive ability testing. In *Contemporary Intellectual Assessment: Theories, Tests, and Issues,* ed. DP Flanagan, JL Genshaft, PL Harrison, pp. 517–32. New York: Guilford. 598 pp.

Heurtin-Roberts S, Snowden L, Miller L. 1997. Expressions of anxiety in African Americans: ethnography and the Epidemiological Catchment Area studies. *Cult. Med. Psychiatry* 21:337–63

Hopper K. 1991. Some old questions for the new cross-cultural psychiatry. *Med. Anthropol. Q.* 5:299–330

Horwath E, Johnson J, Hornig CD. 1993. Epidemiology of panic disorder in African-Americans. *Am. J. Psychiatry* 150:465–69

Ivanović M, Vuletić Z, Bebbington P. 1994. Expressed emotion in the families of patients with schizophrenia and its influence on the course of illness. *Soc. Psychiatr. Epidemiol.* 29:61–65

Jablensky A, Sartorius N, Ernberg G, Ankar M, Korten A, et al. 1992. Schizophrenia: manifestations, incidence and course in different cultures. *Psychol. Med.* 20(Suppl.):1–97

Jenkins JH. 1988a. Conceptions of schizophrenia as a problem of nerves: a cross-cultural comparison of Mexican-Americans and Anglo-Americans. *Soc. Sci. Med.* 26:1233–43

Jenkins JH. 1988b. Ethnopsychiatric interpretations of schizophrenic illness: the problem of *nervios* within Mexican-American families. *Cult. Med. Psychiatry* 12:303–31

Jenkins JH. 1991. Anthropology, expressed emotion, and schizophrenia. *Ethos* 19:387–431

Jenkins JH. 1993. Too close for comfort: schizophrenia and emotional overinvolvement among Mexicano families. In *Ethnopsychiatry,* ed. AD Gaines, pp. 203–21. Albany, NY: State Univ. NY Press

Jenkins JH, Karno M. 1992. The meaning of expressed emotion: theoretical issues raised by cross-cultural research. *Am. J. Psychiatry* 149:9–21

Karno M, Jenkins JH, de la Selva A, Santana F, Telles C, et al. 1987. Expressed emotion and schizophrenic outcome among Mexican-American families. *J. Nerv. Ment. Dis.* 175:143–51

Kavanaugh D. 1992. Recent developments in expressed emotion and schizophrenia. *Br. J. Psychiatry* 160:601–20

Keane EM, Dick RW, Bechtold DW, Manson SM. 1996. Predictive and concurrent validity of the suicidal ideation questionnaire among American Indian adolescents. *J. Abnorm. Child Psychol.* 24:735–47

King LM. 1978. Social and cultural influences on psychopathology. *Annu. Rev. Psychol.* 29:405–33

Kirmayer LJ. 1998. Editorial: the fate of culture in DSM-IV. *Transcult. Psychiatry* 35:339–42

Kirmayer LJ, Young A, Hayton BC. 1995. The cultural context of anxiety disorders. *Psychiatr. Clin. North Am.* 18:503–19

Kleinman A. 1988. *Rethinking Psychiatry: From Cultural Category to Personal Experience.* New York: Free. 237 pp.

Kleinman A, Eisenberg L, Good B. 1978. Culture, illness, and care: clinical lessons from anthropologic and cross-cultural research. *Ann. Intern. Med.* 88:251–58

Kleinman A, Good BJ, eds. 1985. *Culture and Depression.* Berkeley: Univ. Calif. Press. 535 pp.

Kleinman A, Kleinman J. 1991. Suffering and its professional transformations: toward an ethnography of experience. *Cult. Med. Psychiatry* 15:275–301

Kleinman AM. 1977. Depression, somatization and the "New Cross-Cultural Psychiatry." *Soc. Sci. Med.* 11:3–10

LaFromboise T, Coleman HLK, Gerton J. 1993. Psychological impact of biculturalism: evidence and theory. *Psychol. Bull.* 114:395–412

Lambert MC, Weisz JR, Knight F. 1989. Over- and undercontrolled clinic referral problems of Jamaican and American children and adolescents: the culture-general and the culture-specific. *J. Consult. Clin. Psychol.* 57:467–72

Leff JP, Vaughn CE. 1985. *Expressed Emotion in Families.* NY: Guilford. 241 pp.

Lefley H, ed. 1998. *Families Coping with Mental Illness: The Cultural Context.* San Francisco: Jossey-Bass. 115 pp.

Lewis-Fernandez R, Kleinman A. 1994. Culture, personality and psychopathology. *J. Abnorm. Psychol.* 103:67–71

Lewis-Fernandez R, Kleinman A. 1995. Cultural psychiatry: theoretical, clinical and research issues. *Psychiatr. Clin. North Am.* 18:433–48

Liebowitz MR, Salmán E, Jusino CM, Garfinkel R, Street L, et al. 1994. Ataque de nervios and panic disorder. *Am. J. Psychiatry* 151:871–75

Lin KM, Kleinman AM. 1988. Psychopathology and clinical course of schizophrenia: a cross-cultural perspective. *Schizophr. Bull.* 14:555–67

Lin KM, Poland RE, Anderson D. 1995. Psychopharmacology, ethnicity and culture. *Transcult. Psychiatry* 32:3–40

López SR, Nelson K, Polo A, Jenkins JH, Karno M, Snyder K. 1998. *Family warmth, attributions, and relapse in Mexican American and Anglo American patients with schizophrenia.* Presented at Appl. Psychol. Meet., San Francisco

López SR, Nelson K, Snyder K, Mintz J. 1999. Attributions and affective reactions of family members and course of schizophrenia. *J. Abnorm. Psychol.* 108:307–14

López S, Núñez JA. 1987. The consideration of cultural factors in selected diagnostic criteria and interview schedules. *J. Abnorm. Psychol.* 96:270–72

Manson SM, Ackerson LM, Kick RW, Baron AE, Fleming CM. 1990. Depressive symptoms among American Indian adolescents: psychometric characteristics of the Center for Epidemiologic Studies Depression Scale (CES-D). *Psychol. Assess.* 2:231–37

Manson SM, Shore JH, Bloom JD. 1985. The depressive experience in American Indian

communities: a challenge for psychiatric theory and diagnosis. In *Culture and Depression,* ed. A Kleinman, BJ Good, pp. 331–68. Berkeley, CA: Univ. Calif. Press

Markus HR, Kitayama S. 1991. Culture and the self: implications for cognition, emotion, and motivation. *Psychol. Rev.* 98:224–53

Marsella AJ. 1980. Depressive experience and disorder across cultures. See Triandis & Draguns 1980, pp. 237–89

Marsella AJ, Friedman MJ, Gerrity ET, Scurfield RM, eds. 1996. *Ethnocultural Aspects of Posttraumatic Stress Disorder: Issues, Research, and Clinical Applications.* Washington, DC: Am. Psychol. Assoc. 576 pp.

Maser JD, Dinges N. 1992/93. The co-morbidity of depression, anxiety and substance abuse among American Indians and Alaska Natives. *Cult. Med. Psychiatry* 16:409–577 (Whole issue)

Mezzich JE, Kirmayer LJ, Kleinman A, Fabrega H, Parron DL, et al. 1999. The place of culture in DSM-IV. *J. Nerv. Ment. Dis.* 187:457–64

Mezzich JE, Kleinman A, Fabrega H, Parron DL, eds. 1996. *Culture and Psychiatric Diagnosis: A DSM-IV Perspective.* Washington, DC: Am. Psychiatr. Assoc. 360 pp.

Mezzich JE, Kleinman A, Fabrega H, Parron DL, Good BJ, et al. 1997. Cultural issues for DSM-IV. In *DSM-IV Sourcebook,* ed. TA Widiger, AJ Frances, HA Pincus, R Ross, MB First, W Davis, 3:861–1016. Washington, DC: Am. Psychiatr. Assoc. 1048 pp.

Neal AM, Lilly RS, Zakis S.1993. What are African American children afraid of? *J. Anxiety Disord.* 7:129–39

Neal AM, Turner SM. 1991. Anxiety disorders research with African Americans: current status. *Psychol. Bull.* 109:400–10

Neighbors HW, Jackson JS, Campbell L, Williams D. 1989. The influence of racial factors on psychiatric diagnosis: a review and suggestions for research. *Commun. Ment. Health* 25:301–10

Nuckolls CW. 1992. Toward a cultural history of the personality disorders. *Soc. Sci. Med.* 35:37–47

O'Nell T. 1989. Psychiatric investigations among American Indians and Alaska Natives: a critical review. *Cult. Med. Psychiatry* 13:51–87

O'Nell T. 1993. "Feeling worthless": An ethnographic investigation of depression and problem drinking at the Flathead reservation. *Cult. Med. Psychiatry* 16:447–69

O'Nell T. 1996. *Disciplined Hearts: History, Identity and Depression in an American Indian Community.* Berkeley, CA: Univ. Calif. Press. 252 pp.

O'Nell T, Mitchell CM. 1996. Alcohol use among American Indian adolescents: the role of culture in pathological drinking. *Soc. Sci. Med.* 42:565–78

Paris J. 1997. Social factors in the personality disorders. *Transcult. Psychiatry* 34:421–52

Regier DA, Myers JK, Kramer M, Robins LN, Blazer DG, et al. 1984. The NIMH Epidemiologic Catchment Area program. *Arch. Gen. Psychiatry* 41:934–41

Reiss D, Plomin R, Hetherington EM. 1991. Genetics and psychiatry: an unheralded window on the environment. *Am. J. Psychiatry* 148:283–91

Roberts RE, Roberts CR, Chen YR. 1997. Ethnocultural differences in prevalence of adolescent depression. *Am. J. Commun. Psychol.* 25:95–110

Rogler LH. 1989. The meaning of culturally sensitive research in mental health. *Am. J. Psychiatry* 146:296–303

Rogler LH. 1994. International migrations: a framework for directing research. *Am. Psychol.* 49:701–8

Rogler LH. 1996. Framing research on culture in psychiatric diagnosis: the case of the DSM-IV. *Psychiatry* 59:145–55

Rogler LH, Malgady RG, Rodriguez O. 1989. *Hispanics and Mental Health: A Framework for Research.* Malabar, FL: Krieger. 163 pp.

Rudorfer MV. 1996. Ethnicity in the pharmacologic treatment process. *Psychopharmacol. Bull.* 32:181–82 (Special issue)

Sack WH, Beiser M, Phillips N, Baker-Brown G. 1993. Co-morbid symptoms of depression and conduct disorder in First Nations children: some findings from the Flower of Two Soils Project. *Cult. Med. Psychiatry* 16:471–86

Salgado de Snyder VN, Diaz-Perez M, Bautista E. 1998. Pathways to mental health services among inhabitants of a Mexican village with high migratory tradition to the United States. *Health Soc. Work* 23:249–61

Salgado de Snyder VN, Diaz-Perez MJ, Ojerda V. 1999. The prevalence of nervois and associated symptomatology among inhabitants of Mexican rural communities. *Cult. Med. Psychiatry.* In press

Salmán E, Liebowitz M, Guarnaccia PJ, Jusino CM, Garfinkel R, et al. 1998. Subtypes of ataques de nervios: the influence of coexisting psychiatric diagnosis. *Cult. Med. Psychiatry* 22:231–44

Sartorius N, Jablensky A, Korten A, Ernberg G, Anker M, et al. 1986. Early manifestations and first-contact incidence of schizophrenia in different cultures. *Psychol. Med.* 16:909–28

Sashidharan SP. 1993. Afro-Caribbeans and schizophrenia: the ethnic vulnerabilitiy hypothesis re-examined. *Int. Rev. Psychiatry* 5:120–44

Schneider BH. 1998. Cross-cultural comparison as doorkeeper in research on social and emotional adjustment of children and adolescents. *Dev. Psychol.* 34:793–97

Shweder RA. 1991. Suffering in style: on Arthur Kleinman. In *Thinking Through Cultures: Expeditions in Cultural Psychology,* pp. 313–31. Cambridge, MA: Harvard Univ. Press. 404 pp.

Shweder RA, Bourne EJ. 1984. Does the concept of the person vary cross-culturally? In *Culture Theory: Essays on Mind, Self and Emotion,* ed. RA Shweder, RA LeVine, pp. 158–99. Cambridge: Cambridge Univ. Press. 359 pp.

Suarez-Orozco C, Suarez-Orozco M. 1995. Transformations. In *Migration, Family Life, and Achievement Motivation Among Latino Adolescents.* Palo Alto, CA: Stanford Univ. Press. 266 pp.

Sue S, Fujino DC, Hu L, Takeuchi D, Zane N. 1991. Community mental health services for ethnic minority groups: a test of the cultural responsiveness hypothesis. *J. Consult. Clin. Psychol.* 59:533–40

Sue S, Sue D, Sue L, Takeuchi D. 1995. Asian American psychopathology. *Cult. Diversity Ment. Health* 1:39–51

Takeuchi DT, Chung RCY, Lin KM, Shen H, Kurasaki K, et al. 1998. Lifetime and twelve-month prevalence rates of major depressive episodes and dysthymia among Chinese Americans in Los Angeles. *Am. J. Psychiatry* 155:1407–14

Triandis HC. 1989. The self and social behavior in differing cultural contexts. *Psychol. Rev.* 96:506–20

Triandis H, Draguns J, eds. 1980. *Handbook of Cross-Cultural Psychology: Psychopathology.* Vol. 6. Boston: Allyn & Bacon. 370 pp.

Vaughn CE, Leff JP. 1976. The influence of family and social factors on the course of psychiatric illness. *Br. J. Psychiatry* 129:125–37

Vaughn CE, Snyder KS, Jones S, Freeman WB, Falloon IR. 1984. Family factors in schizophrenic relapse: replication in California of British research on expressed emotion. *Arch. Gen. Psychiatry* 41:1169–77

Vega W, Khoury EL, Zimmerman RS, Gil AG, Warheit GJ. 1995. Cultural conflicts and problem behaviors of Latino adolescents in home and school environments. *J. Commun. Psychol.* 23:167–79

Vega WA, Kolody B, Aguilar-Gaxiola S, Aldrete E, Catalano R, Caraveo-Anduaga J. 1998. Lifetime prevalence of DSM-III-R psychiatric disorders among urban and rural Mexican Americans in California. *Arch. Gen. Psychiatry* 55:771–78

Ware N, Kleinman A. 1992. Culture and somatic experience: the social course of illness in neurasthenia and chronic fatigue syndrome. *Psychosom. Med.* 54:546–60

Weine AM, Phillips JS, Achenbach TM. 1995. Behavioral and emotional problems among Chinese and American children: parent and teacher reports for ages 6 to 13. *J. Abnorm. Child Psychol.* 23:619–39

Weisman A. 1997. Understanding cross-cultural prognostic variability for schizophrenia. *Cult. Diversity Ment. Health* 3:3–35

Weisner TS. 1984. Ecocultural niches of middle childhood: a cross-cultural perspective. In *Development During Middle Childhood: The Years from Six to Twelve,* ed. WA Collins, pp. 335–69. Washington, DC: Nat. Acad. Sci. 434 pp.

Weisz JR, Chaiyasit W, Weiss B, Eastman KL, Jackson EW. 1995. A multimethod study of problem behavior among Thai and American children in school: teacher reports versus direct observation. *Child Dev.* 66:402–15

Weisz JR, McCarty CA, Eastman KL, Chaiyasit W, Suwanlert S. 1997. Developmental psychopathology and culture: ten lessons from Thailand. In *Developmental Psychopathology: Perspectives on Adjustment, Risk, and Disorder,* ed. SS Luthar, JA Burack, D Cicchetti, JR Weisz, pp. 568–92. Cambridge: Cambridge Univ. Press

Weisz JR, Sigman M, Weiss B, Mosk J. 1993a. Parent reports of behavioral and emotional problems among children in Kenya, Thailand, and the United States. *Child Dev.* 64:98–109

Weisz JR, Suwanlert S, Chaiyasit W, Weiss B, Achenbach TM, Eastman KL. 1993b. Behavioral and emotional problems among Thai and American adolescents: parent reports for ages 12–16. *J. Abnorm. Psychol.* 102:395–403

Weisz JR, Suwanlert S, Chaiyasit W, Weiss B, Achenbach TM, Trevathan D. 1989. Epidemiology of behavioral and emotional problems among Thai and American children: teacher reports for ages 6–11. *J. Child Psychol. Psychiatry* 30:471–84

Weisz JR, Suwanlert S, Chaiyasit W, Weiss B, Achenbach TM, Walter BR. 1987a. Epidemiology of behavioral and emotional problems among Thai and American children: parent reports for ages 6 to 11. *J. Am. Acad. Child Adolesc. Psychiatry* 26:890–97

Weisz JR, Suwanlert S, Chaiyasit W, Weiss B, Jackson EW. 1991. Adult attitudes toward over- and undercontrolled child problems: urban and rural parents and teachers from Thailand and the United States. *J. Child Psychol. Psychiatry* 32:645–54

Weisz JR, Suwanlert S, Chaiyasit W, Weiss B, Walter B. 1987b. Over- and undercontrolled referral problems among children and adolescents from Thailand and the United States: The *wat* and *wai* of cultural differences. *J. Consult. Clin. Psychol.* 55: 719–26

Weisz JR, Weiss B. 1991. Studying the "referability" of child clinical problems. *J. Consult. Clin. Psychol.* 59:266–73

World Health Organization. 1979. *Schizophrenia: An International Follow-Up Study.* New York: Wiley. 438 pp.

Zheng YP, Lin KM, Takeuchi D, Kurasaki KS, Wang Y, Cheung F. 1997. An epidemiological study of neurasthenia in Chinese-Americans in Los Angeles. *Compr. Psychiatry* 38:249–59

Annu. Rev. Psychol. 2000. 51:599–630

MEMORY SYSTEMS IN THE BRAIN

Edmund T. Rolls

*Department of Experimental Psychology, University of Oxford, Oxford OX1 3UD,
England, e-mail: Edmund.Rolls@psy.ox.ac.uk*

Key Words   emotion, hunger, taste, orbitofrontal cortex, amygdala, dopamine,
reward, punishment, object recognition, inferior temporal cortex,
episodic memory, hippocampus, short term memory, prefrontal
cortex

■ **Abstract**   The operation of different brain systems involved in different types of
memory is described. One is a system in the primate orbitofrontal cortex and amygdala
involved in representing rewards and punishers, and in learning stimulus-reinforcer
associations. This system is involved in emotion and motivation. A second system in
the temporal cortical visual areas is involved in learning invariant representations of
objects. A third system in the hippocampus is implicated in episodic memory and in
spatial function. Fourth, brain systems in the frontal and temporal cortices involved
in short term memory are described. The approach taken provides insight into the
neuronal operations that take place in each of these brain systems, and has the aim of
leading to quantitative biologically plausible neuronal network models of how each
of these memory systems actually operates.

CONTENTS

Introduction 600
Representations of Rewards and Punishers; Learning about Stimuli
Associated with Rewards and Punishers; Emotion and Motivation 600
 Representation of Primary (Unlearned) Rewards and Punishers 602
 The Representation of Potential Secondary (Learned) Reinforcers 605
 Stimulus-Reinforcement Association Learning 607
 Output Systems 612
 Neural Networks for Stimulus-Reinforcer Association Learning 614
The Learning of Invariant Representations 615
The Hippocampus and Memory 619
 Effects of Damage to the Hippocampus and Connected Structures on Memory 619
 Neurophysiology of the Hippocampus and Connected Areas 620
 Hippocampal Models 622
Short Term Memory 623
Conclusion 623

0084–6570/00/0201–0599$12.00

INTRODUCTION

Neuroscience has reached the stage where it is possible to understand how parts of the brain actually work, by combining approaches from many disciplines. Evidence on the connections and internal connectivity of each brain region, of the biophysical properties of single neurons (Koch 1999), on what is represented by neuronal activity in each brain region, and on the effects of lesions, all provide the foundation for a computational understanding of brain function in terms of the neuronal network operations being performed in each region (Rolls & Treves 1998). Crucial brain systems to understand are those involved in memory, but in addition, learning mechanisms are at the heart of how the brain processes information, for it is by modifying the synaptic connection strengths (or weights) between neurons that useful neuronal information processors for most brain functions, including perception, emotion, motivation, and motor function, are built. The application of this approach to understanding not only what functions are performed, but also how they are performed, is described here for a number of different brain systems.

A major reason for investigating the actual brain mechanisms that underlie behavior is not only to understand how our own brains work, but also to have the basis for understanding and treating medical disorders of the brain. Because of the intended relevance to humans, emphasis is placed here on research in nonhuman primates. This is important because many brain systems, including systems in the temporal lobes and the prefrontal cortex, have undergone considerable development in primates. The elaboration of some of these brain areas has been so great in primates that even evolutionarily old systems such as the taste system appear to have been reconnected (compared to rodents) to place much more emphasis on cortical processing taking place in areas such as the orbitofrontal cortex. In primates, there has also been great development of the visual system, and this itself has had important implications not only for perceptual but also for memory and emotional systems in the brain.

REPRESENTATIONS OF REWARDS AND PUNISHERS; LEARNING ABOUT STIMULI ASSOCIATED WITH REWARDS AND PUNISHERS; EMOTION AND MOTIVATION

Brain systems involved in rewards and punishers are important not only because they are involved in emotion and motivation, but also because they are important in understanding many aspects of brain design, including what signals should be decoded by sensory systems, how learning about the stimuli that are associated with rewards and punishers occurs, and how action systems in the brain must be built (Rolls 1999a). These ideas are introduced next.

Emotions can usefully be defined as states elicited by rewards and punishers (Rolls 1990, 1999a, 2000a). A reward is anything for which an animal will work. A punisher is anything an animal will work to escape or avoid. An example of an emotion might thus be happiness produced by being given a reward, such as a pleasant touch, praise, or winning a large sum of money; another example is fear produced by the sight of a painful stimulus. Frustration, anger, or sadness can be produced by the omission of an expected reward or the termination of a reward, such as the death of a loved one. In contrast, relief can be produced by the omission or termination of a punishing stimulus, such as the removal of a painful stimulus. These examples indicate how emotions can be produced by the delivery, omission, or termination of rewarding or punishing stimuli, and go some way to indicate how different emotions could be produced and classified in terms of the rewards and punishments received, omitted, or terminated (Rolls 1999a).

Rewards and punishers can be more formally defined as instrumental reinforcers, i.e. stimuli or events which, if their occurrence, termination, or omission is made contingent upon the making of a response, alter the probability of the future emission of that response. Some stimuli are unlearned, or primary, reinforcers (e.g. pain or the taste of food if the animal is hungry), whereas others may become reinforcing by learning, through their association with primary reinforcers, thereby becoming secondary reinforcers. This type of learning may thus be called stimulus-reinforcement association learning. For example, fear is an emotional state that might be produced by a sound (the conditioned stimulus) that has previously been associated with a painful stimulus (the primary reinforcer).

Part of the adaptive value of emotional (and motivational) states is to allow a simple interface between sensory inputs and action systems (Rolls 1999a). The essence of this idea is that goals for behavior are specified by reward and punishment evaluation. When an environmental stimulus has been decoded as a primary reward or punishment, or (after previous stimulus-reinforcer association learning) as a secondary rewarding or punishing stimulus, then it becomes a goal for action. The animal can then perform any action (instrumental response) to obtain the reward, or to avoid the punisher. Thus, there is flexibility of action, and this is in contrast with stimulus-response, or habit, learning, in which a particular response to a particular stimulus is learned. The emotional route to action is flexible not only because any action can be performed to obtain the reward or avoid the punishment, but also because the animal can learn in as little as one trial that a reward or punishment is associated with a particular stimulus by stimulus-reinforcer association learning. Animals must be built during evolution to be motivated to obtain certain rewards and avoid certain punishers. Indeed, primary, or unlearned, rewards and punishers are specified by genes that effectively specify the goals for action. Rolls (1999a) proposes that this is the solution that natural selection has found for how genes can influence behavior to promote their fitness (as measured by reproductive success), and for how the brain could flexibly interface sensory systems with action systems.

We now turn to address the brain mechanisms that implement these processes, by considering where primary rewards and punishers are represented in the brain, which parts of the brain are involved in learning associations of stimuli to rewards and punishers, and how they do this. Some of the pathways described here are shown on a lateral view of a primate brain in Figure 1 and schematically in Figure 2.

Representation of Primary (Unlearned) Rewards and Punishers

For primary reinforcers, the reward decoding may occur only after several stages of processing, as in the primate taste system, in which reward is decoded only after the primary taste cortex. By decoding, I mean making explicit some aspect of the stimulus or event in the firing of neurons. A decoded representation is one in which the information can be read easily, for example by taking a sum of the synaptically weighted firing of a population of neurons (Rolls & Treves 1998). Processing as far as the primary taste cortex (Figure 2) represents what the taste is, whereas in the secondary taste cortex, in the orbitofrontal cortex, the reward value of taste is represented. This is shown by the fact that when the reward value of the taste of food is decreased by feeding it to satiety, the responses of neurons in the orbitofrontal cortex, but not at earlier stages of processing in primates, decrease to the food as the reward value of the food decreases (Rolls 1997a, 1999a). This functional architecture enables the taste representation in the primary cortex to be used for purposes that are not reward dependent. One example might be learning where a particular taste can be found in the environment, even when the taste is not pleasant because the primate is not hungry. The representation of taste reward in the primate orbitofrontal cortex is very rich, in that there are ensemble encoded representations of sweet, salt, bitter, sour, and umami (protein taste, exemplified by glutamate) tastes, with the neuronal representation of each well separated, as shown by multidimensional scaling (Rolls 1997a). Moreover, this representation is supplemented by representations of astringency (Critchley & Rolls 1996c) (important for detecting tannin-like substances in foods, which impair the absorption of protein), and of the fat content of food (Rolls et al 1999a), both of which activate orbitofrontal cortex neurons through the somatosensory pathways. The representation of reward in the orbitofrontal cortex is made much richer even than this, by incorporating olfactory information to build by olfactory-to-taste learning (see below) representations of the flavor of food, and by also incorporating visual information about food using visual-to-taste association learning (see below). Further evidence that this is a reward mechanism for food is that electrical brain-stimulation reward occurs in this region of the orbitofrontal cortex and is hunger dependent (Rolls 1999a), and that lesions of the orbitofrontal cortex lead to much less discriminating selection of foods and other items to eat (Baylis & Gaffan 1991).

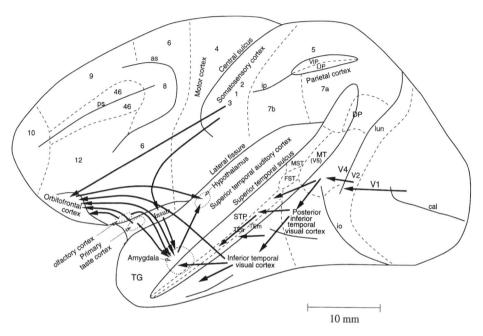

Figure 1 Some of the pathways involved in emotion described in the text are shown on this lateral view of the brain of the macaque monkey. Connections from the primary taste and olfactory cortices to the orbitofrontal cortex and amygdala are shown. Connections are also shown in the ventral visual system from V1 to V2, V4, the inferior temporal visual cortex, etc, with some connections reaching the amygdala and orbitofrontal cortex. In addition, connections from the somatosensory cortical areas 1, 2, and 3 that reach the orbitofrontal cortex directly and via the insular cortex, and that reach the amygdala via the insular cortex, are shown. Abbreviations: as, arcuate sulcus; cal, calcarine sulcus; lun, lunate sulcus; ps, principal sulcus; io, inferior occipital sulcus; ip, intraparietal sulcus (which has been opened to reveal some of the areas it contains); FST, visual motion processing area; LIP, lateral intraparietal area; MST, visual motion processing area; MT, visual motion processing area (also called V5); PIT, posterior inferior temporal cortex; STP, superior temporal plane; TE, architectonic area including high order visual association cortex, and some of its subareas, TEa and TEm; TG, architectonic area in the temporal pole; V1–V4, visual areas 1–4; VIP, ventral intraparietal area; TEO, architectonic area including posterior temporal visual association cortex. The numerals refer to architectonic areas and have the following approximate functional equivalence: 1, 2, 3, somatosensory cortex (posterior to the central sulcus); 4, motor cortex; 5, superior parietal lobule; 7a, inferior parietal lobule, visual part; 7b, inferior parietal lobule, somatosensory part; 6, lateral premotor cortex; 8, frontal eye field; 12, part of orbitofrontal cortex; 46, dorsolateral prefrontal cortex. (After Rolls 1999a:Figure 4.1)

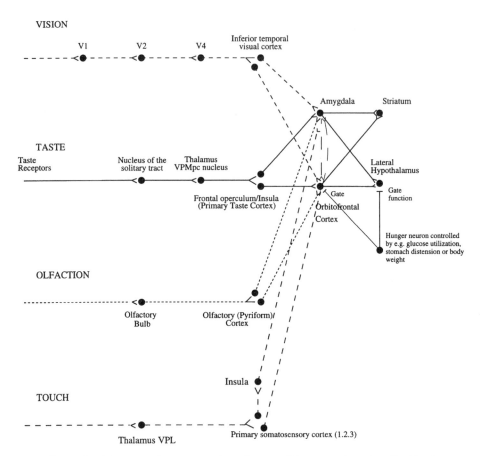

Figure 2 Diagrammatic representation of some of the connections described in the text. V1, striate visual cortex; V2 and V4, cortical visual areas. In primates, sensory analysis proceeds in the visual system as far as the inferior temporal cortex and the primary gustatory cortex; beyond these areas, for example in the amygdala and orbitofrontal cortex, the hedonic value of the stimuli, and whether they are reinforcing or are associated with reinforcement, is represented (see text). The gate function refers to the fact that in the orbitofrontal cortex and hypothalamus the responses of neurons to food are modulated by hunger signals. (After Rolls 1999a: Figure 4.2)

A principle that assists the selection of different behaviors is sensory-specific satiety, which builds up when a reward is repeated for a number of minutes. An example is sensory-specific satiety for the flavor of food, whereby if one food is eaten to satiety and becomes no longer rewarding, other foods may still remain rewarding and be eaten (Rolls 1997a, 1999a). The mechanism for this is implemented in the primate orbitofrontal cortex, in that sensory-specific satiety mirrors the sensory-specific decrease in orbitofrontal neuronal responses to a food that is being fed to satiety (Critchley & Rolls 1996a, Rolls et al 1989), and no decrease is found at earlier stages of processing in the primary taste cortex (Rolls et al 1988) or inferior temporal visual cortex (Rolls et al 1977). The neurophysiological basis proposed for this is in part a type of learning involving habituation with a time course of several minutes of stimulation at the orbitofrontal stage of processing (where reward is represented), but not at earlier stages of processing (where sensory-specific satiety does not modulate neuronal responses) (Rolls et al 1989c, 1999a).

Another primary reinforcer, the pleasantness of touch, is represented in another part of the orbitofrontal cortex, as shown by observations that the orbitofrontal cortex is much more activated (measured with functional magnetic resonance imaging, fMRI) by pleasant relative to neutral touch than is the primary somatosensory cortex (Francis et al 1999). Although pain may be decoded early in sensory processing, in that it utilizes special receptors and pathways, some of the affective aspects of this primary negative reinforcer are represented in the orbitofrontal cortex, in that damage to this region reduces some of the affective aspects of pain in humans (Rolls 1999a), and painful stimuli activate parts of the human orbitofrontal cortex (ET Rolls, J O'Doherty, S Francis, F McGlone, R Bowtell, in preparation).

From the orbitofrontal cortex there are connections to the amygdala and lateral hypothalamus, in both of which there are neurons that respond to reinforcers such as the taste of food. The hypothalamic neurons only respond to the taste of food if the monkey is hungry, and indeed reflect sensory-specific satiety, thus representing the reward value (Rolls 1999a). The evidence on modulation by hunger is less clear for amygdala neurons (Rolls 2000b). There is a connected network in these areas concerned with reward in primates, in that at each site (orbitofrontal cortex, lateral hypothalamus/substantia innominata, and amygdala), electrical stimulation is rewarding, and in that in each site neurons are activated within a few ms by brain-stimulation reward of the other sites, and in many cases also by food reward (Rolls et al 1980).

The Representation of Potential Secondary (Learned) Reinforcers

For potential secondary reinforcers (such as the sight of a particular object or person) in primates, analysis generally proceeds to the level of invariant object representation before reward and punishment associations are learned. For vision, this level of processing is the inferior temporal visual cortical areas, where there are view-, size-, and position-invariant representations of objects and faces that are not affected by the reward or punishment association of visual stimuli (Rolls 1999a, Gross 1992, Wallis & Rolls 1997, Booth & Rolls 1998, Rolls et al 1977). The utility of invariant representations is to enable correct generalization to other transforms (e.g. views, sizes) of the same or similar objects, even when a reward or punishment has previously been associated with one instance. The representation of the object is (appropriately) in a form that is ideal as an input to pattern associators, which allow the reinforcement associations to be learned. The representations are appropriately encoded, in that they can be decoded in a neuronally plausible way (e.g. using a synaptically weighted sum of the firing rates); they are distributed so allowing excellent generalization and graceful degradation; and they have relatively independent information conveyed by different neurons in the ensemble, providing high capacity and allowing the information to be read off quickly, in periods of 20–50 ms (Rolls et al 1997b,c; Rolls & Treves 1998; Rolls 1999a). The utility of representations of objects that are independent of reward associations (for vision, in the inferior temporal cortex) is that they can be projected to different neural systems and then used for many functions independently of the motivational or emotional state. These functions include recognition, recall, forming new memories of objects, episodic memory (e.g. to learn where a food is located, even if one is not hungry for the food at present), and short term memory (Rolls & Treves 1998).

In nonprimates, including for example, rodents, the design principles may involve less sophisticated features because the stimuli being processed are simpler. For example, view-invariant object recognition is probably much less developed in nonprimates, and the recognition that is possible is based more on physical similarity in terms of texture, color, simple features, etc (Rolls & Treves 1998:Sect. 8.8). It may be because there is less sophisticated cortical processing of visual stimuli in this way that other sensory systems are also organized more simply, for example with some (but not total, only perhaps 30%) modulation of taste processing by hunger early in sensory processing in rodents (Scott et al 1995). Moreover, although it is usually appropriate to have emotional responses to well-processed objects (e.g. the sight of a particular person), there are instances, such as a loud noise or a pure tone associated with punishment, in which it may be possible to tap off a sensory representation early in sensory processing that can be used to produce emotional responses. This may occur in rodents, in which the subcortical auditory system provides afferents to the amygdala (LeDoux 1992, 1995; Rolls 1999a).

Especially in primates, it may be important to keep track of the reinforcers received from many different individuals in a social group. To provide the input to such reinforcement-association learning mechanisms, there are many neurons devoted to providing an invariant representation of face identity in macaque cortical areas TEa and TEm in the ventral lip of the anterior part of the superior temporal sulcus. In addition, there is a separate system that encodes facial gesture, movement, and view, as all are important in social behavior, for interpreting whether specific individuals, with their own reinforcement associations, are producing threats or appeasements. In macaques many of these neurons are found in the cortex in the depths of the anterior part of the superior temporal sulcus (Baylis et al 1987; Hasselmo et al 1989a,b; Rolls 1997c; Wallis & Rolls 1997).

Stimulus-Reinforcement Association Learning

After mainly unimodal processing to the object level, sensory systems then project into convergence zones. Those especially important for reward, punishment, emotion, and motivation are the orbitofrontal cortex and amygdala, where primary reinforcers are represented. Pattern associations between potential secondary and primary reinforcers are learned in these brain regions. They are thus the parts of the brain involved in learning the emotional and motivational value of stimuli. Progress on understanding the operation of these systems is considered next.

The Amygdala   Some of the connections of the primate amygdala are shown in Figures 1 and 2 (see also Amaral et al 1992, Rolls 1999a). Not only does the amygdala receive information about primary reinforcers (such as taste and touch), but it also receives inputs about stimuli (e.g. visual ones) that can be associated by learning with primary reinforcers. In primates such inputs come mainly from the ends of cortical processing streams for each modality; for example, for vision the inferior temporal cortex and the cortex in the superior temporal sulcus, and for audition the superior temporal auditory association cortex.

Recordings from single neurons in the amygdala of the monkey have shown that some neurons do respond to visual stimuli, with latencies somewhat longer than those of neurons in the temporal cortical visual areas. Some of these neurons respond primarily to reward-related visual stimuli (e.g. in a visual discrimination task to a triangle that signifies a taste reward can be obtained), and some others respond primarily to visual stimuli associated with punishment (e.g. with the taste of saline) (Sanghera et al 1979, Wilson & Rolls 1993, Ono & Nishijo 1992, Rolls 2000b, FAW Wilson & ET Rolls, in preparation). Although the responses of such neurons reflect previously learned reward or punishment associations of visual stimuli, it is not clear that they reverse their responses rapidly (i.e. in a few trials) when the visual discrimination is reversed (Sanghera et al 1979, Rolls 2000b, Ono & Nishijo 1992). The crucial site of the stimulus-reinforcement association learning that underlies the responses of amygdala neurons to learned reinforcing stimuli is probably within the amygdala itself, and not at earlier stages of processing, because neurons in the inferior temporal cortical visual areas do not reflect the reward associations of visual stimuli, but respond to visual stimuli based on their physical characteristics (see above). Association learning in the amygdala may be implemented by associatively modifiable synapses (Rolls & Treves 1998) from visual and auditory neurons onto neurons receiving inputs from taste, olfactory, or somatosensory primary reinforcers. Consistent with this, Davis (1994, Davis et al 1994) has found in the rat that at least one type of associative learning in the amygdala can be blocked by local application to the amygdala of an NMDA (n-methyl-d-aspartate) receptor blocker, which blocks long-term potentiation (LTP), a model of the synaptic changes that underlie learning (Rolls & Treves 1998). Further, evidence that the learned-incentive (conditioned reinforcing) effects of previously neutral stimuli paired with rewards are mediated by the amygdala acting through the ventral striatum, is that amphetamine injections into the ventral striatum enhanced the effects of a conditioned reinforcing stimulus only if the amygdala was intact (Everitt & Robbins 1992, Everitt et al 2000). The lesion evidence in primates is also consistent with a function of the amygdala in reward- and punishment-related learning, for amygdala lesions in monkeys produce tameness, a lack of emotional responsiveness, excessive examination of objects, often with the mouth, and eating of previously rejected items such as meat (Rolls 1999a). There is evidence that amygdala neurons are involved in these processes in primates, for amygdala lesions made with ibotenic acid impair the processing of reward-related stimuli, in that when the reward value of a set of foods was decreased by feeding it to satiety (i.e. sensory-specific satiety), monkeys still chose the visual stimuli associated with the foods with which they had been satiated (Malkova et al 1997; see further Rolls 2000a).

Further evidence that the primate amygdala processes visual stimuli derived from high-order cortical areas and is of importance in emotional and social behavior is that a population of amygdala neurons has been described that responds primarily to faces (Leonard et al 1985). Each of these neurons responds to some but not all of a set of faces, and thus across an ensemble conveys information about the identity of the face. These neurons are found especially in the basal accessory nucleus of the amygdala, a part of the amygdala that develops markedly in primates (Amaral et al 1992). This part of the amygdala receives inputs from the temporal cortical visual areas in which populations of neurons respond to the identity of faces and to facial expression. This is probably part of a system that has evolved for the rapid and reliable identification of individuals from their faces, and of facial expressions, because of their importance in primate social behavior.

LeDoux and colleagues (1992, 1995, 1996) have traced a system from the medial geniculate directly to the amygdala in rats and have shown that there are associative synaptic modifications in this pathway when pure tones are associated with footshock. The learned responses include typical classically conditioned responses such as heart-rate changes and freezing to fear-inducing stimuli (LeDoux 1995), and also operant responses (Gallagher & Holland 1994). In another type of paradigm, it has been shown that amygdala lesions impair the devaluing effect of pairing a food reward with (aversive) lithium chloride, in that amygdala lesions reduced the classically conditioned responses of the rats to a light previously paired with the food (Hatfield et al 1996; see further Everitt et al 2000). However, the subcortical pathway in which learning occurs, studied by LeDoux and colleagues (see LeDoux 1995), though interesting to study as a model system, is unlikely to be the normal pathway used for reward- and punishment-association learning in primates, in which a visual stimulus will normally need to be analyzed to the object level (to the level e.g. of face identity, which requires cortical processing) before the representation is appropriate for input to a stimulus-reinforcement evaluation system such as the amygdala or orbitofrontal cortex. Similarly, it is typically to complex auditory stimuli (such as a particular person's voice, perhaps making a particular statement) that emotional responses are elicited. The point here is that emotional and motivational responses are usually elicited to environmental stimuli analyzed to the object level (including other organisms), and not to retinal arrays of spots or pure tones. Thus, cortical processing to the object level is required in most normal emotional situations, and these cortical object representations are projected to reach multimodal areas such as the amygdala and orbitofrontal cortex, where the reinforcement label is attached using stimulus-reinforcer pattern-association learning to the primary reinforcers represented in these areas.

Some amygdala neurons that respond to rewarding visual stimuli also respond to relatively novel visual stimuli and they may implement the reward value that novel stimuli have (FAW Wilson & ET Rolls, in preparation; Rolls 1999a, 2000b).

The outputs of the amygdala (Amaral et al 1992) include projections to the hypothalamus and also directly to the autonomic centers in the medulla oblongata, providing one route for cortically processed signals to reach the brainstem and produce autonomic responses. Another interesting output of the amygdala is to the ventral striatum, including the nucleus accumbens, because via this route information processed in the amygdala could gain access to the basal ganglia and thus influence motor output (see Figure 2; Everitt & Robbins 1992). Neurons with reward- and punishment-related responses have been found in the primate nucleus accumbens and other parts of the ventral striatum (Rolls & Williams 1987, Williams et al 1993, Schultz et al 1992). In addition, mood states could affect cognitive processing via the amygdala's direct backprojections to many areas of the temporal, orbitofrontal, and insular cortices from which it receives inputs (Rolls & Treves 1998). Cortical arousal may be produced by conditioned stimuli via the central nucleus of the amygdala outputs to the cholinergic basal forebrain magnocellular nuclei of Meynert (see Kapp et al 1992; Wilson & Rolls 1990a,b,c; Rolls & Treves 1998; Rolls 1999a:Ch. 7). Not only are different amygdala output pathways involved in different responses (broadly instrumental, autonomic, and neuroendocrine effects of conditioned reinforcers), but also there is some specialization within the amygdala for subsystems involved in these different responses (see Everitt et al 2000).

The role of the amygdala in implementing behavior to the reinforcing value of facial expressions has been investigated. Extending the findings on neurons in the macaque amygdala that responded selectively for faces and social interactions (Leonard et al 1985, Brothers & Ring 1993), Young et al (1995, 1996) have described a patient with bilateral damage or disconnection of the amygdala who was impaired in matching and identifying facial expression but not facial identity. Adolphs et al (1994) also found facial expression but not facial identity impairments in a patient with bilateral damage to the amygdala. Although in studies of the effects of amygdala damage in humans, greater impairments have been reported with facial or vocal expressions of fear than with some other expressions (Adolphs et al 1994, Scott et al 1997), and in functional brain imaging studies greater activation may be found with certain classes of emotion-provoking stimuli (e.g. those that induce fear rather than happiness) (Morris et al 1996), it has been suggested (Rolls 1999a) that it is unlikely that the amygdala is specialized for the decoding of only certain classes of emotional stimuli, such as those that produce fear. This emphasis on fear may be related to the research in rats on the role of the amygdala in fear conditioning (LeDoux 1992, 1995, 1996). Indeed, it is clear from single-neuron studies in nonhuman primates that some amygdala neurons are activated by rewarding stimuli, some by punishing stimuli (see above), and others by a wide range of different face stimuli (Leonard et al 1985). Moreover, lesions of the macaque amygdala impair the learning of both stimulus-reward and stimulus-punisher associations, though there is a need for further research with neurotoxic lesions of the amygdala and the learning of an association between a visual stimulus and a primary reinforcer such as taste (Rolls 2000a). Further, electrical stimulation of the macaque and human amygdala at some sites is rewarding, and humans report pleasure from stimulation at such sites (Rolls 1975, Rolls et al 1980, Sem-Jacobsen 1976, Halgren 1992). Thus, any differences in the magnitude of effects between different classes of emotional stimuli that appear in human functional brain–imaging studies (Morris et al 1996, Davidson & Irwin 1999) or even after amygdala damage (Adolphs et al 1994, Scott et al 1997) should not be taken to show that the human amygdala is involved in only some emotions. Indeed, in current fMRI studies we are finding that the human amygdala is activated perfectly well by the pleasant taste of a sweet (glucose) solution (in the continuation of studies reported by Francis et al 1999), showing that reward-related primary reinforcers do activate the human amygdala.

The Orbitofrontal Cortex   The orbitofrontal cortex receives inputs about potential secondary reinforcers, such as olfactory and visual stimuli, as well as about primary reinforcers (see Figures 1 and 2). Some neurons in the orbitofrontal cortex, which contains the secondary and tertiary taste and olfactory cortical areas, respond to the reward value of olfactory stimuli, in that they respond to the odor of food only when the monkey is hungry (Critchley & Rolls 1996b). Moreover, sensory-specific satiety for the reward of the odor of food is represented in the orbitofrontal cortex (Critchley & Rolls 1996b). In addition, some orbitofrontal cortex neurons combine taste and olfactory inputs to represent flavor (Rolls & Baylis 1994), and the principle by which this flavor representation is formed is by olfactory-to-taste association learning (Rolls et al 1996).

The primate orbitofrontal cortex also receives inputs from the inferior temporal visual cortex, and is involved in visual stimulus–reinforcer association learning: Neurons in the orbitofrontal cortex learn visual stimulus-to-taste reinforcer associations in as little as one trial. Moreover, and consistent with the effects of damage to the orbitofrontal cortex that impair performance on visual discrimination reversal, Go/NoGo tasks, and extinction tasks (in which the lesioned macaques continue to make behavioral responses to previously rewarded stimuli), orbitofrontal cortex neurons reverse visual stimulus-reinforcer associations in as little as one trial (Thorpe et al 1983, Rolls et al 1996). Also, a separate population of orbitofrontal cortex neurons responds only on nonreward trials (Thorpe et al

1983). There is thus the basis in the orbitofrontal cortex for rapid learning and updating by relearning or reversing stimulus-reinforcer (sensory-sensory, e.g. visual to taste) associations. In the rapidity of its relearning/reversal, the primate orbitofrontal cortex may effectively replace and perform better some of the functions performed by the amygdala. In addition, some visual neurons in the primate orbitofrontal cortex respond to the sight of faces. These neurons are likely to be involved in learning which emotional responses are currently appropriate to particular individuals, in keeping track of the reinforcers received from each individual, and in making appropriate emotional responses given the facial expression (Rolls 1996a, 1999a).

The evidence thus indicates that the primate orbitofrontal cortex is involved in the evaluation of primary reinforcers, and also implements a mechanism that evaluates whether a reward is expected and generates a mismatch (evident as a firing of the nonreward neurons) if reward is not obtained when expected. These neuronal responses provide further evidence that the orbitofrontal cortex is involved in emotional responses, particularly when these involve correcting previously learned reinforcement contingencies in situations that include those usually described as involving frustration.

It is of interest and potential clinical importance that a number of the symptoms of ventral frontal lobe damage (including the orbitofrontal cortex) in humans appear to be related to this type of function, of altering behavior when stimulus-reinforcement associations alter. Thus, humans with ventral frontal lobe damage can show impairments in a number of tasks in which an alteration of behavioral strategy is required in response to a change in environmental reinforcement contingencies (see Rolls 1990, 1996a, 1999a; Damasio 1994). Some of the personality changes that can follow frontal lobe damage may be related to a similar type of dysfunction. For example, the euphoria, irresponsibility, lack of affect, and lack of concern for the present or future that can follow frontal lobe damage may also be related to a dysfunction in assessing correctly and altering behavior appropriately in response to a change in reinforcement contingencies.

Some of the evidence supporting this hypothesis is that when the reinforcement contingencies unexpectedly reversed in a visual discrimination task performed for points, patients with ventral frontal lesions made more errors in the reversal (or in a similar extinction) task, and completed fewer reversals, than control patients with damage elsewhere in the frontal lobes or in other brain regions (Rolls et al 1994a). The impairment correlated highly with the socially inappropriate or disinhibited behavior of the patients, and also with their subjective evaluation of the changes in their emotional state since the brain damage. The patients were not impaired in other types of memory task, such as paired associate learning. Bechara and colleagues also have findings that are consistent with these in patients with frontal lobe damage when they perform a gambling task (Bechara et al 1994, 1996, 1997; see also Damasio 1994). The patients could choose cards from four decks. The patients with frontal damage were more likely to choose cards from a deck which gave rewards with a reasonable probability but also had occasional very heavy penalties. The net gains from this deck were lower than from the other deck. In this sense, the patients were not affected by the negative consequences of their actions: They did not switch from the deck of cards that though providing significant rewards, also led to large punishments.

To investigate the possible significance of face-related inputs to the orbito-frontal visual neurons described above, the responses of the same patients to faces were also tested. Tests of face (and also voice) expression decoding were included because these are ways in which the reinforcing quality of individuals is often indicated. The identification of facial and vocal emotional expression was found to be impaired in a group of patients with ventral frontal lobe damage who had socially inappropriate behavior (Hornak et al 1996, Rolls 1999c). The expression identification impairments could occur independently of perceptual impairments in facial recognition, voice discrimination, or environmental sound recognition. This provides a further basis for understanding the functions of the orbitofrontal cortex in emotional and social behavior, in that processing of some of the signals normally used in emotional and social behavior is impaired in some of these patients. Imaging studies in humans show that parts of the prefrontal cortex can be activated when mood changes are elicited, but it is not established that some areas are concerned only with positive or only with negative mood (Davidson & Irwin 1999). Indeed, this seems unlikely, in that the neurophysiological studies show that different individual neurons in the macaque orbitofrontal cortex respond to either some rewarding or some punishing stimuli, and that these neurons can be intermingled (Rolls 1999a).

Output Systems

The orbitofrontal cortex and amygdala have connections to output systems such as the striatum through which different types of emotional response can be produced, as illustrated schematically in Figure 2. The outputs of the reward and punishment systems must be treated by the action system as being the goals for action. The action systems must be built to try to maximize the activation of the representations produced by rewarding events and to minimize the activation of the representations produced by punishers or stimuli associated with punishers (Rolls 1999a). Drug addiction produced by psychomotor stimulants such as amphetamine and cocaine can be seen as activating the brain at the stage where the outputs of the amygdala and orbitofrontal cortex, which provide representations of whether stimuli are associated with rewards or punishers, are fed into the ventral striatum and other parts of the basal ganglia as goals for the action system (see Robbins et al 1989, Rolls 1999a, Everitt et al 2000).

Dopamine can be released into this system by aversive as well as by rewarding stimuli (Gray et al 1997). Thus, although Schultz and colleagues (Schultz 1998, Schultz et al 1993, Mirenowicz & Schultz 1996) have argued that dopamine neurons may fire to stimuli that are rewarding or to stimuli that predict reward, such neurons might just respond to the earliest stimulus in a trial that indicates

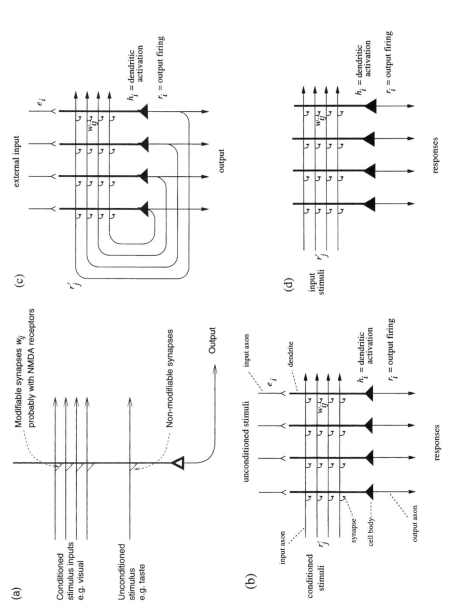

Figure 3 Three neural network architectures that use local learning rules. (a) Pattern association introduced with a single output neuron; (b) pattern association network; (c) autoassociation network; (d) competitive network. (After Rolls & Treves 1998, Figure 1.7)

613

that an action should be made or that preparation for action should begin (see Rolls 1999a, 2000a; Rolls et al 1983). A crucial test here will be whether dopamine neurons fire in relation to active avoidance of aversive stimuli. It is noted in any case that if the release of dopamine does turn out to be related to reward, then it apparently does not represent all the sensory specificity of a particular reward or goal for action, which instead is represented by neurons in brain regions such as the orbitofrontal cortex (see further Rolls 1999a, 2000a).

Emotion may also facilitate the storage of memories. One way this occurs is that episodic memory (i.e. one's memory of particular episodes) is facilitated by emotional states. This may be advantageous because storing many details of the prevailing situation when a strong reinforcer is delivered may be useful in generating appropriate behavior in similar situations in the future. This function may be implemented by the relatively nonspecific projecting systems to the cerebral cortex and hippocampus, including the cholinergic pathways in the basal forebrain and medial septum, and the ascending noradrenergic pathways (see Rolls 1999a, Rolls & Treves 1998). A second way in which emotion may affect the storage of memories is that the current emotional state may be stored with episodic memories, providing a mechanism for the current emotional state to affect which memories are recalled. A third way that emotion may affect the storage of memories is by guiding the cerebral cortex in the representations of the world that are set up. For example, in the visual system it may be useful for perceptual representations or analyzers to be built that are different from each other if they are associated with different reinforcers, and for these to be less likely to be built if they have no association with reinforcement. Ways in which backprojections from parts of the brain important in emotion (such as the amygdala) to parts of the cerebral cortex could perform this function are discussed by Rolls & Treves (1998).

Neural Networks for Stimulus-Reinforcer Association Learning

The neural networks appropriate for this type of learning are pattern associators, in which the forcing or unconditioned stimulus is the primary reinforcer that must activate the neurons through nonmodifiable synapses, and the to-be-associated stimulus activates the output neurons through Hebb modifiable synapses (Figure 3a,b). Nonlinearity in the neurons (requiring as little as a threshold for firing, a property of all neurons), some heterosynaptic long-term depression as well as long-term potentiation, and sparse representations (i.e. distributed representations with a somewhat low proportion of the neurons active) enable large numbers of memories to be stored in such pattern association neural networks. The number of such pattern pairs p that can be associated is proportional to the number of modifiable synaptic connections C (used for the conditioned stimuli) onto each neuron, and is given by

$$p \gg C/[a_0 \log(1/a_0)],$$

where a_0 is the sparseness of the representation of the output neurons produced by the unconditioned stimulus (for binary neurons the sparseness is simply the proportion of neurons active to any one stimulus) (see Rolls & Treves 1998). For a network with 10,000 connections per neuron, and a sparseness a_0 of 0.02, the number of such pattern associations is in the order of 36,000 (Rolls & Treves 1998).

THE LEARNING OF INVARIANT REPRESENTATIONS

There is strong evidence that some neurons in the inferior temporal cortex and cortex in the superior temporal sulcus have representations of faces and objects that show considerable invariance with respect to changes in position on the retina (shift or translation invariance), size, and even view (Gross 1992; Hasselmo et al 1989b; Rolls 1992, 1997b; Logothetis et al 1995; Booth & Rolls 1998; Rolls & Treves 1998; Wallis & Rolls 1997). There is considerable interest in how these invariant representations might be set up. One hypothesis is that they are set up by a learning process (which must be incorporated in the correct neural architecture). This process involves what is essentially a simple Hebbian associative learning rule, but which includes a short memory trace of preceding neuronal activity (in e.g. the postsynaptic term) (Földiàk 1991, Rolls 1992, Wallis & Rolls 1997, Rolls & Treves 1998). The underlying idea is that because real objects viewed normally in the real world have continuous properties in space and time, an object might activate neuronal feature analysers at the next stage of cortical processing, and when the object is transformed (e.g. to a nearby position, size, view, etc) over a short period (for example 0.5 s), the membrane of the postsynaptic neuron would still be in its "Hebb-modifiable" state, and the presynaptic afferents activated with the object in its new transform would thus be strengthened on the still-activated postsynaptic neuron. It is suggested that the short temporal window (0.5 s) of Hebb-modifiability in this system helps neurons learn the statistics of objects moving and thus transforming in the physical world, and at the same time helps them form different representations of different feature combinations or objects, as these are physically discontinuous and present fewer regular correlations to the visual system. (In the real world, objects are normally viewed for periods of a few hundred milliseconds, with perhaps then saccades to another part of the same object, and finally a saccade to another object in the scene.) It is this temporal pattern with which the world is viewed that enables the network to learn using only a Hebb-rule with a short memory trace. The actual mechanism of the trace might be implemented by relatively long-lasting effects of the activation of NMDA receptors, e.g. relatively slow unbinding of glutamate from the NMDA receptor lasting 100 ms or more. Another suggestion is that a memory trace for what has been seen in the last 300 ms appears to be implemented by a mechanism as simple as continued firing of inferior temporal cortex neurons after the stimulus has disappeared, as has been shown to occur (Rolls & Tovee 1994, Rolls et al 1994b), probably implemented by cortical recurrent collateral associative connections setting up attractor networks (Rolls & Treves 1998).

It is suggested that this process takes place gradually over most stages of the multiple-layer cortical processing hierarchy from V1 (the primary visual cortex) to the inferior temporal cortex (see Figure 1), with each stage receiving inputs from a small part of the preceding stage, so that invariances are learned first over small regions of space, about quite simple feature combinations, and then over successively larger regions. This limits the size of the connection space within which correlations must be sought. It is an important part of this suggestion that combinations of features that bind together in their correct spatial configuration are learned early on in the process, in order to solve the feature binding problem (MCM Elliffe, ET Rolls & M Stringer, in preparation). It is also suggested that each stage operates essentially as a competitive network (see Figure 3d; Rolls & Treves 1998) that can learn such feature combinations, and that the trace rule can then learn invariant representations of such spatially-bound feature combinations (Rolls 1992).

In this functional network architecture, view-independent representations could be formed by the same type of trace-rule learning, operating to combine a limited set of views of objects. Many investigators have proposed the plausibility of providing view-independent recognition of objects by combining a set of different views of objects (Poggio & Edelman 1990, Rolls 1992, Logothetis et al 1995, Ullman 1996). Consistent with the suggestion that the view-independent representations are formed by combining view-dependent representations in the primate visual system, is the fact that in the temporal cortical visual areas, neurons with view-independent representations of faces and objects are present in the same cortical areas as neurons with view-dependent representations (from which the view-independent neurons could receive inputs) (Hasselmo et al 1989b, Perrett et al 1987, Booth & Rolls 1998).

This hypothesis has been tested in a simulation, VisNet, which has a 4-layer architecture that incorporates convergence from a limited area of one stage to the next and feedforward competitive nets trained by a trace rule within each stage. The synaptic learning rule used in VisNet is as follows:

$$\mathrm{d}w_{ij} = km_i r'_j \tag{1}$$

and

$$m_i^{(t)} = (1 - \eta)r_i^{(t)} + \eta m_i^{(t-1)}, \tag{2}$$

where r'_j is the jth input to the ith neuron, r_i is the output of the ith neuron, w_{ij} is the jth weight on the ith neuron, η governs the relative influence of the trace and the new input (it takes values in the range 0–1 and is typically 0.4–0.6), and m_i^0 represents the value of the ith cell's memory trace at time t. To train the network to produce a translation invariant representation, one stimulus is placed successively in a sequence of positions across the input (or "retina"), then the next stimulus is placed successively in the same sequence of positions across the input, and so on through the set of stimuli. To train on view invariance, different views of the same object are shown in succession, then different views of the next object are shown in succession, and so on. The network is able to learn translation and view-invariant representations of objects, provided that it is trained with the trace rule (Wallis & Rolls 1997). In control tests, it is shown not to learn invariant representations when trained with just a Hebbian rule.

There have been a number of recent investigations to further explore this type of learning. In one investigation, Parga & Rolls (1998) incorporated the associations between exemplars of the same object in the recurrent synapses of an autoassociative (attractor) network, so that the techniques of statistical physics could be used to analyze the storage capacity of a system implementing invariant representations in this way. They showed that such networks did have an object phase in which the presentation of any exemplar (e.g. view) of an object would result in the same firing state as other exemplars of the same object, and that the number of different objects that could be stored is proportional to the number of synapses per neuron divided by the number of views of each object. Rolls & Milward (1999) explored the operation of the trace learning rule used in the VisNet architecture further, and showed that the rule operated especially well if the trace incorporated activity from previous presentations of the same object but there was no contribution from the current neuronal activity being produced by the current exemplar of the object. The explanation for this is that this temporally asymmetric rule (the presynaptic term from the current exemplar and the trace from the preceding exemplars) encourages neurons to respond to the current exemplar in the same way as they did to previous exemplars. ET Rolls & SM Stringer (submitted for publication) went on to show that part of the power of this type of trace rule can be related to gradient descent and temporal-difference (see Sutton & Barto 1998) learning.

Consistent with this hypothesis, there is evidence that rapid learning is implemented in the inferior temporal visual cortex. For example, Rolls et al (1989a) showed that neurons rapidly adjusted their responses (in 1–2 s for each stimulus) into a profile of firing to a new set of faces, which enabled the neurons to discriminate between the faces, and Tovee et al (1996) showed that neurons came to respond to ambiguous black and white images that contained faces with just a few seconds of viewing the same pictures in greyscale images in which the faces could be clearly seen. In studies aimed to investigate the neural basis of semantic memory, Miyashita and colleagues (see Miyashita 2000, Higuchi & Miyashita 1996) have shown that inferior temporal cortex neurons can have similar responses to pairs of visual stimuli that regularly occur separated from each other by 1–3 sec, and that the learning of these associations may depend on the perirhinal cortex, which has backprojections to the inferior temporal visual cortex, and which could help to produce maintained firing in response to a stimulus in the inferior temporal visual cortex (Figure 4). The delays involved in these exper-

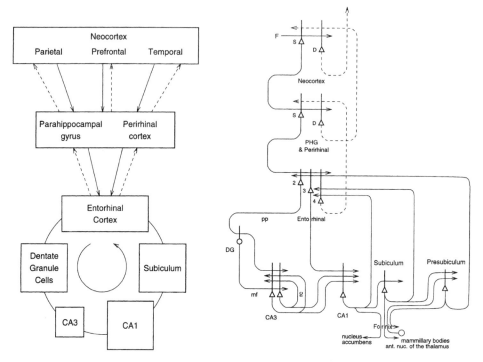

Figure 4 Forward connections (*solid lines*) from areas of cerebral association neocortex via the parahippocampal gyrus and perirhinal cortex, and entorhinal cortex, to the hippocampus; backprojections (*dashed lines*) via the hippocampal CA1 pyramidal cells, subiculum, and parahippocampal gyrus to the neocortex. There is great convergence in the forward connections down to the single network implemented in the CA3 pyramidal cells, and great divergence again in the backprojections. *Left:* block diagram. *Right:* more detailed representation of some of the principal excitatory neurons in the pathways. Abbreviations: D, deep pyramidal cells; DG, dentate granule cells; F, forward inputs to areas of the association cortex from preceding cortical areas in the hierarchy; mf, mossy fibres; PHG, parahippocampal gyrus and perirhinal cortex; pp, perforant path; rc, recurrent collateral of the CA3 hippocampal pyramidal cells; S, superficial pyramidal cells; 2, pyramidal cells in layer 2 of the entorhinal cortex; 3, pyramidal cells in layer 3 of the entorhinal cortex. The *thick lines* above the cell bodies represent the dendrites.

iments are longer than those needed for learning invariant representations of objects (in which the time taken to transform from one view to another might be 100–500 ms), but nevertheless the fact that at least entorhinal cortex neurons can help to bridge delay periods by maintaining firing for a short period after a stimulus has disappeared (Suzuki et al 1997) may be useful in the learning of view-invariant representations. Indeed, Buckley et al (1998) have shown that perirhinal lesions may impair the learning of new view-invariant representations of objects.

THE HIPPOCAMPUS AND MEMORY

Partly because of the evidence that anterograde amnesia occurs in humans with bilateral damage to the hippocampus and nearby parts of the temporal lobe (Squire 1992, Rempel-Clower et al 1996), there is continuing interest in how the hippocampus and connected structures operate in memory. The effects of damage to the hippocampus indicate that the very long-term storage of information is not in the hippocampus, at least in humans. On the other hand, the hippocampus does appear to be necessary to learn certain types of information, which have been characterized as declarative, or knowing that, as contrasted with procedural, or knowing how, which is spared in amnesia. Declarative memory includes what can be declared or brought to mind as a proposition or an image. Declarative memory includes episodic memory (memory for particular episodes) and semantic memory (memory for facts) (Squire 1992, Squire & Knowlton 1995).

Effects of Damage to the Hippocampus and Connected Structures on Memory

In monkeys, damage to the hippocampus or to some of its connections, such as the fornix, produces deficits in learning about where objects are and where responses must be made (Rolls 1996b). For example, macaques and humans with damage to the hippocampus or fornix are impaired in object-place memory tasks in which not only the objects seen, but where they were seen, must be remembered (Gaffan & Saunders 1985, Parkinson et al 1988, Smith & Milner 1981). Such object-place tasks require a whole-scene or snapshot-like memory (Gaffan 1994). Also, fornix lesions impair conditional left-right discrimination learning, in which the visual appearance of an object specifies whether a response is to be made to the left or the right (Rupniak & Gaffan 1987). A comparable deficit is found in humans (Petrides 1985). Fornix-sectioned monkeys are also impaired in learning on the basis of a spatial cue for which object to choose (e.g. if two objects are on the left, choose object A, but if the two objects are on the right, choose object B) (Gaffan & Harrison 1989a). Further, monkeys with fornix damage are also impaired in using information about their place in an environment. For example, Gaffan & Harrison (1989b) found learning impairments when the position of the monkey in the room determined which of two or more objects the monkey had to choose. Rats with hippocampal lesions are impaired in using environmental spatial cues to remember particular places (Jarrard 1993), and it has been argued that the necessity to utilize allocentric spatial cues (Cassaday & Rawlins 1997), to utilize spatial cues or bridge delays (Jackson et al 1998), or to perform relational operations on remembered material (Eichenbaum 1997) may be characteristic of the deficits.

One way of relating the impairment of spatial processing to other aspects of hippocampal function (including the memory of recent events or episodes in humans) is to note that this spatial processing involves a snapshot type of memory, in which one whole scene with its often unique set of elements must be remembered. This memory may then be a special case of episodic memory, which involves an arbitrary association of a set of spatial and/or nonspatial events that describe a past episode. For example, the deficit in paired-associate learning in humans (Squire 1992) may be especially evident when this involves arbitrary associations between words, for example window and lake.

It appears that the deficits in recognition memory (tested, for example, for visual stimuli seen recently in a delayed match to sample task) produced by damage to this brain region are related to damage to the perirhinal cortex, which receives from high order association cortex and has connections to the hippocampus (Figure 4) (Zola-Morgan et al 1989, 1994; Suzuki & Amaral 1994a,b). Given that some topographic segregation is maintained in the afferents to the hippocampus through the perirhinal and parahippocampal cortices (Amaral & Witter 1989; Suzuki & Amaral 1994a,b), it may be that these areas are able to subserve memory within one of these topographically separated areas; whereas the final convergence afforded by the hippocampus into a single network in CA3 that may operate by autoassociation (see Figure 4 and below) allows arbitrary associations between any of the inputs to the hippocampus, e.g. spatial, visual object, and auditory, which may all be involved in typical episodic memories (see below and Rolls 1996b, Rolls & Treves 1998).

Neurophysiology of the Hippocampus and Connected Areas

In the rat, many hippocampal pyramidal cells fire when the rat is in a particular place, as defined, for example by the visual spatial cues in an environment such as a room (O'Keefe 1990, 1991; Kubie & Muller 1991). There is information from the responses of many such cells about the place where the rat is in the environment. When a rat enters a new environment B connected to a known environment A, there is a period in the order of 10 minutes in which, as the new environment is learned, some of the cells that formerly had place fields in A develop place fields in B instead. It is as if the hippocampus sets up a new spatial representation that can map both A and B, keeping the proportion of cells active at any one time approximately constant (Wilson & McNaughton 1993). Some rat hippocampal neurons are found to be more task-related, responding, for example to olfactory stimuli to which particular behavioral responses must be made (Eichenbaum 1997), and some of these neurons may show place-related responses in different experiments.

It was recently discovered that in the primate hippocampus, many spatial cells have responses not related to the place where the monkey is, but instead related to the place where the monkey is looking (Rolls et al 1997a, Rolls 1999b). These are called spatial view cells. These cells encode information in allocentric (world-related, as contrasted with egocentric) coordinates (Georges-François et al 1999, Rolls et al 1998). They can in some cases respond to remembered spatial views, in that they respond when the view details are obscured, and use idiothetic cues, including eye position and head direction, to trigger this memory recall operation (Robertson et al 1998). Another idiothetic input that drives some primate hippocampal neurons is linear and axial whole body motion (O'Mara et al 1994), and in addition, the primate presubiculum has been shown to contain head direction cells (Robertson et al 1999).

Part of the interest in spatial view cells is because they could provide the spatial representation required to enable primates to perform object-place memory, for example remembering where they saw a person or object, which is an example of an episodic memory, and indeed similar neurons in the hippocampus respond in object-place memory tasks (Rolls et al 1989b). Associating such a spatial representation with a representation of a person or object could be implemented by an autoassociation network implemented by the recurrent collateral connections of the CA3 hippocampal pyramidal cells (Rolls 1989, 1996b, Rolls & Treves 1998). In the object-place memory task some other primate hippocampal neurons respond to a combination of spatial information and information about the object seen (Rolls et al 1989b). Further evidence for this convergence of spatial and object information in the hippocampus is that in another memory task for which the hippocampus is needed—learning where to make spatial responses when a picture is shown—some primate hippocampal neurons respond to a combination of which picture is shown, and where the response must be made (Miyashita et al 1989, Cahusac et al 1993).

These primate spatial view cells are thus unlike place cells found in the rat (O'Keefe 1979, Muller et al 1991). Primates, with their highly developed visual and eye movement control systems, can explore and remember information about what is present at places in the environment without having to visit those places. Such spatial view cells in primates would thus be useful as part of a memory system, in that they would provide a representation of a part of space that would not depend on exactly where the monkey or human was, and that could be associated with items that might be present in those spatial locations. An example of the utility of such a representation in humans would be remembering where a particular person had been seen. The primate spatial representations would also be useful in remembering trajectories through environments, of use for example in short-range spatial navigation (O'Mara et al 1994, Rolls 1999b).

The representation of space in the rat hippocampus, which is of the place where the rat is, may be related to the fact that with a much less developed visual system than the primate, the rat's representation of space may be defined more by the olfactory and tactile as well as distant visual cues present, and may thus tend to reflect the place where the rat is. An interesting hypothesis on how this difference could arise from essentially the same computational process in rats and monkeys is as follows (see Rolls 1999b). The starting assumption is that in both the rat and the primate, the dentate granule cells and the CA3 and CA1 pyramidal cells respond to combinations of the inputs received. In the case of the primate, a combination of visual features in the environment will over a typical viewing angle of perhaps 10–20 degrees result in the formation of a spatial view cell, the effective trigger for which will thus be a combination of visual features within a relatively small part of space. In contrast, in the rat, given the extensive visual field that may extend over 180–270 degrees, a combination of visual features formed over such a wide visual angle would effectively define a position in space, that is a place. The actual processes by which the hippocampal formation cells would come to respond to feature combinations could be similar in rats and monkeys, involving, for example competitive learning in the dentate granule cells, autoassociation learning in CA3 pyramidal cells, and competitive learning in CA1 pyramidal cells (Rolls 1989, 1996b; Treves & Rolls 1994; Rolls & Treves 1998). Thus, spatial view cells in primates and place cells in rats might arise by the same computational process but be different by virtue of the fact that primates are foveate and view a small part of the visual field at any one time, whereas the rat has a very wide visual field. Although the representation of space in rats may therefore be in some ways analogous to the representation of space in the primate hippocampus, the difference does have implications for theories, and modeling, of hippocampal function.

In rats, the presence of place cells has led to theories that the rat hippocampus is a spatial cognitive map and can perform spatial computations to implement navigation through spatial environments (O'Keefe & Nadel 1978, O'Keefe 1991, Burgess et al 1994). The details of such navigational theories could not apply in any direct way to what is found in the primate hippocampus. Instead, what is applicable to both the primate and rat hippocampal recordings is that hippocampal neurons contain a representation of space (for the rat, primarily where the rat is, and for the primate, primarily of positions "out there" in space), which is a suitable representation for an episodic memory system. In primates, this would enable one to remember, for example, where an object was seen. In rats, it might enable memories to be formed of where particular objects (for example those defined by olfactory, tactile, and taste inputs) were found. Thus, in primates, and possibly also in rats, the neuronal representation of space in the hippocampus may be appropriate for forming memories of events (which in these animals usually have a spatial component). Such memories would be useful for spatial navigation, for which according to the present hypothesis the hippocampus would implement the memory component but not the spatial computation component. Evidence that what neuronal recordings have shown is represented in the non-human primate hippocampal system may also be present in humans is that regions of the hippocampal formation can be activated when humans look at spatial views (Epstein & Kanwisher 1998, O'Keefe et al 1998).

Hippocampal Models

These neuropsychological and neurophysiological analyses are complemented by neuronal network models of how the hippocampus could operate to store and retrieve large numbers of memories (Rolls 1989, 1996b; Treves & Rolls 1994; Rolls & Treves 1998). One key hypothesis (adopted also by McClelland et al

1995) is that the hippocampal CA3 recurrent collateral connections provide a single autoassociation network that enables the firing of any set of CA3 neurons representing one part of a memory to be associated with the firing of any other set of CA3 neurons representing another part of the same memory (cf Marr 1971). Another key part of the quantitative theory is that not only can retrieval of a memory to an incomplete cue be performed by the operation of the associatively modified CA3 recurrent collateral connections, but also that recall of that information to the neocortex can be performed via CA1 and the hippocampo-cortical and cortico-cortical backprojections (Treves & Rolls 1994, Rolls 1996b, Rolls & Treves 1998). This and other computational approaches to hippocampal function are included in Hippocampus 6 (6) (1996).

SHORT TERM MEMORY

A common method the brain uses to implement a short term memory is to maintain the firing of neurons during a short memory period after the end of a stimulus. In the inferior temporal cortex this firing may be maintained for a few hundred ms even when the monkey is not performing a memory task (Rolls & Tovee 1994, Rolls et al 1994b, 1999b; cf Desimone 1996). In more ventral temporal cortical areas such as the entorhinal cortex the firing may be maintained for longer periods in delayed match to sample tasks (Suzuki et al 1997), and in the prefrontal cortex for even tens of seconds (see Fuster 1997). In the dorsolateral and inferior convexity prefrontal cortex the firing of the neurons may be related to the memory of spatial responses or objects (Goldman-Rakic 1996, Wilson et al 1993) or both (Rao et al 1997), and in the principal sulcus/frontal eye field/arcuate sulcus region the neurons may be related to the memory of places for eye movements (Funahashi et al 1989). The firing may be maintained by the operation of associatively modified recurrent collateral connections between nearby pyramidal cells producing attractor states in autoassociative networks (Amit 1995, Rolls & Treves 1998; Figure 3c). For the short term memory to be maintained during periods in which new stimuli are to be perceived, there must be separate networks for the perceptual and short term memory functions, and indeed two coupled networks, one in the inferior temporal visual cortex for perceptual functions, and the other in the prefrontal cortex for maintaining the short term memory during intervening stimuli, provide a precise model of the interaction of perceptual and short term memory systems (Renart et al 1999).

CONCLUSION

It is now possible not only to delineate brain systems involved in different types of memory, but also to have some insight into the neuronal operations that take place in each of these brain systems, and thus to be able to produce quantitative biologically plausible neuronal network models of how each of these memory systems actually operates, as described more fully by Rolls & Treves (1998). Moreover, this start of a fundamental understanding through a neurocomputational approach of how the brain actually operates quantitatively to implement memory provides the promise of understanding not only how parts of the brain involved in memory operate, but also how many other parts of the brain perform their functions—including sensory information processing to the level of the invariant representation of objects, processing involved in motivation and emotion, and the processing involved in initiating and controlling actions (Rolls & Treves 1998, Rolls 1999a).

ACKNOWLEDGMENTS

The author has worked on some of the research described here with GC Baylis, LL Baylis, MCA Booth, MJ Burton, HC Critchley, P Georges-François, ME Hasselmo, CM Leonard, F Mora, J O'Doherty, DI Perrett, RG Robertson, MK Sanghera, TR Scott, SM Stringer, SJ Thorpe, and FAW Wilson. Their collaboration is sincerely acknowledged. Some of the research described was supported by the Medical Research Council, PG8513790, and by the Human Frontier Science Program.

Visit the Annual Reviews home page at www.AnnualReviews.org.

LITERATURE CITED

Adolphs R, Tranel D, Damasio H, Damasio A. 1994. Impaired recognition of emotion in facial expressions following bilateral damage to the human amygdala. *Nature* 372:669–72

Aggleton JP, ed. 1992. *The Amygdala.* Chichester, UK. Wiley

Aggleton JP, ed. 2000. *The Amygdala: A Functional Analysis.* Oxford: Oxford Univ. Press. In press

Amaral DG, Price JL, Pitkanen A, Carmichael ST. 1992. Anatomical organization of the primate amygdaloid complex. See Aggleton 1992, pp. 1–66

Amaral DG, Witter MP. 1989. The three-dimensional organization of the hippocampal formation: a review of anatomical data. *Neuroscience* 31:571–91

Amit DJ. 1995 The Hebbian paradigm reintegrated: local reverberations as internal representations. *Behav. Brain Sci.* 18:617–57

Baylis GC, Rolls ET, Leonard CM. 1987. Functional subdivisions of temporal lobe neocortex. *J. Neurosci.* 7:330–42

Baylis LL, Gaffan D. 1991. Amydalectomy and ventromedial prefrontal ablation produce similar deficits in food choice and in simple object discrimination learning for an unseen reward. *Exp. Brain Res.* 86:612–22

Bechara A, Damasio AR, Damasio H, Anderson SW. 1994. Insensitivity to future consequences following damage to human prefrontal cortex. *Cognition* 50:7–15

Bechara A, Damasio H, Tranel D, Damasio AR. 1997. Deciding advantageously before knowing the advantageous strategy. *Science* 275:1293–95

Bechara A, Tranel D, Damasio H, Damasio AR. 1996. Failure to respond autonomically to anticipated future outcomes following damage to prefrontal cortex. *Cereb. Cortex* 6:215–25

Booth MCA, Rolls ET. 1998. View-invariant representations of familiar objects by neurons in the inferior temporal visual cortex. *Cereb. Cortex* 8:510–23

Brothers L, Ring B. 1993. Mesial temporal neurons in the macaque monkey with responses selective for aspects of socal stimuli. *Behav. Brain Res.* 57:53–61

Buckley MJ, Booth MCA, Rolls ET, Gaffan D. 1998. Selective visual perception deficits following perirhinal cortex ablation in the macaque. *Soc. Neurosci. Abstr.* 24:18

Burgess N, Recce M, O'Keefe J. 1994. A model of hippocampal function. *Neural Netw.* 7:1065–81

Cahusac PMB, Rolls ET, Miyashita Y, Niki H. 1993. Modification of the responses of hippocampal neurons in the monkey during the learning of a conditional spatial response task. *Hippocampus* 3:29–42

Cassaday HJ, Rawlins JN. 1997. The hippocampus, objects, and their contexts. *Behav. Neurosci.* 111:1228–44

Critchley HD, Rolls ET. 1996a. Olfactory neuronal responses in the primate orbitofrontal cortex: analysis in an olfactory discrimination task. *J. Neurophysiol.* 75:1659–72

Critchley HD, Rolls ET. 1996b. Hunger and satiety modify the responses of olfactory and visual neurons in the primate orbitofrontal cortex. *J. Neurophysiol.* 75:1673–86

Critchley HD, Rolls ET. 1996c. Responses of primate taste cortex neurons to the astringent tastant tannic acid. *Chem. Senses* 21:135–45

Damasio AR. 1994. *Descartes' Error.* New York: Putnam

Davidson RJ, Irwin W. 1999. The functional neuroanatomy of emotion and affective style. *Trends Cogn. Sci.* 3:11–21

Davis M. 1994. The role of the amygdala in emotional learning. *Int. Rev. Neurobiol.* 36:225–66

Davis M, Rainnie D, Cassell M. 1994. Neurotransmission in the rat amygdala related to fear and anxiety. *Trends Neurosci.* 17:208–14

Desimone R. 1996. Neural mechanisms for visual memory and their role in attention. *Proc. Natl. Acad. Sci. USA* 93:13494–99

Eichenbaum H. 1997. Declarative memory: insights from cognitive neurobiology. *Annu. Rev. Psychol.* 48:547–72

Epstein R, Kanwisher N. 1998. A cortical representation of the local visual environment. *Nature* 392:598–601

Everitt BJ, Cardinal RN, Hall J, Parkinson JA, Robbins TW. 2000. Differential involvement of amygdala subsystems in appetitive conditioning and drug addiction. See Aggleton 2000. In press

Everitt BJ, Robbins TW. 1992. Amygdala-ventral striatal interactions and reward-related processes. See Aggleton 1992, pp. 401–30

Földiàk P. 1991. Learning invariance from transformation sequences. *Neural Comput.* 3:193–99

Francis S, Rolls ET, Bowtell R, McGlone F, O'Doherty J, et al. 1999. The representation of the pleasantness of touch in the human brain, and its relation to taste and olfactory areas. *NeuroReport* 10:453–59

Funahashi S, Bruce CJ, Goldman-Rakic PS. 1989. Mnemonic coding of visual space in monkey dorsolateral prefrontal cortex. *J. Neurophysiol.* 61:331–49

Fuster JM. 1997. *The Prefrontal Cortex.* New York: Raven Press. 3rd ed. 333 pp.

Gaffan D. 1994. Scene-specific memory for objects: a model of episodic memory impairment in monkeys with fornix transection. *J. Cogn. Neurosci.* 6:305–20

Gaffan D, Harrison S. 1989a. A comparison of the effects of fornix section and sulcus principalis ablation upon spatial learning by monkeys. *Behav. Brain Res.* 31:207–20

Gaffan D, Harrison S. 1989b. Place memory and scene memory: effects of fornix transection in the monkey. *Exp. Brain Res.* 74:202–12

Gaffan D, Saunders RC. 1985. Running recognition of configural stimuli by fornix transected monkeys. *Q. J. Exp. Psychol.* 37B:61–71

Gallagher M, Holland PC. 1994. The amygdala complex: multiple roles in associative learning and attention. *Proc. Natl. Acad. Sci. USA* 91:11771–76

Georges-François P, Rolls ET, Robertson RG. 1999. Spatial view cells in the primate hippocampus: allocentric view not head direction or eye position or place. *Cereb. Cortex* 9:197–212

Goldman-Rakic PS. 1996. The prefrontal landscape: implications of functional architecture for understanding human mentation and the central executive. *Philos. Trans. R. Soc. London Ser. B* 351:1445–53

Gray JA, Young AMJ, Joseph MH. 1997. Dopamine's role. *Science* 278:1548–49

Gross CG. 1992. Representation of visual stimuli in inferior temporal cortex. *Philos. Trans. R. Soc. London Ser. B* 335:3–10

Halgren E. 1992. Emotional neurophysiology of the amygdala within the context of human cognition. See Aggleton 1992, pp. 191–228

Hasselmo ME, Rolls ET, Baylis GC. 1989a. The role of expression and identity in the face-selective responses of neurons in the temporal visual cortex of the monkey. *Behav. Brain Res.* 32:203–18

Hasselmo ME, Rolls ET, Baylis GC, Nalwa V. 1989b. Object-centered encoding by face-selective neurons in the cortex in the superior temporal sulcus of the monkey. *Exp. Brain Res.* 75:417–29

Hatfield T, Han JS, Conley M, Gallagher M, Holland P. 1996. Neurotoxic lesions of basolateral, but not central, amygdala interfere with Pavlovian second-order conditioning and reinforcer devaluation effects. *J. Neurosci.* 16:5256–65

Higuchi S, Miyashita Y. 1996. Formation of mnemonic neuronal responses to visual paired associates in inferotemporal cortex is impaired by perirhinal and entorhinal lesions. *Proc. Natl. Acad. Sci. USA* 95:739–43

Hornak J, Rolls ET, Wade D. 1996. Face and voice expression identification in patients with emotional and behavioural changes following ventral frontal lobe damage. *Neuropsychologia* 34:247–61

Jackson PA, Kesner RP, Amann K. 1998. Memory for duration: role of hippocampus and medial prefrontal cortex. *Neurobiol. Learn Mem.* 70:328–48

Jarrard EL. 1993. On the role of the hippocampus in learning and memory in the rat. *Behav. Neural Biol.* 60:9–26

Kapp BS, Whalen PJ, Supple WF, Pascoe JP. 1992. Amygdaloid contributions to conditioned arousal and sensory information processing. See Aggleton 1992, pp. 229–45

Koch C. 1999. *Biophysics of Computation. Information Processing in Single Neurons.* Oxford, UK: Oxford Univ. Press. 562 pp.

Kubie JL, Muller RU. 1991. Multiple representations in the hippocampus. *Hippocampus* 1:240–42

LeDoux JE. 1992. Emotion and the amygdala. See Aggleton 1992, pp. 339–51

LeDoux JE. 1995. Emotion: clues from the brain. *Annu. Rev. Psychol.* 46:209–35

LeDoux JE. 1996. *The Emotional Brain.* New York: Simon & Schuster. 384 pp.

Leonard CM, Rolls ET, Wilson FAW, Baylis GC. 1985. Neurons in the amygdala of the monkey with responses selective for faces. *Behav. Brain Res.* 15:159–76

Logothetis NK, Pauls J, Poggio T. 1995. Shape representation in the inferior temporal cortex of monkeys. *Curr. Biol.* 5:552–63

Malkova L, Gaffan D, Murray EA. 1997. Excitotoxic lesions of the amygdala fail to produce impairment in visual learning for auditory secondary reinforcement but interfere with reinforcer devaluation effects in rhesus monkeys. *J. Neurosci.* 17:6011–20

Marr D. 1971. Simple memory: a theory for archicortex. *Philos. Trans. R. Soc. London Ser. B* 262:23–81

McClelland JL, McNaughton BL, O'Reilly RC. 1995. Why there are complementary learning systems in the hippocampus and neocortex: insights from the successes and failures of connectionist models of learning and memory. *Psychol. Rev.* 102:419–57

Mirenowicz J, Schultz W. 1996. Preferential activation of midbrain dopamine neurons by appetitive rather than aversive stimuli. *Nature* 279:449–51

Miyashita Y. 2000. Visual associative long-term memory: encoding and retrieval in inferotemporal cortex of the primate. In *The Cognitive Neurosciences,* ed. M Gazzaniga, 27:379–92. Cambridge, MA: MIT Press

Miyashita Y, Rolls ET, Cahusac PMB, Niki H, Feigenbaum JD. 1989. Activity of hippocampal neurons in the monkey related to a conditional spatial response task. *Behav. Brain Res.* 33:229–40

Morris JS, Frith CD, Perrett DI, Rowland D, Young AW, et al. 1996. A differential neural response in the human amygdala to fearful and happy facial expressions. *Nature* 383:812–815

Muller RU, Kubie JL, Bostock EM, Taube JS, Quirk GJ. 1991. Spatial firing correlates of neurons in the hippocampal formation of freely moving rats. See Paillard 1991, pp. 296–333

O'Keefe J. 1979. A review of the hippocampal place cells. *Prog. Neurobiol.* 13:419–39

O'Keefe J. 1990. A computational theory of the cognitive map. *Prog. Brain Res.* 83:301–12

O'Keefe J. 1991. The hippocampal cognitive map and navigational strategies. See Paillard 1991, pp. 273–95

O'Keefe J, Burgess N, Donnett JG, Jeffery KJ, Maguire EA. 1998. Place cells, navigational accuracy, and the human hippocampus. *Philos. Trans. R. Soc. London Ser. B* 353:1333–40

O'Keefe J, Nadel L. 1978. *The Hippocampus as a Cognitive Map.* Oxford, UK: Clarendon. 570 pp.

O'Mara SM, Rolls ET, Berthoz A, Kesner RP. 1994. Neurons responding to whole-body motion in the primate hippocampus. *J. Neurosci.* 14:6511–23

Ono T, Nishijo H. 1992. Neurophysiological basis of the Kluver-Bucy syndrome: responses of monkey amygdaloid neurons to biologically significant objects. See Aggleton 1992, 167–90

Paillard J, ed. 1991. *Brain and Space.* Oxford, UK: Oxford Univ. Press. 499 pp.

Parga N, Rolls ET. 1998. Transform invariant recognition by association in a recurrent network. *Neural Comput.* 10:1507–25

Parkinson JK, Murray EA, Mishkin M. 1988. A selective mnemonic role for the hippocampus in monkeys: memory for the location of objects. *J. Neurosci.* 8:4159–67

Perrett DI, Mistlin AJ, Chitty AJ. 1987. Visual neurons responsive to faces. *Trends Neurosci.* 10:358–64

Petrides M. 1985. Deficits on conditional associative-learning tasks after frontal- and temporal-lobe lesions in man. *Neuropsychologia* 23:601–14

Poggio T, Edelman S. 1990. A network that learns to recognize three-dimensional objects. *Nature* 343:263–66

Rao SC, Rainer G, Miller EK. 1997. Integration of what and where in the primate prefrontal cortex. *Science* 276:821–24

Rempel-Clower NL, Zola SM, Squire LR, Amaral DG. 1996. Three cases of enduring memory impairment after bilateral damage limited to the hippocampal formation. *J. Neurosci.* 16:5233–55

Renart A, Parga N, Rolls ET. 1999. A distributed recurrent model of the mechanisms of interaction between perception and memory in delay tasks. *Advances in Neural Inf. Proc. Syst.* 10:In press

Robbins TW, Cador M, Taylor JR, Everitt BJ. 1989. Limbic-striatal interactions in reward-related processes. *Neurosci. Bio-Behav. Rev.* 13:155–62

Robertson RG, Rolls ET, Georges-François P. 1998. Spatial view cells in the primate hippocampus: effects of removal of view details. *J. Neurophysiol.* 79:1145–56

Robertson RG, Rolls ET, Georges-François P, Panzeri S. 1999. Head direction cells in the primate pre-subiculum. *Hippocampus* 9:206–19

Rolls ET. 1975. *The Brain and Reward.* Oxford, UK: Pergamon. 115 pp.

Rolls ET. 1989. Functions of neuronal networks in the hippocampus and neotcortex in memory. In *Neural Models of Plasticity: Experimental and Theoretical Approaches,* ed. JH Byrne, WO Berry, 13:240–65. San Diego, CA: Academic. 438 pp.

Rolls ET. 1990. A theory of emotion, and its application to understanding the neural basis of emotion. *Cogn. Emot.* 4:161–90

Rolls ET. 1992. Neurophysiological mechanisms underlying face processing within and beyond the temporal cortical visual areas. *Philos. Trans. R. Soc. London Ser. B* 335:11–21

Rolls ET. 1996a. The orbitofrontal cortex. *Philos. Trans. R. Soc. London Ser. B* 351:1433–44

Rolls ET. 1996b. A theory of hippocampal function in memory. *Hippocampus* 6:601–20

Rolls ET. 1997a. Taste and olfactory processing in the brain and its relation to the control of eating. *Crit. Rev. Neurobiol.* 11:263–87

Rolls ET. 1997b. A neurophysiological and computational approach to the functions of the temporal lobe cortical visual areas in invariant object recognition. In *Computational and Psychophysical Mechanisms of Visual Coding,* ed. M Jenkin, L Harris 9:184–220. Cambridge, UK: Cambridge Univ. Press. 361 pp.

Rolls ET. 1999a. *The Brain and Emotion.* Oxford, UK: Oxford Univ. Press. 367 pp.

Rolls ET. 1999b. Spatial view cells and the representation of place in the primate hippocampus. *Hippocampus* 9:467–80

Rolls ET. 1999c. The functions of the orbitofrontal cortex. *Neurocase* 5:301–12

Rolls ET. 2000a. Précis of the brain and emotion. *Behav. Brain Sci.* In press

Rolls ET. 2000b. Neurophysiology and functions of the primate amygdala, and the neural basis of emotion. In *The Amygdala: A Functional Analysis,* ed. JP Aggleton. Oxford, UK: Oxford Univ. Press. In press

Rolls ET, Baylis LL. 1994. Gustatory, olfactory and visual convergence within the primate orbitofrontal cortex. *J. Neurosci.* 14:5437–52

Rolls ET, Baylis GC, Hasselmo ME, Nalwa V. 1989a. The effect of learning on the face-selective responses of neurons in the cortex in the superior temporal sulcus of the monkey. *Exp. Brain Res.* 76:153–64

Rolls ET, Burton MJ, Mora F. 1980. Neurophysiological analysis of brain-stimulation reward in the monkey. *Brain Res.* 194:339–57

Rolls ET, Critchley HD, Browning AS, Hernadi A, Lenard L. 1999a. Responses to the sensory properties of fat of neurons in the primate orbitofrontal cortex. *J. Neurosci.* 19:1532–40

Rolls ET, Critchley H, Mason R, Wakeman EA. 1996. Orbitofrontal cortex neurons: role in olfactory and visual association learning. *J. Neurophysiol.* 75:1970–81

Rolls ET, Hornak J, Wade D, McGrath J. 1994a. Emotion-related learning in patients with social and emotional changes associated with frontal lobe damage. *J. Neurol. Neurosurg. Psychiatry* 57:1518–24

Rolls ET, Judge SJ, Sanghera M. 1977. Activity of neurones in the inferotemporal cortex of the alert monkey. *Brain Res.* 130:229–38

Rolls ET, Milward T. 1999. A model of invariant object recognition in the visual system: learning rules, activation functions, lateral inhibition, and information-based performance measures. *Neural Comput.* In press

Rolls ET, Miyashita Y, Cahusac PMB, Kesner RP, Niki H, et al. 1989b. Hippocampal neurons in the monkey with activity related to the place in which a stimulus is shown. *J. Neurosci.* 9:1835–45

Rolls ET, Robertson RG, Georges-François P. 1997c. Spatial view cells in the primate hippocampus. *Eur. J. Neurosci.* 9:1789–94

Rolls ET, Scott TR, Sienkiewicz ZJ, Yaxley S. 1988. The responsiveness of neurones in the frontal opercular gustatory cortex of the macaque monkey is independent of hunger. *J. Physiol.* 397:1–12

Rolls ET, Sienkiewicz ZJ, Yaxley S. 1989c. Hunger modulates the responses to gustatory stimuli of single neurons in the caudolateral orbitofrontal cortex of the macaque monkey. *Eur. J. Neurosci.* 1:53–60

Rolls ET, Thorpe SJ, Maddison SP. 1983. Responses of striatal neurons in the behaving monkey. 1. Head of the caudate nucleus. *Behav. Brain Res.* 7:179–210

Rolls ET, Tovee MJ. 1994. Processing speed in the cerebral cortex and the neurophysiology of visual masking. *Proc. R. Soc. London Ser. B* 257:9–15

Rolls ET, Tovee MJ, Panzeri S. 1999b. The neurophysiology of backward visual masking: information analysis. *J. Cogn. Neurosci.* 11:335–46

Rolls ET, Tovee MJ, Purcell DG, Stewart AL, Azzopardi P. 1994b. The responses of neurons in the temporal cortex of primates, and face identification and detection. *Exp. Brain Res.* 101:474–84

Rolls ET, Treves A. 1998. *Neural Networks and Brain Function.* Oxford, UK: Oxford Univ. Press. 418 pp.

Rolls ET, Treves A, Robertson RG, Georges-François P, Panzeri S. 1998. Information about spatial view in an ensemble of primate hippocampal cells. *J. Neurophysiol.* 79:1797–1813

Rolls ET, Treves A, Tovee MJ. 1997b. The representational capacity of the distributed encoding of information provided by populations of neurons in the primate temporal visual cortex. *Exp. Brain Res.* 114:149–62

Rolls ET, Treves A, Tovee M, Panzeri S. 1997c. Information in the neuronal representation of individual stimuli in the primate temporal visual cortex. *J. Comput. Neurosci.* 4:309–33

Rolls ET, Williams GV. 1987. Neuronal activity in the ventral striatum of the primate. In *The Basal Ganglia II. Structure and Function—Current Concepts,* ed. MB Carpenter,

A Jayamaran, pp. 349–56. New York: Plenum. 548 pp.

Rupniak NMJ, Gaffan D. 1987. Monkey hippocampus and learning about spatially directed movements. *J. Neurosci.* 7:2331–37

Sanghera MK, Rolls ET, Roper-Hall A. 1979. Visual responses of neurons in the dorsolateral amygdala of the alert monkey. *Exp. Neurol.* 63:610–26

Schultz W. 1998. Predictive reward signal of dopamine neurons. *J. Neurophysiol.* 80:1–27

Schultz W, Apicella P, Ljungberg T. 1993. Responses of monkey dopamine neurons to reward and conditioned stimuli during successive steps of learning a delayed response task. *J. Neurosci.* 13:900–13

Schultz W, Apicella P, Scarnati E, Ljungberg T. 1992. Neuronal activity in the ventral striatum related to the expectation of reward. *J. Neurosci.* 12:4595–610

Scott SK, Young AW, Calder AJ, Hellawell, DJ, Aggleton JP, Johnson M. 1997. Impaired auditory recognition of fear and anger following bilateral amygdala lesions. *Nature* 385:254–57

Scott TR, Yan J, Rolls ET. 1995. Brain mechanisms of satiety and taste in macaques. *Neurobiology* 3:281–92

Sem-Jacobsen CW. 1976. Electrical stimulation and self-stimulation in man with chronic implanted electrodes. Interpretation and pitfalls of results. In *Brain-Stimulation Reward,* ed. A Wauquier, ET Rolls, pp. 505–20. Amsterdam: North-Holland. 622 pp.

Smith ML, Milner B. 1981. The role of the right hippocampus in the recall of spatial location. *Neuropsychologia* 19:781–93

Squire LR. 1992. Memory and the hippocampus: a synthesis from findings with rats, monkeys and humans. *Psychol. Rev.* 99:195–231

Squire LR, Knowlton BJ, eds. 1995. *Memory, Hippocampus, and Brain Systems.* Cambridge, MA: MIT Press

Sutton RS, Barto AG. 1998. *Reinforcement Learning,* Cambridge, MA: MIT Press. 322 pp.

Suzuki WA, Amaral DG. 1994a. Perirhinal and parahippocampal cortices of the macaque monkey—cortical afferents. *J. Comp. Neurol.* 350:497–533

Suzuki WA, Amaral DG. 1994b. Topographic organization of the reciprocal connections between the monkey entorhinal cortex and the perirhinal and parahippocampal cortices. *J. Neurosci.* 14:1856–77

Suzuki WA, Miller EK, Desimone R. 1997. Object and place memory in the macaque entorhinal cortex. *J. Neurophysiol.* 78:1062–81

Thorpe SJ, Rolls ET, Maddison S. 1983. Neuronal activity in the orbitofrontal cortex of the behaving monkey. *Exp. Brain Res.* 49:93–115

Tovee MJ, Rolls ET, Ramachandran VS. 1996. Rapid visual learning in neurones of the primate temporal visual cortex. *NeuroReport* 7:2757–60

Treves A, Rolls ET. 1994. A computational analysis of the role of the hippocampus in memory. *Hippocampus* 4:374–91

Ullman S. 1996. *High-Level Vision. Object Recognition and Visual Cognition.* Cambridge, MA: Bradford/MIT Press. 412 pp.

Wallis G, Rolls ET. 1997. Invariant face and object recognition in the visual system. *Prog. Neurobiol.* 51:167–94

Williams GV, Rolls ET, Leonard CM, Stern C. 1993. Neuronal responses in the ventral striatum of the behaving macaque. *Behav. Brain Res.* 55:243–52

Wilson FAW, Scalaidhe SPO, Goldman-Rakic PS. 1993. Dissociation of object and spatial processing domains in primate prefrontal cortex. *Science* 260:1955–58

Wilson FAW, Rolls ET. 1990a . Learning and memory are reflected in the responses of reinforcement-related neurons in the primate basal forebrain. *J. Neurosci.* 10:1254–67

Wilson FAW, Rolls ET. 1990b. Neuronal responses related to reinforcement in the primate basal forebrain. *Brain Res.* 509:213–31

Wilson FAW, Rolls ET. 1990c. Neuronal responses related to the novelty and familiarity of visual stimuli in the substantia innominata, diagonal band of Broca and periventricular region of the primate. *Exp. Brain Res.* 80:104–20

Wilson FAW, Rolls ET. 1993. The effects of stimulus novelty and familiarity on neuronal activity in the amygdala of monkeys performing recognition memory tasks. *Exp. Brain Res.* 93:367–82

Wilson MA, McNaughton BL. 1993. Dynamics of the hippocampal ensemble code for space. *Science* 261:1055–58

Young AW, Aggleton JP, Hellawell DJ, Johnson M, Broks P, Hanley JR. 1995. Face processing impairments after amygdalotomy. *Brain* 118:15–24

Young AW, Hellawell DJ, Van de Wal C, Johnson M. 1996. Facial expression processing after amygdalotomy. *Neuropsychologia* 34:31–39

Zola-Morgan S, Squire LR, Amaral DG, Suzuki WA. 1989. Lesions of perirhinal and parahippocampal cortex that spare the amygdala and hippocampal formation produce severe memory impairment. *J. Neurosci.* 9:4355–70

Zola-Morgan S, Squire LR, Ramus SJ. 1994. Severity of memory impairment in monkeys as a function of locus and extent of damage within the medial temporal lobe memory system. *Hippocampus* 4:483–94

Annu. Rev. Psychol. 2000. 51:631–664

PERSONNEL SELECTION: Looking Toward the Future—Remembering the Past

Leaetta M. Hough and Frederick L. Oswald

The Dunnette Group, St. Paul, Minnesota 55102; e-mail: Leaetta@msn.com
Department of Psychological Sciences, Purdue University, West Lafayette, Indiana 47907; e-mail: oswald@psych.purdue.edu

Key Words   job performance, assessment, validity, adverse impact, personality

■ **Abstract**   This chapter reviews personnel selection research from 1995 through 1999. Areas covered are job analysis; performance criteria; cognitive ability and personality predictors; interview, assessment center, and biodata assessment methods; measurement issues; meta-analysis and validity generalization; evaluation of selection systems in terms of differential prediction, adverse impact, utility, and applicant reactions; emerging topics on team selection and cross-cultural issues; and finally professional, legal, and ethical standards. Three major themes are revealed: (a) Better taxonomies produce better selection decisions; (b) The nature and analyses of work behavior are changing, influencing personnel selection practices; (c) The field of personality research is healthy, as new measurement methods, personality constructs, and compound constructs of well-known traits are being researched and applied to personnel selection.

CONTENTS

Introduction 632
Job and Work Analysis 632
Criteria.. 633
   Taxonomic Issues 633
   Measurement Issues 634
   Dynamic Criteria 634
Predictors 634
   Cognitive Abilities and Job Knowledge 634
   Personality.. 636
   Multiple Predictor Domains 640
Assessment Methods 641
   Interview 641
   Assessment Centers.. 642
   Biodata.. 643
Measurement Issues and Validation Strategies 644
   Measurement Issues 644

0084–6570/00/0201–0631$12.00

Meta-Analysis and Validity Generalization 645
Evaluation of Selection Systems 645
    Differential Prediction 645
    Adverse Impact 646
    Utility 647
    Applicant Reactions 647
Emerging Topics 648
    Team Member Selection 648
    Cross-Cultural Selection Issues 649
Professional, Legal, and Ethical Standards 650
    Professional 650
    Legal 650
    Ethical 651
Parting Remarks 651

INTRODUCTION

Global, widespread, and diverse forces impact today's economies and marketplaces, with important implications for personnel selection (Dunnette 1997, Howard 1995, Ilgen & Pulakos 1999, Kraut & Korman 1999a, Pearlman & Barney 1999, Schmitt & Chan 1998). Indeed, Herriot & Anderson (1997) call for new selection methods. Our personnel selection review identifies emerging topics, covers traditional ones, and suggests new avenues for research and practice.

JOB AND WORK ANALYSIS

Recognizing the changing nature of work, many researchers and practitioners conduct "work" analysis, focusing on tasks and cross-functional skills of workers, rather than "job" analysis with its focus on static jobs (Cascio 1995, Nelson 1997, Pearlman 1997, Sanchez & Levine 1999). Perhaps the O*NET, the computerized delivery system for the *Dictionary of Occupational Titles* (*DOT*), has made the greatest operational strides in addressing this shift (Peterson et al 1999). The O*NET is a flexible database containing occupational information structured around a "content model" linking work behaviors to worker attributes, much in line with Dunnette's call to bridge these "two worlds of behavioral taxonomies" (1976, p. 477). As information on work (e.g. jobs, organizational contexts, and work characteristics) and the worker (e.g. knowledge, skills, interests, and motivation) changes, the computerized nature of the O*NET allows an equally responsive change in its database. Collecting and using such information to select individuals for jobs, tasks, or roles is becoming more critical than ever (Campbell 1999).

Work/job analysis now includes personality variables alongside traditional cognitive, behavioral, and situational variables. The National Skill Standards Board (K Pearlman, unpublished manuscript) and O*NET (Peterson et al 1999) both incorporate personality-based work requirements. One personality-based job analysis instrument generates job profiles along seven personality scales (Hogan & Rybicki 1998). Another personality-based job analysis evaluated 260 jobs, meaningfully distinguishing 12 *DOT*-based job clusters (Raymark et al 1997).

Sixteen potential cognitive and social sources of rating inaccuracy in job analysis may influence different dimensions and psychometric properties of job analysis (Morgeson & Campion 1997). Type of job data and method for clustering jobs affect similarities and distinctions between jobs (Colihan & Burger 1995), and Q-factor analysis of rated task importance for two job titles shows meaningful within-title variation (Sanchez et al 1998). Future job analysis studies might identify substantive sources of variance attributable to types of raters, workers, or both.

CRITERIA

Taxonomic Issues

Job performance constitutes all measurable work behaviors relevant to organizational goals and within the individual's control (Campbell et al 1996). Job performance is complex, dynamic, and multidimensional, and consequently personnel selection systems might predict individual differences for several types of job performance (e.g. task proficiency and leadership behaviors). Models incorporating multiple predictors and multiple criteria first apply rational weights to performance criteria and then derive least-squares optimal weights for the predictors. Meta-analytic correlations between ability, conscientiousness (predictors), individual task performance, and organizational citizenship (criteria) illustrate how validity can vary greatly depending on criterion weights (Murphy & Shiarella 1997). Absent criterion data for establishing regression weights, rational weighting of a selection battery increases appropriateness and legal defensibility. Weights could multiply job analysis ratings of importance, time spent, consequences of errors, and time-to-proficiency (Arthur et al 1996).

Contextual performance, or organizational citizenship behavior, is a relatively new and multifaceted job performance construct (Borman & Motowidlo 1997). Coleman & Borman (1999) classified organizational citizenship behaviors into three broad categories: interpersonal citizenship behavior (benefiting employees), organizational citizenship performance (benefiting organizations), and job/task conscientiousness (benefiting work itself). Hierarchical regression analyses suggest that interpersonal facilitation is a part of contextual performance, but job dedication (similar to job/task conscientiousness within the organizational citizenship framework) is a part of task performance (Van Scotter & Motowidlo

1996). Organizations clearly require both task and contextual performance (Kiker & Motowidlo 1999).

Measurement Issues

Regarding criterion reliability, interrater reliability coefficients are more appropriate to use than intrarater (coefficient alpha) or test-retest reliabilities, and interrater reliabilities of supervisory ratings of overall and dimensional job performance are higher than peer ratings (Viswesvaran et al 1996). A greater understanding of "unreliable" criterion variance is needed to address biases in measures of constructs (Schmitt et al 1995). Similarly, criterion range restriction (or enhancement) may be a legitimate organizational phenomenon affecting criterion-related validities and not merely a statistical artifact (James et al 1992). Organizational climate, for instance, does not always attenuate correlations between procedural fairness and customer-perceived performance relationships (Burke et al 1996). Further research should investigate how individual differences, job types, and their interactions influence the mean and variance of criterion measures (see Hattrup & Jackson 1996).

Dynamic Criteria

Job performance and the relative contributions of its determinants (job knowledge, skill, and motivation) change, calling for longitudinal models of reliability and validity (Tisak & Tisak 1996). The nature of performance change (e.g. systematic vs random change or reversible vs irreversible change) and how constructs relate between individual and group levels are critical theoretical and methodological issues (Chan 1998a,b). Nonlinear mixed-effects models simultaneously estimate individual and group levels of change (Cudeck 1996), accommodating missing data, prespecified error structures (see DeShon et al 1998a), and individuals not measured at the same time points. For a review and tutorial of quadratic and linear models of longitudinal change, see Chan (1998a).

Personality items predicted change in eight consecutive quarters of securities sales performance, with a curvilinear group mean increase over time (i.e. greater increase initially) and different rates of increase for each individual (Ployhart & Hakel 1998). Psychomotor ability predicted initial piece-rate performance of sewing machine operators, and cognitive ability predicted performance change. Individuals with less experience and lower levels of initial performance changed more (Deadrick et al 1997).

PREDICTORS

Cognitive Abilities and Job Knowledge

Self-selection on cognitive ability may precede personnel selection. Job seekers may select into or "gravitate" toward jobs with ability requirements commensurate with the seekers' own general cognitive ability (Wilk & Sackett 1996).

Ability self-evaluations might lead to seeking coaching and practice on ability tests. Firefighter applicants with lower cognitive ability scores are likely to attend a free test preparation program, although the program's effects on raising ability test scores (reading, listening, and spelling) are minimal (Ryan et al 1998b).

General Cognitive Ability   Various cognitive ability tests (e.g. verbal, numerical, and spatial tests) intercorrelate positively, and the common variance often operationalizes *g,* a single general cognitive ability factor. For many jobs and practical work outcomes (job knowledge acquisition, training performance, and job performance), *g* predicts well (e.g. Levine et al 1996). For prediction in less complex jobs or in later stages of complex learning, *g* is less useful but rarely useless (Gottfredson 1997). Greater understanding of *g* is needed (Campbell 1996), as its determinants and theoretical meaning are debated (see Lubinski 2000). Individuals higher in *g* show lower intercorrelations between specific abilities (Legree et al 1996). Matching individuals' specific abilities (or ability profiles) to particular jobs may therefore be especially important for individuals with higher *g* (Lubinski & Benbow 1999). Item response theory and computerized adaptive testing have clarified relationships between *g* and specific abilities contributing to it (Sands et al 1997, Segall 1999). Developers of good cognitive ability selection tests cannot rely on knowledge of *g* alone.

Ability and Job Knowledge   Multiple-ability test battery data from 3000 Air Force enlistees supported a hierarchical ability structure (Carretta & Ree 1996) that fit the data well, considerably better than two nonhierarchical models or a *g*-only model (see also Carretta et al 1998). Men and women show similar hierarchical ability structures (Carretta & Ree 1997).

Carretta & Doub (1998) tested the mediating effect of prior mechanical and electrical knowledge on the relationship between *g* and subsequent job knowledge of Air Force trainees. Comparing racial groups (White, Black, and Hispanic) resulted in little moderating effect. Comparing gender groups prior job knowledge mediated subsequent job knowledge for males but not for females. The effect of *g* was weaker in individuals with more prior job knowledge; conversely, *g* was stronger in individuals with less prior job knowledge. It seems that *g* predicts the rate of job knowledge acquisition, which in turn has a larger direct influence on performance ratings than the indirect effect of *g* (Ree et al 1995).

Academic Achievement and Language Proficiency   Meta-analysis found that undergraduate college grade point average (GPA) predicted job performance across many types of organizations, especially for job performance measured closer in time to the GPA (Roth et al 1996). Another meta-analysis reported substantial criterion-related validities for aptitude tests predicting GPA in graduate school. Subject-specific tests (possibly a job knowledge analog) had higher validities than verbal and mathematical tests, but both were of useful magnitude (Kuncel et al 1999).

Increasing immigration and concomitant workforce diversity suggest measuring English language proficiency when selecting for certain jobs. For entry-level meat trimmers ($N = 87$) whose native language was not English, a written and spoken English proficiency test was internally consistent and clearly linked to job analysis information. The test predicted supervisory ratings of overall job performance (Chan et al 1999). Spoken English proficiency assessment is now possible via real-time computer processing and analysis of human speech (Bernstein 1999).

Adverse Impact   Cognitive ability measures tend to show nontrivial racial-group mean differences. Helms' (1992) hypothesis states that White-Black mean differences might be reduced by couching ability test content within a social context. An expert panel modified abstract ability items to reflect everyday organizational, social, and life situations. Contrary to the hypothesis, marked White-Black differences remained under the new test format, even under large-sample replication and parallel test forms (DeShon et al 1998b). Research needs to expand the number and types of items, explore different administration formats, and examine other specific abilities.

Short-term memory tests (digit span and digit-symbol substitution) show promise as an alternative or supplement to traditional ability tests, with lower adverse impact and good validities with job performance. Meta-analysis estimated White-Black mean differences on short-term memory tests at 0.48 SD, about half the 1.0 SD difference typically found in general cognitive ability tests. Short-term memory tests are reliable and correlate with training performance and job performance [$r \approx 0.45$ (Verive & McDaniel 1996)]. Lower adverse impact combined with respectable overall criterion-related validity encourages future research in this area.

The Armed Services Vocational Aptitude Battery (ASVAB) and an experimental ability test battery predicted training performance criteria in 17 military jobs (Sager et al 1997), showing some necessary tradeoffs. One cannot completely (a) minimize adverse impact for all subgroups compared (see Hoffman & Thornton 1997 for this issue in utility context), (b) maximize both criterion-related validity within jobs and classification efficiency across jobs, or (c) satisfy both (a) and (b). A selection strategy aimed at minimizing adverse impact may differ somewhat from a selection strategy aimed at maximizing mean predicted performance (Sackett & Roth 1996).

Personality

Personality Taxonomies and Constructs   The Five Factor Model (FFM), consisting of Extraversion, Agreeableness, Conscientiousness, Neuroticism (Adjustment), and Openness to Experience (see Wiggins & Trapnell 1997), enjoys considerable support. Factor analysis supports the robustness and generalizability of the FFM across different theoretical frameworks, assessments, rating sources, and cultures (see Hogan & Ones 1997b, Saucier & Goldberg 1998, Wiggins & Trapnell 1997). The model is useful for summarizing information and guiding theory and research (e.g. Mount & Barrick 1995, Tokar et al 1998).

The FFM yields information about the higher-order factor structure of personality; however, it ignores, confounds, or otherwise obscures understanding of variables combined into five broad factors (Hough 1997, 1998b; Hough & Schneider 1996). FFM factors contain facets with high and low criterion-related validities, diluting the criterion-related validity of the factors. A review of meta-analyses concluded the FFM factors do not correlate highly with job performance (Matthews 1997). As alternatives, researchers are turning to nonhierarchical models such as the circumplex (Plutchik & Conte 1997) and other hierarchies. Hough (1997, 1998b) argues for a more refined taxonomy, distinguishing achievement from conscientiousness and extraversion and affiliation from extraversion. Meta-analyses demonstrate the importance of these distinctions for predicting managerial performance (Hough et al 1998) and sales performance (Vinchur et al 1998). Ghiselli's (1966) personality framework was compared with the FFM framework in the Barrick & Mount (1991) meta-analysis: the median uncorrected validity in the Ghiselli meta-analysis was 0.24; the highest mean uncorrected validity for an FFM variable in the Barrick & Mount (1991) study was 0.15 (Hough 1997). Several important personality constructs not within the FFM have been used for predicting work behavior:

Emotionality   Emotionality, or affectivity, consists of two bipolar dimensions at the most general level: negative-positive and aroused-unaroused (Averill 1997, Russell & Carroll 1999). A state measure of emotionality did not correlate with job performance, but a dispositional measure did (Wright & Staw 1999). In social welfare workers, negative affectivity correlated positively with emotional exhaustion or "burnout," and emotional exhaustion correlated negatively with job performance (Wright & Cropanzano 1998).

Social Competence   Social competence is a compound variable consisting of social insight, social maladjustment, social appropriateness, social openness, social influence, warmth, and extraversion (Schneider et al 1996). Reliable self-report measures of social insight (e.g. Gough 1968) and empathy (e.g. Hogan 1968) have a long history, as do situational judgment measures of social intelligence (e.g. Moss et al 1955). Variables subsumed under social competence might increment predictive validity for criteria emphasizing interpersonal effectiveness.

Conscientiousness   Many claim that conscientiousness, a FFM factor, is a valid predictor across organizations, jobs, and situations (Hogan & Ones 1997b, Mount & Barrick 1995, Salgado 1997a, 1998). Others question this wholesale conclusion (Hough 1997, 1998b; Robertson & Callinan 1998). Whether or in what direction conscientiousness predicts performance obviously depends on the criterion construct and how conscientiousness is defined and operationalized. Based on the

Hogan & Ones' (1997) definition of conscientiousness as conformity and socially prescribed impulse control, conscientiousness would likely not predict performance across organizations, jobs, or situations in which creativity or innovation is important (Hough 1997, 1998b; Hough et al 1998).

Integrity Tests   Meta-analyses of relations between integrity tests and FFM variables indicate that integrity tests are compound variables consisting primarily of conscientiousness, agreeableness, and adjustment (Ones & Viswesvaran 1998b). Four themes account for most of the variance in overt and personality-based integrity tests: punitive attitudes, admissions of illegal drug use, reliability, and admissions of theft (Hogan & Brinkmeyer 1997). Importantly, integrity tests differ from tests of deception (Murphy & Luther 1997). Sackett & Wanek (1996) provided an insightful and thorough review of integrity testing that dealt with construct- and criterion-related validity evidence; moderator variables; social desirability and applicant reactions; and legal, professional, and governmental evaluations. Meta-analysis indicates that integrity and conscientiousness tests usefully supplement general cognitive ability tests when predicting overall job performance (Schmidt & Hunter 1998). Converging evidence exists for the construct, criterion-related, and incremental validity of integrity tests (Miner & Capps 1996, Ones & Viswesvaran 1998b), but considerable variability may accompany the overall findings.

For example, criteria often used in integrity-testing research are problematic. Self-report or admission of counterproductive behavior confounds reliability with validity for overt integrity tests and underestimates the extent of counterproductive work behaviors, as do more direct measures (e.g. detected theft). Moreover, counterproductivity is not a unitary construct (Ashton 1998, Sackett & Wanek 1996). Two recent meta-analyses summarized correlations between integrity test scores and two facets of counterproductivity: reported drug abuse [$r = 0.21$ (Schmidt et al 1997)] and number of job-related accidents [$r = 0.52$ (Ones & Viswesvaran 1998b)]. Workplace violence, a facet of counterproductivity, tends to be better predicted by narrow measures such as aggression and violence scales than by broad honesty tests. Meta-analysis indicates that the validity for predicting workplace violence is higher for violence scales than for integrity tests [$r = 0.48$ vs 0.26 (Ones et al 1994)]. A physical-aggression measure predicted aggressive penalty minutes ($r = 0.33$) in high school hockey games, but not nonaggressive penalty minutes ($r = 0.04$) (Bushman & Wells 1998).

Customer Service Orientation   Meta-analysis finds that customer service orientation is a compound variable consisting of agreeableness ($r = 0.70$), adjustment ($r = 0.58$), and conscientiousness ($r = 0.43$) (Ones & Viswesvaran 1996), and customer service scales correlate with performance in customer service jobs ($r = 0.31$) (Frei & McDaniel 1998).

Core Self-Evaluation   Core self-evaluation is a compound variable consisting of self-esteem, generalized self-efficacy, locus of control, and emotional stability (Judge et al 1998). Meta-analysis estimated the validity of core self-evaluation for predicting job performance at 0.30 (TA Judge & JE Bono, submitted for publication). A much larger meta-analysis suggests that self-efficacy, a facet of core self-evaluation, correlates higher with job performance than does core self-evaluation as a whole [$r = 0.38$ (Stajkovic & Luthans 1998)].

Other Meta-Analyses   Meta-analysis of the Five Factor Model validities in U.S. studies from 1992 through 1997 produced results similar to past U.S. meta-analyses (Anderson & Viswesvaran 1998), but meta-analyses involving only European samples produced somewhat different results (Salgado 1997a, 1998). Both conscientiousness and emotional stability correlated positively with job performance across occupational groups, and both contributed incremental variance beyond general mental ability in predicting overall job performance. Other meta-analyses of validities of FFM factors indicate that agreeableness, as well as conscientiousness and emotional stability, predicts performance in jobs involving interpersonal interaction (Mount et al 1998). Managerial potential scales predict overall managerial job performance [$r \approx 0.40$ (Ones et al 1998)], although meta-analytic validities tend to be low for FFM factors predicting overall managerial performance (Hough et al 1998). Some FFM facets had much higher validities, shedding light on how facet-level variables might combine to form managerial potential scales with high criterion-related validity. Many of these meta-analytic researchers corrected study correlations for predictor range restriction by using national norm SDs from personality test manuals. This practice of using norm SDs appears warranted, because SDs of job applicants on personality measures are about 2%–9% less than those based on national norms (Ones & Viswesvaran 1999).

Conditional Reasoning   Pioneered by James (1998, 1999), conditional reasoning assumes that individuals' personalities are differentiated by the type of logical reasoning used to justify their actions. For example, people who score high on achievement motivation tend to attribute success to internal rather than external sources and consider demanding tasks challenging rather than frustrating. An achievement conditional reasoning scale correlated positively with scholastic criteria, in-basket performance, and other achievement scales (James 1998, Migetz et al 1999a, Smith et al 1995). An aggression conditional reasoning scale correlated negatively with overall job performance (Hornick et al 1999, James 1998) and positively with counterproductive work behavior (Burroughs et al 1999, Migetz et al 1999b, Patton et al 1999). This approach appears to overcome many problems related to intentional distortion.

Intentional Distortion   Not surprisingly, meta-analysis shows large mean-score differences between honest and directed-faking conditions (Viswesvaran & Ones

1999). The amount of distortion in naturally occurring applicant settings is uncertain however. Rosse et al (1998) found that applicants (N = 197) scored on average 0.69 SD higher than incumbents (N = 73) on FFM facet-level scales. In contrast, three separate samples involving over 40,500 applicants and over 1700 incumbents found significantly less distortion on similar scales (Hough 1998a). Ability and motivation to fake may be key determinants in the amount of distortion found in applicant settings (Snell et al 1999). Meta-analysis indicates that explicit warnings not to distort do reduce distortion [0.23 SD (Dwight & Donovan 1998)].

A slew of recent studies has investigated intentional distortion effects on criterion-related validities. Many assert that distortion does not tend to moderate, mediate, suppress, or attenuate the criterion-related validities of personality scales (Barrick & Mount 1996; Hogan 1998; Hough 1997, 1998a,b; Ones & Viswesvaran 1998b,c; Ones et al 1996). Others, such as Douglas et al (1996), Snell & McDaniel (1998), and Zickar & Drasgow (1996), contend that distortion seriously reduces criterion-related validity. Hough (1998a) resolved the apparent conflict by stratifying results by employment setting. In directed-faking settings, self-report scale scores have dramatically lower criterion-related validities than those obtained in applicant or incumbent settings; in applicant settings, self-report scale scores have the same or slightly lower criterion-related validities than those obtained from job incumbents in research-only settings. Similarly, construct validity may be negatively affected in directed-faking studies (Ellingson et al 1999a), but the effect does not seem to be as serious in applicant settings (Collins & Gleaves 1998, Ellingson et al 1999b, Ones & Viswesvaran 1998c).

Coaching individuals on personality tests potentially threatens the effectiveness of traditional social desirability scales. Subtle items can be more resistant to coaching and distortion than obvious items (Alliger et al 1996). Theory-driven approaches to scale development and validity data to refine items produce subtle items resistant to distortion and with excellent validity (Gough 1994).

Race and Ethnic Background Similar personality factor structures for Blacks and Whites are found (Collins & Gleaves 1998). Meta-analyses of White, Black, Hispanic, and Native American groups indicate minimal group mean differences for three overt integrity tests (Ones & Viswesvaran 1998a) and for FFM factors, although Hispanics scored 0.60 SD higher than Whites on social desirability scales (Hough 1998b). Personality variables have little adverse impact against minorities, if any. Score correction strategies using social desirability scales to correct distortion in content scale scores might affect Hispanics more than others.

Multiple Predictor Domains

Applied psychology has long postulated that ability and motivation interact in predicting job performance: High performers must have the requisite ability and effort to do the job; neither ability nor effort alone suffices. However, regression analyses of data across job samples, performance criteria, and different ability and motivation measures have yielded nonexistent or very slight incremental ability-motivation interaction effects (Sackett et al 1998). A combined meta-analysis of ability-personality correlations and review of the empirical findings on ability-interest and personality-interest relationships have produced an integrated model identifying four categories or "trait complexes": science/math, clerical/conventional, social, and intellectual/cultural (Ackerman & Heggestad 1997). A vocational interest structure was empirically linked to Gottfredson's (1986) ability-based job classification framework, yielding four similar categories (Oswald & Ferstl 1999). Linking different predictor domains to a common job classification framework may clarify the constellations of predictors that are useful for selection into various types of jobs (see Arthur & Bennett 1995, Hattrup et al 1998, Johnson et al 1997, Mael et al 1996b, Vinchur et al 1998) and may improve synthetic validity efforts.

ASSESSMENT METHODS

Interview

Interview Structure Compared with unstructured interviews, structured employment interviews define content more explicitly. Their successes are therefore more likely to replicate, and they are better analyzed and meta-analyzed to determine their transportability to other jobs and work settings. Nonetheless, organizations still prefer unstructured interviews by a wide margin (Graves & Karren 1996). A comprehensive review indicates that various components of structured interviews influence the interview's psychometric properties, legal defensibility, and applicant/interviewer reactions (Campion et al 1997). Recent research offers at least three other compelling reasons for structuring the core of the interview (see also the Dipboye 1997 review).

Reliability Structured interviews tend to have higher interrater reliability than unstructured interviews. Meta-analysis reports average interrater reliabilities of 0.67 for high structure vs 0.34 for low structure (Conway et al 1995).

Standardization Standardized interviews place more burden on the instrument than any particular interviewer's interviewing and assessment skills. A highly standardized situational interview, in which applicants respond to hypothetical critical work incidents, can be less susceptible to rating biases (Kataoka et al 1997). Computerized phone interviews have efficiently obtained standardized applicant information, with validity coefficients similar to those for traditional interviews (Schmidt & Rader 1999). Interviewer experience and training further standardize the interview (Conway et al 1995, Campion et al 1997, Huffcutt & Woehr 1999). Training in note taking improves attention, encoding, recall, and evaluation of interview information focusing on work behaviors (Burnett et al 1998).

Fairness Structured interviews treat applicants in a consistent manner. Mean differences by race are more likely reduced in highly structured interviews containing content related to noncognitive constructs, especially for high-complexity jobs (Huffcutt & Roth 1998). Court outcomes on disparate impact and disparate treatment have favored organizations high on three interview characteristics: standardized administration, high job relatedness, and multiple raters (Williamson et al 1997).

Interpersonal and Nonverbal Behavior Interviewee characteristics (e.g. gaze, hand movement, and physical attractiveness) can predict several dimensions of managerial effectiveness (leadership, teamwork, and planning/organization), even when characteristics are coded independently of the content (Burnett & Motowidlo 1998; see also Motowidlo & Burnett 1995). The convergent and discriminant validities between interpersonal behavior in the interview and different job performance criteria should be considered.

Assessment Centers

Assessment centers (ACs) have long been haunted by evidence of content- and criterion-valid ratings lacking construct validity (Arthur et al 1999, Spychalski et al 1997, Woehr & Arthur 1999). Confusion about the constructs being measured, rating errors, type and form of rating procedures, and participant inconsistencies in behavior across exercises are possible explanations (Arthur & Tubre 1999, Guion 1998). Features improving AC ratings include having (a) only a few conceptually distinct constructs, (b) concrete, job-related construct definitions, (c) frame-of-reference assessor training with evaluative standards, (d) cross-exercise assessment, and (e) several psychology-trained assessors (Lievens 1998, Woehr & Arthur 1999). An AC designed and implemented on the basis of research and professional-practice guidelines (see Task Force on Assessment Center Guidelines 1989) produced construct-valid AC ratings. Generalizability theory facets associated with individuals and constructs accounted for 60% of the total variance, and facets associated with assessors and exercises accounted for 11% of the total variance (Arthur et al 1999).

ACs are expensive and prone to cost-benefit comparisons with other predictors. AC ratings have significant incremental validity over personality variables, and vice versa, when predicting managerial performance (Goffin et al 1996, with $N = 68$). AC ratings also have incremental validity over cognitive ability, although some AC exercise validities are founded primarily on their cognitive component (Goldstein et al 1998). By using policy capturing and meta-analysis, overall AC ratings have been predicted from both cognitive ability and personality variables [$R = 0.77$ (Collins et al 1999)]. The key question is whether policy-captured predictors predict job performance better than AC ratings (Howard 1999). Black-White mean exercise score differences have ranged from 0.03 to 0.40 SDs, with Blacks scoring lower (Goldstein et al 1999). Exercises emphasizing interpersonal skills more than cognitive ability have resulted in less or no adverse impact for Blacks (Goldstein et al 1999, Bobrow & Leonards 1997).

Biodata

Several researchers have focused on much-needed construct-oriented approaches to biodata (biographical information). CN MacLane (submitted for publication) refined the federal government's Individual Achievement Record biodata scales, which measure social and cognitive abilities (see Gandy et al 1994). Personality-based biodata scales predict leadership (Stricker & Rock 1998) and life insurance sales (McManus & Kelly 1999). A review of eleven studies examined the validity of biodata scales based on Mumford & Stokes' (1992) rigorous construct-oriented item-generation procedures. Scales were content and construct valid, with criterion-related validities similar to those for traditional empirical keying (Mumford et al 1996).

Biodata theory relies heavily on the principle that past behavior is the best predictor of future job performance (i.e. the "consistency" principle). Failure or negative life experiences also explain why biodata predict performance (Russell 1999). Moxie (i.e. courage or "ego-resiliency") may moderate how negative life experiences influence development and subsequent job performance (Dean et al 1999, Muchinsky 1999). "Negative" is often in the eye of the beholder, however. Both positive and negative responses to elements of a broader life-events taxonomy may be needed.

Conclusions about the effectiveness of rational, empirical-keying, and factor-analytic biodata scale development strategies are inconsistent. Rational scales have predicted sales performance at least as well as empirically keyed and factor-analytic scales (Stokes & Searcy 1999). Factor-analytic and rational scales have predicted several customer service criteria much better than empirical keying (Schoenfeldt 1999). A meta-analysis found similar levels of criterion-related cross-validities across all three scale construction strategies (Hough & Paullin 1994). Rational, empirical-keying, and factor-analytic scale strategies need not be executed and compared separately; the strategies may iteratively inform one another.

Regarding the generalizability of biodata, the reliability, factor structure, and validity of biodata keys appear stable across two English-speaking countries (Dalessio et al 1996). Validity for a biodata inventory predicting managerial progress generalized across organizations and educational levels (Carlson et al 1999). "Contemporary" items tend to be more valid than "future/hypothetical" or "historical" items, and items that ask respondents about others' opinions of them are more valid than direct self-report items (Lefkowitz et al 1999). Meta-analysis found that the amount and task-level specificity of work experience correlated most highly with job performance (Quiñones et al 1995). Rational biodata scales may produce inadequate levels of validity for separate racial/ethnic groups, but empirical item analysis can be used to produce a scale valid across groups (Schmitt & Pulakos 1998, Schmitt et al 1999). Whitney & Schmitt (1997) discovered differential item functioning between racial subgroups in about one quarter of the biodata items they examined.

MEASUREMENT ISSUES AND VALIDATION STRATEGIES

Measurement Issues

Many published studies in personnel selection continue to suffer from low statistical power due to small sample sizes (Mone et al 1996, Salgado 1998). Confidence intervals directly convey the impact of sample size on the accuracy of statistics (Hunter 1997). A computer program calculates confidence intervals on correlation coefficients corrected for measurement unreliability and range restriction (Salgado 1997b). Formulas are accurate in the large-sample case; for the small-sample case, the bootstrap method (i.e. calculating a distribution of correlations by resampling data with replacement) has generated accurate confidence intervals for ability-training performance validities (Russell et al 1998). Instead of confidence intervals, Murphy & Myors (1999) provide noncentral F tables and real-world examples that test minimum-effect null hypotheses for t-tests, correlations, and ANOVAs.

Measurement error variance can distort patterns of research results and mislead conclusions. Circumstances in 26 applied-research situations show when to correct validities for such error by using the appropriate reliability coefficient (Schmidt & Hunter 1996). Structural equation modeling can test the statistical significance of corrected correlation coefficients and the difference between two such correlations (Hancock 1997). Recent studies considered maximizing the reliability of a linear composite by weighting the constituent variables as a function of their reliabilities (Cliff & Caruso 1998, Li et al 1996, Raykov 1997, Wang 1998).

Estimation formulas for the population validity (expected prediction in the entire population) and cross-validity (expected prediction in other independent samples) were thoroughly reviewed (Raju et al 1997), and formulas were compared in a Monte Carlo study with data from a large sample of Air Force enlistees (Raju et al 1999). Generally, the Ezekiel, Smith, and Wherry procedures all provided good squared population validity estimates, and Burket's formula best estimated the squared population cross-validity. In stepwise regression, results showed that the sample size-to-predictor ratio had to be relatively large (10:1 at least) to yield good cross-validity estimates. All cross-validity estimation formulas performed similarly well; none was clearly superior (Schmitt & Ployhart

1999). Instead of stepwise regression, researchers often judge the relative size of regression weights to decide on the important variables within a particular model. A new type of relative importance weights enhances the interpretability of regression results when predictors are highly intercorrelated (Johnson 1999).

Finally, personnel selection research must often deal with missing data. Generally, pairwise deletion is better than listwise deletion, and estimating missing scores via regression is better than substituting missing scores with their unconditional mean (Roth et al 1996). Personnel selection would profit from understanding substantive processes underlying "missingness." Job promotions or transfers, emotional exhaustion from work, and organizational redesign all may reflect different types of longitudinal and cross-sectional attrition processes.

Meta-Analysis and Validity Generalization

Meta-analysis has had a far-reaching impact on policymaking, real-world application, and academic research (Hunter & Schmidt 1996) and is a useful quantitative tool for summarizing large bodies of personnel selection research (Murphy 1997). The meta-analytic mean effect size across studies (e.g. mean correlation coefficient) tends to be fairly accurate. In contrast, estimates of the variance of effect sizes (after correcting for statistical artifacts) can deviate from their actual population values by practically significant amounts (Oswald & Johnson 1998), which may affect meta-analytic conclusions about selection research. Variance estimates can be downwardly biased if one ignores the fact that individuals were selected on a variable correlated with the variables in the meta-analysis [i.e. incidental range restriction (Aguinis & Whitehead 1997)]. Statistical homogeneity tests of the variance have low statistical power and tend to discourage the search for moderator effects (Sánchez-Meca & Marín-Martínez 1997).

Meta-analysis is one of many lines of evidence supporting the use of a selection test. In addition to meta-analytically averaging correlations, researchers might consider what predicts group or organizational mean differences on predictors and criteria (Ostroff & Harrison 1999). Hierarchical linear modeling (HLM) has been advocated for this purpose; Hofmann (1997) presented some practical organizational examples. Synthetic validity evidence may provide additional validity information (Hoffman & McPhail 1998).

EVALUATION OF SELECTION SYSTEMS

Differential Prediction

A selection test with equal regression slopes across subgroups (e.g. race, gender, and age groups) does not necessarily measure a latent construct the same way across subgroups. Only data conforming to a special set of mathematical constraints will show a lack of differential prediction and latent construct equivalence simultaneously (Millsap 1995, 1997). To the extent that these constraints are violated, this finding may challenge previous selection research suggesting a lack of differential prediction (e.g. cognitive ability research).

Aguinis & Stone-Romero (1997) examined range restriction effects on the statistical power of moderated multiple regression for detecting differential prediction. Range restriction often mistakenly led to concluding no differential prediction when validity differences were moderate (0.4 correlation units). Larger validity differences were detected, and smaller differences were not, regardless of range restriction. Computer software for estimating the statistical power of differential prediction in moderated multiple regression is available (Aguinis & Pierce 1998b). Future software could incorporate violations of the assumption of equal error variances between subgroup regression models. Assumption violations occur when larger subgroup sample sizes are paired with the smaller subgroup validity coefficient (e.g. Aguinis & Pierce 1998a, DeShon & Alexander 1996), but for some organizational data, violations are not severe enough to affect statistical inferences from moderated multiple regression (Oswald et al 1999). Error variance in the independent variables affects differential prediction (Terris 1997), and errors-in-variables regression addresses this problem. Errors-in-variables regression detected differential prediction more accurately than moderated multiple regression when reliability coefficients were >0.65 and sample sizes were >250 (Anderson et al 1996).

Adverse Impact

Common sense might assert that combining low-adverse-impact predictors with a high-adverse-impact predictor improves adverse impact over using the high-adverse-impact predictor alone. However, Sackett & Ellingson (1997) presented tables illustrating reduced subgroup differences for some composites but increased differences for others. Composite measures invariably reduce subgroup differences less than expected. In particular, the "four-fifths rule" set out in the Uniform Guidelines (U.S. Equal Employment Opportunity Commission et al, 1978) is usually met only under very high selection ratios (≥ 0.90) or very slight composite group-mean differences ($d \leq 0.20$).

Similar conclusions came from meta-analytic estimates of criterion-related validities for a cognitive ability measure, a noncognitive composite (interview, biodata, and conscientiousness), and a composite of both, all independently predicting overall job performance. Selection batteries excluding cognitive ability almost always satisfied the four-fifths rule; batteries that included cognitive ability alone or in a composite almost never satisfied the rule (Schmitt et al 1997). Findings are echoed in two large-sample studies of firefighter and police officer job applicants selected on cognitive ability and personality measures (Ryan et al 1998a). Bobko et al (1999) updated the Schmitt et al (1997) meta-analytic matrix, discovering that even a noncognitive composite could violate the four-fifths rule when selection ratios were $\leq 50\%$. Group-mean differences on noncognitive composites should be determined before assuming they reduce adverse impact. Also, adverse impact is partly a function of the criteria chosen and how they are weighted (Hattrup et al 1997).

Alternative forms of administration potentially reduce adverse impact and increase overall validity. Videotaped versions of situational judgment test material can reduce adverse impact and have greater face validity than paper-and-pencil versions. Presumably, validity improves because the content in the video format is preserved, and irrelevant variance related to reading comprehension is removed (Chan & Schmitt 1997). Similar conclusions come from comparing a video-based ability test to a traditional ability test (Pulakos & Schmitt 1996).

Banding Given subgroup differences on selection tests (most notably cognitive ability tests), statistical banding can fulfill important goals such as maintaining workforce diversity and improving perceptions of process and outcome fairness in a selection procedure (Truxillo & Bauer 1999). Linearly transforming bands on predicted criterion scores into bands on predictor scores (Aguinis et al 1998) may improve banding because criterion differences tend to matter more to organizations than predictor differences (see Campbell 1996, Gottfredson 1999). Further advances in banding might consider that reliable predictors tend to produce smaller statistical bandwidths, in which differences larger than the band may still not be practical differences or translate into practical criterion differences.

Utility

A few recent studies focus on how utility information communicates the effectiveness of a selection system to organizational stakeholders. Whyte & Latham (1997) replicated the counterintuitive results of Latham & Whyte (1994), discovering that communicating positive utility information can actually decrease managers' intentions to use a selection system. Utility information may prove beneficial as supplementary information, not delivered face-to-face as a "hard sell" (Cronshaw 1997). Communicating utility in terms of multiple outcomes (e.g. dollars, job performance, and organizational effectiveness) may lead to greater acceptance of the utility message by different stakeholders (Roth & Bobko 1997). Considering and balancing all particular stakeholder positions is difficult but beneficial to organizations (Austin et al 1996).

Applicant Reactions

Positive applicant reactions increase the chances of hiring the best applicants, facilitate the ability to recruit effectively, avoid the possibility of costly litigation, and contribute to the organization's reputation (Gilliland & Steiner 1999, Ryan & Greguras 1998, Schmitt & Chan 1999). Selection systems can be viewed as socialization mechanisms imparting job information to applicants and affecting their work-related thoughts, attitudes, and behaviors (Anderson & Ostroff 1997). Managing applicant reactions does not imply making the organization attractive to all individuals; accurate perceptions can lead to applicant withdrawal. Black-

White test-taking attitude differences may not affect group differences in applicant withdrawal (Schmit & Ryan 1997), but they might, which would add to adverse-impact concerns (Chan 1997).

Chan et al (1998) discovered that (a) pretest reactions affected cognitive ability test performance, and test performance affected posttest reactions, and (b) personality test performance was unrelated to either pretest or posttest reactions. Integrity test results paralleled the personality test conclusions, and the overt integrity test had greater perceived job relatedness than the personality-based test (Whitney et al 1999).

Test outcome (passing or failing) contributes strongly to subsequent applicant reactions. Applicants passing a test for a clerical position rated organizational attractiveness, intentions to work for the organization, and test fairness higher than their initial reactions (Bauer et al 1998). Test outcome affects the perceived fairness of the hiring decision much more than the selection ratio (Thorsteinson & Ryan 1997). Ployhart et al (1999) determined that fairness perceptions of cognitive and job knowledge tests increased with a positive selection outcome and with sensitively conveyed personal and procedural information regardless of outcome. Selected applicants' self-perception improved with personal or procedural information; rejected applicants' self-perception declined. Sensitive explanations amplified this result, implying that providing information about the selection procedure would increase fairness and organizational perceptions but be counterbalanced by lower self-perceptions for rejected applicants.

Invasiveness of personnel selection measures has been investigated. Verifiable, impersonal, and face-valid biodata items tend to be perceived as less invasive, especially for individuals who understand the general purpose of biodata (Mael et al 1996a). Ways to obtain potentially invasive information without violating applicants' needs for privacy have been offered [e.g. explaining the job relevance of the item (Mael 1998)].

EMERGING TOPICS

Team Member Selection

Organizations increasingly use team-based structures for organizing, motivating, and performing work (see Guzzo & Salas 1995, Howard 1995, Kehoe 1999, Klimoski & Zukin 1999, Kraut & Korman 1999b, O'Neil 1997, Sundstrom 1999). Much has been learned about factors affecting team performance and effectiveness (see reviews by Cohen & Bailey 1997, and West & Allen 1997), but more work remains for personnel selection. Selection systems need to consider differences between team selection and traditional selection methods, particular work team circumstances (task type, role differentiation, and resources), and selection into new versus preexisting work teams.

Individual characteristics and types of tasks interact within a team to influence team performance and effectiveness. On a creative problem-solving task, a mid-range of extraverts appears best; too many or too few depress performance ratings slightly. Conscientiousness did not predict team performance on the creative task (Barry & Stewart 1997), as Hough (1992) found at the individual level of analysis. In other team studies (LePine et al 1997, Barrick et al 1998), conscientiousness did predict task performance. Given a designated leader and group members each with unique expertise, team decision-making accuracy over time tends to be best when all members are high in conscientiousness and general cognitive ability (LePine et al 1997). Barrick et al (1998) found that conscientiousness, general cognitive ability, and extraversion all predicted overall team performance ratings in manufacturing work teams, where team members contributed independently to the outcome. Team agreeableness predicted teamwork for those tasks in which intergroup conflict was possible. One disagreeable team member was often enough to disrupt team performance, indicating the importance of interpersonal skills when selecting for some teams. Negotiation, an interpersonal skill, was validly measured with a simulation exercise (O'Neil et al 1997a,b). Significant advances in team selection research await good taxonomies of "team difference" variables (the analog of individual-difference variables for individuals) and situational variables relevant to teams.

Cross-Cultural Selection Issues

With their expanding global markets, culturally diverse work teams, and expatriate work assignments, international and multinational organizations place new demands on selection processes and measurement tools. Validities of domestic selection instruments may not generalize to international sites, because different predictor and criterion constructs may be relevant, or, if the constructs are the same, the behavioral indicators may differ. Interpersonal skill, open-mindedness, and adaptability are important factors for expatriate success, and family situation is the most commonly cited reason for failure (Arthur & Bennett 1995, Nyfield & Baron 1999). The vast majority of companies base their expatriate selection decisions on technical competence alone (Aryee 1997), so finding a very high failure rate among expatriates is unsurprising [between 15% and 40% (Shackleton & Newell 1997)]. A clear need for improving expatriate selection exists.

Several personality inventories originally developed in English have demonstrated similar psychometric properties across languages and cultures (see Katigbak et al 1996, McCrae & Costa 1997, Nyfield & Baron 1999). The International Committee on Test Standards produced a set of stringent standards for translating tests into another language (see Hambleton 1999). Psychologists from many different cultures might be involved in all phases of inventory development and validation, a strategy used to develop the Global Personality Inventory (Schmit et al 1999). Cultural variables likely moderate the validity of selection procedures. The House et al (1997) review concluded that Hofstede's (1980) four constructs (power distance, uncertainty avoidance, individualism vs collectivism, and masculinity vs femininity) described and differentiated cultures most usefully.

PROFESSIONAL, LEGAL, AND ETHICAL STANDARDS

Professional

Three initiatives sponsored by the American Psychological Association provide guidelines and policies regarding test-taker rights and responsibilities, test standards, and test-user qualifications. First, the American Psychological Association is in the final stages of approving 10 test-taker rights and corresponding responsibilities (Joint Committee on Testing Practices 1999). Second, the "Standards for Educational and Psychological Testing" (unpublished manuscript) revises and updates standards for psychological tests and for psychological measurement in general. All parties involved in employment decisions involving psychological assessment should become familiar with these new standards. Third, the "Test User Qualifications" document is currently under review (Fox 1999). These three documents will impact personnel selection practices and have significant legal and ethical implications.

Legal

Over the past 20 years or so, more employment litigation has been brought under common-law torts than under federal or state equal employment opportunity statutes (Highberger 1996). Nevertheless, legal challenges to personnel selection decisions are often based on the Civil Rights Acts, Americans with Disabilities Act (ADA), and Age Discrimination in Employment Act. In the vast majority of these cases, the Equal Employment Opportunity Commission is typically not involved (Sharf & Jones 1999), although commission guidelines provide important compliance information for the public and the courts. Unstructured interviews account for the majority of federal court cases involving selection tools, followed by cognitive ability tests, and physical ability tests; together, they were judged to be discriminatory in about 40% of the cases, with cognitive tests faring somewhat better (Terpstra et al 1999). For important practical guidance and discussions of the many issues, risks, and myths regarding fair employment as well as trends in employment litigation, see Barrett (1996, 1998), Jeanneret (1998), and Sharf & Jones (1999).

The U.S. Supreme Court significantly limited the scope of ADA, ruling that impairments should be evaluated in their corrected or "mitigated" state (*Sutton vs United Airlines* 1999, *Murphy vs United Parcel Service* 1999). The U.S. Equal Employment Opportunity Commission (1999) answered 46 frequently asked questions pertaining to employers' legal obligations and the rights of the disabled in both the application and employment settings. Tippins (1999) provided practical ADA guidance for several testing scenarios, and Bruyére (1999) outlined the psychologist's role in upholding ADA provisions in all phases of the employment process.

Affirmative Action and Reverse Discrimination   Although individuals differ greatly in their perceptions of affirmative action programs (Kravitz et al 1997), negative consequences consistently occur when employees or applicants believe hiring is based on group membership rather than merit (Heilman 1996, Heilman et al 1998, Kravitz et al 1997, Stanush et al 1998). Affirmative action programs are associated with slight improvement in employment conditions for women and racial minorities and appear to have virtually no effect on organizational effectiveness (Kravitz et al 1997).

No general agreement exists on how to prevent discrimination or remedy past discrimination (Campbell 1996). Reverse-discrimination court cases have clarified that race or other job-irrelevant class membership can not be used when making employment-related decisions. Therein lies a conflict: The Uniform Guidelines indicate that organizations should seek out valid non- or less-discriminating predictors, yet developing a selection system with such measures requires attention to class membership. In *Hayden vs County of Nassau* (1999), the claim that an entrance exam designed to minimize discriminatory impact on minority job candidates necessarily discriminated against nonminority job candidates was ruled to be without merit. This case sets a precedent in affirming the reasonableness of designing selection systems to minimize adverse impact against protected groups.

Ethical

Ethical issues in personnel selection are complex, context-specific, and relative to each concerned party. We refer the reader to two important new sources in the field. Lowman (1998) authored an updated ethics casebook for human resource professionals practicing within organizations, and Jeanneret (1998) discussed ethical issues involved in individual assessment, detailing the responsibilities for both assessors and organizations.

PARTING REMARKS

New areas in personnel selection are unfolding, and traditional areas continue to improve. (*a*) Greater conceptual and methodological attention has been devoted to understanding and predicting how organizationally relevant criteria might change over time. Given the present and future state of rapid change in the world of work, this line of research is critically important for improving personnel selection and overall organizational effectiveness. (*b*) Personality theory and measurement within a personnel selection context have burgeoned. New personality constructs and compound constructs of well-known traits are being brought into the fold. (*c*) Applicant reactions to personnel selection procedures have been energetically studied. (*d*) Team member and cross-cultural selection issues have drawn greater research attention. (*e*) Refined taxonomic structures are being developed across many different domains in personnel selection, both from the worker and work perspectives. We predict that selection systems will become more complex as a consequence of all this work; selection systems will mirror today's realities and prove to be more effective and rewarding for individuals and organizations alike. We also predict that Guion's (1998) book on personnel selection will fast become a classic. It is readable, practical, thoughtful, and thorough, and it assures its readers that much has been learned in personnel selection. Although the turn of the millennium marks a distinct ending and beginning, personnel selection theory and practice remain in constant process, looking toward the future while remembering the past.

Visit the Annual Reviews home page at www.AnnualReviews.org.

LITERATURE CITED

Ackerman PL, Heggestad ED. 1997. Intelligence, personality, and interests: evidence for overlapping traits. *Psychol. Bull.* 121:219–45

Aguinis H, Cortina J, Goldberg E. 1998. A new procedure for computing equivalence bands in personnel selection. *Hum. Perform.* 11:351–65

Aguinis H, Pierce CA. 1998a. Heterogeneity of error variance and the assessment of moderating effects of categorical variables: a conceptual review. *Organ. Res. Methods* 1:296–314

Aguinis H, Pierce CA. 1998b. Statistical power computations for detecting dichotomous moderator variables with moderated multiple regression. *Educ. Psychol. Meas.* 58:668–76

Aguinis H, Stone-Romero EF. 1997. Methodological artifacts in moderated multiple regression and their effects on statistical power. *J. Appl. Psychol.* 82:192–206

Aguinis H, Whitehead R. 1997. Sampling variance in the correlation coefficient under indirect range restriction: implications for validity generalization. *J. Appl. Psychol.* 82:528–38

Alliger GM, Lilienfeld SO, Mitchell KE. 1996. The susceptibility of overt and covert integrity tests to coaching and faking. *Psychol. Sci.* 7:32–39

Anderson GD, Viswesvaran C. 1998. *An update of the validity of personality scales in personnel selection: a meta-analysis of studies published between 1992–1997.* Presented at Annu. Meet. Soc. Ind. Organ. Psychol., 13th, Dallas

Anderson LE, Stone-Romero EF, Tisak J. 1996. A comparison of bias and mean squared error in parameter estimates of interaction effects: moderated multiple regression versus errors-in-variables regression. *Multivariate Behav. Res.* 31:69–94

Anderson N, Herriot P, eds. 1997. *International Handbook of Selection and Assessment*, Vol. 13. Chichester, UK: Wiley. 652 pp.

Anderson N, Ostroff C. 1997. Selection as socialization. See Anderson & Herriot 1997, pp. 413–40

Arthur W, Bennett W. 1995. The international assignee: the relative importance of factors perceived to contribute to success. *Pers. Psychol.* 48:99–114

Arthur W, Doverspike D, Barrett GV. 1996. Development of a job analysis-based procedure for weighting and combining content-related tests into a single test battery score. *Pers. Psychol.* 49:971–85

Arthur W, Tubre T. 1999. The assessment center construct-related validity paradox: a case of construct misspecification? See Quiñones 1999

Arthur W, Woehr DJ, Maldegen R. 1999. Convergent and discriminant validity of assessment center dimensions: a conceptual and empirical re-examination of the assessment center construct-related validity paradox. *J. Manage.* In press

Aryee S. 1997. Selection and training of expatriate employees. See Anderson & Herriot 1997, pp. 147–60

Ashton MC. 1998. Personality and job performance: the importance of narrow traits. *J. Organ. Behav.* 19:289–303

Austin JT, Klimoski RJ, Hunt ST. 1996. Dilemmatics in public sector assessment: a framework for developing and evaluating selection systems. *Hum. Perform.* 9:177–98

Averill JR. 1997. The emotions: an integrative approach. See Hogan et al 1997, pp. 513–41

Barrett RS, ed. 1996. *Fair Employment Strategies in Human Resource Management.* Westport, CT: Quorum Books. 319 pp.

Barrett RS. 1998. *Challenging the Myths of Fair Employment Practices.* Westport, CT: Quorum Books. 190 pp.

Barrick MR, Mount MK. 1991. The Big Five personality dimensions and job performance: a meta-analysis. *Pers. Psychol.* 44:1–26

Barrick MR, Mount MK. 1996. Effects of impression management and self-deception on the predictive validity of personality constructs. *J. Appl. Psychol.* 81:261–72

Barrick MR, Stewart GL, Neubert MJ, Mount MK. 1998. Relating member ability and personality to work-team processes and team effectiveness. *J. Appl. Psychol.* 83:377–91

Barry B, Stewart GL. 1997. Composition, process, and performance in self-managed groups: the role of personality. *J. Appl. Psychol.* 82:62–78

Bauer TN, Maertz CP Jr, Dolen MR, Campion MA. 1998. Longitudinal assessment of applicant reactions to employment testing and test outcome feedback. *J. Appl. Psychol.* 83:892–903

Bernstein J. 1999. *Computer-based assessment of spoken language.* Presented at Annu. Meet. Soc. Ind. Organ. Psychol., 14th, Atlanta

Bobko P, Roth PL, Potosky D. 1999. Derivation and implications of a meta-analytic matrix incorporating cognitive ability, alternative predictors, and job performance. *Pers. Psychol.* 52:1–31

Bobrow W, Leonards JS. 1997. Development and validation of an assessment center during organizational change. *J. Soc. Behav. Pers.* 12(5):217–36

Borman WC, Motowidlo SJ, eds. 1997. Organizational citizenship behavior and contextual performance. *Hum. Perform.* 10:67–192

Bruyére S. 1999. Disability nondiscrimination in the employment process: the role for psychologists. See Ekstrom & Smith 1999. In press

Burke MJ, Rupinski MT, Dunlap WP, Davison HK. 1996. Do situational variables act as substantive causes of relationships between individual difference variables? Two large-scale tests of "common cause" models. *Pers. Psychol.* 49:573–98

Burnett JR, Fan C, Motowidlo SJ, Degroot T. 1998. Interview notes and validity. *Pers. Psychol.* 51:375–96

Burnett JR, Motowidlo SJ. 1998. Relations between different sources of information in the structured selection interview. *Pers. Psychol.* 51:963–83

Burroughs SM, Bing MN, James LR. 1999. Reconsidering how to measure employee reliability: an empirical comparison and integration of self-report and conditional reasoning methodologies. See Williams & Burroughs 1999

Bushman BJ, Wells GL. 1998. Trait aggressiveness and hockey penalties: predicting hot tempers on the ice. *J. Appl. Psychol.* 83:969–74

Campbell JP. 1996. Group differences and personnel decisions: validity, fairness, and affirmative action. *J. Vocat. Behav.* 49:122–58

Campbell JP. 1999. The definition and measurement of performance in the new age. See Ilgen & Pulakos 1999, pp. 399–429

Campbell JP, Gasser MB, Oswald FL. 1996. The substantive nature of job performance variability. See Murphy 1996, pp. 258–99

Campion MA, Palmer DK, Campion JE. 1997. A review of structure in the selection interview. *Pers. Psychol.* 50:655–702

Carlson KD, Scullen SE, Schmidt FL, Rothstein H, Erwin F. 1999. Generalizable biographical data validity can be achieved without multi-organizational development and keying. *Pers. Psychol.* 52:731–55

Carretta TR, Doub TW. 1998. Group differences in the role of *g* and prior job knowledge in the acquisition of subsequent job knowledge. *Pers. Individ. Differ.* 23:585–93

Carretta TR, Ree MJ. 1996. Factor structure of the Air Force officer qualifying test: analysis and comparison. *Mil. Psychol.* 8:29–42

Carretta TR, Ree MJ. 1997. Negligible sex differences in the relation of cognitive and psychomotor abilities. *Pers. Individ. Differ.* 22:165–72

Carretta TR, Retzlaff PD, Callister JD, King RE. 1998. A comparison of two U.S. Air Force pilot aptitude tests. *Avation, Space, Environ. Med.* 69:931–35

Cascio WF. 1995. Whither industrial and organizational psychology in a changing world of work? *Am. Psychol.* 50:928–39

Chan D. 1997. Racial subgroup differences in predictive validity perceptions on personality and cognitive ability tests. *J. Appl. Psychol.* 82:311–20

Chan D. 1998a. The conceptualization and analysis of change over time: an integrative approach incorporating longitudinal mean and covariance structures analysis (LMACS) and multiple indicator latent growth modeling (MLGM). *Organ. Res. Methods* 1:421–83

Chan D. 1998b. Functional relations among constructs in the same content domain at different levels of analysis: a typology of composition models. *J. Appl. Psychol.* 83:234–46

Chan D, Schmitt N. 1997. Video-based versus paper-and-pencil method of assessment in situational judgment tests: subgroup differences in test performance and face validity perceptions. *J. Appl. Psychol.* 82:143–59

Chan D, Schmitt N, Jennings D, Sheppard L. 1999. Developing measures of basic job-relevant English proficiency for the prediction of job performance and promotability. *J. Bus. Psychol.* In press

Chan D, Schmitt N, Sacco JM, DeShon RP. 1998. Understanding pretest and posttest reactions to cognitive ability and personality tests. *J. Appl. Psychol.* 83:471–85

Cliff N, Caruso JC. 1998. Reliable component analysis through maximizing composite reliability. *Psychol. Methods* 3:291–308

Cohen SG, Bailey DE. 1997. What makes teams work: group effectiveness research from the shop floor to the executive suite. *J. Manage.* 23(3):239–90

Coleman V, Borman W. 1999. Investigating the underlying structure of the citizenship performance domain. *Hum. Resour. Res. Rev.* In press

Colihan J, Burger GK. 1995. Constructing job families: an analysis of quantitative techniques used for grouping jobs. *Pers. Psychol.* 48:563–86

Collins JM, Gleaves DH. 1998. Race, job applicants, and the five-factor model of personality: implications for black psychology, industrial/organizational psychology, and the five-factor theory. *J. Appl. Psychol.* 83:531–44

Collins JM, Schmidt FL, Sanchez-Ku M, Thomas LE, McDaniel M. 1999. Predicting assessment center ratings from cognitive ability and personality. See Quiñones 1999

Conway JM, Jako RA, Goodman DF. 1995. A meta-analysis of interrater and internal consistency reliability of selection interviews. *J. Appl. Psychol.* 80:565–79

Cronshaw SF. 1997. Lo! The stimulus speaks: the insider's view on Whyte and Latham's "The futility of utility analysis." *Pers. Psychol.* 50:611–15

Cudeck R. 1996. Mixed-effects models in the study of individual differences with repeated measures data. *Multivariate Behav. Res.* 31:371–403

Dalessio AT, Crosby MM, McManus MA. 1996. Stability of biodata keys and dimensions across English-speaking countries: a test of the cross-situational hypothesis. *J. Bus. Psychol.* 10:289–96

Deadrick DL, Bennett N, Russell CJ. 1997. Using hierarchical linear modeling to examine dynamic performance criteria over time. *J. Manage.* 23:745–57

Dean MA, Russell CJ, Muchinsky PM. 1999. Life experiences and performance prediction: toward a theory of biodata. In *Research in Personnel and Human Resources Management,* Vol. 17, ed. G Ferris. Greenwich, CT: JAI. In press

DeShon RP, Alexander RA. 1996. Alternative procedures for testing regression slope homogeneity when group error variances are unequal. *Psychol. Methods* 1:261–77

DeShon RP, Ployhart RE, Sacco JM. 1998a. The estimation of reliability in longitudinal models. *Int. J. Behav. Dev.* 22:493–515

DeShon RP, Smith MR, Chan D, Schmitt N. 1998b. Can racial differences in cognitive test performance be reduced by presenting problems in a social context? *J. Appl. Psychol.* 83:438–51

Dipboye R. 1997. Structured selection interviews: Why do they work? Why are they underutilized? See Anderson & Herriot 1997, pp. 455–73

Douglas EF, McDaniel MA, Snell AF. 1996. The validity of non-cognitive measures decays when applicants fake. In *Proc. Acad. Manage.,* ed. JB Keyes, LN Dosier, pp. 127–31. Madison, WI: Omnipress. 594 pp.

Dunnette M. 1976. Aptitudes, abilities, and skills. In *Handbook of Industrial and Orga-*

nizational Psychology, ed. M Dunnette, pp. 473–520. Chicago: Rand McNally. 1740 pp.

Dunnette MD. 1997. Emerging trends and vexing issues in industrial and organizational psychology. *Appl. Psychol. Int. Rev.* 47(2):129–53

Dwight SA, Donovan JJ. 1998. *Warning: Proceed with caution when warning applicants not to dissimulate (revised).* Presented at Annu. Conf. Soc. Ind. Organ. Psychol., 13th, Dallas

Ekstrom R, Smith D, eds. 1999. *Assessing Individuals with Disabilities: a Sourcebook.* Washington, DC: Am. Psychol. Assoc. In press

Ellingson JE, Sackett PR, Hough LM. 1999a. Social desirability corrections in personality measurement: issues of applicant comparison and construct validity. *J. Appl. Psychol.* 84:155–66

Ellingson JE, Smith DB, Sackett PR. 1999b. Investigating the influence of social desirability on personality factor structure. *J. Appl. Psychol.* In press

Fox HR. 1999. Task force describes test user qualifications. *Score Newsl.* 21(3):3–4

Frei RL, McDaniel MA. 1998. Validity of customer service measures in personnel selection: a review of criterion and construct evidence. *Hum. Perform.* 11:1–27

Gandy JA, Dye DA, MacLane CN. 1994. See Stokes et al 1994, pp. 275–309

Ghiselli EE. 1966. *The Validity of Occupational Aptitude Tests.* New York: Wiley & Sons. 155 pp.

Gilliland SW, Steiner DD. 1999. Causes and consequences of applicant perceptions of unfairness. In *Justice in the Workplace,* ed. R Cropanzano, Vol. 2 Mahwah, NJ: Lawrence Erlbaum. In press

Goffin RD, Rothstein MG, Johnston NG, 1996. Personality testing and the assessment center: incremental validity for managerial selection. *J. Appl. Psychol.* 81:746–56

Goldstein H, Riley Y, Yusko KP. 1999. Exploration of Black-White subgroup differences on interpersonal constructs. *Subgroup dif-*

ferences in employment testing. Symp. Annu. Meet. Soc. Ind. Organ. Psychol., 14th, Atlanta

Goldstein HW, Yusko KP, Braverman EP, Smith DB, Chung B. 1998. The role of cognitive ability in the subgroup differences and incremental validity of assessment center exercises. Pers. Psychol. 51:357–74

Gottfredson LS. 1986. Occupational Aptitude Patterns map: development and implications for a theory of job aptitude requirements. J. Vocat. Behav. 29:254–91

Gottfredson LS. 1997. Why g matters: the complexity of everyday life. Intelligence 24:79–132

Gottfredson LS. 1999. Skills gaps, not tests, make racial proportionality impossible. Psychol. Public Policy Law. In press

Gough HG. 1968. The Chapin Social Insight Test Manual. Palo Alto, CA: Consult. Psychol. Press. 14 pp.

Gough HG. 1994. Theory, development, and interpretation of the CPI Socialization scale. Psychol. Rep. 75:651–700 (Suppl.)

Graves LM, Karren RJ. 1996. The employee selection interview: a fresh look at an old problem. Hum. Res. Manage. 35:163–80

Guion RM. 1998. Assessment, Measurement, and Prediction for Pers. Decisions. Mahwah, NJ: Lawrence Erlbaum Assoc. 690 pp.

Guzzo AR, Salas E, eds. 1995. Team Effectiveness and Decision Making in Organizations. San Francisco: Jossey-Bass. 413 pp.

Hakel M, ed. 1998. Beyond Multiple Choice: Evaluating Alternatives and Traditional Testing for Selection. Hillsdale, NJ: Erlbaum. 221 pp.

Hambleton RK. 1999. Guidelines for adapting educational and psychological tests. Bull. Int. Test Commiss.

Hancock GR. 1997. Correlation/validity coefficients disattenuated for score reliability: a structural equation modeling approach. Educ. Psychol. Meas. 57:598–606

Hattrup K, Jackson SE. 1996. Learning about individual differences by taking situations seriously. See Murphy 1996, pp. 507–41

Hattrup K, O'Connell MS, Wingate PH. 1998. Prediction of multidimensional criteria: distinguishing task and contextual performance. Hum. Perform. 11:305–19

Hattrup K, Rock J, Scalia C. 1997. The effects of varying conceptualizations of job performance on adverse impact, minority hiring, and predicted performance. J. Appl. Psychol. 82:656–64

Hayden vs County of Nassau. No. 98–6113, 1999. WL 373636 (2nd Cir June 9, 1999)

Heilman ME. 1996. Affirmative action's contradictory consequences. J. Soc. Issues 52(4):105–9

Heilman ME, Battle WS, Keller CE, Lee RA. 1998. Type of affirmative action policy: a determinant of reactions to sex-based preferential selection? J. Appl. Psychol. 83:190–205

Helms JE. 1992. Why is there no study of cultural equivalence in standardized cognitive ability testing? Am. Psychol. 47:1083–101

Herriot P, Anderson N. 1997. Selecting for change: How will personnel and selection psychology survive? See Anderson & Herriot 1997, pp. 1–34

Highberger W. 1996. Current evidentiary issues in employment litigation. Empl. Relat. Law J. 22(1):31–56

Hoffman CC, McPhail SM. 1998. Exploring options for supporting test use in situations precluding local validation. Pers. Psychol. 51:987–1003

Hoffman CC, Thornton GC III. 1997. Examining selection utility where competing predictors differ in adverse impact. Pers. Psychol. 50:455–70

Hofmann DA. 1997. An overview of the logic and rationale of hierarchical linear models. J. Manage. 23:723–44

Hofstede G. 1980. Culture's Consequences: International Differences in Work-Related Values. Thousand Oaks, CA: Sage

Hogan J, Brinkmeyer K. 1997. Bridging the gap between overt and personality-based integrity tests. Pers. Psychol. 50:587–99

Hogan J, Ones DS. 1997. Conscientiousness and integrity at work. See Hogan et al 1997, pp. 513–41

Hogan J, Rybicki SL. 1998. *Performance Improvement Characteristics Job Analysis.* Tulsa, OK: Hogan Assessment Systems

Hogan R. 1968. Develoment of an empathy scale. *J. Consult. Clin. Psychol.* 33:307–16

Hogan R. 1998. Reinventing personality. *J. Soc. Clin. Psychol.* 17:1–10

Hogan R, Johnson J, Briggs S, eds. 1997. *Handbook of Personality Psychology.* San Diego: Academic. 987 pp.

Hornick CW, Fox KA, Axton TR, Wyatt BS. 1999. The relative contribution of conditional reasoning and multiple intelligence measures in predicting firefighter and law enforcement officer job performance. See Williams & Burroughs 1999

Hough LM. 1992. The 'Big Five' personality variables—construct confusion: description versus prediction. *Hum. Perform.* 5(1&2):139–55

Hough LM. 1997. The millennium for personality psychology: new horizons or good old daze. *Appl. Psychol. Int. Rev.* 47(2):233–61

Hough LM. 1998a. Effects of intentional distortion in personality measurement and evaluation of suggested palliatives. *Hum. Perform.* 11:209–44

Hough LM. 1998b. Personality at work: issues and evidence. See Hakel 1998, pp. 131–59

Hough LM, Ones DS, Viswesvaran C. 1998. Personality correlates of managerial performance constructs. See Page 1998

Hough LM, Paullin C. 1994. Construct-oriented scale construction: the rational approach. See Stokes et al 1994, pp. 109–45

Hough LM, Schneider RJ. 1996. Personality traits, taxonomies, and applications in organizations. See Murphy 1996, pp. 31–88

House RJ, Wright NS, Aditya RN. 1997. Cross-cultural research on organizational leadership: a critical analysis and a proposed theory. In *New Perspectives on International Industrial/Organizational Psychology,* ed. PC Earley, M Erez, pp. 535–625. San Francisco: New Lexington Press. 790 pp.

Howard A, ed. 1995. *The Changing Nature of Work.* San Francisco: Jossey-Bass. 590 pp.

Howard A. 1999. Discussant comments. See Quiñones 1999

Huffcutt AI, Roth PL. 1998. Racial group differences in employment interview evaluations. *J. Appl. Psychol.* 83:179–89

Huffcutt AI, Woehr DJ. 1999. Further analysis of employment interview validity: a quantitative evaluation of interviewer-related structuring methods. *J. Organ. Behav.* 20(4):549–60

Hunter JE. 1997. Needed: a ban on the significance test. *Psychol. Sci.* 8:3–7

Hunter JE, Schmidt FL. 1996. Cumulative research knowledge and social policy formulation: the critical role of meta-analysis. *Psychol. Public Policy Law* 2:324–47

Ilgen DR, Pulakos ED. 1999. *The Changing Nature of Performance: Implications for Staffing, Motivation, and Development.* San Francisco: Jossey-Bass. 452 pp.

James LR. 1998. Measurement of personality via conditional reasoning. *Organ. Res. Methods* 1(2):131–63

James LR. 1999. *Use of a conditional reasoning measure for aggression to predict employee reliability.* Presented at Annu. Meet. Soc. Ind. Organ. Psychol., 14th, Atlanta

James LR, Demaree RG, Mulaik SA, Ladd RT. 1992. Validity generalization in the context of situational models. *J. Appl. Psychol.* 77:3–14

Jeanneret R. 1998. Ethical, legal, and professional issues for individual assessment. In *Individual Psychological Assessment: Predicting Behavior in Organizational Settings,* ed. R Jeanneret, R Silzer, pp. 88–131. San Francisco: Jossey-Bass. 495 pp.

Johnson JW. 1999. A heuristic method for estimating the relative weight of predictor variables in multiple regression. *Multivariate Behav. Res.* In press

Johnson JW, Schneider RJ, Oswald FL. 1997. Toward a taxonomy of managerial performance profiles. *Hum. Perform.* 10:227–50

Joint Committee on Testing Practices. 1999. *Test Taker Rights and Responsibilities: Guidelines and Expectations.* Washington, DC: Am. Psychol. Assoc. In press

Judge TA, Erez A, Bono JE. 1998. The power of being positive: the relation between positive self-concept and job performance. *Hum. Perform.* 11:167–87

Kataoka HC, Latham GP, Whyte G. 1997. The relative resistance of the situational, patterned behavior, and conventional structured interviews to anchoring effects. *Hum. Perform.* 10:47–63

Katigbak MS, Church AT, Akamine TX. 1996. Cross-cultural generalizability of personality dimensions: relating indigenous and imported dimensions in two cultures. *J. Person. Soc. Psychol.* 70:99–114

Kehoe JF, ed. 1999. *Managing Selection Strategies in Changing Organizations.* San Francisco: Jossey-Bass. In press

Kiker S, Motowidlo S. 1999. Main and interaction effects of task and contextual performance on supervisory reward decisions. *J. Appl. Psychol.* 84:602–09

Klimoski R, Zukin LB. 1999. Selection and staffing for team effectiveness. See Sundstrom 1999, pp. 63–91

Kraut AI, Korman AK. 1999a. The "DELTA Forces" causing change in human resource management. See Kraut & Korman 1999b, pp. 3–22

Kraut AI, Korman AK, eds. 1999b. *Evolving Practices in Human Resource Management.* San Francisco: Jossey-Bass. 376 pp.

Kravitz DA, Harrison DA, Turner ME, Levine EL, Chaves W, et al. 1997. *Affirmative Action: a Review of Psychological and Behavioral Research.* Bowling Green, OH: Soc. Ind. Organ. Psychol. 50 pp.

Kuncel NR, Hezlett SA, Ones DS. 1999. Comprehensive meta-analysis of the predictive validity of the graduate record examinations: implications for graduate student selection and performance. *Psychol. Bull.* In press

Latham GP, Whyte G. 1994. The futility of utility analysis. *Pers. Psychol.* 47:31–46

Lefkowitz J, Gebbia MI, Balsam T, Dunn L. 1999 Dimensions of biodata items and their relationships to item validity. *J. Occup. Organ. Psychol.* In press

Legree PJ, Pifer ME, Grafton FC. 1996. Correlations among cognitive abilities are lower for higher ability groups. *Intelligence* 23:45–57

LePine JA, Hollenbeck JR, Ilgen DR, Hedlund J. 1997. Effects of individual differences on the performance of hierarchical decision-making teams: much more than *g. J. Appl. Psychol.* 85:803–11

Levine EL, Spector PE, Menon S, Narayanan L, Cannon-Bowers J. 1996. Validity generalization for cognitive psychomotor, and perceptual tests for craft jobs in the utility industry. *Hum. Perform.* 9:1–22

Li H, Rosenthal R, Rubin DB. 1996. Reliability of measurement in psychology: from Spearman-Brown to maximal reliability. *Psychol. Methods* 1:98–107

Lievens F. 1998. Factors which improve the construct validity of assessment centers: a review. *Int. J. Select. Assess.* 6:141–52

Lowman RL, ed. 1998. *The Ethical Practice of Psychology in Organizations.* Washington, DC: Am. Psychol. Assoc. 299 pp.

Lubinski D. 2000. Scientific and social significance of assessing individual differences: "Sinking shafts at a few critical points." *Annu. Rev. Psychol.* 51:405–44

Lubinski D, Benbow C. 1999. States of excellence: a psychological interpretation of their emergence. *Am. Psychol.* In press

Mael FA. 1998. Privacy and personnel selection: reciprocal rights and responsibilities. *Empl. Responsib. Rights J.* 11:187–214

Mael FA, Connelly M, Morath RA. 1996a. None of your business: parameters of biodata invasiveness. *Pers. Psychol.* 49:613–50

Mael F, Kilcullen R, White L. 1996b. Soldier attributes for peacekeeping and peacemaking. In *Reserve Component Soldiers as Peacekeepers,* ed. R Phelps, B Farr, pp. 29–

57. Alexandria, VA: U.S. Army Res. Inst. Behav. Sci. 449 pp.

Matthews G. 1997. The Big Five as a framework for personality assessment. See Anderson & Herriot 1997, pp. 475–92

McCrae RR, Costa PT Jr. 1997. Personality trait structure as a human universal. *Am. Psychol.* 52:509–16

McManus MA, Kelly ML. 1999. Personality measures and biodata: evidence regarding their incremental predictive value in the life insurance industry. *Pers. Psychol.* 52:137–48

Migetz DZ, James LR, Ladd RT. 1999a. *A validation of the conditional reasoning measurement.* Presented at Annu. Meet. Soc. Ind. Organ. Psychol., 14th, Atlanta

Migetz DZ, McIntyre M, James LR. 1999b. Measuring reliability among contingent workers. See Williams & Burroughs 1999

Millsap RE. 1995. Measurement invariance, predictive invariance, and the duality paradox. *Multivariate Behav. Res.* 30:577–605

Millsap RE. 1997. Invariance in measurement and prediction: their relationship in the single-factor case. *Psychol. Methods* 2:248–60

Miner JB, Capps MH. 1996. *How Honesty Testing Works.* Westport, CT: Quorum Books. 192 pp.

Mone MA, Mueller GC, Mauland W. 1996. The perceptions and usage of statistical power in applied psychology and management research. *Pers. Psychol.* 49:103–20

Morgeson FP, Campion MA. 1997. Social and cognitive sources of potential inaccuracy in job analysis. *J. Appl. Psychol.* 82:627–55

Moss FA, Hunt T, Omwake KT, Woodward LG. 1955. *Social Intelligence Test Manual.* Washington, DC: Cent. Psychol. Serv. 4 pp.

Motowidlo SJ, Burnett JR. 1995. Aural and visual sources of validity in structured employment interviews. *Organ. Behav. Hum. Decis. Process.* 61(3):239–49

Mount MK, Barrick MR. 1995. The Big Five personality dimensions: implications for research and practice in human resource management. *Res. Pers. Hum. Resour. Manage.* 13:153–200

Mount MK, Barrick MR, Stewart GL. 1998. Five-factor model of personality and performance in jobs involving interpersonal interactions. *Hum. Perform.* 11:145–65

Muchinsky PM. 1999. Biodata: a mirror of moxie. See Stennett et al 1999. In press

Mumford MD, Costanza DP, Connelly MS, Johnson JF. 1996. Item generation procedures and background data scales: implications for construct and criterion-related validity. *Pers. Psychol.* 49:361–98

Mumford MD, Stokes GS. 1992. Developmental determinants of individual action: theory and practice in the application of background data measures. In *Handbook of Industrial and Organizational Psychology,* ed. MD Dunnette, LM Hough, 2:61–138. Palo Alto, CA: Consult. Psychol. Press. 957 pp. 2nd ed.

Murphy vs United Parcel Service, Inc. No. 97–1992 (119 S Ct 2133, June 22, 1999)

Murphy KR, ed. 1996. *Individual Differences and Behavior in Organizations.* San Francisco: Jossey-Bass. 606 pp.

Murphy KR. 1997. Meta-analysis and validity generalization. See Anderson & Herriot 1997, pp. 323–42

Murphy KR, Luther N. 1997. Assessing honesty, integrity, and deception. See Anderson & Herriot 1997, pp. 369–88

Murphy KR, Myors B. 1999. Testing the hypothesis that treatments have negligible effects: minimum-effect tests in the general linear model. *J. Appl. Psychol.* 84:234–47

Murphy KR, Shiarella AH. 1997. Implications of the multidimensional nature of job performance for the validity of selection tests: multivariate frameworks for studying test validity. *Pers. Psychol.* 50:823–54

Nelson JB. 1997. The boundaryless organization: implications for job analysis, recruitment, and selection. *Hum. Resour. Plan.* 20(4):39–49

Nyfield G, Baron H. 1999. Cultural context in adapting selection practices across borders. See Kehoe 1999. In press

O'Neil HF Jr, ed. 1997. *Workforce Readiness: Competencies and Assessment.* Mahwah, NJ: Erlbaum. 467 pp.

O'Neil HF Jr, Allred K, Dennis RA. 1997a. Use of computer simulation for assessing the interpersonal skill of negotiation. See O'Neil 1997, pp. 205–28

O'Neil HF Jr, Allred K, Dennis RA. 1997b. Validation of a computer simulation for assessment of interpersonal skills. See O'Neil 1997, pp. 229–54

Ones DS, Hough LM, Viswesvaran C. 1998. Personality correlates of managerial performance constructs. See Page 1998

Ones DS, Viswesvaran C. 1996. *What do pre-employment customer service scales measure? Explorations in construct validity and implications for personnel. selection.* Presented at Annu. Meet. Soc. Ind. Organ. Psychol., 11th, San Diego

Ones DS, Viswesvaran C. 1998a. Gender, age, and race differences on overt integrity tests: results across four large-scale job applicant data sets. *J. Appl. Psychol.* 83:35–42

Ones DS, Viswesvaran C. 1998b. Integrity testing in organizations. In *Dysfunctional Behavior in Organizations: Vol. 2, Nonviolent Behaviors in Organizations,* ed. RW Griffin, A O'Leary-Kelly, JM Collins, pp. 243–76. Greenwich, CT: JAI. 318 pp.

Ones DS, Viswesvaran C. 1998c. The effects of social desirability and faking on personality and integrity assessment for personnel selection. *Hum. Perform.* 11:245–69

Ones DS, Viswesvaran C. 1999. Job-specific applicant pools and national norms for personality scales: implications for range restriction corrections in validation research. *J. Appl. Psychol.* In press

Ones DS, Viswesvaran C, Reiss AD. 1996. Role of social desirability in personality testing for personnel selection: the red herring. *J. Appl. Psychol.* 81:660–79

Ones DS, Viswesvaran C, Schmidt FL, Reiss AD. 1994. *The validity of honesty and violence scales of integrity tests in predicting violence at work.* Presented at Annu. Meet. Acad. Manage., Dallas

Ostroff C, Harrison D. 1999. Meta-analysis, level of analysis, and best estimates of population correlations: cautions for interpreting meta-analytic results in organizational behavior. *J. Appl. Psychol.* 84:260–70

Oswald FL, Ferstl KL. 1999. Linking a structure of vocational interests to Gottfredson's (1986) Occupational Aptitude Patterns map. *J. Vocat. Behav.* 54:214–31

Oswald FL, Johnson JW. 1998. On the robustness, bias, and stability of statistics from meta-analysis of correlation coefficients: some initial Monte Carlo findings. *J. Appl. Psychol.* 83:164–78

Oswald FL, Saad SA, Sackett PR. 1999. The homogeneity assumption in differential prediction analysis: Does it really matter? *J. Appl. Psychol.* In press

Page RC, chair. 1998. In *Personality determinants of managerial potential performance, progression and ascendancy.* Symp. Annu. Meet. Soc. Ind. Organ. Psychol., 13th, Dallas

Patton TW, Walton W, James LR. 1999. Measuring personal reliability via conditional reasoning: identifying people who will work reliably. See Williams & Burroughs 1999

Pearlman K. 1997. Twenty-first century measures for twenty-first century work. In *Transitions in Work and Learning: Implications for Assessment,* ed. A Lesgold, MJ Feuer, A Block, pp. 136–79. Washington, DC: Natl. Acad. Press. 283 pp.

Pearlman K, Barney MF. 1999. Selection for a changing workplace. See Kehoe 1999. In press

Peterson NG, Mumford MD, Borman WC, Jeanneret PR, Fleishman EA. 1999. *An Occupational Information System for the 21st Century: the Development of O*NET.* Washington, DC: Am. Psychol. Assoc. 319 pp.

Ployhart RE, Hakel MD. 1998. The substantive nature of performance variability: predicting interindividual differences in intraindividual performance. *Pers. Psychol.* 51:859–901

Ployhart RE, Ryan AM, Bennett M. 1999. Explanations for selection decisions: applicants' reactions to informational and sensitivity features of explanations. *J. Appl. Psychol.* In press

Plutchik R, Conte HR, eds. 1997. *Circumplex Models of Personality and Emotions.* Washington, DC: Am. Psychol. Assoc. 484 pp.

Pulakos ED, Schmitt N. 1996. An evaluation of two strategies for reducing adverse impact and their effects on criterion-related validity. *Hum. Perform.* 9:241–58

Quiñones MA, chair. 1999. *Assessment centers, 21st century: new issues, and new answers to old problems.* Symp. Annu. Meet. Soc. Ind. Organ. Psychol., 14th, Atlanta

Quiñones MA, Ford JK, Teachout MS. 1995. The relationship between work experience and job performance: a conceptual and meta-analytic review. *Pers. Psychol.* 48:887–910

Raju NS, Bilgic R, Edwards JE, Fleer PF. 1997. Methodology review: estimation of population validity and cross-validity, and the use of equal weights in prediction. *Appl. Psychol. Meas.* 21:291–305

Raju NS, Bilgic R, Edwards JE, Fleer PF. 1999. Accuracy of population validity and cross-validity estimation: an empirical comparison of formula-based, traditional empirical, and equal weights procedures. *Appl. Psychol. Meas.* 23:99–115

Raykov T. 1997. Estimation of composite reliability for congeneric measures. *Appl. Psychol. Meas.* 21:173–84

Raymark PH, Schmit MJ, Guion RM. 1997. Identifying potentially useful personality constructs for employee selection. *Pers. Psychol.* 50:723–36

Ree MJ, Carretta TR, Teachout MS. 1995. Role of ability and prior job knowledge in com-

plex training performance. *J. Appl. Psychol.* 80:721–30

Robertson I, Callinan M. 1998. Personality and work behaviour. *Eur. J. Work Organ. Psychol.* 7:321–40

Rosse JG, Stecher MD, Levin RA, Miller JL. 1998. The impact of response distortion on preemployment personality testing and hiring decisions. *J. Appl. Psychol.* 83:634–44

Roth PL, Bobko P. 1997. A research agenda for multi-attribute utility analysis in human resource management. *Hum. Resource Manage. Rev.* 7:341–68

Roth PL, Campion JE, Jones SD. 1996. The impact of four missing data techniques on validity estimates in human resource management. *J. Bus. Psychol.* 11:101–12

Russell CJ. 1999. Toward a model of life experience learning. See Stennett et al. 1999. In press

Russell CJ, Dean MA, Broach D. 1998. *Guidelines for Bootstrapping Validity Coefficients in ATCS Selection Research.* Norman, OK: Univ. Okla. 58 pp.

Russell JA, Carroll JM. 1999. On the bipolarity of positive and negative affect. *Psychol. Bull.* 125:3–30

Ryan AM, Greguras GJ. 1998. Life is not multiple choice:reactions to the alternatives. See Hakel 1998, pp. 183–202

Ryan AM, Ployhart RE, Friedel LA. 1998a. Using personality testing to reduce adverse impact: a cautionary note. *J. Appl. Psychol.* 83:298–307

Ryan AM, Ployhart RE, Greguras GJ, Schmit MJ. 1998b. Test preparation programs in selection contexts: self-selection and program effectiveness. *Pers. Psychol.* 51:599–621

Sackett PR, Ellingson JE. 1997. The effects of forming multi-predictor composites on group differences and adverse impact. *Pers. Psychol.* 50:707–21

Sackett PR, Gruys ML, Ellingson JE. 1998. Ability-personality interactions when predicting job-performance. *J. Appl. Psychol.* 83:545–56

Sackett PR, Roth L. 1996. Multi-stage selection strategies: a Monte Carlo investigation of effects on performance and minority hiring. *Pers. Psychol.* 49:549–72

Sackett PR, Wanek JE. 1996. New developments in the use of measures of honesty, integrity, conscientiousness, dependability, trustworthiness, and reliability for personnel selection. *Pers. Psychol.* 49:787–829

Sager CE, Peterson NG, Oppler SH, Rosse RL, Walker CB. 1997. An examination of five indexes of test battery performance: analysis of the ECAT battery. *Mil. Psychol.* 9:97–120

Salgado JF. 1997a. The five factor model of personality and job performance in the European community. *J. Appl. Psychol.* 82:30–43

Salgado JF. 1997b. VALCOR: a program for estimating standard error, confidence intervals, and probability of corrected validity. *Behav. Res. Methods Instrum. Comput.* 29:464–67

Salgado JF. 1998. Big Five personality dimensions and job performance in army and civil occupations: a European perspective. *Hum. Perform.* 11:271–88

Sanchez J, Levine E. 1999. Is job analysis dead, misunderstood, or both? New forms of work analysis and design. See Kraut & Korman 1999b, pp. 43–68

Sanchez J, Prager I, Wilson A, Viswesvaran C. 1998. Understanding within-job title variance in job-analytic ratings. *J. Bus. Psychol.* 12:407–19

Sánchez-Meca J, Marín-Martínez F. 1997. Homogeneity tests in meta-analysis: a Monte Carlo comparison of statistical power and Type I error. *Qual. Quant.* 31:385–99

Sands WA, Waters BK, McBride JR. 1997. *Computerized Adaptive Testing.* Washington, DC: Am. Psychol. Assoc. 292 pp.

Saucier G, Goldberg LR. 1998. What is beyond the Big Five? *J. Pers.* 66:495–524

Schmidt FL, Hunter JE. 1996. Measurement error in psychological research: lessons from 26 research scenarios. *Psychol. Methods* 1:199–223

Schmidt FL, Hunter JE. 1998. The validity and utility of selection methods in personnel psychology: practical and theoretical implications of 85 years of research findings. *Psychol. Bull.* 124:262–74

Schmidt FL, Rader M. 1999. Exploring the boundary conditions for interview validity: meta-analytic validity findings for a new interview type. *Pers. Psychol.* 52:445–64

Schmidt FL, Viswesvaran V, Ones DS. 1997. Validity of integrity tests for predicting drug and alcohol abuse: a meta-analysis. In *Meta-Analysis of Drug Abuse Prevention Programs,* ed. WJ Bukoski, pp. 69–95. Rockville, MD: NIDA National Institute on Drug Abuse Press. 263 pp.

Schmit MJ, Kilm JA, Robie C. 1999. Refining a personality test to be used in selection across several cultures. In *Personality and Performance: Boundary Conditions for Measurement and Structural Models,* chair WC Borman, Symp. Annu. Meet. Soc. Ind. Organ. Psychol., 14th Atlanta

Schmit MJ, Ryan AM. 1997. Applicant withdrawal: the role of test-taking attitudes and racial differences. *Pers. Psychol.* 50:855–76

Schmitt N, Chan D. 1998. *Personnel Selection.* Thousand Oaks, CA: Sage. 378 pp.

Schmitt N, Chan D. 1999. The status of research on applicant reactions to selection tests and its implications for managers. *Int. J. Manage. Rev.* In press

Schmitt N, Jennings D, Toney R. 1999. Can we develop measures of hypothetical constructs? *Hum. Resour. Manage. Rev.* In press

Schmitt N, Nason E, Whitney DJ, Pulakos ED. 1995. The impact of method effects on structural parameters in validation research. *J. Manage.* 21:159–74

Schmitt N, Ployhart RE. 1999. Estimates of cross-validity for stepwise regression and with predictor selection. *J. Appl. Psychol.* 84:50–57

Schmitt N, Pulakos ED. 1998. Biodata and differential prediction: some reservations. See Hakel 1998, pp. 167–82

Schmitt N, Rogers W, Chan D, Sheppard L, Jennings D. 1997. Adverse impact and predictive efficiency of various predictor combinations. *J. Appl. Psychol.* 82:719–30

Schneider RJ, Ackerman PL, Kanfer R. 1996. To "act wisely in human relations": exploring the dimensions of social competence. *Pers. Individ. Differ.* 21:469–81

Schoenfeldt LF. 1999. From dust bowl empiricism to rational constructs in biographical data. *Hum. Resour. Manage. Rev.* In press

Segall DO. 1999. General ability measurement: an application of multidimensional adaptive testing. Presented at Meet. Natl. Council Meas. Educ., Montreal, Canada

Shackleton V, Newell S. 1997. International assessment and selection. See Anderson & Herriot 1997, pp. 81–95

Sharf JC, Jones DP. 1999. Employment risk management. See Kehoe 1999. In press

Smith M, DeMatteo JS, Green P, James LR. 1995. *A comparison of new and traditional measures of achievement motivation.* Presented at Annu. Meet. Am. Psychol. Assoc., 103rd, New Orleans

Snell AF, McDaniel MA. 1998. *Faking: getting data to answer the right questions.* Poster presented at Annu. Meet. Soc. Ind. Organ. Psychol., 13th, Dallas

Snell AF, Sydell EJ, Lueke SB. 1999. Towards a theory of applicant faking: integrating studies of deception. *Hum. Resour. Manage. Rev.* In press

Spychalski A, Quiñones M, Gaugler BB, Pohley K. 1997. A survey of assessment center practices in organizations in the United States. *Pers. Psychol.* 50:71–90

Stajkovic AD, Luthans F. 1998. Self-efficacy and work-related performance: a meta-analysis. *Psychol. Bull.* 124:240–61

Stanush P, Arthur W, Doverspike D. 1998. Hispanic and African American reactions to a simulated race-based affirmative action scenario. *Hispanic J. Behav. Sci.* 20(1):3–16

Stennett RB, Parisi AG, Stokes GS, eds. 1999. *A Compendium: Papers Presented at the First Biennial Biodata Conference.* Athens, GA: Univ. Georgia. In press

Stokes GS, Mumford MD, Owens WA, eds. 1994. *Biodata Handbook.* Palo Alto, CA: Consult. Psychol. Press. 650 pp.

Stokes GS, Searcy CA. 1999. Specification of scales in biodata form development: rational vs. empirical and global vs. specific. *Int. J. Select. Assess.* 7:72–85

Stricker LJ, Rock DA. 1998. Assessing leadership potential with a biographical measure of personality traits. *Int. J. Select. Assess.* 6:164–84

Sundstrom E, ed. 1999. *Supporting Work Team Effectiveness.* San Francisco: Jossey-Bass. 388 pp.

Sutton vs United Airlines, Inc. No. 97–1943, 119 S. Ct. 2139, (June 22, 1999)

Task Force on Assessment Center Guidelines. 1989. Guidelines for ethical considerations. *Public Pers. Manage.* 18:457–70

Terpstra DE, Mohamed AA, Kethley B. 1999. An analysis of federal court cases involving nine selection devices. *Int. J. Select. Assess.* 7:26–34

Terris W. 1997. The traditional regression model for measuring test bias is incorrect and biased against minorities. *J. Bus. Psychol.* 12:25–37

Thorsteinson TJ, Ryan AM. 1997. The effect of selection ratio on perceptions of the fairness of a selection test battery. *Int. J. Select. Assess.* 5:159–68

Tippins NT. 1999. The Americans with Disabilities Act and employment testing. See Ekstrom & Smith 1999. In press

Tisak J, Tisak MS. 1996. Longitudinal models of reliability and validity: a latent curve approach. *Appl. Psychol. Meas.* 20(3):275–88

Tokar DM, Fischer AR, Subich LM. 1998. Personality and vocational behavior: a selective review of the literature, 1993–1997. *J. Voc. Behav.* 53:115–53

Truxillo DM, Bauer TN. 1999. Applicant reactions to test score banding in entry-level and promotional contexts. *J. Appl. Psychol.* 84:322–39

U.S. Equal Employment Opportunity Commission. 1999. *Enforcement Guidance: Reasonable Accommodation and Undue Hardship under the Americans with Disabilities Act.* Washington, DC: Equal Empl. Opportun. Comm.

U.S. Equal Employment Opportunity Commission, Civil Service Commission, Department of Labor, and Department of Justice. 1978. Uniform guidelines on employee selection procedures. *Fed. Regist.* 43:38290–315

Van Scotter JR, Motowidlo SJ. 1996. Interpersonal facilitation and job dedication as separate facets of contextual performance. *J. Appl. Psychol.* 81:525–31

Verive JM, McDaniel MA. 1996. Short-term memory tests in personnel selection: low adverse impact and high validity. *Intelligence* 23:15–32

Vinchur AJ, Schippmann JS, Switzer FS, Roth PL. 1998. A meta-analytic review of predictors of job performance for salespeople. *J. Appl. Psychol.* 83:586–97

Viswesvaran C, Ones DS. 1999 Meta-analyses of fakability estimates: implications for personality measurement. *Educ. Psychol. Meas.* 59:197–210

Viswesvaran C, Ones DS, Schmidt FL. 1996. Comparative analysis of the reliability of job performance ratings. *J. Appl. Psychol.* 81:557–74

Wang T. 1998. Weights that maximize reliability under a congeneric model. *Appl. Psychol. Meas.* 22:179–87

West M, Allen N. 1997. Selecting for teamwork. See Anderson & Herriot 1997, pp. 493–506

Whitney DJ, Diaz J, Mineghino ME, Powers K. 1999. Perceptions of overt and personality-based integrity tests. *Int. J. Select. Assess.* 7:35–45

Whitney DJ, Schmitt N. 1997. Relationship between culture and responses to biodata employment items. *J. Appl. Psychol.* 82:113–29

Whyte G, Latham G. 1997. The futility of utility analysis revisited: when even an expert fails. *Pers. Psychol.* 50:601–10

Wiggins JS, Trapnell PD. 1997. Personality structure: the return of the Big Five. See Hogan et al 1997, pp. 737–65

Wilk SL, Sackett PR. 1996. Longitudinal analysis of ability-job complexity fit and job change. *Pers. Psychol.* 49:937–67

Williams LJ, Burroughs SM, chairs. 1999. *New developments using conditional reasoning to measure employee reliability.* Symp. Annu. Meet. Soc. Ind. Organ. Psychol., 14th, Atlanta

Williamson LG, Campion JE, Malos SB, Roehling MV, Campion MA. 1997. Employment interview on trial: linking interview structure with litigation outcomes. *J. Appl. Psychol.* 82:900–12

Woehr DJ, Arthur W Jr. 1999. The assessment center validity paradox: a review of the role of methodological factors. See Quiñones 1999

Wright TA, Cropanzano R. 1998. Emotional exhaustion as a predictor of job performance and voluntary turnover. *J. Appl. Psychol.* 83:486–93

Wright TA, Staw BM. 1999. Affect and favorable work outcomes: two longitudinal tests of the happy-productive worker thesis. *J. Organ. Behav.* 20:1–23

Zickar MJ, Drasgow F. 1996. Detecting faking on a personality instrument using appropriateness measurement. *Appl. Psychol. Meas.* 20:71–87

Annu. Rev. Psychol. 2000. 51:665–697

EMOTION, REGULATION, AND MORAL DEVELOPMENT

Nancy Eisenberg

Department of Psychology, Arizona State University, Tempe, Arizona 85287–1107;
e-mail: nancy.eisenberg@asu.edu

Key Words   aggression, empathy, guilt, prosocial behavior, shame

■ **Abstract**   Research and theory on the role of emotion and regulation in morality have received considerable attention in the last decade. Much relevant work has concerned the role of moral emotions in moral behavior. Research on differences between embarrassment, guilt, and shame and their relations to moral behavior is reviewed, as is research on the association of these emotions with negative emotionality and regulation.

Recent issues concerning the role of such empathy-related responses as sympathy and personal distress to prosocial and antisocial behavior are discussed, as is the relation of empathy-related responding to situational and dispositional emotionality and regulation. The development and socialization of guilt, shame, and empathy also are discussed briefly. In addition, the role of nonmoral emotions (e.g. anger and sadness), including moods and dispositional differences in negative emotionality and its regulation, in morally relevant behavior, is reviewed.

CONTENTS

The "Moral" Emotions... 666
    The Self-Conscious Moral Emotions... 666
    Empathy-Related Responding.. 671
    The Development of Guilt, Shame, and Empathy... 678
    The Socialization of Guilt, Shame, and Empathy.. 680
Relations of Nonmoral Emotions to Morally Relevant Behavior................ 682
    Mood.. 683
    Individual Differences in Emotionality and Regulation................................ 684
Summary.. 688

For millennia, philosophers have debated whether emotions can be moral and whether emotion contributes to higher-level moral judgment and behavior. Emotions, by their very nature, express a personal, polarized, and biased perspective. Thus, emotion has been viewed as biasing one's evaluations and cognitions and as disrupting rational, moral thought. More recently, philosophers have argued that biased emotional reactions are justified and that emotions help people

665

to distinguish moral features in specific contexts, to motivate moral behavior, and to undercut immoral behavior. In addition, emotions can play a communicative role by revealing our moral values and concerns to others and ourselves (Ben-Ze'ev 1997, Blum 1980).

Philosophers' changing view of the role of emotion in morality is consistent with the predominant view of emotion in psychology today. As is discussed, higher-order emotions such as guilt and sympathy are believed to motivate moral behavior and to play a role in its development and in moral character (e.g. Hoffman 1998, Walker & Pitts 1998). Moreover, in the 1990s there has been considerable interest in the role of basic emotions (i.e. those that are probably universal and involve less cognitive complexity), such as anger and fearfulness, in moral behavior (Eisenberg et al 1999a, Kochanska 1997).

In this chapter, recent issues and findings concerning the role of emotion and emotion-related regulation in moral functioning are reviewed. Behaviors of moral relevance as viewed by others, regardless of their motivation, are the primary foci of interest; the difference between behaviors that are truly moral and those motivated by nonmoral factors is discussed primarily in the context of differentiating between moral and nonmoral emotional reactions (e.g. sympathy vs personal distress). First, issues and findings pertaining to several moral emotions (guilt, shame, and empathy-related responding) are reviewed. Then the role of situational emotion (mood) in moral behavior is discussed briefly. Next, the relations of individual differences in emotionality and regulation to morally relevant behaviors are examined. Finally, research on the prediction of morally relevant behavior from the combination of emotionality and regulation is considered.

THE "MORAL" EMOTIONS

Several emotions, including guilt, shame, and empathy, have been viewed as playing a fundamental role in morality. Although pride is a self-evaluative emotion that can stem from moral behavior, research on pride usually has concerned achievement. Thus, pride is not discussed further.

The Self-Conscious Moral Emotions

Guilt and shame frequently have been implicated in theories of morality, with guilt being a quintessent moral emotion. Both are considered "self-conscious emotions," as is embarrassment. These emotions are labeled "self-conscious" because the individual's understanding and evaluation of the self are fundamental to these emotions.

Embarrassment Keltner & Buswell (1997) argued that embarrassment is an emotion distinct from guilt and shame in that it involves antecedents, experience, and nonverbal displays that are different from those of other emotions. Recent research is consistent with the conclusion that embarrassment, in comparison to shame and guilt, is the least negative, least serious, and most fleeting emotion; it is the least related to moral implications and moral transgressions; it involves less anger at the self and less interest in making amends; and it tends to involve surprising and accidental events for which people feel less responsible (Miller & Tangney 1994; JP Tangney, D Marschall, K Rosenberg, DH Barlow & P Wagner, unpublished data). Rather than playing a role in morality, embarrassment may serve to appease others for one's transgressions of social convention by eliciting light-hearted emotion (Keltner 1995) or may prevent loss of face and serve to assure adherence to important social norms (Leary et al 1996, Miller & Leary 1992). Thus, there generally is consensus that embarrassment plays at most a minor role in moral behavior.

Guilt and Shame   Guilt has been defined in a variety of ways. In classic psychoanalytic theory, it is viewed as a superego response to one's own unacceptable impulses, often based on anxiety caused by childhood conflicts over such issues as abandonment and punishment by parents. This type of guilt generally is seen as causing psychological distress and problems with adjustment, and today it is not viewed as playing much of a role in moral behavior. In contrast, in developmental and social psychology, guilt often refers to regret over wrongdoing. For example, it has been defined as "an agitation-based emotion or painful feeling of regret that is aroused when the actor actually causes, anticipates causing, or is associated with an aversive event" (Ferguson & Stegge 1998:20). The guilty actor accepts responsibility for a behavior that violates internalized standards or causes another's distress and desires to make amends or punish the self (Ferguson & Stegge 1998, Hoffman 1998, Tangney 1991). It is this type of guilt that is most relevant to a discussion of moral emotion.

Shame often has been used as a synonym for guilt and has received much less theoretical attention in the past. More recently it has been defined as " . . . a dejection-based, passive, or helpless emotion aroused by self-related aversive events. The ashamed person focuses more on devaluing or condemning the entire *self,* experiences the self as fundamentally flawed, feels self-conscious about the visibility of one's actions, fears scorn, and thus avoids or hides from others" (Ferguson & Stegge 1998:20).

The topic of guilt, although important in psychoanalytic theory and in early discussions of socialization, was virtually ignored by social and developmental psychologists in the 1970s and 1980s (Baumeister et al 1994). However, in the 1990s, there has been a flurry of research on these self-conscious emotions.

Differences Between Guilt and Shame   Many researchers and theorists now agree that guilt and shame (at least as defined above) are two distinct emotions and that an important difference between them is in the degree of focus on the self (Lewis 1971, Tangney 1998). When a person experiences shame, the entire self feels exposed, inferior, and degraded. Adults report that shame experiences are more painful and intense than are guilt experiences and are associated with a preoccupation with others' opinions. In contrast, guilt generally is less painful and devastating than shame because, when one experiences guilt, the primary concern is with a particular behavior, somewhat distinct from the self (Ferguson et al 1991, Tangney 1998). Guilt involves feelings of tension, remorse, and regret, but does not affect one's core identity. Shame is associated with the desire to undo aspects of the self, whereas guilt is reported to involve the desire to undo aspects of behavior (Niedenthal et al 1994). Similarly, shame, but not guilt, is related to discrepancies between one's beliefs about the self and beliefs about what the self ought to be or what the ideal self would be (Tangney et al 1998).

It is important to note that guilt often has been operationalized as a response that involves concern about others' feelings and with reparation (e.g. Tangney 1991). It is likely that guilt that is less reparation oriented, based on irrational or illogical assessments of responsibility, or that is not resolved can affect feelings about the self over time and may have more maladaptive effects. Moreover, guilt and shame often co-occur; children may be especially prone to the combination (Ferguson et al 1999).

Guilt vs Shame: Links to Empathy and Moral Behavior   Based on adults' reports, shame and guilt both involve a sense of responsibility and the feeling that one has violated a moral standard (JP Tangney, D Marschall, K Rosenberg, DH Barlow & P Wagner, unpublished data). Moreover, both emotions can be responses to the same situations, and both can arise from concerns about the effects of one's behavior on others (Tangney 1992; JP Tangney, D Marschall, K Rosenberg, DH Barlow & P Wagner, unpublished data). Nonetheless, guilt appears to be the more moral emotion of the two. Shame, but not guilt, is likely to arise from nonmoral situations and issues (e.g. failure in performance situations or socially inappropriate behavior), and only shame seems to involve concern about others' evaluations (Ferguson et al 1991, Tangney 1992). Shamed people are relatively unlikely to try to rectify their transgression. Probably because guilt is focused more on the transgression than the self, guilt seems to motivate restitution, confession, and apologizing rather than avoidance (Tangney 1998; JP Tangney, D Marschall, K Rosenberg, DH Barlow & P Wagner, unpublished data). However, it should be kept in mind that, in much of this work, guilt has been defined as a reparative response, so these associations are not surprising.

Moreover, shame and guilt appear to be differentially related to empathy-related responding. Tangney (1991) found that guilt was associated with adults' self-reported, other-oriented empathic responsiveness, whereas shame was negatively associated, especially when controlling for guilt. Shame was especially associated with personal distress reactions (i.e. aversive, self-focused reactions to others in need or distress). When providing autobiographical accounts of shame and guilt experiences, people conveyed more empathy in guilt than in shame descriptions, although this association was somewhat stronger among adults than children (JP Tangney, D Marschall, K Barlow & DH Wagner, unpublished data). Nonetheless, because shame and guilt are substantially correlated and these analyses were part correlations controlling for one another, it is likely that the distinction between guilt and shame is not quite as clear cut as these findings suggest.

Guilt and Shame as Predictors of Externalizing Behavior   Tangney also has found that shame generally is more consistently and highly correlated than is guilt with externalizing problems, including aggression. Findings of this sort, if consistent, are important because problems with aggression are viewed as a component of antisocial behavior. When part correlations were used to assess relations of problem behavior with adults' guilt-free shame and shame-free guilt, shame still was consistently positively related to externalizing problems, whereas guilt generally was unrelated (Tangney et al 1992; also see Tangney et al 1996a). Similar results have been obtained for children in some studies (Ferguson et al 1997; JP Tangney, PE Wagner, SA Burggraf, R Gramzow & C Fletcher, unpublished data), although even shame-free guilt has been associated with externalizing problems for girls [but not for boys (Ferguson et al 1999)]. Among children, adolescents, and adults, guilt-free shame has been linked with direct, indirect, and displaced aggression, whereas shame-free guilt has been negatively related to these types of responding (Tangney et al 1996b).

Tangney's work has been conducted with nonclinical populations and usually has involved a measure of guilt in response to specific events (as assessed with brief vignettes). Moreover, in this work guilt was defined as an adaptive response such as taking responsibility or wanting to make reparations. It appears that dispositional guilt (or shame) that is more global, ruminative, and chronic and guilt assessed with a projective measure (as well as lack of guilt) are positively related to children's and adults' psychopathology, including externalizing problems (Ferguson et al 1996, 1999; Harder et al 1992; O'Connor et al 1999; Sorenson et al 1997). In addition, it appears that girls high in shame-free guilt sometimes may be prone to externalizing behavior, even when guilt is assessed by measures that tap concern with adhering to standards, expressing empathy, and taking appropriate responsibility (Ferguson et al 1999; Zahn-Waxler & Kochanska 1990). Ferguson et al (1999) suggested that the relation between guilt and externalizing problem behavior may hold because girls experience anger at being held to stricter standards of behavior than boys but also realize that failure to express guilt will reap negative consequences.

In discussing the differences in findings across measures, Tangney (1996) argued that her situational measure of guilt is the more valid way to assess the construct of guilt, especially shame-free guilt. Other measures of guilt often (*a*) rely on respondents' abilities to differentiate verbally between guilt and shame, (*b*) do not assess emotional reactions in specific contexts, and (*c*) likely tap a combination of guilt and shame. However, it is possible that guilt often is not as distinct from shame or as adaptive as operationalized in Tangney's work, especially in childhood. In any case, initial findings support the view that one gets different results with measures that focus on specific behaviors (and are unlikely to reflect ruminative guilt) and with measures of more global, chronic, and unresolved guilt (Eyre & Ferguson 1997, Ferguson & Stegge 1998, Quiles & Bybee 1997, Tangney et al 1995). It is quite possible that scenario measures of guilt in specific contexts—which are correlated with the personality trait of agreeableness in adulthood—tap empathy-based guilt, whereas other commonly used measures of guilt tap anxiety-based guilt (Einstein & Lanning 1998). Moreover, it is possible that there is a continuum of guilt proneness and that very low levels of guilt are related to externalizing problems, whereas very high levels of guilt are related to shame and irrational guilt.

The Relation of Guilt and Shame to Negative Emotionality and Regulation   It is likely that dispositional (personality or temperamental) characteristics of people play a role in the proclivities to experience guilt and shame. Because of the intrinsic role of emotion in these responses and the role of regulation in both managing emotion and in moral behavior, dispositional emotionality and regulation are likely correlates of the tendencies to experience guilt and shame.

In fact, guilt and shame have been linked to fear, hostility, anxiety, and sadness in adulthood (Forgas 1994, Harder et al 1992, O'Connor et al 1999, Watson & Clark 1992) and childhood (Zahn-Waxler & Robinson 1995). The degree to which shame and guilt are differentially related to negative emotion likely varies with the measure used. In some studies with adults (JP Tangney, D Marschall, K Rosenberg, DH Barlow & P Wagner, unpublished data) or toddlers (Zahn-Waxler & Robinson 1995), there were few differences in the patterns of relations for guilt and shame. In contrast, in another study with adults, shame and anxious guilt were positively correlated with negative emotionality (i.e. neuroticism on a measure of the "Big Five" personality factors), whereas situational guilt (which often may be based on empathy) was not (Einstein & Lanning 1998). Moreover, some researchers have found that guilt, especially situationally based guilt, is unrelated or weakly related to various negative emotions, especially when the effects of shame are controlled in the correlations, whereas shame is associated with anger and anxiety, even when guilt is controlled in the correlations (Tangney et al 1992, 1996a; JP Tangney, PE Wagner, SA Burggraf, R Gramzow & C Fletcher, unpublished data). Until situational guilt based on situational empathy is differentiated from chronic guilt, findings are likely to be inconsistent.

During the toddler and early-childhood years, the link between guilt or shame and other negative emotions appears to occur primarily in girls (Kochanska et al 1994), with the exception that fear has been related to guilt in male, but not female, toddlers (Zahn-Waxler & Robinson 1995). However, because mothers sometimes provided the data on children's guilt and emotionality, it is possible that the sex difference is based on something related to mothers' beliefs about girls' and boys' emotions. Although there is some evidence that females show shame more than do males, it is not clear that there are sex differences in guilt (Ferguson & Eyre 1999). Moreover, it is quite possible that displays of guilt in very young children actually reflect a combination of shame, guilt, and fear and that guilt in the very young has a different significance than does guilt in older children and adults (who better understand notions of responsibility and causality).

The relation of guilt and shame to individual differences in dispositional regulation seldom has been examined. Emotionally well-regulated children would be expected to manage their emotional arousal so that they are not overwhelmed by feelings of shame; moreover, behavioral regulation would be expected to underlie some markers of guilt such as reparation. Consistent with these expectations, Rothbart et al (1994) found that mothers' ratings of 7-year-olds' regulatory capacities (effortful control, including the abilities to voluntarily shift and focus attention and inhibit behavior) were positively correlated with mothers' reports of their children's guilt/shame (combined). In a study with 2- to 6-year-old children, regulatory capacities were associated with affective discomfort after wrongdoing, but only for girls (Kochanska et al 1994). Although, as is discussed below, measures of conscience often are associated with dispositional regulation, these measures do not necessarily tap guilt. Thus, although well-regulated children might be expected to experience relatively high levels of situationally and age-appropriate guilt, links between regulation and both guilt and shame have been insufficiently examined.

Summary In the 1990s, there has been an increase in research on guilt and shame, the difference between the two, their relation to morally relevant behaviors, and their socialization correlates. Findings often vary as a function of the index of guilt. Salient issues to be addressed include the meaning of various measures of guilt, gender differences in guilt and in the relation of guilt or shame to moral behavior, and the role of regulatory capacities in guilt vs shame. In addition, it is important to determine whether different negative emotions are differentially related to chronic vs empathy-based guilt or shame, for example, whether anxiety and anger are related more closely to shame than guilt.

Empathy-Related Responding

Empathy-related reactions can be other- or self-related or sometimes neither. Eisenberg and colleagues (e.g. Eisenberg et al 1994a) have defined empathy as an affective response that stems from the apprehension or comprehension of another's emotional state or condition and is similar to what the other person is feeling or would be expected to feel. If a child views a sad person and consequently feels sad (even though the child differentiates his or her own and the other person's emotional states or situations at a rudimentary level), that child is experiencing empathy.

In Eisenberg's view, pure empathy is not other-oriented. However, with further cognitive processing (assuming that the individual is old enough to differentiate between one's own and others' internal states), an empathic response usually turns into either sympathy, personal distress, or some combination (perhaps alternating) thereof. Sympathy is an emotional response stemming from the apprehension or comprehension of another's emotional state or condition, which is not the same as what the other person is feeling (or is expected to feel) but consists of feelings of sorrow or concern for the other. Thus, if a girl sees a sad peer and feels concern for the peer, she is experiencing sympathy. A sympathetic reaction often is based upon empathic sadness, although sympathy also may be based on cognitive perspective taking or encoded cognitive information relevant to another's situation accessed from memory. Personal distress is a self-focused, aversive, affective reaction to the apprehension of another's emotion (e.g. discomfort or anxiety), such as the distress of a person feeling anxious when viewing someone who is sad.

About two decades ago, Batson (1998) proposed that sympathy (which he has called empathy) is associated with other-oriented motivation, whereas personal distress is associated with the motive to alleviate one's own aversive affective state. Thus, sympathy is viewed as an other-oriented moral emotion fostering altruism. In contrast, personal distress is hypothesized to lead to prosocial behavior only when that is the easiest way to reduce one's own aversive emotional state (e.g. in a situation in which one cannot escape dealing with the person causing one's distress). Thus, sympathy is viewed as a moral emotion, whereas personal distress is believed to result in egoistically motivated behavior.

In the 1980s, there was considerable interest in why people sometimes help others at a cost to themselves and whether truly selfless altruism exists. These questions stimulated numerous empirical studies demonstrating a positive relation between sympathy and prosocial behavior and a negative relation—or sometimes a lack of a relation—between personal distress and prosocial behavior, both in adults (Batson 1998) and in children (Eisenberg & Fabes 1991, 1998). Work on this topic has continued into the 1990s. Another emerging issue in recent years has been the role of emotionality and regulation in empathy-related responding.

Empathy-Related Responding and Prosocial/Antisocial Behavior   Researchers have continued to demonstrate empirical relations between prosocial behavior and both situationally induced and dispositional empathy-related responding. In the social psychological literature, sympathy and personal distress generally have been elicited in laboratory situations and then examined in relation to prosocial behavior directed toward the target of that emotion. In general, the positive relation between sympathy and prosocial behavior has been replicated (Batson 1998, Batson et al 1997b, Trobst et al 1994). Among children, markers of empathy and sympathy in specific situations, such as their facial, behavioral, and physiological reactions to viewing others in need or distress, also have been associated with situational or dispositional prosocial behavior (Denham et al 1994; Fabes et al 1993; Hastings & Zahn-Waxler 1998; Holmgren et al 1998; Zahn-Waxler et al 1992, 1995). In addition, situational markers of personal distress generally have been negatively related or unrelated to children's prosocial behavior (e.g. Holmgren et al 1998, Fabes et al 1993, Miller et al 1996), although self-distress has been positively related to toddlers' prosocial behavior when the toddlers caused the other person's distress [so the self-distress may have reflected a rudimentary guilt reaction (Zahn-Waxler et al 1992)]. The diversity of methods used in various studies with children enhances one's confidence that the relation between situational sympathetic concern and prosocial behavior is real, albeit sometimes modest in magnitude.

In research with adults, investigators have demonstrated that sympathy may not only motivate moral behavior in specific contexts (Batson et al 1997b), but it may also cause enduring changes in an individual's concern about others' welfare (Batson et al 1995). For example, people who are induced to experience sympathy for a member of a stigmatized group actually develop more benign attitudes toward those individuals weeks later (Batson et al 1997a). However, sympathy, like egoism, also can undermine concern with the welfare of a group if an individual has to choose between allocating resources to the group or to someone with whom they were induced to sympathize (Batson et al 1999).

The central focus in much of the social psychological research on empathy is an issue that has been debated fiercely for two decades—whether prosocial behavior induced by empathy (or sympathy) is really motivated by altruism (a pure other-orientation) rather than egoism. The most recent challenge to the notion of true altruism is the argument that sympathy for another leads to a greater sense of self-other overlap, with the consequence that helping is not selfless but is directed toward both the other person and the self [i.e. to make oneself feel better (Cialdini et al 1997)]. Empirical data both for and against this argument have been published (Batson et al 1997b, Cialdini et al 1997), and the debate continues (Batson 1997, Neuberg et al 1997). In this literature, Cialdini et al (1997) assessed merging of self-other boundaries with a measure of "oneness" (i.e. adults' reports that they would use the term "we" to define their relationship with the target of sympathy and their selection of circles drawn close to each other to indicate the closeness of their relationship with the other person). However, it is possible that their measures of oneness reflect the awareness that they feel concern for the person or close to the person but not a merging of boundaries. It is difficult to imagine actual merging of boundaries when the study participants were responding to hypothetical situations.

Other researchers have been concerned with the relation of the dispositional tendency to experience sympathy and/or personal distress (rather than situationally induced empathy-related responding) to such prosocial behaviors as providing support, volunteering, or helping. In general, links between dispositional sympathy and prosocial behavior have been demonstrated, albeit to various degrees, in research with both adults (e.g. Carlo et al 1999, Penner & Finkelstein 1998, Trobst et al 1994) and children and adolescents (e.g. Carlo et al 1998; Eisenberg et al 1991c, 1995a; also see Estrada 1995, Roberts & Strayer 1996, Eisenberg & Fabes 1998). It is likely that sympathy is most closely linked to modes of prosocial behavior that are other-oriented, such as spontaneously emitted sharing behaviors in preschoolers (Eisenberg et al 1999c). In addition, dispositional sympathy and empathy have been associated with low levels of aggression and externalizing problems in adolescence (Carlo et al 1998, Cohen & Strayer 1996, Hastings & Zahn-Waxler 1998, Tremblay et al 1994).

Relations between sympathy/empathy (situational or dispositional) and prosocial behavior generally have been modest to moderate, and sometimes, when measures of the two constructs have not been obtained from the same reporter or in the same setting, they have been weak. Thus, an important issue is to identify factors that moderate the degree of this association. When predicting prosocial behavior, Miller et al (1996) found an interaction between level of moral judgment and situational sympathy such that children's helping of a distressed peer (shown in a videotape) was highest if children were high in both needs-oriented (rudimentary other-oriented) moral reasoning and in reported sympathy. Similarly, Knight et al (1994) found that the combination of high dispositional sympathy, high perspective taking, and the ability to understand units and the value of money predicted high helping of a peer in need (although sympathy alone also was associated with helping). Studies such as these support the need to identify dispositional and situational moderators of the strength of the relation between empathy-related responding and prosocial (or antisocial) behavior.

The Relation of Empathy-Related Responding to Emotionality and Regulation   The differing relations of personal distress and sympathy to prosocial behavior are consistent with the conclusion that the subjective experiences of sympathy and personal distress are different. Eisenberg et al (1994a) hypothesized that empathic overarousal in situations involving negative affect results in an aversive, overaroused emotional state, which leads to a focus on one's one needs and, consequently, personal distress (also see Hoffman's 1982 discussion of empathic overarousal). In support of this view, investigators have found that negative emotional arousal, especially for reflective affective states such as sadness (Green & Sedikides 1999), is associated with a focus on the self (Wood et al 1990) and that people exhibit higher physiological arousal and sometimes report more distress in situations likely to elicit person distress in contrast to sympathy (Eisenberg & Fabes 1991; Eisenberg et al 1991a,b).

Regulation   Conceptualizing sympathy and personal distress in the above manner led to the prediction that people who can regulate their emotions and emotion-related behavior should be relatively likely to experience sympathy rather than personal distress. Empirical findings in studies of adults have been somewhat consistent with this prediction. In several studies, various measures of behavioral and attentional regulation (e.g. attention shifting) have been negatively correlated with dispositional personal distress (Eisenberg et al 1994a, Eisenberg & Okun 1996, Okun et al 1999). Sometimes dispositional regulation has been positively related to adults' sympathy (Eisenberg & Okun 1996), although in two studies this relation was significant only when individual differences in negative emotionality were controlled (Eisenberg et al 1994a, Okun et al 1999). In a longitudinal study with children, adults' reports of children's dispositional regulation were positively related to teachers' or children's reports of children's dispositional sympathy, both in concurrent analyses and over time (Eisenberg et al 1996c, 1998; Murphy et al 1999). In addition, Rothbart and colleagues (1994) found that mothers' ratings of 7-year-old children's empathy were related to children's effortful control (an index of regulation), as rated by mothers. Thus, there appears to be a positive relation between regulation and sympathy/empathy, especially in childhood, and a consistent negative relation between personal distress and regulation in adulthood (also see Davies et al 1998).

Relations between situational measures of empathy-related responding and measures of dispositional regulation are considerably weaker than are analogous relations for dispositional empathy-related responding. In a study with adults, self-reported sympathy, sadness, and distress in response to empathy-inducing films all were negatively related to a self-report measure of emotion regulation. Facial reactions of sadness, distress, concern, and disgust to the empathy-inducing films were unrelated to measures of regulation, and men's heart rate acceleration during an evocative portion of the film (an index of personal distress) was negatively related to self-reported emotion regulation [but primarily for men exposed to the relatively evocative film (Eisenberg et al 1994a)]. Thus, the relations of measures of situational empathy-related responding to regulation varied with the specific measure and sex of the individual.

Somewhat more consistent relation between situational sympathy and dispositional regulation have been found for children. Ungerer et al (1990) found that 4-month-olds who were low in self-regulation were prone to personal distress at 12 months of age. In two studies with preschoolers or school-aged children, positive relations were found between markers of sympathy (heart rate, facial, or self-reported) or empathic facial sadness and adults' ratings of children's attentional and/or behavioral regulation (Eisenberg & Fabes 1995, Guthrie et al 1997). However, findings sometimes were obtained for only one sex, and often they were weak. Thus, although situational measures of empathy-related responding tend to be associated with regulation, especially for children, the findings are complex and relatively modest in magnitude. Given that empathic responding in any particular context may not be a reliable index of general empathy-related dispositions, it is not really surprising that the relations between situational measures of empathy-related responding and regulation are relatively small.

Cardiac vagal tone, which is substantially correlated with heart rate variance, is considered to be an index of physiological emotion regulation and is believed to promote calm and prosocial behavior [because of its inhibitory effect on sympathetic pathways to the heart (Porges 1997)]. Relations of these measures to children's empathy-related responding have been inconsistent. Some researchers have found that high vagal tone is negatively associated with indices of sympathy and prosocial behavior (Zahn-Waxler et al 1995); others have found positive (Fabes et al 1993), mixed (Eisenberg et al 1996c), or no (Eisenberg et al 1998) relations. The sample for which negative relations were found was selected to include children at risk for externalizing problems, and the relation of vagal tone or heart rate variance [both of which are correlated with lack of behavioral inhibition for boys (Kagan 1998)] to empathy-related responding may vary with characteristics of the sample, as well as sex (Eisenberg et al 1996c, Fabes et al 1993).

Emotionality   Because people prone to experience negative emotions would be expected to be susceptible to vicariously induced emotion, Eisenberg & Fabes (1992) and Eisenberg et al (1999a) hypothesized that people prone to intense emotions (especially emotions such as sadness or distress rather than anger) are prone to both sympathy and personal distress. In addition, because people who are content may be less preoccupied with their own needs and better able to respond to the needs of others, sympathy is hypothesized to be associated with positive emotionality. In general, adults' reports of dispositional sympathy and personal distress, as well as empathy, have been positively related to intensity and frequency of negative emotions (Davies et al 1998, Davis 1994, Eisenberg et al 1994a, Eisenberg & Okun 1996, Okun et al 1999). Moreover, adults' self-reports of sympathy, empathic sadness, and personal distress to an empathy-inducing film (the latter of which may have reflected sympathy to some degree), as well as their facial reactions and heart rate (for men), generally have been positively correlated with intensity of self-reported dispositional emotionality and sadness, but not frequency of negative emotionality (Eisenberg et al 1994a). In addition, positive emotional intensity has been positively associated with sympathy and unrelated or negatively related to personal distress (Eisenberg et al 1994a).

Findings for children differ from those for adults and vary with the measure of empathy-related responding (i.e. empathy or sympathy) and emotion. Rothbart et al (1994) found that mothers' ratings of 7-year-olds' dispositional empathy (rather than sympathy) were uncorrelated with anger/frustration in infancy but positively related to high fearfulness. Empathy was positively related to negative emotionality (especially sadness) at age 7 when other aspects of temperament (including regulation) were controlled in the analysis. Anger at age 7 was negatively related to empathy when regulation was controlled.

In a longitudinal study of children's *dispositional* sympathy, Eisenberg and colleagues (Eisenberg et al 1996c, 1998; Murphy et al 1999) found that parents' and teachers' reports of school children's intense and frequent negative emotions tended to be negatively correlated with (or unrelated to) children's dispositional sympathy (as reported by teachers and sometimes the children). It is likely that the adults' reports of negative emotionality often reflected problematic negative emotions such as anger or anxiety that might undermine sympathy over time. In the same study, boys' physiological arousal (heart rate and skin conductance) when exposed to a relatively distressing film clip was related to low dispositional sympathy. Thus, boys prone to physiological overarousal appeared to be low in dispositional sympathy (Eisenberg et al 1996c; also see Strayer 1993).

Findings for *situational* measures of empathy/sympathy in children suggest an association between empathy-related responding and both positive and negative emotionality. In a study of toddlers, children who sustained a high level of empathy and concern in response to simulated distress incidents (the measure appeared to tap empathy, sympathy, and/or prosocial behavior) from 14 to 20 months of age were observed to express more negative emotion and reported to express more positive emotion at 14 months of age than did those who dropped in empathy/sympathy. Those who increased in empathy/sympathy expressed more positive emotions than those who remained low in empathy (Robinson et al 1994).

In studies of preschool or school-aged children, situational sympathy has been negatively related to adults' reports of children's negative emotionality, whereas facial expressions or self-reports of children's situationally induced empathic sadness have been associated with adults' reports of children's emotional intensity in general or intensity of negative emotions (Eisenberg & Fabes 1995, Guthrie et al 1997). Children's situational personal distress responses sometimes have been positively correlated with negative emotionality (Guthrie et al 1997). Thus, it appears that situational empathic distress and sadness tend to be positively related with negative emotionality and emotional intensity in childhood (also see Roberts & Strayer 1996), whereas situational measures of sympathy are related to low negative emotionality, at least as rated by adults. It is likely that markers of situational sympathy have been negatively related to negative emotionality because the latter reflected adults' perceptions of nonconstructive negative emotions (e.g. anger or anxiety) and sympathetic children are too regulated to express high levels of such emotion.

In brief, there is some evidence that sympathy is positively related to intensity of dispositional emotional responding and some kinds of negative emotions (sadness), especially among adults (who generally provide self-report data). This does not mean that people who respond with sympathy necessarily react intensely to empathy-inducing stimuli; as was discussed above, there is evidence that sympathetic individuals are relatively well regulated. Moreover, reports of frequent negative emotionality tend to be associated with low levels of sympathy. Dispositional personal distress and empathy have been positively related to negative emotional intensity and/or frequency of negative emotionality. It is likely that empathy, personal distress, and sympathy relate somewhat differently to negative emotionality and that it is important to differentiate among different types of negative emotions (e.g. anger and sadness) and intensity vs frequency of negative emotionality when examining these relations.

Interaction of Emotional Intensity and Regulation   Eisenberg & Fabes (1992) hypothesized that emotional intensity in general (i.e. with valence of emotion unspecified) or for negative emotions such as sadness would be moderately associated with sympathy, although optimally regulated people were expected to be somewhat sympathetic regardless of level of emotional intensity. If people can modulate their emotions as needed, their dispositional emotionality should not be an important contributor to empathy-related responding. In contrast, people high in intensity of negative emotions would be expected to be prone to personal distress if they lack the ability to regulate themselves because they will become overwhelmed by their vicariously induced negative feelings.

These predictions have been tested in moderational analyses. Although these predictions have not been supported in studies of adults (Eisenberg et al 1994a, Okun et al 1999), they have received some empirical support in research with children. When participants in a longitudinal study were age 6–8, there was an interaction between general emotional intensity and regulation when predicting teacher-reported sympathy in children. Unregulated children were low in sympathy regardless of their general emotional intensity; such children were likely to be overwhelmed by their vicarious emotion when it was experienced. In contrast, for children who were moderate or relatively high in their regulation, sympathy increased with the level of general emotional intensity. Thus, children who were likely to be emotionally intense were sympathetic if they were at least moderately regulated.

Two years later, children's sympathy was predicted by a similar interaction between behavioral regulation and general emotional intensity, but only for boys. In addition, at this age, attention focusing was associated with sympathy for children who were relatively low in emotional intensity. For children who are not predisposed to experience intense emotions, the ability to focus on events outside themselves may enhance sympathy by facilitating the intake of information about others and, consequently, cognitive perspective taking (Eisenberg et al 1998).

Summary   Research on empathy-related responding has remained a focus in the study of prosocial behavior. Although it is clear that sympathy is associated with prosocial behavior whereas personal distress reactions tend to be negatively or unrelated to prosocial action, there still is debate regarding the nature of sympathetic motivation. Another focus of interest has been the relation of empathy-related responding to emotionality and regulation, especially dispositional differences in these aspects of temperament or personality. The emerging body of research indicates that negative emotionality is related to empathy-related responding, but that relations vary with the type of empathy-related response and with the dimension (intensity or frequency) and type of negative emotion. More work on the ways that individual differences in emotionality and regulation interact in predicting empathy-related responding will be necessary to understand the role of emotion and its regulation in empathy-related responding.

The Development of Guilt, Shame, and Empathy

There has been some disagreement about the age at which guilt emerges (and relatively little discussion about the emergence of shame). M Lewis (1998) has argued that shame and guilt emerge at about age three, once children (*a*) can clearly recognize the self as different from other people, (*b*) have developed some standards of behavior, and (*c*) are able to use these standards to evaluate their own behavior. Others (e.g. Barrett 1998) have suggested that the precursors of guilt or shame are observed during the second and third years of life. Hoffman (1998) described a developmental sequence in which prosocial actions and reparative behaviors (which often are viewed as evidence of guilt) both emerge from early empathic capacities. Based on his theory, in the second year of life, as children increasingly develop the ability to differentiate between their own and others' internal states, they are capable of becoming empathically involved in others' distress. In Hoffman's view, young children initially respond to others' distress with self-oriented distress, but they are increasingly able in the early years to respond with other-oriented sympathetic concern. Empathy for a victim, combined with an awareness that one has caused another's distress, is believed to result in guilt, which motivates attempts at reparative behavior. Moreover, empathy or sympathy often motivates prosocial actions, even if the child did not cause another's distress or needy condition.

Consistent with the hypothesizing of Barrett and Hoffman, there is evidence that 2-year-olds have some awareness of right and wrong and that they engage in reparative behaviors (see Barrett 1995). Children 34 months old have some understanding of the difference between moral and social conventional transgressions (Smetana & Braeges 1990). Empathic responding is observed in the second year of life (Zahn-Waxler et al 1979, 1992), and children 2 to 3 years old frequently show emotional reactions indicative of empathy and engage in reparative behavior in response to mishaps (Cole et al 1992). Moreover, parents report that guilt increases from 14 to 24 months of age (Zahn-Waxler & Robinson 1995), that remorse increases from 14–18 to 30–40 months (Stipek et al 1990), and that discomfort about wrongdoing, apologizing, compliance with standards of conduct, and concern about others' wrongdoing increase from 21–33 months to 34–46 months (Kochanska et al 1994). Thus, it appears that precursors or rudimentary forms of guilt are evident before age three and that guilt increases with age in the early years. Empathy continues to increase with age in childhood (see Eisenberg & Fabes 1998), but it is unclear whether these age-related changes are reflected in developmental changes in guilt past the early years.

There also is evidence of a difference between shame and guilt responses in 2-year-olds. Barrett and colleagues (1993) observed toddlers' reactions when they were playing alone with an experimenter's rag doll and a leg fell off. Some toddlers (avoiders) displayed a shame-relevant pattern; they avoided the experimenter and delayed telling the experimenter about the mishap. Other children (amenders) showed a guilt-relevant pattern of behavior. They repaired the doll quickly, told the experimenter about the mishap shortly after the experimenter returned, and showed relatively little avoidance of the experimenter (e.g. gaze avoidance or active avoidance). The parents of amenders reported that their toddlers showed more guilt relative to shame at home than did parents of avoiders.

As might be expected, the development of conscience is associated with moral behavior. For example, Kochanska et al (1994) found that children 26–41 months old who exhibited evidence of a conscience (i.e. were reported by mothers to feel affective discomfort over transgressions and to display evidence of spontaneous reparation, confession, attempts to regulate their behavior, and concern over others' wrongdoing) transgressed less than their peers in an experimental context. Moreover, during contrived mishaps, these children's violations of standards were associated with behavioral and affective responses indicative of guilt [e.g. acceptance of responsibility, apologies, focus on reparation, and distress (Kochanska et al 1995)]. This association between evidence of conscience and moral behavior also has been found in studies with preschoolers and elementary school children (e.g. Lake et al 1995).

The Socialization of Guilt, Shame, and Empathy

Recently there has been a small burst of activity in assessing parental practices and parenting styles associated with children's guilt or conscience. In early work on guilt, children's guilt was linked to parental use of inductive-reasoning techniques [i.e. reasoning with the child about his/her behavior, e.g. "You made Doug cry. It's not nice to bite" (Zahn-Waxler et al 1979)] and relatively low power assertion [e.g. use of punishment or threats thereof (Hoffman 1977)]. Parental use of induction is believed to foster sympathy, an other-orientation, and optimal levels of attention to and learning about parental expectations and the reasons for behaving in a moral manner (Hoffman 1983), especially if inductions are delivered with emotion and are used by loving parents (Hoffman 1977). Recently researchers have replicated the findings pertaining to power assertion and inductions (Ferguson & Stegge 1995, Kochanska et al 1996b, Krevans & Gibbs 1996). For example, Krevans & Gibbs (1996) found that children tended to be high on empathy/sympathy and on the combination of empathy and guilt—which is likely to reflect other-oriented, empathy-based guilt—when their parents used relatively high amounts of inductive discipline. Moreover, it was found (DJ Laible & RA Thompson, submitted for publication) that mothers' references to feelings, needs, or intentions and moral evaluative statements (e.g. "good boy;" "this was a nice thing to do") during conversations with their 4-year-olds were associated with mothers' reports of children's guilt, remorse, and related reactions to a transgression or mishap, as well as with internalized compliance.

Findings concerning the relation of empathy and guilt to love withdrawal are somewhat less consistent, both in the past (Hoffman 1983) and in recent work. For example, Krevans & Gibbs (1996) found no relation between empathy/sympathy (combined) or guilt and parental use of love withdrawal as discipline, whereas Ferguson & Stegge (1995) found that love withdrawal was associated with high loadings in a canonical correlation on both guilt and shame reactions. It is likely that Ferguson & Stegge's index of guilt reflected the general tendency to evaluate oneself rather than empathy-based guilt. Moreover, these researchers found that guilt, controlling for shame, was associated with the presence of parental anger in negative situations and parental pride reactions in positive encounters.

Kochanska and colleagues demonstrated that the relation between parental socialization and the development of conscience often is moderated by characteristics of the child. They typically have operationalized conscience as some combination of guilt-related affect, an orientation toward reparation, and internalized compliance (which conceptually is less clearly linked to guilt). Kochanska (1991) found that 8- to 10-year-olds' affective/moral orientation (reflecting, in part, their report of empathy and guilt when completing vignettes about transgressions) and children's concern with reparation were positively related to maternal behavior deemphasizing the use of power assertion (based on both self-reports and observed maternal behavior) when the children were toddlers. However, these relations held primarily for children with a fearful/anxious temperament (Kochanska 1991). This finding was replicated in another sample at two ages (Kochanska 1995, 1997). Kochanska (1995) argued that, for fearful/anxious children, gentle maternal discipline deemphasizing power results in an optimal, moderate level of anxious arousal. A moderate level of arousal during disciplinary encounters is viewed as motivating and optimal for the processing of information and not so overwhelming that the child cannot attend to the information provided in the disciplinary encounter (Hoffman 1983).

Investigators also have found an association between mutual positive affect or a secure attachment between mother and child and children's conscience or guilt (Kochanska & Aksan 1995; DJ Labile & RA Thompson, submitted for publication) and empathy or sympathy (Kestenbaum et al 1989, Waters et al 1986; see Eisenberg & Fabes 1998). This pattern of findings is consistent with the view that a mutual interpersonal orientation between parent and child enhances the socialization process. However, a positive cooperative interactive set, as reflected in a secure attachment between parent and child and maternal responsiveness, seems to be especially important for the development of guilt in relatively fearless children (Kochanska 1995, 1997), a finding consistent with the notion that children's temperament moderates the association between parental socialization-related behaviors and the development of conscience.

Moreover, the development of sympathy in children has been associated with (a) parents being high in sympathy, (b) parents allowing their children to express negative emotions that do not harm others, (c) low levels of hostile emotion in the home, (d) parental practices that help children to cope with negative emotions, and (e) parental practices that help children to focus on and understand others' emotions (Eisenberg et al 1991a, 1992; Fabes et al 1994; see Eisenberg & Fabes 1998). It is unclear whether parental practices that are supportive and help children to understand and deal with their emotions also foster empathy-based guilt past the early years of life.

Although researchers seldom have differentiated between shame and guilt in research on parental socialization, relatively recent findings suggest that the two may be differentially related to parental socialization practices. Ferguson & Stegge (1995) found that shame (when guilt was low) was predicted by high parental anger and the absence of any discipline, including the absence of parental induction, love withdrawal, and power assertion. Shame also was associated with parents' not responding positively to appropriate behavior. The combination of shame and guilt was predicted by an array of socialization responses by parents (especially induction, but also including love withdrawal and, to a lesser extent, power assertion). In contrast, in a study of children's parenting experiences at age 5 and self-criticism at age 12, Koestner et al (1991) found that reports by 12-year-olds of feeling "guilty," of perceived incompetence, and of not living up to their own standards were associated with same-sex parents' restrictiveness and rejection at age 5. Given the focus on chronic and global deficiencies of the self in the measure of self-criticism, it is likely that these authors tapped shame as much as guilt and that there is a positive relation between the development of shame in children and parental anger, rejection, or the lack of appropriate discipline.

Other work suggests that chronic and unjustified guilt can develop in children, especially girls, in families with depressed mothers. For example, Zahn-Waxler et al (1990) found that 5- to 9-year-old children of depressed mothers expressed aberrant, distorted, and unresolved themes when responding to a semiprojective procedure involving vignettes developed to elicit children's narratives about inter-personal conflict and distress. Guilt responses are likely to be fused with shame and may represent misplaced assignment of responsibility to the self when children's guilt is assessed with responses to vignettes about negative events in which the child is not unambiguously responsible (Ferguson et al 1999). Misplaced responsibility may be based on a merging of guilt and empathy in young children, especially daughters of depressed mothers, which makes them particularly vulnerable to false beliefs about their responsibility and blameworthiness for others' problems (Zahn-Waxler & Robinson 1995). Depressed mothers, in comparison with well mothers, experience more guilt and irritability in their relationships with their young children, so their children frequently are exposed to these emotions. Moreover, repeated exposure to a sad caregiver may increase the likelihood that children will feel responsible for negative events simply because they are there. In addition, depressed mothers may model a negative attributional style ("it's my fault"), and their children may experience more love withdrawal when their mothers become less involved and emotionally unavailable because of their depression (Zahn-Waxler & Kochanska 1990). However, there is little research in which the reasons for guilt in children of depressed mothers have been tested directly.

RELATIONS OF NONMORAL EMOTIONS TO MORALLY RELEVANT BEHAVIOR

In recent research, a variety of primary, nonmoral emotions such as happiness, sadness, and anger have been examined as predictors or correlates of moral behavior. Some of this research has pertained to situationally induced emotion, whereas other research concerns dispositional emotion.

Mood

In the 1970s and 1980s, a popular topic of research was the relation between temporary mood states (often experimentally induced) and such morally relevant behavior as prosocial behavior and aggression. In this work, the focus was on the typical effects of mood (across individuals) rather than on individual differences in the effects of mood. Researchers found that positive mood is consistently related to enhanced prosocial behavior and that a variety of mechanisms might explain this association (Carlson et al 1988). In addition, in a meta-analytic review, Carlson & Miller (1987) found an association between negative emotion and helping, which varied with the degree to which attention was focused on the self vs others, with helpers' feelings of responsibility for the mood-lowering event, and with a high level of objective self-awareness (i.e. the focusing of attention on the self as an object).

In recent work, researchers' focus has been primarily on the processes that underlie the effects of positive and negative mood (e.g. Forgas 1995). For example, Wegener & Petty (1994) found that people in positive moods, in comparison with those in sad or neutral states, tend to choose activities based on their affective (hedonic) consequences for the self. This research has direct implications for the type of helping behaviors people will engage in and their motives for assisting in a positive mood. For example, such findings support the view that people in positive moods often help to maintain their positive mood (see Carlson et al 1988). Moreover, it appears that when adults experience negative emotional states elicited by threatening stimuli (aversive slides such as mutilation, starvation, a plane crash, or a battered woman) or events (stress of impending exams), they make decisions based on short-term outcomes regardless of possible long-term consequences. These findings can be interpreted as indicating that threat-related negative emotional states undermine the quality of cognitive processing and, as a consequence, regulatory capacities (Gray 1999). Given the relation of regulation to moral behavior (which is discussed shortly), negative moods owing to threatening stimuli likely predict impaired moral functioning.

Some recent work pertaining to temporary mood states and moral behavior or cognition relates to feelings associated with perceived injustice. Anger and other negative emotions (e.g. disgust and sadness) tend to be substantially linked with the perception of injustice and immorality (Mikula et al 1998, Scher 1997). Although appraisals of injustice often may elicit anger reactions, it also has been argued that the experience of justice-related negative emotions such as guilt or anger frequently leads to consideration of justice issues (Scher & Heise 1993; also see Hoffman 1998, on empathic anger).

Situationally induced, directly experienced anger also has been associated with morally relevant behavior and cognition. As is discussed below, situational and trait anger predict externalizing problems (e.g. aggression). In addition, priming anger increases adults' punitive attributions and judgments of others in fictional tort cases (Lerner et al 1998). People induced to feel anger also are likely to attribute responsibility or blame to others (Dix et al 1990, Keltner et al 1993), which could increase the probability of aggressive behavior.

Thus, it is clear that temporary mood has some effect on a range of morally relevant aspects of functioning. However, the role of mood in morally relevant behavior has not received as much attention in the previous decade.

Individual Differences in Emotionality and Regulation

Emotionality   Recently investigators interested in morality and emotion, especially developmentalists, have focused more on the role of individual differences in emotionality in morality than on the effects of situational moods. Much of the recent relevant work on the topic has pertained to aggression and externalizing behavior. In general, children prone to intense and frequent negative emotions (usually operationalized as a mix of different negative emotions such as dysphoria, anger, and anxiety) tend to exhibit relatively high levels of aggression and externalizing problems (e.g. bullying, stealing, and lying) (Eisenberg et al 1996a, Stice & Gonzales 1998). An association between temperamental negative emotionality and externalizing problems has been found across time and reporters (Eisenberg et al 1995b, 1997a, 1999b), as well as when uncontaminated measures of the constructs have been used [i.e. when overlapping items were removed (Lengua et al 1998)]. Moreover, children prone to intense negative emotions tend to deal nonconstructively with their anger (Eisenberg et al 1994b), and those prone to intense externalizing and internalizing emotions (combined) may be low in prosocial behavior (Eisenberg et al 1996b; see Eisenberg & Fabes 1998 for a review). In addition, individual differences in intensity and frequency of negative emotionality predict adolescent substance abuse/use, which sometimes is considered an externalizing behavior (Chassin et al 1993, Cooper et al 1995; cf. Stice & Gonzales 1998).

Anger/frustration appears to be especially linked to externalizing problems. Anger proneness in infancy as rated by mothers (Goldsmith 1996) or observed in the laboratory (Rothbart et al 1994) has predicted aggression in the preschool or early school years. Individual differences in typical intensity of anger reactions have been related to the degree to which young children's reactions to anger are constructive (Eisenberg et al 1994b). Moreover, self-reported anger among high school seniors predicted delinquency 9 months later, even controlling for earlier levels of delinquency (Colder & Stice 1998). In another study, incarcerated juvenile offenders' dispositional anger predicted aggressive behavior over the subsequent 3 months (Cornell et al 1999; also see Carlo et al 1998). In adulthood, frustration in the workplace has been linked to antisocial behavior (Spector 1997). Moreover, in situations involving provocation or harm, self-reported individual differences in feelings of anger are associated with adults' blaming others (Quigley & Tedeschi 1996) and have been found to mediate between attributions of intentionality and nonconstructive aggression reactions to the provocateur (Graham et al 1997, 1992).

Some types of emotional and physiological reactivity may buffer children from externalizing problems. Elevated levels of cortisol responding in novel settings are, if associated at all, negatively related to externalizing problems in children (Stansbury & Gunnar 1994). Cortisol reactions in these situations likely reflect an emotional response to stress. Moreover, children and adolescents who are high in their baseline physiological responding tend to be relatively low in delinquency and other measures of externalizing problems (Mezzacappa et al 1997, Pine et al 1998, Raine 1993). In addition, children prone to internalizing emotions such as fear are prone to low levels of aggression (e.g. Ladd & Profilet 1996, Rothbart et al 1994) and are easily socialized on measures of conscience (e.g. Kochanska 1997). Thus, negative emotions such as fear or anxiety may serve to inhibit externalizing behavior, perhaps because individuals prone to these emotions are less likely to find the stimulation and emotion associated with externalizing behavior pleasurable and are likely to experience more negative emotion (anxiety, guilt, and perhaps empathy) than other people when they engage in inappropriate behavior. Indeed, the tendency to be unemotional sometimes has been linked to antisocial behavior. For example, although children with psychopathic traits may be prone to anger, they also are characterized as low in guilt and empathy, as callous, and as shallow in their emotional responding (Frick 1998).

Regulation   Attention to temperamental/personality regulation and its correlates has increased substantially in recent years. Most measures of regulation pertain to the control of overt (often emotionally induced) behaviors; others tap the regulation of attention or cognitions related to emotion or stress (see Eisenberg et al 1999a). Attentional modes of regulation are believed to be heavily involved in the process of modulating emotional arousal, whereas capabilities such as the ability to inhibit and activate behavior are believed to be particularly important for modulating and regulating the behavioral expression of emotion.

An emerging body of work supports the assumption that individual differences in regulatory behavior play a role in morally relevant behavior, as well as in social competence more generally. In childhood, behavioral regulation has been associated with low externalizing problem behavior in numerous studies, sometimes even when information about regulation and outcome variables was obtained from different sources and when behavioral measures of regulation were obtained [e.g. persistence on a task or delay of gratification (Eisenberg et al 1996a; Huey & Weisz 1997; Krueger et al 1996; Lynam 1997; Oosterlaan & Sergeant 1996, 1998)]. In infancy and early childhood, the ability to inhibit and control one's behavior has repeatedly been associated with a range of measures of conscience and committed (internalized) compliance (e.g. following commands wholeheartedly, making reparation, cheating, and resistance to temptation), concurrently and over time (Kochanska et al 1996a, 1997, 1998; Stifter et al 1999). Behavioral regulation (including low impulsivity) also has been linked to low levels of adolescents' substance abuse (e.g. Block et al 1988, Colder & Chassin 1997). In adulthood, disinhibition, which involves impulsivity and low behavioral control, is associated with antisocial behavior, antisocial personality problems, and substance abuse (e.g. Clark & Watson 1999). Thus, temperamental or personality traits such as impulsivity and voluntary behavioral inhibition appear to be intimately related to the development of conscience and antisocial behavior.

The ability to regulate attentional processes also seems to play an important role in the development and enactment of morally relevant behavior. Attentional regulation has been associated with high social competence and prosocial behavior (Eisenberg et al 1993, 1999a, 1997b; Ladd & Profilet 1996) and with low problem behavior (Eisenberg et al 1996a, Ladd & Profilet 1996), as have composites of behavioral and attentional regulation (Eisenberg et al 1995b, Rothbart et al 1994; also see Fabes et al 1997). Problems in attentional regulation, as tapped by measures of executive cognitive functioning, have been linked to conduct disorders (Moffitt 1993) and psychopathy (O'Brien & Frick 1996, Patterson & Newman 1993). Concentration problems in childhood also have been associated with lower-level moral judgment in adolescence (Hart et al 1998).

Recently several groups of researchers identified personality types that reflect undercontrolled, overcontrolled, and optimal styles of functioning in children from Iceland (Hart et al 1997), the United States (Robins et al 1996), and New Zealand (Newman et al 1997). In general, the well-adjusted (optimal) children were resilient, self-assured, not emotionally labile, and in two samples (Hart et al 1997, Newman et al 1997), attentionally and/or behaviorally regulated. Of most relevance, the adjusted children were not prone to externalizing problems (Hart et al 1997, Newman et al 1997). However, undercontrolled individuals, who tended to be low in regulation and sometimes irritable and impulsive, were prone to externalizing problem behaviors concurrently or later in adolescence or adulthood. In these three studies, the items used to classify children into the three personality groups included ratings of a wide variety of social behaviors and/or items pertaining to both regulation and emotionality. Thus, the investigators did not examine individual differences in regulation and emotionality separate from each other, from their social consequences, or from other temperamental or personality characteristics. Nonetheless, their findings converge with other research in demonstrating an association between regulation and morally relevant behaviors.

Prediction of Morally Relevant Behavior from the Combination of Emotionality and Regulation   The combination of negative emotionality and low regulation may be especially problematic in regard to externalizing problems. In two major longitudinal studies, researchers have used composite measures of combined negative emotionality and low regulation/impulsivity to predict externalizing problems over time. In the Dunedin, New Zealand, longitudinal sample, emotional lability and negative emotionality at age three, when combined with lack of regulation (e.g. a short attention span and restlessness), predicted aggressive behavior problems, criminality and conduct disorders, and antisocial behavior (but not socialized delinquency) in adolescence (Caspi et al 1995) and antisocial behavior (Newman et al 1997), criminality (Henry et al 1996), and antisocial personality (Caspi et al 1996) in adulthood. For example, children identified as undercontrolled (i.e. emotionally labile, restless, with short attention spans, and high in approach and negativism) at age 3 were 2.9 times as likely as adults to be diagnosed with antisocial personality disorder, 2.2 times as likely to be recidivistic offenders, and 4.5 times as timely to be convicted for a violent offense (Caspi et al 1996). Similarly, Pulkkinen (1996) and Pulkkinen & Hamalainen (1995) assessed low self-control in childhood by using a measure that appeared to tap emotionality as well as low regulation. Scores on low self-control tended to predict proactive aggression (aggression without provocation) in adolescence (particularly for boys) and criminal offenses in adulthood.

Often individual differences in emotionality and regulation predict unique, additive variance in externalizing problem behavior, even though emotionality and regulation obviously are correlated (Derryberry & Rothbart 1988, Eisenberg et al 1993). For example, Eisenberg et al (1996a) found that both low regulation and high negative emotionality provided significant, unique prediction of externalizing problem behavior (also see Eisenberg et al 1995b, 1997a). Rothbart and colleagues (1994) obtained less evidence of additive effects, but they controlled another aspect of temperament (surgency) in the regressions they used to assess the unique effects of emotionality and regulation on aggression and defiant behavior (also see Lengua et al 1998).

In addition to main effects, both Rothbart & Bates (1998) and Eisenberg & Fabes (1992) have emphasized the importance of examining moderational relations when assessing the prediction of adjustment from such aspects of temperament/personality as emotionality and regulation. Eisenberg and colleagues (1999a) argued that emotionality, particularly negative emotionality, might have fewer negative implications for behavior if the individual is well regulated.

Some research is consistent with this view, despite the difficulty of obtaining interaction effects in small or moderately sized samples. For example, Eisenberg et al (1996a) found that children who were low in negative emotionality (frequency and intensity) were low in externalizing problem behavior, regardless of their level of regulation (attentional and behavioral regulation combined). However, for children who were more prone to negative emotion, higher regulation often predicted less externalizing problems, sometimes even across reporters (i.e. when reports of emotionality/regulation and externalizing behavior were obtained from different adults). Similarly, Colder & Stice (1998) found that anger was related to concurrent delinquency at higher but not lower levels of impulsivity (although the relation was marginally significant even at lower levels of impulsivity). However, this interaction was not significant when predicting adolescents' delinquency 9 months later. In addition, somewhat similar interactions have been obtained for both socially competent (Eisenberg et al 1995b) and prosocial behavior (Eisenberg et al 1996b) in other samples, although not in small samples for which the power to detect interaction effects was quite low (Eisenberg et al 1997a). Furthermore, there is some evidence, albeit not entirely consistent, that emotionality and regulation sometimes interact when predicting substance abuse problems in adolescence (Colder & Chassin 1997, Colder & Stice 1998; see Eisenberg et al 1999a, for a review).

Few researchers have used longitudinal designs and statistics that optimize the investigator's ability to make inferences about causality from correlational data. In a follow-up of the longitudinal sample of Eisenberg et al (1996b), similar moderational relations were found 2 years later with structural equation modeling. At two ages, negative emotionality moderated the relation of attentional regulation to children's externalizing problems. The relation of attentional regulation to low externalizing problems was stronger for children who were low rather than high in regulation. Findings for behavioral regulation were in the same direction, but the moderating effect was weak and nonsignificant in the best structural equation model (so behavioral regulation predicted low externalizing behavior for all children). Of particular interest, the aforementioned pattern of relations in children in grades 3 to 6 held even when the effects of externalizing behavior from 2 years earlier were taken into consideration. Thus, consistency over time in externalizing problems did not account for the relation between emotionality/regulation and externalizing problems at the 2-year follow-up (Eisenberg et al 1999b).

Thus, it appears that behaviors of moral relevance are predicted not only by regulation or emotionality (especially negative emotionality) in isolation, but also by the combination of the two. Findings such as these suggest that individual differences both in the tendency to experience negative emotions and in the ability to modulate emotional arousal should be considered when theorizing about and predicting moral development and behavior.

SUMMARY

Recent research highlights the importance of emotionality and emotion-related regulation in the study of moral development and behavior. Currently, relevant work is scattered throughout different bodies of literature and generally has not been integrated. As the construct of emotion continues to permeate psychological theory and research, knowledge about the role of emotion and its regulation in morality is likely to increase. Moreover, empirical work in the field is starting to move from attention to mere correlation to concern about moderating influences, mediational processes, and the direction of causality between morally relevant variables and emotionality and regulation. An important problem with the existing literature is the confounding of measures in the research (i.e. overlap of items measuring the various constructs), and this issue also is beginning to receive attention (e.g. Lengua et al 1998, Sanson et al 1990). Thus, it is likely that research on the contributions of emotionality and regulation to moral development and behavior will be conceptually and methodologically stronger in the next decade and will be increasingly integrated with our developing knowledge of the role of emotion in human functioning.

ACKNOWLEDGMENTS

The writing of this chapter was supported by a Research Scientist Award (K05 M801321) and a grant (1 R01 HH55052) from the National Institutes of Mental Health.

Visit the Annual Reviews home page at www.AnnualReviews.org.

LITERATURE CITED

Barrett KC. 1995. A functionalist approach to shame and guilt. In *Self-Conscious Emotions,* ed. JP Tangney, KW Fischer, pp. 25–63. New York: Guilford

Barrett KC. 1998. The origins of guilt in early childhood. In *Guilt and Children,* ed. J Bybee, pp. 75–90. San Diego: Academic

Barrett KC, Zahn-Waxler C, Cole PM. 1993. Avoiders versus amenders—implication for the investigation of guilt and shame during toddlerhood? *Cogn. Emot.* 7:481–505

Batson CD. 1997. Self-other merging and the empathy-altruism hypothesis: reply to Neuberg et al. (1997). *J. Pers. Soc. Psychol.* 73:517–22

Batson CD. 1998. Altruism and prosocial behavior. In *The Handbook of Social Psychology,* ed. DT Gilbert, ST Fiske, G Lindzey, 2:282–316. Boston: McGraw-Hill

Batson CD, Ahmad N, Yin J, Bedell SJ, Johnson JW, et al. 1999. Two threats to the common good: self-interested egoism and empathy-induced altruism. *Pers. Soc. Psychol. Bull.* 25:3–16

Batson CD, Polycarpou MP, Harmon-Jones E, Imhoff HJ, Mitchener EC, et al. 1997a. Empathy and attitudes: Can feelings for a member of a stigmatized group improve feelings toward the group? *J. Pers. Soc. Psychol.* 72:105–18

Batson CD, Sager K, Garst E, Kang M, Rubchinsky K, Dawson K. 1997b. Is empathy-induced helping due to self-other merging? *J. Pers. Soc. Psychol.* 73:495–509

Batson CD, Turk CL, Shaw LL, Klein TR. 1995. Information function of empathic emotion: learning that we value the other's welfare. *J. Pers. Soc. Psychol.* 68:300–13

Baumeister RF, Stillwell AM, Heatherton TF. 1994. Guilt: an interpersonal approach. *Psychol. Bull.* 115:243–67

Ben-Ze'ev A. 1997. Emotions and morality. *J. Value Inq.* 31:195–212

Block J, Block JH, Keyes S. 1988. Longitudinally foretelling drug usage in adolescence: early childhood personality and environmental precursors. *Child Dev.* 59:336–55

Blum LA. 1980. *Friendship, Altruism, and Morality.* London: Routledge & Kegan Paul. 234 pp.

Carlo G, Allen JB, Buhman DC. 1999. Facilitating and disinhibiting prosocial behavior behaviors: the nonlinear interaction of trait perspective taking and trait personal distress on volunteering. *Basic Appl. Soc. Psychol.* In press

Carlo G, Roesch SC, Melby J. 1998. The multiplicative relations of parenting and temperament to prosocial and antisocial behaviors in adolescence. *J. Early Adolesc.* 18:266–90

Carlson M, Charlin V, Miller N. 1988. Positive mood and helping behavior: a test of six hypotheses. *J. Pers. Soc. Psychol.* 55:211–29

Carlson M, Miller N. 1987. Explanation of the relation between negative mood and helping. *Psychol. Bull.* 102:91–108

Caspi A, Henry B, McGee RO, Moffitt TE, Silva PA. 1995. Temperamental origins of child and adolescent behavior problems: from age three to age fifteen. *Child Dev.* 66:55–68

Caspi A, Moffitt TE, Newman DL, Silva PA. 1996. Behavioral observations at age 3 predict adult psychiatric disorders. *Arch. Gen. Psychiatry* 53:1033–39

Chassin L, Pillow DR, Curran PJ, Molina BSG, Barrera M Jr. 1993. Relations of parental alcoholism to early adolescent substance use: a test of three mediating mechanisms. *J. Abnorm. Psychol.* 102:3–19

Cialdini RB, Brown SL, Lewis BP, Luce C, Neuberg SL. 1997. Reinterpreting the empathy-altruism relationship: when one into one equals oneness. *J. Pers. Soc. Psychol.* 73(3):481–94

Clark LA, Watson D. 1999. Temperament: a new paradigm for trait psychology. In *Handbook of Personality,* ed. L Pervin, O John. San Francisco: Guilford. In press. 2nd ed.

Cohen D, Strayer J. 1996. Empathy in conduct-disordered and comparison youth. *Dev. Psychol.* 32:988–98

Colder CR, Chassin L. 1997. Affectivity and impulsivity: temperament risk for adolescent alcohol involvement. *Psychol. Addict. Behav.* 11:83–97

Colder CR, Stice E. 1998. The moderating effect of impulsivity on the relationship between anger and adolescent problem behavior: cross-sectional and prospective findings. *J. Youth Adolesc.* 27:255–74

Cole PM, Barrett KC, Zahn-Waxler C. 1992. Emotion displays in two-year-olds during mishaps. *Child Dev.* 63:314–24

Cooper ML, Frone MR, Russell M, Mudar P. 1995. Drinking to regulate positive and negative emotions: a motivational model of alcohol use. *J. Pers. Soc. Psychol.* 69:990–1005

Cornell DG, Peterson CS, Richards H. 1999. Anger as a predictor of aggression among incarcerated adolescents. *J. Consult. Clin. Psychol.* 67:108–15

Davies M, Stankov L, Roberts RD. 1998. Emotional intelligence: in search of an elusive construct. *J. Pers. Soc. Psychol.* 75:989–1015

Davis MH. 1994. *Empathy: A Social Psychological Approach.* Madison, WI: Brown & Benchmark

Denham SA, Renwick-DeBardi S, Hewes S. 1994. Emotional communication between mothers and preschoolers: relations with emotional competence. *Merrill-Palmer Q.* 40:488–508

Derryberry D, Rothbart MK. 1988. Arousal, affect, and attention as components of temperament. *J. Pers. Soc. Psychol.* 55:958–66

Dix T, Reingold DP, Zambarano RJ. 1990. Mothers' judgments in moments of anger. *Merrill-Palmer Q.* 36:465–86

Einstein D, Lanning K. 1998. Shame, guilt, ego development, and the five-factor model of personality. *J. Pers.* 66: 555–82

Eisenberg N, Carlo G, Murphy B, Van Court P. 1995a. Prosocial development in late adolescence: a longitudinal study. *Child Dev.* 66:911–36

Eisenberg N, Fabes RA. 1991. Prosocial behavior and empathy: a multimethod, developmental perspective. In *Review of Personality and Social Psychology,* ed. M Clark, 12:34–61. Newbury Park, CA: Sage

Eisenberg N, Fabes RA. 1992. Emotion, regulation, and the development of social competence. In *Review of Personality and Social Psychology: Emotion and Social Behavior,* ed. MS Clark, 14:119–50. Newbury Park, CA: Sage

Eisenberg N, Fabes RA. 1995. The relation of young children's vicarious emotional responding to social competence, regulation, and emotionality. *Cogn. Emot.* 9:203–29

Eisenberg N, Fabes RA. 1998. Prosocial development. In *Handbook of Child Psychology. Social, Emotional, and Personality Development,* ed. W Damon, N Eisenberg (ser. ed). 3:701–78. New York: Wiley & Sons

Eisenberg N, Fabes RA, Bernzweig J, Karbon M, Poulin R, Hanish L. 1993. The relations of emotionality and regulation to preschoolers' social skills and sociometric status. *Child Dev.* 64:1418–38

Eisenberg N, Fabes RA, Carlo G, Troyer D, Speer AL, et al. 1992. The relations of maternal practices and characteristics to children's vicarious emotional responsiveness. *Child Dev.* 63:583–602

Eisenberg N, Fabes RA, Guthrie IK, Murphy BC, Maszk P, et al. 1996a. The relations of regulation and emotionality to problem behavior in elementary school children. *Dev. Psychopathol.* 8:141–62

Eisenberg N, Fabes RA, Guthrie IK, Reiser M. 1999a. Dispositional emotionality and regulation: their role in predicting quality of social functioning. *J. Pers. Soc. Psychol.* In press

Eisenberg N, Fabes RA, Karbon M, Murphy BC, Wosinski M, et al. 1996b. The relations of children's dispositional prosocial behavior to emotionality, regulation, and social functioning. *Child Dev.* 67:974–92

Eisenberg N, Fabes RA, Murphy B, Karbon M, Maszk P, et al. 1994a. The relations of emotionality and regulation to dispositional and situational empathy-related responding. *J. Pers. Soc. Psychol.* 66:776–97

Eisenberg N, Fabes RA, Murphy B, Karbon M, Smith M, Maszk P. 1996c. The relations of children's dispositional empathy-related responding to their emotionality, regulation, and social functioning. *Dev. Psychol.* 32:195–209

Eisenberg N, Fabes RA, Murphy M, Maszk P, Smith M, Karbon M. 1995b. The role of emotionality and regulation in children's social functioning: a longitudinal study. *Child Dev.* 66:1239–61

Eisenberg N, Fabes RA, Nyman M, Bernzweig J, Pinuelas A. 1994b. The relations of emotionality and regulation to children's anger-related reactions. *Child Dev.* 65:109–28

Eisenberg N, Fabes RA, Schaller M, Carlo G, Miller PA. 1991a. The relations of parental characteristics and practices to children's vicarious emotional responding. *Child Dev.* 62:1393–408

Eisenberg N, Fabes RA, Schaller M, Miller PA, Carlo et al. 1991b. Personality and socialization correlates of vicarious emotional responding. *J. Pers. Soc. Psychol.* 61:459–71

Eisenberg N, Fabes RA, Shepard SA, Murphy BC, Guthrie IK, et al. 1997a. Contemporaneous and longitudinal prediction of children's social functioning from regulation and emotionality. *Child Dev.* 68:642–44

Eisenberg N, Fabes RA, Shepard SA, Murphy BC, Jones J, Guthrie IK. 1998. Contemporaneous and longitudinal prediction of children's sympathy from dispositional regulation and emotionality. *Dev. Psychol.* 34:910–24

Eisenberg N, Guthrie IK, Fabes RA, Reiser M, Murphy BC, et al. 1997b. The relations of regulation and emotionality to resiliency and competent social functioning in elementary school children. *Child Dev.* 68:295–311

Eisenberg, N, Guthrie, IK, Fabes RA, Shepard S, Losoya S, et al. 1999b. Prediction of elementary school children's externalizing problem behaviors from attentional and behavioral regulation and negative emotionality. *Child Dev.* In press

Eisenberg N, Guthrie IK, Murphy BC, Shepard SA, Cumberland A, Carlo G. 1999c. Consistency and development of prosocial dispositions: a longitudinal study. *Child Dev.* In press

Eisenberg N, Miller PA, Shell R, McNalley S, Shea C. 1991c. Prosocial development in adolescence: a longitudinal study. *Dev. Psychol.* 27:849–57

Eisenberg N, Okun MA. 1996. The relations of dispositional regulation and emotionality to elders' empathy-related responding and affect while volunteering. *J. Pers.* 64:157–83

Estrada P. 1995. Adolescents' self-reports of prosocial responses to friends and acquaintances: the role of sympathy-related cognitive, affective, and motivational processes. *J. Res. Adolesc.* 5:173–200

Eyre HL, Ferguson TJ. 1997. *Do you see what I see? Self- and other-reports of guilt and shame.* Presented at Am. Psychol. Assoc., Washington, DC

Fabes RA, Eisenberg N, Eisenbud L. 1993. Behavioral and physiological correlates of children's reactions to others' distress. *Dev. Psychol.* 29:655–63

Fabes RA, Eisenberg N, Karbon M, Bernzweig J, Speer AL, Carlo G. 1994. Socialization of children's vicarious emotional responding and prosocial behavior: relations with mothers' perceptions of children's emotional reactivity. *Dev. Psychol.* 30:44–55

Fabes RA, Shepard S, Guthrie I, Martin CL. 1997. The roles of temperamental arousal and same-sex play in children's social adjustment. *Dev. Psychol.* 33:693–702

Ferguson T, Sorenson C, Bodrero R, Stegge H. 1996. *(Dys)functional guilt and shame in developmental perspective.* Presented at Bienn. Meet. Int. Soc. Study Behav. Dev. Quebec City, Canada

Ferguson TJ, Eyre HL. 1999. Engendering gender differences in shame and guilt: stereotypes, socialization, and situational pressures. In *Gender and Emotion,* ed. A Fischer. Cambridge, UK: Cambridge Univ. Press. In press

Ferguson TJ, Eyre HL, Stegge H, Sorenson CB, Everton R. 1997. *The distinct roles of shame and guilt in childhood psychopathology.* Presented at Soc. Res. Child Dev., Washington, DC

Ferguson TJ, Stegge H. 1995. In *Self-Conscious Emotions,* ed. JP Tangney, KW Fischer, pp. 174–97. New York: Guilford

Ferguson TJ, Stegge H. 1998. Measuring guilt in children: a rose by any other name still has thorns. In *Guilt and Children,* ed. J Bybee, pp. 19–74. San Diego: Academic

Ferguson TJ, Stegge H, Damhuis I. 1991. Children's understanding of guilt and shame. *Child Dev.* 62:827–39

Ferguson TJ, Stegge H, Miller ER, Olsen ME. 1999. Guilt, shame, and symptoms in children. *Dev. Psychol.* 35:347–57

Forgas JP. 1994. Sad and guilty? Affective influences on the explanation of conflict in close relationships. *J. Pers. Soc. Psychol.* 66:56–68

Forgas JP. 1995. Mood and judgment: the affect infusion model (AIM). *Psychol. Bull.* 117:39–66

Frick PJ. 1998. Callous-unemotional traits and conduct problems: applying the two-factor model of psychopathy to children. In *Psychopathy: Theory, Research and Implications for Society,* ed. DJ Cooke, A Forth, RD Hare, et al, pp. 161–87. Amsterdam: Kluwer Academic

Goldsmith HH. 1996. Studying temperament via construction of the toddler behavior assessment questionnaire. *Child Dev.* 67:218–35

Graham S, Hudley C, Williams E. 1992. Attributional and emotional determinants of aggression among African-American and Latino young adolescents. *Dev. Psychol.* 28:731–40

Graham S, Weiner B, Zucker, GS. 1997. An attributional analysis of punishment goals and public reactions to O.J. Simpson. *Pers. Soc. Psychol. Bull.* 23:331–46

Gray JR. 1999. A bias toward short-term thinking in threat-related negative emotional states. *Pers. Soc. Psychol. Bull.* 25:65–75

Green JD, Sedikides C. 1999. Affect and self-focused attention revisited: the role of affect orientation. *Pers. Soc. Psychol. Bull.* 25:104–19

Guthrie IK, Eisenberg N, Fabes RA, Murphy BC, Holmgren R, et al. 1997. The relations of regulation and emotionality to children's situational empathy-related responding. *Motiv. Emot.* 21:87–108

Harder DW, Cutler L, Rockart L. 1992. Assessment of shame and guilt and their relationships to psychopathology. *J. Pers. Assess.* 59:584–604

Hart D, Hofmann V, Edelstein W, Keller M. 1997. The relation of childhood personality type to adolescent behavior and development: a longitudinal study of Icelandic children. *Dev. Psychol.* 33:195–205

Hart D, Keller M, Edelstein W, Hofmann V. 1998. Childhood personality influences on social-cognitive development: a longitudinal study. *J. Pers. Soc. Psychol.* 74:1278–89

Hastings PD, Zahn-Waxler C. 1998. *Psychophysiological and socialization predictors of empathy and externalizing problems in middle childhood.* Presented at the annual conference of the Am. Psychol. Assoc. August 98, San Francisco

Henry B, Caspi A, Moffitt TE, Silva PA. 1996. Temperamental and familial predictors of violent and nonviolent criminal convictions: age 3 to age 18. *Dev. Psychol.* 32:614–23

Hoffman ML. 1977. Moral internalization: current theory and research. In *Advances in Experimental Social Psychology,* ed. L Berkowitz, 10:86–135. New York: Academic

Hoffman ML. 1982. Development of prosocial motivation: empathy and guilt. In *The Development of Prosocial Behavior,* ed. N Eisenberg, pp. 281–313. New York: Academic

Hoffman ML. 1983. Affective and cognitive processes in moral internalization. In *Social Cognition and Social Development: A Sociocultural Perspective,* ed. ET Higgins, DN Ruble, WW Hartup, pp. 236–74. Cambridge, UK: Cambridge Univ. Press

Hoffman ML. 1998. Varieties of empathy-based guilt. In *Guilt and Children,* ed. J Bybee, 4:91–112. New York: Academic

Holmgren RA, Eisenberg N, Fabes RA. 1998. The relations of children's situational empathy-related emotions to dispositional prosocial behavior. *Int. J. Behav. Dev.* 22:169–93

Huey SJ, Weisz JR. 1997. Ego control, ego resiliency, and the five-factor model as predictors of behavioral and emotional problems in clinic-referred children and adolescents. *J. Abnorm. Psychol.* 106:404–15

Kagan J. 1998. Biology and the child. In *Social, Emotional and Personality Development. Handbook of Child Psychology,* ed.

W Damon (ser. ed.), N Eisenberg (vol. ed.), 3:177–235. New York: Wiley & Sons

Keltner D. 1995. The signs of appeasement: evidence for the distinct displays of embarrassment, amusement, and shame. *J. Pers. Soc. Psychol.* 68:441–54

Keltner D, Buswell B. 1997. Embarrassment: its distinct form and appeasement functions. *Psychol. Bull.* 122:250–70

Keltner D, Ellsworth PC, Edwards K. 1993. Beyond simple pessimism: effects of sadness and anger on social perception. *J. Pers. Soc. Psychol.* 64:740–52

Kestenbaum R, Farber EA, Sroufe LA. 1989. Individual differences in empathy among preschoolers: relation to attachment history. In *New Directions for Child Development,* Vol. 44. *Empathy and Related Emotional Responses,* ed. N Eisenberg, pp. 51–64. San Francisco: Jossey-Bass

Knight GP, Johnson LG, Carlo G, Eisenberg N. 1994. A multiplicative model of the dispositional antecedents of a prosocial behavior: predicting more of the people more of the time. *J. Pers. Soc. Psychol.* 66:178–83

Kochanska G. 1991. Socialization and temperament in the development of guilt and conscience. *Child Dev.* 62:1379–92

Kochanska G. 1995. Children's temperament, mothers' discipline, and security of attachment: multiple pathways to emerging internalization. *Child Dev.* 66:597–615

Kochanska G. 1997. Multiple pathways to conscience for children with different temperaments: from toddlerhood to age 5. *Dev. Psychol.* 33:228–40

Kochanska G, Aksan N. 1995. Mother-child mutually positive affect, the quality of child compliance to requests and prohibitions, and maternal control as correlates of early internalization. *Child Dev.* 66:236–54

Kochanska G, Casey RJ, Fukumoto A. 1995. Toddlers' sensitivity to standard violations. *Child Dev.* 66:643–56

Kochanska G, DeVet K, Goldman M, Murray K, Putnam SP. 1994. Maternal reports of conscience development and temperament in young children. *Child Dev.* 65:852–68

Kochanska G, Murray K, Coy KC. 1997. Inhibitory control as a contributor to conscience in childhood: from toddler to early school age. *Child Dev.* 68:228–42

Kochanska G, Murray K, Jacques TY, Koenig AL, Vandegeest KA. 1996a. Inhibitory control in young children and its role in emerging internalization. *Child Dev.* 67:490–507

Kochanska G, Padavich DL, Koenig AL. 1996b. Children's narratives about hypothetical moral dilemmas and objective measures of their conscience: mutual relations and socialization antecedents. *Child Dev.* 67:1420–36

Kochanska G, Tjebkes TL, Forman DR. 1998. Children's emerging regulation of conduct: restraint, compliance, and internalization from infancy to the second year. *Child Dev.* 69:1378–89

Koestner R, Zuroff DC, Powers TA. 1991. Family origins of adolescent self-criticism and its continuity into adulthood. *J. Abnorm. Psychol.* 100(2):191–97

Krevans J, Gibbs JC. 1996. Parents' use of inductive discipline: relations to children's empathy and prosocial behavior. *Child Dev.* 67:3263–77

Krueger RF, Caspi A, Moffitt TE, White J, Stouthamer-Loeber M. 1996. Delay of gratification, psychopathology, and personality: Is low self-control specific to externalizing problems? *J. Pers.* 64:107–29

Ladd GW, Profilet SM. 1996. The Child Behavior Scale: a teacher-report measure of young children's aggressive, withdrawn, and prosocial behaviors. *Dev. Psychol.* 32:1008–24

Lake NL, Lane S, Harris PL. 1995. The expectation of guilt and resistance to temptation. *Early Dev. Parenting* 4:63–73

Leary MR, Landel JL, Patton KM. 1996. The motivated expression of embarrassment following a self-presentational predicament. *J. Pers.* 64:619–36

Lengua LJ, West SG, Sandler IN. 1998. Temperament as a predictor of symptomatology in children: addressing contamination of measures. *Child Dev.* 69:164–81

Lerner JS, Goldberg JH, Tetlock PE. 1998. Sober second thought: the effects of accountability, anger, and authoritarianism on attributions of responsibility. *Pers. Soc. Psychol. Bull.* 24:563–74

Lewis HB. 1971. *Shame and Guilt in Neurosis.* New York: Int. Univ. Press

Lewis M. 1998. Emotional competence and development. In *Improving Competence Across the Lifespan,* ed. D Pushkar, WM Bukowski, AE Schwartzman, DM Stack, DR White, pp. 27–36. New York: Plenum

Lynam DR. 1997. Pursuing the psychopathy: capturing the fledgling psychopath in a nomological net. *J. Abnorm. Psychol.* 106:425–38

Mezzacappa E, Tremblay R, Kindlon D, Saul J, Arseneault L, et al. 1997. Anxiety, antisocial behavior, and heart rate regulation in adolescent males. *J. Child Psychiatry Psychol.* 38:457–69

Mikula G, Scherer KR, Athenstaedt U. 1998. The role of injustice in the elicitation of differential emotional reactions. *Pers. Soc. Psychol. Bull.* 24:769–83

Miller PA, Eisenberg N, Fabes RA, Shell R. 1996. Relations of moral reasoning and vicarious emotion to young children's prosocial behavior toward peers and adults. *Dev. Psychol.* 32:210–19

Miller RS, Leary MR. 1992. Social sources and interactive functions of emotion: the case of embarrassment. In *Emotion and Social Behavior,* ed. MS Clark, 8:202–21. Newbury Park, CA: Sage

Miller RS, Tangney JP. 1994. Differentiating embarrassment and shame. *J. Soc. Clin. Psychol.* 13:273–87

Moffitt TE. 1993. The neuropsychology of conduct disorder. *Dev. Psychopathol.* 5:135–51

Murphy BC, Shepard SA, Eisenberg N, Fabes RA, Guthrie IK. 1999. Contemporaneous and longitudinal relations of young adolescents' dispositional sympathy to their emotionality, regulation, and social functioning. *J. Early Adolesc.* 29:66–97

Neuberg SL, Cialdini RB, Brown SL, Luce C, Sagarin BJ, Lewis BP. 1997. Does empathy lead to anything more than superficial help-ing? Comment on Batson et al (1997). *J. Pers. Soc. Psychol.* 73:510–16

Newman DL, Caspi A, Moffitt TE, Silva PA. 1997. Antecedents of adult interpersonal functioning: effects of individual differ-ences in age 3 temperament. *Dev. Psychol.* 33:206–17

Niedenthal PM, Tangney JP, Gavanski I. 1994. "If only I weren't" versus "If only I hadn't": distinguishing shame and guilt in counterfactual thinking. *J. Pers. Soc. Psychol.* 67:584–95

O'Brien BS, Frick PJ. 1996. Reward domi-nance: associations with anxiety, conduct problems, and psychopathy in children. *J. Abnorm. Child Psychol.* 24:223–39

O'Connor LE, Berry JW, Weiss J. 1999. Inter-personal guilt, shame, and psychological problems. *J. Soc. Clin. Psychol.* In press

Okun MA, Shepard SA, Eisenberg N. 1999. The relations of emotionality and regulation to dispositional empathy-related respond-ing among volunteers-in-training. *Ind. Dif-fer.* In press

Oosterlaan J, Sergeant JA. 1996. Inhibition in ADHD, aggressive, and anxious children: a biologically based model of child psycho-pathology. *J. Abnorm. Child Psychol.* 24:19–36

Oosterlaan J, Sergeant JA. 1998. Effects of reward and response cost on response inhi-bition in ADHD, disruptive, anxious, and normal children. *J. Abnorm. Child Psychol.* 26:161–74

Patterson CM, Newman JP. 1993. Reflectivity and learning from aversive events: toward a psychological mechanism for the syn-dromes of disinhibition. *Psychol. Rev.* 100:716–36

Penner L, Finkelstein MA. 1998. Dispositional and structural determinants of volunteer-ism. *J. Pers. Soc. Psychol.* 74:525–37

Pine D, Wasserman G, Miller L, Coplan J, Bagiella E, et al. 1998. Heart period vari-ability and psychopathology in urban boys at risk for delinquency. *Psychophysiology* 35:521–29

Porges SW. 1997. Emotion: an evolutionary by-product of the neural regulation of the autonomic nervous system. *Ann. NY Acad. Sci.* 807:62–77

Pulkkinen L. 1996. Proactive and reactive aggression in early adolescence as precur-sors to anti- and prosocial behavior in young adults. *Aggress. Behav.* 22:241–57

Pulkkinen L, Hamalainen M. 1995. Low self-control as a precursor to crime and acci-dents in a Finnish longitudinal study. *Crim. Behav. Ment. Health* 5:424–38

Quigley BM, Tedeschi JT. 1996. Mediating effects of blame attributions on feelings of anger. *Pers. Soc. Psychol. Bull.* 22:1280–88

Quiles Z, Bybee J. 1997. Chronic and predis-positional guilt: relations to mental health, prosocial behavior, and religiosity. *J. Pers. Assess.* 69:104–26

Raine A. 1993. *The Psychobiology of Crime.* New York: Academic

Roberts W, Strayer J. 1996. Empathy, emo-tional expressiveness, and prosocial behav-ior. *Child Dev.* 67:449–70

Robins RW, John OP, Caspi A, Moffitt TE, Stouthamer-Loeber M. 1996. Resilient, overcontrolled, and undercontrolled boys: three replicable personality types. *J. Pers. Soc. Psychol.* 70:157–71

Robinson JL, Zahn-Waxler C, Emde RN. 1994. Patterns of development in early empathic behavior: environmental and child consti-tutional influences. *Soc. Dev.* 3:125–45

Rothbart MK, Ahadi SA, Hershey KL. 1994. Temperament and social behavior in child-hood. *Merrill-Palmer Q.* 40:21–39

Rothbart MK, Bates JE. 1998. Temperament. In *Handbook of Child Psychology.* Vol. 3. *Social, Emotional, Personality Develop-ment,* ed. W Damon (ser. ed.), N Eisenberg (vol. ed.), 3:105–76. New York: Wiley & Sons

Sanson A, Prior M, Kyrios M. 1990. Contam-ination of measures in temperament research. *Merrill-Palmer Q.* 36:179–92

Scher SJ. 1997. Measuring the consequences of injustice. *Pers. Soc. Psychol. Bull.* 23:482–97

Scher SJ, Heise DR. 1993. Affect and the perception of injustice. *Adv. Group Proc.* 10:223–52

Smetana JG, Braeges JL. 1990. The development of toddlers' moral and conventional judgments. *Merrill-Palmer Q.* 36:329–46

Sorenson CB, Ferguson TJ, Eyre HL. 1997. *ASC and ye shall find: measuring shame and guilt.* Presented at the Eastern Psychol. Assoc., Washington, DC

Spector PE. 1997. The role of frustration in antisocial behavior at work. In *Anti-Social Behavior in Organizations,* ed. RA Jiacalone, J Greenberg, pp. 1–17. Thousand Oaks, CA: Sage

Stansbury K, Gunnar MR. 1994. Adrenocortical activity and emotion regulation. *Mongr. Soc. Res. Child Dev.* 59(240):108–134

Stice E, Gonzales N. 1998. Adolescent temperament moderates the relation of parenting to antisocial behavior and substance use. *J. Adolesc. Res.* 13:5–31

Stifter CA, Spinrad TL, Braungart-Reiker JM. 1999. Toward a developmental model of child compliance: the role of emotion regulation in infancy. *Child Dev.* 70:21–32

Stipek D, Gralinski H, Kopp C. 1990. Self-concept development in the toddler years. *Dev. Psychol.* 26:972–77

Strayer J. 1993. Children's concordant emotions and cognitions in response to observed emotions. *Child Dev.* 64:188–201

Tangney JP. 1991. Moral affect: the good, the bad, and the ugly. *J. Pers. Soc. Psychol.* 61:598–607

Tangney JP. 1992. Situational determinants of shame and guilt in young adulthood. *Pers. Soc. Psychol. Bull.* 18:199–206

Tangney JP. 1996. Conceptual and methodological issues in the assessment of shame and guilt. *Behav. Res. Ther.* 34:741–54

Tangney JP. 1998. How does guilt differ from shame? In *Guilt and Children,* ed. J Bybee, pp. 1–17. San Diego: Academic

Tangney JP, Burggraf SA, Wagner PE. 1995. Shame-proneness, guilt-proneness, and psychological symptoms. In *Self-Conscious Emotions: The Psychology of Shame, Guilt,*

Embarrassment, and Pride, ed. JP Tangney, KW Fischer, pp. 343–67. New York: Guilford

Tangney JP, Miller RS, Flicker L, Barlow DH. 1996a. Are shame, guilt, and embarrassment distinct emotions? *J. Pers. Soc. Psychol.* 70:1256–69

Tangney JP, Niedenthal PM, Covert MV, Barlow DH. 1998. Are shame and guilt related to distinct self-discrepancies? A test of Higgin's (1987) hypotheses. *J. Pers. Soc. Psychol.* 75:256–68

Tangney JP, Wagner P, Gramzow R. 1992. Proneness to shame, proneness to guilt, and psychopathology. *J. Abnorm. Psychol.* 101:469–78

Tangney JP, Wagner PE, Hill-Barlow D, Marschall DE, Gramzow R. 1996b. Relation of shame and guilt to constructive versus destructive responses to anger across the lifespan. *J. Pers. Soc. Psychol.* 70:797–809

Tremblay RE, Pihl RO, Vitaro F, Dobkin PL. 1994. Predicting early onset of male antisocial behavior from preschool behavior. *Arch. Gen. Psychiatry* 51:732–39

Trobst KK, Collins RL, Embree JM. 1994. The role of emotion in social support provision: gender, empathy and expressions of distress. *J. Soc. Pers. Relat.* 11:45–62

Ungerer JA, Dolby R, Waters B, Barnett B, Kelk N, Lewin V. 1990. The early development of empathy: self-regulation and individual differences in the first year. *Motiv. Emot.* 14:93–106

Walker LJ, Pitts RC. 1998. Naturalistic conceptions of moral maturity. *Dev. Psychol.* 34:403–19

Waters E, Hay D, Richters J. 1986. Infant-parent attachment and the origins of prosocial and antisocial behavior. In *Development of Antisocial and Prosocial Behavior: Research, Theories, and Issues,* ed. D Olweus, J Block, M Radke-Yarrow, pp. 97–125. Orlando, FL: Academic

Watson D, Clark LA. 1992. Affects separable and inseparable: on the hierarchical arrangement of the negative affects. *J. Pers. Soc. Psychol.* 62:489–505

Wegener DT, Petty RE. 1994. Mood management across affective states: the hedonic contingency hypothesis. *J. Pers. Soc. Psychol.* 66:1034–48

Wood JV, Saltzberg JA, Goldsamt LA. 1990. Does affect induce self-focused attention? *J. Pers. Soc. Psychol.* 58:899–908

Zahn-Waxler C, Cole PM, Welsh JD, Fox NA. 1995. Psychophysiological correlates of empathy and prosocial behaviors in preschool children with problem behaviors. *Dev. Psychopathol.* 7:27–48

Zahn-Waxler C, Kochanska G. 1990. The origins of guilt. *Annu. Nebr. Symp. Motiv. Socioemot. Dev.,* 36th, Lincoln, pp. 183–258. Lincoln: Univ. Nebr. Press

Zahn-Waxler C, Kochanska G, Krupnick J, McKnew D. 1990. Patterns of guilt in children of depressed and well mothers. *Dev. Psychol.* 26:51–59

Zahn-Waxler C, Radke-Yarrow M, King RA. 1979. Child rearing and children's prosocial initiations toward victims of distress. *Child Dev.* 50:319–30

Zahn-Waxler C, Radke-Yarrow M, Wagner E, Chapman M. 1992. Development of concern for others. *Dev. Psychol.* 28:126–36

Zahn-Waxler C, Robinson J. 1995. Empathy and guilt: early origins of feelings of responsibility. In *Self-Conscious Emotions,* ed. JP Tangney, KW Fischer, pp. 143–73. New York: Guilford

Annu. Rev. Psychol. 2000. 51:699–725

Neural Basis of Hearing in Real-World Situations

Albert S. Feng and Rama Ratnam

Department of Molecular and Integrative Physiology, and Beckman Institute, University of Illinois at Urbana-Champaign, Urbana, Illinois 61801; e-mail: a-feng@uiuc.edu

Key Words multisource sounds, neuroethology, sound localization, sound pattern recognition

■ **Abstract** In real-world situations animals are exposed to multiple sound sources originating from different locations. Most vertebrates have little difficulty in attending to selected sounds in the presence of distractors, even though sounds may overlap in time and frequency. This chapter selectively reviews behavioral and physiological data relevant to hearing in complex auditory environments. Behavioral data suggest that animals use spatial hearing and integrate information in spectral and temporal domains to determine sound source identity. Additionally, attentional mechanisms help improve hearing performance when distractors are present. On the physiological side, although little is known of where and how auditory objects are created in the brain, studies show that neurons extract behaviorally important features in parallel hierarchically arranged pathways. At the highest levels in the pathway these features are often represented in the form of neural maps. Further, it is now recognized that descending auditory pathways can modulate information processing in the ascending pathway, leading to improvements in signal detectability and response selectivity, perhaps even mediating attention. These issues and their relevance to hearing in real-world conditions are discussed with respect to several model systems for which both behavioral and physiological data are available.

CONTENTS

Introduction 700
Behavioral Aspects of Hearing 701
   Humans 701
   Frogs 702
   Bats 703
   Birds 705
   Summary 706
Physiological Aspects of Hearing 706
   Sound Pattern Recognition 707
   Sound Localization 709
   Spatially Mediated Release from Masking 711

0084–6570/00/0201–0699/12.00

Cortical Encoding of Complex Sounds..712
Temporal Dynamics of Auditory Processing..714
Gating Mechanisms and Descending Control..714
Summary..717
Conclusion..717

INTRODUCTION

Sounds in real-world situations seldom occur in isolation. Rather, the auditory environment typically contains more than one source, each producing distinct sounds that overlap in time and spectrum. The eardrums vibrate to the sum total of all sounds so that at the periphery all sounds are mixed. The task of grouping and segregating the neural representation of these sounds, to make sense of the what and where of the auditory environment, is carried out by the brain; that is, the brain performs auditory scene analysis (Bregman 1990).

Auditory scene analysis has elements in common with visual scene analysis (Bregman 1990, Julesz & Hirsh 1972). Both tasks involve the grouping and segregation of elemental features to extract distinct perceptual objects. However, auditory objects are not persistent. Instead, the brain must rely entirely on the time evolution of the sound waveform to perform scene analysis, and it appears to do so by means of sequential and spectral integration. Additionally, whereas there is a representation of space in the retina, sound source location must be computed centrally in audition.

In this article we describe recent advances in the neural basis of hearing in real-world situations. This description is limited to a few issues of hearing in such conditions and a few animals for which both behavioral and neural data exist. The limitation in coverage is necessary because the issues addressed are rather broad and represent a coming together of numerous ideas from ethology to physiology. Also, owing to space limitations the data presented are selective and are used to illustrate what is known of the principles of neural processing and what needs to be investigated in the future. The results emerging from these studies suggest that the neural representation of sounds is transformed systematically along the ascending auditory pathway, leading to integration in the time, frequency, and space domains and allowing the extraction of behaviorally relevant features. However, this ascending series of transformations by itself may not be sufficient for creating unitary percepts of objects. Increasingly, physiologists are beginning to appreciate the role of descending (centrifugal) pathways in extraction of signals in difficult listening conditions. Such descending control may form the basis for attention, giving organisms the ability to acquire information about one or two auditory objects while ignoring others. Thus, hearing is an active process. At the same time, signal emitters are known to adjust their vocalizations so that a receiver has a better chance of hearing under adverse conditions.

Previous reviews appearing in this series have focused on auditory psycho-physics and perception, particularly with reference to spectral and temporal anal-ysis, pitch perception, binaural hearing (de Boer & Dreschler 1987, Hirsh & Watson 1996, Trahiotis & Robinson 1979), sound localization (Middlebrooks & Green 1991) and speech perception (Miller & Eimas 1995). Reviews on physi-ology have addressed cochlear processes (Teas 1989) and sound localization (Phillips & Brugge 1985) in quiet environments. This review represents an exten-sion of previous work to more challenging listening conditions.

BEHAVIORAL ASPECTS OF HEARING

Behavioral and psychophysical studies of hearing are well established for humans, frogs, bats, and birds. We first review these studies to place subsequent discussions of physiology in the proper context. At the outset, however, it is important to note that most studies of humans and many other animals have used dichotic paradigms in which the stimuli are delivered to the ears through headphones (i.e. closed-field stimulation). In contrast, hearing in real-world conditions involves listening in a multisource environment where both ears are stimulated differentially (i.e. free-field stimulation). Although psychophysical and physiological results from dichotic paradigms have led to much understanding of auditory processing and the limits to auditory performance, dichotic-stimulus conditions are not always easily related to hearing in the real world.

Humans

In humans, hearing in complex acoustic environments is exemplified by the cock-tail party effect (Cherry 1953). It involves the task of attending to and understand-ing what one person is saying when there are other people speaking at the same time. The problems with hearing under such conditions have all the essentials of the topics discussed in this article. Auditory psychophysicists have examined the phenomena from the viewpoint of sound source determination (Yost 1992) and sound source segregation (Bregman 1990).

It has been shown that the cocktail party effect involves listening with two ears (i.e. binaural hearing) and that performance degrades rapidly when one ear is nonfunctional (Zurek 1992, Hawley et al 1999). Further, the threshold for comprehending speech improves when the sound sources are widely separated in space (Cherry 1953, Hirsh 1950, Plomp & Mimpen 1981). These experiments suggest that there is a close link between sound identification and the ability to separate sound sources in space. Indeed, in humans sound detection thresholds are highest when noise and sound sources originate from the same location, but thresholds are lowered by as much as 10–18 dB when the angular separation between the two sources is increased (Gatehouse 1987, Saberi et al 1991). It is presumed that the separation of the two sounds in space assists in decomposing the auditory scene into its component sound sources. This, in turn, can reduce detection thresholds.

The segregation of concurrent sounds into individual auditory streams is also facilitated if the sounds (*a*) are spectrally separated, (*b*) have uncorrelated waveform envelopes, (*c*) start and stop asynchronously, and (*d*) have harmonics with different fundamentals (Bregman 1990). These conditions make it easier to localize the individual sound sources and to identify the contents from these sources.

There is evidence that the cocktail party effect involves attentional mechanisms because a person can switch to listening to another talker without necessarily moving the head or body. Cherry (1953) used a selective attention paradigm for studying this issue. When the listener was asked to attend to one message delivered to one ear while a different message was delivered to the other ear, Cherry observed that the unattended message could not be recalled. However, when the messages were split between the ears, or mixed and presented monaurally, very little of either message could be determined. How many messages a person can attend to at the same time and what aspects of unattended messages can be processed are major issues yet to be resolved. Almost all of the theories of selective attention are drawn from visual processing and applied to dichotic listening conditions (see Jones & Yee 1993 for a review). They are not easily applicable to auditory information processing in the real world, where competing sounds reach both ears.

Frogs

Anurans (frogs and toads) produce species-specific and somewhat stereotypical vocal signals from a limited repertoire. These include mating, territorial, release, warning, rain, and distress calls (Capranica 1965; see Gerhardt 1988, Rand 1988 for reviews). Each of these calls is distinct. The mating call is well separated spectrally and/or with respect to its temporal pattern from those of sympatric species inhabiting the same breeding pond. In most instances it serves as a species-isolating mechanism and is a salient cue for mate selection by females.

Although anurans have a limited repertoire, they are prodigious callers. In a typical breeding pond in the southeastern United States, a large number of males from as many as 15–25 species may chorus simultaneously on any given night at levels exceeding 120 dB SPL (sound pressure level with reference to 20 µPa). These choruses and other sources of biotic and abiotic sounds give rise to a broadband background noise that can extend beyond 5 kHz (Narins & Zelick 1988). Despite the high level of noise, females can recognize conspecific mating calls in the chorus, localize a conspecific male, and then move toward him. This requires good localization ability and the ability to discriminate conspecific sounds from heterospecific sounds.

The cues used for call discrimination have been well characterized. Most of the behavioral studies have taken an ethological approach, using the evoked calling paradigm (Capranica 1965) or selective phonotaxis paradigm (Gerhardt 1978a,b). There are fewer psychophysical studies designed to test the perceptual abilities of hearing in anurans (Megela-Simmons et al 1985), in part because of difficulties in training these animals (Simmons & Moss 1995). Early work by Capranica (1965) showed that bullfrogs responded to conspecific mating calls while ignoring the calls of other species. He found that the salient feature in bullfrog calls is the power spectrum. Because the bullfrog's ear is most sensitive to the dominant frequency bands of the species mating call, he suggested that the auditory periphery functions as a matched filter. However, from studies of female choice in treefrogs, Gerhardt (1978a,b) provided evidence that a matching spectrum alone is sometimes insufficient and that a call must have the proper temporal structure to attract a female. Temporal attributes important for call discrimination include the calling rate, pulse number, pulse duration, and envelope rise time (see Feng & Schellart 1999, Gerhardt 1988, Wells 1988 for reviews).

Other field experiments have demonstrated that frogs can accurately localize sound (Feng et al 1976, Rheinlaender et al 1979). This has been tested in two-alternative, forced-choice phonotactic experiments in which one call was a conspecific mating call and the second was a sympatric or heterospecific call (Gerhardt 1978b, Oldham & Gerhardt 1975), and in more complex situations in which multiple sounds were broadcast simultaneously (Ehret & Gerhardt 1980, Schwartz & Gerhardt 1995). These studies show that call detection, discrimination, and phonotaxis can be elicited in the presence of multiple interfering sources even though interfering sounds severely degrade the signal of interest by reducing the signal-to-noise ratio (SNR) (Ehret & Gerhardt 1980, Gerhardt & Klump 1988, Narins & Zelick 1988, Schwartz 1994, Schwartz & Wells 1983, Simmons 1988). As in humans (see previous section), there is evidence to suggest that thresholds for discriminating calls improve when sound sources are separated in space (Schwartz & Gerhardt 1989).

In noisy environments where numerous species are calling, selection has favored callers (emitters) that use strategies for enhancing detection of their emitted sounds. These include producing calls that occupy nonoverlapping frequency bands (Narins & Capranica 1976) and calling separately in time, such as at different times of the day or during moments when calling activity from nearby frogs is less interfering, for example, antiphonal calling (Awbrey 1978; Zelick & Narins 1982, 1983, 1985). Reducing call overlap also offers the advantage of preserving fine temporal structure and makes it possible to estimate the intensity of neighbors' calls and, hence, maintain adequate male-male spacing (Schwartz 1987). Other strategies include increasing the call intensity to improve the SNR and increasing the calling rate. Alternatively, the receiver can optimize signal reception by having an auditory system that is well tuned to species-specific vocalizations, for example, matched filtering.

Bats

Many species of bats (and dolphins) have evolved a special mechanism for exploration of the world around them. They produce sonar signals and rely on analysis of echoes from objects along their flight paths to gain information about their surroundings and to navigate and hunt in the dark (Griffin 1958). In essence, bats perform image analysis using echolocation sounds. They can detect, identify, and localize individual targets in the presence of clutter in the environment, even though clutter generates multiple echoes that overlap in time (Neuweiler et al 1988, Simmons 1989). Additionally, bats appear to have the ability to resolve reflections of a pulse from different parts of the same object. These reflections, known as glints, result in the strengthening and weakening of various components of the echoes owing to overlaps in the microsecond range (Simmons 1989).

Echolocating bats can be divided into two groups by their biosonar signal: CF/FM and FM bats. CF/FM bats produce a long constant-frequency (CF) component followed by a brief downward frequency-modulated (FM) sweep and show a preference for hunting in wooded habitats around dense vegetation. FM bats have only a brief downward FM component and prefer to hunt in open areas free from the clutter of vegetation. The difference in complexity of the acoustic signals is thought to be an adaptation to habitat (Fenton 1995, Neuweiler & Fenton 1988).

Echoes provide information about target range, position, size, shape, and texture, as well as the target's dynamic characteristics, such as the frequency and pattern of beating wings if the target is an insect (Kober & Schnitzler 1990, Neuweiler 1990). The sonar system of bats (and dolphins) exemplifies the close interplay between active motor control during echolocation and sensory processing, an interplay that is not immediately apparent in passive listening. While pursuing flying insects, a bat dynamically alters its pattern of sonar emissions by adjusting the rate, duration, bandwidth, and intensity of sonar pulses. While searching for prey, it emits either a CF pulse (CF/FM bats) or a shallow FM sweep (FM bats) at a low emission rate (3–20 pulses/s). Such signals are optimal for long-distance target detection. While tracking and closing in on the prey, the bat reduces its sonar pulse duration to prevent pulse-echo overlap, increases the bandwidth of the FM sweep to enhance target identification, increases pulse rate to increase the sampling rate, and reduces the pulse intensity to keep the perceived amplitude of the echoes essentially constant.

Another remarkable adaptational mechanism is used by CF/FM bats (such as mustached and horseshoe bats). These bats shift the frequency of the sonar pulse to compensate for Doppler shifts resulting from the approach to a target, such that the returned echo remains at a reference frequency to which the bats auditory neurons are maximally sensitive (Pollak et al 1972; Schnitzler 1973; Suga & Jen 1975, 1976). It has been suggested that Doppler shift compensation is useful for evaluating the relative velocity of a target (Pollak et al 1972; Simmons et al 1975; Schnitzler 1973; Suga & Jen 1975, 1976). This behavior is a compelling example of how active control of emissions can be used to improve hearing so that the bat can focus on signals of importance. Other mechanisms that filter out unnecessary information are also present in central auditory circuits and are described later.

Many families of bats, such as Hipposideridae, Rhinolophidae, Megadermatidae, Phyllostomidae, and others, have distinct facial ornaments that appear to be correlated with the duty cycle, bandwidth, and intensity of their sonar signals

(Fenton 1995). These flexible leaflike structures on the face can shape the sonar beam dynamically. Additionally, large and independently maneuverable pinnae are useful for optimal amplification of echoes or for improving target localization, especially in the vertical plane, by keeping track of the prey (Mogdans et al 1988, Obrist & Wenstrup 1998). While audio-motor control is an important aspect of active listening, it is beyond the scope of this review and is not dealt with further.

Birds

As described earlier, the spatial location of sound sources must be centrally computed in the auditory system. The ability to localize sound is crucial for survival and for effective communication in natural situations in many animals. The behavioral aspects of sound localization and its neural basis have been the focus of intensive investigations for many years. Of the many model systems studied, the most is known about the neural mechanisms that subserve sound localization in the barn owl (Konishi 1992), an animal that hunts in the dark by listening to the rustling sounds made by terrestrial prey (Payne 1971).

Sound localization in all vertebrates, including humans, generally involves comparing the differences between the sounds reaching the two ears. Such differences, called binaural or interaural disparities, are created by the different path lengths to the two ears and result in time and intensity differences that may be used to compute sound location. This computation is carried out in central auditory pathways. In barn owls, a unique asymmetry of the ears in the vertical plane allows independent localization along the azimuth and elevation (Konishi 1992). Interaural time difference (ITD) serves as the cue to determine sound source azimuth, and interaural intensity difference (IID) is used for determining elevation. This specialization gives barn owls a high degree of accuracy in localization in both planes: $1.5° \pm 1.6°$ (mean $\pm$ SD) in azimuth and $1.6° \pm 1.2°$ in elevation (Knudsen et al 1979). It is noted that prey-generated sounds are likely to be faint and embedded in background noise. Thus, barn owls normally confront the problem of signal detection in the presence of competing sounds.

The general problem of acoustic communication in noisy environments is especially relevant to songbirds. There is a considerable body of psychophysical work on how birds detect signals in noise (see Dooling 1982, Klump 1996 for reviews). Here we review one thread in this substantial body of work. European starlings (*Sturnus vulgaris*) congregate in large, noisy semicolonial groups (Feare 1984). There is evidence that adults can discriminate between the songs of two or more starlings in such environments (Hulse et al 1997). Specifically, starlings can discriminate and identify a sample of one song when it is presented simultaneously with a sample of another species' song and also when it is presented with a mixture of songs such as in a dawn chorus. Further, starlings trained to discriminate between exemplars of two conspecific individuals can maintain the discrimination in the presence of distractor songs and also form auditory categories (Wisniewski & Hulse 1997). This capacity seems to be generalizable to arbitrary acoustic events, because starlings can also segregate two synthetic pure-tone sequences of different frequencies (MacDougall-Shackleton et al 1998). Previously, only humans had been shown to have this ability (Bregman & Campbell 1971).

Recently, Klump & Langemann (1995) reported that European starlings, like humans, experience a phenomenon called comodulation masking release. That is, improvement in detection of a pure-tone signal embedded in a narrow-band masker centered at the signal frequency (i.e. on-frequency) when noise at other frequencies is added, with the proviso that the added noise is correlated with the on-frequency noise (Hall et al 1984, Schooneveldt & Moore 1987). Also, similar to humans, the degree of release from masking is related to the bandwidth of the masker and the amplitude modulation rate. This observation indicates that birds can exploit temporal correlations in background noise to increase signal detectability. At present, whereas there are some data on the power spectrum of background noise in bird colonies (Klump 1996) and frog choruses (Narins & Zelick 1988), there seem to be no data on the temporal structure of noise. It is likely that both frogs and birds may be able to take advantage of such correlations if they exist.

As indicated earlier, the cocktail party effect in humans and frogs is facilitated by sound source separation. The only study conducted in birds is a study of the budgerigar, in which Dent et al (1997) reported a maximum of 12 dB of improvement at the best frequency in the audiogram ($\sim$3 kHz). However, behavioral data in this area for model systems other than humans are scarce.

Summary

Psychophysical and behavioral studies in frogs, bats, and birds have established that animals other than humans have the capability to perform auditory scene analysis. There is also evidence for auditory categorization and stream segregation in birds. These animals are therefore good model systems for investigation of the physiological basis of hearing in complex environments. As mentioned earlier, listening in complex and noisy environments involves many processes and cues: sound source directionality, sound-source segregation, and attentional mechanisms. The last two areas are not as well developed as the first, and more behavioral data are needed. The utility and importance of the results from various model systems lie in the physiological investigations that complement the behavioral data. This aspect is taken up next.

PHYSIOLOGICAL ASPECTS OF HEARING

Complex sounds can be characterized by the instantaneous distribution of sound energy in different frequency bands and by how the energies in different bands change with time. In the time domain, most vocalizations contain a number of discrete components, appropriately ordered in time, each having specific spectral and temporal characteristics. This section describes what is known of the neural basis of perception of complex sounds in real-world situations. The general principles underlying processing of individual complex sounds are presented first, e.g. recognition of sound pattern and localization. This is followed by a discussion of issues encountered in natural listening conditions.

Sound Pattern Recognition

The neural basis of sound pattern recognition has been studied extensively. These studies have used a number of experimental model systems, but most of these have focused on signal processing at one or two levels of the auditory system. As such, our understanding is far from complete. Most of our knowledge has been gained from the studies in frogs, birds, and bats. Below we describe selective results from these studies.

Frequency Processing   Anurans (frogs and toads) posses two separate hearing organs: the amphibian papilla, which is innervated by two populations of auditory fibers, one tuned to low- and the other to mid-level frequencies; and the basilar papilla, which is tuned to high frequencies (Feng et al 1975). Since the vocalization apparatus appears to have coevolved with the receiving apparatus, one or more of these three populations of fibers are maximally sensitive to the dominant frequencies in the species mating call (Capranica 1965, Capranica & Moffat 1983, Wilczynski & Capranica 1984). The frequency tuning curves (FTCs) of auditory fibers are V shaped (as in mammals), but only fibers tuned to low frequencies exhibit two-tone suppression (TTS, which is a response suppression when an excitatory tone is paired with a tone that is outside the excitatory FTC). For anurans, the best inhibitory frequency is located on the high-frequency flank of the excitatory FTC.

The frequency-tuning characteristics change in an orderly fashion along the ascending auditory pathway. At the level of the cochlear nucleus (CN), cells also have V-shaped excitatory FTCs, and, like auditory nerve fibers, only low-frequency neurons demonstrate TTS by higher-frequency tones (Fuzessery & Feng 1983). In the superior olivary nucleus (SON), more complex tuning curves are evident, and all neurons demonstrate TTS with inhibitory tuning curves along one or both flanks of the excitatory FTC (Fuzessery & Feng 1983). This suggests that there is a convergence of differently tuned CN neurons onto SON neurons. Although FTCs are shaped by TTS originating in the periphery, there is evidence that central mechanisms also play a role in shaping the FTCs along the auditory pathway (Hall 1994). At the level of the anuran inferior colliculus (IC), frequency tuning is highly complex (Fuzessery & Feng 1982). All neurons exhibit prominent inhibitory flanks. Furthermore, 14% of recorded neurons are sensitive to two distinct frequency regions of the call spectrum, responding only (or most markedly) when both regions of the spectrum are presented simultaneously (Fuzessery

& Feng 1982). At the auditory thalamus, temporal (see below) and spectral processing is mediated by two distinct structures. The posterior thalamic nucleus seems to be specialized for processing spectral features of sounds, whereas the central thalamic nucleus is best suited for processing temporal features (Hall & Feng 1987). More specifically, in the posterior thalamus, some 30% of neurons respond to tone combinations in the species mating call and do not respond (or respond poorly) to the individual frequency components alone. The presence of such neurons, called AND neurons for obvious reasons, is a nice illustration of neural integration that facilitates sound pattern recognition. Thus, the progressive change in frequency selectivity from the simple V-shaped FTC in the periphery to the complex FTCs seen in the thalamus suggests that neurons at higher levels are increasingly more selective to spectral features of complex sounds.

Temporal Processing   When stimulated with a tone burst, auditory nerve fibers typically give a pronounced phasic discharge that is followed by a sustained firing with a rate that decays in time owing to adaptation (Megela 1984). Auditory nerve fibers show robust phase-locked response to the envelope of amplitude-modulated (AM) stimuli. They function as envelope detectors (Feng et al 1991, Rose & Capranica 1985) and are capable of encoding the trills and modulations present in anuran vocalizations. Neurons at higher levels show diverse temporal-discharge characteristics that include primary-like firing patterns (resembling the discharge patterns of auditory nerve fibers), a variety of phasic response patterns such as onset and phasic burst responses, and chopper patterns (Condon et al 1995, Gooler & Feng 1992, Hall & Feng 1990). There is a progressive increase in the number of phasic units on ascending the auditory pathway, from ~10% in the CN (Fuzessery & Feng 1983) to ~35%–45% in the IC (Gooler & Feng 1992, Ratnam & Feng 1998). As discussed below, an increase in the number of phasic neurons has implications for temporal processing, sound localization, and signal detection in noise.

In the CN and SON, phasic neurons, as opposed to primary-like neurons, are better suited for encoding temporal patterns—they show more robust phase-locked discharges to the envelope of AM stimuli, as measured by spike count or response synchrony (Feng & Lin 1994, Hall & Feng 1991). In general, the response synchrony code that is prominent in the periphery (Hillery & Narins 1984) is gradually replaced by a rate code at higher levels (see also Rose & Capranica 1984). Whereas auditory nerve fibers show precise time locking to AM stimuli, well into the hundreds of hertz, IC neurons can rarely follow AM stimuli beyond 50 Hz. In response to pulsatile AM stimuli (sounds having a temporal composition similar to frog natural calls), ~25% of all neurons in the CN and SON show a high degree of selectivity and respond only to a narrow range of pulse rates; that is, they show band pass response. In the IC, selectivity for pulse rate appears to improve (Epping & Eggermont 1986, Walkowiak 1984). The proportion of neurons showing band-pass responses to AM rate is higher in the central thalamic nucleus, suggesting that this region may be specialized for AM processing.

Another salient feature of anuran calls is their duration and/or the duration of individual notes in the call. There is evidence that this information, owing to its importance in perception, is computed systematically along the central auditory pathway, leading to the emergence of duration-selective neurons in the IC. In the periphery, auditory nerve fibers uniformly demonstrate long-pass response, that is, monotonically increasing response to an increase in duration. In the CN, primary-like neurons show long-pass response, but phasic neurons give all-pass response; that is, they respond by and large equally to all durations. In the SON, a small number of neurons demonstrate short-pass characteristics, preferring durations that are shorter than some cut-off durations. In the IC, neurons that are tuned to specific stimulus durations are first observed (Gooler & Feng 1992), and this feature is preserved in the thalamus, in particular the central thalamic nucleus.

These findings indicate that the anuran auditory system is initially organized hierarchically at the brainstem, culminating in parallel processing of spectral and temporal information in the thalamus. Neurons from the periphery to the IC demonstrate both spectral and temporal selectivity. However, neurons at the level of the thalamus are suddenly, as it were, specialized for either spectral or temporal filtering. Because peripheral neurons do not make this distinction, sensitivity to various acoustic parameters of anuran vocalizations must be centrally constructed, but it is not known how this is done. Two other areas of research deserve investigation. First, where does auditory grouping take place? In other words, where do spectral information and temporal information from the two thalamic nuclei come together, and where are these types of information integrated with information on sound source location? Second, thalamic processing in anurans in the context of competing sounds has so far not received any attention. Thus, the significance of thalamic specializations for spectral and temporal processing is not known for either auditory grouping or scene analysis under noisy conditions.

Sound Localization

The barn owl sound localization mechanism provides another example of how the nervous system processes information in parallel and later integrates two or more parameters to create higher-level features. We discussed earlier the role of ITD and IID cues in sound localization in the barn owl. ITD information and IID information are processed in functionally independent and anatomically parallel pathways in the lower brainstem. Neurons in these pathways respond selectively only to ITD or IID. The two pathways converge in the IC (Takahashi & Konishi 1988a,b) where they synapse on to neurons that act like AND gates, responding only to sounds originating from a specific region of auditory space, that is, to combinations of specific ITD-IID pairs (Knudsen & Konishi 1978a,b). Further, they are arranged systematically to form a topographical map of auditory space. Thus, information from each cue is processed independently and then both types are brought together in the midbrain to create combination specificity, that is, selectivity to azimuth and elevation.

A difference in azimuthal separation between two sound sources will result in different ITDs (and IIDs) for the two sounds. Can the nervous system localize two (or more) separate sound sources, and what sort of neural circuitry is required to achieve this? This issue is best examined by an ITD network (Jeffress 1948). Such a network has been shown to be implemented neurally by means of coincidence detectors in the barn owl nucleus laminaris, where azimuthal location is mapped topographically within the structure, with individual neurons responding only to a narrow range of ITDs (Carr & Konishi 1990; see also Yin & Chan 1988 for ITD processing in cats). Such a tapped-delay network can presumably represent multiple sound sources provided that frequency information from the sounds is used to resolve phase ambiguities. Phase ambiguities arise when an ITD to a pure tone differs from another ITD by integer multiples of the tone period, thus signaling multiple locations for a sound source, each providing the same phase difference.

In the barn owl, phase ambiguity is eliminated along the ITD pathway. As a result, space-specific neurons in the IC respond exclusively to interaural time disparities independent of stimulus frequency (Fujita & Konishi 1991), and therefore IC neurons could conceivably resolve spatially segregated sound sources without ambiguity. Takahashi & Keller (1994) showed that two spatially separated sound sources can indeed be resolved in the IC if the sounds have nonoverlapping frequencies or are uncorrelated noise bursts. For identical sounds, however, neural responses depend on the delays between the two sounds. When delays are in the range of 0–1 ms, summing localization is observed (Keller & Takahashi 1996b); that is, a single phantom source is perceived between the two sources, with the location of this perceived source being closer to the leading source. For longer delays (up to 5.0 ms), the response to the lagging sound is suppressed (Keller & Takahashi 1996a). These investigators suggest that, for longer delays, a phenomenon parallel to the precedence effect (Blauert 1983) is applicable. In a recent study, Litovsky & Yin (1998) showed that, in the cat IC, the suppression of the lagging response depends on the location of the leading source. A majority of cat IC units show strongest suppression to the lagging response when the leading stimulus is placed in the neuron's responsive area (as compared with a lead in the neuron's unresponsive area). Thus, reverberations can be suppressed so that the location of the leading sound is not smeared.

The more general question of analyzing scenes containing sounds from multiple sources is still not satisfactorily resolved. Takahashi & Keller (1994) reported that, in the barn owl, even if two or more sources were resolved, the activity in the space map was less than that generated by a single source. Hence, it would appear that a single source is clearly resolved, but adding more sources seems to tax the ability of the space map to localize sounds. Although speculative, it is possible that the descending auditory pathway may selectively facilitate the neural image of a sound source being attended to, while it suppresses others. This is discussed in greater detail below with reference to bats. A recent modeling study (C Liu, BC Wheeler, WD O'Brien Jr, RC Bilger, D Jones, CR Lansing, AS Feng, submitted for publication) shows that an ITD neural network can accurately locate azimuths of 4–6 sources of speech sounds with overlapping spectrums. For this, however, a stencil filter (constructed by using the predictable ambiguity functions at different frequency bands) is required to remove the phase ambiguities. At present it is unclear whether the brain possesses a similar filter, given that the brain mechanism for removing phase ambiguity (Fujita & Konishi 1991) does not appear to be adequate, at least insofar as the data from the IC is concerned.

Spatially Mediated Release from Masking

As described earlier, the ability to localize sounds and analyze sound patterns in the presence of noise is crucial for the reproductive success of frogs. We also indicated that while much has been learned about the spectral and temporal processing of sounds as well as the processing of directional information, we do not know how directional information and spectral and temporal information are integrated in the brain to create a unitary percept of auditory objects in space. One approach towards solving this complex problem is to ask a simpler question; for example, how is sound pattern analysis affected when there is a competing sound presented from different locations in space? Surprisingly, very little is known about this aspect also. The initial studies of Cherry (1953) (see above) showed that increasing the angular separation between two sound sources improves the detectability of sounds in humans (Gatehouse 1987, Hirsh 1950, Plomp & Mimpen 1981, Saberi et al 1991), frogs (Schwartz & Gerhardt 1989), and budgerigars (Dent et al 1997). Ratnam & Feng (1998) directly tested the above hypothesis in the frog IC and found that increasing azimuthal separation between a broadband noise source and an AM stimulus (with an SNR of −6 dB) indeed leads to improvement in signal detection, that is, in terms of an increase in the response to the AM stimulus. For many neurons in the frog IC, the improvement in sound detection thresholds could be ≥6 dB for an angular separation of 45°. Ratnam & Feng reported that most neurons demonstrating spatially mediated release from masking had phasic discharge patterns, suggesting that phasic units are well suited for detection of signal under challenging listening conditions.

Recently, the physiology of release from masking was compared at two levels of the frog auditory system, using the frog's natural call as a probe stimulus (at an SNR of −6 dB), positioned at the neuron's best receptive field (contralateral 90° in the IC and ipsilateral 90° in the eighth nerve) (AS Feng & WY Lin, unpublished observations). These researchers found that whereas the release from masking for auditory nerve fibers averages 3.9 dB, the average for IC neurons is 11.9 dB. The difference in the results at the two levels indicates that central processing may be responsible for improving signal detection. However, the evidence for this conclusion is indirect. Further studies are required to obtain direct evidence and determine whether the improvement in signal detectability observed in the IC neurons is caused by ascending or descending pathways. As discussed in detail below, descending pathways most likely play an important role in improving signal detectability.

The above studies of Feng and coworkers on release from masking assumed that spectral and locational cues alone are important. However, there is psychophysical evidence that, in realistic situations, significant cues may be provided by spectro-temporal correlations, such as those demonstrated in comodulation masking release (see above). In a typical frog chorus, background noise is often significantly correlated in time because of the repetitive nature of their vocalizations and of insect sounds and other abiotic sounds. Hence, as Klump (1996) has suggested, spectro-temporal correlations in background noise may have a major impact on signal detection. In general, this is an area in which physiology has not kept pace with psychophysics. Physiological investigations of this phenomenon in birds or frogs are necessary to gain insights into the neural processing of sounds in complex acoustic environments.

Cortical Encoding of Complex Sounds

The auditory cortex of bats is among the most extensively studied of all mammals. In particular, studies of the auditory cortex of the mustached bat (a long CF/FM bat) give the best illustration of functional organization in the neocortex and how this organization may be used to analyze behaviorally relevant sound features in parallel (Suga 1984).

The auditory cortex (AC) of the mustached bat has one major tonotopic field (AI) surrounded by as many as seven secondary fields. The tonotopic field has a large central area overrepresenting the dominant CF_2 component of the sonar signal (the subscript represents the second of four harmonics of the constant-frequency component of the echolocation call). This field is called the Doppler-shifted constant-frequency processing area (Suga & Jen 1976). Within the Doppler-shifted constant frequency area, isofrequency axes are circular (Suga & Jen 1976), and amplitude is represented radially (Suga & Manabe 1982). Further, Manabe et al (1978) showed that binaural excitatory-excitatory neurons with large receptive fields were found in the region having lowest best amplitudes, and binaural inhibitory-excitatory neurons, which are sensitive to IID, were found in the region with higher best amplitudes. These workers suggested that excitatory-excitatory neurons are better suited for target detection and that inhibitory-excitatory neurons are better suited for target localization.

A notable feature of the mustached bat AC is the presence of a number of nontonotopic areas that contain neurons that respond to complex spectral and temporal features. These are similar to the combination-sensitive neurons described in frogs and birds, which respond to a combination of signal features but are unresponsive (or respond poorly) to the features presented alone. Additionally, feature-selective neurons are represented systematically in these areas.

An example is the systematic representation of the time interval (or delay) between a pulse and an echo in the FM/FM area. This delay represents information on target range. The response selectivity to echo delay appears to be created first in the inferior colliculus (Mittmann & Wenstrup 1995). At the periphery, neurons respond to both pulse and echo. In the IC and beyond, delay sensitive neurons respond only to a particular pulse-echo pair presented with a particular delay (Feng et al 1978, Mittmann & Wenstrup 1995, O'Neill & Suga 1979, 1982, Olsen & Suga 1991a,b). In the AC, there are three FM-FM fields: FM_1/FM_2, FM_1/FM_3, and FM_1/FM_4 (the subscripts represent the first through fourth harmonics of the frequency-modulated component of the echolocation signal). Neurons in any of the fields respond to FM_1 component of the pulse and FM_n component of the echo (where n is either 2, 3, or 4) at particular delays of the echo. The temporal structure of the paired signals is important because these neurons do not respond if the sweep direction of either FM_1 or FM_n is reversed (Suga et al 1983). Neurons in a vertical column are tuned to a particular echo delay, and along the cortical surface there is a delay axis; that is, target range is represented topographically.

In a neighboring region (the CF/CF area), neuronal responses are facilitated by a combination of two constant-frequency tones. There are two fields in this area of the cortex: CF_1/CF_2 and CF_1/CF_3, containing neurons tuned to a combination of pulse CF_1 and Doppler-shifted CF_2 and CF_3, respectively (Suga et al 1983). The frequency axes are arranged along the cortical surface so that cells in a column (into the cortex) are tuned to a particular combination of frequencies. When there is a Doppler shift, the deviation from the harmonic (based on CF_1) can be calculated if CF_2 (or CF_3) is known. From this, relative velocity can be calculated.

In both FM-FM and CF/CF fields, the common harmonic component is the first harmonic, which is weaker than the second harmonic by about 30–40 dB. Suga & O'Neill (1979) suggest that this can serve as a private channel that is unavailable to other bats, thus reducing the likelihood of jamming (or masking) of the target-ranging and the relative-velocity systems by conspecific sounds.

As with frogs and birds, the presence of combination-specific neurons in bats that are tuned to specific features of complex sounds provides a tantalizing view of how the auditory system can extract sounds in real-world conditions. We say tantalizing because the major unsolved problem is to understand how a target, such as a moth, is represented as a unitary object. Further, it is not known how much more specialized neurons can get. For instance, whether there are neurons sensitive to a combination of range, azimuth, elevation, and velocity or whether there is a different principle by which target image is created, such as the synchronized activity of specialized areas (see Singer & Gray 1995).

Combination specificity and representation of complex sounds by synchronized activation of groups of neurons have been observed in the song system of birds (Margoliash & Fortune 1992, Margoliash et al 1994). At what level of complexity certain features are represented in single neurons (such as combination specific neurons) while others are represented across groups of synchronized neurons appears to be an important and unresolved issue.

Temporal Dynamics of Auditory Processing

Under natural listening conditions, many sounds including echolocation sound pulses occur in rapid sequence. Most auditory physiological studies have used sound stimulus in isolation to assure physiological isolation of the stimulus. More recently, there is evidence that stimulation rate can influence processing of sound amplitude and frequency in the FM bat *Myotis lucifugus* (Galazyuk & Feng 1998, 1999). About one half of IC neurons in this bat exhibit dramatic increases in amplitude and frequency selectivities when the repetition rate of sound pulses is increased or when presented with a train of sound pulses whose temporal order resembles the sonar emission of a bat pursuing flying insects. That is, selectivity for a particular acoustic parameter may be dependent on the context or on the rate of stimulation. This is an important finding suggesting that acoustic processing is temporally dynamic. The underlying mechanisms, however, are not known.

In addition to basic processing of sound frequency and amplitude, some neurons in the FM-FM area (in both CF/FM and FM bats) do not respond with a stable best delay as do other neurons. Rather, these neurons exhibit best delays that become shorter as the pulse repetition rate is increased (Suga et al 1978; see Wong et al 1992 for an example in an FM bat). Because bats increase their pulse repetition rate during approach to a target (see above), these neurons can provide a mechanism for tracking a target.

Studies on encoding of AM stimuli in bats have also shed light on feature extraction in complex environments. Neurons in the IC (Condon et al 1994), medial geniculate body (Llano & Feng 1999), and auditory cortex (Condon et al 1997) are particularly sensitive to a train of sound pulses at high rates showing variations in pulse amplitude (such as a series of echoes elicited by flying insects). When the amplitude of sound pulses within the train is constant, such as echoes from stationary background targets, neurons respond poorly. It appears the neurons are particularly sensitive to a dynamic target (to amplitude-modulated pulse trains); this sensitivity may serve to draw attention to potential targets of interest. At present, the neural mechanisms underlying differential sensitivities to modulated and unmodulated pulse trains are not clear. Llano (1999) hypothesized that a simple feed-forward inhibitory circuit, coupled with slow $GABA_B$-mediated inhibition, is sufficient to reproduce the differential responses to the two types of pulse trains. Whether such a mechanism is involved in the bat's auditory system remains to be determined.

Gating Mechanisms and Descending Control

Gating Mechanisms for Sensory Acquisition   In bats, vocalization (sonar emission) influences auditory processing in two ways. Sometimes the influence may be purely mechanical, as in the middle-ear muscle reflex, which reduces auditory sensitivity during vocalization (Suga & Jen 1975). However, there are also neural gating mechanisms that can attenuate responses to self-stimulation. Suga & Schlegel (1972) showed that there is an attenuation of 25 dB in the auditory sensitivity of neurons in the lateral lemniscus (with reference to auditory nerve) after a bat's vocalization. They speculated that the inhibition is controlled by vocal centers that activate the descending auditory system, which in turn suppresses the ascending auditory system. On the other hand, responsiveness of neurons in a time window after vocalization can be improved. Schuller (1979) showed that response of an IC neuron to an artificial stimulus is stronger when the stimulus immediately follows electrically elicited vocalizations. For some of these neurons, enhanced responses to pure tones with Doppler-shifted frequencies were observed after vocal activity. Thus, vocalization serves to prepare the auditory system for incoming echoes, by providing a time window after onset of sonar emission when auditory neurons are more sensitive. These results support behavioral experiments that show that horseshoe bats compensate for Doppler shifts only when the echo arrives within a certain time after the onset of sonar emission (Schuller 1977). Thus, under realistic conditions, internal reference signals may be available to enhance auditory signal processing.

More recently, electrophysiological recordings via telemetry in a songbird (Nieder & Klump 1999) showed that frequency selectivity can depend on the acoustic background. In particular, the selectivity can improve over time as the background persists. This has implications for signal detection and discrimination because selectivity for auditory parameters can be improved in a noisy background, perhaps in a context-dependent manner. Such techniques are welcome additions to physiological studies in behaving animals.

Influence of Descending Pathways on Hearing   Information flow along the ascending auditory pathway is subject to modulation by a descending auditory pathway that runs from the cortex to the cochlea. Neurons in the deep layers of the auditory cortex project to the medial geniculate body (MGB), the IC, and subcollicular nuclei (Diamond et al 1969, Saldana et al 1996; see also Huffman & Henson 1990, Winer 1992 for reviews). In general, each central auditory nucleus receives descending projections from one or more higher-processing centers. Ultimately the projections reach the cochlea via the olivocochlear bundle (OCB) (anatomy reviewed in Warr 1992).

At lower levels of the auditory system, the significance of descending pathways may be to improve hearing performance in noise because stimulation of the OCB reduces masking in single auditory fibers (Winslow & Sachs 1987). However, behavioral studies have suggested that the effect may be to improve discrimination between two signals in noise (Dewson 1968) rather than detection of single sounds in noise (Trahiotis & Elliott 1970). The role of the OCB in auditory attention is much less clear because it appears that the OCB does not gate sensory attention (Michie et al 1996, Oatman 1988) but may act to block out irrelevant auditory stimuli during visual attention tasks (Lukas 1981, Meric & Collet 1994).

More evidence is required to unequivocally demonstrate that the OCB is involved in attentional mechanisms.

At the CN, centrifugal pathways assist in detecting signals in noise by controlling critical bandwidth, suggesting that frequency processing is affected (Pickles 1976, Pickles & Comis 1973). Gating of auditory input was also observed by Comis & Whitfield (1968) because CN neurons lowered their threshold by as much as 15 dB when the superior olive was stimulated. At higher levels, descending influence appears to modulate the dynamic processing of information in the ascending auditory pathway and also serves to modify long-term frequency tuning properties in subcortical structures. Only the dynamic modulation of ascending auditory activity via corticofugal pathways is dealt with here, whereas the interested reader is referred to the recent work by Gao & Suga (1998) on the role of descending influence on associative learning.

Stimulating the auditory cortex of a cat produces both inhibitory and excitatory post-synaptic potentials in IC neurons that project to the MGB (Mitani et al 1983). In the MGB, although an inhibitory influence from cortical neurons has been suggested (Watanabe 1966), a powerful facilitatory effect of corticofugal volleys is routinely observed on single neurons (Andersen et al 1972). Because descending cortical fibers project directly onto the same MGB neurons that project to the cortex (Diamond et al 1969, Morest 1975), the facilitatory effect may be caused by the closed corticogeniculate loop, which could set up reverberations seen in many MGB neurons (Ryugo & Weinberger 1976). In contrast, the cortico-collicular loop is not closed because cortical fibers project to areas in the IC that do not receive direct ascending input (Rockel & Jones 1973a,b). The implications of corticofugal circuits for auditory information processing are becoming clear from a number of studies in bats (Jen et al 1998, Suga et al 1997). A cortical neuron tuned to a selected feature, such as a particular echo delay or frequency, can excite neurons matching the same feature in subcortical areas while inhibiting unmatched neurons (Yan & Suga 1996, Zhang et al 1997). Thus, the stimulation of auditory cortex produces a focused positive feedback effect on subcortical neurons that is associated with widespread lateral inhibition (Zhang et al 1997). This is supported by another study demonstrating that corticofugal mechanisms enhance the response of some neurons while decreasing the response of others (Jen et al 1998). The functional role of these mechanisms is not very clear. Jen et al (1998) suggest that, because of the differences in latencies between IC and cortical neurons, the cortex may regulate responses of IC neurons to subsequent sounds. Bats may also use corticofugal facilitation to enhance target detection during early stages of the hunt sequence, whereas they may use corticofugal inhibition to attenuate response to incoming echoes during pursuit and capture.

At present, there are no conclusive data to indicate that the corticofugal system plays a role in auditory attention. However, considerable interest has been generated by the role of the thalamic reticular nucleus (TRN) in recent years, particularly with respect to its possible role in attentional mechanisms (Crick 1984, Guillery et al 1998). The TRN lies between the auditory thalamus and cortex.

Neurons in the TRN receive synapses from both thalamocortical and cortico-thalamic neurons, while they project back onto thalamic relay cells. It has been suggested that TRN could play a role in controlling the firing pattern of thalamocortical relay cells by switching them between burst and tonic modes of firing (McCormick & Feeser 1990). In the tonic mode of firing, information goes straight through to the cortex without modification, whereas in the burst mode the system reacts to changes in input rather than transmitting information to the cortex. A change in firing pattern can be used to change the focus of attention across the cortex (Guillery et al 1998), thus functioning as an attentional searchlight (Crick 1984). Insofar as we can verify, the role of TRN in auditory information processing is completely unknown. This is clearly a gap in our knowledge base.

Summary

Over the last three decades, significant progress has been made in unraveling the mechanisms by which a complex sound is analyzed by the nervous system. Whereas various sound parameters are mixed at the periphery, the brain uses parallel-processing channels to extract various behaviorally important features. Within each of these processing channels, appropriate sound parameters in the time, frequency, and/or space domains are combined in a hierarchical manner to form feature-selective neurons. At present, it is unclear how feature-selective neurons from different processing channels combine to form a unitary percept of auditory objects, especially in real-world listening conditions where the presence of multiple auditory objects confounds the processing of sounds. This review describes some of the issues that are important for hearing in real-world conditions. Most of the issues addressed physiologically have been those that are more tractable than the larger problem of scene analysis. Clearly, physiological investigations of neural mechanisms of scene analysis are still in their infancy, and gaps in our understanding are profound. Additionally, physiological observations should be coupled to psychophysics or behavior to test for perceptual phenomena such as grouping and segregation of auditory streams or to test for attentional mechanisms. In this regard, it is important that the studies are carried out in appropriate animal model systems in which the behavior is characterizable.

CONCLUSION

Nearly 50 years after Cherry (1953) described the cocktail party problem, his most important question remains unanswered: How do humans listen to and understand what one person is saying when there are many people speaking at the same time? But, in the intervening period, a great deal has been added to our understanding. For instance, we know that spatial hearing is important for selective extraction of speech, but by itself it is not sufficient. Other processes such as sound source segregation and grouping of acoustic information, as well as attentional mechanisms, are of equal if not greater importance. Recent physiological studies are offering a glimpse of the neural basis of some of the simpler auditory tasks in scene analysis. Moreover, because most living organisms listen actively in complex environments and use strategies to optimally transmit and receive sounds, future experiments ideally should be conducted in actively behaving animals or at least in unanesthetized preparations. Finally, the auditory system is adaptive, dynamic, and plastic. The system can "learn" to improve its performance through experience. Therefore, it is important to keep in mind that the processing of sounds by biological systems is unlikely to be a static process.

Visit the Annual Reviews home page at www.AnnualReviews.org.

LITERATURE CITED

Andersen P, Junge K, Sveen O. 1972. Cortico-fugal facilitation of thalamic transmission. *Brain Behav. Evol.* 6:170–84

Awbrey FT. 1978. Social interaction among chorusing Pacific tree frogs, *Hyla regilla. Copeia* 1978:208–14

Blauert J. 1983. *Spatial Hearing.* Cambridge, MA: MIT Press. 427 pp.

Bregman AS. 1990. *Auditory Scene Analysis.* Cambridge, MA: MIT Press. 773 pp.

Bregman AS, Campbell J. 1971. Primary auditory stream segregation and perception of order in rapid sequences of tones. *J. Exp. Psychol.* 89:244–49

Capranica RR. 1965. *The Evoked Vocal Response of the Bullfrog: A Study of Communication in Anurans.* Cambridge, MA: MIT Press

Capranica RR, Moffat AJM. 1983. Neurobehavioral correlates of sound communication in anurans. In *Advances in Vertebrate Neuroethology,* ed. JP Ewert, RR Capranica, DJ Ingle, pp. 701–30. New York: Plenum

Carr CE, Konishi M. 1990. A circuit for detection of interaural time differences in the brain stem of the barn owl. *J. Neurosci.* 10:3227–46

Cherry EC. 1953. Some experiments on the recognition of speech, with one and two ears. *J. Acoust. Soc. Am.* 25:975–79

Comis SD, Whitfield IC. 1968. Influence of centrifugal pathways on unit activity in the cochlear nucleus. *J. Neurophysiol.* 31:62–68

Condon CJ, Chang SH, Feng AS. 1995. Classification of the temporal discharge patterns of single auditory neurons in the superior olivary nucleus of the leopard frog. *Hear. Res.* 83:190–202

Condon CJ, Galazyuk A, Feng AS. 1997. Neurons in the auditory cortex of the little brown bat exhibit selectivity for complex-amplitude modulated signals that mimic echoes from fluttering insects. *Audit. Neurosci.* 3:269–87

Condon CJ, White KR, Feng AS. 1994. Processing of amplitude modulated signals that mimic echoes from fluttering targets in the inferior colliculus of the little brown bat, *Myotis lucifugus. J. Neurophysiol.* 71:768–84

Crick F. 1984. Function of the thalamic reticular complex: the searchlight hypothesis. *Proc. Natl. Acad. Sci. USA* 81:4586–90

de Boer E, Dreschler WA. 1987. Auditory psychophysics: spectrotemporal representation of signals. *Annu. Rev. Psychol.* 38:181–202

Dent ML, Dooling RJ, Larsen ON. 1997. Free-field binaural unmasking in budgerigars (*Melopsittacus undulatus*). *Behav. Neurosci.* 111:590–98

Dewson JH. 1968. Efferent olivocochlear bundle: some relationships to stimulus discrimination in noise. *J. Neurophysiol.* 31:122–30

Diamond IT, Jones EG, Powell TPS. 1969. The projection of the auditory cortex upon the diencephalon and the brain stem of the cat. *Brain Res.* 15:305–40

Dooling RJ. 1982. Auditory perception in birds. In *Acoustic Communication in Birds,* Vol. 1, ed. DE Kroodsma, EH Miller, pp. 95–130. New York: Academic

Ehret G, Gerhardt HC. 1980. Auditory masking and effects of noise on responses of the green treefrog (*Hyla cinerea*) to synthetic mating calls. *J. Comp. Physiol. A* 141:13–18

Epping WJM, Eggermont JJ. 1986. Sensitivity of neurons in the auditory midbrain of the grassfrog to temporal characteristics of sound. II. Stimulation with amplitude modulated sound. *Hear. Res.* 24:55–72

Feare C. 1984. *The Starling.* Oxford, UK: Oxford Univ. Press

Feng AS, Gerhardt HC, Capranica RR. 1976. Sound localization behavior of the green treefrog (*Hyla cinerea*) and the barking treefrog (*H. gratiosa*). *J. Comp. Physiol. A* 107:241–52

Feng AS, Hall JC, Siddique S. 1991. Coding of temporal parameters of complex sounds by frog auditory nerve fibers. *J. Neurophysiol.* 65:424–45

Feng AS, Lin WY. 1994. Phase-locked response characteristics of single neurons in the frog "cochlear nucleus" to steady-state and sinusoidally-amplitude modulated tones. *J. Neurophysiol.* 72:2209–21

Feng AS, Narins PM, Capranica RR. 1975. Three populations of primary auditory fibers in the bullfrog (*Rana catesbeiana*): their peripheral origins and frequency sensitivities. *J. Comp. Physiol.* 100:221–29

Feng AS, Schellart NAM. 1999. Central auditory processing in fish and amphibians. In *Comparative Hearing: Fish and Amphibians,* ed. RR Fay, AN Popper, pp. 218–68. New York: Springer-Verlag. 438 pp.

Feng AS, Simmons JA, Kick SA. 1978. Echo detection and target-ranging neurons in the auditory system of the bat *Eptesicus fuscus. Science* 202:645–48

Fenton MB. 1995. Natural history and biosonar signals. In *Hearing by Bats,* ed. AN Popper, RR Fay, pp. 37–87. New York: Springer-Verlag. 515 pp.

Fritzsch B, Ryan MJ, Wilczynski W, Hetherington TE, Walkowiak W, eds. 1988. *The Evolution of the Amphibian Auditory System.* New York: Wiley & Sons. 705 pp.

Fujita I, Konishi M. 1991. The role of GABAergic inhibition in processing of interaural time difference in the owl's auditory system. *J. Neurosci.* 11:722–40

Fuzessery ZN, Feng AS. 1982. Frequency selectivity in the anuran auditory midbrain: single unit responses to single and multiple tones. *J. Comp. Physiol. A* 146:471–84

Fuzessery ZN, Feng AS. 1983. Frequency selectivity in the anuran medulla: excitatory and inhibitory tuning properties of single neurons in the dorsal medullary and superior olivary nuclei. *J. Comp. Physiol. A* 150:107–19

Galazyuk AV, Feng AS. 1998. *Rate of acoustic stimulation influences the response selectivity of inferior colliculus neurons to sound amplitude.* Presented at Annu. Meet. Int. Cong. Neuroethol., 5th, San Diego

Galazyuk AV, Feng AS. 1999. *Temporal effects on central auditory processing.* Presented at Annu. Meet. Assoc. Res. Otolaryngol., 22nd, St. Petersburg

Gao E, Suga N. 1998. Experience-dependent corticofugal adjustment of midbrain frequency map in bat auditory system. *Proc. Natl. Acad. Sci. USA* 95:12663–70

Gatehouse RW. 1987. Further research on free field masking. *J. Acoust. Soc. Am.* 82:S108 (Suppl.)

Gerhardt HC. 1978a. Discrimination of intermediate sounds in a synthetic call continuum by female green treefrogs. *Science* 199:1089–91

Gerhardt HC. 1978b. Mating call recognition in the green treefrog (*Hyla cinerea*): significance of some fine-temporal properties. *J. Exp. Biol.* 74:59–73

Gerhardt HC. 1988. Acoustic properties used in call recognition by frogs and toads. See Fritzsch et al 1988, pp. 455–83

Gerhardt HC, Klump GM. 1988. Phonotactic responses and selectivity of barking treefrogs (*Hyla gratiosa*) to chorus sounds. *J. Comp. Physiol.* A 163:795–802

Gooler DM, Feng AS. 1992. Temporal coding in the frog auditory midbrain: the influence of duration and rise-fall time on the processing of complex amplitude modulated stimuli. *J. Neurophysiol.* 67:1–22

Griffin DR. 1958. *Listening in the Dark.* New Haven: Yale Univ. Press

Guillery RW, Feig SL, Lozsadi DA. 1998. Paying attention to the thalamic reticular nucleus. *Trends Neurosci.* 21:28–32

Hall JC. 1994. Central processing of communication sounds in the anuran auditory system. *Am. Zool.* 34:670–84

Hall JC, Feng AS. 1987. Evidence for parallel processing in the frog's auditory thalamus. *J. Comp. Neurol.* 258:407–19

Hall JC, Feng AS. 1990. Classification of the temporal discharge patterns of single neurons in the dorsal medullary nucleus of the northern leopard frog. *J. Neurophysiol.* 64:1460–73

Hall JC, Feng AS. 1991. Temporal processing in the dorsal medullary nucleus of the northern leopard frog (*Rana pipiens pipiens*). *J. Neurophysiol.* 66:955–73

Hall JW, Haggard MP, Fernandes MA. 1984. Detection in noise by spectro-temporal pattern analysis. *J. Acoust. Soc. Am.* 76:50–56

Hawley ML, Litovsky RY, Colburn HS. 1999. Speech intelligibility and localization in a multisource environment. *J. Acoust. Soc. Am.* 105:3436–48

Hillery CM, Narins PM. 1984. Detection of amplitude-modulated tones by frogs: implications for temporal processing mechanisms. *Hear. Res.* 14:129–43

Hirsh IJ. 1950. The relation between localization and intelligibility. *J. Acoust. Soc. Am.* 22:196–200

Hirsh IJ, Watson CS. 1996. Auditory psychophysics and perception. *Annu. Rev. Psychol.* 47:461–84

Huffman RF, Henson OW Jr. 1990. The descending auditory pathway and acousticomotor systems: connections with the inferior colliculus. *Brain. Res. Rev.* 15:295–323

Hulse SH, MacDougall-Shackleton SA, Wisniewski AB. 1997. Auditory scene analysis by songbirds: stream segregation of birdsong in European starlings (*Sturnus vulgaris*). *J. Comp. Psychol.* 111:3–13

Jeffress LA. 1948. A place theory of sound localization. *J. Comp. Physiol. Psychol.* 41:35–39

Jen PH-S, Chen QC, Sun XD. 1998. Corticofugal regulation of auditory sensitivity in the bat inferior colliculus. *J. Comp. Physiol.* A 183:683–97

Jones MR, Yee W. 1993. Attending to auditory events: the role of temporal organization. In *Thinking in Sound: The Cognitive Psychology of Human Audition,* ed. S McAdams, E Bigand, pp. 69–112. Oxford, UK: Oxford Univ. Press. 354 pp.

Julesz B, Hirsh IJ. 1972. Visual and auditory perception—an essay in comparison. In *Human Communication: A Unified View,* ed. EE David Jr, PB Denes. New York: McGraw-Hill. 458 pp.

Keller CH, Takahashi TT. 1996a. A precedence effect in the owl's auditory space map? *J. Comp. Physiol.* A 178:499–512

Keller CH, Takahashi TT. 1996b. Binaural cross-correlation predicts the responses of neurons in the owl's auditory space map under conditions simulating summing localization. *J. Neurosci.* 16:4300–9

Klump GM. 1996. Bird communication in the noisy world. In *Ecology and Evolution of Acoustic Communication in Birds,* ed. DE Kroodsma, EH Miller, pp. 321–38. Ithaca, NY: Cornell Univ. Press. 587 pp.

Klump GM, Langemann U. 1995. Comodulation masking release in a songbird. *Hear. Res.* 87:157–64

Knudsen EI, Blasdel GG, Konishi M. 1979. Sound localization by the barn owl (*Tyto alba*) measured with the search-coil technique. *J. Comp. Physiol. A* 133:1–11

Knudsen EI, Konishi M. 1978a. Center surround organization of auditory receptive fields in the owl. *Science* 202:778–80

Knudsen EI, Konishi M. 1978b. Space and frequency are represented separately in auditory midbrain of the owl. *J. Neurophysiol.* 41:870–84

Kober R, Schnitzler H-U. 1990. Information in sonar echoes of fluttering insects available for echolocating bats. *J. Acoust. Soc. Am.* 87:882–96

Konishi M. 1992. The neural algorithm for sound localization in the owl. *Harvey Lect. Ser.* 86:47–64

Litovsky RY, Yin TCT. 1998. Physiological studies of the precedence effect in the inferior colliculus of the cat. II. Neural mechanisms. *J. Neurophysiol.* 80:1302–16

Llano DA. 1999. *Information processing in the auditory thalamus of the echolocating bat, Myotis lucifugus: implications for fluttering target detection.* PhD thesis. Univ. Illinois, Urbana

Llano DA, Feng AS. 1999. Response characteristics of neurons in the medial geniculate body of the little brown bat to simple and temporally-patterned sounds. *J. Comp. Physiol. A* 184:371–85

Lukas JH. 1981. The role of efferent inhibition in human auditory attention: an examination of the auditory brainstem potentials. *Int. J. Neurosci.* 12:137–46

MacDougall-Shackleton SA, Hulse SH, Gentner TQ, White W. 1998. Auditory scene analysis by European starlings (*Sturnus vulgaris*): perceptual segregation of tone sequences. *J. Acoust. Soc. Am.* 103:3581–87

Manabe T, Suga N, Ostwald J. 1978. Aural representation in the Doppler-shifted processing area of the auditory cortex of the mustache bat. *Science* 200:339–42

Margoliash D, Fortune ES. 1992. Temporal and harmonic combination-sensitive neurons in the zebra finch's HVc. *J. Neurosci.* 12:4309–26

Margoliash D, Fortune ES, Sutter ML, Yu AC, Wren-Hardin BD, Dave A. 1994. Distributed representation in the song system of oscines: evolutionary implications and functional consequences. *Brain. Behav. Evol.* 44:247–64

McCormick DA, Feeser HR. 1990. Functional implications of burst firing and single spike activity in lateral geniculate relay neurons. *J. Neurosci.* 39:103–13

Megela AL. 1984. Diversity of adaptational patterns in responses of eighth nerve fibers in the bullfrog, *Rana catesbeiana*. *J. Acoust. Soc. Am.* 75:1155–62

Megela-Simmons A, Moss CF, Daniel KM. 1985. Behavioral audiograms of the bullfrog (*Rana catesbeiana*) and the green treefrog (*Hyla cinerea*). *J. Acoust. Soc. Am.* 78:1236–44

Meric C, Collet L. 1994. Differential effects of visual attention on spontaneous and evoked otoacoustic emissions. *Int. J. Psychophysiol.* 17:281–89

Michie PT, Lepage EL, Solowij N, Haller M, Terry L. 1996. Evoked otoacoustic emissions and auditory selective attention. *Hear. Res.* 98:54–67

Middlebrooks JC, Green DM. 1991. Sound localization by human listeners. *Annu. Rev. Psychol.* 42:135–59

Miller JL, Eimas PD. 1995. Speech perception: from signal to word. *Annu. Rev. Psychol.* 46:467–92

Mitani A, Shimokouchi M, Nomura S. 1983. Effects of stimulation of the primary auditory cortex on the colliculogeniculate neurons in the inferior colliculus of the cat. *Neurosci. Lett.* 42:185–89

Mittmann DH, Wenstrup JJ. 1995. Combination-sensitive neurons in the inferior colliculus. *Hear. Res.* 90:185–91

Mogdans J, Ostwald J, Schnitzler H-U. 1988. The role of pinna movement for the localization of vertical and horizontal wire obstacles in the greater horseshoe bat, *Rhin-*

olophusa ferrumequinum. J. Acoust. Soc. Am. 84:1676–79

Morest DK. 1975. Synaptic relationships of golgi type II cells in the medial geniculate body of the cat. *J. Comp. Neurol.* 162:157–94

Narins PM, Capranica RR. 1976. Sexual differences in the auditory system of the treefrog *Eleutherodactylus coqui. Science* 192:378–80

Narins PM, Zelick RD. 1988. The effect of noise on auditory processing and behavior in amphibians. See Fritzsch et al 1988, pp. 511–36

Neuweiler G. 1990. Auditory adaptations for prey capture in echolocating bats. *Physiol. Rev.* 70:615–41

Neuweiler G, Fenton MB. 1988. Behavior and foraging ecology of echolocating bats. In *Animal Sonar Systems: Processes and Performance,* ed. PE Nachtigall, PWB Moore, pp. 535–50. New York: Plenum

Neuweiler G, Link A, Marimuthu G, Rubsamen R. 1988. Detection of prey in echocluttering environments. In *Animal Sonar Systems: Processes and Performance,* ed. PE Nachtigall, PWB Moore, pp. 613–18. New York: Plenum

Nieder A, Klump GM. 1999. Adjustable frequency selectivity of auditory forebrain neurons recorded in a freely moving songbird via radiotelemetry. *Hear. Res.* 127:41–54

Oatman LC. 1988. Stability of evoked potentials during auditory attention. *Psychobiology* 16:288–97

Obrist MK, Wenstrup JJ. 1998. Hearing and hunting in red bats (*Lasiurus borealis, Vespertilionidae*): audiogram and ear properties. *J. Exp. Biol.* 201:143–54

Oldham RS, Gerhardt HC. 1975. Behavioral isolation mechanism of the treefrogs Hyla cinerea and Hyla gratiosa. *Copeia* 2:223–31

Olsen JF, Suga N. 1991a. Combination-sensitive neurons in the medial geniculate body of the mustached bat: encoding of

relative velocity information. *J. Neurophysiol.* 65:1254–74

Olsen JF, Suga N. 1991b. Combination-sensitive neurons in the medial geniculate body of the mustached bat: encoding of target range information. *J. Neurophysiol.* 65:1275–96

O'Neill WE, Suga N. 1979. Target range-sensitive neurons in the auditory cortex of the mustache bat. *Science* 203:69–73

O'Neill WE, Suga N. 1982. Encoding of target-range information and its representation in the auditory cortex of the mustache bat. *J. Neurosci.* 47:225–55

Payne RS. 1971. Acoustic location of prey by barn owls. *J. Exp. Biol.* 54:535–73

Phillips DP, Brugge JF. 1985. Progress in neurophysiology of sound localization. *Annu. Rev. Psychol.* 36:245–74

Pickles JO. 1976. Role of centrifugal pathways to cochlear nucleus in determination of critical bandwidth. *J. Neurophysiol.* 39:394–400

Pickles JO, Comis SD. 1973. Role of centrifugal pathways to cochlear nucleus in detection of signals in noise. *J. Neurophysiol.* 36:1131–37

Plomp R, Mimpen AM. 1981. Effect of orientation of the speaker's head and azimuth of a noise source on the speech-reception threshold for sentences. *Acoustics* 48:325–28

Pollak G, Henson OW, Novick A. 1972. Cochlear microphonic audiograms in the "pure tone" bat *Chilonycteris parnelli parnelli. Science* 176:66–68

Rand AS. 1988. An overview of anuran acoustic communication. See Fritzsch et al 1988, pp. 415–31

Ratnam R, Feng AS. 1998. Detection of auditory signals by frog inferior collicular neurons in the presence of spatially separated noise. *J. Neurophysiol.* 80:2848–59

Rheinlaender J, Gerhardt HC, Yager DD, Capranica RR. 1979. Accuracy of phonotaxis by the green treefrog (*Hyla cinerea*). *J. Comp. Physiol. A* 133:247–55

Rockel AJ, Jones EG. 1973a. The neuronal organization of the inferior colliculus of the adult cat. I. The central nucleus. *J. Comp. Neurol.* 147:11–60

Rockel AJ, Jones EG. 1973b. The neuronal organization of the inferior colliculus of the adult cat. II. The pericentral nucleus. *J. Comp. Neurol.* 149:301–34

Rose GJ, Capranica RR. 1984. Processing amplitude modulated sounds by the auditory mid-brain of two species of toads: matched temporal filters. *J. Comp. Physiol. A* 154:211–19

Rose GJ, Capranica RR. 1985. Sensitivity to amplitude modulated sounds in the anuran auditory nervous system. *J. Neurophysiol.* 53:446–65

Ryugo DK, Weinberger NM. 1976. Corticofugal modulation of the medial geniculate body. *Exp. Neurol.* 51:377–91

Saberi K, Dostal L, Sadralodabai T, Bull V, Perrott DR. 1991. Free-field release from masking. *J. Acoust. Soc. Am.* 90:1355–70

Saldana E, Feliciano M, Mugnaini E. 1996. Distribution of descending projections from auditory neocortex to inferior colliculus mimics the topography of intracollicular projections. *J. Comp. Neurol.* 371:215–23

Schnitzler H-U. 1973. Control of Doppler-shift compensation in the greater horseshoe bat, *Rhinolophus ferrumequinum. J. Comp. Physiol. A* 82:79–92

Schooneveldt GP, Moore BCJ. 1987. Comodulation masking release (CMR): effects of signal frequency, flanking-band frequency, masker bandwidth, flanking-band level, and monotic versus dichotic presentation of the flanking band. *J. Acoust. Soc. Am.* 82:1944–56

Schuller G. 1977. Echo delay and overlap with emitted orientation sounds and Doppler-shift compensation in the bat *Rhinolophus ferrumequinum. J. Comp. Physiol. A* 114:103–14

Schuller G. 1979. Vocalization influences auditory processing in collicular neurons of the CF-FM bat, *Rhinolophus ferrumequinum. J. Comp. Physiol. A* 132:39–46

Schwartz JJ. 1987. The function of call alternation in anuran amphibians: a test of three hypotheses. *Evolution* 41:461–70

Schwartz JJ. 1994. Male advertisement and female choice in frogs: recent findings and new approaches to the study of communication in a dynamic acoustic environment. *Am. Zool.* 34:616–24

Schwartz JJ, Gerhardt HC. 1989. Spatially mediated release from auditory masking in an anuran amphibian. *J. Comp. Physiol. A* 166:37–41

Schwartz JJ, Gerhardt HC. 1995. Directionality of the auditory system and call pattern recognition during acoustic interference in the gray tree frog, *Hyla versicolor. Auditory Neurosci.* 1:195–206

Schwartz JJ, Wells KD. 1983. The influence of background noise on the behavior of a neotropical treefrog *Hyla ebraccata. Herpetology* 39:121–29

Simmons AM. 1988. Masking patterns in the bullfrog (*Rana catesbeiana*). I. Behavioral effects. *J. Acoust. Soc. Am.* 83:1087–92

Simmons AM, Moss CF. 1995. Reflex modification: a tool for assessing basic auditory function in anuran amphibians. In *Methods in Comparative Psychoacoustics,* ed. RJ Dooling, RR Fay, G Klump, W Stebbins, pp. 197–208. Basel, Boston, Berlin: Birkhauser Verlag

Simmons JA. 1989. A view of the world through the bat's ear: the formation of acoustic images in echolocation. *Cognition* 33:155–99

Simmons JA, Howell DJ, Suga N. 1975. Information content of bat sonar echoes. *Am. Sci.* 63:204–15

Singer W, Gray CM. 1995. Visual feature integration and the temporal correlation hypothesis *Annu. Rev. Neurosci.* 18:555–86

Suga N. 1984. The extent to which biosonar information is represented in the bat auditory cortex. In *Dynamical Aspects of Neocortical Function,* ed. GM Edelman, WE Gall, WM Cowan, pp. 315–73. New York: Wiley & Sons

Suga N, Jen PH-S. 1975. Peripheral control of acoustic signals in the auditory system of echolocating bats. *J. Exp. Biol.* 62:277–311

Suga N, Jen PH-S. 1976. Disproportionate tonotopic representation for representation for processing CF-FM sonar signals in the mustache bat auditory cortex. *Science* 194:542–44

Suga N, Manabe T. 1982. Neural basis of amplitude-spectrum representation in auditory cortex of the mustached bat. *J. Neurophysiol.* 47:225–55

Suga N, O'Neill WE. 1979. Neural axis representing target range in the auditory cortex of the mustached bat. *Science* 206:351–53

Suga N, O'Neill WE, Kujirai K, Manabe T. 1983. Specificity of "combination sensitive" neurons for processing complex biosonar signals in the auditory cortex of the mustached bat. *J. Neurophysiol.* 49:1573–626

Suga N, O'Neill WE, Manabe T. 1978. Cortical neurons sensitive to combinations of information-bearing elements of biosonar signals in the mustached bat. *Science* 200:778–81

Suga N, Schlegel P. 1972. Neural attenuation of responses to emitted sounds in echolocating bats. *Science* 177:82–84

Suga N, Yan J, Zhang YF. 1997. Cortical maps for hearing and egocentric selection for self-organization. *Trends Cogn. Sci.* 1:13–20

Takahashi TT, Keller CH. 1994. Representation of multiple sound sources in the owl's auditory space map. *J. Neurosci.* 14:4780–93

Takahashi TT, Konishi M. 1988a. Projections of the cochlear nuclei and nucleus laminaris to the inferior colliculus of the barn owl. *J. Comp. Neurol.* 274:190–211

Takahashi TT, Konishi M. 1988b. Projections of nucleus angularis and nucleus laminaris to the lateral lemniscal complex of the barn owl. *J. Comp. Neurol.* 274:212–38

Teas DC. 1989. Auditory physiology: present trends. *Annu. Rev. Psychol.* 40:405–29

Trahiotis C, Elliott DN. 1970. Behavioral investigation of some possible effects of sectioning the crossed olivocochlear bundle. *J. Acoust. Soc. Am.* 47:592–96

Trahiotis C, Robinson DE. 1979. Auditory psychophysics. *Annu. Rev. Psychol.* 30:31–61

Walkowiak W. 1984. Neuronal correlates of the recognition of pulsed sound signals in the grass frog. *J. Comp. Physiol. A* 155:57–66

Warr WB. 1992. Organization of olivocochlear efferent systems in mammals. See Webster et al 1992, pp. 410–48

Watanabe T, Yanagisawa K, Kanzaki J, Katsuki Y. 1966. Cortical efferent flow influencing unit responses of medial geniculate body to sound stimulation. *Exp. Brain Res.* 2:302–17

Webster DB, Popper AN, Fay RR, eds. 1992. *The Mammalian Auditory Pathway: Neuroanatomy.* New York: Springer-Verlag. 485 pp.

Wells KD. 1988. The effect of social interactions on anuran vocal behavior. See Fritzsch et al 1988, pp. 433–54

Wilczynski W, Capranica RR. 1984. The auditory system of anuran amphibians. *Prog. Neurobiol.* 22:1–38

Winer JA. 1992. The functional architecture of the medial geniculate body and the primary auditory cortex. See Webster et al 1992, pp. 222–409

Winslow RL, Sachs MB. 1987. Effect of electrical stimulation of the crossed olivocochlear bundle on auditory nerve response to tones in noise. *J. Neurophysiol.* 57:1002–21

Wisniewski AB, Hulse SH. 1997. Auditory scene analysis in European starlings (*Sturnus vulgaris*): discrimination of song segments, their segregation from multiple and reversed conspecific songs, and evidence for conspecific song categorization. *J. Comp. Psychol.* 111:337–50

Wong D, Maekawa M, Tanaka H. 1992. The effect of pulse repetition rate on the delay sensitivity of neurons in the auditory cortex of the FM bat, *Myotis lucifugus. J. Comp. Physiol. A* 170:393–402

Yan J, Suga N. 1996. Corticofugal modulation of time-domain processing of biosonar information in bats. *Science* 273:1100–3

Yin TCT, Chan JCK. 1988. Neural mechanisms underlying interaural time sensitivity to tones and noise. In *Auditory Function: Neurobiological Bases of Hearing,* ed. GM Edelman, WE Gall, WM Cowan, pp. 385–430. New York: Wiley & Sons. 817 pp.

Yost WA. 1992. Auditory image perception and analysis. *Hear. Res.* 56:8–19

Zelick RD, Narins PM. 1982. Analysis of acoustically evoked call suppression behavior in a neotropical treefrog. *Anim. Behav.* 30:728–33

Zelick RD, Narins PM. 1983. Intensity discrimination and the precision of call timing in two species of neotropical treefrogs. *J. Comp. Physiol. A* 153:403–12

Zelick RD, Narins PM. 1985. Characterization of the advertisement call oscillator in the frog, *Eleutherodactylus coqui. J. Comp. Physiol. A* 156:223–29

Zhang Y, Suga N, Yan J. 1997. Corticofugal modulation of frequency processing in bat auditory system. *Nature* 387:900–3

Zurek PM. 1992. Binaural advantages and directional effects in speech intelligibility. In *Acoustical Factors Affecting Hearing Aid Performance,* ed. GA Studebaker, I Hochberg, pp. 225–76. Boston: Allyn & Bacon

AUTHOR INDEX

A

Aamar S, 44
Aaron JD, 81
Abe M, 40
Abel RL, 290
Aber JL, 450, 453, 464
Aber MS, 206, 207
Abraini JH, 242
Abramowitz AI, 150
Abrams D, 559
Abrams JS, 44
Abramson LY, 318, 321, 335
Acermann R, 46
Achenbach TM, 584, 585
Achter JA, 411, 412, 420
Ackerman BP, 502
Ackerman E, 462, 463
Ackerman PL, 178, 406, 409, 422, 424, 425, 637, 641
Ackerman PT, 458, 459
Ackerson LM, 588
Ackil JK, 504, 507
Adair W, 297, 300
Addis A, 258
Adelman A, 450
Adelman HS, 369
Adler N, 299
Adolphs R, 609, 610
Aggleton JP, 609, 610
Agnew CR, 552
Aguilar–Gaxiola S, 587
Aguinis H, 647, 645, 646
Ahadi S, 21
Ahadi SA, 671, 675, 676, 684–87
Ahmad N, 673
Ahn W, 127
Ahren B, 265
Aiken L, 206, 212
Aiken LS, 348

Ajzen I, 548–50
Akamine TX, 649
Akar CA, 33
Aker T, 390
Akins FR, 231, 233, 238
Akkerhuis GW, 585
Akman D, 455
Akoh H, 177
Aksan N, 681
Alanen YO, 397
Alarcon RD, 576, 589
Alba JW, 492, 493, 495, 521
Aldrete E, 587
Alessandri SM, 455, 463, 465
Alexander JE, 418
Alexander RA, 646
Alfonso–Reese LA, 135
Algom D, 486, 490
Alizadeh H, 43
Allan LG, 499
Allchorne A, 42, 43
Allen DM, 457, 458, 463
Allen JB, 673
Allen JD, 178
Allen JP, 450
Allen NJ, 209, 648
Allen RE, 464
Alliger GM, 640
Allison DB, 264
Allison ML, 76
Alloy LB, 318, 321, 335
Allport GW, 95–98, 100, 105, 423, 486, 543
Allred KG, 285, 649
Al–Issa I, 579
Almagor M, 423
Alper JS, 384, 388
Alpert A, 207
Alschuler AS, 184

Altizer AM, 258, 261
Altmaier EM, 210
Altman I, 233, 235–38, 245
Alvarez RM, 154, 155
Alvaro EM, 560
Alwin D, 218
Amador XF, 396, 397
Amann K, 619
Amanzio M, 33
Amaral DG, 607–9, 619, 620
Ambadar Z, 505, 507
Ameglio PJ, 262
Amemiya A, 268
Ames C, 174, 175, 185, 190, 191
Ames R, 190
Amit DJ, 623
Amsel G, 137
Anas A, 499
Anastasi A, 406
Anderman EM, 174, 183
Andersen ES, 132
Andersen P, 716
Andersen SL, 462, 463
Andersen SM, 96, 318
Anderson B, 418
Anderson D, 589
Anderson GD, 639
Anderson JR, 96, 124
Anderson JRL, 230
Anderson LE, 646
Anderson N, 632, 647
Anderson S, 267
Anderson SJ, 486, 487, 511
Anderson SW, 611
Anderson WR, 45
Andreasen NC, 388, 389, 397
Andres D, 206
Andrews CA, 350

Andrews JK, 129
Andrews KM, 265
Andrews LK, 457, 459
Angleitner A, 396
Anglin TM, 448, 459
Angoff WH, 10
Angrist B, 386
Anisman H, 20
Anker M, 572, 582
Ansfield ME, 66, 74
Ansolabehere S, 151, 152, 155, 156, 159–61, 163–65
Ansseau M, 242
Antel JP, 45
Antonovsky A, 229, 240
Antrobus JS, 60
Aou S, 40
Apanovitch AM, 554
Apicella P, 609, 612
Appel AE, 452
Appelbaum PS, 394
Applbaum AI, 291
Aravich PF, 260
Arbuckle B, 322
Arbuckle JL, 217
Arbuckle T, 206
Archbold PG, 356
Archer J, 175, 190
Argiles N, 583
Arias I, 321, 322
Armbruster T, 504
Arndt J, 66, 72, 74
Arnett J, 585
Aronne LJ, 269
Aronson E, 546, 547
Aronson J, 547
Arroyo CG, 180
Arroyo W, 462
Arseneault L, 685
Arthur W, 633, 641, 642, 649, 651
Arthur W Jr, 642
Aryee S, 649
Asch SE, 549
Ashby FG, 135
Ashgar AUR, 48
Ashton MC, 638
Askew W, 392

Aspinwall LG, 556
Asquith P, 332
Asuncion AG, 558
Athenstaedt U, 683
Atkins MS, 448, 456, 461
Atkinson JW, 173, 181, 191
Atran S, 129, 130, 133, 138
Au TK, 125, 136, 137
Austen–Smith D, 162
AUSTIN JT, 201–26; 202, 411, 420, 647
Averill JR, 637
Awbrey FT, 703
Axelrod S, 281
Axton TR, 639
Ayers MS, 495, 503–5
Ayers TS, 457, 459, 463
Azar ST, 330
Azuma H, 334
Azzopardi P, 615, 623

B

Baarda B, 408
Baars BJ, 94
Babcock CJ, 129
Babcock JC, 365, 368
Babcock L, 284, 285
Baber NS, 33
Bachelard C, 230, 231, 237, 238
Bachrach AJ, 228, 232
Baddeley A, 104
Baddeley AD, 512, 513
Baden AD, 328
Bagby RM, 208
Bagdade JD, 265
Bagiella E, 685
Bahrick HP, 495, 511
Bailey DE, 648
Baillargeon R, 136, 137
Baker WE, 284, 459
Baker–Brown G, 588
Baldwin MW, 318, 543
Baldwin RL, 44
Bales R, 296
Ball S, 62, 63, 73
Ball TM, 489

Balla JR, 219
Balle–Jensen L, 585
Ball–Rokeach SJ, 550
Balsam T, 643
Balser GM, 323
Baltes MM, 217
Baltes PB, 212
Banaji MR, 97, 99, 100, 109, 131, 336, 549
Bandura A, 319, 324, 388
Banez GA, 336
Bank LI, 7
Banks J, 162
Barabasz AF, 238
Barabasz M, 242
Baradaran LP, 322
Barahal RM, 464
Barak V, 44
Barbarito M, 230
Barber JG, 182
Barclay CR, 510, 511
Barclay LC, 183
Bargh JA, 65, 74, 78, 96–101, 105, 107–9, 111, 131, 318
Barkley RA, 380, 395
Barling J, 456
Barlow BF, 396
Barlow DH, 396, 668–70
Barnes AE, 514, 515
Barnes CD, 38, 40
Barnes RH, 258
Barnett B, 675
Barnett D, 452, 455, 457, 458, 465, 468
Barney MF, 632
Barocas R, 453
Baron AE, 588
Baron GD, 585
Baron H, 649
Baron RS, 547, 553, 561
Barone C, 457, 459, 463
Barone M, 256, 265
Barr RA, 126
Barrachina MD, 261, 263
Barrera M Jr, 684
Barrett GV, 409, 633
Barrett KC, 678, 679

Barrett RS, 650
Barrick MR, 637, 639, 640, 649
Barron KE, 175
Barry B, 281, 286, 649
Barsade SG, 297
Barsalou LW, 129, 130, 132–35
Barsness Z, 291
Bartels LM, 152, 154–56
Bartlett FC, 482, 484, 485, 487, 488, 493, 494
Barto AG, 617
Barton ME, 127
Basinski M, 266
BASKIN DG, 255–77; 265–68
Basoglu M, 390
Bates DE, 63, 66, 70, 72, 74, 82, 83
Bates EA, 13
Bates J, 21
Bates JE, 6, 14, 318, 322, 451, 464, 465, 467, 687
Batson CD, 672, 673
Battle WS, 651
Bauer PJ, 130
Bauer TN, 647, 648
Baum A, 237, 384
Baum CS, 237, 322
Baumeister RF, 65, 78, 667
Baumgardner MH, 213
Baumgartner FR, 157
Baumgartner H, 204
Baumgartner SW, 49
Baumrind D, 4
Bautista E, 587
Baylis GC, 608–10, 614, 615, 617
Baylis LL, 602, 610
BAZERMAN MH, 279–314; 281–86, 292–94, 301–3
Beach SRH, 321, 322, 393
Beals J, 588
Beare AN, 238
Beattie AE, 134
Beattie MC, 352, 360, 362, 366

Beauvois J, 546
Bebbington P, 582, 583
Bebchuk J, 362, 365
Bechara A, 611
Becher B, 45
Bechtel R, 234, 236, 237
Bechtold DW, 588
Beck AT, 69, 82
Beck JG, 80
Beck PA, 157
Becker PS, 46
Bedell SJ, 673
Beech A, 82
Beery RG, 181
Beevers CG, 60, 69, 80, 83
Begg D, 406, 431
Begg IM, 499
Behl–Chadha G, 131
Behr R, 161
Beiser M, 588
Beitchman JH, 455
Bekerian DA, 505
Belding MA, 354
Bell CC, 449, 452, 468
Bell DW, 551
Bell R, 457, 458
Belli RF, 483, 499, 503, 504
Belsky J, 21, 217, 322
Beltranena R, 180
Beltz J, 583
Benbow CP, 406, 408, 409, 411, 412, 414, 416–18, 420, 426, 429, 635
Bendiksen M, 505, 507
Benedetti F, 33
Benet V, 423
Benhabib S, 165
Benjamin AS, 486, 514
Bennett BL, 234
Bennett DLH, 42
Bennett GJ, 44
Bennett M, 648
Bennett N, 634
Bennett PH, 10
Bennett RJ, 301
Bennett W, 641, 649
Benoit SC, 258, 261
Bensel RT, 460

Benson PJ, 489
Benthem L, 258
Benthin AC, 547
Bentler PM, 202, 206, 212, 216, 219, 348
Bentovim A, 322, 326
Benveniste S, 125
Ben–Ze'ev A, 666
Ben Zur H, 497
Berg RA, 455
Bergan T, 229, 238
Bergeman CS, 13, 433
Berger SA, 495
Berghage TE, 237
Bergin DA, 180, 190
Berglas S, 183
Bergner RM, 378, 381–83, 389
Beriama A, 448
Berkowitz JM, 556
Berlin B, 129
Berman AU, 388
Berman ME, 393
Bernheimer LP, 586
Bernieri F, 433
Berning A, 237
Bernstein DP, 396
Bernstein IL, 387
Bernstein J, 636
Berntson GG, 554
Bernzweig J, 681, 684, 686, 687
Berry CA, 234, 244
Berry JW, 587, 669, 670
Berscheid E, 284
Bersoff DN, 109
Berstein LS, 350, 351, 367
Berthoud HR, 262, 263
Berthoz A, 621
Bertrando P, 583
Bessenoff GR, 95, 105, 106
Bessler A, 395
Best DL, 484
Betancourt H, 289, 573
Betz A, 511–13
Betz AL, 549
Bezirganian S, 396
Bezzi P, 46

Bhargava R, 245
Bialik RJ, 462
Bian D, 33
Bickett LR, 328
Bickman L, 361
Biek M, 554, 557
Bierman EL, 265
Biernat M, 104
Biersner RJ, 238
Bigler ED, 418
Bilder RM, 396
Bilgic R, 644
Billings FJ, 506
Billington CJ, 266
Billman DO, 125
Bills AJ, 495
Bimbela A, 327
Binder–Brynes K, 387, 390
Binet A, 508
Bing MN, 639
Bird HR, 585
Birder L, 48
Birgisdottir AB, 71, 82
Birley JLT, 582, 583
Bisby MA, 44
Bishop S, 76
Bisson T, 242
Bizman A, 283
Bjork RA, 60, 77, 486, 514
Bjorklund DF, 503, 509,
    516, 520
Bjorntorp P, 264
Black AE, 4
Black M, 458
Blackstone T, 543, 544, 559,
    560
Blackwell JM, 482–84, 486,
    501–3
Blair IV, 99, 100, 289
Blair SM, 239
Blair–West J, 267
Blais A, 153, 157, 158
Blake AW, 74–76, 81
Blakley T, 459
Blanchard L, 502
Blanchard R, 395
Blanton H, 547
Blasdel GG, 705

Blauert J, 710
Blazer DG, 572
Bleske AL, 382, 383
Bless H, 555
Blessum KA, 105
Blitstein J, 66, 78
Block J, 413, 423, 686
Block JH, 686
Block N, 12
Bloom HS, 356
Bloom JD, 572
Bloom L, 125
Bloom P, 127, 138
Bloom S, 285
Blount S, 288
Blount White S, 301
Blue J, 322, 326, 337
Blum LA, 666
Blumberg SJ, 75, 76, 81
Blumenfeld PC, 177, 190
Blumler JG, 157
Bluth BJ, 232–37, 243, 244
Bluthe R–M, 38
Bobko P, 646, 647
Bobo L, 109
Bobrow W, 643
Bodamer JL, 495
Boden G, 265
BODENHAUSEN GV,
    93–120; 55, 60, 65, 66,
    72, 74, 77, 79, 95,
    97–106, 108–13, 131
Bodrero R, 669
Bohman M, 20
Bohner G, 551, 560, 561
Boisvert J, 175, 176
Bol JGJM, 37
Boldizar JP, 285, 449, 462
Bolger KE, 465, 468, 469
Bolin LM, 44
Bollen KA, 203, 210, 215
Bonanno GA, 76
Bond GR, 350, 354
Bond MH, 208, 298
Bond R, 542, 562
Bondi KR, 234, 238
Bondy EM, 324, 335
Bonett DG, 219

Boney–McCoy S, 448, 449,
    462, 469
Bono JE, 639
Bontempo RN, 299
Boodoo G, 398, 408, 410,
    416
Boot D, 587
Booth MCA, 605, 614, 615,
    618
Booth RJ, 69, 77
Boozer C, 267
Borden GA, 300
Borgen FH, 420, 421
Borgida E, 109
Boring EG, 435
Borkovec TD, 63, 70
Borkowski JG, 176
Borman WC, 632, 633
Bornstein M, 21
Bornstein MH, 334
Bornstein RF, 499
Boroditsky L, 125
Borthwick L, 44
Boruch RF, 346, 347, 363,
    448
Bostock EM, 621
Bosveld W, 550
Bottom WP, 283, 299
Bouchard C, 264
Bouchard TJ, 396–98, 408,
    410, 416, 418, 419, 421,
    422, 429, 432, 433, 435
Bouffard T, 175, 176
Bourne EJ, 582
Bower GH, 70, 96, 462
Bowerman M, 125
Bowers JM, 505
Bowers KS, 73
Bowlby J, 318, 319, 328
Bowman ML, 387
Bowser R, 66, 74
Bowtell R, 605, 610
Boyes–Braem P, 128–30
Boykin AW, 398, 408, 410,
    416
Boyle MH, 448
Bradburn NM, 151, 513
Bradbury TN, 289

Braden CJ, 359
Bradley EJ, 322
Bradley SJ, 395
Brady HE, 153, 156–58
Braeges JL, 679
Brainerd CJ, 336, 492, 500, 501, 503, 505, 518
Braisby N, 138
Brakke KE, 419, 420
Branco AU, 317, 333
Brand C, 408
Brandenburger AM, 286, 290
Brandon P, 259
Brannick MT, 209
Brannon LA, 157
Bransford JD, 494, 495
Brass DJ, 301
Braucht GN, 347
Braungart–Reiker JM, 685
Braverman EP, 642
Bravo M, 580, 581
Bray GA, 257, 263, 264, 267, 269
Breckenridge C, 262
Breckler SJ, 204
Bredenkamp J, 494
Bregman AS, 700–2, 706
Brehm JW, 546
Breininger JF, 266–68
Breinlinger K, 136
Breitbart W, 47
Brekke JS, 353, 359
Brekke N, 109
Bremner JD, 391, 462
Brennan P, 206
Brennan S, 489
Bressi C, 583
Bretherton I, 318
Brett E, 391
Brett JM, 297–301
Brewer MB, 95, 98, 105, 134, 540, 557
Brewer MT, 39
Brewer WF, 485, 486, 492, 493, 495, 496, 510, 511
Brewin CR, 77
Brians CL, 152, 155
Briggs JE, 266

Brimacombe CAE, 508, 509
Brinkmeyer K, 638
Bristow AF, 39, 41, 42
Bristow PK, 266
Broach D, 644
Broadhurst DD, 447
Brodt SE, 302
Brody CJ, 349
Brody G, 15
Brody GH, 321, 322
Brody LE, 416
Brody N, 398, 408, 410, 416
Broks P, 609
Bronen RA, 462
Bronstein P, 183
Brook JS, 396
Brooks LR, 129
Broome A, 75, 76, 81
Brophy J, 192
Brothers L, 609
Brown A, 75, 76
Brown BR, 280, 281, 283, 303
Brown DM, 397, 505
Brown EG, 324, 335
Brown GW, 582, 583
Brown JD, 285, 499
Brown M, 327
Brown R, 96, 97, 99, 100, 128, 134, 512
Brown RJ, 540, 557
Brown RT, 328
Brown SD, 215
Brown SL, 673
Brown TA, 396
Browne A, 451, 468
Browne MW, 212, 215–19
Brownell KD, 264
Browner CH, 589
Browner D, 231
Browning AS, 628
Bruce CJ, 623
Bruce D, 513
Bruce SE, 448, 453, 457, 459
Bruck M, 504, 506–9, 516
Brugge JF, 701
Bruner J, 95

Bruner JS, 545
Brunhart SM, 556
Brunsman B, 553
Brunswik E, 522
Bruyére S, 650
Bryan TS, 69
Bryant B, 81
Bryant KJ, 385
Bryant RA, 63, 70, 80, 391
Bryk AS, 366
Brynjolfsdottir B, 71, 82
Buckley MJ, 618
Budelmann BU, 43
Budesheim TL, 558
BueVallesky JM, 266
BUGENTAL DB, 315–44; 316, 318, 319, 321, 322, 325–27, 330, 331, 336, 337
Buhman DC, 673
Bukowski TR, 266, 267
Bull R, 508
Bull V, 701, 711
Burbaumer N, 418
Burette F, 34
Burger GK, 633
Burgess N, 622
Burgess P, 104
Burgess PW, 513
Burgett SG, 266
Burggraf SA, 670
Burke L, 460
Burke MJ, 634
Burke PJ, 208
Burks BS, 433
Burks VS, 321
Burman B, 469
Burn P, 266–68
Burnam A, 587
Burnett JR, 642
Burns DD, 396
Burns HJ, 495
Burr RG, 230, 238
Burris CT, 547
Burrough B, 240, 241, 247
Burroughs SM, 639
Burrows L, 108, 318
Burt C, 435

Burton D, 462
Burton MJ, 605, 610
Busceme S, 543, 544, 559, 560
Bushman BJ, 638
Buss DM, 382, 383
Buswell B, 666
Butera F, 561
Butterworth B, 191
Butzlaff RL, 394
Bwanausi C, 462
Byatt G, 489
Bybee D, 351
Bybee J, 670
Byrd M, 497
Byrd RE, 235
Byrne RW, 490

C

Cacioppo JT, 554, 551
Cadenhead C, 457
Cadet P, 46
Cador M, 612
Cadoret RJ, 12, 17, 20
Cahusac PMB, 621
Calam R, 457
Calamari JE, 81
Calder AJ, 609, 610
Calderón RF, 202
Caldji C, 19
Caldwell JI, 499
Calingasan NY, 258
Callaghan M, 461
Callinan M, 637
Callister JD, 635
Calloway JW, 258
Camerer C, 284, 285
Cameron KA, 556
Campbell DT, 113, 209, 347, 348, 358, 361, 413, 414
Campbell JE, 150, 706
Campbell JP, 408, 409, 415, 416, 632, 633, 635, 647, 651
Campbell L, 572
Campbell P, 64, 71
Campfield LA, 259, 266, 267

Campion JE, 635, 641, 642, 645
Campion MA, 633, 641, 642, 648
Camras LA, 464
Canino G, 580, 581, 585
Cannon–Bowers J, 635
Cantor N, 182
Capelli S, 462
Caplan LJ, 126
Capps MH, 638
Capranica RR, 702, 703, 707, 708
Caramazza A, 132
Caraveo–Anduaga J, 587
Cardinal RN, 608, 609, 612
Cardon LR, 211
Carey G, 12
Carey S, 136, 137, 489
Carlo G, 673, 674, 681, 684
Carlson AJ, 259
Carlson EA, 321
Carlson KD, 643
Carlson M, 683
Carlson SL, 48
Carlson–Radvansky LA, 490
Carlton SM, 45
Carmichael ST, 607–9
Carnap R, 433
Carnevale PJD, 281, 283, 285, 289–93, 295, 296
Carpenter PA, 424
Carr CE, 710
Carrére S, 243–45
Carretta TR, 635
Carrey NJ, 462
Carrillo E, 579
Carroll JB, 408–13, 425
Carroll JL, 348
Carroll JM, 637
Carroll JS, 281, 283
Carroll KM, 350–52, 354, 366, 385
Carson TL, 291
Carter SR, 60–62, 66, 73
Carter V, 265
Carter W, 391
Carton EER, 323

Carton JS, 323
Caruso JC, 644
Carver CS, 109, 112, 113, 186
Carver LJ, 460
Cascio WF, 632
Casey L, 125
Casey RJ, 680
Casey S, 552, 559
Caspi A, 396, 406, 408, 417, 431, 685–87
Cassaday HJ, 619
Cassel WS, 503
Cassell MD, 267, 607
Cassidy J, 321
Castelli L, 97–101, 108
Castro GA, 43, 44
Catalano R, 587
Cattell JM, 407
Cattell RB, 412, 422, 425
Cazes G, 231
Ceci SJ, 410, 417, 498, 504, 506–9, 516
Cejka MA, 102, 131, 549
Celentano DD, 362
Celuch K, 557
Cervantes RC, 572
Cesselin F, 33
Chaffee SH, 155
Chagnon YC, 264
Chaiken S, 78, 540–42, 544, 545, 548, 550–52, 554, 557, 558, 561
Chaiyasit W, 331, 337, 584, 585
Chalk R, 348, 355
Chan D, 632, 634, 636, 646–48
Chan JCK, 710
Chan T, 380
Chandler CC, 515
Chang R, 385
Chang SH, 708
Chapin SL, 184
Chapman DI, 283, 284, 303
Chapman M, 672, 673, 679
Charles MA, 10
Charlin V, 683

Charney DS, 462
Chartrand T, 74
Chartrand TL, 108
Chassin L, 207, 684, 686, 688
Chasteen AL, 544
Chatani Y, 42
Chater N, 123
Chatman JA, 297
Chaves W, 651
Chavez M, 261, 262, 265
Chemelli RM, 268
Chen C, 585
Chen H–T, 358–61, 364
Chen IS, 45
Chen M, 108, 318
Chen Q, 349
Chen QC, 716
Chen S, 385, 540–42, 551, 552
Chen X, 265, 558, 560, 561
Chen YR, 588
Cherkes–Julkowski M, 185
Cherry EC, 701, 702, 711, 717
Cherry–Garrard A, 229
Cheung CC, 267
Cheung F, 588
Chih–Mei C, 177, 184
Childress AR, 386, 388
Chipuer HM, 13, 14, 16
Chitty AJ, 615
Choi P, 392
Choi S, 125
Chorney K, 418
Chorney MJ, 418
Chorpita BF, 396
Chou C, 209
Chow YH, 204
Chrisman K, 284
Christal RE, 423, 424
Christensen JM, 233
Christensen MD, 48
Christiaansen RE, 494
Christianson SA, 80
Christie R, 295
Christjansen KN, 268
Christopher JS, 328

Chrousos GP, 460
Chua E, 298
Chua SC, 265
Chung B, 642
Chung RCY, 588
Chung WK, 265
Church AT, 208, 649
Cialdini RB, 540–42, 673
Cicchetti D, 321, 446, 450–53, 455–58, 460, 464, 465, 468
Cioffi D, 74, 76
Civita R, 461
Cladji C, 19
Clark DA, 60, 69, 81, 83
Clark DM, 62, 63, 69, 73
Clark JT, 266
Clark LA, 378, 392, 393, 396, 397, 573–75, 670, 686
Clark MS, 284
Clark NK, 510
Classen C, 391
Clatworthy AL, 43, 44
Clawson RA, 550
Clayton IC, 82
Clearwater YA, 235, 237, 241
Cleary TA, 416
Clerici M, 583
Cliff N, 214, 644
Clifton DK, 267
Clore GL, 555, 556
Coates S, 395
Coblentz CL, 129
Coccaro EF, 388, 393
Codazzi F, 46
Cohen A, 572, 582
Cohen D, 449, 674
Cohen E, 351
Cohen G, 504
Cohen J, 165, 356
Cohen LB, 137
Cohen MD, 293
Cohen NJ, 512
Cohen P, 396
Cohen R, 296, 297, 300
Cohen SG, 648

Cohn DA, 321
Colburn HS, 701
Colburn RW, 41, 43–45, 47
Colbus D, 457, 458
Colder CR, 684, 686–88
Cole PM, 672, 675, 679
Cole SW, 380
Coleman HLK, 587
Coleman JS, 415
Coleman PK, 319, 324
Coleman SC, 209
Coleman V, 633
Coley JD, 113, 123, 129, 130, 133, 137, 138
Colihan J, 633
Coll JH, 492
Coll R, 492
Collet J, 229
Collet L, 715
Collins AF, 486, 487, 511
Collins AM, 96
Collins JC, 499
Collins JM, 640, 642
Collins LM, 207, 347, 364
Collins M, 230, 232, 239
Collins NL, 73
Collins RL, 672, 673
Collins WA, 21
Collins–Eaglin J, 175, 180
Combe C, 38
Comet B, 242
Comis SD, 716
Compas BE, 336
Comuzzie AG, 264
Conaway RL, 328
Conaway WA, 300
Condon CJ, 708, 714
Cone RD, 267
Conforti R, 396
Conger RD, 6, 14, 17, 20
Conley M, 608
Connell JP, 336
Connelly M, 648
Connelly MS, 643
Connors GJ, 350–52, 354, 366
Connors MM, 228, 231, 233, 237, 238, 241

Conrad FG, 126
Considine RV, 265
Conte HR, 637
Conway JM, 641
Conway M, 70, 82, 495
Conway MA, 484, 486, 487, 505, 510–12
Cook TD, 346, 347, 414
Cook WL, 332
Cooke DJ, 589
Cooks HC, 180
Cooney G, 457, 458
Cooney NL, 350–52, 354, 366
Cooper J, 546, 547
Cooper LJ, 331
Cooper ML, 73, 684
Coots J, 586
Coovert MD, 209
Coplan J, 685
Copley–Merriman C, 349
Corbin J, 359
Corcoran KJ, 392
Cordero ML, 501
CORDRAY DS, 345–75; 352–54
Corne PH, 300
Corneille O, 106, 114
Cornelius PE, 236
Cornell DG, 684
Corno L, 406
Corp ES, 262
Corsaro WA, 324
Cortez V, 318, 327
Cortina J, 647
Cosmides L, 136
Costa PT, 208, 241, 423, 425
Costa PT Jr, 649
Costanza DP, 643
Cote LR, 330
Cottington EM, 75, 76
Couceyro PR, 269
Council JR, 73
Coupe P, 491
Courtois CA, 505
Cousins JB, 355
Covert MV, 668

COVINGTON MV, 171–200; 176, 179–82, 185–87, 189, 190, 192
Cowan CP, 321
Cowan G, 544
Cowan PA, 321
Cowan WB, 98
Cowen P, 130
Cox A, 457
Coy KC, 685
Coyle DE, 45, 47
Coyle JT, 262
Craiger JP, 209
Craik FI, 497, 502
Cramton PC, 292
Crandall CS, 104
Crano WD, 558–61
Craske ML, 183
Cravalho MA, 231, 241
Crelia R, 78
Cret J, 153, 157, 158
Crick F, 716, 717
Crilly P, 42
Critchley HD, 602, 605, 610, 628
Critelli JW, 285
Crnic K, 21, 217
Crocker J, 285
Croghan TW, 349
Crombag HFM, 505
Cronbach LJ, 409, 415, 430
Cronen S, 544
Cronshaw SF, 647
Cronbach LJ, —
Cropanzano R, 637
Crosby MM, 643
Croson RTA, 295
Cross MD, 74, 77
Crotteau–Huffman ML, 506, 507
Crowell JA, 321
Crown WE, 349
Cruzcosa M, 322, 326
Csikszentmihalyi M, 230
Cudeck R, 209, 212, 216–19, 634
Culler RE, 186
Cumberland A, 73, 673

Cummings EM, 458, 464, 468, 469
Cunha FDQ, 41, 42
Cunha Q, 41
Cunningham TJ, 205
CURHAN JR, 279–314; 283, 299, 303
Curley MD, 237
Curran P, 207
Curran PJ, 207, 210, 364, 366, 367, 684
Curtis K, 247
Curtner ME, 322
Cushin BJ, 262
Cutler BL, 509, 510
Cutler L, 669, 670
Cutler RB, 384

D

D'Agostino PR, 499
D'Andrade R, 183
DaCosta GA, 455
Daeppen J–B, 385
Dalessio AT, 643
Dallas M, 498
Dalton RJ, 157
Damasio A, 132, 609, 610
Damasio AR, 611
Damasio H, 132, 609–11
Damhuis I, 668
Dammann EJ, 378, 389
Daniel KM, 703
Daniels D, 13, 175
Danko GP, 385
Dantas CM, 317, 333
DaPolito KL, 183
Dapretto M, 125
Darby P, 232
Darby R, 232
Dark VJ, 498
Darley JM, 289, 292
Daro D, 446, 447
Das REG, 42
Dauber S, 416
Dave A, 713
David B, 560

Davids K, 208
Davidson C, 326
Davidson D, 494
Davidson JA, 181, 182
Davidson KC, 364
Davidson RJ, 610, 612
Davidson TL, 258, 261
Davies A, 242
Davies MI, 69, 675, 676
Davies PT, 458, 464, 468, 469
Davis H, 181
Davis M, 607
Davis MH, 676
Davis P, 76
Davis W, 395
Davis WW, 390
Davison HK, 634
Dawes RM, 282, 406, 435
Dawis RV, 406, 407, 414, 416, 420, 422, 425, 426, 434
Dawson K, 672, 673
Dawud S, 458
Dawud–Noursi S, 456, 465
Day SX, 421, 425
Deadrick DL, 634
Deak T, 40, 39, 41, 43, 45
Dean MA, 643, 644
Dearing JW, 157
Deary IJ, 415, 418, 419
Deater–Deckard K, 18, 21
Deaux K, 109
De Bellis MD, 459, 460
Deblinger E, 456, 461
de Boer E, 701
De Bruin–Parecki A, 190
Debusschere M, 302
de Castro JM, 257
Dechman K, 322
Decke E, 263
DeCoster J, 95
De Dreu CKW, 283, 285, 286, 289, 290, 560
Dees JG, 292
Deese J, 500
Deffenbacher KA, 509, 510
DeFries J, 11

DeGarmo DS, 328
De Groot EAM, 190
De Groot EV, 175
Degroot T, 642
Deguzman G, 77, 79, 110–12
DeHarpport T, 283
de Jong P, 62–64
de Jong PF, 63, 64, 66
Dekel R, 389
Dekovic M, 328
De La Cancela V, 579
Delaney HD, 351, 361, 362, 364, 365
Delany PJ, 361
de la Selva A, 583
de Lecea L, 268
DeLeo JA, 41, 43–45, 47
De Leon G, 348
De Leonardis DM, 496–48, 502
Della Sala S, 104
Demaree RG, 634
DeMatteo JS, 639
Dembo MH, 184
de Mendoza JLJ, 242
de Monchaux C, 242
Denham SA, 672
De Nisi A, 181
Dennett DC, 107
Dennis ML, 347, 355
Dennis RA, 649
Dent CW, 347
Dent ML, 706, 711
Denton DA, 267
DePaola SJ, 558
DePaulo BM, 294
Depinet RL, 409
Depreeuw E, 187
Derby KM, 331
Derryberry D, 687
Deschamps A, 583
DeSchepper B, 102
DeShon RP, 634, 636, 646, 648
de Silva P, 82
Desimone R, 618, 623
Desjarlais R, 576–78
Desmarais LB, 427

Detterman DK, 410
Deutsch FM, 291
Deutsch M, 540
Deutsch S, 236
DeVet K, 670, 671, 679
Devine JA, 349
Devine P, 79
Devine PG, 60, 68, 71, 79, 96, 97, 100, 101, 109–12, 131, 553, 554
Devlin JT, 132
Devor E, 12
De Vries H, 362
de Vries J, 260
De Vries NK, 548, 560
Dewey J, 189
Dewson JH, 715
Deyo D, 358
Diamond IT, 715, 716
Diamond MC, 418
Diaz J, 264, 648
Diaz–Perez M, 587
Diaz–Perez MJ, 583
Dick RW, 588
Dickerson M, 70
Dickerson P, 552
Dickson N, 406, 431
Dickstein S, 334
DiClemente CC, 350–52, 354, 362, 366
Diederich N, 46
Diekmann KA, 283–85, 302
Diener E, 381
Diesendruck G, 137, 138
Dietzen L, 350, 354
Dijksterhuis A, 104–6, 108
Dijkstra A, 362
Dillard JP, 557
Dimitri S, 78
Dimitrovsky L, 330
Dimsdale JE, 75, 76
Dinges N, 588
Dinh TT, 258
Dion KL, 97
Dion R, 588
Diorio J, 19
Dipboye R, 641
Dishion TJ, 6, 10, 355

Ditto PH, 553, 554
Diwadkar VA, 490
Dix T, 318, 323, 325, 329, 330, 684
Doan B-J, 393, 396
Doan K, 164
Dobkin PL, 674
Dodder L, 183
Dodge K, 21
Dodge KA, 6, 14, 211, 318, 322, 336, 451, 464, 465, 467
Dodson CS, 497, 498, 504
Doerries LE, 260
Dohanics J, 262
Dohrenwend BP, 587
Dohrenwend BS, 587
Dolby R, 675
Dolen MR, 648
Donaldson SI, 359
Donders J, 208
Donders K, 504
Dong HW, 33
Dong Q, 585
Donnett JG, 622
Donohue EM, 291
Donovan DM, 350–52, 354, 366
Donovan JJ, 640
Donovan WL, 325
Dooling DJ, 494
Dooling RJ, 705, 706, 711
Dorfman J, 492
Doris J, 455, 456, 463, 464
Dorn LD, 460
Dorsey JM, 44
Dossett L, 48
Dostal L, 701, 711
Doty K, 48
Doub TW, 635
Doucet E, 264
Dougherty PM, 45
Douglas EF, 640
Douglas WK, 229, 238, 239
Dourish CT, 33
Doverspike D, 633, 651
Dovidio JF, 96, 97, 100, 101, 109

Downey G, 20
Doyere V, 34
Doyle W, 184
Draguns JG, 572, 576
Drasgow F, 640
Dray L, 180
Dreschler WA, 701
Drews JL, 281
Dripps D, 37
Drolet AL, 294
Druch A, 497
Druckman D, 281
Duan C, 106
Dube MG, 266
Dubner R, 33
Dubowitz H, 458
Dubrovsky VJ, 295, 296
Dubrow N, 446, 449, 452, 468
Duclos CW, 588
Dudgeon P, 202
Duff KJ, 66, 78
Dull V, 134
Dumaret AC, 9
Dumka LE, 355
Dumont N, 462, 463
Duncan SC, 207, 208
Duncan TE, 207, 208
Dunlap WP, 634
Dunlosky J, 514, 515
Dunmore JH, 267
Dunn J, 11, 15, 324
Dunn L, 643
Dunn M, 97, 99, 101
Dunnette MD, 427, 435, 632
Dunning D, 100, 292, 510
Dunton BC, 97, 112
DuRant RH, 457
Durso FT, 498
Duval LL, 543
Duval S, 72
Duyme M, 9
Dweck CS, 106, 173–75
Dwight SA, 640
Dworkin RH, 396
Dyce JA, 396
Dye DA, 643
Dykman RA, 458, 459

Dyskstra C, 41, 43, 45
Dywan J, 498, 518

E

Eagly AH, 540, 541, 544, 550, 551, 554, 558, 561
Earls JH, 236
East MP, 70
Eastman KL, 331, 337, 584, 585
Eastwood JD, 73
Eaton MJ, 184
Ebbesen EB, 521
Ebbinghaus H, 482
Ebeling KS, 137
Eccles J, 180
Eccles JS, 188
Eckenrode J, 455, 456, 463, 464
Eddy JM, 355
Edelman S, 615
Edelstein W, 686
Eder D, 324
Edgar T, 557
Edgerton R, 572, 582
Edholm OG, 242
Edmundson E, 362, 365
Edwards CJ, 82
Edwards CMB, 268
Edwards GL, 262
Edwards JE, 644
Edwards K, 69, 554, 684
Edwards LA, 316, 318
Ee JS, 285
Eftekhari–Sanjani E, 411, 420
Egeland B, 452, 453
Egeland JA, 589
Eggermont JJ, 708
Eggleston TJ, 547
Egli G, 260
Ehlers A, 81
Ehret G, 703
Eich E, 60, 77
Eichenbaum H, 619, 620
Eidelson RJ, 396
Eimas PD, 130, 701

Einbender AJ, 455–58, 463
Einstein D, 670
Einwiller S, 551
Eisenberg AR, 73
Eisenberg L, 572, 576–78
EISENBERG N, 665–97; 67,
  73, 211, 666, 671–79,
  681, 684–88
Eisenbud L, 672, 675, 676
Ek M, 37
Elbert T, 418
Elder GH, 6, 14
Eldridge R, 465
Elias CF, 268
Eliav E, 44
Elie CJ, 501–3
Ellingson JE, 640, 641, 646
Elliot AJ, 109, 112, 175–77,
  187
Elliott DN, 715
Elliott ES, 173
Ellis RS, 433
Ellsworth PC, 510, 684
Elman JL, 13
Elmquist JK, 268
Emans BJM, 289, 290
Embree JM, 672, 673
Embretson S, 417
Emde RN, 321, 334, 677
Emery P, 48
Emery RE, 81, 461
Emmons R, 181
Endresen IM, 229, 234
Engelberg E, 80
Engelhart L, 349
England SL, 70
Enright S, 82
Epping WJM, 708
Epstein AN, 258, 259
Epstein R, 622
Erb HP, 551, 560, 561
Erber R, 65, 67, 74, 75, 110,
  111, 291
Erdelyi MH, 70
Erdfelder E, 494
Erel O, 469
Erez A, 639
Erickson GA, 496

Erickson JR, 503
Erickson MA, 135
Ericsson A, 37
Ericsson KA, 425, 429
Eriksen HR, 241
Erlanson–Albertsson C, 263
Erlebacher AE, 348
Ernberg G, 572, 582
Erwin F, 643
Escobar JI, 587
Eshleman S, 589
Eskilson A, 183
Esparaz J, 10
Espinosa MP, 464
Esses VM, 551
Estes WK, 123, 488
Estin P, 129
Estin PA, 126, 127
Estrada G, 157
Estrada P, 673
Eterno R, 262
Etezadi J, 206
Evans CH, 48
Evans GW, 243–45
Evans N, 96, 97, 100, 101
Even P, 260
Everitt BJ, 608, 609, 612
Everton R, 669
Eyre HL, 669, 670
Eysenck HJ, 406, 412, 416,
  423, 428, 429

F

Fabes RA, 211, 666, 671–79,
  681, 684–88
Fabrega H, 380, 572, 575,
  576, 581
Fabrigar LR, 213, 540, 551,
  553
Faedda G, 392
Fairbank JA, 389
Fairbanks L, 462
Fairchild–Huntress V, 267
Fairfield M, 182
Falkner D, 455
Falloon IR, 583
Fan C, 642

Fang Q, 267
Fantuzzo J, 448
Farah MJ, 132
Faraone SV, 396
Farber EA, 681
Farber ED, 455
Faris PL, 33
Farma T, 583
Farmer HS, 178
Farmer ME, 379
Farrell AD, 448, 453, 457,
  459
Faulkner D, 504
Fauser DJ, 262
Faust IM, 263
Faust ME, 102
Fay D, 504
Fazio RH, 97, 102, 112, 131,
  289, 319, 546, 549
Feare C, 705
Featherman DL, 209
Fedorowicz V, 45
Feeser HR, 717
Feig SL, 716, 717
Feigenbaum JD, 621
Fein S, 97, 99, 101, 106, 555
Feingold A, 415
Feinstein A, 105
Feinstein J, 551
Feldlaufer H, 180
Feldman J, 505
Feldman MW, 12
Feldman RS, 455, 465
Feldman SS, 176, 585
Feliciano M, 715
Felling A, 327
Felstiner WLF, 290
FENG AS, 699–725; 703,
  707–9, 711, 713, 714
Fenton MB, 704, 705
Ferguson SA, 497, 498
Ferguson TJ, 667–70,
  680–82
Fernandes MA, 706
Ferreira SH, 39, 41, 42
Ferstl KL, 641
Festinger L, 546, 559
Fetherstonhaugh D, 552, 559

Fick AC, 447, 462
Fidahusein N, 267
Fiedler K, 504
Fields HL, 33, 34
Fiese BH, 334
Fifield WJ, 397
Figlewicz DP, 261, 266, 267
Figueredo AJ, 346, 454, 456
Finch CE, 462
Fincham FD, 289, 321, 322, 393, 467
Finger K, 506
Finke RA, 498
Finkel D, 211
Finkel SE, 152, 153
Finkelhor D, 446–51, 455, 457, 459, 462, 468, 469
Finkelstein MA, 673
First MB, 385, 390, 391
Fischer AR, 637
Fischhoff B, 495
Fischman MW, 385, 386
Fishbain DA, 384
Fisher L, 392
Fisher RP, 483, 508, 510, 522
Fisher SL, 268
Fishkin J, 165
Fiske AP, 293, 330
Fiske DW, 209, 413, 414, 423
Fiske ST, 79, 95, 96, 98, 101, 103, 105, 106, 109, 111, 114, 134, 135, 317, 318, 489, 496, 523, 540
Fitzgerald J, 386, 388
Fitzpatrick KM, 449, 457, 459, 462
Fivush R, 324
Flanery MA, 135
Flannery DJ, 417
Flavell ER, 68
Flavell JH, 68
Fleck K, 327
Fleer PF, 644
Fleischmann RM, 49
Fleishman EA, 632, 633
Fleming CM, 588

Fleming JE, 448
Fleshner M, 37, 38, 40
Fletcher BW, 361
Fletcher GJ, 495
Fletcher JM, 364
Flicker L, 669, 670
Flier ES, 268
Flier JS, 268, 267
Flin R, 240
Floersch J, 589
Flood JF, 263
Flor H, 418
Florman Y, 48
Floyd DL, 556
Floyd FJ, 208
Flynn JR, 9, 417
Foa E, 456, 461
Földiák P, 614
Folkman S, 318
Follenfant RL, 41, 42

Follett M, 283
Follette WC, 379
Foltin RW, 385, 386
Fong C, 97, 99, 101
Foody R, 325
Forbus KD, 288
Ford JK, 644
Ford ME, 179
Ford RL, 65, 77, 79, 110, 111
Forde EME, 132
Fordham S, 180
Forehand R, 10, 456, 459, 469
Forgas JP, 285, 289, 556, 670, 683
Forgatch MS, 6, 10, 328
Forman DR, 685
Formoso D, 355
Forrester E, 82
Förster J, 514
Fortune ES, 713
Foster D, 266, 267
Foster DA, 298
Foster DP, 516
Foster RA, 507
Foulks EF, 589

Fournier D, 358
Fowler JS, 385, 386
Fox A, 41
Fox HR, 650
Fox KA, 639
Fox NA, 672, 675, 679
Foy DW, 389, 462
Foye PE, 268
Fraley RC, 73
France IM, 125
Frances AJ, 390, 391, 395
Francis D, 19
Francis DJ, 208, 364
Francis S, 605, 610
Franco F, 580
Frank E, 561
Frankiewicz RG, 208
Frankish C, 134
Franklin CH, 154, 155
Franklin PE, 98
Franks B, 138
Franks JJ, 495
Fravel DL, 334
Frederich RC, 267
Frederick C, 462
Freeman HE, 359
Freeman W, 328
Freeman WB, 583
Freeman WS, 328
Freeston M, 71
Frei RL, 638
Freimuth VS, 557
Freud S, 60, 109
Frick PJ, 685, 686
Fried CB, 546, 547
Fried–Buchalter S, 181
Friedel LA, 646
Friedland N, 289
Friedman HS, 294
Friedman JM, 256, 265, 267
Friedman MI, 258
Friedman MJ, 579
Friedman RA, 281
Friedman S, 587
Friedman WJ, 512, 513
Friedrich J, 552, 559
Friedrich WN, 455–58, 463
Frisman L, 359

Frith CD, 609, 610
Frodi A, 468
Froman LA, 293
Frone MR, 684
Frost LA, 95, 105, 106
Fruzzetti AE, 487
Fry WR, 295
Frydel BR, 44, 45
Fryer DM, 482
Fu K, 41, 43
Fujino DC, 588
Fujita I, 710, 711
Fukumoto A, 680
Fukuno M, 283
Fukuota H, 48
Fulero SM, 508, 509
Fuligni A, 586
Fulk J, 294
Fulker D, 11, 18
Funahashi S, 623
Fung T, 446
Funk SC, 183
Fury G, 321
Fuster JM, 623
Fuzessery ZN, 707, 708
Fyock J, 103

G

Gabbard GO, 390
Gable SL, 176
Gabriel MT, 285
Gaertner SL, 109
Gaffan D, 602, 608, 618, 619
Galanter E, 112, 113
Galarza L, 242
Galazyuk A, 714
Galazyuk AV, 714
Galbraith JA, 44
Gales MS, 504
Gallagher D, 265, 552, 559
Gallagher M, 608
Gallimore R, 574, 586
Gallo DA, 502
Gallup P, 359
Galperin C, 334
Galton F, 407, 423, 428, 429
Gammeltoft S, 268

Gamson WA, 301
Gandy JA, 643
Gao E, 716
Gao XB, 268
Garbarino J, 446, 449, 452, 468
Garber J, 209
Garcia T, 175, 181, 190
Gardiner JM, 486
Gardner H, 428, 429
Gardner RC, 202
Gardner WL, 554
Garfinkel BD, 460
Garfinkel R, 580, 581
Garling T, 283
Garmezy N, 453
Garner WR, 416
Garnier H, 586
Garrison CJ, 45
Garry M, 506, 505
Garst E, 672, 673
Garst J, 109, 551
Gaskovski P, 73
Gasser MB, 633
Gastardo–Conaco MC, 558
Gatehouse RW, 701, 711
Gathercole SE, 486, 487, 511
Gati L, 421
Gaudin JM, 463
Gaugler BB, 642
Gauthier I, 129
Gautier JF, 264
Gavanski I, 668
Gaykema RPA, 37, 38
Gazzaniga MS, 500
Ge X, 14, 17, 20
Geary DC, 416
Geary N, 262
Gebbia MI, 643
Gebhart GF, 41, 43–45
Gee NR, 503
Geer JG, 153
Geiger JD, 45
Geis FL, 295
Geiselman RE, 483, 508
Gekker G, 45
Gelfand DM, 319, 324
Geller J, 328, 329

Gelles RJ, 447, 452
Gelman A, 150
Gelman R, 136
Gelman SA, 113, 122, 125, 127, 136–38
Gentile CG, 459, 461
Gentner D, 125, 287, 288, 303
Gentner TQ, 706
George A, 44
George C, 465
Georgescu HI, 48
Georges–François P, 606, 620, 621
Gerard HB, 540
Gerhardt HC, 702, 703, 711
Gernsbacher MA, 102
Gerris JRM, 327, 328
Gerrity ET, 579
Gershenhorn S, 326
Gerton J, 587
Gest SD, 206
Ghiselli EE, 409, 637
Ghisilen MT, 138
Ghosh CM, 452
Giacalone R, 298
Giancola PR, 394
Giannopoulos C, 82
Gibbons FX, 547
Gibbons R, 284
Gibbs J, 261, 262
Gibbs JC, 680
Gibbs RW, 128
Gibson JJ, 522
Gigerenzer G, 522
Gil AG, 588
Gilbert DT, 65, 95–101, 103, 105, 289, 489
Giller EL, 387, 390
Gillespie JJ, 283
Gillette J, 268
Gilliland SW, 647
Gilmer WS, 34
Giner–Sorolla R, 540, 541, 548, 551, 552, 554
Gingerich RL, 265
Ginsburg GS, 183
Girard K, 499, 500

Girotto V, 285
Gist PL, 100
Given E, 265
Glanzmann P, 186
Glascow D, 457
Glass JD, 46
Glassman NS, 96, 318
Gleaves DH, 640
Glisky EL, 497
Glod CA, 461–63
Glod RN, 462
Glodich A, 446
Gluck MA, 130
Godbold LC, 557
Goehler LE, 36–41, 43, 45
Goff LM, 483, 497, 506
Goffin RD, 642
Golan S, 181
Gold DB, 63, 70, 71, 80
Gold DP, 206
Goldberg E, 647
Goldberg JH, 683
Goldberg LR, 423, 637
Goldenberg B, 455, 457, 461
Goldenberg CN, 574, 586
Golding JM, 77
Golding SL, 384
Goldman M, 670, 671, 679
Goldman RS, 396
Goldman–Rakic PS, 104, 623
Goldmeier E, 488
Goldsamt LA, 674
Goldsmith HH, 396, 684
GOLDSMITH M, 481–537; 482–84, 487, 491, 508, 510, 513–17, 519, 521, 522
Goldsmith R, 238
Goldstein AW, 427
Goldstein H, 643
Goldstein HW, 642
Goldstein K, 153
Goldstone RL, 123, 126, 129
Golier J, 460
Golisano V, 555
Gollob HF, 205, 206, 212–14, 356

Gollwitzer PM, 67, 107, 108
Gonnerman LM, 132
Gonzales NA, 355, 684
Gonzalez R, 293
Good B, 572, 576–78, 589
Good BJ, 572, 576, 579
Goodenow C, 180
Goodison T, 261
Goodman DF, 641
Goodman GS, 509
Goodman R, 13
Goodnow JJ, 316, 330, 333
Goodson BD, 350, 351, 367
Goodwin FK, 390
Goodwin KA, 501, 506
Gooler DM, 708, 709
Gopnik A, 125, 136
Gordijn EH, 560
GORDIS EB, 445–79; 452
Gordon CJ, 264
Gordon D, 519
Gordon RA, 406, 408, 416, 431
Gore PA, 215
Goren H, 555
Gorman JM, 380, 396, 397
Gorman–Smith D, 453, 456, 459
Gorter JA, 260
Goshgarian HG, 48
Gotlib IH, 70
Gotowiec A, 588
Gottesman CV, 495
Gottfredson LS, 406, 408–11, 415, 416, 635, 641, 647
Gottfried GM, 113, 137, 138
Gottlieb G, 12
Gottman JM, 323, 460, 468, 469
Gough HG, 637, 640
Gould MS, 585
Grabowski TJ, 132
Grace M, 266
Grace NC, 332
Gracely RH, 44
Grafton FC, 635
Graham JL, 299

Graham JW, 359
Graham M, 268
Graham S, 181, 685
Graham–Berman SA, 456, 458, 465
Grajek S, 14
Gralinski H, 679
Gramzow R, 669, 670
Granger DA, 326
Grannemann BD, 183
Grant I, 241
Graves LM, 641
Gray CM, 713
Gray JA, 612
Gray JR, 683
Gray WD, 128–30
Grayson D, 585
Greco S, 97, 108
Green AH, 459, 461
Green DM, 701
Green FL, 68
Green JD, 674
Green P, 639
Green R, 395
Greenbaum C, 458
Greenbaum PE, 356, 366
Greenberg J, 66, 72, 74, 546
Greenberger E, 585
Greene RL, 501
Greenfield PM, 574, 586
Greenhalgh L, 283, 284, 303
Greenspan D, 174
Greenspan S, 453
Greenwald AG, 97, 109, 131, 213, 336, 549
Gregory RL, 522
Greguras GJ, 635, 647
Griest DL, 10
Griffin DR, 704
Griffin DW, 292, 548
Griffin JW, 46
Griffith TL, 283, 295
Griffiths R, 134
Grigorenko EL, 434
Grill HJ, 258
Grohovaz F, 46
Grose EF, 44
Gross CG, 605, 614

Gross JJ, 76
Grossman SP, 258, 259, 265
Grotevant HD, 334
Grove WM, 406, 423
Groves BM, 449
Grow JG, 464
Grube BS, 396
Gruber AJ, 392
Gruenfeld DH, 561
Grund E, 237
Gruppuso V, 499
Grusec JE, 318, 321, 324, 328–30
Gruys ML, 641
Grych JH, 322, 467
Grzybycki D, 41, 43, 45
Guarnaccia P, 380, 381, 579
GUARNACCIA PJ, 571–98; 572, 574, 579–81, 583, 584, 587
Guarrera J, 455, 457, 461
Gubarev V, 237
Gudykunst W, 298
Gudykunst WB, 298
Gueron J, 347
Guijarro ML, 394
Guilford JP, 421
Guillery RW, 716, 717
Guion RM, 633, 642, 652
Gunderson CG, 391
Gunderson EKE, 236, 238, 240–42
Gunderson J, 392
Gunderson JG, 392
Gunnar M, 460
Gunnar MR, 685
Gunstream JD, 44
Guo M, 585
Gurevitch M, 157
Gurtman MB, 96, 97, 101
Gushin V, 237
Gustafsson J, 411
Gutheil G, 137
Guthrie D, 586
Guthrie IK, 211, 666, 673, 675–78, 684–88
Gutmann A, 165
Guzder J, 396

Guzzo AR, 648

H

Haaga DAF, 76
Hackney A, 502
Haddock G, 545
Hadley SD, 48
Hafer CL, 551, 552
Haggard MP, 706
Hagtvet KA, 185
Hahn TM, 268
Hahn U, 123
Haier RJ, 418
Haines RF, 234
Hakel MD, 634
Halaas JL, 267
Halberstadt JB, 135
Hales R, 391
Hales RE, 384
Halgren E, 610
Hall DG, 138
Hall ET, 297, 298
Hall JC, 707, 708
Hall JF, 495, 608, 609, 612
Hall JW, 706
Hall LK, 495
Hall SM, 48
Haller M, 715
Hallett AJ, 394
Hallin D, 155
Halpern DF, 416
Halpern JJ, 291
Halpin B, 455, 456, 459
Halpin SM, 104
Hamagami F, 211
Hamalainen M, 687
Hamann A, 267
Hambleton RK, 649
Hamby SL, 447
Hamilton DL, 95, 113, 114
Hamilton VL, 177
Hammack SE, 37, 45
Hammer AL, 420, 421
Hammer M, 455, 465
Hammond DC, 505
Hampton J, 123, 138
Hampton JA, 123

Han JS, 33, 608
Hancock GR, 177, 644
Hancock RA, 63, 64
Hanisch KA, 411, 420
Hanish L, 686, 687
Hanks HGI, 322, 326
Hanley JR, 609
Hann DM, 447, 462
Hanna C, 462, 460
Hannover B, 109
Hannula–Bral KA, 559
Hansen C, 395
Hansen DJ, 328
Hansen JC, 420, 421
Hansen M, 45–47
Hansen T, 512
Hansen WB, 359
Hao JX, 33, 48
Happaney KH, 327
Harackiewicz JM, 175, 177, 187
Harder DW, 669, 670
Hardin CD, 97, 131, 542
Har–Even D, 330
Harford T, 207
Harker S, 266
Harkness AR, 417
Harlow RE, 182
Harm DL, 230, 237
Harmon LW, 420, 421
Harmon–Jones E, 546, 547, 673
Harnad S, 129
Harnden JL, 63, 76
Harnish JD, 211
Harrington D, 458
Harrington H, 406, 431
Harris JR, 4, 5, 320, 324, 406, 431, 433
Harris MJ, 433
Harris PL, 680
Harrison AA, 228, 230, 231, 233, 235, 237, 238, 241
Harrison B, 327
Harrison DA, 645, 651
Harrison G, 587
Harrison S, 619
Harsch N, 512, 520

Hart BL, 35, 36, 433
Hart D, 686
Hart J, 460
Hart WB, 157
Harter S, 180
Hartigan JA, 416
Hartman E, 137
Hartman R, 349
Hart–O'Rourke DM, 545
Harvey AG, 63, 70, 80, 391
Harvey T, 418
Harwood RL, 586
Haselton MG, 382, 383
Hasher L, 110, 492, 493, 495, 516, 521
Hashtroudi S, 104, 496–98
Haskett ME, 455, 465
Haslam SA, 99, 558
Hasselmo ME, 606, 614, 615, 617
Hassi J, 237
Hastie R, 103, 283, 287, 288, 291, 495, 549
Hastings P, 321, 324, 328
Hastings PD, 318, 330, 672, 674
Hatano G, 136, 137
Hatch M, 587
Hatfield T, 608
Hatry HP, 353
Hattie J, 176
Hattori A, 42
Hattrup K, 634, 641, 647
Havel PJ, 265
Hawkins SA, 495
Hawley KJ, 94, 96, 106
Hawley ML, 701
Hay DF, 333, 393, 394, 681
Hayden RM, 461
Hayes AM, 60, 69, 80, 83
Hayes KJ, 419
Haynes OM, 334
Hays CE, 335
Haythorn WW, 233, 235, 236, 238
Hayton BC, 382, 389, 579
Hazlett S, 182
He K, 46

Heard DH, 326
Heath WP, 503
Heatherton TF, 667
Hebert KS, 510
Heckman HM, 44
Heckman JJ, 349
Hedberg DA, 66, 78
Hedeker D, 362, 366
Hedges LV, 416, 513
Hedlund J, 649
Heger A, 457
Heggestad ED, 422, 424, 425, 641
Heider F, 489
Heilman ME, 651
Heiman ML, 265
Heinsman DT, 348
Heise DR, 683
Heit E, 123
Heit EJ, 123
Hellawell DJ, 609, 610
Helmers K, 460
Helmreich R, 230, 232–34, 236, 238, 240
Helms JE, 574, 636
Helppie M, 232–37, 243, 244
Henderson B, 41, 42
Henderson RW, 183
Henderson SH, 13, 14
Hendrick JB, 462
Hengerer B, 42
Henkel LA, 502
Henly SJ, 216, 218
Hennessy BL, 129
Henry B, 687
Henry D, 461
Henry GT, 360
Hensley VR, 585
Henson OW Jr, 704, 715
Herdegen T, 32
Herman CP, 76, 542
Hermans HJM, 183
Hernadi A, 628
Herndon F, 510
Herrera C, 465
Herriot P, 632
Herrnstein RJ, 12, 409, 410, 415, 430, 432

Hershberger S, 213
Hershey KL, 671, 675, 676, 684–87
Hertiz–Lazarowitz R, 178
Herzberg U, 44, 45
Hess RD, 177, 184
Hess S, 264
Heston J, 461
Hetherington EM, 6, 11, 13–15, 21, 211, 337, 418, 433, 589
Heumann R, 42
Heurtin–Roberts S, 587
Hewes S, 672
Hewitt D, 47
Hewson G, 262
Hewstone M, 134
Heymsfield SB, 265
Hezlett SA, 635
Hichwa RD, 132
Higgins ET, 64, 70, 78, 177, 319, 542, 543, 545
Higgins RL, 183
Higgs GA, 41, 42
Higham PA, 503, 504
Highberger W, 650
Higuchi S, 617
Hildemann WH, 36, 43
Hilgard ER, 508
Hill DR, 33
Hill JO, 264
Hill RG, 262
Hill–Barlow D, 669
Hillery CM, 708
Hilton JL, 95, 100, 106
Hirsch J, 259, 263, 265
Hirschfeld LA, 113, 122, 136, 138
Hirsh IJ, 700, 701, 711
Hirt ER, 495, 496
Hirvonen MD, 263, 264
Hisamitsu T, 48
Hitzemann R, 386
Hixon JG, 95–101, 103, 105
Hodge C, 544
Hodge D, 506
Hodges SD, 78, 548
Hoffman CC, 636, 645

Hoffman GE, 262
Hoffman HG, 504
Hoffman LW, 13
Hoffman M, 283
Hoffman ML, 666, 667, 674, 679–81, 683
Hoffman–Plotkin D, 455, 465
Hoffrage U, 522
Hofmann DA, 645
Hofmann V, 686
Hofstede G, 297, 649
Hogan J, 420, 422, 424, 633, 637, 638
Hogan R, 420, 422, 424, 637, 640
Hogg MA, 558, 559
Hoggard N, 268, 269
Hohenstein JM, 351, 352, 360, 362
Hokfelt T, 33
Holahan CJ, 186
Holahan CK, 406
Holbrook TM, 153
Holcomb J, 393, 396
Holden GW, 316, 318, 452, 456, 458
Holland AW, 242, 247
Holland C, 238
Holland JL, 420, 421
Holland PC, 608
Hollenbeck JR, 649
Hollenberg D, 63, 64
Hollon SD, 380
Holloway J, 74, 76
Holloway SD, 177
Holmbeck GN, 469
Holmer M, 290
Holmes JB, 511
Holmes JG, 543
Holmgren R, 675, 677
Holmgren RA, 672
Holohan CJ, 206
Holohan CK, 206
Holohan P, 204
Holt K, 175, 177
Holton A, 587
Holtz TH, 389

Holtzman J, 349
Holyoak KJ, 491
Homburg C, 204
Hong S, 216
Honma K, 261
Honma S, 261
Hontebeyrie–Joskowicz M, 48
Hood JE, 70, 455
Hood L, 44
Hooley JM, 394
Hooven D, 323
Hopkins N, 557
Hopper K, 582
Hops H, 208
Hori T, 39, 40
Horn CC, 258
Horn JL, 207, 209, 211, 364
Hornak J, 611, 612
Horne L, 457
Hornick CW, 639
Hornig CD, 587
Horowitz K, 462
Horowitz LA, 468
Horowitz LM, 325
Horselenberg R, 73, 81
Horton MS, 126
Horwath E, 587
Hosoi M, 39, 40
Hostetter AM, 262, 589
Hotaling G, 448
Hough G, 361
HOUGH LM, 631–64; 406, 422, 428, 637–40, 643, 649
Hough RL, 587
Houseal M, 231
Houston CE, 77
Houston DA, 164, 558
Houts AC, 379
Hovland C, 164, 165
Howard A, 97, 632, 643, 648
Howard DJ, 552
Howard JH, 490
Howard KI, 347
Howe GW, 6, 328
Howell A, 70, 82
Howell DJ, 704

Howes C, 464, 465
Howing PT, 463
Hoyle RH, 190, 210, 220
Hrebec D, 283, 288
Hsee CK, 299
Hsieh K, 21, 217
Hsiung S, 348
Hsu H–C, 331
Hu L, 216, 219, 588
Hu S, 45
Hubbard C, 556
Hubbard JJ, 446
Huber VL, 300
Huberman M, 359
Huckfeldt R, 157
Hudley C, 685
Hudson SM, 63, 83
Huebner RB, 353
Huey SJ, 685
Huffcutt AI, 641, 642
Huffman RF, 715
Hughes HM, 456, 458, 467
Hughes J, 33, 262
Hughes TK, 43, 46
Huijser RH, 232
Hulland J, 204
Hulse SH, 705, 706
Hulsebosch CE, 48
Humfleet GL, 351, 352, 360, 362
Humphreys GW, 132
Humphreys K, 349
Humphreys LG, 406, 408, 411, 414–17, 420, 431, 433
Hunt E, 406, 408, 412, 417, 434
Hunt JS, 509
Hunt RR, 502
Hunt ST, 647
Hunt T, 637
Hunter JE, 406, 408, 427, 638, 644, 645
Husband TH, 506
Huszar D, 267
Hutchinson KJ, 558
Hutson–Comeaux SL, 553
Huttenlocher J, 134, 513

Hyatt S, 183
Hyman IE, 506
Hyman IE Jr, 506
Hyman SE, 387–89, 396
Hynes ME, 395
Hysong SJ, 230, 237

I

Iacono WG, 397
Ialongo N, 367
Ilgen DR, 632, 649
Illback RJ, 359
Illich PA, 44
Illingworth KS, 182
Imai M, 125
Imhoff HJ, 673
Inagaki K, 136, 137
Incoll P, 243
Innes–Ker AH, 135
Insko CA, 552
Intons–Peterson MJ, 484,
    502
Intraub H, 495
Irish SL, 393
Irwin DE, 490
Irwin W, 610, 612
Isen AM, 285
Ishida N, 42
Ishii M, 268
Isleib RA, 182
Israel L, 502
Issacharoff S, 284
Ito Y, 462, 463
Ivanović M, 583
IYENGAR S, 149–69; 151,
    152, 155–57, 159–61,
    163–65

J

Ja Z, 46
Jablensky A, 572, 582
Jackson AA, 264
Jackson D III, 406
Jackson EW, 585
Jackson JR, 97
Jackson JS, 572
Jackson JW, 553

Jackson MA, 384
Jackson PA, 619
Jackson PR, 208
Jackson SE, 634
Jacobs JE, 183
Jacobs SC, 378
Jacobson K, 136
Jacobson NS, 356
Jacoby JD, 504, 507
Jacoby LL, 73, 109, 486,
    498–501, 514, 518
Jacques TY, 685
Jaffe P, 451, 452, 456, 458,
    465, 466
Jagacinski CM, 175
Jako RA, 641
James K, 298
James LA, 204
James LR, 204, 634, 639
James W, 107
Jamieson KH, 161
Jamison KR, 429
Janczura GA, 503
Janeck AS, 81
Jang KL, 393, 396, 397
Janis IL, 286
Janjigian M, 44
Janoff–Bulman R, 391, 450
Jansen T, 186
Janssens JMAM, 323, 328
Jarrard EL, 619
Jarry JL, 392
Jarvis B, 551
Jasechko J, 499
Jason LA, 188
Java RI, 486
Jeanneret PR, 632, 633
Jeanneret R, 650, 651
Jeffery KJ, 622
Jeffress LA, 710
Jehn KA, 284, 298
Jekel J, 462
Jemmott JB, 76
Jen PH–S, 704, 712, 715,
    716
Jenkins EJ, 449, 452, 468
Jenkins JH, 582, 583
Jenkins JJ, 415

Jenkins JM, 468, 469
Jennings D, 636, 644, 646
Jennings MK, 159
Jensen AR, 406, 408,
    410–12, 415–18, 429
Jensen JB, 460
Jepson C, 557
Jerome C, 262
Jerusalem M, 185, 186
Jetten J, 66, 74, 79, 110–12
Jewett CS, 588
Jimerson DC, 63, 76
Job R, 132
Joe VC, 323
John OP, 686
John RS, 452, 467, 469
Johnsen MC, 463, 466
Johnson B, 97, 242
Johnson BT, 540, 552
Johnson C, 97
Johnson CC, 243
Johnson D, 41
Johnson DF, 281
Johnson DM, 128–30
Johnson EC, 127, 138
Johnson J, 182, 462, 587
Johnson JF, 643
Johnson JT, 510
Johnson JW, 641, 645, 673
Johnson KE, 129
Johnson LG, 674
Johnson MH, 13, 128, 131,
    609, 610
Johnson MK, 104, 486, 487,
    493, 494, 496–98, 502,
    504, 505, 513, 514, 518
Johnson PD, 458, 469
Johnson PJ, 239, 244, 245
Johnson PR, 263, 265
Johnson RE, 494
Johnson SC, 136, 137
Johnson TE, 289
Johnson–Laird PN, 94
JOHNSTON C, 315–44; 318,
    319, 324, 328, 329, 336,
    337
Johnston L, 63, 83, 108, 134
Johnston NG, 642

Johnston R, 153, 157, 158
Johnston S, 76
Johnston WA, 94, 96, 106, 498
Joiner TE Jr, 328
Jolicoeur P, 130
Jones A, 358
Jones BD, 157
Jones C, 207
Jones DP, 650
Jones EE, 290
Jones EG, 715, 716
Jones JL, 556, 675, 676, 678
Jones MB, 236, 242
Jones MR, 702
Jones RK, 129
Jones S, 122, 137, 583, 684
Jones SB, 137
Jones SD, 635, 645
Jonides J, 95, 106
Jöreskog KG, 203, 206, 216–18
Joseph MH, 612
Joule R, 546
Jouriles EN, 452, 456
Judd CM, 97, 99, 100, 203, 549
Judd LL, 388, 389
Judge ME, 268
Judge SJ, 605
Judge TA, 205, 639
Judice TN, 208
Julesz B, 700
Julian DA, 353, 358
Julka DL, 545
Julnes G, 360
Junge K, 716
Jurgens R, 46
Jusino CM, 580, 581
Just MA, 424

K

Kaelber CT, 379
Kaestner E, 261
Kagan BL, 44
Kagan J, 77, 676
Kahan TL, 498

Kahn JH, 63, 64, 68–71, 73, 112, 210
Kahn KF, 156, 160
Kahneman D, 282, 283
Kaiyala K, 261
Kajander KC, 45
Kalafat J, 359
Kalb M, 154
Kalish CW, 137, 138
Kalra PS, 266
Kalra SP, 266
Kaluzny A, 350
Kamboukos D, 453, 456
Kameda T, 557
Kanas N, 235–37
Kandel ER, 385–87
Kane R, 349
Kanfer R, 178, 637
Kang JD, 48
Kang M, 672, 673
Kanwisher N, 622
Kanzaki J, 716
Kaplan A, 174
Kaplan H, 33
Kaplan SJ, 455, 457, 461
Kapp BS, 609
Karabenick SA, 180, 175
Karbon M, 671, 674–76, 678, 681, 684, 686–88
Karmiloff–Smith A, 13
Karno M, 582, 583, 587
Karraker KH, 319, 324
Karren RJ, 641
Kashy D, 209
KasimKarakas S, 265
Kaslow FW, 393
Kaslow NJ, 321
Kasprow W, 457, 459, 463
Kass J, 235
Kass R, 235
Kassem L, 457
Kassin SM, 507, 510, 543, 555
Kataoka HC, 641
Kates M, 453
Katigbak MS, 649
Katsuki Y, 716
Katz D, 545

Katz LF, 323, 460, 468, 469
Katzell RA, 426
Kaufman J, 455, 465, 466, 469
Kauneckis D, 326
Kavanagh K, 10
Kavanaugh D, 582
Kavoussi RJ, 393
Kawakami K, 97
Kawatani M, 48
Kazdin AE, 351, 352, 457, 458
Keane EM, 588
Keane TM, 389
Keele SW, 492
Keesey RE, 263, 264
Kehoe JF, 648
Keil FC, 127, 128, 136–38
Keim NL, 265
Keith BE, 159
Kelk N, 675
Kellem SG, 367
Keller CE, 651
Keller CH, 710
Keller MB, 392, 686
Kelley CM, 109, 486, 498–501, 514, 518
Kelley HH, 286, 318, 332
Kelley ML, 332
Kellman PJ, 136
Kellstein DE, 33
Kelly AE, 63, 64, 68–71, 73, 112
Kelly DC, 48
Kelly DD, 30, 32
Kelly GA, 172
Kelly JR, 553
Kelly L, 262
Kelly LA, 262
Kelly ML, 643
Kelman HC, 540, 549
Keltner D, 283, 286, 289, 666, 667, 684
Kempton T, 456, 459
Kendall–Tackett K, 446, 450
Kendall–Tackett KA, 455, 457, 459
Kendler KS, 211, 385

Kendrick SA, 416
Kendziora KT, 328
Kennedy A, 489
Kennedy MA, 397
Kenney PJ, 156
Kenny DA, 203, 209, 331, 332
Kent JM, 380
Kent S, 38
Keogh BK, 586
Kerig PK, 326
Kern M, 155
Kernis MH, 183
Kerst SM, 490
Kersten AW, 125
Kesner RP, 619, 621
Kessler RC, 378, 381
Kestenbaum R, 681
Kethley B, 650
Kette G, 289
Kettner PM, 353
Keyes S, 686
Khoury EL, 588
Kick RW, 588
Kick SA, 713
Kiechel KL, 507, 543
Kiechle R, 37
Kiecolt–Glaser JK, 207
Kiernan B, 492
Kiesler S, 295, 296
Kiesler SB, 295, 296
Kihlstrom JF, 104
Kiker S, 634
Kilcullen R, 641
Kilduff TS, 268
Killeya LA, 552
Kilm JA, 649
Kilpatrick DG, 466
Kilpatrick KL, 462
Kim C, 207
Kim J, 209
Kim MS, 268
Kim PH, 286, 301, 561
Kimble CE, 183
Kimble CR, 392
Kimble GA, 434
Kimmel EB, 183
Kinard EM, 457, 459

Kinast C, 455
Kinder DR, 157, 550
Kindlon D, 685
King BJ, 73
King DS, 389
King G, 150
King LA, 389
King LM, 572
King P, 348, 355
King RA, 679, 680
King RE, 635
Kinicki AJ, 210
Kinscheck IB, 33
Kinsey AC, 268
Kintsch W, 492
Kirdus VB, 178
Kirk SA, 379
Kirmayer LJ, 382, 383, 389, 576, 579
Kirsh SJ, 321
Kiser LJ, 461
Kishton JM, 215
Kiss JZ, 267
Kistener JA, 455, 465
Kitayama S, 297, 582
Kitchen S, 46
Klauer KC, 99
Klein DF, 379, 380, 383, 390
Klein DN, 392
Klein RG, 395
Klein SB, 63, 66, 67, 75, 83, 104
Klein TR, 673
Klein WJ, 231
Kleinboelting H, 522
Kleinman A, 381, 382, 571–74, 576–78, 580, 582, 589, 590
Kleinman AM, 571, 572, 579, 582
Kleinman J, 580
Kliewer W, 458, 469
Klimoski RJ, 647, 648
Kline RB, 203
Klocking R, 46
Kluger AN, 181
Kluger MJ, 36, 37
Klumb P, 217

Klump GM, 703, 705, 706, 712, 715
Klungland H, 267
Knauper B, 379
Knight F, 585
Knight GP, 674
Knowler WC, 10
Knowlton BJ, 135, 135, 619
Knudsen EI, 705, 709
Knutson B, 63, 66, 67, 380
Kober R, 704
Koblick IG, 232, 234, 244
Kobrynowicz D, 104
Koch C, 600
Kochanska G, 6, 8, 21, 666, 669–71, 679–82, 685
Koenig AL, 685, 680
Koestner R, 682
Koetzle W, 157
Koffka K, 488
Kohlmann CW, 183
Kohnken G, 508
Kohno T, 40
Kojetin BA, 421
Koka P, 46
Kolb B, 388
Kolko D, 455, 457
Kolody B, 587
Komatsu LK, 123, 127
Komisaruk B, 33
Konishi M, 705, 709–11
Konovalov YV, 238
Koomen W, 105, 108, 550
Koop CE, 446
Koopman C, 391
Kopeikin H, 325, 327
Kopin IJ, 44
Kopp C, 679
Koppula S, 267
KORIAT A, 481–537; 482–84, 486, 487, 491, 497, 508, 510, 513–17, 519, 521, 522
Korman AK, 632, 648
Korten A, 572, 582
Korzilius H, 327
Koss MP, 454, 456
Kosslyn SM, 130, 489

Kostelny K, 446, 449, 452, 468
Kosten TR, 385, 386
Koutstaal W, 80, 482, 486, 487, 492, 493, 497, 500, 502, 514, 516, 518
Koverola C, 457, 460, 462
Kozerenko O, 237
Kozlowski LT, 542
Kramer M, 572
Kramer RM, 283, 285, 300
Krantz J, 318, 327
Kratcoski PC, 451
Krause MS, 347
Kraut AI, 632, 648
Kravitz DA, 651
Krech KH, 318, 329
Krenger W, 41
Krevans J, 680
Kriaucinas A, 265
Kring AM, 286
Krinsky R, 262, 263
Kristensen H, 283
Kristensen P, 268
Kronzon S, 292
Krosnick JA, 157, 548, 552
Krueger RF, 396, 685
Kruglanski AW, 484, 523
Kruglyak L, 397
Krupnick J, 682
Kruschke JK, 135
Krysan M, 109
Krystal JH, 462
Kubie JL, 620, 621
Kubis JF, 233–35, 237, 241
Kuby J, 36, 37, 39–41
Kuczynski L, 330
Kuhar MJ, 269, 262
Kuijper JL, 261, 266, 267
Kuipers L, 582
Kujirai K, 713
Kukla A, 182
Kuklinski MR, 191
Kukta CV, 45
Kulesa P, 550, 554
Kulik J, 512
Kulkosky PJ, 262
Kuller LH, 75, 76

Kumar P, 103
Kuncel NR, 635
Kunda Z, 101, 102, 134, 135
Kupersmidt JB, 465, 468, 469
Kurasaki K, 588
Kurasaki KS, 588
Kurosawa M, 37
Kurtz PD, 463
Kurtzberg TR, 294
Kutchins H, 379
Kuttschreuter M, 408
Kuyken W, 77
Kwak RS, 299
Kwallek N, 244
Kyllonen PC, 424
Kyrios M, 688
Kyrkouli SE, 266

L

Laapio H, 237
Ladd GW, 331, 685, 686
Ladd RT, 634, 639
Ladenheim EE, 262
Ladouceur R, 71
Laferrere B, 269
LaFromboise T, 587
Lahti I, 20
Lai J, 33
Lair TJ, 349
Laird M, 455, 456, 463, 464
Lake NL, 680
Lakoff G, 128
Lall R, 242
Lam S, 204
Lamb ME, 322, 456, 458, 465
Lambert AJ, 544
Lambert MC, 585
Lambert MJ, 356
Lambert PD, 269
Lamberts K, 123, 134
Lampert S, 266
Lampinen JM, 486, 500, 501, 504
Landau B, 137
Landel JL, 667

Lane JD, 66, 74, 78, 79
Lane SM, 503, 504, 680
Langemann U, 706
Langenbucher JW, 378, 390, 397
Langfeld HS, 60
Langhans W, 258–60
Langley J, 406, 431
Langley–Evans SC, 264
Lanning K, 670
Laroche S, 34
Larouche C, 175, 176
Larrick RP, 281, 288
Larsen ON, 706, 711
Larsen PJ, 268
Larsen SF, 511–13
Larwill LK, 499
Lasko NB, 408
Lassaline ME, 130
Last CG, 395
Latham GP, 641, 647
Latkin CA, 362
LaTour MS, 557
Latta K, 589
Lau A, 46
Lau S, 585
Laumann–Billings L, 461
Laux L, 186
Lavine H, 545
La Voie L, 332
Lavy EH, 63, 64
Law P, 236
Lawley DN, 217
Lawrence CB, 262
Laye S, 38
Layzer JI, 350, 351, 367
Lazarus R, 318
LeCompte SH, 452
LeDoux JE, 606, 608, 610
Le WW, 262
Leach C, 237
Leary MR, 667
Leavey MB, 189
Leavitt LA, 325
Lebedev V, 236
Lebowitz K, 137
Leck K, 551, 558–61
Lee AY, 95, 105, 106

Lee C, 268
Lee JE, 38
Lee RA, 651
Lee S, 213
Leeuw I, 81
Leff JP, 582
Lefkowitz J, 643
Lefley H, 584
Lefter L, 460
Leggett EL, 175
Legree PJ, 635
Legrenzi P, 561
Lehane J, 455, 457, 461
Leibold JM, 548, 549
Leibowitz SF, 266
Leichtman MD, 507
Leifer M, 457
Leighton AH, 379
Leighton GE, 262
Leippe MR, 213
Leiter J, 463, 466
Lempereur A, 297, 300
Lenard L, 628
Lengua LJ, 684, 687, 688
Lennox RD, 355, 361
Lent RW, 215
Lenzenweger MF, 396, 397
Leonard CM, 606, 608–10
Leonards JS, 643
Leopold L, 256, 265
Lepage EL, 715
LePine JA, 649
Lepore L, 96, 97, 99, 100
Leport SJ, 458, 469
Lepper MR, 548
Lerner B, 427
Lerner JS, 292, 293, 683
Le Scanff C, 242
Leshner AI, 385, 386, 389
Leshner G, 155
Lester J, 585
Letarte H, 71
Letuchikh VI, 238
Leung K, 281, 296–98, 585
Leung MK, 43
Leve LD, 12
Levendosky AA, 456, 458, 465

Levenson RW, 76
Levin DT, 137
Levin RA, 640
Levine AS, 266
Levine EL, 635, 632, 651
Levine J, 559
Levine SB, 395
Levinson DF, 397
Levinson RW, 70
Levinson SC, 125
Levy A, 542
Levy SR, 106
Levy–Sadot R, 486, 514
Levy–Shiff R, 330
Lewicki RJ, 281, 291
Lewin K, 67
Lewin R, 419
Lewin V, 675
Lewis BP, 673
Lewis CM, 244
Lewis DO, 451
Lewis HB, 667
Lewis IA, 448
Lewis J, 327
Lewis JC, 325, 327
Lewis M, 678
Lewis SA, 295
Lewis–Fernandez R, 381, 382, 574, 589
Lewontin RC, 12
Leyens J–P, 106, 114
Li F, 207
Li H, 644
Liben LS, 492
Liberman A, 550
Liberman D, 208
Lichter SR, 154
Lickel B, 544
Liebowitz MR, 580, 581
Lievens F, 642
Light AR, 41, 43
Lilienfeld SO, 378, 382, 383, 389, 390, 640
Lillard A, 382
Lilly RS, 587
Lim RG, 283
Lin E, 325, 327
Lin KM, 582, 588, 589

Lin L–H, 358, 364
Lin LR, 296, 297
Lin M, 105, 134
Lin WY, 708
Lind A, 219
Lindahl KM, 454
Lindenberger U, 212, 215
Lindenlaub L, 44
Linder CW, 457
Lindholm D, 42
Lindsay DS, 104, 496, 497, 500, 504, 505, 510, 514
Lindsay RCL, 509
Lindzey G, 489
Link A, 704
Linnoila MI, 385
Linville P, 110
Lipovsky JA, 466
Lipowski ZJ, 228
Lippa R, 421
Lippmann W, 105, 106, 164
LIPSEY MW, 345–75; 348, 356, 359, 360
Lish JD, 393
Litovsky RY, 701, 710
Litrownik AJ, 455
Litterer JA, 281, 291
Little TD, 206, 209, 212, 215
Lituchy T, 286
Litz BT, 408
Liu D, 19
Liu S, 265
Liu XG, 33
Livanou M, 390
Livesley WJ, 393, 396, 397
Livingston KR, 129
Ljungberg T, 609, 612
Llano DA, 714
Llewellyn–Smith I, 258
Lockabaugh J, 48
Locke CL, 455
Locke EA, 205
Locke SE, 76
Locke V, 97, 99, 100
Lockhart LK, 554
Loeber R, 6, 393, 394
Loehlin JC, 203, 211, 417
Loevinger J, 414

Loewenstein G, 284, 285, 302
Loewenstein J, 288, 303
Lofquist LH, 425, 426
Loftus EF, 96, 483, 487, 495, 503–8, 513
Loftus J, 104
Loftus ST, 77, 79, 110–12
Logan GD, 98
Loges WE, 550
Logothetis NK, 614, 615
Lohman DF, 411, 412
Lollmann B, 267
Lombardi WJ, 78
Long DL, 77
Long JD, 359
Longabaugh R, 352, 360, 362, 366
Longhofer J, 589
López A, 138
Lopez DF, 206, 215
López Sr, 571–98; 380, 381, 573, 576, 583, 587
Lord CG, 105
Lord RG, 289
Lorenz FO, 14
Lorenzetti BB, 39, 41, 42
Lorig TS, 76
Losey KM, 188
Losoya S, 684
Lotter EC, 258, 263
Love BC, 127
Lovejoy MC, 327, 335
Lovrich NP, 151
Lowell BB, 267, 268
Lowman RL, 651
Lozsadi DA, 716, 717
Lu D, 267
LUBINSKI D, 405–44; 406, 408, 411, 412, 414, 416, 417, 420, 426, 431–33, 635
Luce C, 673
Luce RD, 301
Ludwig DS, 268
Lueke SB, 640
Lugg DJ, 229, 230, 232, 237, 238

Luheshi G, 38
Lui L, 134
Lukas JH, 715
Lundberg GD, 446
Lundeberg T, 37
Lundgren SR, 541–44, 559, 560
Lundquist LM, 328
Lunghofer L, 448, 459
Luo CR, 502
Lupkowski A, 416
Lust J, 557
Luthans F, 639
Luther N, 638
Luthy R, 268
Lutz W, 347
Lutzenberg W, 418
Lykken DT, 406, 414, 419, 421, 429–33
Lynam DR, 395, 396, 398, 685
Lynch CA, 267
Lynch DL, 457, 458
Lynch E, 122, 123, 133, 138
LYNCH EB, 121–47; 129
Lynch ME, 73, 110, 446, 452, 457, 458
Lynn R, 417
Lynn SJ, 485, 486
Lyon J, 325, 327
Lyon JE, 318, 327
Lytle C, 457

M
Ma M, 45
Ma Q–P, 42
MACCALLUM RC, 201–26; 207, 213, 215, 216
MacCallum T, 234, 236
MACCOBY EE, 1–27; 5, 21
MacCorquodale K, 417
MacDonald CJ, 355
MacDougall–Shackleton SA, 705, 706
MacIver D, 175
MacKay EM, 258
MacKinnon CE, 322

MacKinnon–Lewis C, 322
MacLane CN, 643
MacLeod C, 70, 97, 99, 100
MacMillan HL, 448
MacNamara J, 125
Macfie J, 321, 334
Maciejewski PK, 378
Mackesy ME, 291
Mackie DM, 548, 558, 559
Macklin ML, 408
Macomber J, 136
MACRAE CN, 93–120; 60, 65, 66, 72, 74, 77, 79, 95, 97–106, 108–13
Madden NA, 189
Maddison SP, 262, 610, 613
Madison SM, 191
Mae R, 453
Maehr M, 191
Maehr ML, 171, 174, 178, 181, 188, 191, 192
Maekawa M, 714
Mael FA, 641, 648
Maertz CP Jr, 648
Maes CJM, 183
Maffei M, 256, 265
Magleby DB, 159
Magliozzi T, 283
Magluyan P, 258
Maguire EA, 622
Mah WA, 491
Mahtani MM, 397
MAIER SF, 29–57; 30, 32, 33, 35–41, 43, 45–47
Main M, 465
Maio GR, 544, 551, 552, 554
Maital S, 334
Maixner W, 41, 43
Maksimov AL, 238
Malan TP Jr, 33
Malarkey WB, 207
Malcarne V, 336
Maldegen R, 642
Malgady RG, 572
Malhotra A, 41, 45
Malik NM, 454
Malkova L, 608
Malle BF, 325

Malloy P, 395
Mallozzi JS, 285
Mallya G, 391
Malos SB, 642
Malpass RS, 508, 509
Malt BC, 123, 127, 138
Mammone N, 321, 324, 328
Manabe T, 712–14
Mandel F, 455, 457, 461
Mandel FS, 455, 457
Mandell W, 362
Mandler G, 492
Mandler JM, 130, 131, 494
Manly JT, 452, 455–58, 465, 468
Mann TE, 150
Manning CG, 506
Mannix EA, 284, 297, 301, 302
Mannuzza S, 395
Mansbridge J, 165
Manson S, 588
Manson SM, 572, 588
Mansson S, 265
Marans S, 449, 450
Maratos–Flier E, 268
Marburger W, 513
March JG, 284
Marchessault K, 396
Marcoulides GA, 203
Marcus S, 448
Mare RD, 349
Margoliash D, 713
MARGOLIN G, 445–79; 446, 449, 451, 452, 458, 459, 467, 469
Margolis H, 138
Margulis C, 125
Marimuthu G, 704
Marín–Martínez F, 645
Marino L, 378, 382, 383, 389, 390
Markman AB, 128, 288
Markman EM, 125, 126, 128
Markman KD, 496
Markow DB, 125
Marks JL, 267
Markus H, 177

Markus HR, 296, 297, 582
Marmar CR, 238
Marr D, 623
Marschall DE, 669
Marsella AJ, 572, 579
Marsh DJ, 387
Marsh HW, 177, 219
Marsh KL, 545
Marshall H, 192
Marshall JC, 482
Marsiske M, 217
Marti MW, 561
Martin AJ, 182
Martin C, 588
Martin CL, 686
Martin D, 39–41, 43–49
Martin HP, 464
Martin JA, 5
Martin LL, 67, 78, 109, 318, 353
Martin R, 208, 560
Martinez J, 32, 39, 41, 43, 45
Martinez P, 448, 458, 462, 468
Martinez V, 261, 263
Martone MW, 457
Martorell G, 321
Maruyama G, 203, 215
Marwell G, 281
Marziniak M, 44
Maser JD, 588
Mash EJ, 324, 335
Maslow AH, 230
Mason P, 39
Mason R, 610
Mass A, 495
Masson MEJ, 499
Masten AS, 446, 453
Maszk P, 671, 674–76, 678, 684–87
Mather L, 290
Mather M, 502
Mathews AM, 70
Matson CA, 261, 265
Matsui F, 285
Matsuzaki I, 268
Matthews G, 81, 637

Matthews KA, 75, 76
Maude–Griffin PM, 351, 352, 360, 362
Mauland W, 644
Maury R, 283
Maves TJ, 44
Maxwell AE, 217
Maxwell G, 418
May CP, 516
May JG, 281
Mayer DJ, 32, 33
Mayer J, 259
Mayer LS, 367
Mayerson NH, 182
Mayou RA, 81
Mazure C, 462
Mazurick JL, 351
Mazzoni G, 514, 515
McArdle JJ, 206, 207, 209, 211
McArthur JC, 46
McBride JR, 635
McBride–Chang C, 455, 458, 461, 463
McCain AP, 332
McCann CD, 70
McCarthy HD, 264
McCarthy TT, 503, 504
McCartney K, 431, 433
McCarty CA, 331, 337, 584
McCauley MR, 483
McClarty B, 462
McClellan M, 349
McClelland DC, 173, 178, 191
McClelland JL, 94–96, 106, 132, 622
McCloskey AL, 555
McCloskey LA, 454, 456
McCloskey M, 505, 512
McClure RD, 155
McCombs MC, 157
McConkey KM, 485
McConnell AR, 114, 548, 549
McCormick DA, 717
McCormick IA, 229, 238

McCormick M, 137
McCown W, 182
McCrae RR, 208, 241, 396,
    423, 425, 649
McCusker C, 283
McDaniel M, 642
McDaniel MA, 636, 638,
    640
McDermott KB, 483, 485,
    486, 500–2, 504, 506,
    507, 522
McDevitt TM, 177, 184
McDonald HE, 496
McDonald L, 350
McDonald M, 47
McDonald RP, 203, 219
McDonough L, 130, 131
McDowell M, 455, 458, 465
McElgin W, 386, 388
McElree BD, 109
McElroy SL, 391
McFarland C, 495
McFarlane AC, 387
McGarty C, 558
McGee RA, 452
McGee RO, 687
McGillicuddy–deLisi AV,
    316
McGirr KM, 269
McGlone F, 605, 610
McGlynn EA, 350
McGorry M, 32, 33, 37
McGowan MK, 265
McGrath EG, 327, 380
McGrath J, 611
McGraw SA, 362, 365
McGregor HA, 176
McGrew JH, 350, 354
McGue M, 211, 396, 397,
    418, 419, 429, 432
McGue MK, 397
McGuffin P, 418
McGuire JPD, 461
McGuire S, 15, 211
McGuire TW, 296
McGuire WJ, 159, 165
McHugh PR, 262, 263
McInerney DM, 177

McInerney V, 177
McIntosh WD, 67
McIntyre LA, 48
McIntyre M, 639
McKay CP, 235, 237, 241
McKay JM, 263
McKeachie WJ, 175
McKendrick K, 348
McKeon JK, 556
McKersie RB, 284, 293
McKinley SC, 135
McKinney VM, 503
McKnew D, 682
McKnight K, 356
McKnight P, 356
McLanahan AG, 126
McLeer SV, 456, 461
McLellan AT, 354
McLellan K, 502
McLeod PL, 561
McLoyd VC, 14
McMahan S, 556
McMahon SB, 42
McMahon SR, 63, 66, 67
McManus MA, 643
McMillan D, 103, 494
McNalley S, 673
McNally RJ, 63, 71, 76, 408,
    462
McNamara TP, 490, 491
McNaughton BL, 94–96,
    106, 620, 622
McNemar Q, 412, 414
McPhail SM, 645
McPherson B, 458, 459
McQuade J, 262
McQueen DS, 48
McVicar D, 469
Meaney MJ, 19, 20
MEDIN DL, 121–47; 113,
    122–24, 129–30, 133, 138
Medina C, 38
Medsker GM, 204
Meece JL, 175, 177, 190
Meehl PE, 397, 406, 409,
    410, 414, 417, 430, 432
Megela AL, 708
Megela–Simmons A, 703

Mein CG, 265
Melby J, 673, 674, 684
Meldolesi J, 46
Mellenbergh GJ, 366
Meller ST, 41, 43–45
Mels G, 217
Melson GF, 331
Memon A, 505, 508
Menon S, 635
Merali Z, 20
Mercer JG, 262, 268, 269
Merckelbach H, 62–64, 66,
    73, 77, 81
Meredith W, 207, 209, 213,
    364
Meric C, 715
Mermelstein RJ, 362, 366
Merry SE, 290
Merry SN, 457, 459
Mervis CB, 124, 128–30
Messick DM, 284, 285, 289,
    292, 302
Messick S, 414
Metcalfe J, 94, 113, 514
Metzger LJ, 408
Meyer HA, 171, 174
Meyer JP, 209, 556
Meyer M, 42
Meyers RJ, 351, 361, 362,
    364, 365
Mezzacappa E, 685
Mezzich JE, 576
Michalski RS, 123
Michie C, 589
Michie PT, 715
Middlebrooks JC, 701
Middleton MJ, 174, 175
Midgley C, 174, 175, 180,
    181, 183, 191, 192
Migetz DZ, 639
Mikula G, 683
Milberg SJ, 134
Milberg WP, 497
Milburn P, 261
Miles D, 12
Milich R, 328
Mill JS, 165
Millar KU, 67, 557

Millar M, 67
Millar MG, 557
Miller AT, 183
Miller DG, 495
Miller DT, 138, 285
Miller EK, 618, 623
Miller EM, 418
Miller ER, 668, 669, 682
Miller GA, 112, 113, 388, 390
Miller JL, 640, 701
Miller JM, 157
Miller JW, 232, 234, 244
Miller LC, 548, 587, 685
Miller LS, 453, 456
Miller MB, 500
Miller MD, 214
Miller N, 178, 683
Miller PA, 672–74, 681
Miller RS, 667, 669, 670
Miller SA, 316, 318, 328
Miller TQ, 394
Milligan E, 45–47
Milligan ED, 46, 47
Mills RS, 322, 327, 330
Mills TM, 296
Millsap PA, 461
Millsap RE, 210, 213, 645
Milne AB, 65, 66, 72, 74, 77, 79, 95, 97–106, 108, 110–13, 131, 134
Milne R, 508
Milner B, 619
Milner JS, 325, 335
Milstein G, 583
Milward T, 617
Mimpen AM, 701, 711
Minami M, 40
Mineghino ME, 648
Mineka S, 183, 378, 390, 393, 396, 397
Miner JB, 638
Minton JW, 281
Mintz J, 583
Mirenowicz J, 612
Mischel W, 113, 325
Miselis R, 259
Misery L, 48

Mishkin M, 619
Mistlin AJ, 615
Mitani A, 716
Mitchell CM, 588
Mitchell KE, 640
Mitchell KJ, 486, 503, 504
Mitchener EC, 673
Mittmann DH, 713
Miura K, 177
Miyashita Y, 617, 621
Mize J, 324, 335
Moag J, 283, 284, 293, 294
Mocellin JSP, 230, 238
Moes GS, 242
Moffat AJM, 707
Moffitt TE, 396, 408, 417, 685–87
Mogdans J, 705
Mogg K, 70
Mohamed AA, 650
Molina BSG, 684
Molish HB, 237
Monahan J, 393, 394
Moncher FJ, 354
Mone MA, 644
Money KE, 232
Monteith MJ, 60, 68, 71, 79, 109–12
Montgomery JD, 289
Mont–Reynaud R, 585
Mooney DM, 458, 459
Mooney–Heiberger K, 33
Moore BCJ, 706
MOORE DA, 279–314; 283, 294, 303
Moore DW, 447
Moore EA, 380
Moore L, 462
Moore TE, 453
Moos RH, 206, 349
Mora F, 605, 610
Moran TH, 262, 263
Morath RA, 648
Moreland LW, 49
Morely IE, 302
Morest DK, 716
Morf CC, 182
Morgan DGA, 268

Morgan IA, 81
Morgeson FP, 633
Moring J, 20
Morley JE, 263
Morris JF, 236, 237, 245
Morris JS, 609, 610
Morris MW, 126, 281, 285, 294, 299
Morris NM, 291
Morrison T, 300
Morton S, 350
Moscovici S, 558, 560
Moscovitch M, 519
Moser J, 457, 458
Moses LE, 348
Mosk J, 585
Mosk MD, 456, 465
Moskowitz GB, 78, 561
Moskowitz JM, 347
Moss CF, 703
Moss FA, 637
Motowidlo SJ, 633, 634, 642
Mount MK, 637, 639, 640, 649
Mowbray CT, 351
Moyer G, 354
Moyer RS, 490
Mozley PD, 386, 388
Mozzoli M, 265
Muceniece R, 267
Muchinsky PM, 643
Mudar P, 684
Muehlbauer G, 183
Mueller GC, 644
Mueller W, 265
Mugnaini E, 715
Mugny G, 560, 561
Mukerji S, 245
Mulaik SA, 634
Mulder RT, 397
Muller HK, 232
Muller RU, 620, 621
Muller WEG, 46
Multhaup KS, 498
Mulvey EP, 394
Mumford MD, 632, 633, 643
Munoz D, 44
Munoz RF, 380

Munro GD, 553, 554
Munton AG, 326
Murase K, 42
Muraven M, 65
Muris P, 62–64, 66, 73, 77, 81
Murnighan JK, 283, 285, 301
Murphey DA, 316
Murphy BC, 211, 671, 673–78, 684–88
Murphy CM, 456
Murphy GL, 123, 126, 130, 131
Murphy GM, 418
Murphy JM, 379, 419, 420
Murphy KR, 633, 638, 644, 645
Murphy M, 684, 686, 687
Murphy PG, 44
Murphy S, 41, 43, 45
Murray C, 12, 406, 408–10, 415, 432
Murray DM, 347, 510
Murray DW, 326
Murray EA, 608, 619
Murray K, 670, 671, 679, 685
Murray SL, 545
Muthén BO, 203, 207, 210, 218, 364, 366, 367
Mutz DC, 156
Myers JK, 572
Myers KA, 466
Myers RR, 42, 44, 45, 48
Myors B, 644

N

Naarala M, 20
Nadel L, 622
Nader K, 462
Nadler J, 286
Naigles L, 125
Naitoh P, 238
Nakamura GV, 123, 492, 493, 495, 496
Nakamura–Craing M, 41, 42
Nalebuff BJ, 286, 290

Nalwa V, 606, 614, 615, 617
Nancarrow DJ, 397
Narayan S, 95, 106
Narayanan L, 635
Narens L, 513–15
Narins PM, 702, 703, 706–8
Nason E, 634
Nath A, 45
Nathan PE, 378, 390, 397
Naumann U, 504
Nauta A, 285
Nauta MM, 73
Naveh–Benjamin M, 187
Navon D, 68
Neal AM, 579, 587
Neale MA, 282–84, 297, 300, 301
Neale MC, 211, 217, 219
Necowitz LB, 216
Needham A, 137
Needham DR, 499
Neely JH, 96, 98
Neiderhiser J, 11, 13, 17, 20
Neiderhiser JM, 13, 14, 16, 337
Neighbors B, 469
Neighbors C, 580
Neighbors HW, 572
Neilson D, 587
Neisser U, 398, 408, 410, 416, 417, 483, 485, 486, 491, 494, 503, 511, 512, 520, 523
Nelson CA, 460
Nelson CJ, 159
Nelson DE, 546
Nelson DL, 503
Nelson JB, 632
Nelson JM, 132
Nelson K, 510, 583
Nelson PD, 235
Nelson TE, 550
Nelson TO, 513–15
Nemeth CJ, 561
Neria Y, 389
Nesbitt N, 359
Nesselroade JR, 207, 209, 212, 215, 220

Neuberg SL, 95, 98, 103, 105, 134, 208, 299, 673
Neubert MJ, 649
Neugebauer R, 453, 456
Neumann E, 102
Neuschatz JS, 486, 500–3, 506
Neuweiler G, 704
Neville HJ, 8
New M, 319, 336
Newby IR, 521
Newell S, 649
Newhouse JP, 349
Newman DL, 686, 687
Newman FL, 348
Newman JP, 686
Newman LS, 66, 78
Newton E, 283, 285
Newton JEO, 458, 459
Ney P, 446
Nguyen KT, 38, 40, 45–47
Nhouyvanisvong A, 514, 515
Nicholls JG, 174, 175, 189
Nicholls T, 510
Nichols M, 41, 45
Nichols ML, 33
Nicolaidis S, 259, 260
Nicolson M, 265
Niedenthal PM, 135, 668
Nieder A, 715
Niemi RG, 159
Nigg JL, 396
Niki H, 621
Nir A, 334
Nisbett RE, 281, 299
Nishijo H, 607
Nishio O, 46
Nishiyori A, 40
Nix RL, 318, 322
Nixon S, 329
Noddin EM, 232, 235, 242
Noel N, 352, 360, 362, 366
Nolde SF, 496, 497
Nomura S, 716
Norcross JC, 362
Norem JK, 182
Norgren R, 258, 262

Norman DA, 94–96, 102, 107, 108
Norman GR, 129
Norman J, 348
Norman KA, 482, 486, 487, 493, 497, 502, 514, 516, 518, 519
Norman WT, 423
Northcraft GB, 283, 290, 295, 297
Northwood A, 446
Nosofsky RM, 135
Novick A, 704
Novins DK, 588
Novy DM, 208
Nowell A, 416
Nowicki S Jr, 323
Nuckolls CW, 589
Nuki G, 48
Núñez JA, 576
Nyfield G, 649
Nyman M, 684

O
Oakes PJ, 558, 559
Oates K, 455, 458, 465
Oates RK, 457, 458
Oatman LC, 715
Obertynski MA, 551, 552
O'Boyle MW, 418
O'Brien BS, 686
O'Brien CP, 385, 386
O'Brien M, 467
O'Brien WA, 45
Obrist MK, 705
O'Connell MS, 641
O'Connor BP, 396
O'Connor E, 321
O'Connor KM, 286, 291, 292
O'Connor LE, 669, 670
O'Connor TG, 13, 18
Odbert HS, 423
O'Doherty J, 605, 610
O'Donahue TL, 262
Ogbu JU, 180
Ogles BM, 356

Ohbuchi K, 283
Ohtsubo Y, 557
Ojerda V, 583
Oka K, 39, 40
Oka T, 39, 40
Okada S, 263
O'Keefe J, 620–22
O'Keefe M, 454, 456, 458
Okumura T, 297, 299, 300
Okun A, 465
Okun MA, 674, 676, 678
Okun RL, 303
Oldham RS, 703
O'Leary KD, 456
O'Leary SG, 322, 328, 329
Olekalns M, 283
Olivardia R, 392
Oliver D, 237
Oliver JE, 466
Oliver JM, 464
Olschowka JA, 48
Olsen JF, 713
Olsen ME, 668, 669, 682
Olson C, 285
Olson JM, 103, 544, 552, 554
O'Mara SM, 621
Omelich CL, 185–87, 189, 190
Omwake KT, 637
O'Neil HF Jr, 648, 649
O'Neil R, 320
O'Neill WE, 713, 714
O'Nell T, 588
Ones DS, 634, 635, 637–40
Ono T, 607
Onorato RS, 558
Oosterlaan J, 685
Opie J, 324
Opie P, 324
Opp M, 46
Oppenheim D, 334
Oppler SH, 636
O'Reilly RC, 94–96, 106, 622
O'Rourke MF, 262
Orr E, 159
Ortiz de Montellano BR, 589

Ortony A, 138
Ortseifen M, 46
Orwin RG, 354
Osgood DW, 366–68
Oskin D, 458, 469
Osofsky JD, 447, 449, 450, 462, 464, 468
Ossipov MH, 33
Ostroff C, 645, 647
Ostrom TO, 549
Ostwald J, 705, 712
OSWALD FL, 631–64; 633, 641, 645, 646
O'Toole BI, 457, 458
O'Toole BJ, 408
Ottati V, 556
Oudji S, 579
Ouellette J, 543, 544, 559, 560
Overall JE, 208
Owen JM, 355
Owen MJ, 418
Owens D, 587
Owens SM, 40
Oxley ZM, 550
Oziemkowska M, 362

P
Padavich DL, 680
Padilla AM, 572
Page MS, 74–76, 81
Paglia DE, 234, 236
Paice JA, 34
Pajares F, 214
Paker M, 390
Palacios J, 324, 333, 334
Palinkas LA, 230, 231, 235, 238, 241
Palkovits M, 267
Pallota GM, 328
Palmer CF, 129
Palmer DK, 641
Palmer LG, 301
Palmeri TJ, 135
Palmiter RD, 387
PANSKY A, 481–537; 491, 516

Panter AT, 220
Panzeri S, 620, 621, 623
Pape D, 62, 63, 73
Pappas T, 137
Paradis CM, 587
Pardo C, 449, 452, 468
Parga N, 617, 623
Paris J, 396, 589
Parisi D, 13
Park B, 97, 99, 100, 549
Park CR, 258, 261
Parke RD, 320, 321
Parker JDA, 208
Parker JG, 465
Parkinson D, 456, 458
Parkinson JA, 608, 609, 612
Parkinson JK, 619
Parra P, 583
Parrish ME, 48
Parron DL, 576
Pascoe JP, 609
Passik S, 47
Patenaude R, 328
Paterson DG, 415
Patterson CJ, 465, 468, 469
Patterson CM, 686
Patterson D, 392
Patterson GR, 6, 7, 10, 13,
    320
Patterson TE, 155
Patton KM, 667
Patton TW, 639
Paullin C, 643
Pauls J, 614, 615
Paunonen SV, 208
Pavelchak MA, 318
Pavelka K, 48
Pawson R, 360
Payne DG, 482–84, 486,
    500–3
Payne RS, 705
Payza K, 33
Peacock W, 46
Pearlman K, 632
Pearson J, 321
Pease BS, 460
Pechman PS, 44
Pederson N, 211

Pekkarinen A, 237
Pekrun R, 187
Pelcovitz D, 455, 457, 461
Pelleymounter MA, 268
Pendergrast RA, 457
Pendry LF, 98, 101, 104,
    105, 134
Peng K, 299
Pennebaker JW, 69, 76, 77,
    109, 110, 505
Penner L, 673
Penrod S, 508–10
Pentland J, 506
Pentz MA, 209
Pepler D, 453
Perdue CW, 96, 97, 101
Perez JA, 561
Perfect TJ, 510
Peri A, 230, 241, 244
Perkins MN, 48
Perl HI, 354
Perlis T, 348
Perovic S, 46
Perrett DI, 489, 609, 610,
    615
Perrott DR, 701, 711
Perry B, 459, 461
Perry KE, 180
Persinger MA, 462
Pertenoy R, 47
Pertovaara A, 33
Perusse L, 264
Peters JC, 264
Peters RD, 322
Peterson C, 318, 321, 335
Peterson CS, 684
Peterson E, 302
Peterson NG, 632, 633, 636
Peterson PK, 45
Peterson RS, 292, 293, 561
Petrausch S, 44
Petrides M, 619
Petrie KJ, 69, 77
Petrocik JR, 151, 152, 159,
    160
Pettit DJ, 10
Pettit G, 21

Pettit GS, 6, 14, 318, 322,
    324, 335, 451, 464, 465,
    467
Petty RE, 109, 540, 542,
    545, 546, 548, 551,
    554–56, 683
Peyron C, 268
Peyton HJ, 262
Pezdek K, 506
Pfau M, 552
Phares V, 585
Phibbs CS, 349
Phillips A, 136
Phillips DP, 701
Phillips JS, 585
Phillips KA, 391, 392
Phillips N, 588
Pick AD, 129
Pickles JO, 716
Pickrell JE, 505, 507
Pierce C, 75, 76
Pierce CA, 646
Pierce JC, 151
Pierson DL, 232
Pifer ME, 635
Pihl RO, 674
Pike A, 337
Pillemer DB, 512
Pilloff D, 66, 74
Pillow DR, 684
Pillutla MM, 285
Pincus AL, 393
Pincus HA, 385, 390, 391,
    395
Pinderhughes EE, 318, 322
Pine D, 685
Pinker S, 125, 282
Pinkley RL, 283, 290
Pintrich PR, 174–76, 181,
    188, 190
Pinuelas A, 684
Pion GM, 352–54
Piper M, 268
Pi–Sunyer FX, 269
Pitkanen A, 607–9
Pitman RK, 387, 390
Pitts RC, 666
Plant EA, 112

Plomin R, 6, 11, 13–16, 18, 19, 211, 418, 433, 589
Plomp R, 701, 711
Plotnick CA, 557
Plotsky PM, 19
Ployhart RE, 634, 635, 644, 646, 648
Plunkett K, 13
Plutchik R, 637
Poggio T, 614, 615
Pohley K, 642
Pokay P, 177
Poland RE, 589
Polewko J, 327
Polivy J, 75, 76
Pollak G, 704
Pollard R, 459
Polo A, 583
Polonsky BD, 265
Polster MR, 497
Polycarpou MP, 673
Polzer JT, 297, 301, 302
Pomerantz EM, 548
Pommerenke PL, 283, 285
Pool GJ, 546, 548, 551, 558–61
Pool K, 73
Poole DA, 509
Poole MS, 290
Poole S, 39, 41–43, 47
Pope HG, 392
Popkin BM, 264
Popkin SL, 156
Popovich PG, 48
Porges SW, 675
Porreca F, 33
Porte D Jr, 261, 263, 265–69
Portin P, 397
Posavac EJ, 356
Posluszny DM, 384
Posner MI, 492
Postman LJ, 486
Postmes T, 108
Potosky D, 646
Poulin R, 684, 686, 687
Pound J, 457
Powell TPS, 715, 716
Power TG, 326

Powers K, 648
Powers TA, 682
Powley TL, 258, 261, 263
Pradere D, 486, 501, 502
Prager I, 633
Pratkanis AR, 213, 560
Pratto F, 105
Prediger DJ, 421
Premack D, 419
Prentice DA, 138
Prentice–Dunn S, 556
Prescott CA, 211
Pribram KH, 112, 113
Price JL, 607–9
Price RA, 10
Price V, 550
Priester JR, 548, 551
Priestley JV, 42
Prigerson HG, 378
Prins AJA, 260
Prinz RJ, 354
Prior M, 688
Prislin R, 541, 542, 546, 548
Probst TM, 293
Prochaska JO, 362
Proenca R, 256, 265
Proffitt JB, 138
Profilet SM, 685, 686
Pruitt DB, 461
Pruitt DG, 281, 290, 295, 296
Prussia GE, 210
Pugh RH, 209
Pulakos ED, 632, 634, 644, 647
Pulkkinen L, 687
Pulliam L, 46
Purcell DG, 615, 623
Purdie N, 176
Purdon C, 60, 69, 80, 81, 83
Puro P, 190
Purvis D, 551, 558, 560, 561
Putnam FW, 455, 458–61, 463, 468
Putnam L, 290
Putnam LL, 290
Putnam SP, 670, 671, 679
Pynoos R, 462

Pynoos RS, 446, 450, 462, 466, 468
Pyszczynski T, 66, 72, 74

Q

Qu DQ, 268
Quigley BM, 684
Quiles Z, 670
Quillian F, 77
Quinn PC, 130, 131
Quiñones MA, 642, 644
Quirk GJ, 621

R

Rabe C, 555
Rabiner D, 322
Rabinowitz JC, 502
Racchetti G, 46
Rachman S, 69
Racine C, 502
Rader M, 641
Radke–Yarrow M, 672, 673, 679, 680
Radloff R, 230, 232–34, 236, 238, 240
Radvansky G, 110
Radvansky GA, 490
Rady P, 46
Rae DS, 379
Ragan P, 385
Ragsdale K, 348
Raia CP, 285
Raiffa H, 282, 301
Raine A, 685
Rainer G, 623
Rainnie D, 607
Rajaram S, 511
Raju NS, 644
Rallis SE, 353
Ralphe D, 456, 461
Ramachandran VS, 617
Ramer MS, 44
Ramirez E, 392
Ramponi C, 486
Ramsay DS, 264
Ramus SJ, 620
Rand AS, 702

Rand N, 48
Randall ER, 462
Rank S, 551, 560, 561
Ransmayr C, 229
Rao CR, 207
Rao SC, 623
Rao U, 321
Rashotte CA, 214
Rasmussen JE, 235
Rassin E, 77
Ratakonda S, 396, 397
Ratcliff K, 281
RATNAM R, 699–725; 708, 711
Ratner H, 187
Rattermann MJ, 288
Raudenbush SW, 366
Ravussin E, 10, 264
Rawlins JN, 619
Raye CL, 498
Raykov T, 207, 208, 220, 644
Raymark PH, 633
Raymond LW, 237
Raymond P, 291
Rayner DV, 268, 269
Raz N, 498
Read JD, 485, 502, 510
Read SJ, 548
Rebert CS, 462
Rebok GW, 367
Recce M, 622
Reder LM, 495, 496, 503–5, 514, 515
Redford EJ, 48
Redinidel–Negro C, 34
Redmond C, 364
Redshirt R, 588
Ree MJ, 635
Reeve AJ, 41
Regier DA, 379, 572
Rehm LP, 380
Reichardt CS, 205, 206, 209, 212–14, 347, 353, 356
Reicher S, 557
Reichert F, 48
Reidelberger RD, 262
Reiffman A, 468

Reilly PM, 351, 352, 360, 362
Reimers TM, 331
Reingold DP, 684
Reinhard MA, 561, 551
Reinhold DP, 325, 329
Reinitz MT, 497
Reise SP, 209, 219
Reiser BJ, 489
Reiser M, 211, 666, 676, 684–88
Reiss AD, 638, 640
Reiss C, 327
Reiss D, 6, 11, 13–15, 211, 337, 418, 433, 589
Reivich M, 386, 388
Relles DA, 349
Relton JK, 37, 39
Rempel–Clower NL, 619
Ren K, 33
Renart A, 623
Rende R, 211
Rendel A, 260
Renwick–DeBardi S, 672
Resnick HS, 387, 390
Retzlaff PD, 635
Reyes O, 188
Reyna VF, 336, 492, 500, 501, 503, 505, 518
Reynolds AJ, 348, 349
Reynolds CF, 378
Reynolds K, 551, 552
Reynolds M, 73, 75
Reynolds S, 328, 378
Reyome ND, 456, 463
Reznick JS, 77
Rheaume J, 71
Rheinlaender J, 703
Rhodes G, 489
Rhodewalt F, 182
Ribel U, 268
Ribordy SC, 464
Ricciardi JN, 63, 71
Rice KG, 205
Richard R, 548
Richards HC, 82, 684
Richards JC, 82
Richardson DE, 32

Richardson PM, 44
Richardson–Klavehn A, 486
Richman BA, 137
Richters JE, 318, 448, 458, 462, 468, 681
Ridge B, 21
Riedy CA, 261
Rieg TS, 260
Riemann R, 396
Rienick CB, 521
Rifkin A, 126
Riker WH, 157
Riley DA, 488
Riley Y, 643
Rimsza ME, 455
Rinaman L, 262
Ring B, 609
Rippe JM, 264
Rips LJ, 123, 124, 126, 127, 138, 151, 513
Risley TR, 433
Ritchie KL, 456, 458
Ritov I, 283
Ritter RC, 38, 40, 258, 261, 262
Ritter S, 38, 40, 258
Rivera M, 580
Rivolier J, 229, 231, 238, 240
Rixon RH, 260
Rizley R, 450
Robbins PC, 394
Robbins TW, 608, 609, 612
Roberts BW, 420, 422, 424
Roberts CR, 588
Roberts GC, 174
Roberts MJ, 502
Roberts MW, 323
Roberts RD, 675, 676
Roberts RE, 588
Roberts W, 673, 677
Robertson I, 637
Robertson RG, 606, 620, 621
Robertson RK, 499
Robie C, 649
Robins LN, 572
Robins RW, 686
Robinson B, 294

Robinson DE, 701
Robinson J, 321, 334, 670, 682
Robinson JL, 677
Robinson KJ, 485, 486, 501, 502, 506
Robinson M, 154
Robinson MD, 510
Robinson RD, 229
Robinson RJ, 283, 289, 291
Rocchi P, 502
Roche LA, 177
Rocher S, 113
Rock DA, 643
Rock J, 647
Rockart L, 669, 670
Rockel AJ, 716
Rockstroh B, 418
Roddy S, 264
Rodet L, 129
Rodriguez O, 572, 574
Roe A, 428
Roediger HL III, 482–86, 497, 500–2, 504, 506, 507

Roehling MV, 642
Roemer B, 33, 40
Roemer L, 63, 70
Roesch R, 384
Roesch SC, 673, 674, 684
Roese NJ, 103
Roeser RW, 181, 190
Rog DJ, 353, 358
Rogers EM, 157
Rogers J, 561
Rogers MJ, 469
Rogers PJ, 361
Rogers RW, 556
Rogers W, 646
Rogier A, 114
Rogler LH, 379, 572, 575, 576, 587
Rogoff B, 324
Rogosch FA, 321, 334, 453, 464
Rohan MJ, 319
Rohrbaugh M, 68, 83
Roijackers J, 362

Rolfhus EL, 425
ROLLS ET, 599–630; 262, 601–15, 617–24, 628
Roman RJ, 78
Romero AA, 552
Romo LF, 137
Roney C, 177
Roper DW, 63, 70, 73, 82
Roper–Hall A, 607
Rosario M, 455, 465
Rosch E, 124, 128–30
Rose GJ, 708
Rose R, 12, 13
Roseborough ME, 296
Rosen BC, 183
Rosen JC, 392
Rosen MJ, 502
Rosenbaum M, 259, 265
Rosenbaum PR, 349
Rosenberg MS, 451, 452, 456, 464, 467
Rosenfeld B, 47
Rosengren K, 137
Rosenheck R, 359
Rosenthal DA, 176, 585
Rosenthal R, 7, 289, 356, 644
Roskos–Ewoldsen DR, 164
Rosnet E, 242
Rosomoff HL, 384
Rosomoff RS, 384
Ross B, 131
Ross DF, 485, 504
Ross HE, 232, 238, 244
Ross L, 281, 283–85, 288, 289, 292, 299, 302
Ross M, 285, 487, 495, 496, 521
Ross R, 391, 395
Rosse JG, 640
Rosse RL, 636
Rossi D, 46
Rossi M, 268
Rossi PH, 354, 359
Rossman BBR, 451, 452, 467
Rotfeld HJ, 557
Roth AE, 293

Roth L, 636
Roth PL, 635, 637, 641, 642, 645–47
Rothbart M, 21, 113, 138
Rothbart MK, 671, 675, 676, 684–87
Rothblum ED, 236, 237, 245
Rothman AJ, 131, 545, 552
Rothman S, 409, 411
Rothstein H, 643
Rothstein MG, 642
Rothwell NJ, 38
Rotshenker S, 44, 48
Rotter JB, 318
Rounds J, 211, 421, 425
Rounds JB, 421
Rouner D, 554
Rounsaville BJ, 385
Rouse D, 76
Rouse WB, 291
Routhieaux BC, 497
Rowbotham MC, 34
Rowe D, 4, 5, 11
Rowe DC, 406, 417, 422, 431
Rowe EA, 262
Rowe–Hallbert A, 323
Rowland D, 609, 610
Rozman B, 48
Roznowski M, 216, 425
Rubchinsky K, 672, 673
Rubel AJ, 589
Rubin DB, 356, 644
Rubin DC, 512, 513
Rubin JZ, 280, 281, 283, 303
Rubin KH, 330
Rubio–Stipec M, 580, 581, 585
Ruble DN, 329
Rubsamen R, 704
Ruckel J, 137
Ruda MA, 44
Rudorfer MV, 589
Ruffini M, 230
Rule BG, 289
Rumbaugh D, 419
Runyan D, 447
Rupinski MT, 634

Rupniak NMJ, 619
Rusbult CE, 286
Ruscher JB, 543
Russell CJ, 634, 643, 644
Russell CW, 392
Russell DW, 210
Russell JA, 637
Russell M, 684
Rusting CL, 555
Rutkowski M, 41, 43, 45
Rutledge JH III, 63, 64
Rutledge JN, 418
Rutledge PC, 63, 64, 71, 82
Rutter ER, 294
Rutter M, 13, 18
Rutter ML, 390, 397
Ruvolo A, 177
Ryan AM, 635, 646–48
Ryan I, 265
Rybicki SL, 633
Rydell SM, 509
Ryugo DK, 716

S

Saad SA, 646
Sabato L, 155
Saberi K, 701, 711
Sacco JM, 634, 648
Sacco WP, 82, 326
Sachdeva U, 245
Sachs MB, 715
Sack W, 588
Sack WH, 588
Sackett PR, 427, 634, 636,
  638, 640, 641, 646
Sacks S, 348
Sadeh A, 461
Sadler JZ, 381
Sadralodabai T, 701, 711
Saemundsdottir I, 63, 64, 81
Safieh–Garabedian B, 42, 43
Sagal M–C, 242
Sagarin BJ, 673
Sagen J, 44, 45
Sager CE, 636
Sager K, 672, 673
Sahu A, 266

Said G, 48
Sakurai T, 268
Salas E, 648
Saldana E, 715
Salgado JF, 637, 639, 644
Salgado de Snyder VN, 572,
  583, 587
Salkovskis PM, 64, 69, 71,
  73, 75, 82
Sally DF, 294
Salmán E, 580, 581
Salnitskiy V, 237
Salovey P, 545
Salter JM, 262
Saltzberg JA, 674
Salyers M, 350, 354
Salzinger S, 455, 457, 465
Sam D, 587
Samaltedinov I, 235
Sameroff AJ, 334, 453
Samuels SM, 284, 285, 302
Samuelson CD, 285
Samuelson WF, 283
Sanacora G, 267
Sanchez J, 632, 633
Sanchez–Ku M, 642
Sánchez–Meca J, 645
Sandal G, 238
Sandal GM, 234, 236–38
Sanders CE, 414
Sandkuhler J, 32, 33
Sandler IN, 684, 687, 688
Sands WA, 635
Sanghera M, 605
Sanghera MK, 607
SANKIS LM, 377–404
Sanson A, 688
Santana F, 583
Santilli G, 455, 456, 459
Santy PA, 235, 240–42
Saper CB, 268
Sapir E, 125
Sapolsky RM, 462
Sarat A, 290
Saris WH, 264
Sartori G, 132
Sartorius N, 572, 582
Sashidharan SP, 587

Satoh M, 40
Saucier G, 423, 637
Saudino KF, 211
Saul J, 685
Saunders BE, 466
Saunders DM, 281
Saunders RC, 619
Savage–Rumbaugh S, 419,
  420
Savickas ML, 420, 421
Sawyer JD, 356
Sayer A, 207
Sayer AG, 207, 364, 366
Scalaidhe SPO, 623
Scalera G, 258
Scalia C, 647
Scarlata C, 230
Scarnati E, 609
Scarr S, 5, 14, 422, 431–33,
  435
Scepansky JA, 554
Schaaf JM, 509
Schacter DL, 80, 95, 482–87,
  492, 493, 497, 500–2,
  507, 514, 516, 518, 519,
  521–23
Schadron G, 106, 113
Schafers M, 44
Schaie KW, 406, 408, 417,
  431
Schaller M, 674, 681
Scharrer E, 258, 260
Schechter D, 541, 542
Scheeringa MS, 450
Scheflin AW, 505
Scheibel AB, 418
Scheier MF, 109, 112, 113,
  186
Scheirer MA, 353, 359
Schellart NAM, 703
Schelling R, 232
Scher SJ, 683
Scherer KR, 683
Scheurink AJW, 258
Schiff MH, 49
Schiffman SS, 261
Schioth HB, 267
Schippmann JS, 637, 641

Schlegel P, 715
Schlichting CL, 234
Schloerscheidt AM, 95, 97, 103, 104, 108
Schmalhofer F, 492
Schmalzle K, 560, 561
Schmeidler J, 387, 390
Schmidt C, 44
Schmidt DB, 414
Schmidt FL, 356, 406, 408, 427, 634, 638, 641, 642, 644–45
Schmidt NB, 390
Schmit MJ, 633, 635, 648, 649
Schmitt DR, 281
Schmitt N, 632, 634, 636, 646–48
Schmitz J, 294
Schneider BH, 586
Schneider BS, 427
Schneider DJ, 60–63, 66, 67, 73
Schneider RJ, 178, 637, 641
Schneider W, 509, 516, 520
Schnitzler H–U, 704, 705
Schoenfeld D, 75, 76
Schoenfeldt LF, 643
Schooler JW, 492, 504, 505, 507
Schooneveldt GP, 706
Schrauben B, 175
Schroeder ML, 393
Schroth HA, 283, 286
Schuckit MA, 385
Schul Y, 555
Schuller G, 715
Schultz J, 138
Schultz LO, 10
Schultz W, 609, 612
Schumacher A, 183
Schumacker RE, 203
Schuman H, 109
Schunk DH, 175, 177, 190
Schuurman M, 560
Schwab–Stone ME, 457, 459, 463
Schwalm DE, 348

Schwartz B, 32, 33
Schwartz BL, 486, 487, 510, 514
Schwartz GJ, 262, 263
Schwartz JJ, 703, 711
SCHWARTZ MW, 255–77; 257, 263, 265–69
Schwarz N, 109, 113, 499, 516, 552, 555, 556
Schwarzer C, 185
Schwarzer R, 185, 186
Schweitzer ME, 291
Schwerin MJ, 392
Schwetje FK, 235
Schyns PG, 129
Sclafani A, 260, 261
Scolton KL, 321
Scott SK, 609, 610
Scott TR, 605, 606
Scott WD, 60, 69, 80, 83, 406
Scriven M, 361
Scullen SE, 643
Scully S, 268
Scurfield RM, 579
Seamon JG, 502
Searcy CA, 643
Sears RR, 406
Sebenius JK, 283
Sechrest L, 346, 352, 356
Sedikides C, 674
Sedlack AJ, 447
Seelau EP, 509
SEELEY RJ, 255–77; 257, 258, 261, 263, 265–69
Seese N, 418
Segal ZV, 70
Segall DO, 635
Seidenberg MS, 132
Seifer R, 453
Seiger A, 33, 48
Seilheimer SD, 295
Sekaquaptewa D, 95, 106
Seligman C, 554
Seligman MEP, 229, 318, 321, 335
Sellars DE, 362, 365
Sellman JD, 397

Sells SB, 233
Selye H, 295
Semetko H, 157
Senghas A, 125
Sem–Jacobsen CW, 610
Sentis KP, 284, 285
Sergeant JA, 685
Seta JJ, 78
Sethi S, 281
Sethna BN, 295
Sevcik RA, 419, 420
Shackelford TK, 382, 383
Shackleton V, 649
Shadish WR, 346, 348
Shaffer D, 395
Shafir E, 285
Shah J, 177
Shah PP, 283, 284
Shallice T, 94–96, 102, 104, 107, 108, 132, 513
Shanks DR, 123
Shapiro DL, 292, 300
Shapiro JP, 457
Sharf JC, 415, 650
Shargill NS, 263
Sharma K, 510
Sharma S, 19
Sharpe MR, 231
Sharpless NE, 45
Shaver PR, 73
Shaw BF, 70
Shaw DR, 153
Shaw JS III, 506
Shaw LL, 673
Shea C, 673
Shear MK, 378
Sheehan M, 154
Shell P, 424
Shell R, 672–74
Shelton DL, 42
Shelton JR, 132
Shen H, 588
Sheng WS, 45
Shepard RN, 486
Shepard SA, 673–76, 678, 684, 686–88
Sheppard L, 636, 646
Sher KJ, 378, 380, 396

Sherman DA, 100
Sherman DK, 397
Sherman JW, 60, 68, 71, 72, 77, 79, 95, 105, 106, 109–13
Sherman SJ, 113, 114, 506, 548, 549
Shestowsky D, 553
Shevell SK, 151, 513
Shiarella AH, 633
Shih JH, 392
Shikhirev P, 297, 300
Shimada M, 268
Shimokouchi M, 716
Shin C, 364
Shipherd JC, 80
Shnayder L, 262
Shoben EJ, 124
Shoda Y, 325
Shoham V, 68, 83
Shooter EM, 44
Shore JH, 572
Shortell S, 350
Shortt JW, 74–76, 81
Showers L, 557
Shulman S, 330
Shultz TR, 548
Shutter JR, 268
Shweder RA, 572, 582
Shyi GC, 498
Sia T, 105
Sidani S, 359
Siddique S, 708
Sidman M, 419
Siegel AW, 520
Siegel J, 296
Siegel S, 261
Sienkiewicz ZJ, 605
Siever LJ, 387, 390
Sigel IE, 316
Sigman M, 585
Sigurjonsdottir H, 63, 64, 81
Silberg J, 13
Silbert L, 39, 41, 43, 45
Silbey S, 290
Silva PA, 396, 417, 686, 687
Silver JE, 44
Silver LA, 73, 110

Silvester J, 319, 322, 326, 336
Sim DLH, 285
Simansky KJ, 262
Simmens SJ, 6
Simmons AM, 703
Simmons JA, 704, 713
Simon A, 152, 165
SIMON AF, 149–69; 155, 157, 160, 162, 164
Simon HA, 282, 284
Simon L, 66, 72, 74, 546
Simonoff E, 13
Simons DJ, 137
Simons R, 14
Simonton DK, 428
Simpson JC, 396
Sinclair L, 102
Singer JE, 237
Singer JL, 60, 76
Singer LK, 258
Singer MI, 448, 459
Singer W, 713
Singer–Koegler LK, 258
Sinha MK, 265
Sipols AJ, 261, 265, 267
Sisk D, 32, 33
Sivers S, 462
Skaalvik E, 174
Skeem JL, 384
Skelly JJ, 558, 559
Skinner EA, 336
Skodol A, 396
Skowronski JJ, 511–13, 549
Skurnik I, 547
Slart R, 34
Slater MD, 554
Slavens G, 457
Slavin RE, 189
Slep AMS, 322
Sloman SA, 123, 127
Slusser PG, 258
Small CJ, 268
Small M, 508, 509
Smari J, 63, 64, 71, 81, 82
Smart L, 65, 72, 74, 79
Smetana JG, 330, 332, 468, 679

Smith AM, 322, 329
Smith B, 352
Smith CA, 209, 448, 453, 466
Smith D, 175
Smith DB, 427, 640, 642
Smith DH, 293
Smith EE, 122, 124, 506, 507, 554
Smith EM, 43
Smith ER, 95, 96, 98, 102, 131, 502, 548, 549
Smith FJ, 259
Smith GL, 366–68
Smith GP, 258, 261, 262
Smith GT, 262
Smith JE, 289, 351, 361, 362, 364, 365
Smith KJ, 48
Smith KP, 40
Smith LB, 137
Smith LC, 36, 43, 122, 137
Smith MA, 468, 469, 639, 675, 676, 684, 686, 687
Smith MB, 545
Smith MC, 98
Smith ML, 619
Smith MR, 636
Smith PB, 559, 542, 562
Smith SM, 123, 233–38, 551
Smith TL, 385
Smith TW, 42, 394
Smith VL, 504, 510
Smith WM, 236, 242
Smith Y, 269
Snell AF, 640
Snidman N, 77
Sniezek JA, 553
Snow CP, 407, 425, 434, 435
Snow RE, 406, 408, 409, 411, 412, 424, 425
Snowden L, 587
Snyder K, 583
Snyder KS, 583
Snyder ML, 177, 290, 545
Snyderman M, 409, 411
Sobel E, 359
Sode J, 237

Soini S, 237
Soja NN, 137
Solomon GEA, 136, 137
SOLOMON KO, 121–47;
  122, 123
Solomon S, 66, 72, 74
Solomon SK, 494
Solomon Z, 389
Solowij N, 715
Sommer C, 44
Sommers SR, 555
Sondak H, 284
Song LY, 448, 459
Song Y, 125
Sonnefeld LJ, 354
Sörbom D, 203, 216–18
Sorenson C, 669
Sorenson CB, 669
Sorkin LS, 34, 42, 44, 45, 48

Sorokin AA, 238
Sorrentino R, 177
Soulez–Larivieres C, 242
Southwick SM, 462
Spaccarelli S, 467
Spanos NP, 506
Spearman C, 409, 410, 418,
  424
Spears R, 99, 108
Spector PE, 209, 635, 684
Speer AL, 681
Speer DC, 348, 356, 366
Spelke ES, 136, 137
Spencer SJ, 97, 99, 101, 106
Spencer WD, 498
Spicer CV, 60, 79, 111
Spiegel D, 391
Spinrad TL, 73, 685
Spitzer RL, 379, 385
Spokane AR, 420, 421
Sporer SL, 509, 510
Spoth R, 210, 364
Sprafkin J, 321
Springer JE, 48
Springer K, 137
Sproull L, 295, 296
Spychalski A, 642

Squire LR, 135, 135, 619,
  620
Sroufe LA, 321, 681
Srull TK, 95, 103, 486
Staab JP, 390
Stadler DR, 547
Stafford D, 326
Stahl SM, 380
Stahlberg D, 495
Staib L, 462
Staines GL, 348
Stajkovic AD, 639
Stallings WM, 188
Stallone DD, 257, 263
Stangor C, 103, 106, 494
Stanislaw T, 9
Stankov L, 675, 676
Stanley BG, 266
Stanley EZ, 260
Stanley JC, 347, 406, 408,
  409, 416, 417
Stansbury K, 685
Stanush P, 651
Stapel DA, 105, 108, 109
Stark KL, 268
Stark N, 291
Starr J, 297, 299
Staw BM, 637
Steadman HJ, 393, 394
Steblay NM, 509
Stecher BM, 350
Stecher MD, 640
Steeh C, 109
STEEL GD, 227–53; 230,
  235, 237, 238, 241, 242
Steele CM, 546, 547
Stefano GB, 43
Stefanovic–Racic M, 48
Steffens AB, 258
Stegge H, 667–70, 680–82
Steiger JH, 217, 219
Stein JA, 206, 212, 348
Stein LM, 336
Stein MB, 460, 462
Steinberg A, 462
Steiner DD, 647
Steiner RA, 267, 365, 368
Steinfield CW, 294

Steinmetz SK, 452
Steinverg L, 21
Ste. Marie L, 387
Stephens TW, 265, 266
Stephenson GM, 510
Stern A, 457, 458
Stern C, 609
Stern JS, 265
Stern LB, 510
Sternberg KJ, 454, 456, 458,
  465
Sternberg RJ, 410, 434
Stettner L, 187
Stevenage VS, 508
Stevens AL, 287, 491
Stevenson JAF, 260
Stevenson–Hinde J, 334
Stewart AL, 615, 623
Stewart BJ, 356
Stewart GL, 639, 649
Stice E, 207, 684, 687, 688
Stifter CA, 685
Stiksrud A, 185, 186
Stillinger C, 283
Stillwell AM, 667
Stipek D, 175, 679
Stoeber J, 70
Stokes BT, 48
Stokes GS, 643
Stokols D, 243–45
Stolowitz ML, 44
Stolzenberg RM, 349
Stone EJ, 362, 365
Stone J, 546, 547
Stone S, 258
Stoneman Z, 15
Stone–Romero EF, 646
Stoolmiller M, 13, 207, 355
Stout R, 352, 360, 362, 366
Stouthamer–Loeber M, 685,
  686
Stowe RP, 232
St. Pierre RG, 350, 351, 367
Strack F, 109, 514
Strage A, 183
Strange RE, 231, 242
Strassberg Z, 325, 328, 335
Stratton P, 322, 326

Straus MA, 447, 448, 452
Strauss A, 359
Strayer J, 673, 674, 676, 677
Street L, 580
Streit R, 183
Stricker EM, 262
Stricker LJ, 643
Strodtbeck FL, 296
Stroessner SJ, 72, 77, 79, 102, 106, 110–13
Strom GA, 455, 456, 459
Stroud JN, 504
Strub H, 243
Strubbe JH, 260, 261, 265
Strudler A, 291
Strycker LA, 207
Studt A, 283
Stuebing KK, 364
Stunkard AJ, 257, 263
Sturges JW, 556
Stuster J, 229–31, 233, 236–38, 240, 242–45
Su SK, 281
Suarez–Orozco C, 587
Suarez–Orozco MM, 188, 191, 587
Subich LM, 637
Suchman EA, 361
Sue D, 588
Sue L, 588
Sue S, 588
SUEDFELD P, 227–53; 228, 230, 231, 235–39, 241, 242, 244, 245
Suengas AG, 486, 497
Suga N, 704, 712–16
Sugawara HM, 215
Suh EM, 381
Sullivan MJL, 76
Sullivan PF, 397
Summerfeldt LJ, 208
Summers G, 218
Summit J, 230
Sun XD, 716
Sundstrom E, 648
Suomi SJ, 19
Supple WF, 609
Surrey J, 462

Susenaar M, 81
Sutter ML, 713
Sutton RS, 617
Suwanlert S, 331, 337, 584, 585
Suzuki WA, 618, 620, 623
Sveen O, 716
Svenson O, 285
Swann WB, 523
Swanson B, 34
Sweitzer SM, 41, 43, 45
Swett C, 462
Switzer FS, 637, 641
Sydell EJ, 640
Szakmary GA, 261

T

Tache Y, 261, 263
Tajfel H, 557
Takahashi TT, 709, 710
Takeshige C, 48
Takeuchi D, 588
Takeuchi DT, 588
Takezawa M, 557
Talbot JM, 233
Talbott E, 75, 76
Tanaka E, 42
Tanaka H, 714
Tanaka JM, 129
Tanenbaum RL, 321
Tang NM, 33
Tang–Christensen M, 268
Tangney JP, 667–70
Tannenbaum B, 19
Tanner J, 183
Tanner JM, 412
Taraban R, 123
Tardif TZ, 125, 137
Tarnowski K, 457, 458, 463
Tarpley WR, 547
Tarr MJ, 129
Tartaglia N, 37
Tataranni PA, 264
Taube JS, 621
Taussig HN, 455
Taylor AJW, 229–31, 235, 236, 238

Taylor JR, 612
Taylor L, 369
Taylor M, 113, 129, 138
Taylor SE, 285, 317
Teachout MS, 209, 635, 644
Teas DC, 701
Tedeschi JT, 684
Teel KM, 185, 190
Teicher MH, 461–63
Tellegen A, 419, 421, 423, 424, 429, 432
Teller SA, 487
Telles C, 583, 587
Temple JA, 348, 349
Tenbrunsel AE, 283–86, 291, 292
Terkildsen N, 556
ter Laak JF, 183
Terman L, 435
Terpstra DE, 650
Terr L, 461, 462
Terris W, 646
Terry L, 715
Tesser A, 67, 318
Test MA, 353
Teti DM, 319, 324
Tetlock PE, 292, 293, 683
Tewksbury D, 550
Thagard P, 101, 134
Theodor L, 98
Therme P, 242
Theuns P, 123
Thibaut JW, 286
Thiele TE, 268, 387
Thilbaut J, 129
Thim L, 268
Thoenen H, 42
Thomas AM, 456, 459
Thomas DW, 259
Thomas LE, 642
Thomas SP, 75–77
Thomas–Hunt MC, 561
Thompson CP, 511–13
Thompson D, 165
Thompson EP, 78
Thompson L, 281–88, 291, 295, 299, 301–3
Thompson LL, 293, 294, 301

Thompson MM, 548
Thompson NM, 364
Thompson RA, 8
Thompson T, 181–83, 420, 433
Thorkildsen TA, 174
Thorn TMJ, 97–101
Thornberry TP, 453, 466
Thorndike R, 411
Thorndike RL, 409
Thorndyke PW, 490
Thornton GC III, 636
Thornton JE, 267
Thorpe PK, 176
Thorpe SJ, 69, 610, 613
Thorsteinson TJ, 648
Thun F, 46
Thurstone LL, 414, 435
Thynn L, 63
Tice DM, 65
Tienari P, 20
Tilders FJH, 37, 38
Tilley N, 360
Tindall EA, 49
Tingate TR, 232
Ting-Toomey S, 298
Tinker E, 125
Tinsley C, 298–300
Tipper SP, 102
Tippins NT, 650
Tisak J, 207, 209, 211, 364, 634, 646
Tisak M, 211
Tisak MS, 634
Tjebkes TL, 685
Tobias S, 186
Todd HF, 290
Toglia MP, 485, 501, 504, 506
Tokar DM, 637
Tolan P, 453, 456, 459
Toland HK, 504
Toland K, 487
Tomasello M, 125
Tomer A, 220
Tomiki K, 183, 184
Tomlinson TM, 555
Toney R, 644

Tong L, 455, 458, 465
Tooby J, 136
Tooman GD, 60, 79, 111
Toomey R, 396
Topman RM, 186
Topping ME, 183
Torchia MG, 462
Tordoff MG, 258
Torgeson JK, 214
Torrance EP, 241
Toth JP, 500
Toth SL, 321, 334, 446, 451, 456–58
Tougas G, 263
Tovee MJ, 606, 615, 617, 623
Toyka KV, 44
Tracey KJ, 41, 43, 45
Tracey TJ, 211, 421
Trahiotis C, 701, 715
Trakowski JH, 390
Tranel D, 132, 609–11
Trapnell PD, 636, 637
Trayhurn P, 268, 269
Tremblay A, 264
Tremblay PF, 202
Tremblay R, 685
Tremblay RE, 674
Tremewan T, 489
Treneer CM, 263
Trevathan D, 585
Treves A, 600, 601, 606, 607, 609, 613–16, 620–24
Triandis HC, 297, 582
Trickett PK, 455, 457–61, 463, 464, 468, 469, 606, 617
Triebwasser J, 392
Trinder H, 71
Tripp ML, 385
Tritos NA, 268
Trobst KK, 672, 673
Troome N, 448
Trost MR, 540, 541
Troyer D, 681
Truax P, 356
Trull TJ, 378, 380, 383, 393, 396

Truxillo DM, 647
Tsai GE, 385
Tsuang MT, 396
Tsui ZC, 33
Tsujii S, 263, 267
Tubre T, 642
Tucker JA, 182
Tucker LR, 207
Tulving E, 95, 486, 502, 510
Tun PA, 502
Tupes EC, 423
Turco RM, 551
Turdiev A, 238
Turk CL, 673
Turken AU, 135
Turkheimer E, 12
Turner CW, 394
Turner JC, 549, 557–60
Turner ME, 560, 651
Turner SM, 579, 587
Turtle JW, 520
Tusel DJ, 351, 352, 360, 362
Tussing AA, 501
Tversky A, 282, 285
Tversky B, 491
Twentyman CT, 455, 465
Tykocinski O, 545
Tyler LE, 406
Tyler RB, 96, 97, 100, 101
Tyor WR, 46
Tyring S, 46

U

Uchino BN, 213
Uleman JS, 78
Ullman S, 615
Ulrich P, 41, 43, 45
Undheim JO, 411
Ungerer JA, 675
Uno H, 462
Unze MG, 129
Urban L, 41
Urdan TC, 174, 181, 183
Ursin H, 229, 234, 236–38, 241, 242
Useda JD, 393, 396
Ushijima H, 46

V

Vaernes RJ, 234, 236–38
Vage DI, 267
Vaid J, 123
Vakkur M, 589
Valdéz G, 191
Valencia ME, 10
Valente E, 211
Valentino N, 160
VALLEY KL, 279–314; 283, 284, 293, 294
Valsiner J, 317, 333
van Avermaet E, 302
Van Breukelen G, 362
Van Court P, 673
Vandegeest KA, 685
Vandello JA, 553
van den Bergh LC, 232
Van den Boom DC, 10
VandenBos GP, 380
van den Brink WP, 366
van den Hout MA, 62–64, 73
Van der Pligt J, 548
van de Vliert E, 285, 289, 290
Van de Wal C, 609
van Dijk G, 258
Van Dijk WW, 548
van IJzendoorn MH, 319, 320
van Knippenberg A, 104–6, 108
van Knippenberg D, 558
van Koppen PJ, 505
Van Lange PAM, 286
van Loon JJ, 232
Vanman EJ, 548
Van Mechelen I, 123
van Pelt M, 513
Van Ryzin GG, 365
Van Scotter JR, 633
Van Slyke DA, 209
Vargas P, 95, 106
Vargo M, 456, 458
Vasko MR, 34
Vasselli JR, 261, 263
Vaughn CE, 582, 583
Vazsonyi AT, 417

Vechia SE, 269
Vega W, 588
Vega WA, 587
Veldhuijzen JP, 232
Verbalis JG, 262
Verda MR, 335
Verdin E, 45
Verfaellie M, 486, 497, 501, 502
Verhulst FC, 585
Verity AN, 44
Verive JM, 636
Vermeulen D, 105
Vernon PA, 393, 396, 397, 418
Vernon PE, 412
Veroff J, 178
Veronen LJ, 466
Vesce S, 46
Vespo JE, 333
Vezeau C, 175, 176
Vicent D, 268
Vig S, 453, 466
Vigilante D, 459
Villeponteaux LA, 466
Vincent KR, 208
Vinchur AJ, 637, 641
Vispoel W, 178
Visser PS, 552
Viswesvaran C, 633, 634, 637–40
Vitaro F, 674
Vitiello MV, 261
Vito R, 184
Vlahov D, 348, 362
Vogelaar R, 550
Volkow NR, 385, 386
Volling BL, 322
Volterra A, 46
Vondra J, 457, 458
Voyce C, 457, 459, 463
Vrang N, 268
Vuchinich RE, 182
Vuletíc Z, 583

W

Wacker DP, 331
Wade D, 611, 612

Wade GS, 510
Wade–Benzoni KA, 284–86, 292
Wagenaar WA, 505
Wagner E, 672, 673, 679
Wagner KD, 328
Wagner PE, 669, 670
Wagner R, 42, 44, 45, 48
Wagner RK, 214
Wagner SH, 459
Wagstaff GF, 510
Wakefield JC, 382, 383, 378, 379, 381–83, 389, 391
Wakeman EA, 610
Wakugawa Y, 40
Waldron EM, 135
Walford RL, 234, 236
Walker CB, 636
Walker E, 20
Walker I, 97, 99, 100
Walker LJ, 666
Walker LS, 209
Walker MJK, 41
Walker NE, 509
Walkowiak W, 708
Wall TD, 208
Wallen J, 461
Waller JH, 433
Waller NG, 421, 423
Wallis G, 605, 606, 614, 617
Walls EK, 258, 261
Walsh RO, 325
Walster E, 284
Walster GW, 284
Walter BR, 584
Walters ET, 43, 44
Walther E, 504
Walton RE, 284, 293
Walton W, 639
Wamboldt FS, 334
Wan KC, 298
Wanek JE, 638
Wang CT, 446, 447
Wang CX, 48
Wang G–J, 385, 386
Wang JCS, 358, 364
Wang L, 261, 263
Wang T, 644

Wang XM, 33
Wang Y, 588
Ward A, 288, 289
Ward T, 63, 83
Ward TB, 123
Ware N, 574
Warheit GJ, 588
Warncke M, 238
Warr WB, 715
Warren S, 334
Warrington EK, 132
Warwick ZS, 260, 261
Washburn DA, 419
Wasserman EA, 419
Wasserman GA, 453, 456, 685
Watanabe T, 716
Waterman JW, 464
Waterman S, 519
Waters BK, 635, 675
Waters E, 681
Waters HS, 511
WATKINS LR, 29–57; 30, 32, 33, 35–41, 43, 45–47
Watson CS, 701
Watson D, 378, 393, 396, 397, 670, 686
Watson EL, 510
Wattenberg MP, 152, 155
Wattenmaker WD, 133
Watts FN, 70
Waxman SR, 125
Weaver CA, 512
Weaver DH, 157
Weber EU, 299
Weber LJ, 234, 236
Webster CD, 384
Webster–Stratton C, 318
Wegener DT, 109, 213, 540, 545, 546, 551, 553–56, 683
Wegener I, 99
WEGNER DM, 59–91; 60–63, 65–67, 70–81, 83
Wei JY, 261
Wei P, 48
Weigle DS, 261, 267

Weinberg–Eliezer A, 491, 516
Weinberger NM, 716
Weine AM, 585
Weine S, 462
Weiner B, 182, 318
Weiner M, 455, 457
Weingardt KR, 504
Weingart LR, 301
Weingarten HP, 261
Weinger B, 685
Weinman J, 70
Weinstein CE, 174
Weinstein RS, 180, 191
Weinstock JS, 236, 237, 245
Weisman A, 582
Weisner T, 586
Weisner TS, 574, 586
Weiss B, 331, 584, 585
Weiss CH, 358–62
Weiss DS, 238, 395
Weiss J, 669, 670
Weiss MJS, 459
Weiss SE, 296, 299, 300
Weisz JR, 326, 331, 337, 584, 585, 685
Wekerle C, 331
Weldon E, 298
Weldon MS, 520
Wellman HM, 136, 137, 510
Wells A, 69
Wells GL, 508–10, 520, 638
Wells KC, 10
Wells KD, 703
Welsch D, 492
Welsh JD, 672, 675, 679
Wenstrup JJ, 705, 713
Wentzel KR, 175, 178–80, 188
WENZLAFF RM, 59–91; 60, 63, 66, 67, 69, 70, 72–75, 80, 82, 83
Wesman A, 416
West DB, 264
West DM, 155
West M, 648
West SG, 208, 348, 684, 687, 688

West T, 502
Westlye MC, 154, 159
Wewers S, 447, 462
Weybrew BB, 232, 235, 237, 242
Whalen PJ, 609
Whang PA, 177
Wheaton B, 218
Wheeler V, 77, 79, 110–12
Whetstone T, 74, 77
Whishaw IQ, 388
White F, 230
White JD, 267, 685
White KG, 238
White KR, 714
White LT, 509, 641
White PH, 554, 555
White RT, 513
White RW, 545
White S, 455, 456, 459
White TL, 60–62, 66, 73
White W, 706
Whitehead R, 645
Whitehouse K, 498, 499
Whitfield IC, 716
Whitney DJ, 634, 644, 648
Whittlesea BWA, 498–500, 514
Wholey JS, 358, 361
Whyte G, 283, 641, 647
Wiater MF, 261
Wible CG, 512
Wibrowski CR, 176
Wichman H, 228, 294
Wickett A, 446
Wicklund RA, 67, 72
Widaman KF, 208, 209, 215, 216, 219
WIDIGER TA, 377–404; 378, 383, 390, 391, 393, 395, 396, 398
Widom CS, 466
Wiedenhaupt S, 180
Wiegand AW, 546, 547
Wiegman O, 408
Wiertelak EP, 32, 33, 39, 40
Wiesenfeld–Hallin Z, 48
Wigdor AK, 416

Wigfield A, 178, 179, 188
Wiggins JS, 393, 636, 637
Wikberg JE, 267
Wilcox T, 137
Wilczynski W, 707
Wildering WC, 260
Wiley MG, 183
Wilk SL, 427, 634
Wilke H, 558
Wilkinson CW, 258
Willerman L, 406, 418
Willett JB, 207, 364, 366
Willett WC, 264
Williams CJ, 97
Williams D, 572
Williams E, 296, 685
Williams GV, 609
Williams JBW, 385
Williams LD, 499, 514
Williams LJ, 204
Williams LM, 455, 457, 459, 462
Williams WM, 417
Williamson LG, 642
Willis SL, 408
Willis WD, 33–35, 40, 43, 45
Wilson A, 633
Wilson DB, 348
Wilson EO, 420, 429, 434
Wilson FAW, 607–10, 623
Wilson JQ, 430
Wilson MA, 620
Wilson S, 451, 456, 458, 466
Wilson SK, 452, 465
Wilson TD, 109, 548
Windschitl PD, 503
Winer JA, 715
Winfrey SE, 503
Wing JK, 582, 583
Wingate PH, 641
Wingfield A, 502
Winkielman P, 499
Winograd E, 484–86, 496, 512, 520, 523
Winship C, 349
Winslow RL, 715
Winter J, 42

Winterbottom MR, 183
Winton E, 63
Winton M, 81
Wirtz PW, 352, 360, 362, 366
Wisnieski BJ, 44
Wisniewski AB, 705
Wisniewski EJ, 125, 128, 130
Witte K, 556
Wittenbrink B, 97, 99, 100, 549
Witter MP, 620
Wodarski JS, 463
Woehr DJ, 641, 642
Wokutch RE, 291
Wolfe CT, 97, 99, 101
Wolfe DA, 331, 452, 456, 459, 461, 465
Wolfe DS, 451, 466
Wolfe DW, 456, 458
Wolfe T, 230, 234, 239, 240
Wolfe VV, 459, 461
Wolfinger RE, 159
Wolfle LM, 202
Wolk M, 555
Wolkowitz OM, 380
Wollmers G, 321
Woloshyn V, 498, 500, 501
Wolters CA, 176
Wong D, 714
Wong M, 448
Wood J, 230, 237
Wood JL, 355
Wood JV, 674
WOOD W, 539–70; 540, 543, 544, 548, 551, 554, 557–61
Woodcock RW, 211
WOODS SC, 255–77; 258, 260–69
Woodward AL, 125, 136
Woodward LG, 637
Woodworth RS, 173, 488
Woody EZ, 73
Woolf CJ, 41–43, 47
Worling JR, 493
Worsham N, 336

Worth LT, 558
Wosinski M, 684, 687, 688
Wothke W, 217
Wrathall JR, 48
Wren–Hardin BD, 713
Wright DB, 503, 504
Wright JD, 349
Wright MO, 446
Wright TA, 637
Wu P, 348
Wulf F, 488
Wu–Peng XS, 265
Wyatt BS, 639
Wyer NA, 72, 79, 111–13
Wyer RS Jr, 95, 103, 486
Wynne LC, 20

X

Xiao WH, 42, 44, 45
Xu F, 125, 137
Xu XJ, 33, 48

Y

Yabuuchi K, 40
Yagaloff KA, 268
Yager DD, 703
Yaksh TL, 32, 34
Yale SA, 396, 397
Yan J, 606, 716
Yanagisawa K, 716
Yang H–YT, 33
Yang R–K, 387, 390
Yaniv I, 516
Yao G, 411, 420
Yates W, 17, 20
Yaxley S, 605
Yeaton WH, 354
Yee W, 702
Yehuda R, 387, 390, 460
Yeung M, 46
Yin J, 673
Yin RK, 353
Yin TCT, 710
Yngvesson B, 290, 297, 299
Yoon K, 561
York DA, 262, 263
Yoshihara T, 261

Yost WA, 701
Young A, 382, 383, 389, 579
Young AMJ, 612
Young AW, 609, 610
Young LV, 104
Young MB, 205
Young RC, 261, 262
Youngman SA, 242
Yu AC, 713
Yu AL, 34
Yu SL, 176
Yusko KP, 642, 643
Yzerbyt VY, 106, 113, 114

Z

Zacks RT, 110, 516
Zaglul H, 81
Zaharia MD, 20
Zahn–Waxler C, 333, 669,
    670, 672–75, 677, 679,
    680, 682
Zaitchik D, 136, 137
Zajonc RB, 295
Zak L, 452, 456, 458, 465
Zaki S, 135
Zakis S, 587

Zaller J, 159, 161
Zambarano RJ, 325, 329,
    684
Zanakos S, 65, 72, 73, 75,
    81, 82
Zane N, 588
Zanis DA, 354
Zanna MP, 103, 319, 545,
    548, 554
Zapf PA, 384
Zaragoza MS, 486, 503–5,
    507
Zárate MA, 98, 131
Zarnoth P, 553
Zax M, 453
Zeanah CH, 450
Zeedyk MS, 330
Zeelenberg M, 548
Zeichner A, 394
Zeigarnik B, 67
Zelick RD, 702, 703, 706
Zelkowitz P, 396
Zeller JM, 34
Zhang S, 216
Zhang Y, 265, 716
Zhang YF, 716

Zhang YY, 256, 265
Zhao X, 155
Zheng YP, 588
Zhong C, 33
Zickar MJ, 640
Zigler E, 180, 466, 469
Zimbardo PG, 295
Zimmer–Gembeck MJ, 336
Zimmerman BJ, 174
Zimmerman RS, 588
Zimmermann M, 32
Zimny S, 492
Zinbarg RE, 396
Zingraff MT, 466
Zola SM, 619
Zola–Morgan S, 620
Zonderman AB, 208
Zucker GS, 685
Zucker KJ, 455
Zuckerman B, 449
Zuckerman H, 428, 429
Zukin LB, 648
Zukow PG, 324
Zurek PM, 701
Zuroff DC, 682
Zuwerink JR, 109, 112, 553,
    554

SUBJECT INDEX

A

Abilities
assessing individual
differences and, 405,
407–15
goal theory, motivation,
and school achievement,
185–89
Abnormal environments
environmental psychology
of capsule habitats and,
228
Aborigines
goal theory, motivation,
and school achievement,
177
Aboutness
psychology of memory
accuracy and, 484
Abstract concepts
kinds of concepts and, 128
psychology of memory
accuracy and, 494
Abuse
assessing individual
differences and, 433
children's exposure to
violence and, 445–70
emotion, regulation and
moral development, 683
parental and child
cognitions in context of
family, 321, 335
structural equation
modeling and, 210
thought suppression and,
77
Academia
goal theory, motivation,
and school achievement,
174–78

personnel selection and,
635–36
Accuracy-oriented research
psychology of memory
accuracy and, 481–523
Achievement
goal theory, motivation,
and school achievement,
171–93
Acquired immunodeficiency
syndrome (AIDS)
cytokines and pain, 47
Adaptation
environmental psychology
of capsule habitats and,
227
Addiction
adult psychopathology
and, 385–86, 388
Adiposity signals
food intake and body
weight regulation, 255,
263–66
Adjusted goodness of fit
index
structural equation
modeling and, 219
Adolescents
children's exposure to
violence and, 462–63
cultural psychopathology
and, 577, 585–86
emotion, regulation and
moral development, 669,
673–674, 684–88
kinds of concepts and, 131
parenting and its effect on
children, 7, 15
structural equation
modeling and, 205, 210

Adoption studies
parenting and its effect on
children, 1, 4, 9, 11–13,
18, 20–21
Adult Attachment Interview
parental and child
cognitions in context of
family, 320, 324
Adult psychopathology
conclusions, 398
construct of
psychopathology, 378–84
cultural relativity, 380–82
diagnostic boundaries,
391–93
dimensional vs categorical
classification, 396–98
discussion, 387–90
domains of
psychopathology, 390–98
dyscontrol, 382–84
etiology, 384–90
harmful dysfunction,
382–84
introduction, 378
life span psychopathology,
394–96
normal vs abnormal
functioning, 378–80
pathology, 384–90
posttraumatic stress
disorder, 386–87
substance dependence,
385–86
Adversaries
goal theory, motivation,
and school achievement,
190
Adverse impact

769

personnel selection and,
631, 646–647
Advertising
political communication
and campaign effects,
152, 161, 164–65
Ad watch journalism
political communication
and campaign effects,
162–63
Affect
attitude change and, 539,
555–57
cultural psychopathology
and, 590
emotion, regulation and
moral development, 674
parental and child
cognitions in context of
family, 315–37
Affirmative action
personnel selection and,
651
Africa
cultural psychopathology
and, 577
negotiation and, 298
African Americans
children's exposure to
violence and, 457, 459
cultural psychopathology
and, 572, 579, 587–88
structural equation
modeling and, 205
Afro-Caribbean immigrants
cultural psychopathology
and, 587
Age
children's exposure to
violence and, 445
cultural psychopathology
and, 580
emotion, regulation and
moral development,
678–82
kinds of concepts and,
131, 136

psychology of memory
accuracy and, 498, 504–5
social cognition and, 95,
98, 101
Agenda control
political communication
and campaign effects,
149–65
Aggression
adult psychopathology
and, 393–94
children's exposure to
violence and, 454–57
emotion, regulation and
moral development, 665,
669, 683–87
parental and child
cognitions in context of
family, 322–23
parenting and its effect on
children, 10, 12
Agreement
attitude change and,
540–44
Alaska
cultural psychopathology
and, 588
Alcohol use
environmental psychology
of capsule habitats and,
245
Allodynia
cytokines and pain, 29,
33–35, 41–42, 45, 47, 49
Altruism
emotion, regulation and
moral development,
672–74, 679
Amish
cultural psychopathology
and, 589
AMOS program
structural equation
modeling and, 217–18
Amygdala
memory systems in the
brain and, 599–624
Analgesia

cytokines and pain, 30,
32–33
Analysis of change
evaluation methods for
social intervention and,
345–69
Analytical cognitions
parental and child
cognitions in context of
family, 318, 321–23
Anger
adult psychopathology
and, 393–94
children's exposure to
violence and, 464
emotion, regulation and
moral development, 665,
669, 676–77, 682–84
thought suppression and,
75
Anglo Americans
cultural psychopathology
and, 583
goal theory, motivation,
and school achievement,
176, 180
Animal studies
neural basis of hearing in
real-world situations,
699–718
parenting and its effect on
children, 19–20
Antarctica
environmental psychology
of capsule habitats and,
228–32, 235–37, 240–41,
243–45
Antianalgesia
cytokines and pain, 32–33
Antisocial behavior
emotion, regulation and
moral development, 665,
672–74
Anurans
neural basis of hearing in
real-world situations,
702–3
Anxiety

adult psychopathology
and, 390
assessing individual
differences and, 430
children's exposure to
violence and, 457
cultural psychopathology
and, 571, 579–81, 587,
590
emotion, regulation and
moral development, 672,
681, 685
environmental psychology
of capsule habitats and,
245
goal theory, motivation,
and school achievement,
186–87
thought suppression and,
69, 73, 76, 81
Aplysia spp.
cytokines and pain, 43–44
Applicant reactions
personnel selection and,
631, 647–48
Aptitude by treatment
interactions
evaluation methods for
social intervention and,
352
Aptitude complexes
assessing individual
differences and, 426
Arctic
environmental psychology
of capsule habitats and,
228, 236
Armed Services Vocational
Aptitude Battery
personnel selection and,
636
Artifacts
adult psychopathology
and, 385
kinds of concepts and,
127–28

parental and child
cognitions in context of
family, 336
Asia
assessing individual
differences and, 415–16
cultural psychopathology
and, 572, 577–88
kinds of concepts and, 131
negotiation and, 297–98
social cognition and,
98–99
thought suppression and,
77
Assessment centers
personnel selection and,
631–33, 641–44
Assimilation effects
social cognition and, 105
Ataque de nervios
cultural psychopathology
and, 571, 579–81, 583,
590
Attack advertising
political communication
and campaign effects, 161
Attentional regulation
emotion, regulation and
moral development,
685–86, 688
Attention deficit
hyperactivity disorder
(ADHD)
parental and child
cognitions in context of
family, 329
Attitude change
affect and influence,
555–57
bias correction, 554–55
cognitive dissonance
theory, 546–48
cognitive response
mediation, 552–53
conclusions, 561–62
dual-mode processing
models of persuasion,
551–55

fear appeals, 556–57
functional theories,
544–45
group and self-identity,
557–60
group identity, 559–60
influence, 549–57
introduction, 540
mood, 555–56
motivated processing,
554–55
motives for agreeing with
others, 540–44
motives in persuasion
research, 544–48
multiple attitudes, 548–51
multiple motives instigated
by groups, 559–60
opinion minority and
majority groups, 560–61
public vs private influence,
542–44
social consensus, 558
social identity theory,
557–60
social influence, 553
validity of information,
558–59
Attraction
thought suppression and,
61
Attraction-selection-attrition
model
assessing individual
differences and, 427
Attributional atyle
parental and child
cognitions in context of
family, 315, 321–23
Auditory cortex
neural basis of in real-
world situations,
spatially-mediated release
from masking, 712–14
Auditory environments
complex neural basis of
hearing in real-world
situations and, 699–718

Australia
cultural psychopathology
and, 585
goal theory, motivation,
and school achievement,
177
Austria
negotiation and, 298
Autobiographical memory
psychology of memory
accuracy and, 481,
510–13
Automatic category
activation
social cognition and,
96–98
Automatic priming
social cognition and, 108
Autoregressive models
structural equation
modeling and, 206

B
Balance of control/power
parental and child
cognitions in context of
family, 326–27
Banding
personnel selection and,
647
Bandwagons
political communication
and campaign effects, 156
Bargaining
negotiation and, 279,
294–96
Basic level concepts
kinds of concepts and,
128–31
Bats
neural basis of hearing in
real-world situations,
703–5
"Battleground" states
political communication
and campaign effects, 153
Behavior

assessing individual
differences and, 405–36
children's exposure to
violence and, 454–57
cytokines and pain, 29
emotion, regulation and
moral development,
665–88
negotiation and, 279
neural basis of hearing in
real-world situations and,
699–718
parental and child
cognitions in context of
family, 315–37
personnel selection and,
631
social cognition and, 110,
107–9
Behavioral decision
perspective
negotiation and, 282
Behavior genetics
parenting and its effect on
children, 1–23
Belgium
negotiation and, 298
Beliefs
parental and child
cognitions in context of
family, 315–37
Benefits
environmental psychology
of capsule habitats and,
227
Best practices
evaluation methods for
social intervention and,
359
Bias
assessing individual
differences and, 414
attitude change and, 539,
554–55
children's exposure to
violence and, 451

evaluation methods for
social intervention and,
368
kinds of concepts and, 138
negotiation and, 303
parental and child
cognitions in context of
family, 322, 327, 329,
335, 337
personnel selection and,
641
social cognition and, 104,
109–10
structural equation
modeling and, 210, 213
thought suppression and,
74, 78
"Big eye"
environmental psychology
of capsule habitats and,
231
Big Five model
emotion, regulation and
moral development, 670
environmental psychology
of capsule habitats and,
241
Bigots
social cognition and, 100
Biodata assesment methods
personnel selection and,
631–33, 643–44
Birds
neural basis of hearing in
real-world situations,
705–6
Blacks
personnel selection and,
635, 640
Black/White contrasts
assessing individual
differences and, 416
Blame
emotion, regulation and
moral development, 684
goal theory, motivation,
and school achievement,
186

parental and child
cognitions in context of
family, 326, 335, 337
Blood
food intake and body
weight regulation, 255
Bodily cues
environmental psychology
of capsule habitats and,
232–33
Body weight
regulation of
food intake and, 255–69
Boomerang shifts
attitude change and, 556,
560
Boredom
environmental psychology
of capsule habitats and,
231, 234, 238, 244–45
Boundary conditions
social cognition and, 111
Boy's Town follow-up study
evaluation methods for
social intervention and,
367
Brain
adult psychopathology
and, 386–89
assessing individual
differences and, 418
cytokines and pain, 29–49
food intake and body
weight regulation, 255
kinds of concepts and,
132, 135
memory systems and
amygdala, 607–10
conclusions, 623–24
emotion, 600–14
hippocampus, 619–23
learned reinforcers,
605–6
learning of invariant
representations,
614–18
motivation, 600–14

neural networks for
stimulus-reinforcer
association learning,
613–14
neurophysiology,
620–23
orbitofrontal cortex,
610–12
output systems, 612–13
potential secondary
reinforcers, 605–6
primary rewards, 602–5
representations, 600–18
rewards and punishers,
600–14
short-term memory, 623
stimulus-reinforcement
association learning,
607–12
unlearned rewards,
602–5
neural basis of in real-
world situations,
behavioral aspects of
hearing, 699–718
social cognition and, 94
Break-off phenomenon
environmental psychology
of capsule habitats and,
234

C

California
cultural psychopathology
and, 583
political communication
and campaign effects,
153, 162
Call discrimination
neural basis of hearing in
real-world situations,
702–3
Campaign effects
political communication
and, 149–65
Canada

cultural psychopathology
and, 589
environmental psychology
of capsule habitats and,
236
political communication
and campaign effects, 157
Capsule habitats
environmental psychology
of
applications of
psychology, 239–45
capsule isolation,
233–34
choosing, 240–42
communication, 236
confinement, 234
conflict, 235
countering boredom,
244–45
cycles, 238
definitions, 228–29
density, 233
duration, 237–38
environmental design,
243–44
introduction, 227–28
miscellaneous issues,
246–47
monotony, 234–35
personality paradox, 242
physical stressors,
231–33
positive capsule
psychology, 229–30
postmission reentry, 239
psycho-environmental
factors, 233
psychologically relevant
aspects of capsule
environment, 230–33,
235–39
recommended research
topics, 246
scheduling, 238–39
screening, 239–40
selecting in, 240–42
selecting out, 239–40

sex, 236–37
social factors, 234–37
social monotony,
234–35
social roles, 235–36
temporal factors,
237–39
Captive populations
political communication
and campaign effects,
163–64
Caribbean
cultural psychopathology
and, 579
Categorical classification
adult psychopathology
and, 396–98
Categorical thinking
social cognition and,
93–114
Categorization
kinds of concepts and,
121–38
social cognition and,
96–113
Caucasians
assessing individual
differences and, 416
cultural psychopathology
and, 587
personnel selection and,
635, 640
structural equation
modeling and, 205
Causality
assessing individual
differences and, 432–33
Causal order
attitude change and, 552
Central America
goal theory, motivation,
and school achievement,
188, 191
Central nervous system
(CNS)
cytokines and pain, 29–49

food intake and body
weight regulation, 255,
264–65
Change
attitude change and,
539–62
evaluation methods for
social intervention and,
360–66
parental and child
cognitions in context of
family, 329–31
Child abuse
children's exposure to
violence and, 445–70
Children
assessing individual
differences and, 431–32
cultural psychopathology
and, 571, 584–86, 588
emotion, regulation and
moral development,
668–88
evaluation methods for
social intervention and,
350, 367
family and community
effects on
aggression, 454–57
behavior problems,
454–57
caveat regarding
adaptive vs
maladaptive outcomes,
466
cognitive consequences,
462–64
conclusions, 469–70
consequences of
exposure to violence
and, 454–65
depression, 457–59
introduction, 446–49
mediating and
moderating variables,
467–69
methodological issues,
452–54

peer relations, 464–65
posttraumatic stress
disorder, 461–62
psychobiological
effects, 459–61
summary of long-range
outcomes, 466–67
vulnerability as related
to development,
449–52
kinds of concepts and, 136
parental and child
cognitions in context of
family, 315–37
parenting and its effect on
children, 1–23
psychology of memory
accuracy and, 509
Chimpanzees
assessing individual
differences and, 419–20
China
cultural psychopathology
and, 586, 588
negotiation and, 298
Chinese Americans
goal theory, motivation,
and school achievement,
177
Cholecystokinin (CCK)
food intake and body
weight regulation, 255,
263
Chunks
of perceptual experience
kinds of concepts and,
125
Cigarette smoking
environmental psychology
of capsule habitats and,
245
thought suppression and,
75–76
Circadian rhythms
environmental psychology
of capsule habitats and,
238, 244

Classroom incentive
structures
goal theory, motivation,
and school achievement,
184–91
Cocaine dependence
adult psychopathology
and, 385–86, 388
evaluation methods for
social intervention and,
351
Cocktail party effect
neural basis of hearing in
real-world situations,
701–2, 706, 717
Cognition
assessing individual
differences and, 407–15
children's exposure to
violence and, 445,
462–64
emotion, regulation and
moral development, 678
kinds of concepts and,
121–38
parental and child
cognitions in context of
family, 315–37
personnel selection and,
631–36
social, 93–114
structural equation
modeling and, 175–78
Cognitive dissonance theory
attitude change and, 539,
546–48
Cognitive response
mediation
attitude change and,
552–53
Cold emotions
negotiation and, 286
Cold flame
thought suppression and,
70
Collaborative negotiation

parental and child
cognitions in context of
family, 315–37
Colombia
negotiation and, 297
Common fate
parental and child
cognitions in context of
family, 334
Communication obsession
environmental psychology
of capsule habitats and,
236
Communications media
negotiation and, 279,
293–96
Community game
negotiation and, 288
Community resource
approach
evaluation methods for
social intervention and,
362, 365
Community violence
children's exposure to,
445–70
Comodulation masking
release
neural basis of hearing in
real-world situations, 706
Competing messages
political communication
and campaign effects,
149–65
Complex sounds
neural basis of hearing in
real-world situations,
712–14
Compound constructs
personnel selection and,
631
Comprehensive Child
Development
Program
evaluation methods for
social intervention and,
350
Concepts

kinds of
abstract concepts, 128
artifacts vs natural
kinds, 127–28
basic level vs
subordinate and
superordinate
concepts, 128–31
candidates for kinds of
concepts based on
content, 125–38
category processing and
the brain, 135
category structure and
the brain, 132
common taxonomic vs
goal-derived
categories, 132–33
content-laden principles,
124–25
count nouns vs mass
nouns, 125–26
criteria for kinds of
concepts, 123–25
domain specificity,
136–38
hierarchies vs
paradigms, 131
introduction, 122–23
isolated and interrelated
concepts, 126
miscellaneous
distinctions, 135
nouns vs verbs, 125
objects vs mental
events, 126–27
processing differences,
124
social information
processing and
individuation, 133–34
stereotypes, subtypes,
and subgroups, 134–35
structural differences,
123–24
Concerns with self
attitude change and,
539–62

Conditional reasoning
personnel selection and,
639
Confession
emotion, regulation and
moral development, 680
Confidence-accuracy relation
psychology of memory
accuracy and, 509–10
Confinement
environmental psychology
of capsule habitats and,
227–47
Confirmatory factor models
structural equation
modeling and, 208–9
Conflict
environmental psychology
of capsule habitats and,
229, 235
parental and child
cognitions in context of
family, 322–23, 335
Conformation bias
structural equation
modeling and, 213
Confounds
assessing individual
differences and, 432–33
Confusions
source
psychology of memory
accuracy and, 497–98
Conscientiousness
personnel selection and,
637–39
Consilience
assessing individual
differences and, 405,
433–36
Consistency principle
personnel selection and,
643
Constant error
assessing individual
differences and, 414
Constellations

assessing individual
differences and, 424–31
Construct validation
assessing individual
differences and, 414
measurement studies and,
208–9
Content analysis
political communication
and campaign effects,
149, 164–65
Content-laden principles
kinds of concepts and,
124–25
Contextual organization
parental and child
cognitions in context of
family, 329–31
Contrast effects
social cognition and, 105
Control
parental and child
cognitions in context of
family, 323, 325–27
Controlled inhibition
social cognition and, 100
Cool cognitive processes
social cognition and, 113
Coping strategies
attitude change and, 556
environmental psychology
of capsule habitats and,
227, 246
Correctness
methodological
political communication
and campaign effects,
153
Correlation matrices
assessing individual
differences and, 413
structural equation
modeling and, 217–18
Correspondence
memory
psychology of memory
accuracy and, 481,
483–87, 517–19

Cortical encoding
of complex sounds
neural basis of hearing in
real-world situations,
712–14
Count nouns
kinds of concepts and,
125–26
Counterstereotypic
processing
expectancy
social cognition and, 99,
103
Courage
personnel selection and,
643
Covariance structures
parenting and its effect on
children, 17–19
structural equation
modeling and, 201,
217–18
Cravings
adult psychopathology
and, 388
thought suppression and,
75–76
Creativity
assessing individual
differences and, 428–30
Criminality
assessing individual
differences and, 405,
430–31
emotion, regulation and
moral development, 684,
687
parenting and its effect on
children, 20
Cross-cultural issues
negotiation and, 296–300
personnel selection and,
631, 649–50
Cross-national differences
cultural psychopathology
and, 571–90
"Crud"

assessing individual
differences and, 414
Cued monitoring
thought suppression and,
62
Cultural psychopathology
anxiety, 579–81
childhood disorders,
584–86
conceptual contributions,
573–76
conclusions, 589–90
definition of culture,
573–75
disorder-related research,
579–86
DSM-IV, 576–79
emerging trends, 587–89
goal of cultural research,
575–76
immigration, 587
introduction, 571–73
key developments, 573–76
miscellaneous research,
589
schizophrenia, 581–84
US ethnic minority
groups, 587–89
World Mental Health
Report, 576–79
Cultural relativity
adult psychopathology
and, 380–82
Culture
assessing individual
differences and, 434–35
attitude change and, 562
negotiation and, 279,
296–300
parental and child
cognitions in context of
family, 330, 333–34
personnel selection and,
631, 649–50
Culture and Diagnosis Task
Force
DSM-IV

cultural
psychopathology and,
571, 576–79
Customer service orientation
personnel selection and,
638–39
Cycles
environmental psychology
of capsule habitats and,
238, 244
Cytokines
pain and
allodynia, 33–35
analgesia, 32–33
antianalgesia, 32–33
central nervous system
trauma, 45–47
future research, 49
human pain conditions,
47–49
hyperalgesia, 33–35
immune system role in
pain, 41–47
immune-to-brain
communication, 35–39
infection, 41–47
inflammation, 41–47
introduction, 30
nerve trauma, 43–45
pain modulation, 30–35
sickness response,
35–41
skin trauma, 41–43

D
Danger seeking
assessing individual
differences and, 430
Deception
negotiation and, 291–92,
294
Deep cognitive activation
thought suppression and,
74
Deep shafts
assessing individual
differences and, 407

Defiant behavior
emotion, regulation and
moral development, 687
Delay of gratification
phenomena
assessing individual
differences and, 431
Delinquency
assessing individual
differences and, 405
emotion, regulation and
moral development, 687
Denmark
cultural psychopathology
and, 585
negotiation and, 298
Density
environmental psychology
of capsule habitats and,
233
Depression
children's exposure to
violence and, 457–59
cultural psychopathology
and, 572, 589
emotion, regulation and
moral development, 682
thought suppression and,
70, 73, 81–83
Descending control
neural basis of hearing in
real-world situations,
714–17
Descriptive cognitions
parental and child
cognitions in context of
family, 317–18, 320–21
Design
environmental
environmental
psychology of capsule
habitats and, 243–44
Despondency
thought suppression and,
69
Detail
psychology of memory
accuracy and, 491–93

Development
children's exposure to
violence and, 445–70
emotion, regulation and
moral development,
665–89
goal theory, motivation,
and school achievement,
183–84
intellectual
assessing individual
differences and,
431–32, 424–26
*Diagnostic and Statistical
Manual-IV (DSM-IV)*
cultural psychopathology
and, 571, 576–79
Diary studies
psychology of memory
accuracy and, 510–11
Dieting
thought suppression and,
76
Differential prediction
personnel selection and,
631, 645–46
Differential psychology
assessing individual
differences and, 405–36
Dilemma of differences
negotiation and, 299
Dimensional classification
adult psychopathology
and, 396–98
assessing individual
differences and, 411–12
Discipline
emotion, regulation and
moral development,
681–82
Discomfort
emotion, regulation and
moral development, 672
Discrimination
neural basis of hearing in
real-world situations, 705
Disequilibrium of tastes

political communication
and campaign effects, 157
Disgust
emotion, regulation and
moral development, 683
Disinhibition
emotion, regulation and
moral development, 686
Dispositional emotionality
emotion, regulation and
moral development, 665,
676
Dissociation
thought suppression and,
73
Distortion
memory
psychology of memory
accuracy and, 481,
489–91
Distracter associations
thought suppression and,
66–67
Distress
emotion, regulation and
moral development, 665,
674–77, 679, 682
Domain specificity
adult psychopathology
and, 390–98
assessing individual
differences and, 405
kinds of concepts and,
121, 124–25, 136–38
parental and child
cognitions in context of
family, 330
personnel selection and,
640–41
Dominance
mental
social cognition and,
102
Donald Duck effect
environmental psychology
of capsule habitats and,
236
Dopamine

memory systems in the
brain and, 599–624
Drinking
thought suppression and,
75
Drive theory
goal theory, motivation,
and school achievement,
191, 193
Drug abuse
evaluation methods for
social intervention and,
351
structural equation
modeling and, 210
Drunkard's search syndrome
political communication
and campaign effects, 153
Dual-mode processing
models
attitude change and, 539,
551–55
Duration
environmental psychology
of capsule habitats and,
237–38
Dyscontrolled maladaptivity
adult psychopathology
and, 382–84, 393–94
Dysphoria
thought suppression and,
82

E

Eating
thought suppression and,
75–76
ECVI index
structural equation
modeling and, 216
Educational choices
assessing individual
differences and, 405
Effective practices
evaluation methods for
social intervention and,
359

Efficacy-prescriptive
   cognitions
   parental and child
   cognitions in context of
   family, 319
Egalitarians
   social cognition and, 100
Egocentrism
   negotiation and, 279,
   284–85
Ego resiliency
   personnel selection and,
   643
Elaboration likelihood model
   attitude change and, 551
Elderly
   social cognition and, 98,
   101, 103
Elections
   political communication
   and campaign effects,
   149–65
Embarrassment
   emotion, regulation and
   moral development,
   666–67
Eminence
   assessing individual
   differences and, 405,
   428–30
Emotions
   adult psychopathology
   and, 394
   emotion, regulation and
   moral development,
   665–89
   memory systems in the
   brain and, 599–624
   negotiation and, 279,
   285–86
   personnel selection and,
   637
   thought suppression and,
   59–84
Empathy
   emotion, regulation and
   moral development,
   665–66, 668–69, 671–85

Emptying the head
   thought suppression and,
   61–62
"Empty" time
   environmental psychology
   of capsule habitats and,
   238
Enclosed habitats
   environmental psychology
   of capsule habitats and,
   227–47
Encoding flexibility model
   social cognition and, 106
Energy homeostasis
   food intake and body
   weight regulation, 255–69
England
   assessing individual
   differences and, 435
   political communication
   and campaign effects, 157
Entativity
   social cognition and, 113
Entity theory
   social cognition and, 107
Environmental factors
   assessing individual
   differences and, 431,
   433–34
   capsule habitats and,
   227–47
   environmental psychology
   of capsule habitats and,
   227, 243–44
   parenting and its effect on
   children, 1, 10–22
   political communication
   and campaign effects, 158
   social cognition and, 108
Episodic memory
   memory systems in the
   brain and, 599–624
   social cognition and, 94
Equity games
   goal theory, motivation,
   and school achievement,
   189–91
Essentialism bias

kinds of concepts and, 138
Ethics
   negotiation and, 279,
   291–93
   personnel selection and,
   631, 650–51
Ethnicity
   assessing individual
   differences and, 408, 433
   children's exposure to
   violence and, 466
   cultural psychopathology
   and, 571–90
   kinds of concepts and, 134
   personnel selection and,
   635, 640, 644
   political communication
   and campaign effects, 163
   social cognition and,
   95–96, 102
Europe
   cultural psychopathology
   and, 586
   environmental psychology
   of capsule habitats and,
   241–42
   negotiation and, 298
Evaluation methods
   social cognition and, 110
   social intervention and,
   345–69
Evaluative-prescriptive
   cognitions
   parental and child
   cognitions in context of
   family, 318, 323–24
Event-dependent cognitions
   parental and child
   cognitions in context of
   family, 327–31
Evocative covariance
   parenting and its effect on
   children, 17
Excitation
   social cognition and, 102
Executive cognitive
   functioning

social cognition and, 103–4

Exemplar models
kinds of concepts and, 126

Exhaustion
thought suppression and, 63

Exotic environments
environmental psychology of capsule habitats and, 228

Experience-producing drives theory
assessing individual differences and, 419

Expressed emotion
adult psychopathology and, 394

"Expression" method
thought suppression and, 62

Extended parallel process model
attitude change and, 556

Externalizing problems
children's exposure to violence and, 445, 453, 468
cultural psychopathology and, 571, 584
emotion, regulation and moral development, 669–70, 674–75, 684–85, 687–88
parenting and its effect on children, 6

Extracurricular services
evaluation methods for social intervention and, 351

Extreme and unusual environments (EUEs)
environmental psychology of capsule habitats and, 228

Eyewitness memory

psychology of memory accuracy and, 481, 507–10

F

Face-to-face communications
negotiation and, 294–96

Failure
fear of
goal theory, motivation, and school achievement, 186–87

Fairness
negotiation and, 279–303
personnel selection and, 642

False recall/recognition
psychology of memory accuracy and, 481, 499–503, 505–7

Families
children's exposure to violence and, 445–70
cognition in
analytical cognitions, 318, 321–23
attributional style, 321–23
balance of control or power, 326–27
capabilities of children, 329–30
change, 330–31
common fate, 334
conceptualization of cognitions, 317–20
conclusions, 334–37
contextual organization, 329–31
control attributed to others, 326
descriptive cognitions, 317–18, 320–21
domains, 330
efficacy cognitions, 319

evaluative-prescriptive cognitions, 318, 323–24
event-dependent cognitions, 327–31
family cognitions as interdependent or joint constructions, 331–34
family-relevant events and characteristics, 327–31
future research, 334–37
goals, 330
interdependent influences, 332
introduction, 316–17
linear links, 319–25
linkages across cognitions, 324–25
locus of control, 323
methodological issues, 336–37
moderators, 325–27
mutual influences, 332–34
owness, 328
parental states, 329
problematic behavior, 328–29
relevant cognitive levels, 317
remediation, 337
restricted focus within family, 335–36
schematic cognitions of individual family members, 319–27
self-efficacy cognitions, 324
self-perceived control, 325–26
subject matter of cognitive constructs, 334–35
theoretical issues, 336–37
topical concerns of cognitions, 317–19

transition, 330–31
cultural psychopathology
and, 586, 590
Fast-learning system
social cognition and, 94
Fat
body
food intake and body
weight regulation,
255–69
Fathers
parental and child
cognitions in context of
family, 336
Fear
adult psychopathology
and, 390
attitude change and,
556–57
emotion, regulation and
moral development, 670,
681, 685
Feedback control
social cognition and, 112
Feelings-as-information
account
attitude change and,
555–56
"Few can influence many"
paradox
attitude change and, 560
Field experiments
evaluation methods for
social intervention and,
345–69
Finland
parenting and its effect on
children, 20
Five Factor Model
personnel selection and,
636, 638–40
Flagging
environmental psychology
of capsule habitats and,
239
Flashbulb memories
psychology of memory
accuracy and, 512

Flathead Indians
cultural psychopathology
and, 588
Flexibility
social cognition and, 95
Fluency misattributions
psychology of memory
accuracy and, 481,
498–500
Flynn effect
assessing individual
differences and, 417
parenting and its effect on
children, 9
Folk biology/psychology
assessing individual
differences and, 424
kinds of concepts and,
137–38
Food intake
environmental psychology
of capsule habitats and,
244
regulation of body weight
and
adiposity regulation,
263–66
adiposity signals,
265–66
central control
mechanisms, 266
correlates of meal onset,
259–60
energy homeostasis,
256–57
introduction, 256
learning, 260–61
meal intitation, 258–61
meal size control,
261–63
patterns of food intake,
257–58
Forgetting
psychology of memory
accuracy and, 484
Four-fifths rule
personnel selection and,
646

France
assessing individual
differences and, 435
environmental psychology
of capsule habitats and,
236, 245
negotiation and, 298
parenting and its effect on
children, 9
political communication
and campaign effects, 157
Frequency processing
neural basis of hearing in
real-world situations,
707–8
Frogs
neural basis of hearing in
real-world situations,
702–3
Frontal cortex
memory systems in the
brain and, 599–624
Frustration
emotion, regulation and
moral development, 676

G

G x E interactions
parenting and its effect on
children, 19–21
Game theory
political communication
and campaign effects,
161–62, 165
Gating mechanisms
neural basis of hearing in
real-world situations,
714–15
Gender
assessing individual
differences and, 416, 418,
421
children's exposure to
violence and, 453,
459–60, 463, 466
cultural psychopathology
and, 577–78, 580–81, 584

emotion, regulation and
moral development,
669–72, 675–77, 687
environmental psychology
of capsule habitats and,
237
kinds of concepts and, 131
parental and child
cognitions in context of
family, 330
political communication
and campaign effects, 160
social cognition and, 95,
98–101, 105
structural equation
modeling and, 205
thought suppression and,
77, 80–82
General intelligence *(g)*
assessing individual
differences and, 408–10,
412–15, 418–20
General psychology
assessing individual
differences and, 405
Generative mechanisms
evaluation methods for
social intervention and,
360
Genetics
adult psychopathology
and, 389–97
assessing individual
differences and, 431–32
cultural psychopathology
and, 589
parenting and its effect on
children, 1–3, 8, 22–23
structural equation
modeling and, 211
Germany
assessing individual
differences and, 435
negotiation and, 298
Gestalt approach
kinds of concepts and, 136

psychology of memory
accuracy and, 481,
488–89
Gist
memory for
psychology of memory
accuracy and, 481,
491–93
Glia
cytokines and pain, 29, 35,
38–39, 41, 43, 45–49
Goal-derived categories
kinds of concepts and,
132–33
Goal interruption
thought suppression and,
67
Goal theory
motivation, and school
achievement
ability games, 185–89
academic goals, 174–78
achievement goal
theory, 174–80
classroom incentive
structures, 184–91
cognitionsachievement,
176
developmental
dynamics, 183–84
dynamics of
achievement failure,
185–87
equity games, 189–91
future research, 191–93
goalscognitions, 175–76
goalscognitions
achievement, 176–78
implications, 187–89
introduction, 171–74
motives as drives, 173
motives as goals,
173–74
prosocial goals, 178–80
self-processes, 180–84
self-protective
mechanisms, 181–83
self-worth theory, 181

parental and child
cognitions in context of
family, 330
social cognition and, 108
structural equation
modeling and, 175–76
Goodness of fit index
structural equation
modeling and, 219
Gravity
environmental psychology
of capsule habitats and,
232–33, 243, 246
Great Britain
cultural psychopathology
and, 587
negotiation and, 297
Great Depression
parenting and its effect on
children, 14–15
Group identity
assessing individual
differences and, 415
attitude change and,
557–61
social consensus, 559–60
Groupiness
social cognition and, 113
Group interaction changes
environmental psychology
of capsule habitats and,
227
Growing apart
assessing individual
differences and, 433
Growth curve models
structural equation
modeling and, 207–8, 211
Guatemala
kinds of concepts and, 129
Guilt
emotion, regulation and
moral development,
665–71, 678–82, 685

H

Habitats
capsule

environmental
psychology and,
227–47
Happiness
emotion, regulation and
moral development, 682
Hard-fought race
political communication
and campaign effects, 156
Hard sell
personnel selection and,
647
Harmful dysfunction
adult psychopathology
and, 382–84
Health risk behaviors
assessing individual
differences and, 405, 431
Hearing
neural basis of in real-
world situations
bats, 703–5
behavioral aspects of
hearing, 701–6
birds, 705–6
conclusions, 717–18
cortical encoding of
complex sounds,
712–14
descending control,
714–17
frequency processing,
707–8
frogs, 702–3
gating mechanisms for
sensory acquisition,
714–15
humans, 701–2
introduction, 700–1
physiological aspects of
hearing, 706–17
sound localization,
709–11
sound pattern
recognition, 707–9

spatially-mediated
release from masking,
711–12
temporal processing,
708–9, 714
Helping
emotion, regulation and
moral development, 673
Heterosexuality
environmental psychology
of capsule habitats and,
237
Heuristic/systematic model
attitude change and,
551–52, 554
Hierarchical linear modeling
evaluation methods for
social intervention and,
366
Hierarchies
assessing individual
differences and, 411–12
kinds of concepts and, 131
Hippocampal learning/
memory system
memory systems in the
brain and, 599–624
social cognition and, 94
Hispanics
personnel selection and,
635, 640
political communication
and campaign effects, 156
Holland
cultural psychopathology
and, 585
Holocaust survivors
adult psychopathology
and, 387–88
Home Observation for
Measurement of the
Environment
(HOME)
assessing individual
differences and, 433
Home office

environmental psychology
of capsule habitats and,
236
Homosexuality
environmental psychology
of capsule habitats and,
237
social cognition and, 77,
111
thought suppression and,
77
Hopelessness
feelings of
goal theory, motivation,
and school
achievement, 186
thought suppression and,
69
Horizontal inquiry
assessing individual
differences and, 417–18
Hormones
cytokines and pain, 29
food intake and body
weight regulation, 255–69
Horse-race coverage
political communication
and campaign effects, 154
Hostility
adult psychopathology
and, 393–94
Hot cognitive proceeses
social cognition and, 113
Hot emotions
negotiation and, 286
Hot flame
thought suppression and,
70
Human capital
assessing individual
differences and, 427
Human immunodeficiency
virus (HIV)
cytokines and pain, 46–47
evaluation methods for
social intervention and,
362
Humanistic psychology

environmental psychology
of capsule habitats and,
230
Humanitarians
social cognition and, 100
Hunger
memory systems in the
brain and, 599–624
Hyperaccesibility
social cognition and,
110–11
Hyperalgesia
cytokines and pain, 29–30,
33–35, 39–42, 44–45, 47,
49
Hypervigilance
children's exposure to
violence and, 451, 459,
461
Hypodermic model
political communication
and campaign effects,
149, 158, 161
Hypothalamus
food intake and body
weight regulation, 255
Hypothetical constructs
assessing individual
differences and, 417–18

I

Identifications
attitude change and,
557–60
Illusions
psychology of memory
accuracy and, 481,
498–500, 514–15
Image appeals
political communication
and campaign effects, 155
Imagination inflation
psychology of memory
accuracy and, 506
Immigration
cultural psychopathology
and, 587

Immune-to-brain
communication
pain and, 29–49
Implantation
memory
psychology of memory
accuracy and, 505–6
Implementation assessment
evaluation methods for
social intervention and,
353–54
"Implemented as plannned"
end state
evaluation methods for
social intervention and,
353
Impression formation
thought suppression and,
78–79
Impulsivity
emotion, regulation and
moral development,
685–86
Incentives
goal theory, motivation,
and school achievement,
184–191
Income
assessing individual
differences and, 405
Incompetency
fears of
goal theory, motivation,
and school
achievement, 186
India
negotiation and, 298
Individual differences
assessing
"big five", 422–23
"big seven", 423–24
causality, 432–33
causal modeling, 432
cognitive abilities,
407–15
confounds, 432–33
consilience, 433–36
constellations, 424–31

creativity, 428–30
crime, 430–31
dimensionality, 411–12
eminence, 428–30
Flynn effect, 417
future directions, 424
general intelligence (g),
408–20
group differences, 415
health risk behavior,
431
horizontal inquiry,
417–18
intellectual
development, 424–26
interests, 420–22
interpretation, 424
introduction, 406–7
life span development,
431–32
literature review, 407
methodological issues,
432–33
organization, 411–12
personality, 422–24
race differences, 416
sex differences, 416
total evidence rule, 433
vertical inquiry, 417–18
vocational adjustment,
426–27
work performance,
427–28
emotion, regulation and,
guilt, 684–88
Individual growth modeling
evaluation methods for
social intervention and,
366–68
Individually-held mental
models
negotiation and, 287–89
Individuation
kinds of concepts and,
133–34
Infants
children's exposure to
violence and, 450

emotion, regulation and
moral development, 676,
684
kinds of concepts and,
136–37
parental and child
cognitions in context of
family, 325–26, 330
Infection
cytokines and pain, 29, 31,
33, 37, 41–48
Inferior-temporal cortex
memory systems in the
brain and, 599–624
Inflammatory response
cytokines and pain, 29–49
Influence
attitude change and,
539–62
Information processing
attitude change and,
539–62
Inhibition
emotion, regulation and
moral development, 686
social cognition and, 93,
100–2, 110, 112
Insomnia
polar
environmental
psychology of capsule
habitats and, 231
Instructed suppression
thought suppression and,
71–72
Insulin
food intake and body
weight regulation, 255,
266–67
Integration
psychology of memory
accuracy and, 495
Integrity tests
personnel selection and,
638
Intellectual development
assessing individual
differences and, 424–26

Intelligence quotient (IQ)
adult psychopathology
and, 398
assessing individual
differences and, 414, 430
parenting and its effect on
children, 9–10
Intensity
emotion, regulation and
moral development,
677–78, 684
Intent
parental and child
cognitions in context of
family, 335
Intentional distortion
personnel selection and,
639–40
Interdependent influences
parental and child
cognitions in context of
family, 331–32
Interests
assessing individual
differences and, 420–22
Interleukin 1 (IL-1)
cytokines and pain, 29,
36–37, 39–49
Internalizing problems
children's exposure to
violence and, 445,
457–59, 468
cultural psychopathology
and, 571, 584
emotion, regulation and
moral development,
684–85
International Space Station
environmental psychology
of capsule habitats and,
235
Interparental violence
children's exposure to,
445–70
Interpersonal behavior
environmental psychology
of capsule habitats and,
231

personnel selection and,
642
thought suppression and,
59, 78–79
Interrelated concepts
kinds of concepts and, 126
Interruptions
negotiation and, 298
Intervening variables
assessing individual
differences and, 417–18
Interventions
parenting and its effect on
children, 10–11
political communication
and campaign effects, 152
social, 345–69
Interview
personnel selection and,
631–33, 641–42
Intrusive thoughts
thought suppression and,
59–84
Invariant representations
of objects
memory systems in the
brain and, 599–24
Ironic process theory
thought suppression and,
59, 67–68
Isolated concepts
kinds of concepts and, 126
Isolated, confined
environment (ICE)
environmental psychology
of capsule habitats and,
227–28, 233, 237
Israel
negotiation and, 298
Issue appeals
political communication
and campaign effects,
155, 160
Item response theory
cultural psychopathology
and, 589
Itzaj tribe
kinds of concepts and, 129

J

Japan
  adult psychopathology
    and, 382
  environmental psychology
    of capsule habitats and,
    240–42
  goal theory, motivation,
    and school achievement,
    176–77
  negotiation and, 298–99
Jealousy
  environmental psychology
    of capsule habitats and,
    237
Jewish populations
  assessing individual
    differences and, 415–16
Job knowledge
  personnel selection and,
    631–36
Joint constructions
  parental and child
    cognitions in context of
    family, 331–34
Judgments
  social cognition and,
    103–6, 110

K

Korea
  negotiation and, 298

L

Lability
  emotion, regulation and
    moral development,
    686–87
"Lamppost"
  political communication
    and campaign effects, 153
Language
  kinds of concepts and, 125
  proficiency
    personnel selection and,
    635–36
Latent curve models

structural equation
  modeling and, 207–8, 211
Latent variable models
  structural equation
    modeling and, 202–3,
    206–7, 215, 218
Latinos
  children's exposure to
    violence and, 457
  cultural psychopathology
    and, 572, 577, 579–83,
    587–89
Learned reinforcers
  memory systems in the
    brain and, 605–6
Learning
  food intake and body
    weight regulation, 260–61
  memory systems in the
    brain and, 613–18
  political communication
    and campaign effects,
    149–65
Legal standards
  personnel selection and,
    631, 650–51
Leptin
  food intake and body
    weight regulation, 255,
    266–67, 269
Lexical approach
  assessing individual
    differences and, 423
Life span
  adult psychopathology
    and, 394–96
  development
    assessing individual
      differences and,
      431–32
Linear links
  parental and child
    cognitions in context of
    family, 319–25
Linear separability
  kinds of concepts and, 133
Lineup studies

psychology of memory
  accuracy and, 508–9
LISREL program
  structural equation
    modeling and, 201, 217
Local vertical cues
  environmental psychology
    of capsule habitats and,
    232
Locus of control
  parental and child
    cognitions in context of
    family, 323
Logic models
  evaluation methods for
    social intervention and,
    353, 358
"Long eye"
  environmental psychology
    of capsule habitats and,
    231, 234
Longitudinal designs
  measurement studies,
    208–10
  structural equation
    modeling and, 205–8
Long-term memory
  social cognition and, 95,
    107
Low-anxiety IQ
  assessing individual
    differences and, 430

M

Main effects
  political communication
    and campaign effects, 163
Majority/minority group
  influence
    attitude change and, 539,
    560–61
Maladaptation
  adult psychopathology
    and, 382–84
Malleability
  social cognition and, 109
Manipulation check

evaluation methods for
social intervention and,
364
Marital conflict
children's exposure to
violence and, 445–70
parental and child
cognitions in context of
family, 322–23
"Masculine" issues
political communication
and campaign effects, 160
Masking
spatially-mediated release
from, neural basis of
hearing in real-world
situations, 711–12
Mass nouns
kinds of concepts and,
125–26
Massachusetts
political communication
and campaign effects, 154
Masturbation
environmental psychology
of capsule habitats and,
237
Matching Alcoholism
Treatments to Client
Heterogeneity
(MATCH)
evaluation methods for
social intervention and,
352
Meals
individual
food intake and body
weight regulation,
255–69
Measured variable models
structural equation
modeling and, 202–3,
207, 212, 215
Measurement invariance
measurement studies,
209–10
Measurement issues

personnel selection and,
631, 634, 644–45
Memory
assessing individual
differences and, 436
kinds of concepts and, 135
memory systems in the
brain and, 599–624
social cognition and,
93–114
thought suppression and,
59–84
Memory accuracy
psychology of
abstraction, 494
accuracy-oriented
correspondence
conception, 483–85
age differences, 498,
504–5
autobiographical
memory, 510–13
children's testimony,
509
confidence-accuracy
relation, 509–10
correspondence
conception, 485–87,
517–19
diary studies, 510–11
distortion, 489–91
experimental paradigms
and assessment
procedures, 519–21
eyewitness memory,
507–10
false recall and
recognition, 499–503
flashbulb memories, 512
Gestalt approach to
memory changes over
time, 488–89
illusions stemming from
fluency
misattributions,
498–500
imagination inflation,
506

integration, 495
interpretation, 494–95
introduction, 482–85
lineup studies, 508–9
memory accuracy and
error within broader
functional perspective,
521–23
memory for gist vs
detail, 491–93
memory for source,
496–97
memory implantation,
505–6
metacognitive
processes, 513–16
metamemory illusions,
514–15
metatheoretical issues,
516–23
methodological issues,
516–23
misinformation effect,
503–5
misleading postevent
information, 503–5
monitoring the
correctness of one's
own knowledge,
514–15
persistence over time,
501–2
phenomenological
studies, 511–12
quality of memories,
504
quantity-oriented
storehouse conception,
483
questioning procedures,
508
real-life false memories,
505–7
reconstruction, 495–96
repeated testing, 506–7
schema-based effects,
493–96
selection, 494

source confusions,
497–98
source monitoring,
496–98
spatial memory, 489–91
strategic regulation of
memory accuracy,
515–16
temporal context,
512–13
theoretical issues,
516–23
true memories, 502–7
Mental control
social cognition and, 102,
109–10
thought suppression and,
59–84
Mental disorders
adult psychopathology
and, 378–98
cultural psychopathology
and, 571–90
Mental events
kinds of concepts and,
126–27
Mental models
negotiation and, 279,
287–91
Mental representation
kinds of concepts and,
121–38
"Mention" control
thought suppression and,
62
Message-based persuasion
attitude change and,
539–562
political communication
and campaign effects, 149
Meta-analysis
adult psychopathology
and, 394
assessing individual
differences and, 415
emotion, regulation and
moral development, 683

parenting and its effect on
children, 12
personnel selection and,
631, 636–37, 639–42,
645–46
Metacognition
psychology of memory
accuracy and, 481,
513–16
social cognition and, 106
thought suppression and,
68–69
Meta-emotion philosophy
parental and child
cognitions in context of
family, 323
Metamemory illusions
psychology of memory
accuracy and, 514–15
Metaphors
memory
psychology of memory
accuracy and, 481
Methods variance
assessing individual
differences and, 414
Mexico
cultural psychopathology
and, 582–89
goal theory, motivation,
and school achievement,
177
Microcontexts of power
cultural psychopathology
and, 580
Microgravity
environmental psychology
of capsule habitats and,
232, 246
Middle East
negotiation and, 298
Migration studies
parenting and its effect on
children, 10
Mind control
social cognition and,
109–10
Misinformation effect

psychology of memory
accuracy and, 503–5
Misleading information
postevent
psychology of memory
accuracy and, 503–5
Mismatch theory
social cognition and, 106
Missingness
personnel selection and,
645
Moderators
parental and child
cognitions in context of
family, 325–27
Molestation
children's exposure to
violence and, 466
Monitoring
psychology of memory
accuracy and, 481,
496–98, 514–15
Monotony
environmental psychology
of capsule habitats and,
234–35
Mood
attitude change and,
555–56
emotion, regulation and,
guilt, 683–84
Moral development
emotion, regulation and
antisocial behavior,
672–74
embarrassment, 666–67
emotionality, 674–77,
684–88
emotional intensity,
677–78
empathy, 668–69,
671–82
externalizing behavior,
669–70
guilt, 667–71, 678–81
individual differences,
684–88
introduction, 665–66

mood, 683–84
negative emotionality,
    670–71
nonmoral emotions vs
    morally relevant
    behavior, 682–88
prosocial behavior,
    672–74
regulation, 670–71,
    674–78, 684–88
self-conscious moral
    emotions, 666–71
shame, 667–71, 678–82
summary, 688–89
social cognition and, 109
Mothers
emotion, regulation and
    moral development, 671,
    675–76, 679–82, 684
parental and child
    cognitions in context of
    family, 325–26, 329–30,
    334, 336
Motivated illusions
negotiation and, 279, 285
Motivated processing
attitude change and,
    540–48, 554–55
Motivation
kinds of concepts and, 135
memory systems in the
    brain and, 599–624
school achievement, goal
    theory and, 171–93
social cognition and, 102,
    105
Multiparty negotiation
negotiation and, 279,
    300–2
Multiple attitudes
attitude change and,
    548–51
Multiple category
    memberships
social cognition and,
    101–2
Multiple effects

political communication
    and campaign effects,
    154–56
Multiple motives
social consensus, 559–60
Multiple predictor domains
personnel selection and,
    640–41
Multisource sounds
neural basis of hearing in
    real-world situations and,
    699–718
Multitrait-multimethod
    studies
measurement studies, 209
Muslim culture
adult psychopathology
    and, 382
Mutual influences
parental and child
    cognitions in context of
    family, 332–34
Mutual responsivity
parenting and its effect on
    children, 8
Myotis lucifugus
neural basis of hearing in
    real-world situations, 714

N

National Skills Standards
    Board
personnel selection and,
    633
Native Americans
cultural psychopathology
    and, 572, 588
goal theory, motivation,
    and school achievement,
    177
personnel selection and,
    640
Natural kinds
kinds of concepts and,
    127–28
Natural suppression targets

thought suppression and,
    70–71
Navaho
goal theory, motivation,
    and school achievement,
    177
Negative advertising
political communication
    and campaign effects,
    152, 164
Negative emotionality
emotion, regulation and
    moral development, 665,
    670–71, 676–78, 681–88
Negative reinforcers
goal theory, motivation,
    and school achievement,
    184
Negative valence
assessing individual
    differences and, 423
Negativity/conflict
parenting and its effect on
    children, 6
Neglect
children's exposure to
    violence and, 463
Neglected aspect
fallacy of
    assessing individual
        differences and, 433
Negotiation
bargaining, 294–96
behavioral decision
    perspective, 282
changing the game,
    299–300
communications media,
    293–96
conclusions, 302–3
cross-cultural issues,
    296–300
early social psychology of
    negotiations, 280–81
egocentrism, 284–85
emotion, 285–86
ethics, 291–93

face-to-face
 communications, 294–96
 history, 280–81
 individual differences, 281
 individually-held mental
  models, 287–89
 introduction, 280
 mental models, 287–93
 motivated illusions, 285
 multiparty negotiation,
  300–2
 parental and child
  cognitions in context of
  family, 315–37
 psychological definition of
  negotiation game,
  286–302
 rebirth of social
  psychology of
  negotiation, 283–86
 sacredness, 291–93
 shared mental models,
  289–91
 social relationships in
  negotiation, 283–84
 structural variables, 281
 within-cultural negotiation,
  296–99
Neocortical learning/memory
  system
 social cognition and, 94
Nerve growth factor (NGF)
 cytokines and pain, 29,
  41–44
The Netherlands
 negotiation and, 297
Neural signals
 food intake and body
  weight regulation, 255–69
Neurasthenia
 cultural psychopathology
  and, 588
Neuroethology
 neural basis of hearing in
  real-world situations and,
  699–718
Neuronal network models

memory systems in the
  brain and, 599–24
Neuropeptides
 adult psychopathology
  and, 387–88
 food intake and body
  weight regulation, 255,
  266–67, 269
Neurophysiology
 memory systems in the
  brain and, 620–23
New look approach
 attitude change and, 546
New Zealand
 emotion, regulation and
  moral development, 686
Niche building
 assessing individual
  differences and, 407, 435
Niche picking
 parenting and its effect on
  children, 17, 23
Noise
 environmental psychology
  of capsule habitats and,
  232
Nonattitudes
 attitude change and, 548
Nonmoral emotions
 emotion, regulation and,
  guilt, 682–88
Non-normed fit index
  (NNFI)
 structural equation
  modeling and, 219
Nonobject concepts
 object concepts and,
  121–38
Nonverbal behavior
 personnel selection and,
  642
"Norman's five"
 assessing individual
  differences and, 423
North America
 negotiation and, 298
Nouns

kinds of concepts and,
  125–26, 132

O
Object concepts
 kinds of concepts and,
  121, 126–27
Object recognition
 memory systems in the
  brain and, 599–624
Obsession
 thought suppression and,
  69, 73
Obsessive-compulsive
  disorder (OCD)
 thought suppression and,
  80–82
Occupation
 environmental psychology
  of capsule habitats and,
  227
 kinds of concepts and,
  131, 134
 social cognition and,
  101–3
Ocean depths
 environmental psychology
  of capsule habitats and,
  227
Oneness
 emotion, regulation and
  moral development, 673
O*NET database
 personnel selection and,
  632–33
Ontology
 kinds of concepts and,
  136–37
Opinion
 group
  attitude change and,
   560–61
Opportunities
 environmental psychology
  of capsule habitats and,
  227
Orbitofrontal cortex

memory systems in the
brain and, 599–624
Organization
assessing individual
differences and, 411–12
Organizational change
evaluation methods for
social intervention and,
361–62
Other-orientation
emotion, regulation and
moral development,
673–74, 679
Other-related characteristics
environmental psychology
of capsule habitats and,
241
Outcome variables
evaluation methods for
social intervention and,
354–57
Output boundedness
psychology of memory
accuracy and, 484
Output systems
memory systems in the
brain and, 612–13
Overstrivers
goal theory, motivation,
and school achievement,
187
Ownness
response to
parental and child
cognitions in context
of family, 328

P

Pacific Rim
cultural psychopathology
and, 577
Pain
adult psychopathology
and, 384
immune-to-brain
communication and,
29–49

thought suppression and,
76–77
Pakistan
negotiation and, 297
Panic disorder
adult psychopathology
and, 390
Paradigms
evaluation methods for
social intervention and,
357
kinds of concepts and, 131
Parent Attribution Test
parental and child
cognitions in context of
family, 326–27
Parenting
and its effects on children
challenge from behavior
genetics, 9–17
claim for substantial
genetic effects, 11–12
environmental factors,
12–17, 19–21
experimental
interventions with
parents, 10–11
focus on variation, 9–11
G x E interactions in
adoption studies,
20–21
G x E interactions in
animal studies, 19–20
interpreting parent-child
covariance, 17–19
introduction, 1–5
overview, 22–23
shared environmental
effects, 13–17
strength of connection
between parent and
child behaviors, 5–9
temperament, 21
unshared environmental
effects, 13–17
assessing individual
differences and, 432

children's exposure to
violence and, 445–70
cultural psychopathology
and, 585
emotion, regulation and
moral development, 671,
675–76, 679–82, 684
parental and child
cognitions in context of
family, 315–37
Past
perception of
psychology of memory
accuracy and, 484
Peer relations
children's exposure to
violence and, 445,
464–65, 469, 585–86
emotion, regulation and
moral development, 672,
674
People interests
assessing individual
differences and, 435
Perception
psychology of memory
accuracy and, 484
social cognition and,
93–114
Performance/avoidance
students
goal theory, motivation,
and school achievement,
187
Performanca criteria
personnel selection and,
631–33
Persistence over time
psychology of memory
accuracy and, 501–2
Personal consequences
thought suppression and,
75–77
Personality
assessing individual
differences and, 405,
422–24

environmental psychology
of capsule habitats and,
227
social cognition and, 108
Personality paradox
environmental psychology
of capsule habitats and,
242
Personality predictors
personnel selection and,
631, 634–41
Personnel selection
academic achievement,
635–36
adverse impact, 646–47
affirmative action, 651
applicant reactions,
647–48
assessment centers,
642–43
assessment methods,
641–44
banding, 647
biodata, 643–44
cognitive abilities, 634–36
conclusions, 651–52
conditional reasoning, 639
conscientiousness, 637–39
criteria, 633–34
cross-cultural selection
issues, 649–50
customer service
orientation, 638–39
differential prediction,
645–46
emerging topics, 648–50
emotionality, 637
ethical standards, 650–51
evaluation of selection
systems, 645–48
fairness, 642
general cognitive ability,
635
integrity tests, 638
intentional distortion,
639–40
interpersonal behavior,
642

interview, 641–42
introduction, 632
job and work analysis,
632–33
job knowledge, 634–36
language proficiency,
635–36
legal standards, 650–51
measurement issues, 634,
644–45
meta-analysis, 639, 645
multiple predictor
domains, 640–41
nonverbal behavior, 642
personality predictors,
634–40
personality taxonomies
and constructs, 636–37
predictors, 636–40
professional standards,
650–51
race and ethnic
background, 640
reliability, 641
reverse discrimination, 651
social competence, 637
standardization, 641–42
structure, 641
taxonomy, 633–34,
636–37
team member selection,
648–49
utility, 647
validation strategies,
644–45
Person perception
social cognition and,
93–114
Perspective taking
emotion, regulation and
moral development, 678
Persuasion
attitude change and,
539–62
Phenomenological studies
psychology of memory
accuracy and, 511
Philippines

negotiation and, 298
Physical abuse
children's exposure to
violence and, 455, 458,
461, 463, 465
cultural psychopathology
and, 577–78
emotion, regulation and
moral development, 683
parental and child
cognitions in context of
family, 321
Physical stressors
environmental psychology
of capsule habitats and,
227, 231–33
Physiology
neural basis of hearing in
real-world situations, 669,
706–17
Plasticity
parenting and its effect on
children, 8
social cognition and,
94–95
Polarization effect
political communication
and campaign effects, 159
Polar regions
environmental psychology
of capsule habitats and,
227–29, 231–32, 235–37,
240–45
Policy capturing
personnel selection and,
642
Political communication
campaign effects and
agenda control, 156–58
beyond survey methods,
163–65
bypassing roadblocks,
154–58
conceptual and
methodological
roadblocks, 151–54
conclusions, 165
content analysis, 164–65

experimentation,
163–64
introduction, 150–51
learning, 154–56
multiple effects, 154–56
new theoretical
perspectives, 158–63
resonance model,
158–60
strategic model, 161–63
Portion control
food intake and body
weight regulation, 261–63
Positive emotionality
emotion, regulation and
moral development, 676,
683
Positive valence
assessing individual
differences and, 423
Postevent information
psychology of memory
accuracy and, 481, 503–5
Postmission reentry
environmental psychology
of capsule habitats and,
227, 239
Postsuppression rebound
thought suppression and,
62–64
Posttraumatic stress disorder
(PTSD)
adult psychopathology
and, 386–91
children's exposure to
violence and, 445,
459–62
thought suppression and,
80–81
Potential secondary
reinforcers
memory systems in the
brain and, 605–6
Power
parental and child
cognitions in context of
family, 326–27, 330, 337
PPIK model

assessing individual
differences and, 425–26
Predictive bias
structural equation
modeling and, 210
Predisposition
political communication
and campaign effects, 149
Prefrontal cortex
memory systems in the
brain and, 599–624
Prejudice
social cognition and, 100,
112
thought suppression and,
61, 79
Preparedness
assessing individual
differences and, 424
Preschoolers
emotion, regulation and
moral development, 675,
677, 680
Primary rewards
memory systems in the
brain and, 602–5
Private influence
attitude change and,
542–44
Processing
kinds of concepts and, 124
Professional standards
personnel selection and,
631, 650–51
Program drift
evaluation methods for
social intervention and,
350
Proinflammatory cytokines
pain and, 29–49
Prosocial behavior
emotion, regulation and
moral development, 665,
672–75, 677, 679, 683,
687
Prosocial goals
structural equation
modeling and, 178–80

Protection
goal theory, motivation,
and school achievement,
171
Psychiatric disorders
parenting and its effect on
children, 20
Psychobiology
children's exposure to
violence and, 445,
459–61
Psychological risks
environmental psychology
of capsule habitats and,
227
Psychopathy
emotion, regulation and
moral development,
685–86
Psychophysiology
thought suppression and,
59, 76–77, 80–83
Public health risks
assessing individual
differences and, 431
Public influence
attitude change and,
542–44
Puerto Rico
cultural psychopathology
and, 579, 581, 585
Punishment
attitude change and,
539–62
emotion, regulation and
moral development, 680
memory systems in the
brain and, 599–624

Q

Quality of memories
psychology of memory
accuracy and, 504
Quantity-oriented storehouse
conception
psychology of memory
accuracy and, 481, 483

Quasi-experiments
evaluation methods for
social intervention and,
345–69

R

Race differences
assessing individual
differences and, 416
RAMONA program
structural equation
modeling and, 217
Random assignment
evaluation methods for
social intervention and,
347–48
Rape
children's exposure to
violence and, 466
thought suppression and,
80
Rapid inference generation
social cognition and, 105
Rating bias
personnel selection and,
641
Rational choice
political communication
and campaign effects, 165
Raven matrices
assessing individual
differences and, 417
Reactivity
parenting and its effect on
children, 19
Reality
valid understanding of
attitude change and,
539–62
Real-life false memories
psychology of memory
accuracy and, 505–7
"Real people"
political communication
and campaign effects, 164
Real-world situations

neural basis of hearing in,
699–718
Rebound effect
social cognition and, 111
thought suppression and,
59, 62–64
Recall
psychology of memory
accuracy and, 481,
499–503
priority
thought suppression and,
74
Receivers' predispositions
political communication
and campaign effects, 149
Reception gaps
political communication
and campaign effects, 161
Recognition
false
psychology of memory
accuracy and, 481,
499–503
Recollections
social cognition and, 110
Reconstruction
psychology of memory
accuracy and, 495–96
Recovered memory
assessing individual
differences and, 436
Recreation
environmental psychology
of capsule habitats and,
227
Reform
school, goal theory,
motivation, and school
achievement, 171
Regulation
emotion, regulation and
moral development,
665–89
Reinforcement effect
political communication
and campaign effects, 159
Rejection

emotion, regulation and
moral development, 682
Relative group change
evaluation methods for
social intervention and,
364–66
Reliability
personnel selection and,
641
Religion
assessing individual
differences and, 433
Remediation
parental and child
cognitions in context of
family, 337
Renegotiation
parental and child
cognitions in context of
family, 315–37
Reparative behavior
emotion, regulation and
moral development,
679–81, 685
Resistance
attitude change and,
539–62
Resonance model
political communication
and campaign effects,
149, 158–60
Restricted focus
parental and child
cognitions in context of
family, 335–36
Reverse discrimination
personnel selection and,
651
Revolving door
advertisement
political communication
and campaign effects, 163
Reward/punishment
attitude change and,
539–62
goal theory, motivation,
and school achievement,
184

memory systems in the brain and, 599–624
RIASEC themes
  assessing individual differences and, 420–21
Risk factors
  environmental psychology of capsule habitats and, 227
Root mean square of approximation
  structural equation modeling and, 219
Rumination
  social cognition and, 108
Russia
  environmental psychology of capsule habitats and, 235–37, 240, 245

S

Sacredness
  negotiation and, 291–93
Sadness
  emotion, regulation and moral development, 665, 671–72, 674–77, 682–83
Sample size
  structural equation modeling and, 215–16
Sample surveys
  political communication and campaign effects, 149
Satiety
  food intake and body weight regulation, 255–69
Scale refinement
  measurement studies, 208–9
Scandinavia
  negotiation and, 298
Scheduling
  environmental psychology of capsule habitats and, 238–39
Schema theory

psychology of memory
  accuracy and, 481, 493–96
Schematic cognitions
  parental and child cognitions in context of family, 319–27
Schizophrenia
  cultural psychopathology and, 571–72, 581–84, 587
  parenting and its effect on children, 20
School reform
  goal theory, motivation, and school achievement, 171
Scotland
  cultural psychopathology and, 589
Screening
  environmental psychology of capsule habitats and, 239–40
SEALAB II
  environmental psychology of capsule habitats and, 233
Selection bias
  evaluation methods for social intervention and, 348, 368
Selection criteria
  environmental psychology of capsule habitats and, 227, 239–42
Self-categorization theory
  attitude change and, 559
Self-consciousness
  emotion, regulation and moral development, 666–71, 679–80, 685
Self-directed attention
  social cognition and, 112
Self-efficacy cognitions
  parental and child cognitions in context of family, 324
Self-identity

attitude change and, 557–60
Self–other boundaries
  emotion, regulation and moral development, 673
Self-perceived control
  parental and child cognitions in context of family, 325–26
Self-processes
  goal theory, motivation, and school achievement, 180–84
Self-protective mechanisms
  goal theory, motivation, and school achievement, 171, 181–83
Self-related characteristics
  environmental psychology of capsule habitats and, 241
Self-report bias
  thought suppression and, 74
Self-sabotage
  goal theory, motivation, and school achievement, 186–87
Self-selection
  personnel selection and, 634
Self-worth theory
  goal theory, motivation, and school achievement, 171, 181
Semantic memory
  social cognition and, 94, 98, 107
Sensation seeking
  assessing individual differences and, 430
Sentence unscrambling
  thought suppression and, 74
SEPATH program
  structural equation modeling and, 217
Sex

assessing individual
differences and, 408, 416
environmental psychology
of capsule habitats and,
236–37
thought suppression and,
75, 79
Sexism
social cognition and, 100
Sexual abuse
children's exposure to
violence and, 452,
455–58, 460–61, 463–66,
468
cultural psychopathology
and, 578
parental and child
cognitions in context of
family, 321
thought suppression and,
77
Shame
emotion, regulation and
moral development,
665–82
goal theory, motivation,
and school achievement,
185–86
Shared environmental effects
parenting and its effect on
children, 13–17
Shared mental models
negotiation and, 289–91
Shared positive affect
parenting and its effect on
children, 8
Short-term memory
memory systems in the
brain and, 599–624
Siblings
assessing individual
differences and, 432–33
parenting and its effect on
children, 14–17, 23
Sickness response
cytokines and pain, 29–49
Simplex models

structural equation
modeling and, 206
Simplification
social cognition and, 93,
96
Situational emotionality
emotion, regulation and
moral development, 665,
676–77
Skin trauma
cytokines and pain, 29,
41–43, 48
Skylab 4 crew
environmental psychology
of capsule habitats and,
238
Sniper attack
children's exposure to
violence and, 462
Social change
evaluation methods for
social intervention and,
362–63
Social cognition
category activation
automatic category
activation, 96–98
determinants, 98–102
behavioral domain,
107–9
conditions, 105–7
forms, 103–5
future research, 113–14
introduction, 93–96
ironic consequences of
stereotype suppression,
110–12
mind control, 109–10
spontaneous stereotype
suppression, 112–13
parental and child
cognitions in context of
family, 315–37
Social factors
assessing individual
differences and, 430
attitude change and,
539–62

emotion, regulation and
moral development,
680–82
environmental psychology
of capsule habitats and,
235–36
negotiation and, 279
parental and child
cognitions in context of
family, 315–37
parenting and its effect on
children, 2–23
personnel selection and,
637
Social identity theory
attitude change and, 539,
557–60
Social information
processing
kinds of concepts and,
133–34
Social interventions
evaluation methods for
aptitude by treatment
interactions, 352
change, 360–63
conclusions, 368–69
delayed, incomplete, or
failed program
implementation, 350
differentiation of
treatment and control
conditions, 352–53
elaboration of
experimental
paradigm, 357
evaluating effects, 356
explanation and the
many roles of theory,
357–63
extracurricular services,
351
how to measure
outcomes, 355–56
implementation
assessment, 353–54
individual engagement
in services, 351

individual growth
  modeling, 366–68
integrating theory,
  design, and analysis,
  363–64
introduction, 346–47
organizational change,
  361–62
outcome variables,
  354–57
problems and progress
  in experimental
  methods, 347–57
random assignment,
  347–48
relative group change,
  364–66
selection modeling,
  348–49
social change, 362–63
statistical modeling,
  363–68
what effects to measure,
  355
within-program
  variation, 349–54
Social judgeability approach
  social cognition and, 106
Social monotony
  environmental psychology
  of capsule habitats and,
  234
Social relationships
  negotiation and, 279,
  283–84
Socioeconomic status
  assessing individual
  differences and, 405
Somatype
  social cognition and, 101
Sound localization
  neural basis of hearing in
  real-world situations, 699,
  709–11
Sound pattern recognition
  neural basis of hearing in
  real-world situations, 699,
  707–9

Source memory
  social cognition and, 104
Source monitoring
  psychology of memory
  accuracy and, 481,
  496–98
South America
  negotiation and, 297–98
Space crews
  environmental psychology
  of capsule habitats and,
  227, 230–32, 234, 238–45
Spatial function
  memory systems in the
  brain and, 599–24
Spatially-mediated release
  from masking
  neural basis of hearing
  in real-world
  situations, 711–12
Spatial memory
  psychology of memory
  accuracy and, 481,
  489–91
Speaking simultaneously
  negotiation and, 298
Spider-related thoughts
  thought suppression and,
  81
Spinal cord
  cytokines and pain, 29–35,
  40–41, 43, 45–49
Spontaneous suppression
  stereotype
  social cognition and,
  112–13
  thought suppression and,
  71–72
Spousal violence
  children's exposure to
  violence and, 445–70
Stability
  social cognition and,
  94–95
Stability-of-alienation
  example
  structural equation
  modeling and, 218

Standardization
  personnel selection and,
  641–42
Statistical modeling
  evaluation methods for
  social intervention and,
  363–68
Stereotypes
  kinds of concepts and,
  134–35
  political communication
  and campaign effects, 160
  social cognition and,
  93–114
  thought suppression and,
  74, 79
Stigmatization
  emotion, regulation and
  moral development, 673
Stimulus-reinforcer
  associations
  memory systems in the
  brain and, 599–624
Strategic model
  political communication
  and campaign effects,
  161–63
Streamlining
  social cognition and, 93,
  96
Stressful environments
  children's exposure to
  violence and, 467
  emotion, regulation and
  moral development, 683,
  685
  environmental psychology
  of capsule habitats and,
  227–28, 231–33, 244, 246
Stroop test
  social cognition and, 98
  thought suppression and,
  64–65, 74
Structural differences
  kinds of concepts and,
  123–24
Structural equation modeling
  conclusions, 220

confirmation bias, 213
construct validation, 208–9
correlation vs covariance
matrices, 217–18
cross-sectional designs,
205
current review, 204
experimental studies, 210
generalizability of
findings, 211–13
interpretation of results,
218–19
introduction, 202
latent variable vs
measured variable
models, 215
literature review, 203–4
longitudinal designs,
205–8
measurement invariance,
209–10
measurement studies,
208–10
miscellaneous areas of
application, 211
model specification,
design, and analysis
issues, 215–19
multitrait-multimethod
studies, 209
overview, 202–3
previous reviews of
applicants, 203–4
problematic areas in
applications, 211–20
psychological research,
204–10
reporting of results,
219–20
sample size, 215–16
scale refinement, 208–9
strategy, 216–17
time issue, 213–14
twin studies, 211
Sturnus vulgaris
neural basis of hearing in
real-world situations,
705–6

Subjective essentialism
social cognition and, 113
Subordinate concepts
kinds of concepts and,
128–31
Substance abuse
cultural psychopathology
and, 577
emotion, regulation and
moral development, 684,
688
personnel selection and,
638
Substance cravings
thought suppression and,
75–76
Substance dependence
adult psychopathology
and, 385–86
Subtypes/subgroups
kinds of concepts and,
134–35
Superordinate group
memberships
social cognition and, 103,
128
Support
emotion, regulation and
moral development, 673
Suppression
thought, 59–84
Survival
environmental psychology
of capsule habitats and,
227
Sweden
structural equation
modeling and, 211
Swiss Army knife metaphor
social cognition and, 106
Switzerland
negotiation and, 298
Sympathy
emotion, regulation and
moral development,
665–66, 671–78, 680–81
Systematic ambient noise

assessing individual
differences and, 414
Systematic bias
assessing individual
differences and, 414

T
Taboo tradeoffs
negotiation and, 292–93
Tacit inferences
social cognition and, 100
Taiwan
negotiation and, 297
Target issues
political communication
and campaign effects, 155
Taste
memory systems in the
brain and, 599–624
Taxonomy
assessing individual
differences and, 426
kinds of concepts and,
128–29, 131–33
personnel selection and,
631, 633–34, 636–37
Teacher ratings
assessing individual
differences and, 419
Team member selection
personnel selection and,
631, 648–49
Temperament
parenting and its effect on
children, 21
Temporal cortex
memory systems in the
brain and, 599–624
Temporal factors
assessing individual
differences and, 419
environmental psychology
of capsule habitats and,
227, 231, 237–39
evaluation methods for
social intervention and,
366

negotiation and, 300
psychology of memory
accuracy and, 501–2,
512–13
social cognition and, 109
structural equation
modeling and, 213–14
Temporal processing
neural basis of hearing in
real-world situations,
708–9, 714
Texas
thought suppression and,
61
Thailand
cultural psychopathology
and, 584–85
Theory of work adjustment
assessing individual
differences and, 426–27
"Think like a burglar" group
thought suppression and,
78
Third force psychology
environmental psychology
of capsule habitats and,
230
Thought
categorical
social cognition and,
93–114
Thought suppression
assessment of thinking,
73–74
conclusions, 83–84
depression, 82–83
distracter associations,
66–67
emotional reactions, 75
emotional valence, 69–70
"emptying the head",
61–62
enhanced accessibility
during suppression, 64–66
goal interruption, 67
immedediate enhancement
with load, 65–66

immedediate enhancement
without load, 64–65
impression formation,
78–79
individual differences,
72–73
instructed suppression,
71–72
interpersonal
consequences, 78–79
introduction, 60–61
ironic process theory,
67–68
key variables, 69–74
memory, 77
metacognition, 68–69
natural suppression targets,
70–71
obsessive-compulsive
disorder, 81–82
pain, 76–77
personal consequences,
75–77
phenomena, 61–66
postsuppression rebound,
62–64
prejudice, 79
psychopathology, 80–83
psychophysiology, 76–77
spontaneous suppression,
71–72
stereotyping, 79
substance cravings, 75–76
target characteristics,
69–71
theoretical accounts,
66–69
trauma, 80–81
treatment implications, 83
Threatening stimuli
emotion, regulation and
moral development, 683
Toddlers
emotion, regulation and
moral development, 670,
672, 681
Total evidence rule

assessing individual
differences and, 405, 433
Trait complexes
assessing individual
differences and, 426
personnel selection and,
641
Transition
parental and child
cognitions in context of
family, 329–31
Trauma
thought suppression and,
80–81
Treatment effectiveness
evaluation methods for
social intervention and,
345–69
True memories
psychology of memory
accuracy and, 502, 507
Tumor necrosis factor (TNF)
cytokines and pain, 29,
36–37, 39–45, 48–49
Tuning
assessing individual
differences and, 424
"20-foot stare in the 10-foot
room"
environmental psychology
of capsule habitats and,
231
Twin studies
assessing individual
differences and, 418, 433
parenting and its effect on
children, 1, 4, 9, 11–13,
20
structural equation
modeling and, 211
"Two cultures"
assessing individual
differences and, 407, 434
Type-like psychopath
assessing individual
differences and, 430
Typical intellectual
engagement

assessing individual differences and, 425

U

Unconscious listening
environmental psychology of capsule habitats and, 232
Undersea habitats
environmental psychology of capsule habitats and, 229, 232, 242
United States
children's exposure to violence and, 449
cultural psychopathology and, 572, 579, 582–89
environmental psychology of capsule habitats and, 235–36, 241–43
goal theory, motivation, and school achievement, 176–77, 180, 188
kinds of concepts and, 129
negotiation and, 297–99
parenting and its effect on children, 10
political communication and campaign effects, 157, 164–65
structural equation modeling and, 211
Unlearned rewards
memory systems in the brain and, 602–5
Unshared environmental effects
parenting and its effect on children, 13–17
Unusual environments
environmental psychology of capsule habitats and, 227–47
Unwanted thoughts
thought suppression and, 59–84

"Usual care" controls
evaluation methods for social intervention and, 352
Utility
personnel selection and, 631, 647

V

Valence
emotional
thought suppression and, 69–70
Validity
attitude change and, 558–59
personnel selection and, 631, 644–45
Values
negotiation and, 279–303
Variation
focus on
parenting and its effect on children, 9–11
Venezuela
negotiation and, 298
Verbal labels
social cognition and, 101
Verbs
kinds of concepts and, 125, 132
Vertebrates
neural basis of hearing in real-world situations and, 699–718
Vertical inquiry
assessing individual differences and, 417–18
Vietnam
cultural psychopathology and, 588
negotiation and, 298
Visual cues
environmental psychology of capsule habitats and, 232–33

Vocational adjustment
assessing individual differences and, 405, 426–27
Volunteering
emotion, regulation and moral development, 673
Vote choice
political communication and campaign effects, 149–63

W

Wall space
environmental psychology of capsule habitats and, 243
Wall Street game
negotiation and, 288
Western cultures
adult psychopathology and, 382
Western Europe
negotiation and, 298
White bear experiments
thought suppression and, 61–62, 67, 69–72, 75, 82
Winter-over syndrome
environmental psychology of capsule habitats and, 231
Wishful thinking
goal theory, motivation, and school achievement, 186
Within-program variation
evaluation methods for social intervention and, 349–54
Word completion
thought suppression and, 74
Word-recognition task
thought suppression and, 67

Work performance
  assessing individual
    differences and, 405,
  427–28

World Mental Health Report
  cultural psychopathology
    and, 571, 576–79

Z
Zeigarnik effect
  thought suppression and,
    67

CUMULATIVE INDEXES

CONTRIBUTING AUTHORS, VOLUMES 41–51

A

Abramov I, 45:451—85
Adair JG, 47:341—70
Ader R, 44:53—85
Adler N, 45:229—59
Arabie P, 43:169—203
Artz N, 45:131—69
Arvey RD, 49:141—68
Asmus C, 47:485—512
Austin JT, 51:201—26

B

Badura LL, 41:81—108
Baltes PB, 50:471—507
Banaji MR, 45:297—332
Banks WP, 42:305—31
Barlow DH, 43:235—67
Bartoshuk LM, 45:419—49
Baskin DG, 51:255—77
Baum A, 50:137—63
Bazerman MH, 51:279—314
Beach SRH, 50:47—77
Beauchamp GK, 45:419—49
Bechara A, 48:85—114
Bell PA, 47:485—512
Bentler PM, 47:563—92
Benton AL, 45:1—23
Berscheid E, 45:79—129
Bertenthal BI, 47:431—59
Bettman JR, 43:87—131
Betz N, 44:343—81
Birren JE, 46:329—53
Bodenhausen GV, 51:93—120
Bond MH, 47:205—35
Borman W, 48:299—337

Boysen ST, 50:683—705
Brédart S, 43:505—29
Breedlove SM, 45:389—418
Brewin CR, 47:33—57
Brody GH, 49:1—24
Brown TA, 43:235—67
Bruck M, 50:419—39
Bugental DB, 51:315—44
Busby PL, 47:485—512
Buss DM, 42:459—91
Butcher JN, 47:87—111
Butters N, 46:493—523

C

Cacioppo JT, 50:191—214
Capaldi EA, 50:651—82
Carnevale PJ, 43:531—82
Carpenter PA, 46:91—120
Carpintero H, 45:51—78
Carretero M, 46:155—81
Carroll JM, 48:61—83
Ceci SJ, 50:419—39
Chakravarti D, 41:243—88
Chase MH, 41:557—84
Christensen A, 50:165—90
Clark LA, 46:121—53;
    49:377—412
Clinkenbeard PR, 49:117—39
Cohen JB, 41:243—88
Cohen N, 44:53—85
Cohen S, 47:113—42
Collins WA, 41:387—416
Compas BE, 46:265—93
Cook TD, 45:545—80
Cooke ADJ, 49:447—77

Cooper CR, 49:559—84
Cordray DS, 51:345—75
Covington MV, 51:171—200
Cowan N, 44:383—425
Cox MJ, 48:243—67
Coyne JC, 42:401—25
Craig JC, 50:305—31
Culhane SE, 46:433—65
Curhan JR, 51:279—314

D

Darley JM, 41:525—56
Delis DC, 46:493—523
Denner J, 49:559—84
Derrick BE, 47:173—203
Dickson MW, 47:307—38
Digman JM, 41:417—40
Dodge KA, 44:559—84
Dornbusch SM, 47:401—29
Downey G, 42:401—25
Dudgeon P, 47:563—92

E

Egeth HE, 48:269—97
Eichenbaum H, 48:547—72
Eimas PD, 46:467—92
Eisenberg M, 44:613—44
Eisenberg N, 51:665—97
Ericsson KA, 47:273—305
Estes WK, 42:1—28
Everitt BJ, 48:649—84

F

Fabrigar LR, 48:609—47
Fahrbach SE, 50:651—82
Falmagne J-Cl, 45:517—44

Falmagne RJ, 46:525—59
Fassinger RE, 41:355—86
Feng AS, 51:699—725
Fernández-Ballesteros R,
    45:51—78
Field T, 47:541—61
Figueredo AJ, 44:645—74
Fincham FD, 50:47—77
Fisher LM, 46:329—53
Fiske ST, 44:155—94
Fitzgerald LF, 44:343—81
Flavell JH, 50:21—45
Foa EB, 48:449—80
Fowles DC, 43:303—36
Frable DES, 48:139—62
Fried CS, 50:387—418

G

Gabrieli JDE, 49:87—115
Galambos NL, 49:413—46
Gallagher JJ, 45:171—95
Gallagher M, 48:339—70
Gardner WL, 50:191—214
Geen RG, 42:377—99
Gelman SA, 43:337—75
Gelso CJ, 41:355—86
Gerhardt CA, 46:265—93
Glanzman DL, 46:585—624
Glasgow KL, 47:401—29
Gluck MA, 48:481—514
Goldfried MR, 41:659—88
Goldman BD, 41:81—108
Goldsmith M, 51:481—537
Goldstone RL, 49:585—612
Gonsalves J, 46:525—59
Gordis EB, 51:445—79
Gordon J, 45:451—85
Gottman JM, 49:169—97
Graesser AC, 48:163—89
Green DM, 42:135—59
Greenberg LS, 41:659—88
Guarnaccia PJ, 51:571—98
Gunnar MR, 41:387—416
Gurman AS, 46:27—57
Guzzo RA, 47:307—38

H

Hanson M, 48:299—37
Hartup WW, 46:655—87
Hay D, 48:371—410
Healy AF, 47:143—72
Heavey CL, 50:165—90
Hedge J, 48:299—337
Heller K, 41:141—68
Hellige JB, 41:55—80
Henderson JM, 50:243—71
Herbert TB, 47:113—42
Hertz RM, 43:235—67
Higgins ET, 44:585—612
Hilgard ER, 42:79—107
Hilton JL, 47:237—71
Himes GT, 50:683—705
Hinden BR, 46:265—93
Hintzman DL, 41:109—39
Hirsh IJ, 47:461—84
Hodapp RM, 42:29—50
Hollingworth A, 50:243—71
Holyoak KJ, 44:265—315
Hood DC, 49:503—35
Hough LM, 51:631—64
Howard KI, 50:441—69
Howell WC, 44:231—63
Hubert LJ, 43:169—203
Hunter JE, 43:627—70

I

Imhoff AR, 48:31—59
Iyengar S, 51:149—69

J

Jackson SE, 46:237—64
Jacoby J, 49:319—44
Jagielo JA, 41:169—211
Janssen P, 43:505—29
Jenkins JM, 43:55—85
Johar GV, 49:319—44
Johnson EJ, 43:87—131
Johnson-Laird PN, 50:109—
    35
Johnston C, 51:315—44
Judd CM, 46:433—65
Just MA, 46:91—120

K

Karniol R, 47:593—620
Karoly P, 44:23—52
Kaufman JC, 49:479—502
Kazdin AE, 41:21—54
Kelley HH, 43:1—23
Kenny DA, 47:59—86
Kessler RC, 48:191—214
Kim JJ, 44:317—42
Kinchla RA, 43:711—42
Knowlton B, 44:453—95
Knutson JF, 46:401—31
Kohler SS, 45:261—96
Kolb B, 49:43—64
Komorita SS, 46:183—207
Kopta SM, 50:441—69
Koriat A, 51:481—537
Koutstaal W, 49:289—318
Krajicek D, 42:305—31
Kramer RM, 50:569—98
Krasne FB, 46:585—624
Krosnick JA, 50:537—67
Krumhansl CL, 42:277—303

L

Ladd GW, 50:333—59
Landy FJ, 45:261—96
Langenbucher JW, 50:79—
    107
Lavond DG, 44:317—42
Lazarus RS, 44:1—21
Leary DE, 42:79—107
LeDoux JE, 46:209—35
Lebow JL, 46:27—57
Lehmann AC, 47:273—305
Leon M, 43:377—98
Lerner RM, 49:413—46
Levine JM, 41:585—634;
    44:585—612
Levine M, 44:525—58
Light LL, 42:333—76
Lin I-C, 47:401—29
Lindenberger U, 50:471—
    507
Lipsey MW, 51:345—75
Loeber R, 48:371—410
Lopes LL, 45:197—227

López SR, 51:571—98
Lubinski D, 51:405—44
Lucas JA, 46:493—523
Luce RD, 46:1—26
Lueger RJ, 50:441—69
Lynch EB, 51:121—47

M

MacCallum RC, 51:201—26
Maccoby EE, 51:1—27
MacCoun RJ, 49:259—87
MacIver DJ, 46:375—400
MacLeod C, 45:25—50
Macrae CN, 51:93—120
MacWhinney B, 49:199—227
Magnusson D, 44:427—52
Maier SF, 51:29—57
Main SR, 46:375—400
Maratsos M, 45:487—516
Margolin G, 51:445—79
Marmar C, 41:659—88
Martinez JL Jr, 47:173—203
Massaro DW, 44:383—425
Matheny L, 45:487—516
Mathews A, 45:25—50
Matthews K, 45:229—59
McClelland GH, 46:433-65
McDonald JL, 48:215—41
McFall RM, 50:215—41
McGuire CB, 42:239—76
McGuire GR, 42:79—107
McGuire WJ, 48:1—30
McKoon G, 49:25—42
McNamara DS, 47:143—72
Meadows EA, 48:449—80
Medin DL, 51:121—47
Mellers BA, 49:447—77
Middlebrooks JC, 42:135—59
Miller GA, 50:1—19
Miller JL, 46:467—92
Miller JS, 41:169—211
Miller RR, 48:573—607
Millis KK, 48:163—89
Milner PM, 43:443—71
Mineka S, 49:377—412

Mischel W, 49:229—58
Misumi J, 41:213—41
Mitchell G, 42:239—76
Miyake A, 46:91—120
Moore DA, 51:279—314
Morales FR, 41:557—84
Moreland RL, 41:585—634
Morrin M, 49:319—44
Mowday RT, 44:195—229
Murphy KR, 49:141—68
Musen G, 44:453—95
Myers CE, 48:481—514

N

Nader K, 48:85—114
Nathan PE, 50:79—107
Nelson RJ, 41:81—108
Newell KM, 42:213—37
Norman KA, 49:289—318
Nosofsky RM, 43:25—53

O

Oatley K, 43:55—85
O'Leary KD, 42:191—212
Olson JM, 44:117—54
Ones DS, 43:627—70
O'Reilly CA III, 42:427—58
Oswald FL, 51:631—64
Ozer DJ, 45:357—88

P

Paivio A, 47:341—70
Paley B, 48:243—67
Palincsar AS, 49:345—75
Palmer C, 48:115—38
Pansky A, 51:481—537
Parks CD, 46:183—207
Pavel M, 45:517—44
Payne JW, 43:87—131
Perkins DV, 44:525—58
Peterson MF, 41:213—41
Pettigrew TF, 49:65—85
Petty RE, 48:609—47
Phillips SD, 48:31—59
Pincus AL, 43:473—504
Plomin R, 42:161—90
Porras JI, 42:51—78

Posluszny DM, 50:137—63
Prentice DA, 45:297—332
Prieto JM, 45:51—78
Pruitt DG, 43:531—82

Q

Quinn RE, 50:361—86

R

Raaijmakers JGW, 43:205—34
Raichle ME, 45:333—56
Rapp PR, 48:339—70
Ratcliff R, 49:25—42
Ratnam R, 51:699—725
Reise SP, 45:357—88
Rende R, 42:161—90
Repetti RL, 48:411—47
Reppucci ND, 50:387—418
Resnick LB, 44:585—612
Reuman DA, 46:375—400
Revelle W, 46:295—328
Reynolds S, 46:121—53
Richelle M, 43:505—29
Rips LJ, 41:321—53
Ritchie P, 47:341—70
Robbins TW, 48:649—84
Robertson I, 41:289—319
Robinson A, 49:117—39
Robinson GE, 50:651—82
Roitblat HL, 43:671—710
Rollman GB, 50:305—31
Rolls ET, 51:599—630
Rose RJ, 46:625—54
Rosenzweig MR, 47:1—32
Ross M, 47:593—620
Rouse SV, 47:87—111
Rousseau DM, 48:515—46

S

Saegert S, 41:441—77
Sandoval J, 46:355—74
Sankis LM, 51:377—404
Saunders SM, 50:441—69
Scarr S, 44:613—44
Schacter DL, 49:289—318
Schlenker BR, 43:133—68

Schmidt FL, 43:627—70
Schmitt N, 41:289—319
Schneider DJ, 42:527—61
Schuler RS, 46:237—64
Schwartz A, 49:447—77
Schwartz MW, 51:255—77
Sechrest L, 44:645—74
Seeley RJ, 51:255—77
Seeman T, 48:411—47
Shadish WR, 45:545—80
Shaffer DR, 41:479—523
Shaffer JP, 46:561—84
Shankster LJ, 45:261—96
Shapley R, 41:635—58
Sher KJ, 47:371—400
Shiffrin RM, 43:205—34
Shoda Y, 49:229—58
Shultz TR, 41:525—56
Shweder RA, 44:497—523
Silvers RC, 42:51—78
Simon AF, 51:149—69
Simon HA, 41:1—19
Smith DA, 42:191—212
Smith PB, 47:205—35
Snow RE, 43:583—626
Snyder M, 50:273—303
Solomon KO, 51:121—47
Spear NE, 41:169—211
Spellman BA, 44:265—315
Squire LR, 44:453—95
Staudinger UM, 50:471—507
Steel GD, 51:227—53
Stern PC, 43:269—302
Sternberg RJ, 49:479—502
Stukas AA Jr, 50:273—303
Suedfeld P, 51:227—53

Sullivan JL, 50:625—50
Sullivan MA, 44:497—523
Sundstrom E, 47:485—512
Suppes P, 45:517—44
Sutton RI, 44:195—229
Swanson J, 43:583—626

T
Tannenbaum SI, 43:399—441
Taylor SE, 48:411—47
Tees RC, 50:509—35
Tesser A, 41:479—523
Tetlock PE, 42:239—76
Thompson RF, 44:317—42
Timberlake W, 44:675—708
Törestad B, 44:427—52
Toro PA, 44:525—58
Transue JE, 50:625—50
Treat TA, 50:215—41
Trull TJ, 42:109—33;
   47:371—400
Tybout AM, 45:131—69

V
Valley KL, 51:279—314
van der Kooy D, 48:85—114
VanLehn K, 47:513—39
van Lieshout CFM, 46:655—87
von Fersen L, 43:671—710
von Hippel W, 47:237—71
Voss JF, 46:155—81

W
Wahlsten D, 50:599—624
Wang Z-M, 44:87—116

Wasserman EA, 48:573—607
Watkins LR, 51:29—57
Watson CS, 47:461—84
Watson D, 46:121—53;
   49:377—412
Wegener DT, 48:609—47
Wegner DM, 51:59—91
Weick KE, 50:361—86
Weigold MF, 43:133—68
Weinstein CS, 42:493—525
Wellman HM, 43:337—75
Wenzlaff RM, 51:59—91
Werker JF, 50:509—35
Whishaw IQ, 49:43—64
White NM, 43:443—71
Wickens TD, 49:537—57
Widiger TA, 42:109—33;
   51:377—404
Wiggins JS, 43:473—504
Wiley J, 46:155—81
Wilpert B, 46:59—90
Winkel GH, 41:441—77
Wood W, 51:539—70
Woods SC, 51:255—77
Woolard JL, 50:387—418

Y
Yantis S, 48:269—97
Yukl G, 43:399—441

Z
Zanna MP, 44:117—54
Zigler E, 42:29—50
Zinbarg RE, 43:235—67
Zwaan RA, 48:163—89

CHAPTER TITLES, VOLUMES 41–51

PREFATORY CHAPTER

Invariants of Human Behavior	HA Simon	41:1–19
Cognitive Architectures from the Standpoint of an Experimental Psychologist	WK Estes	42:1–28
Common-Sense Psychology and Scientific Psychology	HH Kelley	43:1–23
From Psychological Stress to the Emotions: A History of Changing Outlooks	RS Lazarus	44:1–21
Four Tensions Concerning Mathematical Modeling in Psychology	RD Luce	46:1–26
Aspects of the Search for Neural Mechanisms of Memory	MR Rosenzweig	47:1–32
Creative Hyppothesis Generating in Psychology: Some Useful Heuristics	WJ McGuire	48:1–30
On Knowing a Word	GA Miller	50:1–19
Parenting and Its Effects on Children: On Reading and Misreading Behavior Genetics	EE Maccoby	51:1–27

ATTENTION

Attention	RA Kinchla	43:711–42

BIOLOGICAL BASES OF BEHAVIOR

The Pain of Being Sick: Implications of Immune-to-Brain Communication for Understanding Pain	LR Watkins, SF Maier	51:29–57
Food Intake and the Regulation of Body Weight	SC Woods, MW Schwartz, DG Baskin, RJ Seeley	51:255–77
Memory Systems in the Brain	ET Rolls	51:599–630

BIOLOGICAL PSYCHOLOGY

Hemispheric Asymmetry	JB Hellige	41:55–80
The Atonia and Myoclonia of Active (REM) Sleep	MH Chase, FR Morales	41:557–84
Visual Sensitivity and Parallel Retinocortical Channels	R Shapley	41:635–58
Human Behavioral Genetics	R Plomin, R Rende	42:161–90
The Neurobiology of Filial Learning	M Leon	43:377–98
Psychoneuroimmunology: Conditioning and Stress	R Ader, N Cohen	44:53–85
Mammalian Brain Substrates of Aversive Classical Conditioning	DG Lavond, JJ Kim, RF Thompson	44:317–42
Images of the Mind: Studies with Modern Imaging Techniques	ME Raichle	45:333–56
Sexual Differentiation of the Human Nervous System	SM Breedlove	45:389–418
Genes and Human Behavior	RJ Rose	46:625–54
Long-Term Potentiation and Learning	JL Martinez Jr, BE Derrick	47:173–203
The Use of Animal Models to Study the Effects of Aging on Cognition	M Gallagher, PR Rapp	48:339–70
Psychobiological Models of Hippocampal Function in Learning and Memory	MA Gluck, CE Myers	48:481–514
Central Cholinergic Systems and Cognition	BJ Everitt, TW Robbins	48:649–84
Brain Plasticity and Behavior	B Kolb, IQ Whishaw	49:43–64
The Cognitive Neuroscience of Constructive Memory	DL Schacter, KA Norman, W Koutstaal	49:289–318
Single-Gene Influences of Brain and Behavior	D Wahlsten	50:599–624

807

CHEMICAL SENSES
  See SENSORY PROCESSES

CLINICAL AND COUNSELING PSYCHOLOGY (See also PSYCHOPATHOLOGY)
  Social and Community Intervention   K Heller   41:141–68
  Individual Psychotherapy: Process and Outcome   MR Goldfried, LS Greenberg,   41:659–88
                                                              C Marmar
  Diagnosis and Clinical Assessment   TA Widiger, TJ Trull   42:109–33
  Marital Interactions   KD O'Leary, DA Smith   42:191–212
  Cognitive-Behavioral Approaches to the Nature and   RE Zinbarg, DH Barlow,   43:235–67
    Treatment of Anxiety Disorders   TA Brown, RM Hertz
  Schizophrenia: Diathesis-Stress Revisited   DC Fowles   43:303–36
  Social and Community Interventions   M Levine, PA Toro, DV Perkins   44:525–58
  Research Assessing Couple and Family Therapy   JL Lebow, AS Gurman   46:27–57
  Clinical Assessment of Memory Disorders in Amnesia and   N Butters, DC Delis, JA Lucas   46:493–523
    Dementia
  Theoretical Foundations of Cognitive-Behavioral Therapy for CR Brewin   47:33–57
    Anxiety and Depression
  Psychosocial Treatments for Posttraumatic Stress Disorder: A EB Foa, EA Meadows   48:449–80
    Critical Review
  Cognitive Neuroscience of Human Memory   JDE Gabrieli   49:87–115
  Conflict in Marriage: Implications for Working with Couples FD Fincham, SRH Beach   50:47–77
  Interventions for Couples   A Christensen, CL Heavey   50:165–90
  Quantifying the Information Value of Clinical Assessments RM McFall, TA Treat   50:215–41
    with Signal Detection Theory
  Social, Community, and Preventive Interventions   ND Reppucci, JL Woolard,   50:387–418
                                                              CS Fried
  Individual Psychotherapy Outcome and Process Research: SM Kopta, RJ Lueger,   50:441–69
    Challenges Leading to Greater Turmoil or a Positive   SM Saunders, KI Howard
    Transition?

COGNITIVE PROCESSES
  Reasoning   LJ Rips   41:321–53
  Behavioral Decision Research: A Constructive Processing   JW Payne, JR Bettman, EJ Johnson 43:87–131
    Perspective
  Thinking   KJ Holyoak, BA Spellman   44:265–315
  Information Processing Models: Microscopes of the Mind   DW Massaro, N Cowan   44:383–425
  Representations and Models in Psychology   P Suppes, M Pavel, J-Cl Falmagne 45:517–44
  Language Comprehension: Sentence and Discourse   PA Carpenter, A Miyake, MA Just 46:91–120
    Processing
  Deductive Inference   RJ Falmagne, J Gonsalves   46:525–59
  Cognitive Skill Acquisition   K VanLehn   47:513–39
  Discourse Comprehension   AC Graesser, KK Millis,   48:163–89
                                                              RA Zwaan
  Language Acquisition: The Acquisition of Linguistic   JL McDonald   48:215–41
    Structure in Normal and Special Populations
  Visual Attention: Control, Representation, and Time Course HE Egeth, S Yantis   48:269–97
  Memory-Based Language Processing: Psycholinguistic   G McKoon, R Ratcliff   49:25–42
    Research in the 1990s
  Judgment and Decision Making   BA Mellers, A Schwartz,   49:447–77
                                                              ADJ Cooke
  Deductive Reasoning   PN Johnson-Laird   50:109–35
  Are There Kinds of Concepts?   DL Medin, EB Lynch,   51:121–47
                                                              KO Solomon
  Toward a Psychology of Memory Accuracy   A Koriat, M Goldsmith, A Pansky 51:481–537

COMPARATIVE PSYCHOLOGY, ETHOLOGY, AND ANIMAL BEHAVIOR
  Comparative Cognition: Representations and Processes in   HL Roitblat, L von Fersen   43:671–710
    Learning and Memory
  Animal Behavior: A Continuing Synthesis   W Timberlake   44:675–708
  Current Issues and Emerging Theories in Animal Cognition ST Boysen, GT Himes   50:683–705

CONSUMER BEHAVIOR
   Consumer Behavior: A Quadrennium   J Jacoby, GV Johar, M Morrin   49:319–44

COUNSELING (See also EDUCATION AND COUNSELING; CLINICAL AND COUNSELING PSYCHOLOGY)
   Individuality and Diversity: Theory and Research in   NE Betz, LF Fitzgerald   44:343–81
   Counseling Psychology

DEVELOPMENTAL PSYCHOLOGY
   Social and Personality Development   WA Collins, MR Gunnar   41:387–416
   Memory and Aging: Four Hypotheses in Search of Data   LL Light   42:333–76
   Cognitive Development: Foundational Theories of Core   HM Wellman, SA Gelman   43:337–75
     Domains
   Social Foundations of Cognition   JM Levine, LB Resnick,   44:585–612
     ET Higgins
   Child Care Research: Issues, Perspectives, and Results   S Scarr, M Eisenberg   44:613–44
   Language Specificity and Elasticity: Brain and Clinical   M Maratsos, L Matheny   45:487–516
     Syndrome Studies
   Adolescent Development: Pathways and Processes of Risk   BE Compas, BR Hinden,   46:265–93
     and Resilience   CA Gerhardt
   Aging and Speed of Behavior: Possible Consequences for   JE Birren, LM Fisher   46:329–53
     Psychological Functioning
   Origins and Early Development of Perception, Action, and   BI Bertenthal   47:431–59
     Representation
   Attachment and Separation in Young Children   T Field   47:541–61
   Families as Systems   MJ Cox, B Paley   48:243–67
   Key Issues in the Development of Aggression and Violence   R Loeber, D Hay   48:371–410
     from Childhood to Early Adulthood
   Sibling Relationship Quality: Its Causes and Consequences   GH Brody   49:1–24
   Models of the Emergence of Language   B MacWhinney   49:199–227
   Adolescent Development: Challenges and Opportunities for   RM Lerner, NL Galambos   49:413–46
     Research, Programs, and Policies
   Cognitive Development: Children's Knowledge About the   JH Flavell   50:21–45
     Mind
   Peer Relationships and Social Competence During Early and   GW Ladd   50:333–59
     Middle Childhood
   Lifespan Psychology: Theory and Application to Intellectual   PB Baltes, UM Staudinger,   50:471–507
     Functioning   U Lindenberger

EDUCATION AND COUNSELING
   Counseling Psychology: Theory and Research on   CJ Gelso, RE Fassinger   41:355–86
     Interventions
   The Classroom as a Social Context for Learning   CS Weinstein   42:493–525
   Instructional Psychology: Aptitude, Adaptation, and   RE Snow, J Swanson   43:583–626
     Assessment
   Teaching and Learning: New Models   JJ Gallagher   45:171–95
   Teaching in Subject Matter Areas: Science   J Sandoval   46:355–74
   Social Structuring of the School: Studying What Is,   DJ Mac Iver, DA Reuman,   46:375–400
     Illuminating What Could Be   SR Main
   The Social Structure of Schooling   SM Dornbusch, KL Glasgow,   47:401–29
     I-C Lin
   Women and Career Development: A Decade of Research   SD Phillips, AR Imhoff   48:31–59
   Social Constructivist Perspectives on Teaching and Learning   AS Palincsar   49:345–75
   Giftedness: An Exceptionality Examined   A Robinson, PR Clinkenbeard   49:117–39

EDUCATIONAL PSYCHOLOGY
   GOAL THEORY, MOTIVATION, AND SCHOOL   MV Covington   51:171–200
     ACHIEVEMENT: An Integrative Review

EMOTION
   Emotion   JT Cacioppo, WL Gardner   50:191–214

ENVIRONMENTAL PSYCHOLOGY
  Environmental Psychology   S Saegert, GH Winkel   41:441–77
  Environmental Psychology 1989-1994   E Sundstrom, PA Bell, PL Busby,   47:485–512
                                                                   C Asmus
  The Environmental Psychology of Capsule Habitats   P Suedfeld, GD Steel   51:227–53

GENETICS OF BEHAVIOR
  See BIOLOGICAL PSYCHOLOGY

GERONTOLOGY (MATURITY AND AGING)
  See DEVELOPMENTAL PSYCHOLOGY

HEALTH PSYCHOLOGY
  Health Psychology: Why Do Some People Get Sick and   N Adler, K Matthews   45:229–59
    Some Stay Well?
  Health Psychology: Psychological Factors and Physical   S Cohen, TB Herbert   47:113–42
    Disease from the Perspective of Human
    Psychoneuroimmunology
  Health Psychology: What Is an Unhealthy Environment and   SE Taylor, RL Repetti, T Seeman   48:411–47
    How Does it Get Under the Skin
  Health Psychology: Mapping Biobehaviorial Contributions to   A Baum, DM Posluszny   50:137–63
    Health and Illness

HEARING
  See SENSORY PROCESSES

HUMAN ABILITIES
  Human Abilities   RJ Sternberg, JC Kaufman   49:479–502

HUMAN DEVELOPMENT
  Parental and Child Cognitions in the Context of the Family   DB Bugental, C Johnston   51:315–44
  The Effects of Family and Community Violence on Children   G Margolin, EB Gordis   51:445–79
  Emotion, Regulation, and Moral Development   N Eisenberg   51:665–97

INDUSTRIAL PSYCHOLOGY
  See PERSONNEL-ORGANIZATIONAL PSYCHOLOGY

LEARNING AND MEMORY
  Human Learning and Memory: Connections and   DL Hintzman   41:109–39
    Dissociations
  Animal Memory and Learning   NE Spear, JS Miller, JA Jagielo   41:169–211
  Models for Recall and Recognition   JGW Raaijmakers, RM Shiffrin   43:205–34
  Mammalian Brain Substrates of Aversive Classical   D Lavond, JJ Kim, RF Thompson   44:317–42
    Conditioning
  The Structure and Organization of Memory   LR Squire, B Knowlton, G Musen   44:453–95
  Acquiring Intellectual Skills   JF Voss, J Wiley, M Carretero   46:155–81
  What We Can Learn from Invertebrate Learning   FB Krasne, DL Glanzman   46:585–624
  Verbal Learning and Memory: Does the Modal Model Still   AF Healy, DS McNamara   47:143–72
    Work?
  Expert and Exceptional Performance: Evidence of Maximal   KA Ericsson, AC Lehmann   47:273–305
    Adaptation to Task Constraints
  Declarative Memory: Insights from Cognitive Neurobiology   H Eichenbaum   48:547–72
  What's Elementary About Associative Learning?   EA Wasserman, RR Miller   48:573–607
  Perceptual Learning   RL Goldstone   49:585–612
  Neuroethology of Spatial Learning: The Birds and the Bees   EA Capaldi, GE Robinson,   50:651–82
                                                                 SE Fahrbach

MOTIVATION
Mechanisms of Seasonal Cycles of Behavior   RJ Nelson, LL Badura,   41:81–108
     BD Goldman
Social Motivation   RG Geen   42:377–99
Human Emotions: Function and Dysfunction   K Oatley, JM Jenkins   43:55–85
The Psychobiology of Reinforcers   NM White, PM Milner   43:443–71
Emotion: Clues from the Brain   JE LeDoux   46:209–35
The Motivational Impact of Temporal Focus: Thinking About   R Karniol, M Ross   47:593–620
     the Future and the Past
Neurobiological Constraints on Behavioral Models of   K Nader, A Bechara,   48:85–114
     Motivation   D van der Kooy

PERCEPTION
Perception   WP Banks, D Krajicek   42:305–31
High-Level Scene Perception   JM Henderson, A Hollingworth   50:243–71
Influences on Infant Speech Processing: Toward a New   JF Werker, RC Tees   50:509–35
     Synthesis

PERSONALITY
Social and Personality Development   WA Collins, M Gunnar   41:387–416
Personality Structure: Emergence of the Five-Factor Model   JM Digman   41:417–40
Evolutionary Personality Psychology   DM Buss   42:459–91
Personality: Structure and Assessment   JS Wiggins, AL Pincus   43:473–504
A Holistic View of Personality: A Model Revisited   D Magnusson, B Törestad   44:427–52
Personality Assessment   DJ Ozer, SP Reise   45:357–88
Personality Processes   W Revelle   46:295–328
Personality Development in Social Context   WW Hartup, CFM van Lieshout   46:655–87
Personality: Individual Differences and Clinical Assessment   JN Butcher, SV Rouse   47:87–111
Reconciling Processing Dynamics and Personality   W Mischel, Y Shoda   49:229–58
     Dispositions
SCIENTIFIC AND SOCIAL SIGNIFICANCE OF   D Lubinski   51:405–44
     ASSESSING INDIVIDUAL DIFFERENCES: "Sinking
     Shafts at a Few Critical Points"

PERSONNEL-ORGANIZATIONAL PSYCHOLOGY
Consumer Psychology   JB Cohen, D Chakravarti   41:243–88
Personnel Selection   N Schmitt, I Robertson   41:289–319
Organization Development and Transformation   JI Porras, RC Silvers   42:51–78
Organizational Behavior: Where We've Been, Where We're   CA O'Reilly III   42:427–58
     Going
Training and Development in Work Organizations   SI Tannenbaum, G Yukl   43:399–441
Personnel Selection   FL Schmidt, DS Ones, JE Hunter   43:627–70
Organizational Behavior: Linking Individuals and Groups to   RT Mowday, RI Sutton   44:195–229
     Organizational Contexts
Engineering Psychology in a Changing World   WC Howell   44:231–63
Consumer Psychology   AM Tybout, N Artz   45:131–69
Personnel Selection and Placement   FJ Landy, LJ Shankster, SS Kohler   45:261–96
Organizational Behavior   B Wilpert   46:59–90
Understanding Human Resource Management in the Context   SE Jackson, RS Schuler   46:237–64
     of Organizations and Their Environments
Teams in Organizations: Recent Research on Performance   RA Guzzo, MW Dickson   47:307–38
     and Effectiveness
Human-Computer Interaction: Psychology as a Science of   JM Carroll   48:61–83
     Design
Personnel Selection   W Borman, M Hanson, J Hedge   48:299–337
Organizational Behavior in the New Organizational Era   DM Rousseau   48:515–46
Performance Evaluation in Work Settings   RD Arvey, KR Murphy   49:141–68
Organizational Change and Development   KE Weick, RE Quinn   50:361–86
Trust and Distrust in Organizations: Emerging Perspectives,   RM Kramer   50:569–98
     Enduring Questions

PERSONNEL PSYCHOLOGY
    PERSONNEL SELECTION: Looking Toward the Future–   LM Hough, FL Oswald   51:631–64
    Remembering the Past

PSYCHOLINGUISTICS
    See COGNITIVE PROCESSES

PSYCHOLOGY AND CULTURE
    Cultural Psychology: Who Needs It?   RA Shweder, MA Sullivan   44:497–523
    Cross-Cultural Social and Organizational Psychology   MH Bond, PB Smith   47:205–35
    Comorbidity of Anxiety and Unipolar Mood Disorders   S Mineka, D Watson, LA Clark   49:377–412
    Theories Linking Culture and Psychology: Universal and   CR Cooper, J Denner   49:559–84
    Community-Specific Processes

PSYCHOLOGY IN OTHER COUNTRIES
    Psychology in Japan   J Misumi, MF Peterson   41:213–41
    Psychology in Belgium   M Richelle, P Janssen, S Brédart   43:505–29
    Psychology in China: A Review Dedicated to Li Chen   Z-M Wang   44:87–116
    Contemporary Psychology in Spain   JM Prieto, R Fernández-   45:51–78
        Ballesteros, H Carpintero
    Psychology in Canada   JG Adair, A Paivio, P Ritchie   47:341–70

PSYCHOPATHOLOGY (See also CLINICAL AND COUNSELING PSYCHOLOGY)
    Psychotherapy for Children and Adolescents   AE Kazdin   41:21–54
    Social Factors and Psychopathology: Stress, Social Support,   JC Coyne, G Downey   42:401–25
    and Coping Processes
    Social-Cognitive Mechanisms in the Development of Conduct   KA Dodge   44:559–84
    Disorder and Depression
    Cognitive Approaches to Emotion and Emotional Disorders   A Mathews, C MacLeod   45:25–50
    Diagnosis and Classification of Psychopathology: Challenges   LA Clark, D Watson, S Reynolds   46:121–53
    to the Current System and Future Directions
    Methodological Issues in Psychopathology Research   KJ Sher, TJ Trull   47:371–400
    The Effects of Stressful Life Events on Depression   RC Kessler   48:191–214
    Key Issues in the Development of Aggression and Violence   R Loeber, D Hay   48:371–410
    from Childhood to Early Adulthood
    Psychopathology: Description and Classification   PE Nathan, JW Langenbucher   50:79–107
    ADULT PSYCHOPATHOLOGY: Issues and Controversies   TA Widiger, LM Sankis   51:377–404
    CULTURAL PSYCHOPATHOLOGY: Uncovering the   SR López, PJ Guarnaccia   51:571–98
    Social World of Mental Illness

PSYCHOPHARMACOLOGY
    See BIOLOGICAL PSYCHOLOGY

RESEARCH METHODOLOGY
    Similarity Scaling and Cognitive Process Models   RM Nosofsky   43:25–53
    Combinatorial Data Analysis   P Arabie, LJ Hubert   43:169–203
    Program Evaluation   L Sechrest, AJ Figueredo   44:645–74
    Social Experiments: Some Developments Over the Past 15   TD Cook, WR Shadish   45:545–80
    Years
    Data Analysis: Continuing Issues in the Everday Analysis of   CM Judd, GH McClelland,   46:433–65
    Psychological Data   SE Culhane
    Multiple Hypothesis Testing   JP Shaffer   46:561–84
    The Design and Analysis of Social-Interaction Research   DA Kenny   47:59–86
    Covariance Structure Analysis: Statistical Practice, Theory,   PM Bentler, P Dudgeon   47:563–92
    and Directions
    Categorical Data Analysis   TD Wickens   49:537–57
    Survey Research   JA Krosnick   50:537–67
    Applications of Structural Equation Modeling in   RC MacCallum, JT Austin   51:201–26
    Psychological Research
    Evaluation Methods for Social Intervention   MW Lipsey, DS Cordray   51:345–75

SENSATION AND PERCEPTION
  Neural Basis of Hearing in Real-World Situations — AS Feng, R Ratnam — 51:699–725

SENSORY PROCESSES
  Sound Localization by Human Listeners — JC Middlebrooks, DM Green — 42:135–59
  Chemical Senses — LM Bartoshuk, GK Beauchamp — 45:419–49
  Color Appearance: On Seeing Red–Or Yellow, Or Green, Or — I Abramov, J Gordon — 45:451–85
    Blue
  Speech Perception: From Signal to Word — JL Miller, PD Eimas — 46:467–92
  Auditory Psychophysics and Perception — IJ Hirsh, CS Watson — 47:461–84
  Music Performance — C Palmer — 48:115–38
  Lower-Level Visual Processing and Models of Light — DC Hood — 49:503–35
    Adaptation
  Somesthesis — JC Craig, GB Rollman — 50:305–31

SLEEP
  See BIOLOGICAL PSYCHOLOGY

SOCIAL PSYCHOLOGY
  Social and Personality Development — WA Collins, M Gunnar — 41:387–416
  Attitudes and Attitude Change — A Tesser, DR Shaffer — 41:479–523
  Progress in Small Group Research — JM Levine, RL Moreland — 41:585–634
  Social Cognition — DJ Schneider — 42:527–61
  Interpersonal Processes Involving Impression Regulation and — BR Schlenker, MF Weigold — 43:133–68
    Management
  Negotiation and Mediation — PJ Carnevale, DG Pruitt — 43:531–82
  Attitudes and Attitude Change — JM Olson, MP Zanna — 44:117–54
  Social Cognition and Social Perception — ST Fiske — 44:155–94
  Interpersonal Relationships — E Berscheid — 45:79–129
  The Self in Social Contexts — MR Banaji, DA Prentice — 45:297–332
  Interpersonal Relations: Mixed-Motive Interaction — SS Komorita, CD Parks — 46:183–207
  Stereotypes — JL Hilton, W von Hippel — 47:237–71
  Gender, Racial, Ethnic, Sexual, and Class Identities — DES Frable — 48:139–62
  Attitudes and Attitude Change — RE Petty, DT Wegener, — 48:609–47
    LR Fabrigar
  Intergroup Contact Theory — TF Pettigrew — 49:65–85
  Psychology and the Study of Marital Processes — JM Gottman — 49:169–97
  Interpersonal Processes: The Interplay of Cognitive, — M Snyder, AA Stukas Jr. — 50:273–303
    Motivational, and Behavioral Activities in Social
    Interaction
  Thought Suppression — RM Wenzlaff, DM Wegner — 51:59–91
  Social Cognition: Thinking Categorically about Others — CN Macrae, GV Bodenhausen — 51:93–120
  New Perspectives and Evidence on Political Communication — S Iyengar, AF Simon — 51:149–69
    and Campaign Effects
  Negotiation — MH Bazerman, JR Curhan, — 51:279–314
    DA Moore, KL Valley
  ATTITUDE CHANGE: Persuasion and Social Influence — W Wood — 51:539–70

SPECIAL TOPICS
  Moral Judgments: Their Content and Acquisition — JM Darley, TR Shultz — 41:525–56
  Behavioral Functioning in Individuals with Mental — E Zigler, RM Hodapp — 42:29–50
    Retardation
  History of Psychology: A Survey and Critical Assessment — ER Hilgard, DE Leary, — 42:79–107
    GR McGuire
  Motor Skill Acquisition — KM Newell — 42:213–37
  Psychological Perspectives on Nuclear Deterrence — PE Tetlock, CB McGuire, — 42:239–76
    G Mitchell
  Music Psychology: Tonal Structures in Perception and — CL Krumhansl — 42:277–303
    Memory
  Psychological Dimensions of Global Environmental Change — PC Stern — 43:269–302
  Mechanisms of Self-Regulation: A Systems View — P Karoly — 44:23–52
  Neuropsychological Assessment — AL Benton — 45:1–23
  Psychology and Economics: Perspectives on Risk, — LL Lopes — 45:197–227
    Cooperation, and the Marketplace

Psychological Characteristics of Maltreated Children: Putative Risk Factors and Consequences	JF Knutson	46:401–31
Women and Career Development: A Decade of Research	SD Phillips, AR Imhoff	48:31–59
The Effects of Stressful Life Events on Depression	RC Kessler	48:191–214
Psychobiological Models of Hippocampal Function in Learning and Memory	MA Gluck, CE Myers	48:481–514

TIMELY TOPICS

Biases in the Interpretation and Use of Research Results	RJ MacCoun	49:259–87
The Suggestibility of Children's Memory	M Bruck, SJ Ceci	50:419–39
The Psychological Underpinnings of Democracy: A Selective Review of Research on Political Tolerance, Interpersonal Trust, and Social Capital	JL Sullivan, JE Transue	50:625–50

VISION
    See SENSORY PROCESSES